Bingham's
Motor Claims Cases

I hold every man a debtor to his profession; from the which as men of course do seek to receive countenance and profit, so ought they of duty to endeavour themselves by way of amends to be a help and ornament thereunto.

Francis Bacon (1561–1626)
Maxims of the Law Preface.

Bingham's Motor Claims Cases

Ninth edition

J.A. Taylor, LL B (LOND)
Solicitor

London
Butterworths
1986

United Kingdom	Butterworth & Co (Publishers) Ltd, 88 Kingsway, LONDON WC2B 6AB and 61A North Castle Street, EDINBURGH EH2 3LJ
Australia	Butterworths Pty Ltd, SYDNEY, MELBOURNE, BRISBANE, ADELAIDE, PERTH, CANBERRA and HOBART
Canada	Butterworth & Co (Canada) Ltd, TORONTO and VANCOUVER
New Zealand	Butterworths of New Zealand Ltd, WELLINGTON and AUCKLAND
Singapore	Butterworth & Co (Asia) Pte Ltd, SINGAPORE
South Africa	Butterworth Publishers (Pty) Ltd, DURBAN and PRETORIA
USA	Butterworth Legal Publishers, ST PAUL, Minnesota, SEATTLE, Washington, BOSTON, Massachusetts, AUSTIN, Texas and D & S Publishers, CLEARWATER, Florida

First Edition	1946
Second Edition	*March* 1951
Reprint	*June* 1952
Third Edition	*February* 1955
Reprint	*June* 1956
Fourth Edition	*August* 1960
First Reprint	*April* 1961
Second Reprint	*May* 1962
Fifth Edition	*June* 1964
Reprint	*March* 1967
Sixth Edition	*July* 1968
Seventh Edition	*March* 1973
Reprint	*June* 1975
Eighth Edition	*July* 1980

© Butterworth & Co (Publishers) Ltd 1986

British Library Cataloguing in Publication Data
Bingham, Leonard
 Bingham's motor claims cases. —— 9th ed.
 1. Liability for traffic accidents ——
 Great Britain —— Cases
 I. Title.   II. Taylor, J.A. (John Arthur)
 344.106′86232014′0264   KD1980.A8

ISBN 0-406-11813-2

Typeset by Colset Private Ltd, Singapore
Printed in Great Britain by Billings of Worcester

Preface

The main impulse for the production of this new edition of *Bingham* was the need to incorporate the considerable changes in the law of accident claims brought about by the Administration of Justice Act 1982. The awkward concept of damages for loss of expectation of life in fatal cases has, after nearly half a century, been laid to rest, and with it the more recent enlargement, following *Pickett*'s case, to award damages for loss of earnings during the 'lost years'. The current law on fatal claims is to be found in Chapter 13, though the backlog of pending cases has made it necessary to preserve the decisions relevant to pre-1983 claims in Appendix A of this edition (pp 943 to 964). Important amendments have also been made to the Fatal Accidents Act 1976 (pp 488–490). The 1982 Act has in addition given the quietus to those ancient anomalous causes of action for damages for loss of consortium and servitium. More recently the provisions of the Act for the award of provisional damages have been brought into force (pp 425–426).

In the book as a whole more than two hundred new cases have been added — more, perhaps, on damages and points of practice than on liability. The standardisation of traffic signs and of driving techniques over the past twenty years has made obsolete (and therefore expunged) some of the older decisions. The comment of the Court of Appeal in *Foskett v Mistry* (p 76) on citation of authorities is relevant; nevertheless there is value in reported cases, even those turning largely on fact, by indicating the attitude likely to be taken in the courts to particular types of accident. On general principles useful guidance was given in *Kite v Nolan* (p 75).

The law on limitation of actions continues to engender many reportable decisions, stringent or merciful, dependent on point of view. The application of section 33 of the Limitation Act 1980 (and its predecessor, section 2D of the 1939 Act) deserves special note (pp 539 to 549). Important also is *Pirelli v Faber* and the neat illustration of its effect in *Dove v Banhams* (p 535).

The gradual extension of the scope and range of damages for 'shock' and change of personality is illustrated in some new cases of which *McLoughlin v O'Brian* (p 465) and *Brice v Brown* (p 469) are of significance. The case of *Meah v McCreamer* (p 455) which subsequently achieved some public notoriety, came before the Court again on the question of insurance indemnity and is to be found reported on that point in the Times newspaper for 12 December 1985.

Brief notes of cases reported after completion of the manuscript have been inserted during proof-reading but inevitably there are even later matters to be added. A useful decision on a driver's standard of care in an emergency is reported in the Times of 13 November 1985 (*Chief Constable of Avon v Jones*). When a vehicle is capable of being 'used' was considered in

Thomas v Hooper ((1985) Times, 25 October). A case on s 11 of the Limitation Act 1980 (*Pattison v Hobbs*) came before the Court of Appeal and was reported in the Times for 11 November 1985. Two useful cases on service of a writ (*Abu Dhabi Helicopters v International Aeradio* and *Hodgson v Hart D. C.*) are reported in the Times for 25 November 1985. A plaintiff seeking an interim payment against all the defendants must satisfy the court that he would recover substantial damages against the defendant against whom the order is sought (*Breeze v McKennon* (1985) Times, 23 November). In the same issue of the Times is *Eastman v London Country Bus Services* on the effect of delay on the limitation period.

The Court of Appeal's decision in *Samuelson's* case (p 837) is now fully reported at [1985] 2 Lloyds Rep 541, and *A B Maritrans v Comet Shipping Co* (p 14) is reported at [1985] 3 All ER 442. *Ward v Cannock Chase* (p 373) is now reported at [1985] 3 All ER 537 and *Muirhead v Industrial Tank Specialities* (p 377) at [1985] 3 All ER 705. *Harper v Gray and Walker* [1985] 2 All ER 507 is a case on contribution among joint tortfeasors. Finally, RSC Order 62 on costs (p 611) is to be replaced as from 28 April 1986 by a new order, making the two cases following it obsolete.

Users of earlier editions of this book may notice that the decision has at last been taken to put the name of each case at the beginning of the case digest and not at the end. An attempt has also been made to augment, helpfully it is hoped, the practical notes on procedure, limitations and the Motor Insurers Bureau Agreements. The text of the Agreements is printed by permission of Her Majesty's Stationery Office.

Appendix B, containing specimen awards of damages for personal injuries, has been specially prepared by P J Hughes Esq LLB, MA from case digests in Halsburys Laws of England Current Service.

It remains for me to say that I am again indebted to my wife for her great help in typing the considerable amount of new matter and for much other secretarial help for this new edition.

January 1986   J A T

Contents

Appendices

Table of statutes

Page references printed in **bold** type indicate where the section of an Act is set out in part or in full. Page numbers printed in *italic* type refer to pages of the Appendix.

List of Cases

Page references to case summaries are followed by an asterisk. Numbers printed in *italics* refer to the pages of the Appendices.

PART 1

Liability

CHAPTER 1
Negligence

1 LIABILITY FOR NEGLIGENCE

CONSTITUENTS IN ACTION FOR NEGLIGENCE

There are, in addition to damage, two constituents in a cause of action for negligence:

1 a careless act; and
2 a duty to the person injured.

There is a duty on the driver of a motor car to observe ordinary care or skill towards persons using the highway whom he could reasonably foresee as likely to be affected.

Before the liability of a defendant to pay damages for the tort of negligence can be established in an action brought by or on behalf of an injured man, three things have to be proved — (1) that the defendant failed to exercise due care; and (2) that the defendant owed to the injured man a duty to exercise due care; and (3) that the defendant's failure was the 'cause' of the injury in the proper sense of that term: per Viscount Simon in *Woods v Duncan* [1946] AC 401, [1946] 1 All ER 420, [1947] LJR 120, 174 LT 296, 62 TLR 283, HL.

Due care

Negligence is the omission to do something which a reasonable man, guided upon those considerations which ordinarily regulate the conduct of human affairs, would do, or doing something which a prudent and reasonable man would not do: *Blyth v Birmingham Waterworks Co* (1856) 11 Ex 781, 25 LJ Ex 212, 4 WR 204.

If the possibility of danger emerging is reasonably apparent, then to take no precautions is negligence; but if the possibility of danger emerging is only a mere possibility which would never occur to the mind of a reasonable man, then there is no negligence in not having taken extraordinary precautions: per Lord Dunedin in *Fardon v Harcourt-Rivington* (1932) 146 LT 391, 48 TLR 215, 76 Sol Jo 81.

I am far from saying that everyone is entitled to assume, in all circumstances, that other persons will be careful. On the contrary a prudent man will guard against the possible negligence of others when experience shows such negligence to be common: per Lord du Parcq in *Grant v Sun Shipping Co* [1948] AC 549.

The legal fiction of a 'reasonable man' is intended to eliminate the personal factor and strike a fair balance between those who are 'unduly timorous' and those who 'nonchalantly disregard' obvious dangers: per Lord Macmillan in *Glasgow Corpn v Muir* (p 586, below).

In running down accidents, when two parties are so moving in relation to one another as to involve risk of collision, each owes to the other a duty to move with due care, and that is true whether they are both in control of vehicles, or both proceeding on foot, or whether one is on foot and the other controlling a moving vehicle. A pedestrian crossing the road owes a duty to the owner of a vehicle, e g if his rashness causes the vehicle to pull up so suddenly as to damage its mechanism, or as to result in following traffic running into it from behind, or in damage to the vehicle itself by contact with the pedestrian. When a man steps from the kerb into the roadway, he owes a duty to traffic which is approaching him with risk of collision to exercise due care: *Nance v British Columbia Electric Rly Co Ltd* [1951] AC 601, [1951] 2 All ER 448, [1951] 2 TLR 137, 95 Sol Jo 543, PC.

Paraphrasing the words of Lord Uthwatt in *London Passenger Transport Board v Upson* [1949] AC 155, [1949] 1 All ER 60, [1949] LJR 238, 65 TLR 9, 93 Sol Jo 40, HL, a driver is not bound to foresee every extremity of folly which occurs on the road. Equally, he is certainly not entitled to drive upon the footing that other users of the road, either drivers or pedestrians, will exercise reasonable care. He is bound to anticipate any act which is reasonably foreseeable, which the experience of road users teaches that people do, albeit negligently: per Slade J in *Berrill v Road Haulage Executive* [1952] 2 Lloyd's Rep 490.

Note—See also *Nettleship v Weston*, p 69, below on the duty of care of a driver.

To whom a duty of care is owed

The rule that you are to love your neighbour becomes in law, you must not injure your neighbour; and the lawyer's question, who is my neighbour? receives a restricted reply. You must take reasonable care to avoid acts or omissions which you can reasonably foresee would be likely to injure your neighbour. Who, then, in law is my neighbour? The answer seems to be — persons, who are so closely and directly affected by my act that I ought reasonably to have them in contemplation as being so affected when I am directing my mind to the acts or omissions which are called in question: per Lord Atkin in *Donoghue v Stevenson* [1932] AC 562, [1932] All ER Rep 1, 101 LJPC 119, 147 LT 281, 48 TLR 494, HL.

It is not true to say that wherever a man finds himself in such a position that unless he does a certain act another person may suffer, or that if he does something another person will suffer, then it is his duty in the one case to be careful to do the act and in the other case to be careful not to do the act. Any such proposition is much too wide. There has to be a breach of a duty which the law recognises, and to ascertain what the law recognises regard must be had to the decisions of the courts: per du Parcq LJ in *Deyong v Shenburn* [1946] KB 227, [1946] 1 All ER 226, 115 LJKB 262, 174 LT 129, 62 TLR 193, 90 Sol Jo 139, CA.

The famous passage in Lord Atkin's opinion in *Donoghue v Stevenson* has been criticised as too wide: but not its essential principle, namely, that the duty of 'diligence' — which word we use as correlative of 'negligence' — is to be measured by such degree of skill and care as is requisite in the circumstances (which the actor knows or would know if he thought about it) for the purpose of safeguarding the interest of the potential plaintiff — the actor's 'neighbour' in Lord Atkin's passage: per Scott LJ in *Anglo-Saxon Petroleum Co v The Admiralty* [1947] KB 794, [1947] 2 All ER 465, [1948] LJR 153, 80 Ll L Rep 459, CA.

Through the trilogy of cases in this House, *Donoghue v Stevenson*, (above), *Hedley Byrne v Heller & Partners Ltd* [1964] AC 465, [1963] 2 All ER 575, [1963] 3 WLR 101, 107 Sol Jo 454, HL, and *Home Office v Dorset Yacht Co Ltd* (p 372, below) the position has now been reached that in order to establish that a duty of care arises in a particular situation, it is not necessary to bring the facts of that situation within those of previous situations in which a duty of care has been held to exist. Rather the question has to be approached in two stages. First one has to ask whether, as between the alleged wrongdoer and the person who has suffered damage there is a sufficient relationship of proximity or neighbourhood such that, in the reasonable contemplation of the former, carelessness on his part may be likely to cause damage to the latter, in which case a prima facie duty of care arises. Second, if the first question is answered affirmatively, it is necessary to consider whether there are any considerations which ought to negative, or to reduce or limit the scope of the duty or the class of person to whom it is owed or the damages to which a breach of it may give rise: per Lord Wilberforce in *Anns v Merton London Borough Council* [1978] AC 728, [1977] 2 All ER 492, [1977] 2 WLR 1024, 141 JP 526, 121 Sol Jo 377, 75 LGR 555, 243 Estates Gazette 523, 591, HL.

The true question in each case is whether the particular defendant owed to the particular plaintiff a duty of care having the scope which is contended for and whether he was in breach of that duty with consequent loss to the plaintiff. A relationship of proximity in Lord Atkin's sense must exist before any duty of care can arise but the scope of the duty must depend on all the circumstances of the case. . . . So in determining whether or not a duty of care of a particular scope was incumbent on a defendant it is material to take into consideration whether it is just and reasonable that it should be so: per Lord Keith in *Peabody Donation Fund Governors v Sir Lindsay Parkinson & Co* [1984] 3 All ER 529, [1984] 3 WLR 953, 128 Sol Jo 753, 83 LGR 1, HL.

It is not enough that the event should be such as can reasonably be foreseen. The further result that injury is likely to follow must also be such as a reasonable man would contemplate before he can be convicted of actionable negligence. Nor is the remote possibility of injury occurring enough. There must be sufficient probability to lead a reasonable man to anticipate it. The existence of some risk is an ordinary incident of life, even when all due care has been, as it must be, taken: per Lord Porter in *Bolton v Stone* [1951] AC 850, [1951] 1 All ER 1078, [1951] 1 TLR 977, HL.

In order to establish a coherent chain of causation it is not necessary that the precise details leading up to the accident should have been reasonably foreseeable: it is sufficient if the accident which occurred is of a type which should have been foreseeable by a reasonably careful person: per Lord Guest in *Hughes v Lord Advocate* [1963] AC 837, [1963] 1 All ER 705, [1963] 2 WLR 779, 107 Sol Jo 233, HL.

In all these cases you will find that the three questions, duty, causation and remoteness run continually into one another. It seems to me that they are simply three different ways of looking at one and the same problem. Starting with the proposition that a negligent person should be liable within reason, for the consequences of his conduct, the extent of his liability is to be found by asking the one question: Is the consequence fairly to be regarded as within the risk created by the negligence? If so, the negligent person is liable for it: but otherwise not: per Denning LJ in *Roe v Minister of Health* [1954] 2 QB 66, [1954] 2 All ER 131, [1954] 2 WLR 915, 98 Sol Jo 319, CA.

The truth is that all these three — duty, remoteness and causation — are all devices by which the courts limit the range of liability for negligence or nuisance. . . . The law has to draw a line somewhere. Sometimes it is done by limiting the range of the persons to whom duty is owed. Sometimes it is done by saying that there is a break in the chain of causation. At other times it is done by saying that the consequence is too remote to be a head of damage. But ultimately it is a question of policy for the judges to decide: per Lord Denning in *Lamb v Camden London Borough Council* (p 372, below).

Cases on duty of care: foreseeability

Hay (or Bourhill) v Young
[1943] AC 92, [1942] 2 All ER 396, 111 LJPC 97, 167 LT 261, 86 Sol Jo 349, HL.
A woman was at the front of a stationary tramcar on the offside loading a creel on to her back. A motor cyclist passed on the near side of the tramcar and collided with a car 45 to 50 feet ahead. The woman did not see the impact but merely heard the noise of the collision. She alleged shock caused by the noise of the collision. It was admitted that her terror did not involve

any element of reasonable fear of immediate bodily injury to herself.
HELD: The motor cyclist owed no duty to the woman as he could not reasonably have foreseen the likelihood that she could be affected by his negligent act. She was outside the area of potential danger. The question was one of liability, not remoteness of damage. The mere accidental and unknown presence of a person upon the same street as, and somewhere within earshot of, the occurring of an accident in mid-carriageway, does not per se create any relationship of duty raising liability — some other and special element of immediacy is required.

Per Lord Wright: The breach of duty must be vis-à-vis the plaintiff. The plaintiff must sue for a wrong to herself. She cannot build on a wrong to somebody else. A blind or deaf man who crosses the traffic on a busy street cannot complain if he is run over by a careful driver who does not know of and could not be expected to observe and guard against the man's infirmity. These questions go to culpability, not compensation.

Per Lord Thankerton: The duty is to take such reasonable care as will avoid the risk of injury to such persons as he can reasonably foresee might be injured by failure to exercise such reasonable care.

Per Lord Macmillan: The duty to take care is the duty to avoid doing or omitting to do anything the doing or omitting to do which may have as its reasonable and probable consequence injury to others, and the duty is owed to those to whom injury may reasonably and probably be anticipated if the duty is not observed.

Note—See also *McLoughlin v O'Brian*, p 465, below.

Awad v Pillai
[1982] RTR 266, CA
Awad took his car to Pillai to be resprayed. The second defendant had taken her own car to him for the same purpose but it was not yet finished. Pillai lent her Awad's car representing that it was his own and that it was insured for her driving. She had an accident due to her negligent driving and the car was a total loss. Awad sued her for the amount of his loss. She denied liability to him on the ground that as she did not know it was his car and believed Pillai had authority to say she was properly insured, Awad was not a person to whom she owed a duty of care: he was not her 'neighbour' within Lord Atkin's famous words in *Donoghue v Stevenson*.
HELD: This was not right. The first person who was closely and directly affected by the second defendant's negligent driving was the owner of the car, Awad. He was a person to whom she owed a duty of care, and she was liable to him for the damage.

Farrugia v Great Western Rly Co
[1947] 2 All ER 565, CA
Defendants' lorry loaded with a large container attempted to drive under a low railway bridge. The container struck the bridge and was thrown off and injured the plaintiff. The plaintiff had been on the lorry as a trespasser, had just got off and was running along the highway to get on it again.
HELD: The vehicle and load were a potential danger to anyone on the highway in the near neighbourhood, and defendants owed such person a duty whether there lawfully or unlawfully. The plaintiff was within the area

of potential danger referred to in *Bourhill v Young* and might reasonably be expected to be injured. The plaintiff was lawfully on the highway; he was not trespassing on the defendants' vehicle. Judgment for plaintiff upheld.

Connelly v A. and W. Hemphill Ltd
[1949] WN 191, HL
A dock labourer and his mate were trucking goods unloaded from a ship into a shed. The truck was pushed alongside a stationary lorry from the rear to about halfway along the lorry and then turned away from the lorry. When turning the truck the plaintiff inadvertently placed his foot immediately in front of the rear wheel of the lorry. The lorry driver had started his engine, walked round the lorry, checked the load, ascertained that no one was near the rear wheels and then without warning drove forward slowly.

Plaintiff alleged failure to keep a proper look-out, starting from rest without warning and without ascertaining that it was safe. The Lord Ordinary found no negligence of the driver. The Second Division affirmed this decision.

HELD, ON APPEAL to the House of Lords: The plaintiff knew the lorry was ready to move off. The lorry driver was under no legal duty to give warning to the plaintiff that he was about to move off, which duty would only arise if he knew or ought reasonably to have known that danger to others might result. He neither knew nor ought reasonably to have known. Finding of no negligence upheld.

Setchell v Snowdon
[1974] RTR 389, CA
Snowdon and Ashton were acquainted with each other by being members of the same football team. Ashton asked Snowdon, who owned a car, to teach him to drive but Snowdon declined. When at a club together on the evening of that day Ashton asked Snowdon to lend him the key of his car, which was parked nearby, so that he could sit in it with a girl he had met. Ashton said expressly he did not want to drive the car. Snowdon lent him the key which was also the ignition key. When Ashton and the girl were in the car Ashton decided to drive it and, losing control, crashed it, severely injuring the girl. She sued Snowdon saying he should have realised Ashton might drive off in the car and was thereby negligent, knowing Ashton had not learned to drive. The judge accepted Snowdon's evidence that it never crossed his mind that Ashton would drive.

HELD: Snowdon was not liable. The test was: would a reasonable man in all the circumstances have realised that there was a real risk of Ashton driving the car? The answer was no; Snowdon had no reason to anticipate that Ashton would do something contrary to what he had promised and which would be in more than one respect a criminal offence.

Blind persons

Pritchard v Post Office
[1950] WN 310, 94 Sol Jo 404, CA
Post Office workmen opened a man-hole in the pavement and placed the

usual light wooden guard round the hole, which was adequate warning and protection to ordinary people. A woman totally blind walked along the pavement alone, collided with the guard which gave way and she fell in the hole.

HELD: Reasonable precautions had been taken for ordinary members of the public who could see. Post Office not liable.

Haley v London Electricity Board
[1965] AC 778, [1964] 3 All ER 185, [1964] 3 WLR 479, 129 JP 14, 108 Sol Jo 637, 63 LGR 1, HL.

The defendant's employees were searching for a cable in a trench dug along the pavement. They had put a punner-hammer in a sloping position across the pavement to stop pedestrians walking along it and make them walk in the road. Any person with ordinary sight would see it and walk in the roadway. The plaintiff, who was blind, was walking alone on the pavement. His stick passed over the hammer, giving him no warning of the danger and he fell into the trench.

HELD: The duty owed by those who engage in operations on the pavement of a highway is to take reasonable care not to act in a way likely to endanger other persons who may reasonably be expected to walk along the pavement. That duty is owed to blind persons if the operators foresee or ought to have foreseen that blind persons may walk along the pavement and is in no way different from the duty owed to persons with sight, though the carrying out of the duty may involve extra precautions in the case of blind pedestrians. It is common to find blind persons walking along pavements in London. The punner-hammer was not an adequate protection because the handle was low at one end and a blind person's stick feeling for obstructions could pass over it. But elaborate or expensive precautions were not necessary. A light fence two feet high (such as the respondents normally used and which they would have used had not work been started before the fence arrived) across the end of the trench would have been adequate to discharge the respondent's duty of care to the appellant. The respondents were liable.

Exceptional circumstances

Overseas Tankship (UK) Ltd v The Miller Steamship Co Pty (The Wagon Mound (No. 2))
[1967] 1 AC 617, [1966] 2 All ER 709, [1966] 3 WLR 498, 110 Sol Jo 447, PC.

As the result of the same fire as gave rise to the action and appeals in *Overseas Tankship (UK) Ltd v Morts Dock* (p 360, below) a ship belonging to the Miller Steamship Co Pty was damaged. On trial of their action the judge found that: (1) the officers of the *Wagon Mound* who allowed the oil to escape would regard furnace oil as very difficult to ignite on water; (2) in their experience this had very rarely happened; (3) they would have regarded it as a possibility which could become an actuality only in very exceptional circumstances. He held that the damage was not reasonably foreseeable by them.

HELD, ON APPEAL to the Privy Council: A risk cannot be regarded as not reasonably foreseeable merely because it is remote. If a real risk exists but is one that could only happen in very exceptional circumstances the defendant is not justified in dismissing the risk from his mind and doing nothing about it in circumstances where action to eliminate it presents no difficulty, involves no disadvantage and requires no expense. A reasonable man would weigh the risk against the difficulty and expense of eliminating it. In the present case no question of balancing advantages and disadvantages arose: it was both the interest and duty of the appellant defendants' servants to stop the discharge of oil immediately. In *The Wagon Mound (No 1)* the Board were not concerned with degrees of foreseeability because the finding there was that the fire was not foreseeable at all. In the present case the findings of fact showed some risk of fire would have been present to the mind of a reasonable man in the shoes of the defendants' servants. The defendants were liable.

Carmarthenshire County Council v Lewis

[1955] AC 549, [1955] 1 All ER 565, [1955] 2 WLR 517, 119 JP 230, 99 Sol Jo 167, 53 LGR 230, HL.

A schoolmistress in charge of a nursery school allowed a boy aged four years to stray. The child and another were in a room the door of which was not locked and could be opened by them. This door led into a yard which had a gate or door which also was not locked and could be opened by them. The gate opened on to a lane which led to a fairly busy street. The boy ran into the road in front of a lorry. The driver swerved violently to avoid the boy. The lorry struck a telegraph post and the driver was killed. There was no evidence as to the actual accident because the case proceeded on the basis that the deceased was driving carefully and that the only cause of his death was his effort to avoid injuring the child. The driver's widow sued the school authority.

HELD: There is a duty on the occupiers of premises adjoining a highway to prevent children of tender years unable to take care for their own safety, and whom a prudent parent would not allow to go into a street unaccompanied, from escaping on to the highway so as to endanger other persons lawfully passing upon it. The rule relating to domestic animals has no application. The escape of the child (which had not been explained) raised a presumption of negligence on the part of the authority which had not been rebutted. The consequences were foreseeable and the authority were liable in damages to the widow of the deceased.

Per Lord Goddard: I cannot think that it could be considered negligent in a mother to leave a child dressed ready to go out with her for a few moments and then, if she found another of her children hurt and in need of immediate attention, she could be blamed for giving it, without thinking of the child who was waiting to go out with her might wander off into the street.

Note—Their Lordships were careful to point out that the case did not purport to place an unlimited duty of care on mothers to prevent the escape of their children as they could not be expected to exercise continual supervision. In each case the question of what was reasonable depended on the circumstances (71 LQR 163).

70 LQR 6 commented on the decision of the Court of Appeal as follows: The present case is concerned with the duties of a school teacher to see that one of her charges does not stray into the highway. It has, however, wider implications, for it

is obvious that there must be a similar duty of care on the part of the parents. Would a mother who leaves a four-year-old child unattended in the street be liable if the child caused an accident? The answer would seem to be yes, because in these matters there cannot be a stricter duty of care for a teacher than there is for a parent.

It seems doubtful whether in any future case a defendant will concede that the driver was not negligent.

Volunteer

Sherrard v British Gates Ltd
(1984) Times, 25 February (Kilner Brown J)
The plaintiff sustained injuries in an accident while helping the defendants to load and move logs with his tractor.
HELD: He was legally a volunteer and some duty of care was owed him by the defendants as a 'neighbour', namely, to ensure there was a safe system of working and not to expose the plaintiff to risk of injury. On the facts, the plaintiff being an expert tractor driver, there was no breach of duty because no reasonably foreseeable risk of injury.

CONTRIBUTORY NEGLIGENCE

In order to establish the defence of contributory negligence, the defendant must prove, first, that the plaintiff failed to take 'ordinary care for himself' or, in other words, such care as a reasonable man would take for his own safety, and, second, that his failure to take care was a contributory cause of the accident: Per du Parcq LJ in *Lewis v Denye* [1939] 1 KB 540, [1939] 1 All ER 310, 108 LJKB 217, 160 LT 224, 55 TLR 391, 83 Sol Jo 192, CA.

The failure to take care

A plea of contributory negligence should be treated as setting up want of care by the plaintiff for his own safety, whether in the circumstances of the accident the plaintiff owed a duty to the defendant or not.

The statement that, when negligence is alleged as the basis of an actionable wrong, a necessary ingredient in the conception is the existence of a duty owed by the defendants to the plaintiff to take due care, is, of course, indubitably correct. But when contributory negligence is set up as a defence, its existence does not depend on any duty owed by the injured party to the party sued, and all that is necessary to establish such a defence is to prove that the injured party did not in his own interest take reasonable care of himself, and contributed, by that want of care, to his own injury. Where a man was part author of his own injury, he could not call on the other party to compensate him in full: *Davies v Swan Motor Co* (p 200, below) followed; *Nance v British Columbia Electric Rly Co Ltd* [1951] AC 601, [1951] 2 All ER 448, [1951] 2 TLR 137, 93 Sol Jo 543, PC.

The test of contributory negligence in the case of a pedestrian is not whether he is under a duty of care towards the defendant, but whether he was acting as a reasonable man and with reasonable care: per Denning LJ in *Davies v Swan Motor Co.*

Note—See note following *Dawrant v Nutt*, p 201, below.

The effect of contributory negligence

LAW REFORM (CONTRIBUTORY NEGLIGENCE) ACT 1945

(8 & 9 Geo 6 c 28)

1 Apportionment of liability in case of contributory negligence   (1) Where any person suffers damage as the result partly of his own fault and partly of the fault of any other person or persons, a claim in respect of that damage shall not be defeated by reason of the fault of the person suffering the damage, but the damages recoverable in respect thereof shall be reduced to such extent as the court thinks just and equitable having regard to the claimant's share in the responsibility for the damage:
   Provided that —
(a) this subsection shall not operate to defeat any defence arising under a contract;
(b) where any contract or enactment providing for the limitation of liability is applicable to the claim, the amount of damages recoverable by the claimant by virtue of this subsection shall not exceed the maximum limit so applicable.
(2) Where damages are recoverable by any person by virtue of the foregoing subsection subject to such reduction as is therein mentioned, the court shall find and record the total damages which would have been recoverable if the claimant had not been at fault.
(3) (*Repealed by the Civil Liability (Contribution) Act 1978, s 9(2).*)
(4) (*Replaced by the Fatal Accidents Act 1976, s 5: see note, below.*)
(5) Where, in any case to which subsection (1) of this section applies, one of the persons at fault avoids liability to any other such person or his personal representative by pleading the Limitation Act 1939, or any other enactment limiting the time within which proceedings may be taken, he shall not be entitled to recover any damages from that other person or representative by virtue of the said subsection.
(6) Where any case to which subsection (1) of this section applies is tried with a jury, the jury shall determine the total damages which would have been recoverable if the claimant had not been at fault and the extent to which those damages are to be reduced.

2 (*Replaced by the National Insurance (Industrial Injuries) Act 1946, s 89 (1) and Sch 9.*)

3 Saving for Maritime Conventions Act 1911, and past cases   (1) This Act shall not apply to any claim to which section one of the Maritime Conventions Act 1911, applies and that Act shall have effect as if this Act had not been passed.
(2) This Act shall not apply to any case where the acts or omissions giving rise to the claim occurred before the passing of this Act.

4 Interpretation   The following expressions have the meanings hereby respectively assigned to them that is to say —
'court' means, in relation to any claim, the court or arbitrator by or before whom the claim falls to be determined;
'damage' includes loss of life and personal injury;
'dependant' means any person for whose benefit an action could be brought under the Fatal Accidents Acts 1846 to 1959;
'fault' means negligence, breach of statutory duty or other act or omission which gives rise to a liability in tort or would, apart from this Act, give rise to the defence of contributory negligence.
. . . .

7 Short title and extent   This Act may be cited as the Law Reform (Contributory Negligence) Act 1945.

Note—In respect of causes of action arising from deaths on or after 1 September 1976, s 1(4) of the 1945 Act had been replaced by the Fatal Accidents Act 1976, s 5, which is as follows:

'**5 Contributory Negligence**   Where any person dies as the result partly of his own fault and partly of the fault of any other person or persons, and accordingly if an action were brought for the benefit of the estate under the Law Reform (Miscellaneous Provisions) Act 1934 the damages recoverable would be reduced under section 1 (1) of the Law Reform (Contributory Negligence) Act 1945, any damages recoverable in an action brought for the benefit of the dependants of that person under this Act shall be reduced to a proportionate extent.'

As from the same date the definition of 'dependant' in s 4 of the 1945 Act was repealed and was replaced by the definition in the Fatal Accidents Act 1976, s 1(3). In respect of deaths after 1982 that definition was itself replaced by the definition in s 1(3) of the 1976 Act substituted by the Administration of Justice Act 1982, s 3 (p 488, below). The words 'brought for the benefit of the dependants of that person' are to be omitted where the death occurred on or after 1 January 1983 (Administration of Justice Act 1982, s 4(2)).

The effect of the Act

Note—Before the Law Reform (Contributory Negligence) Act 1945 a plaintiff who was guilty of contributory negligence could recover no damages at all. The courts, having to decide between all or nothing, developed rules of causation intended to ascertain the 'sole effective cause' of the damage in cases where common logic might have led to the conclusion that there were two or more effective causes. The 1945 Act (above), in providing for apportionment of damages where the plaintiff's injury was partly his own fault has, in practice, rendered the old cases and tests obsolete.

Per Denning LJ in *Davies v Swan Motor Co* (p 200, below): Speaking generally, the questions in road accidents are simply these: What faults were there which caused the damage? What are the proportions in which the damages should be apportioned having regard to the respective responsibilities of those in fault?
   Questions of negligence and contributory negligence are pure questions of fact for the court, and the court finding of fact is binding if there is evidence to support it.

Basildon District Council v J. E. Lesser (Properties) Ltd
[1985] 1 All ER 20, [1984] 3 WLR 812, 128 Sol Jo 330, [1984] NLJ 330
(Judge Newey Q C Official Referee.)
On a clear and exact analysis of ss 1 and 4, the Law Reform (Contributory Negligence) Act 1945 does not apply to contracts.

Note—But see *Artingstoll v Hewens Garages Ltd*, p 248, below.

Maritrans (AB) v Comet Shipping Co Ltd
(1985) Times, 19 March (Neill L J)
A provision in a charterparty made the owners liable for bad stowage save
to the extent they were able to show that the charterers had by some intervention caused the loss or damage. On the facts of the case the charterers
were entitled to succeed in full unless the provisions of the 1945 Act entitled
the owners to claim an apportionment.
HELD: The 1945 Act was not applicable. The opening words of s 1(1) of
the Act were directed to tortious liabilities alone and were not apt to cover
breaches of contractual duties of care, even if they were described as negligent breaches of contract.

Last opportunity

Reference is still sometimes made to the supposed principle that the party
whose negligence was last in point of time, and who, therefore, could last
have avoided the accident, was liable.
    Denning, LJ in *Davies v Swan Motor Co* (p 200, below), said:

'The doctrine of "last opportunity", as a doctrine of law, was dead before the Law
Reform (Contributory Negligence) Act 1945, though it remained in use by some as
a practical test. Since the Act, it is no longer a practical test, and should disappear
from the books. It was not a principle of law, but a test of causation. It was a fallacious test, because the efficiency of the causes does not depend on their proximity
in point of time, but it held sway because it enabled the courts to mitigate the harsh-
ness of the doctrine of contributory negligence. It was superseded by the simple
test: What was the cause, or what were the causes, of the damage? Now the
doctrine has no place even as a test of causation.'

Note—See also *Chisman v Electromotion (Export) Ltd*, p 217, below.

Contributory negligence: children

Gough v Thorne
[1966] 3 All ER 398, [1966] 1 WLR 1387, 110 Sol Jo 529, CA.
Per Lord Denning MR: A very young child cannot be guilty of contributory negligence. An older child may be, but it depends on the circumstances. A judge should only find a child guilty of contributory negligence if
he or she is of such an age as to be expected to take precautions for his or her
own safety: and then he or she is only to be found guilty if blame should be
attached to him or her. A child has not the roadsense or the experience of
his or her elders. He or she is not to be found guilty unless he or she is
blameworthy.

Minter v D & H Contractors (Cambridge) Ltd
(1983) Times 30 June (Tudor Evans J)
The plaintiff, aged nine, ran into a pile of hardcore when riding his bicycle
and was injured. The hardcore had been negligently left in the roadway by
the defendants.
HELD: The degree to which an infant plaintiff could be capable of contri-

butory negligence was a question of fact in each case. The plaintiff, said in evidence to be 'a good rider', was not in the category of infants who were incapable of any contributory negligence. He was guilty of contributory negligence to the extent of 20%.

Note—See also p 72, below and *Jones v Lawrence*, p 74, below.

Identification

Note—The principle formerly known as the doctrine of identification is now exploded.

Oliver v Birmingham and Midland Motor Omnibus Co
[1933] 1 KB 35, 102 LJKB 65, 147 LT 317, 48 TLR 540, Div Ct
An infant, four years old, was crossing a road in the charge of his grandfather. He was struck by a motor omnibus and injured. The jury found that the accident occurred through the negligence of the driver and the contributory negligence of the grandfather.
HELD: The doctrine of identification was no longer part of the law of England and the infant was entitled to recover.

Note—And see *Morgan v Aylen*, p 41, below.

Contributory negligence of servant

Thompson v Bundy
(1938) Times 5 May
The plaintiff was a passenger in a car driven by her servant which collided with the defendant's car. The court found that the defendant's driver was negligent and that the plaintiff's servant was also negligent and his negligence contributed to the accident. In those circumstances there was no doubt as to the law. It was quite plain that, although a passenger in a vehicle was not identified with the driver, a person responsible for the acts of the driver might be disabled from recovering damages from another person for negligence if the accident was contributed to by the negligence of the driver for whom the passenger in the vehicle was responsible. In this case the plaintiff was, so to speak, driving a car through her appointed agent for whose negligence she was in law responsible vis-à-vis third parties.

Note—Contributory negligence not being, since the 1945 Act, a complete bar to the recovery of damages, the plaintiff would now have had her damages reduced by an amount proportionate to her servant's share of the blame.

Negligence requires reduction

Boothman v British Northrop
(1972) 13 KIR 112, CA
The plaintiff, injured in a factory accident, was held by the judge to have been negligent and his damages were reduced by 25%. On appeal counsel

submitted that even if the plaintiff was negligent it was not 'just and equitable' on the facts to reduce the damages.

HELD: The words of the Law Reform (Contributory Negligence) Act 1945, s 1(1) do not entitle a court which has found a plaintiff guilty of contributory negligence to disregard that negligence and make no deduction in the damages on the ground that it would be 'just and equitable' not to do so.

100% contributory negligence

Jayes v IMI (Kynoch) Ltd
[1984] LS Gaz R 3180, CA
The plaintiff, a production supervisor, was injured when he attempted to wipe grease off a moving belt with a rag. The rag was drawn in and his finger with it. He lost the end of his finger. He agreed that what he did was 'a crazy thing to do'. The judge assumed there was a breach of statutory duty by the employers under the Operation at Unfenced Machinery Regulations but held the plaintiff was entirely to blame.
HELD ON APPEAL: There was no principle of law that where there was a breach of statutory duty there could not be an award of 100% contributory negligence. The judge was entitled to decide in the way he did.

Responsibility for the damage

Note—See under 'Apportionment of Blame', p 23, below.

PLAINTIFF MOTOR CYCLIST NOT WEARING CRASH HELMET

Note—The Road Traffic Act 1962, s 41 (now the Road Traffic Act 1972, s 32) empowering the Minister of Transport to make regulations requiring persons driving or riding on motor cycles to wear protective headgear was brought into force as from 1 October 1971 by the Road Traffic Act 1962 (Commencement No 7) Order 1971 (S I 1971/1335).

The wearing of helmets by riders of motor cycles, scooters and mopeds was made compulsory by the Motor Cycles (Wearing of Helmets) Regulations (S I 1973/180) which came into force on 1 June 1973. Paragraph 29 of the 1978 Highway Code says 'when on a motorcycle, scooter or moped you must wear a safety helmet of approved design.' A Sikh is excused from wearing a helmet while he is wearing a turban (Motor Cycle Crash Helmets (Religious Exemption) Act 1976).

O'Connell v Jackson
[1972] 1 QB 270, [1971] 3 All ER 129, [1971] 3 WLR 463, 115 Sol Jo 742, CA
The plaintiff was riding his moped to work along a busy street when the defendant drove out in his car from a side street and collided with him. The plaintiff was thrown off and struck his head violently on the roadway sustaining a severe fracture of the skull. He was not wearing a crash helmet: he had intended buying one but had not done so. There was evidence from three doctors that the injury would have been less serious had he been wearing one. The judge held the defendant solely to blame for the accident. He also found that if the plaintiff had been wearing a helmet it would have

reduced the gravity of the head injuries but he declined to hold that the failure to wear one was contributory negligence.

HELD, ON THE DEFENDANTS' APPEAL: The Law Reform (Contributory Negligence) Act 1945 required damages to be reduced according to 'the claimant's share in the responsibility for the damage.' In *Jones v Livox Quarries* (p 201, below) Denning LJ had said a person was guilty of contributory negligence if he ought reasonably to have foreseen that if he did not act as a reasonably prudent man he might be hurt himself, and in his reckonings he must take into account the possibility of others being careless. Applying this test the plaintiff ought to have foreseen when travelling through a busy traffic area the possibility of an accident occurring even though he himself drove carefully and that he could well sustain greater hurt if he failed to wear a helmet. He knew as was clear from his own evidence, that it was a sensible practice to wear one. The plaintiff was partly to blame for the additional injury he sustained by not wearing a helmet and the reduction of damages should amount to 15% of the whole.

Note—See also 'Seat belts', p 204, below.

Contributory negligence not pleaded

Fookes v Slaytor
[1979] RTR 40, CA
The plaintiff, driving his car at night, collided with a stationary unlighted lorry and was injured. He sued the driver of the lorry in the county court. The driver filed no defence, did not attend on the trial and was not represented. The judge awarded damages to the plaintiff but reduced them by one-third on the ground that he was contributorily negligent.

HELD, ON APPEAL: The judge was not entitled to find contributory negligence against the plaintiff when it had not been pleaded. The damages should not have been reduced.

TRESPASS

Note—Attempts have sometimes been made by pleading a cause of action in trespass to avoid some disadvantage from having to prove, or establish a cause of action in, negligence. The following cases show that, in motor claims at least, no advantage is to be gained. See also *Winfield and Jolowicz on Tort* (12th edn) pp 116–119.

Gayler and Pope Ltd v Davies
[1924] 2 KB 75, 93 LJKB 702, 131 LT 507, 40 TLR 591, 68 Sol Jo 685
The plaintiffs, shopkeepers with premises adjoining the highway, claimed damages for negligence or trespass against the owner of a runaway pony and van which dashed into the shop window.

On the question whether an action for trespass lay irrespective of negligence, McCardie J stated that the practice for 30 years had been that where a horse and cart or motor car came upon the plaintiff's premises adjoining a highway, the defendant is not liable in the absence of negligence, and held that the plaintiff could not recover on the ground of trespass, and that the plaintiff must prove negligence.

Fowler v Lanning
[1959] 1 QB 426, [1959] 1 All ER 290, 103 Sol Jo 157 (Diplock J)
The plaintiff sued for trespass to the person. The statement of claim alleged that the defendant shot the plaintiff. It was stated this occurred at a shooting party when a shot from a gun fired by the defendant injured the plaintiff. It was not suggested the shooting was intentional. The defence pleaded that the statement of claim disclosed no cause of action as the plaintiff did not allege that the shooting was either intentional or negligent. An order was made that the point of law should be heard and disposed of before the trial of the issues of fact in the action.

The questions raised were whether the onus lies on the plaintiff to prove that the defendant was negligent, and to plead particulars of the negligence (RSC Ord XIX, r 25, now replaced by Ord 18, r 7), or whether it lay on the defendant to prove that he was not negligent.
HELD: (1) Trespass to the person does not lie if the injury to the plaintiff, although the direct consequence of the act of the defendant, was caused unintentionally and without negligence on the defendant's part. (2) Trespass to the person on the highway does not differ in this respect from trespass to the person committed in any other place. (3) Where the injury is the result of neither intention nor carelessness, the plaintiff takes upon himself the risk of inevitable injury. (4) The onus of proving negligence, where the trespass is not intentional, lies on the plaintiff, whether the action be framed in trespass or in negligence.

The statement of claim as delivered disclosed no cause of action. Leave to amend.

Letang v Cooper
[1965] 1 QB 232, [1964] 2 All ER 929, [1964] 3 WLR 573, 108 Sol Jo 519, [1964] 2 Lloyd's Rep 339, CA
On 10 July 1957 the plaintiff, on holiday in Cornwall, lay sunbathing on a piece of grass where cars were parked. The defendant entered the car park in his car, failed to see the plaintiff and drove over her legs causing her injury. On 2 February 1961 she issued a writ against him for damages for injury caused by (1) his negligent driving, (2) the commission by him of a trespass to the person. Under the Law Reform (Limitation of Actions, &c.) Act 1954 the limitation period was three years for 'actions for damages for negligence, nuisance or breach of duty (whether the duty exists by virtue of a contract or of provision made by or under a statute or independently of any contract or any such provision)' where the damages were claimed for personal injuries. On trial of a preliminary issue whether the action was statute-barred Elwes J held that a cause of action in trespass results from a direct injury actionable per se without proof of damage and is different from a cause of action in negligence: the latter is descended from the form of action known as trespass on the case and gives the plaintiff no action until he proves a breach of a particular duty owed to him and damage resulting therefrom. As there was a direct injury to the plaintiff there was a cause of action in trespass: this was not an action for 'negligence, nuisance or breach of duty' and the Act did not apply.

HELD, ON APPEAL: The decision was wrong for two reasons: (1) The distinction between trespass and case is obsolete. Instead of dividing actions for personal injuries into trespass (direct damage) or case (consequential damage) we now divide causes of action according as the defendant did the injury intentionally or unintentionally. If a man does injury unintentionally the plaintiff has no cause of action in trespass: his only cause of action is negligence. The action was thus barred by express provision of the statute. Per Lord Denning MR: The modern law on this subject was well expounded by Diplock J in *Fowler v Lanning*, with which I fully agree. But I would go this one step further: when the injury is not inflicted intentionally, but negligently, I would say that the only cause of action is negligence and not trespass. If it were trespass, it would be actionable without proof of damage; and that is not the law today.

(2) The words 'breach of duty' in the statute cover not only negligence and nuisance and breach of contractual or statutory duty but also a breach of any duty in tort: they are wide enough to comprehend the cause of action for trespass to the person as well as negligence. The action was thus one for 'breach of duty' and barred by the statute.

Note—In *Long v Hepworth* [1968] 3 All ER 248, [1968] 1 WLR 1299, 112 Sol Jo 485 Cooke J held, following *Letang v Cooper*, that even an intentional trespass was a 'breach of duty' for the purpose of the Law Reform (Limitation of Actions, &c.) Act 1954, s 2 (1) — a case in which the plaintiff, a schoolgirl, was hit in the eye by a handful of cement thrown at her by a workman.

Section 2 (1) of the 1954 Act was replaced by the Limitation Act 1939, s 2A contained in the Limitation Act 1975, s 1, preserving the phrase 'breach of duty' (see p 533, below). The phrase 'breach of duty' is again preserved in the Limitation Act 1980, s 11 which replaces s 2A of the 1939 Act.

CONTRIBUTION BETWEEN TORTFEASORS

Note—When an injured party has suffered damage by the negligence of two or more persons, whether acting in concert or not, he may recover the whole of his damage from any one of them, or may sue all of them jointly in the same action. Formerly, joint wrongdoers or those severally liable for the same damage had no right of contribution or indemnity against each other. The rule was altered by the Law Reform (Married Women and Tortfeasors) Act 1935, s 6 which enabled tortfeasors to recover contribution from any other tortfeasor who was, or would if sued have been, liable in respect of the same damage. This section of the 1935 Act was repealed and replaced with effect from 1 January 1979 by the Civil Liability (Contribution) Act 1978. Under this Act contribution may be claimed even if one or both of those concerned is liable to the plaintiff otherwise than in tort.

CIVIL LIABILITY (CONTRIBUTION) ACT 1978

Proceedings for contribution

1 Entitlement to contribution   (1) Subject to the following provisions of this section, any person liable in respect of any damage suffered by another person may recover contribution from any other person liable in respect of the same damage (whether jointly with him or otherwise).

(2) A person shall be entitled to recover contribution by virtue of subsection (1) above notwithstanding that he has ceased to be liable in respect of the damage in question since the time when the damage occurred, provided that he was so liable immediately before he made or was ordered or agreed to make the payment in respect of which the contribution is sought.

(3) A person shall be liable to make contribution by virtue of subsection (1) above notwithstanding that he has ceased to be liable in respect of the damage in question since the time when the damage occurred, unless he ceased to be liable by virtue of the expiry of a period of limitation or prescription which extinguished the right on which the claim against him in respect of the damage was based.

(4) A person who has made or agreed to make any payment in bona fide settlement or compromise of any claim made against him in respect of any damage (including a payment into court which has been accepted) shall be entitled to recover contribution in accordance with this section without regard to whether or not he himself is or ever was liable in respect of the damage, provided, however, that he would have been liable assuming that the factual basis of the claim against him could be established.

(5) A judgement given in any action brought in any part of the United Kingdom by or on behalf of the person who suffered the damage in question against any person from whom contribution is sought under this section shall be conclusive in the proceedings for contribution as to any issue determined by that judgement in favour of the person from whom the contribution is sought.

(6) References in this section to a person's liability in respect of any damage are references to any such liability which has been or could be established in an action brought against him in England and Wales by or on behalf of the person who suffered the damage; but it is immaterial whether any issue arising in any such action was or would be determined (in accordance with the rules of private international law) by reference to the law of a country outside England and Wales.

Note—Subsection (3) gives statutory effect to the decision in *Hart v Hall and Pickles Ltd* (p 635, below) and preserves the effect of such cases as *George Wimpey & Co Ltd v British Overseas Airways Corpn* (p 551, below). Subsection (4) disposes of the difficulty met with by defendants who have settled a plaintiff's claim and seek contribution from another tortfeasor who was not a party to or bound by, the settlement, e g as in *Stott v West Yorks Road Car Co Ltd* (p 604, below). See also *Harper v Gray and Walker* [1985] 2 All ER 507, [1985] 1 WLR 1196.

Logan v Uttlesford District Council
[1984] NLJ 500 (Sheen J)
A third party who had ceased to be liable to the plaintiff by having settled the plaintiff's claim against him is not entitled to have a third party notice and statement of claim against him struck out. The Civil Liability (Contribution) Act 1978, s 1(3) relieves a person from liability to contribute only if he has ceased to be liable by effluxion of time. A settlement did not come within that proviso.

2 Assessment of contribution   (1) Subject to subsection (3) below, in any proceedings for contribution under section 1 above the amount of the contribution recoverable from any person shall be such as may be found by the court to be just and equitable having regard to the extent of that person's responsibility for the damage in question.

(2) Subject to subsection (3) below, the court shall have power in any such proceedings to exempt any person from liability to make contribution, or to direct that the contribution to be recovered from any person shall amount to a complete indemnity.

(3) Where the amount of the damages which have or might have been awarded in respect of the damage in question in any action brought in England and Wales by

or on behalf of the person who suffered it against the person from whom the contribution is sought was or would have been subject to —
(a) any limit imposed by or under any enactment or by any agreement made before the damage occurred;
(b) any reduction by virtue of section 1 of the Law Reform (Contributory Negligence) Act 1945 or section 5 of the Fatal Accidents Act 1976; or
(c) any corresponding limit or reduction under the law of a country outside England and Wales;
the person from whom the contribution is sought shall not by virtue of any contribution awarded under section 1 above be required to pay in respect of the damage a greater amount than the amount of those damages as so limited or reduced.

3 Proceedings against persons jointly liable for the same debt or damage
Judgement recovered against any person liable in respect of any debt or damage shall not be a bar to an action, or to the continuance of an action, against any other person who is (apart from any such bar) jointly liable with him in respect of the same debt or damage.

4 Successive actions against persons liable (jointly or otherwise) for the same damage If more than one action is brought in respect of any damage by or on behalf of the person by whom it was suffered against persons liable in respect of the damage (whether jointly or otherwise) the plaintiff shall not be entitled to costs in any of those actions, other than that in which judgement is first given, unless the court is of the opinion that there was reasonable ground for bringing the action.

Limitation period

A tortfeasor who wishes to recover contribution from another tortfeasor who is liable for the same damage must bring the action for contribution within two years from the date on which the judgment or award was made against him or on which he admitted liability for the amount in respect of which he claims contribution: Limitation Act 1980, s 10. See p 550, below.

Statutory duty: common law

Dooley v Cammell Laird & Co Ltd
[1951] 1 Lloyd's Rep 271 (Donovan J)
The plaintiff was a crane driver employed by shipbuilders, and the crane and plaintiff as driver were loaned to contractors working on the ship. The contractors supplied the sling and rope. The sling was unsuitable and the rope defective and the rope broke and plaintiff was injured.
   The contractors contended that as the liability of the shipbuilders was for breach of statutory duty and that of the contractors was breach of common law, they were not joint tortfeasors and there was no liability to contribute. HELD: There was no authority for such a proposition, and it made no difference to the right to contribute what was just and equitable.

Nature of right to contribution

Ronex Properties Ltd v John Laing Construction Ltd
[1983] QB 398, [1982] 3 All ER 961, [1982] 3 WLR 875, 126 Sol Jo 727, CA
A building built for the plaintiffs in 1972 began to show defects in 1974.

They issued a writ in 1978 against the builders and the architects. In 1979 the architects issued third-party proceedings against consulting engineers for indemnity or contribution under the Law Reform (Married Women and Tortfeasors) Act 1935, s 6 and at common law alleging breach of contract and/or negligence. The sole surviving partner of the firm of architects died in 1980: the plaintiffs obtained an order to carry on against his personal representatives. The third parties then applied to strike out the third-party notice on the ground that it disclosed no reasonable cause of action, since any right to recover contribution under the 1935 Act had been extinguished by the death of the architect. The third parties' argument was that the Law Reform (Miscellaneous Provisions) Act 1934, s 1 provided for the survival against the estate of a deceased person only of 'causes of action' and the architects had no cause of action until (which had not yet happened) they were found liable, or admitted liability, to the plaintiffs; and that the maxim *actio personalis moritur cum persona* applied to destroy any right in the architects to claim contribution.

HELD: It was no doubt right that no right to contribution arose under the 1935 Act unless the defendant was found liable to the plaintiff and that there was no subsisting cause of action in the architect at the time of his death which the 1934 Act could preserve, but it was not the case that the right to claim contribution died with him. It was a defined inchoate right and not a mere hope or expectation. The rule that a personal action dies with the person does not apply to that right, which passed to his personal representatives for the benefit of his estate under the law of succession.

Absence of person possibly liable

Maxfield v Llewellyn
[1961] 3 All ER 95, [1961] 1 WLR 1119, 105 Sol Jo 550, CA
The plaintiff's husband was killed when riding as a pillion passenger on a motor cycle. The motor cyclist was also killed. The plaintiff alleged that the accident was caused by the negligent parking of vehicle A and the negligent driving of vehicle B. She sued the owners and drivers of the two vehicles, but not the personal representatives of the motor cyclist, though there was evidence that he may have been travelling too fast. The Court having held the owners and drivers of both vehicles liable it was argued on behalf of the owners of vehicle A that the Law Reform (Married Women and Tortfeasors) Act 1935, s 6(2) did not empower the Court to apportion blame and order contribution as between the defendants when a person whose negligence may have contributed to the accident was not a party to the action.

HELD: The argument could not be supported. The duty of the Court was to apportion blame for the accident as between the defendants before the Court. The section would otherwise be unworkable. The Court must first consider whether the defendants were liable and then make such apportionment as may be 'just and equitable having regard to the extent of that person's responsibility for the damage'. That meant as between the defendants before the Court. The defendants could bring a separate action, if they thought it was worthwhile, asking for contribution against the personal representatives of the motor cyclist.

APPORTIONMENT OF BLAME

Note—The words in s 2 (1) 'such as may be found by the court to be just and equit-able having regard to the extent of that person's responsibility for the damage in question' present the same problem of interpretation as the words in the Law Reform (Contributory Negligence) Act 1945, s 1 (p 12, above) 'to such extent as the court thinks just and equitable having regard to the claimant's share in the responsibility for the damage'. Should proportions be assessed by reference to the extent to which the negligent acts of the parties caused the damage, or should the division depend on the relative blameworthiness of the parties? The conclusion to be drawn from the decided cases is that whilst causation is not to be ignored the degree of blameworthiness is the more important factor. The following cases include decisions on both Acts.

Croston v Vaughan
[1938] 1 KB 540 at 565
Per Scott LJ: In spite of the illogical details of the language of subsection (2) [of the 1935 Act, s 6] I think that that section should be read as giving the judge, on the evidence that he has heard, complete jurisdiction to assess the blame of each tortfeasor just as if he had held them liable as defendants to the plaintiff only for that portion of the blame.

Davies v Swan Motor Co
[1949] 2 KB 291, [1949] 1 All ER 620, 65 TLR 278, CA
Per Denning LJ: While causation is the decisive factor in determining whether there should be a reduced amount payable to the plaintiff, never-theless the amount of the reduction does not depend solely on the degree of causation. The amount of the reduction is such an amount as may be found by the court to be 'just and equitable' having regard to the claimant's 'share in the responsibility' for the damage. This involves a consideration, not only of the causative potency of a particular factor, but also of its blame-worthiness. The fact of standing on the steps of the dustcart is just as potent a factor in causing damage, whether the person standing there be a servant acting negligently in the course of his employment or a boy in play or a youth doing it for a 'lark' but the degree of blameworthiness may be very different.

Daniel v Rickett Cockerell & Co Ltd
[1938] 2 KB 322
Per Hilbery J: When I see the words ['just and equitable'] are coupled with 'having regard to the extent of that person's responsibility' I think the meaning of the subsection is that exercising a judicial discretion in the matter I am intended to do that which I think is right between the parties, having regard to what I think, on the true facts of the case, is the fair division of responsibility between them.

Note—The view taken by the same judge in *Collins v Hertfordshire County Council* ([1947] KB 598) that 'responsibility' had a causative connotation was considered and rejected by Hallett J in *Weaver v Commercial Process Co Ltd*:

Weaver v Commercial Process Co Ltd
(1947) 63 TLR 466 (Hallett J)

The second defendants supplied the first defendants with a jar of nitric acid which was cracked, and which broke when being handled by a young employee of the first defendants, injuring the plaintiff.

HELD: Both defendants were liable in damages, which were to be apportioned under s 6 (2) of the 1935 Act. In *Collins's* case Mr Justice Hilbery appeared to have come to the view that the contribution must be apportioned not according to the relative negligence, that is culpability, of the two tortfeasors but according to the relative effect of their acts in causing the damage. The same judge's decision in *Daniel's* case (above) was preferable — to exercise a judicial discretion so as to do what is right between such parties having regard to what appears, on the facts, to be the fair division of the responsibility between them. By far the greater responsibility for the casualty should be laid on the shoulders of the second defendants. They were the suppliers of the cracked jar of nitric acid to the first defendants who were entitled to rely on them to supply a jar that was safe to handle. Apportionment 90% second defendants.

Cavanagh v London Transport Executive
(1956) 222 LT Jo 333, (1956) Times, 23 October (Devlin J)

The deceased was crossing the Strand, and stepped off a centre refuge behind a stationary taxi-cab, and was knocked down by a bus. The deceased neither saw nor heard the bus, but the driver braked and nearly avoided an accident.

HELD: If the sole test was 'causative potency' the assessment would be approximately an equal division of responsibility; if 'blameworthiness' were the only test, the driver's responsibility would be assessed at 20%. Giving effect to both tests, the defendant's contribution was one-third.

Brown v Thompson
[1968] 2 All ER 708, [1968] 1 WLR 1003, 112 Sol Jo 464, CA

Mrs Brown was injured when a car driven by her husband collided with the rear of the defendant's lorry. The accident occurred at about 3 am in winter on an unlighted road. The lorry had no lights and was without reflectors. Mr Brown did not see the lorry until just before the accident and was turning out to avoid it when he hit it. The judge apportioned liability 80% to the defendant and 20% to Mr Brown. The defendant appealed contending that 50% responsibility should be apportioned to Mr Brown.

HELD: Dismissing the appeal, regard must be had not only to the causative potency of the acts or omissions of each of the parties but to their relative blameworthiness (citing *The Miraflores* (below)). The act of driving in such a manner that the driver failed to turn out and ran into the back of a stationary vehicle was in a high degree potently causative of the injuries suffered by Mrs Brown. Equally it was potently causative of the collision that the lorry was left in the position it was without lights. But when one looked at the blameworthiness then it seemed plain that Mr Brown's fault was really quite small.

Note—See also *Baker v Willoughby*, p 87, below.

Palser v Grinling
[1948] AC 291, [1948] 1 All ER 1 (Lord Simon)
The words 'have regard to' in the Law Reform (Contributory Negligence)
Act 1945, s 1 (1) call for the exercise of a broad judgment and any arithmetical conclusion is qualified by what is deemed to be fair and reasonable.

Note—See also *Newport Borough Council v Monmouthshire County Council* [1947] AC
520, [1947] 1 All ER 900, HL.

Gregory v Kelly
[1978] RTR 426 (Jones J)
The defendant was driving his mini car at a time when the footbrake was
completely inoperative because part of the hydraulic system was missing.
The plaintiff, a passenger in the defendant's car, knew the brakes did not
work; furthermore he was not wearing the seat belt provided. The defendant, driving at about 40 mph on a narrow country road was confronted,
on rounding a bend, with a vehicle parked partly on the roadway on his
nearside. Being unable to brake he pulled out to overtake and crashed into
a car coming in the opposite direction.
HELD: (1) The defendant's negligence was of a high order in driving too
fast and in so driving when he knew he had no footbrake; (2) the plaintiff
was negligent in not wearing a seat belt and additionally in travelling in the
car as a passenger when he knew from the start it had no operative footbrake. In assessing the respective fault or blameworthiness of the two
parties it would not be right to assess the percentages of negligence or contributory negligence separately and add them up. The matter must be
looked at generally. Apportionment of blame 60% on the defendant, 40%
on the plaintiff.

More than two parties to blame: principles of assessment

The Miraflores and The Abadesa
[1967] 1 AC 826, [1967] 1 All ER 672, [1967] 2 WLR 806, 111 Sol Jo 211,
HL
The *Miraflores* and the *Abadesa* collided in the River Scheldt. The *George
Livanos*, following the *Miraflores*, was presented with a difficulty and, failing
to take action in time to avoid it, ran aground. In actions to determine liability for the damage caused to the vessels the judge first apportioned liability for the collision between the *Miraflores* and *Abadesa* at one-third and
two-thirds respectively. Then to ascertain liability for damage to the *George
Livanos* due to grounding he treated the negligence of the other two vessels
leading to the collision as one unit and the negligence of the *George Livanos* in
running aground as the other. Finding the *George Livanos* one-half to blame
for the grounding he awarded the owners one-half of their damage to be
paid two thirds by the *Abadesa* and one-third by the *Miraflores*.
HELD, ON APPEAL: The 'unit approach' was wrong. In assessing degrees
of fault blameworthiness as well as causation must be considered — it is
necessary to weigh the fault of each negligent party against each of the
others separately and not conjunctively: by putting the several acts of negligence of the *Abadesa* and *Miraflores* into one characterless 'unit' the judge

did not measure their respective blameworthiness against the blameworthiness of the *George Livanos*. The proportions of fault in the other two ships for the grounding of the *George Livanos* should be assessed at two-fifths to the *Abadesa* and one-fifth to the *Miraflores*.

Per Lord Pearce: The Law Reform (Contributory Negligence) Act 1945, s 1 does not give any support to the unit approach. Its intention was to allow the plaintiff, though negligent, to recover damages reduced to such an extent as the Court thinks just and equitable, having regard to his share in the responsibility for the damage (s 1 (1)). But that share can only be estimated by weighing his fault against that of the defendant or, if there are two defendants, against that of each defendant. It is true that apportionment as between the defendants comes theoretically at a later stage (under the Law Reform (Married Women and Tortfeasors) Act 1935). But as a matter of practice the whole matter is decided at one time and the Court weighs up the fault of *each* in assessing liability as between plaintiff and defendants themselves. And I see nothing in the 1945 Act to show that it intends the Court to treat the joint defendants as a unit whose joint blameworthiness could only, one presumes, be the aggregate blameworthiness of its differing components.

Contribution may be 100%

Ryan v Fildes
[1938] 3 All ER 517
Per Tucker J: The section contemplates a contribution amounting to 100%, which is in effect an indemnity.

Whitby v Burt, Boulton and Hayward Ltd
[1947] KB 918, [1947] 2 All ER 324, [1947] LJR 1280, 177 LT 556, 111 JP 481, 63 TLR 458, 91 Sol Jo 517 (Denning J)
A workman was injured whilst employed by building contractors engaged on repairing a factory. The occupiers of the factory were held liable for failing to provide safe means of access under the Factories Act 1937, s 26; the employers were held liable for unsafe system. The occupiers were granted indemnity against the employers. *Ryan v Fildes* (100% contribution) followed.

Lavender v Diamints Ltd
[1948] 2 All ER 249, 92 Sol Jo 362 (Denning J)
The duty of the court in deciding the plaintiff's share of responsibility under s 1 (1) of the 1945 Act is similar to that under the 1935 Act, and the decision in *Whitby v Burt, Boulton and Hayward* above is relevant. The 1935 Act expressly mentions a complete imdemnity but the 1945 Act does not, but the plaintiff's share may be, for all practical purposes, the whole responsibility.

Note—See now the Civil Liability (Contribution) Act 1978, s 2 (2).

Appeal against apportionment

Note—Appellate courts have expressed divergent views on the question whether, as a matter of principle, the apportionment of blame determined by the trial judge should be altered. The restrictive rule adopted by the House of Lords in *British Fame v MacGregor* (below) was not adopted in *Quintas v National Smelting Co* and some later cases (p 29, below).

'BRITISH FAME' CASES

British Fame v MacGregor
[1943] AC 197, [1943] 1 All ER 33, 112 LJP 6, 168 LT 193, 59 TLR 61, 86 Sol Jo 367, 74 Ll L Rep 82, HL
The decision of the Court of Appeal in *The Testbank* [1942] P 75, [1942] 1 All ER 281, that the apportionment was open to the same right of appeal as any other conclusion of fact by the judge was overruled on the ground that the statement is too wide.

The House of Lords decided that the finding of the trial judge as to the degrees of blame to be attributed to two or more tortfeasors involves an individual choice or discretion and will not be interfered with on appeal save in very exceptional circumstances, e g if the trial judge has misapprehended a vital fact (per Viscount Simon LC), or there is some error in law or in fact in his judgment (*The Otranto* [1931] AC 194) or he has misinterpreted a rule of navigation (*The Peter Benoit* (1915) 84 LJP 87).

The apportionment of damages is unlike an ordinary finding of fact, and the rules applicable to one are not applicable to the other. It is a question, not of principle or of positive findings of fact or law, but of proportion, of balance and relative emphasis, and of weighing different considerations. It involves an individual choice or discretion.

Mulligan v Holmes
[1971] RTR 179, CA
Per Salman LJ: In considering what proportion of blame they should bear one has to consider the degree of blameworthiness and causative effect attaching to the negligence of the respective parties. This court interferes only in the most exceptional cases with an apportionment of blame. It is not enough for us to say: 'Well, if we had been trying this case we would have apportioned the blame rather differently from the way in which the judge apportioned it.' It is only if we come to a clear conclusion that the apportionment of blame is quite unreasonable and cannot be defended that we are entitled to interfere.

Ingram v United Automobile Service Ltd
[1943] KB 612, [1943] 2 All ER 71, CA
A lorry of the first defendants was left near a bend on an icy road in the black-out. A bus of the second defendants in passing ran into a bridge and a passenger was injured and sued both defendants. The trial judge found both defendants liable and apportioned two-thirds of the liability to the lorry owners and one-third to the bus owners.
HELD, ON APPEAL: The Court of Appeal should not interfere with the

apportionment. The same rule applies as in collisions at sea: *British Fame v MacGregor* was applied.

Hardy v Walder
[1984] RTR 312, CA
The plaintiff, riding a motor cycle, overtook a car at 55 to 60 mph on a blind corner just before reaching a junction with a minor road on the left. The defendant, driving a car, came out of the minor road across dotted white lines without stopping; he looked both ways initially but was looking to his left as he entered the major road and the plaintiff crashed into the side of the car. The judge held the plaintiff two-thirds to blame: he appealed. It was argued on his behalf that the blind overtaking and the excessive speed were irrelevant since he was so near the car when it came out that a collision could not have been avoided whatever his speed.
HELD, DISMISSING THE APPEAL: It was impossible to say that the accident was caused otherwise than by the negligence of both parties. There was no reason to interfere with the judge's apportionment of blame.

Admiralty Commissioners v North of Scotland etc Co Ltd
[1947] 2 All ER 350, HL
An appellate court should not undertake to alter the proportions fixed by the judge who tried the case save as in exceptional circumstances such as· were indicated in *British Fame v MacGregor* (above) and no such exceptional circumstances are shown to exist here.

Johnson v Stockland Garage
(1949) 99 LJ 315, [1949] CLY 2646
The Court of Appeal will not interfere with an apportionment made by a county court of liability as between two defendants. The apportionment is a matter for the judge and his decision could not be interfered with if supported by the evidence.

Brown v Thompson
[1968] 2 All ER 708, [1968] 1 WLR 1003, 112 Sol Jo 464, CA
In a case where liability had been apportioned 80/20 it was argued on behalf of the appellant that where some blame had been attributed to a party by the trial judge the appellate court was at liberty to substitute its own opinion on the proportion.
HELD: This was quite wrong. The principle was, as Lord Wright said in *British Fame v MacGregor* (above) that it would require a very strong case to justify any review of or interference with the question of apportionment. There should be no interference with the judge's view where no error of principle is alleged and no misapprehension of the fact on the part of the judge is suggested.

'QUINTAS' CASES

Stapley v Gypsum Mines Ltd
[1953] AC 663, [1953] 2 All ER 478, 97 Sol Jo 486, HL

A miner in a gypsum mine, and a fellow workman of equal status, neither being in charge of the other, were directed by a foreman to bring down the roof of a stope, where they were intending to work, as it was unsafe and likely to fall. They tried to bring it down, without success, and then jointly agreed to stop and resume their ordinary work. The miner went to work in the stope but the fellow workman did other work. Both men were in breach of the Metalliferous Mines General Regulations 1938, reg 15. The deceased was killed by a fall of roof.

HELD: In obeying the foreman's order, both were equally negligent and in breach of their duty, and their negligence was so 'mixed up' that the fault of the fellow workman contributed to the accident, and his employers were liable. The negligence of the deceased contributed more to the accident than the negligence of the fellow workman. Deceased's share of responsibility, 80%; employers', 20%.

Quintas v National Smelting Co Ltd
[1961] 1 All ER 630, [1961] 1 WLR 401, 105 Sol Jo 152, CA

The plaintiff appealed against a finding that he was 75% to blame.

Per Sellers LJ: The question arises whether it is just and equitable to deprive the plaintiff of so much. The difference between one-quarter and one-half to blame is over £2,000 and I do not think that we are obliged to hold that a plaintiff to whom such a sum would be very substantial should be deprived of an effective appeal on apportionment if this Court thought the apportionment to be wrong. In *Stapley v Gypsum Mines Ltd* the House of Lords altered the apportionment and since then this Court has from time to time also done so on similar grounds to those on which it would alter an assessment of damages.

Kerry v Carter
[1969] 3 All ER 723, [1969] 1 WLR 1372, 113 Sol Jo 704, CA

In an appeal on apportionment in an action for damages for personal injury sustained by an agricultural apprentice on his employer's farm *Brown v Thompson* (above) was referred to. Lord Denning MR said he would prefer in cases of apportionment to get away from the test in Admiralty cases and say simply that if the Court was satisfied that apportionment was clearly wrong it should intervene and alter it.

Husband and wife

Mallet v Dunn
[1949] 2 KB 180, [1949] 1 All ER 973, 65 TLR 307 (Hilbery J)

The plaintiffs, husband and wife, were walking along a road when the wife was struck and injured by a car driven by the defendant. The defendant was held three-quarters to blame, the wife one-quarter, and her damages reduced proportionately under the Law Reform (Contributory Negligence) Act 1945. The husband claimed special damages for loss and expense incurred by him arising from the injuries to his wife. It was argued for the defendant that either the 1945 Act did not apply to the husband's claim and his wife's contributory negligence destroyed it, or that his claim should be reduced by the same amount as hers.

HELD: The husband and wife was entitled to succeed in full. His cause of action was quite separate from that of his wife. A husband had always had at common law a remedy, enforced by an action on the case, for an injury done to him by an interference with his right of consortium and for the consequential damage done to him. The wife's own negligence was immaterial. The husband had merely to show that the defendant was negligent in a way which was partly the cause of the injury to his wife and he was entitled to succeed without reduction of the damages. As the husband's cause of action was separate and distinct from the claim made by his wife it followed that the 1945 Act did not apply to it, since the Act applies only to a case where the claimant suffers damage 'as the result partly of his own fault' (s 1).

Note—For 'consortium' see now Administration of Justice Act 1982, s 2, p 417, below.

Indemnity before supplying evidence

Note—A motorist is sometimes asked by a third party to supply evidence against another motorist. To provide against being dragged in as a second defendant it is prudent to require an indemnity in the following form:

Indemnity

I/We hereby undertake that no claim or allegation of negligence will be made by me/us or action be
brought against...or their servants in connection with
an occurrence at ....on the.....................................day of...................................

Signed...................................

Costs on apportionment

The Trivia
[1952] 1 Lloyd's Rep 548 (Wilmer J)
The procedure in Admiralty is different from the QBD where defendant can pay in. The principle in respect of costs is therefore different.

Note—Hence shipping cases are no guide to apportionment of costs in motor cases.

MacCarthy v Raylton Productions
[1951] WN 376, 95 Sol Jo 381, CA
Collision between two motor vehicles; the trial judge held plaintiff alone to blame. On appeal, the Court of Appeal held plaintiff two-thirds to blame and defendant one-third. Defendant contended costs should be apportioned in the same proportions.

HELD: Costs were in the discretion of the court. Where a case raised several distinct issues, it might be a proper exercise of discretion to apportion costs, but the practice is, costs follow the event. Here, all the facts had to be gone into, whether the claim was for the whole of the damages suffered or was limited to a part of them. Plaintiff awarded costs in Court of Appeal and below.

Note—The plaintiff is usually awarded the whole of his costs, even if he is held partly to blame, unless he has failed to recover more than the defendant had paid into court. It is the procedure of payment into court which is now the effective factor in determining the award of costs. See pp 659–666, below, and the following:

Waller v Levoi
(1968) 112 Sol Jo 865, Times 16 October, CA
In a claim for damages arising from a road accident the county court judge found the plaintiff 80% to blame and the defendant 20% and awarded the plaintiff £24. He ordered him to pay four-fifths of the defendant's costs on Scale 3 and ordered the defendant to pay one-fifth of the plaintiff's costs on the same scale.
HELD, ON APPEAL: This order could not stand. There had been no payment into court or counterclaim nor any misconduct on the plaintiff's part. In these circumstances it was wrong to deprive a successful plaintiff of his costs or order him to pay the defendant's costs. The right order where a plaintiff was successful, even though guilty of contributory negligence, was that he should recover costs on the scale appropriate to the amount of damages awarded to him. The plaintiff had been awarded £24 and should have his costs of the action on Scale 2.

Contribution proceedings

Note—See ch 16, pp 603–604, below.

Two defendants

Hanson v Wearmouth Coal Co and Sunderland Gas Co
[1939] 3 All ER 47, 55 TLR 747, 83 Sol Jo 397, CA
Plaintiff sued two defendants and recovered judgment against one only. The unsuccessful defendant appealed. The plaintiff did not appeal against the successful defendant.
If the appeal succeeds, the Court of Appeal have power to give judgment against both defendants and to order contribution.

County court jurisdiction

Kelly v Stockport Corpn
[1949] 1 All ER 893, CA
An infant (by his father as next friend) and his mother as plaintiffs brought an action in the county court. The special damages claimed were £26 10s 6d, and the mother claimed £13 10s 0d for loss of wages. The total claimed

was £200 (at that time the limit of the court's jurisdiction). The county court judge assessed the total damages at £300, found the infant plaintiff one-third to blame and the defendant two-thirds, and awarded a total of £200, being £190 to the infant and £10 to the mother.

HELD: (1) The damages recoverable under s 1 (1) and (2) of the 1945 Act were limited to the court's jurisdiction of £200, and it was that figure which had to be reduced. It is not the damage sustained but the damages recoverable which must be taken into account. The sum which the court must find and record as total damages must be a sum within the jurisdiction of the court and not in excess of the jurisdiction. (2) A party cannot recover more damages than he claims in any civil court.

---

2 CONDITIONS OF NO LIABILITY

ACT OF GOD

Nugent v Smith
(1876) 1 CPD 423
A direct, violent, sudden and irresistible act of nature, which could not, by any reasonable care, have been foreseen or resisted.

Trent and Mersey Navigation Co v Wood
(1785) 4 Doug KB 287
The act of God is natural necessity, as winds and storms, which arise from natural causes, and is distinct from inevitable accident.

Greenock Corpn v Caledonian Rly Co
[1917] AC 556
Circumstances which no human foresight can provide against, and of which human prudence is not bound to recognise the possibility.

Accident: definition

Fenton v Thorley & Co
[1903] AC 443, HL
An unlooked-for mishap or an untoward event which is not expected or designed. Any unintended and unexpected occurrence which produces hurt or loss, or such hurt or loss apart from its cause especially if the cause is not known.

R v Morris
[1972] 1 All ER 384, [1972] 1 WLR 228, 136 JP 194, 116 Sol Jo 17, Div Ct
'Accident' in the present context [The Road Safety Act 1967, s 2 (2)]
means an unintended occurrence which has an adverse physical result.

Chief Constable of the West Midlands Police v Billingham
[1979] 2 All ER 182, [1979] 1 WLR 747, 123 Sol Jo 98, [1979] RTR 446,
QBD
It would not be right to treat the definition of 'accident' in *R v Morris*
(above) as if it were written into the statute (now the Road Traffic Act 1972,
s 8 (2)). Where a man deliberately entered a police car, released the brake,
steered it round a parked car and then let it run downhill and crash down an
embankment 25 feet deep there was an 'accident' for the purposes of the
section. The test was whether an ordinary man would say in the circumstances that an accident had occurred.

Chief Constable of Staffordshire v Lees
[1981] RTR 506, QBD
The defendant deliberately drove his car through a locked gate, smashing it.
HELD: Applying *West Midlands Police v Billingham* (above) an 'accident'
could be said to have occurred within the meaning of the RTA 1972,
s 8 (2). It was relevant to note that among the meanings to be found in the
Oxford English Dictionary is 'an unfortunate event, a mishap'.

Death of driver

Ryan v Youngs
[1938] 1 All ER 522, CA
Driver died whilst driving lorry, which ran on and injured the plaintiff.
Driver appeared to be in sound health but suffered from fatty degeneration
of the heart. Medical examination would not have indicated any liability to
sudden collapse.
HELD: (1) The man appeared to be in good health; medical examination
would not have disclosed any defect; the defendant was under no obligation
to have the driver medically examined; and the defendant was not negligent. (2) There was no defect in the lorry and it was not a nuisance. (3) The
accident was due to an act of God.

Waugh v James K. Allan Ltd
[1964] 2 Lloyd's Rep 1, 1964 SC (HL) 102, 1964 SLT 269, HL
The driver of a lorry was suddenly disabled by an attack of coronary thrombosis which killed him. The lorry mounted the pavement and struck the
appellant injuring him. Fifteen minutes before the accident the driver had
been taken ill when loading the lorry but had recovered, at least partially,
and had driven off. He had driven a quarter of a mile when the accident
occurred. He had had gastric attacks from time to time in the past but had
otherwise enjoyed good health.

HELD: A motor vehicle is potentially a dangerous and lethal instrument; there rests upon every driver of such a vehicle a serious duty owed to his fellow human beings not to drive the vehicle in a public highway if he has or should have any reasonable ground for thinking that, from illness or otherwise, his skill or judgment as a driver may have been impaired. Nevertheless, on the facts of this case, the driver was not negligent in taking the lorry out; he had no reason to suppose that his illness was not another gastric attack which, when it passed off, had left no serious disability. The respondents, his employers, were not liable.

Note—See also *Jones v Dennison*, p 36, below.

Wind records

A report on weather conditions, temperatures and wind force at any time or place can be obtained from the Meteorological Office, London Road, Bracknell, Berks. Alternatively application may be made for reports on the weather to the London Weather Centre, 284–6 High Holborn, WC1, or the Manchester Weather Centre 56 Royal Exchange, Manchester, 2, or the Southampton Weather Centre, 160 High St, Below Bar, Southampton, Hants.

AGONY OF THE MOMENT

Brandon v Osborne, Garrett & Co
[1924] 1 KB 548, 93 LJKB 304, 130 LT 670, 40 TLR 235, 68 Sol Jo 460 (Swift J)
Where a person or a third party is placed in danger by the wrongful act of the defendant, that person is not negligent if he exercises such care as may reasonably be expected of him in the difficult position in which he is so placed. He is not to blame if he does not do quite the right thing in the circumstances.

Note—See also *Tocci v Hankard*, p 85, below.

ALTERNATIVE DANGER

Note—This is a somewhat similar principle to 'agony of the moment'. See the cases of *Jones v Boyce* (p 190, below), *Adams v Lancashire and Yorkshire Rly Co* (p 196, below) and *Tocci v Hankard* (p 85, below).

INEVITABLE ACCIDENT

Note—See also 'Act of God', p 32, above.

In an unreported case where a wasp entered a car and settled on the driver's eye (*Gilson v Kidman* 28 October 1938), Mr Justice Lewis adopted the definition of inevitable accident of Sir James Colville in *The Marpesia* (1872) LR 4 PC 212. Nothing was done or omitted to be done which a person exercising ordinary care, caution and maritime skill, in the circumstances, either would not have done, or would not have left undone, as the case may be.

The judge held that the defence of inevitable accident had not been made out and gave a verdict for the plaintiff.

Per Lord Justice Fry (in *The Merchant Prince* [1892] P 179): The burden rests on the defendants to show inevitable accident. To sustain that, the defendants must do one of two things. They must either show what was the cause of the accident, and show that the result of that cause was inevitable; or they must show all the possible causes, one or other of which produced the effect, and must further show with regard to everyone of these possible causes that the result could not have been avoided. Unless they do one or other of these two things, it does not appear to me that they have shown inevitable accident.

The principles were followed in *The St Angus* [1938] P 225.

McBride v Stitt
[1944] NI 7 (Andrews CJ)
'Inevitable accident' was defined by Dr Lushington in the Admiralty case of *The Virgil* (1843) 2 Wm Rob 201 in terms which have since received general acceptance — 'that which the party charged with the offence could not possibly prevent by the exercise of ordinary care, caution and maritime skill'. Omitting the word 'maritime' the definition is as applicable to Courts of Common Law as to the Court of Admiralty.

Pleading inevitable accident

Rumbold v London County Council
(1909) 25 TLR 541, 53 Sol Jo 502, CA
Where in an action claiming damages for negligence, the defence denies negligence, the defendant may give evidence that the accident was an inevitable accident. In such a case the defence of inevitable accident need not be specifically pleaded.

Note—In view of an Irish decision, the above statement was formerly doubted, but it is accepted in the *Supreme Court Practice*, 1985, see p 273, notes to Ord 18, rr 8 and 12. Nevertheless when inevitable accident is relied upon the invariable practice is to plead it.

INVOLUNTARY ACT

Driver overcome by sleep

Kay v Butterworth
(1945) 173 LT 191, 61 TLR 452, 89 Sol Jo 381
The driver of a motor car who had been working all night until 7.45 am at an aircraft factory was driving a car at about 9 am, and was overcome by sleep or drowsiness and ran into the rear of a party of soldiers marching in column in the same direction. The police prosecuted under the Road Traffic Act 1930, ss 11 and 12 (now the Road Traffic Act 1972, ss 2 and 3). HELD, by Divisional Court, allowing appeal from justices: If a driver allows himself to drive while he is asleep, he is guilty of driving without due care and attention, because it is his business to keep awake; if drowsiness overtakes him whilst at the wheel, he should stop and wait until he shakes it off and is wide awake again. If a person through no fault of his own becomes unconscious while driving, eg, by being struck by a stone, or being taken ill, he ought not to be held liable at criminal law. The respondent must have known that drowsiness was overtaking him.

Henderson v Jones
(1955) 119 JP 304, Div Ct
Defendant was charged with driving without due care and attention. She contended she was not 'driving' the car because she was admittedly asleep, she had no control over her actions.
HELD: Driving while asleep was at least driving without due care and attention. Being asleep was no excuse.

Loss of consciousness

Jones v Dennison
[1971] RTR 174, CA
The defendant was driving his car when it ran out of control on to the pavement, striking the plaintiff and injuring her. His defence to her claim for damages was that he had temporarily lost control due to a 'blackout' ie a loss of consciousness. His medical history included a coronary thrombosis six years earlier and a slight cerebral thrombosis. His doctor had not advised he should not drive. He had also had four short blackouts in the previous ten months but had been unaware of them: his wife knew of them but did not tell him of them until after the accident. In the court below the judge accepted the defendant's evidence that he did not know of the blackouts before the accident and held that he had discharged the burden of proof on him. His wife was not called to give evidence because of illness. On appeal it was argued that without the wife's evidence as to when where and how the blackouts had taken place it was an undefended case.
HELD: The judge had properly directed himself that the real issue was whether the defendant ought to have realised from what had happened in the past that he ought not to have been driving. On the evidence of the defendant and his doctor there was no ground for saying he ought reasonably to have suspected that he was or might be subject to an attack such as

he had. The onus was on the defendant and he had established his case. Appeal dismissed.

STATE OF AUTOMATION

Watmore v Jenkins
[1962] 2 QB 572, [1962] 2 All ER 868, 126 JP 432, 106 Sol Jo 492, 60 LGR 325, Div Ct

The defendant was a diabetic. Whilst driving home in the evening he was seen at several points en route to be swerving about in the road and finally collided with a parked car. He remembered nothing of the last five miles of the journey. He had injected himself with a normal dose of insulin that morning but medical investigation showed that he was suffering from a hypoglycaemic episode due to the effects of recovery from a recent illness. The episode resulted from an excess of bodily and injected insulin. When the episode overtook him he was driving his car and continued to perform the functions of driving after a fashion until the accident happened. He was charged with (1) driving a vehicle on a road whilst unfit to drive through drugs; (2) dangerous and careless driving. The charges were dismissed. On the first charge the justices held that the defendant's unfitness to drive was not directly due to the dose of insulin: on the other charges they held that the defendant had been driving in a state of automatism.

HELD: On case stated (1) the justices were entitled on the evidence to entertain a reasonable doubt whether the injected insulin was more than a predisposing or historical cause of the hypoglycaemic episode; (2) the justices had not defined 'a state of automatism'. The expression is no more than a catch phrase to connote the involuntary movement of the body or limbs of a person. It was not reasonable to conclude that the defendant's condition was such that throughout the five miles when he was 'driving after a fashion' the whole of such performance was involuntary or unconscious. There must be a conviction on the charge of dangerous driving.

Roberts v Ramsbottom
[1980] 1 All ER 7, [1980] 1 WLR 823, 124 Sol Jo 313, [1980] RTR 261, (Neill J)

The defendant, a man of 73, was driving his car when it collided with a parked van. He continued on his journey and shortly afterwards collided with a stationary car, injuring the plaintiffs. He told the police 'I felt a bit queer before I ran into the van. I went away and felt all right. After that I felt a bit queer again and I hit the other car'. He was found on medical examination to have suffered a stroke just before starting his journey. The defendant had no previous symptoms or warning signs. After its onset his consciousness was impaired, but he was sufficiently in possession of his faculties to have some awareness of his surroundings and of traffic conditions and to make deliberate and voluntary though inefficient movements of hands and legs to manipulate the controls. He was not aware that he was unfit to drive.

HELD: In civil as well as in criminal matters (following *Watmore v Jenkins* (above)) a state of automatism means in law a complete loss of consciousness; a driver will escape liability only if his actions at the relevant time were wholly beyond his control. If he retained some control, albeit imperfect, he remains liable. The defendant was liable on this ground, and liable also in having continued to drive when he should have been aware of his unfitness.

Moses v Winder
[1981] RTR 37, QBD

The defendant drove his car into collision with another in circumstances justifying a conviction for careless driving. He pleaded automatism, being a diabetic of 20 years' duration. He called no medical evidence.

HELD: (1) Cases must be exceedingly rare where a defence of automatism can succeed without medical evidence; (2) the defendant was well aware of the danger of his going into a coma. He felt he was about to have an attack and took sugar sweets to ward it off; he then drove off and the attack became worse. In those circumstances he failed to take those precautions which he should both in his own interest and in the interest of public safety. The justices must convict.

Farrell v Stirling
[1978] Crim LR 696 (Sheriff Ct)

After a collision with another car the defendant continued to drive his car for a distance of four miles and collided with two other cars. His defence to a charge of careless driving was that he was diabetic and had been in a state of hypoglycaemia.

HELD: The test to determine whether he was 'driving' was whether at the material time he was in conscious control and whether his movements were voluntary. On the evidence he was convicted but given an absolute discharge.

FIT OF EPILEPSY

Balmer v Hayes
1950 SC 477, 1950 SLT 388, Ct of Sess, Scot

A motor omnibus collided with a motor lorry and a passenger in the motor omnibus was injured. She brought an action against the driver of the omnibus, who averred that immediately before the accident he suffered a temporary loss of consciousness owing to a fit of epilepsy. The pursuer replied averring that it was the driver's duty when applying for a driving licence to disclose that he suffered from lapses of consciousness which were likely to cause his driving to be a danger to the public.

The Road Traffic Act 1930, s 5(1) enacts that an applicant for a licence shall make a declaration as to whether or not he is suffering from any such disease or physical disability specified in the form or any other disease or physical disability which would be likely to cause his driving to be a source of danger to the public. Subsection (2) allows an application for a test except in prescribed cases. The Motor Vehicles (Driving Licences) Regulations 1947, reg 5 prescribes as an exception epilepsy, liability to sudden attacks of disabling giddiness or fainting.

Section 112 (2) of the 1930 Act provides a penalty for false statement on application for a licence and for a false statement or withholding of material information on application for a certificate.

HELD: Breach of the section and the Regulations did not give a right of action and the averments relevant to an alleged breach of statutory duty should be excluded from probation: *Phillips v Britannia Laundry* (p 245, below) and *Clarke v Brims* (p 215, below) followed.

Note—The Road Traffic Act 1930, ss 5 and 112 have been replaced, so far as they affect this case, by the Road Traffic Act 1972, ss 87 and 170 respectively.

PEDESTRIAN

Green v Hills
(1969) 113 Sol Jo 385, Times, 22 April (James J)
The plaintiffs, man and wife, were injured when they were knocked off their moped by the defendant, a woman, who stepped off the kerb in a state of automatism after an attack of *petit mal*. She suffered from two different forms of epileptic attacks, major attacks of which she received warning and which occurred once or twice a year, and minor attacks which were more frequent and some of which were accompanied by periods of time when she was not conscious of what was going on or afterwards of what had gone on. She remembered going out on the afternoon of the accident and going into a shop but did not remember the accident. She had not been advised by her doctor not to go out alone. A neurologist said in evidence he did not think it reasonable to forbid a person such as the defendant from going into the street.
HELD: The defendant was not liable. She had first to satisfy the court on the balance or probabilities that she was in a state of automatism: on her own evidence she had discharged this burden. The issue was then whether it was reasonable for her to have gone out alone. Clearly there was some risk but one could not 'chain' an epileptic person to his house. A reasonable person, knowing her life history, would be prepared to balance the risk of causing injury with the need to go out and live as normal a life as possible.

LATENT DEFECT

Note—See ch 6, pp 240–243, below.

RISKS OF HIGHWAY

River Wear Comrs v Adamson
(1877) 2 App Cas 743, 47 LJQB 193, 37 LT 543, 42 JP 244, 26 WR 217
Property adjoining a spot on which the public have a right to carry on traffic is liable to be injured by that traffic. In this respect there is no difference between a shop, the railings or windows of which may be broken by a carriage on the road, and a pier adjoining to a harbour or navigable river or the sea, which is liable to be injured by a ship. In either case the owner of the injured property must bear his own loss, unless he can establish that some third person is in fault and liable to make it good. And he does not establish this against a person merely by showing that he is the owner of the carriage or ship which did the mischief, for the owner incurs no liability merely because he is the owner.

Fletcher v Rylands

1866 LR 1 Exch 265, 4 H & C 263, 35 LJ Ex 154, 14 LT 523, 30 JP 436, 12 Jur NS 603, 14 WR 799 (Blackburn J)

Traffic on the highways whether by land or sea, cannot be conducted without exposing those whose persons or property are near to it to some inevitable risk; and that being so, those who go on the highway or have their property adjacent to it may well be held to do so subject to their taking upon themselves the risk of injury from that inevitable danger, and such persons could not recover without proof of want of skill occasioning the accident.

Note—See *Gayler and Pope v Davis*, p 58, below and *Maitland v Raisbeck*, p 218, below.

Volenti non fit injuria

Note—A person who has expressly or impliedly assented to an act cannot claim for its consequences, but the principle is *volenti*, not *scienti*, that it, consent as distinct from mere knowledge.

Winnik v Dick

1984 SLT 185, Ct of Sess

The plaintiff accepted a lift from a friend who he knew was drunk. En route an accident occurred, injuring the plaintiff. The defendant driver pleaded *volenti non fit injuria*.

HELD: The maxim did not negative negligence: it merely absolved a party from the consequences of his negligence. In the present case the plaintiff had to be taken as having appreciated and consented to the defendant's lack of reasonable care. However, the Road Traffic Act 1972, s 148(3) expressly provided that the fact that a passenger had willingly accepted the risk that the driver may be negligent was not to be treated as negativing the driver's liability. The subsection excluded the operation of the maxim. The plaintiff was entitled to damages subject to 50% deduction for contributory negligence.

Cutler v United Dairies (London) Ltd

[1933] 2 KB 297, 102 LJKB 663, 149 LT 436, CA

A man who, without being under any duty, went into a field to help to catch a runaway horse, was held to be a volunteer.

Haynes v Harwood

[1935] 1 KB 146, 104 LJKB 60, 152 LT 121, 51 TLR 100, 78 Sol Jo 801, CA

If the act of the plaintiff is pursuant to duty, or is a reasonable act to avoid injury to others, the principle does not apply. The plaintiff, a police constable, was on duty inside a police station in a street in which, at the material time, were a large number of people, including children. Seeing the defendants' runaway horses with a van attached coming down the street he rushed out and eventually stopped them, sustaining injuries in consequence, in respect of which he claimed damages.

HELD: (1) That on the evidence the defendant's servant was guilty of negligence in leaving the horses unattended in a busy street; (2) that as the defendants must or ought to have contemplated that someone might attempt to stop the horses in an endeavour to prevent injury to life and limb, and as the police were under a general duty to intervene to protect life and property, the act of, and injuries to, the plaintiff were the natural and probable consequences of the defendants' negligence; (3) that the maxim *volenti non fit injuria* did not apply to prevent the plaintiff recovering.

Note—Followed in *The Gusty and The Daniel M* [1940] P 159, 109 LJP 71, 164 LT 271, 56 TLR 785, 84 Sol Jo 454.

Morgan v Aylen
[1942] 1 All ER 489 (Cassels J)
The plaintiff was escorting a child of three-and-a-half years, and when they reached a cross-road, the child was a little way in front of her and ran forward and began to cross the road. The defendant was riding a motor cycle along the road about 7 feet from the near side. He was about 7 yards from the corner when the child ran into the road and about 5 yards from the child. The plaintiff ran out to save the child. If the plaintiff had been alone, an attempt by her to cross the road in front of the defendant might have been negligent. Here the circumstances were different. The American rule is that the doctrine of the assumption of risk does not apply where the plaintiff has, under an exigency caused by the defendants' wrongful misconduct, consciously and deliberately faced a risk, even a death, to rescue another from imminent danger of personal injury or death, whether the person endangered is one to whom he owes a duty of protection, as a member of his family, or is a mere stranger to whom he owes no such special duty. What the plaintiff did here was, in the circumstances, natural and proper. The initial wrongful act was on the part of the defendant, who was approaching the cross-roads as too great a speed. The plaintiff saw the danger and ran out to save the child, which was a natural and proper thing to do, and there was no contributory negligence on her part. The defendant was in law solely responsible for the accident.

Note—See also 'Rescue cases', p 43, below.

White v Blackmore
[1972] 2 QB 651, [1972] 3 All ER 158, [1972] 3 WLR 296, 116 Sol Jo 547, CA
The defendants organised a race meeting for jalopy cars. The plaintiff's husband took his car and entered his name as a competitor. He brought his wife, child and mother-in-law to the meeting as spectators. He competed in a race but during the next race, in which he was not a competitor, he stood near a post to which safety ropes were fastened talking to his family. The ropes were faultily arranged and on being fouled by a car in that race, pulled out the post and caused the plaintiff's husband injuries from which he died. He had seen the notices around the track: 'Warning to the Public. Motor racing is dangerous. It is a condition of admission that all persons having connection with the promotion and/or organisation and/or conduct of the meeting are absolved from all liabilities arising out of accidents

causing damage or personal injury (whether fatal or otherwise) howsoever caused to spectators or ticketholders.'

HELD: (1) The deceased was at the time of the accident a spectator not a competitor; (2) the defence of *volenti non fit injuria* was available only against one who had impliedly agreed, with full knowledge of the nature and extent of the risk, to incur it. It was not obvious to the deceased that he was standing in a particularly dangerous place and the defence of *volenti* did not apply; (3) the warning notice applied to the deceased as a spectator at the time of the accident and the action failed.

Latchford v Spedeworth International Ltd
(1984) 134 NLJ 36 (Hodgson J)

The plaintiff was a competitor at a 'hot rod' car racing stadium. He had often raced there and was aware of the danger presented to drivers by two concrete flower beds within the area of the race track. He was not aware until the evening of the accident of the organiser's practice of marking the edge of the track with small tyres. The organiser (the defendant company) knew that the practice was potentially hazardous and that larger tyres would have been safer. The plaintiff did not know this. During a race another competitor dislodged some of the tyres of which one jammed under the back axle of the plaintiff's car causing him to crash into one of the concrete flowerbeds. He was seriously injured.

HELD: The accident resulted from the defendant's negligence with regard to the tyres and as the plaintiff was unaware of that danger the defence of *volenti non fit injuria* could not avail in respect of it. The defendant had also pleaded that the plaintiff was on his own admission aware of the danger presented by the flowerbeds and had consented to run that risk. However, the defendant had failed to prove that the plaintiff actually had a full appreciation of the nature and extent of the risk. The plea of *volenti non fit injuria* thus failed entirely.

Drunken driver

Note—See also *Owens v Brimmell* and cases following it, p 202, below.

Dann v Hamilton
[1939] 1 KB 509, [1939] 1 All ER 59, 83 Sol Jo 155 (Asquith J)

The plaintiff was injured while travelling as a non-paying passenger in a car driven by one H. Prior to the accident H had been drinking, and this had markedly affected his driving, which thereafter was fast and erratic. During a stop to let down a passenger, the plaintiff, who by then knew that H, while far from being dead drunk, was not sober, and that there was a certain danger in being a passenger in a car driven by him, had an opportunity of leaving the car, but elected to continue the journey. Shortly afterwards, the accident occurred, and it was contended for the defence that the maxim *volenti non fit injuria* applied.

HELD: The plaintiff was entitled to succeed. By voluntarily travelling in the car with knowledge that through drink H had materially reduced his capacity for driving safely, she did not impliedly consent to, or absolve H from liability for, any subsequent negligence on his part which might cause injury to the plaintiff.

Note—Comments on this decision in 55 LQR 184 and 65 LQR 20 and elsewhere suggested that even if the plea of '*volenti*' did not apply, there was a cast-iron defence on the ground of contributory negligence. Lord Asquith wrote (69 LQR 317) that contributory negligence was not pleaded and counsel for the defendant declined a suggestion from the judge that he should apply for leave to amend and add this plea. The Law Reform (Contributory Negligence) Act 1945 was still in the future. See also the Road Traffic Act 1972, s 148 (3), p 213, below. See also 'Consent to Drunken Driving' 17 NLJ 1079.

In *Slater v Clay Cross Co Ltd* [1956] 2 QB 264, [1956] 2 All ER 629, [1956] 3 WLR 232, 100 Sol Jo 450, Denning LJ said of the judgment of Asquith J in *Dann v Hamilton* and of the note written by Lord Asquith, 'In so far as he decided that the doctrine of *volenti* did not apply, I think the decision was quite correct. In so far as he suggested that the plea of contributory negligence might have been available, I agree with him.' Parker and Birkett LJJ agreed.

See also *Dawrant v Nutt*, p 201, below.

PLEADING DRUNKENNESS

Roe v Robert McGregor & Sons Ltd
[1968] 2 All ER 636, [1968] 1 WLR 925, 112 Sol Jo 235, CA
Per Salmon LJ: If it is going to be part of a defendant's case — or of a plaintiff's case for that matter — that the other party is guilty of negligence because he has driven when he was under the influence of drink, that ought to be expressly alleged in the pleading. It would be grossly unfair to confront a man at the trial for the first time with an allegation that he was driving under the influence of drink and thereby committing a criminal offence, If, however, such an allegation is pleaded, the man against whom it is made will have the opportunity of meeting it. He will go to trial prepared perhaps to prove that he was completely sober. If, however, the issue does not appear on the pleadings he will obviously not bring any witnesses as to the state of his sobriety because he will think, rightly, that that is not in issue.

Rescue cases

Baker v T. E. Hopkins & Son
[1959] 3 All ER 225, [1959] 1 WLR 966, 103 Sol Jo 812
Defendants, builders and contractors, had arranged to clean out a well at a farm. Two workmen in defendants' employ went down the well and were overcome by poisonous gases. A doctor was summoned by telephone, and, though warned of the danger, went down the well to see what he could do for them. He was overcome and died.

The court held the defendants liable in negligence in respect of the deaths of the two workmen. Defendants contended that they owed no duty to the doctor; that his conduct was unreasonable and amounted to a *novus actus interveniens*; and it was a case of *volenti non fit injuria*.

HELD, ON APPEAL: It was natural and proper consequence of the defendants' negligence that someone would attempt to rescue, and the defendants should have foreseen that consequence; accordingly the defendants were in breach of duty towards the doctor (*Donoghue v Stevenson*).

It was not a case of *novus actus interveniens*. The act in question was the very kind of thing that was likely to happen as a result of the negligence.

The maxim *volenti non fit injuria* could not be successfully invoked as a defence by a person who had negligently placed others in a situation of such peril that it was foreseeable that someone would attempt their rescue. Appeal dismissed.

Videan v British Transport Commission

[1963] 2 QB 650, [1963] 2 All ER 860, [1963] 3 WLR 374, 107 Sol Jo 458, CA

Per Lord Denning: The right of the rescuer is an independent right, and is not derived from that of the victim. The victim may have been guilty of contributory negligence — or his right may be excluded by contractual stipulation — but still the rescuer can sue. Foreseeability is necessary, but not foreseeability of the particular emergency that arose. Suffice it that he ought reasonably to foresee that, if he did not take care, some emergency or other might arise, and that someone or other might be impelled to expose himself to danger in order to effect a rescue. Whoever comes to the rescue, the law should see that he does not suffer for it. It seems to me that, if a person by his fault creates a situation of peril, he must answer for it to any person who attempts to rescue the person who is in danger. He owes a duty to such a person above all others. The rescuer may act instinctively out of humanity or deliberately out of courage. But whichever it is, so long as it is not wanton interference, if the rescuer is killed or injured in the attempt, he can recover damages from the one whose fault has been the cause of it.

Harrison v British Railways Board

[1981] 3 All ER 679 (Boreham J)

The plaintiff was the guard on a passenger train. At a station en route he gave the ready-to-start signal to the driver and the train began to move. An off-duty member of the station staff, Howard, then attempted to board the train by seizing the handrail at the guard's door. The plaintiff saw him but failed to apply the emergency brake as he could and should have done. Instead he attempted to help Howard in by grasping his arm. The train, gathering speed, pulled Howard off his feet and he fell between the train and the platform, causing the plaintiff to fall down with him. The plaintiff was injured.

HELD: As an experienced railwayman, Howard was negligent in attempting to board the train when it was moving. Moreover he knew the plaintiff had seen him and would try to help him if he got into trouble. He should have foreseen that by intervening the plaintiff would probably endanger himself. A duty is owed to a rescuer if his intervention is reasonably foreseeable even if the defendant owes no duty to the person being rescued (*Videan v British Transport Commission* (above)). A duty must likewise be owed to a rescuer when the person being rescued is the person who created the peril. Howard was liable to the plaintiff; but he was himself guilty of contributory negligence to the extent of 20 % in failing to apply the emergency brake and thus reduce the chance of injury to himself.

Note—See also *Chadwick v British Transport Commission*, p 464, below and *Hyett v Great Western Rly Co*, p 45, below.

The Occupiers' Liability Act 1957

Note—By s 2(5) of the Act an occupier is under no obligation to a visitor in respect of risk willingly accepted by the visitor.

Not volens

Clayards v Dethick
(1848) 12 QB 439
Commissioners of sewers made a trench in the only outlet from some mews, leaving only a narrow passage on which they heaped sand and gravel. A cab proprietor, in order to get his horse out of the mews led it over the heaped up gravel, which gave way and the horse slipped into the trench, causing its death. He recovered damages on the principle that where the inconvenience is great and the risk is not so great that no sensible man would have incurred it, the principle of *volenti* does not apply.

Voluntary assistance

Lomas v Jones & Son
[1944] KB 4, [1943] 2 All ER 548, 113 LJKB 193, 170 LT 139, 60 TLR 28, CA
A farmer contracted with a firm of carriers for the conveyance in their motor cattle lorry of a heifer to his farm. The farmer gave unsolicited assistance to defendants' driver in unloading the heifer and closing the two doors of the lorry. The first door had been closed but the driver failed to shoot the bolt properly. When plaintiff was stooping to raise the second door, the first door fell on him. Defendants contended the assistance of plaintiff was without their consent and that the driver in accepting assistance was acting outside the scope of his employment.
HELD: The effective cause was the negligence of the driver in not shooting the bolt properly, and defendants were liable for his negligence. Consent was immaterial.

Property

Note—The principle of *Haynes v Harwood* (p 40, above) has been extended to the rescue of property.

Hyett v Great Western Rly Co
[1948] 1 KB 345, [1947] 2 All ER 264, [1947] LJR 1243, 177 LT 178, 63 TLR 411, Sol Jo 434, CA
The plaintiff was employed by a firm of wagon repairers and was working on the sidings of the defendants. He saw some smoke coming from a wagon of the defendants. He climbed into the wagon which contained drums of paraffin oil and found flames on the floor. Plaintiff tried to get some of the drums out of the wagon when a drum exploded and injured him.
HELD: The plaintiff was an invitee and defendants' duty was to take

reasonable steps to see that the premises were reasonably safe. The defendants ought to have known that paraffin was leaking; that engines might emit sparks and men might be smoking, and were guilty of negligence.

Adopting *Haynes v Harwood* and *Steel v Glasgow Iron and Steel Co* (1944 SC 237), there was no *novus actus interveniens*. The plaintiff's act was the kind of act the defendants might reasonably have anticipated as likely to follow from their act of negligence.

Crossley v Rawlinson
[1981] 3 All ER 674, [1982] 1 WLR 369, 125 Sol Jo 865, [1982] RTR 442 QBD

The defendant was the owner and driver of a lorry. Whilst he was driving the vehicle a tarpaulin, negligently placed by him too near the exhaust, caught fire. He drew in to the side of the road and stopped. The plaintiff, an AA patrolman, saw the blaze from 100 yards away and ran towards it along the grass verge with a fire extinguisher. About one-third of the way to the lorry his foot went into a hole concealed by grass and he fell, sustaining injury. He continued to the fire and put it out but, his injury proving serious, he claimed damages from the defendant on the ground that he was owed a duty of care as a rescuer.

HELD: The plaintiff could not succeed. Whilst it is correct that in 'rescue' cases the precise nature of the injury does not have to be foreseen there comes a point at which the judge has to decide where the limit is to be put on the range of liability for negligence. A sensible approach will produce 'an instinctive feeling that the event or act being weighed in the balance is too remote to sound in damages for the plaintiff' (per Watkins LJ in *Lamb v Camden London Borough Council*, p 372, below. In such cases as *Haynes v Harwood*, (p 40, above) and *Videan v British Transport Commission*, (p 44, above) the accident was caused by the original negligence itself, the victim being actually engaged in a rescue operation at the scene of the danger. That was not so here. It was not reasonably foreseeable that the plaintiff would suffer this or any other injury while running along the path.

Master and servant cases

Bowater v Rowley Regis Corpn
[1944] KB 476, [1944] 1 All ER 465, 113 LJKB 427, 170 LT 314, 60 TLR 356, CA

A workman complied after protest with a direction to take out a horse known to make attempts to run away. The horse ran away and he was injured.

HELD: The maxim did not prevent the workman from recovering damages from his employers. The defence hardly ever applies between master and servant.

Passenger: exclusion notice

Bennett v Tugwell
[1971] 2 QB 267, [1971] 2 All ER 248, [1971] 2 WLR 847, 115 Sol Jo 289, [1971] 1 Lloyd's Rep 333, [1971] RTR 211 (Ackner J)

The plaintiff was injured when a passenger in a car driven by the defendant. The car belonged to the defendant's father. It was insured against passenger claims but the defendant did not know this: seven months before the accident he had bought and fixed to the dashboard of the car a notice saying 'Passengers travelling in this vehicle do so at their own risk'. The plaintiff had often seen it and had once had a conversation with the defendant agreeing that he probably could not sue him in the event of an accident. He said in evidence that he had thought nevertheless he would be able to sue the insurance company.

HELD: (1) The effect of the notice was to exclude liability on the part of the defendant for negligent driving; (2) whether the defendant could rely on the defence of *volenti non fit injuria* was to be decided objectively on what the parties' words and conduct evidenced, not by a subjective examination of their thoughts. It was immaterial that the plaintiff thought he had a remedy against the insurers or that the defendant had no intention of depriving him of such a remedy. Nor was it necessary that there should be a contract: all that was required was assent by the plaintiff to being carried at his own risk. Such an assent was clearly to be inferred in the present case. Judgment for the defendant.

Note—See also next three cases and note following *Geier v Kujawa*, p 48, below.

A plea of *volenti* may be relevant in a claim by a driving instructor who has been injured by the negligence of his pupil. See *Nettleship v Weston*, p 69, below, but note also Road Traffic Act 1972, s 148(3).

Infant

Buckpitt v Oates
[1968] 1 All ER 1145 (John Stephenson J)

The plaintiff and defendant were aged 17, and each owned a car. Neither was insured against passenger risks. It was their custom from time to time to ride in each other's cars as passengers. The plaintiff was injured when riding in the defendant's car, due to the defendant's negligent driving. About three weeks earlier the defendant had fixed a notice in his car opposite the passenger seat 'Warning. Passengers ride in this vehicle at their own risk. Neither the owner nor the driver will be liable for loss of life or personal injury or other loss or damage howsoever caused. Passengers are not covered by insurance.' The plaintiff saw this on the day it was fixed. He knew the defendant had no passenger insurance. On the occasion of the accident the plaintiff had persuaded the defendant to take him on the journey by contributing ten shillings to the cost of petrol.

HELD: (1) The payment of ten shillings did not make any legally binding contract between the parties. It was merely a friendly arrangement not amounting to contract. Any rights and obligations were those which the general law imposed. (2) There was no rule that a plea of *volenti non fit injuria* could not be raised against an infant. Like contributory negligence it was a plea which was less likely to succeed as the age and experience of the infant diminished, but this infant plaintiff appreciated what the terms of the notice were and realised that he was riding in the car as a passenger at his own risk. He impliedly assented to the position and agreed to exempt the defendant from liability. Judgment for the defendant.

Birch v Thomas

[1972] 1 All ER 905, [1972] 1 WLR 294, [1972] RTR 130, CA

The defendant, aged 19, was unable to get passenger insurance. He stuck a notice to his windscreen opposite the passenger seat: 'Passengers ride at their own risk and on the condition that no claim shall be made against the driver or owner.' During a social evening he gave the plaintiff a lift: the plaintiff could have travelled instead in someone else's vehicle but chose to go with the defendant, who had said it was 'up to him'. The defendant also pointed out the notice and said it was 'to do with the insurance'. An accident occurred for which the defendant was to blame and the plaintiff was badly injured.

HELD: The defendant was not liable. He had done all that was reasonably necessary to bring to the plaintiff's notice that he was uninsured and that the plaintiff rode at his own risk.

Note—See note following *Geier v Kujawa*, below.

Consent must be real

Geier v Kujawa

[1970] 1 Lloyd's Rep 364 (Brabin J)

The plaintiff, a German girl with little knowledge of English, was a passenger in the defendant's car in which a notice was displayed 'Passengers ride at their own risk.' She was injured in an accident caused by the defendant's negligent driving. The judge was referred to *Buckpitt v Oates* (above).

HELD: Adopting what was said in that case, the Court must consider with great care whether a particular plaintiff had the means and the knowledge and experience to appreciate fully and freely the risk and what she was consenting to. In the present case she did not consent. She could not read the notice, she knew nothing about the risks in respect of vehicles not carrying passenger insurance and, on the facts, consented to nothing.

Note—As from 1 December 1972 exclusion notices of the type displayed in the four preceding cases are of no effect when the vehicle is being used in circumstances in which compulsory passenger insurance is required. See the Road Traffic Act 1972, s 148(3), p 213, below and s 143(1), p 704, below.

See also 'Passenger insurance', p 748, below.

3 RES IPSA LOQUITUR

Note—And see 'Skidding', p 112, below.

PURPOSE OF DOCTRINE

Cole v De Trafford
[1918] 2 KB 523
The doctrine of *res ipsa loquitur* means that an accident may by its nature be more consistent with its being caused by negligence for which the defendant is responsible than by other causes, and that in such a case the mere fact of the accident is prima facie evidence of such negligence. In such a case the burden of proof is on the defendant to explain and to show that it occurred without fault on his part.

Scott v London and St Katherine's Docks Co
(1865) 3 H & C 596, 34 LJ Ex 220, 13 LT 148, 11 Jur NS 204
Merchandise being lowered in a crane slipped out of its fastenings and fell upon the plaintiff.
HELD: That where the thing is shown to be under the management of the defendants or his servants, and the accident is such as in the ordinary course of things does not happen if those who have the management use proper care, it affords reasonable evidence, in the absence of explanation by the defendant, that the accident arose from want of care.

Woods v Duncan
[1946] AC 401, [1946] 1 All ER 420n, [1947] LJR 120, 174 LT 286, 62 TLR 283, HL
Per Viscount Simon: That principle only shifts the onus of proof, which is adequately met by showing that the defendant was not in fact negligent. He is not to be held liable because he cannot prove exactly how the accident happened.

Per Lord Simonds: To apply the principle is to do no more than shift the burden of proof. A prima facie case is assumed to be made out which throws upon the defendant the task of proving that he was not negligent. This does not mean that he must prove how and why the accident happened; it is sufficient if he satisfies the court that he personally was not negligent. It may well be that the court will be more easily satisfied of this fact if a plausible explanation which attributes the accident to some other cause is put forward on his behalf; but this is only a factor in the consideration of the probabilities. The accident may remain inexplicable, or at least no satisfactory explanation other than his negligence may be offered: yet, if the court is satisfied by his evidence that he was not negligent, the plaintiff's case must fail. The defendant can by an affirmative proof that he was not negligent discharge the burden that lies upon him without satisfying the court how otherwise the accident happened, and I think he has done so.

Turner v Mansfield Corpn
(1975) 119 Sol Jo 629, CA

The driver of a dustcart was injured when the tipping body of the dustcart inexplicably rose when the vehicle was being driven and struck a railway bridge.

HELD: Not a case of *res ipsa loquitur*. The vehicle was not under the control of the defendants but under the joint control of the plaintiff and defendants. *Res ipsa loquitur* was not a doctrine but a rule as to the weight of evidence from which negligence could be inferred.

Defendant's onus of proof

Barkway v South Wales Transport Co Ltd
[1950] AC 185, [1950] 1 All ER 392, 66 TLR 597, 94 Sol Jo 128, HL

Per Asquith LJ: The onus is on the defendants to show either a specific cause not connoting their negligence or that they used all reasonable care, it being insufficient merely to show that the accident could have happened without negligence on their part.

Note—For facts, see p 60, below.

Bennett v Chemical Construction (GB) Ltd
[1971] 3 All ER 822, [1971] 1 WLR 1571, 115 Sol Jo 550, CA

The plaintiff, a foreman steel erector, was supervising the installation of electrical control panels. One of the panels started to topple and the plaintiff rushed forward to steady it; as he was doing so another panel next to it fell on him, causing injuries. At the trial the plaintiff was unable to show what caused the panel to fall, nor could the defendants suggest any explanation for the accident. The judge said the panels could not have fallen unless their stability had been interfered with or unless there was some lack of care by the workmen working on the first panel. He accordingly held the defendants negligent.

HELD, ON APPEAL: On the evidence before him the judge could not have come to any other conclusion. It was a classic case of *res ipsa loquitur*. It was not necessary for that doctrine to be pleaded when it was proved that the accident could not have happened without negligence on the part of the defendants.

Walsh v Holst & Co Ltd
[1958] 3 All ER 33, [1958] 1 WLR 800, 102 Sol Jo 545, CA

Contractors were working on a high four-storey building in a street 15 feet wide with a narrow pavement on each side. The plaintiff was walking along the opposite pavement when he was struck and injured by a half-brick which fell from the building. The work involved dislodging of bricks and the building in of new brickwork. The contractors erected elaborate tubular scaffolding, found to be the best of its kind, which covered the entire side of the building; at ground level steel shuttering 7 feet high; above that, wire netting 4 feet higher; and above that an apron or canopy at an angle upwards and outwards for about 5 feet to catch falling debris; wire netting was erected at the two storeys where the word was being done, and tarpaulin sheeting round the pneumatic drill which was being used to prevent debris going down the scaffold. It remained possible that material might be projected into the street or ricochet from the scaffold, and for that reason a man was posted in the street to warn passers-by. They also made inspections when the workmen finished work to make sure no loose bricks had been left.

The trial judge found the contractors had discharged the onus of proving no negligence and dismissed the claim.

HELD, ON APPEAL: The plaintiff had established a prima facie case, but the defendants had by the evidence satisfied the court there was no negligence, that is to say, that they had taken all reasonable steps in the performance of the work to prevent injury to persons using the highway. Although there was no explanation of the accident, the defendants were entitled to succeed if they could prove that there was no negligence on their part.

Aspin v Bretherton
See p 232, below.
It the defendants give an explanation consistent with negligence or no negligence, the onus of proof of negligence passes to the plaintiff.

The defendants are not required to prove exactly how the accident happened. It is sufficient for them to give an explanation which is consistent with no negligence.

Note—See also *Ludgate v Lovett*, p 55, below.

Swan v Salisbury Construction Co Ltd
[1966] 2 All ER 138, [1966] 1 WLR 204, 109 Sol Jo 195, PC
The plaintiff was employed by the defendants as a labourer on pile-driving, which was done by means of a crane. In the course of the work the crane toppled over and the plaintiff was injured. At the trial the judge accepted the evidence of another servant of the defendants' that the cause of the crane falling was that the ground gave way under one of the wheels of the crane and the wheel bolts sheared as a result of the jolt. The judge also found that having regard to the work which had already been done it was not reasonable to anticipate that the ground would give way or that extra precautions should have been taken against it. He gave judgment for the defendants.

HELD, ON APPEAL: There had been no failure on the part of the judge to apply the principles summarised in the phrase '*res ipsa loquitur*'. When once the plaintiff had proved he was injured by the collapse of the crane he was well on the way to proving his care — *res ipsa loquitur*. But the mere fact that the crane fell did not establish that the case must inevitably succeed: it was then for the defendants to show that they had not been negligent. The judge had decided on the evidence what caused the crane to fall over and that the defendants had taken reasonable care in positioning it. This was a conclusion of fact and not based on any error in law. Appeal dismissed.

VEHICLE COLLISIONS

Inference of negligence

Hummerstone v Leary
[1921] 2 KB 664, Div Ct
A collision between two cars raises an inference of negligence and the onus is on the defendants.

Plaintiffs, who were injured in a collision between a motor lorry, in which they were passengers, and a motor car, brought an action in the county court claiming damages, making the owners of both vehicles defendants. Plaintiffs' evidence appeared to make it probable that the driver of the car rather than the driver of the lorry was to blame, but they could do no more than state what they observed just before the collision occurred. Their evidence did not affirmatively or conclusively show that the driver of the lorry was not to blame. At the close of plaintiffs' case counsel for the owner of the lorry submitted that there was no evidence against him and the county court judge took this view and dismissed that defendant from the action. The case then proceeded against the other defendant, whose witnesses threw all the blame on the driver of the lorry, and the county court judge found that the driver of the car was not negligent, and accordingly entered judgment for the second defendant.
HELD: As a state of facts was proved by the plaintiffs from which the reasonable inference to be drawn was that, prima facie, one, if not both, of defendants was negligent, the county court judge should not have dismissed first defendant, the owner of the lorry, from the action at the close of plaintiffs' case, but should have heard the case against both defendants before coming to a decision, and therefore, there must be a new trial.

Baker v Market Harborough Co-operative Society
Wallace v Richards (Leicester) Ltd
[1953] 1 WLR 1472, 97 Sol Jo 861, CA
A motor lorry and a motor van, in the hours of darkness, descending hills in opposite directions, met at the bottom. The two vehicles had collided whilst the offside front wheel of one or other, or perhaps both, was over the 'cat's eyes' which demarked the centre of the road. Both drivers were killed. The widow of each sued the employers of the other. One action was dismissed by Ormerod J on the ground that the plaintiff had failed to prove negligence. In the second, Sellers J differed from Ormerod J in the inference to be drawn from the same facts and held both drivers equally to blame. Appeals in both cases were taken together.
HELD: The inference was that both drivers were negligent in not keeping a proper look-out and hugging the centre of the road. In the absence of evidence that one was more to blame that the other, the blame should be apportioned equally. Assuming that one vehicle was over the centre line a few inches, and thus to blame, why did not the other pull in more to its nearside? The absence of any avoiding action makes that vehicle also to blame. It was not necessary to prove that the other vehicle was over the cat's eyes. It was sufficient to show that the defendant should have taken avoiding action.

W. and M. Wood (Haulage) Ltd v Redpath

[1967] 2 QB 520, [1966] 3 All ER 556, [1966] 3 WLR 526, 110 Sol Jo 673
(Ashworth J)

Shortly before midnight a lorry and a car collided on the Great North Road. There was no other traffic, visibility was clear and from the point of collision it was possible to see in both directions for 350 yards. The occupants of the car were killed and the lorry driver died later. There were no other witnesses. There was some police evidence as to marks on the road which was inconclusive.

HELD: It was not possible to say with confidence which of the vehicles was over the centre line. In these circumstances the case fell within the principle applied in *Baker v Market Harborough Co-op Society*. There was no cogent evidence suggesting that one driver was more to blame than the other and the drivers must be held equally to blame.

Davison v Leggett

(1969) 133 JP 552, 113 Sol Jo 409, CA

The plaintiff driving his van on a straight main road overtook a car. The defendant riding a motor cycle in the opposite direction also overtook a car. The van and motor cycle collided in the middle of the road. The judge said he could find no indication who began overtaking first and who was in the wrong: it was feasible that neither was negligent. He dismissed both claim and counterclaim.

HELD, ON APPEAL: Following *Baker v Market Harborough* (above) where one or both parties were to blame and the court could not decide which, the inference was that both were equally to blame. The principle was not confined to cases where both drivers were dead or could not remember.

France v Parkinson

[1954] 1 All ER 739, [1954] 1 WLR 581, 98 Sol Jo 214, CA

Two motor cars collided at cross-roads of equal status. The driver of the plaintiff's car had hired the car under a false name and disappeared after the accident. The plaintiff's only evidence was that of a police officer from whose evidence it was reasonably plain that both cars were on the right side of their respective roads and they collided somewhere where the two cross roads met. He also gave evidence that the defendant said — 'I was going along the road and we met in the middle.' The defendant called no evidence and the judge dismissed the plaintiff's claim.

HELD, ON APPEAL: Following *Baker's* case, the balance of probabilities was in favour of both drivers having been negligent, particularly having regard to the place of collision and the statement to the police officer. There was a prima facie case against the defendant on which the court should have found him negligent in the absence of any evidence given by him. Appeal allowed.

Shiner v Webster

(1955) Times, 27 April

A motor cyclist was riding along a main road in broad daylight at 40 mph, and the rider of an auto-cycle was proceeding in the opposite direction and presumably was turning into a side road on his off side. A collision occurred and the auto-cyclist was killed and the motor cyclist suffered severe concussion and was unable to recollect anything about the accident. The only witness was the driver of a motor car following the auto-cyclist. This witness was certain that the deceased was intending to cross the road as he made a circular turn up to the middle of the road, showing that he was going to turn into the side road. It looked to him as though both acted as though the other was not on the road at all.

Finnemore J held there was not enough evidence to show whose negligence caused the accident and as in neither case had it been proved before him that there had been negligence, he gave judgment for the defendant in each of the two actions of the deceased's administrator against the motor cyclist and of the motor cyclist against the administrator. The administrator appealed.

HELD: A court cannot say — we do not know whose fault it was and therefore there is no remedy for anyone. It was impossible to take the view that neither saw the other. The trial judge was wrong in thinking that it was not proved that either were negligent. There was evidence of negligence on the part of both. Appeal allowed and, by a majority, both held equally to blame.

Howard v Bemrose
[1973] RTR 32, CA

On a country road in the dark a motor cycle and car collided at a bend. The car driver did not remember anything of the accident; the motor cyclist was killed. Marks and débris on the road and the final positions of the vehicles were the only evidence. The judge said that having examined all the facts and argument as put to the court he was unable to say whether or not (as had been argued) the car was on its offside of the road or not at the moment of impact. He therefore considered the right course to adopt was to apply the *Baker v Market Harborough Co-op* principle and hold the parties equally to blame. The motor cyclist's personal representative appealed.

HELD: The judge was entitled so to hold. What he was saying was that it was no more probable that the collision took place on the car driver's wrong side than that it took place in the centre of the road at the bend. As he was quite unable without independent evidence to say whether it was caused by the negligence of the motor cyclist rather than of the car driver he was right to divide the blame between them equally.

Bray v Palmer
[1953] 2 All ER 1499, [1953] 1 WLR 1455, 97 Sol Jo 830, CA

A motor cyclist with a pillion passenger was proceeding on the main road from Gloucester to Bristol and a small motor car with passengers was proceeding in the opposite direction. The time was about midday on 6 August 1951. The road was approximately 26 feet wide. There was no other traffic. There was a pool of water on the car's nearside. The car turned to the off to avoid this pool. The motor cycle also turned to its off side and there was a collision in the middle of the road. Both vehicles were proceeding at a reasonable speed. The motor cyclist alleged that the car turned so far to its off side that he had to turn to the off to avoid a collision.

The judge decided that the accident was due either to the sole negligence of the car driver or the sole negligence of the motor cyclist and was not prepared to find both to blame. He was unable to decide which was the right story, and on the principle that the claimant must prove his case he dismissed the claim of the motor cyclist and the counterclaim of the motor car driver.

HELD: The possibility of both to blame should not have been excluded. Until a judge has decided that an accident has happened in some particular way, he is not in a position to decide. New trial ordered.

Note—Distinguished in *Salt v Imperial Chemical Industries* (1958) Times, 1 February.

Price v Price
(1954) Times, 12 February, CA
In March 1949, the plaintiff was a pillion passenger on a motor cycle driven by his son and was injured in a collision with a Wallasey Corporation omnibus. On 19 April 1950, Mr Justice Oliver dismissed an action by the plaintiff against the Corporation, finding the son alone to blame.

The father then brought an action against the son. Mr Justice Devlin dismissed the claim and gave judgment for the son.

In both actions the plaintiff had given evidence that the son was not to blame.

HELD, ON APPEAL: The plaintiff had only himself to blame for not suing both parties in the first action. Appeal dismissed.

Defendant electing not to give evidence

Chapman v Copeland
(1966) 110 Sol Jo 569, Times, 7 May, CA
The plaintiff's husband was crossing the first lane of a dual carriageway on his moped when he was struck and killed by a car driven by the defendant. The evidence brought on behalf of the plaintiff was that her husband had waited for a time at the side of the road and had crossed 17 feet of the 24 feet wide lane when hit. A police officer gave evidence of marks on the road 184 feet long made by the car. The defendant by his counsel elected to give no evidence, maintaining that there was no evidence of negligence against him on behalf of the widow. The judge held the defendant wholly to blame.

An appeal was dismissed. In such a case as this the defendant was not under an obligation to give evidence, but if he chose not to do so he could not complain if on a narrow balance of probability the evidence justified the court in drawing the inference of negligence against him. On the slender evidence of the length of the brake marks the inference was sufficient for the court's purposes. On the question of contributory negligence it was for the defendant to prove it and again he had not done so.

Failure to discharge onus

Ludgate v Lovett
[1969] 2 All ER 1275, [1969] 1 WLR 1016, 113 Sol Jo 369, CA
The defendant hired a motor van from the plaintiff. It was in good condition with no mechanical defects. When the defendant was driving it

along a motorway at speed it suddenly swerved to right and left and turned over. The plaintiff sued for the damage done, pleading *res ipsa loquitur*. The county court judge accepted the defendant's evidence that he did not go to sleep nor fail to pay attention and that he was not negligent. The judge suggested an explanation of the accident which was not supported by any evidence and dismissed the claim.

HELD, ON APPEAL: The plaintiff was entitled to succeed. In a *res ipsa loquitur* case it is open to the defendant to satisfy the court that he took all reasonable precautions and was not negligent even though he cannot explain why or how the accident happened. But in the present case the presumption of negligence from the facts of the accident was too strong to be overcome merely by the defendant's denial that he had done anything negligent. The judge had accepted the defendant's evidence of no negligence only by advancing an explanation of his own. As this was not acceptable it remained that the defendant had not discharged the onus placed upon him by the plea *res ipsa loquitur*.

McBride v Stitt
[1944] NI 7, CA

The plaintiff's daughter was killed by a lorry owned by one of the defendants and driven on the public road by the other defendant. At the trial of an action brought by the plaintiff claiming damages for the negligent driving of the lorry no eye-witness of the accident was called and the principal evidence consisted of certain statements made by the defendants to the effect that two little boys having run from behind a motor car travelling in the opposite direction, the driver of the lorry was obliged to swerve in order to avoid hitting them, and in doing so struck the plaintiff's daughter who was cycling from a side street on to the road on which the lorry was travelling. At the close of the plaintiff's case the trial judge held that the statements were not admissions of negligence, that they pointed to inevitable accident, and that the plaintiff had not discharged the onus of proof, and gave judgment for the defendants.

HELD: By the Court of Appeal that the plaintiff had established a prima facie case of negligence of which no satisfactory explanation had been given by the defendants; and that the statements of the defendants whether in favour of the plaintiff or the defendants were admissible in evidence in toto; and that there should be a new trial of the action.

EVENTS IMPLYING NEGLIGENCE

Sudden stop or swerve

O'Hara v Central Scottish Motor Traction Co Ltd
1941 SC 363

Pulling up suddenly and violently is prima facie evidence of negligence (*Mars v Glasgow Corpn* 1940 SC 202) and so is a violent swerve.

Ballingall v Glasgow Corporation
1948 SC 160, Scot
Sudden braking of a tramcar to avoid a collision with a motor van going in
the opposite direction did not per se establish negligence of the driver.
Mars's case and *O'Hara's* case distinguished.

Doonan v Scottish Motor Traction Co
1950 SC 136, 1950 SLT 100, Ct of Sess
The fact that a bus struck a fence after a swerve raised a presumption of the
driver's negligence despite the explanation that the swerve was due to a
child's sudden running across the road.

Note—In the above three cases the plaintiff was a passenger in the defendant's
vehicle.

Ritchie's Car Hire Ltd v Bailey
(1958) 108 L Jo 348, Epsom CC (Gordon Clarke J)
Defendant hired a car from plaintiffs on terms that he was liable for damage
to the car unless he could show that such damage was not due to his act or
default. He was driving in an empty suburban street about 36 feet wide at
4.40 am. He was neither tired nor sleepy, driving under 30 mph about a
yard from the kerb when a cat suddenly ran out very near the car from the
near side. He instinctively swerved and hit a kerb tree almost simulta-
neously. He had no time to apply his brakes. The plaintiff sued defendant
for the damage to the car.
HELD: There might be a school of thought which said that a driver should
subordinate the interests of animals to the safety of his passengers, or even
of a vehicle, but such a doctrine had never been expressed by Parliament or
in the Highway Code. Nowhere was it stated that a driver was at fault in
swerving to avoid an animal. The defendant had apparently no time for
thought, but it could not be said that his action would have been a correct
one had he had time to reflect on it, yet in the particular circumstances it
could not also be said that what the defendant did was unreasonable.
Judgment for defendant.

Gussman v Gratton-Storey
(1968) 112 Sol Jo 884, CA
The defendant was driving her car along a country road in daylight when a
pheasant dashed out in front of the car. She instinctively braked hard and
swerved to avoid it. The plaintiff who was driving close behind her ran into
the back of her car. The county court judge in the plaintiff's claim for £62
damages said the defendant was negligent in braking and swerving for a
pheasant when there was a car behind and gave judgment for the plaintiff.
HELD, ON APPEAL: As the amount was under £200 there was no appeal on
fact and as the judge's view was a perfectly tenable one it could not be said
there was no evidence on which he could so decide. Appeal dismissed.

Note—Contrast *Ritchie's Car Hire Ltd v Bailey*, above, and *Parkinson v Liverpool Corpn*,
p 191, below.

Car on footpath

Ellor v Selfridge
(1930) 46 TLR 236, 74 Sol Jo 140
Where a motor van gets on to a pavement intended for foot passengers and
injures persons standing there, these facts, in the absence of explanation,
constitute evidence of negligence.

McGowan v Stott
(1923) 99 LJKB 357, 142 LT 217
Plaintiff was walking along a well defined footpath. Defendant's motor
vehicle mounted the footpath and struck plaintiff. This was considered
sufficient evidence of negligence.

Vehicle overlapping pavement

Laurie v Raglan Building Co
[1942] 1 KB 152, [1942] 3 All ER 332, 111 LJKB 292, 166 LT 63, 86 Sol Jo
69, CA
Where a portion of the vehicle sweeps across the pavement, the facts raise a
prima facie case of negligence just as much as where the wheels mount the
pavement. It is a position where it has no right to be. No vehicle has a right
so to manoeuvre itself that its tail or its radiator, or whatever it may be,
projects over the pavement to the injury of pedestrians lawfully there.

Watson v Thomas S. Whitney & Co Ltd
[1966] 1 All ER 122, [1966] 1 WLR 57, 110 Sol Jo 73, CA
Shortly after midnight the plaintiff was walking along the pavement about
six inches from the edge and with the roadway on his left. The defendants'
van turned in suddenly from the middle of the road to draw in alongside the
pavement for a passenger to alight. In doing so it struck the plaintiff's left
arm with the projecting handle of a door, causing him slight injury. The
registrar of the Liverpool Court of Passage held the defendant's driver not
to blame: he had difficulty in seeing the plaintiff whom he would not expect
to be there.
HELD, ON APPEAL: The registrar was wrong. There was no blame to be
attached to the plaintiff in walking close to the edge of the pavement. The
pavement should give security to those who use it from vehicles using the
road. There was clear liability on the driver where, as here, the vehicle
overlapped the footpath.

Note—See also *Chapman v Post Office* p 90, below.

Car in shop window

Gayler and Pope Ltd v Davies
[1924] 2 KB 75, 93 LJKB 702, 131 LT 507, 40 TLR 591, 68 Sol Jo 685
(McCardie J)

When a pony and van (or a motor vehicle) wholly unattended dash into plaintiff's shop window adjoining a highway there is a prima facie case of negligence.

Car on hill

Martin v Stanborough
(1924) 41 TLR 1, 69 Sol Jo 104
To leave a motor car unattended on a fairly steep slope in a public highway, with the brakes out of order and with only an easily removable block of wood to keep the car in position, so that the car could easily be started downhill by any mischievous person, constitutes evidence of negligence.

Car turning over

Halliwell v Venables
(1930) 99 LJKB 353, 143 LT 215, 74 Sol Jo 264, CA
The defendant was driving a fast small sports car. It was a dark night, dry; broad road; no other traffic, slight bend. The defendant said he was going at 35 mph, driving with one hand only on the wheel as was his usual practice. The car was found to have turned over, possibly twice, and bounced along the road. The passenger was thrown out on the right-hand side of the road and fatally injured. The car was found some way off the road on the left-hand side. On a submission by defendant's counsel in an action brought by the passenger's widow the judge held there was no case to go to the jury.
HELD, ON APPEAL: There was evidence which should have been submitted to the jury. The mere happening of the accident, unexplained, may be and often is in itself evidence of negligence. The facts required explanation by the person driving the car; they constituted an accident which would not usually happen with proper driving. New trial ordered.

Note—See also *Hurlock v Inglis*, p 119, below.

Colliding with stationary vehicle

Randall v Tarrant
[1955] 1 All ER 600, [1955] 1 WLR 255, 99 Sol Jo 184
The plaintiff stopped his car in a lane which was a public highway but only led to a farm occupied by the defendant. The lane was about 15 feet wide. The car was 5 feet 6 ins wide and as close as possible to the near side. The plaintiff trespassed into an adjoining field of the defendant, and while he was there the defendant drove a tractor towing a baler which was 9 feet wide along the lane. On approaching the car, which the defendant thought was unattended, he slowed down. His servant was sitting at the back of the baler and shouted 'I think we can get through, guv'nor'. In attempting to pass, the baler struck the car and damaged it.
HELD: When there is a collision between a moving vehicle and a stationary vehicle which is plainly visible, the onus is on the driver of the moving

vehicle to show that he has taken all reasonable care and the onus had not been discharged. The fact that plaintiff was trespassing on the defendant's field at the time did not make the plaintiff a trespasser on the highway in respect of the car, or that he was committing a nuisance, and the defence based on trespass failed.

Tyre bursting

Barkway v South Wales Transport Co Ltd
[1950] AC 185, [1950] 1 All ER 392, 66 TLR 597, 94 Sol Jo 128, HL
A motor omnibus of the defendants was proceeding along the highway when the off front tyre burst. The omnibus then went to the off side of the road, mounted the pavement, crashed into some railings and fell on its side down an embankment. Four passengers were killed and others injured.

The burst was caused by an impact fracture of the cord of the outer tyre brought about by a blow more severe than in the ordinary course on the external surface of the tyre causing some of the plys to become fractured. The tyre which burst was periodically examined on the rim by an expert fitter of the defendants. He examined it on frequent dates during January and February 1943, the last occasion on 24 February, three days before the accident and on each occasion adjusted the pressure, and he tested the pressure on 20 February and 22 February. There was no evidence when the impact fracture was caused. No instructions were given to drivers to report an unusual and heavy blow on the tyre. There was no examination of the internal surface. A burst in this size of tyre is very rare. The tyre would go in for thorough examination at 25,000 miles. It had not been taken off for examination for nearly 18 months, during which time it had run about 21,750 miles.

HELD, ON APPEAL to the House of Lords:
Per Lord Porter: Adopting the language in *Scott v London and St Katherine's Docks Co* (p 49, above), if the facts are sufficiently known, the question is whether on the established facts, negligence is to be inferred or not.

The decision in favour of the plaintiff depends on one or other of the grounds (1) whether there was negligence in the system of inspection, or (2) of any of the drivers in not reporting a blow severe enough to cause an impact fracture. The evidence established that a competent driver would recognise the difference between a blow heavy enough to endanger the strength of the tyre and a lesser concussion. If this be so, the fact that he would be unlikely to report it would still leave him negligent in not doing so, and for that negligence his employers must answer. In the second place, it was the duty of the respondents, who were fully aware of the possibility of an impact fracture, to instruct their employees as to the effect which a heavy blow may produce, and to impress upon them the necessity of reporting its incidence. An uninstructed driver might not know nor have experience of such a danger, and that difficulty would be surmounted if proper instructions were given. Such an incident is a rare event but the duty of a transport company is to take all reasonable precautions for the safety of their passengers and not to leave them in danger of a risk against which some precautions, at any rate, can be taken. Although the practice of inspection and overhaul of tyres was adequate in other respects, and was in accordance with the practice of companies carrying on a similar occupation, the respondents did not take all the requisite steps to protect their passengers from risk.

Per Lord Normand: The drivers themselves failed to report impacts which they ought to have reported, the respondents failed to instruct their drivers about impact fractures and to require them to report, and the tyre examiners ought to have been, but were not, informed. The defendants were liable.

Note—See also 'Latent Defect', p 240, below.

Elliott v Chiew
(1966), 110 Sol Jo 724, Times, 24 May, CA

The defendant was driving the plaintiff's car on the M1 motorway with the plaintiff as a passenger. When travelling at 70 to 80 mph the defendant felt a swaying of the car over the back wheels. It was corrected after a little distance but the defendant said at some point 'I can't hold the car'. After going all right for a few moments the car began to sway again: the defendant applied the brakes but the car went out of control over an embankment, seriously injuring the plaintiff. A police officer gave evidence that after the accident the rear offside tyre was flat. An expert gave evidence that the tyre had probably deflated gradually and that it should have been possible to bring the car under control. The judge found that the cause of the accident was in all probability a deflated tyre, that when the brakes were applied the car went out of control and that nothing which a reasonably competent driver could have done at that time could have prevented the accident. He dismissed the claim.

HELD, ON APPEAL: It was essentially a matter for the judge who heard the case and saw the witnesses. The principle of *res ipsa loquitur* enabled the plaintiff to get the case on its legs but at the end the judge had to ask himself: was the defendant negligent or not? It was a matter for regret that he had not referred to the expert's evidence but a judgment was not to be criticised because a judge did not refer to everything which no doubt had passed through his mind. Where there was this evidence from the driver and passengers from which the judge could conclude that the driver was not guilty of negligence the Court of Appeal should not interfere.

Door coming open

Note—See *Easson v London and North Eastern Rly Co*, under 'Passengers', p 196, below.

Independent wrongdoer

Ruoff v Long & Co
[1916] 1 KB 148, 85 LJKB 364, 114 LT 186, 32 TLR 82, 60 Sol Jo 323

The principle does not apply where the negligence is wholly that of an independent wrongdoer. A person lawfully leaving his property unattended in a highway must take reasonable means to prevent such mischief as he ought to contemplate as likely to arise from his use of the highway. He is not liable for damage caused by his property through such interference of a third person as he is not bound to anticipate.

Defendant's servants momentarily left stationary but unattended on a highway a steam motor lorry. In order to start the lorry it was necessary to withdraw a hand-pin from the gear lever and then to remove that and two other levers. Two soldiers seeing the lorry mounted it. One tried but failed to set it in motion. The other succeeded in starting it backwards, so that it ran into plaintiff's shop front and did damage, for which the action was brought.

HELD: (1) There was in the circumstances no evidence of negligence in leaving the lorry unattended. (2) Assuming that there was negligence, there was no evidence that it caused the damage.

Inference of negligence rebutted

Knight v Fellick
[1977] RTR 316, CA

In the hours of darkness in an unlighted street the plaintiff, a street sweeper, was injured when knocked over by the defendant's car. The plaintiff remembered nothing of the accident. The defendant did not see the plaintiff before the impact. There was a brief written statement by a witness who had since died but otherwise no account at the trial from an eye witness. The judge concluded from the available evidence including the position of damage to the car that the defendant was not to blame.

HELD, ON APPEAL: The judge's conclusions on a balance of probabilities were justified. It was not a case to which the principles applied in such cases as *Baker v Market Harborough Co-operative* and *Davison v Leggett* (pp 52–53, above) were applicable. That line of cases related to collisions between two vehicles more or less in the centre of the road and were not to be extended beyond that ambit. The inference of negligence from the defendant not having seen the plaintiff before impact had, on the available evidence, been rebutted.

CHAPTER 2
Liability of the driver

THE HIGHWAY CODE

Note—The Highway Code is issued with the authority of Parliament. The Road Traffic Act 1972, s 37(5) provides:

'(5) A failure on the part of a person to observe a provision of the Highway Code shall not of itself render that person liable to criminal proceedings of any kind, but any such failure may in any proceedings (whether civil or criminal . . .) be relied upon by any party to the proceedings as tending to establish or to negative any liability which is in question in those proceedings.'

The current edition of the Highway Code was issued in March 1978. Paragraphs 1 to 25 relate to pedestrians and paras 26 to 128 to 'The road user on wheels'. There are extra rules for cyclists in paras 129 to 137 and for those in charge of animals in paras 138 to 144. Motorway driving is dealt with in paras 145 to 175 and level crossings in paras 176 to 185.

CASES ON HIGHWAY CODE

Crash helmet

Note—See *O'Connell v Jackson*, p 16, above.

Herding animals

Andrews v Watts
[1971] RTR 484 (Karminski LJ)
The owner of some cattle wanted to fetch them from a field some distance
from her farm. She took two men to help her. It was a dark evening in
November. They got the cattle out from the field on to the road, one man
walking at the front and the other at the rear of the herd. Neither man was
carrying a light of any kind. The owner had parked her car in the road at
the gateway with dipped headlights on facing away from the herd. She
stood there herself to warn approaching traffic. A car came along at about
40 mph and the cattle owner waved it down. The driver, a 19-year old girl
took fright; she was dazzled by the headlights and seeing nothing beyond
thought it must be some kind of hold-up. Her own headlights were dipped.
She went on faster and ran into the man at the rear of the herd who by that
time was about 50 yards from the gateway. He was killed.
HELD: On a claim by the widow, both the driver and the cattle-owner were
to blame. The driver should have realised that the waving-down and the
headlights might be a warning of an obstruction; she should have reduced
her speed and put her headlights on full beam. The cattle-owner had
brought the cows on to the road, had failed to provide the men with any
lights (contrary to the advice in the Highway Code) and had pointed the
headlights away from the cattle instead of illuminating them. She was two-
thirds to blame and the driver one-third. The deceased was not to blame at
all.

Keep to the left

THE HIGHWAY ACT 1835, s 78

78 . . . if the driver of any waggon, cart or other carriage whatsoever . . . shall not
keep his waggon, cart or carriage . . . on the left or nearside of the road . . . [he]
shall, in addition to any civil action to which he may make himself liable . . . forfeit
any sum not exceeding five pounds . . .

Nuttall v Pickering
[1913] 1 KB 14, 82 LJKB 36, 107 LT 852, Div Ct
A waggon was being driven so far beyond the centre of the road that when a
motor car approached from behind the waggoner drew further to his offside
and waved to the motorist to overtake on his nearside, which he did. There
were no other vehicles on the road.
HELD: The waggoner was not guilty of an offence under s 78 (above). No
inconvenience was caused to the motorist, who was quite willing to pass on
the nearside and did. When there is no other traffic on a road the driver of a
vehicle is entitled to go on to any part of the road he wishes.

Pluckwell v Wilson
(1832) 5 C & P 375
Per Alderson J: A person is not bound to keep on the ordinary side of the road; but if he does not do so he is bound to use more care and diligence and keep a better look-out than would be requisite if he confine himself to his proper side of the road.

Phillips v Britannia Hygienic Laundry Co
[1923] 1 KB 539, affd. [1923] 2 KB 832, 93 LJKB 5, 129 LT 777, 39 TLR 530, 68 Sol Jo 102
Per McCardie J: So far as I know, it has not been held that a mere breach of [s 78] ipso facto gives a cause of action for damage. On the contrary, it has been held in cases of collision there is no such rule of the road as to make the left always the proper side . . . I think that in spite of s 78 a man may sometimes and without negligence keep on his right hand side, and, indeed, if by so doing he can avoid a collision, it is his duty to do so.

Pleading

Wells v Weeks
[1965] 1 All ER 77, [1965] 1 WLR 45, 108 Sol Jo 1032 (Lawton J)
A statement of claim in an action arising from a road accident included in the particulars of negligence the words 'The plaintiff will also rely on s 74 of the Road Traffic Act 1960 (now s 37 of the Road Traffic Act 1972), and on all the provisions of the Highway Code applicable to the drivers of motor vehicles in so far as the same are applicable in the circumstances', said by counsel to be adapted from *Bullen & Leake* (11th edn) p 537. The judge said pleading in such an imprecise manner invited a request for further and better particulars and he was surprised no request had been made.

CAUSATION: REMOTENESS

Lloyds Bank Ltd v Budd
[1982] RTR 80, CA
A lorry broke down with clutch trouble on the A1 road and was left all night in a lay-by. Early on the following morning, in daylight but in fog, the driver, Lake, with a mechanic returned to the vehicle to repair it. They found it capable of being driven and decided to take it to a place more convenient for them to do the repair. After a short distance had been done, however, it again broke down and came to a halt on the carriageway blocking it. Because of the fog the mechanic went to the rear of the vehicle to warn traffic. A police car leading a line of vehicles came to a stop when he waved it down. The police officers went to the front of the lorry to attach a tow rope. Three or four minutes later there was a series of collisions at the back of the stationary convoy as vehicles came through the fog and failed to pull up in time. A car in which the plaintiff's husband was a passenger struck a stationary vehicle in front of it and was then struck very violently by a lorry driven by the first defendant, Budd. The plaintiff's husband was killed. The judge said it was negligent of Lake to take his lorry out on to the carriageway and that it created a nuisance, but he considered the nuisance

or negligence too remote to be a cause of the accident. He found Budd alone to blame for the death.

HELD, ON APPEAL: Lake's negligence was not too remote. Despite the interval between the convoy coming to a halt and the subsequent collisions the broken down vehicle was a cause of the collisions. Budd was the more blameworthy, however, in driving much too fast in fog. Apportionment of blame: Budd 60%, Lake 40%.

Note—See also *Rouse v Squires*, p 222, below and 'Novus actus interveniens,' pp 371–375, below.

LEADING AND FOLLOWING VEHICLE

Jungnikel v Laing
(1966) 111 Sol Jo 19, CA

Lorry A was travelling in the slow lane of the M1 motorway at night when it was run into from behind by lorry B. As a result of the collision lorry B crossed the central island on to the other carriageway and there turned over. The plaintiff's husband driving a mini-truck ran into it and was killed.

As between the two lorry drivers the judge held the driver of lorry B 90% to blame for not keeping a proper look-out but said the driver of lorry A was 10% to blame because he had effected a sudden reduction of speed without warning, as if changing gear.

HELD, ON APPEAL: The driver of lorry A was not at all to blame. Even on the M1 deceleration without warning is not an act of negligence. If a driver was going to make a sudden heavy stop he was under a duty to give warning to traffic behind, but not if he was merely decelerating. Moreover his failure to warn had no causative effect since the driver of lorry B was not keeping a look-out and would not have seen a signal.

Brown and Lynn v Western Scottish Motor Traction Co Ltd
1945 SC 31, Ct of Sess

A motor lorry was travelling along a public street followed at a distance of 25 to 30 feet by a motor omnibus, the speed of both vehicles being approximately 15 mph. The driver of the lorry, in order to avoid a pedestrian, swerved suddenly to the left and pulled up almost instantaneously, and the driver of the omnibus, when he realised that the lorry was stopping, swerved to the right and applied his brakes, but, although he acted with reasonable promptitude, he did not succeed in avoiding a collision. The driver of the lorry had no time to give any signal, and the driver of the omnibus had not seen, and had no reasonable chance of seeing the pedestrian.

HELD: (Lord Stevenson dissenting): The fact that the driver of the omnibus, although allowing a sufficient space between the vehicles in which to deal with the ordinary exigencies of traffic, had followed the lorry so closely that he could not cope with its exceptionally abrupt stop did not amount to negligence upon his part, and, accordingly, that the owners of the omnibus were not liable to the owners of the lorry for the damage sustained by their vehicle.

Per Lord Cooper: The distance which should separate two vehicles travelling one behind the other must depend upon many variable factors — their speed, the nature of the locality, the other traffic present or to be expected, the opportunity available to the following driver of commanding a view ahead of the leading vehicle, the distance within which the following vehicle can be pulled up, and many other things. The following driver is, in my view, bound, so far as reasonably possible, to take up such a position and to drive in such a fashion, as will enable him to deal successfully with all traffic exigencies reasonably to be anticipated: but whether he has fulfilled this duty must in every case be a question of fact whether, on any emergency disclosing itself, the following driver acted with the alertness, skill and judgment reasonably to be expected in the circumstances.

Scott v Warren
[1974] RTR 104, Div Ct
The defendant was driving a car behind a van, both travelling at about 20 to 25 mph. The van driver braked suddenly to avoid a large piece of metal which dropped off a lorry in front. The defendant did not see the metal fall, his vision being obstructed by the van, and he had no warning that the van driver was about to make an emergency stop. He braked but was unable to avoid colliding with the back of the van. The prosecution, on a charge of driving without due care, presented it as a matter of settled law that if a driver did not leave sufficient space between himself and the vehicle in front to avoid a collision whatever the circumstances, he was guilty of the offence charged; the Highway Code (1968), rr 34 and 35 were relied on.
HELD: The proposition could not be accepted. The words of Lord Cooper in *Brown and Lynn v Western Scottish Motor Traction Co Ltd* (quoted above) indicated a standard to be observed by a following driver appropriate in civil cases. The obligation could not be higher on a criminal charge. In the present case it could not be said the justices were perverse in finding the defendant not guilty of the offence.

Note—The Highway Code (1968), rr 34 and 35 are repeated, with some elaboration, in the Highway Code (1978), rr 46 and 47.

Parnell v Receiver for Metropolitan Police
[1975] 1 Lloyd's Rep 492, CA
The plaintiff was a passenger in a mini-bus being driven about two vehicle lengths behind a large tipper lorry along a road having no crossroads, pedestrian crossings or other interferences. The lorry suddenly stopped for no apparent reason and without warning. The driver of the mini-bus had to brake hard to avoid hitting it and was successful in pulling up 6 feet behind the lorry without his brakes locking. The plaintiff was thrown forward and ricked her neck.
HELD: The test to be applied was that laid down by Lord Cooper in *Brown and Lynn v Western Scottish Motor Traction Co Ltd* (above). The view expressed in *Wooller v London Transport Board* (p 193, below) was relevant to the present case. On the facts the driver was not negligent.

Thompson v Spedding
[1973] RTR 312, CA
The plaintiff was riding her moped in a moving line of traffic. There was a Triumph car ahead of her, and in front of that, a Morris driven by the defendant. The Morris pulled up sharply preparatory to turning right. The Triumph was able to pull up safely without colliding with the Morris but the plaintiff could not pull up in time and in trying to avoid the Triumph collided with it and was injured. The judge held the defendant wholly to blame, saying that the plaintiff was not required to ride her moped on the basis that the defendant was suddenly going to stop and put her and the driver in front in jeopardy.
HELD, ON APPEAL: The judge had failed to express correctly the duty of persons driving in a line of traffic; it was to drive at such a distance behind the car in front as to be prepared for foreseeable emergencies. The plaintiff's blame was equal to that of the defendant.

Sharp v Avery
[1938] 4 All ER 85, CA
A motor cyclist in company with another motor cyclist carrying a pillion passenger was proceeding from London to Southend. The two motor cyclists agreed that one of them, 'A' should lead the other because he knew the way. The other followed at a distance of about 8 yards. The leading motor cyclist mistook the road and drove on to some waste ground. He then applied his brakes and skidded forward gradually slowing down. The second motor cyclist followed on to the waste ground and collided with the first motor cycle and the pillion passenger on the second motor cycle was injured.
HELD: The first motor cyclist was negligent and in the circumstances there was a duty on him not to mislead the motor cyclist who was following. Verdict against 'A' upheld.

Smith v Harris
[1939] 3 All ER 960, 83 Sol Jo 730, CA
Five motor cyclists were engaged in a treasure hunt. P was apparently clever at finding clues, and it was agreed between them that he should lead the hunt. They were proceeding at about 25 to 30 mph and about 8 yards between each. P overshot a turning and braked hard. He did not swerve either to the left or right to give those behind him a chance of avoiding him. O, who was next, was spreadeagled on the ground to the right of P, and M, who was third, was spreadeagled to the left. H, with the plaintiff as pillion passenger, who was fourth, swerved out to avoid M but ran into O and overturned, and plaintiff was injured. The county court judge held that P was negligent in the way he drew up, and H for not having proper control of his machine, and found each equally to blame.
HELD, ON APPEAL: It was a question of fact. The case *Sharp v Avery* above laid down no fresh principle of law. Appeal dismissed.

Motorway concertina collision

Smith v Samuel Williams & Sons

(1972) Times, 3 March (Bristow J)

A recovery vehicle was towing a Scammell lorry in the slow lane of the M1 motorway at about 25 mph at night. Behind was a lorry driven by the plaintiff's husband at 50 mph, followed at two or three lengths by another lorry travelling at the same speed. A concertina collision occurred in which the plaintiff's husband was killed.

HELD: The driver of the rearmost lorry, which had crashed into the back of the deceased's lorry, was undoubtedly negligent in driving much too close, but a careful analysis of the evidence showed that the fatal injuries were those to the deceased's legs, caused by the collision with the Scammell, and that there had been only one blow to the legs. It followed that the first collision was between the deceased's lorry and the Scammell: the subsequent collision had not contributed to the death of the deceased. The action accordingly failed.

LEARNER DRIVER

Provisional driving licence

Note—By Motor Vehicles (Driving Licences) Regulations 1981, SI 1981/952), reg 8, a provisional licence is subject to the condition that the holder shall use it only when under the supervision of a person who holds a licence, not being a provisional licence, authorising him to drive a motor vehicle of the same class as that being driven by the holder of the provisional licence. This person shall, except in the case of a motor cycle or invalid carriage, be present with him in or on the vehicle.

Duty of care

Nettleship v Weston

[1971] 2 QB 691, [1971] 3 All ER 581, [1971] 3 WLR 370, 115 Sol Jo 624, CA

The defendant asked the plaintiff to teach her to drive. He was not a professional instructor. He agreed to do so, having first asked about insurance and been told by the defendant that there was comprehensive insurance which covered him as a passenger. During the defendant's third lesson the plaintiff told her to move off from a halt sign and turn left. She did so but failed to straighten up. Despite the plaintiff's efforts to apply the handbrake and move the steering wheel the car mounted the pavement and struck a lamp-post. The plaintiff was injured. The judge of assize dismissed his claim for damages saying that the only duty the defendant owed him was to do her best and this she had done.

HELD, ON APPEAL: This was not right. The standard of care owed by any driver, whether a learner or not, is that of a driver of skill, experience and care, who is sound in mind and limb, eyesight and hearing, makes no errors of judgment and is free from infirmity. The duty of care is the same to all persons on or near the highway, whether passengers or not and is the same to an instructor, with this exception, that there would be no liability if he had voluntarily agreed to take the risk of injury. The defence of *volenti non fit injuria* is not available unless the plaintiff expressly or impliedly agreed to waive any claim for injury that may befall him. In the present case the plaintiff did not so agree: he asked about insurance to make sure he was covered. But an instructor could be guilty of contributory negligence in for example, not being quick enough to correct errors. Moreover an instructor and learner are jointly concerned in driving the car and together must maintain the same measure of control over the car as an experienced and skilful driver. If an accident happens one or both must have been at fault: in the absence of evidence to distinguish between them they should be held equally to blame. That was the case here and the plaintiff was entitled to half his damages.

Note—Salmon LJ disagreed that the defence of *volenti* was not available against an instructor in the absence of agreement to waive any claim. He held that as an instructor knows the learner has practically no driving experience or skill he is not owed the duty of care to be expected from a skilled driver: the instructor voluntarily agrees to run the risk of injury. But he held that this plaintiff's enquiry about insurance had altered the whole relationship to one in which the defendant accepted responsibility for any injury. Megaw LJ dissented on the question of contributory negligence: he could not see that, on the facts, the plaintiff had done anything wrong.

Rubie v Faulkner
[1940] 1 KB 571, [1940] 1 All ER 285, 109 LJKB 241, 163 LT 212, 104 JP 161, 56 TLR 303, 84 Sol Jo 257, Div Ct
The appellant, while in a motor vehicle driven by the holder of a provisional licence (a 'learner driver') who was driving under his supervision in accordance with the Motor Vehicles (Driving Licences) Regulations 1937, reg 16(3)(a) (see now the Motor Vehicles (Driving Licences) Regulations 1976, reg 8), was in a position to see that the driver was about to overtake another vehicle by pulling considerably to the offside at a pronounced bend of the road, but he neither said nor did anything to prevent it. An accident occurred and the driver was convicted of driving without due care and attention.
HELD: That the appellant was rightly convicted of aiding and abetting the driver in the commission of the offence.

Per Hilbery J: The Regulation is framed to make some provision for the protection of the public against the dangers to which they are exposed through a car being driven on the road by a driver who is still a learner and therefore assumed to be not fully competent. The supervisor must be intended by the Regulation to have the duty, by supervision, of making up as far as possible the driver's incompetence. In other words, it is the supervisor's duty, when necessary, to do whatever can reasonably be expected to be done by a person supervising the acts of another to prevent that other from acting unskilfully or carelessly or in a manner likely to cause danger to others, and to this extent to participate in the driving.

R v Clark
Daily Telegraph 30 May 1950 (Sheriff Substitute, Dundee)
A supervisor of an 'L' driver of a motor lorry was held to be the person in charge of the vehicle and convicted of being under the influence of drink to

such an extent as to be incapable of having proper control. There was a continuing duty on the part of the supervisor to control the learner's driving which was not interrupted because the learner was driving properly. *Rubie v Faulkner* followed.

Gibbons v Priestley
[1979] RTR 4, QBD (Judge Lymbery QC)
After 18 lessons in a driving school car which had dual controls the plaintiff, a woman of 51, went out with the instructor in her husband's car which did not have dual controls. At a T junction the plaintiff came to a halt before turning left. On starting forward and turning left she let the clutch in too fast, failed to straighten up and crashed into a tree. The whole incident from start to stop lasted about five seconds. She sustained injury and sued the instructor for damages, claiming that he was negligent in letting her drive on the highway in a car without dual controls and in failing at the time of the accident to take any proper steps to avoid the collision.
HELD: The instructor was not liable because (1) it was not wrong to allow the plaintiff to drive without dual controls in the light of the knowledge he had of the stage her tuition had reached. (2) The passenger supervisor of a learner driver, whether he is a driving instructor or not is not a passenger purely and simply. He has a responsibility of care jointly with the learner driver to other road users in relation to the safe conduct and control of the car on the road. Further, the supervisor and the learner each has a responsibility to the other in the exercise of control over the car in which they are travelling. Circumstances may vary anywhere between nought and 100% as to the comparative blameworthiness of the one as compared with the other. In the short time available the instructor could not reasonably have done more than he did, namely, to shout 'Brake, brake' and pull on the handbrake. (3) The instructor was negligent in failing to recommend the plaintiff to wear her seat belt but this was not a cause of the collision.

Thompson v Lodwick
[1983] RTR 76, QBD
A learner driver who owned a car asked the defendant to sit with him in the car as a qualified driver. The defendant did not ask about the insurance of the car. He was convicted of 'permitting' the driver to drive without third-party insurance.
HELD, ON APPEAL: The fact that the defendant's presence in the car was necessary to enable the owner to drive lawfully did not mean that he was in a position to permit or refuse the use by the owner of the vehicle. Conviction quashed.

No supervision

Verney v Wilkins
(1962) 106 Sol Jo 879 (Winn J)
The infant plaintiff was injured when riding as a passenger in a car driven by the defendant. The car ran out of control and overturned. The defendant held only a provisional licence and there was no one in the car who was a qualified driver.

HELD: There was no actionable claim against the driver merely on the ground that injury had been caused by him and that at the time he was not a fully licensed driver, or was one who had not passed the driving test.

The statutory requirements with regard to learner drivers did not give rise to any cause of action for damages sustained as a result of his driving, whether or not a more skilful driver might have avoided those consequences. The breach of statutory duty per se was not a cause of action. On the facts, however, the defendant had not discharged the onus on him of disproving negligence and was liable.

Examiner not liable

British School of Motoring Ltd v Simms
[1971] 1 All ER 317, [1971] RTR 190 (Talbot J)
A learner driver was undergoing a driving test by a Ministry of Transport examiner. She approached a road junction governed by a 'Give Way' sign and broken white lines. She failed to see them and drove into the junction. The examiner saw a car approaching and applied the brake. The test car stopped in the path of the other car and was struck, causing another collision with the plaintiffs' car. They sued the learner and examiner, alleging negligence against him on the grounds (1) that he failed to ensure that the learner paid regard to the 'Give Way' sign and lines and failed to apply the brake soon enough and (2) that he applied the brakes when it was unsafe and stopped the car in the path of the other car.
HELD: The examiner was not negligent because (1) he is not in the position of a driving instructor but is there to observe if mistakes are made: he should not interfere with the driving except where it is essential in the interests of safety; (2) his application of the brakes was done in the agony of the moment and following the principle in *Jones v Boyce* (p 190, below) and *The Bywell Castle* (1879) 4 PD 219, he was not to be blamed if what he reasonably did in the circumstances turned out to be wrong.

LIABILITY FOR CHILDREN

Child pedestrians

Gough v Thorne
[1966] 3 All ER 398, [1966] 1 WLR 1387, 110 Sol Jo 529, CA
The plaintiff aged $13\frac{1}{2}$ was waiting with her brothers aged 17 and 10 to cross the road. A lorry stopped to allow them to cross. The driver put his right hand out to warn other traffic and beckoned the children to cross. They had got across just beyond the lorry when a car driven by the defendant came past the lorry at speed and hit the plaintiff. The judge held the defendant negligent but said the plaintiff was one-third to blame for having advanced past the lorry into the open road without pausing to see whether there was any traffic coming from her right.
HELD, ON APPEAL: The plaintiff was not to blame at all. Though there was no age below which it could be said that a child could not be guilty of contributory negligence age was a most material fact to be considered. The question whether the plaintiff could be said to be guilty of contributory

negligence depended on whether any ordinary child of $13\frac{1}{2}$ could be expected to do any more than she did. If she had been a good deal older she might have wondered whether a proper signal had been given and looked to see whether any traffic was coming, but it was quite wrong to suggest that a child of $13\frac{1}{2}$ should go through such mental processes.

Note—See also *Minter v D & H Contractors*, p 14, above.

Andrews v Freeborough
[1966] 2 All ER 721, [1966] 3 WLR 342, 110 Sol Jo, 407, CA
An eight-year old girl and her brother, aged four, were standing on the pavement edge waiting to cross the road. The defendant was driving her car at 15–20 mph close to the kerb (because of oncoming traffic) and saw the children when she was about 40 yards away. She thought they were waiting to cross though they did not look in her direction. She did not slacken speed or sound her horn. As the car passed the children the girl's head came into violent contact with the windscreen. At the trial of the action the defendant said she saw the girl step off the pavement into the side of the car but the judge did not accept this evidence. He held the defendant to blame (1) for not sounding her horn, (2) for failing to reduce her speed and if necessary stop on seeing the children, (3) for driving too close to the kerb. He found no contributory negligence on the part of the child. On appeal, the defendant did not dispute the finding of negligence in not sounding the horn but disputed the judge's other findings including that of no contributory negligence.

The appeal was dismissed.

Per Willmer LJ: I confess I find it quite difficult to appreciate just how the accident happened if the child remained throughout standing on the kerb. But [the judge's] finding that the child did not step off the kerb was a finding of primary fact, based largely on his view of the quality of the evidence he had heard. In my judgment it is not a finding with which this Court could properly interfere . . . I would only add that if I thought that we could properly find that this child did step off the kerb into the road, I should have needed a good deal of persuasion before imputing contributory negligence to the child having regard to her tender age.

Per Davies LJ: So far as concerns the finding that the defendant was negligent in driving too close to the kerb it is not easy to see the justification for it save in the light of the judge's conclusion that the little girl while still on the pavement was caught up by the car. Failure to slow or stop is another matter: in the light of the fact that the defendant had seen the children and had failed to call their attention to her presence the judge was entitled to make this finding. On the question whether, as the judge found, the child was caught up by the car or, as the defendant said, she stepped off from the kerb into the side of the car I am bound to say that I incline to the view that it was more probable that the child did step off the kerb into the side of the car. But it is not necessary to express any decided view on this point for the little girl was only eight years of age. Even if she did step off into the car it would not be right to count as negligence on her part such a momentary, though fatal, act of inattention or carelessness.

Prudence v Lewis
(1966) Times, 21 May (Brabin J)
The infant plaintiff aged just under three was struck by the defendant's car on a pedestrian crossing. His mother had been waiting to cross, holding her youngest child in a push chair poised on the edge of the kerb at the crossing: while she looked round for her third child the plaintiff ran on to the crossing and was hit when about 7 feet from the kerb.
HELD: The defendant was wholly to blame. He had seen the mother and children but, though realising that any child was likely to run out, did not blow his horn, thought that they should wait for him and drove on. A child of just under three was incapable of being guilty of contributory negligence.

Jones v Lawrence
[1969] 3 All ER 267
The plaintiff, a boy aged seven, ran across a street 22 feet wide from behind a parked van. The defendant was riding his motor cycle near the crown of the road and was unable to avoid striking the plaintiff, who had failed to see the motor cycle approaching. There was a 30 mph speed limit but the judge found from independent evidence that the defendant's speed was about 50 mph.
HELD: By travelling at such a speed the defendant had deprived himself of the opportunity to avoid the collision by swerving or braking and was negligent. The plaintiff's behaviour was such as one could expect in a normal child of his age momentarily forgetful of the perils of crossing a road and no finding of contributory negligence could be made against him.

Moore v Poyner
[1975] RTR 127, CA
The defendant was driving his car at 25–30 mph along a street in a poor district in Birmingham on a Sunday afternoon. There was no other traffic. A coach 30 feet long was parked against the nearside pavement and concealed from the defendant an opening between the houses on that side of the road just beyond the front of the coach. As the defendant's car was passing the coach the plaintiff, a child of six, ran from the opening across the front of the coach into the defendant's path and was struck by the nearside front of the car. The judge held the defendant liable: he should have slowed down or sounded his horn.
HELD, ON APPEAL: The defendant was not liable. The test to be applied to the facts was this: would it have been apparent to a reasonable man, armed with commonsense and experience of the way pedestrians, particularly children, are likely to behave in the circumstances such as were known to the defendant to exist in the present case, that he should slow down or sound his horn, or both? What course of action would he have to take if he was going to make quite certain that no accident would occur? Ought he to have slowed down to such an extent that there could have been no possibility of a child's running out at any moment in front of him and his being unable to stop without striking the child? To do so he would have had to slow down to something like 5 mph. Such a duty of care would be unreasonable; the chance that a child would run out at the precise moment he was passing the coach was so slight as not to require him to slow down to that

extent. As for sounding the horn, drivers in traffic are constantly exposed to the danger of pedestrians stepping out in front of parked vehicles. It would be an impossible burden for drivers to sound their horns every time they passed a parked vehicle.

Kite v Nolan
(1982) 126 Sol Jo 821, [1983] RTR 253, CA
The defendant was driving his car on a hot afternoon when he saw an ice-cream van parked on the offside of the road in front of him. He also saw three cars parked on the nearside ahead of the van. He slowed almost to a standstill to allow an approaching car to pass between the van and the parked cars. He then accelerated to about 15 mph. The plaintiff, aged five, ran out in front of him from between the parked cars and was struck by the defendant's car. The judge found that the defendant could not have avoided striking the plaintiff unless travelling at not more than 5 mph. He held that the defendant was not negligent, referring to *Moore v Poyner* (above). On appeal it was argued that the defendant should have realised the serious risk of a child running out bearing in mind the weather and the attraction of the ice-cream van.
HELD: The judge had decided correctly. He had to determine what was a reasonable standard of care in all the circumstances of the particular case. He would have regard to many factors including the following: (1) the likelihood of a pedestrian crossing the road, considering the allurement of the ice-cream van; (2) the nature of the pedestrian likely to cross, child or adult; (3) the likely degree of injury if struck; (4) the adverse consequences to the public and to the defendant of taking whatever precautions are under consideration. The application of the principles must always depend on the particular circumstances of the case; any decision applying the general standard to particular facts is unlikely to, almost cannot, produce a precedent. The judge had not treated *Moore v Poyner* as a precedent. He had correctly applied the general principle.

Davies v Journeaux
[1975] 1 Lloyd's Rep 483, CA
The plaintiff, aged $11\frac{1}{2}$, was struck by the defendant's car when running across the road from the pavement on the defendant's nearside. She had come down a flight of steps to the pavement, which was 3 feet wide. The entrance to the steps was 3 or 4 feet wide. She was struck by the offside front of the car which, after the accident, was parallel with the pavement and 4 feet and 9 ins from it. There was a mark on the road behind the nearside rear wheel 22 feet long indicating heavy application of the brakes. The passenger in the nearside front seat of the car saw the plaintiff as she stood momentarily in the entrance to the steps and then dashed across. The defendant did not see her until she was in the act of dashing across; he was then 50 to 60 feet away, travelling at 20 to 25 mph. The judge held him 40% to blame for having failed to see the plaintiff at the moment when his passenger did and failing to sound his horn.
HELD: The fact that the passenger saw the plaintiff a split second before the defendant did not establish a lack of proper care on the defendant's part; he was driving and needed to switch his eyes from one direction to another. Even if he had seen the plaintiff at the same instant it could not be

said he should then have sounded his horn; what he did do was to apply his brakes heavily. Having regard to the brake marks he had acted promptly and efficiently. The judge's decision seemed to place a duty on motorists to sound the horn virtually whenever they see a pedestrian, regardless of whether the pedestrian is manifesting an intention of leaving the pavement and dashing across the road. Appeal allowed.

Foskett v Mistry
[1984] RTR 1, [1984] LS Gaz R 2683, CA
The plaintiff, a boy of $16\frac{1}{2}$, ran down a parkland slope on to a busy road and collided with the nearside of the defendant's car near the windscreen, sustaining serious injury. The defendant had not seen him before he ran into the car. A driver coming in the opposite direction had seen the plaintiff and thought he was going to run into the road. The judge at first instance dismissed the claim.
HELD, ON APPEAL: The root of liability was negligence, which depended on the facts: reference to authorities in simple running-down cases was unnecessary. Could the defendant be shown to have failed to take reasonable care in all the circumstances? The defendant taking reasonable care ought to have glanced at the open parkland on his left and should have seen the plaintiff when he emerged into his view. A reasonably careful driver would have sounded his horn in the circumstances; if the defendant had seen the plaintiff and sounded his horn probably the accident would have been prevented. The defendant was plainly negligent, though the plaintiff was guilty of contributory negligence to the extent of 75%.
   Appeal allowed.

Allurement to children

Rawsthorne v Ottley
[1937] 3 All ER 902 (Hilbery J)
A tip-up lorry in the charge of a single driver had delivered coke in a school playground, and was driving away when a number of boys jumped on to the rear of the lorry causing the tipping part to tip up. Another boy, the plaintiff, had jumped on to the lorry immediately behind the driver's cab, and when the tipping part of the lorry was suddenly released it came down on the plaintiff and crushed his leg. The headmaster of the school had left the boys to play in the playground and had returned into the school premises before the arrival of the lorry. He did not know of the arrival of the lorry. An action for damages was brought against the managers of the school, the headmaster and the owners of the lorry.
HELD: (1) The headmaster was not negligent in leaving the boys in the playground without supervision, nor ought he to have taken steps to stop the lorry from coming during playtime. The headmaster and the managers were accordingly not liable. (2) The owners of the lorry had sent the lorry in the charge of a reasonable adult, and ought not reasonably to have anticipated interference. (3) The driver was not negligent in not looking to see if the boys had jumped on to the lorry, and he could not have anticipated sufficient weight to tip the lorry. The owners of the lorry were, therefore, not liable. (4) A lorry as such is not an allurement to children.

Creed v John McGeoch & Sons
[1955] 3 All ER 123, [1955] 1 WLR 1005, 99 Sol Jo 563 (Ashworth J)
Defendants were contractors for road making on some spare ground or
waste land which was freely used by the public and children played on it.
They left a two-wheeled trailer fitted with a towing bar used for removing
kerbs, about 6 feet from the roadside kerb. On Saturday afternoon a girl
aged five with three other children were playing on the trailer and the girl
was injured. The defendants were not occupiers and their duty was higher
than that of occupiers on the principle of *Donoghue v Stevenson* (p 228, below)
and *Buckland v Guildford Light & Coke Co* (p 504, below). The defendants
knew that the trailer was attractive and dangerous to children who might
play on the trailer and be injured, and were negligent in not taking precautions to prevent injury to children, and were liable to damages to the
injured girl.

Note—This case, in which a motor vehicle is not concerned, bears some resem-
blance to *Rawsthorne's* case but *Rawsthorne's* case was not cited.

Culkin v McFie
[1939] 3 All ER 613 (Croom-Johnson J)
A motor lorry and trailer was carrying sacks of sugar on the highway and
sugar was leaking from one sack. A boy aged seven ran off the pavement
after the lorry had passed him but not the trailer, and his foot was run over
by the trailer. The accident happened in a street in which there were three
schools, and on a school holiday. The practice of boys running after the
lorries was well known, and the driver of the lorry had frequently had
trouble with the boys. There was an alternative route close by. The defendants did nothing to prevent the sugar escaping on to the roadway.
HELD: The lorry was an allurement to the infant and a concealed danger;
he was lawfully on the highway and was indulging a natural instinct and
not guilty of contributory negligence. Defendants had placed a manifest
allurement to children on the highway with an insufficient number of look-
out men, and were liable.

MAKING HIGHWAY DANGEROUS

Note—See also 'Nuisance on highway', p 309, below.

Lorry dropping acid

Pope v Fraser
(1938) 55 TLR 324, 83 Sol Jo 135
Lorry on highway loaded with carboys of sulphuric acid. Without driver's
knowledge and without negligence, one carboy became cracked and the
acid ran into the road. After going some distance, the driver was told of the
leakage, but did not return for nearly half an hour and took no steps to warn
persons on the highway of the danger. In the interval, plaintiff on a motor
cycle, saw the patch of acid extending across the road, but thought it was
water. His machine skidded in the acid and he fell and was burned.
HELD: The driver could have discovered the leakage when he stopped and
it was his duty to go back and warn traffic, and defendants were liable.

Smoking exhaust

Tysoe v Davis
[1984] RTR 88, [1983] Crim LR 684 (Skinner J)
The defendant was driving a horsebox which was emitting dense clouds of
smoke. A Landrover was travelling behind the horsebox. The plaintiff
riding a moped came up behind the Landrover and thinking it was that
vehicle that was causing the smoke, overtook it. Because of the smoke he
failed to see the horsebox and crashed into it, sustaining injury. He claiming in negligence and public nuisance.
HELD: The defendant was negligent in driving the horsebox when it was
dangerous to do so: it would have been neither difficult nor expensive to
have it towed. As to public nuisance the plaintiff was entitled to sue because
(1) the clouds of smoke made the highway less commodious to other road
users; (2) they were a dangerous obstruction; and (3) the defendant had
acted unreasonably. The plaintiff was 20% to blame for failing to keep a
proper look out.

MOTORWAYS

Note—The motorways are special roads provided under the Special Roads Act
1949, or the Highways Act 1959, limited to certain classes of vehicles. The special
rules applying to traffic on motorways are contained in the Motorways Traffic
(England and Wales) Regulations 1982, SI 1982/1163. The use of motorways is
restricted to traffic of Classes I and II specified in the Second Schedule to the
Special Roads Act 1949, as amended by the Special Roads (Classes of Traffic)
Order 1959 SI 1959/1280.
   The Special Roads Act 1949, s 12, under which the Motorways Traffic Regulations 1959, were made was repealed by the Road Traffic Act 1960, and its provisions are now contained in, s 17 the Road Traffic Regulation Act 1984. Vehicles
excluded from motorways include pedal cycles, motor cycles not exceeding 50 cc
capacity, invalid carriages, certain vehicles carrying oversize loads and agricultural vehicles. Vehicles must be driven in one direction only. Stopping, turning or
reversing on a carriageway are forbidden. If a vehicle has to be stopped for certain
specified emergencies it must be driven on to the nearside verge and shall not
remain there longer than necessary. Learner drivers are forbidden to drive on
motorways. No person must go on foot on a motorway except for certain necessary
purposes. There are exceptions to and relaxation of the rules in certain specified
circumstances, e g to avoid or prevent an accident.
   There is a general speed limit of 70 mph (SI 1974/502).
   The Highway Code, paras 145–175 deal with motorway driving.
   (See also Motorways Traffic (England and Wales) Regulations 1982.)

Wallwork v Rowland
[1972] 1 All ER 53, 136 JP 137, 116 Sol Jo 17, [1972] RTR 86, Div Ct
The defendant stopped on the hard shoulder of a motorway to eat sandwiches. He was charged with unlawfully causing his vehicle to remain at
rest on a 'carriageway'.
HELD: The hard shoulder of a motorway is part of the 'verge' and not of
the 'carriageway'. The 'marginal strip' in the Motorways Traffic Regulations 1959 refers not to the hard shoulder but to the white line which
borders the running surface of the nearside lane.

Rivers v Cutting
[1982] 3 All ER 69, [1982] 1 WLR 1146, 126 Sol Jo 362, [1983] RTR 105,
CA
The plaintiff's car broke down on a motorway; he left it on the verge. A
police officer in exercise of powers granted by SI 1968/43, reg 4 arranged
for it to be towed away by a local garage employee. The plaintiff alleged
that damage was caused thereby in the sum of £716 and sued the police as
being vicariously liable for the negligence of the garage. The regulation
reads '. . . a constable may remove or arrange for the removal of the
vehicle. . .'. The plaintiff claimed that the obligation to ensure the performance of a statutory duty without negligence cannot be discharged by delegating the duty to an independent contractor.
HELD: The constable's duty in exercising the power to arrange for the
removal of the car was merely to exercise reasonable care in the choice of
the garage. The word 'arrange' authorised the appointment of an independent contractor to do the work. The appointment of a contractor to
remove the vehicle was not a delegation of the power but an exercise of the
power itself. The police were not vicariously liable for any negligence of the
garage in doing the work.

NARROW ROAD

Thrower v Thames Valley Bus Co Ltd
[1978] RTR 271, CA
The plaintiff on a dark December evening was driving his car along a
narrow lane when he collided with the offside of the defendants' bus travelling in the opposite direction. The lane was 9 feet wide to the centre line on
the defendants' side and 8 ft 6 ins on the plaintiff's side. The judge found
that the bus may have been an inch or two over the centre line but acquitted
the driver of any negligence. There was a restriction order in force prohibiting vehicles more than 6 ft 6 ins wide from using the road but public
service vehicles were exempted. He held that the defendants were negligent
in failing to give the driver some form of special training or instruction so
that he could take special precautions when driving a bus on this narrow
road.
HELD: The defendants were not negligent. The road was perfectly
adequate to take two vehicles of the width of the two concerned. Other
vehicles ahead of the plaintiff had got past safely and it was perfectly
possible for him to have done so too.

NEGLIGENT PARKING

Parking on a bend

Waller v Levoi
(1968) 112 Sol Jo 865, Times, 16 October, CA
The defendant was driving his car on a main road in daylight when he came
to a left-handed bend where a side road went off to the left. He had been
intending to turn off on to the side road but missed it and went beyond it a
little way. He stopped at the kerb on the nearside of the bend to look back at

the signpost and his car was run into from behind by the plaintiff on a motor cycle. The county court judge found the plaintiff 80% to blame and the defendant 20%.

HELD, ON APPEAL: The judge's apportionment of blame should stand. The plaintiff was negligent in failing to see the car in time. The defendant was to blame in stopping on the bend. It was a distinct bend though not sharp: he could have driven on to a straight part of the road and walked back to see the signpost. A car parked on a bend should not cause danger to a person driving carefully but one also owed a duty to careless drivers. A motorist who drove too fast or was temporarily inadvertent could be put in difficulty by a car parked on a bend.

Chop Seng Heng v Thevannasan s/o Sinnapan
[1975] 3 All ER 572, [1976] RTR 193, PC

At 3 am on a winding road in rather misty conditions A was driving his employer's lorry when he required to stop. He chose a spot about 30 feet beyond the exit from a blind left hand bend. He parked the lorry at the nearside with its lights on. There was plenty of room for other vehicles to pass. B drove a lorry round the bend at about 25 mph and crashed into the back of A's lorry, causing severe injuries to the plaintiff, a passenger in B's lorry. The judge at first instance held A 75% to blame and B 25%. On appeal the Federal Court held by a majority that B was wholly to blame. The dissenting member considered A wholly to blame.

HELD, ON APPEAL to the Privy Council: (1) The proposition that a driver who parks a vehicle at night with its lights on where there is room to pass cannot be guilty of negligence is unacceptable. A was to blame for parking too close to the corner. *Waller v Levoi* (above) applied. (2) B was also to blame for taking the bend too fast. Had he been travelling more slowly the impact would have been less heavy and the plaintiff's injuries less severe. (3) As the judge at first instance had not misdirected himself when apportioning blame his 75:25 apportionment should be restored.

Parking at night

Stevens v Kelland
[1970] RTR 445 (Waller J)

In a quiet street V left his van parked on the inside of a bend without lights. C, without noticing the van, parked his car on the outside of the bend near a street lamp a short distance to the north of the van. The gap between the two vehicles, measured along the road, was about 20 feet S, riding a scooter from the south, saw V's van on his offside and C's car on his nearside and also saw a car driven by Z approaching from the opposite direction on its correct side of the centre line. S saw he could pass C's car safely without himself crossing the centre line and carried on. Z did not see S until he, Z, had pulled over the centre line to pass through the gap. He collided with the scooter as it was passing C's car, jamming it against the car and severely injuring the pillion rider.

HELD: (1) S was not to blame because by the time Z pulled over to pass through the gap he could do nothing to avoid the accident. (2) Z was mainly to blame because he had not seen S in time; he should not have pulled over without ensuring that it was safe to do so. (3) V and C were each partly to blame; V for having parked his van near the elbow of the bend where it blocked the view and was a potential cause of danger, C because by parking his car where he did without noticing the van he had created a hazard. (4) Apportionment of blame was 60% to Z and 20% each to V and C.

Watson v Heslop
[1971] 115 Sol Jo 308, RTR 308, CA
The defendant parked his car by the nearside kerb of a busy main road 22 feet wide in the hours of darkness. There were no street lights and no speed restrictions. He turned out the lights of the car except for a parking light on the offside. The plaintiff driving his car at 40 mph with dipped headlights failed to see the defendant's car because of the dazzling headlights of approaching traffic and drove straight into it from the rear. The judge of assize held the defendant solely to blame.
HELD, ON APPEAL by the defendant: He was negligent in parking his car there where traffic was passing at speed in both directions: he could foresee that a stationary car might well put traffic in a difficulty. But the plaintiff was also to blame. When he found himself dazzled by approaching head-lights he should at once have slowed down to a very slow pace in case there should be someone or something in his path. Moreover, if he had been keeping a proper look-out he should have seen the parking light. He was 30% to blame.
Per Sachs LJ: The defendant should have put his car at least partly on the footway. A parking light was not as good as normal lights.

OPENING DOOR OF VEHICLE

Note—Claims for damages for personal injury or for damage to passing vehicles caused by the opening of the offside door of a stationary car are extremely common but, perhaps because the negligence is self-evident, they rarely result in a reported decision. For examples where a passenger was to blame, see *Brown v Roberts* (p 706, below), *Trivett v Harding* (p 186, below) and *Daimler Hire v Gomez* (p 186, below).
Prosecutions were at one time laid under the Highway Act 1835, ss 72 or 78. They are now brought under the Motor Vehicles (Construction and Use) Regulations 1978, reg 125, which provides:

'No person shall open or cause or permit to be opened any door of a motor vehicle or trailer on a road so as to cause injury or danger to any person.'

The regulation does not give a right of action to a person injured by the breach — see *Barkway v South Wales Transport* and *Phillips v Britannia Laundry*, p 245, below. For a case in which justices were held on a prosecutor's appeal to the Divisional Courts to have been entitled to hold that there was a doubt whether opening a car door had caused danger see *Sever v Duffy* [1977] RTR 429.

OVERTAKING

Overtaking: sounding horn

Holdack v Bullock Bros (Electrical) Ltd
(1964) 108 Sol Jo 861, affd (1965) 109 Sol Jo 238, CA
In daylight on a straight road a motor scooter was overtaking a motor van
when the van swerved to the offside and the scooter collided with the offside
front wing of the van. The van driver had not seen the scooter in spite of
having two outside mirrors and an interior mirror. The judge held the van
driver was negligent in changing course without warning when it was
extremely dangerous to do so, but held the scooter rider one-third to blame
for having failed to hoot to show his intention to overtake. The scooter rider
appealed.
HELD: There was no ground on which the Court of Appeal should interfere. In the ordinary way if a motor scooter was overtaking another vehicle
which was going straight along a road there was no need for the scooter to
hoot before overtaking if the scooter was giving reasonable clearance. In
this case the judge must have come to the conclusion that the movement of
the van was such as to put the scooter rider on enquiry as to what the van
was going to do.

Distracting driver

Rothwell v Davies Bros (Haulage) Ltd
(1963) 107 Sol Jo 436, CA
The second defendant was in his stationary car when it was struck and
damaged by the first defendant's lorry which did not stop. The second
defendant, incensed, followed the lorry trying to attract the driver's attention. He drove alongside the lorry flashing his lights, sounding his horn and
shouting. The lorry driver's attention was distracted and as a result the
lorry collided with the plaintiff's car and injured the plaintiff. The judge
found the lorry driver one-quarter to blame and the second defendant
three-quarters.
HELD, ON APPEAL by the second defendant: The apportionment could not
be disturbed. Motorists must not distract the attention of a driver of a
heavy vehicle on a busy road. The second defendant's conduct, though
understandable, was foolish and was the substantial cause of the accident.

Note—See also 'Signalling and turning', p 105, below.

Jumping the queue

Powell v Moody
(1966) 110 Sol Jo 215, Times, 10 March, CA
Riding his motorcycle along a busy road the plaintiff came up to the tail of a
stationary line of traffic consisting of vehicles two abreast which were held
up. He proceeded along the offside of the line of traffic, overtaking the
stationary vehicles. The defendant, driving a car, came out of a side road
on the nearside of the line of traffic to pass through a gap and turn right to
go along the main road in the opposite direction. He was given a signal by

the driver of a milk tanker to come out and as he was inching his way out the plaintiff, who had not seen the side road, collided with him. The judge held both parties to blame but attributed 80% of the blame to the plaintiff.

HELD, ON APPEAL by the plaintiff: The judge's apportionment was reasonable. Any vehicle which jumped a queue of stationary vehicles was undertaking an operation fraught with great hazard and which had to be carried out with great care. There was always difficulty in such circumstances of seeing what was happening especially emerging from gaps.

Note—Whether any member of the Court expressly mentioned the Highway Code (1959), para 29, 'In traffic hold-ups do not "jump the queue" ', is not clear from the report. Paragraph 29 is repeated in the Highway Code (1978), para 72.

Clarke v Winchurch
[1969] 1 All ER 275, [1969] 1 WLR 69, 112 Sol Jo 909, CA

The first defendant's car was parked on its offside of the road, facing the direction in which the first defendant wished to travel. A continuous line of traffic was travelling in the opposite direction and he had to pass through this to proceed on his way. The third defendant, a bus driver driving the second defendants' bus, saw that the first defendant wished to come out and stopped to allow him to do so. The bus driver flashed his headlights at the first defendant who then came out slowly across the front of the bus. When the front of the car was about a yard beyond the offside of the bus the car was struck by a moped ridden by the plaintiff who had overtaken the bus on the offside. The bus driver had looked in his mirror but had not seen the plaintiff. The judge of assize accepted the first defendant's evidence that he was only just crawling out and acquitted him of any blame. He found the plaintiff two-thirds to blame and the bus driver one-third for not giving a hand signal to warn the plaintiff as he said he would have done if he had seen him.

HELD, ON APPEAL: The plaintiff was to blame but the first defendant and the bus driver were not. A cyclist or moped rider is entitled to overtake stationary traffic but to do this warrants a very high degree of care and he must ride in such a way that he can immediately deal with an emergency. When he saw that the bus had stopped the plaintiff ought to have realised that something was going on in front of it and driven accordingly. With regard to the bus driver his flashing his headlights meant merely 'Come on so far as I am concerned'. Having stopped he was under no duty to do anything else and the flashing of the headlights was not a representation that it was clear for the car driver to pull out beyond the offside of the bus. Nor was the bus driver under a duty to give a signal to the moped rider. With regard to the first defendant the judge's finding that he was moving very, very slowly and that he could not have done more justified his being acquitted of negligence.

Note—In a dissenting judgment Russell LJ said the car driver should have stopped with only the tip of his bonnet showing beyond the bus as an indication to overtaking traffic of his presence and should then have paused and listened for any horn sounding before going any further out. He would have held him 20% to blame. The other members of the court also felt there was a good deal of difficulty in finding no blame on the part of the driver but were unwilling to hold that there was anything more the driver could do once the judge's finding was accepted that he

came out very, very slowly. In *Worsfold v Howe* (below) the Court of Appeal held
that *Clarke v Winchurch* laid down no principle of law.

Leeson v Bevis and Tolchard Ltd
[1972] RTR 373, CA

The defendant's garage was on the north side of Upper Richmond Road
with access by an exit 11 feet wide. Their van was being driven out of the
exit across the eastbound traffic stream which was at a standstill. A lorry
driver had stopped his vehicle so as to leave a substantial gap and had
gestured to the defendants' driver to come out. The plaintiff was riding his
motor cycle at about 15 mph along the offside of the line of traffic, overtaking the stationary vehicles. As the defendant's van came through the
gap, turning right, there was a collision between the motorcycle and the
nearside front of the van. The judge held the plaintiff and the van driver
equally to blame.

HELD, ON APPEAL: The decision should stand. The plaintiff was doing
nothing wrong in overtaking the line of stationary vehicles, but doing that
and being aware of this exit and others on to Upper Richmond Road he
should have been proceeding with the greatest care and keeping an effective
look-out. The van had almost completed its turn when hit and if the
plaintiff had been alert he could have swerved away to avoid it. The van
driver had to perform a difficult and dangerous manoeuvre and very great
care was needed: he should have made quite sure that nobody was going
across his path in an easterly direction. It was important to realise that the
lorry-driver's gesture merely meant that he was giving way to the van
emerging and not that if the van crossed beyond the shelter of the lorry it
would be safe: *Clarke v Winchurch* and *Powell v Moody* (above) were distinguishable on the facts.

H. L. Motorworks (Willesden) Ltd v Alwahbi
[1977] RTR 276, CA

The plaintiffs' driver stopped at the mouth of a side road, waiting to turn
right into the main road. Two cars were stationary side by side in the main
road on his right. The driver of one of these waved to him to come out. He
drove out across the front of the two cars and when about on the middle line
was run into by the defendant's car overtaking the two stationary cars.

HELD: The plaintiffs's driver was not to blame.

   Per Cairns LJ: If the driver of one of the cars has given the signal inviting
him to come forward, what is he to do? Is he to stay in the mouth of [the side
road] disregarding the invitation to come out and wait until there is a
complete clearance in both directions in [the main road]? I think that he is
entitled to assume that no vehicle will come along on its wrong side of the
road making a third line of traffic and overtaking two stationary cars.

Worsfold v Howe
[1980] 1 All ER 1028, [1980] 1 WLR 1175, 124 Sol Jo 646, CA

At a part of a busy city street where for the northbound traffic the road led
to traffic lights at a road junction the nearside lane was for traffic intending
to go straight on and the offside lane for traffic intending to turn right at the

junction. The plaintiff was riding his motor cycle in the offside lane; on his left was a line of stationary vehicles held up at the lights. One of the vehicles was a large tanker with a gap ahead of it to allow vehicles to enter the roadway from a railway yard on the left. As the plaintiff overtook the stationary tanker the defendant drove his car across the front of it very slowly so as to cross the northbound lanes and turn right. As his car entered the traffic lane beyond the tanker the plaintiff travelling at a speed more than 10 but less than 30 mph ran into the nearside front of the car which was at an angle. The judge said he would have found the parties equally to blame — the plaintiff for travelling too fast and the defendant for having gone beyond the line of his vision — but for the decision in *Clarke v Winchurch* (p 83, above) which he considered to be on all fours with the present case. He dismissed the plaintiff's claim.

HELD ON APPEAL, and adopting the dictum of Cairns LJ in *Garston Warehousing v Smart* (p 134, below): The judge was not bound by *Clarke v Winchurch*, which laid down no principle of law. The apportionment of 50–50 suggested by the judge should be accepted.

Overtaking at road junction

Tocci v Hankard
(1966) 110 Sol Jo 835, CA

The plaintiff was riding his moped in a main London street when the defendant's vehicle coming in the opposite direction swerved across the road and struck him. The reason the defendant swerved was that he was in the act of overtaking a scooter travelling in the same direction as himself when the scooter swung to the right to enter a side road. The scooter rider did not stop and could not be identified.

HELD, ON APPEAL: The defendant was not to blame. The rule in the Highway Code not to overtake at road junctions did not apply to side roads such as this of which there were so many in London. One ought not to be critical of what was done on the spur of the moment when a dangerous situation had been created by someone else.

Overtaking horse

Burns v Ellicott
(1969) 113 Sol Jo 490 (Paull J)

The plaintiff was riding her horse on a path at the side of a narrow road. Her right leg was over the edge of the kerb. The defendant driving his car in the same direction as the plaintiff saw another car approaching from the opposite direction. He slowed down and passed the plaintiff almost brushing her horse. The horse took fright and reared or turned catching its hooves under the front bumper of the defendant's car. It was badly injured and had to be destroyed.

HELD: The defendant was negligent. If a horse was being ridden in a narrow road a car driver must exercise great caution in passing it. His duty was to slow down and give the horse a wide berth. If he could not do that because a car was coming from the other direction his duty was to wait until the other car had passed.

Haimes v Watson
[1981] RTR 90, CA
The defendant counterclaimed for damages sustained when his car collided with a horse ridden by the plaintiff. He was driving along a road 20 feet wide at about 30 mph. The horse was being ridden in the same direction in the nearside gutter when it shied and moved broadside across the road: the collision was unavoidable. The plaintiff admitted that the shy took the horse temporarily out of his control. There was no plea of scienter in the counterclaim.
HELD: The defendant could not succeed. He had established that the horse had suddenly moved sideways across his bows, and that called for an explanation; but the plaintiff had given one which was adequate to negative any inference of negligence. The county court judge's view that a rider must so control his horse that it will not move sideways if startled and that not so to control the horse was negligence was not the law.

Carryfast Ltd v Hack
[1981] RTR 464 (Ralph Gibson J)
The defendant, an experienced horsewoman, was riding her horse along the narrow grass verge on the nearside of a main road 21 feet wide. The plaintiffs' van was being driven by their employee in the same direction at about 30 mph. When the van had almost reached the horse the driver saw the horse begin to 'dance'; he swerved to the offside, crashing into a lorry approaching from the opposite direction. The plaintiffs claimed against the defendant for the damage to the van. She admitted in evidence that her horse was nervous in traffic but said she could keep the animal under control and that it was on the grass verge all the time before the accident.
HELD: She was not liable. The accident was caused by the plaintiffs' driver's negligence in not being able to slow down sufficiently and stop when he saw the horse 'dancing'. Every case turns on its own facts. It is not negligent of a rider to go on the highway on a horse simply because the rider knows that the horse does not like some traffic noises and may on occasion act as if unsettled, but such a rider may be negligent in taking a horse on to the highway if there is a reasonable risk of the horse getting out of control.

PEDESTRIANS

Rights

Boss v Litton
(1832) 5 C & P 407
All persons, paralytic as well as others, have a right to walk on the road and are entitled to the exercise of reasonable care on the part of persons driving carriages upon it.

Duty of driver

Note—See *Kite v Nolan*, p 75, above.

Kayser v London Passenger Transport Board
[1950] 1 All ER 231, 114 JP 122 (Humphreys J)
A bus driver stopped at a compulsory stop some distance from a pedestrian crossing near where two wide thoroughfares joined the main road. There were two trolley buses ahead, and as the traffic lights turned green, he followed the trolley buses. When about one and a half lengths of an omnibus from the traffic lights, he saw plaintiff, a girl of 14, another girl, and a man, hurrying across the road diagonally, holding hands and talking. It was obvious they would have crossed the road before he reached them and he went on. An air raid shelter obstructed his vision and he proceeded very slowly in first gear. The pedestrians scattered but he just caught the plaintiff. According to the evidence, the plaintiff was half-way across, when she suddenly ran back, probably as the result of traffic in the opposite direction, and ran into the omnibus. She was just off the crossing.
HELD: Where the driver of a vehicle is satisfied that persons who are lawfully entitled to cross the road, whether they are on a pedestrian crossing or not, are out of danger from him if he goes on in the normal course, he is entitled to do so but only at such a pace as will enable him to stop almost immediately should the persons who are crossing do anything dangerous or negligent.

There was no negligence on the part of the driver. Judgment for defendants.

Note—Cf *Foskett v Mistry*, p 76, above.

Baker v Willoughby
[1970] AC 467, [1969] 3 All ER 1528, [1970] 2 WLR 50, 114 Sol Jo 15, HL
The plaintiff wished to cross a main road 33 feet wide in open country. He saw a car approaching from his right about 100 yards away and assumed he had time to cross. He walked out into the centre of the road, paused to look left, and was struck by the defendant's car coming from his right. The defendant had overtaken two other cars at least 200 yards before the point of collision and had the plaintiff in view over that distance. The judge found both parties to blame: the defendant three-quarters because, having the plaintiff in view for 200 yards and taking no evasive action he must have been either driving too fast or not keeping a proper look-out; the plaintiff one-quarter for not waiting for the approaching cars to pass and not looking to his right a second time. The Court of Appeal altered the apportionment to 50–50 on the ground that each party had a view of each other throughout the time the plaintiff was crossing the road to the point of collision and neither did anything about it.
HELD, ON APPEAL to the House of Lords: The judge's apportionment of blame should be restored. There were two elements in an assessment of liability, causation and blameworthiness. A pedestrian had to look to both sides as well as forwards. He was going at perhaps three miles an hour and was rarely a danger to anyone else. A motorist had not got to look sideways and if he was going at a considerable speed must not relax his observation otherwise the consequences might be disastrous. It was quite possible for a motorist to be very much more to blame than the pedestrian.

Mulligan v Holmes
[1971] RTR 179, CA

Two pedestrians began to cross a wide brightly-lit street at night. The distance from the kerb to the central island was 35 feet. There was no satisfactory evidence whether they looked to their right or not. Two cars were approaching. The driver of the first, travelling at 30–40 mph, saw the pedestrians begin to cross when he was about 60 yards away. He slowed slightly but they presented no problem to him and passed across his front. The second car driven by the defendant at a very fast speed, overtook the first car when it was 10 to 15 yards from the pedestrians. The defendant had not seen them before though he could have seen them from 100 yards away if he had looked. They were by that time quite near the central island. They were struck by his car and injured, one fatally. The judge at first instance held that the pedestrians could not have looked to their right and were 50% to blame.

HELD, ON APPEAL: The proportion of contributory negligence should be reduced to 20%. The evidence did not warrant the conclusion that the pedestrians did not look to their right. Nevertheless, they were not blameless: if they had exercised all reasonable care they would have realised that the second car was being driven very quickly and that there was a risk that the driver might not see them and would run them down.

Hurt v Murphy
[1971] RTR 186 (Talbot J)

The plaintiff's wife began to cross the road at a place where her visibility to her left was restricted by a bend to 100 yards. There was no vehicle in sight when she left the pavement. She walked across, looking ahead. The defendant driving his car at a speed very much greater than the 30 mph limit came round the bend and though he applied his brakes he was unable to avoid striking and killing her. She was then just beyond the centre of the road. The defendant admitted his own negligence but alleged contributory negligence.

HELD: The plaintiff's wife was not negligent when she left the pavement because there was then nothing in sight, but there was lack of care on her part in not looking to her left again as she was crossing the road. She was one-fifth to blame.

Williams v Needham
[1972] RTR 387, QBD

The plaintiff at night but in a well-lighted street parked her car with its nearside to the kerb so that she could cross to a shop on the other side. She stood in the roadway on the offside of the car with her back to it and looked to her right. She saw nothing approaching and then looked to her left. She saw three cars approaching and waited until they had passed. Then without looking again to her right she stepped forward to cross the road and was at once hit by the defendant's car coming from her right. The defendant had seen her standing by her car looking away from him and had guessed that she intended crossing the road. He assumed she would look to her right before beginning to cross and he took no precautions against her not doing so. When she stepped forward he was too near to avoid hitting her.

HELD: The plaintiff must bear two-thirds of the blame but one-third must rest on the defendant. He knew that people did sometimes begin to cross without looking and, realising the plaintiff was about to cross, should have drawn her attention to the presence of his car or taken some other precautions against the possibility of her taking a risky step.

Crossing at traffic lights

Shepherd v H. West & Son Ltd
(1962) 106 Sol Jo 391 (Paull J)
The plaintiff and her 13-year-old daughter wished to cross the road at a junction controlled by traffic lights. They ensured that the traffic lights were showing red and then began to cross in front of a bus which was stationary at the traffic light on the nearside of the road. Whilst they were passing in front of the bus the light changed to red-amber and the bus driver 'revved-up' his engine preparatory to moving off. This alarmed the plaintiff who looked to her right along the offside of the bus and took a step forward to clear the bus in case it moved forward. She was at once struck by the defendant's lorry which was overtaking the bus. The lorry driver's evidence was that the traffic lights were red when he approached, changed to red-amber before he reached the bus and to green as he came alongside it.
HELD: The lorry driver was clearly negligent. A reasonable driver in such circumstances would not have let the front wheels of his lorry get level with the bus until the bus had got half-way across the crossing. To pass a stationary vehicle under such circumstances was a dangerous practice: the danger ought to be realised by all motorists. It was natural for the plaintiff to have tried to get out of the way of the bus when she heard its engine 'revving-up': she could not have taken more than one step forward and was not in any way negligent.

Note—An appeal was dismissed
See also *Frank v Cox*, p 128, below.

Narrow pavement

Adamson v Roberts
(1951) 101 LJ 511, Ct of Sess
A pedestrian was walking in daylight along a pavement at a point where it was narrowed by a projecting building, and had to put one foot over the edge of the pavement into the gutter in order to pass other pedestrians. As she did so, she was struck from behind by a motor van. The van did not encroach upon or over the kerb. In the Outer House of the Court of Session the action was dismissed ((1951) 101 LJ 330).
HELD, ON APPEAL: In the circumstances a special duty was imposed upon the driver in relation to the speed at which he travelled, the warning which he gave and the part of the road on which he directed his vehicle. Appeal allowed.

Note—See also 'Vehicle overlapping pavement' p 58, above.

Standing on kerb

Chapman v Post Office
[1982] RTR 165, CA
The plaintiff was struck by the projecting driving-mirror of a passing vehicle when standing on the kerb at a bus stop. She sustained a severe blow to her arm. At the trial of her claim for damages the judge said she must have been leaning over the carriageway and found her equally to blame with the driver of the vehicle.
HELD, ON APPEAL: She was not at all to blame. A person standing on a kerb is not guilty of negligence if struck even if leaning out or having her back to the traffic, nor even if she went an inch or two into the roadway.

Not using pedestrian crossing

Snow v Giddins
(1969) 113 Sol Jo 229, CA
The plaintiff began to cross the road near a road junction and not far from a pedestrian crossing which had a central refuge. He threaded his way through the northbound traffic, which was stationary and then stood in the middle of the road just over the centre line looking to his left for any approaching south-bound traffic. Whilst standing there he was struck from his right by a motor cycle ridden by the defendant, who was travelling north overtaking the stationary vehicles. The county court judge held the defendant wholly to blame, rejecting, inter alia, a suggestion that the plaintiff was negligent in not using the pedestrian crossing.
HELD, ON APPEAL: The plaintiff was not negligent in failing to use the pedestrian crossing but he was negligent in taking on himself the hazard of being marooned in the centre of the road at the mercy of on-coming traffic instead of crossing where there was a central refuge. He was 25% to blame. A pedestrian who elected not to use a crossing took upon himself a higher standard of care.

Pedestrians running

Brophy v Shaw
(1965) Times, 25 June, CA
Shortly before midnight the plaintiff and a friend had taken part in a street brawl and the plaintiff had struck and injured an elderly man. The police being about to apprehend them the plaintiff and friend ran away. They ran along the pavement past a bus which was just pulling away from a stop and shortly afterwards darted out into the carriageway, running across at an angle of 45 degrees. The road had dual carriageways and the defendant was driving his car at about 30 mph keeping close to the offside. He failed to see the men crossing from his left, even though his headlights were on, until they had got a substantial way across the road. They ran right across in front of his car and were hit by it. The plaintiff was seriously injured and his friend killed.
HELD: The defendant was not liable. It had been alleged that he should have seen the men running along the pavement, but his duty, like that of any other road user, was to exercise reasonable care. He was not under a

duty to be a perfectionist. It was going too far to say he should have observed the negligence and irresponsible action of the two men earlier than he did.

Walking on road at night

Powell v Phillips
[1972] 3 All ER 864, 116 Sol Jo 713, CA
The plaintiff and a friend were walking along a poorly-lit street at night on the left-hand pavement. From time to time because of snow and slush on the pavement they walked in the roadway near the kerb. Whilst so doing the plaintiff was hit from behind by the defendant's car, which was travelling at speed and did not stop. It was argued for the defendant that the plaintiff was guilty of 25% contributory negligence because she was not complying with the rules for pedestrians in the Highway Code: she was walking next to the kerb with her back to traffic, not wearing or carrying anything white.
HELD: She was not, on the facts, guilty of contributory negligence. Though the Road Traffic Act 1960, s 74(5) (now replaced by s 37(5) of the 1972 Act) enables a party to rely upon a breach of the Highway Code as tending to establish or negative liability, a breach creates no presumption of negligence calling for an explanation, still less a presumption of negligence contributing to causing an accident or injury. A breach is just one of the circumstances on which a party can rely in establishing the negligence of the other and its contribution to causing the accident or injury. It must not be elevated into a breach of statutory duty. In the present case, the plaintiff had not failed to take reasonable care for her own safety in walking a few feet out in the road for about 20 yards when it got too slushy; even if it did amount to negligence it made no real contribution to the accident.

Parkinson v Parkinson
[1973] RTR 193, CA
The defendant was driving his car along a straight unlighted road at night. He saw ahead of him on the nearside of the road two women pedestrians walking in the same direction as he was travelling but failed to see until too late two men walking about 20 yards behind them, the outer about 4 ft 6 ins from the edge of the road. His car struck both men killing one and seriously injuring the other. The road was 25 feet wide. There was a grass verge on the left of the road but only a hedge on the right. The judge found the defendant wholly to blame. On appeal it was argued that the pedestrians were negligent in not following the advice in the Highway Code to walk on the right of the road so as to face the oncoming traffic.
HELD: There were no grounds for finding contributory negligence. Even if the outside pedestrian was 4 ft 6 ins out it did not amount to negligence when the road was 25 feet wide. It is depriving pedestrians of their natural rights as highway users to say they must walk on the right and are not entitled to walk on the nearside. The mere fact that a pedestrian walks on the left side of a country road is not necessarily negligent; it depends on the circumstances. In the present case there was a grass verge on the left on to which one could move in an emergency but only a hedge on the right.

Kerley v Downes
[1973] RTR 188, CA
The plaintiffs were father and son, the latter aged 13. At night they left the lighted entrance to a fairground adjoining a straight country road and walked along a grass verge alongside the road for a distance and then along the left hand edge of the road for 20 yards or so preparatory to crossing to the other side at a place where there was an isolated street lamp. Before they reached it they were struck from behind by the defendant's car. The judge declined to find the plaintiff father negligent either for his own safety or in respect of his son's.
HELD: The judge was right. Following *Parkinson v Parkinson* (above) and *Powell v Phillips* (above) a mere contravention of the recommendation in the Highway Code to walk on the right of the road and not to walk with your back to the traffic did not create a presumption of negligence.

Duty of child pedestrians

Note—See 'Liability for children', p 72, above.

Pedestrian liable to motorist

Eames v Cunningham and Capps
(1948) 82 Sol Jo 314, *Eastern Daily Press*, 1 June (Croom-Johnson J)
At 5.10 pm on 20 November 1946, a motor cyclist with pillion passenger collided with a pedestrian and the pillion passenger, a plasterer, was killed. His widow sued the motor cyclist and the pedestrian. A witness who was walking with the pedestrian gave evidence that when he saw the lights of the motor cycle approaching, he shouted 'Look out!' and stepped back. He had taken about one step into the road and the pedestrian was about to step in front of him. The pedestrian, who had a dog on a lead, seemed to hesitate for about a second and was struck by the motor cycle. Another witness said the pedestrian seemed to hesitate when the motor cyclist sounded his hooter, turned round as if to speak to the first witness and then took another step forward. There was a good headlight on the motor cycle.

The motor cyclist said the pedestrian walked into the road, hesitated and then stepped forward. He was travelling slowly and had sounded his hooter. He could have avoided the pedestrian if he stood still or stepped back like the other man. The pedestrian said he saw a light but thought it was a bicycle, not a motor cycle. He tried to make for the opposite pavement. If he had known it was a motor cycle he would have stopped till it had gone by.
HELD: The motor cyclist was not guilty of negligence; the pedestrian and the first witness stepped off the pavement with their minds on something else and got into the way of the motor cyclist. Judgment against pedestrian with costs; judgment for motor cyclist without costs.

Barry v MacDonald
(1966) 110 Sol Jo 56, Times, 15 January (MacKenna J)
The plaintiff's husband, riding a motor scooter, was killed when he collided with the defendant and his infant son when they were walking across the

road. The defendant's statement to the police was 'I stepped off the kerb without looking and the next thing I was flying. It was entirely my fault.' In evidence he said he looked to his right but could not explain why he did not see the scooter.

HELD: The defendant was to blame in stepping from the footpath without ensuring it was safe to do. It had been suggested that the plaintiff's husband was riding too close to the nearside and should have been nearer the middle of the road in case a pedestrian should step off the grass verge. It was not certain how close he was to the verge but if he were within a few feet it could not be said he was negligent. The defendant's negligence was the sole cause of the accident.

Note—See also *Green v Hills*, p 39, above.

PEDESTRIAN CROSSINGS

Note—The Road Traffic Regulation Act 1984, s 25 (replacing earlier enactments) provides for power to make regulations with respect to the precedence of vehicles and foot passengers respectively.

THE 'ZEBRA' PEDESTRIAN CROSSINGS REGULATIONS 1971
SI 1971/1524

1 These Regulations shall come into operation on 29 September, 1971 and may be cited as the 'Zebra' Pedestrian Crossings Regulations 1971.
2 [Revocation of 1954 regulations and savings.]
3 (1) In these Regulations, unless the context otherwise requires, the following expressions have the meanings hereby respectively assigned to them:—
'carriageway' does not include that part of any road which consists of a street refuge or central reservation, whether within the limits of a crossing or not;
'central reservation' means any provision, not consisting of a street refuge, made in a road for separating one part of the carriageway of that road from another part of that carriageway for the safety or guidance of vehicular traffic using that road;
'crossing' means a crossing for foot passengers established either —
(a) by a local authority in accordance with the provisions for the time being in force of a scheme submitted and approved under s 21 of the Act of 1967, or
(b) in the case of a trunk road, by the appropriate Secretary of State in the discharge of the duty imposed on him by s 22 of the Act of 1967;
but does not include a 'Pelican' crossing within the meaning of the 'Pelican' Pedestrian Crossings Regulations 1969;
'dual-carriageway road' means a length of road on which a part of the carriageway thereof is separated from another part thereof by a central reservation;
'give-way line' has the meaning assigned to it by paragraph 2 of Schedule 3;
'one-way street' means any road in which the driving of all vehicles otherwise than in one direction is prohibited at all times;
'stud' means a mark or device on the carriageway, whether or not projecting above the surface thereof;
'zebra controlled area' means, in relation to a zebra crossing, the area of the carriageway in the vicinity of the crossing and lying on both sides of the crossing or only one side of the crossing, being an area the presence and limits of which are indicated in accordance with Schedule 3;
'zebra crossing' means a crossing the presence and limits of which are indicated in accordance with the provisions of Schedule 2;
'uncontrolled zebra crossing' means a zebra crossing at which traffic is not for the

time being controlled by a police constable in uniform or by a traffic warden.

(2) Any reference in these Regulations to a numbered Regulation or Schedule is a reference to the Regulation or Schedule bearing that number in these Regulations except where otherwise expressly provided.

(3) Any reference in these Regulations to any enactment shall be construed as a reference to that enactment as amended by any subsequent enactment.

(4) The Interpretation Act 1889 shall apply for the interpretation of these Regulations as it applies for the interpretation of an Act of Parliament, and as if for the purposes of s 38 of that Act these Regulations were an Act of Parliament and the Regulations revoked by Regulation 2 were Acts of Parliament thereby repealed.

4 (1) The provisions of Part I of Schedule 2 shall have effect for regulating the manner in which the presence and limits of a crossing are to be indicated by marks or studs on the carriageway for the purpose of constituting it a zebra crossing.

(2) The provisions of Part II of Schedule 2 shall have effect as respects the size, colour and type of the traffic signs which are to be placed at or near a crossing for the purpose of constituting it a zebra crossing.

5 (1) Subject to para (3) of this Regulation, the provisions of Schedule 3 shall have effect as respects the size, colour and type of the traffic signs which shall be placed in the vicinity of a zebra crossing for the purpose of constituting a zebra controlled area in relation to that crossing and of indicating the presence and limits of that area.

(2) A give-way line (included among the said signs) shall, where provided, also convey to vehicular traffic proceeding towards a zebra crossing the position at or before which a driver of a vehicle should stop it for the purpose of complying with Regulation 8.

(3) [Appropriate authority may dispense with a 'zebra controlled area' where impracticable.]

6 [Permissible variations in dimensions.]

7 [Appropriate authority is empowered to provide lamps for illumination of pedestrians where desirable.]

8 Every foot passenger on the carriageway within the limits of an uncontrolled zebra crossing shall have precedence within those limits over any vehicle and the driver of the vehicle shall accord such precedence to the foot passenger, if the foot passenger is on the carriageway within those limits before the vehicle or any part thereof has come on the carriageway within those limits.

For the purpose of this Regulation, in the case of such a crossing on which there is a street refuge or central reservation the parts of the crossing which are situated on each side of the street refuge or central reservation as the case may be shall each be treated as a separate crossing.

9 (1) The driver of a vehicle shall not cause the vehicle or any part thereof to stop within the limits of a zebra crossing unless either he is prevented from proceeding by circumstances beyond his control or it is necessary for him to stop in order to avoid an accident.

(2) No foot passenger shall remain on the carriageway within the limits of a zebra crossing longer than is necessary for the purpose of passing over the crossing with reasonable despatch.

10 The driver of a vehicle while it or any part of it is in a zebra controlled area and it is proceeding towards the limits of an uncontrolled zebra crossing in relation to which that area is indicated (which vehicle is in this and the next succeeding Regulation referred to as 'the approaching vehicle') shall not cause the vehicle, or any part of it—

(a)   to pass ahead of the foremost part of another moving motor vehicle, being a vehicle proceeding in the same direction wholly or partly within that area, or

(b)   subject to the next succeeding Regulation, to pass ahead of the foremost part of a stationary vehicle on the same side of the crossing as the approaching vehicle, which stationary vehicle is stopped for the purpose of complying with Regulation 8.

For the purposes of this Regulation—
(i) the reference to another moving motor vehicle is, in a case where only one other motor vehicle is proceeding in the same direction in a zebra controlled area, a reference to that vehicle, and, in a case where more than one other motor vehicle is so proceeding, a reference to such one of those vehicles as is nearest to the limits of the crossing;
(ii) the reference to a stationary vehicle is, in a case where only one other vehicle is stopped for the purpose of complying with Regulation 8, a reference to that vehicle and, in a case where more than one other vehicle is stopped for the purpose of complying with that Regulation, a reference to such one of those vehicles as is nearest to the limits of the crossing.

11 (1) For the purposes of this Regulation, in the case of an uncontrolled zebra crossing, which is on a road, being a one-way street, and on which there is a street refuge or central reservation, the parts of the crossing which are situated on each side of the street refuge or central reservation as the case may be shall each be treated as a separate crossing.

(2) Nothing in paragraph (b) of the last preceding Regulation shall apply so as to prevent the approaching vehicle from passing ahead of the foremost part of a stationary vehicle within the meaning of that paragraph, if the stationary vehicle is stopped for the purpose of complying with Regulation 8 in relation to an uncontrolled zebra crossing which by virtue of this Regulation is treated as a separate crossing from the uncontrolled zebra crossing towards the limits of which the approaching vehicle is proceeding.

12 (1) For the purposes of this Regulation and the next two following Regulations, the expression 'vehicle' shall not include a pedal bicycle not having a sidecar attached thereto, whether additional means of propulsion by mechanical power are attached to the bicycle or not.

(2) Save as provided in Regulations 14 and 15, the driver of a vehicle shall not cause the vehicle or any part thereof to stop in a zebra controlled area.

13 [Transitional provision.]

14 A vehicle shall not by Regulation 12 or 13 be prevented from stopping in any length of road on any side thereof—
(a) if the driver has stopped for the purpose of complying with Regulation 8 or Regulation 10 (b);
(b) if the driver is prevented from proceeding by circumstances beyond his control or it is necessary for him to stop in order to avoid an accident; or
(c) for so long as may be necessary to enable the vehicle, if it cannot be used for such purpose without stopping in that length of road, to be used for fire brigade, ambulance or police purposes or in connection with any building operation, demolition or excavation, the removal of any obstruction to traffic, the maintenance, improvement or reconstruction of that length of road, or the laying, erection, alteration, repair or cleaning in or near to that length of road of any traffic sign or sewer or of any main, pipe or apparatus for the supply of gas, water or electricity, or of any telegraph or telephone wires, cables, posts or supports.

15 A vehicle shall not by Regulation 12 be prevented from stopping in a zebra controlled area—
(a) if the vehicle is stopped for the purpose of making a left or right turn;
(b) if the vehicle is a public service vehicle, being a stage carriage or an express carriage being used otherwise than on an excursion or tour within the meaning of s 159(1) of the Transport Act 1968, and the vehicle is waiting, after having proceeded past the zebra crossing in relation to which the zebra controlled area is indicated, for the purpose of enabling persons to board or alight from the vehicle.

Schedule 2, Part I provides that a crossing and its limits shall be indicated by two lines of studs and that the carriageway within the limits of the crossing shall be marked with a pattern of alternate black and white stripes. Part II of Schedule 2 requires the crossing to be indicated by globes illuminated by flashing lights.

Schedule 3 prescribes the manner in which the 'zebra controlled area' is to be indicated, namely, by a transverse white broken line (the 'give-way line') one metre from and parallel with the nearer line of studs indicating the limits of the crossing, and two or more longitudinal white broken lines (the 'zig-zag lines') placed on the carriageway and extending away from the crossing.

Precedence of foot passenger

Note—Regulation 8 gives precedence to foot passengers only on an 'uncontrolled zebra crossing', ie a zebra crossing not controlled for the time being by a policeman or traffic warden. 'Pelican' crossings are provided for by different regulations (see p 102, below). The following cases deal with uncontrolled crossings.

Regulation 4, both of the 1954 Regulations and of the 1951 Regulations, was in similar terms to reg 8 of the 1971 Regulations (p 94, above).

Leicester v Pearson
[1952] 2 QB 668, [1952] 2 All ER 71, 116 JP 407, [1952] 1 TLR 1537, 96 Sol Jo 397, Div Ct

A pedestrian on a crossing was struck by a car. The lighting was poor, it was raining, the road surface wet and in poor condition, one side of the road flanked by trees causing shadows and the other side lighted from shop windows, and the pedestrian was crossing from the darker to the lighter side. The magistrate found the driver was exercising all due care, keeping a proper look-out, and driving without negligence and the accident happened because the car skidded and it was not his fault that he did not accord precedence. The prosecutor appealed.

HELD: The Pedestrian Crossings (General) Regulations 1951, reg 4 (see now reg 8 of the 1971 Regulations), although it appears in terms to be absolute, does not impose an absolute duty, but a duty to take reasonable steps to let the foot passenger have precedence. A driver might do everything required of him but might skid or be pushed forward by a car. It is not a regulation prohibiting the doing of some specific act but one for controlling the order of traffic and indicating precedence. Although it would only be in an exceptional case that a magistrate would be able to find the failure to see a foot passenger was not due to failure to keep a proper look-out, it might be inevitable or due to some circumstance over which the driver had no reasonable or possible control. The finding of the magistrate of no negligence was by itself an answer. Appeal dismissed.

Note—This decision can be misleading unless the following seven cases are also read.

Gibbons v Kahl
[1956] 1 QB 59, [1955] 3 All ER 345, [1955] 3 WLR 596, 120 JP 1, 99 Sol Jo 782, Div Ct

A trolley bus driver pulled up at a pedestrian crossing because three children stepped on to the crossing when he was 20 or 25 yards away. He signalled following traffic to slow down, stopped and waved the children to cross. A motorist proceeding in the same direction as the bus saw the driver's signal but did not see the children and struck one of the children who was 22 feet across on a 33 feet road. He was prosecuted for driving without due care and attention and failing to accord precedence to a pedestrian. The justices dismissed both summonses as they were not satisfied he was negligent.

HELD, ON APPEAL: The appeal court would not interfere on the first decision as they could not say the finding was perverse. There must be a conviction on the second charged. A breach of the regulations does not necessarily mean careless driving: *Leicester v Pearson* (above) was a very special case on very peculiar facts.

It is the duty of any motorist approaching a pedestrian crossing to approach it in such a way that he can deal with the situation on the crossing when he gets there. He must be in such a position and driving at such a speed that if anybody is on the crossing he is in a position to stop.

Note—Overtaking at zebra crossings was not then an offence, as it is now under reg 10 of the 1971 Regulations.

Lockie v Lawton

(1959) 124 JP 24, 103 Sol Jo 874, 57 LGR 329, Div Ct QBD

The defendant, driving a trolley-bus, approached an uncontrolled crossing. A lorry reversing out of a side street on his offside of the road obscured at least half his view of the crossing. An old man, partially blind and deaf, was making his way over the crossing from the offside of the road. The defendant did not see the man until he had reached the crown of the road. Though the defendant then applied his brakes violently he was unable to avoid striking the man. The magistrates dismissed a charge of failing to give precedence to the foot-passenger contrary to reg 4 (of the 1954 Regulations: now reg 8 of the 1971 Regulations).

HELD, ON APPEAL: The magistrates should convict. *Leicester v Pearson* (above) was a decision that the duty under reg 4 is a duty only to take reasonable steps to let the pedestrian have precedence, but it was a case on very special facts. What are and what are not reasonable steps must be viewed in the light of the clear duty which arises from reg 4, namely the duty laid down in *Gibbons v Kahl* (p 96, above) to drive at such a speed that one can stop if there is in fact a pedestrian there, albeit he is hidden from one's view. On the facts of the present case it was the driver's duty to drive at such a speed as to be able to stop when the old man emerged from behind the lorry.

Scott v Clint

(1960) Times, 28 October, Div Ct

A lorry was approaching a pedestrian crossing at 15–20 mph. When it was only 10 yards from the crossing two children stepped on to the crossing without looking to their right and started to cross. The driver did his best to avoid them but was unable to avoid hitting one of them.

HELD: Regulation 4 of the Pedestrian Crossing Regulations 1954 laid down an absolute duty. Once a pedestrian is on a crossing the driver of any vehicle approaching that crossing must accord him precedence, however unexpectedly or suddenly he crosses. The driver was guilty of an offence.

Neal v Bedford

[1966] 1 QB 505, [1965] 3 All ER 250, [1965] 3 WLR 1008, 129 JP 534, Div Ct

Two pedestrians began to walk across a pedestrian crossing. When they were about a third of the way across they stopped to allow a car coming from their right to pass over the crossing in front of them. The defendant was driving a car behind the one which the pedestrians had allowed to pass and he began to follow it over the crossing. As he did so the pedestrians started to walk forward again and one was struck by his car on the crossing. A charge against him of failing to accord precedence to the pedestrians on the crossing was dismissed, the magistrates being of the opinion that the pedestrians had waived their precedence. The prosecutor appealed.

HELD: Regulation 4 imposed an absolute duty on motorists to accord precedence to pedestrians on an uncontrolled crossing. The justices had taken the view that the defendant was misled into thinking that the pedestrians had stopped to let him pass. Whether he genuinely thought they would let him pass was irrelevant. His absolute duty was to allow the pedestrians to cross. They had not waived their precedence by signalling him to pass; they had started walking. There must be a conviction.

Note—Regulation 4: see now reg 8 of the 1971 Regulations.

Hughes v Hall

[1960] 2 All ER 504, [1960] 1 WLR 733, 124 JP 411, 104 Sol Jo 566, Div Ct

The respondent was driving a car at a reasonable and proper speed towards a pedestrian crossing. He had passed over the studs indicating the approach to the crossing when a woman stepped off the nearside pavement on to the crossing without looking to right or left and began to walk over the crossing. The respondent applied his brakes at once but was unable to pull up in time to avoid hitting her. On a charge under the Pedestrian Crossings Regulations 1954, reg 4 the respondent pleaded that (1) in passing over the approach studs he had come within the limits of the crossing before the woman stepped on to it and there was no case to answer; (2) on the authority of *Leicester v Pearson* (p 96, above) the duty imposed by reg 4 was not absolute.

HELD: (1) The limits are not the approach studs but the studs which border the striped crossing; (2) on the latest decisions of the Divisional Court reg 4 imposes an absolute duty and it is quite immaterial whether there is any evidence of negligence or failure to take reasonable care. Offence proved.

Moulder v Neville

[1974] RTR 53, Div Ct

The defendant was driving his car towards an uncontrolled (ie 'zebra') crossing and was within the area marked by the zig-zag lines when a pedestrian stepped on to the crossing. The defendant continued over the crossing, missing the pedestrian by a foot. On a charge of failing to give precedence he claimed that the area between the zig-zag lines was part of the crossing and that when a vehicle was within the controlled area (ie between the zig-zag lines) no pedestrian should move on to the crossing.

HELD: This was a similar contention to that made under the 1954 Regulations in *Hughes v Hall* (above) and was wrong. The roadway between the zig-zag lines was not part of the crossing. If a pedestrian gets on to the striped area before the car gets on to the striped area the driver must give the pedestrian priority.

Levy v Hockey
(1961) 105 Sol Jo 157 (Nield J)
The plaintiff was knocked down and injured on an uncontrolled pedestrian crossing by a car driven by the defendant who overtook three other cars that were slowing down. The defendant pleaded that his failure to pull up in time was due to a latent defect in the braking system of his car, not discoverable by the exercise of reasonable care, so that the brakes failed to operate properly when he applied them.
HELD: In so far as the claim was based on a breach of the Pedestrian Crossings Regulations 1954, reg 4, the question arose of impossibility. If the Court were satisfied that, owing to a latent defect, a situation arose in which it was impossible for a driver to accord precedence to a foot passenger there would be no breach of the statutory duty so as to give rise to a right to damages. On the particular facts of this case, however, there was no latent defect.

Note—See note after *Gibbons v Kahl* (p 96, above). Regulation 4 of the 1954 Regulations has been replaced by reg 8 of the 1971 Regulations (p 94, above).

Burns v Bidder
[1967] 2 QB 227, [1966] 3 All ER 29, [1966] 3 WLR 99, 130 JP 342, 110 Sol Jo 430, Div Ct
The defendant was charged with failing to accord precedence to a pedestrian on a pedestrian crossing contrary to reg 4. When driving his car he had overtaken a bus which was waiting at a pedestrian crossing for people to cross, and had gone straight over the crossing without stopping, striking a pedestrian. He alleged that his brakes had failed, though a police officer testing them afterwards found nothing wrong. The magistrate said he was not satisfied the brakes had not failed but that the duty under the regulation was absolute and the defendant was guilty of the offence charged.
HELD, ON APPEAL: Regulation 4 does not impose an absolute duty come what may; there is no breach of the obligation under the regulation in circumstances where the driver fails to afford precedence to a pedestrian on the crossing solely because his control of the vehicle is taken from him by the occurrence of an event which is outside his possible or reasonable control and in respect of which he is in no way at fault. As Nield J said in *Levy v Hockey* (above) reg 4 must be read subject to the principle as to impossibility. Examples include a driver stung by a swarm of bees or suffering a sudden epileptic form of disabling attack, or a vehicle being knocked forward on to the crossing by another vehicle hitting it from behind, or a sudden removal of control occasioned by a latent defect of which the driver did not and could not reasonably know. But beyond that limited sphere the obligation of the driver can properly be described as

absolute. *Gibbons v Kahl* (p 96, above), *Scott v Clint* (p 97, above) and *Hughes v Hall* (p 98, above) were all cases where the driver was in control of the vehicle as a driver and no special feature had occurred to take control of the vehicle out of his hands. *Leicester v Pearson* (p 96, above) had not been overruled but it remained a very special case. In the present case the magistrate was not satisfied the brakes had not failed and the conviction must be quashed.

Note—See note following previous case.

Crank v Brooks
[1980] RTR 441, QBD
A person who is walking across a pedestrian crossing pushing a bicycle having started on the pavement on one side on foot and pushing the bicycle with both feet on the ground is a 'foot passenger' within the meaning of the 'Zebra' Pedestrian Crossings Regulations 1971.

Negligence of pedestrian

Note—In view of the considerable changes in the Pedestrian Crossings Regulations since 1951 cases decided before that date are of little value. The following cases are a guide to present law and practice where the pedestrian plaintiff is guilty of negligence.

Regulation 4 of the 1954 Regulations referred to in the following cases has been replaced by reg 8 of the 1971 Regulations which is in similar terms (p 94, above).

Kozimor v Adey
(1962) 106 Sol Jo 431 (Megaw J)
The plaintiff, a woman of 40, ran on to an uncontrolled pedestrian crossing in front of the defendant's car. The car was travelling at about 25 mph and was about 15 yards away when the plaintiff began to cross. The defendant applied his brakes and swerved to the right but was unable to avoid hitting the plaintiff.
HELD: (1) The defendant was not guilty of any negligence from the point when the plaintiff ran on to the crossing. (2) Having collided with the plaintiff when she was crossing he was guilty of a breach of the Pedestrian Crossing Regulations 1954, reg 4. Under those regulations there was an absolute duty on a driver to drive at such a speed and keep such a look-out that he might be able to allow uninterrupted crossing to any pedestrian who set foot on the crossing intending to cross. He could only be certain of avoiding a breach by approaching the crossing at such a slow speed that he could stop in time to avoid any pedestrian however unexpected and however foolish. (3) His breach of the regulations was a cause of the plaintiff's injuries but another cause was the plaintiff's failure to take care for her own safety, and the Court had to consider how far, if at all, the breach was the cause of the injury. Because of the policy behind the regulations there was a measure of moral responsibility on the defendant because his duty was to anticipate and provide against even so unexpected an occurrence. The proportion of responsibility was 75% to the plaintiff and 25% to the defendant.

Maynard v Rogers
[1970] RTR 392 (Mocatta J)
Shortly after midnight in a not-very-well-lit street the plaintiff, aged 19, stepped on to a pedestrian crossing without first looking to her right. She was hit by the defendant's car coming from her right. She was not far from the pavement she had left and the defendant had very little opportunity of avoiding the accident. The plaintiff must have been able to see his car if she had looked.
HELD: Although the major portion of the blame must rest on the plaintiff it was possible that if the defendant had sounded his horn she might have been able to jump back. Moreover (following *Kozimor v Adey* (above)) there was a breach of statutory duty, namely, reg 4 of the 1954 Regulations, inasmuch as the plaintiff when struck was on an uncontrolled pedestrian crossing. Plaintiff two-thirds to blame, defendant one-third.

Lawrence v W. M. Palmer (Excavations) Ltd
(1965) 109 Sol Jo 358 (Phillimore J)
The plaintiff, aged 77 and deaf, was crossing the road on a pedestrian crossing when she was struck by the rear nearside of the defendants' lorry, which came from her right. She was found after the accident lying on the road 11 feet from the pavement she had left and eight or nine feet from the crossing.
HELD: Her injuries indicated a considerable impact from which one might have expected her to be thrown to some extent backwards in the direction she had come. The accident could not have happened in the way it had if the driver had been keeping a proper look-out since she must have been on the crossing before the lorry came on to it. Under the regulations she was entitled to precedence and accordingly there was an element of negligence and breach of statutory duty for which the defendants were liable. The plaintiff was guilty of some contributory negligence in failing to see the lorry and proceeding without regard to whether there was other traffic on the road. Defendants two-thirds to blame, plaintiff one-third.

Clifford v Drymond
[1976] RTR 134, CA
Whilst walking across the road on a zebra crossing the plaintiff was struck by a car coming from her right. She was thrown or carried 45 feet and sustained serious injuries. She was 10 feet on to the crossing when hit. The judge found on the available evidence that the car, travelling not more than 30 mph had been about 75 feet away when the plaintiff began to cross. He considered whether the plaintiff was guilty of contributory negligence in stepping on to the crossing when the approaching car was within 75 feet to 80 feet and decided she was not.
HELD, ON APPEAL: The plaintiff should bear 20% of the blame. Rules 13 and 14 of the 1968 Highway Code require a pedestrian not only to allow vehicles plenty of time to slow down or stop before starting to cross but also to look right and left while crossing. If the plaintiff did not look at the approaching car she was negligent; if she did look she should have seen the car was near enough to make it doubtful whether it would pull up. She must also have been guilty of a measure of negligence in having failed to keep the

car under observation as she proceeded to cross the road. If she had she would have seen it was not going to stop and could have allowed it to pass.

Note—For the Highway Code (1968), rr 13 and 14 see now the 1978 Code, rr 11 and 12.

Bassett v Victoria Wine Co
(1958) Times, 6 February, CA

A woman pedestrian aged 60 was crossing the road on a zebra pedestrian crossing. On her right was a parked car between the crossing and the line of studs, contrary to reg 6 [which was similar in effect to reg 9 of the 1971 Regulations, p 94, above]. Whilst on the crossing she was struck by a van, the driver of which could not see the plaintiff because of the stationary car. She looked to the right before crossing and saw nothing. She was struck in the middle of the crossing. She claimed against the owners of the van, but no reliance was placed on reg 4. The claim was based on common law negligence and nothing more. The county court judge held the van driver was not negligent. The plaintiff appealed.

HELD: This was a matter of common law and the plaintiff must prove the defendants at fault. Drivers could not be expected to stop when they got to crossings if their view was obscured, but they must drive at a speed which took into consideration that a person might emerge from behind the stationary vehicle and that such person had precedence under the regulations. The county court judge found there was no evidence of excessive speed. It was a question of degree what was a proper speed in the circumstances and this was eminently a matter for the judge. Appeal dismissed.

Jankovic v Howell
[1970] CLY 1863 (Ormerod J)

The plaintiff, crossing a road by a pedestrian crossing, walked over the central island without pausing and on to the other half of the crossing, where he was struck by the defendant's scooter.

HELD: It was superfluous to hoot or take evasive action every time a pedestrian approaches a refuge. Judgment for the defendant.

Push button controlled crossing

Note—The 'Pelican' Pedestrian Crossings Regulations and General Directions 1969, SI 1969/888, contain rules governing precedence at pedestrian crossings where a pedestrian may operate traffic lights by a push button control so as to require vehicular traffic to come to a stop. By reg 6(1)(c) a driver of a vehicle is prohibited from driving on to the crossing when a vehicular traffic light signal is showing a red light. By reg 6(1)(d) every foot passenger on the carriageway within the limits of the crossing has precedence over any vehicle whilst the vehicular traffic light signal is showing a flashing amber light. The effect is that a pedestrian has precedence during both the red and flashing amber periods of the vehicular traffic light signal.

Oakley-Moore v Robinson
[1982] RTR 74, Div Ct
The defendant's car ran out of petrol. He stopped it within the limits of a Pelican crossing and went away. He was convicted of leaving it within the approach limits of the crossing. On appeal he contended he had been 'prevented from proceeding by circumstances beyond his control' (the 'Pelican' Pedestrian Crossings Regulations, reg 9(2)).
HELD: Though a latent defect unknown to the driver could be a defence, as indicated in *R v Spurge* (p 243, below) and *Burns v Bidder* (p 99, above), the present case was not one of latent defect. The amount of petrol is indicated by a gauge of some sort; moreover the quantity of petrol in a motor car is something which is at all times plainly within the control of the driver.

School crossings

Note—(Road Traffic Regulation Act 1984, ss 26, 27 and 28, replacing earlier enactments.)
    Operate between 8 am and 5.30 pm
    Patrol appointed by the authority (s 28) may require a vehicle to stop by exhibiting prescribed sign.
    The School Crossing Patrol must be in uniform.
    Signs prescribed by SI 1982/859.

Hoy v Smith
[1964] 3 All ER 670, [1964] 1 WLR 1377, 129 JP 33, 108 Sol Jo 841, 62 LGR 661, Div Ct
'Exhibiting' does not necessarily mean that the sign should be held full face to the oncoming traffic; it is sufficient if the sign is held in such a way that the driver can see the words 'Stop children crossing' on the sign.

Toole v Sherbourne Pouffes Ltd
[1971] RTR 479, CA
The plaintiff, aged six, came out of school, which was beside a busy main road, and was taken by a teacher with other children to a pedestrian crossing. At the crossing was a school crossing patrol, an elderly man. He stood at the side of the road with the children, waiting until he could step forward with his sign board to stop the traffic. The first defendant's van was approaching. The driver saw the patrol waiting at the side of the crossing so he carried on to pass over the crossing at about 30 mph. Suddenly the plaintiff darted across the road on the crossing and was hit by the van. The judge held the first defendants' driver free from blame and held the second defendants, the school authority who employed the patrol, liable by reason of his negligence.
HELD: Dismissing the appeal, the patrol man had not done enough to keep the children under control. If he had been really exercising proper charge and keeping them back the plaintiff would not have made the sudden dart into the road. Moreover, the second defendants, on this most critical part of the case, had not called the patrol man to give evidence.

Franklin v Langdown
[1971] 3 All ER 662, 135 JP 615, 115 Sol Jo 688
When the crossing patrol is correctly displaying the 'Stop: children cross-ing' sign a motorist must stop and not move on again until the sign has been removed.

Wall v Walwyn
[1974] RTR 24, [1973] Crim LR 376.
An offence is committed if the driver fails to stop whether the children are impeded or not.

RACE

O'Down v Fraser-Nash
[1951] WN 173, 95 Sol Jo 269 (McNair J)
The course of a road race in Jersey and the regulations were approved by the RAC. The deceased, a doctor, gave his services as a first aid official. He was provided with an RAC handbook for officials giving warning not to set foot on the course, the pavement or road except where their duty required them to do so.

On a practice run the deceased took up a position on the pavement at a road junction opposite to a bend where the course took a sharp right-hand bend. The brakes of a car failed and the deceased was killed. There had been no neglect to maintain the car in a fit condition. There was no negli-gence of the driver. The organisers had performed their duty of protecting their officials against reasonably foreseeable perils. There was no inade-quacy in any of their arrangements. The warning in the handbook was adequate. It was a case of familiarity having bred contempt.

The claim against the organisers and the driver failed.

REVERSING

Liddon v Stringer
(1967) Times, 15 April, Div Ct
At the end of its journey a bus had to be reversed into a side road. The conductor stood on the nearside pavement about level with the rear of the bus facing the front and signalled with his arms. The driver watched the conductor and the nearside kerb through his nearside wing mirror and began to reverse at about 3 mph. The conductor walked backwards keeping level with the rear of the bus. When it had moved about 5 yards the conductor signalled to the driver to stop, which he did. The reason for the conductor's signal was that a woman trying to get across to the kerb behind the bus had been knocked down. The driver was convicted by the magistrates of driving without due care and attention.
HELD: Where someone was using someone else as his eyes he was under a duty to see that those eyes were in a position to see what they ought to see. On what was written in the case stated it was difficult to see why the driver had been convicted, but it could not be said that a reasonable bench of justices, who saw the witnesses, could not have reached the conclusion that

the driver had not taken steps to see that his 'eyes' were in a position to see. There was no error in law: Per Lord Parker CJ. Appeal dismissed.

Wilks v Cheltenham Home Guard Motor Cycle and Light Car Club
[1971] 2 All ER 369, [1971] 1 WLR 668, 115 Sol Jo 309, CA

The plaintiff was a spectator at a motor-cycle scramble when he was struck and injured by a machine of a competitor, the second defendant. The machine and rider somehow surmounted a 'wrecking rope', crossed a space of 10 feet and then went under or over another rope barrier before striking the plaintiff. The judge of assize acquitted the organisers (the first defendants) of any blame but held the second defendant negligent on the ground that he lost control of his machine because of excessive speed, inadequate skill or reckless driving. The second defendant appealed.

HELD, ON APPEAL: He was not to blame. A competitor in a race must use reasonable care — but as a competitor he is expected to go all out to win and the degree of care required is that which a reasonable competitor would take in those circumstances. In a race a reasonable man would do everything he could to win but he would not be foolhardy, that is, so conduct himself as to evince a reckless disregard of the spectators' safety. There was no evidence of greatly excessive speed on the part of the second defendant. The fact that he had somehow crossed the two rope barriers did not bring into play the doctrine of *res ipsa loquitur*; the circumstances were vastly different from a case such as *Ellor v Selfridge* (p 58, above) where a motorist mounts the pavement. Appeal allowed.

Harrison v Vincent
[1982] RTR 8, CA

In a motor cycle and combination race the plaintiff was a sidecar passenger. At a point on the course the machines had to be brought down from speeds of 100 mph or more to 30 mph to negotiate a hairpin bend. The rider of the machine applied the brake but due to a defect it failed adequately to slow the machine which went off the course into an escape road. It struck a vehicle projecting into the road injuring the plaintiff severely. The vehicle was placed there to clear away any broken-down equipment. The plaintiff sued the rider and the organisers.

HELD: He was entitled to succeed, (1) against the rider of the machine, since he owed the normal duty of care to the plaintiff, the defect in the brake being one which should have been rectified beforehand, and (2) against the race organisers for not keeping the escape road clear of obstruction.

Note—See also *White v Blackmore* (p 41), above and *Latchford v Spedeworth International*, p 42, above.

SIGNALLING AND TURNING

Pratt v Bloom
(1958) Times, 21 October, Div Ct

Per Streatfeild J: The duty of a driver changing direction is (1) to signal, and (2) to see that no one was incommoded by his change of direction and the duty is greater if he first gives a wrong signal and then changes it.

Overtaking turning vehicle

Sorrie v Robertson
1944 JC 95, Ct Jus

The Road Traffic Act 1930, s 12, made it an offence to drive 'a motor vehicle on a road without due care and attention or without reasonable consideration for other persons using the road'.

The driver of a motor lorry, who knew that he was being overtaken gradually by a motor cycle, signalled in the appropriate manner that he was about to turn across the road to his right — his intention being to enter a garage 50 yards further on. At that moment he saw the cyclist in his driving mirror, but after giving the signal he concentrated his whole attention on turning into the garage. He took no steps to ascertain whether his signal had been observed, and, when he made the turn, the cyclist, who had not observed the signal, was about to pass him, so that a collision resulted. The lorry driver having been convicted of an offence under s 12 of the Act of 1930.

HELD: That the conviction was warranted, in respect that the accused, in view of his knowledge of the overtaking cycle, had a duty to observe whether his own signal had been appreciated.

Note—Similar provisions to those in the Road Traffic Act 1930, s 12 are now contained in the Road Traffic Act 1972, s 3.

Clark v Wakelin
(1965) 109 Sol Jo 295 (Roskill J)

The plaintiff on a pedal cycle turned right from the nearside of the road and was struck by the defendant who was about to overtake on a motor cycle. The plaintiff's statement to the police was 'I looked behind me, let a car go by, put out my hand and turned right'. The defendant said he was about to overtake when the plaintiff put out his hand, turned and never gave him a chance to avoid the accident. No claim was made for a year: a writ was issued after a further year and the action was tried ten months later. The plaintiff said in evidence that the car he let go by was coming towards him from the opposite direction. He relied on the provision in the Highway Code 'Never overtake unless you know you can do so without danger to yourself and others'.

The judge said it was the plaintiff who was in danger from the delay in bringing the action since he had to prove his case. The defendant's version of the accident was to be accepted. A driver was entitled to assume that he could overtake without danger if what he was overtaking gave not the slightest sign that it was going to do something other than what another ordinary careful motorist or motor cyclist might expect. The plaintiff was solely to blame.

Note—See also *Dyer v Bannell*, p 117, below.

Goke v Willett
[1973] RTR 422, CA

On a busy three-lane road in daylight a mini van pulled out into the centre lane to overtake a lorry and trailer travelling in the nearside lane. The mini driver whilst still in the centre lane decided to enter a service station on the offside of the road. He put on his offside indicator and braked, slowing down fairly sharply to enter the further of the two entrances; he had already passed the first entrance before braking. The mini van was then struck from behind by a heavily-laden lorry which had been following the mini van in the centre lane. The lorry driver had been about 100 yards behind the mini van when it braked but the driver had not seen the mini's brake light or trafficator. The mini driver was unaware of the presence behind him of the lorry until after the impact.

HELD: The mini driver was engaged in a most undesirable manoeuvre, turning off the centre lane of a fast road into the second entrance of a service station on the offside. It behoved him to make certain he did it without risk to following or oncoming traffic. In the particular circumstances of this case he ought to have given a hand signal; if he had the lorry driver would probably have seen it and avoided a collision. The Highway Code, insofar as it appears to say that hand signals need never be used when trafficators and brake lights are in good working order, contains unwise advice. There may still be circumstances, as in this case, where the utmost warning to other traffic of one's intentions should be resorted to and a hand signal called for. Proportions of blame: mini driver one-third, lorry driver two-thirds.

Note—But see now the Highway Code (1978), p 49.

Turning out of minor road

Harding v Hinchcliffe
(1964) Times, 8 April, CA
In open flat country early in the morning the plaintiff was riding his motor cycle to school along a class B road and came up behind a bus travelling in the same direction. The bus driver signalled his intention to turn left into a minor road. The plaintiff, wishing to go on along the main road, overtook the bus as it was turning. He was hit by the defendant's car which came out of the minor road as the bus turned into it. The defendant had stopped at the mouth of the lane, intending to turn right into the main road. He had seen the bus approaching for about 150 yards and had waited but when the bus driver showed he was going to turn into the lane the defendant had driven out. He had not seen the plaintiff, who had been masked by the bus until the moment of collision, nor had the plaintiff seen the defendant. The judge held that the defendant had not been negligent, since he could not have anticipated a motor cyclist being masked by the bus for all that time and distance.

HELD, ON APPEAL: Coming out from a lane into a major road the defendant ought to have waited the few extra seconds necessary to let the bus get completely into the lane because there was always the possibility of a vehicle being masked by the bus. The proper inference was that he was negligent and the boy was not negligent at all.

MacIntyre v Coles
[1966] 1 All ER 723, [1966] 1 WLR 831, 130 JP 189, 110 Sol Jo 315, CA
On a Sunday morning in pouring rain the defendant was driving a heavy

lorry along Spon End in the city of Coventry towards a Y junction where The Butts forked off to the right and Spon Street to the left. He intended bearing right into The Butts. There were no road signs indicating the relative importance of these streets but the defendant passed along this route regularly and knew that traffic entering Spon End from Spon Street on his left usually paused at the mouth of Spon Street where there was a 'Keep Left' sign. The plaintiff's husband who did not know the district was riding a motor cycle along Spon Street towards the junction intending to bear right into Spon End along which the defendant was approaching. The plaintiff's husband rode out of Spon Street across the path of the defendant's lorry, which was taking the right fork into The Butts, and was struck by it and killed. The judge of assize held the defendant to be free from blame.

HELD, ON APPEAL: The plaintiff could not succeed. The defendant had given a proper signal that he was turning right, had seen the plaintiff's husband and was proceeding round in the ordinary way. Although it was most unfortunate there were no road signs to indicate how traffic should manoeuvre, the configuration of the road and the 'Keep Left' sign in the mouth of Spon Street did indicate that traffic on Spon End should have priority. Moreover the deceased had the lorry coming from his right: it is a well-recognised and conventional practice that where there is a doubt as to priority, the vehicle which has the other on its right-hand side is the give-way vehicle.

Note—Lang v London Transport Executive was not cited.

The alleged 'well recognised and conventional practice' of giving way to vehicles on the right was said not to exist by Streatfeild J in the case reported on p 139, below but this, like *Lang's* case, was apparently not brought to the attention of the Court.

Turning into minor road

Patel v Edwards
[1970] RTR 425, CA

At a crossroads in town the plaintiff on a pedal cycle wished to turn off the main road into the minor road on his right. He looked behind him and saw a car signalling a left turn and slowing down. He moved towards the centre of the road to make his turn just as the defendant, on a motor cycle, overtook the car, which was then almost stationary. The defendant ran into the plaintiff knocking him on to the pavement on the far corner. The plaintiff had not seen the defendant, nor did the defendant see the plaintiff until he came out in front of him; by that time the defendant was already level with the rear side window of the car. The trial judge said the parties were equally to blame; the plaintiff for his failure to make absolutely certain that it was safe to cross by coming out gently, the defendant overtaking the car when he could not see what was happening ahead of it.

HELD, ON APPEAL: The blame should be apportioned two-thirds to the plaintiff, one-third to the defendant. The judge had not given sufficient weight to the factor that the pedal cyclist was moving in front of a substantially stationary car across a main and important road. Anyone making such a move must naturally take special care to see that he does not get into the path of other traffic. Failure to take such care imports a high degree of culpability.

Simpson v Peat

[1952] 2 QB 24, [1952] 1 All ER 447, [1952] 1 TLR 469, 96 Sol Jo 132, Div Ct

The driver of a motor car in a main road turned to enter a road on his offside and a collision occurred with a motor cyclist coming in the opposite direction. He was prosecuted for driving without due care and attention. The justices found that the defendant had committed an error of judgment in thinking he had left room for the motor cyclist to get through. The defendant contended he could not be guilty for a mere error of judgment, and was acquitted. The prosecutor appealed.

HELD: The expression 'error of judgment' was not a term of art and was of the vaguest possible description. It could mean either a negligent act or one which, though mistaken, is not negligent. A driver might not be using due care and attention although his lack of care may be due to something which could be described as an error of judgment. If he is driving without due care and attention it is immaterial what caused him to do so. The question was whether he was exercising that degree of care and attention which a reasonable and prudent driver would exercise in the circumstances. The question was one of fact and not of law. On the facts, the defendant was cutting across the line of traffic coming from the opposite direction. It was for him to take care that he could execute the manoeuvre in safety.

Case remitted to justices with a direction to convict.

Challoner v Williams and Croney

[1975] 1 Lloyd's Rep 124, CA

At night on an unlighted road Williams was driving the first of three cars the other two being driven by friends whom he was leading. He discovered he had taken the wrong route and, seeing a turning on the right, put on his offside flashing indicator preparatory to turning into it so as to go back in the opposite direction. He slowed and moved towards the centre of the road. He looked in his driving mirror when he indicated he was going to turn and looked in the mirror again before he turned. He began to turn into the road on the right without actually stopping; when he was about half-way across the offside half of the road his car was struck by a car driven by Croney which had overtaken both the other cars, Croney not having seen Williams's car ahead until too late. The judge held both drivers equally to blame: he said Williams should have satisfied himself that there was no car overtaking the other two and should have stopped before crossing the offside half of the road.

HELD, ON APPEAL: Williams had done nothing wrong; Croney was wholly to blame.

Brake lights and hand signals

Flack v Withers

(1960) Times, 22 March, CA (reported on another point at [1961] 3 All ER 388, HL)

The infant plaintiff was riding his pedal cycle behind a car driven by the defendant W when the latter pulled up to allow the defendant S to pass him in the opposite direction. The plaintiff ran into the rear bumper of W's car, was thrown to the right and was hit by S's car, sustaining severe injuries. W gave evidence that he looked into his inside mirror but not the wing mirror as he was slowing down, but did not see the plaintiff or any other traffic. His car was fitted with the usual red lights at the back which came on as soon as any pressure was applied to the brake pedal. He had not regarded a hand signal as necessary in the circumstances particularly having regard to his slow speed. At the trial the jury found W 17% to blame for the accident. HELD, ON APPEAL: There was no evidence to support a finding of negligence against W. A driver could not give more than an occasional glance into his driving mirror. As to the lack of hand signal, W's car was fitted with the usual red lights at the back. It was difficult to accept the view that that might properly be regarded by a jury as evidence of want of care on W's part. The onus of proof on the plaintiff had not been discharged.

Note—The 1978 edition of the Highway Code accepts that stop light signals can be used to mean 'I am slowing down or stopping' without the use of a hand signal (p 48).

Misleading signal

Another v Probert
[1968] Crim LR 564, Div Ct
The defendant was driving a car along a main road: the 'left turn' indicator was flashing. A police car waiting in a side turning moved out into the main road in reliance on the flashing signal. The defendant drove straight on, colliding with the police car. He defended a charge of careless driving on the ground that the police driver should not have relied on the indicator signal.
HELD: On the prosecutor's appeal, it was careless driving to give misleading signals: the justices must convict.

Note—The Ministry of Transport Driving Manual (1969) warns against reliance on a left turn indicator in such circumstances. It might mean merely that the driver is intending to stop on the left before or *after* the junction as authorised by the 1968 Highway Code (p 34).
   The Highway Code (1978), para 87 says 'when waiting to emerge at a junction do not assume that a vehicle approaching from the right which is signalling with its left-hand direction indicator *will* turn left. Wait to make sure'.

Wadsworth v Gillespie
[1978] CLY 2534 (Sir Basil Nield)
The defendant, driving a car, came along a minor road to a major road at a junction governed by a 'Give Way' sign. She twice looked to her right along the major road and saw the plaintiff approaching on a motor cycle, his flashing indicator signalling an intended left turn. In reliance on the signal she moved out on to the major road; the plaintiff drove straight on and crashed into her car. He had accidentally turned the indicator on and was unaware it was flashing.
HELD: The defendant was negligent in not looking again to make sure the plaintiff was in fact turning left. The plaintiff was negligent in driving along the main road giving a misleading signal. Liability apportioned two-thirds to the defendant, one-third to the plaintiff.

Overtaking signal

Note—The Highway Code formerly contained a hand signal denoting that the driver was ready to be overtaken. The signal was omitted from the 1959 and subsequent editions of the Highway Code, but as some drivers still use it the following case may sometimes be useful.

White v Broadbent and British Road Services
(1957) Times, 29 November, CA
A woman was walking along the pavement at 3.30 pm on a wet and misty afternoon when she was overtaken by a lorry travelling at about 15 mph. She thought it was going to turn into a side street but it drew out to the white line in the centre of the road and stopped as the woman came abreast of it. She crossed the road in front of the stationary lorry and came into the path of a van which was overtaking and passing the lorry. She tried to step back but slipped and fell and was struck by the van and injured. When the lorry driver stopped, he looked to his front and saw the road was clear, and in his mirror to see if any traffic was coming from behind. The mirror was misty and he wiped it and looked again, saw the van and gave the 'passing' signal to an overtaking driver. He had not seen the woman who had actually started to cross the road when he gave the signal.

The county court judge found the plaintiff one-third to blame; of the remaining two-thirds, the lorry driver 80% and the van driver 20%. The lorry owners appealed.
HELD: The overtaking signal did not amount to an authority to the van driver to pass, but it was probable the van driver would proceed, and with greater confidence. The lorry would to some extent obscure the view of pedestrians seeking to cross. The lorry driver's duty was to be on the look-out for pedestrians before he gave the signal. Appeal dismissed; no interference with the apportionment.

Grange Motors Ltd v Spencer
[1969] 1 All ER 340, [1969] 1 WLR 53, 112 Sol Jo, 908, CA
The defendant in his car was approaching a bend in the road. A Post Office van was parked at the bend partly on the roadway. A postman crossed the road towards the van from a house opposite and stood close to it facing the driver's door. The defendant saw him look in the opposite direction and then make a gesture or signal to him which he took to mean that it was safe for him to pass. To do so, giving the postman three feet clearance, the defendant had to go over the centre line of the road. The plaintiff's vehicle came round the bend in the opposite direction and the defendant was unable to avoid colliding with it. The county court judge held the postman wholly to blame for the accident.
HELD, ON APPEAL: He was entitled so to find. The postman owed a duty of care to the defendant, whose car was coming on and he was negligent in giving an invitation to pass at a time and in a position when it was unsafe to give such an invitation. As was said in *White v Broadbent* (above) the driver of a vehicle on a road who makes a signal to another vehicle must have regard to other users of the road before giving that signal and owes a duty to the other driver to that effect, though the extent to which the driver to whom the signal is addressed is entitled to rely on it is a question of fact and

degree according to the case. The question must always be, did the driver act with reasonable care?

SKIDDING

Note—And see 'Res ipsa loquitur', p 49, above.

A defence of skidding is sometimes raised in answer to a prima facie case of negligence, but the modern tendency is to regard a skid as placing a heavy onus of proof on the defendant. The older cases must be regarded as of doubtful value since *Richley v Faull* (p 114, below).

Defendant held not liable

Hunter v Wright
[1938] 2 All ER 621, CA

The defendant was driving a motor car when it skidded and subsequently mounted the pavement and injured the plaintiff, who was walking thereon. It was found that the skid was not due to any negligence on the part of the defendant, but it was contended that she had been negligent (1) in steering the wrong way to correct the skid, and (2) in accelerating after the skid. Shortly before the accident she had practically stopped at a pedestrian crossing, and was accelerating when the skid occurred. The speed of the car was estimated at 16 to 20 mph, and the car travelled 13 to 20 feet between the skid and the pavement.

HELD, ON APPEAL: The time and space at the disposal of the defendant in which to remedy the skid was so short that it being proved that the skid was not due to any fault of hers, she had discharged the onus of showing how her car came to be on the pavement, and could not be said to have been in any way to blame for the accident. It was decided many years ago that a skidding vehicle is not in law a nuisance, nor is the skidding in itself any evidence of negligence on the part of the driver. There are also cases which have decided that the mounting of a car upon the pavement is prima facie evidence of negligence upon the part of the driver. Here the combination of these matters is considered, and the result is that, when a car mounts the pavement by reason of skid not due to negligence on the part of the driver, there is no fault for which the driver is responsible, and no action lies in respect of such a skid. Appeal dismissed.

Browne v De Luxe Car Services
[1941] 1 KB 549, [1941] 1 All ER 383, 110 LJKB 369, 165 LT 175, 57 TLR 346, 85 Sol Jo 165, CA

A motor car which knocks over a cyclist and carries on into a garage raises a prima facie case of negligence and shifts the onus on to the driver. Where the driver is using skill and care and proceeds to carry out an ordinary simple and perfectly normal manoeuvre, but because of the condition of the road most unexpectedly gets into a skid, the driver is not liable. A skid in itself does not excuse an accident. It may be caused by bad driving, careless driving or over-rapid driving, and the onus is on the driver to prove that the skid was not brought about by one of these causes.

The judge found the treacherous surface was due to long use and wear on granite sets, giving them a highly polished surface which, in wet weather and sometimes in dry weather, became slippery. The highway authority held liable, not the driver.

Custins v Nottingham Corpn
[1970] RTR 365, CA

The plaintiff was waiting for a bus; it was freezing weather and the road was covered with snow. She was standing not on the pavement but about three feet out in the road. The bus driver saw her when he was 70 yards away; he was moving at only 10 mph and slowed down gradually to the place where the plaintiff was standing. He applied slight pressure to the brake and managed to stop the bus, but then it slid sideways and knocked the plaintiff down. The Commissioner of Assize held that as the bus had stopped without difficulty and then slipped sideways the driver had failed to keep the bus under control and was negligent.

HELD: It was impossible to draw an inference of negligence from the evidence accepted by the Commissioner. What more could the driver have done than drive very slowly, keep a proper look-out and apply his brakes gently? There was a camber on the road; when a vehicle starts to skid on an icy road it may take the most unpredictable of courses. It is common knowledge that if you are unlucky when you are driving on an icy road, whatever care you may take, it sometimes by mischance occurs that the vehicle does slide and gets out of control. In these circumstances it does not mean that there is any negligence on the part of the driver. Appeal allowed.

Driver held liable

Liffen v Watson
(1939) 161 LT 351 (Stable J)

The driver of a taxi-cab which was travelling fast suddenly applied his brakes on a wet road causing the cab to skid, and collide with a street refuge. The driver admitted that at this speed a sudden application of the brakes on this wet road was very likely to cause a skid. He gave an explanation of the accident which the court did not accept.

HELD: Where a passenger was injured by a sudden application of the brakes a presumption was raised of negligence or lack of skill. The obiter dictum of Fletcher-Moulton LJ, in *Wing v London General Omibus Co* [1909] 2 KB 652, 78 LJKB 1063, 101 LT 411, 73 JP 429 CA that the mere occurrence of such an accident was not in itself evidence of negligence, and that the fact that an accident had happened either to or through a particular vehicle was by itself no evidence that the fault, if any, which led to it was committed by those in charge of the vehicle went too far. The principle to be applied is stated by Scrutton LJ in *Halliwell v Venables* (p 59, above) that the facts required explanation by the driver of the motor car. The facts in this case required an explanation. The driver's explanation was unacceptable and the passenger was entitled to judgment.

Laurie v Raglan Building Co
[1942] 1 KB 152, [1941] 3 All ER 332, 111 LJKB 292, 166 LT 63, 86 Sol Jo 69, CA

In daylight a heavily laden ten-wheeled lorry was driven at 10 to 12 mph on a broad good road and skidded. The road was in an extremely dangerous condition, as it had snowed and frozen and the surface was like glass. The lorry had no chains on the wheels.

Skidding is not of itself sufficient to displace the prima facie presumption of negligence arising from the vehicle being in a position where it has no right to be. The skid by itself is neutral. It may or may not be due to negligence. If it is shown that the skid happened without the fault of the driver, the prima facie presumption is clearly displaced but merely establishing the skid is not sufficient.

HELD: In the circumstances it was negligent to drive at 10 to 12 mph without chains. It might be unsafe to go at more than foot pace or possibly to proceed at all. If roads are in such a condition that a motor car cannot safely proceed at all, it is the duty of the driver to stop.

Note—Also noted under 'Res ipsa loquitur,' p 58, above.

Richley v Faull
[1965] 3 All ER 109, [1965] 1 WLR 1454, 129 JP 498, 109 Sol Jo 937 (MacKenna J)

On a road which was wet, but not slippery from any other cause, the defendant was driving his Bentley car when it went into a skid. It skidded across the road, turning as it went, into the path of a Hillman car in which the plaintiff was a passenger. The Hillman collided with the Bentley and the plaintiff was injured. The defendant gave no explanation of the reason why his car skidded. He said the same thing had happened two years before when he was driving the same car: he could not explain why.

HELD: The collision was caused by the defendant's negligence. Adopting Lord Greene's reasoning in *Laurie v Raglan Building Co* (above), where a vehicle moves on to the wrong side of the road into the path of another car there is a prima facie case of negligence which is not displaced merely by proof that the defendant's car skidded. But Lord Greene's dictum that a skid by itself is neutral is not acceptable; the unexplained and violent skid is in itself evidence of negligence. It is hardly consistent to hold that the skid which explains the presence of the vehicle on the wrong side of the road is neutral but that the defendant must fail unless he proves that this neutral event happened without his default. On either view, however, the conclusion is the same: the defendant fails if he does not prove that the skid which took him to the wrong place happened without his default.

Butty v Davey
[1972] RTR 75, Div Ct

The defendant was charged with driving without due care and attention. He was the driver of a lorry which skidded to the offside of the road on a shallow left hand bend, colliding with a lorry coming in the opposite direction. The justices, having heard that his speed was not excessive accepted his submission that the accident must have been caused by some unexpected slipperiness of the road due to rain and dismissed the charge.

HELD: On a case stated, the justices had applied their minds to the question whether the lorry was being driven at a reasonable speed in the conditions prevailing and there was no reason to interfere with their decision. *Richley v Faull* (above) had shown that where negligence was concerned proof of a skid was not sufficient to exonerate a driver, but the test in a criminal case was inevitably different. Appeal dismissed.

Brayshaw v Pratt
(1947) B No 759. Leeds Assizes, 20 January 1949
Court of Appeal, 15 June 1949
Unreported, extracted from the shorthand notes of judgments
The defendant's car was turning a very slight right-hand bend when it suddenly skidded and turned to the right across the road and on to the pavement on the wrong side of the road. The defendant sustained concussion and was unable to give any evidence as to how the accident happened or to what had caused her to go on to the pavement. The car was being driven at average speed and in the proper part of the road. There was no reason to account for the sudden turn to the right.
HELD, ON APPEAL (per Tucker LJ): It is clear from the authorities that the presence of a vehicle on the footpath implies negligence unless and until evidence is given which would entitle the court to infer that notwithstanding the occurrence the driver had in fact been exercising all reasonable care. There was no explanation given as to how or why the vehicle became out of control; or what had caused the driver to apply the brake if the brake was applied before the skid; or that any effort had been made to get out of the skid if the skid started without any application of the brakes; nor any evidence that defendant had not momentarily taken her eye off the road for some reason or other which caused her to get into a position of difficulty or danger or which might have caused her to apply her brakes. There was a complete absence of any evidence negativing negligence except possibly with regard to the one factor of speed. The defendant had failed to discharge the onus of establishing that the accident happened without any negligence on her part.

London Transport Executive v Foy, Morgan & Co
(1953) L 1572. 7 July 1955
Unreported, extracted from the pleadings and shorthand note of judgment
The plaintiff's coach had just pulled up on a particularly bad winter night when there had been ice on the road because of previous snow. It had been snowing and the snow had turned to a certain degree of sleet. It was freezing as well and the road was in such a condition that a police officer had some difficulty in standing. It was a very bad and a very dangerous road. The defendant was driving at 25 mph. He realised that he was on a dangerous road and he was coming to a bend and he had no chance. He was therefore driving in a way that was not showing the care which he ought to have been showing and in such a way as would reasonably avoid a skid.

Per Lord Goddard CJ: People are apt to think that if only they can show that their car skidded, because of certain decisions given a very long time ago, there is an end of the matter. When the cases are examined carefully, it will always be seen that it is only where the skid occurs unavoidably that the driver cannot be held responsible. If he is driving in a way which is asking for a skid, then he is liable.

Plea in defence

The matters complained of by the plaintiff were caused by unavoidable accident.

Particulars

The defendant's car suddenly and without warning skidded upon the wet and greasy road and became uncontrollable, with the result that the defendant although exercising all due care and skill was unable to avoid a collision.

SPEED

Note—There is a general speed limit of 70 mph on dual carriageway roads (not being motorways), and a general speed limit of 60 mph on single carriageway roads (not being motorways) (SI 1978/1548).

The speed limit of 30 mph on restricted roads is imposed by the Road Traffic Regulation Act 1984, s 81. A restricted road is a road with street lamps 'placed not more than two hundred yards apart' (s 82(1)) but the section provides for various exceptions.

Speed limits on roads other than restricted roads are authorised by s 84, and for vehicles of different classes by s 86. The speed limits at present applicable to various classes of vehicle are contained in the Road Traffic Regulation Act 1984, Sch 5.

Exceeding speed limit not in itself negligence

Barna v Hudes Merchandising Corpn
(1962) 106 Sol Jo 194, CA
The plaintiff, driving his car, wished to turn right from a minor road into a major road. Another car was waiting on the crown of the major road to turn into the minor road. The plaintiff's view to his right was obscured by parked cars. He moved out slowly at a time when the defendant's car was approaching from his right at a speed between 30 and 40 mph, though the road was subject to a 30 mph speed limit. The defendant was unable to pull up in time and ran into the plaintiff's car.
HELD: The defendant was not to blame for the accident. To exceed the speed limit, though an offence, was not in itself negligence imposing civil liability. In the circumstances the defendant's speed was not excessive. He had no reason to suppose that the road would be blocked as it was.

Tribe v Jones
(1961) 105 Sol Jo 931, 59 LGR 582, Div Ct QB
At 7.20 am when traffic was light the defendant drove his car over half a mile at speeds between 45 and 65 mph. The road was wide, well-surfaced and bounded by common land, but it was subject to a 30 mph speed limit. No accident occurred nor was there evidence of any actual danger to others. The defendant was charged with driving at a speed dangerous to

the public contrary to the Road Traffic Act 1960, s 2(1) (now the Road Traffic Act 1972, s 2).

HELD, ON APPEAL (from a dismissal of the charge by the justices): A fast speed was not automatically dangerous although in many cases it might well be so. The justices were entitled to find as they did.

High speed alone not negligence

Quinn v Scott
[1965] 2 All ER 588, [1965] 1 WLR 1004, 109 Sol Jo 598 (Glyn-Jones J)
On a straight level main road 32 feet wide the defendant was driving his Jaguar car at 70 to 75 mph. He was overtaking another car when he saw, 50 yards ahead, a tree falling across the road from the left. He instinctively swerved to the offside towards the thinner part of the tree, applying his brakes. He crashed into the foliage and lost control of the car due to the windscreen breaking, the car being filled with leaves and the steering wheel spinning out of his hands. The plaintiff driving a minibus from the opposite direction had seen the tree falling and had pulled up about 40 yards from the centre of the tree. The defendant, coming through the tree out of control, collided with the minibus and the plaintiff was injured.

HELD: The defendant was not negligent. High speed alone is not evidence of negligence unless the particular conditions at the time preclude it. There were no conditions present to make the defendant negligent in overtaking the two cars on his nearside at a speed of 70 to 75 mph. 50 yards was not at that speed sufficient distance in which to pull up when the tree began to fall: the 'thinking distance' shown on the diagrams on the back of the Highway Code could not be applied as a universal rule of thumb where so alarming an event occurs as the unexpected fall of a tree.

Hurlock v Inglis
(1963) 107 Sol Jo 1023 (Havers J)
The defendant was driving at a speed of 100 mph or more along the M1 motorway when his car got out of control and struck the plaintiff's lorry, causing him injuries. There were skid and tyre marks over 950 feet long. The defendant said he was about to overtake a car travelling in the centre lane when a van swerved in front of it: in trying to avoid the car he was unable to avoid striking the plaintiff's lorry.

The judge found the defendant liable. It was not in itself negligent to drive on the M1 at 100 mph but the defendant had not satisfactorily explained what happened. He had for some reason jammed on his brakes when he was in the outside lane and his car got out of control and for a considerable distance went backwards. Some explanation was called for to account for this extraordinary behaviour. In the absence of a satisfactory explanation he must be held to have been negligent.

Police vehicles

Dyer v Bannell
(1965) 109 Sol Jo 216 (Glyn-Jones J)
The plaintiff was injured when a van she was driving was struck by a police

car driven by the defendant, a police constable. It was night time but visibility was good and there was ordinary street lighting. The plaintiff wished to turn right from a main road into a side turning. She switched on her flashing indicators and also made a hand signal. She saw in her driving mirror a taxi cab some distance behind and the reflection of the defendant's car lights behind that. She then began to turn. The defendant was answering a call and was travelling at 45 mph in a built-up area. He overtook the taxi and collided with the plaintiff's van as she turned across his path.

HELD: It was not negligent of a police officer in the execution of his duty to drive at a fast speed; if there was nothing against the defendant except the fact that he was driving at 45 mph or more then it was not negligent. But he must exercise a degree of care and skill proportionate to the speed at which he was driving. He must remember that the ordinary road user in a built-up area would not expect vehicles to drive at that speed and should give audible warning of approach or otherwise make known the presence of a police car. The defendant had not apprehended what the van was doing as quickly as he should have done: he was guilty of want of what was a very high standard of care and skill demanded of a driver at 45 mph in a built-up area. The plaintiff as a reasonable motorist was entitled to suppose it was safe to turn as she had seen that the next vehicle behind her, the taxi cab, would not be embarrassed by her turn. She need not contemplate that a vehicle still further away would be travelling at such a speed that it would be dangerous to turn. She was not guilty of any contributory negligence. Judgment for the plaintiff.

Note—The Road Traffic Regulation Act 1984, s 87 provides:

'No statutory provision imposing a speed limit on motor vehicles shall apply to any vehicle on an occasion when it is being used for fire brigade, ambulance or police purposes, if the observance of that provision would be likely to hinder the use of the vehicle for the purpose for which it is being used on that occasion.'

Gaynor v Allen
[1959] 2 QB 403, [1959] 2 All ER 644, [1959] 3 WLR 221, 103 Sol Jo 677 (McNair J)
A pedestrian was injured by a police motor cyclist who was on a road where a 40 mph speed limit was in force. He was travelling at 60 mph or more and was killed as a result of the accident. The case raised the question on which the judge said there appeared to be no authority, of the extent to which the section affected the civil liability of the driver. The defendant contended that there was a difference between a police officer and an ordinary motor cyclist, but the Court negatived this contention. The driver was to be judged in exactly the same way as any other driver. He owed a duty to the public to drive with due care and attention and without exposing members of the public to undue danger. The defendant was guilty of negligence and so was the plaintiff, to a lesser extent; apportioned one-third to plaintiff.

Wood v Richards
[1977] RTR 201, Div Ct
A police patrol driver on a motorway when answering an emergency call

decided to overtake a large vehicle by driving on the hard shoulder. In doing so he collided with a lorry standing on the hard shoulder. He was convicted of driving without due care contrary to the Road Traffic Act 1972, s 3. On appeal he claimed that a special standard was applicable to a police officer driving to an emergency.

HELD: Not so. If the Act had meant a different standard to apply it would have said so — as does the Road Traffic Regulation Act 1984 on speed limits by s 87 — and it does not.

Marshall v Osmond

[1983] QB 1034, [1983] 2 All ER 225, [1983] 3 WLR 13, 127 Sol Jo 309, [1983] RTR 475, CA

The plaintiff with other men was a passenger in a car which he knew was stolen. A police car set off in pursuit and stopped alongside the stolen car when the occupants were getting out and running away. The plaintiff was struck by the police car and sustained injury which he claimed was caused by the negligent driving of the defendant, the driver of the police car. The defendant did not intend to injure him.

HELD: He was not entitled to succeed. A police officer driving a car in hot pursuit of a person or persons whom he rightly suspects of having committed an arrestable offence does not owe that person the same duty of care which he owes to a lawful and innocent user of the highway going about his lawful occasions; though he must not deliberately injure such a person unless it is reasonably necessary to do so in order to arrest him.

An appeal was dismissed. Per Sir John Donaldson M R: I do not believe that the defence of *volenti non fit injuria* is really applicable in the case of the police pursuing a suspected criminal. I think that the duty owed by a police driver to the suspect is . . . the same duty as that owed to anyone else, namely to exercise such care and skill as is reasonable in all the circumstances. The vital words in that proposition of law are 'in all the circumstances' and of course one of the circumstances was that the plaintiff bore all the appearance of having been somebody engaged in a criminal activity for which there was a power of arrest.

Fire engine

Wardell-Yerburgh v Surrey County Council

[1973] RTR 462 (Brabin J)

On a three-lane road in fog which limited visibility to 50 yards the plaintiff's husband was driving a mini-van in the centre lane, slowly overtaking a lorry and trailer 52 feet long. He was following at least one other car. The defendants' emergency tender (fire engine) was being driven in the opposite direction in the centre lane at 50 mph with headlights on and blue light flashing. It was taking tools to rescue trapped persons in crashed vehicles some distance away. A car ahead of the tender moved into its nearside lane to let it through, as did the car ahead of the mini. The tender and the mini collided in the centre of the road, killing the plaintiff's husband. It was argued by the defendants that the tender on such an errand could justifiably be driven in a way which in an ordinary vehicle would be regarded as reckless.

HELD: Following *Gaynor v Allen* (above) the driver of the tender owed to the public the same duty of care as any other driver: he was negligent in driving too fast in fog and not keeping a proper look-out. But the mini driver was the more to blame in the manner of his overtaking. To overtake as the last of three in a fog is liable to result in an accident. He should have delayed overtaking until he could see what was ahead of him. Instead he was moving forward at a slow differential speed in relation to the lorry he was overtaking and could move neither to right nor left when the tender came in sight. All this happening in a second or two he had placed himself in the worst possible position. He was two-thirds to blame, the defendants' driver one-third.

TABLE SHOWING DISTANCE COVERED IN ONE SECOND AT VARIOUS SPEEDS

Miles per hour	*Feet per second*
10	14.66
15	22.00
20	29.33
25	36.66
30	44.00
35	51.33
40	58.66
45	66.00
50	73.33
60	88.00

BRAKING TESTS

Appropriate minimum stopping distances
Four-wheel brakes, pneumatic tyres

	Stopping Distances in feet				
Road Surface	*Dry Smooth*	*Macadam*	*Asphalt*		*Low Adhesion Surface*
	Concrete	Dry	Dry	Wet	(Wet)
Co-efficient of Friction	0.9	0.8	0.7	0.5	0.4
SPEEDS WHEN BRAKES APPLIED IN MPH					
20	15	17	19	27	33
25	23	27	30	42	52
30	33	38	43	60	75
35	45	50	59	82	102
40	60	67	76	107	133
45	75	85	97	135	170
50	93	105	120	167	207
55	112	127	145	202	251
60	134	152	172	240	298

Time lag not allowed for.

Two-wheel brakes approximately double the distance, subject to correction for weight distribution.

Smooth types — add about 25%.

Solid types — add about 33%.

Note—The Highway Code gives the following stopping distances in perfect conditions, ie good weather — broad daylight — good dry roads.

Speed	Thinking distance	Braking distance	Overall stopping distance
mph	ft	ft	ft
70	70	245	315
60	60	180	240
50	50	125	175
40	40	80	120
30	30	45	75
20	20	20	40

On wet roads, for all vehicles, allow twice the normal.

STATUTORY LIABILITY WITHOUT NEGLIGENCE

Note—Damage to public utility installations and local authority property in streets was formerly made recoverable without proof of negligence by various statutory provisions. The tendency in recent legislation has been to make liability depend on fault but some of the older Acts still remain in force.

The point does not seem to have been the subject of express decision, but presumably all these Acts are subject to the Magistrates' Courts Act 1980, s 127, which provides that in all cases where no time is fixed, complaint or information shall be laid within six calendar months from the time when the matter of such complaint or information respectively arose, and by s 58(1) gives power to make an order on complaint for the payment of any money recoverable summarily as a civil debt.

Gas equipment

Note—The Gas Act 1972, Sch 4, para 20 provides as follows:

'20 (1) If any person wilfully fraudulently or by culpable negligence injures or suffers to be injured any pipes, meter or fittings . . . he shall (without prejudice to any other right or remedy for the protection of the Corporation . . .) be liable for each offence on summary conviction to a fine not exceeding £100.

(2) The prosecution of any such offence shall not prevent the Corporation from recovering the amount of any damage caused to them by the offence . . .'

HIGHWAYS ACT 1980

131 Penalty for damaging highway etc (1) If a person, without lawful authority or excuse,—

(a) lights a fire . . . within fifty feet from the centre of a highway which consists of or comprises a carriageway, and in consequence thereof the highway is damaged, he shall be guilty of an offence.

161 Penalties for causing certain kinds of danger or annoyance   (2) If a person, without lawful authority or excuse, lights any fire . . . within fifty feet of the centre of a highway which consists of or comprises a carriageway, and in consequence thereof a user of the highway is injured, interrupted or endangered, that person shall be guilty of an offence.

Bucks County Council v Bradley's Transport Co
(1936) 5 June, Aylesbury CC (Judge Crawford), unreported
The above sections replace a similar provision in the Highway Act 1835, s 72, and the Highways Act 1959 claimed by some local authorities to render an owner of a motor car liable for damage if the car took fire.

On such a claim a verdict was given for the defendant and it was held that the injury was not caused by person but by fire.

Tunnicliffe v Pickup
[1939] 3 All ER 297, Div Ct
Appellant was the driver of a motor lorry with a load of cotton which caught on fire without any negligence on his part and the fire damaged the highway. He was convicted under the Highway Act 1835, s 72, and ordered to pay damages and costs. The justices held it was not necessary to prove that the damage was wilfully caused or to prove mens rea.
HELD: Reversing the justices' decision, the appellant was perfectly innocent of what happened; he was not guilty of any wilful act or omission, nor of anything causing the fire.

Telegraph posts and apparatus

Note—The Telegraph Act 1878 (as amended by the British Telecommunications Act 1981), provides:

'**8** Where any undertakers, body, or person, by themselves or by their agents, destroy or injure any telegraphic line of the Postmaster-General, such undertakers, body, or person shall not only be liable to pay to the Postmaster-General such expenses, if any, as he may incur in making good the said destruction or injury, but also, if the telegraphic communication is carelessly or wilfully interrupted, shall be liable to a fine not exceeding £20 per day for every day during which such interruption continues.
2 The expression "telegraphic line" means telegraphs, posts, and any work (within the meaning of the Telegraph Act 1863) and includes any portion of a telegraphic line as defined by this Act.'

Postmaster-General v Beck and Pollitzer
[1924] 2 KB 308, CA
Defendants' servant while driving their motor lorry along a public highway caused it, without any negligence on his part, to come into collision with a fire alarm post belonging to the Postmaster-General and thereby injured the post. An action was brought by the Postmaster-General under Telegraph Act 1878, s 8, to recover the expenses of making good the injury.
HELD: The word 'person' must be read, not as limited to persons who had special statutory rights in the highway which might come into conflict with

the corresponding rights of the Postmaster-General, but in its natural and unrestricted sense as including all persons exercising their common law right of passage. Defendants were liable to make good the damage done.

Postmaster-General v James Lee & Sons
1968 SLT 52 Sh Ct
The defendants borrowed a crane from one company and a driver from another. Whilst the crane was being driven it damaged telegraph wires belonging to the Post Office who claimed the cost of replacement under the Telegraph Act 1878, s 8. It was not suggested that the driver was a servant of the defendants but that he was their agent as referred to in s 8.
HELD: The definition of 'agents' in s 2 of the Act includes 'contractors and also the officers, engineers, workmen or servants, as well of the Postmaster-General, undertakers, bodies or person as of his or their contractors'; it is very wide and takes the term right out of its usual proper meaning. The driver was driving the crane with the express authority of the defendants and for the purposes of the Telegraph Act 1878 was their agent. The defendants were liable.

Postmaster-General v Liverpool Corpn
[1923] AC 587, 92 LJKB 791, 130 LT 41, 87 JP 157, 39 TLR 598, 67 Sol Jo 701, 21 LGR 553, HL
A claim for sums due by statute for injury to a telegraph line failed where the damage was due to the Postmaster-General's own negligence or that of persons for whom he was responsible.

Post Office v Hampshire County Council
[1980] QB 124, [1979] 2 All ER 818, [1979] 2 WLR 907, 123 Sol Jo 421, CA
Employees of the defendants damaged Post Office telephone cables by plunging a crowbar into the grass verge of a highway to clear away flood water. Post Office employees at the scene had indicated that the cables were under the roadway, not the verge.
HELD: Once it is shown that by his voluntary act a servant of the defendants has damaged the cable then the requirements of s 8 have been fulfilled. It is not correct, as appears to be the effect of *Postmaster-General v Liverpool Corpn* (above), that s 8 does not apply where the person damaging the cable was not at fault and there has been negligence on the part of the Post Office. The true ratio of the *Liverpool* case is that the section does not apply where the damage was caused not by the defendant but by the Post Office. In the present case the section did apply but by reason of the negligence of the Post Office employees the defendants could plead circuity of action — they could set up the negligence of the Post Office or its servants in mitigation of the claim. Whether it should be done by way of defence or by way of counterclaim was a pure pleading matter. As the negligence of the Post Office employees in the information given to the defendants' employees had led to the damage being caused the defendants would have been entitled in law to recover from the Post Office as damages for negligence the sum claimed against them by the Post Office. It was a classic example of circuity of action. The plaintiff's claim failed.

Note—A similar view on the true ratio decidendi of the *Liverpool Corpn* case was expressed by Willis J in *Post Office v Mears Construction Ltd* [1979] 2 All ER 813.

Waterworks

Note—The Water Act 1945, by s 67 of Sch 3 provides—

'If any person either — (a) wilfully and without the consent of the undertakings; or (b) negligently turns on, opens, closes, shuts off or otherwise interferes with any valve cock or other work or apparatus . . . he shall be liable to a fine not exceeding £200 and whether proceedings be taken against him in respect of his offence or not the undertakers may recover from him summarily as a civil debt the amount of any damage sustained by them.'

For '£200' must now be substituted 'level 3 on the standard scale': the Criminal Justice Act 1982, s 46. There is therefore no statutory liability without negligence.

TRAFFIC LIGHTS

Note—The current regulations providing for traffic light signals are the Traffic Signs Regulations 1981, SI 1981/859, of which reg 31 describes the size colour and type and reg 34 sets out their significance.

Vehicle crossing against red light

Eva Ltd v Reeves
[1938] 2 KB 393, [1938] 2 All ER 115, CA
At a crossing controlled by traffic lights, R approached on offside at 25 to 30 mph and lights changed to green when he was 20 to 30 yards away. Nearside was occupied by traffic and R passed these vehicles on offside of road just as they were starting to move. A van was crossing from his left against the red lights. R could not avoid collision.
HELD: R not negligent. He owed no duty to traffic crossing against red light beyond a duty, if in fact he saw such traffic, to take reasonable care to avoid a collision. He was entitled to assume no traffic would be crossing against the lights and could therefore overtake on offside provided no danger to traffic in opposite direction or to traffic turning right. The Traffic Signs Regulations provide that the red signal shall be taken as prohibiting vehicular traffic to proceed until the green signal is shown. Highway Code — 'Never overtake at cross roads' — distinguished where traffic is regulated by lights.

Note—Though criticised from time to time this decision has never been overruled. It has been considered or explained in the following two cases.
    See also *Godsmark v Knight Bros*, p 127, below.

Knight v Wiper Supply Services Ltd
(1965) 109 Sol Jo 358 (Havers J)
The plaintiff was riding his moped along Brixton Hill when he came to traffic lights controlling a junction with a road on his left. When he passed the traffic light, the judge found, it was at green but immediately

afterwards turned to amber. The defendant's vehicle came out of the side road and struck the plaintiff, injuring him.

HELD: As the light had only just turned amber it must still have been showing red for the defendant's driver when he came out and he was therefore negligent. On the issue of contributory negligence *Eva v Reeves* (above) decided that the driver of a motor vehicle entering a cross-roads with the traffic lights in his favour was not guilty of contributory negligence in colliding with a vehicle entering the cross-roads with the lights against it, since the driver with the lights in his favour was not under any obligation to assume that a driver might be entering the crossroads with the lights against him. The decision had never been criticized in any subsequent decision and accordingly it was unnecessary in this case to consider any question of contributory negligence. The defendants were solely liable.

Davis v Hassan
(1967) Times, 13 January, CA

The plaintiff drove across a junction controlled by traffic signals with the green light in her favour. The defendant drove out from the road on her left against a red light and there was a collision. The county court judge held himself bound by *Eva v Reeves* to find wholly in favour of the plaintiff but said that if he had not been so bound he would have held the plaintiff one-third to blame.

HELD, ON APPEAL: (1) It was not necessary in this case to consider whether *Eva v Reeves* was right or wrong. Every case of negligence and certainly every case of traffic accidents had to be decided on its own particular facts. The judge was wrong in thinking himself bound by *Eva v Reeves*. (2) On the facts the judge's finding of the blame against the plaintiff was not justified. The question was whether having the green light in her favour the plaintiff was negligent in not seeing the defendant's car come out of the road on the left. Her attention was focussed on the lights and it was a very large junction: it would be wrong to hold her guilty of negligence merely because she did not see the car until the last moment.

Note—Lord Justice Willmer said he wished to make it clear that he was approaching the matter as a jury question and not seeking to lay down a proposition of law. The effect of the decision seems to be that cases which might formerly have been regarded as governed by the principle of *Eva v Reeves* are now simply to be treated as questions of fact.

Sudds v Hanscombe
[1971] RTR 212, CA

The defendant's car entered a crossroads from the east when the traffic lights were in his favour. He passed the primary light but before reaching the centre of the crossroads he had to stop because of an altercation between the drivers of two cars which had stopped there. Those two cars were eventually driven away and the defendant then drove forward to continue over the crossroads. Meanwhile the traffic lights had changed and were red for the road along which he was travelling. The plaintiff's car came to the crossroads from the south: when it was about 10 yards short of the crossing the traffic lights changed to green and he drove straight on. He did not see the defendant's car which had begun to move forward again and there was a collision. The county court judge found against the defendant and held there was no contributory negligence on the part of the plaintiff.

HELD, ON APPEAL: The plaintiff was entitled to assume when approaching lights which had already changed in his favour that no fresh traffic would enter the junction from the east because the lights there must have been red. On the other hand he was not discharged from his duty of looking to his front to see where he was going and to look out for traffic already in the junction which might obtrude into his path. The crucial question was whether or not the defendant was in a position where a reasonably careful motorist in the plaintiff's position might regard him as a hazard. On the evidence the judge was right in holding that the defendant was far enough back from the centre of the crossing that the plaintiff would not suppose he would continue over the junction.

Note—No cases were referred to in the judgments nor were any cited in argument.

Hopwood Homes Ltd v Kennerdine
[1975] RTR 82, CA

The plaintiff, driving a lorry, approached a cross roads where he intended to turn right. The traffic lights were green for him and changed to amber just as he passed the primary light. He came to a stop in the centre of the junction angled to the right ready to continue to make his turn. He looked to his left and saw the defendant's car approaching about 25 yards away. Knowing the traffic lights had turned to red and seeing the car had time to pull up he began to move forward. The car did not stop but continued on past the red light and collided with the lorry. The county court judge held the plaintiff 10% to blame for not having apprehended that the car might not stop at the lights.

HELD, ON APPEAL: The plaintiff was not at all to blame. He had good reason to suppose the car would pull up at the traffic signal. Although as Lord du Parcq said in *Grant v Sun Shipping Co* (p 4, above), 'a prudent man will guard against the possible negligence of others when experience shows such negligence to be common', one's experience does not lead one to think that it is a common folly for a driver who has time to pull up at traffic lights to fail to do so. The plaintiff was correct in his assessment when he first saw that car that it had time to stop at the lights which were at red and that it was safe for him to move forward.

Miller v Evans
[1975] RTR 70, CA

Travelling west along the Great West Road, which had dual four-lane carriageways, Miss Pouleuf driving a small Citroen wished to turn right at a cross-roads controlled by traffic lights. Having passed the primary light at green she took up a position in the gap between the two ends of the central reservation, at an angle to cross the eastbound carriageway when it should be safe to do so. When the lights changed to amber and red for eastbound traffic three cars slowed down and stopped. A fourth car driven by Evans travelling in the lane nearest the central reservation drove past the red light at speed and collided with the front of the Citroen. The judge held Miss Pouleuf 15% to blame for the collision on the ground that she must have moved forward, having seen the other cars stop and not having seen Evans's car. She strongly denied having moved at all.

HELD, ON APPEAL: (1) On the evidence, Miss Pouleuf had not moved and was not negligent; (2) even if she had moved forward into the path of Evans's car she was not negligent. Knowing from the fact that the other cars had stopped that the lights had changed to red for eastbound traffic she was under no duty to see if there was traffic in the fourth lane and whether if there were any, it was travelling at such a speed as to be unlikely to stop at the lights. The clear inference of a reasonably careful motorist would have been that there was no reason to think that a car in the fast lane would come across against the lights. *Hopwood Homes Ltd v Kennerdine* (above) followed. *Sudds v Hanscombe* (above) supported this view.

Duty of drivers when lights changing

Godsmark v Knight Brothers (Brighton) Ltd
(1960) Times, 12 May (Barry J)
A, driving a large lorry over 30 feet long, and B, driving a car, were approaching a cross-roads controlled by traffic lights. A from the south, B from the east. When A was well short of the stop line the lights changed from green to amber. He could not safely stop on or short of the line, however, and carried on, though the stop line was about 40 feet from the crossroad and he could have pulled up within the 40 feet. As B approached the cross-roads the lights changed from red to red-and-amber and were showing green when he entered the cross-roads. Thus neither driver disobeyed the rules in the Traffic Signs Regulations as to the significance of light signals. The two vehicles collided at the cross-roads.

HELD: A was two-thirds and B one-third to blame. It must have been obvious to A when the lights changed to amber before he reached the stop line that, if he proceeded, he would for a considerable time be blocking traffic on the east-west road which had received the green light. He should have taken steps to avoid obstruction of traffic lulled into a sense of security by green lights.

B relied entirely on *Eva Ltd v Reeves*. That case did not apply here since it dealt with a vehicle which had entered the cross-roads against the red lights. It might well be that a time arrived when drivers on roads to which green was shown might cease to have any obligation to look left or right to see whether any vehicle was ignoring the regulations. When amber had just been shown to them the position was different. Here the lights had just turned green in favour of B. There was an obligation on B to see that no other vehicles had entered the cross-roads while the lights were amber. B was bound to contemplate that some vehicle which had properly entered the cross-roads might still be passing across, although the lights had changed to green.

Radburn v Kemp
[1971] 3 All ER 249, [1971] 1 WLR 1502, 115 Sol Jo 711, CA
The plaintiff, riding a bicycle, came to a large road junction controlled by traffic lights. He wished to enter a street on the opposite side of the junction but the lights were at red. It was a murky wet evening. When the lights

changed to green he started forward but by the time he had reached a point about two-thirds of the way over the junction (which was 127 feet across) he noticed the light at the mouth of the street he was aiming for had changed to amber. He was then struck by the defendant's car which had emerged from a street on his left. The defendant had started from this street when the light there changed to green: he had not seen the plaintiff at all. It was admitted that he was negligent but the judge of assize also held the plaintiff to blame to the extent of 50% because he had not seen the defendant's car and if he had, could have stopped.

HELD, ON APPEAL: The plaintiff was not at all to blame. As in *Godsmark v Knight* (above) the defendant, for whom the light had just changed to green, was under a duty to see that there were no vehicles on the crossing which might still be passing across. He had no business, despite the light being in his favour, to enter the junction at all unless he was satisfied that it was safe for him to do so. Once having entered it he had no right to proceed further without taking the utmost care to save harmless people who rightly were already on the junction before he entered it. The defendant had failed to prove that the plaintiff if he had seen the car before the collision could have done anything effective to avoid it.

Smithers v H & M Transport
(1983) 133 NLJ 558 (Stocker J)

The defendant's van was stationary in a crossroads junction controlled by traffic lights, waiting to turn right when the lights should change. A motor cyclist was approaching from the opposite direction. The lights had changed for him from green to amber as he crossed the stop line. The van moved into his path and there was a collision.

HELD: The van driver was liable. He had not seen the motor cycle until a split second before impact though he could have seen it if he had looked. It must have been visible before the van was driven off from its angled and stationary position. He should not have driven forward at all so long as the lights were green for traffic coming from the opposite direction over the cross roads.

Duty to pedestrian at traffic lights

Frank v Cox
(1967) Times, 11 May, CA

At a crossroads controlled by traffic lights Frank began walking across the road on the south side from east to west. The traffic lights had changed and were in his favour. Cox was in his car in the road at the west side of the junction. As soon as the lights changed he drove into the junction and turned right, knocking down Frank who had then almost reached the centre refuge.

HELD: Cox's driving was not only careless: it verged on the monstrous, and Frank was not at all to blame. There is a paramount duty on motorists turning at junctions when the lights showed in their favour to be sure that no pedestrians were crossing the road they were entering. They must observe para 26 of the Highway Code [now the Highway Code (1978), para 60] which requires them when turning at junctions to give precedence to pedestrians who are crossing.

Note—See also *Shepherd v West*, p 89, above.

Presumption that lights are working correctly

Wells v Woodward
(1956) 54 LGR 142, Div Ct
Where a court finds that traffic lights are showing green one way, the court is entitled to infer, unless the contrary is proved, that they are showing red the other way.

Tingle Jacobs & Co v Kennedy
[1964] 1 All ER 888, [1964] 1 WLR 638, 108 Sol Jo 196, CA
At a crossroads controlled by traffic lights a car belonging to the plaintiffs collided with a car owned and driven by the defendant. In evidence the plaintiff's driver said that when travelling westwards he saw the traffic light was green in his favour and was crossing the junction when the defendant's car came across his path from the south and ran into it. Two independent witnesses supported the plaintiff's driver's evidence that the light was green in his favour when he entered the crossing. The defendant and his wife gave evidence that they saw the light in their road change from red to amber and then green and they then went forward into the crossing. There was evidence from a police officer of inspections of the lights on dates before and after the accident when they were working properly. The county court judge accepted that both parties were telling the truth and concluded that the traffic lights could not have been working properly. He apportioned liability equally on the ground that the drivers had failed to keep a proper look-out.
HELD, ON APPEAL: It was plain that one side or the other must have been mistaken. The police evidence was that there had been no trouble with the lights. When you have a device of this kind set up for the public use in active operation the presumption should be that it is in proper working order unless there is evidence to the contrary and there was none here. The case must be decided on the basis that the lights were working properly and there must be a new trial.

Lights not working correctly

Ramoo Son of Erulapan v Gan Soo Swee
[1971] 3 All ER 320, [1971] WLR 1014, 115 Sol Jo 445, PC
At a crossroads controlled by traffic lights a lorry was approaching from the east and a taxi-cab (in which the plaintiff was a passenger) from the north. The lights were not functioning properly: those facing the lorry were showing only a green-amber-green sequence with no red phase; those facing the cab were changing in normal sequence but too rapidly. The lorry driver said he first looked at the lights when he was 40 to 50 feet away and saw them at green only; he was unaware of any malfunction. The plaintiff said he first saw the lights facing the cab when it was 15 feet away and they were green. The cab driver did not give evidence. Both vehicles drove on to the junction at speed and the cab was hit by the lorry, injuring the plaintiff.
HELD: The question was whether either driver should have realised the

lights were not working properly and that he must proceed with caution. *Eva v Reeves* (p 124, above) was of no relevance; it merely showed that a driver who enters properly on to a crossing when the lights are in his favour is under no duty to anticipate that another driver may enter the crossing improperly against the lights facing him. The cab driver should have noticed that the lights were changing rapidly and have realised that they were out of order. He should have slowed down but did not. The natural inference in the absence of evidence from him was that he was not keeping a proper look-out. If the lorry driver did not, as he said, see the lights until he was 40 to 50 feet away he too was not keeping a proper look-out. He could not shelter behind the possibility that even if he had looked at them much earlier he may not have been able to deduce that they were out of order. Both drivers were negligent.

Crossing stop line

Ryan v Smith
[1967] 1 All ER 611, [1967] 2 WLR 390, 131 JP 193, 110 Sol Jo 854, Div Ct
At a crossroads controlled by traffic lights the defendant, driving a bus, passed the primary light and its associated stop line when the light was at green. Before the whole of his bus had passed over the stop line he stopped to allow a vehicle coming in the opposite direction to turn across his front into the road on his left. By the time the road was clear again the traffic light which he had just passed and the secondary light facing him on the far side of the crossroads, had changed to red. He nevertheless started forward and crossed over the junction. The evidence showed that if he had remained stationary in the position in which he first came to a stop he would not have obstructed traffic wishing to cross the junction from right to left or vice versa. He was convicted of failing to conform to an indication given by the traffic lights, since the Traffic Signals Regulations 1964, reg 34(1)(a) provides that 'the red signal shall convey the prohibition that vehicular traffic shall not proceed beyond the stop line', and the rear end of his bus had crossed the stop line after the light changed to red.
HELD, ON APPEAL: The defendant was rightly convicted. The prohibition relates to any vehicle or any part of any vehicle and is infringed if any part of a vehicle moves forward from one side of the line to the other.

Fire Brigade, Ambulance and Police

Ward v London County Council
[1938] 2 All ER 341 (Charles J)
A fire engine came to a light controlled crossing with the lights against it. The driver had been sounding his gong, seeing no vehicle crossing, proceeded against the red light. A car was entering the crossing from his left with the green light in its favour, turning to its right, and collided with the fire engine.
HELD: The driver of the fire engine was alone to blame. The fact that other traffic gave way to a fire engine was no excuse. The red light was an absolute prohibition.

TRAFFIC SIGNS

Note—See also 'White lines', p 139, below.

The Road Traffic Regulation Act 1984, s 65, replacing the Road Traffic Act 1960, s 52, authorises a highway authority to place traffic signs, and s 22(1) of the 1972 Act makes it an offence for the driver of any vehicle who fails to conform to the sign.

The Road Traffic Regulation Act 1984, s 64 deals with traffic signs and defines the expression, which includes any line or mark on a road.

Regulations

Note—The current traffic signs regulations are the Traffic Signs Regulations and General Directions 1981, SI 1981/859, replacing earlier regulations which came into effect as from 1 January 1965. The principle of these regulations is to use symbols to replace words wherever possible in traffic signs. The symbols adopted are, in general, those in use on the continent of Europe.

To understand some of the older cases it is necessary to know that 'Stop' replaces the old 'Halt at Major Road Ahead' sign. It appears on a minor road where traffic emerges into a major road and requires every vehicle (a) to stop at the major road and (b) not to proceed into the major road 'in such a manner or at such a time as is likely to cause danger to the driver of any other vehicle on the major road or as to necessitate the driver of any such other vehicle to change its speed or course in order to avoid an accident with the first mentioned vehicle'.

'Give Way' replaces the old 'Slow Major Road Ahead' sign. Its meaning is the same as that of the 'Stop' sign with the omission of requirement (a).

The Traffic Signs (Speed Limits) Regulations and General Directions 1969, SI 1969/1487, deal with traffic signs relating to speed limits.

Breach not actionable without negligence

Kelly v WRN Contracting Ltd
[1968] 1 All ER 369, [1968] 1 WLR 921, 112 Sol Jo 465 (Ashworth J)
Burke parked his car on a bend opposite double white lines in the road; by so doing he was in breach of the Traffic Signs Regulations 1964, reg 23 [now reg 23 of the 1981 Regulations]. Its nearside wheels were on the pavement and only 3 feet of the width of the car projected into the roadway. It was visible to approaching traffic for at least 100 yards and there was plenty of room for vehicles to pass. O'Connor driving a lorry too fast and possibly failing to see the car until too late got out of control and crashed into a wall injuring the plaintiff, his passenger. O'Connor admitted liability to the plaintiff but claimed a contribution from Burke.
HELD: There was no common law negligence on the part of Burke. There was a breach of reg 23 and as the accident would not have occurred but for parking the car where it was it had a causative effect on the accident. The regulations were designed to avoid accidents and therefore to prevent injury. A breach of the regulations gave rise to civil liability to a person injured by reason of the breach. Liability apportioned 90% to O'Connor, 10% Burke.

Note—But see next case.

Coote v Stone
[1971] 1 All ER 657, [1971] 1 WLR 279, 115 Sol Jo 79, CA
The Various Trunk Roads (Prohibition of Waiting) (Clearways) Order 1963, art 4 provides that 'no person shall . . . cause or permit any vehicle to wait on' a clearway. On a straight stretch of main road which had been designated a clearway the defendant stopped his car close in to the nearside to attend to his small daughter who was feeling sick. After two minutes or so the plaintiff came along in his car from the same direction as the defendant. Being dazzled by the sun he failed to see the defendant's car and crashed into the back of it. The judge held the defendant in breach of the regulation, and said that as the collision would not have occurred if he had not stopped there he was liable.
HELD, ON APPEAL: That was not right. As in *Clarke v Brims* (p 215, below) and *Phillips v Britannia Laundry* (p 245, below) the question was whether the regulation was intended to give a civil remedy to a person injured by the breach or whether it imposed only a public duty. The primary object of the Clearways Regulations was to facilitate the passage of traffic, and though this object is not unconnected with the avoidance of danger it was not intended to give rise to any private liability. *Kelly v WRN Contracting Ltd* (above) was wrongly decided and should not be followed.

Effect of traffic sign

Brazier v Alabaster
(1962) Times, 16 January, Div Ct QBD
A motorist approached a roundabout on a dual-track road. The central intersection of the road ended 62 ft 9 in from the roundabout. Instead of going round the roundabout the motorist made a U-turn between the end of the intersection and the roundabout to get on to the other track of the road. There was a 'Keep Left' sign on the roundabout. He was convicted of failing to conform to an indication given by a traffic signal contrary to s 14 of the Road Traffic Act 1960 (now the Road Traffic Act 1972, s 22).
HELD, ON APPEAL: The conviction could not stand. A traffic sign could only indicate that if a motorist were to pass it he must obey it. As there was not a 'No Entry' sign in the intersection the motorist had the right to use that part of the highway.

No warning sign

James v Parsons
[1975] 1 Lloyd's Rep 178 (Kilner Brown J)
Travelling at 40 mph or more in the dark a car driven by the defendant entered an S-bend at the end of which was a hump-backed bridge. There was no warning sign of the bridge, which came as a surprise to the defendant. The car lost contact with the road in passing over the bridge and the plaintiff, a passenger, was injured. It was argued for the defendant that he was not to blame for the result of meeting an unsuspected hazard in the road in these circumstances.
HELD: The defendant should have seen the bridge before he hit it even though not warned about it and should have been driving in such a way

that, once he did hit the hump he could have controlled the car and so prevented it from leaving the road.

Slow sign

Buffel v Cardox
[1950] 2 All ER 878, CA
A cyclist crossing a main road was injured by a lorry on the main road. About 95 yards from the crossing there were in the main road three warning signs consisting of studs in the road with the word 'slow', a cross-road sign and a flashing beacon. The lorry did not slow down before the crossing. Parker J held the cyclist alone to blame.
HELD, ON APPEAL:
    Per Bucknill LJ: I do not think that 'slow' means any more than 'proceed with caution' — 'proceed at such a speed that you can stop if, when you get to the crossing, you find somebody, or something, in the process of crossing, or about to cross.'
    Per Singleton LJ: It is not easy to define the word 'slow'. Its meaning must depend on a variety of circumstances. That which may appear slow to some motorists may strike a pedestrian as fast. I think the fairest way to look on it is that the sign is an indication to the motorist that he is approaching a place of potential danger, and that, therefore, he ought to be driving more slowly than he would drive on a normal open road without any such sign. In other words, his speed ought to be such that he can pull up fairly quickly if someone or something appears from one or other of the crossroads. Appeal allowed.

Traffic entering major road from minor road

Brown v Central Scottish Motor Traction
1949 SC 9, 1949 SLT 66, Ct of Sess
A motor cyclist with pillion passenger was proceeding along a minor road which had a 'Slow, Major Road Ahead' sign and formed the left arm of a Y junction with a major road. He collided with a bus proceeding along the major road at about 25 mph. Each vehicle should have been clearly visible to the other driver. The bus driver did not slow down until the motor cycle emerged from the minor road, when he at once braked and swerved. The pillion passenger was killed, and his father brought proceedings against the bus company. The jury found the bus driver negligent.
HELD, ON APPEAL: There was no evidence of negligence of the bus driver. On the evidence, the bus driver had no opportunity of observing what the motor cyclist was going to do.

Note—Compare *Lang v London Transport Executive* (below).
    See also *MacIntyre v Coles*, p 107, above.

Lang v London Transport Executive
[1959] 3 All ER 609, [1959] 1 WLR 1168 (Havers J)
A motor cyclist was riding along a minor side road and approaching a

major main road. The minor road continued the line of the major road
from the junction, where the major road changed direction. About 180 feet
from the junction there was a 'Slow, Major Road Ahead' sign. Traffic on
the major road was clearly visible from the side road for a distance of 40
yards from the junction. The motor cyclist was proceeding at a speed of 20
mph and he did not slow down but continued at that speed straight out on to
the major road. A bus was being driven along the major road at a speed of
about 20 mph. There was a 'Slow' sign painted on the major road about
190 feet away from the junction. Just after passing the 'Slow' sign, the bus
driver glanced in the direction of the side road and saw some cyclists, but
did not look in the direction of the side road again. The bus driver was
aware of the 'Slow' sign in the minor road, and he knew that people would
suddenly emerge from a side road when it was unwise to do so. The motor
cyclist was killed, and his widow sued the bus driver and his employers.
HELD: The deceased was guilty of a high degree of negligence. The bus
driver was negligent in not taking the precaution of looking at the traffic in
the side road. The judge found the deceased was two-thirds to blame and
the bus driver one-third.

Note—See comments of Sachs LJ in *Watkins v Moffat*, p 136, below.

Walsh v Redfern
[1970] RTR 201 (Lyell J)
The defendant was driving an Army lorry and trailer along the main Bath
Road late at night. His speed was 35 mph. A car containing six people was
being driven along a narrow lane at great speed towards the Bath Road
from his left. The defendant saw from the light cast by the car's headlight
on the tall hedges on each side of the lane that a car was approaching but
owing to the rain and darkness he could form no clear impression of speed
and gave no further thought to it. The driver of the car did not stop or slow
down but drove straight out on to the main road at speed. The defendant
was unable to avoid the car and in the collision four of its occupants were
killed.
HELD: The defendant was not at all to blame. There was nothing he could
have done to avoid the collision short of slowing right down to such a speed
that he could have stopped the lorry and let the car pass across its front
when he saw it emerge from behind the hedge. It would be unreasonable to
expect him to do so. He was driving on one of the main trunk roads from
London to the West of England; it is common knowledge that every minor
road which debouches on to a road of this importance has warning signs to
approach the major road at slow speed. There was nothing known to the
defendant to put him on guard against a lunatic driver who would wholly
disregard the warning signs.

Garston Warehousing Co v O F Smart (Liverpool) Ltd
[1973] RTR 377, CA
On a November evening after dark the plaintiffs' car was being driven out
of a side street across a main road, which was 26 feet wide and well-lighted,
into a street opposite. The main road was a one-way street with traffic
travelling only from the car driver's right. As he was about to leave the side
street there was on his immediate right against the kerb in the main road a

bus which obscured his view to the right. The bus driver gave a flash of his headlights and a hand signal to the car driver to come on. After looking along the nearside of the bus and seeing nothing approaching the car driver switched on his headlights and drove out slowly across and beyond the front of the bus without stopping. When about to enter the street opposite the car was struck violently on its offside by the defendants' van which had over-taken the bus. The van driver had not seen the car until he was 12 to 15 feet away, nor had he noticed a slow-down signal given by the bus-driver. The judge held the van driver two-thirds to blame for driving at a speed excessive in the circumstances and failing to see the car earlier; he held the car driver one-third to blame for not stopping when the car was just past the bus and when he would have seen the van approaching.

HELD, ON APPEAL: The apportionment should not be disturbed.

Cross-roads collisions

MAJOR ROAD DRIVER 25% TO BLAME

Williams v Fullerton
(1961) 105 Sol Jo 280, CA
A was driving a car along Richmond Avenue, near King's Cross, London: B was driving a car along Hemingford Road, a minor road which crosses Richmond Avenue at an ordinary cross-roads junction. Hemingford Road had a sign 'Slow — Major Road Ahead'. Despite this B drove on to the cross-roads at a speed estimated between 30 and 60 mph and collided with A's car causing fatal injuries to a passenger. A had approached the junc-tion, which had a conventional cross-road sign, at a reasonable speed, looked right and left and did not see anything. The trial judge held A 25% to blame and B 75%. A appealed. It was argued on his behalf that a driver on a major road approaching a crossing had no duty to keep a look-out except to see what might reasonably be seen and that there was no obliga-tion to look out for what travelled at an excessive speed.

HELD: The trial judge's finding could not be disturbed. If A's failure had consisted merely in failing to take into account the outrageous driving of B it was at least doubtful if he could be considered negligent. But although he had looked left and right at the crossing he had not, as indicated by the Highway Code, looked right again. Had A looked at the right time or looked properly he must have seen the other car and could have taken avoiding action.

Per Ormerod LJ: If a driver exercised proper care he approached a crossing with his foot off the accelerator and ready to brake and deal with any traffic from the minor road by slowing down or stopping.

Note—For comment on this decision see *Humphrey v Leigh*, p 136, below.

Butters v J. H. Fenner & Co Ltd
(1967) Times, 17 February (MacKenna J)
At a cross-roads in a built-up area the first defendant's servant was driving a car along a minor road. He failed to see a 'Slow, Major Road Ahead' sign and a large 'Slow', painted on the roadway. He drove straight on to the cross-roads where the car was hit by the second defendant's lorry travelling

on the major road. The lorry driver had not looked to his offside as he crossed the junction nor had he slowed down.

HELD: The lorry driver was 25% to blame. He should have looked to his right and slowed down before entering the junction. If he had done so he would have been able to avoid the collision or at least reduce its force.

MAJOR ROAD DRIVER NOT TO BLAME

Note—See *Brown v Central Scottish Motor Traction*, p 133, above.

Watkins v Moffatt
(1967) 111 Sol Jo 719, CA

The plaintiff, a passenger, was injured in a crossroads collision between a Ford van in which he was travelling and an Austin car. The Ford was travelling on the minor road on which there was a 'Slow, Major Road Ahead' sign. The Austin was on the major road. The judge held that the Ford driver was guilty of a high degree of negligence in coming out faster than he should have done but the possibility of danger should have been reasonably apparent to the driver of the Austin if he had been keeping a proper look-out. He held the Austin driver one-third to blame.

HELD, ON APPEAL: It could not be inferred that the driver of the Austin was not keeping a proper look-out. The Ford was on a side road with 'Major Road Ahead' signs and must have been coming so fast that the driver of the Austin, keeping a reasonable look-out on both sides of the road might well not have seen it, and he was not to blame.

Per Sachs LJ: The case is another in which the authority of *Lang v London Transport Executive* (p 133, above) is prayed in aid on behalf of a driver of a vehicle emerging from a side road on to a main road. Whatever may be the correct view of that case on its own facts, a matter on which I would wish to reserve judgment, *Lang's* case is not a charter in favour of motorists emerging from a side road at speed. That would entail a somewhat unrealistic view of the way reasonably driven traffic uses main roads and would derogate from the great responsibility of those emerging from side roads in relation to main road traffic.

Humphrey v Leigh and Roe
[1971] RTR 363, CA

The second defendant was driving his car at a steady pace up Gipsy Hill in South London when the first defendant drove out of a side road to cross into a road opposite without stopping or slowing down. There was a collision resulting in injury to the plaintiff. There were no road signs to show that Gipsy Hill was the major road but there was no doubt that it was and that traffic in the side road would as a matter of course slow down and stop. The judge attributed all the blame to the first defendant, who appealed.

HELD: The appeal should be dismissed — the second defendant was in no way negligent.

Per Russell LJ: The question is whether it can be propounded as a matter of law that a person in the position of the second defendant has a duty, if he is to avoid a charge of negligence every time he comes across a side road of this kind leading out of Gipsy Hill, to take his foot off the accelerator and poise his foot over the brake, being prepared to stop short of the crossing. In so far as anything to that effect was said by Lord Justice Ormerod in the case of *Williams v Fullerton* (p 135, above) it was an obiter dictum and I personally would not follow it at all; otherwise you would approach in situation in which no traffic moves about the country at any reasonable speed whatsoever.

Watson v Everall and Tebbett
(1960) 12 July, CA, unreported
In the hours of darkness a motor coach and a van collided at a crossroads where a main road was crossed by a subsidiary road. The van was being driven along the main road and the coach along the subsidiary road, which had a 'Halt' sign and stop line at the point where the coach emerged on to the main road. Due to his injuries the driver did not remember the actual collision but he remembered turning on his headlights as he left the lights of a town some distance from the crossroads: they would have been visible to the coach driver for at least 70 yards before the crossing. The court found that the coach driver did not halt at the main road but was crossing it at some speed, and without looking out for other traffic, when the van struck the coach on its offside in front of the rear wheel. There was no evidence as to what the van was doing before the impact either as to speed or position on the road, nor did it leave any brake marks on the road. The judge of assize held the drivers equally to blame.
HELD: Allowing the van driver's appeal, the coach driver was wholly to blame.
Per Sellers LJ: It depicts the typical case of a vehicle coming out from the side road directly in front of the van which had the right to use that main road expecting that traffic coming out from the side road on the left would conform with the requirements of the law that it should halt and the further requirement that being a side road it should give way to traffic passing on the main road.

Note—The above is taken from a transcript of the full judgment.

Brooks v Graham
(1964) 12 March, CA, unreported
At a crossroads in a built-up area a van was travelling north and a car was travelling west. There was a 'Halt' sign in the van-driver's road, but he did not stop. He drove straight out on to the crossroads at about 20 mph, colliding with the nearside of the car which was travelling at about 15 mph. Neither party saw the other before the collision. The car driver said he looked into the turning on his left as he approached but saw no vehicle at the halt line and carried on. The judge found that car driver 25% to blame for driving at an excessive speed and not keeping a proper look-out.
HELD, ON APPEAL: The driver of the car was not to blame at all. It was impossible to support the judge's conclusion without taking a wholly unrealistic view of traffic conditions as they are. The relative speeds of the vehicles showed that at the moment the car reached the actual crossroads the van could not have reached the halt line. If the car driver had seen it coming towards the crossing he might justifiably have assumed that it

would halt when it reached the halt line. The judge had treated the case as though it were one of a collision at an uncontrolled crossroads or a crossroads subject only to a 'Slow' sign. Where there is a 'Halt' sign wholly different considerations apply. If a vehicle on a major road is to approach such a crossroads in such a way that it can stop dead if a vehicle on a minor road fails to observe the 'Halt' sign, it would mean that it would have to slow down to little more than a walking pace and for all practical purposes bring traffic on the major road to a standstill.

Note—Taken from full transcript of judgment.

Barclays Bank Ltd v Gaughan and Toole
(1970) 8 June (James J), unreported.
Approaching a crossroads in a rural area in daylight the second defendant was driving his car along the main road at 25 to 30 mph. He knew the minor road on his left had a 'Halt' sign at its mouth. From a point about 35 yards from the junction there was a view through an open fence along the minor road for a similar distance from the junction. The first defendant approaching the crossroads along the minor road at about 50 mph ignored the 'Halt' sign and drove straight on to the junction striking the second defendant's car and killing a passenger. The second defendant, who was paying attention to some horses approaching from the far side of the junction, said he had only a fleeting glimpse of the other car before the collision.
HELD: The second defendant was not at all to blame. He was driving quietly and sensibly on a main road with knowledge of the 'Halt' sign in the minor road. He was faced with the presence of the horses. His obligation was to behave reasonably. It was doubtful whether he would have seen anything in the minor road but he had every reason to believe a car in the minor road would stop. The sole responsibility for the accident lay on the first defendant.

Gooder v Taylor and Yorkshire Tar Distillers Ltd
(1966) Times, 18 October, CA
At a crossroads where a minor road crossed a major road a van was travelling along the minor road and a tanker along the major road. As the van approached the crossroads the driver slowed down almost to a stop. He looked along the major road but saw nothing coming, pressed the accelerator again and proceeded to cross. The tanker-driver had seen the van approaching the crossroads. He took his foot off the accelerator but, seeing the van slow down as if to stop, put his foot on again to go over the crossroads. When at the last moment the van moved forward on to the crossroads the tanker driver was unable to avoid hitting it. The judge of assize held the van driver five-sixths to blame for the collision and the tanker driver one-sixth.
HELD: Allowing the tanker-driver's appeal, he was not to blame at all. He had seen the van slow down and was justified in thinking that the van driver had seen him and was going to let him pass. For the same reason he was not negligent in not sounding his horn. The tanker driver was not negligent in not reducing his speed, for only by slowing down to a very considerable

extent could he have avoided the consequences of the van pulling out at the last moment. As he had seen the van slow down as if to allow him to pass he was under no duty to take such drastic action.

Traffic from right

There is no rule or custom in this country requiring a driver approaching cross-roads to give way to traffic on his right and allowing him to take precedence over traffic on his left. It would be quite disastrous if some users of the highway observed that practice while others did not. Users of roads of equal importance which crossed one another owed a duty to each other to take care. Even the driver on a major road was not acquitted altogether of the duty of taking care, even though there might be a greater duty on the driver on the minor road. The question of negligence is one of fact.

(1954) 98 Sol Jo 380, Times, 29 May (Streatfeild J)

White lines

Note—And see 'Traffic signs', p 131, above.

The Road Traffic Regulation Act 1984, s 64 provides that 'In this Act "traffic sign" means . . . any line or mark on a road for' conveying to traffic on roads warnings, information, requirements, restrictions or prohibitions of any kind specified by regulations.

Kirk v Parker
(1938) 60 Ll L Rep 129

If the offside wheels of the defendant's lorry were a little over an imaginary central white line, that is not necessarily negligence if, by driving a car in that position, it is clear you will avoid any collision with vehicles coming in the opposite direction.

Day v Smith
[1983] 133 NLJ 726, QBD

The plaintiff was injured when the car he was driving collided with another on a bend. The deceased's administrator counter-claimed, alleging negligence on the part of the plaintiff. There were no eye witnesses of the accident but there was evidence of some marks on the road. The bend on which the accident occurred was a left hand bend for the plaintiff, the road being 24 feet wide divided by a single central white line.

HELD: On the evidence the plaintiff's car was 3 to 4 feet on the wrong side of the white line at the time of collision. He was negligent in allowing that to happen and the deceased was not to blame. Judgment for the defendant administrator on the counter-claim.

Dotted lines across mouth of road

Note—The Traffic Signs Regulations 1981 provide by regs 21 and 22 that transverse broken white lines across the mouth of a road at a road junction have the

effect of a 'Give Way' sign whether or not used in conjunction with a sign.
See *Hardy v Walder*, p 28, above.

Murray v Nicholls

1983 SLT 194 (Outer House)

There was a collision of cars at the junction of a major and a minor road. There had been white lines at the junction but these had not been renewed after roadworks.

HELD: The fact that there had been white lines before was relevant to the issue of foreseeability but not to the existence of a duty. To hold there was such a duty would expose highway authorities to a wide range of liabilities. In any event there was no evidence that either driver was influenced by the existence of the markings at an earlier date. Action dismissed.

Note—But see *Bird v Pearce*, p 288, below.

Double white lines

Note—The Traffic Signs Regulations and General Directions 1981, reg 23 contains the rules of the 'double white line' system of traffic control. Vehicles must not stop on any length of road having a double white line, nor must a vehicle cross a continuous line when it is on the left of a dotted or continuous line as viewed in the direction of travel of the vehicle. There are exceptions to the rule against stopping, including a stop for a person to board or alight, or for the purposes of loading or unloading. It is permissible to cross a continuous line for, inter alia, the purpose of passing a stationary vehicle or entering another road. When the dotted line is on the left a vehicle may cross it provided it is seen by the driver to be safe to do so.

West v Buckinghamshire County Council

(1984) Times, 13 November (Caulfield J)

The plaintiff driver, while overtaking, collided with an oncoming vehicle causing the death of the driver of that vehicle, whose personal representatives recovered £160,000 damages. In the present action the plaintiff claimed indemnity from the defendants, the highway authority, for having failed to place double white lines on the road pursuant to their power to do so under the Road Traffic Regulation Act 1967, s 55(1). The Department of Transport had in 1964 recommended that roads less than 20 feet wide should not carry double white lines. At that time the defendants had decided that double white lines were not desirable as the road was less than 20 feet wide. When measured after the accident in 1979 it was found to be more than 20 feet wide. The plaintiff urged that the defendants should have foreseen a gradual widening of the road due to piecemeal repairs and should have measured it after repairs and supplied double white lines, as was done after the accident.

HELD: The defendants were not liable. Although a public body exercising powers given it by statute could owe a duty of care and be liable in damages (per Lord Wilberforce in.*Anns v Merton London Borough Council* [1978] AC 728 [1977] 2 All ER 492, [1977] 2 WLR 1024, 121 Sol Jo 377, 75 LGR 555, 243 Estates Gazette 523, 591, HL) a policy decision made pursuant to such statutory powers was a matter of discretion which could not be attacked in the courts. In the present case the defendants had exercised their discretion bona fide and no duty of care arose.

R v Blything Justices, ex parte Knight
[1970] RTR 218, Div Ct
The defendant was following two cars and an articulated lorry. He decided to overtake. He did not know he was approaching the beginning of a double white line. He was unable to get back to the nearside until he had driven 40 or 50 yards on the offside of the double white line. He was charged with failing to comply with the Traffic Signs Regulations 1964, reg 23 (now reg 23 of the 1981 Regulations). He said the first of the two cars had accelerated and prevented him from getting back to the nearside in time and that this was an accident giving him a defence under reg 23(4)(a). The magistrate's clerk advised the bench that this defence was not available to a driver who had not first had the double white lines on his offside before crossing them. He was convicted.
HELD, ON APPEAL: The conviction should stand because a driver could not, after putting himself in the wrong by beginning to overtake in such circumstances, claim that he had to continue in the wrong because of some accident. Even so, the magistrate's clerk's advice had been too narrow and was bad. There may be cases (eg when overtaking stationary vehicles) when a man through no fault of his own approaches the double white line on the wrong side of it and never gets back on to his nearside until some distance of the white line has been passed.

TREES

Colliding with branch

Radley v London Passenger Transport Board
[1942] 1 All ER 433, 166 LT 285, 106 JP 164, 58 TLR 364, 86 Sol Jo 147 (Humphreys J)
On a country road an overhanging branch of a tree on the side of the road broke a window in a bus and injured a passenger. The accident occurred at midday, and the tree was clearly visible along the road. A witness said he had seen the defendants' buses brush against the trees on the road on several occasions. The defendants submitted no case and called no evidence.
HELD: Prima facie case of negligence and defendants were liable. It was immaterial that the obstruction was not on the ground. It was visible to the driver. It might be different if a branch broke off suddenly in a gale.

Hale v Hants and Dorset Motor Services Ltd
[1947] 2 All ER 628, CA
Plaintiff was a passenger on top of a bus. Just after the bus moved off from a stop, the near side upper deck came in contact with the branches of a tree standing on the edge of the pavement and glass on the upper deck was broken. A splinter entered plaintiff's eye, which had to be removed. He sued the bus company and the corporation.

The judge of assize held that the corporation ought to have contemplated that a bus would pull close to the tree near a bus stop, and should have pruned a badly shaped tree leaning towards the highway. The road camber caused the bus to tilt slightly, but the bus would hit the overhanging branch apart from the camber.

He held the corporation two-thirds, and the bus company one-third, to blame.

Both defendants appealed. On appeal it appeared from the evidence that the projection of the branches was $7\frac{1}{2}$ and $6\frac{1}{2}$ ins respectively. It was at night. There was a brilliant street lamp between the driver and the tree as he came round a roundabout.

HELD, ON APPEAL: The corporation had planted the tree on the side of the highway under the provisions of the Road Improvement Act 1925, s 1(1) (now replaced by the Highways Act 1980, s 96) which empowers a highway authority to cause trees to be planted in any highway maintainable by them. Section 1(2) (now replaced by the Highways Act 1980, s 96(6)) is as follows: 'No such tree . . . shall be placed, laid out or allowed to remain in such a situation as to hinder the reasonable use of the highway by any person entitled to the use thereof.'

HELD: The passengers on the omnibus were persons entitled to the use of the highway, the omnibus was making reasonable use of it, the tree hindered reasonable use and the corporation had allowed the tree to remain in that position. It was not unreasonable for the driver to drive very close to the kerb. It was only the tree which made the danger. The driver was not to be blamed for not observing and estimating the overhang, but he knew the trees were potential sources of danger and should have acted on the footing that it might overhang and give it a wide berth. Both appeals dismissed.

Note—Cases of claims by motorists against land owners or occupiers are in ch 9, below.

CHAPTER 3
Vicarious Liability

1 MASTER AND SERVANT

It is a rule that an employer, though guilty of no fault himself, is liable for damage done by the fault or negligence of his servant acting in the course of his employment: Per Lord Reid *Staveley Iron Co Ltd v Jones* [1956] AC 627, [1956] 1 All ER 403, [1956] 2 WLR 479, 100 Sol Jo 130.

Who is a servant? A servant may be defined as any person employed by another to do work for him on the terms that he, the servant, is to be subject to the control and directions of his employer in respect of the manner in which his work is to be done: *Salmond on Torts* (15th edn) p 647.

Note—MacKinnon LJ in *Hewitt v Bonvin* (p 181, below) said that this definition can 'hardly be bettered'.

Servant distinguished from independent contractor

Note—A servant is one whose work is under the control of another. He must be distinguished from an independent contractor, 'who undertakes to produce a given result, but so that in the actual execution of the work he is not under the order or control of the person for whom he does it, and may use his own discretion in things not specified before hand': *Winfield on Tort* (9th edn) p 734 quoting *Pollock on Torts* (15th edn) p 62.

Ready Mixed Concrete Ltd v Ministry of Pensions
[1968] 2 QB 497, [1968] 1 All ER 433, [1968] 2 WLR 775, 112 Sol Jo 14
(MacKenna J)

The owner of a lorry worked for the appellant company under a written contract which described him as an independent contractor. It required him to make his lorry available for the purpose of carrying concrete for the company, to maintain it in good order at his own expense and to hire a driver to drive it when he himself was not available to do so: he was to be paid per mile for the concrete he delivered.

HELD: A contract of service existed if three conditions were fulfilled (1) an agreement by the servant to provide his own work and skill to perform some service in consideration of remuneration; (2) agreement that in performance of the service he would be subject to control sufficiently to make the other the master, (3) the other provisions of the contract are consistent with a contract of service. In classifying the contract a judge might take into account other matters besides control. In the present case the driver had ownership of the assets, the chance of profit and the risk of loss. He had sufficient freedom in the performance of the obligations under the contract to qualify as independent contractor. He was a 'small businessman' and not a servant.

Note—See also *Ready Mixed Concrete Ltd v Yorkshire Traffic Licensing Authority*, p 166, below.

Global Plant Ltd v Secretary of State
[1972] 1 QB 139, [1971] 3 All ER 385, [1971] 3 WLR 269, 115 Sol Jo 506
(Lord Widgery CJ)

For a period up to 1968 the appellants, a company which hired out earthmoving machines with drivers, employed Summers as a driver at a weekly wage and on terms which amounted to a contract of service. In that year he asked to be self-employed as a sub-contractor. Thereafter he stamped his own insurance card at the self-employed person's rate, paid his own income tax under Sch D and was paid at a much enhanced hourly rate, but without travelling allowances, sick pay or provision for holidays. He drove the company's machines as before on sites selected by them under the control of the site foreman or agent. He was not expressly under any duty to work at all but the intention was that he should work exactly as he had before. A determination was made by the Secretary of State for Social Services under the National Insurance Act 1965 that Summers was still a person employed under a contract of service.

HELD: There was no error in law in the Minister's decision.

Note—After commenting that 'the idea of the degree of control exercised by the employer over the servant being a decisive factor in this question has been very largely modified', Lord Widgery quoted with approval a passage from Cooke J's judgment in *Market Investigations Ltd v Minister of Social Security* [1969] 2 QB 173, [1968] 3 All ER 732, [1969] 2 WLR 1, 112 Sol Jo 905: 'factors which may be of importance are such matters as whether the man performing the services provides his own equipment, whether he hires his own helpers, what degree of financial risk he takes, what degree of responsibility for investment or management he had and whether and how far he has an opportunity of profiting from sound management in the performance of his task'.

Ferguson v Dawson
[1976] 1 Lloyd's Rep 143 (Boreham J)
The plaintiff was a building worker 'on the lump'. He was injured when working for the defendants who were building contractors. Both the plaintiff and the defendants regarded and named him as a 'self-employed labour only contractor'. The plaintiff paid his own national insurance stamp as a self-employed person and his wages were paid free of tax.
HELD: Where all the other indicia mentioned by MacKenna J in *Ready Mixed Concrete v Ministry of Pensions* (p 144, above) point to the relationship being that of master and servant then it was in reality a contract of service.

Massey v Crown Life Insurance Co Ltd
[1978] 2 All ER 576, [1978] 1 WLR 676, 121 Sol Jo 791, CA
From 1971 to 1973 the appellant worked as branch manager for the respondent insurance company which treated him as a servant, paying him wages and deducting tax. From 1973 onwards he carried on doing the same job but as an independent contractor under a new agreement at his own instance to enable him to be taxed under Sch D. Later he was dismissed and sought compensation for unfair dismissal.
HELD: He was not an employee and could not claim compensation. Where a perfectly genuine agreement had been entered into at his instance and for his benefit he could not afterwards claim the relationship was something other that what the agreement stated. *Ferguson's* case (above) was different; there the contract was so unspecific that the way the parties had acted was the only thing to go by.

Challinor v Taylor
[1972] ICR 129, 116 Sol Jo 141, 7 ITR 104
A taxi driver had an agreement with the owner of a taxi whereby he paid to the owner 65% of the fares registered on the clock plus the cost of an employee's national insurance stamp. The owner paid for fuel and maintenance. The driver kept the balance of the takings plus all the tips. He was assessed income tax under Sch D as a self-employed person. No memorandum of the terms of employment was supplied to him under the Contracts of Employment Act 1963. The owner never exercised any control over where or for how long the driver plied for hire. When the owner sold the cab the driver claimed a redundancy payment under the Redundancy Payments Act 1965 as an 'employee'.
HELD: He was not an employee. In deciding whether someone was an employee or an independent contractor many factors had to be taken into account of which actual control or the right to control the way in which the work was performed was only one. Whether the contract was one of service depended in the last resort on whether an ordinary person would so consider it in the light of his experience and knowledge.

Roberts v Warne
[1973] RTR 217, Div Ct
Roberts, a hire-car driver, made an agreement with Davies, who ran a hire-car booking office, having the following elements: Roberts would

drive Davies's car for the purpose of carrying passengers who booked in at Davies's Need-a-cab office; Roberts would be on call or attend at the office regularly at agreed times on every weekday except Fridays and Saturdays and would then drive a car as directed by Davies's office; Davies would ensure that Roberts was covered by Davies's own insurance; Roberts would be entitled to 50% of the takings from passengers whom he drove and would pay his own national insurance contributions and income tax. HELD: The question whether Roberts was employed by Davies under a contract of service or not could be decided by asking: Whose business was it that was being carried on? What they had agreed was that Davies was to supply the car and booking facilities and Roberts was to do the work and they were to split the proceeds 50–50; the answer to the question was that it was the business of both of them. It was not a contract of service, it was a co-adventure.

Egginton v Reader
[1936] 1 All ER 7 (Lewis J)
A commercial traveller who owned a car worked for a company under an oral agreement subject to one week's notice. He received no salary but was paid £1 a week towards running expenses of the car and 6% commission on sales. He worked for no one except the company. He called on his own customers but he also sometimes called on firms whose names were given him by the manager of the company, although under no obligation to do so. When an accident occurred, he was on his way to see a customer and had in his car goods of the company to show those customers. He was at liberty to refuse to call on anyone if he did not wish and could travel when and where he liked, and need not work at all unless he chose.
HELD: The company not liable for his negligence.

SCOPE OF EMPLOYMENT

Joel v Morison
(1834) 6 C & P 501
The plaintiff was knocked down and injured by the defendant's horse and cart driven by his servant when a considerable distance from its usual route.

Per Parke B: The master is only liable where the servant is acting in the course of his employment. If he was going out of his way against his master's implied commands when driving on his master's business he will make his master liable, but if he was going on a frolic of his own, without being at all on his master's business, the master will not be liable.

Verdict for the plaintiff.

Note—See also *Aitchison v Page Motors Ltd*, p 162, below.

Whether driving on employer's business

Rayner v Mitchell
(1877) 2 CPD 357
Defendant's carman, without his master's permission and for a purpose of his own wholly unconnected with his master's business, took out defendant's horse and cart and on his way home negligently ran against plaintiff's cab and damaged it. The course of the employment of the carman was that with defendant's horse and cart he took out beer to customers of defendant, a brewer, and in returning to the brewery he called for empty casks wherever they would be likely to be collected, for which he received from the defendant a gratuity of 1d each. At the time of the accident the carman had with him two casks which he had picked up on his return journey at a public house which his master supplied, and for which he afterwards received the customary 1d.
HELD: The carman had not re-entered upon his ordinary duties at the time of the accident and therefore the master was not liable.

Storey v Ashton
(1869) LR 4 QB 476, 10 B & S 337, LLQB 223 (Lush J)
Defendant, a wine merchant, sent his carman and clerk with a horse and cart to deliver some wine, and bring back some empty bottles; on their return, when about a quarter of a mile from defendant's offices, the carman, instead of performing his duty and driving to defendant's offices, depositing the bottles, and taking the horse and cart to the stable in the neighbourhood, was induced by the clerk, it being after business hours, to drive in quite another direction on business of the clerk's; and whilst they were thus driving, plaintiff was run over, owing to the negligence of the carman.
HELD: Defendant was not liable, for the carman was not doing the act, in doing which he had been guilty of negligence, in the course of his employment as servant. The question on all such cases as the present is whether the servant was doing that which the master employed him to do.

A & W Hemphill v Williams
[1966] 2 Lloyd's Rep 101, HL
The defendants sent their lorry and driver to fetch a party of boys, of whom the plaintiff was one, from Benderlock in Argyll, where the boys had been camping, back home to Glasgow. Impliedly, the driver's orders were to return by the most direct route. Some of the boys asked him to return through Stirling which required a detour: the driver asked the adult in charge of the boys (who was not returning in the lorry) but was refused permission. On the journey some of the boys (but not the plaintiff) persuaded the driver to go to Stirling and then to Dollar before returning to Glasgow. An accident occurred on the way to Dollar in which the plaintiff was seriously injured. The boys' object in going via Stirling and Dollar was to see some Girl Guides who had been camping near to the boys and who were returning home to Dollar by train on the same day. The defendants denied they were vicariously liable for the driver's negligent driving on the ground that he was acting outside the scope of his employment.

HELD: It is a question of fact and degree in each case whether the deviation is sufficiently detached from the master's business to constitute a frolic of the servant unconnected with the enterprise for which he was employed. In *Storey v Ashton* (above) the continued presence in the cart of the master's empty wine bottles was not considered a compelling factor in deciding the question of degree as to how far the deviation could be held to absolve the master from vicarious responsibility: had the property in the cart been some more important or valuable or dominant cargo the result might well have been different. In the present case the presence of passengers whom the servant as such was charged to drive to their ultimate destination made it impossible (at all events, provided they were not all parties to the plans for deviation) to say that the deviation was entirely for the servant's own purposes. Their presence and transport was a dominant purpose of the authorised journey and although they were transported deviously continued to play an essential part. The defendants remained liable for the driver's negligence.

Note—The form of a plea in defence can be as follows:

'The driver was in the general employment of the defendants as a . . . but at the time of the occurrence complained of he was not driving for or on behalf of or with the authority of the defendants nor within the scope of his employment by them but was using the vehicle for his own purposes.

CONDUCTOR DRIVING — DRIVER ABSENT

Beard v London General Omnibus Co
[1900] 2 QB 530, 69 LJQB 895, 83 LT 362, 16 LTR 499
At the end of a journey, the conductor of an omnibus belonging to defendants, in the absence of the driver, and apparently for the purpose of turning the omnibus in the right direction of the next journey, drove it through some by-streets at a considerable pace, and while so doing negligently ran into and injured plaintiff. Plaintiff gave no evidence that the conductor was authorised by defendants to drive the omnibus in the absence of the driver. HELD: Plaintiff had not discharged himself from the burden cast upon him of showing that the injury was due to the negligence of a servant of defendants acting within the scope of his employment, and defendants were entitled to judgment.

Note—If the conductor had merely been turning the vehicle round at the terminus in preparation for the next journey in the circumstances of the driver's absence it is doubtful whether the decision, at least in these days, would have gone the same way: Per Sellers LJ in *Kay v ITW*, p 156, below.
    See also *Ricketts v Tilling*, p 159, below.

DRIVER GOING FOR FOOD

Hilton v Thomas Burton Ltd
[1961] 1 All ER 74, [1961] 1 WLR 705, 105 Sol Jo 322 (Diplock J)
The plaintiff's husband was killed when riding in a lorry driven by the second defendant who was an employee of the first defendants, the owners of the lorry. The accident was caused by the negligent driving of the second

defendant. The plaintiff's husband was a foreman in charge of a gang of men engaged on demolition some miles from the employer's premises. After working for some time, four of the men including the plaintiff's husband and the second defendant decided to go in the lorry to a café seven miles away to have some tea. Before arriving there they decided there was not enough time as they had to pick up some other men who were still working at the site. They turned round and were on the return journey when the accident happened. A director of the first defendants gave evidence that he permitted the employees to use the lorry for any reasonable purpose including going to get refreshment: the second defendant was an authorised driver.

HELD: Following *Higbid v R. C. Hammett Ltd* (below), the second defendant was not at the time of the accident doing something he was employed to do. He, the plaintiff's husband and the other men in the lorry were out on a frolic of their own and the first defendants were not vicariously liable for his negligent driving.

Elleanor v Cavendish Woodhouse Ltd
[1973] 1 Lloyd's Rep 313, CA

The second defendant was a salesman employed by the first defendants. He worked ordinary business hours in his employers' shop in Darlington but was also required to do some canvassing during evenings within the radius of thirty miles, using his own car. Sometimes he went with another salesman, a practice known to their employers which led to better results. One evening he took another salesman Smith on canvassing some distance from Darlington. The canvassing finished by 8 pm and they then called at one or more public houses for food and drink. On the way home there was an accident at about 9.30 pm caused by the second defendant's negligence.

HELD: The employers were vicariously liable. On the evidence the second defendant was under a duty as an employee to bring his fellow-salesman back to Darlington and was therefore doing something which he was employed to do.

Crook v Derbyshire Stone Ltd
[1956] 2 All ER 447, [1956] 1 WLR 432, 100 Sol Jo 302 (Pilcher J)

The driver of a motor lorry on a journey stopped shortly before 8 am and crossed the road to a café on the other side. A motor cyclist collided with him and both were injured. The practice of drivers stopping at wayside cafés to obtain refreshment was well known to the driver's employers and impliedly sanctioned by them.

HELD: The driver was not employed on the employer's business. When he left the lorry he had no further duty to perform on his employer's account until he returned to the lorry and resumed his journey. The employers were not liable for his negligence.

Century Insurance Co case distinguished.

Note—This case was distinguished in the case of *Staton v National Coal Board* (below). See also *British Transport Commission v Maxine & Co Ltd*, p 158, below.

ACCIDENT IN DINNER HOUR

Higbid v R. C. Hammett Ltd

(1932) 49 TLR 104, CA

Delivery boy employed by firm of butchers used employers' cycle with their permission to ride home to his dinner and negligently rode into plaintiff. HELD: Under Shop Acts employers had no power to say how servant should use his dinner hour. Servant was using cycle for his own purposes and not doing something in the course of employers' business and (reversing judgment of Roche J and a common jury) employers were not liable.

WORKMAN STILL ON EMPLOYER'S PREMISES

Staton v National Coal Board

[1957] 2 All ER 667, [1957] 1 WLR 893, 101 Sol Jo 592 (Finnemore J)

A workman was in regular employ of a colliery as a first-aid man. He was on night shift from 10.30 pm to 8 am. Friday afternoon between 1 pm and 5 pm was the proper time for the men employed at the colliery to collect their week's wages. On Friday he finished his shift at 8.30 am. In the afternoon he proceeded to the colliery for his wages. He called at the Time Office in the colliery premises and then proceeded on his cycle to the General Office where the pay office was situated. On the left-hand side of the road was a bus park where some buses were parked waiting to take home the miners who had finished the day shift. The workman left the road to proceed across the bus park and decided to ride through the space between the second and third buses.

A miner employed by the colliery who had finished his work on the day shift, was seated in one of the buses, when he suddenly remembered something which required him to go back across the road to one of the offices. He came round the front of the bus and was knocked down in collision with the cycle, and sustained injuries from which he died.

HELD: The accident arose in the course of the employment of the first-aid man rendering his employers liable to the defendants of the injured man. He had finished his manual work and was riding his cycle across the employers' premises to collect the wages the employers had contracted to pay him and was still in the course of his employment. There had been nothing to break the course of his employment. It was in the interests of the employer as well as the employee that a workman should receive his wages and receive them at a convenient place and at a convenient time. He was not on the Queen's highway on his way to his place of employment to get his wages but was actually on his employers' premises going to the place which the employers had said was the place to which he was required to come in order to draw his wages. The case of *Crook v Derbyshire Stone Ltd* (p 149, above) was quite different on the facts.

SEMBLE: If a workman was off the employer's premises, e g on the Queen's highway on his way to his place of employment, he would not be in the course of his employment.

Note—See also *British Transport Commission v Maxine & Co Ltd*, p 158, below.

Compton v McClure
[1975] ICR 378 (May J)
The first defendant was employed at the second defendants' factory. On arriving at work and in attempting to clock on in time he drove too fast and on the wrong side of the factory road to the car park and knocked the plaintiff down. The second defendants had imposed a speed limit and the first defendant had been warned several times for speeding.
HELD: (1) The accident was caused by the first defendant's negligent driving; (2) the second defendants had not been negligent as they had taken reasonable precautions to protect persons using the roadway; (3) the second defendants were vicariously liable for the first defendant's negligent driving because he was acting in the course of his employment in entering the factory gates to clock on for the purposes of his employers' business.

Coult v Szuba
[1982] ICR 380, [1982] RTR 376, QBD, Div Ct
While driving his car from the clocking on point to his place of work two miles away the defendant had an accident on a private road. It was alleged for the purpose of a prosecution under the Health and Safety at Work etc Act 1974 that he was 'in the course of his employment'.
HELD: The phrase was not easily defined. The precise meaning of the words had to be extracted by looking at the facts in each case in the context of the legislation. It was not a matter of law that once the defendant had clocked on his course of employment must have started. The finding of the justices that he was not in the course of his employment could not be said to be wrong in principle.

British Transport Commission v Ministry of Supply
(1951) R 1007, Nottingham Summer Assizes, 25 June 1956
The driver of a railway locomotive at the defendant's depot drove his engine to the canteen in his lunch hour. On the way be negligently ran into and damaged the plaintiffs' lorry.
HELD: He was acting within the scope of his employment. He had a meal break and had to have a meal at the canteen built for that purpose. He was doing what he was employed to do — driving a locomotive. *Higbid's* case (p 150, above) distinguished. In that case the servant had left work and gone home: Per Finnemore J.

Note—The case is not reported but is mentioned in *The Times* and other papers of 26 June 1956.

Authorised act done in unauthorised way

'If the unauthorised and wrongful act . . . is not so connected with the authorised act as to be a mode of doing it, but is an independent act, the master is not responsible: for in such a case the servant is not acting in the course of his employment, but has gone outside of it': *Salmond on Torts* (15th edn) p 621.

Croft v Alison
(1821) 4 B & Ald 590
If a driver for some purpose of his own wantonly strikes the horse of another, the master is not liable, but if, in performance of his orders he strikes, but injudicially and in order to extricate himself from a difficulty, the master is liable.

Limpus v London General Omnibus Co Ltd
(1862) 1 H & C 526, 32 LJ Ex 34, 7 LT 641
Defendants' driver, in breach of his instructions not to hinder or obstruct other omnibuses, purposely pulled across the road to stop another omnibus passing.
HELD: A case of improper driving in the course of the employment and the master was liable.

Note—See also *Ilkiw v Samuels*, p 159, below.
    And see citation in *McKean's* case, below.

McKean v Raynor Brothers
[1942] 2 All ER 650, 167 LT 369, 86 Sol Jo 376
A servant who was a general utility hand was instructed by his employer to take and drive one of the employer's lorries and meet a convoy and deliver a message to them. Without permission from his employer, he used his father's private car and was involved in an accident. He had used a private car on other occasions on the employer's business, and had never been told not to use a private car for those purposes.
HELD: The workman was doing an authorised act in an unauthorised but not a prohibited way, and the employer was liable. Hilbery J cited *Bayley v Manchester Rly Co*:

'Where a servant is acting within the scope of his employment, and in so acting does something negligent or wrongful, the employer is liable even though the acts done may be the very reverse of that which the servant was actually directed to do.'

He also cited *Limpus v London General Omnibus Co*, above.

'The law casts upon the master a liability for the act of the servant in the course of his employment; and the law is not so futile as to allow a master, by giving secret instructions to his servant, to discharge himself from liability.'

Note—Followed in *Harvey v O'Dell*, p 177, below. See also *CPR v Lockhart*, p 155, below.

ASSAULT BY SERVANT

Greenwood v Seymour
(1861) 4 LT 835
A passenger was expelled from an omnibus by the conductor for what the latter regarded as improper conduct with such violence as to cause injury. The employers were held responsible. There was evidence that the servant was obeying the commands of the master.

Keppel Bus Co Ltd v Sa'ad bin Ahmad
[1974] 2 All ER 700, [1974] 1 WLR 1082, [1974] RTR 504, PC
In the course of a bus journey the conductor, a servant of the appellant bus company, spoke sharply to a lady passenger and was reproved for doing so by another passenger, the respondent. An altercation then broke out between the conductor and respondent in which they aimed blows at each other, but they were separated by other passengers. Later, whilst collecting fares, the conductor abused the respondent, using a very rude Chinese expression. The respondent stood up, told the conductor not to use the expression and sat down again. The conductor then hit him with the ticket-punch causing serious injury to his eye. The respondent was awarded damages against the appellants as vicariously liable for the conductor's act on the ground that he was acting, even though in a high-handed manner, in the course of his duty to keep order among the passengers.
HELD, ON APPEAL to the Privy Council: The appellants were not vicariously liable. To describe the conductor's act as quelling disorder was impossible on the evidence; if anyone was keeping order in the bus it was the passengers. The evidence fell far·short of establishing an implied authority in the conductor to take violent action where none was called for, nor was there present in the bus an emergency situation calling for forcible action justifiable upon any express or implied authority with which the appellants could be said on the evidence to have clothed him.

Bayley v Manchester, Sheffield and Lincolnshire Rly Co
(1873) LR 8 CP 148, 42 LJCP 78, 28 LT 366
A railway passenger was pulled violently out of a railway carriage by a porter under the erroneous impression that the passenger was in the wrong carriage. The byelaws did not authorise any such action. Employers held liable.
Per Willes J: A person who puts another in his place to do a class of acts in his absence, necessarily leaves him to determine, according to the circumstances that arise, when an act of that class is to be done, and trusts him for the manner in which it is done; and consequently he is held answerable for the wrong of the person so intrusted either in the manner of doing such an act, or in doing such an act under circumstances in which it ought not to have been done; provided that what was done was done, not from any caprice of the servant, but in the course of the employment.

Note—Hilbery J in *Warren's* case, below, pointed out that the words 'in the course of the employment' should be read in the light of the judgment of Scrutton LJ, in *Poland's* case.

Poland v John Parr & Sons
[1927] 1 KB 236, 96 LJKB 152, 136 LT 271, CA
A carter employed by defendants was walking behind a wagon driven by one of the defendants carrying bags of sugar. The carter honestly thought a boy of twelve, walking beside the wagon, was pilfering the sugar, struck the boy on the neck which knocked him under the wagon.
HELD: Master liable: the servant had implied authority to protect his master's property; the method was mistaken and excessive, and even amounted to a crime; it was not so excessive as to take it outside the

authority; it was an unauthorised mode of doing an authorised act.

Per Bankes LJ: A master is not responsible for a wrongful act done by his servant unless it is done in the course of his employment. It is deemed to be so done if it is either (a) a wrongful act authorised by the master, or (b) a wrongful and unauthorised mode of doing some act authorised by the master.

Per Scrutton LJ: to make an employer liable for the act of a person alleged to be his servant the act must be one of a class of acts which the person was authorised or employed to do. If the act is one of that class the employer is liable, though the act is done negligently or, in some cases even if it is done with excessive violence. But the excess may be so great as to take the act out of the class of acts which the person is authorised or employed to do.

Stitt v Woolley
(1971) 115 Sol Jo 708, CA

Stitt, Woolley and another man G, were members of a local authority fire brigade and were required by their terms of service 'to attend promptly at the station in response to a call at any time'. On the night in question the fire bells rang in their homes. Woolley went, as usual, in his car, with G in the front passenger seat and Stitt in the back. On the way to the fire station G suddenly grasped the steering wheel. There was a struggle: the car crashed into a bridge and Stitt was injured. He claimed not only against Woolley but against the local authority as being vicariously liable for Woolley's or G's negligence.

HELD: Woolley was not negligent. In respect of the local authority's liability for G's acts the men were, in the special circumstances of the case, on duty once they left their homes in answer to an emergency call since it was part of their duty to get to the station as quickly as possible. It was different from the case of a man going to work and was an exception to the rule that a workman was not usually employed until he reached his place of business. It was a case like *Blee v LNER* (p 746, below). But it could not be said that G's extraordinary action was within the course of his employment and the employers were not liable for it.

Warren v Henlys Ltd
[1948] 2 All ER 935, [1948] WN 449, 92 Sol Jo 706 (Hilbery J)

The plaintiff driving one vehicle and his servant driving a second vehicle called at a garage for petrol. After the first vehicle was supplied, the plaintiff drove a short distance to allow the second vehicle across to the pump. The attendant ran after the plaintiff, swore at him and accused him of trying to get away without paying or surrendering coupons. The attendant refused to supply petrol to the second vehicle and they repaired to the cash desk where the plaintiff paid and gave up coupons. The plaintiff then noticed a police car was passing, drove after it, and brought a police constable back, apparently thinking the police could take action. Finding this was not so, the plaintiff told the attendant he would report him to his employers. The attendant then assaulted the plaintiff.

HELD: The plaintiff's business with the defendants had ended, and going for the police was a matter personal to the plaintiff and the attendant. The employers were not liable.

Prohibited act within scope of employment

Canadian Pacific Rly Co v Lockhart
[1942] AC 591, [1942] 2 All ER 464, PC

The plaintiff was a child who was knocked down by a car driven by one of the defendant's employees. The defendants were a railway company and the employee was a handyman who used to do various repair jobs at different railway stations. On the day of the accident he was required by his employers to take a newly-made key to a station a few miles away and see if it would fit the lock it was made for. He could have travelled by rail, and was expected to do so, but instead he chose to go in his own car. The employers did not object to employees using their own cars, but had twice issued a firm instruction that they must not use a car if it was not covered by third-party insurance. On this occasion the employee's car was not covered by third-party insurance.

HELD: The employers were liable. The principles were set out in *Salmond on Torts*: A master, as opposed to the employer of an independent contractor, is liable even for acts which he has not authorised provided they are so connected with acts which he has authorised that they may rightly be regarded as modes — although improper modes — of doing them. In other words, a master is responsible not merely for what he authorises his servant to do, but also for the way in which he does it. On the other hand, if the unauthorised and wrongful act of the servant is not so connected with the authorised act as to be a mode of doing it, but is an independent act, the master is not responsible; for in such a case the servant is not acting in the course of his employment but has gone outside it.

The first consideration is the ascertainment of what the servant was employed to do. The existence of prohibitions may, or may not, be evidence of the limits of the employment. If the prohibition had absolutely forbidden the servant to drive his motor car in course of his employment it might well have been maintained that he was employed to do carpentry work and not to drive a motor car, and that, therefore, the driving of a motor car was outside the scope of his employment, but it was not the acting as driver that was prohibited but the non-insurance of the motor car, if used as a means incidental to the execution of the work which he was employed to do. It follows that the prohibition merely limited the way in which, or by means of which, the servant was to execute the work which he was employed to do, and that breach of the prohibition did not exclude the liability of the master to third parties.

Note—The above quotation from *Salmond on Torts* was adopted by the Court of Appeal in the following case:

London County Council v Cattermoles (Garages) Ltd
[1953] 2 All ER 582, [1953] 1 WLR 997, 97 Sol Jo 505, CA

At a garage a workman was employed as a general garage hand, including moving cars by pushing them or giving guidance to the drivers, e g when reversing. He was not competent to drive, had no licence, and had been forbidden to do so. A van was stationary at the petrol pumps and he moved the van to enable two lorries to obtain petrol. He got into the van, started the engine, drove the van and went on to the highway. He had not intended to go on the highway, but to keep inside the garage, but did so intending to return behind the lorries. On the highway he collided with the plaintiff's van.

HELD: The terms of the employment were not precise. The prohibition about driving was not a limitation of the scope of the employment but a subsequent prohibition when the employers discovered he had no qualification for driving and his employment could not be limited to pushing cars by hand and not by other means including driving them. The use of the van's own engine to do shunting was not something independent of the job of shunting but was an unauthorised or prohibited means of doing an authorised job. The fact that the workman did not intend to go on to the highway but this was accidental did not alter the result even though the servant was doing something unlawful, having no licence. The job was not something quite different in its nature and character from the driving of motor cars. The employers were liable.

Mulholland v William Reid and Leys
1958 SC 290, 1958 SLT 285 (Ct of Sess, Inner House)
An apprentice working with a journeyman, both in the employ of the defenders, offered to move a van which was in the way. He had never driven a vehicle before and had no authority to do so, but the journeyman made no objection. He started up the van and fatally injured the husband of the pursuer.

HELD: He was acting within the scope of his employment and his employers were liable. *London County Council v Cattermoles (Garages) Ltd* followed.

Iqbal v London Transport Executive
(1974) 16 KIR 329, CA
The plaintiff, a bus driver employed by the defendants, found he could not get his bus out of the garage to begin work until the bus behind it had been moved. He asked his conductor, Carberry, to get someone from the engineering department to move the other bus. Instead, Carberry, who had never driven a bus before, tried to move it himself. He started it and it crushed the plaintiff, who was standing between it and his own bus. There was a clear instruction, adequately published, 'In no circumstances is a conductor allowed to drive a bus'.

HELD: The defendants were not vicariously liable for Carberry's negligence. It was not a case within the principle set out in *Salmond on Torts* (quoted in *Canadian Pacific Rly v Lockhart* (above)) of his having improperly done what he was authorised to do. The defendants' prohibition did not merely deal with conduct within the sphere of employment; it was a prohibition which limited the sphere of his employment.

Kay v ITW Ltd
[1968] 1 QB 140, [1967] 3 All ER 22, [1967] 3 WLR 695, 111 Sol Jo 351, CA
The defendants employed a man named Ord to drive small trucks inside their works. A large diesel lorry belonging to another company came to the works for loading and was parked on a ramp with its back facing the closed

doors of a warehouse. The plaintiff (a storeman in the defendants' employment) and the lorry driver were loading the lorry. Ord came to the ramp
with a fork lift truck to take it into the warehouse where it was normally
kept. Without asking or even looking for the driver he got into the cab of the
lorry and turned the key to start the engine: his intention was to move the
lorry so that he could drive the fork lift into the warehouse. The lorry had
been left in reverse gear and at once started backwards pinning the plaintiff
against the warehouse doors. The defendants' case was that Ord was acting
outside the scope of his employment in trying to move the lorry: they
conceded that he was entitled to move light or small obstructions.

HELD: Ord was acting in the scope of his employment and the defendants
were liable. Though his entering the cab and starting the engine was foolhardy and unnecessary the question was whether, as in *Lockhart v CPR*, it
was a mode, though an improper one, of doing the work he was employed
to do. It was not conclusive that what he was doing was in the employers'
interest or was done during working hours. It was a border-line case but he
was trying to move the lorry so as to take the fork lift truck into the warehouse and his conduct was not so gross or exteme as to take the act outside
what he was employed to do.

Note—See also *East v Beavis Transport*, p 160, below and *Harrison v Michelin Tyre Co
Ltd* [1985] 1 All ER 918.

Spencer v Curtis Brothers
(1962) 106 Sol Jo 390, CA

The plaintiff, a farmer, was helping the defendant, who was a neighbour of
his, to harvest grain on the defendant's farm. The plaintiff was driving his
own combine harvester on which the defendant's employee H was riding
for the purpose of filling bags with grain: this was part of the operation of
using the harvester. H had been shooting earlier that day and had his gun
with him. The defendant realising the danger of carrying the gun on the
machine, told H not to do so: in disobedience of this order H had nevertheless put his gun on the floor of the machine. As the plaintiff was driving the
machine the gun went off and he was seriously injured. Negligence on the
part of H was admitted. It was contended for the defendant that the taking
of the gun on the machine was not an act in the scope of H's employment
but was something entirely independent.

HELD: In taking the gun on the machine H had added an additional
danger to the risks of the work and the defendant was liable. It had been
said that *Jefferson v Derbyshire Farmers Ltd* (below) and *Century Insurance Co Ltd
v Northern Ireland Road Transport Board* (p 167, below) were distinguishable
because the act which caused the damage in those cases was one which
could be done while the proper work was being carried on, but there was no
real distinction. The true test was defined by Lord McNaghten in *Lloyd v
Grace Smith & Co* [1912] AC 716, when he said that the words 'scope of
employment . . . must be used liberally'.

Note—And see *Harvey v O'Dell*, p 177, below.

Servant causing fire

SMOKING

Jefferson v Derbyshire Farmers Ltd
[1921] 2 KB 281, 90 LJKB 1361, 124 LT 755, CA

The owner of a motor garage leased it to a firm of motor engineers, who agreed with defendants to give them the use of it as a garage for motor lorries. A youth employed by defendants in the garage, while drawing motor spirit from a drum into a tin, struck a match, lit a cigarette and then threw the match on the floor. This set light to some oil and petrol lying about the floor; the fire spread to the motor spirit flowing from the drum and the garage and its contents were consumed. An action was brought by the owner and the lessees of the garage against defendants for the negligence of their servant.

HELD: The servant being engaged in an act which was within the scope of his employment and required special caution, and having failed to exercise caution, was guilty of negligence in the course of his employment and defendants were liable for the resulting damage.

Note—In Williams v Jones (1865) 3 H & C 602 the defendant's carpenter while working in plaintiff's shed lighted a pipe from a match with a shaving which he accidently dropped and the shed was burned down. It was there held that the negligent act was not within the scope of the employment. This case is now overruled by *Jefferson's* case.

British Transport Commission v Maxine & Co Ltd
(1963) 107 Sol Jo 1024 (McNair J)

Premises held by the defendants on licence from the plaintiffs were damaged by fire caused by the defendants' workman who had carelessly thrown down a lighted match. The incident occurred on a Friday, the day on which the workman received his pay. He had been given notice in the previous week and his employment was to end on that Friday. He finished his day's work by 4.30 pm and his pay would not be ready for collection until 4.45. While waiting he went to another part of the premises to say goodbye to friends. It was during this call that he threw away the lighted match. The plaintiffs claimed that the defendants were vicariously liable for his negligence.

HELD: He was not acting in the scope of his employment when he threw away the match. The test was whether the negligence arose in the course of work being done for the employer or was incidental to it. Although the workman here was entitled to go to the warehouse to see his friends and although he had to wait for his pay packet it was unrealistic to say that he was then performing any work for his employers or doing any act incidental to it. *Staton's* case (p 150, above) was distinguishable on the basis that there the workman and the employers had an interest in the workman receiving his wages.

Note—See also Century Insurance Co v Northern Ireland Road Transport Board, p 167, below.

MAKING TEA

Dempster v Road Haulage Executive
(1952) 102 L Jo 105, Ct of Sess
A garage had a fire near the entrance used only for heating the garage. Its use for making tea was forbidden. An employee poured paraffin from a tin upon the fire in order to make tea. The paraffin in the tin caught alight and the employee threw it into the adjoining yard and injured a child.
HELD: Employers not liable; the servant's act was outside the scope of his employment.

Presumption from general authority to drive

Laycock v Grayson
[1939] WN 204, 55 TLR 698
A was the proprietor of a garage and employed B as manager and salesman. B had an accident while driving a car belonging to A. A pleaded that at the time of the accident B was acting outside the scope of his employment.

It was proved or admitted that A had given a general authority to B to drive the car for demonstration or business purposes. This raised a presumption that B was acting within the scope of his employment at the material time and the onus was shifted to A to prove that B was acting outside it. A had not rebutted that presumption or discharged the onus, and A was liable.

Driver allowing unauthorised person to drive

Ricketts v Tilling
[1915] 1 KB 644, 84 LJKB 342, 112 LT 137, 31 TLR 17
At the end of a journey the conductor of an omnibus belonging to defendant, in the presence of the driver, who was seated beside him, for the purpose of turning the omnibus in the right direction for the next journey, drove it through some by-streets so negligently that it mounted the foot-pavement and knocked down and seriously injured plaintiff, who was standing there. At the trial the judge upon the authority of *Beard v London General Omnibus Co* (p 148, above) held there was no evidence that the conductor had any authority from defendants to drive the omnibus and entered judgment for defendants.
HELD: There was evidence of negligence on the part of the driver in allowing the omnibus to be negligently driven by the conductor and there must therefore be a new trial.

Ilkiw v Samuels
[1963] 2 All ER 879, [1963] 1 WLR 991, 107 Sol Jo 680, CA
The defendants' lorry was driven to the premises of the plaintiff's employers to load bags of sugar. The defendants' driver Waines put the lorry under a conveyor and then stood in the back of the lorry to load bags from the conveyor. When sufficiently loaded the lorry had to be moved. Samuels, a fellow employee of the plaintiff's and not employed by the

defendants, offered to move it. Waines allowed him to do so without asking whether he could drive. In fact Samuels could not drive and after starting the lorry could not stop it. It crushed the plaintiff, who was working nearby, against another conveyor causing him serious injury. Waines remained in the back of the lorry throughout. He had been expressly forbidden by his employers to let anyone other than himself drive the lorry. HELD: (1) Waines was negligent in allowing Samuels to drive without inquiring whether he was competent: the defendants were vicariously liable for his negligence because it was a mode, though an improper mode, of performing the duties on which he was employed namely, to have charge and control of the lorry. It was therefore a negligent act within the scope of his employment.

Per Willmer LJ: Waines was employed not only to drive but also to be in charge of his vehicle in all circumstances during any such times as he was on duty. That means to say that, even when he was not himself sitting at the controls, he remained in charge of the lorry and in charge as his employers' representative. His employers must remain liable for his negligence so long as the vehicle was being used in the course of their business. As I understand the authorities, the employers escape liability if, but only if, at the time of the negligent act, the vehicle was being used by the driver for the purpose of what had been called a 'frolic' of his own. That is not this case. Here, at the material time, this vehicle was in fact being used in the course of the defendants' business. In those circumstances it appears to me that there is no ground on which the defendants can escape liability for Waines' negligence.

(2) Even if Samuels had been a competent driver but negligent on that occasion, Waines would still have been negligent for the reason give in *Ricketts v Tilling* (above) that it was his duty to prevent another person from driving, or, if he allowed another person to drive, to see that he drove properly. This also was negligence within the scope of his employment.

(3) Per Diplock LJ: It was not necessarily negligent of Waines to allow Samuels to drive; even if it were, the employers would not be vicariously liable since the selection of a person to drive was not part of Waines's duties — indeed he was forbidden to let anyone else drive. But the employers were liable to the plaintiff on the broader ground that the lorry was being driven negligently while being used for the purposes of the defendants' business under the control of their servant Waines, he being employed to take charge and control of the vehicle while engaged on the task being performed when the accident took place. Liability would be the same even if Samuels had been a highly experienced driver, provided his negligent driving on this occasion was the cause of the plaintiff's injuries.

(4) The fact that the defendants had expressly forbidden Waines to let anyone else drive was immaterial since it was no more than a direction as to the mode in which the servant was to perform the duty. *Limpus v LGOC* (p 152, above) followed.

East v Beavis Transport Ltd
[1969] 1 Lloyd's Rep 302, CA
Two lorries stood back to back at Boston docks being loaded with produce by dockers and others. It was required to move one of them, owned by Beavis, to let the tail board down. Beavis's driver Rose gave permission to Sellars, a docker employed by Andersons, to move it. Sellars reversed into

the other lorry, squashing the plaintiff against it and injuring him.

HELD: Rose was negligent because he was in charge of the lorry and even if it was in order for a docker to move the lorry he should have directed him. He was responsible for the movements of the lorry and Beavis were vicariously liable. Sellars was equally negligent because he could not see properly when reversing and made no arrangement with Rose to direct him. His employers Andersons were vicariously liable for his negligence because although they did not employ him to drive lorries his act had a close connection with what he was employed to do, namely, the loading of lorries (following *Kay v ITW Ltd*, p 156, above.)

Breach of duty of safe custody

Central Motors Glasgow Ltd v Cessnock Garage Co
1925 SC 796

The plaintiffs entrusted their car to the defendants, who were garage proprietors, for a single night for custody for reward. The defendants' night watchman, in defiance of express orders, took the car out on a frolic of his own, became intoxicated, and smashed up the car. The defendants pleaded the servant was acting outside the scope of authority.

HELD: Defendants were liable.

Per Lord Cullen: A person who is a servant has always a purely personal and independent sphere of life and action and at any particular time may be acting in that sphere and not in his sphere of service and if he is so acting his master cannot be responsible for what he does. This is simple enough; but what is often so difficult is to determine in a question with a third party within which sphere a particular act falls. The question is not to be answered merely by applying the test whether the act in itself is one which the servant was employed or ordered or forbidden to do. The employer has to shoulder responsibility on a wider basis; and he may and often does become responsible to third parties for acts which he has expressly or implicitly forbidden the servant to do. A servant is not a mere machine continually directed by his master's hand but is a person of independent volition and action; and the employer when he delegates to him some duty which he is himself under an obligation to discharge must take the risk of the servant's actions being misdirected when he is, for the time, allowed to be beyond his master's control. It remains necessary that the servant's act be one done within the sphere of his service but it may have that character although it consists in doing something the very opposite of what the servant has been intended or ordered to do, and which he does for his own private ends. The servant is a bad servant who has not faithfully served, but has betrayed, his master. Still, *quoad* the third party injured, his dishonest act may fall to be regarded as an ill way of executing the work assigned to him and which he has been left with power to do — well or ill.

Note—This decision can be misleading if regarded merely as a case of the liability of an employer for a prohibited act. The judgment in *Adams (Durham) Ltd and Day v Trust Houses Ltd* (p 328, below) shows that the essence of this case was that the contract was one of custody. The defendants had delegated the safekeeping of the car to their servant and were liable for his betrayal of that duty. The position of a third party injured by the servant's negligent driving might have been different.

The correctness of this view is supported by the following case:

Morris v C. W. Martin & Sons Ltd
[1966] 1 QB 716, [1965] 2 All ER 725, [1965] 3 WLR 276, 109 Sol Jo 451,
[1965] 2 Lloyd's Rep 63, CA
The plaintiff's mink fur was sent to the defendants for cleaning. They
delegated the task of cleaning it to an employee, who stole it. It was not
recovered and the plaintiff sued for its value. The county court judge held
that the employee was not acting in the scope of his employment in stealing
the fur and that the defendants were not liable for his wrongful act.
HELD, ON APPEAL: The defendants had accepted the fur as bailees for
reward in order to clean it. They put the employee as their agent to clean
the fur and take charge of it whilst doing so. The manner he conducted
himself in doing that work was to convert it: it was done in the scope or
course of his employment and the defendants were liable for his wrongful
act.

Lord Denning MR drew attention to the fact that if the owner of a car
takes it to a garage to be repaired and it is repaired by a garage hand who
then takes it out on a 'frolic of his own' and collides with a motor cycle the
owner of the car can sue the garage proprietor for any damage to the car (as
in *Central Motors v Cessnock*, above) but the motor cyclist cannot sue the
garage proprietor for damage to the motor cycle (citing *Storey v Ashton*,
p 147, above). He continued: I ask myself, How can this be? How can the
servant, on one and the same journey, be acting both within and without
the course of his employment? Within *qua* the car owner. Without *qua* the
motor cyclist. It is time we got rid of this confusion. And the only way to do
it, so far as I can see, is by reference to the duty laid by the law on the
master. The duty of the garage proprietor to the owner of the car is very
different from his duty to the motor cyclist. He owes to the owner of the car
the duty of a bailee for reward, whereas he owes no such duty to the motor
cyclist on the road. He does not even owe him a duty to use care not to
injure him. If you go through the cases on this difficult subject, you will find
that, in the ultimate analysis, they depend on the nature of the duty owed
by the master towards the person whose goods have been lost or damaged.

Aitchison v Page Motors
(1935) 154 LT 128, 52 TLR 137 (Macnaghten J)
The defendants were a garage company who sent the plaintiff's car to the
makers' works at Fulham for repair. The defendants' service manager collected the car at 7 pm on Friday evening to deliver it to the plaintiff at
Epsom. At 11 pm on Friday, driving the car with two friends as passengers,
he collided with a bus at Balham; all three were killed, and the plaintiff's car
was destroyed.
HELD: The manager was acting in the course of his employment and
within the scope of his authority when he took delivery of the car. In breach
of his duty he used it for some private purpose of his own, and whilst he was
so using it the accident happened. The defendants as his employers were
liable to the plaintiff for the manner in which he conducted himself in
performing the service of delivering the car.

Prohibited act outside scope of employment

Wright v International Tea Co
(1943) 27 October, unreported (Croom-Johnson J)
The driver of a trade vehicle which had no provision for passengers in the ordinary sense gave a lift to a pedestrian, who sat on a sort of continuation of the driver's seat. The driver had been warned on two occasions by his employers that he must not take up passengers, and on one occasion that it would cause some difficulty about the insurance policy.
HELD: The driver's act was in defiance and disobedience of a precise prohibition. The scope of the authority must be measured by reference to the ordinary duties of such a man. He had no authority from his employers nor had he been held out by anybody as having authority to pick up passengers, and no such authority was to be implied. The plaintiff ought to have known she had no authority to get into the van and must take the consequences of her own neglect. The case was one of a prohibition which limited the sphere of employment and not a prohibition of conduct within the sphere of employment. In his judgment the judge referred to the two following cases:

Houghton v Pilkington
[1912] 3 KB 308, 82 LJKB 79, 107 LT 235, 28 TLR 492, 56 Sol Jo 633
Plaintiff at the request of a servant of defendant, got into defendant's cart, which was then in charge of the servant, in order to render assistance to another servant of defendant who had been rendered unconscious by an accident. Plaintiff fell out of the cart and was injured through the negligence of the servant in charge of the cart causing the horse to start.
HELD: The existence of the emergency gave no implied authority to the servant to invite plaintiff into the cart and defendant was not liable.

Lygo v Newbold
(1854) 9 Exch 302, 23 LJ Ex 108
Plaintiff, a person of full age, contracted with defendant to carry certain goods for her in his cart. Defendant sent his servant with the cart, and plaintiff, by the permission of the servant, without defendant's authority, rode in the cart with her goods. The cart broke down and plaintiff was injured.
HELD: The defendant had not contracted to carry the plaintiff, and as she had ridden in the cart without his authority, he was not liable. The plaintiff had no business to get up into the cart without defendant's permission.

Twine v Bean's Express Ltd
(1946) 175 LT 131, 62 TLR 458, CA
Defendants provided a motor van and driver for a bank on terms that they accepted no liability for passengers other than employees of the defendants. The driver was forbidden to take any such passengers and a notice was on the dashboard of the van. The driver took a passenger an employee of the bank, first informing him it was at his own risk.
HELD: Defendants were not liable; they owed no duty to the passenger;

it was outside the scope of the driver's employment to extend the liability of the defendants to the passenger who was a trespasser: Per Uthwatt J ([1946] 1 All ER 202, 174 LT 239).

ON APPEAL: Only limited classes of persons were entitled to be carried on this van and it was clear that the deceased was not one of the those persons. The driver, in giving the lift to T, was clearly not acting within the scope of his employment and his employers were consequently not liable.

Note—See also *Baker v Provident Accident* [1939] 2 All ER 690, 64 Ll L Rep 14, 83 Sol Jo 565

Conway v George Wimpey & Co
[1951] 2 KB 266, [1951] 1 All ER 363, 95 Sol Jo 156, [1951] 1 TLR 587, CA

Defendants were the main contractors for the building of an aerodrome and provided motor lorries to convey their workmen to their place of work. In the cab was a notice as follows: 'The driver of this vehicle has strict orders to carry no passengers other than employees of G. Wimpey & Co Ltd during the course of and in connection with their employment. Any other person travelling on this vehicle does so at his own risk.' The driver had also received express instructions to carry defendants' men only.

A workman of another contractor on the same site hailed the lorry and was permitted by the driver to ride on it, and was injured by the driver's negligence. It was not unusual for men not employed by defendants to get lifts on defendants' lorries but it was not established that the drivers in general knowingly carried men other than defendants' servants, or that the driver in this case knew that the plaintiff was not in the defendants' employ. The defendants themselves were not aware of such use by other men.

HELD: The fact that in *Twine's* case (above) the plaintiff was informed by the driver that he had no right to travel on the van was immaterial. The argument that the plaintiff could not be a trespasser unless he knew he was one was unfounded in law. It is elementary that if A, professedly acting on behalf of B, purports to give leave to enter on B's land, and A has no actual authority to do so, the person receiving permission who acts on the permission is a trespasser, and none the less so because he does not know of A's want of authority. To establish an apparent authority binding on the driver's employers the plaintiff must show, (1) knowledge of the defendants of a practice by their drivers of disregarding the prohibition; (2) acquiescence by the defendants in the practice, (3) acquiescence in such a manner as to represent to the plaintiff that the driver's authority was not limited to carrying the defendants' men. There was no evidence to establish the first proposition, apart from the others. The fact that four of the defendants' workmen gave evidence that they knew of the practice did not impute knowledge to the defendants; nor that a practice of this kind must inevitably grow up. There was clear evidence that they did not know. The plaintiff never ceased to be a trespasser.

On the contention that the driver's act was within the scope of his employment, it was pointed out by Uthwatt J in *Twine's* case that the driver's act was outside the scope of his employment. Taking men other than the defendants' employees on the vehicle was not merely a wrongful mode of performing an act of the class which the driver was employed to perform, but was the performance of an act of a class which he was not

employed to perform at all. The act was outside the scope of the employment for the same reason as in *Twine's* case. The case of *Limpus v London
General Omnibus Co* did not apply. The case of *Hay (or Bourhill) v Young* (p 6,
above) mentioned by the trial judge had nothing to do with the responsibility of employers for the acts of their servants. Appeal dismissed.

Rose v Plenty
[1976] 1 All ER 97, [1975] 1 WLR 141, 119 Sol Jo 592, CA

The second defendant employed the first defendant as a milkman. Notices
at the depot made it clear that roundsmen were not allowed to take children
on vehicles. Despite this the first defendant took the plaintiff, a boy of 13,
on his milk float, paying him a few shillings for help in delivering milk.
Whilst being carried on the vehicle the plaintiff was injured by the first
defendant's negligence.

HELD, ON APPEAL (Lawton LJ diss): There was vicarious liability on the
second defendant. The prohibited act, namely taking the boy on the float to
help him deliver milk was done by the milkman in the course of his service
and for the employer's purposes. *Twine v Bean's Express* and *Conway v
Wimpey* (above) were cases where a driver had given a lift to someone else
contrary to a prohibition and not for the purposes of the employers. The
prohibition on the milkman against employing boys to help him was not
one which defined or limited his sphere of employment, which was to go
round the rounds delivering milk. This distinguished it from such cases as
Iqbal v London Transport (p 156, above).

Licensee, not trespasser

Young v Edward Box & Co
[1951] 1 TLR 789, CA

The plaintiff was employed by the defendants in unloading at a quarry. It
was the plaintiff's business to make his own way to the place of work. It was
necessary to work on Sundays and it was difficult for the plaintiff and other
workmen to get to and from the place on a Sunday. The defendants'
foreman arranged for a lorry of the defendants, driven by the defendants'
driver, to pick up workmen to take to work and take them home from work,
and this took place for some seven or eight Sundays before the accident.
The place where the plaintiff was picked up was on the lorry's normal
route. On a Sunday the plaintiff whilst a passenger on the lorry was injured
by the negligence of the lorry driver. Defendants' traffic manager denied
that he had given any instructions for the men to be carried, and the foreman had no authority to do so.

HELD (per Somervell and Singleton LJ): The plaintiff was a licensee on the
lorry and not a trespasser; he was there by permission of the foreman and
this was plainly within the ostensible authority of the foreman.

Per Denning LJ: The foreman had no authority to let the men travel on
the lorry and the men were therefore trespassers so far as the employers
were concerned; but the defendants were liable because the driver was
acting in the course of his employment in giving the plaintiff a lift. It would
not have been in the course of his employment to give a lift to a hitch-hiker,
but it was to give a lift to the men on the job.

Defendants held liable to the plaintiff caused by negligence of the driver.

Miller v Liverpool Co-operative Society
[1940] 4 All ER 367 (Stable J), affd. [1941] 1 All ER 379n
Plaintiff had been in the habit of waking up a driver who in return gave him
a lift to his place of work. The owner knew this, had seen him on a number
of occasions, had not taken the slightest exception and had acquiesced in
what had become an established practice. The owner had not given express
permission. The passenger was not a trespasser but a licensee; the driver
was on the owner's business and the owner was liable.

LOAN OF SERVANT

Note—In the case of a servant being loaned, the question whether the employer
who lent the servant, or the employer who hired him, is liable for the servant's
negligence, depends upon the question of fact who has the power of control, and as
a rule the employer who engages, pays and has the right to discharge the servant, is
liable.

Parker v Miller
(1926) 42 TLR 408 (Scrutton LJ)
Ever since *Quarman v Burnett* (1840) 6 M & W 499, the law had been that
right to control, not actual physical control, was the test of agency in cases
of negligence.

Fenlon v Rea
(1944) 77 Ll L Rep 8 (Hallett J)
The presumption is all against the transfer of the man's services from the
general employer to the temporary employer.

Ready Mixed Concrete v Yorkshire Traffic Licensing Authority
[1970] 2 QB 397, [1970] 1 All ER 890, [1970] 2 WLR 627, 134 JP 293, 114
Sol Jo 111, Div Ct
The appellants had a contract with a haulage contractor for collection,
carriage and delivery of their goods to customers. He was bound by terms
of the contract to abide by all reasonable directions from the appellants for
deliveries and to keep his vehicle clean and in good condition. He could,
with the appellants' consent employ another suitable person to drive the
vehicle, for whose acts the contractor would be responsible.
   The contractor was ill for a month during the period of contract and
unable to drive. The appellants sent Stacey, one of their own employees,
to drive the truck during his illness. Stacey was given the keys by the
contractor who told him to look after the vehicle. He could have refused to
have Stacey drive it if he wished. The appellants continued to pay Stacey's
wages, stamp and SET. They deducted 15s a load from the payments to the
contractor being an agreed amount to cover all expenses.
HELD: Stacey was throughout the servant of the appellants. Although
prima facie the owner of a vehicle is the person who has the authority to give
directions as to how it is to be driven it is not the sole or decisive test. There
is a presumption against transfer of a servant to a temporary employer. In
the present case the appellants whilst continuing to pay Stacey lent him to

the contractor to perform particular deliveries. It was not a case of a transfer of the servant but merely of the use and benefit of his work.

General employer liable

Century Insurance Co v Northern Ireland Road Transport Board
[1942] AC 509, [1942] 1 All ER 491, 111 LJPC 138, 167 LT 404, 72 Ll L Rep 119, HL
A Board entered into a written contract with distributors to supply tankers, with driver, who should accept and obey the orders of the distributors regarding delivery to their customers: the Board should dismiss any employee disregarding or failing to obey such orders; the distributors provided garage accommodation; the tankers were painted and the drivers wore uniform to identify them with the distributors.

Per Lord Simon: Applying *Donovan v Laing* [1893] 1 QB 629, the test is in whose employment the man was at the time when the acts complained of were done, in the sense that by the employer is meant the person who has a right at the moment to control the doing of the act. And applying *Moore v Palmer* (1886) 2 TLR 781 the great test was this — whether the servant was transferred or only the use and benefit of his work.

Per Lord Wright: This was a contract for carriage and delivery with their own servants and not for the hiring out of lorries and men or lending them to the distributors to enable them to effect delivery. The question is, who is the 'superior' in the particular instance? The facts of one case can never rule another case. The contractor may contract to do the work, the means being left to him, or he may place his servants and plant under the control of another, that is, he may lend them and in that case he does not retain control of the work. Citing *Quarman v Burnett* (1840) 6 M & W 499: A job-master contracted with two ladies to send horses and a driver for their coach. The ladies were intended to direct the times when and the places to and from which they took their drives. That was certainly a measure of control, but what was there transferred was the use and benefit of the coachman's work. The coachman did not become the servant of the ladies. The authority of that case had never been questioned. Following Lord Herschell in *Cameron v Nystrom* [1893] AC 308: Has there been a transfer of the man's services from his general employer to the other who is said to be his temporary employer? It is, I think, clear that the presumption is all against there being such a transfer.
HELD: The Board were independent contractors undertaking by the use of their own vehicles and by the activities of their own servants to make the deliveries, and not that of people lending vehicles and drivers for the hirers to direct.

Note—For facts see p 259, below. See also *Harris v Continental Express Ltd* [1961] 1 Lloyd's Rep 251.

Marney v Campbell Symonds & Co Ltd
(1946) 175 LT 283, 62 TLR 324, 90 Sol Jo 467 (Hilbery J)
The Minister of War Transport under the Defence Regulations requisitioned a motor car belonging to garage proprietors and directed them to deliver the car to a specified address and provide a driver and fuel for that

purpose. Directions were given in case of breakdown and forms of request to traders to supply requisites and to the police to assist, the cost being chargeable to the officer commanding the unit to which the vehicle was consigned. As the car had no road licence, a disc was provided in lieu, 'On His Majesty's Service only'.

HELD: Following *Century Insurance Co v Northern Ireland Transport Board* and *Hewitt v Bonvin*, there was no transfer of service. The driver remained the servant of the garage proprietors.

Nicholas v F. J. Sparkes & Sons
[1945] KB 309n, CA (reported with *Dowd* and *McFarlane's* cases, below)
Plaintiff's employers, Curran's Industries Ltd, hired from defendants from two to nine lorries per week, by telephoning and saying how many lorries they required a week. The drivers were told to work for a week at Currans. A driver was told to work there and accept orders as other lorry drivers and had been working only for Currans for three months or more with the same lorry. Defendants could take him away or give him a holiday. Plaintiff was injured on a private roadway of Currans premises by defendants' lorry. The county court judge held the driver was under the control of Currans and the defence of common employment succeeded.

HELD, ON APPEAL reversing the county court decision: Where the particular employer directs the driver as to time and place but has no control over the driver's art of driving, the general employer is liable. If, however, the particular employer has detailed control over the manner in which the servant does the work, complying with his orders and not acting except on his orders, the particular employer is liable.

The driver was exercising his own discretion as driver, and Currans had nothing to do with the mistake he made as driver.

The onus is on the general employer. This is particularly so in the case of a vehicle where the driver is in sole charge and he alone is allowed to drive. It is placed under his control by the general employer who relies on him to use his own skill and exercise his own discretion in driving.

O'Reilly v Imperial Chemical Industries
[1955] 3 All ER 382, [1955] 1 WLR 1155, 99 Sol Jo 778, CA
A driver's employers had a contract with customers whereby they set aside lorries and drivers for almost exclusive use of the customers. The lorries were painted a special colour and bore the name and trade mark of the customers.

HELD: Adopting the judgment of Lord Porter in *Mersey Docks & Harbour Board v Coggins and Griffiths* (p 169), the driver remained in the employ of the general employers. The temporary employer had got the right to dictate not only what the servant was to do but also how he was to do it.

Dowd v W. H. Boase & Co Ltd
[1945] KB 301, [1945] 1 All ER 605, 61 TLR 308, 78 Ll L Rep 383, CA
McFarlane v Coggins and Griffiths (Liverpool) Ltd
[1945] KB 301, [1945] 1 All ER 605, 61 TLR 308, 78 Ll L Rep 383, CA
It was a common practice for master stevedores to supply bogies and

drivers to other master stevedores as required. There was no written agreement. Defendants supplied a bogie and driver to plaintiff's employers. Plaintiff was injured by the negligence of the driver. Defendants pleaded the driver was under the control of the particular employer and relied on defence on common employment.

McFarlane's case: Stevedores hired from Dock Authority mobile crane and driver. The Regulations stated that 'the drivers so provided shall be the servants of the applicants'. A third party was injured by the negligence of the driver and the issue was between the general and the particular employer.

HELD: In each case the particular employer could tell the driver where to go, what to transport and where to deliver, but not in regard to the manner of driving. The driver had entire control of the actual driving and was the only man who had any right to drive or manipulate the controls (brakes, steering, etc) in the exercise of his own discretion as a driver, the discretion being vested in him by the general employer, and the general employer was liable. Applying the test in *Nicholas'* case, in each case the general employer had not discharged the onus.

In *McFarlane's* case, the Regulation did not effect a transfer of the service of the driver without the consent of the driver, and could not affect the rights of a third party. It was only a matter between the parties to the contract.

Note—Followed in *Burkey v Mersey Dock Board* (1945) 79 Ll L Rep 12, CA

Mersey Docks and Harbour Board v Coggins and Griffiths (Liverpool) Ltd

[1947] AC 1, [1946] 2 All ER 345, HL

Coggins and Griffiths hired from the Dock Board a crane and driver who was engaged and paid by the Board. A third party employed by a firm of forwarding agents was injured by the negligence of the crane driver and obtained judgment against the Board. The Board appealed.

Per Viscount Simon: In applying the doctrine of *respondeat superior*, prima facie the responsibility for the negligence of servants engaged and paid by a general employer or permanent employer is on that employer, and the burden of proving that the responsibility has shifted to the hirer rests on the general employer. That burden is a heavy one and can only be discharged in quite exceptional circumstances. I prefer, instead of the test applied by the Court of Appeal following *Nicholas'* case, the test where the authority lies to direct, or to delegate to, the workman, the manner in which the vehicle is driven. It is this authority which determines who is the workman's 'superior'.

In this case, the servant was exercising his own discretion as driver, a discretion vested in him by his general employers, and the mistake he made had nothing to do with the hirers. If, however, the hirers had intervened to give directions how to drive and the driver *pro hac vice* had complied with them the hirers might have been liable, as joint tortfeasors.

The contract between the parties provided that the hirers of the crane and workman must take all risks and the workman shall be the servant of the hirers. This contract does not affect the rights of third parties. Appeal dismissed.

Per Lord Macmillian: The stevedores could tell the crane driver where to go, what parcels to lift, and where to take them, but not how he was to handle the crane in doing his work. His negligence was not the result of any order of the stevedores but in driving the crane as work for the general employers.

Per Lord Porter (quoted in *Chowdhary's* case (p 171, below)): Many factors have a bearing on the result. Who is paymaster, who can dismiss, how long the alternative service lasts, what machinery is employed — all these questions have to be kept in mind.

In determining this question it has to be borne in mind that the employee's position is an important consideration. A contract of service is made between master and man and an arrangement for the transfer of his services from one master to another can only be effected with the employee's consent, express or implied. His position is determined by his contract. No doubt, by finding out what his work is and how he does it and how he fulfils the task when put to carry out the requirements of an employer other than his own, one may go some way towards determining the capacity in which he acts, but a change of employer must always be proved in some way, not presumed.

Nor is it legitimate to infer that a change of masters has been effected because a contract has been made between the two employers declaring whose servant the man employed shall be at a particular moment in the course of his general employment by one of the two. A contract of this kind may of course determine the liability of the employers inter se, but it has only an indirect bearing upon the question which of them is to be regarded as master of the workman on a particular occasion.

In the present case, if the appellants' contention were to prevail, the crane driver would change his employer each time he embarked on the discharge of a fresh ship. Indeed, he might change it from day to day, without any say as to who his master should be and with all the concomitant disadvantages of uncertainty as to who should be responsible for his insurance in respect of health, unemployment and accident. I cannot think that such a conclusion is to be drawn from the facts established.

Per Lord Simonds: The general employers had vested in their servant a direction in the manner of carrying out the directions of the hirers. The driver's evidence was, 'I take no orders from anybody', ie he was a skilled man and knew his job and would carry it out in his own way.

Per Lord Uthwatt: The hirer must be shown to have authority to control the manner in which the workman does his work. The position of a craftsman entrusted for the hirer's purpose with the management of a machine of his employers, requiring technical skill and judgment, differs from the hire of an agricultural labourer for general work.

Treadaway v Dike and Ramsgate Corpn
[1967] 1 Lloyd's Rep 564

Per Paull J: In my judgment, the law is reasonably simple. It is this: if I hire a machine together with its driver, who from the essence of the case is an expert, and must be an expert in the driving of the machine, and there are no special terms with regard to what shall be the position between the driver and the firm to whom he is hired, then so long as he is driving that crane or that machine the person from whom it is hired is liable for the driver's negligence.

County Plant Hire Ltd v Jackson
(1970) 114 Sol Jo 263, CA

The defendant, a quarry owner, hired an excavator and driver from the plaintiffs who substituted an excavator and driver hired by them from the third parties. The driver was given orders for his work by the defendant but in negligently carrying them out damaged some equipment of the defendant. The plaintiffs sued for unpaid hire charges whereupon the defendant counterclaimed for the damage to his equipment and made the same claim against the third parties. The judge held that the defendant could not succeed in either claim because he was the person giving orders to the driver.

HELD: When the driver was driving the excavator he was acting in the course of that employment by the third parties: the mere fact that directions were given by the defendant as to what to do did not take the matter out of the course of that employment. If he had given wrong directions it might amount to contributory negligence. Judgment for the defendant against the third parties.

Chowdhary v Gillot
[1947] 2 All ER 541, 63 TLR 569 (Streatfeild J)

The plaintiff for 10 or 12 years had been a valued customer of the Daimler Co. He was in the habit of taking his Daimler car to their works and leaving it with them for servicing and repairs. Before the war the Daimler Co drove the plaintiff to the nearest railway station as a courtesy service in their own car with their own driver. During the war, their servant drove the plaintiff in his own car to the station and would then drive the car back to the works. On the way to the station an accident occurred by the negligence of the servant, and the plaintiff and a third party were injured.

HELD: Although the burden of proof of transfer of a servant is not so heavy when the servant alone is hired, as opposed to the man plus the machine, it remains a heavy burden. The burden of proof was on the plaintiff to show that he had abandoned his right to control or had contracted himself out of that right.

(1) The Daimler Co were in possession of the car as bailees, (2) plaintiff had no right to control the bailees' servant; (3) plaintiff was doing no more than receive courtesy service; (4) plaintiff was not in a position to exercise control.

The fact that he could have ordered him to drive more carefully if he was driving dangerously, or more slowly if at an uncomfortable or dangerous speed would be no more than the common prudence that a hirer would exercise towards a taxi driver, who is not the servant of the fare. He could not have ordered the driver to stop and wait half an hour, or deviate and wait while he visited a patient, or drive to a more distant place for his own purposes. If the Daimler Co had a regulation limiting the driving of customer's cars to a speed of, say, 20 mph and plaintiff had ordered the driver to drive faster to catch a train, the driver could have refused.

Distinguishing *Pratt v Patrick* (p 179, below) and *Samson v Aitchison* (p 179, below), the driver remained the servant of the Daimler Co.

Loaned servant injured

Savory v Holland, Hannen and Cubitts (Southern) Ltd
[1964] 3 All ER 18, [1964] 1 WLR 1158, 108 Sol Jo 479, CA
The defendants, building contractors, were clearing a large site to build a factory. They encountered rock, and engaged sub-contractors to blast it out. The sub-contractors sent the plaintiff, a skilled blaster, to do the job. He brought his own equipment but the defendants provided flagmen. The sub-contractors employed him, paid him and had power to dismiss him. The defendants could decide what rock they wanted him to blast but had no right to dictate to him how the actual blasting should be done. He was injured when he slipped whilst walking down a bank after acting as a flagman. He claimed damages on the grounds that the defendants had not provided enough flagmen nor a ladder to climb the bank in spite of his having asked for both. The judge held that he was a servant for the time being of the defendants and that they were liable.
HELD, ON APPEAL: The plaintiff was not a servant of the defendants either for the time being or at any time. He remained throughout the servant of the sub-contractors, his general employers, and the defendants were not liable.
   Per Diplock LJ: The doctrine of master and servant *pro hac vice* today seems to me to be relevant only to a question of vicarious liability: it is a mere adjunct of the doctrine of *respondeat superior* for determining whether A is the superior of B.

Note—See also *Garrard v A E Southey & Co and Standard Telephones and Cables Ltd* [1952] 2 QB 174, [1952] 1 All ER 597, [1952] 1 TLR 630, 96 Sol Jo 166 and *Johnson v A H Beaumont* [1953] 2 QB 184, [1953] 2 All ER 106, [1953] 2 WLR 1153, 97 Sol Jo 389, [1953] 1 Lloyd's Rep 546

Legal position of loaned servant

Denham v Midland Employers Mutual Assurance Ltd
[1955] 2 QB 437, [1955] 2 All ER 561, [1955] 3 WLR 84, 99 Sol Jo 417, [1955] 1 Lloyd's Rep 467, CA
Eastwoods Ltd, brickmakers, contracted with Le Grand Co, arterial well engineers, to perform work on their property, and agreed to provide one unskilled labourer to assist two skilled drillers of Le Grand Co free of charge. The labourer was selected by and paid by Eastwoods; they alone could suspend or dismiss him; they kept his insurance cards and paid for his insurance stamps. He was not asked nor did he consent to a transfer of his contract of service; if he was not paid his wages, or was wrongfully dismissed, he could sue Eastwoods and no one else; if he failed to turn up, Eastwoods alone could sue him. The labourer was killed in circumstances whereby Le Grand Co were liable to his widow by reason of negligence of Le Grand Co or their servants.
   Le Grand Co had a policy of insurance against employers' liability with the first defendants indemnifying them in respect of injury to any person under a contract of service with them by accident arising out of and in the course of his employment by them. They also had a public liability policy with the second defendants, which excluded liability in respect of any person under a contract of service with them by accident arising out of and

in the course of employment by them. Each insurer contended the other was liable to indemnify.

HELD, ON APPEAL: There was no contract of service with Le Grand and they were not entitled to recover from the first insurers. The contract of service was with Eastwoods. The second defendants were liable under the public liability policy.

THEFT BY SERVANT

United African Co v Saka Owoade
[1955] AC 130, [1957] 3 All ER 216, [1955] 2 WLR 13, 99 Sol Jo 26, [1954] 2 Lloyd's Rep 607, PC

A transport contractor authorised a customer to hand goods to his driver and clerk, who received goods for carriage. The goods were never delivered and the clerk and driver were convicted of stealing the goods.

HELD: The goods were converted in the course of the employment and the contractor was liable to the customer.

Grundy (Teddington) v Fulton
[1981] 2 Lloyd's Rep 666 (Stuart-Smith J); affd. [1983] 1 Lloyd's Rep 16, CA

The plaintiff company claimed under an insurance policy which covered theft of goods from its premises. The goods had been stolen by drivers deviating from their routes and failing to make deliveries.

HELD: The plaintiffs could not succeed. 'Theft' in the policy of insurance must be given the same meaning as in criminal law and in that law the theft took place when the driver deviated from his route.

Note—See also *Morris v C. W. Martin & Sons Ltd* p 162, above.

Employer's duty on engaging servant

Adams (Durham) Ltd and Day v Trust Houses Ltd
[1960] 1 Lloyd's Rep 380

The manager of a hotel at Chester engaged a night porter on information supplied by the man himself. He also telephoned a hotel at Wolverhampton where the man had previously been employed and spoke to a woman without ascertaining who she was and asked if the man was good at the job, sober and honest. He received a satisfactory answer. In fact the man had five convictions.

HELD: The manager had made insufficient enquiry having regard to the responsibility falling on the night porter.

Note—For full facts see p 328, below. See also *Nahhas v Pier House (Cheyne Walk) Management Ltd* (1984) 270 Estates Gazette 328, 134 NLJ 657 on liability for dishonest servant.

Employer not liable

Grey v Gee Cars Ltd
(1940) Times, 27 July
The defendants were garage proprietors and had engaged a car washer through the labour exchange. The servant was interviewed and produced two documents as references, which were satisfactory, but the defendants did not take up the references. In the press of work it was necessary to employ the servant as a chauffeur. The plaintiff hired a motor car and chauffeur to take her to Torquay. The plaintiff's luggage was loaded into the car, when an air raid warning was sounded, and plaintiff went to a shelter. Whilst there, the servant drove away with the car and the plaintiff's luggage and jewellery.
HELD: Defendants were entitled to assume a servant was honest until proved otherwise; it was not negligent to employ a car washer without taking up his references; he had given satisfaction in that job, and it was not negligent to employ him as a driver. Defendants were not liable to the plaintiff for the loss.

Homecraft Weavers v Ewer, Welsh Third Parties
(1945) 78 Ll L Rep 496 (Lawrence LJ, sitting in KB), CA
The third parties, haulage contractors, engaged as driver a young man aged twenty-one whose real name was Kennedy, who had two criminal convictions, one as a juvenile and one as an adult. When he applied for work, the third parties asked for and received a series of documents such as workmen now carry, and they gave him a trial and he proved an efficient driver. He produced his identity card in the name of Heiden; a new unemployment book because it was his first engagement; a discharge from the Army with character 'good'; and his driving licence, all in the name of Heiden, and all apparently signed in the same handwriting. The third parties demanded he should produce a green card from the Labour Exchange to notify his engagement. They therefore had information that the Labour Exchange recognised him as Heiden.
   The man gave his address but the third parties did not go to the address until after the larceny.
   The man stole or assisted in stealing goods on the third parties' lorry belonging to and being carried for their customer, and on enquiry the third parties learned Heiden was in the Army.
HELD: An ordinary reasonable person would be satisfied with this evidence of his identity and would not 'check up' on it; there was no negligence of third parties as haulage contractors in engaging Kennedy, and they were not liable to their customer for the theft of the goods.

Note—See also *Transmotors Ltd v Robertson Buckley & Co*, p 331, below.

SERVANT'S LIABILITY TO MASTER

Note—Smith's *Master and Servant* (7th edn, 1922) p 69, contained the following note:

'A servant is also liable to an action at the suit of his master, where a third party has brought an action, and recovered damages against the master, for injuries sustained in consequence of the servant's negligence or misconduct; and in such action against the servant, the verdict against the master, in the action brought against him, is evidence as to the quantum of damages, though not as to the fact of the injury. (*Green v New River Co* (1792) 4 Term Rep 589.)'

It was upon this ground that formerly in an action against a master for an injury caused by the negligence of his servant, the servant was not a competent witness for his master without a release.

Ryan v Fildes
[1938] 3 All ER 517 (Tucker J)
A schoolmistress, the servant of the school managers, boxed the ears of a schoolboy and caused injury. The boy sued the schoolmistress and the school managers and recovered against both defendants. The managers recovered 100% contribution from the schoolmistress.

Jones v Manchester Corpn
[1952] 2 QB 852, [1952] 2 All ER 125, [1952] 1 TLR 1589, CA
Per Singleton LJ: It may well be that in the ordinary simple case a servant must indemnify his master against his wrongful acts for which the master is made liable. A chauffeur who, through negligence, causes damage for which his employer is held responsible may well be liable to his master. On the other hand, if the chauffeur is young and inexperienced, and is suddenly told to drive another and bigger car, or lorry, which he does not understand, and an accident follows, it is by no means certain that the employer would be entitled to an indemnity. The statement in Salmond on the *Law of Torts* (15th edn) p 620, that a master should generally be able to sue his servant for indemnity cannot apply if the master has himself contributed to the damage or if some other employee has contributed to the damage.

Semtex Ltd v Gladstone
[1954] 2 All ER 206, [1954] 1 WLR 945, 98 Sol Jo 438 (Finnemore J)
The defendant was a driver employed by the plaintiffs. By the negligent driving of the defendant, personal injuries were caused to other workmen of the plaintiffs. The plaintiffs, by the insurers of their employers' liability policy, settled claims amounting to £9,360, and sued the defendant for that sum. The defendant was indemnified by the plaintiffs' motor policy, and these insurers were the real defendants. The employers claimed from the servant driver indemnity at common law or contribution of 100% under the Law Reform (Married Women and Tortfeasors) Act 1935, s 6(2).
HELD: It was clear law that a master could sue his servant for negligence. This right applies to moneys paid by the master for such negligence to other parties as well as to the master himself as in *Digby v General Accident* (p 860, below), whether treated as a breach of contract by the servant, or a case of contribution of 100%. It was immaterial whether the plaintiff's claim was based on a breach of the contract of service which placed the driver under a duty to drive carefully, or whether as between tortfeasors, for in either event they were entitled to recover the whole of the damages which they had been forced to pay owing to his negligence.

The servant's argument based on *Gregory v Ford* (p 716, below), of an implied contract that the servant should not be required to do an unlawful act broke down, because the Road Traffic Act 1930, s 35(1), does not provide that the driver, if a servant or agent, shall be insured. There is no implied term in the contract of service that the master shall take out a policy of insurance which indemnifies the driver. Any implied term is satisfied by a policy which complies with the Road Traffic Act 1930, s 35(1).

Note—(1) Section 35(1) of the Road Traffic Act 1930 has been replaced by s 143(1) (p 704, below) of the Road Traffic Act 1972. The Law Reform (Married Women and Tortfeasors) Act 1935, s 6 has been replaced by the Civil Liability (Contribution) Act 1978.

(2) This case was said to be rightly decided in the House of Lords in the case of *Lister v Romford Ice and Cold Storage Co*, below.

(3) The position which arose in the *Semtex* case only applies when the policy indemnifies the driver treated as an unqualified insured. The position is different when the policy wording is apt to exclude indemnity of the driver in respect of servants of the same employer.

A specimen wording is the following:

'That no indemnity is provided to such person in respect of any claim which if made against the Insured would not have been the subject of indemnity under this policy.'

Lister v Romford Ice and Cold Storage Co Ltd
[1957] AC 555, [1957] 1 All ER 125, [1957] 2 WLR 158, 101 Sol Jo 106, [1956] 2 Lloyd's Rep 505, HL
The driver of a motor lorry went to a yard off the highway to collect goods. His father, in the same employ, went with him. In the yard the father was injured whilst the driver was backing the lorry. The father sued the employers and recovered damages. The employers sued the driver claiming indemnity in contract and in negligence.
HELD: The employers were entitled to an indemnity from the driver.

Per Viscount Simonds: In my opinion the case of *Semtex Ltd v Gladstone* (above) was rightly decided. It is clear that it was an implied term of the contract that the appellant would perform his duties with proper care (*Harmer v Cornelius* (1858) 5 CBNS 236). This includes a servant employed to drive a lorry. There is no distinction between possessing skill and exercising it. Skill embraces care. In this case it is immaterial whether the cause of action lies in contract or in tort. The servant owes a contractual duty of care to his master, and breach founds an action for damages for breach of contract. A single act of negligence may give rise to a claim either in tort or for breach of a term express or implied in a contract. The respondents are entitled to recover the damage for breach of contract, unless the damage is too remote or there is some other intervening factor which precludes recovery. The damages are not too remote. With regard to the implication of some implied term, I cannot accept the implication that the respondents would indemnify the appellant for any act in the course of his employment, nor that the appellant would receive the benefit of any contract of insurance effected by them, nor that the employer was bound as a reasonable man to effect such an insurance. The fact that one party to a contract is insured is to be disregarded.

Harvey v R. G. O'Dell Ltd (Galway, Third Party)
[1958] 2 QB 78, [1958] 1 All ER 657, [1958] 2 WLR 473, 102 Sol Jo 196, [1958] 1 Lloyd's Rep 273 (McNair J)

The plaintiff was in the employ of the defendant company. Galway was also in the company's employ as a storekeeper at their works. The defendant company were builders and repairers of barges with works at Battersea, but also did general work away from the works. If the outside work necessitated the use of substantial materials, or heavy tools, the men were conveyed by the company's lorry or van, but in other cases the men made their own arrangements for travel and were reimbursed the cost of travel by public transport, whether they used it or not. Galway owned a motor cycle combination which he used to travel to and from work, from time to time on the employers' business to collect materials, and sometimes for travelling to and from an outside repairing job. He paid his own money for petrol and maintenance but when on business was allowed a travelling allowance based on the cost of public transport. The plaintiff was Galway's assistant. The defendants' manager told Galway he would like him to go the following day to repair a fence round a caravan at Hurley, some five to six miles from Maidenhead, and to take the plaintiff with him. Galway was free to refuse, but agreed. The same evening he told the plaintiff to make arrangements with Galway to accompany him. On 29 February 1952, Galway collected a brace and bit and some tools from the store, put them in the sidecar and proceeded with the plaintiff to Hurley, where they worked for four or five hours, and Galway then told the plaintiff they would have to go to Maidenhead for more tools and materials. At Maidenhead the plaintiff got out at a café and Galway rejoined him about half-an-hour later, where they both had a meal of coffee and sandwiches. On the way back to Hurley the combination collided with a car, and Galway was killed. The accident was due in part of the negligence of Galway.

The judge held (1) Galway was using the combination on behalf of his employers; (2) Galway was acting within the scope of his employment in the journey from London to Hurley; (3) the journey from Maidenhead to Hurley was fairly incidental to the work.

The defendants sued Galway's administratrix in third party proceedings for an indemnity.

HELD: The authorities, including *Lister v Romford Ice and Cold Storage Co Ltd*, were cases where the servant was employed as a driver. Galway was engaged as a storekeeper. Making his motor cycle available to his employers from time to time as a concession, did not imply into his contract of employment a term that he would use reasonable care and skill in driving or that he had impliedly agreed to indemnify his employers against liability arising from his negligent driving. There is no right to indemnity on the facts in this case.

But there was a right to contribution as a joint tortfeasor under the Law Reform (Married Women and Tortfeasors) Act 1935, s 6(1) (c). The right of contribution between tortfeasors is a right *sui generis* conferred by statute. They are not proceedings in respect of a cause of action in tort. The claim of the plaintiff against the company and Galway's administratrix was as against joint tortfeasors. The company's liability is purely vicarious, and the company was entitled to judgment for 100% contribution, ie an indemnity against their liability under the judgment in action, with costs of action and third party proceedings.

Note—In place of s 6(1) (c) of the 1935 Act see the Civil Liability (Contribution) Act 1978, p 19, above.

2 OWNER'S LIABILITY FOR DRIVER

Prima facie liable

Note—An owner of a vehicle incurs no liability for damage caused by it merely by being the owner: see *River Wear Commissioners v Adamson*, p 39, above, and du Parcq LJ in *Hewitt v Bonvin*, p 181, below.

Barnard v Sully
(1931) 47 TLR 557
Where a plaintiff in an action for negligence proved that damage has been caused by defendant's motor car, the fact of ownership of the motor car is prima facie evidence that the motor car, at the material time, was being driven by the owner, or by his servant or agent.

Per Scrutton LJ: The more usual fact is that a motor car is driven by the owner or the servant or agent of the owner and therefore the fact of ownership is some evidence fit to go to the jury that at the material time the motor car was being driven by the owner of it or by his servant or agent. But it is evidence which is liable to be rebutted by proof of the actual facts.

Note—Applied in *Elliott v Loake* [1983] Crim LR 36, a criminal case.

Rambarran v Gurrucharran
[1970] 1 All ER 749, [1970] 1 WLR 556, 114 Sol Jo 244, PC
The defendant owned a car which he allowed his sons to use at any time. He himself did not drive. An accident occurred when his son Leslie was driving. The defendant gave evidence at the trial, accepted by the trial judge, that he did not know Leslie was out in the car on the day in question: it had not been used for his own purposes on that day and he was not at his home where the car was kept. The Guyana Court of Appeal by a majority held that the defendant had not rebutted the prima facie case of agency arising from the fact of ownership of the car, as in *Barnard v Sully* (above), since he had left the court without evidence as to the journey during which the accident occurred.

HELD, ON APPEAL to the Privy Council: The defendant was not liable. A plaintiff must establish, if he is to make the owner liable, that the driver was driving the car as the servant or agent of the owner and not merely on his own concerns. Although in the absence of other evidence an inference can be drawn from ownership that the driver was the servant or agent of the owner there was evidence from the defendant that the car was not being used for his purposes on the day of the accident and this was sufficient to rebut the inference. It was not necessary additionally that he should prove what Leslie's object was in using the car: once he had proved that Leslie was not driving as his servant or agent then Leslie's actual purpose on that day was irrelevant. Appeal allowed.

OWNER IN CAR

Samson v Aitchison
[1912] AC 844, 82 LJPC 1, 107 LT 106
Where the owner of a vehicle, being himself in possession and occupation of it, requests or allows another person to drive, this will not of itself exclude his right and duty of control, and therefore, in the absence of further proof that he has abandoned that right by contract or otherwise, the owner is liable as principal for damage caused by the negligence of the person actually driving.

In his judgment which was approved by the Privy Council, the trial judge said: 'I think that where the owner of an equipage, whether a carriage and horses or a motor, is riding in it while it is being driven, and has thus not only the right to possession but the actual possession of it, he necessarily retains the power and the right of controlling the manner in which it is to be driven, unless he has in some way contracted himself out of his right, or is shown by conclusive evidence to have in some way abandoned his right. If any injury happen to the equipage while it is being driven, the owner is the sufferer. In order to protect his own property if, in his opinion, the necessity arises, he must be able to say to the driver, "Do this," or "Don't do that." The driver would have to obey, and if he did not the owner in possession would compel him to give up the reins or the steering wheel. The owner, indeed, has a duty to control the driver. . . . The duty to control postulates the existence of the right to control. If there was no right to control there could be no duty to control. No doubt if the actual possession of the equipage has been given by the owner to a third person — that is to say, if there has been a bailment by the owner to a third person — the owner has given up his right of control'. (Quoted in *Chowdhary's* case.)

Pratt v Patrick
[1924] 1 KB 488, 93 LJKB 174, 130 LT 735 (Acton J)
Defendant was in his motor car, with him, on his invitation, being two friends, E and P. E drove the car and, owing to his negligence, it collided with another vehicle and P sustained injuries from which he died. P's widow sued defendant under the Fatal Accidents Acts for damages.
HELD: As defendant was in the car, and there was no evidence that he had abandoned his right of control, he was liable notwithstanding that by a casual delegation he had entrusted its actual physical management and mechanical control to E.

Note—In that case [*Pratt v Patrick*] there was a delegation of the control of the car by the owner to a casual driver while the owner himself remained in the car ready to control, if he was so minded, or to direct the driver. There was no question of the car having been handed over to anybody. There was no evidence there of any abandonment by the owner of his right to control it: Per Streatfeild J in *Chowdhary's* case (p 171, above).

The Trust Co Ltd v de Silva
[1956] 1 WLR 376, 100 Sol Jo 262, [1956] 1 Lloyd's Rep 309, PC
Insurers employed canvassers on commission but no salary, and field

officers with a small salary and overriding commission who supervised their canvassers. Either selected a doctor to examine proposers for life insurance. A doctor was a passenger with a field officer in a car of the field officer driven by a canvasser, and was injured.

HELD: The field officer was a servant of insurers and was acting in the course of and for the purposes of his employment; he had the right to exercise control over the driver and was in control of the car. Insurers were liable to the doctor for injuries caused by the negligent driver of the canvasser.

Bailee in car

Haydock v Brown

(1939) Times, 24 May, *Manchester Guardian*, 24 May, (Croom-Johnson J)
The owner of a car gave permission to A (her son) to drive the car. A was in the car which was being driven by B. A was bailee of the car and had the right to possession of it. There is no difference whether the right to possession is as owner, hirer, or gratuitous bailee. If he is in the car, he must be taken to have retained his right of control, and if he has the right of control, he is liable for a person who must be deemed to be driving on his behalf and under his control.

OWNER NOT IN CAR

Loan of car

Britt v Galmoye and Nevill

(1928) 44 TLR 294, 72 Sol Jo 122
A had been in the employment of B as a van driver. B lent A his private car after the day's work was finished to take A's friends to a theatre. A, by his negligent driving, injured the plaintiff.

HELD: As the journey was not on the master's business, and the master was not in control, he was not liable for his servant's act.

Hillman v Walls

(1938) 5 LJCCR 167
Defendant owned a car and lent it to a fellow servant H to go home to lunch. H returned by other means. At the owner's request H brought the car back to work next morning, and on the way injured the plaintiff. H disappeared and the plaintiff sued the defendant alleging defendant had the right to control.

HELD: Following *Higbid v Hammett* (p 150, above), defendant was not in control and H was not his servant or agent.

Driving with consent — owner not liable

Hewitt v Bonvin

[1940] 1 KB 188, 109 LJKB 223, 161 LT 360, 56 TLR 43, 83 Sol Jo 869, CA

A son was driving his father's car with the consent of the father. Lewis J, held that as he was driving with the consent of the father, he was the father's agent on that journey. The Court of Appeal reversed the decision.

Per MacKinnon LJ: A man may, of course, be temporarily employed as a servant without remuneration. If I say to a friend, or to my son, 'the chauffeur is ill and cannot come. Will you drive me in my car to the station?' he is no doubt *pro tempore* my servant, and he is doing my work for me. But a servant must at the moment of his act be doing work for his employer. The plaintiff must establish (1) that the son was employed to drive the car as his father's servant, and (2) that he was, when the accident happened, driving the car for the father, and not merely for his own benefit and for his own concerns.

Per du Parcq LJ: It is plain that the ownership of the car cannot of itself impose any liability on the owner. The owner, without further information, is prima facie liable, because the court is entitled to draw the inference that the car was being driven by the owner, his servant or agent, but when the facts are given in evidence the court is not left to draw an inference. The owner is liable if the driver had authority, express or implied, to drive on the owner's behalf. This depends not on ownership, but on the delegation of a task or duty. Permission to drive the car is consistent with a mere loan or bailment. The relationship of father and son is not of itself evidence of agency.

HELD: The father was not liable.

Note—See also *Rambarran v Gurrucharran*, p 178, above. The following is a form of a Plea in a Defence denying agency:

'The driver of the defendant's car was not the servant or agent of the defendant. The defendant lent the car to the said driver, who was driving the car merely for his own benefit and for his own concerns and was not driving the car for the defendant. The defendant disclaims all legal liability for the acts of the said driver.'

Klein v Caluori

[1971] 2 All ER 701, [1971] 1 WLR 617, 115 Sol Jo 228, [1971] 1 Lloyd's Rep 421, [1971] RTR 354 (Lyell J)

The defendant's car was borrowed and driven away without his knowledge or consent by a friend. An hour or two later the friend telephoned the defendant and told him he had taken his car. The defendant told him curtly to bring it back. On the way back the car collided with the plaintiff's stationary car and damaged it. The plaintiff claimed that the defendant was vicariously liable on the ground that his friend was his agent in driving the car because in bringing it back he was driving for the purposes of the owner, the defendant.

HELD: The return journey was part and parcel of the whole enterprise, namely, the borrowing of the car. A mere permission to drive a car does not make the driver the agent of the person giving permission. Whether or not the borrowing had been with consent the return journey was for the purposes of the borrower only. It could make no difference that the defendant told the friend to bring the car back: it was merely a reminder of his duty to do so.

Common interest — spouses

Morgans v Launchbury
[1973] AC 127, [1972] 2 All ER 606, [1972] 2 WLR 1217, 116 Sol Jo 396, HL

Mrs Morgans, the defendant, owned a car which was registered and insured in her name. Both she and her husband regularly used it, he more than she. She regarded it as being their car jointly, rather than hers. He used it for going to work. One evening he telephoned her from his place of work, saying he was going out for the evening. He visited various public houses and at one of them, conscious that he ought not to drive, asked a friend named Cawfield to act as his chauffeur for the rest of the evening. Later he and Cawfield left a public house in the car with the plaintiffs as passengers and were travelling to a town some miles away, not in a homeward direction, when an accident occurred due to Cawfield's negligent driving. The defendant's husband and Cawfield were killed, the plaintiffs injured. The defendant had been promised by her husband that if ever he had had too much to drink when out with the car he would get someone who was sober to drive. The Court of Appeal held the defendant vicariously liable for Cawfield's negligent driving on the grounds inter alia that it was a 'family car' and that she had an 'interest and concern' in the purpose for which it was being driven.

HELD: Allowing the appeal, there was no authority for accepting the 'interest and concern' or 'family car' arguments, which have no validity in English law. An owner's vicarious liability for the negligence of the driver was correctly and accurately stated by MacKinnon LJ and du Parcq LJ in *Hewitt v Bonvin* (p 181, above). The understanding between Mr and Mrs Morgans that when unfit he would get someone else to drive was no basis for holding that Cawfield had been delegated to drive as agent for her, and she was not vicariously liable for his negligence.

Norwood v Navan
[1981] RTR 457, CA

Mrs Navan had her husband's consent to use his car. She went out in it for the afternoon with two friends to a neighbouring town, first to visit a fortune-teller and then on a shopping expedition. On the return journey by her negligent driving she caused injury and loss to the plaintiff. He claimed damages against both Mr and Mrs Navan. She allowed judgment against her to go by default but her husband denied any vicarious liability for her negligence. The county court judge held he was liable in that the shopping she had done was in the interests and for the purpose of both of them. There was a sufficient use of the car for his purposes to make her his agent: he was vicariously liable for her negligent driving.

HELD, ON APPEAL: This was not right. The idea of a 'matrimonial car' formulated by Lord Denning in *Launchbury v Morgans* (above, sub nom *Morgans v Launchbury*) had been rejected by the House of Lords. The law there laid down by the Lords is based on proper proof of agency. The facts in the present case did not amount to such proof. Mrs Navan was at very most doing only general shopping. It would be absurd in such a case for the court to have to examine the contents of her shopping basket to see what she had bought. There was no vicarious liability on Mr Navan.

Driving on owner's business

Smith v Moss
[1940] 1 KB 424, [1940] 1 All ER 469, 109 LJKB 271, 162 LT 267, 56 TLR 305, 84 Sol Jo 115 (Charles J)
B bought a car which was garaged at her son's house and the son was the only driver. The car was used to convey the mother, son and son's wife home from a party. The mother was taken to her house and the son drove the wife in the car to the son's house. The wife was injured and sued the mother.
HELD: The driver was the agent of the owner. It was by her direction that he took her to the party, and it was by her direction that he took her back from the party. He had not ceased to be acting for her. The wife was entitled to recover.

Ormerod v Crosville Motor Services Ltd
[1953] 2 All ER 753, [1953] 1 WLR 1120, 97 Sol Jo 570, CA
The owner of a car who was taking part in the Monte Carlo rally arranged with a friend for the friend to drive the car, with the friend's wife as passenger, in the friend's own time and manner, and meet him at Monte Carlo before the end of the rally, after which the car would be used for a holiday in Switzerland of these three persons. A suitcase belonging to the owner was carried in the car. On the journey in England the car was involved in a collision and the owner of the other vehicle sued the car owner for damages caused by the negligent driving of the friend.
HELD: The friend driving was not the servant of the owner. To render the owner liable there must be something more than the granting of the mere permission but it is not necessary to show a legal contract of agency. It is, however, sufficient where there is a social or moral obligation (per du Parcq LJ in *Hewitt v Bonvin* (above)), to drive the owner's car. A request to the friend to drive the car, and compliance with the request, makes the friend the agent of the owner, since the owner has an interest in the request being complied with. The driving was for the owner's benefit, and the owner is liable for the driver's negligence.

Per Singleton LJ: Mere consent is not proof of agency. Here the purpose was that the car should be used by the owner or for the joint purposes of the plaintiff and the owner when it reached Monte Carlo. The male plaintiff was driving for the purposes of the owner or the joint purposes of the owner and himself.

Per Denning LJ: An owner may be liable although the driver is not his servant. The owner is also liable if the driver is, with the owner's consent, driving the car on the owner's business or for the owner's purposes. Here it was partly for the driver's own purposes and partly for the owner's purposes. The contention that because the driver started two or three days earlier for his own purposes the owner is not liable fails. The law puts an especial responsibility on the owner who allows it to go on the road in charge of someone else. If it is being used wholly or partly on the owner's business or for the owner's purposes, the owner is liable. He only escapes when it is to be used for purposes in which he has no interest or concern (*Hewitt v Bonvin*). The trip to Monte Carlo must be considered as a whole.

Carberry v Davies
[1968] 2 All ER 817, [1968] 1 WLR 1103, 112 Sol Jo 445, CA

The owner of a car was a coal-merchant who had three lorries for delivery of coal one of which was driven by his employee H, who was a servant at a wage. The owner also had a Ford car which he regarded as the family car and which he wanted all his family to use as far as practicable. But he would not allow anyone to drive it except himself and H. When his son aged 16 wanted to go out in the car he could do so provided H drove it. On one such occasion it collided with the plaintiff and H was held to blame. Was the car-owner vicariously liable for H's negligence?

HELD: The principle was stated by Singleton LJ in *Ormerod v Crosville Motor Services* (above): 'the driver of a motor car must be doing something for the owner of the car to become an agent of the owner'. The present case turned on how the arrangement was made. Did the car-owner make the arrangement with H, so that his son could have the use of the car or was it the son who made the arrangement and simply asked his father's permission? On the facts it was the father who made the arrangement and he was liable for H's negligent driving.

Vandyke v Fender
[1970] 2 QB 292, [1970] 2 All ER 335, [1970] 2 WLR 929, 134 JP 487, 114 Sol Jo 205, CA

On the facts set out on p 743, below, the Court of Appeal held, following *Ormerod v Crosville Motor Services* (above) that Fender was the agent of the second defendants when driving the car owned by them for a purpose in which they had an interest and they were vicariously liable for his negligent driving whether or not he was driving in the course of his employment.

BUT NO LIABILITY WITHOUT DELEGATION

Norton v Canadian Pacific Steamships Ltd
[1961] 2 All ER 785, [1961] 1 WLR 1057, 105 Sol Jo 442, CA

The plaintiff claimed damages for injuries he received by the negligent driving of an electric bogie by a porter named Morris on the Prince's landing stage at Liverpool. Morris was one of 180 porters plying for hire on the landing stage. Though requiring a licence from the Liverpool City Council to act as such the porters were an independent body of men not in the general employment of anyone. The defendants were ship owners whose vessels used the landing stage for the disembarkation of passengers. They paid for the porters' services in handling passengers' luggage by a single payment per ship to the senior head porter who was responsible for distributing the money among the porters in whatever manner they had agreed. The electric bogie was one of the seven in use by the porters. Four had been provided by the defendants and the Cunard Line jointly and three by the manufacturers of the bogies. They were all used indiscriminately by the porters. The bogie Morris was driving at the time of the accident happened to be one of the four belonging to the defendants and the Cunard Line. The accident occurred when Morris was using it to transfer luggage from the defendant's ship to a conveyor on the landing stage. In the Court of first instance the plaintiff alleged that Morris was a servant of the defendants, but the judge held that he was not. This finding was not appealed against. The judge found in favour of the plaintiff on the ground that the bogie belonged to the defendants (as joint owners with the Cunard Line) and that in the circumstances Morris was driving as their agent at the time of the accident, following *Ormerod v Crosville Motor Services Ltd* (above).

HELD, ON APPEAL: The defendants were not liable. Morris never lost his independence as a licensed porter and was in complete control of the services he was rendering: he was using the bogie purely for the better or easier performance of the duties for which he was engaged and paid. The defendants had not assumed any obligation or undertaken any task of driving and using the bogies and had not delegated such task to the porters. There was clear and emphatic evidence that the defendants did not exercise any control or have any right to control the licensed porters in respect of the manner in which they were to move the luggage or use the bogies. Ownership of the bogie was insufficient in itself to create liability for its negligent use. The principle in *Ormerod's* case is that of the delegation of a task or duty as in *Hewitt v Bonvin* (p 181, above). The owner of a car who takes or sends it on a journey for his own purposes owes a duty of care to other road users and is liable for the negligent driving of the car whether by himself or by an agent to whom he had delegated the driving. In the present case there was no such delegation.

Principal not the owner of vehicle

Nottingham v Aldridge
[1971] 2 QB 739, [1971] 2 All ER 751, [1971] 3 WLR 1, 115 Sol Jo 328, [1971] 1 Lloyd's Rep 424 (Eveleigh J)
The plaintiff and the first defendant were apprentices employed by the Post Office (the second defendants). They were required by the terms of their service to attend a residential course of training some distance from home. They were allowed home for the weekend but had to be back at the training centre by Sunday night. They were returning on Sunday evening in a car driven by the first defendant when an accident occurred in which the plaintiff was injured. The car belonged to the first defendant's father. In accordance with Post Office regulations the first defendant was entitled to be, and was, paid 3d per mile for the cost of travel by car and an additional 1d per mile for conveying the plaintiff. The plaintiff claimed that the Post Office were vicariously liable for the first defendant's negligence either (1) as their servant or (2) as their agent, driving the car for their benefit.
HELD: (1) Although the first defendant was the servant of the Post Office in that he had with them a contract of service he was not at the relevant time acting as such and the relationship of master and servant did not exist. (2) The Post Office were not so involved in the carriage of the plaintiff as to make the first defendant their agent. While ownership of motor vehicle is not essential in all cases to make a principal liable for the acts of his agent in driving it for his benefit the fact of ownership is of value in determining whether or not the driver was driving independently or on behalf of the principal. Where (as here) the principal is not the owner of the vehicle it

must be established that the driver was driving in a genuinely representative capacity, that is, as an agent for and on behalf of the principal and as one to whom there has been a delegation of a task or duty. That was not the case here and the Post Office were not liable.

Driving by repairer

McManus v Weinbert
(1940) *Post Magazine* 11 May 621
W's policy was O.O.D. Repairers sent driver who was driving car from W's house to repairers when plaintiff was injured. Lewis J held that W had no right to control the driver. The right of control remained with the repairers who were the employers of the driver on the journey and repairers were liable.

Note—Referred to in *Nottingham v Aldridge* (above).

PASSENGERS

Liability for negligence of passenger

Trivett v Harding and Watkin
Liverpool Assizes, Trinity Sittings (Streatfeild J), unreported
Watkin, a taxi driver, was travelling in another taxi (but not as a fare-paying passenger) owned and driven by Harding. Watkin opened the nearside rear door before Harding had brought the vehicle to a standstill and knocked down the plaintiff, a pedestrian. Plaintiff sued the owner-driver and the passenger jointly, but Streatfeild J said that he could not understand why Harding had been brought into the action at all, as the passenger, Watkin, was alone responsible for the accident. He gave judgment against Watkin solely for £1,250 plus costs. Trivett was ordered to pay the costs of Harding.

Note—See also *Brown v Roberts*, p 706, below.

Daimler Hire v Gomez
(1953) 15 January, Westminster CC
A passenger who opened the offside door of a hired car in front of a passing taxi was ordered to pay £127 17s 6d.

Note—Most private motor car policies now cover passengers against claims against them for negligence. Commercial vehicle policies normally do not.

Liability of passenger for negligence of driver

Scarsbrook v Mason
[1961] 3 All ER 767, 105 Sol Jo 889 (Glyn-Jones J)
The defendant was a passenger in a car which, due to the negligence of the

driver, ran off the road and injured the plaintiffs who were standing on the footway. The judge found that the defendant had joined the other occupants of the car for a trip to Southend: he had paid 4s towards the cost of petrol and he was accepted by the others as an equal member of the party, all equally concerned in the trip, one of whom was to drive on behalf of all the others. The owner was not present, the car having been driven away by someone without his consent about three days previously.

HELD: The members of the party were jointly and severally liable for the manner in which the car was driven and the plaintiffs were entitled to succeed against the defendant as a member of the party, on the ground that the driver was acting as agent for each and all the members of that party.

Bown v Chatfield
[1963] CLY 2348, CC

The defendant and another man took the plaintiff's car from a car park without his consent. The car was damaged whilst being driven by the other man with the defendant as a passenger. The plaintiff relied on *Scarsbrook v Mason* (above). The defendant gave evidence that he was drunk when the car was taken from the car park and remembered nothing of the journey. The judge held that the driver is agent for the passengers only when they are equal members of the venture. On the facts the defendant was not an equal member and was not liable.

TAXI-CAB

Liability of proprietor for negligence of driver in London

Keen v Henry
[1894] 1 QB 292, 63 LJQB 211, 69 LT 671, 58 JP 262, 10 TLR 96, Sol Jo 77, CA

Gates v Bill
[1902] 2 KB 38, 71 LJKB 702, 87 LT 288, 50 WR 546, 18 TLR 592, 46 Sol Jo 498, CA and other cases

Under the London Hackney Carriage Act 1843, so far as the public is concerned, the registered proprietor, and also the actual proprietor, of a hackney carriage is responsible for the acts of the driver whilst he is plying for hire, as if the relationship of master and servant exists between them, even though it does not in fact exist.

Liability of proprietor for negligence of driver outside London

Bygraves v Dicker
[1923] 2 KB 585, 92 LJKB 1021, 129 LT 688, Div Ct

Outside London the Town Police Clauses Act 1847, provides that the registered proprietor must be treated as the employer of the driver for the purpose of claims by members of the public in respect of damage by the negligence of the driver.

Note—By the London Cab Order 1934, dated 11 December 1934, S R & O 1934/1346, made pursuant to the Metropolitan Public Carriage Act 1869 (32 & 33 Vict, c 115) and the London Cab and Stage Carriage Act 1907 (7 Edw 7, c 55), which applies by para 2 to a motor cab in the City of London and Metropolitan Police District, it is provided by r 8 as follows:

'**8** (1) The liability to third parties to which this paragraph relates is any liability (other than a contractual liability) incurred by the owner or driver of a cab, as a consequence of the user of the cab, in respect of

(a)   the death or bodily injury to any person, other than a person employed by the owner of the cab whose death or injury arises out of and in the course of his employment, and

(b)   damage to animals or to property not belonging to the cab-owner or cab-driver nor held in trust by him nor under his charge or control not being conveyed in the cab, and not being damage to any bridge, weighbridge, viaduct, or road, or any property thereunder.

(2) Subject as hereinafter provided there shall be in force in relation to every cab a policy of insurance issued by an insurer approved by the [Assistant Commissioner] which insures the owner of the cab and any other person who drives the cab with his permission in respect of any liability to third parties to which this paragraph relates: provided that

(a)   a policy of insurance or a security complying with Part II of the Road Traffic Act 1930, as amended by any subsequent Act, shall be a sufficient fulfilment of the requirements of this paragraph in respect of so much of the liability as it covers, and

(b)   any other liability to which this paragraph relates shall not be required to be covered for an amount in excess of £10,000 in respect of any claim or series of claims arising out of any one accident or occurrence.

(3) The [Assistant Commissioner] may, in any case where he is satisfied that the financial position of the owner of a cab is such as to enable him and the cab-driver to meet without insurance any liability to third parties to which this paragraph relates, or any part of that liability, direct that the requirements of this paragraph (not being requirements of Part II of the Road Traffic Act, 1930, as amended by any subsequent Act) either shall not apply in relation to that cab or shall apply with such modifications as he may direct, and in any such case those requirements shall either have no effect or have effect as so modified as the case may be.'

Minicab service

Rogers v Night Riders
[1983] RTR 324, CA

The defendants were a firm operating a minibus service, holding themselves out to the general public as a car hire firm. The plaintiff telephoned them for a car to take her to Euston station. A car was sent and the plaintiff travelled in it. En route a door flew open, struck a parked vehicle and bounced back, injuring the plaintiff's hand. The car belonged to the driver; he was not the defendants' employee and the defendants had no control over the management of the car. The county court judge found that there had been a failure to maintain the car properly but also that the driver was an independent contractor for whose negligence the defendants were not liable.

HELD, ON APPEAL: This was not right. It was not a case of vicarious liability; it was a case of a primary duty on the part of the defendants. They had undertaken to provide a car and driver to take the plaintiff to her destination and they owed her a duty to take care to see that the vehicle was safe and reasonably fit for that purpose. It was immaterial whether the duty was put in contract or in tort: it was a duty the defendants could not delegate. The situation would have been different if the true nature of the defendants' business had been known to the plaintiff, but it was not.

PARENTS

Donaldson v McNiven
[1952] 2 All ER 692
Parents are not responsible for the torts of their children.

Bebee v Sales
(1916) 32 TLR 413
They are only responsible when they have themselves done something wrong, e g if they have been guilty of lack of that supervision to be expected of reasonable and prudent parents.

Note—See *Carmarthenshire County Council v Lewis*, p 10, above.

CHAPTER 4
Passengers

DUTY TO PASSENGERS

No absolute duty

Ludditt v Ginger Coote Airways Ltd
[1947] AC 233, [1947] 1 All ER 328, [1947] LJR 1067, 177 LT 334, 63 TLR 157, PC

The liability of a common carrier of passengers was settled by the decision of *Readhead v Midland Rly Co* (p 240, below). It is more limited than that of a common carrier of goods. His obligation is to carry 'with due care'. One reason, no doubt, is that the carrier of goods is a bailee of the goods but not of passengers (citing *Grand Trunk Rly Co of Canada v Robinson* [1915] AC 740, 84 LJPC 194, 113 LT 350, 31 TLR 395). In the case of a railway company a breach can be regarded as a breach of an implied contract, or of a duty imposed by the general law and in the latter case as in form a tort. This general duty, subject to any statutory restrictions, can be superseded by a specific contract. The carrier is not precluded from making a special contract with his passengers.

Jones v Boyce
(1816) 1 Stark 493, 18 RR 812

A passenger in a coach was, by negligence of the coach proprietor in failing to provide proper means of conveyance placed in a perilous position, and he leaped from the coach and was injured. This is the result of the negligence of the coach proprietor in providing a coupling rein that was defective.

Joint enterprise for crime

Ashton v Turner
[1981] QB 137, [1980] 3 All ER 870, [1980] 3 WLR 736, 124 Sol Jo 792, [1981] RTR 54 (Ewbank J)
After an evening of heavy drinking in public houses and clubs, Ashton, Turner and McLune returned to McLune's home in his car, driven by Turner. There Ashton suggested going out to burglarise a shop. Turner agreed but McLune said he would have nothing to do with it and went to bed. The other two then drove off in McLune's car. They chose a suitable shop, smashed the window and stole goods from it. They went back to the car and Turner drove it, Ashton in the passenger seat. They were pursued by a taxi and in travelling at a high speed to get away from the taxi, skidded and crashed. Ashton was badly injured. He sued Turner for damages for negligent driving.
HELD: (1) The law of England may in certain circumstances not recognise the existence of a duty of care by one participant in a crime to another participant in the same crime in relation to an act done in connection with the commission of that crime; the law is based on public policy. In the present case no duty of care existed between Turner and Ashton during the course of the burglary and the subsequent flight in the get-away car. (2) The maxim *volenti non fit injuria* could on the facts of this case, where two burglars had been drinking and were fleeing in a get-away car, apply to give a complete defence; and this was so despite the Road Traffic Act 1972, s 148(3). (3) If (1) and (2) were wrong the plaintiff would still on the facts be guilty of contributory negligence to the extent of 50%.

PASSENGERS ON PUBLIC TRANSPORT

Driver's duty

Glasgow Corpn v Sutherland
[1951] WN 111, 95 Sol Jo 204, HL
A passenger boarded a tramcar at a stopping place and soon after it moved off a dog which had been running alongside darted in front. The driver applied his magnetic brake and brought the car to a sudden stop. The passenger had not had time to take her seat and was thrown to the ground and injured.
   Per Lord Simonds: It was a question of fact whether the driver had acted with the skill and care of a reasonable driver and the findings showed that he had not. This opinion did not either doubt or affirm *Parkinson's* case, below.

Parkinson v Liverpool Corpn
[1950] 1 All ER 367, [1950] WN 43, 66 TLR 262, 94 Sol Jo 161, CA
The driver of an omnibus applied his brakes with some suddenness to avoid running over a dog. The dog came from the nearside and the driver saw it about 20 yards away. It appeared to be crossing in front of the bus and the driver took his foot off the accelerator and passed behind the dog. Having cleared the bus, the dog suddenly came back across the front of the bus when the driver was some 5 or 6 yards away, whereupon the driver applied

his brakes with some suddenness and stopped the bus. A male passenger aged 65 had risen from his seat to be ready to alight and was walking along the gangway. He was thrown to the floor and broke two ribs. The conductor was also thrown to the floor but the seated passengers were not inconvenienced.

Pritchard J held the test was not whether the driver owed a duty to the dog and a greater duty to the passengers. The test was — Did the driver act reasonably or unreasonably by doing something which a reasonable person would do? The judge held that the driver acted as a reasonable person in an emergency and there was no negligence.

HELD, ON APPEAL: If there had been no explanation there was a prima facie inference of negligence but the driver had given an explanation. The proper test had been applied of an ordinary, reasonable, careful driver. The argument based upon *Sutherland's* case (above) that there was a paramount duty to the passengers and that it is not an answer to say it was to avoid a dog, was not accepted. There were two differences on the facts, (1) the passengers had not had time to get to their seats; (2) it was a case of a magnetic brake on a tramway car which has extremely sudden consequences. Although drivers act instinctively they are required to go through some process of reasoning. The driver's evidence was that he would try to save the animal's life without endangering anybody else. He had applied his mind to the question of endangering anyone else when faced with an emergency of this kind. Appeal dismissed.

Barry v Greater Manchester Passenger Transport Executive
(19 January 1984, unreported: taken from full transcript), CA
As the driver of a bus approached a bus stop where he intended to stop he saw ahead on the pavement three girls with two dogs, one on a lead, the other not. He was driving slowly, at about 15 mph, because he was approaching the stop. Just as he was about to pass the girls and dogs one of the dogs dashed out into the road in front of him. Instinctively he stepped on the brake; the plaintiff passengers who had risen from their seats intending to alight were thrown to the floor and injured. The judge held the driver not to blame: he had acted on instinct — the instinct to preserve life whether of a dog or of a child or of whatever it may be. 'Anybody who had driven for any length of time knows perfectly well that when such an emergency arises you go for the brakes'. It was argued on appeal that the judge should not have equated the attitude of a driver to a dog as it should be to a child; the driver should have taken a conscious decision as he approached the group that if a dog ran out he would drive on rather than risk injuring his passengers.

HELD: This would be a totally unrealistic expectation utterly divorced from the way in which reasonable people conduct their affairs. Three young people and two dogs standing on a pavement do not call for any special adjustment of the driving of a bus. A dog suddenly dashing out is an uncovenanted happening. The judge approached the case on the right lines: the driver was taken by surprise and reacted instinctively. Passengers on public transport take the risk that the driver may effect emergency braking causing inconvenience. Although the facts in *Parkinson's* case (above) were different the judge was right to have regard to that decision as a guide. Appeal dismissed.

Challen v Bell and London Transport Executive
[1954] Times, 6 February (Pilcher J)
A pedestrian stepped in front of an omnibus causing it to stop suddenly. The plaintiff was a passenger and was thereby injured. The plaintiff sued London Transport Executive and the pedestrian. Pedestrian found alone to blame; judgment against pedestrian and for LTE.

Wooller v London Transport Board
[1976] RTR 206, CA
The defendants' bus was being driven along Lewisham Way in the rush hour at about 25 mph. It was about half a bus-length behind a lorry. Some passengers in the bus, of whom the plaintiff was one, were standing ready to get off at a stop 150 yards ahead. Suddenly a pedestrian stepped off the pavement on to a pedestrian crossing in front of the lorry. The lorry pulled up suddenly and the bus driver applied his brakes hard and stopped without hitting the lorry. The plaintiff, who was not holding on, was thrown over by the sudden stop and injured. The judge held the bus driver two-thirds to blame for driving too close to the lorry.
HELD, ON APPEAL: The bus driver was not to blame at all. It was a case like *Parkinson v Liverpool Corpn* (above). The bus was a reasonable distance behind the lorry and the driver was able to pull up in this emergency without hitting it. The suggestion that the bus should keep such a distance from the lorry that it could pull up without having to brake suddenly was a counsel of perfection which ignored modern traffic conditions.

ENTERING VEHICLE

Guinnear v London Passenger Transport Board
(1984) 92 Sol Jo 350, Times, 10 April (Lynskey J)
The plaintiff signalled a Green Line bus to stop at a request stop in Limpsfield. The bus driver slowed down and drew in towards the plaintiff, but signalled to him that he was going to stop farther on. The plaintiff failed to see the signal and attempted to board the bus while it was still moving at 3 or 4 miles an hour. The bus then accelerated and the plaintiff fell from it into a trench, which had been dug in the road just in front of the request stop, and suffered personal injuries.
HELD: The driver of the bus was negligent in accelerating before he had made sure of the plaintiff's safety, and the plaintiff was negligent in boarding a moving bus; each party was equally to blame. Award one-half of assessed damage.

Davies v Liverpool Corpn
[1949] 2 All ER 175, 93 Sol Jo 373, CA
Five women were waiting to board a tramcar at a request stop. Three of them had boarded it and the plaintiff had one foot on the step, when an unidentified and unauthorised passenger rang the bell to restart the car and the plaintiff was injured. The conductor was collecting fares on the upper deck. The judge found that the conductor made no endeavour to come from the top deck for the purpose of restarting the car, and notwithstanding

the number of persons waiting to board it, showed gross indifference to the safety of the passengers. The car was stopped for an appreciable time and the conductor could have come down to see that it was safe, and in breach of his admitted duty and without sufficient excuse was absent from the place where he should have been.

HELD, ON APPEAL: It is desirable, unless there are some special circumstances which make it impracticable or impossible, for the conductor to be on the platform at a stopping place, because he is the only person authorised to give the starting signal. The conductor might reasonably have foreseen such a happening if he did not come down quickly. Appeal dismissed.

Geeves v London General Omnibus Co
(1901) 17 TLR 249, 190 LT Jo 15

A passenger was starting to go upstairs on an omnibus when the conductor asked him whether all was well. The passenger replied, 'Yes, go on.' The vehicle started with a jerk and the passenger fell. The passenger was held entitled to recover.

McLaughlin v Glasgow Corpn
1963 SLT (Sh Ct) 53 (Sheriff Court)

The defenders' bus started as the pursuer was boarding it and before she had reached a position of safety on the platform. A witness said in evidence that the conductress had rung the bell for the driver to proceed, and it was argued for the defenders that it could not be negligent for him to do so.

HELD: A bell from the conductress only authorised the driver to proceed and did not absolve him from a duty to exercise reasonable care. So far as he was able to do so from his position and with the assistance of his mirrors, he must still take care. In any event it had not been established that the bell had been rung and for the bus to start while the pursuer was in the act of boarding was negligent.

Degan v Borough of Dundee
(1940) 190 LT Jo 15

A passenger was thrown off his balance by a number of workmen who boarded an omnibus as he was making his way towards a seat. The court held the bus company not liable. The plea that the presence in an omnibus of 20 or 30 workmen placed on the bus company a duty for special measures of caution by police or a special staff was fantastic.

Note—See also *Glasgow Corpn v Sutherland*, p 191, above.

EN ROUTE

Western Scottish Motor Traction v Allam
[1943] 2 All ER 742, 60 TLR 34, 87 Sol Jo 399, HL

A passenger was standing in a motor omnibus near the doorway which was in the forward part just behind the driver's cabin. The door had not been closed. There were no vacant seats, but he was not holding on to any part of the vehicle. The vehicle was not provided with rails or straps. He was thrown through the doorway into the road while it was being driven round a curve.

HELD: The driver was negligent in driving round the bend at high speed and there was no contributory negligence. The decision was upheld in the House of Lords.

Per Viscount Simon LC: The driver was not entitled to sway round the corner at what speed he liked so long as that speed was safe for passengers who were seated or holding on to some portion of the vehicle. The duty of reasonable care owed by the driver to those on board extends to all passengers whether they are 'holding on' or not. There may well be a case, e g of a person with baby in his arms, where a standing passenger had no free hand with which to hold on.

Wragg v Grout and London Passenger Transport Board
(1966) Times, 22 April, CA

The plaintiff boarded a bus at a request stop and decided to go upstairs. As she was mounting the stairs the conductor rang the bell and the bus started. It had covered about 40 yards and had reached a speed of about 20 mph when on rounding a slight right-hand bend it swayed to the left. The plaintiff had not quite reached the top of the stairs; she was not holding on and fell back down the stairs breaking her leg. The road had a camber so that as the bus started from the bus stop it would tend to be leaning to the left. On passing the mouth of a side road it would straighten up and would sway to the left again after passing the side road and on entering upon the right-hand bend.

HELD: It must be common knowledge that when a bus was being driven in a normal fashion movements of the body of the bus could be felt and that as it went round the bend even at a moderate speed it would not be unusual for it to sway to the left. Anyone standing or just about to sit down would be inconvenienced by the sway and might momentarily lose his balance; that was even more true of anyone mounting the stairs whilst holding two bags in one hand as the plaintiff did and momentarily not holding on to the rail. It was impossible to say that if a person did fall down that that was evidence of negligence against the bus driver. If there was evidence of an extraordinary swerve or sway, that might be evidence of negligence on the basis of *res ipsa loquitur*. *Western Scottish Motor Traction v Allam* (above) was no authority for saying that if there was any movement of the bus while people were standing or walking to their seats it was evidence that the driver was not driving the bus carefully. In the absence of a finding that the driver was driving too fast or that the movement or sway was wholly exceptional there was no ground for holding the driver negligent. *Allam's* case was quite different. In that case the bus was going too fast.

Johnstone v Western Scottish Motor Traction Co Ltd
(1955) 105 L Jo 762, Outer House, Ct of Sess

A man was killed when he was flung through the open door of the defenders' omnibus in which he was travelling as a passenger. The omnibus was a single decker to which access was obtained through a doorway at the front end of the nearside, the open doorway being fitted with a folding door which opened inwards and forwards. When the deceased and his wife (who was the pursuer in this action) entered the bus there was standing room only and the deceased took his position inside the bus but near the doorway. He stood with his back against the forward partition without apparently holding on. About 170 yards from the bus stop the road turned to the left, passed under a railway bridge and then turned to the right. The accident occurred as the bus was emerging from the railway bridge and was steering on a right lock. The pursuer contended inter alia that the fact of the deceased's accidental exit from the omnibus while in motion, being something that did not happen in the ordinary course of things, amounted prima facie to evidence of fault on the part of the defenders and she prayed in aid the maxim *res ipsa loquitur*. Reference was also made to *Western Scottish Motor Traction Co Ltd v Allam.*

In rejecting the contention Lord Walker observed that in the case referred to it was proved independently that the omnibus had been driven at too great a speed. The only useful proposition extractable from the decision related to the standard of care required of a driver. The driver, it was held, must exercise care to avoid ejecting a passenger even although that passenger was standing without holding on. The decision was not, however, in his Lordship's opinion, an authority for the view that the fact of a passenger's accidental exit from an omnibus in motion was prima facie evidence of negligence on the part of the driver or conductor.

Note—See also *Scottish Omnibuses v Wyngrove*, p 199, below.

Shutting door

Adams v Lancashire and Yorkshire Rly
(1869) LR 4 CP 739, 20 LT 850, 17 WR 884
If the passenger's position is one of inconvenience only, where the door of a railway carriage flies open and he is injured trying to shut it, he is not entitled to recover.

Drury v North Eastern Rly Co
[1901] 2 KB 322, 70 LJKB 830, 84 LT 658, Div Ct
A passenger, when the train was stopped at a station and another passenger had alighted, put out his hand and the door of the carriage was shut by a railway servant who came from behind the passenger, and the passenger's hand was injured. There was no indication that the train was about to start and no warning was given before the door was shut.
HELD: No evidence of negligence of railway company.

Door coming open

Easson v London and North Eastern Rly Co
[1944] KB 421, [1944] 2 All ER 425, 170 LT 234, CA
A boy aged four went alone along the corridor of a train and fell through a door which was later found open.

HELD: The principle of *res ipsa loquitur* applied when the thing which caused the accident was at the time wholly under the control of the defendant. The doors of an express train were not continuously under the sole control of the company, and the mere fact that a door came open was not of itself evidence of negligence.

Note—For similar cases see *O'Connor v British Transport Commission* [1958] 1 All ER 558, [1958] 1 WLR 346, 102 Sol Jo 214 and *Inglis v London Midland and Scottish Rly* 1941 SC 551.

ALIGHTING

Holland v North Metropolitan Tramway Co
(1886) 3 TLR 245, 190 LT Jo 15
It is negligence for a tram conductor to start his vehicle whilst a passenger is getting off.

Hall v London Tramways Co
(1896) 12 TLR 611, 190 LT Jo 15
If after a bell is rung, the driver slows down 'almost to a standstill' he is bound to look round and see whether the passenger is safe.

Note—208 LTJ 15 adds that the plaintiff asked the conductor to stop; he rang his bell and went upstairs, but the tram never came to a standstill and the driver accelerated suddenly, jerking the plaintiff off. This was a case of a horse tram. The Court of Appeal said there was no rule that a passenger must sit still until the vehicle actually stops.

Folkes v North London Rly Co
(1892) 8 TLR 269
A passenger who stood by an open door of a tram as it slowed down and was thrown out because it stopped with a jerk was held not entitled to recover.

Note—This case was afterwards doubted but not reversed, 190 LTJ 15.

Baird v South London Tramways Co
(1886) 2 TLR 756, 190 LT Jo 15
A conductor who calls out the name of a stopping place which a tramcar is approaching does not thereby invite a passenger to alight.

Mottram v South Lancashire Transport Co
[1942] 2 All ER 452, 86 Sol Jo 321, CA
About 10.30 pm on 7 September 1941, the plaintiff followed a male passenger down the stairs from the upper deck of a bus to dismount at a request stop. The male passenger rang the bell once, and the bus slowed down, but just as he was getting off, he rang the bell twice (the signal to proceed). The plaintiff proceeded to alight after him but the bus did not

stop and gathered speed, and plaintiff was thrown and injured. The conductress was collecting fares on the upper deck.

HELD: No negligence of conductress; it was putting the duty too high to say that she should go down to the platform to see people off in safety.

Askew v Bowtell
[1947] 1 All ER 883, 63 TLR 316, 91 Sol Jo 249, 45 LGR 476, Div Ct

A tramcar approaching a compulsory stop slowed down to a speed of one mile per hour. An elderly woman, believing the tramcar had come to a standstill, began to alight. The driver did not stop but accelerated, and she was thrown off and injured.

The conductor was on top of the tramcar collecting fares, and was unaware that any passenger wished to alight and took no steps to ascertain.

The police prosecuted the conductor for unlawfully endangering the safety of a passenger through negligence (the Stage Carriage Act 1832, s 48).

HELD: The conductor was entitled to assume that the driver would stop at a compulsory stop, and that passengers would not get off before the tram stopped. Once it had stopped, his duty was not to start again until passengers were safely on or off. The conductor was not negligent. The accident was due solely to the negligence of the driver.

Prescott v Lancashire United Transport Co
[1953] 1 All ER 288, [1953] 1 WLR 232, 97 Sol Jo 64, CA

The plaintiff and her husband were passengers on the defendants' single-decker bus, which was full. All the seats were occupied and some five or eight people were standing. The door was at the front. The husband told the conductor that they wished to alight at the next request stop. The conductor rang the bell and told them to wait until the bus stopped. Owing to road works, marked with red lights, and driving conditions, the bus stopped 20 or 25 yards short of the request stop right into the kerb. Unknown to the driver and conductor, but known to the plaintiff and her husband, it had for some time been customary for other buses to stop for passengers to alight at that point short of the request stop on account of the road works. The plaintiff and her husband assumed the bus had stopped for them to alight. The husband alighted and as the plaintiff was alighting, the bus re-started and the plaintiff was injured. The driver was unaware of the accident. The conductor had closed the door at the previous stop and had not noticed anyone opening the door.

HELD: There was no evidence of negligence of the driver. The conductor was negligent. His statement to the husband to 'wait until the bus stops' was a clear invitation to the plaintiff and her husband to alight when the bus did stop. When the bus stopped short of the request stop, the conductor ought either to have warned the passengers or communicated with the driver. The conductor could see the husband had got off and that there were others waiting to get off.

Adopting the statement of Goddard LJ in *Mottram's* case:

'After the man had given the signal for the bus to stop, and if the bus had stopped, it would have been the duty of the conductress to see that no one else was getting off before giving the signal for the bus to start again. In this case the bus never did stop.

Before it could stop, the officious passenger gave the signal for the bus to start again.

The conductor was negligent and the defendants were liable.

Hett v McKenzie
1939 SC 350
A passenger, while getting out of the rear of a car, put his hand on the pillar between the rear and front door. The driver slammed the front door and injured the passenger's fingers, not knowing they were there. The driver was held liable.

Massie v Edinburgh Corpn
(1950) 100 L Jo 665, Ct of Sess
A man boarded a bus which had a door at the front, and sat beside a friend on the front nearside seat next the gangway. In front of him was a metal shield and an upright stretching to the roof for passengers to hold on to. He got up to leave, holding the upright with his left hand, and, as the bus turned a corner, he fell out of the open door and was killed.
HELD: The conductor was not under an absolute obligation to keep the door shut; he had no reason to anticipate that the deceased might fall through the open door, there being no standing passengers. Nor was there evidence that it should have been apparent to the conductor that the deceased was unwell and might fall. The owners of the bus were under no liability.

Scottish Omnibuses Ltd v Wyngrove
1966 SC (HL) 47
The appellants' bus was of a type having a rear door which gave access from and to a rear platform. The doorway was 3 ft 3 in wide. The door was kept open along parts of the route where stops were frequent. There was no central pillar in the doorway but there were nine handholds available to passengers on the platform. The respondent's husband came on to the platform ready to alight at the next stop. The door was open. There were two handholds on the right but he failed to grasp either and fell out. The bus was being driven smoothly at the time. In the courts below the judges took the view that if there had been a central pillar the accident would have been prevented and the appellants were negligent.
HELD, ON APPEAL: The well established principles of law on the duty of a person towards passengers showed that he must take all precautions for their safety and anticipate such degree of inadvertence on their part as experience showed to be not uncommon. But he was entitled to have regard to his own experience and that of others in a similar situation with regard to what precautions had been found hitherto to be adequate. It was clearly foreseeable that a person leaving his seat in a moving bus may lose his balance and, if near the door, may fall out. The recognised means of enabling him to save himself was to provide handholds, of which there were nine on the platform of this bus. Over a period of years no accident had been attributed to the absence of a central pillar and it would have been unreasonable to fit one. Appeal allowed.

Jude v Edinburgh Corpn
1943 SC 399, Ct of Sess
In an action against the owners and operators of an omnibus service for
damages in respect of injuries sustained through falling from one of their
omnibuses, the pursuer averred that, as the omnibus approached the
stopping place at which she wished to alight, she was standing on the upper
of two steps below the platform, holding the handrail, preparatory to
alighting. Instead of stopping, the omnibus suddenly and without warning
swerved violently, first to the right and then to the left, in order to pass
another omnibus already at the stopping place. As a result of this swerve,
the pursuer was thrown onto the roadway and injured. The conductress,
who saw where the pursuer was standing, did not suggest that she should
leave the step, the stance usually taken by passengers intending to alight,
and the only one from which a notice warning passengers against alighting
before the omnibus stopped was legible.
HELD: That the pursuer's averments disclosed that she had been guilty of
contributory negligence in placing herself in a position of danger on the
step of a vehicle in motion; and action dismissed.

Kilpatrick v Christchurch Tramway Board
[1933] NZLR Supp 170
It had been held in New Zealand that when a vehicle stops between the
fixed stages, this is not necessarily an invitation to alight.

CONTRIBUTORY NEGLIGENCE OF PASSENGER

Davies v Swan Motor Co
[1949] 2 KB 291, [1949] 1 All ER 620, 65 TLR 278, CA
A workman was riding on steps on the offside of his employers' dust lorry,
contrary to regulations. An overtaking omnibus collided with the lorry and
the workman sustained fatal injuries. His widow sued the bus company,
who joined the employers and their driver as third parties. The judge held
the bus company were negligent; that the deceased was not negligent; that
the lorry owners were not liable by reason of the doctrine of common
employment; and that the lorry driver was not liable because deceased was
in the position of a trespasser.
HELD, ON APPEAL: The deceased, the bus driver and the lorry driver,
were all negligent; the bus driver for overtaking on a bend in a narrow lane
without warning and before receiving a signal; the lorry driver for turning
suddenly across the road without making proper use of his mirror and
without giving sufficient warning; the deceased for taking up a dangerous
position by riding on the offside step. The plaintiff contended that the
deceased owed no duty to the bus driver not to stand on the step, and that
the bus driver had the last opportunity of avoiding the accident, and that
the plaintiff's damages should not be apportioned as against the bus
company.
HELD: Deceased owed a duty to the bus driver as his act rendered it more
difficult for the bus to pass and increased the risk of collision (*Donoghue v
Stevenson*), and there was contributory negligence apart from this breach of
duty by failing to exercise reasonable care for his own safety (*Caswell v*

Powell Duffryn Associated Collieries). Last opportunity had ceased to be of any practical effect since the 1945 Act, if it had not ceased to exist before.

Per Bucknill LJ citing Charlesworth on the *Law of Negligence* (2nd edn) p 464, and Atkin LJ in *Ellerman Lines Ltd v Grayson* [1919] 2 KB 514, affd in HL sub nom, *H. & C. Grayson v Ellerman Line Ltd* [1920] AC 466, 123 LT 65:

'The doctrine of contributory negligence cannot, I think, be based upon a breach of duty to the negligent defendant. It is difficult to suppose that a person owes a duty to anyone to preserve his own property. He may not recover if he could reasonably have avoided the consequences of the defendant's negligence.'

Apportionment between plaintiff and defendants; lorry driver four-fifths to blame; deceased one-fifth; of the four-fifths between defendants (adopting that of trial judge) lorry driver two-thirds to blame' bus driver one-third.

Dawrant v Nutt
[1960] 3 All ER 681, [1961] 1 WLR 253, 105 Sol Jo 129 (Stable J)
The plaintiff was a passenger in the side-car of a motor cycle combination driven by her husband when it collided with a car driven by the defendant. The accident happened at a dark part of the road after 9 pm on 30 August. Due to some defect neither the headlight nor the side light on the motor-cycle combination was alight: both the plaintiff and her husband had been aware of this for some time before the collision. The plaintiff was injured and her husband was killed. In actions, heard together, for damages for the plaintiff's personal injuries and as administratrix of her husband's estate for damages under the Fatal Accidents and Law Reform Acts the judge held the defendant and the plaintiff's husband equally to blame for the collision. On the question of the plaintiff's own contributory negligence in knowingly riding in an unlighted vehicle:
HELD: It was sufficient to say that it was unwise of the plaintiff to travel in a motor vehicle which she knew to be improperly lighted. That would not amount to a defence unless there was a legal duty imposed on the plaintiff, vis-à-vis other possible users of the highway, not to do so; in other words, a legal duty to take reasonable care for her own safety. Having regard to *Dann v Hamilton* (see p 42, above) and the reason behind it, the plaintiff did owe a duty and was in breach of it in knowingly travelling in an unlighted combination. But the proportion of negligence to be attributed to the driver and passenger of an unlighted vehicle was not necessarily the same. On the facts of the present case, the plaintiff's share of the blame vis-à-vis the defendant was one-quarter.

Note—G. H. L. Fridman points out (117 NLJ at 1079) that the plaintiff's contributory negligence could not consist in a breach of a duty to other road users not to travel in an unlighted vehicle, for she owed none. It consisted in her disregard for her own safety.
See also *Dann v Hamilton*, p 42, above.

Jones v Livox Quarries
[1952] 2 QB 608, [1952] 1 TLR 1377, 96 Sol Jo 344, CA
A workman in a quarry proceeding to the canteen jumped on the back of a

traxcavator (which did work similar to an excavator) and stood on the towbar at the back holding on to two uprights. In so doing, he was acting in defiance of orders. A dumper ran into the back of the traxcavator and the plaintiff was injured. Hallett J held the driver of the dumper was negligent and plaintiff contributed to extent of 15%. Both parties appealed and both appeals were dismissed.

Per Denning LJ: Contributory negligence depends on foreseeability and the plaintiff must take into account the possibility of others being careless. The consequences did not depend on foreseeability but on causation. The question in every case was: what faults were those which caused the damage? Was the plaintiff's fault one of them? That necessity was shown by the word 'result' in s 1(1) of the 1945 Act. There was no clear guide to causation. It was a matter of common sense depending on the facts. Foreseeability was not the decisive test of causation though it was often a relevant factor. The plaintiff's injury was due in part to the fact that he chose to ride on the towbar instead of walking. His position was similar to that of the plaintiff in *Davies'* case. One of the causes was the plaintiff's negligence in riding on the towbar.

When drivers affected by drink

Note—See *Dann v Hamilton* (p 42, above) and the note following it. See also *Winnik v Dick*, p 40, above.

Owens v Brimmell
[1977] QB 859, [1976] All ER 765, [1977] 2 WLR 943, 21 Sol Jo 338, [1977] RTR 82 (Tasker Watkins J)
The plaintiff and defendant were friends, both about 20 years of age, who at times drank together in public houses and clubs. One evening they went together visiting various public houses and a club, which they left in the defendant's car at about 2 am. But that time each had drunk about eight pints of beer. A short distance from the club the defendant overtook another car and in bringing his car to the nearside lost control and ran into a lamp post. The plaintiff was very seriously injured.
HELD: (1) It must be inferred that the effect of alcohol on the defendant's ability to drive was the cause of his losing control; (2) it was a clear case of contributory negligence on the part of the plaintiff either on the ground that the minds of both parties behaving recklessly were so befuddled by drink as to rid them of clear thought and perception or that the plaintiff should have foreseen the risk of being hurt by riding as a passenger with the defendant. But in such a case the driver, who alone controls the car and therefore has it in him whilst in drink to do great damage must bear by far the greater responsibility. The plaintiff's damages would be reduced by 20%.

Buckingham v D'Souza
18 July 1978, unreported (taken from full transcript)
The plaintiff aged $16\frac{1}{2}$ and the defendant aged 19 went out together for the evening in the defendant's car. Despite his being the younger the plaintiff was the dominant partner in the expedition; they were out to find girls.

After pints of lager in two public houses they went to a dance hall at about 10 pm. Between bouts of dancing they bought drinks and sat at a table drinking. They had further pints of lager as well as vodka and lime. They left the hall at 2 am, two girls in the back of the car. On a clear road with no other traffic present the car, driven by the defendant, ran off the road and overturned: the plaintiff suffered injury causing permanent paralysis below neck level. At about 5.30 am a blood test showed the defendant's alcohol level to be 150 mg. At trial expert evidence was given that it must have been at least 190 at the time of leaving the dance hall.

HELD: The amount the boys had had to drink by the time they left the dance hall was enough to have considerably affected the defendant's ability to drive and for it to be visible to anyone who was watching out for it. A passenger knows, or should know, that any drinking substantially beyond the permitted limit is likely to result in an accident. The plaintiff must bear some responsibility: his damages should be reduced by 20%. If it had been a case of two boys setting out on a pub-crawl a higher degree of contributory negligence would have been appropriate: per Jupp J.

Traynor v Donovan
[1978] CLY 2612 (Sheldon J)

The plaintiff suffered severe injuries when travelling as a front seat passenger in a car driven by the defendant. She had first met him in a public house only half an hour previously. The defendant was found to have a blood/alcohol level of 168 milligrammes but she had not noticed before accepting a lift any sign that his driving ability might be impaired. She called police evidence to confirm that symptoms of such excessive consumption of alcohol were not necessarily apparent to a lay person. There was medical evidence that her injuries had she been wearing a seat belt would have been different but no less serious.

HELD: There should be no deduction for contributory negligence from the plaintiff's damages.

Thomas v Fuller
(7 February 1977 (Cantley J), unreported (taken from full transcript of judgment))

The plaintiff, defendant and a friend spent an evening at a public house drinking. They were all habitual drinkers there, and on this evening, just before Christmas, they drank even more than usual, mainly spirits, amounting to about £45 worth. The plaintiff and defendant in the course of the evening began to think it a good idea to drive to Scotland on the M1. They borrowed the friend's car. They called at the plaintiff's house where they had more to drink and then set off. A few miles along the M1 the car ran into the back of a lorry. Each man said the other was driving: the driver was in fact the defendant. The plaintiff was seriously injured.

HELD: The cause of the accident was drink and the parties were on a drunken frolic. In putting himself as a passenger in a car driven by his drinking companion at the end of such an evening the plaintiff showed recklessness for his own safety. But although it was a joint venture it would be wrong to apportion the damages equally between them. The driver of a car is in control and it is he who is primarily responsible for its being properly driven. A fair adjustment even though this was a bad case of its type would be to hold the plaintiff 25% to blame for his injuries.

Malone v Rowan
[1984] 3 All ER 402 (Russell J)

At about 8.15 pm the defendant was driving his small van with five friends as passengers when he lost control of the vehicle. One of his passengers, the plaintiff's husband, was thrown out and killed. The party had been out since morning. Between 12.30 and 3.30 pm they had been in public houses where the defendant drank four pints of lager: in the evening he had a further three half-pints. A blood-alcohol test showed that at the time of the accident he would have had at least 148 mg per 100 ml of blood. The surviving passengers said in evidence they knew the defendant had been drinking but not how much; they did not consider him unfit to drive and said there was nothing unusual in his manner of driving.

HELD: The facts were far removed from those of *Owens v Brimmell* (above). There was no direct evidence of the deceased's knowledge of what the defendant had consumed or whether he appreciated the risk he was running. The burden of proof was on the defendant. There should be no reduction of damages for contributory negligence.

Meah v McCreamer
[1985] 1 All ER 367, [1985] NLJ Rep 80

The plaintiff was seriously injured when a car in which he was a passenger, driven by the defendant, crashed into a tree. The two men had been out drinking before the accident: the plaintiff ought to have realised that the defendant was unfit to drive. The defendant was tested and found to have excess alcohol in his blood. Subsequently he disappeared and could not be found; his insurers through their solicitor contested the action. They pleaded that the plaintiff was negligent in accepting a lift when he knew the defendant was drunk. It was argued on behalf of the plaintiff that the plea was an admission of a criminal offence on the part of the defendant and that as the solicitor had perforce received no express instructions from him he was not able to make such a plea.

HELD: The insurance policy gave the insurers 'full discretion' in the conduct of proceedings. Although *Groom v Crocker* (p 898, below) showed that a solicitor was nevertheless bound in such case by a general duty to his client it was not inconsistent with that duty to plead contributory negligence. It was merely a plea that if the defendant were found to have been negligent the plaintiff was negligent in accepting a lift: indeed not so to plead would be inconsistent with the duty to the defendant not to incur more damages than justice required. The plaintiff's damages should be reduced by 25%.

SEAT BELTS

Not wearing seat belt

Note—The question whether the omission to wear a seat belt was a reason for reducing a plaintiff's damages was argued in a number of cases heard in courts of first instance and gave rise to considerable conflict of opinion among the judges. The question eventually came before the Court of Appeal in *Froom v Butcher* (below), decided on 21 July 1975. The following are cases at first instance:

Geier v Kujawa
[1970] 1 Lloyd's Rep 364 (Brabin J)
In June 1964 the defendant took the plaintiff, a German girl newly arrived in England, as a passenger in his car. He had had seat belts fitted and wore his. The plaintiff had not seen a seat belt before. Due to the defendant's negligent driving there was a collision with another vehicle and she was injured. He claimed she was negligent in not wearing the seat belt.
HELD: Whatever factors may arise in an appropriate case at a later date this plaintiff was not negligent because it was the first seat belt she had ever seen and the defendant did not explain how to use it.

Damages reduced

Toperoff v Mor
[1973] RTR 419 (Judge Dean QC)
By the defendant's admitted negligence his car, in which the plaintiff was a passenger, overturned and the plaintiff was thrown out, suffering injuries which would probably not have been inflicted if he had been wearing the seat belt. He had worn it at the instance of the defendant (who was wearing his) for 30 miles or so but had neglected to fasten it again after a short stop.
HELD: His damages should be reduced by 25%.

Pasternack v Poulton
[1973] 2 All ER 74, [1973] 1 WLR 476, [1973] 1 Lloyd's Rep 439, QBD
The plaintiff, aged 19, was a front seat passenger in the defendant's car, not wearing a seat belt, when due to his negligence it struck a lamp-post and she sustained facial injuries by being thrown against the windscreen. She knew of the use of seat belts and had used them in other cars but was unaware that there was one available for her in the defendant's car. He had said nothing about seat belts and was not wearing his. The accident took place on a short journey in city streets late at night. Evidence was given by a statistician that the risk of injury was substantially reduced by seat belts and that there was no difference in this respect between accidents occurring within built-up areas and those outside.
HELD: (1) The plaintiff ought reasonably to have foreseen the possibility of the car being involved in an accident and of her suffering injury as a result; (2) she ought to have found out for herself that the seat belt was available; (3) it was known to the plaintiff (as enjoined by the Highway Code) that it was sensible to wear seat belts, (4) there was a clear connection between her failure to wear a seat belt and the injury she suffered; (5) the defendant's duty of care to the plaintiff involved not merely a duty to drive and control the car with reasonable care and skill but also to take some step towards seeing that the plaintiff wore the seat belt; since he did nothing to see that she wore it and was in addition careless in driving and controlling the car by far the greater share of overall blame was his. The plaintiff's damages would be reduced by 5%.

Parnell v Shields
[1973] RTR 414 (Wien J)
The plaintiff's husband was killed when thrown from his van after a collision caused entirely by the defendant's negligence. He was not wearing a seat belt: if he had done so he would probably not have been killed.
HELD: The damages should be reduced by one-fifth. A prudent driver guards against the possible negligence of others. A driver in the position of the deceased need not anticipate folly in every form but likewise he was not entitled to reject all the teachings of recent years about the desirability of wearing a seat belt.

McGee v Francis Shaw & Co Ltd
[1973] RTR 409 (Kilner Brown J)
Plaintiff, riding as passenger in his employer's car was injured in the face and head by striking the windscreen when the car ran into a stationary vehicle. He had travelled in the same car before and worn a seat belt. He did not wear the cross-brace on this occasion because it was uncomfortable. Had he been wearing it he would have sustained no injury at all. Damages reduced by one-third.

Drage v Smith and Drage
[1975] 1 Lloyd's Rep 438 (Stabb J)
The plaintiff suffered bad facial injuries when a passenger in her husband's car. She may have escaped injury if wearing a seat belt. They were on a short journey in town; she wore a seat belt on a long journey but not on a short one because she thought the risk slight.
HELD: A person travelling in a vehicle on a road is inevitably subject to some risk of injury; the plaintiff ought reasonably to have anticipated injury to herself through any negligence on the part of any driver. *Challoner v Williams, Smith v Blackburn, Chapman v Ward* (below) not followed. She knew it would have been wiser to wear a seat belt. Damages reduced by 15%.

Damages not reduced

Challoner v Williams
[1974] RTR 221 (Shaw J)
Plaintiff injured when a passenger in Williams' car (for facts see Court of Appeal decision, p 109, above). The defendants were found not to have proved either that the plaintiff was not wearing a seat belt nor that his injuries would have been worse if he had not. Obiter, it was unreasonable to require someone to take steps to protect himself against a vague and distant contingency; travelling in a car does not yet involve the incidence of imminent risk to life and limb.

Smith v Blackburn
[1974] 2 Lloyd's Rep 229 (O'Connor J)
The plaintiffs, driver and passenger, sustained injuries in a collision

between their car and the defendant's. They were not wearing seat belts. HELD: It was for the defendant to show that if the plaintiffs had been wearing seat belts they would have been less severely injured. He had not discharged the onus. Obiter, the law does not require a driver in Mr Smith's position on a one way flyover driving absolutely normally to foresee that a madman would drive up the flyover in the wrong direction at high speed; the idea that the insurers of a grossly negligent driver should be relieved in any degree from what is proper compensation for the injuries because the occupants were not wearing seat belts is an idea which offends ordinary decency.

Note—Similar views to those expressed in the obiter dicta in the two cases above are to be found in several other decisions at first instance including *Lertora v Finzi* [1973] RTR 16, *Chapman v Ward* [1975] 1 Lloyd's Rep 309 and *Freeborn v Thomas* [1975] RTR 16. They must be taken to have been superseded by the decision in *Froom v Butcher* (below) and the views therein expressed.

The Transport Act 1981, s 27 adds s 33A to the Road Traffic Act 1972, which makes it an offence punishable by fine to drive or ride in a motor vehicle on a road when not wearing a seat belt. Section 28 adds a further section to the 1972 Act numbered 33B making it an offence to drive a motor vehicle on a road when there is in the front of the vehicle a child under the age of 14 years who is not wearing a seat belt. Section 33A provides for regulations to be made excepting from the offence users of delivery vehicles on local deliveries, drivers of vehicles 'while performing a manoeuvre which includes reversing', and any person holding a medical certificate to the effect that it is inadvisable on medical grounds for him to wear a seat belt. Motor Vehicles (Wearing of Seat Belts) Regulations 1982, SI 1982/1203, were made, and came into force on 31 January 1983.

Froom v Butcher

Froom v Butcher
[1976] QB 286, [1975] 3 All ER 520, [1975] 3 WLR 379, 119 Sol Jo 613, CA

A head-on collision occurred, wholly by the negligence of the defendant, between his car and a car driven by the plaintiff. The injuries sustained by the plaintiff included an abrasion of the scalp, fracture of the fourth right rib and fracture of a bone in the right hand. He was not wearing the seat belt fitted in the car for his use. He said he did not like wearing one and had heard of cases where belts had caused danger. The judge held on the medical evidence that the injuries might have been slighter if the belt had been worn; the issue was whether the driver's omission to wear the belt constituted negligence or lack of care. There were two bodies of opinion of which the dominant opinion was that belts should be worn. Nevertheless proper respect should be paid to the minority view; the courts were not justified in invading the freedom of choice of a motorist by holding it to be negligence or lack of care or fault to act on an opinion firmly and honestly held and shared by many other sensible people. The plaintiff's damages should not be reduced ([1974] RTR 528).

HELD, ON APPEAL: The judge's view was not right. In determining responsibility the law took no notice of the views of the particular individual. It required everyone to exercise all such precautions as a man of ordinary prudence would observe. As it is compulsory for every motor car to be fitted with seat belts Parliament must have thought it sensible to wear them. The material before the court about the value of wearing a seat belt showed plainly that everyone in the front seats of a car should wear one. The Highway Code advised wearing them. Wearing them only when there was a high risk as on a motorway in a fog was not enough; every time a car went out on the road there was a risk of accident. Forgetfulness was no excuse but there might be exceptional cases where a person might be excused from wearing a belt — for example, an unduly fat man or pregnant women. Apart from such cases a person failing to wear a seat belt should accept some share of responsibility for the damage if it could have been prevented or lessened by wearing one. The question how much the share should be should not be prolonged by an expensive enquiry into the degree of blameworthiness. If the injuries would have been prevented altogether by wearing a seat belt the reduction should be 25%. If the evidence merely showed that the injuries would have been a good deal less by wearing a belt damages should be reduced by 15%. In the present case 20% would be right. In the case of passengers a driver might have a duty to invite his passenger to fasten the seat belt but adult passengers should know they ought to wear a seat belt without being told.

Patience v Andrews
[1983] RTR 447, CA (Croom-Johnson J)
Where a plaintiff who was not wearing a seat belt suffered injuries the court had to examine the injuries actually suffered, assess compensation and then make a deduction depending on the extent to which those injuries had been caused or contributed to by the failure to wear the seat belt. It was not open to the court to reduce that percentage by speculating upon what other injuries the plaintiff might have suffered had he been wearing a seat belt, otherwise there would be 'an imponderable diminution' of the effect of the rule set out in *Froom v Butcher* (above).

Salmon v Newland
(1983)Times, 16 May (Michael Davies J)
The plaintiff suffered a perforating injury to the right eye resulting in total loss of useful vision in that eye, multiple facial injuries resulting in scarring and a continuing anxiety state. The injuries were sustained in a head-on collision of cars in one of which she was a passenger. She was not wearing a seat belt.
HELD: She was guilty of contributory negligence. Even though there was no medical evidence on the point, her injuries would have been a good deal less severe if she had been wearing one. Although Lord Denning had said in *Froom v Butcher* (above) that 15% was an appropriate reduction in such cases it was not high enough in this case: the reduction should be 20%. Additionally the cost of a convalescent holiday was recoverable in damages when, without it, her general condition might now be a good deal worse. Award for pain suffering and loss of amenity £18,500: loss of future earnings £54,000, special damages £11,414 all subject to 20% reduction for contributory negligence.

An 'exceptional case'

Condon v Condon
[1978] RTR 483 (Bristow J)
The plaintiff, a front seat passenger in the defendant's car, sustained injury to her right eye when the car struck a telephone pole. She was not wearing a seat belt. In a medical report a doctor said she would probably not have sustained such a severe injury had she been wearing a seat belt. The defendant called no evidence on the point. The plaintiff said she could not bear to wear a seat belt because of her fear of being trapped in the event of an accident.

HELD: If the defence wished to rely on a seat belt contributory negligence plea then in the absence of a clear admission it must elicit some evidence at the trial to enable the court to form a conclusion about it. The doctor had not said on what basis he expressed his opinion. On the available evidence it was unlikely that not wearing a seat belt had anything to do with the eye injury at all. Even it if had the damages should not be reduced because the plaintiff's phobia made her an 'extraordinary case' such as Lord Denning had visualised in *Froom v Butcher* (above). Her not wearing a seat belt was not a failure on her part to take reasonable care for her own safety.

No seat belts fitted

Hoadley v Dartford District Council
(1979) 123 Sol Jo 129, [1979] RTR 359, CA
The plaintiff, driving his 1963 Ford van, was injured when it was forced into a lamp post following a collision with the defendant's vehicle. He was awarded damages. The van was not fitted with seat belts as there was no statutory obligation to do so: the relevant Vehicle (Construction and Use) Regulations did not call for seat belts in vehicles registered before 1966. The defendants appealed, contending that the plaintiff ought to have fitted his van with seat belts.

HELD: It would not be right to extend the principle in *Froom v Butcher* (above) to hold that a person was failing to take proper care for his own safety by not having had seat belts fitted to a vehicle in respect of which there was no statutory obligation to do so. *Froom's* case merely applied the principle that the law required everyone to exercise all such precautions as a man of ordinary prudence would observe. Such a man would not necessarily fit a belt to his vehicle when the law did not require that to be done, or not drive his car until seat belts were fitted. Appeal dismissed.

Tripping on seat belt

Donn v Schacter
[1975] RTR 238 (Phillips J)
The defendant's car had seat belts for the front seats, fitted in the usual position on the central door pillar on each side. They were rarely used and were normally left hooked up on each pillar. The plaintiff when being given a lift home by the defendant was travelling in the rear offside seat; at the end of the journey when alighting she caught her foot in the nearside seat belt and fell, sustaining injury.

HELD: The defendant was not liable. On the evidence that the seat belt was probably hooked up the driver was not in breach of duty to the passenger either in allowing it to remain in that condition or failing to warn the plaintiff about it. Even if the belt was not hooked up but was on this isolated occasion lying loose on the floor there was no obligation on the driver to make a visual check or to warn the passenger to make sure the seat belt was satisfactory.

McCready v Miller
[1979] RTR 186, CA
The plaintiff, a woman of 53, travelled home at night in the defendant's minicab. She occupied the rear nearside seat. The car was an ordinary saloon car with a seat belt on the nearside central pillar properly hooked up out of use. When alighting at the end of the journey the plaintiff's left foot caught in the belt and she fell out on to the pavement, breaking her ankle. The street lighting was poor and the interior light of the car was not on. The judge held that the defendant was under no duty to see that the seat belt was not loose or warn the plaintiff or switch the interior light on, but was entitled to assume that a passenger would do what was necessary to avoid the hazard.
HELD, ON APPEAL: This was not right. The driver of a car carrying passengers has a duty to take reasonable care to provide a vehicle which is safe for them when getting into it, riding in it and getting out of it. The duty depends on the circumstances but it cannot be lower than the common duty of care defined in the Occupiers Liability Act 1957, s 2(2) and may be higher on a driver who carries passengers for hire. The decision in *Donn v Schacter* (above) may have been right on the facts but is no authority for saying that the driver's duty does not include a duty to see that the hazard or obstruction caused by a seat belt is avoided or reduced. The defendant was under a duty to reduce the reasonably foreseeable risk by switching on the interior light or by warning the plaintiff or both.

CONTRACTING OUT OF LIABILITY

PUBLIC PASSENGER VEHICLES ACT 1981

29 Avoidance of contracts so far as restrictive of liability in respect of death of or injury to passengers in public service vehicles   A contract for the conveyance of a passenger in a public service vehicle shall, so far as it purports to negative or to restrict the liability of a person in respect of a claim which may be made against him in respect of the death of, or bodily injury to, the passenger while being carried in, entering or alighting from the vehicle, or purports to impose any conditions with respect to the enforcement of any such liability, be void.

1 Definition of 'public service vehicle'   (1) Subject to the provisions of this section, in this Act 'public service vehicle' means a motor vehicle (other than a tramcar) which —
(a) being a vehicle adapted to carry more than eight passengers, is used for carrying passengers for hire or reward, or
(b) being a vehicle not so adapted, is used for carrying passengers for hire or reward at separate fares in the course of a business of carrying passengers.

2 Classification of public service vehicles as stage, express or contract carriages (1) for the purposes of this Act —

(a) a 'stage carriage' is a public service vehicle being used in the operation of a local service.

(b) an 'express carriage' is a public service vehicle being used in the operation of an express service; and

(c) a 'contract carriage' is a public service vehicle being used to carry passengers otherwise than at express fares.

Note—Similar provisions (repealed) were contained in the Road Traffic Acts 1930 and 1960. Compare the Road Traffic Act 1972, s 148(3) (p 213, below).

Note also in the context of the following cases the provisions of the Unfair Contract Terms Act 1977 (p 338, below).

Wilkie v London Passenger Transport Board
[1946] 1 All ER 650, 175 LT 331, 110 JP 215, 62 TLR 327, 90 Sol Jo 249 (Lord Goddard CJ); [1947] 1 All ER 258, [1947] LJR 846, 177 LT 71, 111 JP 89, 63 TLR 115, 45 LGR 170, CA
Plaintiff was a clerk in the employ of the LPTB and was given a free pass for use on their omnibuses. The pass contained the following condition. 'No 6. It is issued and accepted on condition that neither the London Passenger Transport Board not their servants are to be liable to the holder or his or her representative for loss of life, injury or delay or other loss of or damage to property howsoever caused.' The pass was subject to the right of the Board at any moment to cancel it if they thought fit. The condition did not apply in the case of an employee while using the pass in the course of his or her employment or on the business of the Board.

Plaintiff was injured as a passenger whilst on vacation.

HELD: There was no contract and the Road Traffic Act 1930, s 97 (which was in the same terms as the Public Passenger Vehicles Act 1981, s 29 p 210, above) did not apply. The pass was a mere privilege or licence and no part of the plaintiff's contract of employment.

HELD, ON APPEAL: The condition came into operation as soon as the plaintiff began to enjoy any of the benefits and included taking such steps as would enable him to obtain those benefits and included boarding the bus. There was no contractual animus in the pass. It was nothing but a licence subject to a condition and s 97 had no application.

Per Bucknill LJ: There must be some limitation on the wide terms of the condition. It would be reasonable that it should only apply when the pass-holder is using the pass.

Cosgrove v Horsfall
(1945) 175 LT 334, 62 TLR 140, CA
An omnibus driver in the employ of the Board was travelling for his own purposes as passenger on one of the Board's buses with a similar pass. He sued and recovered against the driver. The condition did not avail the driver who was not a party to the contract nor were the Board his agents in making the contract.

Per du Parcq LJ: It is, to say the least, doubtful whether the deposit under s 35(4) of the 1930 Act (now the Road Traffic Act 1972, s 144(1) p 705, below) can be made available to meet the judgment.

Genys v Matthews

[1965] 3 All ER 24, [1966] 1 WLR 758, 110 Sol Jo 332 (Liverpool Court of Passage)

The Liverpool Corporation granted the plaintiff a free pass on Corporation buses on the following conditions: 'The pass is issued and accepted on the understanding that it merely constitutes and grants a licence to the holder to travel on the Liverpool Corporation's buses with and subject to the conditions that neither the Liverpool Corporation nor any of their servants or agents . . . are to be liable to the holder . . . for . . . injury . . . ' The plaintiff was injured when travelling on a Corporation bus due to the negligence of the defendant, the driver of the bus, who was a servant of the Corporation.

HELD: Following *Cosgrove v Horsfall* (above) the defendant was not protected by the terms on which the pass was issued. Even though the pass may be only a licence and not a contract the condition could only be enforced by a party to it. This was the effect of, inter alia, *Scruttons v Midland Silicones* (p 343, below) and *Adler v Dickson* [1955] 1 QB 158, [1954] 3 All ER 397, [1954] 3 WLR 696, 98 Sol Jo 787, [1954] 2 Lloyd's Rep 267, CA

Gore v Van der Lann

[1967] 2 QB 31, [1967] 1 All ER 360, [1967] 2 WLR 358, 110 Sol Jo 928, CA

The plaintiff was an old-age pensioner who had been given a free pass by the Liverpool Corporation to travel on its buses. The defendant was a bus conductor employed by the Corporation. Due to his negligence the plaintiff was injured when boarding a bus. The Corporation intervened in the action claiming an order to stay on the ground that the free pass was issued on the express condition that the Corporation and its servants should be under no liability for injury to the plaintiff.

HELD: (1) The free pass in this case, unlike that in *Wilkie v LPTB* (above) was a contract. It was issued in response to a written application, was couched in the language of contract, calculated to impress upon the plaintiff that she was entering into a legally binding agreement. Consequently the exclusion of liability was void under the Road Traffic Act 1960, s 151; (2) a stay could be granted (under the Supreme Court of Judicature (Consolidation) Act 1925, s 41) only if the prosecution of the action amounted to a fraud on the Corporation either (a) because the plaintiff had agreed with the Corporation for good consideration not to bring the action or (b) because the Corporation would in law be obliged to indemnify the defendant against liability to the plaintiff. As to (a) no express or implied agreement had been made out. As to (b) there was no such legal obligation on the Corporation. They were not entitled to a stay.

Note—The Road Traffic Act 1960, s 151 is repealed and is repeated in the Public Passenger Vehicles Act 1981, s 29. The provisions of the Supreme Court of Judicature (Consolidation) Act 1925, s 41 relating to a stay of proceedings are now contained in the Supreme Court Act 1981, s 49(3).

Mayor v Ribble Motor Services Ltd

(1958) Times, 16 October, CA

A bus conductress was injured whilst a passenger in an omnibus belonging to her employers by the negligence of the bus driver. She was a member of a darts team and was being carried gratuitously subject to the express condition that the employers should be under no duty to carry her with care or safety and were to be free from all liability to her arising from personal injuries or loss or damage to her property, however caused. They had agreed to provide transport for sporting events.

HELD: Section 97 (of the 1930 Act) did not apply, since there was no contract. The document containing the condition used the word 'agreed' but this did not of itself have a contractual import and did not make the document a term of the plaintiff's contract of employment. It merely expressed willingness to provide transport, and was not taking any obligation on itself. The same defence applied to the claim based on the Law Reform (Personal Injuries) Act 1948, s 1(3)

Note—The provisions of the Road Traffic Act 1930, s 97 are now contained in the Public Passenger Vehicles Act 1981, s 29.

Passenger's dependants

Nunan v Southern Rly Co

[1923] 2 KB 703 (Swift J), affd [1924] 1 KB 223, 93 LJKB 140, 130 LT 131, 40 TLR 21, 68 Sol Jo 139, CA

A passenger purchased a workman's ticket containing a condition that the liability of the railway company under any claim to compensation for injury or otherwise is limited to a sum not exceeding £100. The passenger was killed and his widow sued under the Fatal Accidents Acts.

HELD: The right of action under the Acts was a different right of action from that which the deceased would have had if he had survived. It was necessary to show that the deceased would have had certain rights if he had lived. If he had destroyed his cause of action, e g if he had contracted to the effect that no personal injury would give him a cause of action (*Griffiths v Earl of Dudley* (1882) 9 QBD 357, 51 LJQB 543, 57 LT 10), or accepted a sum in settlement of his claim (*Read v Great Eastern Rly Co* (1868) LR 3 QB 555, 37 LJQB 278, 9 B & S 714, 18 LT 822), there is no cause of action. In this case the deceased at the time of his death had a cause of action; there was no bargain as to the rights of his executor or widow. The statute gives the right to the beneficiaries. A bargain made by deceased as to the amount of compensation for personal injury does not affect the claim of the widow to compensation for his death.

EXCLUSION OF PASSENGER LIABILITY INEFFECTIVE

Road Traffic Act 1972, s 148(3)

148 Avoidance of certain exceptions of policies or securities and of certain agreements, etc, as to risks required to be covered thereby (3) Where a person uses a motor vehicle in circumstances such that under s 143 of this Act there is required to be in force in relation to his use of it such a policy of insurance or security as is mentioned in subs (1) of that section, then, if any other person is carried in or upon the vehicle while the user is so using it, any antecedent agreement or understanding between them (whether intended to be legally binding or not) shall be of no effect so far as it purports or might be held —

(a) to negative or restrict any such liability of the user in respect of persons carried in or upon the vehicle as is required by s 145 of this Act to be covered by a policy of insurance; or

(b) to impose any conditions with respect to the enforcement of any such liability of the user;

and the fact that a person so carried has willingly accepted as his the risk of negligence on the part of the user shall not be treated as negativing any such liability of the user.

For the purposes of this subsection references to a person being carried in or upon a vehicle include references to a person entering or getting on to, or alighting from, the vehicle, and the reference to an antecedent agreement is to one made at any time before the liability arose.

Note—This subsection is operative from 1 December 1972. It re-enacts the Motor Vehicles (Passenger Insurance) Act 1971, s 1(2) which did not come into force. As the first words of the subsection show, it applies only in circumstances in which compulsory insurance against passengers claims is required by s 143(1) (p 704, below). Section 145 (p 742, below) requires the user of a vehicle to be insured in respect of liability for the death of or bodily injury to any person caused by the use of the vehicle on a road (as defined in s 196 of the Act (p 733, below)), other than persons in the employment of the insured where the death or bodily injury arose out of and in the course of that employment. See pp 743–749, see also *'Passenger: exclusion notice'*, p 46, above.

In *Gregory v Kelly* (p 25, above) a defence of *volenti* was raised. Kenneth Jones J said 'I can deal with that very shortly because it is now agreed between counsel, as I understand it, and I certainly so judge, that s 148(3) of the Road Traffic Act 1972 has the effect of depriving the defendant of that defence'. In *Ashton v Turner* (p 191, above) Ewbank J declined to accept that the subsection deprived the owner of the car of the defence of *volenti* having regard to the special facts of that case, namely 'two burglars who had been drinking and were fleeing in a getaway car'.

See also *Winnick v Dick*, p 40, above.

CHAPTER 5
Lighting of vehicles

LIGHTS ON VEHICLES

Parking without lights

Note—As from 30 April 1972 all rules and regulations relating to parking without lights were standardised throughout the whole of Britain. Cars, motor cycles and goods vehicles under 20 cwt unladen weight may be parked without lights on roads provided that:
(1) the road is subject to a speed limit of 30 mph or less;
(2) the vehicle is parked close to the kerb and parallel to it, and, except in one-way streets, with its nearside to the kerb; and
(3) no part of the vehicle is within 10 metres of a road junction.
The current regulations are the Road Vehicles Lighting Regulations 1984, SI 1984/812, reg 21(2).

Lighting-up time

Note—For the lighting-up time at any particular place and date, apply to Royal Greenwich Observatory, Hurstmonceux, Nr Hailsham, Sussex.

No civil remedy for breach

Clarke v Brims
[1947] KB 497, [1947] 1 All ER 242 (Morris J)
On the night of 14 October 1944, the plaintiff was driving his car along the Colnbrook By-pass when he ran into the back of the defendant's car, which was stationary without rear lights on the nearside. The defendant was changing the nearside front wheel of his car. The defendant's car had been overhauled shortly before. It was a very dark night and black-out restrictions were in operation. The plaintiff was driving with side-lights and a regulation masked headlamp.

215

The judge found that the rear lights of the car were on when the defendant stopped his car and walked round it to find the trouble, but between that time and the moment of impact, the rear lights for some reason failed. HELD: (1) In the circumstances the fact that the rear lights were not lit could not be imputed to the defendant as negligence; (2) the defendant was not liable on the basis of causing a nuisance; (3) the plaintiff was not guilty of negligence; and (4) the breach of the Road Transport Lighting Act 1927 did not give a right to damages for breach of statutory duty.

Claim and counter-claim dismissed and no order as to costs. *Phillips v Britannia Co* and *Badham v Lambs* followed.

Note—See Regulations, p 244, below; 'Nuisance on highway', p 309, below. See also *Balmer v Hayes*, noted at p 38, above.

Checking lights

Sieghart v British Transport Commission
(1956) 106 L Jo 185 (Finnemore J)
On a dark and rainy night the defendants' driver stopped his lorry for the purpose of adjusting his windscreen wiper. He stopped on a straight length of road with a visibility of not less that 20 to 30 yards and parked correctly on his nearside. The driver did not know and had no reason to suspect that at the time his rear lamp was unlit. The lorry had been checked at the depot a few miles back. Having glanced in both directions and seen that no traffic was approaching the driver descended from his cab. As he reached up to move the windscreen wiper, the car driven by the male plaintiff struck the back of the lorry and he and his wife, the second plaintiff, received injuries. HELD: The statement regarding stopping at night in the Highway Code (p 65 in 1978 edn) 'see that your side and tail lamps are alight' did not require that a driver who was stopping only for a minute or two and had no reason to suspect that his lamps were not alight should, immediately he stopped, examine the vehicle's rear lights, and that in the circumstances the lorry driver was not guilty of negligence and had not created a nuisance on the highway. Judgment for defendants.

Headlights not dipped

Saville v Bache
(1969) 113 Sol Jo 228, Times, 28 February, CA
The first defendant was driving along an unlighted B road at night, using dipped headlights. The second defendant was approaching in the opposite direction, also on dipped headlights. When he was about 100 yards from the first defendant he (as the judge found) turned his headlights on to main beam. The first defendant was dazzled and collided with the plaintiff whom he had not seen and who was standing with his bicycle at the side of the road. The second defendant denied that he had put his headlights on full beam: he said they were dipped all the time. The judge, rejecting his evidence, held him one-third to blame. HELD: Dismissing his appeal, it was good manners and good driving to approach another vehicle with headlights dipped. There could be circumstances when a driver had to put his lights on full beam but the second

defendant was negligent unless he had a good reason for doing so. He had not given a reason; he had merely denied it.

Headlights in fog

Burgess v Hearn
(1965) Guardian, 25 March, CA
The plaintiff, riding a motor cycle combination, was injured when he collided with the offside wing of the defendant's car, which was travelling in the opposite direction. The accident happened in thick fog with visibility of 10 to 15 yards. The plaintiff was travelling at 25 mph and the defendant at 15 mph. The plaintiff had a dipped headlight on but the defendant was showing sidelights only. There had been a collision shortly before on the plaintiff's side of the road between a van and a car. The plaintiff ignored the wave of a man who had come to wave people down and had to swerve round the car and then pass the van. It was at this point when the bulk of his motor cycle was on the wrong side of the road that he saw the defendant's car at very short range. The judge found the parties equally to blame, holding the defendant negligent for not having his headlights on and the plaintiff for his speed and for blindly pulling out on to the wrong side of the road.
HELD, ON APPEAL by the defendant: (1) The judge was justified in finding the defendant negligent in not having dipped headlights on. Paragraph 111 of the Highway Code (1978) recommended headlights in mist or fog and though not of statutory force it was of assistance in assessing proper road usage. Moreover there was evidence that it was police policy to use headlights in fog and other road users at the trial had said they were using dipped headlights. But (2) even if the defendant had had his headlights on it would not have prevented the accident since the vehicles were so far apart when the plaintiff pulled out on to the wrong side of the road that he would not have been able to see the headlights. Appeal allowed.

Note—The use of headlamps in poor daytime visibility is now compulsory. See Road Vehicles Lighting Regulations 1984, SI 1984/812, regs 21(1) and 22(1)(b). Conditions adversely affecting visibility include 'fog, smoke, heavy rain or spray, snow, dense cloud'.
   The use of sidelights only is not a compliance with the regulations: see *Swift v Spence* [1982] RTR 116.

Parked with headlights on

Chisman v Electromotion (Export) Ltd
(1969) 113 Sol Jo 246, CA
In the hours of darkness on a straight main road the defendant's lorry was parked on the wrong side of the road with its headlights on. It was visible 700 yards away. The plaintiff driving a mini struck the lorry full tilt. The judge said it was a case of almost maximum negligence on the part of both parties and apportioned liability equally.
HELD, ON APPEAL: The court declined to alter the judge's decision. The attempt to plead that the plaintiff should be found wholly to blame was just one more attempt to bring into the law the doctrine of last opportunity. The court would decline to administer the kiss of life to that doctrine. To put a

lorry with its lights on on the wrong side of the road was plain and obvious negligence. There was also negligence on the part of the plaintiff. The court had the power to apportion the damages if it was satisfied that the apportionment was wrong but started with the presumption that the judge was right. In this case he was.

Stationary lorry on clearway

Butland v Coxhead
(1968) 112 Sol Jo 465, Times, 8 May (Browne J)
The plaintiff, a learner, was riding a scooter on a clearway on the main London-Portsmouth road in the hours of darkness when he ran into the back of the defendants' stationary lorry. The lorry had broken down and could not be moved. Before the plaintiff's accident another vehicle had collided with the lorry's offside rear and damaged the rear lamp, but the lamp had been repaired and when the plaintiff ran into the lorry both rear lamps were on and visible from a reasonable distance.
HELD: The defendants were not liable. Though a stationary lorry, even with normal tail lights, was a danger to traffic on a fast road and on a bad night, the lorry could not move after it had broken down and the defendants were not negligent in not parking in a side road or on the verge. There was no evidence of a practice among lorry owners to provide torches or flashing lamps. The case of *Moore v Maxwells* (p 220, below) was stronger than the present case. It would be a very good thing if heavy lorries were required to carry some form of warning lamp but no regulation existed to that effect; there was no negligence on the part of the defendants.

UNLIGHTED VEHICLES

Cases before Law Reform (Contributory Negligence) Act 1945

Note—Before 1945 contributory negligence was a complete defence to a claim for damages in negligence. Since the Law Reform (Contributory Negligence) Act 1945 most claims arising from collisions with unlighted vehicles have been treated as cases for apportionment of blame. See *Henley v Cameron* (p 219, below) *Hill-Venning v Beszant* (p 219, below) and *Harvey v Road Haulage Executive* (p 221, below). The pre-1945 decisions digested in earlier editions of this work, including such cases as *Baker v Longhurst*, *Tart v Chitty* and *Ware v Garston Haulage Co* must now be regarded as obsolete.

Unlighted vehicle not a nuisance

Maitland v Raisbeck
[1944] KB 689, [1944] 2 All ER 272, 113 LJKB 549, 171 LT 118, 60 TLR 521, CA
On a dark night a motor omnibus overtook and collided with a lorry which was moving slowly. The rear light of the lorry had gone out. The driver had had the tail light attended to and it was working all right when he first put the lights on, and he was unaware that it had gone out. A passenger in the omnibus brought proceedings against the owners of both vehicles. The

county court judge found that the omnibus driver had not been negligent, and that the lorry owners and their driver had not been guilty of negligence or nuisance.

HELD: If the driver of a vehicle was exercising due care and something happened to him which caused an obstruction to the highway but was in no way referable to his fault, that did not ipso facto and immediately create a nuisance. A nuisance would be created if an obstruction was allowed for an unreasonable time or in unreasonable circumstances, but the mere fact of an obstruction did not create a nuisance. That depended on the facts of each case. The driver of a vehicle is not an insurer of latent defects. Accidents happened on highways when both parties had been reasonable and a person injured must put up with it.

Note—See also *Dymond v Pearce*, p 311, below.

Cases after 1945 Act

FAILURE OF LIGHTS

Henley v Cameron
[1948] WN 468, [1949] LJR 989, 65 TLR 17, CA
Defendant's car ran out of petrol on the road from Market Drayton to Newcastle about midnight. By 1 am the batteries had run down and there were no lights on the car. The road was 19 feet wide with 3 inch kerb and a 5 feet grass verge in a cutting with hedges and trees 15 feet high. The car was left with its rear near wheel close to the kerb and front near wheel about 1 foot out, the front wheels being turned in slightly to the off. There was a turning into a lane 20 or 30 yards away. Lighting up time was 4.20 pm to 7.50 am. At about 6 am deceased riding a motor cycle combination collided with the car. A police officer said the car could have been placed in the mouth of the lane or on the verge. Henn Collins J found the deceased alone to blame.

HELD, ON APPEAL:

Per Tucker LJ: Defendant was negligent in leaving the car unlighted in that position in the hours of darkness when it could have been moved, and the car constituted a nuisance. The absence of a light was prima facie a cause contributing to the accident. The fact that a car driver runs into a stationary unlighted vehicle does not establish that he is solely to blame. It is a question of fact depending on the particular circumstances.

Per Singleton LJ: There was evidence of two witnesses of the difficulty of seeing a car in that position. The negligence of both continued up to the time of the accident.

HELD by a majority: defendant two-thirds; deceased one-third to blame.

Hill-Venning v Beszant
[1950] 2 All ER 1151, [1950] WN 538, 66 (Pt 2) TLR 921, 94 Sol Jo 760, CA
A motor cyclist was riding along the road from Guildford to Farnham when his lights failed. He thought it would only mean changing the bulb in the headlight, but discovered that the tail light was also out, and that there was

a fault in the electric wiring. Still thinking the fault could be quickly repaired, he did not move his motor cycle, which was standing with its offside some three feet from a wide grass verge. The road was wide and straight and he would have had no difficulty in removing it on to the verge which was level with the highway. While repairing the wiring, he observed some five minutes after stopping, the light of a vehicle coming from behind, which was a dipped headlight of the plaintiff's motor cycle. The plaintiff failed to see the defendant's motor cycle in time to avoid it. It was not disputed that the plaintiff was negligent, but the plaintiff contended the defendant was negligent in not removing the motor cycle on to the grass verge and leaving an obstacle on the road. Parker J held the defendant had not been guilty of negligence.

HELD, ON APPEAL:

Per Cohen LJ: It might not have been negligent not to have moved the motor cycle merely to change the bulb, but when he found the breakdown in the electric wiring, it was his duty to move it on to the grass verge, and when he saw a light and knew a vehicle was coming, he should have taken the precaution of moving it off the road. A court has to be very careful before taking the view that there is no negligence in leaving an obstacle on the road after lighting up time when it is not plainly visible to approaching vehicles without the aid of full headlights and when it could easily be moved off the road. I think the defendant was responsible to the extent of one-third.

Per Denning LJ: It is clear beyond controversy that his unlighted motor cycle was a danger on the road. Any unlighted bicycle on a fast motor road is a danger to traffic. This is a proposition not of law, but of common sense. It is prima facie evidence of negligence and the onus is on him to show it came to be unlighted and why he could not move it out of the way or give warning to on-coming traffic. I should have been inclined to apportion the responsibility two-thirds to the unlighted vehicle as in *Henley v Cameron*, but in deference to my brothers I do not dissent from the proportions suggested by Cohen LJ.

Appeal allowed.

Moore v Maxwells of Emsworth Ltd

[1968] 2 All ER 779, [1968] 1 WLR 1077, 112 Sol Jo 424, CA

On a clear evening in the hours of darkness the defendants' lorry was being driven along an unlit dual-track road by their driver when a passing motorist signalled that there was something wrong. The driver stopped at the nearside of the road and found his rear light was out. In checking whether a plug was connected he fused all the obligatory lights. He began to repair the plug whilst his mate stood at the back of the lorry to warn approaching vehicles. The plaintiff driving a chassis failed to see the lorry until too late and crashed into the back of it. The defendants' driver had checked his lights before starting the journey and again at lighting-up time and found them working properly.

HELD: The defendants were not liable. The presence of an unlighted vehicle on the highway called for an explanation from the defendants and to that extent the onus of proof was on them, but the driver had given an explanation, namely, the failure of the lighting system. There was no further onus of proving regular servicing of the vehicle. Nor were the defendants negligent in not supplying torches or flashing warning lights, there being no evidence that it was customary to do so. The driver was not negligent in not driving on to the verge as it was soft and the lorry heavy. He acted reasonably in assuming it would not take long to mend the fuse rather than drive on with no lights to a place where there was street lighting.

Note—See also *Brown v Thompson* p 24, above and *Parish v Judd*, p 225, below. And see *Jordan v North Hampshire Plant Hire*, p 223, below.

Lee v Lever
[1974] RTR 35, CA
The plaintiff's car developed an electrical fault and as a result came to a stop at night by the nearside verge (to which the plaintiff had steered it) of a well-lighted road which was a clearway. There were no lights on the car; he took the battery to a garage on the other side of the road for recharging. Twenty minutes later the defendant driving his car at about 30 miles an hour did not see the plaintiff's car in time and crashed into the back of it. The county court judge held the plaintiff wholly to blame: he said the plaintiff had not discharged the onus of proof placed on him by Denning LJ's ruling in *Hill-Venning v Beszant* (quoted above).
HELD, ON APPEAL: The plaintiff was negligent in failing to borrow a red lamp from the garage to put by his car and perhaps (as the county court judge held) for failing earlier to see the warning red light on the dashboard and failing to push the car on to the verge; but the defendant was also to blame for not seeing the plaintiff's car in time to pull up. The proper proportions of blame were 50–50.

Per Buckley LJ: I do not think normal experience leads one to the conclusion that it is safe to assume that no one will ever park in a part of the roadway which is classified as a 'Clearway', and it is incumbent upon every user of such a roadway to drive in a way which enables him to meet an emergency or hazard presented by the fact that someone has parked — it may be for unavoidable reasons, such as a breakdown — in the 'Clearway'.

Ill-lit lorry across highway

Harvey v Road Haulage Executive
[1952] 1 KB 120, 95 Sol Jo 759, CA
On a foggy morning in November 1949, shortly after sunrise, the defendants' lorry, 22 feet long and 7 feet wide was towed from a car park on to the highway in order to start the engine. The towing vehicle left, and the lorry remained standing with the engine running for about five minutes to warm up. The road was 30 feet wide, divided into three 10 foot strips by two white lines. The lorry was on the slant athwart the road, the near rear wheel being 5 feet from the nearside kerb, the near front wheel 7 feet from this kerb and the off front wheel 14 feet out into the road nearly half-way across, straddling across the nearside white line. Visibility only extended to 11 or 12 yards. The plaintiff riding a motor cycle at 18 or 20 mph along the nearside white line, came from behind, saw the lorry when within 11 or 12 yards and thought it was moving. It was impossible to overtake it on the offside, since he could not see a clear way through on-coming traffic. There

was a dispute whether the red rear light was on, and without coming to a firm conclusion, the judge assumed the light was on. Slade J found the plaintiff was driving too fast in the fog and that he was also negligent in failing to avoid the impact when he had seen the lorry. He made no finding whether the lorry driver was also at fault in leaving the lorry in a dangerous position athwart the road. Assuming he was, this had created a static position which the plaintiff could have avoided. He dismissed the action. HELD, ON APPEAL: The lorry driver was at fault. He ought to have brought the lorry wholly within the nearside lane. The finding below seemed a reversion to the doctrine of 'last opportunity' which was obsolete. If a motorist saw an obstruction on the road and purposely and recklessly ran into it, he could not recover, but if he were merely negligent in not taking steps to avoid it, the damage was the result partly on his own fault and also partly the fault of the person leaving the obstruction on the road. Both parties were equally to blame.

Barber v British Road Services
(1964) Times, 18 November, CA
The defendants' driver, stopping at a lorry driver's cafe on the Oxford-Banbury road at 3 am on a dark and rainy morning, decided to turn his lorry round and back it into the car-park. The lorry was 30 feet long and the road 32 feet wide. The manoeuvre took one and a half minutes and involved having the lorry at right angles covering the whole road in both directions. Whilst the lorry was across the road the plaintiff driving a lorry from Banbury failed to see it in time and crashed into it, sustaining serious injuries. The judge of assize held that the defendants' driver was not negligent.
HELD, ON APPEAL: If at night there was an obstruction across a fast main road, that was prima facie evidence of negligence and it was up to the person who put it there to explain how it came there without negligence. The defendants' driver had not given any sufficient explanation. The length of time required to reverse a lorry of this size made the manoeuvre inevitably dangerous. The defendants were not entitled to assume that any person driving along that road at that time of the night would be driving at a moderate speed and keeping a good look out. Permanent lights showing sideways were contrary to the law but some temporary lateral light could have been shown either by torches carried by someone from the café or at the side of the vehicle. Blame should be apportioned as to two-thirds to the plaintiff and one-third to the defendants.

Rouse v Squires
[1973] QB 889, [1973] 2 All ER 903, [1973] 2 WLR 925, 117 Sol Jo 431, CA
On the M1 motorway at night an articulated lorry driven by Allen got out of control and came to a stop in a position blocking the middle and fast lanes. A car collided with it in the centre lane and remained there with rear lights on. Another lorry stopped in the nearside lane short of Allen's lorry with its headlights on to illuminate the stationary vehicles. Squires then came along driving his employer's lorry; he saw the vehicles ahead when 400 yards away but did not realise two lanes were obstructed. At 150 yards

away he saw the vehicle in the nearside lane, braked and moved into the centre lane. He then realised that lane was also blocked; he applied the brake harder, went into a skid and hit the lorry on the nearside, killing the plaintiff's husband who was standing in front of it. The judge held Squires wholly to blame; the fact that Allen caused an obstruction was not, bearing in mind the circumstances, a factor which contributed to the fatal accident. HELD, ON APPEAL: There was no break in the chain of causation between the negligent driving of Allen and the death of the plaintiff's husband. If a driver so negligently manages his vehicle as to obstruct the highway and constitute a danger to other road users including those who are driving too fast or not keeping a proper look-out (but not those who deliberately or recklessly drive into an obstruction as in *Dymond v Pearce* (p 311, below)) then the first driver's negligence may be held to have contributed to the causation of an accident of which the immediate cause was the negligent driving of a vehicle which collided with it. Where a party guilty of prior negligence has created a dangerous situation which is still continuing to a substantial degree at the time of the accident which would not have happened but for the continuing danger he is responsible as well as the party subsequently negligent. *Harvey v Road Haulage Executive* (p 221, above) and *Barber v British Road Services* (p 222, above) followed. Allen held 25% to blame.

Jordan v North Hampshire Plant Hire Ltd
[1970] RTR 212, CA

After a stop at a café on the west side of a fast and busy main road in the hours of darkness the defendants' driver wished to resume his journey south. The lorry was an articulated vehicle 35 feet long. It had a flashing light on the cab roof but no other lights showing to the side. There were three reflectors on the side of the trailer. The driver had to drive slowly across the road which had double white lines in the middle and then turn right using the grass verge on the other side to get enough room to make the turn. The manoeuvre would take 10 to 15 second during which the lorry would block the carriageway. The plaintiff, driving his car from the south at about 60 mph approached the scene round a slight left hand bend which limited visibility to about 300 yards. He failed to see the lorry in time and struck the back end of the trailer. The county court judge found the two drivers equally to blame. The defendants appealed. HELD, BY THE COURT OF APPEAL: (1) It was quite wrong for the defendants' driver to have pulled into a café on his offside of the road when the curve was such that only rarely, if at all, could he pull out again without creating grave risks; (2) the lorry was quite insufficiently lit to give proper warning to a driver coming from the south. The flashing light might confuse, and at the time of the accident was in the other traffic lane; the three reflectors had swung round by the time the plaintiff arrived and would not show, and there was no other light which showed; (3) the lorry driver's mate could have flashed a torch as a warning. There have been changes in outlook since *Moore v Maxwells* (above) and the defendants were negligent in not using warning lights in such circumstances as the present. The appeal was hopeless. The plaintiff (who had not cross-appealed) was unlucky to have had his damages docked by as much as one-half.

Note—Barber v BRS (above) was not cited.

Lancaster v H. B. and H. Transport Ltd

[1979] RTR 380, CA

The defendants' driver had to deliver a lorry load of potatoes to a farm on the east side of the A1 road. To do so he came to the A1 from the west on a side road and wished to cross to a road on the opposite side of the double carriageway. It was early on a February morning, still getting light. Mist reduced visibility to between 50 and 100 yards; the roadway was wet. The articulated lorry had its headlights on but only a small marker light and orange reflector on the side. It crossed the north-bound carriageway and stopped in the intersection to allow cars to pass before starting to cross the southbound carriageway. When he started forward the driver could see no headlights to his left but when part-way over he saw the headlights of a car approaching at quite a fast speed. He thought it best to continue; the car did not stop but crashed into and underneath the trailer. It left no brake marks. The car driver was killed. The lorry would take 12 seconds to cross the carriageway. The judge at first instance considered the lorry driver not to blame.

HELD, ON APPEAL: The lorry driver was negligent in taking the lorry across the A1 in such poor conditions of visibility. He knew that vehicles coming towards him and which he could not see — even 150 yards away at 30 mph — would be on him before he could get clear of the carriageway. He could have found out, had he asked, that he could cross the A1 by slip roads and a bridge a couple of miles to the north. Allegations of contributory negligence on the grounds of excessive speed and the car driver's failure to brake were not adequately established by the defendants' evidence. It was too much to expect of the car driver that he should realise that disembodied headlights passing from the right to left across his front indicated no less than 50 feet of a slow moving vehicle blocking the carriageway.

Unlighted vehicle on road: duty of care

Hill v Phillips

(1963) 107 Sol Jo 890, CA

The plaintiff was injured when a car in which she was a passenger collided with a stationary trailer during the hours of darkness. The trailer had broken down and had been pushed by the driver of the towing lorry on to a 4 ft 6 in grass verge. As the trailer was 8 feet wide it protruded 3 ft 6 in into the roadway. The lorry driver had gone in the lorry to find a garage and left the trailer unlighted. The driver of the car, driving with dipped headlights at 30 mph, did not see the trailer until he was a car's length away. The judge held the lorry driver wholly to blame, saying that a motorist was not negligent if he did not see what was not visible.

On appeal, the drivers were held equally to blame. The car driver was plainly negligent in failing to keep a proper look-out. When driving with dipped headlights in country roads motorists should drive so that they could see unlighted obstructions. Although unlighted obstructions should not be on country roads their presence was to be anticipated, eg cyclists without lights or men in dark clothes.

The lorry driver was negligent in leaving an unlighted obstruction which was a danger to oncoming traffic. He should have done something to illuminate the trailer; he could have left the lorry behind it with the lights on. It might be that drivers of heavy lorries should have lamps with them as a precaution in case their lights failed.

Parish v Judd
[1960] 3 All ER 33, [1960] 1 WLR 867, 124 JP 444, Sol Jo 664, CA

On a dark night at about 10 pm the defendant was driving along a main road when without negligence on his part the lighting system of his car failed completely. A passing lorry stopped and the driver offered him a tow to a service station. The defendant accepted and the lorry began to tow the defendant's car. Before reaching the service station the lorry driver stopped to see if the defendant was all right. He chose a place just beyond a street lamp, which illuminated the rear of the defendant's car. When the two vehicles had been stationary about a minute a car driven by the plaintiff's husband ran into the back of the defendant's car and the plaintiff, who was a passenger, was injured.

HELD: (1) The mere fact that an unlighted vehicle is found at night on a road is not sufficient to constitute a nuisance; there must also be some fault on the part of the person responsible for the vehicle; (2) the presence on a dark road at night of a wholly unlit vehicle is prima facie evidence of negligence on the part of the person responsible for the vehicle; (3) the whole basis of the claim, both in negligence and in nuisance, must be the existence of danger. On the facts, no danger was presented by the presence of the defendant's motor car on that road at that place at that time.

Fotheringham v Prudence
[1962] CLY 2036, CA

The defendant was driving a lorry after dark when a wheel came off. He had to draw in on the nearside of the road just past a bridge. There were no rear lights on the lorry and no reflectors. The nearest street lamp was 12 yards away on the other side of the road. The plaintiff riding a motor cycle at 10 to 12 mph ran into the back of the stationary lorry and was injured. Elwes J found the defendant wholly to blame. The Court of Appeal refused to disturb the finding: there was ample evidence of negligence and causation and the plaintiff was not guilty of contributory negligence.

Drew v Western Scottish Motor Traction Co
1947 SC 222

On a dark morning in December, just before daybreak and the end of lighting-up time, a bread van was delivering bread at a shop situated on a main road in a built-up area. The van was drawn up facing west close to the south kerb. Although its rear lamp was lit, it was completely obscured by the lower half of the open back door which folded downwards. An omnibus coming from the east ran into the back of the van and inflicted fatal injuries on a boy who was unloading bread. The court found the owners of the omnibus to blame in respect that their driver had failed to maintain a proper look-out, and the van owners in respect that they had allowed their vehicle to be on the road during lighting-up time with a rear light which was invisible; proportions 50–50.

Hannam v Mann
(1984) RTR 252, CA

The plaintiff, riding a motor cycle in the hours of darkness, followed a car out of a side road turning left into a well-lit major road. When in the major road the car's offside traffic indicator light came on. The plaintiff, watching the car and thinking it about to turn right, took his eyes momentarily off the road ahead and crashed into the defendant's car parked without lights against the nearside kerb. The car driver was not turning right; he was merely indicating to show that he was moving out to pass the defendant's car. Although the defendant's car was illuminated by a street lamp opposite it was illegally parked since it was only 5 yards from a road juction, contrary to the Road Vehicles Lighting (Standing Vehicles) (Exemption) General Regulations 1975, reg 4. The judge found the defendant 25% to blame on the ground that if the rear lights of his car had been on they might just have drawn the plaintiff's attention to the car and enabled him to avoid it. The defendant appealed.

HELD: The appeal should be dismissed. The car, unlit and in the position where it was, constituted a nuisance. The judge had asked himself the right question, would the accident have been avoided if the car had been lit? He was entitled to draw the inference that it might and it would be wrong to interfere with that decision or, in the Court of Appeal, to alter the assessment of the degree of blame.

Young v Chester
[1974] RTR 70, CA

The defendant was driving his car on a fast, wide road at night when the engine stopped and he came to a standstill by the nearside verge but not on it. He then attempted to re-start the engine by operating the self-starter. The plaintiff driving his van in the nearside lane from the same direction at 45 to 50 mph saw the two rear lights of the defendant's car when he was about 400 yards away and they seemed to him to disappear. He thought the car must have turned off on to a slip road. He did not see it again until he was quite close. He applied his brakes heavily but struck the car, pushing it 57 feet. The judge concluded that the apparent disappearance of the car's rear lights was due to the defendant's use of the self-starter, causing the lights to dim or go out and that the defendant was 60% to blame.

HELD, ON APPEAL by the defendant: The judge was entitled to find as he did.

PROSECUTIONS

Jarvis v Fuller
[1974] RTR 160, Div Ct

The defendant was driving in the dark at about 50 mph with dipped headlights when his car struck a pedal cyclist travelling in the same direction. The cyclist was in dark clothing and had no rear light on his cycle. The defendant did not see him until within 6 to 8 feet to him. It was contended by the prosecutor on a charge of driving without due care that as the defendant was in breach of para 34 of the Highway Code then by reason of the Road Traffic Act 1972, s 37(5) the defendant was guilty of the offence.

HELD: (1) There was a fallacy in the contention at the outset: the fact that the defendant did not see the cyclist until 6 to 8 feet away did not mean he could not see beyond 8 feet. There were many possible explanations of a failure to see him before he did. (2) Whether or not a driver is driving in contravention of s 3 of the Act must be a question of fact in every case. A breach of para 34 could have no more positive effect than provided in s 37(5), namely, that it was evidential. On the facts it could not be said that the justices were perverse in holding that the offence was not proved.

Note—Highway Code (1968), para 34 provides: 'Never drive so fast that you cannot stop well within the distance you can see to be clear.' It is repeated in the Highway Code (1978) para 46.

Webster v Wall
[1980] RTR 284, QBD

The defendant was charged with driving without due care and attention in that in the hours of darkness he had, on his motor cycle, collided with a stationary motor car. The car was unlit; it was parked in a street where the nearest street light was 35 feet away. There was heavy rain; the defendant's headlight was dipped. He was riding at about 28 mph, the speed limit being 40 mph. It was argued by the prosecution that a collision having occurred between a moving and a stationary vehicle there was a presumption that the defendant was not maintaining a proper lookout to his front. The justice dismissed the charge.

HELD: On the prosecutor's appeal, the justices' finding could not be said to be perverse. The facts were very similar to those in *Jarvis v Fuller* (above). It was a pure question of fact with no point of law for decision.

CHAPTER 6
Defective vehicles

1 LIABILITY AT COMMON LAW

The rule in Donoghue v Stevenson

Donoghue v Stevenson
[1932] AC 562, [1932] All ER Rep 1
Per Lord Atkin: A manufacturer of products, which he sells in such a form as to show that he intends them to reach the ultimate consumer in the form in which they left him with no reasonable possibility of intermediate exam-ination and with the knowledge that the absence of reasonable care in the preparation or putting up of the products will result in an injury to the consumer's life or property, owes a duty to the consumer to take that reasonable care.

Note—'The principle has been extended from manufacturers to include repairers, fitters, erectors, assemblers, in other words to persons who have done something active to create the danger' — *Winfield and Jolowicz on Tort* (12th edn) pp 248-9.

Junior Books Ltd v Veitchi Co Ltd
[1983] 1 AC 520, [1982] 3 All ER 201, [1982] 3 WLR 477, 126 Sol Jo 538, HL
The appellants were specialist contractors in the laying of flooring. The respondents had had a factory built for them by main contractors with whom the appellants contracted to lay the flooring. There was no privity of contract between the appellants and the respondents. Three years after the floors were laid defects were alleged by the respondents to have developed as a result of the appellants' negligent workmanship or materials, causing

loss and expense to the respondents by the need to have repairs done. It was not alleged that the defects were such as to cause danger to life or limb or to property of other persons or that there was financial loss other than that resulting from repairing or replacing the flooring. It was conceded by the appellants that if the flooring had been so badly constructed that the respondents had had to expend money on renewing it to avoid imminent danger to others they could have recovered the cost of so doing. Were they entitled to recover the cost where there was merely a need, not immediate or pressing, to repair the floor?

HELD: The appellants were liable. The question to be decided was whether the relevant Scots and English law (which in this respect are identical) now extends the duty of care in tort beyond a duty to prevent harm being done by faulty work to a duty to avoid such faults being present in the work itself. The answer lay not in asking whether the proper remedy lay in contract or tort but in establishing the relevant principles. Adopting Lord Wilberforce's two tests in *Anns v Merton London Borough Council* (above, p 5), (1) was there a sufficient relationship of proximity and (2) were there any considerations negativing, reducing or limiting the scope of the duty or the class of person to whom it was owed or the damages to which a breach of duty may give rise? In the present case the facts inter alia that the appellants were specialists and were alone responsible for the composition and construction of the flooring and were aware that the respondents relied on their skill and experience, and that the relationship was as close as it could be short of privity of contract, established a sufficient degree of proximity. On the second test there was nothing to restrict the duty of care arising from that proximity.

But see *Muirhead v Industrial Tank Specialities* [1985] 3 All ER 705, [1985] 3 WLR 993, 129 Sol Jo 855.

MANUFACTURER AND REPAIRER

Malfroot v Noxal
(1935) 51 TLR 551, 74 Sol Jo 610 (Lewis J)
While the male plaintiff, the owner of a motor cycle to which a few days previously the defendants had fitted a side-car, was driving the combination along a public road, the side-car became detached from the motor cycle. Both the male plaintiff and the female plaintiff who was a passenger in the side-car, sustained personal injuries. An action was brought for damages.

HELD: That the defendants were guilty of negligence in fitting the side-car to the motor cycle, that they were liable to the male plaintiff in contract and in tort, and to the female plaintiff in tort. The principles enunciated in *Donoghue v Stevenson* were applied: per Lewis J.

Lambert v Lewis: Lexmead (Basingstoke) Ltd (third party)
[1982] AC 225, [1981] 1 All ER 1185, [1981] 2 WLR 713, 125 Sol Jo 310, [1981] 2 Lloyd's Rep 17, [1981] RTR 346, HL
The first defendant was the owner of a Landrover and trailer being driven by his employee the second defendant when the trailer became detached and ran out of control into collision with a car in which the plaintiffs were travelling. The coupling which failed had been designed and manufactured

by the third defendants and sold to the first defendant by retailers, the
fourth defendants. The judge found, on the evidence, that the coupling was
defective in design and dangerous in use and that the defects were readily
foreseeable by an appropriately skilled engineer; the manufacturers were
negligent and liable to the plaintiffs in tort for the personal injuries
sustained. He also found the owner liable in that he had allowed the coupling to be used for some months in a damaged condition without having it
repaired or even finding out if it was safe to use in such condition. Apportionment: 75% blame on the manufacturers, 25% on the owner. The
retailers were not liable to the plaintiffs because (1) the coupling in question
was a standard fitting for a Landrover and the defects would call for a
knowledge of design they did not possess, and (2) when servicing the
vehicle they were not required without specific mention to inspect the
coupling.

In third party proceedings the owner claimed indemnity from the
retailers for breach of the Sale of Goods Act 1893, s 14, the retailers having
supplied the coupling as fit and suitable for the owner's requirements. The
judge held that there was a breach of sub-s 14 (1) of the 1893 Act in that the
coupling was unsuitable and unfit for the purpose but the owner's act in
continuing to use the coupling when he realised, or ought to have realised,
that it was broken was not within the contemplation of the parties when the
contract was made. *Mowbray v Merryweather* [1895] 2 QB 640 was authority
for saying that the owner's liability to pay damages to the plaintiffs was a
natural consequence of the breach of s 14 and entitled the owner to
indemnity, but not where the damage was also due to an act not within the
contemplation of the parties, namely, the use of the coupling in a damaged
condition. The owner's claim against the retailers failed. The Court of
Appeal disagreed, holding that as the owner's conduct was not so
unreasonable as to be beyond the contemplation of the retailers there was
no break in the chain of causation and the dealers were liable to indemnify
him.
HELD in the House of Lords: This was not right. The first inquiry to be
made was what were the terms of the warranty which was said to have been
broken? It was that the coupling as fixed to the Landrover should be
reasonably fit for towing trailers fitted with the appropriate type of
attachment. This warranty was continuing up to the time when the owner
learnt of its damaged condition. After this damage became apparent to him
the only warranty he could have relied on was one which warranted that the
coupling could continue to be safely used even in a damaged state — an
obvious impossibility. The issue of causation on which the owner's claim
against the dealers depended was whether it resulted from the dealer's
breach of warranty, and manifestly it did not; it resulted from his own
negligence in using the coupling in a damaged state.

Herschtal v Stewart and Ardern Ltd
[1940] 1 KB 155, [1939] 4 All ER 123, 161 LT 331, 56 TLR 48, 84 Sol Jo
79 (Tucker J)
The plaintiff, who was a director of, and had a controlling interest in, a
company known as UP Ltd acquired on its behalf a reconditioned motor
car from a company known as S & A Services Ltd. The latter company
acquired the car from the defendants for the purpose of hiring it out on hire
purchase terms to UP Ltd. The defendants knew that the car was going to

be used chiefly by the plaintiff, and they knew that it was going to be so used immediately. On the morning after the delivery of the car, before it had been driven more than a few miles, and while it was being driven by the plaintiff, the nearside rear wheel came off, whereby the plaintiff suffered damage. There was no evidence that anything had happened between the time when the car was delivered by the defendants and the time of the accident. At the time of delivery the plaintiff had signed, for and on behalf of UP Ltd, a form of receipt stating that the car was accepted as being in good condition and as seen, tried and approved.

HELD: (1) The form of receipt did not protect the defendants in a claim of negligence by the plaintiff, however it might affect their contractual liability with UP Ltd. (2) The defendants were liable in negligence under the rule in *Donoghue v Stevenson*, because, although the plaintiff was given an opportunity to examine the car for the purpose of discovering any defects, yet the defendants never anticipated that there would be any such examination.

Note—In the above case, the Motor Vehicles (Construction and Use) Regulations 1937, reg 67, and the Road Traffic Act 1934, s 8 were referred to, but counsel for the plaintiff conceded the plaintiff could not succeed without proof of negligence in view of *Phillips v Britannia Hygienic Laundry* (p 245, below). See also *Andrews v Hopkinson*, p 239, below.

Opportunity of intermediate examination

Stennett v Hancock and Peters
[1939] 2 All ER 578, 83 Sol Jo 379 (Branson J)
The owner of a motor lorry took the wheel of the lorry, the flange of which had come off, to a motor repairer with instructions to reassemble it. The repairer's assistants reassembled and replaced it on the lorry, and the lorry owner's servant drove the lorry away. An hour or two later, the flange came off while the lorry was being driven on the highway by the lorry owner's servant, and, bowling along the road, it mounted the pavement and hit the female plaintiff, injuring her. There was no evidence that anything had happened between the time when the lorry was taken out of the garage and the time of the accident which might have caused the wheel to become dislodged.

HELD: (1) Following *Phillips v Britannia Hygienic Laundry* (p 245, below) the lorry owner having entrusted the repair of the lorry to a competent repairer, he was not liable for either negligence or nuisance to a person who suffered injury upon the road by reason of the competent repairer having been negligent. (2) The lorry owner, or the person who was going to take the vehicle on the road, was not under a duty to ascertain for himself, in so far as his capabilities allowed him to do so, whether the competent repairer had competently repaired the lorry. (3) Following *Donoghue v Stevenson* and distinguishing *Earl v Lubbock* ([1905] 1 KB 253) the repairer was liable to the persons who suffered injury on the road as a result of his negligence, as he was in the same position as that of the manufacturer of an article sold by a distributor in circumstances which prevented the distributor or ultimate purchaser or consumer from discovering by inspection any defect in the article.

Vaile Brothers v Hobson Ltd
[1933] 149 LT 283, [1933] All ER Rep 447, Div Ct
The plaintiffs had sent a carburettor to the defendants for repair. In use one of the connecting rods broke, the engine raced out of control, the flywheel broke and extensive damage was done. The county court judge found that the engine switch was not connected to the dashboard, with the result that the damage could not be prevented by switching off the engine. He held this to be contributory negligence and absolved the defendants from liability. On appeal, this was reversed and it was held that the repairer could not escape liability for a defective repair by pointing to another defect for which he was not liable.

Aspin v J. Bretherton & Sons
(1947) *Policy Holder Law Supplement*, 24 December (Streatfeild J)
On 24 June 1946, the owners sent their lorry to the repairers to have the brakes relined which involved dismantling, reassembling and replacement as necessary. The following day the repairers fixed a new drum and replaced roller bearings. On 22 July 1946, the owners sent the lorry to the repairers for special greasing. The owners did the maintenance work and greased once a week and tested for end play. On 24 July 1946, the lorry had travelled 2,059 miles, when the front offside wheel came off causing the lorry to collide with a bus. A passenger in the bus was injured and sued the lorry owners and the repairers.
HELD: The owners' explanation excluded them from liability. The lorry driver was not negligent. The condition of the thrust washer put the repairers on enquiry. There was no anticipation of examination by the owners and they were not bound to inspect after 2,059 miles and within a month. Time and distance were questions of fact. The repairers were negligent and were liable to the passenger.

The time factor

EIGHT YEARS

Sharpe v E. T. Sweeting & Son Ltd
[1963] 2 All ER 455, [1963] 1 WLR 665, 107 Sol Jo 666
A house was built by the defendants in 1951 for the Middlesbrough Corporation and was provided according to the Corporation's design with a canopy over the front door. In July 1959 the canopy fell, injuring the plaintiff who was the wife of the tenant. The canopy fell because reinforcing wire had not been fixed in the right position.
HELD: The defendants were liable. There was a sufficiently proximate relationship to come within the principle in *Donoghue v Stevenson*.
   Per Nield J: It is true that it might be difficult after a lapse of years to know whether a dangerous defect in a house was due to age or interference or negligent building. But that difficulty should surely be capable of being met by applying the general principles of the onus of proof under which the plaintiff would be required to prove that the dangerous defect in a house was due to negligent building and by excluding other cases.

Chain of causation

Donnelly v Glasgow Corpn
1953 SC 107, 1953 SLT 161
An omnibus belonging to a local authority overturned owing to a broken front spring. In an action of damages arising out of the accident, the local authority sought to blame the manufacturers of the spring, on the ground that two usual and normal safety devices connected with the spring had been omitted in the construction of the chassis.
HELD: The defect was clearly one which could have been detected by an examination of the bus after it came into the hands of the local authority, they having competent mechanics expert in the maintenance of public service vehicles. As a result the chain of causation between the manufacturers and the persons injured was broken, since there had been an opportunity for intermediate examination. No fault, therefore, could be placed at the door of the manufacturers. The contention of the local authority rejected.

Clay v A. J. Crump & Sons Ltd
[1964] 1 QB 533, [1963] 3 All ER 687, [1963] 3 WLR 866, 107 Sol Jo 664, 187 Estates Gazette 835, CA
Per Ormerod LJ: The important question is to decide first whether the plaintiff comes within the class of persons entitled to recover damages if they suffer loss as a result of another person's negligence and then to decide whether in law that loss has indeed been suffered as a result of the negligence or has been suffered, for example, because of the intervening negligence of some other person. It may well be that in the case of manufactured articles made up in such a way that they are not intended to be examined it is simpler to decide whether they come within the class; but it is nonetheless the duty of the court to inquire into the facts of other cases, and to determine whether the injury suffered is something which can in law be related to the breach of duty of some particular person.

Knowledge of dangerous condition

Hurley v Dyke
[1979] RTR 265, HL
The defendant was a garage owner near Malvern. On 28 September a man named Halford driving an old Reliant three-wheeled car called at the garage because the carburettor was leaking. Both looked at the car and noticed it was down on one side. The defendant said Halford could not drive it like that. Halford said he would scrap the car and the defendant then paid him £10 for it. On 8 October, the carburettor having been repaired, the defendant took the car to a car auction at Tewkesbury, putting a reserve of £40 on it. It was offered for sale at auction on the terms 'To be sold as seen and with all its faults and without warranty'. Jones, a motor dealer, bought it for £40 intending to use it for spares, but after the sale Nigel Clay, a young man who had tried unsuccessfully to bid for the car, offered Jones a further £10 and Jones sold it to him. Clay drove it to Coventry where he lived and a week later to Surrey to see a friend. On

16 October he was driving the car with the plaintiff as passenger when the nearside of the chassis collapsed causing the car to go out of control. Clay was killed and the plaintiff very seriously injured. The judge at first instance held the defendant liable on the ground that, knowing the car was dangerous to drive, he had not ensured that the auctioneer made it clear that what was being sold was an unroadworthy vehicle. The Court of Appeal held there was no liability on the defendant. The warning given by the auctioneer was sufficient to bring home to the mind of any reasonable immediate buyer from the defendant that the car should not be put upon the road without intermediate examination. The defendant's duty did not extend beyond any first buyer from him.

HELD, ON APPEAL to the House of Lords: The defendant was not liable. The case turned on the question of fact as to the extent of the defendant's knowledge of the nature of the defect in the car when he put it up for auction. The highest that the defendant's knowledge could be put was an awareness of the possible danger of driving the car without further examination. The warning given at auction that it was to be sold 'as seen and with all its faults' was adequate to satisfy any duty of care owed by the defendant to the plaintiff.

Safety glass

Grenfell v Meyrowitz
[1936] 2 All ER 1313, CA
'Safety glass' means made from laminated glass, and there is no warranty of absolute safety in these words.

Evans v Triplex Glass Co
[1936] 1 All ER 283 (Porter J)
The plaintiff bought a motor car in June 1934, with a windscreen made of 'Triplex Toughened Safety Glass'. The windscreen was fitted by the Vauxhall Motor Co. On 27 July 1935, whilst he was driving the car, the windscreen, suddenly and for no apparent reason, broke into many fragments and injured the second plaintiff, wife of the first plaintiff. The plaintiffs brought an action in negligence against the defendants. There was no claim in contract against the vendors of the car.

HELD: A number of causes might have brought about the disintegration. The suppliers of the car had every opportunity to examine the windscreen. I do not find any negligence proved against the defendants. Verdict for defendants with costs.

Limits of duty to inspect

Davie v New Merton Board Mills
[1959] AC 604, [1959] 1 All ER 346, [1959] 2 WLR 331, 103 Sol Jo 177, [1959] 2 Lloyd's Rep 587, HL
The plaintiff, a maintenance fitter in the employ of the first defendant, was injured when using a drift, a tool for separating pieces of metal. At the second blow by a hammer, a particle of metal flew off the head of the drift

and entered his left eye resulting in the loss of all useful vision in that eye. The accident occurred on 8 March 1953. The drift had been purchased by the employers from a reputable firm of suppliers in 1946, who had purchased it in 1946 from a firm of reputable and old established tool makers. The drift appeared to be in good condition but was excessively hard for its purpose owing to negligence in its manufacture. The employers were unaware of the defect and could not reasonably have discovered it. HELD: The employers were not liable. No intermediate examination of the tool between the time of its manufacture and the time of its actual use was reasonably to be expected. It was unreasonable to expect an employer to test a drift for hardness before issuing it to his employee. No examination short of a test would have revealed the danger existing in this particular drift.

Note—The duty of an employer to a workman is admittedly higher than the owner of a car to a passenger, but the decision may be a guide to the defence of a car owner.

The Employer's Liability (Defective Equipment) Act 1969 (which came into force on 25 October 1969), s 1(1)-(3) provides as follows:

'**1 Extension of employer's liability for defective equipment**   (1) Where after the commencement of this Act —

(a) an employee suffers personal injury in the course of his employment in consequence of a defect in equipment provided by his employer for the purposes of the employer's business; and

(b) the defect is attributable wholly or partly to the fault of a third party (whether identified or not),

the injury shall be deemed to be also attributable to negligence on the part of the employer (whether or not he is liable in respect of the injury apart from this sub-section), but without prejudice to the law relating to contributory negligence and to any remedy by way of contribution or in contract or otherwise which is available to the employer in respect of the injury.

(2) In so far as any agreement purports to exclude or limit any liability of an employer arising under subsection (1) of this section, the agreement shall be void.

(3) In this section —

"business" includes the activities carried on by any public body;

"employee" means a person who is employed by another person under a contract of service or apprenticeship and is so employed for the purposes of a business carried on by that other person, and "employer" shall be construed accordingly;

"equipment" includes any plant and machinery, vehicle, aircraft and clothing;

"fault" means negligence, breach of statutory duty or other act or omission which gives rise to liability in tort in England and Wales or which is wrongful and gives rise to liability in damages in Scotland; and

"personal injury" includes loss of life, any impairment of a person's physical or mental condition and any disease.'

Clarkson v William Jackson & Sons Ltd

(1984) Times, 21 November, CA

The Employer's Liability (Defective Equipment) Act 1969 does not give employees a new cause of action. The scheme of the Act is to prevent an employer escaping liability when the fault in the equipment was the fault of the supplier or manufacturer and not of the employer.

Repairer: duty in contract

G. H. Myers & Co v Brent Cross Service Co
[1934] 1 KB 46, [1933] All ER Rep 9, 103 LJKB 123, 150 LT 96, Div Ct
(Swift and du Parcq JJ)
The owner of a motor car in October 1932, handed his car to repairers to cure a 'knock' in the engine and renew any part which in their opinion required replacement. The repairers obtained from the manufacturers six connecting rods which they fitted to the engine. On 9 November 1932, one of the rods broke causing extensive damage to the engine. The owner claimed £62 18s 0d for the cost of repairing the car and consequential damage. The county court judge found that one connecting rod was defective but was due to an undiscoverable latent defect.
HELD: This was not a contract for the sale of goods but a contract for work and labour in the course of which goods were supplied. The liability of a person supplying goods in the course of doing work and labour is certainly not less than the liability of the person selling goods. He warrants that the material which he uses will be of good material and reasonably fit for the purpose for which he is using them, unless the contract excluded any such warranty, and the person is liable if there is any defect in the materials supplied, even if it was one which reasonable care could not have discovered.

The case was remitted to the county court judge to decide whether the defendants were contracting in such a way as to bind themselves to exercise their own skill and judgment with reference to the selection of the material, or whether they were bound to get the materials from the original manufacturers of the car.

Stewart v Reavell's Garage
[1952] 2 QB 545, [1952] 1 All ER 1191, [1952] 1 TLR 1266, 96 Sol Jo 314
(Sellers J)
The plaintiff was the owner of a Bentley speed model and took the car to defendants, who were experienced car repairers to whom the car was well known, to have the brake-drums and brake-shoes relined. This was specialist's work which to the knowledge of the plaintiff the defendants did not undertake. Plaintiff suggested that the work should be done by a firm who advertised cast-iron linings for Bentley brake-drums and informed the defendants that a cast-iron sleeve, which would be cut from a tube with no weld, would be preferable. The price quoted by this firm was too high and the defendants with the plaintiff's consent obtained a quotation from a firm who normally did this work for them. Defendants recommended this firm to plaintiff and plaintiff accepted their advice without knowing that this method involved welding, which was not suitable for this make of car. The sub-contractors did not fit the offside front brake lining properly. The day after the car was delivered to the plaintiff, the faulty lining caused an accident and the car was damaged. The defendants contended that their only duty was to take reasonable care to employ a suitable sub-contractor and that they were entitled to assume without further detailed examination that their work would be satisfactory.
HELD: The contract was for work done and materials supplied. The standard of care in the case of a sale of goods was stated by Lord Wright in

Cammell Laird & Co Ltd v Manganese Bronze and Brass Co Ltd [1934] AC 402, [1934] All ER Rep 1, 103 LJKB 289, 151 LT 142. The standard of proof was equally applicable in this case. The law was also stated by du Parcq J in *G. H. Myers & Co v Brent Cross Service Co* (above). There might be an implied warranty of absolute fitness for the intended purpose if the circumstances showed that the particular purpose was made known to the repairer, and that the work of repair was of the type which the repairer held himself out to perform, either by himself or sub-contractor, and if the circumstances showed that the purpose was made known so as to show that the customer relied on the repairer's skill and judgment. Such a reliance must be brought home to the mind of the repairer that he was relying on him in such a way that the repairer must be taken to have contracted on the footing that the reliance was to be the basis of the contract. It was their duty in the circumstances to provide good workmanship, materials of good quality, and a braking system reasonably fit for its purpose, and they failed to do so by reason of the faulty offside front brake-drum lining. In fact, though unwittingly, they handed over to the plaintiff a highly dangerous vehicle. Judgment for the plaintiff for £283 3s 4d.

Note—68 LQR 297 points out that a repairer will be protected if he uses replacement material supplied by the makers of the car because he is entitled to assume it will be suitable, but if obtained from an independent contractor, it is his duty to see that it is adequate for its purpose. He is being paid for expert supervision, which is not properly performed if all he does is to rely on the skill of a third person.

3,000 mile service

Taylor v Kiddey
(1968) Times, 1 February, CA
In November 1965 the plaintiff bought a secondhand car from the defendant who warranted that it was 'in tiptop condition and really roadworthy'. On 3 February 1966 the defendant gave the car a routine 3,000-mile service, one item of which was checking the steering. On 4 April 1966 while the plaintiff was driving, the nearside front wheel came off because the securing bolts had been insufficiently tightened; she was injured and the car wrecked. She claimed damages. There was no evidence that anything had happened, such as the changing of a wheel, between November 1965 and the accident which might have caused the wheel bolts to be left insufficiently tightened.
HELD: The plaintiff was entitled to damages because (1) on the evidence it was clear that the bolts had been loose when the car was sold by the defendant and he was thus in breach of warranty; (2) it was part of the duty of a garage when carrying out a service which included checking the steering to test the front wheels to ensure that the securing bolts were tight.

HIRER

Hire: implied warranty

Spear v Self Motoring Ltd
(1947) S No 27, 15 March 1948 (Mr Commissioner Sachs KC)
Plaintiff hired from defendants, whose business was to let out private cars on hire a 1938 h p car to drive from Norwich to Cambridge, a distance of 61 miles. After driving 54 miles, the steering gear failed and the car swerved across the road into an oncoming vehicle. The plaintiff was very seriously injured. The car was eight years old and had been in heavy use. The accident was due to the steering mechanism being defective, whereby a ball joint by which the drag link is joined to the steering side arm (the rear drag link joint) came apart, due to severe wear and strain.
HELD: The car was unsuitable for the purpose for which it was hired, due to the negligence of the defendants in failing properly to examine it and service it. The defendants were liable for breach of implied warranty that the car was reasonably fit for the purpose (even if the defect is latent), and for negligence in failing to take any adequate steps to keep the car in safe and efficient condition. There was not any servicing system. The ball joints had not been properly attended to. Verdict for plaintiff. *Myers's* case p 236, above, followed.

Reed v Dean
[1949] 1 KB 188 (Lewis J)
There is an implied warranty of fitness on the hire of a chattel, that it shall be as fit for the purpose for which it was hired as reasonable care and skill can make it.

Note—See also *Astley v Grimley* (p 347, below).

Hirer of car — insurance

Moon's Motors Ltd v Kiuan Wou
[1952] 2 Lloyd's Rep 80, CA
Defendant hired a car from plaintiffs and received a card showing prices, etc and the card showed that prices included petrol and insurance. Defendant signed an agreement which contained at the bottom the words: 'The terms and conditions of hire can be seen overleaf' in quite clear print. The defendant was never given a copy of the agreement.
　　The agreement started by saying: 'It is agreed that the owner will let subject to the following questions which constitute a proposal for insurance being answered by the hirer to the satisfaction of the owner and the insurance company concerned and the hirer will take on hire . . .'. Clause 8 said: 'The hirer has completed the proposal for insurance incorporated in this agreement and a policy of insurance is in force in relation to the use of the car by the hirer but nothing herein contained shall confer or give rise to any rights against the owner by way of indemnity . . .'.
　　The insurance was for third party only. The car was damaged in an accident and the plaintiffs sued the defendant for the damage. The county court judge found that the defendant never had an opportunity to read the

condition and never read it and it was never brought to his notice.

HELD: The statement that the price included insurance amounted to a warranty that the defendant would be covered against all normal risks. Read together, clauses 7 and 8 had the effect that the hirer is responsible for the cost of repairs but entitled to look to an insurance company in respect of the usual risks on the usual terms. 'A policy of insurance in relation to the use of the car' means a policy covering normal risks. Defendant was not liable.

Hire purchase: implied warranty

Brown v Sheen and Richmond Car Sales

[1950] 1 All ER 1102 (Jones J)

Plaintiff arranged to obtain a car from motor car dealers who represented that the car was in perfect condition. The transaction was completed by a hire-purchase agreement. Plaintiff paid all instalments and the car became his property. He sued the dealers for damages for breach of warranty.

HELD: The warranty had induced the plaintiff to enter into the agreement and the dealers were liable for the difference between the amount paid and the amount plaintiff would have paid if the warranty had not been given.

Andrews v Hopkinson

[1957] 1 QB 229, [1956] 3 All ER 422, [1956] 3 WLR 732, 100 Sol Jo 768 (McNair J)

On 11 September 1952, plaintiff arranged to obtain from defendant, a dealer in secondhand cars, a 1934 car. Plaintiff told defendant that he did not know a great deal about cars. Defendant took plaintiff and a friend for a drive for about 5 miles in the car and said 'It's a good little bus. I would stake my life on it. You will have no trouble with it'. Plaintiff agreed to a price of £150 for the car, payable as to £50 the next day, the balance to be by hire purchase. On 12 September 1952, the £50 was paid and a hire-purchase agreement completed. This agreement provided that acceptance of delivery should be conclusive evidence that the car was complete and in good order and condition and in every way satisfactory, and plaintiff signed the agreement.

On 19 September 1952, the plaintiff was driving the car when it suddenly swerved and collided with a lorry. The car was wrecked and plaintiff seriously injured. Plaintiff sued defendant for damage to car and personal injuries. The judge found the defective condition of the drag-link joint was the cause of the accident.

HELD: The words used amounted to a warranty that the car was in good condition and reasonably safe for use on the highway. There was an implied warranty similar to that implied on a sale of goods and the plaintiff had acted on this warranty in entering into the agreement and could enforce the warranty. *Brown's* case (above) followed. The plaintiff's personal injuries were a direct and natural result of the breach and the plaintiff was entitled to recover on this ground. The defendant was also liable for negligence in delivering the car in a dangerous condition when he could have discovered the condition by reasonable care and he had failed to have the car examined or warn the plaintiff that it had not been examined. *Herschtal's* case followed. Judgment for plaintiff.

LATENT DEFECT

Note—The Occupiers' Liability Act 1957, by s 1 (3) (a), applies the duty of an occupier to his visitors to any person having control of any vehicle.

Readhead v Midland Rly Co
(1869) LR 4 QB 379, 38 LJQB 169
If an accident is due to a latent defect which is not discoverable by reasonable care, there is no negligence.

The contract made by a general carrier of passengers for hire with a passenger is to take due care, including in that term the use of skill and foresight to carry the passenger safely; it is not a warranty that the carriage in which he travels shall be in all respects perfect for its purpose, that is, free from all defects likely to cause peril, even if those defects were such that no skill, care or foresight could have determined their existence.

Note—But there is a high degree of duty on the carrier:

Newberry v Bristol Tramways and Carriage Co Ltd
(1912) 107 LT 801, 29 TLR 177, 57 Sol Jo 172
Plaintiff was a passenger on the outside of an uncovered tramway car belonging to defendants, which was propelled by means of overhead electric traction. The wheel at the head of the trolly arm was detached from the electric wire and the trolly arm was plucked away from the standard at its socket and fell upon plaintiff's head. Such an occurrence was extremely rare and no contrivance had been discovered to prevent it. The system of electric traction adopted by the defendants was the best and most widely used; the apparatus on that particular car on which the accident occured was in perfect order; and there was no negligence on the part of defendant's servants. An action was brought by plaintiff against defendants claiming damages in respect of the injuries sustained by him. The jury, having been directed that plaintiff could only be entitled to recover damages if there was negligence on the part of defendants in carrying him as a passenger, that the defendants were not insurers, and that they were bound to take every reasonable precaution that could be taken to secure the safety of their passengers, but not as insurers, found for plaintiff, but stated that not one of the alleged acts of negligence of defendants was established to their satisfaction.
HELD: That the verdict of the jury showed that defendants discharged the burden which rested upon them; and the only negligence alleged was disproved, notwithstanding plaintiff's prima facie case. As to the standard of care required in the case of a carrier of passengers, it is sufficient that the carrier should adopt the best known apparatus, kept in perfect order and worked without negligence by the servants he employed. If he does that he ought not to be responsible for the consequences of an extremely rare and obscure accident which cannot in a business sense be prevented by any known means.

Hyman v Nye
(1881) 6 QBD 685, 44 LT 919, 45 JP 554
Plaintiff hired from a jobmaster a carriage, pair of horses and driver. During the journey a bolt in the undercarriage broke and the plaintiff was injured. The judge held the jobmaster not liable.
HELD, ON APPEAL: The duty of the owner was to supply a carriage as fit for the purpose for which it was hired as care and skill could render it. He is not responsible for all defects, discoverable or not; he is not an insurer against all defects, nor is he bound to take more care than coach proprietors or railway companies, but he is bound to take as much care as they; and although not an insurer against all defects, he is an insurer against all defects which care and skill can guard against. The breaking throws the onus on the owner. New trial ordered.

Note—And see *Reed v Dean*, p 238, above.
   The form of plea may be as follows:

'The defendants further say that if, which is denied, the said . . . was defective as alleged, such defect was latent and not discoverable by the use of reasonable care, which the defendants exercised.'

Mechanical defect causing accident

Henderson v Henry E. Jenkins & Sons
[1970] AC 282, [1969] 3 All ER 756, [1969] 3 WLR 732, 113 Sol Jo 856, HL
A lorry driver applied the brakes of the lorry on a steep hill but they failed to operate. As a result the lorry struck and killed a man who was emerging from a parked vehicle. His widow sued the lorry owners who denied liability on the ground that the brake failure was due to latent defect not discoverable by reasonable care on their part. The lorry was five years old and had done at least 150,000 miles. The brakes were hydraulically operated. It was found after the accident that the brake failure was due to steel pipe bursting at a point where corrosion had reduced the thickness of the wall of the pipe from .7mm to .1mm. The corrosion had occured where it could not be seen except by removing the pipe completely from the vehicle and this had never been done. Expert evidence showed that it was not a normal precaution to do this if, as was the case, the visible parts of the pipe were not corroded. The corrosion was unusual and unexplained. An expert witness said it must have been due to chemical action of some kind such as exposure to salt from the roads in winter or on journeys near the sea or from leakage of corrosive liquids from particular kinds of loads. The judge of assize held there was no negligence on the part of the lorry owners. The Court of Appeal, by a majority, agreed.
HELD, ON APPEAL to the House of Lords: The defendants had not discharged the burden of proof which lay on them of showing they had taken all reasonable care and that despite this the defect remained hidden. The evidence showed that something unusual must have happened to cause this corrosion: it was caused by some chemical agent. So it was necessary for the defendants to show that they neither knew nor ought to have known of any unusual occurrence to cause the breakdown. They had given no evidence at all of the history of the vehicle or the loads it had

carried. It might have been sufficient for them to prove that they had a proper system for drivers reporting all occurrences but they had not done this. They chose to leave the case in a state where, for all they knew, the lorry might have been carrying carboys of acid regularly or had been coming into contact with sea water or salt frequently or had been engaged in carrying cattle. They had to prove that in all the circumstances of which they knew or ought to have known they had taken all proper steps to avoid danger. They had failed to do that and the plaintiff must succeed.

Note—See also *Barkway v South Wales Transport Co*, p 60, above.

Rees v Saville
[1983] RTR 332, CA

The defendant was driving his car when it suddenly swerved to the right and struck the plaintiff's parked car causing substantial damage for which the plaintiff claimed. The accident was caused by the failure of a ball joint on the steering mechanism of the front offside wheel of the defendant's car. The car was eight years old but he had owned it only a month or less: he had bought it privately. He was not an engineer but he had inspected it before purchase and found no defects. It had an MOT certificate three or four months old. Expert evidence was that the worn condition of the ball joint was not easily discoverable on inspection, but should have been detected on the MOT test. The defendant said in evidence that he had noticed no symptoms of wear on the ball joint which might be shown by uneven tyre wear or otherwise and that 'it was a natural assumption from the MOT certificate that the vehicle was okay'. The judge said the test of negligence was what a reasonable motorist could be expected to do. He held there was no negligence on the part of the defendant.

HELD, ON APPEAL: The judge was entitled so to hold. (1) The question of onus matters only when there is a question of fact on which no evidence is called on one side or the other. In this case credibility of the evidence was established at the trial and it merely remained for the court to decide whether, on the facts proved or admitted, the defendant was negligent. *Henderson v Jenkins* (p 241, above), and *Barkway v South Wales Transport* (p 60, above) were distinguishable. In *Henderson's* case the plaintiff established the cause of the corrosion but the defendants called no evidence. In *Barkway's* case negligence was proved against the defendant's servants or agents. (2) It had been said against the present defendant that he should have placed no reliance on the MOT certificate. A valid MOT certificate was a factor which must be taken into account in deciding whether or not it was necessary for the defendant himself to submit the car to an expert for inspection. On the facts of the present case the defendant was not negligent in failing to have a further inspection of the vehicle.

Pearce v Round Oak Steel Works Ltd
[1969] 3 All ER 680, [1969] 1 WLR 595, 113 Sol Jo 163, CA

The plaintiff, a factory worker, was injured when a piece of a machine fell on his foot. The fall was caused by the breakage of a bolt due to a latent defect not discoverable by reasonable inspection. The plaintiff pleaded *res ipsa loquitur* and called as a witness a metallurgist who said the machine had been made in 1930 and bought by the defendants in 1959. He said there may have been drawings which would have given information about the material from which the bolt was made. The defendants called no evidence. The county court judge said the plaintiff had given sufficient evidence to put the burden on the defendants to show they had taken reasonable precautions. They had called no evidence and the plaintiff was entitled to succeed.

HELD, ON APPEAL: The judge's approach to the problem was right. Even though there is a latent defect the defendants must prove that the accident happened despite all reasonable care on their part: this means reasonable care not only in inspection and maintenance but also when they bought the machine. They must prove that in acquiring the machine and in their dealings with it they had taken reasonable care to see that it was in good order and condition. They ought to have called evidence about the circumstances in which they acquired the machine. Appeal dismissed.

R v Spurge
[1961] 2 QB 205, [1961] 2 All ER 688, [1961] 3 WLR 23, 125 JP 502, 105 Sol Jo 469, CCA

The appellant was driving his sports car round a very sharp and dangerous left hand bend. The car went over the double white lines in the centre of the road and collided with an oncoming motor scooter. His defence was that he decided to take the bend at a snail's pace and applied the brakes somewhat vigorously; the application of the brakes pulled the car on to its wrong side of the road in such a fashion that it was impossible for him to control it. Expert witnesses gave evidence that the brakes were in very bad condition and that vigorous application at 30 mph pulled the car fairly violently to its offside. The appellant had taken delivery of the car only a few days before.

HELD: (1) There is no real distinction between a man being suddenly deprived of all control of a motor car by some sudden affliction to his person and being so deprived by some defect suddenly manifesting itself in the motor car, but (2) cases in which a mechanical defect can be relied on as a defence to a charge of dangerous driving must be rare. The defence has no application where the defect is known to the driver or should have been discovered by him had he exercised reasonable prudence; (3) the appellant could not succeed because he admitted he was aware of the tendency of the car to pull to the right when its brakes were applied.

Hougham v Martins
(1964) 108 Sol Jo 138, Div Ct

The defendant was driving a Ford Anglia car along a main road when it gradually moved over to its offside of the road and collided with a vehicle travelling in the opposite direction. The defendant said she had no recollection of the accident. In answer to a charge of driving without due care and attention it was argued in her favour that the accident might have been caused by a mechanical defect to which modern mass-produced vehicles were prone but which it was not possible to specify. The justices dismissed the information.

On a case stated the Divisional Court directed the justices to convict. The mere suggestion that modern mass-produced vehicles were prone to mechanical defects did not give rise to a reasonable doubt and was merely fanciful.

2 STATUTORY DUTIES

REGULATIONS UNDER ROAD TRAFFIC ACTS

ROAD TRAFFIC ACT 1972, s 40

40 Regulation of construction, weight, equipment and use of vehicles   (1)
The Secretary of State may make regulations generally as to the use of motor
vehicles and trailers on roads, their construction and equipment and the conditions
under which they may be so used, and in particular, but without prejudice to the
generality of the foregoing provisions, may make regulations with respect to any of
the following matters:

(a)   the width, height and length of motor vehicles and trailers and the load
      carried thereby, the diameter of wheels, and the width, nature and condition
      of tyres, of motor vehicles and trailers;

(g)   the number and nature of brakes, and for securing that brakes, silencers and
      steering gear shall be efficient and kept in proper working order;

(gg) lighting equipment and reflectors;

(h)   the testing and inspection, by persons authorised by or under the regula-
      tions, of the brakes, silencers, steering gear, tyres, lighting equipment and
      reflectors of motor vehicles and trailers on any premises where they are,
      subject however to the consent of the owner of the premises;

(5) Subject to the provisions of this section and sections 41 and 42 of this Act, a
person —

(a)   who contravenes or fails to comply with any regulations under this section; or

(b)   who uses on a road a motor vehicle or trailer which does not comply with any
      such regulations or causes or permits a vehicle to be so used;

shall be guilty of an offence.

THE MOTOR VEHICLE (CONSTRUCTION AND USE) REGULATIONS 1978 (SI 1978/1017 (came into force 30 August 1978))

Note—As appears from cases set out below, breach of the regulations does not give
rise to a cause of action for damages. Accordingly no detailed resume of the regulations is called for here. Part II of the Regulations governs the construction, weight
and equipment (eg brakes, tyres, mudguards, seat belts, windscreen wipers,
silencers, safety glass) of motor vehicles. Part III governs the use on roads of motor
vehicles and includes regulations relating to driving and stopping. Among them
are regulations which require that a vehicle must not be driven backwards further
than may be requisite for the safety or reasonable convenience of the occupants or
of other vehicles on the road (reg 120); that during the hours of darkness vehicles
must not stand on a road otherwise than with the nearside of the vehicle as close as
may be to the edge of the carriageway (reg 123); that a motor vehicle not attended
by a person licensed to drive it must (subject to some necessary exceptions) have
the engine stopped and the brake set (reg 124); and that no person shall open any
door of a motor vehicle so as to cause injury or danger to any person (reg 125). Part
IV consists of reg 145 which gives power to a police officer or vehicle examiner to
test and inspect the brakes, silencers, steering gear, tyres, lighting equipment and
reflectors either on 48 hours notice or in any event within 48 hours of an accident in
which the vehicle had been involved.

No cause of action for breach

Winter v Cardiff Rural District Council

[1950] 1 All ER 819, 114 JP 234, 49 LGR 1, HL

Per Lord Porter: The statement of claim also contained an allegation that the respondents had been guilty of a breach of statutory duty in that the requirements of the Motor Vehicles (Construction and Use) Regulations 1941, reg 67 (now reg 101·of the 1978 Regulations) had not been complied with. This last contention, however, was not persisted in save as providing a standard with reference to which the requisite care to be observed could be estimated. So regarded, it merges in the question whether the respondents were guilty of negligence for which the responsibility was theirs, though the actual immediate cause of the injury was the negligence of a fellow servant.

Barkway v South Wales Transport Co Ltd

Per Lord Normand: The Regulations give no right of action to persons injured by breach of a regulation:

Note—Noted fully at p 60, above.

Phillips v Britannia Hygienic Laundry

[1923] 2 KB 832, 93 LJKB 5, 129 LT 777, 39 TLR 530, 68 Sol Jo 102, CA

The axle of the defendants' motor lorry broke, causing a wheel to come off and damage the plaintiff's van. He claimed damages for breach of a clause of the Motor Cars (Use and Construction) Order 1904 made under the Locomotives on Highways Act 1896: 'The motor car and all the fittings thereof shall be in such a condition as not to cause . . . danger to any person on the motor car or on any highway.'

HELD: Breach of the regulation did not give rise to a civil cause of action because (per Bankes LJ) it was a rule for the protection of the public at large and not a particular class: the public using the highway is not a class; it is itself the public: per Atkin LJ. Whether a person aggrieved by a breach of the duty has a right of action depends on the intention of the Act. The duty the Regulations were intended to impose was not a duty enforceable by individuals injured, but a public duty only, the sole remedy for which was the remedy provided by way of fine.

Tan Chye Choo v Chong Kew Moi

[1970] 1 All ER 266, [1970] 1 WLR 147, 113 Sol Jo 1000, PC

The respondent bought a taxi as an investment in November 1960. It was driven and maintained by an employee. In October 1961 it was examined by the registrar of motor vehicles who reported that it was satisfactory in all respects. On 28 January 1962 it suddenly swerved out of control when being driven by the respondent's servant, colliding with a car travelling in the opposite direction and killing two of the occupants. The cause of the swerve was the collapse of the nearside ball joint of the steering gear due to excessive strain placed upon it by the modification to the spring seating done when the original petrol engine was replaced by a heavier diesel engine. This modification had been done before the respondent bought the car and was not of a kind which any ordinary inspection would have revealed.

HELD: The respondent had not been negligent and was not liable. On an alternative claim that she was liable in damages for breach of a statutory rule requiring the condition of the car to be at all times 'such that no danger is caused or likely to be caused to any person' the case was impossible to differentiate from *Phillips v Britannia Laundry* (above). The statutory rule was not one which gave a civil cause for action.

Sale of secondhand car

Note—The Road Traffic Act 1930, s 3 (1) (now replaced by s 40 (5) of the 1972 Act), made it unlawful to use a motor vehicle which does not comply with the Regulations as to construction, weight and equipment.

The Road Traffic Act 1934, s 8 (1) (now replaced by s 60 (1) of the 1972 Act), made it unlawful to sell or supply a motor vehicle in such a condition that its use would be unlawful under s 3 of the 1930 Act.

Section 59 of the 1930 Act (now replaced by s 40 (1) of the 1972 Act), empowered the Minister to make regulations as to the number and use of brakes, and for securing their efficiency and maintenance.

Section 113 of the 1930 Act provided penalties for offences under that Act.

Regulations 39 and 68 of the 1947 Regulations (now regs 64 and 101 of the 1978 Regulations) require (1) an efficient braking system, and (2) maintenance in efficient working order, respectively.

Badham v Lambs
[1946] KB 45, [1945] 2 All ER 295, 115 LJKB 180, 173 LT 319, 61 TLR 569, 89 Sol Jo 381 (du Parcq LJ in KBD)
In July 1944, plaintiff bought a secondhand car from defendants, and the contract of sale contained a term eliminating any warranty of quality or fitness. After driving 27 miles plaintiff was involved in a collision owing to a defect in the braking system which caused him loss, and claimed to recover his loss from defendants.
HELD: (1) The contract was a defence apart from breach of statutory duty. (2) There was a breach of statutory duty but the Act had provided a specific remedy, and this deprived the subject of any other form of remedy. Applying *Phillips v Britannia Hygienic Laundry* judgment was given for defendants.

Vinall v Howard
[1954] 1 QB 375, [1954] 1 All ER 458, [1954] 2 WLR 314, 98 Sol Jo 143, CA
Plaintiff sold to defendant a secondhand motor car which had defects in the speedometer, brake and silencer. Both parties were aware of the defects at the date of sale. Defendant gave a cheque in payment but stopped payment of the cheque and plaintiff sued for the amount of the cheque. Streatfeild J held the sale was unlawful under s 8 (1) of the 1934 Act (now replaced by s 60 (1) of the 1972 Act).
HELD, ON APPEAL by the defendant: The defects were not in the original construction and equipment of the car but neglect of proper maintenance, a failure to keep in working order. They did not come under Part II of the Regulations made under s 3 of the 1930 Act but arose under Part III made under s 30 of the 1930 Act. The defects did not fall within s 3 and the contract was not unlawful under s 8 (1) of the 1934 Act.

Note—The Road Traffic Act 1972, s 60 (5) provides: 'Nothing in the foregoing provisions of this section shall affect the validity of a contract or any rights arising under a contract.' There was no such provision in the 1930 Act.

Tests of condition of vehicles

Note—The Road Traffic Act 1972, s 43, replacing the Road Traffic Act 1960, s 65 contains provisions for the purpose of ascertaining whether the prescribed statutory requirements relating to the construction and condition of motor vehicles are complied with. Subsection 2 of the section enables the Secretary of State to make provision by regulations for the examination of vehicles and the issue of test certificates. Section 44 makes it an offence to use on a road a vehicle to which the section applies and in respect of which no test certificate has been issued within the previous 12 months. The section applies to vehicles registered more than ten years but enables the Minister by regulation to substitute a shorter period. The period is at present three years.

The Motor Vehicles (Tests) Regulations, SI 1981/1694, have been made under s 43. They provide, inter alia, for examiners to be authorised to carry out tests at vehicle testing stations, requirements as to vehicles submitted for examinations and the manner of carrying out the examinations. Regulation 14 provides that when a vehicle has been submitted for examination the authorised examiner shall have the same responsibility for loss of or damage to the vehicle or to any other property, or personal injury, arising out of the use of the vehicle in connection with the carrying out of the examination as would rest on a person who had undertaken for payment to accept the custody of the vehicle and to carry out the same examination under a contract making no express provision with respect to the incidence of liability as between the parties thereto for any such loss, damage or injury.

This provision would appear to exclude the operation of any 'owners risk' notices or other exemptions from liability which may be displayed at garages and service stations which are also authorised vehicle testing stations whilst a vehicle is being tested or is in the custody of the examiner for the purpose of carrying out the test.

MOT inspection: civil liability

Rowley v Chatham
[1970] RTR 462 (Shaw J)
On 6 March the defendant, an authorised examiner under the Motor Vehicles (Test) Regulations 1960, issued a test certificate relating to the plaintiff's husband's motor van. On 31 March the plaintiff's husband was driving the van when it steered into the path of an approaching lorry and he was killed. It was found that the upper and lower ball race cages of the steering column had broken down. There was evidence that this state of affairs had existed at the time of the test on 6 March.
HELD: (1) On the evidence adduced by the defendant, the tests required by the 1960 Regulations were properly and duly applied and would not have revealed that there was a fault or defect in the steering. (2) The relationship between the examiner and the owner of the vehicle is a contractual one but the duty owed by the examiner is prescribed by the Regulations and is limited to certifying the condition of the vehicle at the date of the examination. Any representation expressed or implicit in the certificate cannot be relied upon (as in the present case) some weeks

later. The purpose of the Road Traffic Act 1960, s 66 is to protect the public from unroadworthy vehicles, not to provide motorists with a cheap means of being advised on the condition of their own vehicles. Judgment for the defendant.

Note—See also *Rees v Saville*, p 242, above.

Artingstoll v Hewen's Garages Ltd
[1973] RTR 197 (Kerr J)
On 13 December 1967, the plaintiff delivered his car to the defendants, who were authorised examiners for the annual MOT test. After the test they issued a notification of refusal of a certificate saying that the nearside front hub bearing needed renewal. The plaintiff obtained a new bearing and the defendants fitted it. Without further test they then issued a test certificate on 14 December. Five weeks later during which the plaintiff had driven the car 700 miles it suddenly veered across a busy main road and collided with an approaching vehicle, injuring the plaintiff. It was found that steering joints were loose. The plaintiff sued the defendants for damages for personal injury.
HELD: Following *Rowley's* case (above) (1) there is a duty on an examiner in contract to carry out the test properly and with reasonable skill and care and the issue of a test certificate bearing the prescribed wording also imports a warranty that the statutory requirements prescribed by the regulations were complied with at the date of the examination; (2) though a claim for damages either in contract or tort may be difficult to establish because of the lapse of time there is no reason in principle (contrary to the view expressed in *Rowley's* case) why substantial (as distinct from nominal) damages should not be recovered by a plaintiff who can prove a failure to carry out the examination with proper skill and care and the issue of a test certificate which should not have been issued and that loss and damage were thereby caused; (3) if a plaintiff himself was guilty of some degree of carelessness in driving at the time of the accident the court can make an apportionment as between the causative faults under the Law Reform (Contributory Negligence) Act 1945 even if the claim is regarded as lying solely in contract; (4) on the facts of the present case the plaintiff had failed to prove any breach of contract or duty in relation to the brakes or steering. Action dismissed.

Note—But see *Basildon District-Council v Lesser*, p 13, and *Maritrans A B v Comet Shipping*, p 14, above.

OCCUPIER'S LIABILITY ACT 1957

Note—Section 1 (3) (a) applies the duty of an occupier to visitors to the person having control over any vehicle. Section 5 (2) applies that section to vehicles. The motorist is therefore concerned in respect of passengers, and also in respect of damage caused to his vehicle where he visits premises. The relevant sections of the Act are set out below.
The Act abolished the distinction between invitees and licensees, and enacted the same duty to every visitor, a 'common duty of care', which is a duty to take such care as in all the circumstances of the case is reasonable to see that the visitor

will be reasonably safe in using the premises for the purpose for which he is invited or permitted to be there. Note that, in respect particularly of s 2, the Unfair Contract Terms Act 1977 (p 338, below) prohibits the exclusion or restriction by a term of a contract or by notice of liability for death or personal injury resulting from negligence, where such liability arises in the course of business.

Relevant sections of the Act

2 Extent of occupier's ordinary duty   (1) An occupier of premises owes the same duty, the 'common duty of care', to all his visitors, except in so far as he is free to and does extend, restrict, modify or exclude his duty to any visitor or visitors by agreement or otherwise.

(2) The common duty of care is a duty to take such care as in all the circumstances of the case is reasonable to see that the visitor will be reasonably safe in using the premises for the purpose for which he is invited or permitted by the occupier to be there.

(3) The circumstances relevant for the present purpose include the degree of care and of want of care, which would ordinarily be looked for in such a visitor, so that (for example) in proper cases —

(a) an occupier must be prepared for children to be less careful than adults; and

(b) an occupier may expect that a person, in the exercise of his calling, will appreciate and guard against any special risks ordinarily incident to it, so far as the occupier leaves him free to do so.

(4) In determining whether the occupier of premises had discharged the common duty of care to a visitor, regard is to be had to all the circumstances, so that (for example) —

(a) where damage is caused to a visitor by a danger of which he had been warned by the occupier, the warning is not to be treated without more as absolving the occupier from liability, unless in all the circumstances it was enough to enable the visitor to be reasonably safe; and

(b) where damage is caused to a visitor by a danger due to the faulty execution of any work of construction, maintenance or repair by an independent contractor employed by the occupier, the occupier is not to be treated without more as answerable for the danger if in all the circumstances he had acted reasonably in entrusting the work to an independent contractor and had taken such steps (if any) as he reasonably ought in order to satisfy himself that the contractor was competent and that the work had been properly done.

(5) The common duty of care does not impose on an occupier any obligation to a visitor in respect of risks willingly accepted as his by the visitor (the question whether a risk was so accepted to be decided on the same principles as in other cases in which one person owes a duty of care to another).

(6) For the purposes of this section, persons who enter premises for any purpose in the exercise of a right conferred by law are to be treated as permitted by the occupier to be there for that purpose whether they have in fact his permission or not.

3 Effect of contract on occupier's liability to third party   (1) Where an occupier of premises is bound by contract to permit persons who are strangers to the contract to enter or use the premises, the duty of care which he owes to them as his visitors cannot be restricted or excluded by that contract, but (subject to any provision of the contract to the contrary) shall include the duty to perform his obligations under the contract, whether undertaken for their protection or not, in so far as those obligations go beyond the obligations otherwise involved in that duty.

(2) A contract shall not by virtue of this section have the effect, unless it expressly so provides, of making an occupier who has taken all reasonable care answerable

to strangers to the contract for dangers due to the faulty execution of any work of construction, maintenance or repair or other like operation by persons other than himself, his servants and persons acting under his direction and control.

(3) In this section 'stranger to the contract' means a person not for the time being entitled to the benefit of the contract as a party to it or as the successor by assignment or otherwise of a party to it, and accordingly includes a party to the contract who has ceased to be so entitled.

LIABILITY IN CONTRACT

5 Implied term in contracts   (1) Where persons enter or use, or bring or send goods to, any premises in exercise of a right conferred by contract with a person occupying or having control of the premises, the duty he owes them in respect of dangers due to the state of the premises or to things done or omitted to be done on them, in so far as the duty depends on a term to be implied in the contract by reason of its conferring that right, shall be the common duty of care.

(2) The foregoing subsection shall apply to fixed and movable structures as it applies to premises.

(3) This section does not affect the obligations imposed on a person by or by virtue of any contract for the hire of, or for the carriage for reward of persons or goods in, any vehicle, vessel, aircraft or other means of transport, or by virtue of any contract of bailment.

GENERAL

6 Application to Crown   This Act shall bind the Crown, but as regards the Crown's liability in tort shall not bind the Crown further than the Crown is made liable in tort by the Crown Proceedings Act 1947, and that Act and in particular section two of it shall apply in relation to duties under sections two or four of this Act as statutory duties.

The Occupier's Liability Act 1984 requires an occupier of premises 'to take such care as is reasonable in all the circumstances' to see that a person (not being his visitor within the meaning of the 1957 Act) does not suffer injury on the premises by reason of a danger of which the occupier knows or has reasonable grounds to believe exists when he knows or has reasonable grounds to believe the other may be in its vicinity. The duty can be discharged in an appropriate case by a warning. 'Premises' includes any fixed or movable structure and 'movable structure' includes 'any vessel, vehicle or aircraft'. No duty is owed under the Act to persons using the highway.

CHAPTER 7
Fire damage

Note—Liability for damage to property by fire may be founded in negligence; or, where there is an escape of fire due to a non-natural use of land, there may be liability without negligence. If negligence is relied on, the burden of proof is on the plaintiff (Fires Prevention (Metropolis) Act 1774). Both grounds of liability were considered in *Musgrove v Pandelis*, where the fire began in a motor car:

Musgrove v Pandelis
[1919] 2 KB 43, 88 LJKB 915, 120 LT 601, 35 TLR 299, 63 Sol Jo 353, CA
Plaintiff occupied rooms over a garage. Part of the garage was let to defendant, who kept a motor car there. Defendant's servant, who had little skill as a chauffeur, having occasion in the course of his employment to move the motor car, started the engine, and from some unexplained cause, and without negligence on the part of the servant, the petrol in the carburettor caught fire. If the servant had promptly turned off the tap leading from the petrol tank to the carburettor, the fire would have harmlessly burnt itself out. But he failed to do this; and the fire spread and burnt the car, the garage and plaintiff's rooms and furniture. Plaintiff brought an action for damages. Defendant pleaded that the fire accidentally began within the meaning of the above enactment. The judge at the trial found that defendant's servant was negligent in not promptly turning off the petrol tap.
HELD: (1) The Fires Prevention (Metropolis) Act 1774, did not protect a person who brought upon his premises an object likely to do damage if not kept in control, and a motor car ready to start, or such a car in charge of an unskilled chauffeur, was an object of that kind; (2) the fire which caused the damage was not that which took place in the carburettor, but was the fire which spread to the car; and this fire did not begin accidentally but was caused by the negligence of defendant's servant.

Note—The Fires Prevention (Metropolis) Act 1774 (which applies to the whole country) provides that no action shall lie against a person on whose land any fire 'shall accidentally begin'. The Act has been interpreted to mean that such a person shall not be liable merely because the fire began on his premises: if the plaintiff cannot prove negligence he will not succeed unless he can bring his case within the principle of strict liability for the escape of the fire, against which the act gives no protection.

Mason v Levy Auto Parts of England

[1967] 2 QB 530, [1967] 2 All ER 62, [1967] 2 WLR 1384, 111 Sol Jo 234, [1967] 1 Lloyd's Rep 372

The plaintiff's house and garden adjoined the defendants' premises on which they stored large quantities of machinery and spare parts. The machinery was coated in grease and packed in paper and was contained in wooden packing cases. There were quantities of other combustible materials including tarpaulins and inflammable liquids. Fire broke out among this material through no ascertainable cause and spread to the plaintiff's property causing damage.

HELD: The defendants had the protection of the Fires Prevention (Metropolis) Act 1774, against a claim based on their negligence in causing the fire or allowing it to spread: the onus of proof of negligence was on the plaintiff and he had failed to discharge it. But the Act did not give protection to a defendant who in the course of some non-natural use of the land had brought on to it things likely to catch fire and had kept them there in such conditions that if they did catch fire the fire would be likely to spread to the plaintiff's land (*Musgrove v Pandelis*). In the present case having regard to the amount of combustible material, the way in which it was stored and the character of the neighbourhood the defendants' use of their land was non-natural and they were liable for the damage done to the plaintiff's premises by the escape of the fire.

LIABILITY FOR ESCAPE

Sturge v Hackett

[1962] 3 All ER 166, [1962] 1 WLR 1257, 106 Sol Jo 568, 183 Estates Gazette 161, CA

The tenant of a flat forming part of a house wished to destroy a bird's nest in a cornice on the exterior of his flat. He stood on the roof of a porch (not forming part of his flat) below the cornice, lit some paraffin-soaked rags and then applied them at the end of a stick to the nest. The nest caught fire and a piece of burning straw entered the roof-space, setting fire to the house, which was burnt down. In an action arising from the destruction of the house a question arose whether the fire started on the premises (ie the flat) of which he was occupier.

HELD: Following *Musgrove v Pandelis* the relevant fire for the purposes of the old common law liability of allowing fire to escape from one's premises is the fire which gets out of control — not the match or other means used for lighting the fire which gets out of control. The paraffin rag was merely the means by which he ignited the nest. What got out of control and spread was the new fire which he started when he applied the paraffin rag to the base of the nest.

Collingwood v Home and Colonial Stores

[1936] 3 All ER 200, 155 LT 550, 53 TLR 53, 56 Ll L Rep 105, CA

The dicta in the judgments in *Musgrove's* case which suggested that the principle of *Rylands v Fletcher* applied, have been criticised as follows:

Per Lord Wright MR: I confess, however, I find some difficulty about the other ground (than negligence) on which the decision was based though, if it were necessary, I should follow the ruling of the Court of Appeal.

Per Romer LJ: I think at some time it will be desirable if the House of Lords would consider the case of *Musgrove v Pandelis*, so far as the decision in that case was based upon *Rylands v Fletcher* (1) that a motor car is a dangerous thing to bring into a garage, and (2) that the use of one's land for the purpose of erecting a garage and keeping a motor car there, is not an ordinary and proper use of the land, are two propositions which, but for that authority, I should myself respectfully have doubted.

Read v J. Lyons & Co Ltd

[1947] AC 156, [1946] 2 All ER 471, [1947] LJR 39, 175 LT 413, 62 TLR 646, 91 Sol Jo 52, HL

A worker was injured in a munition factory by the explosion of a shell. She claimed that the employers were liable without proof of negligence under the principle of *Rylands v Fletcher*.

HELD: Two conditions were necessary (1) escape from the place of occupation, and (2) non-natural use of the land, and there was no 'escape'.

Per Lord Porter: Furthermore, in *Musgrove v Pandelis* it was held that a motor car brought into a garage with full tanks was a dangerous object, a conclusion which, as Romer LJ pointed out in *Collingwood v Home and Colonial Stores*, involves the propositions that a motor car is a dangerous thing to bring into a garage and that the use of one's land for the purpose of erecting a garage and keeping a motor car there is not an ordinary or proper use of the land.

My Lord, if these questions ever come directly before this House it may be necessary to lay down principles for their determination. For the present I need only say that each seem to be a question of fact . . . and . . . all the circumstances of the time and place and practice of mankind must be taken into consideration so that what might be regarded as dangerous or non-natural may vary according to those circumstances.

The question whether the principle applied to personal injuries was left open. Lord Macmillan did not think it had ever been laid down that it did; and if the foundation was to be found in the injunction *sic utere tuo ut alienum non laedas*, it was manifest it did not apply to personal injuries.

Lord Porter said this point was not in issue and the cases where it had been thought to apply, *Shiffman v Order of St John* [1936] 1 All ER 557, 80 Sol Jo 346 and *Miles v Forest Rock Granite Co (Leicestershire) Ltd* (1918) 34 TLR 500, 62 Sol Jo 634 may some day require examination.

Note—See also *Dunne v North Western Gas Board*, p 298, below.

Leong Bee & Co v Ling Nam Rubber Works
(1970) 114 Sol Jo 806, [1970] 2 Lloyd's Rep 247, PC

A fire started on the respondents' premises at night and spread to the appellants' building 14 feet away. There was no evidence to show how the fire began.

HELD: The burden of proof lay on the appellants (as original plaintiffs) as to both negligence and nuisance. Their task at the trial was to establish (1) that the respondents themselves or some person for whose conduct they were answerable had been guilty of some negligent act or omission which was a cause either of the commencement of the fire or of its spreading to the appellants' premises, or (2) that the respondents had caused or permitted to exist on their premises a source of fire danger giving rise to a reasonably forseeable risk of material injury. On the evidence given at the trial the fire was not caused by the respondents' negligence or nuisance. Their only remaining duty was under the principle explained in *Goldman v Hargrave* (p 256, below) and based on knowledge of the fire, foreseeability of the consequences of not checking it and ability to abate it. Although the respondents' nightwatchman became aware of the fire and could foresee the consequences there was nothing he could then do which would have saved the appellants' building. The respondents were not liable.

Perry v Kendricks Transport Ltd
[1956] 1 All ER 154, [1956] 1 WLR 85, 100 Sol Jo 52, CA

Garage and coach proprietors had left a coach for three months on their parking ground adjoining waste land. People crossing the waste land might go through the vehicle park, though they had no right to do so. When left, the tank was emptied of petrol and the cap of the tank replaced. There was regular inspection of the park and vehicles. A boy aged ten saw two other boys near the coach and went towards them. As he neared them, they jumped away and there was an explosion and he was dreadfully burned. The court concluded that the cap had been removed by someone before the accident and found there was no negligence of the proprietors. It was also contended that the case came within the rule in *Rylands v Fletcher* which contention failed.

HELD, ON APPEAL: Assuming the removal of the cap and the throwing of a lighted match was done by the two boys mischievously and deliberately, it was not something the defendants ought to have anticipated and the rule did not apply to the wrongful acts of third parties over whom the defendants had no control.

Per Parker LJ: Although the decision in *Musgrove v Pandelis* (p 251, above) has been the subject of some criticism, it is still binding on the Court of Appeal, nor do I think it is open to this court to hold that it does not apply to personal injury.

Note—Followed by Pearce J in *Adcock v Loveridge* (1956) Times, 21 June.

H. and N. Emanuel Ltd v Greater London Council
[1971] 2 All ER 835, 115 Sol Jo 226, 218 Estates Gazette 1413, [1971] 2
Lloyd's Rep 36, CA
A demolition contractor was removing prefabricated bungalows under
contract with the Ministry of Works from land belonging to the defendant
council. In breach of a term of his contract with the Ministry he lit a rubbish
fire and negligently allowed sparks to fly on to the plaintiffs' adjoining
property causing fire damage to buildings and vehicles. He had no contract
with the defendants but he was on the site with their permission. Their
foreman had the keys of the prefabs and anyone wanting to do anything
with them had to get his permission. There was evidence that it was a
standard practice of demolition contractors to light fires when clearing
sites.
HELD: It has been the law for centuries that an occupier of premises is
liable for an escape of fire caused by anyone other than a 'stranger', though
since the Fires Prevention (Metropolis) Act 1774 the escape must be negligent. The contractor was negligent: was he a 'stranger' ie a person who
acts in a way contrary to anything which the occupier could anticipate? As
there was a standard practice among demolition men to burn rubbish and
as they were on the site with the leave and knowledge of the defendants they
were not 'strangers'. The defendants were occupiers and had control over
the activities of the contractor. They were liable to the plaintiffs.

Scotland

Sinclair v Juner
(1952) 101 L Jo 706, Ct of Sess First Div
The principles of the Act of 1774 that a fire is deemed to accidentally begin
do not apply to Scotland.

LIABILITY FOR NEGLIGENCE

Onus of proof

Note—*Charlesworth on Negligence* (7th edn) para 13-77 says — 'the burden of
proving negligence rests firmly on the plaintiff. It is not for the defendant to prove
that the fire was accidental in its origin.' The cases cited in support are *Becquet v
Maccarthy* (1831) 2 B & Ad 951, and *Musgrove v Pandelis, Collingwood v Home &
Colonial Stores* and *Williams v Owen* (p 257, below).
But in the case of a bailment the onus is on the bailee. See below, *Hyman v Benedyk*
and *Smith v Taylor*, p 258, below.

Roskill v Cook
(1932) 43 Ll L Rep 511 (de Parcq J)
A fire occurred in the plaintiff's house. The plaintiff suggested that the fire
originated in a wood block in the party wall. The defendant suggested it
arose from an electric installation in the plaintiff's house.
HELD: The plaintiff had failed to discharge the onus of proof of the cause of
the fire.

Sochaki v Sas
[1947] 1 All ER 344 (Lord Goddard CJ)
A lodger went out leaving a fire burning in his room, and was away two or
three hours. There was no evidence that he made up the fire in an unusual
way or built up any enormous fire. While he was out a fire took place,
probably caused by a spark jumping from the fire and setting fire to the
floorboards. There was no fire guard or iron fender. There was an ordinary, natural, proper, everyday use of the fire place.
HELD: No evidence of negligence. The lodger was not liable under *Rylands
v Fletcher*, and the doctrine of *res ipsa loquitur* did not apply. The lodger was
not liable.

Negligence: principles of liability

Balfour v Barty-King
[1957] 1 QB 496, [1957] 1 All ER 156, [1957] 2 WLR 84, 101 Sol Jo 62,
[1956] 2 Lloyd's Rep 646, CA
A large country house had been divided into separate dwelling houses. The
defendant occupied one part and the plaintiff occupied another part which
adjoined and was contiguous to the defendant's part. The water system of
defendant's house became frozen and he employed an independent contractor to do the necessary work. The cisterns were in a loft which
contained combustible material. The contractor's men used a blowlamp,
which set fire to the material. The fire spread to the roof and so to the plaintiff's house and caused considerable damage to it. The trial judge found
that the contractor's men were negligent in using a blowlamp near to
combustible material. He held the defendant was liable to the plaintiff for
the damage. The defendant appealed.
HELD: There was no direct authority. From very early times the law
recognised a special duty to guard against an escape of fire. The curfew was
imposed as a precautionary measure. *Musgrove v Pandelis* (p 251, above)
held that the statutory exception of accidental fire leaves the other heads of
liability at common law untouched. It is clear that at the present day a
person in whose house a fire is caused by negligence is liable if it spreads to
that of his neighbour, whether the negligence is his own or that of his
servant or guest but not a stranger. A trespasser would be a stranger, but an
employed contractor cannot be in any better position than a guest. Here
the defendant had control of the contractor in that he chose him, invited
him to his premises to do the work, and could have ordered him to leave
at any moment. The defendant is liable to the plaintiff for the plaintiff's
damage.

Goldman v Hargrave
[1967] 1 AC 645, [1966] 2 All ER 989, [1966] 3 WLR 513, 110 Sol Jo 527,
[1966] 2 Lloyd's Rep 65, PC
On 25 February a tree on the appellant's land was struck by lightning and
caught fire 84 feet above the ground. The appellant had the tree felled on
the following day to deal with the blaze but instead of putting the fire out
with water, which he could have done on the morning of the 25th at the
latest, he preferred to burn it out. On 1 March the wind rose, reviving the

fire, which then spread to the respondent's adjoining properties causing damage.

HELD: (1) There is a general duty of care on occupiers in relation to hazards occurring on their land, including that of fire, and whether natural or man-made, to remove or reduce such hazards. The duty is based on knowledge of the hazard, ability to foresee the consequences of not checking or removing it, and the ability to abate it. What is reasonable for the occupier to do depends on his circumstances: he should not be held liable unless it is clearly proved that he could, and reasonably in his individual circumstances should, have done more. In the present case it was well within the capacity and resources of the appellant to put the fire out on 26 or 27 February and he was liable to the respondents for not having done so; (2) The Fires Prevention (Metropolis) Act 1774 relieved an owner from liability for a mere escape of fire but not from a claim for damages for negligence — *Musgrove v Pandelis* (p 251, above). In the present case the fire which damaged the respondents' property was that which arose on 1 March as a result of the negligence of the appellant, and the statutory defence failed.

Note—See also *Sturge v Hackett*, p 252, above.

Williams v Owen

[1956] 1 All ER 104, [1955] 1 WLR 1293, 99 Sol Jo 890 (Finnemore J)

Plaintiff was a guest at an hotel and his car was in the hotel garage. The car was destroyed by fire. He sued the hotel keeper for damages for its loss. His claim was based on the responsibility of an innkeeper at common law for the goods of his guests. The defendant claimed to be protected by the Fires Prevention (Metropolis) Act 1774, s 86, which prohibits the bringing of proceedings against a person on whose premises a fire accidentally begins 'any law, usage or custom to the contrary notwithstanding'. In a corner of the garage was a small boiler for heating water for rooms above the garage occupied by the staff. The boiler had a closing door and was surrounded by a concrete wall 7 ft 6 in high, and it was stoked from the far side where there was a ramp. The boiler was lit about noon and stoked until 2.30 pm when it was shut down and the fire allowed to die out, and was usually out by 8 pm. The fire broke out about 11.30 pm.

HELD: That the innkeeper's liability at common law was a custom within the meaning of s 86, and that accordingly the defendant's liability was limited, in the case of damage by fire, to non-accidental fires. The Act of 1774 applied and plaintiff had not proved negligence. Verdict for defendant.

Liability of bailee

I. and J. Hyman (Sales) Ltd v A. Benedyk & Co Ltd

[1957] 2 Lloyd's Rep 601 (Judge Malcolm Wright), Lambeth CC

Rags belonging to the plaintiffs, rag and general merchants, were being processed in defendants' premises by the defendants. Fire broke out on the defendants' premises and the plaintiffs' goods were damaged. It was common ground that the defendants were bailees for reward. The likely cause of the fire was by a cigarette or match carelessly disposed of by defendants' labourer, but the judge did not think this was proved. Defendants contended that, under the 1774 Act, the onus was on the plaintiffs to prove negligence.

HELD: At common law the onus was on defendants as bailees to prove absence of negligence.

The onus was on the defendants to show that the fire was accidental. In *Charlesworth on Negligence* (3rd edn) p 298, it is stated the burden of proving negligence is on the plaintiff (*Willams v Owen*, above.) Apart from innkeeper's liability, that was not a case of bailor and bailee.

When defendants seek to rely on the statute, in a case where the law requires them to prove the absence of negligence, the duty lies on them to prove the defence they have set up. Judgment for plaintiffs.

Smith v Taylor

[1966] 2 Lloyd's Rep 231 (Blain J)

The plaintiff left his car for repair at the defendant's garage. Whilst the mechanic was draining the petrol tank a quantity of petrol spilled on to the floor. A short time later the car burst into flames and was destroyed. The cause of the fire was not ascertained.

HELD: The defendant being a bailee was at common law under a liability to establish that when a vehicle entrusted to his care was damaged that did not happen through negligence on his part or that of his servant or agent. It was therefore, necessary, even when the plaintiff's expert witness could not establish the probable cause of the fire, for the defendant, if he sought to escape liability, to call evidence. The mechanic knew that petrol vapour was dangerous in the presence of an electric lead lamp such as he was using and his failure to take the necessary steps to prevent a quantity of petrol spilling on the floor was negligence. The defendant was liable.

Inference of negligence

Anglo-Saxon Petroleum Co v The Admiralty

[1947] KB 794, [1947] 2 All ER 465, [1948] LJR 153, 80 Ll L Rep 459, CA

An oil tanker during the war stranded in Alexandria Harbour. The naval authorities took complete control of the salvage operations and lightened the ship by forcing petrol by air pressure out of the tanks with the result that there was one-sixteenth of an inch of petrol over two square miles of sea. Two tugs were sent to the stranded vessel. The petrol caught fire. The cause of the fire could not be determined. Probable causes were (1) smoking, both lighting and from burning cigarette ends thrown away; (2) galley fires; (3) sparks from the funnel of the tugs; (4) sparks from any blow of steel against steel; (5) electric sparks from the tug's degaussing coils. The plaintiffs were unable to say which one was the actual cause.

HELD: The plaintiffs were entitled to succeed if they established a balance of probability that the source of the ignition emanated from the tugs rather than from the ship. In one sense it was a new point but it depended on well-established principles. Verdict for plaintiffs upheld.

Servant smoking at work

Note—See also *Jefferson v Derbyshire Farmers Ltd*, p 158, above and *British Transport Commission v Maxine*, p 158, above.

Century Insurance Co v Northern Ireland Road Transport Board

[1942] AC 509, [1942] 1 All ER 491, 111 LJPC 138, 167 LT 404, 72 Ll L Rep 119, HL

Policy covered use of motor tanker including loading and unloading not beyond the limit of the carriageway or thoroughfare. The driver backed a petrol lorry into the garage of a customer, inserted the nozzle of the delivery hose into the manhole of the customer's storage tank and turned on the stopcock at the side of the tanker. While petrol was flowing from the tanker to the tank, he lit a cigarette, and threw the lighted match on the floor of the garage, which ignited material on the floor of the garage and set fire to the petrol at the nozzle. He drove the tanker out of the garage and stopped with the fore-wheels in the water channel and jumped off. An explosion occurred causing damage to the tanker and to property of third parties.

HELD: (1) This was negligence in the discharge of his duties and the master was responsible. It need not be an act for the employer's benefit. (2) The damage was caused by the use of the tanker including loading and unloading.

Paraffin

Mulholland and Tedd Ltd v Baker

[1939] 3 All ER 253, 161 LT 20 (Asquith J)

Asquith J in a case of a 20-gallon drum of paraffin catching fire in the yard of a shop, adopted the decision in *Musgrove v Pandelis* (p 251, above) that it is not necessary to prove negligence where the defendant has brought on his premises an object likely to do damage if it is not kept under control and that object catches fire, but as he had already found negligence of the defendant, his decision was really obiter.

CHAPTER 8
Animals on highway

LIABILITY OF OWNER

THE ANIMALS ACT 1971

Note—The common law rules which formerly determined the liability of owners for damage caused by animals were amended and partially codified by the Animals Act 1971, which came into force on 1 October 1971. The owner of an animal has a duty to take reasonable care so to control or restrain the animal that it does not cause damage or injury to persons using the highway (*Deen v Davies*, p 269, below), but the old common law rule (see *Searle v Wallbank*, p 273, below) that an owner is under no duty to prevent his animals from straying on to the highway is abolished.

Those sections of the Act which are or may be relevant to motor claims are as follows.

1 New provisions as to strict liability for damage done by animals (1) The provision of ss 2 to 5 of this Act replace —
(a) the rules of the common law imposing a strict liability in tort for damage done by an animal on the ground that the animal is regarded as ferae naturae or that its vicious or mischievous propensities are known or presumed to be known;
(b) . . .
(c) . . .
(2) Expressions used in those sections shall be interpreted in accordance with the provisions of s 6 (as well as those of s 11) of this Act.

2 Liability for damage done by dangerous animals (1) Where any damage is caused by an animal which belongs to a dangerous species, any person who is a keeper of the animal is liable for the damage, except as otherwise provided by this Act.
(2) Where damage is caused by an animal which does not belong to a dangerous species, a keeper of the animal is liable for the damage, except as otherwise provided by this Act, if
(a) the damage is of a kind which the animal, unless restrained, was likely to cause or which, if caused by the animal, was likely to be severe; and

260

(b) the likelihood of the damage or of its being severe was due to characteristics of the animal which are not normally found in animals of the same species or are not normally so found except at particular times or in particular circumstances; and

(c) those characteristics were known to that keeper or were at any time known to a person who at that time had charge of the animal as that keeper's servant or, where that keeper is the head of a household, were known to another keeper of the animal who is a member of that household and under the age of sixteen.

5 Exceptions from liability under sections 2 to 4   (1) A person is not liable under ss 2 to 4 of this Act for any damage which is due wholly to the fault of the person suffering it.

(2) A person is not liable under s 2 of this Act for any damage suffered by a person who has voluntarily accepted the risk thereof.

6 Interpretation of certain expressions used in sections 2 to 5   (1) The following provisions apply to the interpretation of ss 2 to 5 of this Act.

(2) A dangerous species is a species —

(a) which is not commonly domesticated in the British Islands; and

(b) whose fully grown animals normally have such characteristics that they are likely, unless restrained, to cause severe damage or that any damage they may cause is likely to be severe.

(3) Subject to subs (4) of this section, a person is a keeper of an animal if —

(a) he owns the animal or has it in his possession; or

(b) he is the head of a household of which a member under the age of sixteen owns the animal or has it in his possession;

and if at any time an animal ceases to be owned by or to be in the possession of a person, any person who immediately before that time was a keeper thereof by virtue of the preceding provisions of this subsection continues to be a keeper of the animal until another person becomes a keeper thereof by virtue of those provisions.

(4) Where an animal is taken into and kept in possession for the purpose of preventing it from causing damage or of restoring it to its owner, a person is not a keeper of it by virtue only of that possession.

(5) Where a person employed as a servant by a keeper of an animal incurs a risk incidental to his employment he shall not be treated as accepting it voluntarily.

8 Duty to take care to prevent damage from animals straying on to the highway   (1) So much of the rules of the common law relating to liability for negligence as excludes or restricts the duty which a person might owe to others to take such care as is reasonable to see that damage is not caused by animals straying on to a highway is hereby abolished.

(2) Where damage is caused by animals straying from unfenced land to a highway a person who placed them on the land shall not be regarded as having committed a breach of the duty to take care by reason only of placing them there if —

(a) the land is common land, or is land situated in an area where fencing is not customary, or is a town or village green; and

(b) he had a right to place the animals on that land.

10 Application of certain enactments to liability under sections 2 to 4   For the purposes of the [Fatal Accidents Act 1976] the Law Reform (Contributory Negligence) Act 1945 and the [Limitation Act 1980] any damage for which a person is liable under ss 2 to 4 of this Act shall be treated as due to his fault.

11 General interpretation   In this Act —

'common land', and 'town or village green' have the same meanings as in the Commons Registration Act 1965;

'damage' includes the death of, or injury to, any person (including any disease and any impairment of physical or mental condition);

'fault' has the same meaning as in the Law Reform (Contributory Negligence) Act 1945;

'fencing' includes the construction of any obstacle designed to prevent animals from straying;

'species' includes sub-species and variety.

12 Application to Crown   (1) This Act binds the Crown, but nothing in this section shall authorise proceedings to be brought against Her Majesty in her private capacity.

(2) Section 38 (3) of the Crown Proceedings Act 1947 (interpretation of references to Her Majesty in her private capacity) shall apply as if this section were contained in that Act.

   [*The Act does not apply to Scotland*].

Wallace v Newton

[1982] 2 All ER 106, [1982] 1 WLR 375, 126 Sol Jo 101, (Park J)

The plaintiff was employed as a groom, handling horses belonging to her employer which were used for show jumping. On an occasion when she was leading a horse into a horsebox it suddenly leaped or lunged forward, crushing her arm against a bar in the trailer. The injury was serious. She claimed damages under the Animals Act 1971, s 2(2).

HELD: By s 2(2)(b) the plaintiff had to establish that the likelihood of the damage was due to characteristics of the animal which were not normally found in horses. This did not mean the horse had to be shown to have a vicious tendency to injure people by attacking them: it was sufficient to show that it had characteristics of a kind not usually found in horses. There was evidence that during the period the plaintiff had the horse in her charge its behaviour was unpredictable and unreliable and that the owner, the defendant, knew of it. The plaintiff was entitled to succeed.

Davies v Davies

[1975] QB 172, [1974] 3 All ER 817, [1974] 3 WLR 607, 118 Sol Jo 717, CA

Alongside a main road was a large area of common land. Owners of a nearby farm were entitled to put animals on the common for grazing and were registered for that purpose under the Commons Registration Act 1965. Sheep got on the road from the common; the plaintiff in his car collided with them without negligence on his part and his car was damaged. The defendant, who was a son of the owner of the farm by whom he was licensed to have sheep on the farm, was charged under the Highways Act 1959, s 135 and pleaded guilty. The plaintiff sued for the damage to his car.

HELD: The defendant was not liable. He had the right to place sheep on the common and so was protected by the Animals Act 1971, s 8(2). A conviction under the Highways Act did not make him liable for a civil offence. Being licensed to put sheep on the common was sufficient to apply s 8(2); the protection was not limited to persons actually having title to the land.

OWNER'S DUTY OF CARE

Deen v Davies
[1935] 2 KB 282 at 295
Per Romer LJ: The general principle is established that the owner of an animal which he brings on to the highway must use all reasonable care to prevent the animal doing damage.

Note—For facts see p 269, below.

Ludlam v Peel
(1939) Times, 10 October
Cattle belonging to a farmer were customarily driven from the farm for about a mile along the Great North Road to a field. Six cows were being driven along the grass verge at the side of the road. A motor car was being driven along the road in the opposite direction. When the car was a few yards away, one cow suddenly ran out across the road in front of the car and a collision occurred. The county court judge based on the judgment of Lord Moncrieff in *Harper v GNR of Scotland* 1886 13 R (Ct of Sess) 1139, held it was not necessary to prove actual negligence, and there was a duty to control the cows on the highway, and the farmer had failed to keep them under proper control.
HELD, ON APPEAL: It was necessary to prove negligence. The owner had employed a competent drover and there was no evidence of failure to take reasonable care. The county court judge had sought to impose an absolute duty which did not exist in law.

Cows

Imrie v Clark
(1939) Times, 24 October (Lord Patrick)
A motor cyclist at 5.45 am whilst it was dark, collided with cattle on the road. The owner of the cattle had opened a gate between the field and the road to allow the cattle to emerge and proceed along the road to the farm. The owner remained in the field and took no steps to warn drivers of vehicles in the road.
HELD: The cattle were entitled to use the road for passage as much as motor cars or pedestrians. The law does not require or custom prescribe that warnings should be given of cattle on the road or that in the dark the cattle owner must place lights on the road or give signals to warn traffic.

Note—But see next case.

Harrison v Jackson
(1947) 14 LJNCCR 242 (Judge Peel KC)
About 5.45 am on 12 October 1946, the plaintiff was driving his motor car along the highway from Kirkby Lonsdale to Carnforth. On the nearside ahead was an open gate to a field, and about 30 or 40 yards inside the gate 'a bunch' of about 30 cows. On the offside nearly opposite the field gate was

the gate from the farm yard to the road. This gate was open. The plaintiff inferred that the cows had just come from the farm to the field. There was no one on the road. A high wall prevented the plaintiff seeing into the farm yard. The plaintiff reduced his speed to 10 or 15 mph in case any other cows emerged. Just short of the farm gate two other cows came out at a fast speed close together and side by side. One cow was probably playing with or molesting the other. The plaintiff applied his brakes. One cow went straight into the car at the offside end of the windscreen and the other landed right across the bonnet. Immediately after the accident a German prisoner who did not understand English was in the farm yard walking towards the gate. What was taking place was a routine operation of the farm. Whether the car had actually come to rest at the moment of impact was immaterial.

HELD: This was not a case of cattle straying on to the highway but of their being put on to and across the highway and of being sent by defendant's men across it. The defendant was not any the less liable by letting his cattle wander back unattended than if they had been driven.

Following Romer LJ's dictum in *Deen v Davies* (quoted on p 263, above) which was approved by Lord Porter in *Searle v Wallbank*, the defendant had failed in his duty to users of the highway to ensure that reasonable care was taken in the control of his cows crossing the highway. It would have been reasonable to have a man on the road to warn approaching traffic, especially as the corner at the gateway was blind. A man placed in the roadway would have been able to prevent the cows dashing out, or halt the plaintiff's car. Judgment for plaintiff.

Note—See also *Andrews v Watts*, p 64, above.

Friend v Facey
(1963) Times, 19 March, CA
The plaintiff was driving his car along the main Ilfracombe-Barnstaple road at about 40 mph when a cow suddenly galloped out of a gateway on his nearside whilst being taken to the farm for milking. He jammed on his brakes at once but struck the cow, injuring it and damaging the car. The county court judge found the farmer to blame for not having two men to take the cows home to milk: it was not sufficient to leave the job to his 17-year-old son as he had done. He found the plaintiff equally to blame for not avoiding the cow by swerving to the offside. The Court of Appeal agreed that the farmer was negligent for the reasons given but held the plaintiff free from blame. His speed was not too fast on that road, the warning he received was nil and it would be asking too much to say he was negligent because he did not swerve.

Martin v Zinn
(1961) Times, 9 March, CA
The plaintiff, riding a 1935 motor cycle with a light which shone for 50 yards, collided in the dark with one of the defendant's cows which was crossing a narrow public road which divided two of the defendant's fields. The defendant's practice was to allow his cows to cross in threes. He stood by the gate holding a lamp until the third cow was in the road, when he would follow behind.

HELD: The plaintiff was to blame for the accident. He was riding an old fashioned motor cycle with a headlamp which for country lanes was inadequate. The defendant had stationed himself by the gateway of his farm and was holding a lamp which could be seen by traffic on the road. The plaintiff knew the locality and should have anticipated that cows might be on the road.

Wright v Callwood
[1950] 2 KB 515, 66 TLR (Pt 2) 72, 94 Sol Jo 420, CA
The defendant, a farmer, drove two calves out of a field on to the highway, then to the right for a few yards along the highway, and then to the left through a gateway into a drive some 14 feet wide and 50 feet long to the farm. A lorry was stationary in the farm yard and the engine was started and frightened the calves which ran back down the drive, the defendant following close behind with a stick attempting to get in front of them. The plaintiff was cycling along the highway passing the gateway. One of the calves ran out about a yard in front of her cycle and the second knocked her off her machine. A veterinary surgeon gave evidence that a calf ran away just like a young horse, and more men were needed to drive them.

The county court judge considered there were special circumstances which imposed a special duty and referred to the judgment of Greer LJ in *Sycamore v Ley* (1939) 147 LT 342; the defendant ought to have closed the gates or had a man to assist, and gave judgment for the plaintiff.
HELD, ON APPEAL: There was no evidence the defendant knew that the motor lorry was in the yard and that its engine might be started; there were no special circumstances. Appeal allowed.

Werry v Andrew
(1951) 101 L Jo 289 (Judge Rawlins)
Animals were being driven out on to a road. Adopting the obiter observation of Goddard LJ in *Hughes v Williams* [1943] 1 KB 574 that 'a different question may arise if he drives animals on to the highway, because there he is doing a deliberate act,' defendant held liable.

Thorp v King Brothers
(1957) Times, 23 February (Stable J)
A cow unloaded from a transport vehicle at Guildford Market ran away without any negligence in the unloading. It turned into a cul-de-sac where it was frightened by a number of people shouting and waving their arms and it turned into the main street and trotted quietly along and turned into a car park. The sound of a motor horn sent it into another road and over a pedestrian crossing. A pedestrian on the crossing was knocked down by the cow and injured. He claimed damages from the owner of the cow and the transporters.
HELD: The cow had never shown any sign of vice. It had been driven frantic by the behaviour of the people.

Verdict for both defendants.

Dogs

Gomberg v Smith

[1963] 1 QB 25, [1962] 1 All ER 725, [1962] 2 WLR 749, 106 Sol Jo 94, CA

At about 6.30 pm at Roman Road, Bow, London, the defendant opened the door of his shop. His dog, a large St Bernard, shot out and ran across the road. The defendant followed, shouting at the dog, which eluded him and ran back across the road, colliding with the plaintiff's van and causing damage. In a solicitor's letter and in his defence in the action the defendant alleged, untruthfully, that he had the dog on a lead. In the county court the judge held, following *Searle v Wallbank* (p 273, below), that there was no liability on the defendant if the dog escaped on to the highway and that there was no evidence either how the dog got out or that the defendant was taking it on to the highway.

HELD, ON APPEAL: The evidence of a witness that the defendant and dog came out together, and the fact that the defendant had not alleged in his defence that the dog escaped, amounted to evidence that he had brought the dog on to the highway. He had failed to keep it under control and was liable, following *Deen v Davies* (p 269, below).

Ellis v Johnstone

[1963] 2 QB 8, [1963] 1 All ER 286, [1963] 1 WLR 176, 106 Sol Jo 1030, CA

The defendant was the occupier of a house on a country road 17 feet wide opposite common land. The drive opened on to the roadway by a gateway the gate of which was never closed. The drive was concealed on one side by a wall and on the other by a hedge. The defendant's dog was in the habit of crossing the road on to the common without restraint: it had no road sense and the defendant had not tried to train it. The plaintiff was driving his car past the gateway when the dog ran across and was struck by the car and killed. The car sustained damage for which the plaintiff claimed in negligence. The county court judge held there was no general duty on the defendant to keep the dog off the highway and no special circumstances giving rise to a duty of care.

HELD, ON APPEAL: (1) A dog is a domestic animal within the rule as laid down in *Searle v Wallbank* (p 273, below) and the owner is under no liability to prevent it from straying on to the highway; (2) special circumstances, including both topographical features and idiosyncracies of the animal itself, might take a particular case out of the rule but in the present case there were none; neither the topography of the scene of the accident nor the dog's habit of running across to the common put the defendant under a duty to take care; (3) the fact that the dog was not confined and was free to pass through the gateway did not make the case one of 'escape' as in *Deen v Davies* (p 269, below).

Per Donovan LJ: The occasions when topography can be a 'special circumstance' must be rare though I would not deny the possibility. Had it been established that the dog frequently bounded out of this gate on to the highway, turning itself for the moment into something more like a missile than a dog, then in my opinion special circumstances would have existed taking the case outside the rule.

Per Pearson LJ: In deciding whether there are 'special circumstances' in the nature and habits and propensities of the particular animal, the situation and character and lay-out of the defendant's land, the nature of the highway, the expected number and speed of passing vehicles and any other relevant factors must be taken into account. There was evidence in the present case on which the defendant could have been held liable for negligence but the question was one of fact on which the county court judge had decided otherwise and his findings could not be disturbed.

Note—To the extent that it turned on the rule in *Searle v Wallbank* (see p 273, below) this case has been made obsolete by the Animals Act 1971, s 8 (p 260, above), but if a dog owner allows his dog to go out alone on the highway it remains an issue whether he was negligent in so doing. See next two cases.

Lister v Vergette

(1964) Times, 12 June (Thompson J)
The plaintiff was injured when he was knocked off his moped by the defendant's dog, which emerged suddenly from the gateway of the defendant's house. It was the dog's habit to accompany the tractor drivers on their rounds to the farm fields. On the day of the accident she had returned to the yard. A tractor was being taken out and she probably thought she was being left out and ran out to join the tractor driver. The plaintiff's case was based on *Brock v Richards* [1951] 1 KB 529 and dicta of Pearson LJ in *Ellis v Johnstone* (above).

The judge found that the defendant was not aware of the dog's 'unwelcome attitude to users of the highway' nor of any previous incidents she may have caused. The plaintiff's claim failed.

Howarth v Straver

(1953) 16 November (Croom-Johnson J)
The plaintiff was riding a motor cycle with a pillion passenger at 10.40 pm on 14 October 1951, along Bagshot Road, Cobham at not more that 40 mph. The defendant's golden retriever dog was loose and uncontrolled and roaming about the road. It ran across the road from the right, swerved to go behind the motor cycle and then came back and hit the motor cycle. The plaintiff in trying to avoid it ran into the hedge on the left-hand side of the road and was injured. He sued the defendant for damages alleging that the dog was of a mischievous nature. The judge found the dog was not vicious in the ordinary sense of the term. Citing *Deen v Davies* (p 269, below) if an animal owner knows that it has a tendency to run into cyclists or other passengers on the highway, it cannot avail him to say that it was not vice, but a frolicsome disposition, or perhaps mere blundering, which caused the harm. A cyclist gave evidence that the dog had previously got in his way, and a woman that the dog ran round bicycles and people and that she had complained to the defendant. The judge found it was a nuisance to people and a potential source of danger and gave a verdict for plaintiff.

Note—The Road Traffic Act 1972, s 31 provides as follows:

'**31 Control of dogs on roads**   (1) A person who causes or permits a dog to be on a designated road without the dog being held on a lead shall be guilty of an offence.
(2) In this section "designated road" means a length of road specified by an order in that behalf of the local authority in whose area the length of road is situated . . .
(3) An order under this section may provide that subsection (1) thereof shall apply

subject to such limitations or exceptions as may be specified in the order, and (without prejudice to the generality of this subsection) the said subsection (1) shall not apply to dogs proved to be kept for driving or tending sheep or cattle in the course of a trade or business, or to have been at the material time in use under proper control for sporting purpose.'

In a case of *Adam v The Chiddingfold Farmers Foxhounds*, a motorist driving at 35 to 40 mph along the Portsmouth Road near Wisley, saw a fox run across the road 20 or 30 yards ahead of him. He did not realise it was a fox until a pack of hounds dashed into the road after it, when he was about 10 or 15 yards away. He could not avoid them and sustained damage to his car and sued for £22 10s 6d. Judge Gordon Clark found that all reasonable precautions had been taken. The huntsmen and hounds were legitimate users of the highway and there was nothing improper in allowing hounds on a road of this sort. Judgment for defendants: (1955) Times, 5 November.

See also Allison v Corby District Council p 286, below.

DOG IN CAR

Fardon v Harcourt-Rivington
(1932) 146 LT 391, [1932] All ER Rep 81, 48 TLR 215, 76 Sol Jo 81, HL
Defendant parked his saloon car in a street with its back against the pavement. The car was left shut with a dog inside it. There was no evidence that the dog had a vicious propensity. When plaintiff, who had parked his car near defendant's car, was walking past defendant's car the dog, which had been barking and jumping about the car, jumped up against a window in the rear of defendant's car, smashing a panel, whereby a glass splinter flew out and entered plaintiff's eye, with the result that plaintiff lost his eye. An action for damages for personal injuries was brought.
HELD: The danger of a piece of glass being knocked by a dog out of a small window at the back of the car and of a splinter of glass hitting a passer-by on the pavement was such an unlooked-for event that no reasonable man could say that a person ought to be convicted of negligence for not taking any precautions against it. A person must guard against reasonable probability of danger; he was not bound to guard against a fantastic possibility.

Hens

Hadwell v Righton
[1907] 2 KB 345, 76 LJKB 891, 97 LT 133, 71 JP 499, 23 TLR 548, 51 Sol Jo 500, 5 LGR 881 (Bray J)
Plaintiff was riding carefully a bicycle on a highway, upon the footpath of which were some fowls belonging to defendant, who occupied premises on the side of the road opposite to the footpath. As plaintiff got abreast of the fowls a dog belonging to a third party frightened the fowls, one of which flew into the spokes of the machine, causing it to upset, whereby plaintiff suffered personal injury and the bicycle was damaged. Defendant knew the fowls were in the habit of straying on the road.
HELD: (1) Even if the fowls were not lawfully on the highway, the damage which happened was not of such a nature as was likely to result from their unlawful presence there, and such damage was too remote. (2) Plaintiff could not recover.

Quaere whether it is unlawful for the occupiers of land adjoining a high-way to allow their poultry to stray upon the highway.

Cases in which plaintiff was the owner of the soil on which the trespass was committed are not in point; for here the cyclist had no interest in the soil of the highway.

Horses

Holmes v Mather
(1875) LR 10 Exch 261, 44 LJ Ex 176, 33 LT 361
Plaintiff was walking along a public street when defendant, seated on the box of his carriage which was drawn by two horses and driven by a man then under his control, came down a cross street. The horses, frightened by the barking of a dog, ran away. The driver was unable to hold them in, but told defendant to leave them to him. Defendant accordingly sat passive, while the driver, trying to turn the horses so as to prevent them from running into a shop window opposite, pulled them aside toward the spot where plaintiff then happened to be, but on nearing her, endeavoured vainly to draw them away from her. They ran against her, and she being hurt, sued defendant for negligence and trespass. The jury found defendant free from negligence, and that the occurrence was a mere accident.
HELD: He was not liable in trespass.

Turner v Coates
[1917] 1 KB 670, 86 LJKB 321, Div Ct
A young unbroken colt belonging to defendant, a farmer, was being taken along a highway on a dark night. It was allowed to go loose behind a mare which was being led and in front of a trap being driven by defendant. Plaintiff, who was riding a bicycle, was coming from the opposite direction when the colt, being startled by the light on the bicycle, suddenly ran across the road and collided with and injured plaintiff. No warning was given by the defendant to plaintiff of the presence of the colt. In an action to recover damages the county court judge found that it was well known, especially to a farmer, that a young unbroken colt when loose on the highway is apt, when startled, to rush about and kick, and to go loose on the highway in the dark; and he held that defendant was guilty of negligence in allowing the colt to be on the highway in the dark without being under proper control, and in failing to give warning to plaintiff of the presence of the colt.
HELD: The county court judge was right in so holding.

Note—Adopted and followed by CA in *Deen v Davies*.

Deen v Davies
[1935] 2 KB 282, [1935] All ER Rep 9, 104 LJKB 540, 153 LT 90, 51 TLR 398, 79 Sol Jo 381, CA
The defendant, a farmer, rode his pony into a neighbouring large town and stabled it there whilst he did business in the town. Instead of tethering it to a staple provided for the purpose he tied it to a piece of wood which he believed to be firmly nailed to the wall of the stable. Whilst he was away the pony broke the piece of wood away from the wall and went out into the

street to return home. Though of docile disposition it caused the plaintiff
to fall when stepping from the pavement and she sustained injury. The
county court found that the pony, whilst not exhibiting any savage
tendencies, had acted in a way in which a pony might be expected to when
unattended on a roadway in a town. The defendant had been negligent in
not tying up the pony properly in the stall and his negligence had led to the
pony getting on to the roadway unattended and injuring the plaintiff. He
awarded the plaintiff damages.

HELD, ON APPEAL: This was not a case of an animal being depastured on
land adjoining the highway and escaping or straying on to it: it was one of a
different class of case in which the owner himself has brought the animal
upon the highway. In this type of case the owner has a duty to take reasonable care that the animal does not damage other parties. Reasonable care in
the country may not be reasonable care in the town. The defendant had
brought his horse upon the highway and rode it into a town. When he
tethered it in the stable he had not secured it properly and thereby failed to
discharge the duty he owed to the public. The duty began when he took the
horse on to the highway and did not come to an end when he tethered it in
the stable. Appeal dismissed.

Aldham v United Dairies
[1940] 1 KB 507, [1939] 3 All ER 522, 109 LJKB 323, CA

Defendant's horse, attached to a milk cart, was left unattended for half an
hour in a main thoroughfare. The horse attacked and injured the plaintiff.
There was evidence that it was the horse's habit to become restive, to put
his forefeet on the pavement and to cause alarm to some persons.

Per du Parcq LJ: The established rules may be stated as follows: (1)
Negligence cannot be established merely by proof that a defendant has
failed to provide against the possibility that a tame animal of mild disposition will do something contrary to its ordinary nature. (2) Even if the defendant's omission to control or secure his horse is negligent, an act on the part
of the horse which is contrary to its ordinary nature cannot be regarded, in
the absence of special circumstances, as being directly caused by such
negligence.

The negligence in this case was the result of leaving an impatient horse
unattended for too long a time, and the plaintiff was entitled to recover.

Rose v Collier Ltd
[1939] WN 19, CA

A mare, known to be of an excitable and nervous disposition, was left
unattended on a towpath, where it kicked a man leading a quiet horse
pulling a barge.

HELD: The owner was liable.

Cox v Burbridge
(1863) 13 CBNS 340, 32 LJCP 89, 11 WR 435

The owner of an animal is answerable for any damage done by it provided
it be of such a nature as is likely to arise from such an animal and the owner
knows it.

Note—Adopted in *Heath's Garage v Hodges* (p 272, below).

Landau v Railway Executive
(1949) 99 L Jo 233, Clerkenwell CC (Judge Earengey)
A railway carman took his horse and cart on his usual collection and delivery round into a manufacturer's yard. The yard was paved with stone sets, and sloped down to an archway, where there was a gatekeeper. The cart was backed up to a loading bank at right angles to the slope, and a nosebag was put on the horse, and a chain on the rear wheel, but without the brake applied. The horse had been bought about two years previously with a warranty that it was quiet. It had been driven frequently by the carman who had never known it to bolt before. After the horse had been left unattended for about five minutes, it ran through the archway into the highway and caused damage.
HELD: The brake was fitted for the obvious purpose of reinforcing the chain on difficult ground, or in cases of emergency, and the yard was clearly dangerous ground. *Deen v Davies* was not doubted by the Court of Appeal in *Brackenborough v Spalding UDC* and was approved by Lord Porter in *Searle v Wallbank*. Railway Co held liable.

Bativala v West
[1970] 1 QB 716, [1970] 1 All ER 332, [1970] 2 WLR 8, 113 Sol Jo 856 (Bridge J)
The defendant, the proprietor of a riding school, organised a gymkhana in a field. The part of the field used was some distance from a road and separated from it first by a rope to control spectators and then by a hedge with an open gateway in it. In a race in which competitors had to saddle their ponies a saddle slipped and caused the pony to bolt, clearing the rope and running out into the road where it collided with the plaintiff's car.
HELD: The defendant was liable. She was aware of the risk; a slipping saddle was a well-known hazard and if this happened the horse would probably run away in fear. Each link in the chain of causation was reasonably foreseeable and she was negligent by ordinary standards. She had relied on the rule as laid down in *Searle v Wallbank* (p 273, below) that there was no duty to prevent the escape of animals on to the highway, but an owner could still be liable if he could be shown to have failed in his duty to take care. Most cases in which the rule in *Searle v Wallbank* had been held to apply were cases in which the animal had strayed from a situation in which it had been properly left to its own devices. Different considerations arose when the animal escaped from a situation in which it was under direct human control. The present case could be decided in accordance with the ordinary principles of negligence and the plaintiffs were entitled to damages.

Annells v Warneford
(1958) Times, 7 May, [1958] CLY 104, CA
Two children were trying to catch a pony which was in a field; but the pony slipped past one of them, ran down a lane and into a main road where it collided with a motor car. The driver of the car sued in negligence.
HELD: Although the children had been under a duty to take reasonable care to prevent the pony going down the lane and into the road they had fulfilled that duty. Appeal dismissed.

Sheep

Frazer v Pate

1932 SC 748, 60 Sc LR 470

A motor cyclist was injured by a collision in daylight with a sheep upon a public road. Pursuer averred that defender was negligent in knowingly failing to keep his fences in such repair as would prevent his sheep from straying on to the road, in any event in allowing his sheep to graze upon the road.

HELD: The accident was not the natural and probable result of the negligence alleged.

Heath's Garage Ltd v Hodges

[1916] 2 KB 370, 85 LJKB 1289, 115 LT 129, 32 TLR 570, 60 Sol Jo 554, CA

An owner or occupier of land adjoining highway (ie putting aside cases where, either by a local Enclosure Act, or by prescription, or otherwise, a duty to fence is imposed) is not bound to fence so as to prevent animals like sheep straying upon the highway.

While plaintiff's motor car was being driven along a highway in the daylight at the rate of 16 to 20 mph, the driver saw in front of him on the road a number of sheep untended. He put on his brakes and almost immediately thereafter two sheep, which had apparently been left behind by the others, jumped from the bank on the near side and one of them ran in front of the car and broke part of the steering gear, in consequence of which the driver lost control, and the car ran into the bank and was damaged. The sheep were the property of the defendant, who was subsequently prosecuted and fined under the Highway Act 1864, s 25, for having allowed them to stray on the highway. In an action against the defendant by the plaintiffs in respect of the damage to the car, the county court judge found (1) the sheep escaped on to the highway from defendant's field owing to a defective hedge; (2) it was the natural tendency of sheep which were untended to run across or otherwise endanger vehicles in a road, and it was common knowledge that when sheep find themselves separated from the flock they have almost a mania for rejoining it, regardless of intervening traffic; (3) defendant had been guilty of negligence, or had committed a nuisance, in allowing sheep to stray on to the highway, and the accident was the natural consequence thereof, and he held the defendant was liable.

HELD, ON APPEAL: (1) Whether the action was sought to be based on negligence or on a nuisance to the highway, it was not breach of duty by defendant, not to keep his sheep from straying on to the highway; (2) an animal like a sheep, by nature harmless, could not fairly be regarded as likely to collide with a motor car, and defendant could not be held liable on that footing; (3) (per Avory J) the tendencies of sheep as found by the county court judge were not a vicious or mischievous propensity within the decided cases.

But see note following *Hoskin v Rogers* on p 273.

McGowan v Gilmore
[1953] CLY 117, Cty Ct
A farmer's ram escaped on to the highway in the hours of darkness. The defendant went in his car in pursuit and, whilst chasing it, the ram collided with and damaged the plaintiff's car.
HELD: Defendant had not brought the ram on to the highway. He was reasonably and properly attempting to take possession and control of it but had not succeeded in doing so at the time of the accident. The defendant was not negligent.

STRAYING ANIMALS

Duty of landowner

Hoskin v Rogers
[1985] LS Gaz R 848, Times, 25 January, CA
The plaintiff motorcyclist was injured when he collided with the body of a heifer killed by another vehicle. It had strayed on to the highway through inadequate fencing from adjoining land owned by the second defendant. The accident occurred in October; the land had been let to the first defendant on a 'grass purchase' agreement since May, when the fence was reasonably stockproof. The judge held the first defendant alone liable.
HELD, ON APPEAL: The duty of care on the second defendants as owners of the land was to take reasonable care to see that the land was fenced adequately so as to prevent stock they knew was going to be on the land from straying on to the highway. There was no breach of that duty by the second defendants in May when the agreement was negotiated. Thus the question was whether it had been shown that by the date of the accident they had been put on notice that the fencing was by then inadequate. The evidence did not establish that that was so; the second defendants were not in breach of their duty of care. Appeal dismissed.

Note—The rule at common law that the owner of animals on land adjoining a highway had no duty to prevent them from straying on to it received its most authoritative statement in *Searle v Wallbank* (below). The rule was abolished as from 1 October 1971 by the Animals Act 1971, s 8(1) (p 260, above) but there are exemptions in sub-s (2).

Searle v Wallbank
[1947] AC 341, [1947] 1 All ER 12, HL
A cyclist was injured by a horse which strayed from a field adjoining the highway through a defective fence.
HELD: (1) The owner of a field abutting on the highway is under no prima facie legal obligation to users of the highway so to keep and maintain his hedges and gates along the highway as to prevent his animals from straying on to it; (2) nor to take reasonable care to prevent his animals (not known to be dangerous) from straying on to the highway.

Note—The cases of *Hughes v Willams* and *Brock v Richards* ((6th edn) pp 210 and 213 respectively) may now be regarded as obsolete. The following case may still be of value:

Fitzgerald v E. D. and A. D. Cooke Bourne (Farms) Ltd
[1964] 1 QB 249, [1963] 2 All ER 36, [1963] 3 WLR 522, 107 Sol Jo 459,
188 Estates Gazette 209, CA
The plaintiff was crossing a field by a public footpath when she was knocked
down by a filly belonging to the defendants. She did not receive serious
physical injury but was frightened and subsequently suffered a nervous
breakdown. The filly was one of two normally pastured in the field. It had
not attacked the plaintiff but galloped up to her, swerving and prancing in a
playful way, striking her with its shoulder and knocking her down. There
was some evidence of similar behaviour to a person on the footpath on a
previous occasion. The judge held that the horses were not vicious but had
a natural propensity to gallop up to people who walked across the field:
their behaviour was what could be expected of young animals of that sort of
breeding. He held that the defendants were liable on the basis that they
knew of the potential danger of the horse doing to the plaintiff what it did.

On the appeal the decision was reversed. The plaintiff's case was put in
two ways (1) that the filly was a dangerous animal to the knowledge of the
defendants and that accordingly they were under strict liability as for an
animal *ferae naturae*; (2) that they were liable in negligence on the ground
that they ought reasonably to have foreseen and guarded against an
accident of the kind that occurred.

HELD: On the first point, the filly was not vicious but was merely indulging its natural propensity to be playful. It was not attacking or showing
hostility. The fact that its conduct was frightening to the plaintiff or others
did not make it a dangerous animal so as to place the defendants under
strict liability. On the second point the footpath was similar to a highway in
the unfenced condition in which highways existed when the common law
developed. *Searle v Wallbank* (p 273, above) made it clear beyond doubt that
the owner of animals pastured in the vicinity had no duty to prevent them
from straying on to the highway, but it was envisaged in that case that an
action for negligence might lie if, in the particular circumstances of the
particular case, the owner of a particular animal ought reasonably to
foresee that, having regard to its peculiar propensities, it may cause injury
otherwise than by merely straying if it escaped on to a highway. To
establish such a case in negligence it was not sufficient to show a 'reasonable possibility' of injury: it must be shown that there was a real likelihood
of injury which ought to have been foreseen. In the present case the
evidence proved nothing against the defendants to show that they ought
reasonably to have foreseen the likelihood of injury except in so far as they
must be taken to have had a general knowledge of the behaviour of fillies of
this class; this was not sufficient to make them liable.

CHAPTER 9

Highways: dangers and obstructions

1 LIABILITY OF HIGHWAY AUTHORITY

DISREPAIR

Note—At common law a highway authority was not liable for damage or injury caused by disrepair of the highway if the disrepair was the result of non-feasance and not misfeasance. It was not liable, that is, for failing to repair the highway but only for doing work negligently and thus causing the danger. This freedom from liability for non-repair came to an end on 3 August 1964 (except in cases where the damage arose from an event occurring before that date), as a result of the Highways (Miscellaneous Provisions) Act 1961, s 1. That section was repealed and replaced in part by s 58 of the Highways Act 1980 as follows:

HIGHWAYS ACT 1980, s 58

58 Special defence in action against a highway authority for damages for non-repair of highway   (1) In an action against a highway authority in respect of damage resulting from their failure to maintain a highway maintainable at the public expense, it shall be a defence (without prejudice to any other defence or the application of the law relating to contributory negligence) to prove that the authority had taken such care as in all the circumstances was reasonably required to secure that the part of the highway to which the action relates was not dangerous for traffic.
(2) For the purposes of a defence under subsection (1) above, the court shall in particular have regard to the following matters,
(a) the character of the highway, and the traffic which was reasonably to be expected to use it;
(b) the standard of maintenance appropriate for a highway of that character and used by such traffic;
(c) the state of repair in which a reasonable person would have expected to find the highway;
(d) whether the highway authority knew, or could reasonably have been expected to know, that the condition of the part of the highway to which the action relates was likely to cause danger to users of the highway;
(e) where the highway authority could not reasonably have been expected to repair that part of the highway before the cause of action arose, what warning notices of its condition had been displayed;
but for the purposes of such a defence it is not relevant to prove that the highway authority had arranged for a competent person to carry out or supervise the maintenance of the part of the highway to which the action relates unless it is also proved that the authority had given him proper instructions with regard to the maintenance of the highway and that he had carried out the instructions.
(3) This section binds the Crown.'

Subsection (4) excludes the operation of the section from damage following the breakage or opening of a street and resulting from an event before the completion of reinstatement required by the Public Utilities Street Works Act 1950, s 7(2).

The rule at common law

Note—Only sufficient cases are quoted here as may explain the old rule. A full digest of the old cases will be found in the 5th edition of this work.

Russell v Men of Devon
(1788) 2 Term Rep 667
No action will lie by an individual against the inhabitants of a county for an injury sustained in consequence of a county bridge being out of repair.

Note—The rule was based solely on the historical reason that in the past it was difficult to levy on the unincorporated inhabitants of the county.

Simon v Islington Borough Council
[1943] 1 KB 188, [1943] 1 All ER 41, CA (Scott LJ)
The principle that a highway authority is not liable for non-feasance is that the immunity descended to it as the lineal successor, first, of the surveyor of highways, and before him, of the inhabitants at large. It is limited to duties

as highway authority. It extends only to damage due solely to the non-repair of the road *qua* road. It does not extend to acts or defaults of the high-way authority in connection with any duties except characteristic highway duties such as that of repairing the road. It does not apply in connection with the public health duties, e g in connection with sewers: nor with the duty of protecting the public from falling into an unfenced pit alongside the high road; nor with duties imposed by the Road Traffic Acts.

Note—For facts see p 290, below.

Burton v West Suffolk County Council
[1960] 2 QB 72, [1960] 2 All ER 26, [1960] 2 WLR 745, 124 JP 273, 104 Sol Jo 349, 58 LGR 175, CA
The plaintiff was injured when his car skidded, without negligence on his part, on a road covered, at the place of the accident, by a thin film of ice. The defendants, who were the highway authority, had carried out some road drainage work some months previously by which the drainage had been improved but there was still a tendency to flooding and the road surface tended to keep damp from water which ran off the adjoining land. If more drainage work had been done this tendency would have been reduced and the accident would probably not have occurred. The plaintiff claimed damages on the grounds (1) that the failure to complete the drainage work amounted to misfeasance; (2) that the defendants failed to give warning of the dangerous state of the road.
HELD: (1) If a highway authority does work on a road by way of repair or reconstruction, it must be done properly and in such a way as not to cause danger on the road, but this does not mean that where some work has been done and done properly to improve the drainage of the road the defendants should be held liable for failing to do further work which would result in further improvement of the drainage. It was not misfeasance but non-feasance. (2) The defendants were under no duty to warn the plaintiff of the icy conditions of the road.

The modern law

BREACH OF STATUTORY DUTY TO MAINTAIN HIGHWAY

HIGHWAYS ACT 1980, s 41(1)

41 (1) The authority who are for the time being the highway authority for a highway maintainable at the public expense are under a duty . . . to maintain the highway.

Griffiths v Liverpool Corpn
[1967] 1 QB 374, [1966] 2 All ER 1015, [1966] 3 WLR 467, 110 Sol Jo 548, CA
The plaintiff was walking along the pavement of a street when she slipped or tripped on a flag-stone and fell, sustaining injury. The flag-stone rocked when walked on and when at rest one of its edges protruded half an inch

above the adjacent flag-stone. She sued the highway authority. The county court judge on the evidence of a surveyor and of a highway superintendent found as a fact that the flag-stone was dangerous. The highway superintendent said there was no system of inspection and that inspection should be done every three months. The reason it was not was that it was not possible to get tradesmen to do the repair work, though there was no difficulty in getting sufficient labourers to do the inspection. If the flag-stone in question had been discovered it could have been made safe even by a labourer.

HELD: The Highways Act 1959, s 44 imposed a duty on the defendants, the highway authority, to keep the pavement in repair. This action was based on a breach of that duty. The Highways (Miscellaneous Provisions) Act 1961, abrogated the old rule exempting highway authorities from liability for non-repair of highways and therefore, since the flag-stone was dangerous, the defendants were liable to the plaintiff absolutely and without proof of negligence unless they could establish a defence under s 1(2) and (3) of the Act. To establish the defence it was not necessary that the highway authority should prove they had taken such care as was reasonably necessary to make the highway safe: it would be sufficient for them to prove that they had taken such care as, in all the circumstances, they reasonably could. If through no fault of theirs they had been unable to take steps to make the highway safe they would escape liability. In the present case the defendants, though unable to get tradesmen, could have employed labourers to deal with dangers such as the one in question and had not established a defence under subss (2) and (3). Judgment for the plaintiff upheld.

Note—The finding of fact that the flag-stone was dangerous was not appealed. All the Appeal Judges expressed doubts whether they themselves would have made such a finding. See *Meggs v Liverpool Corpn* and *Littler v Liverpool Corpn*, p 281, below. The Highways Act 1959 was repealed as from 1 January 1981 by The Highways Act 1980. Section 44(1) of the 1959 Act is re-enacted in s 41(1) of the 1980 Act.

Pitman v Southern Electricity Board

[1978] 3 All ER 901, 143 JP 156, 122 Sol Jo 300, 76 LGR 578, CA

The plaintiff, aged 78, was walking at dusk along the pavement in the village where she lived when she tripped on a metal sheet which the defendants' employees had placed over a hole. It was only $\frac{1}{8}$ inch proud of the surrounding surface. The place was unlighted.

HELD: She was entitled to damages. The difference between this case and those of *Meggs* and *Littler* (above) was that she tripped on an unexpected condition and level of the pavement — unexpected because as an inhabitant of the village she had become accustomed to the state of affairs there and on the evening in question was faced with a new and unexpected hazard.

FLOODING

Burnside v Emerson

[1968] 3 All ER 741, [1968] 1 WLR 1490, 133 JP 66, 112 Sol Jo 565, CA

The plaintiff and first defendant were driving their cars in opposite directions on a main road and were about to pass each other. It had been raining hard for some hours and a pool of water had formed extending half-way across the road on the first defendant's side. He was travelling at about 50 mph. As his car struck the water it swerved across the road into collision with the plaintiff's car. The second defendants were the highway authority. Their attention had been drawn before the accident to the tendency of the road to become flooded at that point in wet weather, due to bad position of a drain and a failure by the second defendants' employees to keep the grips or gulleys in good condition and to keep the ditch cleaned out.

HELD: The second defendants were liable for their failure to fulfil the duty to maintain the highway placed upon them by the Highways Act 1959, s 44(1). An action under the section requires three things: (1) The plaintiff must show the road was dangerous for traffic, that is to say, in a state in which injury may reasonably be anticipated to persons using the highway; foreseeability is an essential element. (2) The plaintiff must prove that the dangerous condition was due to a failure to maintain which includes a failure to repair. (3) If there is a failure to maintain the highway authority is prima facie liable but can escape liability if it proves that it took such care as in all the circumstances was reasonable, having regard to the Highways (Miscellaneous Provisions) Act 1961, s 1(3). The pool of water was admitted by the second defendants' surveyor at the trial to be a danger to traffic and the existence of the pool was due to their failure to maintain the drainage system in a satisfactory condition. They were liable, but the first defendant was also negligent in driving too fast. Blame apportioned two-thirds to the first defendant and one-third to the second defendants.

Tarrant v Rowlands
[1979] RTR 144 (Cantley J)
The first defendant was driving his car at dusk at 40 mph along the A6 road when he ran into a pool of water on the road which he had not seen. He lost control of the steering and crashed head-on into a van driven by the plaintiff. Both were injured. It had been a wet day but the rainfall had not been of exceptional severity. The pool extended about 30 feet along the road and covered it to about the middle on the first defendant's side. It was about 5 inches deep at the deepest. There was evidence that water was usually found lying in that place on the road after a good deal of rain. The supervising foreman of the highway authority, the second defendants, said that there was regular inspection of the road once a month and before the accident he was unaware of any drainage problems in this area of the road.

HELD: The principles to be followed were those laid down in *Burnside v Emerson* (above) applying the Highways Act 1959, s 44 (now Highways Act 1980, s 41) and the Highways (Miscellaneous Provisions) Act 1961, s 1 (now Highways Act 1980, s 58). The evidence that water was frequently found on the road at that place showed that the second defendants 'could reasonably have been expected to know' that the condition of the highway 'was likely to cause danger to users of the highway' (s 1(3)(d) of the 1961 Act). If they did not know then the system of inspection had broken down and they had some responsibility for the accident. The first defendant was also to blame for failing to see the pool. He was driving too fast in the conditions obtaining. Division of responsibility 50–50.

Morris v Thyssen (GB) Ltd
1983 Abr 2418 (Booth J)

A van driver lost control of his vehicle when it hit a large pool of water on the road caused by flooding. He blamed the highway authority.

HELD: The flooding was a serious hazard which was reasonably predictable from the low-lying nature of the road and the weather conditions. The authority had direct knowledge of the serious extent of the flood from the police and their own employees. The one flood sign displayed in a nearby lay-by was not an adequate warning. Authority two-thirds liable, van driver one-third.

DEFECTIVE ROAD-EDGES

Rider v Rider
[1973] QB 505, [1973] 1 All ER 294, [1973] 2 WLR 190, 117 Sol Jo 71, CA

The plaintiff was badly injured when a car in which she was a passenger on a narrow lane at night swung across the road and collided with an approaching vehicle. The lane was commonly used as a secondary traffic route but the highway authority had done no repair work for at least six months. The edges of the tarmac had broken away in places causing gaps where the nearside wheels of vehicles would pass; the judge accepted that the driver's loss of control was due to this state of disrepair. He held the highway authority two-thirds to blame.

HELD: Dismissing the highway authority's appeal, the judge was right. They had failed to perform their statutory duty under the Highways Act 1959, s 44 to keep the highway in repair. They had further failed to discharge the duty implied in the Highways (Miscellaneous Provisions) Act 1961, s 1(2) to maintain the road in such a way as to secure that there was no danger for traffic. Whether part of the highway is a danger for traffic is a question of fact to be decided in a common sense way; but it was not correct that the test of danger is the risk to a careful driver. The duty of maintaining the highway free of danger is owed to all users who use the highway in the way normally to be expected of them — including some who may be rated as negligent. In the present case a finding of one-third negligence on the part of the car driver was justified on the ground that, with knowledge of the state of the lane he should have been going more slowly.

Jacobs v Hampshire County Council
(1984) Times, 28 May (Skinner J)

A cyclist was injured when the front wheel of his cycle went into a hole at the edge of the road caused by water penetration. The highway authority had inspected the road at six-monthly intervals, having regard to the type of area in which the road lay and the likely extent and type of use of the road.

HELD: To establish a defence under the Highways Act 1980, s 58 the authority should have also taken into account in deciding the frequency of inspections, the design of the road. Tarmac adjoining cobbles at the edge made it especially vulnerable to water penetration, capable of causing damage within two months. The defence was not established.

NO BREACH

Meggs v Liverpool Corpn

[1968] 1 All ER 1137, [1968] 1 WLR 689, 132 JP 207, 111 Sol Jo 742, 65 LGR 479, CA

The plaintiff tripped on uneven flag-stones of a pavement in the highway. One of them had sunk three-quarters of an inch. She sued the highway authority. The judge found as a fact that the state of the pavement was not such as to indicate a failure by the highway authority to discharge its duty.

Her appeal was dismissed. The Highways Act 1959, put the duty to maintain on the highway authority and the Act of 1961 had abrogated the non-feasance rule. If a highway was in a dangerous condition so that it was not reasonably safe for traffic or people going along it there was prima facie a breach of the obligation to maintain or repair. But in order to get a claim going the plaintiff must at least show that the highway or pavement was not reasonably safe and that it was dangerous to traffic. The judge had examined the evidence and, having regard to the fact that thousands had used the pavement and no one had reported it, had said he was not satisfied the highway authority was in breach of its duty. That was a finding of fact: everyone had to take account of unevenness in a pavement here and there, and there was no reason for discharging the judge's finding.

Note—Section 44 of the 1959 Act is now replaced by the Highways Act 1980, s 41(1) in similar terms.

Littler v Liverpool Corpn

[1968] 2 All ER 343, 66 LGR 660 (Cumming-Bruce J)

The plaintiff, aged 19, was running along the pavement of a street when he tripped and fell. The pavement was of York stone about 80 years old. The only defect was a triangular depression half-an-inch deep measuring about 3 inches along its longest side. He alleged against the defendants, the highway authority, a failure to maintain contrary to the Highways Act 1959, s 44, and negligence.

HELD: To establish a cause of action for failing to maintain the highway the plaintiff must prove that it was dangerous to relevant traffic (*Meggs's* case (above)). The test is reasonable foreseeability of danger. It is a mistake to isolate and emphasise differences in level between the flagstones of a pavement unless the difference is such that a reasonable person who considered it would regard it as a real source of danger. Differences of about an inch may cause a stumble but they have to be accepted. A pavement is not to be judged by the standards of a bowling green. The evidence in the present case did not establish that the pavement was dangerous.

Note—See also *Ford v Liverpool Corpn* (1972) 117 Sol Jo 167.

Whiting v Hillingdon London B C

(1970) 114 Sol Jo 247, 68 LGR 437 (James J)

In April 1966 the plaintiff was walking along a footpath when, to pass another person, she stepped to the side of the path and sustained injury to her leg on a tree stump hidden by foliage. She sued the defendants, the highway authority, both under the Occupiers' Liability Act 1957 and for breach of the Highways Act 1959, s 44. The defendants had inspected the path in the summer of 1964 and 1965 and repaired it in February 1966 without noticing the tree stump.

HELD: (1) The only basis for the defendants' occupation of the path (of which they were not owners) was their duty of maintenance under the Highways Act 1959, s 44(1) and that did not render them occupiers for the purpose of the 1957 Act. (2) As the defendants' officer could not remember seeing the tree stump in February 1966 the tree must have been cut down after that date. It was not reasonable to expect another inspection between February and April 1966 when the accident happened. Action dismissed.

Haydon v Kent County Council

[1978] QB 343, [1978] 2 All ER 97, [1978] 2 WLR 485, 121 Sol Jo 849, CA
The plaintiff was descending a steep footpath coated with snow and ice when she slipped and broke her ankle. She claimed damages from the highway authority, relying on the duty in the Highways Act 1959, s 44 'to maintain the highway'. Section 295 says ' "Maintain" includes repair'. [The Highways Act 1980, s 329 says ' "maintenance" includes repair and "maintain" and "maintainable" are to be construed accordingly'.]

HELD: The duty under s 44 was to repair and also maintain. The statutory obligation included clearing snow and ice or providing temporary protection by gritting, but whether there had been a breach of that duty was a question of fact and degree on the facts of each case. The plaintiff must prove either that the authority was at fault apart from merely failing to take steps to deal with the ice, or that having regard to the nature and importance of works sufficient time had elapsed to make it prima facie unreasonable for the authority to have failed to take remedial measures. In the present case not sufficient time had elapsed after the onset of the icy conditions having regard to the authority's heavy commitments to keep major roads in its area safe and clear.

Bartlett v Department of Transport

(1985) Times, 8 January (Boreham J)
The plaintiff's husband was killed in a road accident on the A34 road due, at least in part, to the icy, slippery condition of the road surface. The roadway had not been gritted because the defendants were in dispute with the employees, members of the National Union of Public Employees, who had forbidden all work on the A34. The plaintiff alleged a breach of the Highways Act 1959, s 44 (now the Highways Act 1980, s 41(1)).

HELD: The defendants were not liable. An action for breach of s 44 could succeed only if the failure to maintain was related to want of repair or if an obstruction caused or contributed to want of repair. The plaintiff could not complain of any breach of the employees' duty to the defendant unless it was induced or condoned by the employers and, on the facts, this was not the case.

Statutory defence: inspection

Pridham v Hemel Hempstead Corpn

(1970) 114 Sol Jo 884, 69 LGR 523, CA

The plaintiff was pushing a pram along the pavement of a residential road when she caught her foot in a hole and was injured. In answer to her claim for damages for breach of the Highways Act 1959, s 44 the defendants, the highway authority, pleaded the statutory defence in s 1(2) of the 1961 Act. They gave evidence that two men were employed full time on inspection of roads and that residential roads were inspected every three months. The judge concluded on examination of the figures of mileage of roads and hours of work that residential roads could have been inspected monthly and held that the defendants had not established the statutory defence.

HELD, ON APPEAL: It was wrong to depart from the words of the section, in which the test is reasonableness. The system was reasonable and the fact that it was practicable to inspect more frequently did not make the system unreasonable. Appeal allowed.

Bramwell v Shaw

[1971] RTR 167 (Ackner J)

On a busy road carrying heavy commercial traffic at Millwall, London, one-half of the roadway was obstructed by fenced-off roadworks in which the plaintiff was working. An articulated lorry driven by the first defendant had to pull over to the offside lane, which was about 10 feet wide, to pass the obstruction. The road surface was nearing the end of its life and was a patchwork of old cobbles, tarmac, concrete and asphalt. As the first defendant drove through the gap at 15 to 20 mph the offside wheels of the lorry ran into a depression in the road surface 4 to 6 inches deep, causing it to lean over. As a result a container on the lorry struck a tree growing near the edge of the road and fell off on to the plaintiff.

HELD: (1) The first defendant was negligent in that he drove too fast. If he had driven more slowly he would have seen the hole and could have avoided it. (2) The highway authority (the third defendants) were in breach of their statutory duty under the Highways Act 1959, s 44 to maintain the highway. They were unable to rely on the defence afforded by the Highways (Miscellaneous Provisions) Act 1961, s 1(2) because they had failed to take 'such care as in all the circumstances was reasonably required' to make the road safe. The traffic which could be expected to use the road was heavy; at the particular point where the accident occurred there was especially heavy wear and tear and it should have been inspected pretty well daily: if it had been the depression would have been seen in time and could have been repaired. (3) The first defendant was the more to blame: proportions 60% first defendant, 40% third defendants.

Note—For references to the Highways Act 1959, s 44 and Highways (Miscellaneous Provisions) Act 1961, s 1, see notes to pp 278 and 275 above.

Concealed danger

Baxter v Stockton-on-Tees Corpn
[1959] 1 QB 441, [1958] 2 All ER 675, [1958] 3 WLR 275, 102 Sol Jo 562, CA

A motor cyclist at about midnight collided with the kerb of an approach island adjacent to a roundabout on the highway and sustained fatal injuries. His widow sued the defendants as the highway authority alleging negligence in failing to light or give warning of a concealed danger or trap. The highway was constructed between 1938 and 1940 by the Durham County Council under the Development and Road Improvement Funds Act 1909, ss 8 and 10, as amended by the Roads Act 1920, s 4 and Sch 1, as a main road repairable by the inhabitants at large. The Local Government Act 1929, s 29(1), substituted 'county road' for 'main road'. In 1941 the defendants took over the highway from the county council under the Local Government Act 1929, s 32 and thereby became the highway authority and responsible for its maintenance and repair.

HELD: If there had been negligence of the county council in the construction of the road and they were still in charge of it, and a person sustained injury in consequence, there might be liability on the principle of negligence in the performance of statutory powers. The Court of Appeal was not satisfied that such a case could have been made out, but if it could, the defendants could not be liable on that principle, as they were not the constructors of the road. The plaintiff's claim on the basis that if a highway authority place an obstruction on the highway, they have a duty to light or otherwise protect the public, had no application, because the defendants had done no positive act, but merely kept the island as they found it. The theory that the defendants inherited any such duty from the county council is untenable in view of *Nash v Rochford Rural Council*. The defendants could only be liable by virtue of some express words in the Act under which the road became vested in them. There was nothing in s 32 of the Act of 1929 to impose on an urban district council taking over a county road any special obligation as to maintenance so as to exclude the ordinary immunity for mere non-feasance. Appeal of defendants from judgment of Barry J awarding £4,500 to the widow, allowed.

Note—In so far as this decision was based on the immunity of a highway authority from liability for non-feasance it is no longer good law. It is still effective on the point that a highway authority constructing a road for public use under statutory powers owes a duty to the public to take reasonable care to construct the road properly, but the Acts do not make such an authority liable for acts of misfeasance committed by its predecessors.

MISFEASANCE

Unfenced ravine

McClelland v Manchester Corpn
[1912] 1 KB 118, 81 LJKB 98, 105 LT 707, 28 TLR 21 (Lush J)

A street within the district of the defendants, a municipal corporation, was dedicated to the public by its owner. Across the end of the street was an unfenced natural ravine. In 1904 the defendants took over the street under the provisions of a private Act of Parliament similar to those contained in the Public Health Act 1875, and paved and made it up and subsequently maintained it. They also lighted it under their statutory powers, which authorised them to do such act as they should think necessary for lighting their district. In 1910 a motor car containing the plaintiff while being driven along the street at night fell over the ravine in consequence, it was alleged, of the ravine being unfenced and the street being insufficiently lighted. In an action by the plaintiff to recover damages for injuries sustained the jury found that the street as made up and constructed was a danger to persons using it, that the unfenced ravine was a hidden trap, and that the defendants had not take proper care to warn the public of danger. HELD: That the effect of the findings of the jury was that the defendants in taking over and making up the street and leaving it in a dangerous condition had been guilty of misfeasance, and also that they had acted negligently in the performance of their statutory duties with regard to maintaining and lighting the street, and that the plaintiff was, therefore, entitled to judgment.

Note—See also *Burton v W. Suffolk CC*, p 277, above.

Gradient across road

Scottish Omnibuses Ltd v Midlothian County Council
(1955) 105 L Jo 90, Ct of Sess, Outer House
A motor omnibus was proceeding along a road which turned to the right and 90 yards further on, going downhill, crossed a bridge over a river. The outer side of the turn was 2 feet higher than the inner side making a gradient of about one in ten across the road. The road was icebound and at the turn the bus skidded and slipped down the road, collided with the parapet of the bridge and fell into the river.
HELD: The highway authority were under no duty to construct a roadway to prevent such an occurrence.

Negligent repair causing subsidence

Newsome v Darton Urban District Council
[1938] 3 All ER 93, 159 LT 153, 54 TLR 945, 82 Sol Jo 520, CA
In July 1933, the defendants had made a trench in a highway for the purpose of executing certain drainage work. The excavation was filled in, and in 1935, when the surface was tar-sprayed and chippings were rolled in with a steam roller, the surface was said to be level. In 1936, a depression or hole had formed at the place where the work had been done, and the jury found that the highway at this place was dangerous to those using it with due care. The jury also found that, although the original work was executed without negligence, the dangerous condition was due to the work of the defendants, and that the defendants were negligent in not discovering and taking steps to remedy the danger. The plaintiff having been thrown from his bicycle and injured by reason of the subsidence of the road at the place in question, brought an action against the defendants as the highway authority responsible for the repair of the road.

HELD: There was a duty on the defendants to make good the inevitable subsidence from their work in 1933, and they were negligent in not discovering, and in not taking steps to remedy, the danger. The jury had found that the subsidence was due to the excavations made by the highway authority. If the authority interferes with the structure of the road, then the operation of restoring it to the condition in which it was before such interference includes the remedying of a subsequent subsidence, although the subsidence was two years after the excavation and the accident three years after the excavation.

Birmingham v East Ham Corpn
(1962) 60 LGR 111, CA

The plaintiff was injured when walking across a public highway for which the defendants were the appropriate authority. His foot went into a hole 9 inches wide by 6 inches deep. Four days previously the highways superintendent of defendants had noticed a depression at the same spot. He had at once arranged for repairs which had been carried out. The loose earth beneath the surface was taken out until a solid base was reached. The sides of the excavation were made firm and the hole filled and 'punnelled' firm. An asphalt topping was put on and levelled with the wheel of a vehicle. There was evidence that rats were active in the vicinity and that there was a rat run nearby.

HELD: The defendants were not liable. The mere fact that the surface had sunk so soon after the work was done was not conclusive that the work had not been satisfactorily carried out. There was direct evidence that the work had been properly done and there was evidence about the rat run which could provide an explanation how the cavity could arise. The defendants were not under a further duty in the circumstances to take special precautions against the rats, eg by mixing broken glass with the filling.

Dogs on highway

Allison v Corby District Council
(1979) 78 LGR 197, [1980] RTR 111 (Pain J)

In June 1974 in good conditions the plaintiff's husband was riding his motor cycle along a road in the town of Corby when five dogs ran into the roadway in front of him. His machine struck one of the dogs and he fell off. He sustained injuries from which he died. The plaintiff claimed damages from the highway authority on the grounds that (1) they had been negligent in not taking adequate steps to keep the streets of the town clear of stray dogs which were hazardous to road users; (2) they were in breach of their statutory duty under the Highways Act 1959, s 44 to maintain adequately the highway; and (3) they had failed to prevent obstruction of the highway contrary to s 116 of the same Act. In 1971 following a number of accidents on the highway caused by dogs the defendants had obtained an order under the Road Traffic Act 1960, s 220 designating all the streets of Corby as roads on which it was an offence to allow a dog on the road without being held on a lead; they had also appointed a dog catcher and an assistant with a motor van to catch stray dogs and dispose of them and to place stickers on lamp posts saying 'Keep your dog on a leash'. There was evidence that the number of accidents caused by dogs had been much reduced.

HELD: The plaintiff could not succeed for the following reasons: (1) even accepting (as indicated by Lord Wilberforce in *Anns v Merton London Borough Council* (p 5, above) that there was a duty of care on the defendants at common law parallel with their public law duties, the defendants were not in breach of it. They had taken effective measures substantially to reduce the hazard caused by stray dogs; (2) adopting a phrase from Lord Denning in *Burnside v Emerson* (p 278, above) the passage of five dogs across a road was a mere 'transient danger' and s 44 could not possibly be applied to this case; (3) s 116 which lays a duty on the highway authority to prevent the stopping up or obstruction of a highway was designed to impose on the authority a duty to assert its title to the highway to defeat any attempt by someone to obstruct it, and does not relate to maintenance and repair. In the event, five dogs crossing a road cannot be regarded as an obstruction within the meaning of s 116.

Note—Highways Act 1959, s 44 — see note to p 278, above.

Repair work causing danger

Leech v Bristol Corpn
(1932) *Post Magazine*, 6 February
At the Bristol County Court a motor cyclist was awarded damages in his action against the Bristol Corporation in respect of personal injuries and material damages sustained owing to the alleged misfeasance of the Corporation as surveyors of highways in Bristol. The motor cyclist alleged that the Corporation, by servants or agents, repaired a part of a lane by placing loose gravel on the tarred surface in such a manner as to render it dangerous, so that it could not be properly and safely traversed by the public. While driving over the repaired patch of road, the motor cycle skidded, as a result of which he was injured and his machine and clothing were damaged.

The Corporation denied negligence, pleading that if plaintiff had kept a proper lookout he would have seen that part of the road had been recently tarred and covered, and would have escaped the risk of accident, if any. Evidence was given by an omnibus driver to the effect that the chippings were very loose, and where vehicles had gone through them the wheels had caused ridges. Another motor cyclist said in evidence that on the day following the accident he drove over the re-surfaced part of the road, and in turning the bend where the accident happened he had difficulty in controlling his machine. The chippings were loose, and he estimated that there was a depth of about 3 inches of chippings on the road.

Bright v A-G
(1971) 118 Sol Jo 226, [1971] RTR 253, 69 LGR 338, [1971] 2 Lloyd's Rep 68, CA
The plaintiff was riding his motor cycle down a road which had formerly been part of the A1 road when he lost control due to longitudinal ridges on the road surface and was injured. The road had ceased to be a trunk road

about two years earlier and the Ministry of Transport had instructed the local authority as its agent to remove double white lines which had divided two lanes of traffic. The local authority had done so about four months before the accident by covering the lines with asphalt. Summer traffic had compacted the asphalt between the lines, creating the ridges. An expert gave evidence that the groove between the ridges presented a serious and foreseeable danger to motor cycles. The judge at first instance held the Ministry to blame for not having given instructions to the local authority on how the work should be done.

HELD, ON APPEAL: The case turned on its own special facts. The Ministry was not negligent since the local authority was quite capable of doing the work properly. The negligence was that of the workmen who had failed to chip off the lines but had merely covered them up. The local authority was liable for the negligence of its workmen and the Ministry, as principals, must accept responsibility.

Per Lord Denning: If it were not for the special circumstances of this case I would have held the defendant not liable. The law still is that a highway is not to be considered to be dangerous simply because it is uneven, or not level, or has patches or undulations, or has been dug up for pipes and been filled in, or because the surface is bad. Road users cannot expect it to be as level as a bowling green. They must take the rough with the smooth. A highway is only to be considered dangerous when there is something which may be regarded as a trap into which an ordinary careful person may fall.

Note—In *Rider v Rider* (p 280, above) members of the Court of Appeal disagreed with the final sentence of the passage from Lord Denning's judgment in *Bright's* case; they did not accept as a matter of law that a danger for traffic cannot exist unless the road conditions constituting it would be a trap for the careful driver. Highway authorities must not provide only for those who use reasonable care.

Bird v Pearce
[1979] RTR 369, 77 LGR 753, CA

At a crossroads where Downs Lane crossed the Bruton Road the first defendant's car entering the crossroads from Down Lane was struck by the second defendant's car travelling along the Bruton road. Both roads were unclassified. The traffic system laid out by the highway authority gave priority to the Bruton road by double dotted white lines at the mouth of side roads, but at this crossroads the white lines had been obliterated by resurfacing about a month before the accident and not yet repainted. As between the defendants the first defendant was found 90% to blame. In third-party proceedings he sought contribution from the highway authority.

HELD: It was foreseeable that there was a risk of drivers misunderstanding their priorities at a crossroads junction — a greater risk than in the days before there had been any signs at all at the mouths of the side roads along a major road. The highway authority had created a pattern of traffic flow which did not exist before they placed white lines on the roads, a pattern which drivers could be expected to rely on. The highway authority was under a duty of care to the plaintiff to prevent injury from the potentially dangerous situation resulting from the removal of the white lines. They failed to erect any warning sign. The authority should contribute one-third to the damages paid by the first defendant.

Note—See also *Murray v Nicholls*, p 140, above.

Alexander & Sons v Dundee Corpn
1950 SC 123, 1950 SLT 76, Ct of Sess
In an action for negligence against a highway authority, averments that various other road accidents had taken place in the recent past on the stretch of road in question were held relevant and could properly be admitted to proof.

Road not taken over

Coleshill v Manchester Corpn
[1928] 1 KB 776, 97 LJKB 229, 138 LT 537, 44 TLR 258, CA
The defendants in execution of a housing scheme were laying out a new road running eastwards from a certain highway and closed at its eastern end by a quickset hedge. Footpaths had already been laid out and edged with kerb stones; houses were being built on the northern side and heaps of earth and building materials made the footpath on this side impassable; the footpath on the south side was still unfinished, but was traversable; it was bounded by a fence of wooden posts and bars; the middle of the road was levelled but not metalled; across it, for laying an electric cable, the defendants had cut a trench which they left unfenced and by night unlighted. They did not prevent persons, whether intending occupiers of houses or others, from walking down the new road. The plaintiff on a September evening while there was still daylight, walked with a companion down the highway and into the new road along the southern footpath. Through a gap in the fence they went across other land occupied by the defendants to a golf course. They returned somewhat hurriedly when it was growing dark, and the plaintiff fell into the trench and was injured.
HELD: That the trench being apparent to all, there was nothing in the nature of a concealed danger or 'trap', and that therefore the defendants were not liable to the plaintiff, who was a mere licensee.

Adjacent occupier

Macfarlane v Gwalter
[1959] 2 QB 332, [1958] 1 All ER 181, [1958] 2 WLR 268, 122 JP 144, 102 Sol Jo 123, 56 LGR 160, CA
A pedestrian walking along the footpath slipped through an iron grating which formed part of the pavement. The grating was old and in bad condition. The defendant was the occupier of the adjacent building.

The Public Health Acts Amendment Act 1890, s 35(1) (now replaced by the Highways Act 1980, s 180(5), which is in similar terms), provided as follows—

'All vaults, arches, and cellars under any street, and all openings into such vaults, arches, or cellars in the surface of any street, and all cellarheads, gratings, lights and coal holes in the surface of any street, and all landings, flags, or stones of the path or street supporting the same respectively shall be kept in good condition and repair by the owners or occupiers of the same, or of the houses or buildings to which the same respectively belong.'

The grating covered a small open area and its purpose was to provide light for the cellar window of the defendant's premises.

HELD: The defendant was liable under the Act whether the street had been dedicated or not.

Note—And see 'Dedication of highway', p 291, below; 'Adjacent danger', p 303, below.

Scott v Green & Sons
[1969] 1 All ER 849, [1969] 1 WLR 301, 113 Sol Jo 73, CA
A lorry backed on to the pavement outside the defendant's premises cracking a paving stone over the defendants' cellar. A few minutes later the plaintiff, walking along the pavement, stepped on it and it gave way. She was injured and sued for damages for breach of the Highways Act 1959, s 154(5) (now replaced in similar terms by the Highways Act 1980, s 180(5)) which provides 'every vault, arch and cellar under a street . . . and all landings flags or stones . . . by which they are supported . . . shall be kept in good condition and repair by the owner or occupier . . . of the premises to which it belongs'.
HELD: The subsection placed no absolute liability on the occupier in case of a breach. It merely gives control of the flagstone over the cellar to the owner or occupier so as to enable him to repair it whether the pavement had been dedicated to the public or not. Being in control of it he can be liable in negligence or nuisance but where, as here, there was no negligence or nuisance on the part of the defendants at all they were not liable.

Tramways

Browne v De Luxe Car Services
[1941] 1 KB 549, [1941] 1 All ER 383, 110 LJKB 369, 165 LT 175, 57 TLR 346, 85 Sol Jo 165, CA
The Tramways Act 1870, s 28 provides that if the undertaking or any part is abandoned and taken up, the undertakers shall within six weeks fill in and make good to the satisfaction of the road authority and restore to its former condition.
   Undertakers abandoned in 1932. They did not pull up the rails, but everything else connected with the tramway disappeared, and only the steel rails in the ground were left, and these were covered up with tar.
HELD: The tramway still belonged to the Corporation and the track still remained in the road, and there was nothing in the section or the Act to divert them from maintaining the roadway. The Corporation were under a liability for what, apart from the statute, would be a nuisance. They could take up the tram rails and make good the surface and then their obligation as a tramway company would end and be that of a local authority.

Simon v Islington Borough Council
[1943] 1 KB 188, [1943] 1 All ER 41, 112 LJKB 337, 168 LT 65, 59 TLR 87, 87 Sol Jo 92, CA
Undertakers abandoned a tramway and pursuant to the provisions of the London Passenger Transport Act 1933, the defendants took over. By the provisions of the Act they indemnified the undertakers. A cyclist was fatally

injured owing to the defective condition of the tramway track.

HELD, ON APPEAL: The tramway equipment was foreign to the highway. The defendants took over something which was an artificial work. It had become incongruous foreign matter in a modern road, and a mere obstruction to traffic. The principle of non-feasance did not apply and the defendants were liable.

Work by contractor

Penny v Wimbledon Urban Council
[1899] 2 QB 72, 68 LJQB 704, 80 LT 615
A district council, acting under the Public Health Act 1875, s 150, employed a contractor to make up a highway which was used by the public but had not become repairable by the inhabitants at large. In carrying out the work the contractor negligently left on the road a heap of soil, unlighted and unprotected. A person walking along the road after dark fell over the heap and was injured. An action was brought against the district council and the contractors to recover damages for the injuries sustained.

HELD: As, from the nature of the work danger was likely to arise to the public using the road, unless precautions were taken, the negligence of the contractor was not casual, or collateral to his employment, and the district council were liable.

Note—See also *Salsbury v Woodland*, p 304, below.

DEDICATION OF HIGHWAY

Note—The textbook writers accept that there is no liability on the owner of the soil when the public are permitted to use a way over the land. *Salmond on Torts* (18th edn) pp 259–60 says:

'Passengers on a highway across land in private ownership stand in a class apart. Apart from statutory modifications of the common law, a highway is merely a public right of way over land which remains in the occupation of the owner of the land. It is well established that such an occupier is under no responsibility as such towards users of the highway for its safety and is not liable for dangers thereon whether they exist at the time of dedication or come into existence later.'

Citing *Gautret v Egerton* (1867) LR 2 CP 371, 36 LJCP 191, Willes J: If I dedicate a way to the public which is full of ruts and holes, the public must take it as it is.

Right of way

Holden v White
[1982] QB 679, [1982] 2 All ER 328, [1982] 2 WLR 1030, 126 Sol Jo 230
CA
The only means of access to cottages in a row extending at right angles to the highway was over a strip of land belonging to the owner of the cottage nearest the highway. A milkman visiting one of the further cottages was injured on the right of way when his foot went through a defective manhole cover.

HELD: He was not entitled to damages against the owner of the strip of land, whether or not she was the occupier, because he was not her 'visitor' for the purposes of the Occupiers Liability Act 1957. She did not owe the common duty of care to him; it was entirely unreal to regard her, as servient owner, as having in any sense issued any invitation or permission to a person who entered the land in exercise of the dominant owner's right of way.

Note—See also *Greenhalgh v British Railways Board* (p 293, below).

RAILWAY BRIDGES

Swain v Southern Rly Co
[1939] 2 KB 560, [1939] 2 All ER 794, 108 LJKB 827, 160 LT 606, 55 TLR 805, 83 Sol Jo 476, CA
Plaintiff was riding his bicycle on a road, a bridge carrying the road over a railway which was repairable by the railway company pursuant to their private Act. Plaintiff was thrown from his bicycle because the wheels got into a rut about 3 inches deep and from 6 to 9 inches wide, which was a dangerous rut. The accident was caused by the want of repair of the road.
HELD: By the Railways Clauses Consolidation Act 1845, s 46, the railway company were liable for non-feasance as well as misfeasance. The road was in a condition which would have been dangerous to traffic as it was when the bridge was constructed. The duty is to maintain in the state when originally constructed and that necessarily implies an absence of dangerous ruts. The Railway Company were liable.

Lewys v Burnett and Dunbar
[1945] 2 All ER 555, 173 LT 307, 61 TLR 527, 89 Sol Jo 315 (Croom Johnson J)
A road ran under a railway bridge, the headroom of which, by the Act authorising the construction of the railway, was required to be not less than 9 feet, and had been 9 ft 3 in. The road authority had repaired the road and reduced the headroom to 8 ft 9 in and fixed a notice to the bridge '8 ft 9 in headroom'. A passenger on a lorry was killed by his head coming into contact with the bridge.
HELD: The lorry owner was liable for failing to warn, and the highway authority for negligently performing the statutory duty to repair; proportions 50–50.

James v Durkin (Civil Engineering Contractors) Ltd
(1983) Times, 25 May (Michael Davies J)
The driver of a skip lorry owned by the defendants was killed when part of the lorry slightly over 12 feet high struck a bridge of 11 ft 6 ins clearance, causing the vehicle to overturn. There was no notice in the cab of the lorry to indicate the height of the lorry.
HELD: A vehicle of such a height should have a clear warning notice, and the defendants were liable. Damages should be reduced by 50% because the driver approached the bridge at too high a speed having regard to the height of the lorry.

North Staffordshire Rly Co v Dale
(1858) 8 E & B 836
The roadway over a bridge is part of the bridge so that the railway company is obliged not only to maintain the structure of the bridge, but also the road surface going across it.

Note—Followed by CA in *Bury Corpn v London and Yorkshire Rly Co* (1888) 20 QBD 485.

London and North Western Rly Co v Skerton
(1864) 5 B & S 559
A railway company who, in carrying a railway over a highway by a bridge, lowered the level of the highway, were not bound to keep the slope of the road in repair as being a part of the approaches on each side of the bridge.

Greenhalgh v British Railways Board
[1969] 2 QB 286, [1969] 2 All ER 114, [1969] 2 WLR 892, 113 Sol Jo 108, CA.
The plaintiff was walking across the defendants' bridge over their railway when she fell and was injured owing to the bad condition of the road surface. The bridge had been built in 1873 as an accommodation bridge for adjoining landowners under the Railways Clauses Consolidation Act 1845, s 68. In the course of time the public had acquired a right of way across the bridge. The local authority built large housing estates on each side of the railway with good approach roads to the bridge. The plaintiff lived on one of the estates some distance from the bridge.
HELD: (1) The defendants' duty under s 68 was only to 'owners and occupiers of lands adjoining the railway' and the plaintiff was not in that category; (2) the plaintiff was not a 'visitor' on the bridge for the purposes of the Occupiers' Liability Act 1957. A person is a 'visitor' only if at common law he would be regarded as an invitee or licensee. This does not include a person who, like the plaintiff, crosses land in pursuance of a public right of way (citing dictum of Willes J in *Gautret v Egerton*, quoted on p 291, above). Judgment for the defendants.

---

2 STREET WORKS: REINSTATEMENT

THE STREET WORKS CODE

Note—Part I of the Public Utilities Street Works Act 1950, consists of a 'Street Works Code' to regulate relations as to apparatus (ie pipes, cables, sewers, etc) in streets between authorities having statutory powers to place apparatus therein. It deals among other things with breaking open and reinstating streets for any purposes other than road purposes.
  Reinstatement is provided for in s 7(2) of the Act as follows:

'**7 Requirements as to mode of executing major works, and as to reinstatement** (2) Undertakers executing any code-regulated works which involve breaking up or opening the street . . . shall be under obligation to reinstate and make good the street . . . after the completion of the works, and — . . .

(a) . . . to execute it in accordance with any reasonable requirements of any such authority . . . and to execute it to the reasonable satisfaction of . . . such authority . . .

(b) in the case of works which involve breaking up or opening the street . . . to reinstate it and make it good up to what was the surface level before the execution of the works, subject to the provisions of the Third Schedule . . . where the street authority . . . elect thereunder to do the reinstatement and making good at upper levels:. . . .'

See the reference to this subsection in s 58 of the Highways Act 1980, p 276, above.

Subsection (4) provides that if the authority is not satisfied with the reinstatement, it can require the undertakers to remedy the defect.

By s 39(1), 'reinstatement and making good' includes interim restoration.

Schedule 3, para 1(1) empowers the authority to elect to do the permanent reinstatement at upper levels. In that case para 3 limits the liability to interim restoration, or such permanent restoration as is not within the obligation of the authority.

Paragraph 4(1) then puts the liability for permanent reinstatement and making good at surface level on the authority.

Highway authority's obligation — s 7(2)(c)

McNair v Dumfermline Corpn
(1954) 104 LJ 66
The fact that a Gas Board failed to discharge its obligation under s 7(2)(c) to reinstate the pavement does not diminish the responsibility of the highway authority who have the paramount interest.

No cause of action for breach — s 8(1)(a)

Keating v Elvan Reinforced Concrete Co Ltd
[1968] 2 All ER 139, [1968] 1 WLR 722, 112 Sol Jo 193, CA
The plaintiff fell into a trench dug by the defendants and was injured. Part of the barricade and lamps erected by the defendants had been knocked down by someone else and they were in no way to blame. The Public Utilities Street Works Act 1950, s 8(1)(a) required the defendants to ensure that the trench was adequately fenced and guarded and lighted. The plaintiff claimed that this duty was absolute, that the defendants were in breach of it and that he was entitled to damages.

HELD: The plaintiff's contention failed. The section was part of the group of sections which comprised the Street Works Code and it was only in s 8 that provisions for safety were made, provisions little different from those of the common law except for the possibility that they might be absolute. Having regard to the statute as a whole there was no intent to create a cause of action for breach of statutory duty.

An appeal was dismissed. The proper approach to the case, said the Court of Appeal, was to ask whether on a true construction of the statute as a whole the duties were public duties only or whether a right of action by an individual ought to be implied. Examination of ss 3 to 14 of the Act, which comprised the 'Street Works Code' showed that they were enacted for the purpose of providing protection for certain public authorities concerned with streets. There was no suggestion that any part of it was enacted for the protection of individuals who may suffer injury owing to defective precautions taken with regard to excavations in the streets. Moreover s 8(3) provided for a penalty on conviction of undertakers who failed to comply with s 8(1) and subs (4) gave a civil remedy to an authority against undertakers who failed to satisfy an obligation under s 8(1). Neither in subs (3) or (4) was there any mention or suggestion that any private individual would have any remedy or right of action under the section.

Cohen v British Gas Corpn
[1978] CLY 2053 (Judge Lymbery QC)
The defendants temporarily reinstated an excavation which they had made in a public road and gave notice to the local authority under the provisions of the Public Utilities Street Works Act 1950. The excavation was about 5 feet by 3 feet and the filling had sunk causing a depression of about 1 inch. The plaintiff alleged he tripped over the temporary reinstatement.
HELD: Inevitably in a roadway one finds undulations; the surface is not to be judged by the standards of a bowling green. A depression of 1 inch was not dangerous.

Cressy v South Metropolitan Gas Co
(1906) 94 LT 790, Div Ct
Under the Gasworks Clauses Act 1847, undertakers had power to break up roads and reinstate. Under the Metropolis Management Act 1855, s 114 (now repealed), the borough council had power to step in and do repairs.
  A gas company had excavated in a street, and the local authority had stepped in and reinstated. Owing to the negligent filling in of the excavation, a hole was caused and the plaintiff was injured by stepping into the hole. She sued the gas company.
HELD: The legislature before the 1855 Act contemplated a trading company for its own profit interfering with a street and made provision for the protection of the public if the authorised work was not properly done. The effect of the 1855 Act was that this obligation was subject to the provision 'unless the local authority step in and do the work' at the expense of the gas company, which the local authority are entitled to do if they please. This included maintenance, because the Act uses the words 'making good', and it is not made good until it is in a permanent condition so far as practicable. The gas company could not do the work and were not liable.

Note—Similar provisions to those of s 114 of the Metropolis Management Act 1855, are now contained in Sch 3 to the Public Utilities Street Works Act 1950.

Brame v Commercial Gas Co
[1914] 3 KB 1181, 84 LJKB 570, 111 LT 1099, Div Ct
A metropolitan borough council, acting under s 114 of the 1855 Act, passed a resolution to the effect that where the surface of any street in the borough was opened by a gas company, they would themselves undertake

the work of reinstatement. Subsequently to the date of this resolution, a gas company having finished laying their pipes under the pavement of a street in the borough, notified the council that reinstatement was necessary. The plaintiff was injured owing to the pavement being out of repair after such notice had been given. She sued the gas company.

HELD: The resolution of the Borough Council did not release the gas company from its obligations under the Gasworks Clauses Act on the expiration of a reasonable time after they had received notice from the gas company that reinstatement was necessary. Before such a release could be effected, it was necessary that the company should be dismissed from the control of the reinstatement by the council, and the work undertaken by the council.

Sanitary authority

Shoreditch Corpn v Bull
(1904) 90 LT 210, 20 TLR 254
Appellants, who were both the sanitary and the highway authority, dug a trench along a road under their control for the purpose of laying a sewer. When the work was completed they filled in the trench and opened the road for traffic. About a week afterwards respondent was driving along the road in a cab at night. The driver found that the part of the road where the trench had been opened was soft, and crossed on to the other side, and ran into a heap of rubbish, with the result that the cab was overturned and respondent was injured. The rubbish had been wrongfully deposited in the road without the permission of appellants, but they knew it was there, and had not lighted or fenced it. The jury found that the part of the road where the trench had been opened had been properly filled in, but had been rendered soft by subsequent rain, and was dangerous to traffic at the time of the accident.

HELD: Appellants were liable for the injury.

Water Board

Rider v Metropolitan Water Board
[1949] 2 KB 378, [1949] 2 All ER 97 (Devlin J)
On 8 July 1944, undertakers broke the tarred surface of the pavement to repair a stop-cock box and excavated a hole 2 feet square by 18 inches deep. They refilled and consolidated, and also made the surface good temporarily by laying gravel to a depth of 4 inches. On 10 July 1944, they gave notice to the Wandsworth Borough Council under the Waterworks Clauses Act 1847, s 30 that the surface had been broken open and required immediate reinstating. This notice should be three days before starting the work, except in emergency, when it may be given as soon as possible after starting. This occasion was treated as an emergency. On 15 August 1944, the Council did the work of renewing the surface; they removed the temporary surface of gravel and put down tar with a topping of finer material. About 5.30 pm on 29 December 1946, a very foggy night, plaintiff tripped over the lid of the box, which projected and formed a danger due to the negligence of the Council in laying the topping. The Council was acting under the Metropolis Management Act 1855, s 114.

HELD: Following *Cressy's* case and *Brame v Commercial Gas Co*, the undertakers are absolved from all liability under s 32 of the 1847 Act, which is qualified by s 114 of the 1855 Act, and should be read as if subject to the proviso 'unless the local authority step in and do the work', but not until the work is actually taken over by the Council (*Brame's* case). Section 114 applies although the Council only did part of the work, ie reinstatement of the surface, as distinct from filling in a firm base done by undertakers. It applies to both these two operations separately, and so does s 32 of the 1847 Act. (Judgment for defendants.)

Note—See note after *Cressy's* case, p 295, above.

WATER ACT 1945

Third Schedule, Part VI

22 Power to break open streets Subject to the provisions of this Part of this Schedule, the undertakers may within their limits of supply for the purpose of laying, constructing, inspecting, repairing, renewing or removing mains, service pipes, plant or other works, and outside those limits for the purpose of laying any mains which they are authorised to lay and of inspecting, repairing, renewing or removing mains, break open the roadway and footpaths of any street, and of any bridge carrying a street, and any sewer, drain or tunnel in or under any such roadway or footpath, and may remove and use the soil or other materials in or under any such roadway or footpath:

Provided that they shall in the exercise of the powers conferred by this section cause as little inconvenience and do as little damage as may be, and for any damage done shall pay compensation to be determined, in case of dispute, by arbitration.

27 Remedies where undertakers fail to comply with foregoing requirements (1) If the undertakers fail to comply with, or contravene, any of the foregoing provisions of this Part of this Schedule, they shall, without prejudice to their civil liability if any, to a person aggrieved, be liable to a fine not exceeding five pounds, and to a further fine not exceeding five pounds for each day on which the offence continues after notice thereof has been given to them by, or by an officer or agent of, the persons aggrieved.

The fine is increased to 'level 1 on the standard scale' by Criminal Justice Act 1982, s 46.

Wells v Metropolitan Water Board
[1937] 4 All ER 639 (Humphreys J)
The plaintiff was injured through tripping over the cover-plate of a valve-box, belonging to the defendant water board. When the cover of this valve-box was closed it was in no way objectionable or dangerous, but on this occasion someone, presumably a child, had opened the cover and, when open, it projected some 3 inches or 4 inches above the surface of the road. The cover could be opened quite easily, and was not fitted with any locking device, and there was evidence that the fitting of a locking device was both possible and reasonable.
HELD: (Distinguishing *Simpson v Metropolitan Water Board* (1917) 15 LGR 629) the plaintiff's injuries were caused by the negligence of the defendants, and she was entitled to recover.

Longhurst v Metropolitan Water Board
[1948] 2 All ER 834, [1948] WN 418, 112 JP 470, 64 TLR 579, 92 Sol Jo
633, HL
A stopcock below a public footway, belonging to and controlled by water
undertakers, developed a leak. The escaping water dislodged the paving
stones of the footway from their seatings. The practice of the undertakers
was to take up only so much of the highway as was necessary to repair the
leak, make good the surface temporarily, and notify the highway authority
to effect permanent repairs, and until they did so, maintain a warning to
the public of any danger. The work of repairing the leak was completed in a
day, but the undertakers did not think it their duty to render safe the
loosened stones in the pavement which it was not necessary to remove to
repair the leak. They did not give warning to the public of the dangerous
condition of those stones. The local authority received notice about 10 am
the day after the repairs had been completed, but before they had time to
begin the permanent repairs, the plaintiff tripped over a loose paving stone
and was injured.

The Waterworks Clauses Act 1847, s 28 gave the Board power to break
up the pavement and to repair. Section 32 (see now Public Utilities Street
Works Act 1950, s 8) required them to reinstate and to fence or guard and
to light at night to warn passengers and keep in repair for three months.
HELD: The defendants were not liable: there was no evidence or inference
that the undertakers knew or ought to have known of the danger. No negligence being proved, the only remaining basis of claim lay in nuisance.
Even in the case of a private individual liability for nuisance without negligence is not readily established, but statutory authorities acting under
statutory powers are under a more limited liability (*Geddis v Bann Reservoir
Proprietors* (1878) 3 App Cas 430). No action lay for damage caused by
doing an act authorised by the legislature unless done negligently. In *Green
v Chelsea Waterworks Co* (1894) 70 LT 547, 10 TLR 259, undertakers were
not liable for a burst main. The obligation under s 32 only requires the
undertakers to reinstate and repair such portion of the road as they had
taken up.

Per Lord du Parcq: There might be a duty to warn in an emergency
where undertakers knew or had means of knowledge not available to the
highway authority.

Note—The 1847 Act was repealed by the Water Act 1945, but the repeal does not
apply to individual undertakers except by order of the Minister. Sections 30–34 are
now repealed by the Public Utilities Street Works Act 1950. See now the Street
Works Code in that Act. Section 32 was similar to s 8 of the 1950 Act.

Dunne v North Western Gas Board
[1964] 2 QB 806, [1963] 3 All ER 916, [1964] 2 WLR 164, 107 Sol Jo 890,
62 LGR 197, CA
The plaintiffs were injured by a gas explosion in a street in Liverpool. It
was caused by a leakage of gas from a gas main into a sewer due to a leak
from a water main. Both the judge of first instance and the Court of Appeal
held there was no negligence on the part of either the gas board or the water
undertakers, but the judge held the gas board liable in nuisance and the
water undertaker liable under the doctrine in *Rylands v Fletcher*.

HELD, ON APPEAL: The defendants supplied gas and water under statutory authority. If in such cases there was an accident occurring as the result of statutory operations without negligence on the part of the statutory undertakers there could be no liability. Quoting Lord Blackburn in *Geddis v Bann Reservoir Proprietors*, 'No action will lie for doing that which the legislature has authorised, if it be done without negligence, although it does occasion damage.' *Rylands v Fletcher* did not apply; that case imposed liability for the negligence of an independent contractor on a landowner who for his own purposes collected things on his land which escaped. Those were not the facts in the present case.

Note—But see comments of Robert Goff J on *Geddis's* case in *Fellowes v Rother District Council* [1983] 1 All ER 513 at 518-20.

Liability after 12 months

Hartley v Rochdale Corpn
[1908] 2 KB 594, 77 LJKB 884, 99 LT 275, 72 JP 343, 24 TLR 625, 6 LGR 858
A corporation had power to supply and supplied water outside their area. They filled up an excavation, and under the Waterworks Clauses Act their liability to remedy post-work subsidence ceased after 12 months. During the 12 months subsidence occurred and the Corporation employed the local council of the area to repair. Twenty months after the expiry of the 12 months the plaintiff was injured.
HELD: The local council had repaired as agents for the Corporation; the road had been out of repair since the 12 months expired, and the defendant Corporation were liable.

---

3 OBSTRUCTIONS AND DANGERS ON HIGHWAY

STATUTORY

Note—A statutory right may rebut negligence

Great Central Rly Co v Hewlett
[1916] 2 AC 511, 85 LJKB 1705, 115 LT 349, 32 TLR 707, 60 Sol Jo 678, HL
A railway company erected in the public highway certain gate posts from which collapsible steel gates could be run across the road so as to close the entrance to the station yard. These posts were erected by the company in contravention of their special Act and in 1901 were judicially held to be an obstruction to the highway. In 1902 the company obtained an Act which empowered them to 'maintain' the posts and gates and to replace them when necessary on the same site. A licensed taxicab driver, while lawfully

driving his cab on a dark rainy night along the public highway into the station yard, collided with one of these posts, which was practically invisible owing to the darkening of the street in compliance with the Reduction of Lighting Regulations and thereby damaged his cab. The post was in the condition in which it was at the time of the passing of the Act in 1902. An action was brought by the cab driver against the railway company for damages for negligence.

HELD: The accident arose, not from any overt act of the company, but from the existence of the gate post which had been legalised by the Act of 1902, coupled with the diminution of light necessitated by the exigencies of the War; the mere power to maintain the post imposed no obligation on the company to take reasonable precautions to warn the public of its existence; and the company was not guilty of negligence.

Unlighted obstruction in highway

Note—The conflicting decisions on this point were reviewed and the principles applicable were dealt with by the Court of Appeal in *Fisher v Ruislip-Northwood UDC* (below).

Polkinghorn v Lambeth Borough Council
[1938] 1 All ER 339, 158 LT 127, 54 TLR 345, 82 Sol Jo 94, CA
An illuminated bollard at one end of a tram refuge had been damaged in an accident. The defendant council had placed a light upon it, but the light had, for some unexplained reason, gone out. As a result of this, the plaintiff's motor car collided with the bollard, and the plaintiff was injured.
HELD: The defendant council having erected the refuge and bollards, were under a continuing duty to keep them adequately lighted. They were, therefore, liable to the plaintiff in respect of the injury he had sustained. Farwell J said he would prefer to deal with the case as one of negligence rather than as a case of breach of any statutory duty, and held that it was common law negligence.

Fisher v Ruislip-Northwood Urban District Council and Middlesex County Council
[1945] KB 584, [1945] 2 All ER 458, 173 LT 161, 62 TLR 1, 89 Sol Jo 434, CA
The defendant local authority had lawfully erected a surface shelter in the highway under the Civil Defence Act 1939, s 9. There was a warning light at each corner which could be turned on and off by a switch inside the shelter, which it was the duty of the air-raid wardens to switch on at the appointed time. The shelter was sometimes lighted and sometimes not lighted. The plaintiff driving a car in the hours of darkness with due care and on the proper side of the road collided with the shelter which was unlighted. He was a complete stranger to the district and had never been in the road before.
HELD, by the Court of Appeal: On undertakers who were given statutory power to construct works, a legal duty was imposed that reasonable care should be taken so to construct and maintain the works as to render them safe and not dangerous to the public though no such duty was imposed by

the statute itself or by the common law; except in cases where the statute excluded the duty of taking care. The duty to take reasonable care to prevent danger to the public was present throughout; the date of the erection of an obstruction and the purpose for which it was intended to be used (apart from special circumstances or special language in the statute), were immaterial. So long as the streets were properly lit, the duty was ipso facto performed, but when the street lighting was suspended for any reason, whether by lighting restrictions, the exercise of an option on the part of the local authority not to light, or accidental breakdown, it became the duty of the local authority to take such steps to safeguard the public by special danger lights or otherwise, as in the circumstances of the case were reasonably possible.

The respondents were responsible for the shelter and were under a duty to take reasonable steps to warn the public of its existence and that duty was not performed, and they were liable to the appellant. Appeal allowed.

Whiting v Middlesex County Council and Harrow Urban District Council

[1948] 1 KB 162, [1947] 2 All ER 758, [1948] LJR 242, 112 JP 74, 63 TLR 614, 92 Sol Jo 41, 46 LGR 136 (Croom-Johnson J)

A motor cyclist during the hours of darkness when public lighting was unrestricted, collided with an air-raid shelter which was built partially on the footway to the extent of about 1 foot and jutted out into the roadway for about another 6 feet. It was near a street lamp which threw a shadow into the roadway causing a pool of darkness. An electric bulb showing a red light was built in, protected from outside by a wire mesh grill, and inside two screws would have to be removed to remove the red glass covering the lamp. The lamp was for some reason extinguished. The light had been destroyed over and over again by mischievous persons, and other accidents had occurred. The defendants ordered workpeople to put the light back, but it was repeatedly destroyed to the knowledge of the defendants.

HELD: Defendants had not taken reasonable steps. What they did was equivalent to taking no steps at all. The duty is not a duty to light but a duty to take reasonable steps to prevent the obstruction becoming a danger to the public; to ensure that a warning is given. Lighting is no doubt the obvious and simplest measure of precautions during the hours of darkness. It may be the only possible effective precaution. There may be other steps which would be as effective.

'Properly lit' (see *Fisher's* case) applies when the street lighting is effective to fulfil the duty. Here the public lighting resulted in something like a trap and the structure remained a danger. The defendants could not say — we will put the lighting back and until somebody destroys it again, we have performed our duty. Defendants were liable.

ROADWORKS

Lilley v British Insulated Callenders Construction Co Ltd

(1968) 67 LGR 224, CA

The plaintiff was injured when at about 10.50 pm his car collided with an obstruction left in the road by the defendants. The plaintiff said there were no lights or guard rail round the obstruction. The defendants brought evidence that at 8.30 pm barriers were in position and lights were burning.

HELD, ON APPEAL: The real issue was whether the defendants ought to have had a man to inspect the lights periodically during the night. There was evidence that the defendants did so at their main sites, but this accident had taken place in a quiet residential road. The defendants had taken reasonable precautions and were under no obligation to send a man to inspect the site.

Murray v Southwark Borough Council
(1966) 65 LGR 145 (MacKenna J)

In a street in Rotherhithe, London, reasonably well lit by sodium lighting of orange colour the plaintiff saw lines of red lamps dividing the road into two lanes. He was using only the sidelights of his car. He drove into the nearside lane, which was out of use for repairs, and though finding the surface rough drove on for ten yards or so until the front wheels fell into an excavation a foot deep. Some hooligans had removed a trestle and lamps which had been placed across the entrance to the nearside lane by the defendant highway authority to divert traffic into the offside lane.

HELD: The plaintiff was not negligent either in not using headlights or in failing to see the excavation. The defendants were negligent in not providing enough watchmen in an area where hooliganism was common.

Duty to light optional outside metropolis

Note—Outside the Metropolis, the lighting of streets comes under the provisions of the Public Health Act 1875, s 161:

'Any urban authority may contract with any person for the supply of gas, and other means of lighting the streets, market and public buildings in their district, and may provide such lamps, lamp posts and other materials and apparatus as they may think necessary for lighting the same.

Where there is not any company or person (other than the urban authority) authorised by or in pursuance of any Act of Parliament, or any order confirmed by Parliament, to supply gas for public and private purposes, supplying gas within any part of the district of such authority, such authority may themselves undertake to supply gas for such purposes or any of them throughout the whole or any part of their district; and if there is any such company or person so supplying gas, but the limits of supply of such company or person include part only of the district, then the urban authority may themselves undertake to supply gas throughout any part of the district not included within such limits of supply. . . .'

Sheppard v Glossop Corpn
[1921] 3 KB 132, CA

The defendants had placed a lamp on a place which was dangerous when not lighted, but extinguished it every night soon after 9 pm in accordance with a resolution passed by the authority.

HELD: The section confers upon urban authorities a discretion but imposes on them no obligation to light the streets in their districts; consequently the defendants who had begun were not bound to continue to light the street; and having done nothing to make the street dangerous they were under no obligation whether by lighting or otherwise, to give warning of danger.

Note—See also *Burton v W. Suffolk CC* (p 277, above).

Dangerous position of road sign

Levine v Morris
[1971] 1 All ER 144, [1970] 1 WLR 71, 113 Sol Jo 799, [1970] RTR 93, CA
The first defendant driving a car on a main road towards a roundabout in heavy rain got into a skid and crashed into massive concrete columns supporting a road sign erected by the Ministry of Transport, killing a passenger. He was held 75% to blame and the Ministry 25%.

The Ministry's appeal was dismissed. They owed a duty to take reasonable care, when there were sites for signs equally good as regards visibility, not to select the one which involved greater hazards to the motorist. It was well known that at high speeds there was a risk of motorists going off the road in bad weather. The chances of such accidents should always be borne in mind by the Ministry and the extent of such chances assessed. In the present case anyone skilled in road design would foresee that drivers who had not the fullest degree of skill might leave the road. The danger could have been averted by siting the sign where the risk was diminished.

Hughes v Sheppard, Morley v Sheppard
(1940) 163 LT 177, 104 JP 357, 56 TLR 810, 84 Sol Jo 490, 38 LGR 336
The employees of a county council acting as agents for the Minister of Transport were engaged in painting a white line down the centre of a trunk road for which by virtue of the Trunk Roads Act 1936, the Minister was the highway authority. The men having left their work for the midday rest, the newly-painted line was marked by a series of cans filled with sand in which red flags were fixed. A motor driver, having failed to see the cans, collided with the first as he approached, and then with another car coming towards him.

In actions brought against him, and against the county council and Minister of Transport for negligence, it was contended that the council and the Minister were guilty of negligence in not giving clear indication of the presence of the cans and flags and of nuisance.
HELD: (1) The painting of the white lines was, whether or not an 'improvement' within the Trunk Roads Act 1936, within the powers of the Minister as highway authority; it was no more than what was reasonably necessary to the process of painting the line to indicate that such work was in progress by means of the cans and flags; and the placing of the cans and flags did not constitute negligence or nuisance; (2) in any event, even if the placing of the cans and flags along the line constituted a nuisance, the only person liable to plaintiffs was defendant driver by reason of his negligence in failing to see the cans and flags in time to avoid the accident.

OTHER DANGERS

Adjacent danger

Caseley v Bristol Corpn
[1944] 1 All ER 14, CA
The duty of an occupier of land is to fence any dangerous excavation adjoining the highway, and this may extend to a danger close to though not actually adjoining.

A man wandered in a fog from the highway and fell into a dock basin 47 feet from the highway.

HELD: There was no duty to fence unless the danger was so near the highway that a man making a false step, or overcome by temporary giddiness, would fall into the excavation.

Ball from playing field on highway

Hilder v Associated Portland Cement Manufacturers Ltd

[1961] 3 All ER 709, [1961] 1 WLR 1434, 105 Sol Jo 725; 179 Estates Gazette 445 (Ashworth J)

The defendants allowed their field adjoining a busy road to be used as a playing field by children. The field was separated from the road by a three-foot wall and a line of poplar trees. Two boys aged nine and ten were playing with a football using a poplar tree as one goal post and a stick as the other. In the course of the game one of the boys kicked the ball on to the road. The plaintiff's husband was riding by on a motor cycle: he was thrown off by the ball and killed.

HELD: The defendants were liable in negligence. The test was whether the defendants were shown to have failed to take reasonable care in all the circumstances. The relevant circumstances included the situation of the field and the road, the amount of traffic using the road, the ages of the children using the field, the nature of their amusements and the frequency with which the field was used. A reasonable man would come to the conclusion, on the facts given in evidence, that there was a risk of damage to persons using the road which was not so small that he could disregard it.

Danger created by independent contractor

Salsbury v Woodland

[1970] 1 QB 324, [1969] 3 All ER 863, [1969] 3 WLR 29, 113 Sol Jo 327, CA

The first defendant was the owner of a house adjoining a public highway. He wished to have a hawthorn tree removed which stood in the front garden 28 feet from the roadway. His wife found some tree-fellers and engaged one of them (the second defendant) to do the job. He failed to lop the branches sufficiently before bringing the tree down and as a result it fouled and broke two telephone wires running to the house from a post on the other side of the road. The wires hung across the roadway and the plaintiff, a bystander, went to remove them. Before he reached them he saw the third defendant coming in his car at fast speed towards the wires. He flung himself down on the grass verge to avoid being struck by the wires and injured his back. The second defendant did not contest the action. The judge held the first defendant was liable for the second defendant's negligence even though he was an independent contractor. He said that when the very act which is required to be done by the independent contractor contains a risk of injury to others the principal is liable if injury results from negligence in performing it.

HELD, ON APPEAL: The judge's statement of principle was too wide. The first defendant was not himself negligent and could not be liable unless the case was within the special categories of case in which the principal was liable for the contractor's lack of care in doing the work. Only two such categories were relevant to the present case: (1) 'extra hazardous acts' — those acts so hazardous that the law has seen fit to impose direct liability on the principal. The present case did not come into that category. The job if done with elementary caution by skilled men presented no hazard to anyone at all. (2) Dangers created in a highway. Such cases are all found on analysis to be cases where the work being done was in a highway and of a character which would have been a nuisance unless authorised by statute. This case was not one of work done in a highway. There was no sound authority for saying that there is an additional class of case of liability where the principal commissions work to be done *near* a highway.

Fire engine parked

Amos v Glamorgan County Council
(1967) 66 LGR 166, CA
The plaintiff, a youth of 19, was riding his motor cycle when he collided with the defendants' stationary fire engine. The accident happened in broad daylight. The fire engine was properly parked at the kerb, having been called to a fire at a nearby house. It had been there only two minutes or so and had two blue flashing lights on top. The plaintiff had a view of it for at least 80 yards. There was heavy rain and the plaintiff was not wearing his spectacles. The Commissioner of Assize found the defendants one-half to blame for omitting to put a red warning light on the road to give oncoming traffic early warning of the presence of the fire engine.
HELD, ON APPEAL: The defendants were not to blame at all. The fire brigade had to give priority to those in peril from fire and in the circumstances the flashing signal from the fire engine was a sufficient warning of its presence. Bad weather conditions did not justify a motor cyclist for failing to keep a proper look-out: they required him to proceed more carefully.

Ice on road

Manchester Corpn v Markland
[1936] AC 360, [1935] All ER Rep 667, 104 LJKB 480, HL
The Manchester Corporation were the statutory authority for the supply of water. A service pipe in a road burst and caused a pool of water to form in the road. The water lay unheeded for three days. On the third day a frost occurred, the water froze, and on the ice so formed a motor car skidded and knocked down and killed a man. The Corporation were not informed until after this accident that the service pipe had burst.
HELD: The driver of the car was not guilty of negligence, but the Corporation were liable for not having taken prompt steps to attend to the leak and so to prevent the road from becoming dangerous to traffic.

Lambie v Western Scottish Motor Traction Co
1944 SC 415
Ice formed on the pavement from washing of buses in a neighbouring garage. A pedestrian slipped on the ice and was injured.
HELD: The bus company were liable.

Lamp-post

Davies v Carmarthenshire County Council
[1971] RTR 112, CA

The plaintiff was driving her car up a hill at about 17 mph into the setting sun. The road had recently been widened by the defendants who had left a lamp-post in its original position about 5 feet out from the new edge of the road. The plaintiff completely failed to see it and drove straight into it. The county court judge held the defendants wholly to blame. They appealed on the issue of contributory negligence.

HELD: The plaintiff was not so dazzled by the sun that she had no visibility at all: if she were then it was negligent to go ahead except at a minimal pace. She was not driving completely blind and should have seen the lamp-post at the speed she was travelling and avoided it. But the blameworthiness of the defendants in leaving the obstacle in the road without any sufficient warning to motorists was very much greater. Proportion 80% defendants, 20% plaintiff.

Slates on highway

Almeroth v W. E. Chivers & Sons Ltd
[1948] 1 All ER 53, 92 Sol Jo 71, CA

Contractors left a small pile of slates by the kerb which was between 4 and 6 inches high. The pile did not overtop the kerb. The plaintiff crossing the road in daylight tripped over the pile which he had not previously seen and did not notice as he was stepping up on to the kerb, and was injured. There was no evidence that the defendants' work could not be carried on in any other way.

Lewis J held the heap constituted a nuisance but that the accident was due solely to the negligence of the plaintiff because he did not see the pile. HELD, ON APPEAL: A pedestrian is not bound to keep his eyes on the ground or look constantly down to his feet to see whether or not there was any obstacle in his path. The small heap did not cause an obstruction in that it prevented or impeded the flow of traffic or the passage of pedestrians, but it constituted a nuisance which might easily not be noticed by a reasonably careful person. There was no evidence of negligence of the plaintiff. The defendants were guilty of negligence and nuisance. Appeal allowed.

Prince v Gregory
[1959] 1 All ER 133, [1959] 1 WLR 177, 103 Sol Jo 130, CA

Defendant left a pile of lime mortar in the gutter outside his house pending his use of it presumably for repairs. The plaintiff was a boy aged ten. Another boy aged 14 picked up some of the mortar and threw it at the plaintiff and injured him.

HELD: The defendant could not reasonably be expected to apprehend danger to children from the lime mortar being left where it was, pending its use for a useful purpose. Defendant not liable.

Smoke on highway

Holling v Yorkshire Traction Co Ltd

[1948] 2 All ER 662 (Oliver J)

The second defendants were owners of coke ovens on the north side of and about 50 yards from the main road from Sheffield to Manchester. The operations produced masses of steam and smoke about every three-quarters of an hour. In normal weather the clouds of vapour rose and blew over the road at a height which did not inconvenience traffic, but on comparatively rare occasions they passed low and involved vehicles on the road.

On 22 February 1947, about 3 pm, an omnibus of the first defendants and a private car travelling in opposite directions collided in the middle of a particularly dense cloud of grey smoke and steam, which amounted to complete obscurity. The omnibus driver could not see the car even after he had run into it. Two passengers in the car were killed and their widows brought proceedings against both defendants.

HELD: There was no negligence of the driver of the private car.

With regard to the second defendants, the discharge of vapour was a nuisance. It was not an incident of the ordinary and lawful use of land, nor a case of lawful user of the highway. The smoke clouds had persisted all day and were obvious. The second defendants were also negligent. They could have posted a man at each end of the affected area to warn traffic.

As to the first defendants, the accident occurred during one of the most severe winters in human memory. The road surface was extremely treacherous and dangerous demanding the utmost care from drivers. Any sudden application of the brakes unless the speed was very moderate would certainly precipitate a skid. Visibility apart from the smoke was quite good. The omnibus driver was negligent (1) in driving on the wrong side of the road; (2) in going too fast; (3) in failing to observe and guard against the vapour cloud in time to take effective action.

Hall & Co Ltd v Ham Manor Farms Ltd

(1966) 116 L Jo 838, Chichester CC (Judge Talbot)

The plaintiff's lorry collided with another lorry in thick smoke on the main Worthing-Chichester road. The smoke came from the defendants' adjacent field where stubble was being burnt; it was patchy but in one area visibility on the road was reduced practically to nil.

HELD: (1) In so far as the claim lay in negligence it failed because the defendants' servants had taken all reasonable precautions to avoid any dangers and the enveloping of the road with thick smoke was not only foreseen but was of short duration and was a temporary hazard which could be seen by those travelling along the road; (2) if an action lay in nuisance it could do so only as a public nuisance from which the plaintiffs had suffered damage. It was impossible to hold that the thick smoke which covered the road for such a short space of time could be classed as such an interference with the public right as to warrant it being classed as a public nuisance: the facts were wholly different from *Holling v Yorkshire Traction Co Ltd* (above); (3) the rule in *Rylands v Fletcher* was not applicable where the defendants were making an ordinary and proper use of their land. Judgment for the defendants.

Perkins v Glyn
[1976] RTR April p ix, Wimborne CC
The plaintiff, riding a motor cycle, collided with a stationary car when his vision was obscured by smoke from stubble burning in a field owned by the defendant. The smoke was blowing in gusts across the road for a distance of 150 yards or so.
HELD: (1) Burning stubble was not a non-natural user of land. (2) The defendant was not negligent. He could not always wait until the wind was blowing away from the road; warning was not necessary as the smoke was visible a mile away and the plaintiff had already ridden through 100 yards of it. (3) On the question of nuisance, a motorist must expect to be obstructed occasionally and the defendant could not be said to have set a trap. The claim failed. Per Judge Pennant.

Rollingson v Kerr
[1958] CLY 2427
A collision occurred between two vehicles going in opposite directions on a straight stretch of road. Defendant's servant had lit a bonfire of hedge clippings, causing dense smoke to blow across the road, and it was in the midst of this that the collision took place. The judge found the defendant guilty of negligence and the defence of *volenti non fit injuria* failed, and that neither driver was guilty of contributory negligence.

Holling's case followed; *Heywood v London North Eastern Rly Co* (1926) Times, 1 December not followed.

Road repairs

Maher v Hurst
(1969) 113 Sol Jo 167, 67 LGR 367, CA
On the Watford by-pass, a road wide enough to take three lines of traffic, asphalting contractors were spreading asphalte by means of a large machine which spread a strip 10 feet wide. It operated on one lane at a time leaving the other two lanes open for traffic. The contractors had put the usual warning signs out to warn oncoming traffic and so placed as to funnel the traffic into the two open lanes. The plaintiff, an employee of the contractors was standing at the side of the strip being spread, on the road surface of the middle lane which was being used by traffic. A lorry begin to pass the roadworks using the middle lane with the spreader on its nearside. The driver saw a coach approaching at a time when a cloud of steam came up from the hot asphalte. He failed to see the plaintiff and knocked him on to the hot asphalte causing serious injury. The judge said the driver was going too fast but accepted the suggestion that the contractors should have put up a barrier of tripods on the middle lane to protect the plaintiff. He held the contractors three-quarters to blame.
HELD, ON APPEAL: The contractors were not to blame at all. They were carrying out the usual system for such work by which two lanes were left clear for traffic. There was no evidence of similar accidents. If tripods were put in the middle lane traffic on this very important road would be reduced to one line: it would cause such inconvenience to the public that it should not be done unless the risk to the men was so great as to warrant it. There

was no evidence of such risk. The accident was caused solely by the driver's negligence in driving too fast.

Traffic studs

Skilton v Epsom and Ewell Urban District Council
[1937] 1 KB 112, [1936] 2 All ER 50, 106 LJKB 41, 154 LT 700, 52 TLR 494, 80 Sol Jo 345, CA
A traffic stud, placed in a road by authority of the Road Traffic Act 1930, s 48 (now the Road Traffic Regulation Act 1984, s 65), caused an accident through being defective.
HELD: The defective stud was a nuisance and Council was liable.

NUISANCE ON HIGHWAY

DEFINITION OF NUISANCE

Howard v Walker
[1947] KB 860, [1947] 2 All ER 197, [1947] LJR 1366, 177 LT 326, 63 TLR 518, 92 Sol Jo (Lord Goddard CJ)
I can think of no better definition of nuisance than this, given in Winfield's textbook on the *Law of Tort* (3rd edn) p 426: 'Nuisance is the unlawful interference with a person's use or enjoyment of land, or of some right over, or in connection with it.' If a person's right of free passage over a highway is subject to interference he has an action, just as he would have if a private right of way of which he was the grantee was obstructed.

Note—And see *Almeroth v Chivers*, p 306, above.

Harper v G. N. Haden & Sons Ltd
[1933] Ch 298, 102 LJCh 6, 148 LT 303, 96 LP 525, 76 Sol Jo 849, 31 LGR 18, CA
The law relating to the user of highways is in truth the law of give and take. Those who use them must, in doing so, have reasonable regard to the convenience and comfort of others, and must not themselves expect a degree of convenience and comfort only obtainable by disregarding that of other people. They might expect to be obstructed occasionally. It is the price they pay for the privilege of obstructing others.

Jacobs v London County Council
[1950] 2 KB 353, [1950] 1 All ER 727, [1950] WN 170, 66 TLR 659, HL
It will help to keep sight of the differences between cases of nuisance and cases of negligence if two propositions are maintained — (1) that negligence is not necessarily an element in nuisance, and (2) that, where the nuisance in respect of which a private person sues is a 'public nuisance', he has no personal right of action unless he can prove special damage beyond that suffered by other members of the public.

Overseas Tankships (UK) Ltd v Miller Steamship Co Pty (The Wagon Mound (No 2))

[1967] 1 AC 617, [1966] 2 All ER 709, [1966] 3 WLR 498, 110 Sol Jo 447, [1966] 1 Lloyd's Rep 657, PC

Per Lord Reid: Although negligence may not be necessary [to establish nuisance], fault of some kind is almost always necessary and fault generally involves foreseeability, eg in cases like *Sedleigh-Denfield v O'Callaghan* ([1940] AC 880) the fault is in failing to abate the nuisance of which the defendant is or ought to be aware as likely to cause damage to his neighbour. The present case is one of creating a danger to persons or property in navigable waters (equivalent to a highway) and there it is admitted that fault is essential — in this case the negligent discharge of the oil. . . . So in the class of nuisance which includes this case foreseeability is an essential element in determining liability.

Note—The events giving rise to the action were the same as in *Overseas Tankships (UK) v Morts Dock* (p 360, below). In *The Wagon Mound (No 2)* the respondent plaintiffs were owners of two ships damaged by the fire.

Searle v Wallbank

[1947] AC 341, [1947] 1 All ER 12, [1947] LJR 258, 176 LT 104, 63 TLR 24, 91 Sol Jo 83, HL (Lord du Parcq)

An underlying principle of the law of the highways is that all those lawfully using the highway, or land adjacent to it, must show mutual respect and forbearance. The motorist must put up with the farmer's cattle; the farmer must endure the motorist. It is commonly part of a man's legal duty to his neighbour to tolerate the untoward results of his neighbour's lawful acts. These observations are, I think, relevant not only to the issue of negligence, but also to the allegation of nuisance. The stray horse on the road does not seriously interfere with the exercise of a common right, and is no more a nuisance in law, merely by reason of its presence there, than the fallen cart-horse or its modern analogue, the lorry which has temporarily broken down. The same considerations which guided the Court of Appeal in *Maitland v Raisbeck* (p 218, above) are, I think, applicable here.

Note—'A nuisance to a highway consists either in obstructing it or in rendering it dangerous:' *Salmond on Torts* (14th edn) p 124, quoted by Sir Raymond Evershed MR in the following case.

Trevett v Lee

[1955] 1 All ER 406, [1955] 1 WLR 113, 99 Sol Jo 110, CA

Per Sir Raymond Evershed MR: It is well established that a private individual can only sue in respect of a public nuisance if he suffers some special damage as a result of it.

If I make a small hole in the highway difficult to see, or put some greasy substance on it, so that treading in the hole or on the substance is liable to cause a man as a natural consequence to fall, then it may be that I have caused a nuisance to the highway, not by obstructing it, but by rendering it dangerous.

It is not open to doubt that in a claim for damages based on nuisance the defendant may set up and rely on a fault consisting of what is commonly called contributory negligence so as to reduce or extinguish his own liability.

Broken down vehicle

Chesterfield Corpn v Arthur Robinson (Transport) Ltd
(1955) 106 L Jo 61 (Judge Braund)
The defendants, transport contractors, were engaged in transporting by road an excavator weighing 60 tons. They used a transport vehicle aided by an additional tractor. At a sharp rise in the road the wheels of the additional tractor began to slip, throwing the whole of the load on to the transporter tractor. The maximum towing load of the latter as specified by the manufacturers was substantially less than the weight being towed and as a result a half-shaft broke. The whole caravan came to a halt, blocking the road, and could not be moved for three days. The plaintiffs suffered loss because of the necessary diversion of their bus routes.
HELD: The plaintiffs were entitled to damages. Though it was not unreasonable or actionable merely to carry a heavy load on the highway and cause obstruction by breaking down, it was unreasonable to do the job with a vehicle that was not designed to draw such a heavy load. The question was whether the defendants in exercising their undoubted right to use the highway for the purpose they did created an obstruction which was unreasonable in quantum and duration. It was not a reasonable use of the highway to launch upon it a mechanism which the defendants knew or ought to have known would be strained beyond the limits of its endurance. They were liable for the consequences as from when the obstruction occurred. The plaintiffs' damage was not merely 'fleeting and evanescent'.

Note—See also *'Unlighted vehicle not a nuisance'*, p 218, above and *Parish v Judd*, p 225, above.

Vehicle parked on roadway

Dymond v Pearce
[1972] 1 QB 496, [1972] 1 All ER 1142, [1972] 2 WLR 633, 116 Sol Jo 62, [1972] RTR 169, CA
The defendants' driver fetched a large loaded lorry from their depot at 6 pm and parked it near his home ready for an early start next morning. It was parked on the outside of a shallow bend on an urban road having two carriageways each 24 feet wide. Before lighting-up time the driver turned on the lights. The lorry was under a street light and was visible for at least 200 yards to approaching traffic: it was $7\frac{1}{2}$ feet wide leaving at least 16 feet of the carriageway unobstructed. After lighting-up time a motor cyclist, looking round at someone on the pavement, failed to see the lorry and crashed into it. The plaintiff, his passenger, was injured. He based his claim on two grounds: (1) that the lorry was negligently parked and (2) that the lorry was an obstruction and amounted to a common law nuisance, actionable without proof of negligence. The trial judge held that (1) in the manner in which the lorry was parked there was no foreseeable danger and no negligence; (2) the mere parking of the lorry on the nearside of the road where it was not foreseeably dangerous did not amount to

nuisance at common law; (3) the sole cause of the accident was the motor cyclist's failure to look where he was going.

HELD, ON APPEAL: (1) The judge was right in finding that the defendants and their driver had not been negligent in parking the lorry at that place in the way they did; (2) there were two categories of nuisance on a highway, an obstruction which constituted a danger and an obstruction without danger. It was important to remember the two categories when looking at the authorities. In neither category was it necessary to prove negligence as an ingredient, and in both proof of what was prima facie a nuisance laid the onus on the defendant to prove justification. Neither category was actionable unless the plaintiff could prove damage had been caused to him. Leaving aside the special position of frontagers (and the driver in this case was not a frontager) the common law rights of users of the highway were normally confined to use for passage and repassage and incidents reasonably associated with such use. Leaving a large vehicle on the highway prima facie resulted in a nuisance, for it narrowed the highway: in the present case the lorry constituted a nuisance at the time the motor cyclist ran into it but that did not render the defendants liable to the plaintiff because, as the judge had found, the nuisance was not the cause of the accident — the sole cause was the motor cyclist's negligence. In most cases that was an inevitable conclusion once negligence on the part of a stationary vehicle was negatived. Nevertheless (per Edmund Davies LJ) a person creating a highway obstruction must be alert to the possibility that weather changes or the actions of third parties might convert what was originally a danger-free obstruction into a grave traffic hazard. In the present case the lorry parked as it was did not present a danger to those using the highway in the manner in which they could be reasonably expected to use it. Appeal dismissed.

Builder's skip on roadway

Saper v Hungate Builders Ltd
[1972] RTR 380 (Cantley J)

King was driving his car in the hours of darkness along a residential road with the plaintiff as passenger when he collided with a builder's skip which he did not see in time to avoid. The skip had been placed partly on the grass verge and partly on the roadway by the owners who had delivered it on the instructions of the hirers. The hirers were builders doing work on a nearby house. They arranged for the house-owner, their customer, to put a lamp at each offside corner of the skip. Two motorists passing the skip two to three hours before the accident had seen the skip only just in time to swerve and avoid it.

HELD: The provision of two lamps which so many persons failed to see was not adequate lighting. An object like a skip was very dangerous unless proper warning was given by lighting which would be readily and instantly apparent: this skip in its position and condition was a nuisance in the highway. The fact that King failed to see it was not fatal to his claim, but driving at a reasonable speed and being alert as a driver should be at night he should have seen it. He was 40% to blame. The builders were liable as having taken detailed charge of the safety precautions. The owners of the skip were equally to blame with the builders having put the obstruction in the carriageway and left it there; they were under a duty to light it and could not escape liability by delegating the duty to someone else. The house-owner was not liable; he had merely done what he was asked to do.

Note—In *Dymond v Pearce* (above) Sachs LJ considered there were two categories of nuisance: either an obstruction which was not dangerous, or one which was. Edmund Davies LJ in the same case thought an obstruction in a highway did not become a nuisance unless it was shown to be dangerous. This difference of view was alluded to in the following two cases.

Wills v T. F. Martin (Roof Contractors) Ltd
[1972] 116 Sol Jo 145, [1972] RTR 368 (Forbes J)

Riding a moped in the hours of darkness along a residential road which was poorly lit the plaintiff collided with a skip which he had not seen. It was on the nearside of the roadway and the plaintiff said it was unlighted. He was injured and claimed damages in nuisance and negligence against the roofing contractors who had put it there.

HELD: Applying *Dymond v Pearce* (above), you have first to consider whether the presence of the skip on the highway is a nuisance. If the plaintiff satisfies that burden he has still to show, according to Edmund Davies LJ (in *Dymond's* case), that the obstruction was also a dangerous obstruction. The last link in the chain is that the plaintiff must satisfy the court that the obstruction was at least a cause of the accident. A skip placed on a highway is in a different category from a parked vehicle. It has no business to be on the highway at all; to deposit a container of that character on the highway creates a nuisance. The skip was a nuisance because it was occupying a section of the highway which ought not to be obstructed in that way. If unlit in this position on the road it would be potentially dangerous, but on the evidence it was not established that it was unlighted. The sole cause of the accident was the plaintiff's failure to look where he was going and the claim failed.

Drury v Camden Borough Council
[1972] RTR 391 (May J)

The defendant Council had placed a skip against the nearside kerb of a one-way street 35 feet wide. It was 6 feet wide and of much the same colour as the road surface and unlighted: the street lighting was adequate but not good. The plaintiff riding a scooter in the early morning before it was light failed to see the skip in time and collided with it.

HELD: As a matter of law, adopting Sachs LJ's view in *Dymond's* case, the skip was an obstruction and as such constituted a nuisance; it did not matter either that it occupied only 6 feet of a 35 foot-wide road, nor that the street lighting was or was not good. If the view of Edmund Davies LJ in *Dymond's* case was correct, and in any event on the alternative claim in negligence, it was necessary to decided further whether the obstruction was dangerous. On the facts and the evidence it was. The final question was one of causation: did the presence of the skip play any causative part in the occurrence of the accident or was the plaintiff's failure to keep a proper lookout the sole cause? Bearing in mind all the circumstances, the nature of the road, the lighting and the amount of traffic which had avoided the skip, the existence of the nuisance did play a part but the plaintiff was 50% to blame in failing to keep as good a lookout as he should.

Vehicle stationary on a clearway

Coote v Stone
[1971] 1 All ER 657, [1971] 1 WLR 279, 115 Sol Jo 79, [1971] RTR 66, CA
The defendant stopped his car on a clearway contrary to the Various Trunk Roads (Prohibition of Waiting) (Clearways) Order 1963. The plaintiff's car ran into it. The judge held that the defendant's car having stopped on a part of the road which should have been kept clear it was an illegal obstruction and therefore a nuisance: the plaintiff was entitled to damages against the defendant who had created the nuisance.
HELD, ON APPEAL: The judge was wrong. The presence of the car stationary on the highway for a short time was not a nuisance and the fact of being in breach of the relevant regulations did not make it one. There was no right of action for the breach of the statutory duty and the plaintiff could not recover on that ground by calling it a nuisance.

---

4 LEVEL CROSSINGS

Note—Reference should be made to the Highway Code (1978) paras 176 to 185. These contain detailed instructions for the guidance of drivers at all types of railway level crossing.

PUBLIC CROSSINGS

Note—The Railways Clauses Consolidation Act 1845, s 47, provides as follows:

'**47 Provisions in cases where roads are crossed on a level**   If a railway cross any turnpike road or public carriage road on a level, the company shall erect and at all times maintain good and sufficient gates across such road, on each side of the railway, where the same shall communicate therewith, and shall employ proper persons to open and shut such gates; and such gates shall be kept constantly closed across such road on both sides of the railway, except during the time when horses, cattle, carts, or carriages passing along the same shall have to cross such railway, and such gates shall be of such dimensions and so constructed as when closed to fence in the railway, and prevent cattle or horses passing along the road from entering upon the railway; and the person intrusted with the care of such gates shall cause the same to be closed as soon as such horses, cattle, carts, or carriages shall have passed through the same. . . .'

Ellis v Great Western Rly Co
(1874) LR 9 CP 551, 43 LJCP 304, 30 LT 874
Railway companies operate under statutory powers and are not analogous to ordinary road traffic cases.

Stubley v London and North Western
(1865) LR 1 Exch 13, 4 H & C 83, 35 LJEx 3, 13 LT 376, 29 JP 808, 14 WR
133, 11 Jur NS 956
The railway company are bound, as to rate of speed, and signalling or
whistling, or other ordinary precautions, to do everything reasonably
necessary to secure the safety of persons using the crossing. The persons
who cross the line take the risk, but the railway company must not do anything to prevent such persons from taking care of themselves or expose
them to greater peril than that of a level crossing, or they then impose upon
themselves an obligation to take other than the usual precautions (*Cliff v
Midland Rly Co* (1870) LR 5 QB 258, 22 LT 382, 34 JP 357, 18 WR 456).
There is no general duty on railway companies to place watchmen at public
footways crossing the railway on the level.

Liability to railway passengers

Knapp v Railway Executive
[1949] 2 All ER 508, CA
By the Brighton and Chichester Railway Act 1844 (7 & 8 Vict, c 67) and an
Order made under the Act, it was provided that at a level crossing on a
public highway the railway company should maintain gates closed across
each end of the highway except when trains passed across the road, and
employ persons to open and shut the gates so that carriages passing along
the highway should not be exposed to danger or damage by trains. The
Order was made under a proviso in the Act giving power when 'it will be
more conducive to the public safety'. The plaintiff driving a motor car
approached when the gates were closed and stopped about a car length
away, but the car moved slowly down the slope and struck the gate. The
gate was not securely fixed as it should have been and swung across the line,
and was struck by a train and the train driver was injured. The driver sued
the plaintiff who settled the action and claimed contribution from the
railway company.
HELD: The purport of the Act was to protect road users and not persons
travelling on the railway. There was an important difference between the
1844 Act and s 47 of the 1845 Act (above), which is in general terms, and
s 274 of the 1844 Act which was quite clearly for the protection of users of
the highway. Section 68 of the 1845 Act (see *Copps v Payne*, p 316, below),
which requires the railway company to maintain works for the accommodation of owners and occupiers of adjoining lands, does not impose a duty
to fence as to passengers. Citing *Buxton v North Eastern Rly Co* (1868) LR
3 QB 549, 9 B & S 824, 37 LJQB 258, 18 LT 795, a passenger injured
through a truck striking a bullock which had got on to the line through a
defective fence held not entitled to recover from the railway company. The
train driver had no right of action under the Act, and the plaintiff was not
entitled to contribution.

Level crossing replaced by sub-way

Law v Railway Executive and Chigwell Urban District Council
[1949] WN 172, 65 TLR 288, 93 Sol Jo 251 (Hallett J)
A cyclist at 10 pm on 5 October 1949, collided with a pavement and wall

which formed part of a sub-way substituted under statutory authority for a public level crossing. By agreement the county council built the wall and pavement; the railway company were responsible for maintenance of the sub-way and the UDC for lighting.

HELD: The railway company would not have been under any legal liability to light the gates, but that did not apply to the wall and pavement; there was no obligation on the UDC to light the road, the UDC and railway company were partners in the works and therefore shared in any liability. They had not taken all reasonable precautions to render it safe, and were liable. The plaintiff knew the obstruction was there and was also negligent. Apportionment 50–50.

Private accommodation crossing becoming public crossing

Note—The Railways Clauses Consolidation Act 1845, s 68, which deals with accommodation crossing provides:

'The company shall make and at all times thereafter maintain the following works for the accommodation of the owners and occupiers of lands adjoining the railway. . . .'

The works include gates

Section 75 provides a penalty if a person using the gates omits to shut and fasten them.

Copps v Payne
[1950] 1 KB 611, [1950] 1 All ER 246, 66 TLR 217, 94 Sol Jo 147, Div Ct
At the time the railway was built, it crossed an occupation road, and gates were erected as an accommodation crossing. Subsequently the road became a public highway. The defendant opened the gates on both sides of the crossing and he and the carriage under his care passed over the crossing. He failed to close the gates. He was prosecuted under s 75. The justices held the obligation was on the railway company and dismissed the summons.

HELD, ON APPEAL: This did not create a liability on the railway company under s 47 in respect of a public carriage road. Their liability remained limited to that under s 75. The test was the liability at the time of the construction of the railway. Case remitted to justices to convict.

Lloyds Bank Ltd v Railway Executive
[1952] 1 All ER 1248, 96 Sol Jo 313, [1952] 1 TLR 1207, CA
Deceased was killed by a railway train whilst driving his motor car across a railway at C. There were gates at the crossing which had to be operated by those using them and a friend travelling with deceased got out of the car to open the gates. The visibility was bad but the deceased without waiting for his friend to signal him, started to cross the level crossing when a train came into collision with the car. Lloyd-Jacob J held the Railway Executive were in breach of their statutory duty and were negligent at common law, but deceased was guilty of contributory negligence and held the Railway Executive 75% to blame ((1951) Times, 20 December).

HELD, ON APPEAL: Apart from statute the defendants were under a duty at common law to prevent danger at these crossings. As the danger increases, so must their precautions increase. They were not bound to turn the crossing into a public level crossing but they must take all reasonable requirements in the shape of warnings, whistles and so forth. Appeal dismissed.

PRIVATE ACCOMMODATION CROSSINGS

Knight v Great Western Rly Co
[1943] 1 KB 105, [1942] 2 All ER 286 (Tucker J)
There is a duty to take reasonable precautions, but the nature of the precaution and the degree of care required are not the same as for a public crossing and may vary very considerably. The difference is merely in the degree of care which is required in the circumstances. There may be cases where, owing to a sharp turn in the railway or the presence of a large number of trees in a cutting obstructing the view, precautions should be taken, but there is no rule that at any private crossing the railway company is bound to use special precautions of some kind. The distance of vision owing to fog was limited to a space of from 30 to 50 yards, and the engine was proceeding at 30 mph. The driver knew of the crossing and that cows were driven across it daily. He had blown his whistle at the whistle board 440 yards from the crossing. He had received the appropriate fog signal, that the line was clear from the railway point of view.
HELD: It was not negligent that he could not pull up within the distance of his vision.
  Citing *Cliff v Midland Rly Co* (1870) LR 5 QB 258, 22 LT 382:

'The railway company are to work the railway in a reasonably proper manner; and in crossing a footway on a level the company are bound, as to the mode of working their railway, as to the rate of speed, the provision of men to give warning of approach, the position of warning signals such as a whistle board, and signalling or whistling, or other ordinary precautions to do everything reasonably necessary for the safety of persons crossing.'

Liddiatt v Great Western Rly Co
[1946] KB 545, [1946] 1 All ER 731, CA
The plaintiff's servant was driving eight cattle across a private accommodation crossing over a single track railway line. This crossing was 160 yards east of a public level crossing. There was a signal box 1,030 yards and a signal 700 yards west of the public crossing. The public crossing gate and the signal were operated by a crossing keeper. The gate of the accommodation crossing on the south side, but not on the north side, was visible to the crossing keeper. The crossing keeper did not have any regard to the accommodation crossing.
HELD: The railway company were under no duty to place a watchman or keeper at the accommodation crossing; nor was there any evidence that the crossing was so placed as to impose on the railway company the duty to take some great precaution at this spot than is usual in the normal working of a railway. The fact that it was only 160 yards from a public crossing did not enlarge or extend the obligations or duties of the company or the crossing keeper.

Smith v London Midland and Scottish Rly
1948 SC 125, Ct of Sess, SLR 235
A railway company has a duty at every level crossing where members of the public have a right to be to take all reasonable precautions in train operations (and perhaps in other respects) to reduce the danger to a minimum, the nature of the precautions required and the question whether the duty has been fulfilled depending on the circumstances of each case. *Cliff v Midland Rly Co* applied.

Lloyds Bank Ltd v British Transport Commission
[1956] 3 All ER 291, [1956] 1 WLR 1279, 100 Sol Jo 148, CA
A railway built about one hundred years ago crossed a lane to a farm and four cottages and an accommodation crossing was provided for the occupants. Gates were installed, which were regularly closed but were occasionally left open. A ganger who patrolled the line daily inspected the gates and closed them if open. There was a distance of vision to the left for about 350 yards. Owing to the acute angle the car driver would have the difficult task of looking behind across his left shoulder to see if anything was coming along the line.

A car driver when it was quite dark drove his car with his headlights on. The gate had been left open by some unknown person and the driver drove straight through. When crossing the second line of rails the car was hit broadside by a train coming from his left, and the driver killed. His widow sued the railway authorities and contended the crossing had special peculiarities which called for safeguards; that there was negligence in the management of the railway and also negligence of the engine driver; that there ought to have been a whistle board; that the driver ought to have seen the headlights of the car, and that the bend in the railway line and the crossing called for special precautions.

HELD: The railway authority had fulfilled their duty; the engine driver's look-out was properly directing his attention to the signals; he did whistle 175 yards from the crossing; the bend was immaterial as the car driver could see for 350 yards; the driving of a train and of a motor car were two different things. The learned judge was correct in finding that the engine driver was not negligent and that the accident was due solely to the negligence of the car driver in failing to stop in the 30 feet between the gate and the actual line. The facts in the cases of *Smith v London Midland and Scottish Rly Co* (above) and *Lloyds Bank Ltd v Railway Executive* (p 316, above) were different. Appeal dismissed.

Hazell v British Transport Commission
[1958] 1 All ER 116, [1958] 1 WLR 169, 102 Sol Jo 124 (Pearson J)
A farm tractor was being driven across an accommodation crossing, on a single branch line. On a stretch of 16 miles there were 33 level crossings most of which were accommodation crossings. Possibly two or three farm vehicles used the crossing each day. The gates were padlocked except when opened by a user. The crossing was so wide that the tractor could stand between the gates and the railway line. Shortly before the crossing the line ran round a left-hand bend with a slow down gradient of about 1 in 500. In ordinary weather the train could be seen several hundred yards away.

There was a bad fog, visibility varying from place to place. As the tractor was being driven over the line a train ran into it. The train driver had shut off steam and was coasting, there being a station about a mile or one and a half miles ahead, so that the sound of the exhaust blast had ceased; the line was wet so that the train made less noise than usual, and the effect of the fog was to smother the sound to some extent, but the train could have been heard by anyone at the crossing if there was no other noise, and the judge drew the inference that the tractor driver failed to switch off his engine.

HELD: The principle to be applied is that in the absence of special circumstances, the engine driver is not expected to reduce speed or whistle, and the Commission are not expected to erect a whistle-board. An engine driver is not expected to reduce speed to five miles an hour because of fog. If the engine driver is aware of something on, or likely to come on, the line, he must take proper steps to avoid an accident. There are no special circumstances in this case, and no liability on the Commission or the engine driver, and the action fails.

Smith v Smith and Railway Executive
[1948] WN 276, 92 Sol Jo 499 (Hilbery J)

The plaintiff was a passenger in a car driven by the first defendant in a private lane over a railway line of the second defendants at an accommodation crossing. The gates were open to the lane. A train ran into the motor car and the plaintiff was injured. The lane had been regularly used by occupiers of the adjacent land and their servants and visitors. The railway company had constructed the gates to close the lane when a train was approaching and provided a hut for a servant whose duty was to open and shut the gates. The servant left duty at 6 pm and the accident occurred in daylight about 9.40 pm on 10 July 1941. About two years before the accident a swimming pool had been constructed about 100 yards from the crossing and the lane was largely used by private motorists visiting the pool and this must have been known to the railway company's servants, but they took no action to prevent it except to put up a notice near the crossing marked 'Beware of the trains.'

HELD: Citing Pickford J, in *Jenner v South East Rly Co* (1911) 105 LT 131, there was a duty cast on a railway company to take reasonable precautions at an accommodation crossing. The judge rejected the contention of the railway company that their only duty was to refrain from obstructing a right of way. *Johnson v London Midland and Scottish Rly Co* (7 May 1926, unreported) distinguished. In that case the plaintiff was the occupier of land adjacent to the road, knew all about the crossing and was guilty of contributory negligence. The judge found both defendants to blame, and apportioned the blame as to three-fifths to the railway company and two-fifths to the motor driver.

Skeen v British Railways Board
[1976] RTR 281 (Latey J)

Three cottages were reached by crossing a railway at an accommodation crossing approached down a lane from which the railway could not be seen. At the crossing the visibility to the right along the railway was limited to 100 yards by a sharp curve. On 14 June a van was being driven over the crossing when it was hit by a train from the right travelling at about 50 mph. The van driver and passenger were both killed. Though there had been no previous accidents the occupier of one of the cottages had complained to British Railways about seven weeks earlier about the danger at the crossing. A meeting had been held with British Railways representatives when it was agreed that the crossing was dangerous. Various safety precautions were canvassed such as the erection of whistle boards or the provision of a telephone to the signal box, but nothing had been done. The defendants pleaded that both the van driver and passenger were negligent in not having the passenger cross the line on foot and direct the driver from the other side, from which visibility of trains was 200 yards.

HELD: There was a duty on the defendants to take reasonable care not to imperil those using the crossing. What is reasonable depends on the particular circumstances of the crossing, its layout and any special dangers. The fact of there having been no previous accident was immaterial since the danger was admitted seven weeks earlier. Precautionary measures should have been taken as a matter of urgency. The direct telephone to the signal box was the best method as was in fact done after the accident. The defendants were liable in negligence. The passenger was not negligent since decisions are in the hands of the driver of a motor vehicle. The driver was not negligent in not sending the passenger across the line to direct him because the increase in visibility would have reduced the danger so minimally as to be insignificant.

Kemshead v British Transport Commission
[1958] 1 All ER 119, [1958] 1 WLR 173, 103 Sol Jo 122, CA

An accommodation level crossing for a road leading to a farm and some farm cottages had a notice on the gates requiring users to shut and fasten the gates. The plaintiff was a passenger in a car going to the farm. He had used the crossing on at least twenty occasions and knew of the notice. The gates had been left open by some person unknown and apparently the car driver crossed without stopping. It was a foggy morning and as the car crossed the railway lines, a train ran into it. The plaintiff and driver were severely injured and another passenger was killed. The plaintiff alleged that no whistle was sounded and no indication was given of the approach of the train.

HELD: At an accommodation crossing there is no obligation on a railway company to supply watchmen or have signals or bells, nor to whistle unless there are special circumstances where people may reasonably be expected. Citing Scrutton LJ in *Burrows v Southern Rly Co* (unreported, read by Tucker J in *Knight v Great Western Rly Co* (p 317, above)) a sharp turn in the railway, or the presence of a large number of trees in a cutting obstructing the view might call for some reasonable precautions even at a private crossing. There was nothing calling for special precautions. The presence of fog calls for special precautions by the person crossing. There were no special conditions applying to this crossing. There must be judgment for the Commission.

5 TREES

FALLING BRANCH

Noble v Harrison
[1926] 2 KB 332, 95 LJKB 813, Div Ct
A branch of a beech tree growing on the defendant's land overhung a highway at a height of 30 feet above the ground. In fine weather the branch suddenly broke, fell upon the plaintiff's vehicle, which was passing along the highway, and damaged it. In an action by the plaintiff claiming in respect of the damage to his vehicle, the county court judge found that neither the defendant nor his servants knew that the branch was dangerous, and that the fracture was due to a latent defect not discoverable by any reasonably careful inspection, but he held that the defendant was liable (1) upon the principle of *Rylands v Fletcher* and (2) for a nuisance.
HELD (reversing the decision of the county court judge): (1) That the *Rylands v Fletcher* principle had no application, inasmuch as a tree was not in itself a dangerous thing, and to grow trees was one of the natural uses of the soil; (2) that the mere fact that the branch overhung the highway did not make it a nuisance seeing that it did not obstruct the free passage of the highway, and although the branch proved to be a danger the defendant was not liable, inasmuch as he had not created the danger and had no knowledge, actual or imputed, of its existence. (*Barker v Herbert* [1911] 2 KB 633 applied.) (Observations of Best J in *Earl of Lonsdale v Nelson* (1823) 2 B & C 302 and *Tarry v Ashton* (1876) 1 QBD 314, distinguished.)

FALLING TREE

Cunliffe v Bankes
[1945] 1 All ER 459 (Singleton J)
A motor cyclist riding along a road in the dark collided with a tree which had fallen across the road. It was an elm, 50 years old, about 40 feet high, growing about 20 feet inside a park wall 6 feet high. It had been attacked by honey fungus. The estate agent had inspected each year when the trees were in foliage, which was performing his duty, but the tree showed no sign of danger.
HELD: No evidence of negligence. As to nuisance, the defendant was not liable unless (1) he caused the nuisance, or (2) by the neglect of some duty he allowed it to arise, or (3) when it has arisen without his own act or default, he omits to remedy it within a reasonable time after he became or ought to have become aware of it.

Brown v Harrison
[1947] WN 191, 177 LT 281, 63 TLR 484
The plaintiff was walking along the highway when he was injured by the fall of a tree growing in a spinney on the side of the road. At about the time of the accident there was a gust of wind at 58 mph registered at an observatory 10 or 15 miles away, and two other perfectly sound trees in the neighbourhood were blown down.
   The defendant owner of the tree was in the habit of passing the spinney

daily and often in and about it, and it never occurred to him that the tree was a source of danger or he would have removed the danger. It did not occur to anyone that there was any real likelihood of danger.

HELD: The tree was in a defective and therefore dangerous condition. There is no duty on the landowner to have a periodical examination by an expert. It is impossible to define the duty to apply to all cases. On a large timbered estate there may be a duty to call in expert advice and have expert examination, but in the ordinary case a landlord discharges his duty if he takes reasonable steps to remove any dangers of which he becomes aware, but if there is a danger which is apparent, not only to the expert but to the ordinary layman, which the ordinary layman can see with his own eyes if he chooses to use them, and he fails to do so, and injury is occasioned to someone on the highway, the owner is responsible.

The tree had the appearance of being dead at the top for many years. It was not quite dead all the way down, but the leaf in spring was very restricted and less than a normal healthy tree and did not blossom. The ordinary layman with ordinary powers of observation would have noted this, and that it could fall across the highway. In *Noble v Harrison* it was said a tree in decay may become a dangerous object. If the owner knew of the danger and did not remedy it, his liability would be established beyond controversy. This tree by reason of its decay had become a dangerous object, sufficiently apparent to impose on the landowner the duty of taking precautionary measures. The defendant was liable (1946) Birmingham Assizes, 11 December (Stable J).

HELD, ON APPEAL: The landowner's duty was correctly stated that if there was a danger apparent, not only to the expert, but to the ordinary layman, if he chose to notice it, the owner should take precautionary measures. A dying tree at a certain stage became a danger which should be apparent to the ordinary landowner.

Caminer v Northern and London Investment Trust Ltd
[1951] AC 66, [1950] 2 All ER 486, 66 TLR (Pt 2) 184, [1950] WN 361, 94 Sol Jo 518, HL

A large elm tree in the forecourt of a block of flats fell on a car passing along the highway. The wind was blowing in strong squally gusts from time to time but was not exceptional. Defendants became owners in 1940. The tree was a large, well-grown elm between 120 and 130 years old. After it fell it was evident that the base of the tree had been affected by a disease not uncommon in an elm tree of elm butt rot. The disease was of long standing and must have been in the roots long before the defendants became owners. There was nothing in the appearance of the tree to indicate that it was in any way diseased. The tree carried a crown of about 35 feet. It had not been trimmed or lopped for a great many years. Elms are shallow-rooted trees and notoriously treacherous and apt to fall. The owners shortly before the accident had given orders to lop and top the trees in the forecourt and but for the Easter holidays this tree would probably have been pollarded or topped before the accident. There was evidence that elm trees should be inspected every five to seven years.

HELD, ON APPEAL to the House of Lords: The defendants were not liable.

Per Lord Porter: I cannot accept the view that the defendants were negligent merely because they failed to call in an expert to advise as to the possible existence of an unsuspected and undiscoverable disease, even though an expert, if called in, might have recommended topping and lopping.

I do not regard the evidence as establishing that elm trees are so plainly a danger as to require their being lopped and topped lest they should fall, though to all external appearance they are sound and no inspection would raise a doubt as to their general condition.

Per Lord Oaksey: The defendants had performed their duty by employing a well-known firm of estate agents to manage this property and they in turn employed a timber contractor.

Quinn v Scott

[1965] 2 All ER 588, [1965] 1 WLR 1004, 109 Sol Jo 498 (Glyn-Jones J)

At a place where the Doncaster-Nottingham road runs alongside Clumber Park a belt of trees inside the park bordered the road. They included a beech tree about 200 years old having four or five limbs growing 70 feet or so almost vertically from the top of a bole about 20 feet high. On a windy day part of the tree split away from the rest and fell across the road causing a collision of vehicles in which the plaintiff was injured. The tree had reached an age at which decay could be apprehended. There was, before the accident, some appearance of unhealthiness in the thinness of the foliage and indications of die-back, but these had not been reported to the owners, the National Trust.

HELD: (1) A landowner on whose land this belt of trees stood, adjoining a busy highway, was under a duty to provide himself with skilled advice about the safety of the trees; (2) the National Trust had fulfilled this duty by employing a forestry adviser, a land agent, a forester and seven woodmen who inspected the tree several times a year; but (3) there had been a failure to report the signs of decay to the land agent and the Trust should have known of them; (4) a reasonable landowner with knowledge of these signs would have had the tree felled. The National Trust must be held liable.

Lambourn v London Brick Co

(1950) 156 Estates Gazette 146.

The plaintiff's husband was killed in a collision with elm trees that had been blown across a road from the defendants' land.

HELD: There was nothing to indicate to the defendants that the trees were dangerous; defendants not liable.

Damage from pollen

Coachcraft v Lancegays Safety Glass Co

(1938) *City Press*, 15 July, City of London Ct

Repairers placed car under lime tree. Lime pollen fell or was driven on to the car by rain. The acid concentration from the lime pollen pitted and damaged the cellulose and lacquer treatment of the car body.

HELD: Repairers were negligent as bailees and liable for damage.

COLLIDING WITH TREE

J. H. Dewhurst Ltd v Ratcliffe
(1951) 101 L Jo 361 (Judge Reid)
Plaintiffs' motor car in daylight and clear weather was being driven along
a road 16 to 18 feet wide at 20 to 25 mph, when a single-deck omnibus
approached from the opposite direction. The car driver in passing brushed
the hedge on the near side with the car and collided with a tree stump nearly
4 feet high which was 1 or 2 inches inside the hedge and hidden by the leaves
and foliage. Plaintiffs sued the defendant who was the owner and occupier
of the farm adjoining the road. The tree stump was wholly on the defendant's land but did not overhang the road although it was less than 6 inches
clear of it. The defendant trimmed the top and inside of the hedge and the
local council cut back the hedge from the road.
HELD: The claim in negligence failed because defendant owed no legal
duty to the plaintiffs. As regards nuisance, the car driver was not entitled to
brush innocent looking leaves and twigs at the roadside and complain if he
sustained damage because of something lying behind them. Verdict for
defendant.

British Road Services Ltd v Slater
[1964] 1 All ER 816, [1964] 1 WLR 498, 108 Sol Jo 357 (Lord Parker CJ)
A lorry belonging to the plaintiffs was being driven at night along the A41
road at a place where it adjoined farm land belonging to the defendants.
The roadway was 20 feet wide: along the side of it was a strip of gravel a foot
wide beyond which was a grass verge or bank. Standing in the verge about
2 ft 6 in from the gravel edge was an oak tree of considerable age which had
a stout branch growing towards the road for about 2 feet and then turned
upwards. The driver of the lorry on approching this place had to keep well
to the nearside to avoid another of the plaintiff's lorries which was
approaching from the opposite direction. As the first lorry passed the tree a
packing case stacked on the back of the lorry struck the branch causing
another packing case to fall off into the path of the lorry. Damage was
caused both to this lorry and the packing case, for which the plaintiffs
claimed against the defendants on the ground that they had created or
continued a nuisance in the form of the branch of the tree. The defendants
had owned the land on both sides of the road since 1936 but the tree had
been sown long before that, but not before the highway, which was ancient,
had been dedicated. Neither the defendants nor the highway authority nor
the driver of the lorry (who had very frequently passed along the road) had
ever considered the branch to be a hazard.
HELD: (1) Looked at objectively, the branch prevented the convenient use
of the highway and was a nuisance; (2) even though the highway authority
might have a right or duty to remove obstructions the defendants were not
sufficiently dispossessed of the verge or of the tree to exonerate them from
liability for an obstruction created by the branch; (3) although the branch
was a nuisance the defendants could not be presumed to know of it because
no one had ever thought it was a hazard. Only the fortuitous circumstance
that two heavy lorries happened to meet at that point in the dark had shown
this. The defendant had not created the nuisance since the tree was already
there when they acquired the land. They could be liable for continuing it

only if they had knowledge or means of knowledge so that they knew or should have known of the nuisance in time to correct it and obviate its mischievous effects (quoting Lord Wright in *Sedleigh-Denfield v O'Callaghan* [1940] AC 880). This rule was not limited to cases where the nuisance was due to a hidden defect but applied also where, as here, the defendants had no reason to suppose it was a nuisance. The defendants were not liable.

Note—See also *Radley v London Passenger Transport Board* and *Hale v Hants and Dorset Motor Services* (p 141, above).

CHAPTER 10
Bailments and exemption clauses

1 BAILMENTS

Note—Bailment is a delivery of goods from one person, called the bailor, to another person called the bailee, for some purpose, upon a condition, express or implied, that, after the purpose has been fulfilled, they shall be redelivered to the bailor, or otherwise dealt with according to his directions, or kept till he reclaims them.

Bailments are of three kinds:

(1) Those for the exclusive benefit of the bailor, as, if A leaves plate with B to keep safely and securely without reward. He, the bailee, is only responsible in respect of gross negligence

(2) Those for the mutual benefit of bailor and bailee; as, if C lets a horse to D for so much per hour; or if E gives F (a tailor) clothes to repair, in the course of his trade, etc. The bailee must exercise ordinary care.

(3) Those for the exclusive benefit of the bailee; as, if G lends H a book to read, without reward. The bailee is responsible for even slight negligence.

Questions of bailment may arise in the case of a car park, of a carrier, of owner's risk and contracting out of negligence, of garage of cars, and of repairs to car, as well as in keeper cases.

The onus is on the bailee to prove that loss or damage to the goods has occurred without negligence on his part.

BAILEE'S LIABILITY FOR LOSS OR DAMAGE

Repairer

Cooper v Dempsey
(1961) 105 Sol Jo 320, CA

The defendant had a garage, petrol station and café on a main road 12 miles from Plymouth. Behind the premises was a yard used as a car park with access from it to a minor road through a gate. The yard was used for storing the defendant's own vehicles and for parking cars of café patrons and cars brought in for repairs. The plaintiff took his car for repair on 18 October 1959, and left it on the defendant's premises. The defendant left it in the car park with the ignition key in the switch, the doors unlocked and without supervision. Between 5.30 pm and 10 pm on 21 October it was stolen and was later found elsewhere in a damaged condition. The county court judge held that the defendant had done his duty as a custodian of the car.

HELD, ON APPEAL: The test was what a reasonable and prudent man looking after his own property would do. Leaving the car in the yard unsupervised and with the ignition key in the switch was not exercising proper care. The defendant had not discharged the onus of proving that without the absence of reasonable care this car had disappeared. The plaintiff was entitled to damages for the damage to the car which was not too remote. The damage was foreseeable.

Cowan v Blackwill Motor Caravan Conversions Ltd
[1978] RTR 421, CA

The plaintiff took his motor caravan to the defendants for repair. It was difficult to engage any of the forward gears and the reverse gear could not be engaged at all. The defendants told him to leave it in a sidestreet alongside their wired-in compound. He was told they would put it in the compound as soon as possible. The sidestreet was a cul-de-sac; the vehicle was left facing downhill towards the dead end. It was not put in the compound on the following day because other vehicles were put in in preference to the plaintiff's, since it could not be taken away except by pushing it backwards uphill. On the second night there it was stolen.

HELD: The issue was whether the defendants, as bailees of the vehicle, had discharged the onus of showing that the vehicle was lost without negligence on their part. The standard of care required of the defendants was that which was to be expected in the relevant circumstances from a prudent owner, and was no greater than the standard exhibited by thousands of vehicle owners who immobilise their vehicles appropriately by steering locks, locking doors, removing the distributor arm or by other means. On the facts the defendants had not been negligent.

Idnani v Elisha
[1979] RTR 488, CA

The defendant was proprietor of a service station on a main route out of London, comprising a forecourt, two petrol pumps, a kiosk and two repair bays. The enclosed premises where vehicles would be under lock and key could accommodate only three vehicles: the defendant handled many more than this and there were often seven or eight vehicles left out on the forecourt overnight. The plaintiff, a motor dealer for whom the defendant had previously repaired vehicles, took a Jaguar E-type car to him for repair. The defendant removed the cylinder head in the course of the repairs; consequently the car could not be moved under its own power. It was left locked on the forecourt. Overnight someone towed it away; when subsequently recovered it had been severely damaged by the removal of components. The plaintiff sued for the damage done. In the pleadings both parties pleaded contractual terms; the plaintiff that it was an express term of their dealings with each other that no car of his would be left out on the forecourt overnight; the defendant that there was a term to be implied from their dealings that he was at liberty to keep a car entrusted to him by the plaintiff on the forecourt overnight. In the course of the hearing both these pleas were expressly abandoned. The county court judge nevertheless held as a fact that the plaintiff did tell the defendant that he wanted his cars kept in at night. The judge said it was in every way foreseeable that someone would come on the forecourt and help themselves to components from the car. He held that the defendant had not discharged the burden of proof on him to show that he had discharged the duty of care he owed as bailee.

HELD, ON APPEAL: This was not right. The finding of the judge that the plaintiff had asked for his cars to be kept in at night, taken with his express abandonment of the alleged contractual term, must imply that the defendant had not given the plaintiff reason to believe that he would do so. Whether there was negligence or not depended on the circumstances of any particular case; the degree of risk on the one hand had to be balanced against the degree of practicability of taking effective steps to prevent that loss on the other. Was it in all the circumstances reasonably practicable for this car to have been kept under lock and key having regard to the limited lock-up accommodation? The decisive consideration was that the car was not placed inside because it was immobile and difficult to manoeuvre in the morning to get out. The judge had given too little consideration to the practical difficulties confronting the defendant of which the plaintiff was well aware. Appeal allowed. *Cowan v Blackwill Motor Caravan Conversions Ltd* (above) applied.

Note—See also *Smith v Taylor*, p 353, below.

Hotel keeper

Adams (Durham) Ltd and Day v Trust Houses Ltd
[1960] 1 Lloyd's Rep 380

The second plaintiff, driving a car owned by the first plaintiff, arrived at the defendant's hotel some time after 10 pm to stay the night. The night porter unlocked the hotel garage for him and he put the car in. The night porter locked the garage and remained in possession of the keys. There was a charge of 2s for using the garage. During the night the night porter took the car out for some purpose of his own, ran into a traffic island and wrecked it.

HELD: (1) There was a bailment of the car to the defendants, not a mere licence to park the car on the defendant's premises. *Ashby v Tolhurst* (p 331, below) distinguished. (2) As bailees for safe custody for reward the defendants were under a legal obligation to take all reasonable care of the plaintiff's car. They had delegated the safe custody of the car to their night porter and were liable not so much as being vicariously responsible for his torts when driving about the streets, but on the basis that they had entrusted to him the fulfilment of their own contractual duty and that duty was not performed. *Central Motors, Glasgow Ltd v Cessnock Garage Co* (p 161, above), followed. (3) On the facts, clauses excluding liability for the defendants had not been brought to the notice of the second plaintiff and did not form part of the contract, but even if they had, there was a fundamental breach of the contract of bailment bringing it to an end along with any conditions forming part of it.

Note—There is statutory liability on a hotel proprietor under the Hotel Proprietors' Act 1956 to make good loss or damage to a guest's property even when not due to fault of the proprietor or his staff; but by s 2(2) of the Act this liability does not extend to any vehicle or any property left therein.

Coach proprietor

Houghland v R. R. Low (Luxury Coaches) Ltd
[1962] 1 QB 694, [1962] 2 All ER 159, [1962] 2 WLR 1015, 106 Sol Jo 243, CA

The plaintiff was a passenger in the defendant's motor coach on a journey from Southampton to Hoylake. Her suitcase was put with other passengers' luggage in the boot of the coach at Southampton and the boot was locked. When the coach stopped during the journey for the passengers to take tea it could not be restarted. The defendants' driver telephoned the defendants who sent a relief coach. Whilst the driver of the relief coach was having his tea the driver of the first coach with the help of the passengers transferred the luggage from the boot of his coach to the boot of the other which was then locked. When the relief coach arrived at Hoylake the plaintiff's suitcase was not in the boot and could not be found. She claimed the value of the case and contents from the defendants.

HELD: The defendants were liable. They were bailees of the suitcase and had failed to discharge the onus which was on them of proving that the suitcase had been lost without default on their part. It made no difference whether the case was put in detinue or whether it was treated as an action for negligence. It had been admitted in argument that the plaintiff, by proving the delivery of the suitcase at Southampton and its non-return on the arrival of the coach at Hoylake, made out a prima facie case. That prima facie case stood unless and until it was rebutted. The burden was on the defendants to adduce evidence in rebuttal. They could discharge that burden by proving that what in fact did happen happened without any default on their part or by showing that, although they could not put their fingers on what actually did happen to the suitcase, nevertheless, whatever did occur occurred notwithstanding all reasonable care having been exercised by them throughout the journey. The first coach had stood for three hours in the dark waiting for the relief coach and the luggage had then been transferred by passengers and stowed in the relief coach by one driver only, with no supervision at all over the unloading of the first coach. The defendants had failed to discharge the onus of proof on them.

Carrier: liability as bailee

Note—See pp 333–335, below.

Onus of proof on bailee

British Road Services Ltd v A. V. Crutchley & Co Ltd
[1968] 1 All ER 811, [1968] 1 Lloyd's Rep 271, CA

The plaintiffs arranged for the defendants to receive a lorry load of whisky worth £9,000 at their warehouse preparatory to being loaded on board ship for export. The whisky was unloaded from the lorry on to a trailer which was left overnight, with tractor attached, facing the doors of the warehouse ready to be driven to the ship on the following morning. During the night thieves entered the warehouse through a skylight, opened the doors and drove away the whole load. The defendants had a contract with third parties to send a patrolman to the premises from time to time during the night but he had failed to make all the visits required of him.

HELD: The onus was on the defendants to prove that the loss did not result from negligence on their part. (*Coldman v Hill*, below.) On the facts, the defendants' system of protection was not adequate in relation to the special risks involved and they had failed to discharge the burden on them of proving that the loss was not caused by negligence on their part. The defendants must accept responsibility for the negligence of the third party's patrolman even though they were independent contractors. A bailee cannot escape from the responsibility for taking proper care of the goods bailed merely by employing sub-contractors for that purpose.

Coldman v Hill
[1919] 1 KB 443, 88 LJKB 491, 120 LT 412, CA

The plaintiff sent cattle to the defendant for agistment. Two cows were stolen without default of the defendant but he did not report the loss to the plaintiff or the police nor make any effort himself to find them.

HELD: The defendant was liable. He was to blame for not reporting the loss or trying to trace the cows, and it was no defence that the plaintiff could not prove that the cows would have been traced if this had been done. The onus was on the defendant to prove, if he could, that the cows would not have been recovered if he had made enquiries.

Global Dress Co Ltd v Boase & Co Ltd
[1966] 2 Lloyd's Rep 72, CA

The defendants, master porters, received 30 cases of dresses for the plaintiffs at their dockside shed. A few days later one case was found to be missing. The county court judge found that the defendants' security system was good but said he could not understand how the case could have been removed without being seen if the watchman, checkers or others of the defendants' servants were doing their duty properly. He held the defendants had not discharged the onus on them as bailees.

HELD, ON APPEAL: The judge's decision should not be upset. The onus was on the defendants as bailees to show that they had taken reasonable care of the plaintiffs' goods. It was not sufficient for them to prove that their system was to have a watchman on duty. There was evidence on which the judge could find that the watchman had not been sufficiently vigilant but even if he had been left in doubt on this point the defendants still could not have succeeded because the onus was upon them.

Transmotors Ltd v Robertson Buckley & Co Ltd
[1970] 1 Lloyd's Rep 224 (Mocatta J)
The defendants, road hauliers, contracted with the plaintiffs to deliver consignments of food by lorry from Liverpool to places in the London area. The defendants' driver, Davenport, left Liverpool at 5 a m; late in the afternoon he reported to Plumstead Police Station that his lorry and load had been hijacked when he stopped on a lay-by on the A4 near Maidenhead at about 1 pm. He said he had been forced into a van and dumped four hours later at Woolwich. His lorry was found empty at Bow the following day. There was no evidence to corroborate his story but it was not positively disproved. He had been convicted of theft when working as a docker some months earlier and his employers knew of this when they engaged him. His account of his movements up to the time of the hijacking was unsupported by any other evidence. Nine months after the hijacking he was sacked by the defendants after another conviction for theft. The plaintiffs claimed for the loss of the goods.
HELD: If the servant of a bailee in the course of his employment stole goods bailed then the bailee was liable to the bailor for the loss of the goods — *Morris v Martin* (p 162, above). In order for a bailee to escape liability he had to prove he had taken all reasonable care in relation to the goods including proof that the goods had not been stolen by his employees (though it was highly desirable that the bailors should give specific notice of their intention to allege theft, if that was their case, either in the pleadings or otherwise). It was not necessary for the court to decide positively whether Davenport was a party to the theft but merely whether on the balance of probabilities the defendants had exercised reasonable care in regard to the goods and their safety and had negatived Davenport having acted as an accomplice. On the evidence the defendants had not discharged the burden of proof upon them. Judgment for the plaintiffs.

CAR PARK

Liability for loss by theft

Ashby v Tolhurst
[1937] 2 KB 242, [1937] 2 All ER 837, 106 LJKB 783, 156 LT 518, 53 TLR 770, 81 Sol Jo 419, CA
The owner of a car left it on a private parking ground, paid 1s and received a ticket from the attendant headed 'Seaway Car Park, Car Park Ticket' containing receipt for 1s and the provision: 'The proprietors do not take any responsibility for the safe custody of any cars or articles therein nor for any damage to the cars or articles however caused . . . all cars being left in all respects entirely at their owners' risk.'
    The car park attendant handed the car to a man who described himself

as the owner's friend. The car was locked and this man had not the ticket nor the key, but was able to put his hand through the windscreen and free the car. The negligence of the attendant was admitted.

HELD, by Court of Appeal: (1) Relation of parties was licensor and licensee and car park proprietor was under no liability whatever for the car; (2) there was not a misdelivery of the car; (3) assuming there was a contract of bailment and of misdelivery of car, the conditions on the ticket relieved proprietors of all liability; (4) no term could be implied that the car should not be parted with without production of the ticket.

Note—See also *Adams (Durham) Ltd and Day v Trust Houses Ltd*, p 328, above.

BG Transport Service v Marston Motor Co
[1970] 1 Lloyd's Rep 371 (Bean J)

The defendants were owners of a large garage with a car park at the rear enclosed by fencing. Drivers could leave vehicles in the car park on payment or by pre-arrangement. A driver on parking a vehicle paid a charge and received a ticket which bore a printed notice relieving the defendants of liability for all risks and losses and containing the words 'On production of this ticket by any person, the vehicle be released to the bearer. No responsibility can be accepted by us for any delay in releasing the vehicle resulting from the loss of this ticket.' The plaintiff's driver left a loaded van in the car park overnight having paid the charge and received a ticket. On returning the following morning he found the van had gone. The defendant's night watchman, who had come on duty at midnight, said that at about 2 am he was in the petrol pump attendant's office where the keys of parked vehicles were kept when a man knocked and asked for the keys of the vehicle, mentioning the number of the ticket. The man had then taken the keys and driven the vehicle away. He had not surrendered, nor been asked for, the driver's part of the ticket. There was evidence that not all drivers left their keys in the office nor, if they were regular parkers, did they always have tickets. The plaintiffs claimed the value of the load, which was stolen, on the basis that there was a bailment and that the defendants were at fault in parting with the vehicle without receiving or seeing the ticket. They cited an Australian case of *City of Sydney v West* (1965) 144 CLR 481 in which there was held to have been a bailment where the attendant at the exit from a parking station was under a duty not to permit vehicles to proceed out of the parking station except on production of a ticket.

HELD: The present case was one of a licence only and not a bailment. The case of *Ashby v Tolhurst* (above) was on one side of the line between licences and bailments and the Australian case was on the other. The *Ashby v Tolhurst* style of parking, with a nominal payment and no formalities to collect the car, would result in a licence; equally, parking within a bounded area in circumstances under which there is no access to the vehicle except through a special entrance, and where the vehicle can be withdrawn by presentation of a ticket and not otherwise, is a bailment. The present case was similar to *BRS (Contracts) Ltd v Colney Motor Engineering Co Ltd* (p 333, below). The words on the ticket did not mean that a vehicle would only be handed over in exchange for a ticket; nor, on the evidence, did the ticket play but a small part in the running of the car park.

Note—See also *James Buchanan Co Ltd v Hay's Transport Services Ltd* [1972] 2 Lloyd's Rep 535.

Preston v Ascot Central Car Park Ltd
(1954) Times, 28 January (Pilcher J)
The plaintiff on 18 June 1952, went to Ascot races and left his car in the car park of the Ascot Central Park Ltd, to whom he had paid 15s and received a ticket with the words on it 'The proprietor does not hold himself responsible for any damage to the motor car, or loss by fire or theft of any property stored here, but all due care will be taken.' The car was stolen.
HELD: There was no sufficent delivery to constitute a contact of bailment; the plaintiff had locked the doors and closed the windows to prevent the car being tampered with. There was only a licence to park and no duty was owed to the car owner. The words 'all due care will be taken' merely meant that the attendants would be careful in parking and unparking cars, and no more; *Ashby v Tolhurst* followed.

BRS (Contracts) Ltd v Colney Motor Engineering Co Ltd
(1958) Times, 27 November, CA
A lorry which was carrying cigarettes worth £32,000 from Ashton-under-Lyne to London, stopped for the night at the defendants' car park. The place where the lorry had been parked consisted of a large floodlit yard surrounded by a fence 6 feet high, topped with barbed wire. There was an adjacent petrol station, and an attendant was on duty night and day. Whilst the lorry was parked, part of the load, of the value of £312, was stolen. A standard charge of 1s 6d a night was made for parking irrespective of the value of the contents of the lorry, which was locked up by the driver, who kept the keys and who drove away when he liked. At the trial of an action by the lorry owners the judge held the lorry had been bailed and awarded them £312.
HELD, ON APPEAL: The defendants exercised no control over the lorry. There was no bailment. The facts pointed to the place being a car park rather than a place in the nature of a closed garage. Appeal allowed.

Note—See also *Cooper v Dempsey*, p 327, above.

Automatic car park

Note—See *Thornton v Shoe Lane Parking Ltd*, p 353, below.

CARRIERS

Negligence of carrier as bailee

VEHICLE LEFT UNATTENDED

WLR Traders Ltd v B & N Shipping Agency
[1955] 1 Lloyd's Rep 554 (Pilcher J)
Plaintiffs contracted with forwarding agents, who sub-contracted with private carriers, to collect three cartons of nylon stockings from plaintiffs' London warehouse and deliver at Millwall Docks. The goods, with other goods, were taken on an open lorry, which was left by the driver in Euston Road while he went to a near-by shop on a private errand to buy a hammer. He removed the ignition key pursuant to his employers' instructions and

was absent for three or four minutes during which the lorry with its load
was stolen.
HELD: The carriers as bailees of the goods had failed to prove that the loss
occurred without their negligence. Lorries containing goods are often
stolen when left unattended. The driver ought to have anticipated that the
load was probably valuable. He had no reason to stop. He must be taken to
have known that lorry thieves are active in London; that ignition keys are
easily procurable; that removing the ignition key would not foil a thief
for more than half a minute; he might have removed a vital part of the
electrical mechanism. His employers should have taken further precautions by instructions to drivers if obliged to leave their lorries unattended.
The carriers were liable to the plaintiffs for the loss of their goods.

Lee Cooper Ltd v C. H. Jeakins & Sons Ltd

[1967] 2 QB 1, [1965] 1 All ER 280, [1965] 3 WLR 753, 109 Sol Jo 794,
[1964] 1 Lloyd's Rep 300 (Marshall J)
The plaintiffs instructed a firm of shipping agents with whom they
normally did business to forward some goods from London to Eire. For a
part of the journey the shipping agents engaged the defendants, who were
hauliers, to carry the goods in their lorry. The driver stopped on the
journey and left the lorry unattended. As a result the goods were stolen.
The contracts between the plaintiffs and the shippers, and between the
shippers and the defendants, both contained exclusion clauses. The judge
found that the theft was due to the driver's negligence and that, there being
no contractual relationship between the plaintiffs and defendants, the
defendants had no protection from the exclusion clauses, nor were plaintiffs owed any duties by the defendants in contract. Could the plaintiffs
succeed in tort?
HELD: Lord Atkin's famous dictum in *Donoghue v Stevenson* was wide and
flexible and the plaintiff's case was within it. The law of torts exists to
prevent men from hurting one another, whether in respect of their
property, their persons, their reputation or anything else that is theirs. The
defendants were bailees for reward of the plaintiff's goods though their
contractual duty was owed to the shippers. They knew from previous
trading that the shippers were continuously handling their customers'
goods and not their own. They knew from the delivery notes that the
plaintiffs were the owners of the goods. They owed the plaintiffs a duty of
care which was breached by their driver's negligence. Judgment for the
plaintiffs.

Learoyd Brothers & Co v Pope & Sons Ltd

[1966] 2 Lloyd's Rep 142 (Sachs J)
The plaintiffs wished to send 12 bales of worsted from Huddersfield to
London Docks. They contracted for the carriage with Hanson Haulage Ltd
who, for the last stage of the journey hired a lorry and driver from the
defendants. The lorry was loaded with the bales and other goods some of
which were for Mark Brown's Wharf, off Tooley Street. The driver parked
his vehicle in Tooley Street and left it unattended whilst he went to the
wharf office 75 yards away, which he knew would not be open for another

10 minutes or so. When it did open he took 15 minutes to transact his business. When he returned to the place where he had left the lorry it had gone. When it was found later the bales had been stolen.

HELD: (1) The defendants were bailees of the goods in relation to the plaintiffs; (2) whatever were the terms of the contract between Hanson Haulage and the defendants, the driver, so far as the plaintiffs were concerned, remained a servant of the defendants who were liable for his negligence; (3) the driver was negligent in leaving the vehicle when he knew the office was not yet open, not keeping it under observation and locking it properly; (4) the defendants were negligent in not fitting the vehicle with brake lock devices. The defendants were liable to the plaintiffs for the value of the goods lost.

Note—See also *Bontex Knitting Works v St John's Garage* (p 346, below) and *Colverd v Anglo-Overseas Transport Ltd* (p 346, below).

In *Pye Ltd v BG Transport Service Ltd* [1966] 2 Lloyd's Rep 300 Browne J held that a driver who left his lorry unattended in Berner Street, Stepney for 20 minutes was negligent in not operating the 'petro-mag' (an anti-theft device cutting off petrol and ignition) before leaving it, though he locked the cab. By contrast Roskill J in *Presvale Trading Co Ltd v Sutch and Searle Ltd* [1967] 1 Lloyd's Rep 131 held the driver of a lorry who locked the cab when leaving it in a locked garage in Peckham overnight was not negligent merely by leaving the 'Waso' steering lock on the lorry unsecured.

Common carriers

Ludditt v Ginger Coote Airways Ltd

[1947] AC 233, [1947] 1 All ER 328, [1947] LJR 1067, 177 LT 334, 63 TLR 157, PC

A common carrier is one who undertakes to carry goods of all persons indifferently for hire. The question whether the liability of a common carrier has been undertaken in any particular case is one of fact and not of law. A common carrier is an insurer of the goods he carries, but not of passengers. If he is not a common carrier, a carrier is not liable for accidental damage by fire.

By the custom of the realm a common carrier of goods was at common law 'bound to answer for the goods at all events. . . . The law charges this person thus entrusted to carry goods against all events but acts of God and of the enemies of the King': *Readhead v Midland Rly Co* (p 240, above).

The common carrier of goods was at common law free to limit his stringent obligations by special contract. He could insist on making his own terms and refuse to carry except on those terms, subject to any statutory provisions.

Great Northern Rly Co v LEP Transport

[1922] 2 KB 742, 91 LJKB 807, 127 LT 664, 38 TLR 711, CA

The liability of a common carrier for loss, injury, or delay in respect to the goods carrier may be varied by contract. If the contract be such as to obliterate or destroy his character of a common carrier, he must be regarded for the purposes of that particular contract as a private carrier but if the contract does not so obliterate or destroy that character, and merely limits his liabilities in some respects, in all other respects he remains under a common carrier's liability.

LIEN OF REPAIRER

Hatton v Car Maintenance Co Ltd

[1915] 1 Ch 621, 84 LJCh 847, 110 LT 765, 30 TLR 275, 58 Sol Jo 361

The owner of a motor car had an agreement with a company under which the latter were for three years to maintain the car and its accessories, provide a driver who was to be the company's servant, and do the necessary repairs. The owner was to pay the company a fixed annual sum up to a limited mileage and at a rate for every mile beyond the limit. The car when in London was kept at the company's garage, and whether the owner was in London or elsewhere she took the car out when and as she liked. An amount having become due by the owner under the agreement, the company took possession of the car and claimed a lien on it for the amount due.

HELD: (1) Inasmuch as what the company did to the car was not to improve it, but only to maintain it in its former condition, the company had no lien on the car; (2) even if the company had a lien, their lien would have been lost by the arrangement acted on, under which the owner was entitled to take away the car as and when she pleased.

Re Southern Livestock Producers Ltd

[1963] 3 All ER 801, [1964] 1 WLR 24, 108 Sol Jo 15

Per Pennycuick J: It is perfectly clear that unless a bailee can establish improvement he has no lien. If this matter were free from authority it would, I think, be tempting to draw the line in rather a different place so as to cover the case where a person by the exercise of labour and skill prevents a chattel from deteriorating. . . . However, it is quite impossible for me at this time of day to introduce that sort of modification into a well-established principle.

Bailee ordering repairs: lien against owner

Tappenden v Artus

[1964] 2 QB 185, [1963] 3 All ER 213, [1963] 3 WLR 685, 107 Sol Jo 572, CA

The plaintiff, a motor dealer, owned a motor vehicle which A wished to take on hire purchase. Requiring to use it at once on his business and having insufficient cash to pay the necessary deposit, A was allowed by the plaintiff to take it away and use it pending completion of a hire-purchase agreement. It was also stipulated by the plaintiff that A should tax and insure the vehicle and he did so. Two days later A was using the vehicle when it broke down. He arranged for repairers to take it to their garage and repair it. After doing so they rendered an account for £40 to A which was unpaid. After some weeks (the bailment to A having been terminated) the plaintiff traced the vehicle to the repairers who refused to give it up whilst the bill for repairs remained unpaid, claiming to exercise their repairer's lien. The plaintiff sued the repairers for a return of the van and damages for its detention.

HELD: The repairer was entitled to assert his lien against the plaintiff. Where possession of goods is given to a repairer not by the owner but by a bailee the test whether the repairer can assert his lien against the owner is whether the owner authorised the bailee either expressly or as a necessary incident of the bailment to give possession of the goods to the repairer. A had received the vehicle from the plaintiff as a bailee with the right to use it for all reasonable purposes and in all reasonable ways, and among those ways was the right to get the vehicle repaired when necessary (*Bowmaker Ltd v Wycombe Motors* (below) per Goddard CJ). There was consideration for the bailment in that A had taxed and insured the vehicle. On the day in question A lawfully had possession of the vehicle and could not use it for the purposes of the bailment unless he were to have it repaired: the giving of actual and lawful possession of the vehicle to the repairer for the purpose of effecting repairs necessary to render it roadworthy was an act reasonably incidental to his use of the vehicle.

Hire purchase

Green v All Motors Ltd
[1917] 1 KB 625, 86 LJKB 590, 116 LT 189, CA

P was the hirer of a car under a hire-purchase agreement with the plaintiff, one of the terms of which was that he should keep the car in good repair and working condition. The car having been damaged in an accident P sent it to the defendant for repair at a time when no default had been made in the payment of instalments. Before the repairs had been completed the plaintiff as owner demanded the return of the car. The defendant completed the repairs and refused to deliver up the car until they were paid for, claiming a lien.

HELD: The defendant had a valid lien on the car for the cost of the repairs. The hirer of a chattel is entitled to have it repaired so as to enable him to use it in the way in which such a chattel is ordinarily used. In this case there was an additional contractual duty to keep the car in repair. Thus the hirer had by contract a duty as well as a right until the hire was terminated to have the car repaired, with the ordinary consequence of giving the repairer a lien on the car for the proper cost of repairs not only against himself but also against the owner.

Bowmaker Ltd v Wycombe Motors Ltd
[1946] KB 505, [1946] 2 All ER 113, 115 LJKB 411, 175 LT 133, 62 TLR 437, 90 Sol Jo 407, Div Ct

A hire-purchase company determined the hire of a car for default in payment of instalment, but the hirer retained possession of the car. After the determination the hirer instructed repairers to repair the car. Repairers claimed a lien against the hire-purchase company. The hire-purchase agreement contained a condition that the hirer had no authority from the company to create a lien for repairs.

HELD: Whilst the hiring was in existence and the hirer entitled to possession, the lien would have been good, and the condition would not affect the repairer, but when the hire had been determined, the hirer has no right to the car and there is no lien.

---

2 OWNER'S RISK: EXEMPTION CLAUSES

Note—Clauses which exclude liability for loss or damage are a common feature in many types of contract, including those for repair, hire or storage of vehicles or for the carriage of goods. In considering the effect of such clauses the points most commonly met with are:
(1) whether the words of the clause are effective to exclude liability for negligence;
(2) whether there has been a fundamental breach of contract rendering the clause inoperative;
(3) whether the clause has been effectively brought to the notice of the other contracting party;
(4) applicability of the Unfair Contract Terms Act 1977.
The cases relevant to (1) are at pp 339–344, below, (2) at pp 344–350, below, and (3) at pp 351–355, below.

UNFAIR CONTRACT TERMS ACT 1977

Where in respect of contracts made on or after 1 February 1978, or (where non-contractual notices are concerned) liability arises for any loss or damage suffered on or after that date, clauses or notices purport to exclude liability for loss or damage, the provisions of the Unfair Contract Terms Act 1977 will call for consideration. The essence of the Act is contained in sub-ss (1) and (2) of s 2:

'(1) A person cannot by reference to any contract term or to a notice given to persons generally or to particular persons exclude or restrict his liability for death or personal injury resulting from negligence.
(2) In the case of other loss or damage a person cannot so exclude or restrict his liability for negligence except in so far as the term or notice satisfies the requirement of reasonableness.'

The test of 'reasonableness' is explained in s 11. A term of a contract must be 'fair and reasonable . . . having regard to the circumstances which were or ought reasonably have been known to or in the contemplation of the parties when the contract was made'. A non-contractual notice must be 'fair and reasonable . . . having regard to all the circumstances obtaining when the liability arose or (but for the notice) would have risen'. In relation to contracts (other than sale or hire purchase) s 2 applies only to 'business liability', defined in s 1(3): 'liability for breach of obligations or duties arising
(a) from things done or to be done by a person in the course of a business (whether his own business or another's); or
(b) from the occupation of premises used for business purposes of the occupier.'
Contracts of insurance are excluded altogether from the controls in the Act.

REASONABLENESS

Phillips Products Ltd v Hyland
[1985] LS Gaz R 681, (1984) 129 Sol Jo 47, CA
The plaintiffs hired an excavator and driver from the second defendants.
The driver negligently drove the excavator, damaging the plaintiff's buildings. It was a condition of the contract of hire that the driver (who was the
first defendant) would be under the direction and control of the plaintiffs,
the hirers, and that they would be responsible for all the claims arising in
connection with the operation of the plant by the driver.
HELD, ON APPEAL: Having regard to the Unfair Contract Terms Act
1977, s 11(1) the second defendants had to show that the condition was a
fair and reasonable one in the light of the circumstances which were or
ought to have been known to both parties when the contract was made. The
judge had examined all the relevant circumstances and was not satisfied
that it was. The question was not whether the condition was valid or invalid
in any and every contract of hire between hirer and plant owner. The
question was whether the second defendants' exclusion of liability satisfied
the requirement of reasonableness imposed by the Act. The judge was not
plainly or obviously wrong in his conclusion. Appeal dismissed.

Note—See also *Stevenson v Nationwide Building Society* (1984) 128 Sol Jo 875, 272
Estates Gazette — reasonableness of a disclaimer in an application form for a
building society loan.

MEANING OF CLAUSE

Ailsa Craig Fishing Co v Malvern Fishing Co
[1983] 1 All ER 101, [1983] 1 WLR 964, 127 Sol Jo 508, [1983] 1 Lloyd's
Rep 183n, 1981 SLT 130, HL
Per Lord Wilberforce: Whether a condition limiting liability is effective or
not is a question of construction of that condition in the context of the
contract as a whole. If it is to exclude liability for negligence, it must be
most clearly and unambiguously expressed, and, in such a contract as this
(a contract between a security company and owners of a fishing vessel to
provide a security service for the vessel when in harbour), must be construed *contra proferentem*. . . . But I venture to add one further qualification,
or at least clarification: one must not strive to create ambiguities by
strained construction. . . . The relevant words must be given, if possible,
their natural, plain meaning. Clauses of limitation are not regarded by the
courts with the same hostility as clauses of exclusion; this is because they
must be related to other contractual terms, in particular to the risks to
which the defending party may be exposed, the remuneration which he
received and possibly also the opportunity of the other party to insure.

Negligence not expressly mentioned

Rutter v Palmer
[1922] 2 KB 87, CA
The defendant was a garage owner with whom the plaintiff deposited his

car for sale on commission. The contract of bailment included a clause 'Customers' cars are driven by [the defendant's] staff at customers' sole risk'. Whilst being demonstrated to a possible purchaser the car was badly damaged by the negligent driving of the defendant's driver.

HELD: The clause protected the defendant from liability for the damage. Since an ordinary bailee is not liable for the acts of his servants unless they are negligent the clause covered negligent acts because otherwise the words would have no effect.

Per Scrutton LJ: In construing an exemption clause certain general rules may be applied: First the defendant is not exempted from liability for the negligence of his servants unless adequate words are used; second, the liability of the defendant apart from the exempting words must be ascertained; then the particular clause in question must be considered; and if the only liability of the party pleading the exemption is a liability for negligence, the clause will more readily operate to exempt him.

Canada Steamship Lines v R

[1952] AC 192, [1952] 1 All ER 305, 96 Sol Jo 72, [1952] 1 Lloyd's Rep 1, [1952] 1 TLR 261, JC

(1) If the clause contains language which expressly exempts the person in whose favour it is made from the consequences of the negligence of his own servants, effect must be given to that provision.

(2) If there is no express reference to negligence, the court must consider whether the words used are wide enough in their ordinary meaning, to cover negligence on the part of the servants of such person. If a doubt arises at this point, it must be resolved against such person.

(3) If the words used are wide enough for the above purpose, the court must then consider whether 'the head of damage' may be based on some ground other than that of negligence, as stated by Lord Greene in *Alderslade v Hendon Laundry* [1945] KB 189. The 'other ground' must not be so fanciful or remote that such person cannot be supposed to have desired protection against it, but subject to this qualification, which is, no doubt, to be implied from Lord Greene's words, the existence of a possible head of damage other than that of negligence is fatal to such person even if the words are, prima facie, wide enough to cover negligence on the part of his servants.

Note—See also *Clement Shaw & Co v Joseph C. Mount & Co* (p 342, below). For consideration of the three tests see *Smith v South Wales Switchgear Ltd* [1978] 1 All ER 18, [1978] 1 WLR 165, 122 Sol Jo 61, HL. See also (applying the tests) *Lamport & Holt Lines Ltd v Coubro & Scrutton (M & I) Ltd* [1981] 2 Lloyd's Rep 659, [1982] Comm LR 123; affd [1982] 2 Lloyd's Rep 42, CA and *George Mitchell (Chesterhall) Ltd v Finney Lock Seeds Ltd* [1983] QB 284, [1983] 1 All ER 108, especially Kerr LJ at 125, and [1983] 2 AC 803, [1983] 2 All ER 737, [1983] 3 WLR 163, [1983] 2 Lloyd's Rep 272, HL.

Hollier v Rambler Motors (AMC) Ltd

[1972] 2 QB 71, [1972] 1 All ER 399, [1972] 2 WLR 401, 116 Sol Jo 158, [1972] RTR 190, CA

The plaintiff arranged with the defendants by telephone for them to do some repair work to his car. The defendants told him to send it to their works; no other terms were discussed or agreed. The plaintiff sent his car.

Whilst it was in the defendants' works it was damaged by fire caused by their negligence. On three previous occasions over a period of five years the defendants had done work to the plaintiff's car and each time had obtained his signature on an invoice containing the words (which the plaintiff had never read) 'The company is not responsible for damage caused by fire to customers' cars on the premises'. They claimed that this was a course of dealing which imported the exclusion of liability into the oral agreement. HELD: (1) Following *McCutcheon v David MacBrayne Ltd* (p 351, below) there was not such a frequent and consistent course of dealing as could import the term into the oral contract. (2) Even if the words used had formed part of the contract they were not effective to exclude liability. For a clause to exclude liability for negligence the language should be so plain that it clearly bears that meaning. If negligence is not mentioned the question is whether the exemption clause would convey to any ordinary literate and sensible person that the garage was excluding liability for their negligence. It is not correct that if the only liability which could arise would lie in negligence and nothing else the clause *must* be construed as extending to that head of damage (as Lord Greene appeared to say in *Alderslade's* case [1945] KB 189); in such a case the clause would merely, as Scrutton LJ said in *Rutter v Palmer* (p 339, above), '*more readily* operate to exempt him'. In the present case an ordinary man would consider the clause meant that the mere fact that there was a fire would not make the garage liable, not that the defendants were excluding liability for a fire caused by their own negligence. Alternatively the words could be given ample content by construing them as a warning or a statement of fact that the garage was not liable for fire in the absence of negligence. Judgment for plaintiff.

'Any cause whatsoever'

A. E. Farr Ltd v Admiralty
[1953] 2 All ER 512, [1953] 1 WLR 965, 97 Sol Jo 491 (Parker J)
Plaintiffs contracted with the Admiralty for the construction of a jetty. The contract included a clause that the plaintiffs should be responsible for any loss or damage to the works arising from any cause whatsoever. The works were damaged by the negligent navigation of an Admiralty vessel.
HELD: The words 'any cause whatsoever' were as wide as they could be and included negligent navigation of a ship by an Admiralty servant.

Wright v Tyne Improvement Commissioners
[1968] 1 All ER 807, [1968] 1 WLR 336, [1968] 1 Lloyd's Rep 113, CA
The plaintiff was in a railway wagon into which a sling of timber was being lowered by means of a crane when the wagon moved and he was pushed off by the suspended timber, sustaining injury. The wagon was under the control of the first defendants and was moved by their employee, a capstan operator. He should not have moved the wagon at the time of the accident; his negligence was the sole cause of the accident and the plaintiff was awarded damages against the first defendants. The crane from which the timber was suspended had been hired by the first defendants to the second defendants, the plaintiff's employers, by a contract containing the words 'We [the second defendants] hereby agree to bear the risk of and be

responsible for all damages injury or loss whatsoever howsoever and when-soever caused arising directly or indirectly out of or in connection with the hiring or use of the said crane'.

HELD: The words 'whatsoever and whensoever caused' were wide enough to give an indemnity against damage, injury or loss due to negligence of the first defendants' servant and they were entitled to be indemnified by the second defendants.

Clement Shaw & Co v Joseph C. Mount & Co
(1949) 82 Ll L Rep 995 (Lord Goddard CJ)

Defendants were warehousemen and agreed to store motor lorries of the plaintiffs and that they would 'drain the radiators on arrival' and accept the lorries at 'owner's risk'. The printed conditions exempted from liability for negligence, which probably did not add anything to the words 'owner's risk' (see *McCawley v Furness Rly Co* (1872) LR 8 QB 57, considered and applied in *Rutter v Palmer*). The defendants would have been liable for nothing but negligence and the term 'at his own risk' excluded all liability for negligence. The lorries had separate drainage for radiator and cylinder blocks and the latter were not drained. Frost damage ensued.

HELD: Defendants had carried out their contract by draining the radiators. They were unaware of the drainage system of the cylinder blocks. They were not told to drain the cylinder blocks and knowledge could not be imputed to them. There was no negligence and no breach of contract, and if there had been, the exemption clause and the 'owner's risk' term protected them. Breach of contract might arise in the case of a garage proprietor.

Note—Denning LJ in *White v John Warwick & Co* ([1953] 2 All ER 1021, [1953] 1 WLR 1285, 97 Sol Jo 740, CA) pointed out that 'if a transport company expressly stipulates with the plaintiff for exemption from liability for damage, *howsoever caused*, the plaintiff cannot overcome that exemption by suing in negligence instead of contract'.

INDEMNITY CLAUSE

Gillespie Brothers Ltd v Roy Bowles Ltd
[1973] QB 400, [1973] 1 All ER 193, [1972] 3 WLR 1003, 116 Sol Jo 861, CA

A condition of a contract of carriage provided: 'The trader . . . shall keep the carrier indemnified against all claims or demands whatsoever by whomsoever made. . . '. Goods were lost by negligence of the carriers' servant and the owners successfully sued for the amount of their loss. The carriers sought indemnity from the traders.

HELD: If the words of the clause were sufficient to show an express agreement to indemnify the carriers even against claims arising from the negligence of their own servant, effect must be given to them. The use of the word 'whatsoever' in the phrase 'all claims or demands whatsoever' signified an intention that the indemnity was to extend to all claims of whatsoever kind without exception. The first of the requirements propounded in *Canada Steamship Lines v R* (p 340, above) was satisfied and it was unnecessary in this case to apply the second and third.

WORDS NOT EFFECTIVE

Chowdhary v Gillot
[1947] 2 All ER 541, 63 TLR 569

The plaintiff for 10 or 12 years had been a valued customer of the Daimler Co. He was in the habit of taking his Daimler car to their works and leaving it with them for servicing and repairs some three or four times every year. He stated his requirements verbally or brought a rough list, and these were transferred to a 'Repair form', which he signed or which was posted to him for signature. He never read the conditions but supposed they contained ordinary garage contract conditions.

Condition 4 was: If a customer's car and/or chassis shall be driven at any time by one of the company's employees, the employee shall be deemed for all purposes to be the servant of the customer who shall be entitled to all rights and shall discharge all liabilities incident to that relationship.

On 23 November 1944, the plaintiff did not sign any order form. The company's servant drove him in his car to the station, and on the way an accident occurred by the negligence of the servant, and the plaintiff and a third party were injured.

HELD: Plaintiff had not signed the form. Even if he is to be taken to have contracted on the usual terms, condition 4 did not refer to the circumstances. On a repair order, it refers to driving incidental to the repairs, e g, on test or from one garage to another.

EXTENT OF 'OWNER'S RISK'

Michaelides v Henleaze Park Garage (Anstey, Third Party)
(1954) 104 L Jo 412 (H H Judge Paton), Bristol County Court

The plaintiff claimed damages for the damage done to his car by negligence on the part of the defendant's employee when driving a car belonging to the third party, Anstey, on a test run after repairs. The defendants settled the plaintiff's claim and then claimed indemnity from Anstey in third-party proceedings on the basis of a term in the contract for repair to be implied from a notice 'customers' cars garaged and driven at owner's risk'.

HELD: Anstey was not liable. The words 'owner's risk' were appropriate to absolve the defendants for damage *to* Anstey's car but wholly insufficient to fix him with liability for damage done *with* the car.

Exemption not effective against third party

Note—See *Cosgrove v Horsfall*, p 211, above.
Liability for death or personal injury: see now Unfair Contract Terms Act 1977, s 2(1).

THIRD PARTY CANNOT CLAIM BENEFIT OF CLAUSE

Scruttons Ltd v Midland Silicones Ltd
[1962] AC 446, [1962] 1 All ER 1, [1962] 2 WLR 186, 106 Sol Jo 34, [1961] 2 Lloyd's Rep 365, HL

The appellants, who were stevedores, damaged a drum of chemicals belonging to the respondents whilst in transit under a bill of lading with carriers by the terms of which the liability of the carriers for damage was limited to 500 dollars. The word 'carriers' was expressed to include any person acting as carrier or bailee. The agreement between the carriers and the appellants provided that the appellants should have the protection of the 'terms conditions and exceptions of the bill of lading'. The appellants claimed the benefit of the limitation against the respondents.

HELD: As the appellants were not parties to the bill of lading they could not claim the benefit of a term contained in it.

Effect of oral variation

Mendelssohn v Normand Ltd
[1970] 1 QB 177, [1969] 2 All ER 1215, [1969] 3 WLR 139, 113 Sol Jo 263, CA

The plaintiff left his car in the defendants' garage whilst he went away to have lunch. He wanted to lock the car but the garage attendant, employed by the defendants, said it was contrary to the rules and would not let him. He told the attendant there were valuables in the car and gave him the keys on the understanding that he would lock the car after moving it. The plaintiff was given a ticket, as on previous occasions when he used the garage, bearing the printed conditions: '1. The [defendants] will not accept responsibility for any loss or damage sustained by the vehicle its accessories or contents however caused. 6. No variation of these conditions will bind the [defendants] unless made in writing signed by their duly authorised manager.' When the plaintiff reclaimed the car he found it unlocked and some valuables were missing.

HELD: The plaintiff was entitled to damages for the loss. Although the printed terms were part of the contract the promise of the attendant to see that the contents were safe took priority over any printed condition. The oral promise had a decisive influence on the transaction since it induced the plaintiff to contract and it would be unjust to allow the maker to go back on it. The defendants were additionally liable in having deviated from the contract — they had agreed to keep the car locked and had failed to do so.

FUNDAMENTAL BREACH

Note—Note the Unfair Contract Terms Act 1977, s 9:

'Where for reliance upon it a contract term has to satisfy the requirement of reasonableness, it may be found to do so and be given effect accordingly notwithstanding that the contract has been terminated either by breach or by a party electing to treat it as repudiated.'

Suisse Atlantique Société d'Armement Maritime SA v Rotterdamsche Kolen Centrale
[1967] 1 AC 361, [1966] 2 All ER 61, [1966] 2 WLR 944, 110 Sol Jo 367, [1966] 1 Lloyd's Rep 529, HL

A demurrage clause in a contract of charter provided for the calculation of payments for delays in loading and unloading the ship. The shipowners, alleging a fundamental breach of the contract but electing to continue the charter, claimed that damages for the breach were not limited to the payments in the demurrage clause since it was an exemption clause and could not apply where there had been a fundamental breach. The House of

Lords rejected the argument and disapproved of observations of members of the Court of Appeal in *Charterhouse Credit Co Ltd v Tolley* [1963] 2 QB 683, [1963] 2 All ER 432, [1963] 2 WLR 1168, 107 Sol Jo 234, *Karsales (Harrow) Ltd v Wallis* [1956] 2 All ER 866, [1956] 1 WLR 936, 100 Sol Jo 548, *Yeoman Credit Ltd v Apps* [1962] 2 QB 508, [1961] 2 All ER 281, [1961] 3 WLR 94, 105 Sol Jo 567, CA and other cases appearing to assert a rule of law that where there is a fundamental breach of a contract the party in breach can never rely on the terms of an exemption clause contained in the contract. If the other party elects to treat the contract as still in being then the question whether the party in breach can claim the benefit of the terms of the exemption clause depends on the true construction of the clause in its context. Such clauses must be construed strictly and will not normally be found applicable to cases of fundamental breach, but where suitable words are used it is not impossible as a matter of law that such a clause may have effect even where a fundamental breach has occurred.

Photo Production Ltd v Securicor Transport Ltd
[1980] AC 827, [1980] 1 All ER 556, [1980] 2 WLR 283, 124 Sol Jo 147, [1980] 1 Lloyd's Rep 545, HL

Securicor contracted with Photo Production to provide a night patrol at their premises, a factory containing much paper and cardboard. The patrolman employed by Securicor when on his rounds deliberately set fire to some paper in a cardboard box; the fire spread and the factory was burned down. It was conceded by Securicor that in the absence of contractual terms to the contrary they would be liable for the act of the patrolman. They claimed the benefit of two exemption clauses which excluded or reduced their liability.

It was held in the Court of Appeal that the words of the clauses if applicable were effective to protect Securicor but by the patrolman's act they were guilty of a breach which went to the root of the contract; instead of safeguarding the premises they had burned them down. They could not rely on the exemption clauses.

HELD, ON APPEAL to the House of Lords: This was wrong. The question whether, and to what extent, an exclusion clause is to be applied to a fundamental breach, or breach of a fundamental term, or indeed to any breach of contract, is a matter of construction of the contract. This is the correct rule, established in *Suisse Atlantique v Rotterdamsche Kolen* (above). Parties should be left free, when risks are normally borne by insurance, to apportion the risks as they think fit and according to the contractual provisions they have themselves made. In the present case the words of the clause were perfectly clear and relieved Securicor from liability for the patrolman's act.

Note—The effect of the decision was discussed at length in *George Mitchell (Chesterhall) Ltd v Finney Lock Seeds Ltd* [1983] QB 284, [1983] 1 All ER 108, [1982] 3 WLR 1036, 126 Sol Jo 689, [1983] 1 Lloyd's Rep 168, CA.

Per Kerr LJ: Beginning with the *Securicor* case [1980] AC 827, it is in my view perfectly clear that this has wholly laid to rest the doctrine of 'fundamental breach' in one respect at least. It has abrogated the supposed rule, exemplified most signally by the decisions of this court in *Harbutt's Plasticine Ltd v Wayne Tank and Pump Co Ltd* [1970] 1 QB 447, [1983] QB 284, and *Wathes (Western) Ltd v Austins (Menswear) Ltd* [1976] 1 Lloyd's Rep 14, that a breach which can be described as fundamental, or a breach of one of the terms of the contract which can be so described, caused any exemption clause to cease to be applicable and capable of being relied upon; and — further — that this is so whether the innocent party treats the breach as a repudiation of the entire contract or whether it affirms the contract. It is now clear law that, whatever the nature of the breach, an exemption clause can never 'terminate' or 'cease to have effect,' but remains to be construed in order to decide whether or not the parties intended that its terms should apply to the breach in question. Thus, such commonly used expressions as 'the defendants cannot rely on the clause' must now be treated as suspect, unless they mean no more than that the clause, on its true construction, does not apply to the breach in question. Further, as pointed out by Lord Diplock in the *Securicor* case [1980] AC 827, if the expression 'fundamental' is to be retained in any context whatever, it should be confined to cases of anticipatory breach, ie to breaches which entitle the innocent party to treat the contract as at an end and to absolve him from any further performance of its terms; but not in any context which bears on the continuing effect of an exemption clause.

The decision of the Court of Appeal was affirmed in the House of Lords [1983] AC 803, [1983] 2 All ER 737, [1983] 3 WLR 163, [1983] 2 Lloyd's Rep 272, where Lord Bridge said 'The Photo Production case gave the final quietus to the doctrine that a "fundamental breach" of contract deprived the party in breach of the benefit of clauses in the contract excluding or limiting his liability'.

Haulage contracts: vehicles left unattended

Bontex Knitting Works v St John's Garage
[1944] 1 All ER 381n, 60 TLR 253, CA

Plaintiffs, a firm of manufacturers, contracted with defendants, motor contractors, for the hire of a motor van and driver by time or by mileage. The defendants' document contained a clause, 'We do not hold ourselves responsible for the loss or damage to goods while on our lorry.' The plaintiffs instructed the driver as to the parcels to be delivered with addresses and documents. The contract was to deliver forthwith and immediately, and was estimated to take $2\frac{1}{2}$ hours. On the journey the driver parked the van, removed the ignition key, but took no further precautions against theft. From 11 am or 11.15 am to 12 noon or 12.20 pm, he was absent from the van, which disappeared.

HELD, ON APPEAL: As the job was estimated not to occupy more than $2\frac{1}{2}$ hours, and paid for on a time basis, there must be implied a term that the delivery should be forthwith and immediate and should go on continuously. Judgment of Lewis J [1943] 2 All ER 690, 60 TLR 44, in the court below was upheld.

Note—But see *Colverd v Anglo-Overseas Transport*, below.

NOT A FUNDAMENTAL BREACH

Colverd & Co Ltd v Anglo-Overseas Transport Co Ltd
(1961) 105 Sol Jo 1010, [1961] 2 Lloyd's Rep 352 (Barry J)

The defendants were forwarding agents for the importation of watches from Switzerland by the plaintiffs under arrangements first made in 1955. A consignment of watches arrived at London Airport on 17 February 1958 and was collected by the defendants in their vehicle on 21st and taken to a depot at Finsbury. On 24th it was loaded with other cases of goods on another of their vehicles for delivery to the plaintiffs. The driver made various other calls first and still had the plaintiffs' watches in his van when he stopped for lunch near Oxford Street. He parked the van without locking it and was absent 40 minutes. When he returned the van was gone and the plaintiffs' watches were never recovered. There were exclusion clauses in the contract of carriage which it was admitted excluded the defendants' liability unless there could be said to be a fundamental breach of the contract.

HELD: There was no fundamental breach and the defendants were not liable. The driver of the van was negligent but any negligence for which the defendants would, but for the exclusion clauses, have been liable was in the course of carrying out their contract. This was a contract spread over a number of days and included duties other than the delivery of the goods. The isolated lapse on the part of the driver could not be said to go to the root of the contract.

Hire purchase: unusable car

Astley Industrial Trust Ltd v Grimley
[1963] 2 All ER 33, [1963] 1 WLR 584, 107 Sol Jo 474, CA

The defendant, a haulage contractor in a fair way of business, went to a dealer to obtain a tipping lorry on hire purchase. He said he had not done tipping before and that he could afford to take a lorry in the £500–£700 range. The dealer recommended him to take a Bedford lorry, six years old and the defendant agreed to do so. The dealer sold the vehicle to the plaintiffs, a hire-purchase company, from whom the defendant agreed to hire it under a hire-purchase agreement which expressly excluded any warranty as to description, repair, quality or fitness for any purpose. The defendant noticed defects in the clutch, starter and tipping mechanism which the dealer said he would put right. After the lorry had been left with him on two occasions the defects were still not put right and the defendant took the lorry away, under protest, and began to use it for carrying hardcore. He drove it 150 miles to a place where for some weeks he used it to carry hardcore from a quarry. This was very heavy work which could quickly wear out even a new vehicle. A number of defects showed themselves and breakdowns occurred requiring repairs which cost the defendant a total of £55 in three months.

HELD: The plaintiffs were entitled to succeed: there was an implied condition or fundamental term that they were letting on hire a Bedford tipper, but the vehicle, though not free from defects, complied with that description and was capable of use as such. There was no fundamental breach and the plaintiffs were entitled to rely on the express exclusion of warranties in the hire-purchase agreement.

Porter v General Guarantee Corpn
[1982] RTR 384 (Kilner Brown J)

The plaintiff took a secondhand car on hire purchase from motor dealers. The dealers represented that the car was in excellent condition, knowing that he wished to use it as a minicab. The car was not in fact in excellent condition.

HELD: The representation in the context of intended use as a mini-cab was sufficiently important in the minds of both parties to make it a fundamental term, breach of which entitled the plaintiff to repudiate the contract. He was entitled to judgment against the hire purchase company as the contract was between him and them, they having utilised the services of the dealers and being bound by any representations made by them. As the agreement was a consumer credit agreement under the Consumer Credit Act 1974 the hire-purchase company were entitled as creditors to be indemnified by the dealers who were suppliers to the debtor.

G. Montague (Southern) Ltd v Warren
(1965) Times, 5 February, CA

The defendant, a chauffeur, took on hire purchase a Ford car. He paid three monthly instalments and drove the car 1,200 miles before beginning to complain about the condition of the car. His complaint was that he had to keep having the car repaired. He took the car back to the dealers from whom he had obtained it and paid no further instalments. To an action for recovery of arrears he pleaded a fundamental breach in that the condition of the car made it unroadworthy.

HELD: He had driven it 1,200 miles: there was no fundamental breach.

Honest error not fundamental breach

Hollins v J. Davy Ltd
[1963] 1 QB 844, [1963] 1 All ER 370, [1963] 2 WLR 201, 106 Sol Jo 1033 (Sachs J)

The plaintiff garaged his car at the defendants' premises on the terms of a written contract which provided for payment every four weeks and contained conditions excluding the defendants from liability 'for loss of or damage to customer's goods, however caused' and from 'responsibility for loss or misdelivery of . . . any vehicle . . . whilst in our hands . . . arising from any cause including negligence'. A man came to the garage and was allowed by the garage attendant, a servant of the defendants, to drive away the car on his representing that he had been sent by the plaintiff to collect it. He was in fact a thief and the car was lost. It was admitted that the attendant, though acting honestly had been negligent in allowing the man to take it. In this action the plaintiff alleged that the circumstances amounted to a fundamental breach of the contract which disentitled the defendant to rely on the exclusions in the contract.

HELD: The honest error of the attendant leading him to give the permission to take the car away was not a fundamental breach of the contract. A person doing an act honestly intending to do his best to carry out the intent of the contract cannot, merely because he is deceived, be said to be deliberately breaking the contract. In cases of fundamental breach there is a deliberate disregard of bounden obligations. The attendant honestly believed the man represented the plaintiff: if he had known the man had no authority or not actively believed him to have authority the case would have been different. There was both a loss and misdelivery of the car and each was covered by the exemption clause.

Mere negligence not fundamental breach

John Carter (Fine Worsteds) Ltd v Hanson Haulage (Leeds) Ltd
[1965] 2 QB 495, [1965] 1 All ER 113, [1966] 2 WLR 553, 109 Sol Jo 47,
[1965] 1 Lloyd's Rep 49, CA

The defendants were private carriers who accepted goods from the plaintiffs for carriage from Bradford to London Docks subject to the terms of a contract which provided that 'the liability of the contractor in respect of loss of or damage of the goods . . . shall in any case be limited as follows . . . to the sum of £50 per gross cwt and pro rata for any part of a cwt of the goods so lost or damaged'. The goods were taken by the defendants to their London depot and transferred to a lorry driven by a man whom they had taken into employment only two days before. He had given some details of former employment but the defendants had not checked them or asked for a reference. He had a conviction, unknown to the defendants, for breaking and entering and his object in entering the defendants' employment was to steal the first load he was entrusted with. He drove the load including the plaintiff's goods to an arranged meeting place with friends who stole them. The defendants paid the plaintiffs a sum calculated on the terms of the limitation of liability in the contract but the plaintiffs sued for the balance. The county court judge held that the defendants' failure to make proper inquiries about the driver before employing him was negligence amounting to a fundamental breach of the contract and the limitation of liability did not apply.

HELD, ON APPEAL: (1) The defendants were negligent as found by the county court judge, but (2) this negligence could not amount to a fundamental breach. The defendants, in employing the driver, were not abandoning the contract or deviating from the performance of it: they were attempting, albeit negligently, to carry it out. (3) The theft itself did not constitute a fundamental breach of the contract by the defendants since it was not their act but the act of their driver: to amount to a fundamental breach there must be a deliberate breach of the contract which can be imputed to the contracting party personally. (4) The words of the contract limiting liability were effective to cover loss by theft.

Gillette Industries Ltd v W. H. Martin Ltd
[1966] 1 Lloyd's Rep 57, CA

The defendants, who were forwarding agents, contracted with the plaintiffs to collect 19 containers of goods from a ship arriving at Liverpool and to deliver them to Reading. Their normal practice was to arrange transport by employing sub-contractors known to them. Transport of 16 of the containers was arranged in this way but for the last three, being unable to find anyone else, they employed two men who were available for work with a lorry in the Liverpool 'lorry pool', a parking space where lorries and drivers waited for any work that may be available. The defendants saw that the lorry had an 'A' licence bearing the name of a transport company and interviewed the two men though without seeing their driving licences or taking their names and addresses. The two men took the containers but did not deliver them to Reading. The containers were found at Leytonstone a few days later with some of their contents missing. The contract between the plaintiffs and defendants contained a clause exempting the defendants from liability for loss or damage to goods 'unless such loss or damage occurs whilst the goods are in the actual custody of the company [ie the defendants] and under their actual control and unless such loss or damage is due to wilful negligence or default of the company or their own servant'. The plaintiffs sued for damages for the loss of goods, claiming that by handing them over to two unknown men without taking any adequate steps to satisfy themselves as to the bona fides or honesty of the men the defendants were in fundamental breach of the contract and could not rely on the exemption clause.

HELD: Following *John Carter v Hanson Haulage* (p 349, above) any negligence on the part of the defendants in failing to make proper enquiries about the two men amounted to no more than negligence in the performance of the contract and was not a fundamental breach. The defendants were accordingly protected by the exemption clause.

Sub-contract

Davies v Collins

[1945] 1 All ER 247, 114 LJKB 199, 172 LT 155, 61 TLR 218, 89 Sol Jo 152, CA

Where a cleaner of clothes entered into a contract containing an owner's risk clause and limiting liability to ten times the cost of cleaning, the defendant had sent the work to sub-contractors. A contract might be for work to be done by the defendant himself, or by sub-contractors. The wording here that 'every care is exercised in cleaning' referred to the defendant himself. The contract excluded any right to get the work done by sub-contractors, though not for ancillary matters such as a carrier to take the goods back.

HELD: The clause did not relieve from negligence of sub-contractors and the defendant was liable.

Edwards v Newland & Co

[1950] 2 KB 534, [1950] 1 All ER 1072, 66 TLR (Pt 2) 321, 94 Sol Jo 351, CA

B agreed with A for reward to store A's furniture. B stored the furniture with C. C's premises were bombed and C wrote to B advising the removal of the furniture. B wrote to A with the same advice but without informing A that the storage was not with B, and enclosing the account to date. A was on military service and his wife sought to remove the goods but was denied access until the account was paid. When the goods were delivered up, a number of articles were missing.

HELD: (1) B was in breach of his contract ab initio by undertaking to be a bailee and not acting as such; (2) the personal care and skill of B was of the essence of the contract and B was in breach of his contract in employing a sub-contractor.

Denning LJ pointed out that a repairer of a motor car can often reasonably sub-contract and send away a part of it to another firm for repairs; a carrier of goods would be entitled to make a sub-bailment and might need to entrust them to another carrier for part of the journey; a hirer of goods might often lawfully sub-hire. It depends on the circumstances of the particular case.

B held liable to A.

NOTICE OF EXEMPTION CLAUSE

Note—As part of the test of 'reasonableness' the Unfair Contract Terms Act 1977, s 2 includes among relevant matters 'whether the customer knew or ought reasonably to have known of the existence and extent of the terms . . . ' In reference to this s 11(2) expressly 'does not prevent the court or arbitrator from holding, in accordance with any rule of law, that a term which purports to exclude or restrict any relevant liability is not a term of the contract', e g because adequate steps had not been taken by the other party to draw his attention to it.

Ticket cases

Sugar v London, Midland & Scottish Rly Co
[1941] 1 All ER 172, 164 LT 311, 57 TLR 197, 85 Sol Jo 32 (Viscount Caldecote LCJ)
The words on the face of a railway ticket reading 'For conditions see back, Day Excursion', were obscured and blotted out by the date stamp.
HELD: Reasonable notice had not been given and the passenger was not bound.

Thompson v London, Midland and Scottish Rly Co
[1930] 1 KB 41, 98 LJKB 615, 141 LT 382, CA
The plaintiff's niece, who accompanied plaintiff, took an excursion ticket for plaintiff, who could not read.
On the ticket was printed (inter alia) 'Excursion. For conditions see back'. On the back were printed (inter alia) the words 'Issued subject to the conditions and regulations in the company's time tables and notices and excursion and other bills'. On the excursion bill were printed (inter alia) the words, 'Excursion tickets are issued subject to the notices and conditions shown in the company's current time tables'. In the company's time table (which could be obtained for 6d each) were printed the words 'Excursion tickets . . . are subject to the condition that neither the holders nor any other person shall have any right of action against the company . . . in respect of . . . injury (fatal or otherwise), loss, damage or delay however caused'.
HELD: The fact that the plaintiff could not read did not avail her in any degree. Sufficient notice of the condition had been given to the plaintiff and she was bound by it. Appeal against judgment for defendants dismissed.

Note—See now Unfair Contract Terms Act 1977, p 338, above.

McCutcheon v David MacBrayne Ltd
[1964] 1 All ER 430, [1964] 1 WLR 125, 108 Sol Jo 93, [1964] 1 Lloyd's Rep 16
The appellant, McCutcheon, wished to have his car sent from Islay to the Scottish mainland by the respondent's steamship service. The carriage was arranged by his brother-in-law, McSporran, who went to the respondents'

office on Islay and there saw the purser of their vessel, who quoted a freight charge for the journey. McSporran paid the amount of the freight, was given a receipt and delivered the car to the respondents. By an oversight he was not shown or asked to sign the respondents' 'risk note' a document containing an effective exclusion of liability for negligence. McCutcheon and McSporran had each consigned goods on previous occasions. McCutcheon had always signed the risk note though he had not read it; McSporran had sometimes been presented with the risk note to sign (and had signed it) and sometimes not; he had never read it. Both knew the note contained conditions.

The respondent's vessel sank by reason of their servants' negligence and the car was lost. In this action by McCutcheon for its value the respondents contended that by reason of the knowledge of the risk note gained by McCutcheon and McSporran in the previous transactions the appellant was bound by the conditions in it.

HELD: McCutcheon was not bound by the conditions in the risk note which formed no part of the contract. The course of dealing on earlier occasions is often relevant in determining contractual relations but not where, as here, the respondents had omitted to ask the appellant's agent to sign the document which would have been protection. If McSporran had known that the respondents always required a risk note to be signed and knew the purser was simply forgetting to submit it to him the result might be different; but there had been no constant course of dealing. He was offered an oral contract without any reference to conditions and accepted the offer in good faith.

Per Lord Devlin: There can be no conditions in any contract unless they are brought into it by expression, incorporation or implication. They are not brought into it simply because one party has inserted them into similar transactions in the past and has not given the other party any reason to think he will not want to insert them again. . . . If a man is given a blank ticket without conditions or any reference to them, even if he knows in detail what the conditions usually exacted are, he is not, in the absence of any allegation of fraud or of that sort of mistake for which the law gives relief, bound by such conditions.

Note—See also *Hollier v Rambler Motors*, p 340, above.

The 'Eagle'

[1977] 2 Lloyd's Rep 70, QBD (Deputy Judge Mr Michael Ogden, QC)
The plaintiff was injured by the negligence of the defendants when on a cruise on their ship. The booking for the cruise had been made for the plaintiff by a friend. When making the booking he had seen a brochure issued by the defendants drawing attention to the conditions of carriage to be seen in the defendants' offices. When he eventually received the ticket he saw for the first time that there was a condition exempting the defendants from liability for negligence.

HELD: (1) He was agent for the plaintiff and his knowledge was binding on her; but (2) the contract was completed at the time of the booking, not delivery of the tickets, and the ticket was not a contractual document; (3) mere knowledge that there were conditions was not sufficient in the circumstances to make them terms of the contract, and (4) even if that were wrong the brochure did not fairly bring home to passengers the existence of the exemption clause and the plaintiff was not bound by it.

The 'Dragon'
[1979] 1 Lloyd's Rep 257 (Brandon J)
On 19 January 1971 the plaintiff's husband booked passages for himself, the plaintiff and their children on the defendants' vessel for the 7 July through their agents. He was not notified of any conditions of carriage. In June he received the tickets by post together with conditions of carriage exempting the defendants from liability for injury to a passenger. He did not notice or read the conditions.
HELD (following on this point *The 'Eagle'*, above): It would be wrong to hold that there was no concluded contract until the plaintiff's husband received and accepted the tickets sent him in June. The contract was concluded in January when no notice of the conditions was given. The defendant could not subsequently, by issuing a ticket containing the conditions, introduce them into the contract when it was not subject to them originally.

Notice boards

Smith v Taylor
[1966] 2 Lloyd's Rep 231 (Blain J)
The plaintiff's car broke down. He walked to a nearby garage for help. A mechanic came with a breakdown vehicle and towed the car to the garage, the plaintiff steering it. It was towed into a yard at the side of the garage where the plaintiff said 'Do whatever is necessary' and then went away. He was known at the garage, where he had a monthly account, though he had used it in the past solely for the purchase of petrol. He had occasionally entered a small office when paying his petrol account but had not seen a notice displayed in the office window which relieved the garage owner of liability for damage by negligence to cars being repaired. Whilst the plaintiff's car was being repaired it caught fire due to the mechanic's negligence and was destroyed.
HELD: The notice did not apply. There was an onus on the garage owner if he wished to cover himself contractually to display the notice of conditions so as to bring it to the attention of persons who were likely to be making use of the garage in a way to which the conditions were relevant. When the plaintiff had been in the office it was simply for the purpose of paying for petrol and he had not had occasion then to concern himself with his position if he were going to be a regular user of the garage or workshops. When he was towed in to use the garage for the first time as a repair shop he went only in the yard, where there was no such notice. No previous use he had made of the premises was such as to impose on him any duty to make himself aware of what had been shown on the notice on the office window.

Thornton v Shoe Lane Parking Ltd
[1971] 2 QB 163, [1971] 1 All ER 686, [1971] 2 WLR 585, 115 Sol Jo 75, CA
The plaintiff, wishing to park his car, drove it to the defendants' automatic car park. There was a notice outside giving the charges and saying that all

cars were parked at owners' risk. He drove up to the entrance where a machine automatically extruded a ticket which he took. He then drove on further and the car was taken up in a lift. In addition to instructions how to reclaim the car the ticket bore the words in small print 'This ticket is issued subject to the conditions of issue as displayed on the premises'. These (which he could have found if he had looked round for them) included a condition excluding liability for any injury. When he returned to the premises to reclaim the car he sustained personal injuries due to the defendants' negligence.

HELD: The defendants could not claim the protection of the condition because they had not taken adequate steps to bring it to the plaintiff's notice. They should have posted a prominent notice at the entrance, or used something like red ink on the ticket. The first attempt to bring the conditions to his notice was when it was almost impossible for him to leave. Moreover (per Lord Denning) the plaintiff had accepted the offer when he drove into the appropriate line or place; the ticket then issued was merely a receipt which could not alter the terms.

The Humorist
[1944] P 28, 113 LPJ 41, 171 LT 85, 60 TLR 190, 77 Ll L Rep 189 (Pilcher J)

'Notice to barge owners' on a notice board 6 feet by 4 feet 10 inches was exhibited on the wall of a mill adjacent to a wharf. A barge lay alongside the wharf after loading, and was damaged by the defective berth. The writing on the notice board was faded and it was difficult to read. The plaintiff's lightermen had not observed the notice board at all.

HELD: Defendants had not taken reasonable steps to bring the conditions on the board to the notice of casual invitees and plaintiffs were not affected with knowledge of its terms either as constituting a modification of the conditions of the invitation or as a warning to frequenters of the premises.

Cawood, Wharton & Co Ltd v Samuel Williams & Sons, The Cawood III
[1951] P 270, [1951] 1 TLR 924, [1951] 1 Lloyd's Rep 350, 93 Sol Jo 335 (Willmer J)

The plaintiffs, lightermen, contracted with the defendants, wharf owners, to provide a lighter to be loaded by defendants at the defendants' jetty. The lighter was sunk by a projecting bolt of a timber fender at the jetty. A printed clause in the defendants' letter forming part of the contract provided that the defendants should not be liable for damage howsoever caused, even by their negligence, in relation to any goods handled by them. They also relied on a notice exhibited at the jetty that all lighters used the premises solely at their own risk and defendants would not be liable for any damage howsoever caused even by their negligence, and that the owners of lighters would indemnify them against all claims.

HELD: The notice was not a defence. (1) The onus of providing a previous course of business was on the defendants and had not been discharged; (2) it was not proved that any person representing the plaintiffs (other than the lightermen) ever had the terms of the notice brought to their attention, or ever had a fair opportunity of seeing or reading it; a lighterman was not an agent of the plaintiffs to receive such a notice; (3) the defendants had not included a clause in the terms of the notice in the contract; (4) the exceptions in the contract implied that they were the only exceptions. Judgment for plaintiffs.

Note—In some reports *Catwood* for *Cawood*.

Furley v Victoria Garage Co
(1948) 98 L Jo 94, Bristol CC

The exhibition of notices at a garage to the effect that cars are accepted for storage at the owner's risk is not sufficient to limit the common law liability of the garage proprietors as bailees for reward, in the absence of positive evidence that the plaintiff saw and assented to the condition contained in the notices. The notices exhibited by the defendants constituted no defence unless it could be shown that the plaintiff had read one or more of them, and had assented to these terms being incorporated in the contract when he left his car in the defendants' custody. The judge found as a fact that the plaintiff had not at that time seen any one of the notices, and therefore that the restriction on the defendants liability was not a term of the contract.

Hire-purchase agreement

Lowe v Lombank Ltd
[1960] 1 All ER 611, [1960] 1 WLR 196, 104 Sol Jo 210, CA

The plaintiff, a widow aged 65, went to a motor car dealer to buy a second-hand car. She was offered a car at £200 which the dealer said was in perfect condition. She wanted hire-purchase facilities and was required by the dealer to sign a form of hire-purchase agreement issued by the defendants. She signed without reading it. The car was later delivered to her and she signed a delivery receipt. The car turned out to be utterly unroadworthy, though to the plaintiff the defects would not have been apparent on reasonable inspection. The plaintiff sued for damages for breach of the implied condition of fitness in the Hire-Purchase Act 1938, s 8(2).

HELD: (1) Clauses in the hire-purchase agreement which purported to exclude conditions and warranties, express or implied, were not brought to the plaintiff's notice as required by s 8(3) of the Act and the defendants could not rely on them; (2) the plaintiff had made known to the owners the particular purpose for which the goods were required since the agreement itself contained terms appropriate to the use of the car as a means of transport; and (3) there was a breach of the implied warranty of fitness in s 8(2); (4) the plaintiff was not estopped from relying on the defects as proof of the breach of warranty by having signed a delivery receipt acknowledging that the car was in good order and condition, because it was not the case that the defendants had entered into the hire-purchase agreement in reliance on the terms of the receipt.

Note—For implied term as to fitness in hire-purchase agreements see now Supply of Goods (Implied Terms) Act 1973, s 10 as amended by the Supply of Goods and Services Act 1982, s 17.

PART 2
Damages

CHAPTER 11

Damages: general principles and damage to property

FORESEEABLE CONSEQUENCES

Note—A wrongdoer is liable in damages for the natural and direct consequences of his wrongful act, but he is not liable for every damaging consequence, however remote. Difficulty has sometimes arisen in formulating a principle by which a line can be drawn between those consequences for which he is required to compensate the injured party and those indirect and more remote consequences for which he is not. Formerly the accepted principle in actions of tort was that established by the Court of Appeal in *Re Polemis* [1921] 3 KB 560 that a wrongdoer was liable for all the direct consequences of his act including those which could not reasonably have been anticipated. In 1961 this rule was rejected by the Privy Council in *Overseas Tankship (UK) Ltd v Morts Dock and Engineering Co Ltd (The Wagon Mound)* (below). Foreseeability is now the criterion to determine not only the existence of a duty of care but also liability to pay for the results of failing in that duty. A man is not to be made to pay for damage or loss which a reasonable man in the circumstances of the wrongdoer and with his knowledge and means of knowledge would not have foreseen. In practice the rejection of the rule in *Re Polemis* has had only a limited effect. In personal injury cases in particular, such decisions as *Smith v Leech Brain* (p 362, below) and *Warren v Scrutton* (p 362, below) have ensured that a wrongdoer must still take a victim as he finds him, however unlikely and unexpected the result.

The 'Wagon Mound'

Overseas Tankship (UK) Ltd v Morts Dock and Engineering Co Ltd (The Wagon Mound)

[1961] AC 388, [1961] 1 All ER 404, [1961] 2 WLR 126, 105 Sol Jo 85, [1961] 1 Lloyd's Rep 1

The respondents were owners of a wharf which they used for their business of ship repairing. The appellants were charterers of a vessel which was discharging petroleum products and taking in furnace oil at another wharf about 600 feet away. By carelessness of the appellants' servants a large quantity of furnace oil was allowed to spill into the water and spread over the surface, particularly along the foreshore near and under the respondents' wharf. Molten metal from welding operations on the respondents' wharf fell on some cotton waste or rag floating on debris beneath the wharf and set it alight. Flames from the cotton waste ignited the furnace oil on the water, as a result of which a conflagration developed which damaged the respondents' wharf. The appellants did not know and could not reasonably be expected to have known that the furnace oil was capable of being set on fire when spread on water. There was other damage directly caused by the oil but not caused by the fire, though the respondents had not claimed for it. The Supreme Court of New South Wales, following the decision in *Re Polemis*, held that the appellants were liable for the fire damage.

HELD, ON APPEAL to the Privy Council: The respondents were not liable for the fire damage. The *Polemis* decision should no longer be regarded as good law. If a defendant is guilty of negligence he is liable only for those consequences of his act which were reasonably foreseeable. It is, no doubt, proper when considering tortious liability for negligence to analyse its elements and to say that the plaintiff must prove a duty owed him by the defendant, a breach of that duty by the defendant, and consequent damage. But there can be no liability without damage. It is not the act but the consequences on which tortious liability is founded. The test of liability for the consequences of a negligent act is the foreseeability of the damage which in fact happened.

Doughty v Turner Manufacturing Co Ltd

[1964] 1 QB 518, [1964] 1 All ER 98, [1964] 2 WLR 240, 108 Sol Jo 53

In the heat treatment department of the defendants' works was a sodium cyanide bath containing molten liquid at 800°C. Whilst changing electrodes in the bath a workman allowed a cover of asbestos cement to fall into the bath. After a minute or two there was an eruption in the bath and hot liquid was blown off, injuring the plaintiff. No one knew before this accident that asbestos cement caused an explosion of this kind in sodium cyanide. The judge said the defendants were not to blame for not appreciating that the immersion of the cover would produce an explosion but held that the workman was negligent in letting the cover fall into the bath and that the defendants were liable for his negligence.

HELD, ON APPEAL: Even if the act of the workman in allowing the cover to fall in was negligence there was no liability on the defendants because the evidence showed that nobody supposed that the cover could not be safely immersed in the bath. The *Wagon Mound* (above) showed that *Re Polemis* was no longer good law: the essential factor in determining liability was whether the damage was of such a kind as the reasonable man should have foreseen.

SCOPE OF FORESEEABILITY

Stewart v West African Terminals Ltd

(1964) 108 Sol Jo 838, [1964] 2 Lloyd's Rep 371, CA

The plaintiff, a boiler maker, was going aboard a vessel to fetch his tools when he involuntarily put his hand on a derrick wire to support himself whilst pushing aside another wire which was blocking his path. As he did so the derrick wire moved and injured his hand in a block. The stevedores argued that the risk of injury was not reasonably foreseeable.

HELD: There was evidence that the plaintiff's way to his tools was obstructed by the stevedores' negligence. Since *The Wagon Mound* a person was not responsible for the consequences of negligence unless they were reasonably foreseeable — subject to this, that it was not necessary for the precise concatenation of circumstances to be envisaged if the consequence was one which was within the general sphere of contemplation and not of an entirely different kind which no one could anticipate. The plaintiff's accident was within the sphere of contemplation for which the stevedores were liable.

Slatter v British Railways Board

[1966] 2 Lloyd's Rep 395 (Sachs J)

The plaintiff was a wagon examiner at the defendants' goods yard. He was inspecting a broken wagon on a railway line in the yard when he was startled by the noise of a violent crash as three loaded wagons were shunted into the other wagons on the line. He stumbled forward and his hand went on to the line where it was run over by the wheel of the wagon. It was known by the shunter that the plaintiff was in the vicinity.

HELD: The injury was a foreseeable result of allowing the wagons to crash into each other. It was foreseeable that someone would be startled by the crash and it was 'on the cards' that they would jump or stumble and by so doing might well be injured.

UNFORESEEABLE MAGNITUDE OF DAMAGE IRRELEVANT

Vacwell Engineering Co Ltd v BDH Chemicals Ltd

[1971] 1 QB 88, [1969] 3 All ER 1681, [1969] 3 WLR 927, 113 Sol Jo 639 (Rees J)

The defendants supplied a quantity of boron tribromide, a substance which explodes in contact with water, to the plaintiffs for industrial use in glass ampoules. They gave no warning of its explosive character. The plaintiffs put a large number of the ampoules in water to remove the labels. Somehow an ampoule broke causing others to break and bringing about a vast explosion. The defendants could have foreseen that, in the ordinary course of handling, an ampoule might come into contact with water and cause a minor explosion, but a violent and damaging explosion of the size which actually occurred was not reasonably foreseeable.

HELD: Following *Smith v Leech Brain & Co* (below) an explosion and some damage to property being foreseeable it was immaterial that the magnitude of the former and the extent of the latter were not. The defendants were liable for the whole of the damage done.

Note—An appeal was settled before the end of the hearing on the basis that that part of Rees J's judgment dealing with remoteness of damages in negligence should not be challenged. See [1970] 3 All ER 533.

The rule applied to personal injury cases

Smith v Leech Brain & Co Ltd
[1962] 2 QB 405, [1961] 3 All ER 1159, [1962] 2 WLR 148, 106 Sol Jo 77
(Lord Parker CJ)
The plaintiff's husband received a burn on the lip in the course of his work
due to the negligence of the defendants. The burn healed but later became
ulcerated and cancerous. An operation was done to remove the cancer but
secondary cancers developed and after further operations the deceased died
about three years after sustaining the burn. In an action under the Fatal
Accidents and Law Reform Acts the judge found that the burn was the pro-
moting agency of the cancer in tissues which already had a pre-malignant
condition as a result of the deceased's having worked in a gasworks. It was
contended by the defendants that *The Wagon Mound* (p 360, above) disentitled the plaintiff to recover damages since the defendants could not
reasonably have foreseen that the burn would cause cancer and that the
deceased would die.
HELD: In *The Wagon Mound* the Privy Council did not have the 'thin skull'
cases in mind. It has always been the law of this country that a tortfeasor
takes his victim as he finds him: there is not a day goes by where some trial
judge does not adopt that principle. If the Privy Council had any intention
of making an inroad on that principle they would have said so. On the
contrary a distinction was drawn in their advice between type of injury and
extent of damage. The test was not whether the defendants could reasonably have foreseen that a burn would cause cancer and that the deceased
would die: the question was whether the defendants could reasonably
foresee the type of injury which he suffered, namely, the burn. The plaintiff
was entitled to damages for her husband's death.

Warren v Scruttons Ltd
[1962] 1 Lloyd's Rep 497 (Paull J)
The plaintiff, a dockworker, was handling a wire rope when his finger was
pricked by a projecting strand of wire. The wound became poisoned,
causing a generalised poisoning of the system with a high temperature.
Part of the injured finger had to be cut off and there was continuing tender-
ness. In his teens the plaintiff had suffered from ulceration of the right eye
leaving some weakness of vision. The high temperature and poisoning of
the system following the injury to the finger caused a further ulcer with
some resulting deterioration of the vision. The medical evidence was that
an eye which had once suffered ulceration may always get further ulcers if
some condition of the body causes a high temperature. The defendants
having been found liable for the injury to the finger it was argued on their
behalf that (on the principle of *The Wagon Mound*, p 360, above) the eye
condition was not a foreseeable result of the pricking of the finger and
damages for the eye condition should not be awarded against them.
HELD (following *Smith v Leech Brain*, above): The defendant's argument
was not right. You must look to the type of damage to see whether it was
one which could reasonably be anticipated. The type of damage here was a
pricked finger. Once it was found that that damage could have been
reasonably anticipated then any consequence which resulted because the
individual had some peculiarity was a consequence for which the tortfeasor

was liable. Nevertheless the fact that any febrile condition which the plaintiff suffered, eg a high temperature brought on by a very serious cold, would produce the same condition as the accident did must be taken into account in assessing damages. Award £850 plus special damage of £41.

Bradford v Robinsons Rentals Ltd
[1967] 1 All ER 267, [1967] 1 WLR 337, 111 Sol Jo 33, (Rees J)
In very cold weather on roads made difficult by ice and snow the plaintiff was required by his employers, the defendants, to take an old Austin van from Exeter to Bedford, a distance of 240 miles, and bring back a new one. This was not his normal work. Neither vehicle had a heater. The plaintiff protested against having to do the journey in such weather but the defendants insisted. The journey took two days. Owing to the prolonged exposure to very low temperatures the plaintiff sustained injury to his health by 'frost bite' or cold injury. There was no evidence that before the plaintiff started the journey either the plaintiff himself or the defendants actually contemplated that the plaintiff might suffer from 'frost bite' if he were required to carry out the journey.
HELD: Any reasonable employer would know that if the plaintiff were required to carry out the journey he would be subjected to a real risk to his health from prolonged exposure to the exceptional cold — for example a common cold, or pneumonia or chilblains. The law does not require that the precise nature of the injury must be reasonably foreseeable before liability for its consequences is attributed. *Salmond on Torts* (14th edn) p 719 conveniently states the principle to be followed since *The Wagon Mound* (p 360, above): 'It is sufficient if the type, kind, degree or order of harm could have been foreseen in a general way. The question is, was the accident a variant of the perils originally brought about by the defendant's negligence?' In the present case the defendants knew that the plaintiff was being called upon to carry out an unusual task which would be likely to expose him for prolonged periods to extreme cold and considerable fatigue. By sending him on this journey they exposed him to a reasonably foreseeable risk of injury arising from such exposure. He sustained injury from it and was entitled to damages.

Note—See also *Malcolm v Broadhurst*, p 420, below.

Oman v McIntyre
1962 SLT 168
As a result of the collapse of a trench in which he was working the pursuer's husband sustained fractures of the right tibia and fibula. He was admitted to hospital but his condition deteriorated through fat embolism resulting from the fractures. Broncho-pneumonia supervened and he died five days after the accident. The defenders pleaded that as the death was due to a rare complication not reasonably foreseeable there was no liability.
HELD (adopting the test in *Smith v Leech Brain*, p 362, above): It was not necessary for the pursuer to show that the wrongdoer ought to have foreseen the precise type of physical injury suffered. It was sufficient to show in a case of this nature that the wrongdoer ought to have appreciated that if he were negligent someone to whom he owed a duty of care would suffer physical injury. The full effects of such injury do not have to be foreseeable.

Burden v Watson

1961 SLT 67

The driver of a bus which collided with a motor cycle suffered a coronary thrombosis due to shock. It was contended on behalf of the motor cyclist that such an injury was not reasonably foreseeable.

HELD: Though the loss alleged to have been suffered must always be subject to the test of foreseeability it need not be shown that the wrongdoer ought to have foreseen the precise type of physical injury suffered. The position might well be different if the loss sustained as a result of the accident was of a type which a reasonable man would not be expected to foresee, eg through being unable to keep an appointment or attend a meeting.

TYPE OF INJURY NOT FORESEEABLE

Tremain v Pike

[1969] 3 All ER 1303, [1969] 1 WLR 1556, 113 Sol Jo 182 (Payne J)

The plaintiff, a farm worker, contracted Weil's disease by handling materials contaminated by rat's urine. The disease was not a reasonably foreseeable result of rat infestation.

HELD: This was not a case like *Smith v Leech Brain* (p 362, above) or *Bradford v Robinsons Rentals* (p 363, above) in which the risk of injury from a burn or from extreme cold was foreseeable and in which it was only the degree of injury or the development of the sequelae which was not foreseeable. In the present case the risk of the initial infection was not foreseeable and was entirely different in kind from other possible injuries from rat infestation. The plaintiff was not entitled to succeed.

Second accident

Wieland v Cyril Lord Carpets Ltd

[1969] 3 All ER 1006 (Eveleigh J)

The plaintiff, a lady of 57 years of age was a passenger in a bus when she was thrown forward and sustained injury to her neck. She was treated at hospital where, two days later, she was fitted with a collar. On the same day whilst descending some stairs she fell and injured her ankles. The cause of her fall, the judge found, was that whilst wearing the collar she was unable properly to judge the position of the steps when wearing her bifocal lens spectacles. The defendants contended that the injury to the ankles was not due to their negligence; alternatively it was not foreseeable, relying on *The Wagon Mound (No 1)*.

HELD: (1) The fall and resultant injury was caused by the defendants' negligence. The plaintiff's ability to negotiate stairs had been impaired and this caused the fall. It had long been recognised that injury sustained in one accident may be the cause of a subsequent injury, eg the injury sustained by accident victims on the operating table. It is always a question for the court to decide on the facts whether the accident did cause the second injury; *Hogan v Bentinck Collieries* (p 450, below). (2) *The Wagon Mound (No 1)* decided that damages can only be recovered if the injury complained of was an injury of a class or character foreseeable as a possible result of the negligence. 'The injury complained of' means that personal injury, loss or damage which the law requires to constitute the tort of negligence. *The*

Wagon Mound (No 1) is not to be read as dealing with the extent of the injury or the degree to which it has affected the plaintiff, still less as requiring foreseeability of the manner in which that original injury has caused harm to the plaintiff. In determining liability for the possible consequences of the injury it is not necessary to show that each consequence was within the foreseeable extent or foreseeable scope of the original injury in the same way as the possibility of injury must be foreseen when determining whether or not the defendant's conduct gives a claim in negligence. The present case was concerned with the extent of the harm suffered by the plaintiff: the injury and damage suffered because of the second fall were attributable to the original negligence. (3) Another way of putting it is to say that it is foreseeable that one injury may affect a person's ability to cope with the vicissitudes of life and thereby be a cause of another injury. Foreseeability of this general nature will suffice.

A CONTRASTING CASE

McKew v Holland and Hannen and Cubitts (Scotland) Ltd
[1969] 3 All ER 1621,1970 SC(HL) 20, 1970 SLT 68, HL
On 14 February owing to the defender's negligence the pursuer sustained minor injuries to his left leg. On several occasions following the injury his left leg for a short time went numb and he lost control of it. On 7 March as he was about to descend a staircase he felt his leg give way again. To avoid a fall he jumped down the flight of stairs and sustained severe injury.
HELD: The defendant was not liable in damages for the second injury. The pursuer was acting unreasonably in choosing to descend the staircase without taking precautions against the possibility that his leg might give way. His unreasonable conduct was a *novus actus interveniens*.

Per Lord Reid: I do not think that foreseeability (of the defender) comes into this. A defender is not liable for a consequence of a kind which is not foreseeable. But it does not follow that he is liable for every consequence which a reasonable man could foresee. . . . It only leads to trouble if one tries to graft on to the concept of foreseeability some rule of law to the effect that a wrongdoer is not bound to foresee something which in fact he could readily foresee as quite likely to happen. For it is not at all unlikely or unforeseeable that an active man who has suffered such a disability will take some quite unreasonable risk. But if he does he cannot hold the defender liable for the consequences.

Note—See also 'Novus Actus Interveniens', p 448, below.

Contract and tort contrasted

The Heron II, Koufos v C Czarnikow Ltd
[1969] 1 AC 350, [1967] 3 All ER 686, [1967] 3 WLR 1491, 111 Sol Jo 848, HL
The respondents chartered the appellant's ship to carry a cargo of sugar to Basrah. Owing to a deviation amounting to a breach of contract the ship arrived nine days later than anticipated. The price of sugar at Basrah fell during that period and the respondents obtained less for the cargo than if the ship had arrived on time. At the time the contract was made the appellant did not know what the respondents were going to do with the

sugar but he knew there was a market in sugar at Basrah and could have assumed if he thought about it that the sugar would be sold there. The price might have gone up or down — there was an even chance of either happening.

HELD: The loss was not too remote and the appellant was liable for it.

Per Lord Reid: In cases [of contract] like *Hadley v Baxendale* (1854) 9 Exch 341 or the present case it is not enough that in fact the plaintiff's loss was directly caused by the defendant's breach of contract. It clearly was so caused in both. The crucial question is whether, on the information available to the defendant when the contract was made, he should, or a reasonable man in his position would, have realised that such a loss was sufficiently likely to result from the breach of contract to make it proper to hold, that the loss flowed naturally from the breach or that loss of that kind should have been within his contemplation. The modern rule in tort is quite different and it imposes a much wider liability. The defendant will be liable for any type of damage which is reasonably foreseeable as liable to happen even in the most unusual case, unless the risk is so small that a reasonable man would in the whole circumstances feel justified in neglecting it; and there is a good reason for the difference. In contract, if one party wishes to protect himself against a risk which to the other party would appear unusual, he can direct the other party's attention to it before the contract is made. . . . In tort, however, there is no opportunity for the injured party to protect himself in that way, and the tortfeasor cannot reasonably complain if he has to pay for some very unusual but nevertheless foreseeable damage which results from his wrongdoing.

Batty v Metropolitan Realisation Ltd
[1978] QB 554, [1978] 2 All ER 445, [1978] 2 WLR 500, 112 Sol Jo 63, CA
The *ratio decidendi* of *Esso Petroleum Co Ltd v Mardon* ([1976] QB 801, [1976] 2 All ER 5, [1976] 2 WLR 583, 120 Sol Jo 131) necessarily requires that the mere fact the plaintiffs have obtained judgment for breach of contract does not preclude them from the entitlement which would have existed, apart from contract, to have judgment entered in their favour also in tort, assuming, eg that the plaintiffs had established a breach by the defendant of a common law duty of care owed to the plaintiffs.

REPAIRER'S LIABILITY IN CONTRACT

Hargreaves Vehicle Distributors Ltd v Holbrook
[1970] RTR 380, CA
The defendant was acquiring a lorry by hire purchase and was using it as his only means of livelihood. It was badly damaged in an accident and was taken to the plaintiffs' garage for repair on 4 April. An estimate was agreed with the defendant's insurers on 24 April but the plaintiffs did not order essential parts until 17 May. They completed the work on 10 September but did not tell the defendant until 14 October. When he collected it he found the work had not been satisfactorily done. Meanwhile because of the delay he had been unable to keep up his payments to the hire-purchase company who in January repossessed themselves of the vehicle and obtained judgment against the defendant for £418. The plaintiffs sued for £10 excess under his insurance policy: the defendant counterclaimed for the amount of his loss.

HELD: The plaintiffs knew it was a commercial vehicle and that when it was not available there would be loss of profit or other monetary loss to the defendant. They were under a contractual obligation to return the vehicle properly repaired within a reasonable time and the delay of at least two months was a breach of that duty. Whether or not they were aware of the precise circumstances of the hire purchase they were liable to the defendant for the amount of his loss.

Note—See also *Charnock v Liverpool Corpn*, p 884, below.

CAUSATION OF DAMAGE

Note—The test of foreseeability determines liability in damages for the result of a wrongful act. An entirely separate question is whether a particular form of loss is a sufficiently direct result of the wrongful act as to give the plaintiff a right to be compensated for that loss.

Roe v Minister of Health
[1954] 2 QB 66, [1954] 2 All ER 131, [1954] 2 WLR 915, 98 Sol Jo 319, CA
Per Lord Denning LJ: There is first the question whether there was a duty, and the test is what you could foresee. The second question is whether the neglect of duty was a cause, and the test is the same. The chain of causation is broken when there is intervening action which could not reasonably be foreseen or expected. The third question is remoteness of damages and it is necessary that the negligence should be the immediate or precipitating cause of the damage. The question is — Is the consequence fairly to be regarded as within the risk created by the negligence? or it might be simpler and better to ask one question: Is the consequence within the risk? and to answer it by applying ordinary plain common sense.

The Liesbosch
The law cannot take account of everything that follows a wrongful act; it regards some subsequent matters as outside the scope of its selection, because 'it were infinite for the law to judge the cause of causes' (Bacon's *Elements of the Common Laws of England*), or consequences of consequences. Thus, the loss of a ship by collision due to the other vessel's sole fault may force the shipowner into bankruptcy, and that again may involve his family in suffering, loss of education or opportunities in life, but no such loss could be recovered from the wrongdoer. In the varied web of affairs, the law must abstract some consequences as relevant, not perhaps on grounds of pure logic but simply for practical reasons (per Lord Wright).

Note—See p 369, below for facts and references.

Damage must result from the wrongful act

Carslogie SS Co v Royal Norwegian Government
[1952] AC 292, [1952] 1 All ER 20, [1951] WN 609, [1951] 2 TLR 1099, 95 Sol Jo 801, HL
The elementary principle is that it is for the plaintiff in an action for

damages to prove his case; to show affirmatively that damage under any particular head has resulted from the wrongful act of the defendant.

Performance Cars Ltd v Abraham
[1962] 1 QB 33, [1961] 3 All ER 413, [1961] 3 WLR 749, 105 Sol Jo 748, CA

The plaintiffs' car was damaged in a collision with the defendant's car for which the defendant admitted he was to blame. The damage was such that the whole of the lower part of the plaintiffs' car would need to be resprayed to put it right, at a cost of £75. A short time before this accident the plaintiffs' car had been damaged in another collision and needed a re-spray of the whole of the lower part to put that damage right. The respray had not been done at the time of the second accident. A judgment had been obtained for £75 against the person responsible for the first accident but was unsatisfied. The plaintiffs claimed they were entitled to £75 damages from the present defendant as one of two separate tortfeasors who must each be liable for the consequences of his own tortious act.

HELD: The defendant was not liable for the cost of the re-spray. The necessity for re-spraying was not the result of the defendant's wrongful act because the necessity already existed. The second collision had put no extra burden on the plaintiffs in the matter of re-spraying, for the earlier collision had already imposed the burden of re-spraying on them. The rights of the plaintiffs against the person who caused the first collision were not completely collateral and the quotation from *Mayne on Damages* referred to by Asquith LJ in *Shearman v Folland* (p 461, below) did not apply here. The principle to be applied was that adopted by the House of Lords in *Carslogie SS Co v Royal Norwegian Government* (above).

Note—See also *Hodgson v General Electricity Co Ltd* and *Jobling v Associated Dairies Ltd*, p 472, below.

Cutler v Vauxhall Motors Ltd
[1971] 1 QB 418, [1970] 2 All ER 56, [1970] 2 WLR 961, 114 Sol Jo 247, CA

In November 1965 the plaintiff sustained a graze on the right ankle in an accident at work. It healed in a fortnight and he was not off work. In May 1966 he had pain in the right leg. He was found to have a varicose condition of both legs. An ulcer formed on the site of the original graze and because of this he was advised to have an immediate operation on both legs to cure the varicose condition. This was done in September 1966. The varicose condition was not the result of the accident but the ulcer was, and it was also the reason for having the operation done at once, though even if the accident had never occurred the operation would have been necessary by 1970 or 1971. The plaintiff lost wages amounting to £173 when the operation was done. The judge awarded him £10 for the graze but nothing for the discomfort of the operation or the resultant loss of wages.

HELD, ON APPEAL: The judge was right. The task of the court is to assess the totality of the damages to be awarded and to do so the court must have regard to future probabilities. There was no reasonable ground for supposing that if the accident had not happened the plaintiff would not

have survived to 1970 or 1971 and then lose a sum at least equivalent to the
£173. If the plaintiff were awarded £173 in this action the defendants would
be recouping him for a loss which in all probability he would have had to
bear even if the accident had not occurred.

Organic Research Chemicals Ltd v Ricketts
(1961) Times, 16 November

The plaintiffs had handed their car to the defendant to repair when it broke
down. The car was towed to the defendant's garage. Attempts were made
to restart it which caused further extensive damage to the engine. The first
breakdown was due to a broken camshaft which would have cost £30 to
replace. The extensive damage caused by the defendant's attempt to restart
it made necessary the fitting of a re-conditioned engine at a cost of £61. The
county court judge awarded the plaintiffs the whole cost of the engine. On
appeal the Court of Appeal reduced the award to £31 being the difference
between the cost of the re-conditioned engine and the cost of replacing the
camshaft. It was impossible to say that the plaintiffs had suffered £61
damage, since the engine needed £30 spent on it before the damage was
done. What they had suffered was the difference between the £61 for the
re-conditioned engine and the £30 they would have had to pay anyhow. *The
Bernina* 6 Asp M LC 65 and *The Munster* (1896) 12 TLR 264 were distinguishable on the grounds that the pre-existing damage to this car had
rendered it completely immobile.

Impecuniosity

Dredger Liesbosch v Edison SS
[1933] AC 449, 102 LJP 73, 149 LT 49, HL

While the dredger 'L' was lying moored alongside the breakwater at Patras
Harbour the steamship 'E' fouled the dredger's moorings and carried her
out to sea, where she sank and was lost. The owners of the 'E' admitted sole
liability for the loss. The 'L' had been bought in 1927 for £4,000 by her
owners, who had spent a further £2,000 in bringing her to Patras. They
were a syndicate of civil engineers. Under a contract with the Patras
Harbour Commissioners they were engaged in construction work in the
harbour, for which a dredger was necessary and for which they were using
the 'L'. The contract provided for completion of the work within a specified
time. The loss of the 'L' stopped the work and, being unable from want of
funds to purchase any suitable dredger which was for sale, on 4 May 1929,
they hired a dredger, the 'A' which was lying in harbour at Carlo Forte,
Sardinia, to take the place of the 'L'. The 'A' was more expensive in
working than the 'L' and required the attendance of a tug and two hopper
barges. The 'L' was sunk on 26 November 1928. The 'A' got to work on
the harbour on 17 June 1929.

HELD: The measure of damages was the value of the 'L' to her owners as a
profit-earning dredger at the time and place of her loss; and that it should
include: (1) A capital sum made up of (a) the market price on 26 November
1928, of a dredger comparable to the 'L'; (b) the cost of adapting the new
dredger and of transporting and insuring her from her moorings to Patras;
and (c) compensation for disturbance and loss suffered by the owners of the

'L' in carrying out their contract during the period between 26 November 1928, and the date on which the substituted dredger could reasonably have been available for use at Patras, including in that loss such items as overhead charges and expenses of staff and equipment and the like thrown away, but neglecting any special loss or extra expenses due to the financial position of one or other of the parties. (2) Interest upon that capital sum from 26 November 1928.

If the appellants' financial embarrassment is to be regarded as a consequence of the respondents' tort, I think it is too remote; but I prefer to regard it as an independent cause, though its operative effect was conditioned by the loss of the dredger (Lord Wright).

Note—The point was neatly put in arrangement that the defendants were liable for restitution but not to pay for destitution.

It is common to find a plaintiff claiming for continuing loss of use because he had not the means to pay for repairs. It is submitted this cannot be recovered. But see the following cases.

Clements v Bawns Shipping Co
(1948) 81 Ll L Rep 232 (Denning J)
A ship was sold by fradulent misrepresentation. The purchaser sued for damages, including loss of profit-earning capacity. The plaintiff was too poor to be able to expend the money on repairs for two years, nor up to the date of trial.
HELD: The consequences of his own poverty were not damages resulting from the tort of the defendant. The '*Liesbosch*' (above) followed.

The judge allowed for loss whilst the boat was being repaired, whilst arrangements were being made for it, and whilst obtaining the necessary parts for the engine.

Dodd Properties (Kent) Ltd v Canterbury City Council
[1980] 1 All ER 928, [1980] 1 WLR 433, 124 Sol Jo 84, 253 Estates Gazette 1355 CA
A building owned by the plaintiffs was damaged by building work next door carried out by the defendants, who eventually admitted liability to pay damages. The damage was done in 1968 and repairs could have been done in 1970 when they would have cost £11,375. For various reasons, including financial stringency (short of impecuniosity or financial embarrassment) the plaintiffs had not done repairs at the time of the hearing in 1978. By then the cost of repairs had gone up to £30,000.
HELD: Though the general principle is that damages are to be assessed as at the date the damage occurs it is not a universal rule and is subject to many exceptions and qualifications. Where there is a material difference between the cost of repairs at the date of the wrongful act and the cost when the repairs can, having regard to all relevant circumstances, first reasonably be undertaken it is the latter time at which the cost of repairs should be taken in assessing damages. On the facts the plaintiffs had good commercial reasons for not doing the repairs before the case was heard and were entitled to damages based on cost of repairs at £30,000. The decision in the *Liesbosch* case (above) was not applicable: in that case the excess loss flowed directly from the lack of means and not from the tortious act.

See also *London Congregational Union v Harriss & Harriss* [1985] 1 All ER 335.

Perry v Sidney Phillips & Son (a firm)
[1982] 3 All ER 705, [1982] 1 WLR 1297, 126 Sol Jo 626, 263 Estates
Gazette 888, CA
The plaintiff bought a house on the strength of a report from the defendants
that it was sound. In fact it suffered from a number of defects causing him
anxiety and distress for which he claimed damages. It was pleaded for the
defendants that he could have cut his losses by selling or having repairs
done and that if lack of means prevented him from doing this *The Liesbosch*
case was a bar to his recovering.
HELD: Per Kerr LJ: It was reasonable for the plaintiff not to do any repairs
by the time of the trial, and those reasons went beyond his lack of means. In
any event it seems to me that the authority of what Lord Wright said in *The
Liesbosch* is consistently being attenuated in more recent decisions of this
court, in particular in *Dodd Properties v Canterbury CC* (above). . . . If it is
reasonably foreseeable that the plaintiff may be unable to mitigate or
remedy the consequences of the other party's breach as soon as he would
have done if he had been provided with the necessary means to do so from
the other party, then it seems to me that the principle of *The Liesbosch* no
longer applies in its full vigour.

Contract

Robbins of Putney v Meek
[1971] RTR 345 (John Stephenson J)
The defendants ordered from the plaintiffs, motor dealers, a Bentley car at
a price of £7,510. In breach of the contract they refused to accept it and the
plaintiffs had to find another buyer. They were short of liquid capital and
purchase of the car had caused them to exceed the limit of their overdraft.
After two months of advertising it at figures well over £6,000 they sold it to
a dealer at £5,750. In reply to the plaintiffs' claim for loss of profit the
defendants said that because of impecuniosity they had sold too quickly and
should not have sold it until they could get its full value.
HELD: In relation to mitigation of damages (as distinct from measure of
damages) the wrongdoer must take his victim as he is. The plaintiffs, with
the maximum limit fixed for their overdraft and their lack of liquid capital,
had acted reasonably in selling the car as they did and were entitled to
recover from the defendants the amount of the loss.

Interoffice Telephones Ltd v Robert Freeman & Co
[1958] 1 QB 190, [1957] 3 All ER 479, [1957] 3 WLR 971, 101 Sol Jo 958,
CA
With regard to the measure of damages, there is no difference in the
principle applicable between a contract for sale and a contract for hiring.

Novus actus interveniens

INTERVENING ACT OF THIRD PARTY

Note—The chain of causation between the defendant's wrongdoing and the plaintiff's damage may be broken if the immediate cause of the damage was the act of a
third party.

Home Office v Dorset Yacht Co Ltd
[1970] AC 1004, [1970] 2 All ER 294, [1970] 2 WLR 1140, 114 Sol Jo 375,
[1970] 1 Lloyd's Rep 453, HL

A party of borstal trainees were working on Brownsea Island under the
supervision and control of three borstal officers employed by the appellants. During the night seven of the trainees escaped and went on board a
yacht they found nearby. They set it in motion and collided with the
respondent's yacht which was moored in the vicinity, causing damage.

HELD: The appellants were liable for the damage.

Per Lord Reid: The ground of liability is not responsibility for acts of the
escaping trainees; it is liability for damage caused by the carelessness of
these officers in the knowledge that their carelessness would probably result
in the trainees causing damage of this kind. So the question is really one of
remoteness of damage . . . [and] to what extent the law regards the acts of
another person as breaking the chain of causation between the defendants'
carelessness and the damage of the plaintiff. . . . It has never been the law
that the intervention of human action always prevents the ultimate damage
from being regarded as having been caused by the original carelessness.
The convenient phrase *novus actus interveniens* denotes those cases where such
action is regarded as breaking the chain and preventing the damage from
being held to be caused by the careless conduct. But every day there are
cases where, although one of the connecting links is deliberate human
action, the law has no difficulty in holding that the defendant's conduct
caused the plaintiff loss. . . . What then is the dividing line? . . . [The]
cases show that, where human action forms one of the links between the
original wrongdoing of the defendant and the loss suffered by the plaintiff,
that action must at least have been something very likely to happen if it is
not to be regarded as *novus actus interveniens* breaking the chain of causation.
I do not think that a mere foreseeable possibility is or should be sufficient,
for then the intervening human action can be more properly regarded as a
new cause than as a consequence of the original wrongdoing. But if the
intervening action was likely to happen I do not think it can matter whether
that action was innocent or tortious or criminal.

Note—See also *Robinson v Post Office*, p 448, below, and *Lloyds Bank v Budd*, p 65,
above.

Lamb v Camden London B C
[1981] QB 625, [1981] 2 All ER 408, [1981] 2 WLR, 1038, 125 Sol Jo 356,
CA

The plaintiff owned a house in a good neighbourhood. She let it to a tenant
and went to America. Some months later the defendant council in doing
work for renewal of a sewer damaged a water main. Water caused a subsidence of the house: it was not safe to live in and the tenant left. Repair work
was not done until some years later. During the intervening period the
house was locked up but squatters broke in and caused considerable
damage to the interior. The council admitted liability for nuisance. The
plaintiff claimed damages for the cost of repairs made necessary by the subsidence and in addition damages for the cost of making good the damage
done by the squatters.

HELD: The defendants were not liable for the damage done by the squatters: it was too remote. Applying Lord Reid's test in *Home Office v Dorset Yacht Co* (above) the squatters' actions, though 'foreseeable', were not 'likely', the house being in a neighbourhood where squatting had not formerly occurred. But even Lord Reid's test may not be adequate where the fresh damage had been caused by the intervening act of a third party. A court may require a degree of likelihood amounting almost to inevitability before it fixes a defendant with responsibility for the act of a third party over whom he has and can have no control.

Note—Applied in *P. Perl (Exporters) Ltd v Camden London Borough Council* [1984] QB 342, [1983] 3 All ER 161, [1983] 3 WLR 769, 127 Sol Jo 581, CA. See also *Ward v Cannock Chase District Council* [1985] 3 All ER 537.

West v Hughes
[1971] RTR 298 (Mocatta J)
In the hours of darkness the plaintiff, on a bicycle, wished to turn right from a busy road into a side road. When in the centre of the main road before turning he was struck from behind by a van and knocked over. He got up, picked up his bicycle, and was then hit and very severely injured by a car which was following the van. Neither driver saw him before the collisions though they were using headlights and there was nothing to prevent them from seeing him. The judge held both drivers to have been negligent. It was argued for the van driver that (1) the car driver's negligence was a *novus actus*, alternatively (2) as the most serious injuries were caused by the car the car owner should bear the major part of the responsibility.
HELD: (1) Although all the grave injuries were directly caused by the car there was not such a break in the chain of causation that the van driver could be held liable only for nominal damages. If a driver in a line of traffic on a busy road at night negligently knocks down a cyclist it is plainly foreseeable that the next following vehicle may injure the rider. The fact that the following driver could have avoided the cyclist if he had been keeping a proper look-out does not make his negligence a *novus actus*. (2) The negligence of each driver was causative of the plaintiff's injuries: as the van driver had a better opportunity of seeing the plaintiff than the car driver he should bear 55% of the responsibility and the car driver 45%.

Knightley v Johns
[1982] 1 All ER 851, [1982] 1 WLR 349, 126 Sol Jo 101, [1982] RTR 182, CA
Johns was driving his car through a tunnel having two carriageways when it overturned, blocking most of the northbound carriageway. The accident was admittedly due to his negligent driving. The driver of a following car reported the accident by telephone to the police control centre whence a message was transmitted by radio to the plaintiff, PC Knightley, a police officer on a motor cycle. He entered the tunnel, saw the situation, and then left it to radio further information to the control centre. On returning to the scene he found that Inspector Sommerville, the third defendant, had already arrived with other police officers. The inspector said to him and another officer 'I have forgotten to close the tunnel; you go back and do it'. The two officers then rode south, in the opposite direction to the traffic stream. The plaintiff collided with an oncoming car near the entrance and

was injured. There were in existence standing orders presumably known to the inspector (who, though present at the trial, did not give evidence) specifying a procedure and precautions for dealing with accidents in the tunnel. They required, inter alia, the tunnel to be closed at the outset, for officers to go on foot only and for 'emergency vehicles' to be accompanied by an officer only when all traffic had been stopped. The trial judge held that the police officers were not negligent, that the whole sequence of events flowed from Johns's negligence, and that he was liable in damages to the plaintiff.

HELD, ON APPEAL: The decision was not right. The inspector was negligent in not closing the tunnel and in ordering or allowing his subordinates to do a very dangerous thing contrary to standing orders. The question to be answered was whether his negligence was concurrent with the negligence of Johns or whether the acts and omissions of the plaintiff and the inspector were new causes which broke the chain of causation. In considering the effects of carelessness the test is reasonable foreseeability; in this case, whether the whole sequence of events was a natural and probable consequence of Johns's negligence and a reasonably foreseeable result of it. Negligent conduct is more likely to break the chain of causation than conduct which is not; positive acts will more easily constitute new causes than inaction. The inspector's negligence was not a concurrent cause running with Johns's negligence, but a new cause interrupting the effect of it. The judge's decision carried Johns's responsibility too far. The inspector, not Johns, was liable in damages to the plaintiff.

The Oropesa
[1943] P 32, [1943] 1 All ER 211, 112 LJP 91, 168 LT 364, 59 TLR 103, CA

To break the chain of causation it must be shown that there is something which I will call ultroneous, something unwarrantable, a new cause which disturbs the sequence of events, something which can be described as either unreasonable or extraneous or extrinsic. I doubt whether the law can be stated more precisely than that: per Lord Wright.

Two ships collided at sea. Although one ship was badly damaged, her master thought she could be salved. He sent 50 of his crew to the other vessel. About one and a half hours later he decided to go to the vessel and confer with the master. He launched a lifeboat with 16 men. The weather was rough and the boat capsized and nine of the men were drowned. An action was brought by the representatives of one of the deceased men.

HELD: The master had acted reasonably in the emergency; the death was not the result of a *novus actus interveniens*, but was directly caused by the collision.

Note—See also *Rothwell v Caverswall Stone Co* and *Hogan v Bentinck*, p 450, below.

INTERVENING ACT OF PLAINTIFF

Note—See cases at p 450, below, under heading 'Refusal to undergo operation'. See also cases under heading 'Second accident', p 364, above.

Malcolm v Dickson
(1951) 112 *Post Magazine* 249, Ct of Sess
The painter employed in painting premises set fire to the woodwork with a
blowlamp. The deceased, who was living in the house, went upstairs to
save some personal belongings. He was overcome by fumes and collapsed
and was burned to death.
HELD: The death was too remote from the alleged negligence. Logically,
the loss of a battle, or even a kingdom, might be traced on the absence of a
nail in a horse's shoe, but strict logic is not a safe guide. There is a danger of
the courts being driven stage by stage to undue lengths in the direction
of allowing the inclusion of more and more remote consequential items
of loss.

ECONOMIC LOSS

Note—Mere economic loss unaccompanied by damage to the plaintiff's person or
property is irrecoverable in an action for negligence.

Weller & Co v Foot and Mouth Disease Research Institute
[1966] 1 QB 569, [1965] 3 All ER 560, [1965] 3 WLR 1082, 109 Sol Jo 702,
[1965] 2 Lloyd's Rep 414
The defendants allowed foot and mouth virus to escape into the atmosphere. As a result the Minister of Agriculture ordered the Guildford and
Farnham cattle markets to be closed: the plaintiffs were auctioneers there
and lost business by reason of the closure.
HELD: The plaintiffs could not recover damages from the defendants. A
great volume of authority both before and after *Donoghue v Stevenson* (p 228,
above) was to the effect that a plaintiff suing in negligence for damages
suffered as a result of an act or omission of the defendant could not recover
if the act or omission did not directly injure, or at least threaten directly to
injure, the plaintiff's person or property but merely caused consequential
loss, as, for example, by upsetting his business relations with a third party
who was the direct victim of the act or omission. A duty of care which arose
from a direct injury to person or property was owed only to those whose
person or property might foreseeably be injured by a failure to take care. If
the plaintiff could show that the duty was owed to him, he could recover
both direct and consequential loss which was reasonably foreseeable and
there was no reason for saying that proof of direct loss was an essential part
of the claim. The plaintiff had, however, to show he was within the scope of
the defendant's duty to take care. In the present case the duty to take care to
avoid an escape of virus was owed to the owners of cattle which might be
infected by the virus. The plaintiffs were not owners of cattle and had no
proprietary interest in anything that might conceivably be damaged by the
virus if it escaped.

Note—See also *Lee Cooper v C. H. Jeakins & Sons Ltd*, p 334, above.

Brandon Electrical Engineering Co v Wm Press & Son
(1956) 106 L Jo 332 (McKee)
Public works contractors broke water main under highway which put electric cable out of action and plaintiff's factory stopped for some hours. Plaintiffs could not recover damages for wasted wages and loss of production.

Electrochrome v Welsh Plastics
[1968] 2 All ER 205 (Geoffrey Lane J)
The plaintiffs and defendants were tenants of premises about 500 feet apart on a factory estate. A servant of the defendants driving a motor lorry negligently damaged a fire hydrant near their factory and the main water supply had to be turned off for some hours. The plaintiffs suffered loss of production because they could not work without water. The hydrant did not belong to them and was not on their premises.
HELD: The plaintiffs having no proprietary or possessory rights in the hydrant could not recover damages. The contract which the plaintiffs had with the industrial estate had been made less beneficial by the defendants' negligence but this did not give them a cause of action. As in *Weller v Foot and Mouth Disease Research Institute* (above) the defendants were not liable in negligence because as the hydrant did not belong to the plaintiffs they owed no duty of care to them.

CONTRASTING CASES

British Celanese Ltd v Hunt
[1969] 2 All ER 1252, [1969] 1 WLR 959, 113 Sol Jo 368 (Lawton J)
The plaintiffs and the defendants both occupied premises on an industrial estate about 150 yards apart, supplied with electricity from a sub-station about 100 yards from the plaintiffs' premises. Metal foil strips were blown by the wind from the defendants' premises on to busbars at the sub-station and caused a breakdown in the electricity supply to the plaintiffs' factory. Material solidified in their machines which had to be cleaned. They claimed damages for loss of production and profit. Metal foil strips had been blown into the sub-station on a previous occasion and the electricity board had warned the defendants that it could cause a failure of electricity supply to premises on the estate.
HELD: The damages claimed were not too remote. The solidifying of material in the machines was damage to property and the loss claimed for was not merely economic. Unlike the plaintiff in *Weller's* case (above) the present plaintiffs were direct victims of the negligence alleged. In the present case, too, the defendants owed the plaintiffs a duty of care because they foresaw or ought to have foreseen that the interruption of power supplies would injure the plaintiffs' property.

SCM (UK) Ltd v W. J. Whittall & Son Ltd
[1971] 1 QB 337, [1970] 3 All ER 245, [1970] 3 WLR 694, 114 Sol Jo 706, CA
The defendants were digging a trench in a road adjoining a number of factories of which the plaintiffs' was one. In the course of the work the

defendants damaged an electric cable, causing a power failure in the plaintiffs' factory. Molten materials solidified in the machines causing physical damage to the plaintiffs' materials and tools. They claimed damages, confining the claim to the physical damage and to economic loss directly consequential on that physical damage.

HELD: The plaintiffs were entitled to recover. The defendants owed them a duty of care not to damage the cable because they knew that if they damaged it the current would be cut off and damage would be suffered by the factory owners. It was immaterial that the factory was not liable to be directly injured. A man may owe a duty of care to those whom he foresees may be indirectly injured as well as to those whom he foresees may be directly affected. But (per Lord Denning) when the plaintiff has suffered no damage to his person or property, but has only sustained economic loss, the law does not usually permit him to recover that loss; this is not because no duty of care is owed to him but because it is too remote to be a head of damage. *Weller's* case (above) depends on remoteness, not duty of care; similarly *Electrochrome v Welsh Plastics* (above).

Per Winn LJ: There is no liability (except in the special case of negligently uttered false statements) for unintentional negligent infliction of any form of economic loss which is not consequential on foreseeable physical injury or damage to property. *British Celanese Ltd v Hunt* (above) approved.

Spartan Steel and Alloys Ltd v Martin & Co (Contractors) Ltd
[1973] QB 27, [1972] 3 All ER 557, [1972] 3 WLR 502, 116 Sol Jo 648, CA
The plaintiffs' factory was supplied with electricity by a direct cable from the power station. The defendants were doing work in a road about a quarter-mile from the factory and negligently damaged the cable causing the power supply to the factory to be cut off for 14 hours. As a result the plaintiffs suffered loss from (1) damage to metal in an electric furnace; (2) loss of profit on that melt of metal; (3) loss of profit on metal which they would have subsequently melted during the period the power was off.
HELD: The plaintiffs were entitled to damages under heads (1) and (2) but not head (3). The loss under head (3) was economic loss independent of the physical damage to the metal in the furnace when the power failed.

Note—In *Junior Books Ltd v Veitchi Co Ltd* (p 228, above) Lord Roskill commented that there was no reason why 'damage to the pocket' simpliciter should be disallowed when damage to the pocket coupled with physical damage had always been allowed. He asked, was the decision of the majority in *Spartan Steel and Alloys Ltd v Martin & Co* correct or was the dissenting judgment of Lord Justice Edmund Davies to be preferred? The view expressed by Edmund Davies LJ in *Spartan Steel* was that an action lay in negligence for damages in respect of purely economic loss provided it was a reasonably foreseeable and direct consequence of failure in a duty of care. See also *Muirhead v Industrial Tank Specialities* (1985) Times, 6 August, CA.

DUTY TO MINIMISE LOSS

British Westinghouse Co v Underground Electric Railways Co
[1912] AC 673, 81 LJKB 1132, 107 LT 325
In assessing damages in contract, the fundamental basis is compensation for pecuniary loss naturally flowing from the breach, but this is qualified by

plaintiff's duty to take all reasonable steps to mitigate the loss consequent on the breach and he cannot claim any part of the damage which is due to his neglect to take such steps. If the action which he has taken has actually diminished his loss, such diminution may be taken into account even though there was no duty on him to act.

Bellingham v Dhillon

[1973] QB 304, [1973] 1 All ER 20, [1972] 3 WLR 730, 116 Sol Jo 566 (Forbes J)

The plaintiff was a driving school proprietor. In 1967 he was negotiating to instal an electronic simulator to teach driving but because of injuries he had sustained in an accident for which the defendant was responsible the negotiations broke down. A simulator would have cost him £1,824 a year for five years and then £71 per year. In 1971 he was able to, and did, buy one outright secondhand from a company in liquidation. But for this purchase his net loss of profit on simulator teaching would be £2,774; if the defendant was entitled to take the purchase of the secondhand simulator into account the loss was nil. It was argued for the plaintiff that sums which came to him as a result of the tortious act and would not have come to him but for the tort were not to be taken into account.

HELD: The plaintiff had a duty to mitigate his damage by buying equipment just as much when that damage arose in tort as if it had arisen in contract. Applying the principles set out by Lord Haldane in *British Westinghouse v Underground Electric Railways Co* (above) the damages were to be arrived at by subtracting the profits the business earned after the wrong had been suffered from the profits the business would have earned on the hypothesis that the defendant's wrong had not reduced them, looking at the whole of the facts and ascertaining the result. On this basis no loss arose on the simulator venture.

Dunkirk Colliery Co v Lever

(1878) 9 ChD 20

The plaintiff is not under any obligation to take any steps which a reasonable and prudent man would not ordinarily take in the course of his business, but if, though there was no duty on him so to act, he took action which resulted in diminution of the loss, this might be taken into account.

The Pacific Concord

[1961] 1 All ER 106, [1961] 1 WLR 873, 105 Sol Jo 492, [1960] 2 Lloyd's Rep 270

The plaintiffs' vessel was damaged in a collision with the defendants' vessel for which the defendants admitted liability. The repairs (for which there was no urgency) were carried out at London where repair charges were about 50% more than at Newcastle where the plaintiffs could have had them done if they had taken reasonable precautions to give adequate notice to stem a dry dock. Moreover by having the repairs done before the cancellation of a charter party instead of after it they lost £2,319 profit on the charter.

HELD: The plantiffs' duty was to make such arrangements for the repair.

of the damage as a prudent uninsured owner would make for himself. It was an unreasonable decision to have the repairs done when and where the plaintiffs had them done: they were not entitled to recover from the defendants the additional expense by having them done at London, nor the loss of profit on the charter party. *Dunkirk Colliery Co v Lever* (above) applied.

Pomphrey v James A. Cuthbertson
1951 SC 149, 1951 SLT 191, Ct of Sess
Pursuer claimed (1) the cost of a vehicle which he had bought to replace his damaged car; (2) the cost of adapting it to his purposes; and (3) hire charges until replacement; less the scrap value of his damaged car.
HELD: This was the wrong basis; the correct basis being either the cost of repair plus hire charges, or the market value of the damaged car immediately before the accident, plus hire charges until replaced, less its scrap value.

Moore v DER Ltd
[1971] 3 All ER 517, [1971] WLR 1476, 115 Sol Jo 528, [1972] RTR 97, CA
It was the plaintiff's custom to buy a new car every second year. His car was damaged beyond repair when it was 18 months old. Instead of buying a car of similar age secondhand he ordered a new car the delivery of which was expected in two months. It was not in fact delivered for four months. Meanwhile the plaintiff hired a car of the same make and type at £20 per week for the whole period. As a dentist living some distance from his practice he did a lot of driving and needed a reliable car. The county court allowed recovery of only three weeks' hire holding that the plaintiff could and should have bought an 18-month-old car of that type within three weeks.
HELD, ON APPEAL: In mitigating his damage a plaintiff is only required to act reasonably. Whether the plaintiff had acted reasonably is a question of fact not of law. *Darbishire v Warren* (p 382, below) was quite a different case in which the car was a very old one of little value which the plaintiff had repaired out of affection. In the circumstances of the present plaintiff it was sensible and reasonable to buy a new car and it was just unfortunate for everybody concerned that delivery took so long. The plaintiff was entitled to the hire charges for the whole period.

Hiring replacement vehicle

Watson Norie Ltd v Shaw
(1967) 111 Sol Jo 117, CA
The plaintiff company's Jensen car, used by the managing director was damaged by the defendant's negligence. The company hired a Rover and later a Jaguar car for seven weeks at £40 per week whilst it was being repaired, these cars being of equivalent value and prestige to a Jensen. The defendants objected that the amount was unreasonable and the plaintiffs had failed to mitigate their damage. There was evidence that a Triumph Herald could be hired at £17 10s per week or a Ford Zephyr at £25 per

week. The county court judge thought it was not reasonable to expect the plaintiff to use the Triumph but that the Ford would have been suitable. He considered the plaintiffs had been casual in hiring a replacement, not having made enquiries to find out if a suitable car could be obtained more cheaply. He awarded only £25 per week loss of use.

HELD on the plaintiffs' appeal: There was material before the judge that a reasonable substitute could be hired for £25 per week and he was entitled to reach the conclusion he did. Where as here it was necessary to hire a car for only a short period it was not necessarily right that the defendants had to pay the cost of hiring a car equal in value and prestige to the damaged car.

H. L. Motorworks (Willesden) Ltd v Alwahbi
[1977] RTR 276, CA

The plaintiffs were motor repairers. When giving a test run to a customer's car, a Rolls Royce, it was damaged by the defendant's negligence and was off the road 11 days for repairs. The owner hired another Rolls Royce for those 11 days at a cost of £467.55, which the plaintiffs paid. In a claim against the defendant for reimbursement the judge held that it was unnecessary for so great an expense to be incurred and awarded only £160 as being sufficient for hiring a suitable car.

HELD: He should have awarded the whole amount. The owner of the car was entitled to have another Rolls Royce during the 11 days he had been deprived of his own. He was the plaintiffs' customer and it might have been damaging to the relationship to try to cut down the amount of his claim. *Watson Norie Ltd v Shaw* (above) was quite a different case.

Daily Office Cleaning Contractors v Shefford
[1977] RTR 361 (Stabb J)

The plaintiff company supplied its directors with so-called 'prestige' cars for use in their work. One of these, an American-made Rambler car, was damaged in a collision by the defendant's negligent driving. The plaintiffs sent their car to their usual garage by whom it was sent to coachwork repairers who applied to the main suppliers for the necessary parts. Meanwhile the plaintiffs obtained from the garage on hire a Jaguar XJ6 at £75 per week, a concessionary price: the normal price was £100 per week. Because of long delays in obtaining necessary parts repairs were not completed until 25 weeks had elapsed. The plaintiffs claimed 25 weeks' hire at £75 per week. The defendants contended that to hire a Jaguar XJ6 for so long was unreasonable in that a medium-sized car would have sufficed.

HELD: A plaintiff had only to act reasonably when dealing with a situation he finds himself in as a result of the act of a tortfeasor. There was no call for the plaintiffs to shop around to hire a car at a lesser sum from someone with whom they did not normally deal, especially as the Jaguar was supplied at a concessionary rate. Although the repairs took a long time the plaintiffs had pressed the repairers to hasten completion and it would be wrong to blame the plaintiffs for the American Motor Corporation's delay in delivery.

Martindale v Duncan
[1973] 2 All ER 355, [1973] 1 WLR 574, 117 Sol Jo 168, CA

On 27 November the plaintiff's taxi was damaged. He obtained an estimate of the cost of repair on 1 December and claimed the estimated amount from the defendant. He did not instruct the repairers to carry out the repairs, not being able to afford them and believing he had to allow the defendant's insurers to inspect the vehicle and also to get permission from his own insurers. It was not until 26 January that the defendant's insurers wrote agreeing the cost of repairs after an engineer's inspection. The plaintiff then instructed the repairers and the repairs were completed by 25 February. Meanwhile the plaintiff had hired a replacement vehicle for ten weeks, starting a month after the accident. The defendant contested payment of the hire charges on the ground that the repairs should have been put in hand immediately after the accident.

HELD: It was not a case like *The Liesbosch*. The plaintiff was seeking to recover his damages from the defendant's insurers and, if that went wrong, to recover from his own insurers. Until he had authorisation to do the work he could not be certain of being in a good position vis-à-vis the insurance company.

Note—See also *Moore v DER Ltd*, p 379, above.

Repairs costing more than the total loss value

O'Grady v Westminster Scaffolding Ltd

[1962] 2 Lloyd's Rep 238 (Edmund Davies J)

The plaintiff claimed for loss and expense he had sustained by the negligence of the defendants in damaging his car on 13 July 1960. The car was a 1937 MG which he had bought in 1947 for £475. It had been maintained by him in exceptionally good condition at considerable expense: in the year before the accident the plaintiff had spent over £300 on a new engine and coachwork. It was doubtful whether a car of the same type in similar condition could be found on the open market. The plaintiff had the car repaired at a price of £253 and claimed this sum plus hire charges of £207 for cars hired whilst the repairs were being carried out. The defendants contended that the pre-accident value of the car was about £180 and the salvage value £35 to £40 and that the plaintiff had acted unreasonably in having the car repaired.

HELD: The pre-accident market value of chattels affords a guide to the measure of conpensation when, and only when, a similar chattel can be obtained in the open market. The plaintiff acted reasonably in having the car repaired and in hiring other cars whilst the repairs were being done.

Harbutts Plasticine Ltd v Wayne Tank and Pump Co Ltd

[1970] 1 QB 447, [1970] 1 All ER 225, [1970] 2 WLR 198, 114 Sol Jo 29, CA

Per Widgery LJ: The distinction between those cases in which the measure of damages is the cost of repair of the damaged article and those in which it is the diminution in value of the article is not clearly defined. . . . Each case turns on its own facts, it being remembered, first, that the purpose of the award of damages is to restore the plaintiff to his position before the loss occurred, and second, that the plaintiff must act reasonably to mitigate his loss. If the article damaged is a motor car of popular make, the plaintiff cannot charge the defendant with the cost of repair when it is cheaper to buy a similar car on the market. On the other hand if no substitute for the damaged article is available and no reasonable alternative can be provided, the plaintiff should be entitled to the cost of repair.

Darbishire v Warran

[1963] 3 All ER 310, [1963] 1 WLR 1067, 107 Sol Jo 631, [1963] 2 Lloyd's Rep 187, CA

The plaintiff's car was damaged in a collision with a car driven by the defendant, who was wholly to blame. The car was a 1951 Lea Francis shooting brake bought by the plaintiff in 1958 for £300. At the time of the collision in 1962 its market value was £85. The cost of repairing it was considered by engineers to be uneconomic and the plaintiff accepted £80 as a constructive total loss payment from his insurers, being £85 less an excess of £5. Despite this he had the car repaired at a cost of £192 and sued the defendant for the difference between that amount and the payment he had received from his own insurers, plus a loss of use claim. He said that it was worth it to him to have the car repaired since it suited his needs and, having looked after it carefully, he would be unable to buy a car of the same worth to him for less than £192. He admitted in evidence that he had not looked for one. The county court judge held that he had acted reasonably in having the car repaired and awarded him the cost of the repairs less £80. HELD, ON APPEAL: The true question was whether the plaintiff acted reasonably, not merely so far as he himself was concerned, but as between himself and the defendant, having regard to his duty to mitigate the damages. It has come to be settled that in general the measure of damage is the cost of repairing the damaged article; but there is an exception if the cost of repairs greatly exceeds the value in the market of the damaged article. In the latter case the measure is the value of the article in the market provided there is a market in which the article can be bought. If there is none the cost of repairs can still be claimed. In the present case there was evidence that a similar type of car was obtainable in the market at £85 to £100. It was not an irreplaceable article and therefore should be treated as a constructive total loss and the measure of damages was its value. The decision in *O'Grady v Westminster Scaffolding Ltd* (above) was justified by unusual facts which made the car in that case unique so that the standard market value was irrelevant: the present case was quite different. The plaintiff was entitled to recover only £5 excess plus £25 for hire of another car whilst finding a replacement.

Note—See also *Moore v DER Ltd*, p 379, above.

Repairs causing loss of value

Payton v Brooks

[1974] RTR 169, [1974] 1 Lloyd's Rep 241, CA

The plaintiff's car, only four weeks old, was damaged by the defendant. He claimed from her not only the cost of repairs but also the sum of £100 being the estimated loss of market value of the car, even after repair, due to its being a repaired car. The judge awarded only the cost of repairs, finding on the evidence that no diminution in market value had been established by the plaintiff.

HELD, ON APPEAL: The judge's finding of fact must be accepted, but obiter, if the judge had found that the diminution in value had been established the plaintiff would have been entitled to an award. The normal measure of damages is the cost of repair but if, despite good repairs, a reduced market value can be proved, compensation for the reduction can be awarded to the plaintiff, the value of his property as a saleable asset having been reduced.

MEASURE OF DAMAGES: BETTERMENT

Property

Moss v Christchurch Rural District Council
[1925] 2 KB 750, 95 LJKB 81
A cottage was set on fire as the result of the negligence of the defendants. The fabric was seriously damaged and a quantity of the household effects destroyed. The Official Referee assessed the damage sustained by the owner and tenant at the cost of replacement in each case. The defendants appealed contending the damages were limited to the value of the property at the time it was destroyed.
HELD: The measure of damages is not the cost of replacement but is the value to the owner of the property at the time it was destroyed. The true measure of damage is the difference between the money value of the interest before the damage and the money value of the interest after the damage.

Note—Considered in *Hutchinson v Davidson* 1945 SC 395, where the cost of replacement was awarded.

Hole & Sons Ltd v Harrisons
[1973] 1 Lloyd's Rep 345, QBD
The defendants' lorry crashed into a row of three ancient cottages owned by the plaintiff company, causing damage. Two of the cottages were occupied as an office and store by the plaintiffs; the third was occupied by a statutory tenant at a rent of 15s per week and was so badly damaged that she had to move elsewhere, losing her tenancy. The plaintiffs claimed the estimated cost of reinstating all the damaged cottages at a cost of £4,079. At the trial it appeared that the plaintiffs, even before the accident, had intended to demolish the cottages and build new premises in place of them; the departure of the tenant had now enabled them to do this, for which they had obtained planning permission.
HELD: A claim for damage to property was either for cost of reinstatement or diminution in value. The evidence showed that the plaintiffs had no intention of reinstating; the departure of the statutory tenant had increased the value rather than diminished it. The only damages the plaintiffs were entitled to was the cost of a temporary repair already done and an agreed sum for loss of rent.

C. R. Taylor (Wholesale) Ltd v Hepworths Ltd
[1977] 2 All ER 784, [1977] 1 WLR 659, 121 Sol Jo 15, 242 Estates Gazette 631 (May J)
The plaintiffs owned property consisting of a billiard hall and three shops.

The billiard hall had been out of use as such for 30 years and two of the shops were unlet. The plaintiffs had not tried for some time to let or sell; the site was regarded as ripe for redevelopment. By negligence of a servant of the defendants the property caught fire and was damaged. The plaintiffs claimed damages assessed at the amount which it would cost to reinstate the premises, though they were never rebuilt.

HELD: The two basic principles were that (1) damages awarded against a tortfeasor shall be such as will, so far as money can, put the plaintiff in the same position as he would have been had the tort not occurred, but (2) the damages to be awarded are to be reasonable as between the plaintiff on the one hand and the defendant on the other. The plaintiffs had been holding on to the property merely for its development value which lay in the site itself, not the buildings. It would be totally unrealistic as well as unreasonable as between the plaintiffs and the defendants to award the notional cost of reinstating the premises. The measure of damages was the diminution in the value of the property assessed at £2,500 but as it would have cost the plaintiffs more than that to clear the site for redevelopment they were entitled to nothing in respect of that head of damage.

Moss v Christchurch RDC distinguished

Hollebone v Midhurst
[1968] 1 Lloyd's Rep 38 (Norman Richards Esq QC, Official Referee)

The plaintiffs' house was damaged by fire caused by the negligence of the second defendants. The cost of making good the damage was £18,991. The difference in value between the pre-fire value and the value after the fire was £14,850. It was urged on behalf of the defendants that the right measure of damage was the difference in value ie £14,850, not the cost of making good.

HELD: On the authorities there was no firm rule that the diminution in value is the correct measure of damage. In *The Susquehanna* [1926] AC 655 Lord Dunedin said no rigid rule or rules apply and one must consider all the relevant circumstances. These must depend on such matters as the interest which the injured party had in what is damaged, the purpose for which it is used and whether its life is likely to be short or long. In the present case where the property was of a nature that comparable properties were few and far between the cost of repair was the correct measure of damage as providing fair and proper restitution for the damage sustained.

The question remained whether an allowance should be made for 'betterment' on the basis of substitution of new material for old. If an allowance of new for old must always be made this may well prevent a plaintiff from being fairly compensated. It was conceded that the old rafters and floors would have lasted out the life of the house so there could be no betterment for those. In the case of new electrical wiring it had deferred the need for this for 15 to 20 years and there was some benefit to the plaintiffs in this. But it was not a case in which it would be fair to deduct it from the cost of repair.

Damaged machine

Bacon v Cooper (Metals) Ltd
[1982] 1 All ER 397 (Cantley J)
In the course of the plaintiff's business as a scrap metal dealer he used a large and expensive machine, called a fragmentiser, for the purpose of reducing scrap metal to fragments. He purchased a consignment of metal from the defendants which, in breach of the contract of sale, contained a large lump of steel. The rotor of the machine was broken by it and had to be replaced by a new one, costing £41,000. No secondhand rotors were available. A rotor lasted seven years; at the time of the damage the plaintiff's rotor had been in use three and a quarter years. The defendant's contended that the plaintiff ought to give credit for three and a quarter years' use, reducing the claim to £22,232.
HELD: Not so. Each case should depend on its own facts. There was no certainty that the plaintiff would have needed to buy a new rotor at the end of another three and a quarter years if there had been no damage. After that time the fragmentiser may be out of date or the plaintiff may be using a different process or have died or retired from business. It would be wrong to charge the defendants for the whole cost if the damaged rotor had, say, only three months of the seven years to run, but that was not the case. The plaintiff was entitled to recover the whole cost of the replacement rotor.

Irreplaceable loss

Uctkos v Mazetta
[1956] 1 Lloyd's Rep 209 (Ormerod J)
An Admiral's Barge constructed in America was sold after the war in 1947 by the Admiralty for £600. The owner did work on it and it was moored in the Thames at Isleworth and used for visits at weekends. A painter and decorator known to the owner visited it as a purely social arrangement, and helped to recondition the ship presumably in the hope that he would be allowed some use of it. By his negligence on 2 May 1952, the ship was destroyed. The owner claimed £5,000 as the cost of purchasing another ship or replacing it. The ship was quite an unusual type and was irreplaceable. Evidence was given by an agent for the disposal of craft by the Admiralty after the war of the sale of four other ships of a comparatively similar design and construction and performance, that the value of the ship was about £750.
HELD: The owner was not entitled to damages on the basis of the replacement of his ship, but to the reasonable cost of another craft which reasonably meets his needs and in reasonably the same condition. Judgment for £800 plus £108 for fittings.

Note—See also *O'Grady v Westminster Scaffolding Ltd*, p 381, above.

LOSS OF USE

Note—See also *Watson Norie Ltd v Shaw*, p 379, above.

The Mediana

[1900] AC 113, 69 LJP 35, 82 LT 95

The owner of a chattel who is wrongfully deprived of its use may recover substantial damages for the deprivation, though he may have incurred no out of pocket expenses consequent thereon.

'Nominal damages' is a technical phrase, which means that you have negatived anything like real damage, but that you are affirming by your nominal damages that there is an infraction of a legal right, which, though it gives you no right to any real damages at all, yet gives you a right to the verdict or judgment because your legal right has been infringed. But the term 'nominal damages' does not mean small damages: Per Lord Halsbury LC.

Note—See also *The Hebridean Coast*, p 387, below.

Caxton Publishing Co v Sutherland Publishing Co

[1939] AC 178, [1938] 4 All ER 389 (Lord Porter)

Even the loss of the use for a time of a chattel which the owner would not have used during that time may give rise to substantial damages, whether in an action for damages or in any action for conversion.

McAll v Brooks

[1984] RTR 99, CA

The plaintiff had a comprehensive insurance policy in respect of his car with a £50 policy excess. The insurance brokers offered, and he accepted, membership of a scheme whereby for a payment of £5 per annum he would be entitled to the use of a car if his own car was damaged and out of use. In an accident for which the defendant was wholly to blame the plaintiff's car was damaged and, as arranged, he was supplied by the brokers with a car for three weeks. A reasonable hire charge for such a car was £328. In proceedings against the defendant in which he claimed the amount of the excess and £328 as the measure of damages for loss of use the county court judge awarded £50 for the excess but held that he was not entitled to the £328 because (1) he had not lost it, (2) the £5 scheme was insurance business and therefore illegal under the Insurance Companies Act 1974 and there was no right of subrogation; (3) the plaintiff's contract under the scheme was tainted with illegality.

HELD, ON APPEAL: The plaintiff was entitled to recover the sum of £328. It had been accepted that the plaintiff had needed a car when his own was off the road and that £328 was a reasonable hire charge. Following *Donnelly v Joyce* (p 412, below) the plaintiff's need of a car had to be paid for by the wrongdoer and £328 was to cover that need. If the scheme was tainted with illegality and the plaintiff had been a knowing party to that illegality he could not recover, but this was not the case. If there was any taint of illegality on the part of the brokers it was not the concern of the plaintiff. The court was not concerned to consider what the plaintiff was going to do with his money or whether he owed any legal or moral obligation to the brokers or any other third party.

Dixons (Scholar Green) Ltd v Cooper
[1970] RTR 222, 114 Sol Jo 319, CA

The plaintiffs claimed £589 for loss of use of their 9-ton lorry. This figure comprised £1,189 average deficiency in turnover for 11 weeks during which it was off the road for repair less sums for wear and tear, running costs and wages plus further sums for depreciation etc. The defendants though admitting liability contested the figures. The judge said it was for the plaintiffs to establish their financial loss and they had failed to do so to his satisfaction: he accordingly awarded nominal damages of £2.

HELD, ON APPEAL: This could not be right. This was a valuable vehicle in constant demand and it had been off the road 11 weeks. There were difficulties in arriving at an exact figure but having heard the plaintiffs' evidence (the defendants called none) it was the duty of the judge to make the best he could out of the evidence and choose a figure which was a reasonable estimate of the damage suffered by the plaintiffs. The amount awarded, on examination of the figures, should be £450.

Griffin & Co Ltd v De-La-Haye and De-La-Haye Contractors
[1968] 2 Lloyd's Rep 253 (Paull J)

The plaintiff's vehicle was damaged in an accident by the defendants' negligence on 8 November 1966. The plaintiff's solicitors wrote to the defendants on 15 November saying the vehicle was considered to be a 'write-off' but offering an inspection. The defendants' insurers did not reply but their engineer inspected the vehicle in January 1967: he told them it was a 'write-off'. Despite further letters from the plaintiff's solicitors the insurers made no reply to them until 11 May 1967 when they agreed the vehicle was a total loss. Meanwhile the plaintiff had been hiring a vehicle at £12 per week.

HELD: The question was to decide what was a reasonable time after which the plaintiff ought to have mended his vehicle or bought another. The appropriate date was 8 April even though by then he had not heard from the insurance company. The defendants' insurers could not complain in view of their failure to answer the plaintiff's solicitors' letters.

Public authorities

The Greta Holme
[1897] AC 596, 66 LJP 166, 77 LT 231, 13 TLR 552, HL

A steam dredger belonging to trustees was damaged and the trustees were deprived of the use of it for some weeks and the dredging works were delayed. The trustees were charged with the duty of maintaining a harbour and waterway, deriving their funds from rates and not entitled to distribute profits.

HELD: Though the trustees were not out of pocket in any definite sum they were entitled to recover damages for the loss of use of the dredger.

The Hebridean Coast
[1961] AC 545, [1961] 1 All ER 82, 104 Sol Jo 37, [1960] 2 Lloyd's Rep 423, HL

The plaintiffs' vessel was damaged by the defendants'. Liability was admitted. The plaintiffs were the Central Electricity Generating Board, who do not trade for profit, and whose sea-borne coal was carried, as to about one-half in the Board's own ships, and as to the remainder in chartered ships. The damaged vessel was detained for repairs $11\frac{1}{2}$ days as a result of the accident. She would not have been idle but for the damage, but no vessel specifically replaced her by carrying coal which she would have carried: her carrying capacity during the period of detention represented only one thousandth part of the tonnage required by the plaintiffs in the current six months' period. On a claim for damages for loss of use based on freight payable for chartering alternative tonnage:

HELD, ON APPEAL to the House of Lords: The evidence did not establish that the appellants chartered any tonnage to replace the damaged vessel and the claim to special damage must fail. A claim for general damages for loss of use to be ascertained by reference to the sums which the appellants were paying for chartered tonnage as a matter of regular practice could not succeed because general damages could not be awarded for some kind of harm which the shipowners could not prove they had sustained. The appellants were entitled to general damages on the principle which derives from the *Greta Holme* case (p 387, above) of assessing damages on the basis of interest on the value of the damaged vessel.

BUS CASES; REPLACEMENT VEHICLE

Birmingham Corporation v Sowsbery
[1970] RTR 84, 113 Sol Jo 877 (Geoffrey Lane J)

The plaintiff's omnibus was out of use for 69 days for repairs following a collision. They claimed as special damages the cost of maintaining a spare fleet omnibus for 69 days at £4 11s per day.

HELD: (1) If the plaintiffs had hired a replacement vehicle they could have claimed the cost of hire as special damages but as a non-profit making body not needing to hire another vehicle different considerations applied and the claim was one for general not special damage. The maintenance of a stand-by fleet was reasonable and necessary and the whole fleet including the stand-bys must be taken as being in operation at any one time. The plaintiffs had been deprived of the use of a valuable chattel during the relevant period and were entitled to substantial (ie not nominal) general damages for the loss of use. (2) There were two possible methods of arriving at a proper figure to compensate the plaintiffs (a) the cost of maintaining and operating the damaged vehicle (excluding running charges) on the assumption that this figure must represent approximately the value of the vehicle to the operators where the concern is non-profit making, or (b) interest on capital value of the vehicle and depreciation, as in *The Hebridean Coast* (above). If the latter method were used a proper rate of interest to take would be 7% on the value of the bus at the material time plus a sum for depreciation. But this method suffers from possible variations in capital value and interest rates. It is important that there should be as much consistency as possible between awards of general damages. In the present case where £4 11s per day was agreed as an accurate estimate of the standing charges of such a vehicle run by a reasonably efficient organisation the first method of assessment was a proper solution of the problem. Judgment for £313 19s being 60 days at £4 11s per day.

Note—In an unreported case, *Manchester Corpn v Campbell* (Oliver J at Manchester Assizes, 27 April 1950), summarised and discussed in the *Post Magazine* for 31

March 1956, the plaintiffs claimed damages for loss of use of a trolleybus damaged in an accident. The claim was for 90 days at £3 4s 9d per day calculated in accordance with the formula prepared by the Financial Officers' Section of the Municipal Passenger Transport Association. The formula provides for taking the total working expenses of the undertaking and deducting from these the actual cost of running the vehicles on the road. Capital charges in respect of buses and buildings and depreciation of plant and equipment relating to the running of the buses are then added. The total divided by 365 and by the number of buses in the fleet established a figure for the 'charge per day'. This figure multiplied by the number of days' loss of use gives the amount of the claim. The judge accepted the formula and his decision in this respect was not upset on appeal (16 January 1951). The formula is still in use though the amounts are of course now very different.

ADDITIONAL DAMAGE DUE TO DANGEROUS LOAD

Pickfords Ltd v Perma Products Ltd
(1947) 80 Ll L Rep 513 (Hilbery J)
Carriers contracted to carry goods which were dangerous because highly inflammable and the owners of the goods indemnified the carriers against damage arising from the carriage of the goods. In transit the lorry caught fire and because of the inflammable load became a total loss.

The lorry owners claimed under the indemnity for the value of the lorry and for loss of use at £12 per week until the vehicle was replaced a year later under a Ministry of Transport licence. The judge estimated the damage to the lorry if it had not had a dangerous load at £150 and that it would take eight weeks to repair. He allowed the balance of the value of the lorry, and loss of use for the year, less the eight weeks, at £12 per week, ie £614 claimed, less £96, net £518, plus £200 net for the lorry, total £718.

INCOME TAX

Herring v British Transport Commission
[1958] TR 401, 37 ATC 382 (Donovan J)
A lorry owner sued for loss of use claiming that he lost £12 per week profit on the vehicle whilst it was out of use for seven weeks. The defendants contended that tax should be deducted.
HELD: Income tax is not imposed upon particular items in a business account of profits. The £12 per week is not the profit of a business, but is simply the excess of earnings over expenses attributable to one particular use in a mixed business of haulage, scrap dealing, and dealing in vehicles; and when merged with all the other incomings and outgoings of the entire business, it might increase the profits of that business or it might mitigate the loss on the rest of the business. It is a taxable receipt of the plaintiff's business and the rule in *Gourley's* case (p 429, below) does not apply.

Diamond v Campbell-Jones
[1961] Ch 22, [1960] 1 All ER 583, [1960] 2 WLR 586, 104 Sol Jo 249, [1960] TLR 131, 53 R & IT 502 (Buckley J)
In a case in which a dealer in real property claimed damages for breach of a contract for sale of a house which he intended to convert, it was held that he was entitled to a sum equal to the amount of the profit which he would likely to have made. The damages he recovered were liable to attract tax as

part of the profits or gains of his business: *Gourley's* case was distinguished on the grounds that in that case it was conceded that no part of the sum awarded as damages would be subject to tax.

Pryce v Elwood
(1964) 108 Sol Jo 583 (Fenton Atkinson J)

The plaintiff's car which he used for hire-work, was damaged by the defendant's negligence and was out of use for 30 weeks for repair. He claimed damages including an item for loss of trading profit during the period while his car was being repaired. The defendant claimed that a deduction should be made for tax on the profit lost.

HELD: As the damages for loss of profit must be entered in the plaintiff's profit and loss account he would in due course be assessed to tax on them. It would thus be wrong to deduct the amount of the tax in assessing the damages. *Gourley's* case was different in that it was agreed that the damages awarded there would not be subject to tax. *Diamond v Campbell-Jones* (above) followed.

London and Thames Haven Oil Wharves Ltd v Attwooll
[1967] 1 Ch 772, [1967] 2 All ER 124, [1967] 2 WLR 743, 110 Sol Jo 979, CA

A jetty was damaged as a result of negligent navigation of a ship. It was out of use 380 days as a result. The jetty owners recovered damages of which £21,000 was in respect of use of the jetty. They were assessed to tax on the £21,000 under case 1 of Schedule D.

HELD, ON APPEAL: They were rightly assessed. If the damages a trader receives from another person pursuant to a legal right (whether in contract or tort) includes a sum to compensate him for losing money, which, if it had been received would have been credited to the amount of profits arising in any year from the trade carried on by him the compensation is to be treated in the same way for tax purposes as that sum of money would have been had it not been lost. The £21,000 was compensation for the loss of amounts the company would have received from customers for use of the jetty less the expenses they would have incurred in earning those sums during the 380 days. Such amounts would have been credited to profits and the £21,000 was to be treated for income tax purposes in the same way.

Note—Applied in *Raja's Commercial College v Gian Singh & Co Ltd* [1977] AC 312, [1976] 2 All ER 801, [1976] 3 WLR 58, 120 Sol Jo 404, PC

DAMAGES IN FOREIGN CURRENCY

Note—It was formerly the rule that a claim in damages must be made in sterling and the judgment given in sterling. In *Miliangos v George Frank (Textiles) Ltd* [1976] AC 443, [1975] 3 All ER 801 the House of Lords departed from this rule to the extent of holding that in an action for the recovery of money due under a contract (e g the price of goods sold) the court has power to give judgment for payment of the money in a foreign currency. The question whether the same rule should apply to claims for damages for breach of contract or for tort was expressly left open. In an action of tort the question came before the House of Lords in the following case.

The Despina R
[1979] 1 Lloyd's Rep 1, HL
After a collision in which two ships were damaged the owners of one of them incurred expenses of temporary and permanent repairs and other services which had to be paid for in various foreign currencies. All payments were made from a US dollar account in New York; all the expenses incurred in the foreign currencies other that US dollars were met by transferring US dollars from that account. The Court of Appeal, in an action claiming the amount of the expenses from the owners of the negligent vessel, held that the *Miliangos* case entitled the Court to abrogate the former rule and give the money judgment in currency other than sterling.
HELD, ON APPEAL to the House of Lords: An English court had the power to give judgment or make an award in foreign currency. Applying the normal principles in tort of *restitutio in integrum* and reasonable foreseeablility of damage, the award should be made in the 'plaintiff's currency', namely, the currency in which the loss was effectively felt by him, having regard to the currency in which he generally operated or with which he had the closest connection.

Hoffman v Sofaer
[1982] 1 WLR 1350, 126 Sol Jo 611 (Talbot J)
The plaintiff was an American citizen who was injured by negligent medical treatment when on a visit to England. Damages for pain and suffering were assessed at £19,000. The remainder of the damages comprising special damage and future loss related mainly to loss of earnings and future loss as president of a company in the USA, where he lived.
HELD (applying *The Despina R* (above)): The question was: with what currency was the plaintiff's loss closely linked? All the losses in effect for which damages had been awarded other than for pain and suffering were closely linked with the currency of his country, namely, dollars. To meet his losses he would have to pay in dollars: the judgment would be in US dollars with the exception of the £19,000.

INTEREST ON DAMAGES

Note—The Law Reform (Miscellaneous Provisions) Act 1934, s 3 (set out at p 435, below) empowers the court to award interest on damages for which judgment is given. This section has been superseded as from 1 April 1983, so far as it applied to the High Court and county courts, by respectively the Supreme Court Act 1981, s 35A and the County Courts Act 1959, s 97A (now the County Courts Act 1984, s 69). See pp 435–436, below. Section 3 of the 1934 Act (including the subsections added by the Administration of Justice Act 1969, s 22) remains in force in respect of other courts of record, e g the Court of Appeal. Except in cases where judgment is given for damages for personal injuries or death exceeding £200 the award of interest is not mandatory but is at the discretion of the court. The following cases refer to damage claims. For personal injury cases see pp 435–442, below.

Interest: plaintiff insured

Harbutt's Plasticine v Wayne Tank and Pump Co Ltd
[1970] 1 QB 447, [1970] 1 All ER 225, [1970] 2 WLR 198, 114 Sol Jo 29, CA

The plaintiffs' factory was burned down on 6 February 1963. On 8 November 1968 the defendants were held liable and judgment given against them for £146,581 damages. The plaintiffs applied for interest under the 1934 Act. They had received various payments from time to time before trial totalling £143,658 from their insurers who would now be reimbursed. The judge said that in exercising his power to award interest he could not ignore the fact that the plaintiffs had not been kept of all their money until that date but had had their loss reduced by periodical payments from their insurers. He awarded three years' interest on the whole sum at an agreed rate of 6%.

HELD, ON APPEAL: The judge had applied the right principle but had done so rather unscientifically. The basis of the award of interest is that the defendant has kept the plaintiff out of his money, but this reasoning does not apply when he had in fact been indemnified by an insurance company. The judge should award interest from the date when the defendants should have paid the money but only on the balance remaining after payment had been received from the insurers.

Cousins & Co Ltd v D and C Carriers Ltd
[1971] 2 QB 230, [1971] 1 All ER 55, [1971] 2 WLR 85, 114 Sol Jo 882, [1970] 2 Lloyd's Rep 397, CA

In an action for damages for loss of goods a claim was made for interest. The Master awarded interest from the date when the plaintiffs would have been paid if the goods had not been lost until the date when their insurers paid them in full the amount of their loss. The plaintiffs appealed. The defendants said the point was decided beyond argument by *Harbutt's* case (above).

HELD: *Harbutt's* case was decided on the basis, not argued, that the interest would be retained by the plaintiff and not handed over together with the damages to the insurers. In the present case the question had been raised whether interest awarded for the period after the plaintiffs had been indemnified by their insurers could be retained by the plaintiffs or could be claimed by the insurers by subrogation. On the authorities and in particular Brett LJ's wide statement of principle in *Castellain v Preston* (see p 879, below) any recovery of interest after the date of payment under the policy could be claimed by the insurers. It followed that interest should not be limited to the period up to the date of indemnity.

Gardner Steel Ltd v Sheffield Brothers (Profiles) Ltd
[1978] 3 All ER 399, [1978] 1 WLR 916, 122 Sol Jo 488, CA

An order that a plaintiff is entitled to summary judgment under RSC Ord 14 is the determination of an issue and, as such, is a trial. It is therefore a proceeding 'tried in any court of record for the recovery of any debt or damages' for the purposes of the Law Reform (Miscellaneous Provisions) Act 1934, s 3 and the judge or master has jurisdiction to award interest.

Note—This decision now has statutory recognition in High Court cases by the Supreme Court Act 1981, s 35A.

Vehicle and General Insurance Co Ltd v Christie
[1976] 1 All ER 747, QBD
The plaintiffs claimed from the defendants, insurance brokers, money received for insurance premiums. After proceedings were started by writ which included a claim for interest the parties agreed in March 1975, that the amount of premiums due was £314.30. The plaintiffs asked for interest on the agreed amount. The defendants refused saying interest was not payable unless there was a judgment. They paid £314.30 into court. The plaintiffs took the action to trial in October 1975.
HELD: The plaintiffs were entitled to interest and should have the costs of the whole action before and after payment in. Lord Denning had said in *Jefford v Gee* (p 437, below) that a plaintiff who thought the amount paid into court was enough would tell the defendant he was disposed to go to trial to collect the interest. He would not have said this if he thought the plaintiff must necessarily pay all the costs after payment in. The court had discretion as regards costs and where, as here, the parties had come to court on the issue of interest, the amount in court not being in dispute, justice required the discretion to be exercised in the plaintiff's favour.

Note—The claim not comprising damages in respect of personal injuries, the award of interest was not mandatory.

PLEADING CLAIM FOR INTEREST

RSC Ord 18, r 8 reads: 'A party must plead specifically any claim for interest under section 35A of the Act [Supreme Court Act 1981] or otherwise.' See also County Court Rules, Ord 6, r 1A and *Ward v Chief Constable of Avon* (1985) Times, 7 June, CA.

Income tax on interest

The Norseman
[1957] P 224, [1957] 2 All ER 660, 101 Sol Jo 556, [1957] 1 Lloyd's Rep 503 (Lord Merriman P)
The principle is that the payor must ascertain the amount of the deduction for tax, and notify the payee of the deduction and pay him the residue. Otherwise the payor will be taken to have made the payment without deduction. The same principle applies to a payment into court, and therefore where a payment into court includes interest, the form of payment in should make it clear that the money paid in is the residue after deduction of tax on the interest.

Westminster Bank v Riches
[1945] Ch 381, [1945] 1 All ER 466, 114 LJCh 307, 173 LT 148, CA
One partner brought proceedings against the legal personal representative of the other partner for balance of half share of profits fraudulently withheld, and recovered £36,255 and £10,028 interest at 4% under s 3 of the 1934 Act from 14 June 1936, to 14 May 1943. The legal personal representative deducted £5,014 for income tax, claiming it was 'interest of money' under the Income Tax Act 1918, Sch. D, and paid £5,014 in satisfaction of the judgment of £10,028 for interest.
HELD: Entitled to do so; the 1934 Act has not introduced any new principle for interest on a debt.

Per Morton LJ: I doubt whether any distinction can be drawn between interest awarded upon a debt, and interest on damages.

Re Cooper
[1911] 2 KB 550, 80 LJKB 990, 105 LT 273; sub nom *Re Boulter* 55 Sol Jo 554, CA
A judgment debt, though by law carrying interest from the date of the judgment, was not a transaction to which the language of the Income Tax Acts relating to 'yearly interest on money' applied. The Acts exclude cases to which the Judgments Act 1838, applies, and interest on a final judgment is therefore not subject to deduction of tax.

Note—This decision was not referred to in *Riches'* case, presumably because in that case the interest was before judgment. In practice it seems accepted that income tax is not to be deducted from interest after judgment.

LOSS OF NO-CLAIMS BONUS

Ironfield v Eastern Gas Board
[1964] 1 All ER 544, [1964] 1 WLR 112, 108 Sol Jo 691 (Streatfeild J)
The plaintiff was driving his father-in-law's car when it collided with the defendants' lorry due to the defendants' negligence. He was injured and the car was damaged. In a claim for damages for his personal injuries he included a claim for £10 excess insurance and £15 for loss of no-claim bonus.
HELD: (1) The loss of 'no-claim bonus' was a real loss sustained by the assured, the father-in-law, and formed part of the damage which resulted from the accident. He should be put in the same position as if he had not made a claim under the policy at all. (2) Though they were items of loss suffered by the father-in-law and not the plaintiff there was no reason why they should not be dealt with in this action and awarded to the plaintiff on his undertaking to pay them over to his father-in-law.

LOSS OF PREMIUM

Patel v London Transport Executive
[1981] RTR 29, CA
Only a week or so after the plaintiff had paid £222.75 for a year's full comprehensive insurance, his car was damaged beyond repair by negligence of the defendants. He claimed under his policy and his insurers paid him the total loss value of the car. It was a term of the policy that on settlement of a claim on a total loss basis all benefits of the insurance would terminate as from the date of the accident without return of premium. The plaintiff claimed from the defendants £218.47 being the balance of the year's premium from the date of the accident. It was acknowledged by the defendants that the term of the policy was a usual one.
HELD: The plaintiff was entitled to succeed. He had acted reasonably in claiming under his policy instead of incurring the greater delay and expense of claiming for his loss directly against the defendants. The claim

on the policy was foreseeable by the defendants; therefore the loss following from that claim was foreseeable. The case was analogous with *Ironfield v Eastern Gas Board* (above) which was rightly decided.

PROOF OF DAMAGES

Bonham-Carter v Hyde Park Hotel
[1948] WN 89, 64 TLR 177, 92 Sol Jo 154 (Lord Goddard CJ)
Plaintiffs must understand that if they bring actions for damages it is for them to prove their damage; it is not enough to write down the particulars, and, so to speak, throw them at the head of the court, saying: 'This is what I have lost; I ask you to give me these damages.'

Thatcher v Littlejohn
[1978] RTR 369, CA
The plaintiff's car was damaged beyond economic repair in a collision for which the defendant admitted liability. Evidence was given by an engineer that the retail price of such a car at that age would be £795 plus something more for the hardtop and low mileage. The plaintiff had accepted £775 from his insurers. He was unable to find a similar car at less than £875. The county court judge said the correct approach was how much the car was likely to fetch on the open market and assessed the pre-accident value at £700.
HELD, ON APPEAL: This was wrong for two reasons: (1) the correct approach was what would it have cost the plaintiff to put himself back in the position in which he was immediately before the accident, and (2) there was no evidence at all to support the judge's assessment. It should have been based on the evidence, which was all one way. The further argument that the figure of £75 or so was not sufficient to induce the appellate court to interfere could not stand where, as here, the value was a matter of actual figures before the court.

Ashcroft v Curtin
[1971] 3 All ER 1208, [1971] 1 WLR 1731, 115 Sol Jo 687, CA
The plaintiff, a self-employed precision engineer, ran his own business which had a staff of six. He received injuries which disabled him permanently for some activities and might well have a damaging effect on the business. There was evidence which pointed to a decline in the profits. The plaintiff had no skill at bookkeeping and his accounts, as the judge found, were rudimentary and unreliable, but he awarded him £10,500 for estimated financial loss. The defendant appealed, contending that as there were no reliable accounts the award for that item should be nil.
HELD: Whilst it was probable that there had been some loss of profitability it was quite impossible to quantify it and make an award for it. But as there was a risk, though slight, that the plaintiff might at some time be thrown on to the labour market and because of his injuries be unable to do the work for which he had been trained an award of £2,500 for that possibility should be substituted for the item of £10,500.

Macrae v H. G. Swindells
[1954] 2 All ER 260, [1954] 1 WLR 597, 98 Sol Jo 233 (Barry J)
A garage negligently or by breach of contract damaged a customer's car which was with the garage for repairs. The garage lent the customer another car till it was properly repaired. The customer's servant negligently drove the lent car and it was destroyed in an accident. The garage obtained judgment against the customer for the value of the lent car. No other car was offered by the garage and the customer hired another car till he received his car back and sued the garage for the amount of the hire charges incurred.
HELD: The hire was the result of the negligence or breach of contract of the garage and not the result of the negligence of the customer's servant; the reason the lent car ceased to be available was irrelevant.

Jackson v Chrysler Acceptances Ltd
[1978] RTR 474, CA
In April the plaintiff took a new car on hire purchase from the defendants. He made it clear to the defendants' agents, who supplied the car, that he intended using it for a four weeks' holiday in France in July with his family. In the course of the first few months' use, including the holiday, the car developed numerous defects, some serious. The plaintiff complained on numerous occasions and work was done by the agents including supplying new parts without charge. During the holiday the engine overheated and lacked acceleration, a sun visor snapped off and there were other faults. The car was in the agents' hands for three weeks for overhaul on its return. In county court proceedings the judge held that the car 'was not fit for its purpose and was not of merchantable quality' but that having used the car for several months the plaintiff could not have the contract rescinded. He awarded £200 damages for the general shortfall in the quality of the car below what was properly to be expected and £75 for the detrimental effect on the plaintiff's holiday in France.
HELD, ON APPEAL: The damages awarded were much too low. To assess damages one had to look to see what would have been the fair market price for that car at the time of the hire-purchase contract if the inherent defects had been known to the vendor and the purchaser. In the case of the holiday the question was one of degree: how much was spoiled? On the facts, substantially greater compensation was called for than the £75 awarded. Without segregating the two elements the award would be increased to £750.

Commercial vehicles

The *Commercial Motor* publishes annually a book of tables of operating costs for all types of commercial vehicle, petrol, oil, steam and electric goods and passenger carrying, based upon prevailing costs. The publishers are Temple Press Limited of Bowling Green Lane, London EC 1.

These tables afford a basis of calculating in claims for loss of use.

CHAPTER 12
Damages: personal injuries

PRINCIPLES — MEASURE OF DAMAGES

H West & Son Ltd v Shephard
[1964] AC 326, [1963] 2 All ER 625, [1963] 2 WLR 1359, 107 Sol Jo 454, HL
The damages which are to be awarded for a tort are those which 'so far as

money can compensate, will give the injured party reparation for the wrongful act and for all the natural and direct consequences of the wrongful act' (*Admiralty Comrs v Susquehanna (Owners), The Susquehanna*). The words 'so far as money can compensate' point to the impossibility of equating money with human suffering or personal deprivations. A money award can be calculated so as to make good a financial loss. Money may be awarded so that something tangible may be procured to replace something else of like nature which has been destroyed or lost. But money cannot renew a physical frame that has been battered and shattered. All that judges and courts can do is to award sums which must be regarded as giving reasonable compensation. In the process there must be the endeavour to secure some uniformity in the general method of approach. By common assent awards must be reasonable and must be assessed with moderation. Furthermore, it is eminently desirable that so far as possible comparable injuries should be compensated by comparable awards: per Lord Morris of Borth-y-Gest.

The practice of the courts hitherto has been to treat bodily injury as a deprivation which in itself entitles a plaintiff to substantial damages according to its gravity. In *Phillips v London & South Western Rly Co*, Cockburn CJ, in enumerating the heads of damage which the jury must take into account and in respect of which a plaintiff is entitled to compensation said:

'These are the bodily injury sustained; the pain undergone: the effect on the health of the sufferer according to its degree and its probable duration as likely to be temporary or permanent; the expenses incidental to attempts to effect a cure or to lessen the amount of the injury; the pecuniary loss. . . .'

In *Rose v Ford* Lord Roche said: 'I regard impaired health and vitality not merely as a cause of pain and suffering but as a loss of a good thing in itself.' If a plaintiff has lost a leg, the court approaches the matter on the basis that he had suffered a serious physical deprivation no matter what his condition or temperament or state of mind may be. That deprivation may also create future economic loss which is added to the assessment. Past and prospective pain and discomfort increase the assessment. If there is loss of amenity apart from the obvious and normal loss inherent in the deprivation of the limb — if, for instance, the plaintiff's main interest in life was some sport or hobby from which he will in future be debarred, that too increases the assessment. If there is a particular injury to the nervous system, that also increases the assessment. So too with other personal and subjective matters that fall to be decided in the light of common sense in particular cases. These considerations are not dealt with as separate items but are taken into account by the court in fixing one inclusive sum for general damages: per Lord Pearce.

Itemising heads of damage

Watson v Powles
[1968] 1 QB 596, [1967] 3 All ER 721, [1967] 3 WLR 1364, 111 Sol Jo 562, CA
The plaintiff was awarded £8,000 general damages for personal injuries sustained when he was knocked down by a motor scooter. There was a serious permanent disability as well as a continuing loss of earnings at £400 per annum.

HELD, ON APPEAL: It was urged on the plaintiff's behalf that the judge ought to have split up the items of general damage indicating how much for past pain and suffering, how much for past and how much for future loss of earnings. The Court of Appeal rejected the suggestion: an award of damages for personal injuries was essentially a composite one. Though every judge no doubt noted down and calculated what he thought was fair for the various items of damage it was necessary eventually to award a composite general sum because of the many intangibles involved. It was for the same reason undesirable that the award for future loss of earnings should be worked out from actuarial evidence.

Note—See next case.

Kirby v Vauxhall Motors

(1969) 113 Sol Jo 736, CA

On an appeal against the amount of an award of damages for personal injuries the question was raised how far damages should be itemised by a judge in his award and how far an appeal lay against individual items. Lord Denning MR said lest there should be any misunderstanding of his judgment in *Watson v Powles* (above) he would say at once that itemisation was often useful and desirable (1) because the judge had then himself to apply his mind to the various items and show that he had done so and (2) because it was a great help to the Court of Appeal in computing the overall figure. So judges should not be discouraged from itemising by anything said in *Watson*'s case. But the items having been stated and analysed, they still had to be brought together in one award which was fair, reasonable and comparable to other awards in like cases.

Note—The mandatory award of interest on damages normally calls for itemisation.

George v Pinnock

[1973] 1 All ER 926, [1973] 1 WLR 118, 117 Sol Jo 73, CA

Per Sachs LJ: Whatever may have been the differing judicial views up to a few years ago and indeed up to 1970 as to whether a judge should simply award a global sum or whether he should state in his judgment what are the main components in that figure, the modern practice . . . is to adopt the second course. . . . [The] plaintiff and defendant alike are entitled to know what is the sum assessed for each relevant head of damage and thus be able on appeal to challenge any error in the assessments. . . . It is of course always open to a respondent to do something which was not done here; that is, to give a cross-notice [of appeal] that even if one head as awarded by the judge is held to be demonstrably too low, some other head is demonstrably too high and thus seek to produce what is sometimes called a swings and roundabouts position. In other circumstances it seems to me that a court should normally be slow to deal with an appeal on such a basis.

Smith v Manchester City Council

(1974) 118 Sol Jo 597, 17 KIR 1, CA

Per Edmund Davies LJ: Now that the assessment of general damages is required to be divided into damages for pain and suffering and loss of amenities on the one hand and future financial loss on the other I think the two matters have to be considered separately. In the result if the award under one head is clearly wrong it should be interfered with even though ultimately there may be no very substantial variation in the global award.

Adding up heads of damage

Fletcher v Autocar and Transporters Ltd
[1968] 2 QB 322, [1968] 1 All ER 726, [1968] 2 WLR 743, 112 Sol Jo 96, CA
The plaintiff, a quantity surveyor aged 56, was seriously injured in a motor accident. Head injuries had so seriously affected his mental capacity that he had little thought or feeling, was incapable of looking after himself and would never be able to work again. He was partly paralysed. He was dependent on his wife for everyday care but in three years or so would have to go into an institution for the rest of his life. His expectation of life was not reduced and was about 16 years. Before the accident he had been leading a very full and active life. He had an income from his profession of £4,000 a year, tax paid, and spent all of it. He had no savings and would have continued at work at least to the age of 69. At trial the judge assessed the following main heads of damage: (1) special damage £10,000; (2) future loss of earnings after allowing for tax and calculating the loss actuarily as a lump sum, £32,000; (3) additional expense (ie expense he would not have incurred but for the accident) in the future comprising the cost of being looked after by his wife for the next three years and then for the rest of his life at an institution, less a saving on food and laundry at home, £14,000; (4) pain and suffering and loss of amenities £10,000. He added them up and awarded £66,000 damages.
HELD, ON APPEAL: The judge had awarded too much. He was wrong to take each item separately and then just add them up at the end. There is a risk of overlapping if the items are just added up. The plaintiff had spent his income on the pleasures of living and on recreations such as golf, fishing and shooting without saving anything. It was fair to compensate him for the loss of these but not unless account was taken of the fact that he had to pay for them. He should not therefore have been given his full loss of earnings. Another way of looking at it was to say that he should not be given both the full cost of his keep at the institution and also his full salary, for that would mean that he would be saving full salary and spending nothing. Award reduced to £51,000.

Harris v Harris
[1973] 1 Lloyd's Rep 445, CA
The plaintiff was 14 when injured in a road accident. The main damage was to her brain: though she had been able after the accident to complete her education and pass GCE examinations she would not be able to take up a career nor do ordinary domestic tasks, such as cooking. She would probably never marry. She was of good middle-class background and might, but for the injuries, have become a solicitor or civil servant. The judge awarded her £20,000 for pain and suffering and loss of amenities including loss of marriage prospects; £22,500 for loss of future earnings

(15 years at £1,500 p.a.); and £15,974 for the cost of a housekeeper when she would need a place to live of her own.

HELD, on the defendants' appeal: (1) The award of £20,000 for loss of amenities for life was justified. (2) £22,500 for loss of future earnings was too much. She might have married and not have been able to earn so much; damages for loss of marriage prospects were already compensated for in the first item; in any event she might not have earned for any great length of time. (3) On the third item there was doubt whether she would in fact set up in a flat of her own; having regard to the uncertain prospect and the amounts awarded for the other items the right figure for cost of future support was £6,000. It was very important where a judge was following the modern practice of sub-dividing the claim under various headings to avoid overlapping. There was here a serious overlap between the allowance made for loss of plaintiff's prospects of marriage on the one hand and loss of future earnings and the additional cost of domestic assistance on the other.

Moriarty v McCarthy
[1978] 2 All ER 213, [1978] 1 WLR 155, 121 Sol Jo 745 (O'Connor J)
In October 1973 the plaintiff sustained spinal injuries which resulted in complete loss of the power to move or feel from the waist down, with no control of bladder and bowel and no sexual sensation; she would be confined to a wheelchair for the rest of her life. She was then 20 years of age, 24 at the date of assessment of damages, living with her mother and sisters in the Republic of Ireland. Despite some training for sedentary work she had not shown herself capable of any gainful employment.
HELD: Her damages should be assessed under the following heads: (1) Future loss of earnings at a net figure of £1,820 per annum, applying a multiplier of 11 years = £20,000. The multiplier of 11 was taken instead of the 15 years' purchase which would be applicable in the case of a man of the same age so as to allow for the likelihood that the plaintiff would have married and ceased work at least for a number of years. (2) General damages £27,500 plus £7,500 to compensate her for the lost opportunity of marriage and the support of the husband = £35,000. (3) Resident domestic help from someone who would live in, a service that would probably be done many years by her mother, £1,000 per annum at 15 years' purchase = £15,000. (4) The cost of converting or adapting (not buying) an existing house in Ireland, say £8,000. (5) The cost of adapting a suitable car, but not buying one, £70. (6) The cost of future medical expenses in Ireland, £2,500. (7) Telephone on a 15-year multiplier, £820. (8) Agreed special damage, £9,896. The sum of £511 per annum which she was receiving from the Irish State should not be deducted: it was completely non-contributory and a wrongdoer should not have the benefit of it.

Hughes v McKeown
[1985] 3 All ER 284, 1 WLR 963 (Leonard J)
At four and a half years of age in 1973 the plaintiff was struck by the defendant's car and badly injured. Both her prospects of marriage and future earnings were diminished. The case came to trial in December 1984.
HELD: In *Moriarty*'s case (above) O'Connor J applying the decision in

Harris v Harris (p 400, above) had reduced the multiplier in respect of future earnings but had added a sum equal to that by which the future earnings award had been reduced to compensate for lost marriage prospects. In *Carrick v Camden London Borough Council* (unreported) he had adopted an approach from *Martin v Scott* (unreported) which was to consider the plaintiff's economic loss. The simplest method of assessing such loss was to use the multiplier applicable to a man and disregard the intervention of marriage altogether. The plaintiff's net annual loss of earnings was £2,812 and the appropriate multiplier, disregarding the possibility of the plaintiff marrying and having children was 17. This figure should be reduced to 14 to take into account the difficulty she would have in the current economic climate in getting employment.

Lim Poh Choo v Camden and Islington Area Health Authority
[1980] AC 174, [1979] 2 All ER 910, [1979] 3 WLR 44, HL

The plaintiff, after a minor surgical operation, suffered a cardiac arrest caused by the negligence of an employee of the defendants. Extensive and irremedial brain damage resulted leaving her only intermittently conscious, totally dependent on others and not able to appreciate what had happened to her. She was 36 years of age at the time of the incident; her life expectation was unaffected. The judge at first instance awarded £254,765. The defendants' appeals to the Court of Appeal and the House of Lords were dismissed but with small variations after hearing further evidence. On matters of principle—

HELD: (1) The sheer size of the total award was not a reason for reducing it. The burden on the public through insurance premiums or taxes or the availability of National Health Service care were matters for a legislator, not a judge. (2) The award of general damages for pain and suffering and loss of amenities at £20,000 was not too large, either on the ground that the plaintiff was unaware of what had happened to her or that she was not suffering any pain. *Wise v Kaye* (p 473, below) and *West v Shephard* (p 473, below) were rightly decided. Those cases drew a distinction between damages for pain and suffering and damages for loss of amenities. The latter are awarded for the fact of deprivation whether the plaintiff is aware of it or not. (3) It is right to award damages for actual and future loss of earnings, even in a catastrophic case, but care should be taken to avoid duplication or overlap with other heads of damage. Two deductions fall to be made, (a) the expenses of earning the income which has been lost and (b) from damages for the cost of caring for the plaintiff, the living expenses she would have incurred had she not been injured (*Shearman v Folland*, p 461, below). (4) Damages for cost of future care are recoverable but must be assessed on the basis that capital as well as income is to be used in meeting the cost. In the present case a multiplier of 12 applied to the annual cost of the plaintiff's care from date of judgment in the House of Lords would be fair. (5) Only in exceptional cases, where justice can be shown to require it, will the risk of future inflation be brought into account in assessing damages for future loss. It would be unrealistic to refuse to take inflation into account at all, but the better course in the great majority of cases is to disregard it. The victims of tort who receive a lump sum award are entitled to no better protection against inflation than others who have to rely on capital for their future support.

Details of award:	£
Pain, suffering, loss of amenities	20,000
Out of pocket expenses	3,596
Cost of care to date of judgment (HL)	22,689
Loss of earnings to date of trial	14,213
Cost of future care	76,800
Loss of future earnings (incl pension rights)	92,000

£229,298 plus interest

Note—In *Re Crowther & Nicholson Ltd* ((1981) 125 Sol Jo 529, Times, 10 June) directors claimed compensation for the balance of their service agreements, which provided for the company to pay inflation-proofed salaries, received annually. The judge said that in *Lim Poh Choo's* case Lord Scarman had said the correct approach was to assess damages without regard to future inflation, but in that case the claimant had no contractual right to protection against inflation. In the present case the service agreements did provide protection and this must be taken into account in assessing compensation.

Actuarial evidence undesirable

Mitchell v Mulholland (No 2)
[1972] 1 QB 65, [1971] 2 All ER 1205, [1971] 2 WLR 1271, 115 Sol Jo 227, [1971] 1 Lloyd's Rep 462, CA

As a result of a road accident the plaintiff aged 32 was so seriously injured that although his life expectation was normal he was totally unemployable and would have to remain permanently in a nursing home or similar institution. Before the accident he was a planning engineer at an aircraft factory earning about £22 per week. The judge awarded a total of £45,757 damages of which £17,570 was in respect of post-trial loss of earnings: he took a figure of £1,325 for the annual loss after allowing something for the prospects of promotion and multiplied by 14. On appeal it was argued that the judge should have fixed the number of years' purchase by actuarial calculation and that he was wrong in excluding evidence on the prospects and likely effect of inflation.

HELD: (1) Actuarial methods were unsatisfactory for assessing future loss since they may ensnare one into treating as virtual certainties what in truth are mere chances. The judge was right in adopting the conventional method of assessing the loss of the individual plaintiff in the light of experience applied to the particular case by seeking out an appropriate multiplier and multiplicand, though actuarial tables might supply a means of cross-checking the calculation. (2) Though it would be wrong to refuse to take inflation into account it does not follow that evidence specifically directed to the prospect of inflation should be admitted. There may be rare cases in which solid evidence regarding a particular plaintiff would justify the court in considering evidence of the likely impact of inflation on his future but this was not one of them. The judge was right in ruling as inadmissible evidence on the rate of inflation of prices and the effect of likely future increases in productivity per head of population.

Note—See also *Watson v Powles*, p 398, above.

S v Distillers Co (Biochemicals) Ltd
J v the same
[1969] 3 All ER 1412, [1970] 1 WLR 114, 113 Sol Jo 672 (Hinchcliffe J)
It may be convenient if the Court should state at this stage how it regards
the actuarial calculations introduced into these two cases. It is only
comparatively recently that attempts have been made to persuade the
courts that pecuniary loss in the future should be itemised under various
headings and be based on actuarial calculations. The highwater mark of
these cases is *Fletcher v Autocar & Transporters Ltd* (p 400, above) where the
court seems to have based its decision on the actuarial tables put before it
and in respect of various headings which were then added together, the
total of the three headings then being awarded to the plaintiff. This the
Court of Appeal said was wrong. Lord Denning stated that the various
items were not separate heads of compensation and that the actuarial
evidence is only an aid to arriving at fair and reasonable compensation.
. . . What this court will do is to look at [the actuarial] tables, use them as a
guide, exercising great caution, and will do everything it can to avoid any
overlapping. . . . I get the impression that the reformers would like an
alteration in the law so that, in assessing damages, pecuniary loss would be
itemised and based on actuarial calculations. That time has not yet arrived.
In both these cases the court, when assessing the damages, will have regard
to the cost of special care, to the loss of earning capacity and the deprivation
or loss of amenities suffered by each infant plaintiff. But of course these are
not separate heads of compensation. The court will regard them separately
because it will assist the court to reach a global sum which is just and
reasonable.

Sullivan v West Yorkshire Passenger Transport Executive
(1980) Times, 28 June, CA
It is for the parties to decide what evidence to call and for the judge to rule as
to its admissibility. There was nothing to prevent judges from considering
actuarial evidence and it could not be said that such evidence would confuse them.

Objective valuation of injury

Hindmarsh v Henry and Leigh Slater Ltd
(1966) 110 Sol Jo 429, CA
The plaintiff was awarded £22,000 for injuries which included a hideous
disfigurement and a complete change of personality and temperament. He
did not himself appreciate his condition. He had a sense of euphoria or
well-being, not realising the extent of the disaster which had befallen him or
even the extent of his deformity.
HELD, on the defendants' appeal: The fact of the plaintiff's being unaware
of his condition was not a ground for reducing the damages. The so-called
'sleeping beauty' cases showed that you must not reduce the damages that
would otherwise fall to be awarded to an injured plaintiff by reason of that
fact. By parity of reasoning the damages should not be reduced because this
unfortunate man was happy and did not realise the awful things that had
happened to him.

Note—But see next case.

Consciousness of injury

Cutts v Chumley

[1967] 2 All ER 89, [1967] 1 WLR 742, 111 Sol Jo 458 (Willis J)
Woman aged 28 sustained head injury of 'devastating severity'. Complete
personality change, intellectually reduced to level of a child of five, uninhi-
bited in speech, dirty in habits, incontinent, would have to live permanently in a home, charges of which were £1,100 pa. Judge said *West v
Shephard* (p 473, below) was not dissimilar but Mrs Cutts had more awareness of her condition than Mrs West and a much longer expectation of life
and was thus entitled to a much higher award for pain and suffering and
loss of amenities.

Note—The heads of damage were given in *Roach v Yates* [1938] 1 KB 256 as (1) the
actual loss and expenditure; (2) the pecuniary damage which will be incurred;
(3) the pain and suffering; (4) the loss of expectation of life; (5) the mental
suffering to be undergone; and (6) the physical disabilities.

WHEN ITEMS ARE AGREED

Bennett v Chemical Constructions (GB) Ltd

[1971] 3 All ER 822, [1971] 1 WLR 1571, 115 Sol Jo 550, CA
Per Edmund Davies LJ: Where in personal injury cases figures have been
agreed between the parties regarding any of the items of damage, it is
helpful that counsel should state to the court the basis of their calculation so
that it may be recorded and embodied in the judgment. This is helpful not
only to the trial judge but, in the event of an appeal, to the higher court also.
. . . Similarly, where the parties have agreed on a figure for continuing
financial loss, it is desirable to have it stated in clear terms how that figure
was arrived at.

Falling value of money: inflation

Wooding v Wooding

(1967) Times, 17 October, CA
Per Lord Pearson: While it is important from the point of view of public
policy that the general level of damages should be kept moderate rather
than extravagant, a judge must keep up with the times and in particular
with the decline in the purchasing power of money.

Walker v John McLean & Sons Ltd

[1979] 2 All ER 965, [1979] 1 WLR 760, 123 Sol Jo 354, 374, CA
An award must be reasonable, moderate and 'conventional' in the sense
used by Lord Morris in *West v Shephard* (p 473, above) but this did not mean
it should not have a relation to the changing value of money. Where there is
found to be a steady fall in the value of money the victim of the most serious
kind of injury qualifies for protection against it as much as or more than
any other economic group in society.

Note—See also *Senior v Barker & Allen Ltd*, p 458, below, and *Mitchell v Mulholland*
and *Lim Poh Choo* v *Camden and Islington Area Health Authority*, p 402, above. See also
'*Effect of inflation*', p 497, below and *Auty v National Coal Board* [1985] 1 All ER 930,
CA.

APPEALS ON AMOUNT

Greenfield v London and North Eastern Rly

[1945] KB 89, [1944] 2 All ER 438, 171 LT 337, 61 TLR 44 (MacKinnon LJ)

The principle on which the Court of Appeal reviews the assessment of damages, whether too high or too low, is not because the Court of Appeal might have given rather more or rather less, but only (1) if the judge has omitted some relevant consideration or admitted some irrelevant consideration, or (2) if the amount is so excessive, or insufficient, as to be plainly unreasonable.

Flint v Lovell

[1935] 1 KB 354, [1934] All ER Rep 200, 104 LJKB 199, 152 LT 231, 50 TLR 127, 78 Sol Jo 860, CA

Per Greer LJ: I think it right to say that this Court will be disinclined to reverse the finding of a trial judge as to the amount of damages merely because they think that if they had tried the case in the first instance they would have given a lesser sum. In order to justify reversing the trial judge on the question of amount of damages it will generally be necessary that this Court should be convinced either that the judge acted upon some wrong principle of law, or that the amount awarded was so extremely high or so very small as to make it, in the judgment of this court, an entirely erroneous estimate of the damage to which the plaintiff is entitled.

Note—The above statement of the law was adopted by Sir Wilfred Greene MR in *Rook v Fairrie* [1941] 1 KB 507, [1941] 1 All ER 297, 110 LJKB 319, 165 LT 23, 57 TLR 297, 85 Sol Jo 297, CA, by Asquith LJ in *Bull v Vazquez* [1947] 1 All ER 334, [1947] LJR 551, by Lord Wright in *Davies v Powell Duffryn Associated Collieries*, [1942] AC 601 and by the Court of Appeal in *Paris v Stepney Borough Council*, p 461, below.

Wilson v Pilley

[1957] 3 All ER 525, [1957] 1 WLR 1138, 101 Sol Jo 868, CA

Per Lord Evershed MR: Again let me emphasise that interference by this court with an award of damages by the trial judge must be a rare thing, and may I say it should be perhaps even rarer in relatively small cases tried in the county court. No one would suggest that, because this court thought that the damages, small in any case, were rather on the low side, this court could consider for a moment slightly raising the figure or adopting the converse course in a different kind of case. In other words, the onus on an appellant seeking to interfere with an award of damages, particularly within this sort of scale, is a heavy one.

Elliot v Preston Corporation

[1971] 2 Lloyd's Rep 328, CA

Per Salmon LJ: Before we can interfere, there has to be (in the phrase which is hallowed, but has now I think a rather archaic ring) a wholly erroneous estimate of damage. That I have always regarded as meaning that the court has to be satisfied that it is very wrong. If you are satisfied that it is wrong, and seriously wrong, then not only is this court entitled to interfere, but it is its duty to interfere. I would agree . . . that you cannot say, if it is wrong by such and such a per cent you do interfere and if it is not you do not. I think each case stands by itself, and a great deal depends upon the amount of the award.

HONG KONG

Chan Wai Tong v Li Ping Sum
[1985] AC 446, [1985] 2 WLR 396, 129 Sol Jo 153 PC
The plaintiff was awarded HK$90,000 general damages for injury to her back in a road accident and HK$108,000 for loss of future earnings. The defendants appealed to the Privy Council.
HELD: (1) Reference to guidelines laid down by the Hong Kong Court of Appeal (differently constituted) in 1980 was useful and to be encouraged. On the guidelines after allowing for inflation the award of general damages was reasonable and should stand; (2) the damages awarded for future loss of earnings (which had not been originally pleaded and had been inserted in the notice of appeal only by the plaintiff herself) required to be proved and the present value of the future risk properly evaluated as in *Moeliker v Reyrolle* (below, p 459). No evidence at all had been brought on this and the award of HK$108,000 must be deleted; (3) a court should in general, when assessing damages, have regard only to awards in the same jurisdiction or in a neighbouring locality where the relevant conditions are similar.

MALAYSIA

Jamil bin Harun v Yang Kamsiah Bte Meor Rasdi
[1984] AC 529, [1984] 2 WLR 668, 128 Sol Jo 281, PC
At the age of seven the plaintiff sustained very severe injuries in a road accident: the defendant admitted liability. The plaintiff as a result of the accident was mentally retarded and could not learn a useful self-supporting trade. Her life expectation was not reduced. The trial judge awarded $75,000 and declined to itemise it. On appeal the Federal Court increased and itemised the damages as $70,000 for pain suffering and loss of ameni-ties, $33,816 for loss of future earnings and $25,362 for cost of future care. HELD, in the Privy Council:(1) Malaysian law did not forbid itemisation and the Federal Court was not wrong in itemising the damages. (2) The loss of future earnings for a young child was not so speculative that it could not be assessed. It was done in *Croke v Wiseman* and *Joyce v Yeomans* (p 425, below) and there were compelling social reasons why it should be done. Where there was reduced expectation of life assessment of loss of earnings in the 'lost years' was too speculative, but that was not this case. (3) The award for cost of future care by the Federal Court was justifiable.

Court of Appeal will not examine injury

Ellis v Sayers Confectioners Ltd
[1963] 61 LGR 299, CA
The Court of Appeal was invited by counsel to see the appellant's injured leg. The Court declined. Whilst there is no definite rule it is, on the whole, not desirable for the Court of Appeal to see the claimant.

Stevens v William Nash Ltd
[1966] 3 All ER 156, [1966] 1 WLR 1550, 110 Sol Jo 710, CA
The plaintiff's right arm was seriously injured in an accident resulting in permanent weakness and loss of movement both in the arm and in the hand and fingers. At the hearing of his appeal against the amount of an award of damages the Court of Appeal was invited by counsel to see the plaintiff's arm. The Court rejected the invitation.

Per Winn LJ: In general it is probably not wise for this Court to embark on examinations of the physical conditions of appellants — though there may be some cases which call for it. There may be a suggestion of malingering; a man might be tempted to refrain from exerting quite so much movement as he really is capable of. Cases of scarring or shortening are in a different category since they are objective.

Judge should assess damages

Harrison v National Coal Board
[1950] 1 KB 466, [1950] 1 All ER 171, 66 (Pt 1) TLR 300, 94 Sol Jo 145, CA
In cases which involve difficult questions of law and are likely to be taken to appeal, it is always desirable that the trial judge, whether or not he is specifically requested by counsel to do so, should assess the damages provisionally, if his decision is adverse to the plaintiff. Failure to do so frequently results in unnecessary further expense to the parties.

Appeal from jury

Note—Order 59, r 11(4) provides that where the Court of Appeal has power to order a new trial where damages awarded by a jury are excessive or inadequate, the Court may with the consent of all parties, fix the amount; with the consent of the party entitled to receive or liable to pay, reduce or increase by a sum fixed by the Court in respect of any distinct head of damages; but otherwise has no power to reduce or increase damages awarded by a jury.

Morey v Woodfield
[1963] 3 All ER 533n, [1964] 1 WLR 16 n, CA
On an appeal from a judge (which is technically a re-hearing) the duty of the Court of Appeal is to correct judgments unduly divergent from other judicial decisions: on an appeal from a jury's verdict the court has no power to correct. It can set aside verdicts only if satisfied (except in cases of misdirection and mistake) that no reasonable jury could have come to such a verdict. The standard of a reasonable jury must be applied but this is not necessarily the standard of judicial decisions. As Lord Halsbury said in *Metropolitan Rly Co v Wright* (1886) 11 App Cas 152 at 156: 'Thus the question in truth is not whether the verdict appears to the appellate tribunal to be right, but whether it is such as to show that the jury have failed to perform their duty.'

New evidence in Court of Appeal

Jenkins v Richard Thomas and Baldwins Ltd

[1966] 2 All ER 15, [1966] 1 WLR 476, 110 Sol Jo 111, [1966] 1 Lloyd's
Rep 473, CA

The plaintiff was employed by the defendants as a pitman, earning £19 10s
per week. He received an eye injury which prevented him from doing the
work of a pitman and he was employed instead as a labourer at £11 per
week. At the trial of his action for damages the defendants said he could be
trained to work as a grinder and in that job would earn £17 per week. The
judge awarded £3,040 damages of which £1,040 was in respect of future
loss at £2 10s per week. After the trial the plaintiff started working as a
grinder but showed no aptitude for it and continued to earn only £11 per
week. He appealed against the award. The Court of Appeal allowed fresh
evidence to be called including that of two eye surgeons, the plaintiff and a
fellow employee.

HELD: The appeal should be allowed. It was only in very special circumstances that the Court would hear fresh evidence but here the expectation
on which the judge has assessed damages had been entirely falsified by
events: the plaintiff had been told he would get £17 per week and only got
£11. The general rule in actions of this type is that damages have to be
assessed once and for all at the trial. It must not be thought that whenever
the assessment of the plaintiff's future earnings turns out to be wrong one
or other of the parties can appeal for damages to be increased or reduced. In
the present case an exceptional circumstance was that the assessment was
based on what the defendants had genuinely but mistakenly said at the
trial.

Murphy v Stone-Wallwork Ltd

[1969] 2 All ER 949, [1969] 1 WLR 1023, 113 Sol Jo 546, HL

The plaintiff, aged 54, was injured at work on 17 March 1965. Both the
judge at first instance and the Court of Appeal made their awards on the
footing that the rest of his working life would probably be spent in
the employment of the defendants. Within a fortnight of the Court of
Appeal's award the defendants dismissed him from their employment. He
appealed within time to the House of Lords.

HELD: The House had a discretion to take evidence of something which
had occurred after the date of the decision from which the appeal was
brought and which had altered the effect of the order of that Court, especially when as here the appeal was launched within the time allowed. The
defendants, though acting in good faith, had falsified the basis of the
judgment of the Court of Appeal and it was right that the House should
admit the new evidence to enable the damages to be adjusted to the new
situation. It was a power which a court should exercise sparingly: *Curwen v
James* [1963] 2 All ER 619 was rightly decided but *Jenkins v Richard Thomas
& Baldwins* (above) might call for re-consideration, since in that case it was
not the defendants who had caused the change of circumstances.

Mulholland v Mitchell (No 1)

[1971] AC 666, [1971] 1 All ER 307, [1971] 2 WLR 93, 115 Sol Jo 15, HL

At the trial of an action the judge assessed damages for very serious personal injury on the basis that it would be possible for the plaintiff to be looked after at home or alternatively at a nursing home where the charges would be at the rate of £903 a year. The plaintiff appealed and applied for leave to adduce fresh evidence that after the trial it had been found impossible to look after him at home, and that he would have to go to a special nursing home where the charges were £1,827 a year.

HELD: RSC Ord 59, r 10(2) gave the Court of Appeal 'power to receive further evidence on questions of fact . . . but . . . no such further evidence (other than evidence as to matters which have occurred after the date of trial or hearing) shall be admitted except on special grounds'. It is generally undesirable to admit fresh evidence on appeal because there ought to be finality in litigation. The question is largely a matter of degree. Fresh evidence ought not to be admitted when it bears on matters falling within the field or area of uncertainty in which the judge's estimate had previously been made. It may be admitted if some basic assumptions common to both sides have been clearly falsified by subsequent events (particularly if this has happened by the act of the defendant) or when to refuse it would affront commonsense or a sense of justice. The situation in the present case was sufficiently exceptional that it could not be said the Court of Appeal had wrongly exercised its discretion in giving leave.

McCann v Sheppard
[1973] 2 All ER 881, [1973] 1 WLR 540, 117 Sol Jo 323, CA

Because of great pain from his injuries. McCann needed a pain-killing drug, palfrium. By the date of the trial of his action for damages in June 1972 he had become reliant on the drug. He was awarded general damages for pain, suffering and loss of amenities, for loss of future earnings and special damage. The defendants lodged notice of appeal in July 1972. On 18 October McCann was convicted in the magistrates' court of procuring drugs by deception. On 22 October 1972, he was found dead from an overdose of drugs. The hearing of the defendant's appeal was begun on 28 February 1973.

HELD, by the Court of Appeal: (1) Evidence of McCann's death should be admitted. Where notice of appeal has been served within the time prescribed by the rules and an event has taken place at a time reasonably proximate to the date of the trial which falsifies the facts on which judgment proceeded the Court of Appeal should not rehear the matter on the basis of the fiction that the event has not taken place. (2) Damages for future loss of earnings must consequently be reduced from 15 years to 20 weeks.

WRONG OR MISTAKEN EVIDENCE

Beaton v Naylors of Plymouth
(1965) 109 Sol Jo 632, CA

The plaintiff gave evidence on the hearing of his action for damages for personal injuries that he had not been able to work since the accident. On that basis his special damage was agreed at £848. The judge awarded him £1,500 general damages in addition. Subsequent to the trial the defendants obtained evidence to show that the plaintiff had done quite a lot of work between the accident and the trial.

The Court of Appeal ordered a new trial. The tests to be applied were

(1) that the new evidence could not reasonably have been available at the trial, (2) that it was apparently credible, and (3) that it would have had an important influence on the judge. All these tests were satisfied.

Day v Harland and Wolff Ltd
[1967] 1 Lloyd's Rep 301, CA
At the trial of an action in which the plaintiff alleged he injured his wrist by falling over a pile of dunnage judgment was given in his favour for £1,055. Some days later the defendants received a message that the injury had not been caused in the way alleged but in a fight on the evening of the same day. The defendants' solicitors then obtained statements from a publican and two other men to show that the plaintiff had been injured in a fight at a public house. They applied for a new trial.
HELD: There must be a new trial. The evidence could not have been obtained by reasonable diligence for use at the trial and if given it would have been likely to have had an important influence on the result.

Power v Standard Triumph Motor Co Ltd
(1970) Times, 10 December, CA
The plaintiff sustained a head injury at work which, he said, had changed his whole personality. His life had become a misery, he had lost all sense of taste and smell and could not walk properly. He was awarded £17,648 damages. The defendants appealed and applied to adduce fresh evidence relating to matters both before and after trial which would show that so far from being a cripple the plaintiff could walk up ladders, paint his house, move paving stones and chase vandals.
HELD: The Court clearly had power to admit such evidence under Ord 59. Applying *Ladd v Marshall* (p 641, below) the evidence was apparently credible, could have a material influence on the case, and the defendant's solicitors had acted reasonably. Further if the fresh evidence were true the plaintiff had perpetrated a gross fraud and the court should not allow it to succeed. New trial ordered.

BOARD AND LODGING

Liffen v Watson
[1940] 1 KB 556, [1940] 2 All ER 213, 109 LJKB 367, 162 LT 398, 56 TLR 442, 84 Sol Jo 368, CA
Plaintiff before an accident was a domestic servant receiving a weekly wage of £1 plus board and lodging, which was claimed at 25s. It is for the court to assess the value of the board and lodging, but the loss of the board and lodging is damage equally with the cash. The fact that her father provided board and lodging without payment does not alter the fact that she sustained this loss in kind.
Per Goddard LJ: The right to recover does not depend upon whether or not she made a contract with somebody else to give her board and lodging. She has lost it with the cash wages because she lost her work. It does not matter in the least whether she is taken in by her father or whether she is taken in by a friend. She might say to a friend, 'I cannot make a contract to

pay you, but if I get damages I shall pay you something for board and lodging.' These considerations are immaterial. The only consideration is what has she lost. She has lost the value of the board and lodging, just the same as she has lost her wages.

CARE AND NURSING

Note—In claims based on causes of action accruing on or after 1 January 1983 maintenance of a claimant at public expense is to be taken into account in assessing damages. The Administration of Justice Act 1982, s 5 reads:

'**5 Maintenance at public expense to be taken into account in assessment of damages** In an action under the law of England and Wales or the law of Northern Ireland for damages for personal injuries (including any such action arising out of a contract) any saving to the injured person which is attributable to his maintenance wholly or partly at public expense in a hospital, nursing home or other institution shall be set off against any income lost by him as a result of his injuries.'

Haggar v de Placido
[1972] 2 All ER 1029, [1972] 1 WLR 716, 116 Sol Jo 396 (May J)
The plaintiff became tetraplegic as a result of a road accident. His mother, brother and two lodgers in his mother's house looked after him. His mother waived the £4 per week she had formerly received from the lodgers in consideration of their help. His brother took a job at a lower wage so as to have more time to look after him. Later the plaintiff entered into written contracts to pay his mother £12.60 per week and his brother £10 a week to look after him.
HELD: The plaintiff could not claim in his action for damages the £4 per week his mother had waived nor his brother's loss of wages since he was under no legal liability to make good that loss, but he was under a legal liability to pay the amounts he had contracted to pay them and it was reasonable to assess future nursing expenses at £22.60 per week.

Note—See next case.

Donnelly v Joyce
[1974] QB 454, [1973] 3 All ER 475, [1973] 3 WLR 514, 117 Sol Jo 488, CA
The plaintiff, aged six, received injury to his leg in a road accident. After his discharge from hospital his mother gave up her work for six months to look after him. The judge awarded the plaintiff £147 in respect of her loss of earnings. On appeal the defendant argued that the item was not claimable by the plaintiff but that his mother might have recovered it had she been a party to the action.
HELD, ON APPEAL: The loss of the mother's wages was rightly claimed by and awarded to the plaintiff. It was his own loss — the existence of the need for nursing services of his mother, valued for the purposes of damages as the proper and reasonable cost of supplying those needs. It does not matter, so far as concerns the defendant, how or by whom the services have been

provided nor whether the plaintiff has a legal liability to repay the provider. Nor is the existence of a moral obligation a material factor, nor an agreement between the injured person and the provider of the services to pay for them. On this point *Haggar v de Placido* (above) was wrong. *Roach v Yates* [1938] 1 KB 256 was authority for holding that the plaintiff was entitled to recover damages referable to the past and future financial value of voluntary services rendered to a plaintiff by others. *Liffen v Watson* (p 411, above) embodied the same principle. Contrary to the defendant's 'concession' the plaintiff's mother would not have been entitled to recover the loss herself had she been a party.

Note—See *McAll v Brooks*, p 386, above and, or catastrophic injury damages generally, *Housecroft v Burnett* (1985) Times, 7 June.

Cunningham v Harrison
[1973] QB 942, [1973] 3 All ER 463, [1973] 3 WLR 97, 117 Sol Jo 547, CA
The plaintiff's neck was broken in a motor accident, paralysing him for life in all four limbs and his body. He was entirely dependent on others for dressing, bath, evacuation of bowels and feeding. His wife did everything for him for two years, then committed suicide. Trial of his action for damages came three days afterwards. Because of a difficult personality the plaintiff was considered unsuitable to enter a home and would have to live and be looked after in his own home.
HELD, ON APPEAL: Had the plaintiff's wife continued to look after him the value of her nursing services could have been claimed by the plaintiff without his having to make an agreement with her to pay her for them. On recovering such damages he would hold them on trust for her and pay them over to her; the judge's award for the cost of future nursing was too high. There should be moderation in all things, even in a claim for personal injuries. It was not right that the defendant should have to pay extra because of the plaintiff's difficult personality. Moreover it would be difficult to find people to look after him at home all the time and he would sometimes have to use other and state-provided facilities e g under the Chronically Sick and Disabled Persons Act 1970.

Taylor v Bristol Omnibus Co
[1975] 2 All ER 1107, [1975] 1 WLR 1054, 119 Sol Jo 476, CA
The plaintiff was three and a half when injured, nine at the date of trial. Very serious head injuries left him unable to control his limbs properly, unable to walk, unable to speak properly, permanently unemployable. The judge awarded £27,500 for pain and suffering and disability, £18,000 for future nursing and care and £16,000 for potential loss of earnings. With some agreed items the total was £63,000.
HELD, ON APPEAL: On particular points, (1) the item for care and nursing should not be any less if the plaintiff is looked after at home instead of in an institution. It is now settled that compensation can be given in money for services rendered by parents. (2) The fact that at the plaintiff's age calculation of future loss of earnings is extremely speculative is no ground for awarding merely a nominal sum. The present practice is to calculate a likely figure for future loss on present rates of earnings and having regard to the plaintiff's family background.

Rialas v Mitchell
(1984) 128 Sol Jo 704, CA

The plaintiff aged six suffered severe brain damage in a road accident resulting in spastic quadriplegia. He could not speak or feed himself and had to be looked after day and night. Figures for heads of damage if the plaintiff was to be cared for at home were agreed — the cost of a suitable house, future nursing care etc. Evidence was adduced by the defendant that private institutions had homes where the plaintiff could be cared for at substantially less, and that it was unreasonable to compensate him at more than the lower cost.

HELD: Before the accident the plaintiff had been a healthy uninjured child of six living with his parents. He was then in hospital for a year and returned home where he had been looked after for four years. The court was being asked to say that the plaintiff should live in an institution because it would cost less. That was not the true alternative. Once it had been decided by the judge that it was reasonable for the plaintiff to remain at home there was no acceptable reason for saying the defendant should not pay the reasonable cost of caring for him there.

Croke v Wiseman
[1981] 3 All ER 852, [1982] 1 WLR 71, CA

In the case of an infant of nine whose expectation of life was limited to the age of 40, the judge took a multiplier of 16 to 17 years for estimating the cost of future nursing care. On appeal, held, this was too high and should be reduced to 14. The judge's figure made no allowance for the possibility that the infant's life might be ended by accident before reaching the estimated life expectancy.

Davies v Tenby Corpn
[1974] 2 Lloyd's Rep 469, CA

The plaintiff became a quadriplegic as a result of a diving accident. He was completely bedridden and everything had to be done for him by his wife who nursed him with outstanding care and devotion.

HELD: per Lord Denning: In *Cunningham v Harrison* (above) I ventured to say that an award of damages could be made for a wife's services in nursing her injured husband. Even though she had not theretofore been doing paid work, but only domestic duties in the house, nevertheless all extra attendance on him called for compensation. It is not necessary for her to enter into a legal agreement as if she was a paid nurse. Sufficient that she had rendered services which would otherwise have had to be paid for. But I do not think that the award should be as high as that required for outside help. The wife does, after all, fit this extra work into her ordinary household duties and does it out of her wifely duty to keep him in sickness and in health. It is difficult to suggest an appropriate figure but I would suggest £15 a week or £780 a year. . . . His expected life is 10 years from the trial. The present value of this may be taken at £780 multiplied by seven.

CHARITABLE OR VOLUNTARY PAYMENTS

Redpath v Belfast and County Down Rly
[1947] NI 167
A distress fund supported by voluntary contributions from the public was established to assist passengers injured in a railway accident. In an action by a passenger against the railway company claiming damages for negligence, the railway company applied to interrogate the plaintiff as to the amount received by him from the fund.
HELD: The interrogatories were irrelevant. Plaintiff's damages were not to be reduced because plaintiff had received without legal right moneys voluntarily subscribed by third parties.

Dennis v London Passenger Transport Board
[1948] 1 All ER 779, 92 Sol Jo 350 (Denning J)
An injured plaintiff received no wages during disability but the Minister of Pensions and his employers the London County Council paid him approximately the amount of the wages in pension and sick pay. The Minister, without contending there was a legal obligation to refund, said the plaintiff would be expected to refund out of the damages if recovered and the LCC told the plaintiff the same. The plaintiff undertook to repay if he recovered damages.
HELD: The plaintiff was under a moral obligation to repay. A wrongdoer is not to be allowed to reduce damages because other persons have made up the wages. The plaintiff had lost his wages, and prima facie he should be paid them by the wrongdoer. They had been made up to him by other people who expect to be repaid and should be included as damages, subject to the direction that the amounts should be repaid. *Allen v Waters & Co* (see below) followed.

Schneider v Eisovitch
[1960] 2 QB 430, [1960] 1 All ER 169, [1960] 2 WLR 169, 104 Sol Jo 89 (Paull J)
The plaintiff was injured, and her husband killed, in a motor accident in France caused by the defendant's negligence. Immediately after the accident, while the plaintiff was still unconscious, her brother-in-law and his wife flew from England to France to give what help they could. The plaintiff later wished to pay their expenses for so doing and claimed the expenses as part of her special damage.
HELD: She was entitled to recover the expenses from the defendant. Before such a sum can be recovered the plaintiff must (1) show that the services rendered were reasonably necessary as a consequence of the tortfeasor's tort; (2) show that the expenses were reasonable and would have been incurred had the friends not assisted; (3) undertake to pay to those who incurred the expense the amount recovered. *Allen v Waters & Co* ([1935] 1 KB 200 dictum of Goddard J) and *Dennis v LPTB* applied.

Note—But see *Gage v King*, below.

Gage v King
[1961] 1 QB 188, [1960] 3 All ER 62, [1960] 3 WLR 460, 104 Sol Jo 644
(Diplock J)
The plaintiffs, husband and wife, were injured in an accident, the wife
seriously, the husband less so. In an action by the plaintiffs for damages for
personal injuries the defendant was held one-third to blame and the male
plaintiff two-thirds. Expenses incurred for the female plaintiff's injuries
amounted to £449, most of which had been paid by her husband from a
joint bank account on which both were entitled to draw and of which about
$4\frac{1}{2}\%$ of the total came from investments belonging to her, though given to
her by her husband. There was no evidence of any agreement between
them as to the ownership of the balance in the bank account.
HELD: The question which of the two plaintiffs was entitled to claim the
expenses as special damage depended on which of them incurred the legal
liabilities to pay them to the persons who had rendered the services. An
arrangement between husband and wife for a joint banking account is not
intended to have legal consequences while the marriage is still subsisting.
On the facts, the expenses were incurred by the husband and having been
found two-thirds to blame, he was entitled only to one-third of the amount
claimed.

Note—Schneider v Eisovitch, above, not followed.

CITATION OF AWARDS

Note—There is no rule of law or practice to forbid citation of previous awards, at
least when there is no jury, but judges have not shown much enthusiasm for it. The
views of the Court of Appeal were expressed in *Waldon v War Office*, below.

Waldon v War Office
[1956] 1 All ER 108, [1956] 1 WLR 51, 100 Sol Jo 33, CA
In an action for damages for personal injuries plaintiff's counsel wished to
refer the trial judge to decisions of the Court of Appeal and of other judges
of amounts of awards in cases of a like nature. The circumstances were
similar but not quite the same but would have been of help to the judge.
The judge thought the request referred mainly to decisions of the Court of
Appeal and did not think that the Court wished to impose on a judge this
additional burden, and declined the request.
ON APPEAL: The Court of Appeal said they were anxious not to put any
additional burden on a judge, particularly judges on assize. A judge is not
bound to consider other cases. It is for the judge to say whether, in his
discretion, he thinks it will help him or not. He may know the recent cases,
or many of them. It would not be right for the plaintiff's counsel to invite
attention to a number of cases where the amounts were high, and for
defendant's counsel to quote a number where the amounts were low. That
would not be of any help. In this case the injury was not of a common kind.
It would have been of help to look at the judgment in another case. A judge
draws on his own experience, his knowledge of decisions of other judges,
and his ordinary experience in life. The receiving of material of this kind
ought to happen seldom. The discretion is one to be exercised sparingly.
These views are limited to trial by a judge without a jury. Counsel should
refer to other cases only very sparingly.

Singh (an infant) v Toong Fong Omnibus Co Ltd
[1964] 3 All ER 925, [1964] 1 WLR 1382, 108 Sol Jo 818, PC
It need hardly be emphasised that caution has to be exercised when paying heed to the figures of awards in other cases. This is particularly so where cases are merely noted but not fully reported. It is necessary to ensure that in main essentials the facts of one case bear comparison with the facts of another before any comparison between awards in the respective cases can fairly or profitably be made.

DERIVATIVE CLAIMS

Note—There is no general principle of English law which entitles a person to recover damages against someone who has caused physical injury to a third person. Thus, for example, a partner cannot recover damages against a person who has caused him financial loss, however direct, by negligently injuring his partner. See below, *IRC v Hambrook* p 421.

There were at common law two exceptions to this: (1) it was a tort actionable at the suit of a husband negligently to do physical harm to his wife whereby the husband was deprived of her society (loss of consortium) or of her services (loss of servitium); (2) it was similarly a tort actionable at the suit of a master (or of a parent suing in respect of a child's services) negligently to cause bodily harm to his servant or child whereby the master or parent was deprived of his services (loss of servitium). The rule in respect of the master and servant relationship was held to be limited to those of the status of domestic servants (*A-G for New South Wales v Perpetual Trustee Co Ltd* [1955] AC 457, [1955] 1 All ER 846, [1955] 2 WLR 707, 119 JP 312, 99 Sol Jo 233, PC).

These exceptional rights of action have been abolished by the Administration of Justice Act 1982, s 2. The section came into force on 1 January 1983, save in respect of causes of action which accrued before that date, and reads as follows:

'**2** No person shall be liable in tort under the law of England and Wales or the law of Northern Ireland—
(a) to a husband on the ground only of his having deprived him of the services or society of his wife;
(b) to a parent (or person standing in the place of a parent) on the ground only of his having deprived him of the services of a child; or
(c) on the ground only—
   (i) of having deprived another of the services of his menial servant;
   (ii) of having deprived another of the services of his female servant by raping or seducing her; or
   (iii) of enticement of a servant or harbouring a servant.'

The following cases should be read in the light of the above. For other cases on loss of consortium and servitium see the 8th edition of this work, pp 414–22.

Husband and wife

HUSBAND'S OWN LOSSES

Kirkham v Boughey
[1958] 2 QB 338, [1957] 3 All ER 153, [1957] 3 WLR 626, 101 Sol Jo 301 (Diplock J)
On 10 September 1955, the plaintiff husband was driving a car with his wife, also a plaintiff, as passenger, when there was a collision with a car

driven by defendant, due to the admitted negligence of the defendant. The husband sustained trivial injuries but the wife was severely injured. She was in hospital until 1 February 1956, when she returned home and was then able to do light housework. By August 1956, she was able to do most of the housework except heavy lifting.

With regard to the husband's claim for loss of earnings, he was at the time of the accident on a month's leave from a job in Africa expiring at the end of September 1955. The wife and two children aged four and seven years had remained in England. He did not return to Africa because of his anxiety for his wife and the care of the children. He made no attempt to find work in England until the end of November 1955, when he took a job locally as an electrician at £8 a week.

He claimed difference in earnings up to the £30 per week (his salary in Africa) for so long as the court thought it reasonable for him to refuse to go to Africa because of the anxiety as to the condition of his wife and the problem of looking after the children. The claim was not based on loss of consortium, but on a contention that if the husband acted reasonably, he was entitled to any money loss as if the wrong had not been done to him. HELD: The argument that a driver owed a duty to members of the family circle of the party injured, e g father or brother, is unsupported by authority and in direct conflict with the dicta, and possibly the *ratio decidendi* in *Best v Samuel Fox & Co*. Such person has no remedy in law against the driver, because he owes no duty to such person. The husband of an injured wife is in no different position except for loss of consortium and there was no claim for loss of consortium. The fact that the husband was present and was himself injured makes no difference. The loss of wages is not recoverable.

The husband also claimed for medical treatment, convalescence, and cost of visiting the wife in hospital. Such damages may be recoverable either as mitigating damages for loss of consortium, or, as stated by Lord Goddard CJ in *Best's* case, lie in the husband's duty to provide proper maintenance and comfort for his wife. The judge preferred the second ground, which applied also to parent and child, which was a legal duty, but would not apply to medical treatment which he was under no legal duty to provide. With regard to the visits to hospital, the cost is frequently awarded to husbands. They may be a factor in recovery and so mitigate damages for loss of consortium, but if the sole justification is comfort or pleasure to the husband, it is not recoverable.

Walker v Mullen

(1984) Times, 19 January (Comyn J)
The plaintiff was seriously injured in a road accident. He had two spells in hospital during which his father, who worked in Jordan, stayed in England to be with his wife and son.
HELD: Following Diplock J's decision in *Kirkham v Boughey* (above) the father's loss of earnings was not recoverable because such loss would not reasonably have been within the contemplation of the defendant and as thus too remote.

McNeill v Johnstone

[1958] 3 All ER 16, [1958] 1 WLR 888, 102 Sol Jo 602 (Devlin J)
A husband and his wife were both injured in an accident due to the negli-

gence of the defendant. The husband was a United States Air Force officer and was living with his wife at Margate. The wife was French and the parties had only been married two months. The wife spoke English but had only lived in England since the marriage. The wife's injuries necessitated in-patient treatment at a hospital, and the husband sent her to a US Air Force hospital at Swindon, about 160 miles from Margate where she could receive free medical treatment and the hospital charges would be much less than a nursing home or hospital at Margate. The husband took a month's leave without pay so that he could spend time with his wife, but he also travelled to and fro between Margate and Swindon to discharge business in Margate. At Swindon he stayed cheaply at the bachelor officer's quarters.

The husband claimed as his special damages: £24, cost of five visits to Swindon to see the wife; £14 6s 0d cost of his staying in a hotel; £3 15s 0d and £5 1s 0d hotel bills when the wife returned to hospital for check up and further treatment; £6 cost of petrol of journeys to Swindon; £120 loss of earnings through month's leave.

HELD: Part of the damages claimed might be put on the ground that the visits contributed to recovery of the wife, but the legal principle for the claims was damages for loss of consortium. The loss sustained was partly attributable to business not the result of the accident, and a fair apportionment would be to award one-half of the £180 claimed.

Note—The judge referred to the judgment of Diplock J in *Kirkham v Boughey*, above, and agreed with the conclusion of Diplock J on the facts of that case.

McDonnell v Stevens
(1967) Times, 8 April (Swanwick J)
The plaintiffs, husband and wife, were injured in a road accident. The wife was severely injured and the plaintiffs claimed loss of earnings suffered by the husband by staying at home to look after the wife.
HELD: Neither of the plaintiffs could recover this loss. His looking after her had materially helped her recovery but it was not possible to infer any contractual term that his wife had agreed to recompense him for his loss. There was no principle in law which entitled a plaintiff to recover expenses however properly incurred and however enriching a defendant tortfeasor, in order to compensate a third party for services rendered voluntarily and gratuitously.

Note—See *Kirkham v Boughey*, p 417, above.

WIFE HAS NO CAUSE OF ACTION

Best v Samuel Fox & Co Ltd
[1952] AC 716, [1952] 2 All ER 394, 96 Sol Jo 494, HL
The plaintiff's husband, aged 30, suffered serious injuries by the negligence of the defendants. As a result he became impotent. He sued for and recovered substantial damages from the defendants for his own injuries. The plaintiff then sued for damages for loss of consortium by deprivation of normal marital relations.
HELD, ON APPEAL to the House of Lords: She could not succeed. There is no general principle of English law entitling a wife to recover damages for loss of consortium. A husband is entitled to recover damages for loss of

consortium against a person who negligently injures his wife but this is an anomaly founded on old authorities from a time when a husband was regarded as having a quasi-proprietary right in his wife.

Note—See now the Administration of Justice Act 1982, s 2, p 417, above.

HUSBAND INJURED: WIFE'S LOSS OF EARNINGS

Janney v Gentry
(1966) 110 Sol Jo 408 (Milmo J)
The plaintiff, a customs employee aged 37 was injured in a road accident to the extent that he was a permanent invalid, unemployable and wholly dependent on the full-time care and assistance of other people for the rest of his life.
HELD: In assessing damages for the wife's loss of earnings as a result of the need to look after the plaintiff *Kirkham v Boughey* (p 417, above) was direct authority against the wife's bringing a claim herself to recover the loss of her earnings. Distinguishing *Schneider v Eisovitch* (p 415, above) it was not possible to see on what principle the plaintiff in the present case could recover that loss. £6,000 should be awarded for future nursing as part of the general damages.

Wattson v Port of London Authority
[1969] 1 Lloyd's Rep 95 (Megaw J)
After an accident the plaintiff was at home for some weeks immobilised by his injuries and unable to work. His wife gave up work to look after him and lost £150 wages. The plaintiff claimed this amount as part of his special damages.
HELD: He was entitled to recover the amount of his wife's loss. *Liffen v Watson* (p 411, above) was an analogous case in showing that it was not necessary to have a binding contract to repay to enable the husband to claim his wife's loss. The position was covered in substance by the judgment in *Schneider v Eisovitch* (p 415, above) except that in the present case it did not matter that the plaintiff had given no firm undertaking to his wife to repay her.

Note—It does not appear from the report whether *Janney v Gentry* was brought to the attention of the court.

Malcolm v Broadhurst
[1970] 3 All ER 508 (Geoffrey Lane J)
A husband and wife (the plaintiffs) were injured in a road accident for which the defendant was to blame. The husband sustained the more serious injuries and was unable to return to his pre-accident occupation for which his wife had given him some part-time secretarial help. His injuries had made him bad-tempered and difficult to live with. The wife was incapacitated for work due to her own injuries for a year and then had a further six months' incapacity due to the effect of her husband's bad temper on her own unstable temperament. After that she was able to do full-time employment. As her husband was unable to do his old work the part-time secretarial work she had done for him was no longer available and she was not

able to find other part-time work which she could fit in with her full-time job.
HELD: (1) She was entitled to recover her loss of wages for the six months when her husband's behaviour was causing the incapacity. The defendant must take her as he finds her; exacerbation of her nervous depression was a readily foreseeable consequence of injuring her. Once damage of a particular kind can be foreseen the fact that it arises or is continued by an unusual complex of events does not avail the defendant (*Hughes v Lord Advocate*, p 6, above). (2) She was not entitled to recover damages for loss of her former part-time earnings as her husband's secretary. The defendant could not reasonably foresee that by injuring the husband he would be depriving the wife of her only means of part-time employment.

Disfigurement

Lampert v Eastern National Omnibus Co
[1954] 2 All ER 719, [1954] 1 WLR 1047, 98 Sol Jo 493 (Hilbery J)
A wife disfigured in a motor accident alleged that as a result the husband said he was sick of looking at it and left her, and claimed damages under this head. The judge said it was not a claim for loss of consortium. The question was whether it was damage resulting from the accident. If the facts showed the wife did lose anything of value, it might be consequential damage and recoverable, but in this case it was not the reason but only an excuse for deserting her.

Master and servant — servitium

Note—See note under 'Derivative Claims', p 417, above.

EMPLOYER'S CLAIM

IRC v Hambrook
[1956] 2 QB 641, [1956] 3 All ER 338, [1956] 3 WLR 643, 100 Sol Jo 632, CA
A tax officer being an established civil servant, was injured whilst off duty in a collision between his motor cycle and defendant's motor car. During his incapacity the plaintiffs paid him £231 13s 11d and sued defendant for that sum. It was agreed that the defendant was two-thirds responsible and the tax officer one-third.
HELD, by the Court of Appeal: Per Denning LJ: The general principle of law is stated by Lord Parker of Waddington in *Admiralty Comrs v S S Amerika*: 'the loss of A arising out of an injury whereby B is unable to perform his contract is not actionable'. The action *per quod servitium amisit* is an anomaly. If a director of a company or a partner in a firm is injured in an accident, he alone can sue for damages. The company or firm cannot sue for loss of his services. In the eighteenth century the action had become confined to menial servants and apprentices, those who lived in the household as part of the family (*Blackstone* vol I, p 425).
The action lies when the relationship of master and servant exists but only in the realm of domestic relations where a member of the master's household is injured. It does not apply to a tax officer. A payment where the

servant is not entitled to wages whilst sick, ie employed at a weekly wage is a voluntary payment and not recoverable. As stated in *Admiralty Comrs v S S Amerika* ([1917] AC 38), 'No person aggrieved by an injury is by common law entitled to increase his claim for damage by any voluntary act. . . .' The payment by the Crown is a voluntary act but may be evidence of the value of his services.

POLICE OFFICERS

Metropolitan Police District Receiver v Croydon Corpn; Monmouth-shire County Council v Smith

[1957] 2 QB 154, [1957] 1 All ER 78, [1957] 2 WLR 33, 101 Sol Jo 60, CA

(1) A police constable in the Metropolitan Police was injured whilst on duty and incapacitated from duty. The Receiver paid him his full wages and allowances and claimed that the defendants had benefited to the extent of £104 which the constable would have been entitled to recover from the defendants. The Receiver sued for the amount of wages, relying on the decision of Atkinson J in the case of *Metropolitan Police District Receiver v Tatum* [1948] 2 KB 68, [1948] 1 All ER 612, 92 Sol Jo 221. Slade J followed the decision in *Tatum*'s case and found for the plaintiff.

(2) A police constable in the Monmouthshire Constabulary was injured in similar circumstances. The Council claimed £751 18s 0d made up of (1) the full pay and allowances (other than house allowance) paid to him during total incapacity; (2) half of the full pay during partial incapacity; (3) house allowance during total incapacity; (4) half the house allowance during partial incapacity; (5) the pension paid up to the date on which he obtained judgment in an action brought by him against the defendants. The judge decided that the decision in *Tatum*'s case was not correct and dismissed the claim.

HELD: The two appeals raised exactly the same point. In both cases the police authority are obliged to pay a constable his full wages and allowances, although he may be off duty by reason of an injury received in the course of his service. In each case the constable brought an action against the respective defendants, but did not claim for pay and allowances, so that the damages were not so large as if they had been entitled to claim for loss of wages.

The police constable sustained certain damage for which he has been compensated. That damage did not include loss of wages, because he had already been paid his wages. The plaintiffs have not been called upon to pay anything which they would not otherwise have had to pay and are therefore no worse off than if the accidents had never taken place. What they have lost is the services of the constables, and their claim is the old action of *per quod servitium amisit*. In *A-G for New South Wales v Perpetual Trustee Co* ([1955] AC 457, [1955] 1 All ER 846, [1955] 2 WLR 707, 119 JP 312, 99 Sol Jo 233, PC), the Judicial Committee held that the action would not lie in the case of a police constable, and in *Hambrook*'s case the Court of Appeal so held in the case of a civil servant and expressed the view that the action *per quod servitium amisit* must nowadays be confined to the cases of what are generally known as menial servants.

Appeal by Croydon Corporation allowed; appeal by Monmouthshire CC dismissed.

Note—See note below heading 'Derivative Claims' p 417, above.

Employers can guard against a similar result by making it a term of the contract of employment that any payments made during absences from work due to injuries for which the employee has a right of action against a third party are to be treated as a loan. Alternatively where the contract of employment does not make special provision payments can be made expressly on the terms that they are loans to be recovered as part of the wage loss.

DIRECTOR OF COMPANY

Lee v Sheard
[1956] 1 QB 192, [1955] 3 All ER 777, [1955] 3 WLR 951, 99 Sol Jo 888, CA
The plaintiff was one of two directors and shareholders of a limited company. He did the outside work of buying and selling and the other director the inside work of administration. The plaintiff was injured and incapacitated and in consequence the profits of the company were reduced. The judge assessed his personal loss at £1,500.
HELD, ON APPEAL: The loss he had suffered was a real loss and was not too remote. He was not a servant and the company could not claim loss of servitium. The plaintiff was entitled to recover. Appeal dismissed.

DUTY TO MITIGATE

Waterhouse v H. Lange Bell & Co
[1952] 1 Lloyd's Rep 140 (Sellers J)
Amount of loss of earnings, and relative general damages for pain and suffering reduced because the plaintiff could have reduced his claim by taking available work of a lighter nature pending his total recovery.

Barnes v Port of London Authority
[1957] 1 Lloyd's Rep 486 (Byrne J)
A shunter, aged 50, sustained a severe injury to the right foot whereby he lost the outer four toes and a considerable portion of his big toe, and became permanently partially disabled. In February 1956, he was offered work as a night watchman by his employers at a wage which was £2 per week less than his earnings as a shunter, which he refused. At the trial on 28/29 May 1957, the plaintiff said he was now willing to accept the work offered. The judge found that the plaintiff was fit for the work offered in February 1956, and should have accepted the work, and assessed the general damages on that basis.

Luker v Chapman
(1970) 114 Sol Jo 788 (Browne J)
The plaintiff's injuries, caused by the defendant's negligent driving, were such that he was unable to continue his pre-accident job as a telephone engineer. His employers offered him clerical work but he refused it, deciding instead to train as a teacher. He claimed his loss of earnings during the period of his training.
HELD: Though the plaintiff was showing courage in undertaking this training he was under a duty to mitigate his damage and should have accepted the clerical job. The defendant could not be held liable for that loss.

Selvanayagam v University of West Indies
[1983] 1 All ER 824, [1983] 1 WLR 585, 127 Sol Jo 288, PC
The appellant sustained injury to his neck in an accident. There was evidence from a specialist who had treated him that surgical therapy which he had recommended would have reduced his disability and enabled him to resume his professional work. However, the specialist said in evidence that as the appellant was diabetic and knew of the risks of infection it was for him to decide whether to have the operation or not. The judge accepted the appellant's decision not to have the operation as reasonable and awarded damages accordingly.
HELD, on appeal to the Privy Council: The judge was entitled so to decide. The rule that a plaintiff who rejects a medical recommendation of surgery must show that he acted reasonably is based on the principle that a plaintiff is under a duty to act reasonably so as to mitigate his damage. The question is one of fact: whether in all the circumstances, including particularly the medical advice received, the plaintiff acted reasonably in refusing surgery; the burden of reasonableness was on him.

EPILEPSY

Note—The three cases following are of a type to which the procedure under the Supreme Court Act 1981, s 32A would seem now to be appropriate. See below under 'Future disability uncertain'.

Hawkins v New Mendip Engineering Ltd
[1966] 3 All ER 228, [1966] 1 WLR 1341, 110 Sol Jo 633, CA
A fitter aged 27 was struck on the head by a piece of an accumulator which exploded. He was off work seven weeks before resuming his job. There was no fracture of the skull but he developed a minor form of epilepsy. There was a 50–50 chance that he might develop a major epilepsy but it was virtually impossible to tell within five years what the future was likely to be. His present symptoms included headaches, forgetfulness, the feeling known as *déja-vu*, and panosmia. The judge awarded £8,000. The defendants appealed.
HELD: There was no reason to interfere with the judge's award. What had to be quantified was the uncertainty of the future. If major epilepsy did develop it would be a major catastrophe for the plaintiff, virtually ending his working life. The judge was moving in the realm of guesswork and the judge's guess was as good as that of an appellate tribunal.

Prudence v Lewis
(1966) Times, 21 May (Brabin J)
A child of three was struck by a car and sustained a head injury. When trial of his action was reached three years later the doctors said the risk of development of epilepsy was at least 10%. The judge awarded £3,000. The difficulty (he said) in fixing an award in such a case was that, in the future the award must be wrong, because, if in fact the boy was free from epilepsy, the award would appear to the defendant to have been too high, and if the boy did develop it, the award would appear to him to have been too low. A compromise had to be made in fixing the damages before the medical position became certain.

Jones v Griffith
[1969] 2 All ER 1015, [1969] 1 WLR 795, 113 Sol Jo 309, CA
The plaintiff, aged 21, sustained head injuries in a road accident. One result was a liability to attacks of traumatic epilepsy. She had one major epileptic attack and several further attacks not so serious. With suitable medication she might not have any more fits but there remained a liability to an occasional attack. The trial judge awarded £6,000, of which up to £5,000 was in respect of the epilepsy.
HELD: The question was what were the chances of further attacks of epilepsy of a serious nature. Unlike *Hawkins'* and *Prudence's* cases (above) the plaintiff had already suffered attacks. One approach was to consider what figure would be appropriate in a case where future serious attacks were virtually certain (say £10,000 to £11,000) and then discount that figure according to the degree of optimism in the medical reports. In the present case the plaintiff's prospects were a little better than 50–50. On that basis it would not be right to interfere with the judge's award.

Joyce v Yeomans
[1981] 2 All ER 21, [1981] 1 WLR 549, 125 Sol Jo 34, CA
The plaintiff, a boy of ten, was hit by a car, sustaining a head injury, ruptured spleen and a fractured clavicle. Some months later he showed symptoms of epilepsy and during three years had four or five grand mal attacks. The judge accepted a doctor's opinion that the boy would have developed epilepsy by the time he was 14 even without the injuries but that they had caused the epilepsy to appear earlier and to be more disabling. The plaintiff had done poorly at school and had been unable to pass any 'O' level examinations. The judge awarded £7,500 inclusive of loss of future earning capacity which he did not assess separately.
HELD, ON APPEAL: The injuries and epilepsy in themselves justified an award of £6,000, which left too little for loss of earning capacity. It was not appropriate to use the multiplier/multiplicand method to calculate this loss because there were so many imponderables but a proper figure in the circumstances would be £7,500, making a total of £13,500 but with interest on the £6,000 only.

Note—See also *Stephenson v Cook* [1975] 1 Lloyd's Rep 495.

FUTURE DISABILITY UNCERTAIN: PROVISIONAL DAMAGES

The Supreme Court Act 1981, s 32A (added by the Administration of Justice Act 1982, s 6) enables a court to make provisional awards of damages, and to award further damages at a later date, in certain types of case. The section is as follows:

32A Orders for provisional damages for personal injuries (1) This section applies to an action for damages for personal injuries in which there is proved or admitted to be a chance that at some definite or indefinite time in the future the injured person will, as a result of the act or omission which gave rise to the cause of action, develop some serious disease or suffer some serious deterioration in his physical or mental condition.

(2) Subject to subsection (4) below, as regards any action for damages to which the section applies in which a judgment is given in the High Court, provision may be made by rules of court for enabling the court, in such circumstances as may be prescribed, to award the injured person—

(a) damages assessed on the assumption that the injured person will not develop the disease or suffer the deterioration in his condition; and

(b) further damages at a future date if he develops the disease or suffers the deterioration.

(3) Any rules made by virtue of this section may include such incidental, supplementary and consequential provisions as the rule-making authority may consider necessary or expedient.

(4) Nothing in this section shall be construed—

(a) as affecting the exercise of any power relating to costs, including any power to make rules of court relating to costs; or

(b) as prejudicing any duty of the court under any enactment or rule of law to reduce or limit the total damages which would have been recoverable apart from any such duty.

The section was brought into force with effect from 1 July 1985 by SI 1985/846 (Rules of the Supreme Court (Amendment No 2) Order). The rules form rr 7 to 10 of Ord 37. The damages awarded under s 32A sub-s (2)(a) are designated 'provisional' damages; those under sub-s (2)(b) as 'further' damages. The court will not award 'provisional' damages unless (1) satisfied that the action is one to which s 32A applies and (2) the claim for 'provisional' damages has been pleaded (see rr 7 and 8). For a detailed examination of the rules reference may usefully be made to 82 LS Gaz 1835 (26 June 1985). See also *Practice Note* [1985] 2 All ER 895.

By the Administration of Justice Act 1982, s 73(2) 'section 6 above [ie containing s 32A of the 1981 Act] . . . shall apply to actions whenever commenced, including actions commenced before the passing of this Act'. By s 6(3) s 32A 'shall have effect in relation to county courts as it has effect in relation to the High Court, as if references in it to rules of court included references to county court rules'.

HOSPITAL CHARGES

Note—Payment of hospital charges was dealt with in the Road and Rail Traffic Act 1933, s 33 now replaced by the Road Traffic Act 1972, s 154 as follows:

'**154 Payment for hospital treatment of traffic casualties** (1) Where a payment, other than a payment under section 155 of this Act, is made (whether or not with an admission of liability)—

(a) by an authorised insurer, the payment being made under or in consequence of a policy issued under section 145 of this Act, or

(b) by the owner of a vehicle in relation to the use of which a security under this Part of this Act is in force, or

(c) by the owner of a vehicle who has made a deposit under this Part of this Act, in respect of the death of, or bodily injury to, any person arising out of the use of a motor vehicle on a road or in a place to which the public have a right of access, and the person who has so died or been bodily injured has to the knowledge of the insurer or owner, as the case may be, received treatment at a hospital, whether as 'an in-patient or as an out-patient, in respect of the injury so arising, the insurer or owner shall pay the expenses reasonably incurred by the hospital in affording the treatment, after deducting from the expenses any moneys actually received in payment of a specific charge for the treatment, not being moneys received under any contributory scheme:—

Provided that the amount to be paid shall not exceed £200 for each person treated as an in-patient, or £20 for each person treated as an out-patient.

(2) For the purposes of this section 'expenses reasonably incurred' means—

(a) in relation to a person who receives treatment at a hospital as an in-patient, an amount for each day he is maintained in the hospital representing the average daily cost, for each in-patient, of the maintenance of the hospital and the staff thereof and the maintenance and treatment of the in-patients therein; and

(b) in relation to a person who receives treatment at a hospital as an out-patient, reasonable expenses actually incurred.'

In respect of accidents occurring on or after 1 April 1980 £1,250 is substituted for £200 and £125 is substituted for £20 by the Road Traffic Accidents (Payments for Treatment) (England and Wales) Order 1980, SI 1980/111. A 1982 Order of the same name, SI 1982/1194, increases £1,250 to £1,525 and £125 to £152.50 as from 20 September 1982. SI 1985/202 increases £1,525 to £1,777 and £152.50 to £177.70 as from 1 April 1985.

'A payment under the next following section' (sub-(1)) — see s 155 set out on p 772.

Voluntary passengers

Note—The following cases have no relevance to passenger claims which, from 1 December 1972 require insurance cover. See Road Traffic Act 1972, s 145 and s 148(3) and 'Passenger insurance', p 748, below.

Royal Victoria Hospital v London Guarantee and Accident Corpn
[1937] NI 64

The Court of Appeal in Northern Ireland (Andrews and Best LJJ, the Lord Chief Justice dissenting) held (under the Northern Ireland Acts) that where a policy covered passenger risk (of voluntary passengers) and insurers had paid a passenger claim, the insurers were liable for the hospital account, because the policy (as stated in the certificate) was issued under the Act, and insurers had made a payment under the policy.

Lockerbie v Eagle Star Insurance Co
(20 March 1936, unreported)

Insurers are not liable under the certificate to meet a judgment obtained by a voluntary passenger. The words 'being a liability covered by the terms of the policy' are for the protection of insurers who are not liable unless the liability is in fact covered by the policy. The section does not mean 'covered by the policy whether required to be covered or not'.

Barnet Hospital v Eagle Star Insurance Co
[1960] 1 QB 107, [1959] 3 All ER 210, [1959] 3 WLR 610, 123 JP 521, 103 Sol Jo 619, [1959] 2 Lloyd's Rep 335

The policy issued by insurers covered the insured against claims by voluntary passengers. Insurers settled a claim by a passenger and at the date of settlement insurers were not aware that the passenger had received hospital treatment. The hospital claimed from insurers the amount of the hospital charges of £12 12s 6d. The insurers denied liability on two grounds, viz: (1) that the Act did not apply to the case of a voluntary passenger and was limited to cases where the passenger was one who was compulsorily insured: (2) that the insurers had no knowledge that the passenger had received hospital treatment. The judge reserved judgment, and held that the Act applied to a voluntary passenger, but as insurers had no knowledge of the treatment, they were not liable.

Third-party sharing agreement

Glasgow Royal Infirmary v Municipal Mutual Insurance
1953 Glasgow Sheriff's Court, 14 July

A motor vehicle insured with the defenders collided with a Glasgow Corpn tramcar and a passenger in the tramcar was injured, and received treatment at the pursuers' hospital. The passenger sued the Corporation who settled her claim. The defenders had a third-party sharing agreement with the Corporation and under the agreement paid one-half the cost. Pursuers claimed from defenders the hospital charges contending that defenders had made a payment as insurers.

The Sheriff Substitute, whilst regretting that an important matter without helpful authority should be tested in a summary cause, said he found the decision easy. No claim had been made by the passenger against defenders as insurers of the motor vehicle and therefore there had been no payment 'under' the policy. If no claim lies by a third party against the policy, no payment can be exacted by any fourth or other party 'in consequence of' any more than 'under' the policy. Without the agreement there could be no means of approach by the pursuers to the defenders and but for the agreement there would have been no payment by the defenders. The payment was in no way connected with or derived from the policy but solely under a private agreement and was not made either 'under' or 'in consequence of' the policy.

INCAPACITY FOR HOUSEKEEPING

Daly v General Steam Navigation Co
[1980] 3 All ER 696, [1981] 1 WLR 120, 125 Sol Jo 100, [1980] 2 Lloyd's Rep 415, CA

The plaintiff, seriously injured by the defendants' negligence, claimed damages for, inter alia, her inability to do the heavier kind of housework in her home. She was 34 years of age at the time of the injuries, married and lived with her husband and two children. She was not gainfully occupied before the accident nor did she employ any domestic help. Her incapacity would last for the rest of her life. Trial was reached seven years after the accident. The judge held that (1) The partial loss of housekeeping capacity should be treated as a separate head of damage and not merely an element in the general damages for loss of amenities; (2) such damages should be assessed by reference to the cost of employing someone else to do the work, even for the period before trial when no one was employed and the plaintiff's husband acted in part as a substitute housekeeper himself; (3) they should be calculated on a basis of ten hours per week at an average of 90p per hour before date of trial and eight hours per week at £1.40 per hour for the future at a multiplier of 15 years: total £11,427.

On appeal the award was varied. In respect of the award for future partial loss of housekeeping capacity in the figure of £8,736, held, the judge was right in assessing it at the estimated cost of employing some third person to come in and do that which the plaintiff was unable to do. It was not requisite that the plaintiff should satisfy the Court that she had a firm intention in any event that such a person should be employed. It was immaterial whether the plaintiff, having received those damages, should choose to alleviate her housekeeping burden by employing someone to do it, or to spend the damages on luxuries she would otherwise be unable to afford. In respect of the award of £2,691 for loss of housekeeping capacity up to date of trial, however, it was wrong to assess it by reference to the cost of employing domestic help which she had not in fact employed but which had been furnished by her husband and daughter. The judge ought instead to have asked himself to what extent the difficulties which the plaintiff had had to contend with in performing her household duties ought to have increased the award for pain and suffering. The Judge's award of £8,000 for pain and suffering should be increased by the sum of £2,691 from which should be deducted the sum of £930, the husband's partial loss of earnings due to his having to help in the home.

INCOME TAX

Note—The question whether income tax should be deducted from loss of earnings was decided in the case of *Gourley v British Transport Commission* (below). The defendants contended that income tax and surtax should be taken into account and the sum necessary to effect a *restitutio in integrum* should only be a fraction of the gross amount lost.

Before *Gourley*'s case came before the House of Lords the case of *Jordan v Limmer & Trinidad Lake Asphalt Co* [1946] KB 356, [1946] 1 All ER 527, Atkinson J following the decision of du Parcq J in *Fairholme v Firth and Brown Ltd* (1933) 149 LT 332, 49 TLR 470, 77 Sol Jo 485, decided that income tax was not to be deducted from damages. In *Henley v Murray* [1950] 1 All ER 908, [1950] WN 241, 94 Sol Jo 338, in the Court of Appeal, the Crown conceded that in a claim for damages for wrongful dismissal, any damages awarded was not taxable as income. There followed the decision of *Billingham v Hughes* in the Court of Appeal [1949] 1 KB 643, [1949] 1 All ER 684, where the decision was that tax was not to be deducted from damages for personal injuries. Meanwhile in Scotland the cases of *McDaid v Trustees of the Clyde Navigation* (1945) 24 ATC 321, Ct of Sess and *Blackwood v Andre* 1947 SC 333, Ct of Sess were decided. Then in this state of affairs came the case of *British Transport Commission v Gourley*, which is set out below, and which overruled the above six cases.

Gourley's case

British Transport Commission v Gourley
[1956] AC 185, [1955] 3 All ER 796, [1956] 2 WLR 41, 100 Sol Jo 12, [1955] 2 Lloyd's Rep 475, HL
The plaintiff was 65 years of age and was a partner in a firm of civil engineers. He was totally disabled for some time and after returning to

work his earning capacity was reduced. Pearce J awarded £47,720 being £9,000 pain and suffering, £1,000 out of pocket expenses, £15,220 for actual loss of earnings before the end of 1953 and £22,500 for estimated future loss of earnings. The two latter sums (ie £37,720) did not take income tax or surtax into account. If tax had been, the award would have been £6,695, being £4,945 instead of £15,220 and £1,750 instead of £22,000. The parties agreed that one or other of the two sums fixed by the judge should be awarded.

Per Earl Jowitt: It was agreed by counsel on both sides — and I think rightly agreed — that the respondent would incur no tax liability in respect of the award of £37,720 or alternatively £6,695. The broad principle is an award of such sum of money as will put the injured person in the same position as he would have been if he had not sustained the injuries. The principle of *restitutio in integrum* affords little guidance for pain and suffering and impairment but affords some guidance in assessing financial loss and was referred to by Lord Wright (*The Liesbosch*) as 'the dominant rule of law'. There is no distinction between cases under PAYE where tax is deducted before payment, and cases where tax is paid after the money is received. It is fallacious to consider the problem as though a benefit was being conferred on a wrongdoer. The problem is rather for what damages he is liable. He is liable for such damages as, by reason of his wrongdoing, the plaintiff has sustained. The tax element is not too remote and no sensible person regards his net earnings as equivalent to his available income. The assessment of tax liability need not be elaborate, but an estimate formed on broad lines, even rough and ready. Appeal allowed.

Lyndale Fashion Manufacturers v Rich
[1973] 1 All ER 33, [1973] 1 WLR 73, 117 Sol Jo 54, CA
The defendant was awarded £495 damages on a counterclaim for wrongful dismissal, less tax to be decided by the Court. The defendant had earned £1,343 in the tax year, on which he had paid tax of £23. If he had earned the additional £495 as income he would have paid a total of £160 in tax. The plaintiffs contended that the damages of £495 should be reduced by £137 being the additional tax that would have been attracted by £495 treated as the top slice of his income. The defendant claimed that only the average rate of tax between the £495 and the other income should be deducted.
HELD: The plaintiffs' contention was right. The principle in *Gourley*'s case (above) plainly applied. If a comparison was to be made between a given income and that income with something added, the addition must be treated as the top part of the income; it was the increase in the income which attracted the higher rates of tax.

Hartley v Sandholme Iron Co Ltd
[1975] QB 600, [1974] 3 All ER 475, [1974] 3 WLR 445, 118 Sol Jo 702
(Nield J)
The plaintiff was off work for 19 weeks as a result of injury and claimed loss of earnings for that period calculated on the weekly pre-accident wage after deduction of income tax on a PAYE basis. Afterwards he received a tax rebate of £18.70 due to his not having earned wages during the 19 weeks off work.

HELD: Applying the principles of *Gourley*'s case, his claimed loss should be reduced by the amount of the tax rebate. The saving of tax to the plaintiff was not too remote but stemmed directly from the consequences of the accident; it was not *res inter alios acta* nor completely collateral, and the amount of the saving was not a matter of speculation but was accurately quantified.

Duller v South East Lincs Engineers
[1981] CLY 585, QBD
The plaintiff claimed damages for severe personal injuries sustained in an accident. Before the accident in addition to his full time job he had worked as a part-time barman, but had not disclosed his earnings from the part-time job for income tax purposes.
HELD: He was entitled to be compensated for the loss of the part-time earnings. They did not come from any criminal origin but came lawfully into his hands. His unlawful conduct came later and was only with the Inland Revenue, not with the earnings. He did not base his claim on any unlawful act of his and it was not defeated by being tainted with illegality, but deductions must be made in respect of income tax. *Burns v Edman* (p 501, below) distinguished.

Tax on interest

Note—See p 441, below.

Loss of use

Note—See p 385, above.

INCONVENIENCE AND DISCOMFORT

Note—The following cases arise from breach of contract.

Burton v Pinkerton
(1867) LR 2 Ex 340, 36 LJ Ex 137, 17 LT 15
A seaman agreed to serve on board a vessel, which in the course of its voyage, acted as a supply ship to Peruvian men-of-war during hostilities between Peru and Spain, with both of whom England was at peace. He was held entitled to treat this as a breach of contract and to claim not only loss of wages but also damages for the inconvenience suffered when he left the ship at Rio.

Hobbs v London and South Western Rly Co
(1875) LR 10 QB 111, 44 LJQB 49, 32 LT 252
Plaintiff and his family were put on the wrong train and so found themselves at Esher late at night instead of at Hampton Court, as a consequence

of which they had to suffer the inconvenience of walking home in the rain.
HELD: Damages were recoverable; they could have hired a carriage had
one been available and charged the cost as special damage.

Stedman v Swans Tours

(1951) 95 Sol Jo 727, Times, 6 November, CA
Plaintiff contracted with travel agents for transport for a party of six and a
fortnight's accommodation at a first-class hotel with superior rooms with a
sea view. The rooms reserved were very inferior and had no sea view. The
party were unable to obtain accommodation elsewhere. Romer J awarded
£13 15s 0d special damages but no general damages.
HELD, ON APPEAL: General damages could be recovered for appreciable
inconvenience and discomfort caused by breach of contract assessed at £50
by CA. *Bailey v Bullock* followed.

Jackson v Horizon Holidays Ltd

[1975] 3 All ER 92, [1975] 1 WLR 1468, 119 Sol Jo 759, CA
The plaintiff booked a holiday with the defendants for himself, his wife and
their three-year-old twin sons in Ceylon for a month at a cost of £1,450. For
the first fortnight they were housed in a hotel which did not fulfil the
description given in the defendants' brochure. The judge awarded £1,100
damages for (1) the difference in value between what the plaintiff got and
what he bargained for; (2) compensation for distress and disappointment.
HELD, ON APPEAL: The award should stand. The plaintiff was making a
contract for the benefit of the whole family. He could recover damages for
the discomfort, vexation and upset which the whole family suffered.

Note—In *Woodar Investment Development Ltd v Wimpey Construction (UK) Ltd* ([1980]
1 All ER 571, [1980] 1 WLR 277, 124 Sol Jo 184, HL) Lord Wilberforce referred
to *Jackson v Horizon Holidays* and said

'I am not prepared to dissent from the actual decision in that case. It may be
supported either as a broad decision on the measure of damages or possibly as an
example of a type of contract, examples of which are persons contracting for family
holidays, ordering meals in restaurants for a party, hiring a taxi for a group, calling
for special treatment . . . [but] I cannot agree with the basis on which Lord
Denning MR put his decision in that case'.

Jarvis v Swans Tours Ltd

[1973] QB 233, [1973] 1 All ER 71, [1972] 3 WLR 954, 116 Sol Jo 822
The plaintiff booked a skiing holiday in Switzerland on the strength of the
description in the defendants' catalogue promising a houseparty each
week, a wide variety of ski runs, hire of skis, sticks and boots and other facilities. On the second week of the holiday he was the only person in the hotel,
the skiing was disappointing and there was no satisfactory equipment available. The county court judge awarded as damages only one-half of the cost
of the holiday.
HELD, ON APPEAL: This was not the right measure of damages. If the contracting party in a contract for a holiday breaks his contract damages can be
given for the disappointment, the distress, the upset and frustration caused
by the breach. The damages should be increased to £125.

TORT

Ichard v Frangoulis
[1977] 2 All ER 461, [1977] 1 WLR 556, 121 Sol Jo 287 (Peter Pain J)
The plaintiff and defendant were injured when their cars collided on a road in Yugoslavia where both were on holiday. The defendant after hospital treatment continued to Athens where he spent his holiday, though his enjoyment was spoiled by his injuries. The plaintiff conceded he was to blame for the collision.
HELD: On the defendant's counterclaim, the loss of enjoyment was a factor to be taken into account in assessing damages in a claim in tort as it is in contract (e g *Jarvis v Swans Tours* and *Jackson v Horizon Holidays* (above)) provided the damages were foreseeable by the negligent party. Where as here the accident took place in a holiday area much frequented by tourists it was obviously foreseeable.

INFANTS' DAMAGES

Gold v Essex County Council
[1942] 2 KB 293, [1942] 2 All ER 237, 112 LJKB 1, 167 LT 166, 58 TLR 357, 86 Sol Jo 295
Tucker J awarded £125 to an infant aged five, taking into account that the amount would be considerably increased when the time came for it to be handed over. The CA said this was wrong. It held that it ought not to have been taken into account, and awarded £300.

Special damage

Note—It has been common in the past for a parent to be joined as a plaintiff (other than as next friend) in an infant's action for damages for personal injuries, and to claim separately for loss and expense incurred as a result of the child's injuries. It was always doubtful whether such a claim was maintainable except on the basis of *per quod servitium amisit* even though not expressly pleaded as such: see *Hall v Hollander* (1825) 4 B & C 660. Now that the separate tort has been abolished by the Administration of Justice Act 1982, s 2(b) (p 417, above) such a claim ought properly to be made as part of the infant's own case. See e g *Donnelly v Joyce*, p 412, above.

INJURIES TO UNBORN CHILDREN

Note—The Congenital Disabilities (Civil Liability) Act 1976 which came into force on 22 July 1976, provides for children born with a disability to have a remedy in damages in circumstances specified in the Act where the disability can be proved to result from a wrongful act committed by any person. The sections likely to be relevant to motor claims are the following:

'**1 Civil liability to child born disabled** (1) If a child is born disabled as the result of such an occurrence before its birth as is mentioned in subsection (2) below, and a person (other than the child's own mother) is under this section answerable to the child in respect of the occurrence, the child's disabilities are to be regarded as damage resulting from the wrongful act of that person and actionable accordingly at the suit of the child.

(2) An occurrence to which this section applies is one which—

(a) affected either parent of the child in his or her ability to have a normal healthy child; or

(b) affected the mother during her pregnancy, or affected her or the child in the course of its birth, so that the child is born with disabilities which would not otherwise have been present.

(3) Subject to the following subsections, a person (here referred to as ''the defendant'') is answerable to the child if he was liable in tort to the parent or would, if sued in due time, have been so; and it is no answer that there could not have been such liability because the parent suffered no actionable injury, if there was a breach of legal duty which, accompanied by injury, would have given rise to the liability.

(4) In the case of an occurrence preceding the time of conception, the defendant is not answerable to the child if at that time either or both of the parents knew the risk of their child being born disabled (that is to say, the particular risk created by the occurrence); but should it be the child's father who is the defendant, this subsection does not apply if he knew of the risk and the mother did not. . . .

(6) Liability to the child under this section may be treated as having been excluded or limited by contract made with the parent affected, to the same extent and subject to the same restrictions as liability in the parent's own case; and a contract term which would have been set up by the defendant in an action by the parent, so as to exclude or limit his liability to him or her, operates in the defendant's favour to the same, but no greater, extent in an action under this section by the child.

(7) If in the child's action under this section it is shown that the parent affected shared the responsibility for the child being born disabled, the damages are to be reduced to such extent as the court thinks just and equitable having regard to the extent of the parent's responsibility.

2 Liability of woman driving when pregnant　A woman driving a motor vehicle when she knows (or ought reasonably to know) herself to be pregnant is to be regarded as being under the same duty to take care for the safety of her unborn child as the law imposes on her with respect to the safety of other people; and if in consequence of her breach of that duty her child is born with disabilities which would not otherwise have been present, those disabilities are to be regarded as damage resulting from her wrongful act and actionable accordingly at the suit of the child.

4 Interpretation and other supplementary provisions　(1) References in this Act to a child being born disabled or with disabilities are to its being born with any deformity, disease or abnormality, including predisposition (whether or not susceptible of immediate prognosis) to physical or mental defect in the future.

(2) In this Act—

(a) ''born'' means born alive (the moment of a child's birth being when it first has a life separate from its mother), and ''birth'' has a corresponding meaning; and

(b) ''motor vehicle'' means a mechanically propelled vehicle intended or adapted for use on roads.

(3) Liability to a child under s 1 or 2 of this Act is to be regarded—

(a) as respects all its incidents and any matters arising or to arise out of it; and

(b) subject to any contrary context or intention for the purpose of construing references in enactments and documents to personal or bodily injuries and cognate matters,

as liability for personal injuries sustained by the child immediately after its birth.

(4) No damages shall be recoverable . . . in respect of any loss of expectation of life . . . unless . . . the child lives for at least 48 hours.

(5) This Act applies in respect of births after (but not before) its passing, and in respect of any such birth it replaces any law in force before its passing, whereby a

person could be liable to a child in respect of disabilities with which it might be born; but in 1(3) of this Act the expression "liable in tort" does not include any reference to liability by virtue of this Act, or to liability by virtue of any such law.'

The Act binds the Crown and extends to Northern Ireland but not to Scotland.

INTEREST ON DAMAGES

Note—The Law Reform (Miscellaneous Provisions) Act 1934, s 3 empowers any court of record (other than the High Court and County Court — see below) to award interest on damages for which judgment is given. Subsection 1 reads as follows:

'(1) In any proceedings tried in any court of record for the recovery of any debt or damages, the court may, if it thinks fit, order that there shall be included in the sum for which judgment is given interest at such rate as it thinks fit on the whole or any part of the debt or damages for the whole or any part of the period between the date when the cause of action arose and the date of the judgment.

   Provided that nothing in this section:—
(a) shall authorise the giving of interest upon interest; or
[(b) *and* (c) *inapplicable to actions of tort.*]'

Personal injury cases

Note—The Administration of Justice Act 1969, s 22 provides that interest is to be awarded as a matter of course in cases of personal injury. The section reads as follows:

'**22** In section 3 of the Law Reform (Miscellaneous Provisions) Act 1934 (power of courts of record to award interest on debts and damages), after sub-s (1) there shall be inserted the following subsections:—
   "(1A) Where in any such proceedings as are mentioned in subsection (1) of this section judgment is given for a sum which (apart from interest on damages) exceeds £200 and represents or includes damages in respect of personal injuries to the plaintiff or any other person, or in respect of a person's death, then (without prejudice to the exercise of the power conferred by that subsection in relation to any part of the sum which does not represent such damages) the court shall exercise that power so as to include in that sum interest on those damages or on such part of them as the court considers appropriate, unless the court is satisfied that there are special reasons why no interest should be given in respect of those damages.
   (1B) Any order under this section may provide for interest to be calculated at different rates in respect of different parts of the period for which interest is given, whether that period is the whole of the period mentioned in subsection (1) of this section.
   (1C) For the avoidance of doubt it is hereby declared that in determining, for the purposes of any enactment contained in the County Courts Act 1959, [now the County Courts Act 1984] whether an amount exceeds, or is less than, a sum specified in that enactment, no account shall be taken of any power exercisable by virtue of this section or of any order made in the exercise of such a power.
   (1D) In this section 'personal injuries' includes any disease and any impairment of a person's physical or mental condition, and any reference to the County Courts Act 1959 is a reference to that Act as (whether by virtue of the Administration of Justice Act 1969 or otherwise) that Act has effect for the time being." '

From 1 April 1983 the provisions of the Law Reform (Miscellaneous Provisions) Act 1934, s 3, s 35A and the Administration of Justice Act 1969, s 22 so far as they applied to the High Court and county courts ceased to have effect and were superseded by the Supreme Court Act 1981, s 35A and the County Courts Act 1959, s 97A (now the County Courts Act 1984, s 69) respectively. These sections are inserted by the Administration of Justice Act 1982, s 15. The Supreme Court Act 1981, s 35A is as follows:

'**35A Power of High Court to award interest on debts and damages**
(1) Subject to rules of court, in proceedings (whenever instituted) before the High Court for the recovery of a debt or damages there may be included in any sum for which judgment is given simple interest, at such rate as the court thinks fit or as rules of court may provide, on all or any part of the debt or damages in respect of which judgment is given, or payment is made before judgment, for all or any part of the period between the date when the cause of action arose and—
(a) in the case of any sum paid before judgment, the date of the payment; and
(b) in the case of the sum for which judgment is given, the date of the judgment.
(2) In relation to a judgment given for damages for personal injuries or death which exceed £200 sub-s (1) shall have effect—
(a) with the substitution of "shall be included" for "may be included"; and
(b) with the addition of "unless the court is satisfied that there are special reasons to the contrary" after "given", where first occurring.
(3) Subject to rules of court, where—
(a) there are proceedings (whenever instituted) before the High Court for the recovery of a debt; and
(b) the defendant pays the whole debt to the plaintiff (otherwise than in pursuance of a judgment in the proceedings),
the defendant shall be liable to pay the plaintiff simple interest at such rate as the court thinks fit or as rules of court may provide on all or any part of the debt for all or any part of the period between the date when the cause of action arose and the date of the payment.
(4) Interest in respect of a debt shall not be awarded under this section for a period during which, for whatever reason, interest on the debt already runs.
(5) Without prejudice to the generality of s 84, rules of court may provide for a rate of interest by reference to the rate specified in the Judgments Act 1838, s 17 as that section has effect from time to time or by reference to a rate for which any other enactment provides.
(6) Interest under this section may be calculated at different rates in respect of different periods.
(7) In this section "plaintiff" means the person seeking the debt or damages and "defendant" means the person from whom the plaintiff seeks the debt or damages and "personal injuries" includes any disease and any impairment of a person's physical or mental condition.
(8) [Bills of Exchange]'
The County Courts Act 1984, s 69 which repealed and replaced s 97A of the 1959 Act is in similar terms, plus the following sub-s (8) but not including sub-s (5) above:

'(8) In determining whether an amount exceeds—
(a) the county court limit; or
(b) an amount specified in any provision of this Act, no account shall be taken of the provisions of this section or of anything done under it.'

(1) Courts of record other than the High Court and county courts include e g the Court of Appeal when dealing with an appeal in an action for damages. (2) On pleading a claim for interest see *Practice Direction* 24 February 1983 [1983] 1 All ER 934, [1984] 1 WLR 377, 127 Sol Jo 208. See also p 391, above, and Ord 18, r 8(4).

Principles to be applied

Jefford v Gee

[1970] 2 QB 130, [1970] 1 All ER 1202, [1970] 2 WLR 702, 114 Sol Jo 206, CA

The plaintiff sustained severe injuries by accident on the 30 November 1966. At trial on 16 June 1969 the judge awarded special damages (mainly loss of earnings) at £2,131 and general damages at £3,500. On an application for interest under the 1934 Act he allowed no interest on the special damages but awarded $6\frac{1}{2}\%$ on the general damages from the date of the accident to date of trial.

HELD, ON APPEAL: The principle of the 1934 Act (which is unaltered by the 1969 Act) is that interest should be awarded to a plaintiff for being kept out of money which ought to have been paid to him. In detail the principles to be applied in a case of personal injury are as follows:

(1) *Special damages* should be dealt with on broad lines. Medical expenses and damage to clothing etc. are too small to warrant special calculation. Interest on loss of earnings in principle should be calculated on each week's loss from that week to date of trial but that would mean too much detail. In ordinary cases it would be fair to award interest on the total sum of special damages at half the rate allowed on the other damages.

(2) *Loss of future earnings:* no interest should be awarded.

(3) *Pain and suffering and loss of amenities:* interest should run from the date of service of the writ to the date of trial.

(4) *Fatal Accidents Acts and Law Reform damages:* interest should be awarded from date of service of the writ.

(5) *Rate of interest* should be the rate payable on money in court placed on short term investment account. This rate is fixed from time to time by rules made by the Lord Chancellor. Since 1 March 1970 it has been 7%, but over a period which included lower rates a mean or average of the rate obtainable should be taken: in the present case it should be 6%.

(6) *Tax:* the courts should not concern themselves with deduction of tax but merely award a gross sum of interest. The judgment should state the rate of interest and the period for which it is awarded.

(7) *County courts:* the same principles apply.

(8) *Exceptional cases* (e g where a party has been guilty of gross delay) may require the court to depart from the proposals above either in the rate of interest or the period for which it is allowed.

In the present case interest on special damage awarded at 3% from date of accident, on general damages of £2,500 for pain and suffering at 6% from date of service of the writ, on £1,000 general damages for future loss of earnings no interest.

Note—Income tax is not payable on interest awarded on damages for personal injuries. See pp 441–442, below.

On making payments into court, interest calculated up to date of payment in should be included if appropriate: see p 662, below.

In *Cookson v Knowles* ([1977] 1 QB 913, [1977] 2 All ER 820, [1977] 3 WLR 279, 121 Sol Jo 461) Lord Denning in the Court of Appeal said the guideline in *Jefford v Gee* should be changed because of inflation and that no interest should be awarded on the lump sum for pain and suffering and loss of amenities. 'The courts invariably assess the lump sum on the scale for figures current at the date of trial, which is much higher than the figure current at the date of the injury or at the date of the writ. The plaintiff thus stands to gain by the delay in bringing the case to trial. He ought not to gain still more by having interest from the date of service of the writ.' This dictum was disapproved by the House of Lords in *Pickett v British Rail Engineering* (p 444, below). Lord Scarman said it was wrong for two reasons: (1) It was a fallacy to say that because the award at trial was greater than it would have been if assessed at the date of service of the writ therefore it was of greater monetary value; the cash awarded was more but its purchasing power was the same or even less. (2) The Administration of Justice Act 1969, s 22 made the award of interest mandatory in the absence of special reasons why no interest should be given. Inflation was general to society and was not a special reason. However, the Court of Appeal has considered the matter again in the following case:

Birkett v Hayes
[1982] 2 All ER 710, [1982] 1 WLR 816, 126 Sol Jo 399, CA
The plaintiff sustained very serious injury in a road accident on 23 February 1975. She issued a writ for damages on 10 May 1976. On 19 January 1981 the judge assessed her damages for pain and suffering and loss of amenities at £30,000. He added £16,000 interest for the period from service of the writ at the rates available on the short term investment account, reducing the total award by 25% because of her failure to wear a seat belt. The defendant appealed against the amount of interest awarded. HELD: To award the full rate of interest at the high rates of the STI account on the whole of the award was wrong for the following reasons: (1) the damages were assessed on the value of money at the date of the award, not the date of proceedings; (2) interest on damages was tax free (Finance Act 1971, s 19); (3) there may be good reasons for delay in bringing the action on for trial and the defendant should not be penalised by the rate of interest chosen. Though *Pickett's* case decided that to award no interest was wrong it was for the Court to award it 'at such rate as it thinks fit' (Law Reform (Miscellaneous Provisions) Act 1934) so as to arrive at a final figure which will be fair to both parties. The appropriate rate here was 2%.

Wright v British Railways Board
[1983] 2 AC 773, [1983] 2 All ER 698, [1983] 3 WLR 211, 127 Sol Jo 478 HL
In an action for damages for personal injuries the judge awarded general damages for pain suffering and loss of amenity in the sum of £15,000. In awarding interest on these damages he felt himself bound to follow the guideline in *Birkett v Hayes* (above) and awarded interest at the rate of 2% per annum from the date of service of the writ to the date of judgment. On appeal to the House of Lords under the 'leap-frog' procedure (the Administration of Justice Act 1969, s 13):
HELD: There were no grounds for holding the guideline of 2% wrong during a period when inflation was proceeding at a very rapid rate. That guideline should continue to be followed for the time being.

Dexter v Courtaulds
[1984] 1 All ER 70, [1984] 1 WLR 372, 128 Sol Jo 81, CA
The plaintiff was awarded damages for personal injury he sustained on 22 August 1977. Trial of his action was not reached until May 1982. His

damages included sums for loss of wages for four months in 1977 and six weeks in 1978. Interest on these sums was awarded at only half rate from the date of the accident following the method in *Jefford v Gee*. On appeal it was argued on his behalf that as the whole amount of his loss of wages was ascertained as long ago as 1978 he should have interest at the full rate on the loss calculated from the end of each period.

HELD, dismissing the appeal: This was a straightforward case of personal injuries and the *Jefford v Gee* method of awarding half interest on the wage loss from the date of the accident to date of trial was the right one. There may be special circumstances in which the *Jefford v Gee* method would not be fair but this was not such a case. In the case of a high-earning self-employed man for example, off work for three or four months, whose action does not reach trial for four or five years, or where he has paid for an expensive operation out of his own pocket it may be fair to award interest at the full rate but in the generality of cases *Jefford v Gee* should not be departed from. In special cases the plaintiff claiming full interest should set out the special facts in the claim, so as to enable the defendant to make an appropriate calculation of interest for a payment into court.

Chadwick v Parsons

(1971) 115 Sol Jo 127, [1971] 2 Lloyd's Rep 49; affd [1971] 2 Lloyd's Rep 322, CA (Mars-Jones J)

In *Jefford v Gee* (above) the Court of Appeal did contemplate that interest might be awarded from a date earlier than the service of the writ, namely, the date of the letter before action. It may well be that in exceptional cases it would be right for the Court to award interest on general damages from a date even earlier than that; for example, in cases where the plaintiff has not issued proceedings at an earlier date because he has been suffering under some disability, or where the defendant has fraudulently concealed the facts upon which a cause of action might be based.

Slater v Hughes

[1971] 3 All ER 1287, [1971] 1 WLR 1438, 115 Sol Jo 428, CA

The plaintiff was injured on 23 April 1966. On 7 December 1966 she served a writ on the defendant Hughes who on 29 April 1968 served a third-party notice on Jones. On 31 March 1969 the plaintiff joined Jones as a defendant. At the trial liability was found against the defendants in the proportions 40% to Hughes 60% to Jones. The judge awarded interest on the general damages against both defendants from the date of service of the writ on Hughes. Jones appealed against the award of interest against him from 7 December 1966, as he had no notice of the proceedings until 29 April 1968 when he was served with the third-party notice.

HELD: The principle as established in *Jefford v Gee* was that interest should be paid to a plaintiff from the time when the defendant ought to have paid it. It followed that a party ought not to be treated as liable to pay interest until that party received notice of the claim. Interest should be payable by Jones only from 29 April 1968.

Interest on acceptance of money in court

Newall v Tunstall
[1970] 3 All ER 465, [1971] 1 WLR 104, 115 Sol Jo 14, [1970] 2 Lloyd's
Rep 417 (Ashworth J)
In a personal injury claim the defendant paid £1,300 into court in January.
The plaintiff did not then accept but in May she applied to the court for
leave to accept £1,300 and asked for interest on that sum under the 1934
and 1969 Acts on the ground that leave to take the money out was an order
equivalent to a judgment.
HELD: An order giving leave to take money out of court after the expiry of
the 14 days allowed by the rules was not a judgment and no interest was
payable.

Note—The same conclusion was reached by Fisher J on an exactly similar application in *Waite v Redpath Dorman Long Ltd* [1971] 1 QB 294, [1971] 1 All ER 513,
[1970] 3 WLR 1034. The problem which these two cases presented was overcome
by the addition of para (8) to RSC Ord 22, r 1 which provides that the plaintiff's
cause of action in respect of damages shall be construed as a cause of action also for
such interest as might be included in the judgment if judgment were given at the
date of payment in.

Blundell v Rimmer
[1971] 1 All ER 1072, [1971] 1 WLR 123, 115 Sol Jo 15, [1971] 1 Lloyd's
Rep 110 (Payne J)
In an action for damages for personal injury the defendant did not dispute
negligence and make a payment into court. The plaintiff applied to the
district registrar under RSC Ord 27, r 3 and obtained an order that he 'be
at liberty to sign interlocutory judgment on admission and that damages be
assessed by judge alone'.
HELD, ON APPEAL: The interlocutory judgment would be set aside. This
was a further attempt to circumvent the rule in *Jefford v Gee* (above) that on
acceptance of money in court the case ended without payment of interest.
Even if (contrary to the court's view) Ord 27, r 3 did enable the plaintiff to
obtain judgment the court would not exercise its discretion to give leave to
sign judgment in the present case: the rights of the parties were governed
by Ord 22 which entitled the defendant to make the payment in.

Interest on increased damages on appeal

Cook v J L Kier & Co Ltd
[1970] 2 All ER 513, [1970] 1 WLR 774, 114 Sol Jo 207, CA
After being awarded £9,589 damages the plaintiff appealed. The appeal
was reached nearly a year later when the Court of Appeal raised the award
to £15,045. The plaintiff asked for interest on the difference since the
original judgment.
HELD: Interest should be awarded on the amount by which the award was
increased at 5% but credit was to be given against it for 4% which would
automatically be running from the date of the judgment under the Judgments Act 1838.

Interest not stopped by adjournment

May v A G Bassett & Sons Ltd

(1970) 114 Sol Jo 269 (Paull J)

The plaintiff's action for damages under the Fatal Accidents Acts was due to be tried on 7 July 1969 but she asked for an adjournment to which the defendants agreed. She died on 6 September. Her administrator was substituted and the action was heard on 20 March 1970. The defendants opposed an award of interest after 7 July 1969 on the ground that the case would have been heard then but for the plaintiff's request for the adjournment.

HELD: Award of interest was in the discretion of the judge. The deciding factor here was that the defendants had had the advantage of keeping the money during the period of the adjournment and had drawn interest on it. The plaintiff should have interest to actual date of trial. There was no principle that interest should cease to be paid because of an adjournment.

Rate of interest

Note—See *Jefford v Gee*, p 437, above, para (5). The rate payable on money in court on short term investment account is the rate prescribed for the time being under the Supreme Court Funds Rules, r 78(1). See also *Birkett v Hayes* (above).

Income tax and interest

Note—The Finance Act 1971, s 19 reads as follows:

'**19 Exemption of interest on damages for personal injuries** The following section shall be inserted in the Taxes Act after s 375:

375A Exemption of interest on damages for personal injuries (1) The following interest shall not be regarded as income for any income tax purpose—

(a) any interest on damages in respect of personal injuries to a plaintiff or any other person, or in respect of a person's death, which is included in any sum for which judgment is given by virtue of a provision to which this paragraph applies, and

(b) any interest on damages or solatium in respect of personal injuries sustained by a pursuer or by any other person, decree for payment of which is included in any interlocutor by virtue of s 1 of the Interest on Damages (Scotland) Act 1958.

(2) In this section ''personal injuries'' includes any disease and any impairment of a person's physical or mental condition.

''The Taxes Act'' means the Income and Corporation Taxes Act 1970.'

The Finance Act 1981 added sub-s (1A) to s 375A as follows:

'(1A) A payment in satisfaction of a cause of action, including a payment into court, shall not be regarded as income for any income tax purpose to the extent to which it is in respect of interest which would fall within subsection (1) above if included in a sum for which a judgment is given. . . .'

Subsection (1B) applies sub-s (1) to the Law Reform (Miscellaneous Provisions) Act 1934, s 3 the Supreme Court Act 1981, s 35A and the County Courts Act 1959, s 97A (now replaced by the County Courts Act 1984, s 69).

Mason v Harman
[1972] RTR 1
The Finance Act 1971, s 19 by relieving a plaintiff from tax on interest does not call for a reduction in the rate of interest from that which would have been awarded before the 1971 Act in order to produce the same real net situation as was achieved by the *Jefford v Gee* principles before the relief was granted. There was no reason to suppose that s 19 was not intended by Parliament to benefit the recipient.

INTERIM PAYMENTS

The power of the court in actions pending in the High Court to order interim payments of damages is contained in the Supreme Court Act 1981, s 32 which is as follows:

'**32 Orders for interim payment**   (1) As regards proceedings pending in the High Court, provision may be made by rules of court for enabling the court, in such circumstances as may be prescribed, to make an order requiring a party to the proceedings to make an interim payment of such amount as may be specified in the order, with provision for the payment to be made to such other party to the proceedings as may be specified or, if the order so provides, by paying it into court.
(2) Any rules of court which make provision in accordance with sub-s (1) may include provision for enabling a party to any proceedings who, in pursuance of such an order, has made an interim payment to recover the whole or part of the amount of the payment in such circumstances, and from such other party to the proceedings, as may be determined in accordance with the rules.
(3) Any rules made by virtue of this section may include such incidental, supplementary and consequential provisions as the rule-making authority may consider necessary or expedient.
(4) Nothing in this section shall be construed as affecting the exercise of any power relating to costs, including any power to make rules of court relating to costs.
(5) In this section "interim payment", in relation to a party to any proceedings, means a payment on account of any damages, debt or other sum (excluding any costs) which that party may be held liable to pay to or for the benefit of another party to the proceedings if a final judgment or order of the court in the proceedings is given or made in favour of that other party.'

For actions in the High Court rules have been made which comprise Part II of Ord 29 (rr 9 to 18). They enable a plaintiff in action for damages for personal injuries to apply for an interim payment of damages at any time after a writ has been served and the time limited for appearance has expired. No order will be made unless the defendant is insured, or is a public authority or is a person whose means and resources are such as to enable him to make the interim payment.

Fryer v London Transport Executive
(1982) Times, 4 December, CA
The plaintiff was seriously injured in a road accident. In an action for damages against the defendants he applied to the court for an interim payment. The master awarded £20,000, but on appeal the judge awarded £50,000. The defendants appealed against the award on the ground that the plaintiff had disclosed to the master and to the judge that the defendants had already made interim payments and a payment into court. Order 22, r 7 prohibits disclosure to the courts of a payment into court at a trial or hearing. Order 29, r 15 says no communication of an interim payment

whether voluntary or pursuant to an order 'shall be made to the Court at the trial or hearing of any . . . issue as to . . . damages until all questions of liability and amount have been determined'.

HELD: (1) Whether or not an interim payment should be made and how much it should be were not questions or issues as to damages but related to what in interlocutory proceedings should be done to meet the justice of the case. (2) The defendants had made their objections too late. The information in question had been before both the master and the judge and the defendants had not objected: it would be wrong to allow them to do so now. Appeal dismissed.

LOSS OF EXPECTATION OF LIFE

Note—For fatal cases, see under 'Law reform damages', p 524, below.

In respect of causes of action accruing on or after 1 January 1983 claims for damages for loss of expectation of life are abolished in part by the Administration of Justice Act 1982, s 1 which is as follows:

'**1 Abolition of right to damages for loss of expectation of life** (1) In an action under the law of England and Wales or the law of Northern Ireland for damages for personal injuries—
(a) no damages shall be recoverable in respect of any loss of expectation of life caused to the injured person by the injuries; but
(b) if the injured person's expectation of life has been reduced by the injuries, the court, in assessing damages in respect of pain and suffering caused by the injuries, shall take account of any suffering caused or likely to be caused to him by awareness that his expectation of life has been so reduced.
(2) The reference in sub-s (1)(a) above to damages in respect of loss of expectation of life does not include damages in respect of loss of income.'

Sub-section (2) preserves the right to damages for loss of earnings during the 'lost years' for a living plaintiff (but not for the benefit of the estate of a deceased person; see p 523, below).

Loss of prospective earnings in 'lost years'

Oliver v Ashman
[1962] 2 QB 210, [1961] 3 All ER 323, [1961] 3 WLR 669, 105 Sol Jo 608, CA
The plaintiff, a child aged 20 months received very serious head injuries in a road accident. He was aged four years at the time of the trial. As a result of the injuries he had become a low-grade mental defective with a severe traumatic epilepsy. He had ceased to talk and would never be able to earn his living. He would need fairly soon to enter an institution for care and supervision and for such re-education as he was capable of. He would probably spend the rest of his life in a state institution. His expectation of life was reduced from about 60 years to 30 years.

HELD: The matter was concluded by *Benham v Gambling* [1941] AC 157, [1941] 1 All ER 7, 110 LJKB 49, 164 LT 290, 57 TLR 177, 84 Sol Jo 703, HL and the decision of Slade J in *Harris v Bright's Asphalt Contractors* [1953] 1 QB 617, [1953] 1 All ER 395, [1953] 1 WLR 341, 97 Sol Jo 115, 51 LGR 296. There is no authority for distinguishing between the case of a living plaintiff and a dead man's estate. The House of Lords in *Benham v Gambling* showed that the House was intending to settle the problem once and for all, that loss of future wages during the lost years was but an ingredient in the loss of expectation of life and did not fall to be valued as an item on its own.

Pickett v British Rail Engineering Ltd
[1980] AC 136, [1979] 1 All ER 774, [1978] 3 WLR 955, 122 Sol Jo 778, HL

The plaintiff, aged 51, was found to be suffering from mesothelioma caused by the defendants' admitted negligence. His expectation of life was reduced to one year. He claimed damages for loss of expectation of life. The Court of Appeal following *Oliver v Ashman* (above) held that damages for loss of earnings during the 'lost years' were not recoverable.

HELD, ON APPEAL to the House of Lords: *Oliver v Ashman* was wrongly decided. It had been based on a dictum of Lord Simon in *Benham v Gambling* [1941] AC 157: 'No regard must be had to financial losses and gains during the period of which the victim has been deprived'. But in *Benham's* case no claim for loss of earnings had been made and Lord Simon could not be taken to intend that his words should apply to a case where there was such a claim. Though damages for loss of earnings during the 'lost years' should be assessed with moderation they must not be fixed at a conventional figure because, being damages for pecuniary loss, they can be measured in money. In assessing those damages the plaintiff's own living expenses which the plaintiff would have expended during the lost years should be deducted but whether he has dependants or not or whether he would have looked after them is immaterial. Case remitted for damages to be assessed.

Note—In *Harris v Empress Motors Ltd* (below), a fatal case, O'Connor LJ after examining in detail the speeches in *Pickett's* case on the assessment of damages for loss of earnings during the 'lost years', quoted from Lord Scarman's speech 'the loss to the estate is what the deceased would have been likely to have available to save, spend or distribute after meeting the cost of his living at a standard which his job and career prospects at time of death would suggest he was reasonably likely to achieve. Subtle mathematical calculations, based as they must be on events or contingencies of a life which he will not live are out of place; the judge must make the best estimate based on the known facts and his prospects at time of death'. O'Connor LJ then quoted the amendment to the Law Reform (Miscellaneous Provisions) Act 1934, s 1(2)(a) made by the Administration of Justice Act 1982 s 4(2) (p 523, below) and said that the problem of estimating 'living expenses' would remain in future 'to a much more limited extent in cases where a live plaintiff is claiming in respect of loss of earnings during a period of time that his working life has been shortened by the tort of the defendant'. He proceeded to summarise as follows:

Harris v Empress Motors Ltd
[1983] 3 All ER 561, [1984] 1 WLR 212, 127 Sol Jo 647, CA

Three principles emerge from the decisions in *Pickett v British Rail Engineering* and *Gammell v Wilson:* (1) the ingredients that go to make up 'living expenses' are the same whether the victim be young or old, single or married, with or without dependants; (2) the sum to be deducted as living expenses is the proportion of the victim's net earnings that he spends to maintain himself at the standard of life appropriate to his case; (3) any sums expended to maintain or benefit others do not form part of the victim's living expenses and are not to be deducted from the net earnings.

A hidden difficulty arises from principles (2) and (3) when some living expenses are shared with others. In such cases (e g husband and wife) half the cost should be referable to each. The greater the number of persons provided for out of the victim's net earnings the less must be his share of the living expenses, e g where a household consists of four persons provided for by his earnings, one-quarter of the cost of the joint items should be deducted. This differs from the straight Fatal Accidents Act solution applied in the Queen's Bench Division: per O'Connor LJ.

INFANTS

Connolly v Camden and Islington Area Health Authority
[1981] 3 All ER 250 (Comyn J)
When only a few days old the infant plaintiff (four and three-quarters years at the date of trial) suffered serious brain damage when being anaesthetised for a surgical operation. He was left with extensive mental and physical disabilities. His expectation of life, as found by the judge on the evidence, was shortened to $27\frac{1}{2}$ years. Damages were claimed for loss of earnings during the 'lost years'.
HELD: The plaintiff qualified for a 'lost years' payment but the assessment was nil. From *Pickett's* case (above) and *Gammell's* case (p 960, below) it was clear that a young or middle-aged man could rightly expect an award for the financial benefit of the years' earnings which he had lost even though it involved a great deal of guesswork, but those cases show that a child is in a different position. No hard and fast rule can be laid down but a child qualifies under this head of damage dependent on the ability to prove the potential loss. As Lord Scarman said in *Gammell's* case (p 960, below) the lost years of earning capacity will ordinarily be so distant that no estimate is possible, though there may be exceptions — e g that of a child television star. Other possible examples are the son of a father who owns a prosperous business or the son of a farmer who is able to leave the estate to his son. But in the present case on the evidence, though there is a claim, the assessment is nil.

Croke v Wiseman
[1981] 3 All ER 852, [1982] 1 WLR 71, CA
The infant plaintiff when 21 months old suffered a cardiac arrest due to negligence of the defendants. He survived but with severe loss of brain function, paralysis of all four limbs and blindness. His expectation of life was limited to 40 years. Damages were claimed for (inter alia) loss of future earnings during life and during the 'lost years' of life expectation.
HELD: Though it is a task of great difficulty to assess an appropriate sum for a young child it has been frequently done e g in the thalidomide cases. Taking a figure of £5,000 per annum for estimated future loss and a maximum working life of 22 years (i e from 18 to 40) the actuarial figure for the multiplier is 8.876. But this makes no allowance for the receipt of a capital sum at least 11 years before earnings would begin nor for the possibility that the child would never have become an earner. The multiplier should be reduced to five years making a total of £25,000 for future loss of earnings. As for earnings during the lost years there are compelling reasons as in *Pickett's* case (above) for awarding a sum of money to a living plaintiff of mature years which would have been available to spend on his

dependents, but in the case of a child there are no dependents and, if the injuries are catastrophic, there never will be any. In such a case the court should refuse to speculate. No sum should be awarded for the lost years.

SUBSTANTIAL UNEARNED INCOME

See *Adsett v West*, p 964, below (Appendix). Though a fatal case and therefore no longer applicable to fatal cases since 1 January 1983, it may call for consideration in the case of a living plaintiff who claims for loss of earnings during 'lost years' and who has a substantial unearned income in addition to his earned income.

NEUROSIS: HYSTERIA

Griffiths v R. and H. Green and Silley Weir
(1948) 81 Ll L Rep 378 (Birkett J)
A boilermaker, earning £9 per week, aged 32, married, with three young children, was injured on February 1947, the injuries being to the head and causing concussion and resulting in anxiety neurosis. It was agreed by all the medical witnesses that there were no signs of organic lesion or organic disease, but there was every sign of functional nervous disturbance.

For the plaintiff, the medical evidence was that it was unlikely the plaintiff would ever be able to do his work of a boilermaker again, though he would probably be able to do suitable light work. For the defendants, that the plaintiff's condition had become one of hysteria as a consequence of anxiety neurosis. When the case was settled and that anxiety taken away and he did light work, ultimately all would be well.

The plaintiff had been offered work at his own trade but said he could not do it. He was given a job of watchman but complained he could not do it and gave it up. He later failed to take a job in the stockyard for which he had asked. The employers were still willing to find a job.

HELD PER BIRKETT J: The field of functional nervous disturbance is difficult for laymen quite to understand. I suppose that there is none of us quite immune from anxiety of one kind and another in these days, but when people speak of anxiety neurosis when a man is not suffering organically but has hysteria, the ordinary sound, healthy man is apt to look upon that with a little disdain or a little suspicion and to treat it rather lightly and to say: 'Well, if you have a little courage or determination you can overcome it. If you have a little will-power to go back to work and confront the difficulty, that would overcome it.' It is comparatively easy for healthy people to think and to speak like that, but people who have undergone an illness frequently look upon small matters as very important and are fearful and nervous and apprehensive. The plaintiff's complaints were genuine and he was really suffering a serious functional disturbance.

The judge allowed full wages to the date of hearing (62 weeks, £558) less £70 received, net £488. He allowed for six months light work with loss of earnings for that period of £4 and £5 per week (£104 to £130); he took into account pain and suffering to the date of trial, and allowing in addition for the condition of anxiety neurosis, he awarded a total sum of £1,500.

Liffen v Watson
[1940] 1 KB 556, [1940] 2 All ER 213, 109 LJKB 367, 162 LT 398, 56 TLR
442, CA (Slesser LJ)
The neurosis may itself prevent the injured person from making the effort
necessary to make the disability cease. If the plaintiff can avoid the neurotic
pain by not doing certain normal things, then she has been damaged
because she cannot do them. Conversely, if she attempts them, and feels
pain, the pain causes suffering.

Dupey v T. F. Maltby
[1955] 2 Lloyd's Rep 645 (Pearce J)
Plaintiff suffered a slight accident at work and afterwards suffered serious
post traumatic hysteria.
HELD: The accident produced the hysteria. Defendants could not plead
extraneous factors retarding recovery in reduction of damages, but only
causes producing or adding to the hysteria caused by the accident.

Love v Port of London Authority
[1959] 2 Lloyd's Rep 541 (Edmund Davies J)
The plaintiff, a lorry driver, sustained a blow on the head from the swing-
ing chains of a crane on 23 July 1955. He received attention for some minor
cuts, then drove his lorry 12 miles to his depot. On July 25, he had a 'black-
out' and was unfit for work to 20 August 1955. Since 1955, however, until
trial in November 1959, he had never resumed his pre-accident work. He
had done other kinds of work from time to time of a light nature. His
incapacity was due to (1) pre-existing heart trouble; (2) neurosis. The
neurosis was itself not entirely due to the accident: 70% of the neurosis was
due to the heart trouble, 30% to the accident.
HELD: The defendants must take the plaintiff as they find him, that is to
say, with his already vulnerable personality. As far as special damages were
concerned, if the 30% of the neurosis due to the accident made the difference between working and not working then the defendants would have to
recompense the plaintiff for all the special damages arising from the 100%
neurosis. Conversely where the interruption in work would have occurred
in any event no special damages were recoverable. As to general damages
the Court had to try to assess compensation for such precipitation and
aggravation in the functional (ie neurotic) condition as was fully attributable to the accident and which would not have developed without it.
Award, special damages £825, general damages £850.

Effect of delay in litigation

James v Woodall Duckham Construction Co Ltd
[1969] 2 All ER 794, [1969] 1 WLR 903, 113 Sol Jo 225, CA
On 17 March 1962 the plaintiff fell from a ladder and was injured. The
physical injuries were not serious: he was in hospital four days and in June
1962 the hospital declared him fit for work. He did not try any work until
October 1962 when he worked for three days and then gave up. He did no
further work at all. He complained of pains all over his body. The doctors

said there was no physical reason for these but he was not a malingerer. The pains were functional or neurotic. On 18 June 1963 a neuro-surgeon reported to the plaintiff's solicitors that the pains would not clear up until his claim for damages was settled and that the longer the functional illness was allowed to continue the more difficult it would be for him to return to work. The claim did not reach trial until 26 June 1968, when the judge awarded £11,267 damages of which £5,000 was for loss of earnings up to date and £2,500 for estimated future loss.

HELD: The plaintiff's solicitors received the report from the neuro-surgeon in June 1963 as agents for the plaintiff. They should at once have issued a writ with the object of bringing the action on for trial. If they had done this and pursued the action with ordinary diligence it would have been heard in 1965 and the plaintiff would soon thereafter have gone back to his old job. Damages should be limited to the amount the plaintiff would have lost if that had been done plus a fair figure for the pain he had suffered. Award reduced from £11,627 to £4,500.

Batchelor v Rederij A. and L. Polder
[1961] 1 Lloyd's Rep 247 (Megaw J)
The plaintiff was struck on the head by a hawser in an accident at work on 17 October 1957. There was no fracture of the skull or damage to the brain but the plaintiff developed a condition of pseudo dementia which incapacitated him for work and brought about a complete change of personality. Although he had been discharged from the Army in 1946 on account of hysterical amnesia he had recovered and was living a normal active life before the accident. After the accident he had become completely inactive, unable to walk properly, unable to work and unable to conduct his own affairs. It was a matter of guess-work as to what was likely to happen to him in the future. His average pre-accident earnings were £18 13s 4d per week. What had to be taken into account was what the plaintiff would have earned over the years had he not suffered the accident, what amount, if anything, he was likely to earn in the future and to make various other allowances for mortality or illness which might happen to anyone. It was also necessary to take into account the fact that he had suffered from hysterical amnesia earlier in his career and that had predisposed him to attacks.

   Award for future anticipated loss of earnings £7,000.

   Award for pain and suffering £1,500.

NOVUS ACTUS INTERVENIENS

Note—See also pp 371–375, above and under 'Death resulting from accident', p 513, below.

Robinson v Post Office
[1974] 2 All ER 737, [1974] 1 WLR 1176, 117 Sol Jo 915, CA
The plaintiff, a Post Office employee, sustained a wound on his leg when he slipped on an oily rung whilst descending a tower wagon ladder. He visited his doctor who gave him an injection of anti-tetanus serum. A few days later the plaintiff developed symptoms due to an allergy to the serum and

eventually suffered serious brain damage. The judge held the doctor was not negligent in administering the serum and that although he was negligent in failing to give a preliminary test dose it would have made no difference if he had. The Post Office admitted that the accident and injury to the plaintiff's leg was caused by negligence on its part but said it was not liable for the serious results of the injection because they were not reasonably foreseeable.

HELD: (1) The injection of serum by the doctor was not a *novus actus interveniens* which broke the chain of causation between the negligence of the Post Office and the plaintiff's disability caused by the injection. Conduct of the doctor falling short of negligence could not amount to a *novus actus* and such negligence as the judge found against him was of no effect in causing the disability. (2) It was foreseeable both that the plaintiff might slip on an oily rung and sustain injury and that if he did he might well require medical treatment. The only unforeseeable result was the terrible extent of the injury caused by the plaintiff's allergy to the serum; in that respect the Post Office must take their victim as they found him. *Smith v Leech Brain & Co* (p 362, above) followed. If a wrongdoer ought reasonably to foresee that as a result of his wrongful act the victim may require medical treatment he is, subject to the principle of *novus actus interveniens*, liable for the consequences of the treatment applied although he could not reasonably foresee those consequences.

Negligent treatment

Rothwell v Caverswall Stone Co
[1944] 2 All ER 350, 171 LT 289, 113 LJKB 520, 61 TLR 17, CA
A workman met with an accident during employment on 23 March 1943, and suffered a fracture dislocation of his right shoulder. He was treated at the local hospital. His shoulder was not X-rayed and the injury was not correctly diagnosed. If it had been and been correctly treated, he would probably have completely recovered in six to eight weeks. Subsequently, when correctly diagnosed, it was too late for effective treatment and the arm was permanently stiff. On the hearing of an arbitration under the Workmen's Compensation Acts, the county court judge found the then existing incapacity was due to negligent medical treatment and was not the result of the accident.

HELD, ON APPEAL: The workman's condition was due to the negligent treatment and not the accident. No compensation was payable after the date on which he would have recovered if properly treated. The county court judge was bound by authority to come to the conclusion he did on the facts as found by him.

Per du Parcq LJ: In my opinion, the following propositions may be formulated upon the authorities as they stand: first, an existing incapacity 'results from' the original injury if it follows, and is caused by, that injury, and may properly be held so to result even if some supervening cause has aggravated the effects of the original injury and prolonged the period of incapacity. If, however, the existing incapacity ought fairly to be attributed to a new cause which has intervened and ought no longer to be attributed to the original injury, it may properly be held to result from the new cause and not from the original injury, even though, but for the original injury, there would have been no incapacity. Second, negligent or inefficient treatment by a doctor or other person may amount to a new cause and the circumstances may justify a finding of fact that the existing incapacity results from the new cause, and does not result from the original injury. This is so even if the negligence or inefficient treatment consists of an error of omission whereby the original incapacity is prolonged. In such a case, if the arbitrator is satisfied that the incapacity would have wholly ceased but for the omission, a finding of fact that the existing incapacity results from the new cause, and not from the injury will be justified. In stating these propositions I am far from seeking to lay down any new principles of construction. I have sought only to collect, by a process of induction, such general, and necessarily vague, rules as seem to emerge from the decided cases. Such rules do no more than indicate the bounds within which an arbitrator is free to decide — the province of fact. It is constantly being said, and must always be remembered, that the arbitrator is the sole judge of the facts.

Appeal dismissed.

Hogan v Bentinck West Hartley Colleries (Owners) Ltd
[1949] 1 All ER 588, [1949] LJR 865, [1949] WN 109, HL

If a surgeon, by lack of skill or failure in reasonable care, causes additional injury or aggravates an existing injury and so renders himself liable in damages, his intervention is a new cause and the additional injury or aggravation should be attributed to it and not to the original accident. On the other hand, an operation prudently advised and skilfully and carefully carried out should not be treated as a new cause, whatever its consequences may be.

Refusal to undergo operation

McAuley v London Transport Executive
[1957] 2 Lloyd's Rep 500, CA

It cannot be laid down as a general rule that a plaintiff can disregard the advice given by a doctor examining him, even though the doctor examining him is doing so on behalf of the defendant. The question is one of fact in each particular case. Was the advice, and were the prospects of success of the proposed operation or treatment, clearly put to the plaintiff, so that he, as a reasonable man, would appreciate that he was being advised that this treatment or operation would put him right? If the evidence shows that, the plaintiff, as a reasonable person, ought either to accept that advice, or else go to his own doctor and ask for his advice.

Morgan v T. Wallis Ltd
[1974] 1 Lloyd's Rep 165, QBD

Per Browne J: The plaintiff in the present case is not in the slightest degree a malingerer and is a completely honest man who genuinely holds the beliefs about which he has told us in evidence. But in deciding whether the defendants have proved that he had unreasonably refused to have the investigation and operation in question here, it seems to me clear from the authorities to which I have referred [*Steel v Robert George & Co* ([1942] AC 497, [1942] 1 All ER 447), *Marcroft v Scruttons Ltd* ([1954] 1 Lloyd's Rep

395, CA)] that I must apply an objective test, in this sense, would a reasonable man, in all the circumstances, receiving the advice the plaintiff did receive, have refused the operation? I think this question must be considered as at the times when his decision was made and on the basis of the advice he then received. If the plaintiff preferred and prefers to go on as he is rather than have the operation [for removal of a prolapsed intervertebral disc] no one can blame him. But the question I have to consider is not, 'Is the plaintiff to blame for refusing the operation?' but 'Is it fair and reasonable to make the defendants pay for his refusal?'

PENSIONS

Service pensions

Note—The Ministry of Pensions has declared its practice in relation to reduction of a war pension awarded on account of disablement by reference to damages or other compensation recovered. Of the total amount of damages or other compensation recovered 75% is disregarded altogether. The balance after making this deduction is converted into a weekly sum by assessing the amount of a Government annuity for the life of the pensioner which could be purchased therewith, having regard to the price of consols on the date of payment. The war pension is then reduced by this weekly sum. The reduction operates only from the date of payment of the damages.

Payne v Railway Executive
[1952] 1 KB 26, [1951] 2 All ER 910, [1951] 2 TLR 929, [1951] WN 547, 95 Sol Jo 710, CA

Plaintiff was injured in a railway accident whilst serving in the Royal Navy. He received 100% disability pension of £2 5s 0d per week under the Royal Warrant 1946 (Cmd 6489) because he was injured whilst in the service; later reduced to 90% disability of £2 0s 6d, and increased later when he married by 9s for wife and 6s 9d for child; to £2 16s 3d. The railway executive contended that the pension awarded as a result of the accident should be taken into account in assessing damages for loss of future earnings of £3,000. If it had, the judge would have awarded £750.

HELD: The pension did not operate to reduce the damages. The cases under the Fatal Accidents Acts had no application. The position was similar to that of *Bradburn v Great Western Rly Co* (1874) LR 10 Exch 1, 44 LJ Ex 9, 31 LT 464, where Pigott B in refusing to deduct accident insurance money from damages said:

'there is no reason or justice in setting off what the plaintiff has entitled himself to under a contract with third persons, by which he has bargained for the payment of a sum of money in the event of an accident happening to him. He does not receive that sum of money because of the accident, but because he has made a contract providing for the contingency; an accident must occur to entitle him to it, but it is not the accident, but his contract, which is the cause of his receiving it.'

In *Shearman v Folland* (p 461, below), Asquith LJ quoted from *Mayne on Damages*:

'Matter completely collateral, and merely *res inter alios acta*, cannot be used in mitigation of damages. The pension was *res inter alios acta* and would have been paid if defendants had not been liable. No account should be taken of the pension in assessing the loss.'

The defendants appealed. In the Court of Appeal it was pointed out that evidence was given in the court below from the Ministry of Pensions (mentioned at p 451, above) of the present practice that the disability pension was abated by the annuity value of 25% of the damages (less special damages). An opposite conclusion to that of Sellers J would put the Minister in an impossible position. He would not wish to impose a double deduction (a) by the court in assessing damages and (b) by the Minister in adjusting the pension. Appeal dismissed.

Carroll v Hooper

[1964] 1 All ER 845, [1964] 1 WLR 345, 108 Sol Jo 120 (Veale J)

The plaintiff, aged 24, suffered serious injuries including loss of an arm, in a motor cycle accident for which the defendants' husband, who was killed in the accident, was held wholly to blame. At the time of the accident the plaintiff was a National Serviceman in the Royal Corps of Signals. As a result of his injuries he was discharged from the Army and was awarded a service disablement pension of £6 12s 6d per week. The pension was held on the terms of the Pension Appeals Tribunal Act 1943, s 11 under which the award was subject to the power of the Minister of Pensions to vary, revoke or reduce the award in accordance with any provision of the Royal Warrant. The Royal Warrant of 24 May 1949, art 52(1) provided: 'Where the Minister is satisfied that compensation has been or will be paid to . . . a person to . . . whom a pension . . . is being . . . paid . . . The Minister may take the compensation into account against the pension . . . in such manner or to such extent as he may think fit, and may . . . reduce the pension . . . accordingly.'

HELD: *Browning v War Office* (below), was distinguishable since in that case the service pension was held as of right and could not be taken away. The *ratio decidendi* of Singleton LJ in *Payne v Railway Executive* (above) applied here, that it would be unfair to take the pension into account since as soon as the compensation was awarded by the Court the Minister might cut off or cut down the pension. The pension should be disregarded.

Elstob v Robinson

[1964] 1 All ER 848, [1964] 1 WLR 726, 108 Sol Jo 543 (Elwes J)

The plaintiff, a naval rating aged 18, was seriously injured in a road accident for which the defendant was to blame. As a result of his injuries the plaintiff was discharged from the Royal Navy and was awarded a service disability pension of £5 15s 0d per week under an Order in Council dated 29 September 1949 of which art 52(1) was in the same terms as art 52(1) of the Royal Warrant quoted in *Carroll v Hooper* (above). It was the current policy of the Minister of Pensions to exercise his discretion to diminish a pension in such a case as this by deducting from the pension an amount equal to the value of a government life annuity which would be produced by one quarter of the damages awarded. In the present case the appropriate figure for general damages was £11,250 so that the Minister would reduce the pension by £3 1s 8d per week being the value of an annuity based on £2,812 10s 0d, one-quarter of the damages recovered. This would leave a pension of £2 13s 4d per week. Ought this to be taken into account in assessing the damages?

HELD: Following *Carroll v Hooper* (above) it should not. The decision in *Payne v Railway Executive* (p 451, above) that the quantum of damages ought not to be reduced by reference to a disability pension which was not payable as a matter of right was binding on the court. Moreover the same rule applied to special damages for loss already sustained. In the present case £1,477 was recoverable for loss of earnings which would be reduced to £740 if the pension were to be taken into account. The vital distinction between a pension received as of right and a pension received at discretion applies equally whether the damages are precisely calculated retrospectively as special damages or assessed for the future as general damages. There should be no deduction from the sum of £1,477 on account of the pension.

Pensions received as of right

Browning v War Office
[1963] 1 QB 750, [1962] 3 All ER 1089, [1963] 2 WLR 52, 106 Sol Jo 957, [1962] 2 Lloyd's Rep 363, CA
The plaintiff, a Sergeant in the United States Army, was very seriously injured in a road accident. As a result he was discharged from the Army in which his pay had been 450 dollars a month. On discharge he was paid veteran's benefit of 217 dollars per month. This was a payment to which he was entitled as of right by the law of the United States and which he would always receive. He was awarded £32,111 damages of which £25,111 was in respect of loss of army pay, the judge considering himself bound by *Payne v Railway Executive* (p 451, above) to hold that the veteran's benefit could not be taken into account in assessing the loss.
HELD: The amount of the veteran's benefit which the plaintiff was receiving and would receive should be taken into account in assessing the loss of earnings. The general principle is that a plaintiff should be compensated so far as money can do it for the pecuniary loss which he has suffered. He should give credit for all sums which he received in diminution of his loss except where it would not be just or fair to require him to do so. The plaintiff in the present case was already receiving as of right nearly half his pay and regard should be given to this. Damages reduced from £32,111 to £14,411.

Note—Held in *Parry v Cleaver* (p 454, below) to be wrongly decided.

Judd v Hammersmith West London and St Mark's Hospitals
[1960] 1 All ER 607, [1960] 1 WLR 328, 104 Sol Jo 270 (Finnemore J)
The plaintiff claimed damages for injuries he received in an accident. He was a local government officer who had contributed compulsorily for 32 years to a superannuation fund maintained by his employer. Because of his injuries he had to retire from his employment earlier than he would otherwise have done and on retirement was awarded a pension of £300 a year from the superannuation fund.
HELD: In assessing damages for loss of earnings due to the injuries he received in the accident the pension should not be taken into account since it was the service of the plaintiff with the borough council and not the accident that gave rise to the pension.

Parry v Cleaver
[1970] AC 1, [1969] 1 All ER 555, [1969] 2 WLR 821, 113 Sol Jo 147, HL
The plaintiff, a policeman, had to leave the police force because of injury
caused by the defendant's negligence. He was then aged 36. But for the
injury he would not have retired from the force until he was 48 and would
then have been entitled as of right to a pension of £10 per week for life. On
leaving the force at 36 he became entitled as of right to a pension of £3
per week for life. He had contributed to the fund during his service by
payments which were compulsory. The trial judge, following *Judd v
Hammersmith Borough Council* (above) held that in assessing damages the
pension should be ignored during the period up to age 48, when the
plaintiff would have left the force, but should be taken into account
thereafter.
HELD, by the Court of Appeal: This was not correct. The general rule is
that the injured party should give credit for all sums which he received in
diminution of his loss save for exceptional cases such as insurance benefits.
The case was indistinguishable from *Browning v War Office* (above) and the
pension must be taken into account for the whole period.
   The decision of the Court of Appeal was reversed by the House of Lords
who by a majority of three to two restored the decision of the trial judge.
   Lord Reid drew attention to the two types of payments which are
disregarded in assessing damages — benevolent gifts (*Redpath v Belfast and
County Down Railway* (p 415, above)) and moneys coming to the plaintiff
under a contract of insurance (*Bradburn v Great Western Rly Co*). There was
no reason to regard these types of receipt as anomalous. In the case of benevolent payments it would be revolting to a man's sense of justice that the
sufferer should have his damages reduced so that he would gain nothing
from the benevolence of his friends and relatives. In the case of insurance
moneys they are not taken into account because the plaintiff has bought
them, and it would be unjust and unreasonable to hold that the benefit from
the money he had prudently spent on premiums should enure to the benefit
of the tortfeasor. Why should it make any difference that he insured by
arrangement with his employer rather than with an insurance company? If
it did not, then a contributory pension, which is a form of insurance, should
not be taken into account either. There is no relevant difference between a
pension, for which payments are made into a fund to meet future contingencies, and other forms of insurance. The reason the pension was to be
taken into account after age 48 was that in the later period it was a
comparison of like with like. In the period before age 48 the plaintiff was
receiving something different in kind from what he had lost, namely,
wages. *Browning v War Office* (above) was wrongly decided.

PERSONALITY CHANGE

Divorce

Jones v Jones
[1984] 3 All ER 1003, CA
The plaintiff was very seriously injured in a road accident, so much that he
suffered a personality change and his affairs were administered by the
Court of Protection. He was awarded a total of £177,500 damages. At the

time of the accident he had a wife and one child with another expected. As a result of his injuries the marriage broke down; his wife divorced him and lived separately with the two children. It was conceded that the breakdown of the marriage and separation or divorce were reasonably foreseeable by the defendant. The judge at first instance in the light of this concession held there was no reason in principle for refusing to award damages for the extra expense to the plaintiff in maintaining his wife and children in a separate establishment but said at the time of the trial that the plaintiff had not proved any additional loss and expense. After the trial the plaintiff's wife in matrimonial proceedings obtained an order for periodical payments at £2,445 a year and for a lump sum of £25,000 which had been spent on a house for the wife.

HELD: As it was conceded that the particular type of loss was reasonably foreseeable the only issue was quantum (*McLoughlin v O'Brian*, p 465, below). In respect of the periodical payments for maintenance there were so many imponderables it was not proved that such payments were greater than the plaintiff would have had to spend if his wife and family had continued to live with him. But the lump sum payment would not have been necessary if they had continued to live together. On the other hand if she had remained with him he may (or even the Court of Protection on his behalf may) have thought it right to make her a gift for giving up her life to care for him. £10,000 ought to be deducted in respect of this: there should accordingly be an award of a further £15,000 damages additional to the amount awarded in the court below.

Criminal acts: imprisonment

Meah v McCreamer
[1985] 1 All ER 367 (Woolf J)
The plaintiff sustained a close-head injury to the left frontal lobe of the brain in a road accident. Some years before the accident he had shown a pattern of violent behaviour but no serious crime: he had a number of convictions for offences of dishonesty. After the accident he had become violently and sexually aggressive and was, by the time of trial, serving two life sentences for crimes of rape and wounding. There was medical evidence that the frontal lobe injury sustained in the accident had removed the inhibitions formerly restraining his aggressiveness. His condition was untreatable and he had to be kept in prison for the protection of society.

HELD: *Jones v Jones* (above) had shown that awards could be made in head injury cases that at first sight seemed surprising. The plaintiff had shown that, on a balance of probabilities, but for the accident he would not have committed the crimes for which he was now in prison. He was entitled to damages for the resulting imprisonment. The right figure in general damages was £60,000 to be reduced by 25% for contributory negligence.

PLEADING DAMAGE

Special damage must be pleaded

Ilkiw v Samuels
[1963] 2 All ER 879, [1963] 1 WLR 991, 107 Sol Jo 680, CA
The plaintiff was injured in an accident at work in 1958 but his action for damages did not reach trial until 1963. In the Statement of Claim the only loss of earnings claimed as special damage was for four months' absence from work immediately after the accident; this was agreed by the parties at trial at £77. The plaintiff's injuries had reduced his earning capacity, however, and some evidence was admitted to show that he had suffered a loss of earnings since the accident and before trial at about £200 a year. As special damage was agreed no amendment of the Statement of Claim was sought. The judge awarded a sum in general damages which took into account the yearly loss of earnings between the accident and trial.
HELD, ON APPEAL: He should not have done so and the award must be reduced.
    Per Diplock LJ: In my view it is plain law — so plain that there appears to be no direct authority, because everyone has accepted it as being the law for the last hundred years — that one can recover in an action only special damage which has been pleaded and, of course, proved. The evidence about the loss of earnings in excess of £77 was admissible, not as proof of special damage (which had not been pleaded) but as a guide to what the future loss of earnings of the plaintiff might be.

Note—Facts on p 159, above.

Perestrello v United Paint Co Ltd
[1969] 3 All ER 479, [1969] 1 WLR 570, 113 Sol Jo 36, CA
In 1961 the defendants contracted to supply the plaintiffs for a period of five years with information and materials to enable them to make and sell a type of paint in Portugal. In 1963 before they had done anything under the contract they repudiated it and were admittedly in breach. In 1964 the plaintiffs wrote the defendants saying their clients had lost £4,000 in capital and outlay and 'a very considerable sum in respect of net profits'. They issued a specially endorsed writ in July 1964 alleging £4,228 wasted expenditure and ending with the words 'And the plaintiffs claim £4,228 and damages'. No claim was made for loss of profits. In July 1968 the plaintiffs' solicitors wrote the defendants' solicitors saying the claim for damages was in respect of loss of profits, quantifying it at £251,000. A few days before trial they delivered a 51-page document of explanations and figures and at the trial applied to amend the Statement of Claim by adding a claim for £250,000 'loss of profits'. The plaintiffs contended in the alternative that no amendment was necessary as the loss of profit was general damages sufficiently pleaded by the words 'and damages' in the writ. The judge refused to allow the amendment.
HELD, ON APPEAL: (1) Having regard to the difficulties which such a late amendment would cause the defendants it was rightly refused. (2) The plaintiffs were not entitled without amendment to lead evidence of the loss of profits.

Per Lord Donovan: There is plenty of authority for the proposition that a plaintiff need not plead general damage; but since the expressions 'special damage' and 'special damages' are used in such a wide variety of meaning it is safer to approach this question by considering what a plaintiff *is* required to plead rather than what he is not. . . . If a plaintiff has suffered damage of a kind which is not the necessary and immediate consequence of the wrongful act, he must warn the defendant in the pleadings that the compensation claimed will extend to this damage, thus showing the defendant the case he has to meet and assist him in computing a payment into Court. . . . The same principle gives rise to a plaintiff's undoubted obligation to plead and particularise any item of damage which represents out-of-pocket expenses, or loss of earnings, incurred prior to the trial, and which is capable of substantially exact calculation. Such damage is commonly referred to as special damage or special damages but is no more than an example of damage which is 'special' in the sense that fairness to the defendant requires that it be pleaded.

Special circumstances must be pleaded

Domsella v Barr
[1969] 3 All ER 487, [1969] 1 WLR 630, 113 Sol Jo 265, CA
The plaintiff, a steel erector aged 23, sustained head injuries in an accident and was unable to work again as a steel erector, though he was able to do other work. Before the accident he had accepted a contract to work as a steel erector in Nigeria on lucrative terms, and had to give this up. This was pleaded in the Statement of Claim, but at the trial he was permitted also to give evidence of his intention and wish, with help which his father would have given him, to set up in business on his own, if the accident had not occurred, as a steel erector. The judge said that the plaintiff had lost the opportunity of earning very large sums of money and awarded £9,000. The defendants appealed against the amount of the award.
HELD: Where it is proposed to allege that there are any special circumstances which may cause the plaintiff to sustain losses in the future over and above those which in the ordinary ways would reasonably be expected to flow from the accident then those special circumstances should be pleaded. By adverting to the plaintiff's intention to set up business on his own account an entirely new element had been introduced into the case which was not mentioned in the Statement of Claim. The plaintiff had gone outside his pleading and objection might properly have been taken to the leading of such evidence. Lord Donovan's remarks in *Perestrello*'s case (above) quoted with approval. Nevertheless as the evidence had been given it could not be entirely disregarded. Award reduced to £5,750.

POTENTIAL LOSS OF EARNINGS

White v Hutton Bros (Stevedores) Ltd
[1960] 1 Lloyd's Rep 524, CA
A stevedore aged 38 suffered injuries to his back which incapacitated him permanently for heavy work. He had taken other employment of a lighter kind in which he earned £5 a week less than in his pre-accident work. He

had aching in the back and right leg and was unable to do many of the things he could do before the accident. The judge awarded him £2,250 general damages.

HELD, ON APPEAL: The award was too small. A period of 10 years at £260 per year was the least that could be reasonably taken as a basis for the calculation of prospective earnings. £3,500 was the proper figure to award, the balance above £2,600 being for pain and suffering.

Cook v J. L. Kier & Co Ltd

[1970] 2 All ER 513, [1970] 1 WLR 774, 114 Sol Jo 207, CA

A foreman of a cable company, 38 years of age, sustained a serious head injury which reduced him permanently to simply factory work at a wage of £14 per week less than his pre-accident work. The judge took eight years as the multiplier of £14 per week.

HELD, ON APPEAL: Eight years was too low and should be increased to ten.

Senior v Barker and Allen Ltd

[1965] 1 All ER 818, [1965] 1 WLR 429, 109 Sol Jo 178, CA

The plaintiff, a Jamaican, was aged 17 when his right hand was severely injured at work. All four fingers were lost except for the proximal phalanx of the index finger, and the dorsum of the hand had to be skin grafted. The thumb was present and there was a reasonable pinch grip between it and the stump of the index finger. The plaintiff had been unable to find work since the injury except by the defendants as a sweeper and he did not want to do that. He was right-handed. Liability was admitted. The judge awarded him £6,500 general damages plus £504 special damage.

HELD, ON APPEAL: The award could not be said to be a wholly erroneous estimate or as being far too high. It was unfortunate that there was no estimate for loss of future earnings: the judge might well have taken it to be £5 to £6 per week. The usual practice was to take a substantial number of years' purchase, especially for a boy. At, say, 15 years' purchase the sum for future loss of earnings might be £4,000. If the figure for loss of the use of the hand were £2,500 the total of £6,500 general damages could not be too high.

Mulvaine v Joseph

(1968) 112 Sol Jo 927 (Thompson J)

The plaintiff was an American club professional golfer. Whilst playing on a European tour he was injured by the negligence of the defendants. As a result he played badly and cut short his tour. He claimed damages.

HELD: The claim was for damages for loss of opportunity of competing in tournaments, the ensuing loss of experience and prestige which might have resulted in his becoming a tournament professional in America, and loss of a chance of winning prize money. The figure was bound to be speculative. £1,000 would be awarded under that head including damages for disappointment felt by the plaintiff through the frustration of his plans.

Note—See also *Jenkins v Richard Thomas and Baldwins Ltd*, p 409, above and *Batchelor v Rederij A. & L. Polder*, p 448, above.

Value of company car

Kennedy v Bryan
(1984) Times, 3 May (Beldam J)
Where the plaintiff had lost the use of a company car the value should be assessed in the range of £750 to £1,000 a year.

Loss of earning capacity

Smith v Manchester Corpn
(1974) 17 KIR 1, CA
The plaintiff, aged 51, sustained a serious injury to her right elbow in May 1971. She was off work for 14 months. She was then able to resume her work without a drop in earnings and would be able to continue indefinitely, though she was left with severe restriction of movements in the elbow and shoulder which would be permanent. As a result she would be at considerable disability in the competitive labour market should she lose her job, though her employers, the defendants, undertook to continue to employ her so far as they could. The judge awarded £2,000 general damages for pain and disability but only £300 for future financial loss.
HELD, ON APPEAL: The award for future financial loss should be increased to £1,000. An award for loss of future earnings is usually compounded of two elements, (1) actual continuing loss multiplied by the appropriate number of years' purchase, and (2) the weakening of the plaintiff's competitive position in the open labour market; if the plaintiff loses her present employment what are her chances of obtaining comparable employment in the open labour market? If there is a real risk that a plaintiff will lose his or her present employment it calls for real compensation.

See also *Mitchell v Liverpool Area Health Authority* (1985) Times, 17 June.

Moeliker v Reyrolle & Co Ltd
[1977] 1 All ER 9, [1977] 1 WLR 132, 120 Sol Jo 165, CA
In an action for damages for injuries to his left hand sustained at work the plaintiff claimed an award for loss of earning capacity as in *Smith v Manchester Corpn* (above). He was a skilled man, valued by his employers for whom he had worked for 30 years. He had resumed his pre-accident work after the accident and his employers had no intention of ending his employment with them. If he ever lost his job he would be at a disadvantage in getting an equally well paid job because of the permanent injuries to his left index finger and thumb. The judge awarded £750 for loss of earning capacity.
HELD: The award was sufficient. *Smith v Manchester Corpn* laid down no new principle of law. An award for loss of earning capacity had been made in *Ashcroft v Curtin* (p 395, above) three years before *Smith's* case. This head of damage usually arises where a plaintiff is, at the date of trial, in employment but there is a risk of his losing that employment at some time in the future and then because of his injury may be at a disadvantage in getting equally well paid work. It was not correct that whenever a plaintiff establishes a claim under this head the damages must be considerable. Whether

and what to award should be considered in two stages: (1) Is there a 'substantial' or 'real' risk that a plaintiff will lose his present job before the end of his working life? (2) If there is (but not otherwise) the court must assess and quantify the present value of the risk of financial damage which the plaintiff will suffer if the risk materialises. A judge must look at all the relevant factors and do the best he can.

Clarke v Rotax Aircraft Equipment Ltd
[1975] 3 All ER 794, [1975] 1 WLR 1570, 119 Sol Jo 679, CA
The plaintiff contracted dermatitis of the hands as a result of his work with defendants. After two attacks he had to take work away from the irritant substance, resulting in a loss of £9 a week in wages. In addition to special damage the judge awarded £2,700 for future loss (being £9 per week for six years) and £1,250 for loss of earning capacity.
HELD: (1) It was essential to avoid overlap of the awards for loss of future earnings and for loss of earning capacity. If the plaintiff lost his present lower-paid job he would probably be able to find another at similar wages. In these circumstances £1,250 was too much; a nominal award of £250 was adequate. (2) No interest should be added to the award for loss of earning capacity.

Note—See also *Nicholls v National Coal Board* [1976] ICR 266.

Cook v Consolidated Fisheries Ltd
[1977] ICR 635, CA
Following an accident at work in February the plaintiff resumed his pre-accident work in June but gave it up in December partly because he found the heavy work difficult because of the injury. He decided to become a lorry driver though he was not actually working at the date of the trial. There was persisting disability which might affect his working ability within 10–15 years. The judge awarded £3,000 general damages but only £500 for loss of future earning capacity as a total of £3,500 seemed about right.
HELD, ON APPEAL: Loss of future earning capacity should be assessed separately without reference to what was being awarded for general damages. The award of £500 should be increased to £1,500. An award for loss of earning capacity is possible even if the plaintiff is not actually in employment at the time of trial.

Loss of partnership profit

Vaughan v Greater Glasgow Passenger Transport Executive
1984 SLT 44, Ct of Sess
The plaintiff worked in partnership with another man, taking a share of the profits. He was injured by the defendant's negligence and claimed for losing the share of profits which the partnership would have made but for his incapacity after the accident.
HELD: He was entitled to damages for loss of earnings. It made no difference that he was not in salaried employment nor self-employed. He was entitled to claim damages for the diminution in his share of the profits.

PREVIOUS INJURY

Paris v Stepney Borough Council
(1951) Times, 19 January
Workman had sustained injuries in an air raid and could only distinguish light from dark with his left eye. His right eye was injured at work and he lost the sight of the right eye. Lynskey J awarded £5,250. The workman's appeal on amount came before the Court of Appeal who increased the amount to £9,250.

Fowler v A. W. Hawksley Ltd
(1951) 95 Sol Jo 788, CA
Woodworking machinist aged 51 lost tip of left thumb. When three years old he had lost right eye and when 31 had sustained injury resulting in inability to flex left forefinger. Lord Goddard CJ awarded £300.
HELD, ON APPEAL: The pre-existing disabilities should have been taken into account and had not. Award increased to £600. *Paris v Stepney BC* followed.

SET OFF

Shearman v Folland
[1950] 2 KB 43, [1950] 1 All ER 976, 66 TLR 853, 94 Sol Jo 336, CA
Plaintiff, lady aged 67, healthy, active and young for her years; one leg amputated at the thigh and the other permanently unstable and in practice largely useless; unable to walk more than 150 yards and that only on a perfectly even surface; unable without assistance to go up and down stairs or to get into or out of a bath or motor car. The special damages included a claim of £12 12s 0d per week for nursing home fees. Before the accident she resided in hotels in London and paid £7 7s 0d per week for board and lodging. Slade J deducted all or most of the £7 7s 0d from the £12 12s 0d and drastically cut down the claim of £12 12s 0d per week on the ground that it was unreasonable and exorbitant.
HELD, ON APPEAL: The £7 7s 0d could not be set off. The precise style in which she would probably or might have lived was a collateral matter. 'Matter completely collateral and merely *res inter alios acta*, cannot be used in mitigation of damages', *Mayne on Damages*. The expenses of a millionaire accustomed to live at a palatial hotel would far exceed the charges of a nursing home. Could a wrongdoer say in such a case that he was entitled to go scot free? A court would not pursue beyond a certain limit what would have been the position if no accident had occurred. Ordinarily a householder or lodger has fixed expenses or charges which continue. Those parts which do not (e g, food) may be difficult to disengage from the total. *Contra* a claim for extra nourishments by implication concedes that the plaintiff is giving credit for the food for which he would have to pay apart from the accident. No such claim to set off had previously been advanced, let alone succeeded. The defendant is entitled to set off living expenses of some amount, and if evidence had been adduced to show what proportion of the £12 12s 0d had been attributable to living expenses, it would have been open to the judge to make a deduction in respect of that.

Daish v Wauton
[1972] 2 QB 262, [1972] 1 All ER 25, [1972] 2 WLR 29, 115 Sol Jo 891, CA
The plaintiff at the age of four sustained such serious brain damage in a
motor accident that he would never be able to work for a living. In assessing
his damages the judge made only a 'modest allowance' for lost future
earnings because most of them would have been spent on living expenses,
whereas now the plaintiff would be supported entirely in a state institution
free of cost, ie at the expense of the National Health Service.
HELD, ON APPEAL: It was not right to set off the living expenses against the
potential loss of earnings. Comments to the contrary in *Oliver v Ashman*
(p 443, above) should not be followed. In assessing a claim for loss of earnings *Gourley*'s case (p 429, above) must first be considered to compute the
net loss and the *Parry*'s case (p 454, above) to consider whether any particular gain or benefit is to be deducted against net loss. In the latter case it
was said that a benefit would not be deductible if it was not necessarily
intended as a substitute for earning capacity. It was hard to say what the
intention of Parliament was in relation to a case like the present when it had
conferred a right to National Health Service benefits both on contributors
and non-contributors, but it was clear that the effect of the legislation was to
confer the benefits independently of any loss of earning capacity or of any
legal liability in another person to compensate the victim: even a person
injured entirely by his own fault would be entitled to such benefits. Accordingly the fact that the plaintiff would be receiving from the state free board
and lodging should not be reflected in the quantum of damages.

Note—This decision and *Bowker v Rose* (1978) 122 Sol Jo 147, CA have been
effectively overruled by the Administration of Justice Act 1982, s 5. See p 412,
above, under heading 'Care and nursing'.

SHOCK

Note—A cause of action in negligence for damages for nervous shock has the same
constituents as any other personal injury claim: (1) a duty to the plaintiff to take
care, (2) a careless act amounting to a breach of that duty, (3) resultant injury to
the plaintiff. The question whether the plaintiff was within that category of persons
to whom, in the circumstances, the defendant owed a duty of care was considered
in *Hay (or Bourhill) v Young* (p 6, above) and in the following cases.

King v Phillips
[1953] 1 QB 429, [1953] 1 All ER 617, [1953] 2 WLR 526, 97 Sol Jo 171
A boy aged five or six years unaccompanied by any adult, was on his
tricycle on the highway at Birstal Road where it joined Greenfield Road.
The driver of a taxi-cab stopped at the first house in Greenfield Road
beyond the junction with Birstal Road to pick up a passenger. The boy
asked the driver if he was going to take someone for a ride and then, so far
as the driver saw, disappeared. The passenger entered the cab, and the
driver looked round, and thinking the boy had gone some minutes before,
began to back the cab. The boy was just behind the cab and was knocked off
the tricycle which was pushed a short distance. The driver heard a little
shout from behind the cab. He got down and found the tricycle smashed up
and the boy running towards his home some 70 or 80 yards distant on the

other side of Birstall Road. The boy's mother was in her house looking out of an upstairs window when she heard a scream from the end of the road which she identified as that of her boy. She saw the taxi-cab backing into the tricycle and then saw the tricycle under the taxi but could not see the boy. She ran into the road, met the boy running towards her and took him indoors. She found he was injured but the injuries were very slight and transient. The mother claimed damages for shock.

HELD: *Hay (or Bourhill) v Young* (p 6, above) decided that a driver was not liable for shock unless the injury was within that which he ought to have reasonably contemplated as the area of potential danger which would arise as the result of his negligence. Adopting the expression of 'the reasonable hypothetical observer' in that case, the driver could not reasonably have anticipated that to back the taxi in this way, though negligent vis-à-vis the boy, would cause injury to the boy's mother in her house 70 or 80 yards away. She was wholly outside the area or range of reasonable anticipation. Adopting Lord Wright's language, the line should be drawn where the good sense of the jury or judge decides. It would be contrary to common sense to say that the driver ought reasonably to have contemplated that he might cause injury by shock to a woman in a house some 70 or 80 yards distant on the other side of Birstall Road. Judgment for defendant. [1952] 2 All ER 459, [1952] WN 393, [1952] 2 TLR 277, 96 Sol Jo 513 (McNair J). An appeal was dismissed.

Note—Professor Goodhart (69 LQR 347) points out that the three Lords Justices gave conflicting grounds for their decision. Hodgson LJ said that was no reasonably foreseeable risk of physical injury to the plaintiff herself. On this view *Hambrook v Stokes* has been overruled for all practical purposes. Singleton LJ said that the defendant could not have anticipated that the plaintiff would see the accident, and this implies that the defendant had far less foresight than in *Haynes v Harwood* (p 40, above), where the plaintiff was injured a quarter of a mile away. Denning LJ said that the test was not foreseeability of physical injury but foreseeability of emotional shock and the defendant could not reasonably have been expected to have foreseen that the plaintiff would suffer from emotional shock and that the shock was too remote to be a head of damage.

He suggests therefore that the case decides (1) the plaintiff in a shock case need not be within the area of physical injury to himself; (2) that the shock need not be based on fear for oneself; fear for the safety of one's child is sufficient; and in the result that a slight alteration in the facts might lead to a different conclusion. See now *Boardman v Sanderson* and *McLoughlin v O'Brian*, p 465, below.

Dooley v Cammell Laird & Co Ltd
[1951] 1 Lloyd's Rep 271 (Donovan J)

A crane driver was lowering a sling when the rope broke and the load fell, and out of sight of the plaintiff dislodged some scaffolding which crashed into the hold where the plaintiff knew fellow workmen were at work. The plaintiff was thereby put into a state of apprehension and acute anxiety and suffered severe nervous shock.

Defendants contended they owed no duty except in the case of impact upon the claimant, his wife or child, or reasonable fear of such impact.

HELD: There is no duty unless physical injury to the person or his relations or friends is reasonably to be expected, or unless shock was reasonably to be expected to him as a result of defendant's negligence. The fear that fellow workmen may have been injured was not baseless or extravagant and was a consequence reasonably to have been foreseen as likely to cause a nervous shock, which fear was not unreasonable in the circumstances and was not too remote.

Galt v British Railways Board
(1983) 133 N LJ 870

The plaintiff, driving a train at 65 mph in conditions of restricted visibility, suddenly saw two men on the track about 30 yards away. He could not stop and thought (mistakenly as it turned out) they had been killed. He suffered nervous shock bringing on a myocardial infarction, to which he was predisposed by a pre-existing symptomless condition.

HELD: He was entitled to damages, no speed limit having been in force. The injury was reasonably foreseeable and the defendants owed him a duty to take reasonable care not to expose him to injury from nervous shock. They were liable for increased damage caused by the pre-existing disease, applying *The Wagon Mound* (p 360, above) and *Jason v Batten (1930) Ltd* [1969] 1 Lloyd's Rep 281.

Boardman v Sanderson
[1964] 1 WLR 1317, 105 Sol Jo 152, CA

The plaintiff and his son, aged eight, went with the defendant to a garage to collect the defendant's car which had been repaired. At the defendant's request the plaintiff went into the office to pay the bill whilst the defendant got into the car a few yards away to back it out of the garage. The boy was standing very near the car when the defendant backed it out and ran on to his foot. The boy screamed and the plaintiff ran out of the office to see what had happened. He saw the wheel of the car on his son's foot and suffered shock.

HELD: He was entitled to damages for the shock. The defendant knew the boy was in the yard and that any carelessness in driving might result in injury to the boy. He knew the father was within earshot and that he was in such a position that if he heard a scream from the boy he was bound to run out. A duty was owed by the defendant not only to the boy but also to the near relatives of the boy who were, as he knew, on the premises within earshot and likely to come upon the scene if any injury or ill befell the boy. *King v Phillips* (above) was distinguishable since in that case it was unknown to the driver that the mother happened to live nearby. He could not reasonably foresee that if he injured the child the mother would be immediately upon the scene of the accident. *Hay (or Bourhill) v Young* (p 6, above) was no authority for saying that if the plaintiff did not actually see the accident (as distinct from the results) he could not succeed. The father's injury by shock was reasonably foreseeable by the defendant.

Chadwick v British Transport Commission
[1967] 2 All ER 945, [1967] 1 WLR 912, 111 Sol Jo 562 (Waller J)

The plaintiff, a window cleaner aged 41, was at home when a serious railway accident occurred about 200 yards away. He did not see it, but went to help. He spent several hours at the scene helping passengers who had serious and horrifying injuries. Afterwards he fell into a condition of depression and nervousness that was eventually diagnosed as an anxiety neurosis caused by his experiences at the scene of the disaster. He claimed damages against the defendants who admitted the railway accident was their fault but denied liability for the plaintiff's condition.

HELD: (1) Shock, other than caused by fear for oneself or children, may be the subject of a claim for damages; (2) it was reasonably foreseeable by the defendants that if trains collided and people were killed some persons who were physically unhurt might suffer from shock; (3) the defendants owed a duty of care to the plaintiff because they could have foreseen that, if passengers were injured by their negligence, somebody might try and rescue the passengers and suffer injury in the process; (4) the fact that the risk run by the rescuer was not precisely that run by the passengers did not deprive the plaintiff of his remedy; it was sufficient that shock was foreseeable and that rescue was foreseeable.

Judgment for the plaintiff.

McLoughlin v O'Brian

[1983] 1 AC 410, [1982] 2 All ER 298, [1982] 2 WLR, 126 Sol Jo 347, [1982] RTR 209, HL

The plaintiff's husband and three of her children, George aged 17, Kathleen, 7, and Gillian, 3, were in a car which collided with a lorry. The plaintiff was not present: she was at home two miles away. She was told of the accident by a witness who said he thought George was dying. He drove her to hospital where she was told by her second son (who was not in the car) that Gillian was dead. She saw Kathleen crying and her face cut. She heard George shouting and screaming. She saw her husband, head in hands, covered in mud and oil. As a result she suffered severe shock, organic depression and change of personality, with numerous symptoms of a physiological character. She claimed damages against the defendant lorry drivers and owners responsible for the collision. The judge dismissed her claim on the ground that injury by shock was not reasonably foreseeable in the circumstances. The Court of Appeal dismissed her appeal: the Lords Justices held that injury by shock was reasonably foreseeable but that public policy required a limit to be placed on the extent of the duty of care in such cases: it should be limited to those on or near the highway at or near the time of the accident.

HELD, ON APPEAL to the House of Lords: The plaintiff was entitled to succeed. When injury from shock was reasonably foreseeable to the plaintiff the duty of care was not to be limited merely by considerations of public policy. A cause of action for injury by shock had developed through a series of cases: (1) without the need for injury to oneself; (2) by injury or fear of it to a near relative (*Hambrook v Stokes Brothers*, below), *Boardman v Sanderson* (above)); (3) by coming upon the immediate aftermath (*Boardman*'s case); (4) coming upon the scene as a rescuer (*Chadwick v British Transport Commission*, above). If the process of logical progression was followed it was hard to see why this plaintiff should not succeed. Her claim may be upon the margin of what the process of logical progression will allow, but the facts being strong and exceptional her case ought to be assimilated to those which have passed the test. There was no requirement of public policy that the damage to a plaintiff should be on or adjacent to the highway. A defendant's duty of care must depend on reasonable foreseeability and be adjudicated only upon a case-by-case basis.

Note—See also *Baker v Hopkins* (p 43, above) and *Videan v British Transport Commission* (p 44, above).

Remoteness of damage

Hambrook v Stokes Brothers
[1925] 1 KB 141, 94 LJKB 435, 41 TLR 125, CA

Defendants' servant left a motor lorry at the top of a steep and narrow street unattended, with the engine running, and without having taken proper precautions to secure it. The lorry started off by itself and ran violently down the incline. Plaintiff's wife, who had been walking up the street with her children, had just parted from them a little below a point where the street makes a bend, when she saw the lorry rushing round the bend towards her. She became frightened for the safety of her children, who by that time were out of sight round the bend, and who she knew must have met the lorry in its course. She was almost immediately afterwards informed by bystanders that a child answering the description of one of hers had been injured. In consequence of her fright and anxiety she suffered a nervous shock, which eventually caused her death, whereby her husband lost the benefit of her services. In an action by the husband under the Fatal Accidents Acts:

HELD: On the assumption that the shock was caused by what the woman saw with her own eyes as distinguished from what she was told by bystanders, plaintiff was entitled to recover, notwithstanding that the shock was brought about by fear for her children's safety and not by fear for her own safety.

Note—*Hambrook v Stokes Bros* was discussed in *Hay (or Bourhill) v Young* (p 6, above). Lord Thankerton said he preferred the dissenting judgment of Sargent LJ. Lord Wright said he agreed with that decision.

Owens v Liverpool Corpn
[1939] 1 KB 394, [1938] 3 All ER 727, CA

A funeral procession was passing along a street when a tramcar collided with the hearse, broke its glass side and overturned the coffin, so that there was a danger of its being ejected into the road. The plaintiffs, the relatives of the deceased, were in a carriage following the hearse. One of them actually saw the impact, the others saw its effect immediately after it had happened. Each of the plaintiffs received injury in the nature of shock.

HELD: The right to recover damages for mental shock is not limited to cases in which apprehension as to human safety is involved, but extends to every case where injury by reason of mental shock results from the negligent act of the defendant. The plaintiffs were therefore entitled to recover the damages assessed. Mental or nervous shock, if in fact caused by defendant's negligence, gave a cause of action. The shock was not occasioned by fear for human life, but by the imperilment of the coffin containing the corpse of a near relative. The plaintiffs might be peculiarly susceptible to being disastrously disturbed by the accident, but the idiosyncrasies of the victim did not alter the fact that the injury was the result of the accident.

Note—Owens v Liverpool Corpn was discussed in *Hay (or Bourhill) v Young* (p 6, above). Lord Wright said he would have stopped short of judgment for the plaintiff. Lord Porter said he did not think the driver was in breach of any duty to the plaintiff.

Semble: If the case had been contested on liability instead of remoteness of damage, the judgment would have been for defendants.

Schneider v Eisovitch

[1960] 2 QB 430, [1960] 1 All ER 169, [1960] 2 WLR 169, 104 Sol Jo 89 (Paull J)

The plaintiff was injured and rendered unconscious in a motor accident; her husband was killed. She recovered consciousness in hospital and was then told that her husband was dead. She subsequently suffered from a mental condition resulting from three factors: (1) the shock of the accident itself; (2) the shock of discovering in hospital that her husband had been killed; and (3) the continuing mental strain of having to adjust her life after her husband's death.

HELD: (1) and (2) were allowable in awarding damages; (3) was not. With regard to (2) the shock was a direct consequence of the defendant's negligent act. The fact that owing to the unconsciousness a period of time elapsed before the news was heard makes no difference provided that that news was a consequence which flowed directly from the breach of duty towards the plaintiff. The fact that the defendant by his negligence caused the death of the plaintiff's husband did not give the plaintiff a cause of action for the shock caused to her, but the plaintiff having a cause of action for the negligence of the defendant could add the consequences of shock caused by hearing of her husband's death when estimating the amount recoverable on her cause of action.

*Note—*This case was decided before the Privy Council decision in *Overseas Tankship (UK) Ltd v Morts Dock and Engineering Co Ltd ('The Wagon Mound')*, p 360, above.

Tregoning v Hill

(1965) Times, 2 March (Paull J)

The plaintiff and her husband were cycling together when they were run into from behind by the defendant's car. Her husband was dragged along and rolled over and over before being left lying on the road fatally injured. The plaintiff fell off her cycle but did not suffer personal injury. She claimed damages for herself for the shock she suffered at seeing her husband killed in her presence, the depression she suffered as a result of the accident and the loss of her husband's company, especially on cycle tours.

HELD: No damages could at law be awarded for the loss of her husband's company or even for the shock as a result of her husband's death but she was entitled to an amount to cover the difference between the situation where she was at home and heard that her husband had been killed in a cycling accident and the situation where she herself actually witnessed the killing. The fact that she saw him killed did add to her depressed state and £750 was a fair sum for this.

Hinz v Berry
[1970] 2 QB 40, [1970] 1 All ER 1074, [1970] 2 WLR 684, 114 Sol Jo 111, CA

The plaintiff was out for a picnic with her husband and children. Their car was parked and her husband was unloading it when she saw the defendant's car crash into it, killing her husband and injuring the children. She claimed damages for nervous shock. The judge held that the extreme shock of witnessing the exceptionally tragic accident had brought about a morbid state of mind additional to what her condition would have been if she had not witnessed it. He awarded £4,000.

HELD: On the defendant's appeal against the amount of the award, the plaintiff's depressed state arose from five causes: (1) grief and sorrow at losing her husband; (2) anxiety for the welfare of the injured children; (3) financial stress from the loss of the family breadwinner; (4) the need to adjust herself to a new life; (5) shock of witnessing the accident. Only the fifth of these was a proper subject for compensation at law. Was the assessment right for this one factor? There was evidence that the morbid element in her symptoms was due solely to the shock of witnessing the accident and the judge had so found. His figure was high but not so high as to be a wholly erroneous estimate. Appeal dismissed.

Per Lord Denning: Somehow or other the court has to draw a line between sorrow and grief for which damages are not recoverable, and nervous shock and psychiatric illness for which damages are recoverable. The way to do this is to estimate how much the plaintiff would have suffered if, for instance, her husband had been killed in an accident when she was 50 miles away and compare it with what she is now, having suffered all the shock due to being present at the accident.

Note—Referred to and followed in *Allen v Dando* [1977] CLY 738 where the plaintiff was said to be suffering from a morbid depression which was 'a recognisable psychiatric illness' as a result of witnessing the death of his daughter aged 11 in an accident in which he himself sustained slight injuries. He nevertheless at the time of trial four years later had no insomnia, an improved appetite and an active social life; Mrs Hinz's condition was 'far more serious'. Award of damages for nervous shock £2,250. But see *Whitmore v Euroways*, below.

Meaning of 'shock'

Behrens v Bertram Mills Circus Ltd
[1957] 2 QB 1, [1957] 1 All ER 583, [1957] 2 WLR 404, 101 Sol Jo 208 (Devlin J)

The plaintiff was in a booth at a fun fair which was knocked over by an elephant and the shock must have been considerable. The judge said he was satisfied he could not award damages except to the extremely limited extent that the shock resulted in physical or mental harm. The effect of the authorities is that the word 'shock' is used, not in the sense of a mental reaction but in a medical sense as the equivalent of nervous shock. MacKinnon LJ in *Owens v Liverpool Corpn* (p 466, above), refers to it as being 'ascertainable by the physician' and as 'the form of ill-health known as shock'. The judge appreciated that it is now becoming increasingly difficult to define the boundaries of mental ill-health. Without infringing the general principle embedded in the common law that mental suffering caused by grief, fear, anguish and the like is not assessable, *Owens v Liverpool Corpn* goes as far as any court can go and he could not accept the invitation of counsel for the plaintiffs to attempt an extension of what is there said.

Brice v Brown
[1984] 1 All ER 997 (Stuart-Smith J)
The plaintiff, 42 years old at the time of the accident, sustained relatively trivial physical injuries in a road accident. She was a passenger in a hire car with her daughter aged 12, who sustained alarming facial injuries causing the plaintiff both fear and panic. Dating from childhood the plaintiff had a personality disorder which had caused turbulent spells in her married life but it was on the whole well controlled and for a year or so before the accident her home life had been reasonably happy. After the accident and throughout the time to date of trial her behaviour had became wild and disorderly. There were spells when she left home for days or weeks and lived rough; there were several attempts at suicide. At the time of trial she lived in the same house as her husband and family but her conduct was bizarre and she was severely deranged. She was unfit to give evidence. The defendants argued that before the plaintiff could succeed she must prove first that she sustained a psychiatric illness and second that that illness was reasonably foreseeable by the defendants.
HELD: 'Nervous shock' is a convenient phrase to describe mental injury or psychiatric injury to distinguish it from grief and sorrow or from physical or organic injury. The circumstances of the accident had caused or materially contributed to the plaintiff's nervous shock, which was a reasonably foreseeable consequence of the tortfeasor's breach of his duty of care. For this purpose the plaintiff is assumed to be a person of normal disposition — not eg the pursuer in *Hay v Young* (p 6, above) or a person who faints at the sight of a road accident. On establishing these first points the plaintiff is entitled to compensation for nervous shock and for its direct consequences whether or not they were initially reasonably to be foreseen. There is no reason why mental injury should be in a different category from physical: see *Smith v Leech Brain* (p 362, above). The fact that the tortfeasor could not foresee the precise name the psychiatrists were to put on the plaintiff's condition or the precise mental or psychological process that led to that result is immaterial. She was entitled to succeed.

'ORDINARY' SHOCK

Whitmore v Euroways Express Coaches Ltd
(1984) Times, 4 May
The plaintiff was with her husband in a coach which overturned causing her husband serious injuries. She suffered shock by witnessing him in his injured condition and being with him. It was argued by the defendant that she could not recover damages for the shock without adducing medical or psychiatric evidence.
HELD: The plaintiff was claiming for shock in its everyday meaning, not in a medical or psychiatric sense. It was 'ordinary shock' not susceptible of further definition but it was a concept which everyone understood. Damages could be awarded for it without departing from the law that damages for worry, strain and distress occasioned by the continuing effects

of the injury to a spouse were not recoverable. The right figure in the present case was £2,000, bearing in mind that the shock had continued when her husband was in hospital in France and for some weeks afterwards.

SLIGHT INJURIES

Note—The sums awarded in the following two cases are no guide to the level of damages today, but the decisions are not without value on the principles to be followed.

Wilson v Pilley
[1957] 3 All ER 525, [1957] 1 WLR 1138, 101 Sol Jo 868, CA
Plaintiff, married woman aged 21, sustained the following injuries set out in agreed medical evidence.

Penetrating wound of right ankle and minor injuries to left shin; an irregular dirty wound which entered the ankle joint, a few pieces of the external malleolus being torn off, together with further bone injuries; the ligament was reconstituted later and the leg immobilised in a plaster. At a later date a walking plaster was applied which had to be modified because she was developing a sore. That plaster was removed about six weeks after the accident and then she had to attend hospital for exercises. Seven months later she still had a tendency for the right ankle to turn outwards and had been ordered by her doctor an elastic anklet to afford some relief and protect the scar against minor injury. She was always likely to have some discomfort in the right ankle in cold and wet weather but should regain full function within the next six months and her present minor symptoms would have, by then, abated.

The county court judge assessed the general damages at £75. The plaintiff appealed.

ON APPEAL: The Court of Appeal stated that the interference with an award of damages must be a rare thing and perhaps even rarer in relatively small cases tried in the county court. The Court of Appeal would not consider for a moment slightly raising the figure or the converse. The onus on an appellant, particularly in the case of small damages, is a very heavy one. It must be established plainly that the judge proceeded upon a wholly erroneous estimate. In this case, having regard to the modern scale in awarding damages, and the reports of amounts in other cases, and the desirability that there should not be wide disformity in the kind of sums awarded, the sum of £75 would be appropriate only in cases which could be properly classified as such as would be likely to have no further effects of a lasting nature, still less of a permanent character. The injury in this case was not of that character, and the figure of £75 is really a wholly erroneous estimate. The figure was increased to £200, making with the special damages, £255 3s 8d.

Parry v English Electric Co Ltd
[1971] 2 All ER 1094, [1971] 1 WLR 664, 115 Sol Jo 286, CA
The plaintiff's feet were injured by accident on 7 November 1969. There was bruising and grazing of both feet and a fracture of the neck of the fifth

metatarsal of the left foot which she had in a walking plaster for three weeks. By 26 January 1970 when she resumed work there was very little wrong with her. The county court judge assessed general damages for loss of amenity, pain and suffering at £75. She appealed. Lord Evershed's comment in *Wilson v Pilley* (above) that £75 general damages would be appropriate only 'in cases which if not trifling, could be properly classified as slight' was cited.

HELD: The appeal should be dismissed. Lord Evershed did not mean that £75, neither more nor less, was the appropriate award for the kind of slight injury he mentioned. All he was saying was that £75 was only appropriate to slight injuries: it should not be used as a kind of rubber stamp or standard figure for a particular category of injury. In the present case it was on any view a very slight injury and the judge was perfectly entitled to arrive at a figure of £75.

SUBSEQUENT INJURY OR DISEASE

Baker v Willoughby
[1970] AC 467, [1969] 3 All ER 1528, [1970] 2 WLR 50, 114 Sol Jo 15, HL
In September 1964 the plaintiff's left leg was fractured in a road accident caused by the defendant's negligent driving. In a shooting accident in November 1967 the same leg was injured so badly that it had to be amputated. His action for damages for the first injury was heard in February 1968. The judge held that the plaintiff's prospective loss from the defendant's negligence should not be reduced by the fact of the subsequent amputation and awarded damages which included an amount for the prospect of loss of earnings and pain and suffering which the plaintiff would have suffered after 1967 if the amputation had never occurred.

The Court of Appeal said this was wrong. The court must have regard to events which had occurred since the date of the accident and must be guided by those events in so far as they had made certain what would otherwise be uncertain. The award should be restricted to the period up to the shooting incident.

On appeal to the House of Lords the judge's award was restored. Lord Reid said it was not correct that the second injury had submerged or obliterated the effect of the first. A man was not compensated for the physical injury but for the loss he suffered as a result of it. The plaintiff's losses were his inability to lead a full life and earn as much as he used to earn or could have earned if there had been no accident. The second injury did not diminish any of those. Whether injuries received before trial reduced the damages depended on the nature and result of those injuries. If the later injury either reduced the disabilities from the injury for which the defendant was liable or shortened the period during which they would be suffered by the plaintiff the defendant would have to pay less damages. But if the later injuries merely became a concurrent cause of the disabilities caused by the first injury they could not diminish the damages. So far as pain and suffering were concerned if the result of the amputation was that the plaintiff suffered no more pain he could not claim for pain he would never suffer, but the judge's award for pain (as distinct from loss of earnings) subsequent to the amputation was probably only a small part of the award and no deduction from the award should be made for this.

Hodgson v General Electric Co Ltd

[1978] 2 Lloyd's Rep 210 (Latey J)

The plaintiff sustained very serious injuries to his left hand in an accident at work in September 1971. In 1974 liability was agreed at 70%. In mid-1976 a serious heart condition developed making the plaintiff unfit for any work in the future. But for the heart condition his employers would have been able to find him suitable light work. Trial was reached in July 1978. He claimed on the basis of the speeches in *Baker v Willoughby* (above) that he was entitled to compensation for the difference between his pre-accident earnings and the earnings he would have received in such light work during the remainder of his expectation of life. It was accepted that there was no causal connection between the injury to his hand and the heart disease.

HELD: In *Baker's* case the second injury was tortious; in this case not. If what was said in *Baker's* case was meant also to apply to cases where the second injury was non-tortious it was *obiter* and not binding. There was no reason in logic or justice why the defendants should compensate the plaintiff for a consequence for which they were not to blame, namely, loss of earnings due to heart disease which came upon him unconnected with anything the defendants did. An award of damages is not the imposition of a fine or penalty but is made to compensate the victim for consequences of the wrongful act of the defendants and nothing else. The defendants were not liable for loss of earnings from mid-1976 onwards.

Jobling v Associated Dairies Ltd

[1982] AC 794, [1981] 2 All ER 752, [1981] 3 WLR 155, 125 Sol Jo 481, HL

In January 1973 the appellant plaintiff slipped and fell at work in circumstances imposing liability for damages in tort on the respondents, his employers. The accident caused injury to his back which kept him off work for a time and on his resuming work his earning capacity was 50% less than before the accident. In 1976 he became totally disabled by myelopathy a disease not brought on by the accident. At the trial of the action in 1979 the judge, following Lord Reid's views in *Baker v Willoughby* (above) awarded the plaintiff damages for loss of earnings for a period after 1976, considering himself 'bound to leave out of account the disability caused to the plaintiff by the myelopathy in assessing the damages resulting from the 1973 incident'. The Court of Appeal reversed the finding.

HELD: By the House of Lords, dismissing the appeal, the appellant was not entitled to damages for loss of earnings after he became disabled by myelopathy. Where the victim of a tort is overtaken before trial by a wholly unconnected and disabling illness the decision in *Baker v Willoughby* does not apply. No considerations of policy warrant placing liability for loss of earnings on the respondents after the emergence of myelopathy; the onset or emergence of illness is one of the vicissitudes of life relevant to the assessment of damages. Whether the decision in *Baker's* case was correct on its facts (ie as a case of two successive tortious injuries) must be left open, but Lord Reid's *ratio decidendi* in that case could not be accepted. Per Lord Edmund-Davies: I can formulate no convincing juristic or logical principles supportive of the decision of this House in *Baker v Willoughby*.

Note—See also *'Damage must result from the wrongful act'*, p 367, above.

UNCONSCIOUSNESS

Wise v Kaye
[1962] 1 QB 638, [1962] 1 All ER 257, [1962] 2 WLR 96, 106 Sol Jo 14, CA

The plaintiff, aged 20, received serious brain injuries in a road accident and as a result was in a state of unconsciousness which continued both at the date of the trial and of appeal. She had no purposeful movement of her limbs, had to be fed by tube and was in every way completely helpless. She was kept alive by skilful nursing but complications might easily prove fatal. For all practical purposes the situation was permanent. At assize she was awarded damages amounting to £18,279 comprising (1) £879 special damages (loss of earnings to date of trial); (2) £2,000 general damages for loss of probable future earnings based on her expectation of life before the accident; (3) £400 for loss of expectation of life and £15,000 general damages. On appeal against the award:

HELD: (1) Following *Oliver v Ashman* (p 443, above) the award of £2,000 was made on a wrong principle in so far as it included potential loss over the whole of the plaintiff's expectation of life before the accident and should be reduced to £1,500; (2) the award of £15,000 general damages should stand. Neither the fact that the plaintiff was unaware of her condition nor that the award would in all probability never be used for her personal benefit was relevant. The first element of damages is the physical injury itself, which has always been a head of claim which requires in law an award of damages according to the extent, gravity and duration of the injury.

Note—On damages for loss of future earnings *Oliver v Ashman* was overruled in *Pickett v British Rail Engineering*, p 444, above. In respect of loss of expectation of life see now the Administration of Justice Act 1982, s 1.

H West & Son Ltd v Shephard
[1964] AC 326, [1963] 2 All ER 625, [1963] 2 WLR 1359, 107 Sol Jo 454, HL

The plaintiff, aged 41, sustained severe head injuries when knocked down by the defendant's lorry. As a result she was permanently bedridden, only partly conscious, could not use her limbs (except movements of the right hand) could not speak or eat and required skilled nursing to keep her alive. She appeared to recognise relatives and could respond to some questions by hand movements or show likes and dislikes by facial expression. Her expectation of life was about seven years. In assessing damages the trial judge mentioned *Wise v Kaye* (above) and said this case was worse because Mrs Shephard must have some realisation of her condition. He awarded general damage of £17,500, ie £2,500 more than was awarded in *Wise v Kaye* for the same head of damage. An appeal against the amount of the award was dismissed both in the Court of Appeal and in the House of Lords. In the House of Lords the majority held: (1) Damages may properly include an element for mental distress, fear or anxiety resulting from realisation of the deprivation of faculty; the fact of unconsciousness will eliminate those heads of damage which can only exist by being felt or thought or experienced. (2) Except for taking into account the expense of future care or treatment the use to which the damages awarded are to be put or whether the plaintiff can or will ever be able to use the money is irrelevant. (3) It is correct for a judge to approach some matters on an objective and some on a subjective basis but he is not required in making his award to segregate the objective and subjective elements. (4) The decision in *Benham v Gambling* as to the level of awards for loss of expectation of life was not intended to affect the assessment of damages for varying degrees of physical deprivation in a living plaintiff.

Note—On the factor of awareness of injury in assessing damages see *Hindmarsh v Henry*, p 404, above, and *Cutts v Chumley*, p 405, above.

Andrews v Freeborough
[1967] 1 QB 1, [1966] 2 All ER 721, [1966] 3 WLR 342, 110 Sol Jo 407, CA
On 5 February 1962 a girl aged eight was struck by a car and was rendered instantly unconscious. She remained deeply unconscious until she died on 29 January 1963. As administrator of her estate her father was awarded by the Judge of Assize £31 agreed special damage, and £2,000 for the actual injuries and for the loss of amenities during the year of unconsciousness.
HELD, ON APPEAL: There were no grounds for disturbing the award. The father was entitled to recover such damages for her estate as the child herself could have recovered had an action been brought at the moment immediately preceding her death. The only difference between an action brought before and one brought after death is that in the latter the Court is spared the task of estimating the probable duration of life. *Wise v Kaye* was authority for the principle that unconsciousness and therefore ignorance of the injury suffered was irrelevant except as an element in assessing pain and suffering, and was no ground for reducing damages. *West v Shephard* and *Oliver v Ashman* (p 443, above) were to the same effect. *West v Shephard* being a House of Lords decision was binding on the Court. £2,000 for a year of unconsciousness was in line with the award in *Wise v Kaye*.

Gray v Mid Herts Group Hospital Management Committee
(1974) 118 Sol Jo 501 (Waller J)
A child a year old sustained brain damage in the course of a surgical operation. Thereafter he was blind and deaf and did not react to stimuli of light, heat, sound, cold, hunger, comfort and discomfort. He died aged three years ten months. Damages for loss of amenity were assessed at £5,000.

SOCIAL SECURITY PAYMENTS — DEDUCTIONS

National insurance benefits

Note—The Law Reform (Personal Injuries) Act 1948, s 2(1) provides that in an action for damages for personal injuries there shall, in assessing those damages, be taken into account against loss of earnings one-half of the value of any rights in respect of Industrial Injury and Disablement Benefit and Sickness Benefit for a period of five years from accrual of the cause of action. The whole Act as amended by the Social Security (Consequential Provisions) Act 1975 is as follows:

LAW REFORM (PERSONAL INJURIES) ACT 1948

1 Common employment (1) It shall not be a defence to an employer who is sued in respect of personal injuries caused by the negligence of a person employed by him, that that person was at the time the injuries were caused in common employment with the person injured.

(2) Accordingly the Employers' Liability Act 1880, shall cease to have effect, and is hereby repealed.

(3) Any provision contained in a contract of service or apprenticeship, or in an agreement collateral thereto (including a contract or agreement entered into before the commencement of this Act) shall be void in so far as it would have the effect of excluding or limiting any liability of the employer in respect of personal injuries caused to the person employed by the negligence of persons in common employment with him.

2 Measure of damages (1) In an action for damages for personal injuries (including any such action arising out of a contract), there shall in assessing those damages be taken into account, against any loss of earnings or profits which has accrued or probably will accrue to the injured person from the injuries, one-half of the value of any rights which have accrued or probably will accrue to him therefrom in respect of any of the following benefits under the Social Security Act 1975 or the Social Security (Northern Ireland) Act 1975, namely—

sickness benefit
invalidity benefit
non-contributory invalidity pension
injury benefit
disablement benefit

for the five years beginning with the time when the cause of action accrued.

This subsection shall not be taken as requiring both the gross amount of the damages before taking into account the said rights and the net amount after taking them into account to be found separately.

(2) In determining the value of the said rights there shall be disregarded any increase of an industrial disablement pension in respect of the need of constant attendance.

(3) The reference in sub-s (1) of this section to assessing the damages for personal injuries shall, in cases where the damages otherwise recoverable are subject to reduction under the law relating to contributory negligence or are limited by or under any Act or by contract, be taken as referring to the total damages which would have been recoverable from the reduction or limitation.

(4) In an action for damages for personal injuries (including any such action arising out of a contract), there shall be disregarded, in determining the reasonableness of any expenses, the possibility of avoiding those expenses or part of them by taking advantage of facilities available under the National Health Service Act [1977], or the National Health Service (Scotland) Act 1947, or of any corresponding facilities in Northern Ireland.

(5) In assessing damages in respect of a person's death in any action under the Fatal Accidents Act 1846, as amended by any subsequent enactment, or under the Carriage by Air Act 1932, there shall not be taken into account any right to benefit resulting from that person's death.

(6) For the purposes of this section disablement benefit in the form of a gratuity is to be treated as benefit for the period taken into account by the assessment of the extent of the disablement in respect of which it is payable.

3 Definition of 'personal injury' In this Act the expression 'personal injury' includes any disease and any impairment of a person's physical or mental condition, and the expression 'injured' shall be construed accordingly.

4 Application to Crown   This Act shall bind the Crown.

Contracting out (s 1(3))

Smith v British European Airways Corpn
[1951] 2 KB 893, [1951] 2 All ER 737, [1951] 2 TLR 608, 95 Sol Jo 579
(Hilbery J)
The Civil Aviation Act 1946, by s 20(1) enabled the Minister to make regulations to provide pensions for employees and for benefits in case of death.
By SI 1948/2361 a scheme was established from contributions by the
defendants and employees. Membership of the scheme by employees was
compulsory. Deceased was already in the employ of the defendants when
the scheme came into force and was therefore not compelled to join. He had
the right to apply, and did so and was accepted. The scheme provided for a
lump sum payment in the event of death and that the death benefits were in
substitution of any claim for damages for negligence at common law. An
employee was killed in an accident and the sum of £1,508 was paid to the
administratrix who signed a receipt in full discharge of all claims under the
scheme.
HELD: The Law Reform (Personal Injuries) Act 1948, s 1(3) (p 475,
above), rendered the contractual provision void. The deceased was in
common employment with the negligent servant of the defendants. The
section included a provision in an agreement collateral to a contract of
service, which this scheme was.

Social Security Act 1975

Note—Section 50 of the Act provides that where the accident occurs out of and in
the course of the employment there shall be payable (a) injury benefit, (b) disablement benefit, and (c) industrial death benefit. The accident shall be deemed to
arise 'out of' if it arise 'in the course of'.
    Section 52 makes the Act applicable notwithstanding breach of regulations if
done for the purposes of and in connection with the employer's trade or business.
    Section 53 has express reference to vehicles and is as follows.

'**53** (1) An accident happening while an employed earner is, with the express or
implied permission of his employer, travelling as a passenger by any vehicle to or
from his place of work shall, notwithstanding that he is under no obligation to his
employer to travel by that vehicle, be deemed to arise out of and in the course of his
employment, if—
(a) the accident would have been deemed so to have arisen had he been under such
     an obligation; and
(b) at the time of the accident, the vehicle—
        (i) is being operated by or on behalf of his employer or some other person by
             whom it is provided in pursuance of arrangements made with the
             employer; and
        (ii) is not being operated in the ordinary course of a public transport service.
(2) In this section references to a vehicle include references to a ship, vessel,
hovercraft or aircraft.'

To be taken into account

Note—See the Law Reform (Personal Injuries) Act 1948, s 2(1), above.

Life gratuity — proportion to be deducted

Hultquist v Universal Pattern and Precision Engineering Co Ltd

[1960] 2 QB 467, [1960] 2 All ER 266, [1960] 2 WLR 886, 104 Sol Jo 427, CA

On 9 December 1957, the plaintiff sustained injuries at work for which the defendants were liable. He was away from work for 13 weeks during which he lost earnings amounting to £197 18s 6d and received Industrial Injury Benefit amounting to £61 1s 6d. After returning to work he was awarded and Industrial Disablement Gratuity of £210 being an Assessment at 14% from 10 March 1958, for life. His expectation of life was 35 years.

HELD: For the purposes of the deduction required by the Law Reform (Personal Injuries) Act 1948, s 2(1) the amount of the Disablement Gratuity to be taken into account was one-half of such proportion of the gratuity as the five-year period (or the unexpired period thereof) bore to the plaintiff's expectation of life. In the present case the amount was £15. The words 'shall . . . be taken into account' in s 2(1) mean 'shall be deducted' when the benefits have been assessed and are ascertainable. Where the Court has to assess the value of any right which 'probably will accrue' the Court will take them into account by way of an estimated allowance.

Note—The following table is based on the 1971 Census. The decision in *Hultquist v Universal Pattern Co* (above) requires the use of the table for calculation of the proportion of an Industrial Disablement Gratuity, granted for life, to be taken into account in a claim for loss of wages.

MEAN EXPECTATION OF LIFE
(ENGLISH LIFE TABLE — NO 13)

Age	Expectation (years)		Age	Expectation (years)	
	MALES	*FEMALES*		*MALES*	*FEMALES*
0	69.00	75.25	20	51.08	56.89
1	69.39	75.41	21	50.13	55.92
2	68.47	74.49	22	49.19	54.94
3	67.53	73.54	23	48.23	53.96
4	66.57	72.58	24	47.28	52.99
5	65.60	71.61	25	46.32	52.01
6	64.64	70.63	26	45.36	51.03
7	63.66	69.65	27	44.40	50.06
8	62.69	68.67	28	43.44	49.08
9	61.71	67.69	29	42.48	48.11
10	60.74	66.71	30	41.51	47.13
11	59.76	65.72	31	40.55	46.16
12	58.78	64.74	32	39.60	45.19
13	57.80	63.75	33	38.64	44.22
14	56.82	62.76	34	37.68	43.26
15	55.84	61.78	35	36.73	42.29
16	54.87	60.80	36	35.78	41.33
17	53.91	59.82	37	34.83	40.37
18	52.97	58.84	38	33.88	39.42
19	52.02	57.86	39	32.94	38.47

MEAN EXPECTATION OF LIFE — *continued*
(ENGLISH LIFE TABLE — NO 13)

	Expectation (years)			Expectation (years)	
Age	*MALES*	*FEMALES*	*Age*	*MALES*	*FEMALES*
40	32.01	37.52	75	7.32	9.50
41	31.08	36.58	76	6.93	8.95
42	30.16	35.65	77	6.56	8.42
43	29.24	34.72	78	6.21	7.92
44	28.34	33.80	79	5.87	7.44
45	27.44	32.88	80	5.54	6.98
46	26.55	31.97	81	5.23	6.54
47	25.68	31.07	82	4.94	6.13
48	24.81	30.18	83	4.66	5.74
49	23.95	29.29	84	4.39	5.37
50	23.11	28.41	85	4.14	5.02
51	22.28	27.53	86	3.90	4.69
52	21.46	26.66	87	3.68	4.39
53	20.65	25.80	88	3.47	4.10
54	19.86	24.95	89	3.28	3.83
55	19.08	24.10	90	3.09	3.57
56	18.32	23.26	91	2.92	3.34
57	17.56	22.43	92	2.76	3.11
58	16.83	21.61	93	2.61	2.90
59	16.11	20.79	94	2.47	2.70
60	15.41	19.98	95	2.34	2.52
61	14.72	19.19	96	2.22	2.35
62	14.06	18.40	97	2.10	2.19
63	13.41	17.62	98	2.00	2.04
64	12.79	16.86	99	1.91	1.91
65	12.18	16.10	100	1.84	1.79
66	11.60	15.36	101		
67	11.04	14.64	102		
68	10.50	13.93	103		
69	9.99	13.24	104		
70	9.50	12.56	105		
71	9.02	11.91	106		
72	8.57	11.27	107		
73	8.14	10.66			
74	7.72	10.06			

Deduction not limited to period of incapacity

Stott v Sir William Arrol & Co Ltd
[1953] 2 QB 92, [1953] 2 All ER 416, [1953] 3 WLR 166, 97 Sol Jo 439
(Slade J)
The deduction is not confined to the period of incapacity. Accident 15
November 1949; return to work, 22 December 1949; incapacitated for
work for five weeks and his loss of earnings after deducting one-half industrial injury benefit of £2 11s 6d per week was £41 6s 9d, ie £47 15s 6d gross
less one-half of £12 17s 6d. He claimed £41 6s 9d as special damages. After

returning to work he received a further £126 13s 0d for industrial injury or disablement benefit.

HELD: One half of the £126 13s 0d, viz £63 6s 6d, must be taken into account, and this extinguished the claim for £41 6s 9d.

Flowers v Geo Wimpey & Co Ltd
[1956] 1 QB 73, [1955] 3 All ER 165, [1955] 3 WLR 426, 99 Sol Jo 564, [1955] 2 Lloyd's Rep 293 (Devlin J)
The plaintiff, a labourer, was struck on the legs above and below the knee on 29 April 1953. After a fortnight's absence from work a tumour near the right knee joint was found and was removed by operation on 8 July 1953. Later a ganglion appeared in the left leg and was the subject of a minor operation in November 1953. Therapeutic treatment was given following both operations. Recovery was throughout delayed by a mental condition which the doctors called 'compensitis'. The judge found that the only incapacity caused by the accident was between three and four weeks and that neither the tumour nor the ganglion were caused by the accident. He awarded £50 for loss of earnings and £25 for general damages.

The plaintiff was paid industrial benefit at £4 7s 0d per week from 4 May to 30 August when it was reduced to £3 5s 6d per week and continued for the remainder of the 156 days. Before returning to work on 1 May 1954, he claimed disablement benefit, which was provisionally assessed at 10% and he was paid disablement gratuity. On 28 January 1955 another provisional disablement assessment was made and the 10% was increased to 30% and he then received a small weekly pension.

HELD: The loss of earnings could not be more than £68. As a result of the National Health authorities regarding the whole of the incapacity as the result of the accident, the plaintiff had received £178 13s 0d and was still receiving £1 0s 3d per week. One-half of the total of these benefits would extinguish the whole of the claim for loss of earnings. There is no difference between the word 'injury' and 'injuries' in the Act. The 'rights' under the Act are worth what is paid and received and to be received under the statutes, neither more nor less. The words 'taken into account' mean that the court must make as accurate a valuation of the rights of actual and estimated figures. They do not mean that the court has a discretion to limit the amount to the benefits received in respect of the period affected by the loss of earnings. No part of the claim for loss of earnings was recoverable as one-half the value of the rights exceeded £68.

Benefits after five years not deductible

Barnes v Bromley London Borough Council
(1983) Times, 16 November QBD
In an action for damages for personal injuries it was submitted on behalf of the defendants that a plaintiff who had been given credit for half the invalidity benefit and industrial disablement benefits he had received for the five years following the accident (as required by the Law Reform (Personal Injuries) Act 1948, s 2(1)) should in addition give credit for the whole of those benefits which he continued to receive thereafter.

HELD: Not so. Although there was a common law principle that a plaintiff should not recover in damages more than he had lost by the accident, the 1948 Act made specific provision in relation to benefits and had thus abrogated the common law principle insofar as it related to them.

Haste v Sandell Perkins Ltd

[1984] QB 735, [1984] 2 All ER 615, [1984] 3 WLR 73, 128 Sol Jo 334 (Hirst J)

The plaintiff was injured on 3 July 1978. His injuries kept him off work beyond the fifth anniversary of the accident. The continuing wage loss was then £70.96 per week and his total benefits in the nature of industrial injury benefit etc amounted to £72.57 per week. The defendants submitted that the Law Reform (Personal Injuries) Act 1948, s 2 as amended, applied only to the first five years after the accident and as a matter of general principle the whole of the benefits after that period should be deducted from the wage loss.

HELD: This was not right. Section 2(1) of the 1948 Act covers the whole period past and future from the date the cause of action arose, not merely the first five years. By the use of the word 'shall' and the words 'loss of earnings or profits which . . . probably will accrue' the section leaves earnings and profits at large and applies the five-year restriction only to benefits. *Hultquist's* case supports this. *Barnes v Bromley London Borough Council* (above) was rightly decided.

Denman v Essex Area Health Authority

[1984] QB 735, [1984] 2 All ER 621, [1984] 3 WLR 73, 128 Sol Jo 318 (Pain J)

The plaintiff, injured in a road accident, was receiving invalidity and disablement benefits and special hardship allowance amounting to £4,750 per annum more than five years after the cause of action accrued. The defendants argued that the benefits received after the end of the five-year period should be set off in full against the plaintiff's loss of earnings, relying on the common law principle as in *Gourley's* case (p 429, above).

HELD: Not so. *Gourley's* case merely applied the common law to a given set of circumstances. The question to be answered was the intention of Parliament in passing the Law Reform (Personal Injuries) Act 1948, s 2(1). *Hultquist's* case (p 477, above) in limiting the deduction to an amount determined by the proportion that five years bore to the injured person's expectation of life implied that the proportion after the five-year period was not to be taken into account. It followed that no amount of benefit should be deducted from the plaintiff's continuing loss.

Benefit not claimed is not deductible

Eley v Bedford

[1972] 1 QB 155, [1971] 3 All ER 285, [1971] 3 WLR 563, 115 Sol Jo 369 (MacKenna J)

The plaintiff claimed damages for personal injuries, including £904 loss of wages. One-half of the social security benefits actually received amounted to £263 but the defendants claimed that a further £467 should be deducted being one-half of the disablement benefit she would have received if she had claimed in time. Her failure to claim these benefits was due to her ignorance of her entitlement.

HELD: Nothing was deductible in respect of the benefits not received. Following Devlin J's reasoning in *Flowers v Wimpey* (above) the 'value of any rights' in s 2(1) of the 1948 Act is what in fact is paid for them neither more nor less. A right in respect of which nothing is paid is valueless. Her failure to claim and thus mitigate her loss was not a reason for deducting what had not in fact been paid because s 2 is an exhaustive statement of the circumstances in which her damages could be reduced by reason of national insurance benefits.

RATES OF BENEFIT

Note—The number and frequency of the increases in social security benefits makes it impracticable to maintain an up-to-date list of rates in this work. The Social Security Benefits Act 1975, ss 3 and 4 (repealed and replaced by similar provisions in the Social Security Act 1975, ss 124 and 125) give the Secretary of State both a power and a duty to up-rate benefits to keep pace, in effect, with the general level of earnings and prices. Details of the current rates of benefit can be obtained from the offices of the Department of Health and Social Security.

Deduction of unemployment benefits

Parsons v BNM Laboratories Ltd
[1964] 1 QB 95, [1963] 2 All ER 658, [1963] 2 WLR 1273, 107 Sol Jo 294, CA

The plaintiff claimed damages for wrongful dismissal. When assessing damages the master of the Queen's Bench held that unemployment benefit received by the plaintiff should be disregarded.

HELD, ON APPEAL: This was wrong. Per Harman LJ: Unemployment insurance is a sum receivable by contract made by the employed man and his employer each of whom contributes to the State on the footing that if and when the servant is unemployed the State will make good part of his earnings to him. . . . This is a contribution which he is bound to make with the very object of mitigating the damage which inability to work will do him. . . . The loss he suffers is pro tanto diminished and therefore cannot be charged against the wrongdoer. Per Pearson LJ: The effect of the dismissal was not to deprive him of all income but to reduce his income by substituting unemployment benefit for his salary. It would be unrealistic to disregard the unemployment benefit, because to do so would confer on the plaintiff . . . a fortuitous windfall in addition to compensation.

Fitzpatrick v Moore
[1962] NI 152 (Lord MacDermott LCJ)

In an action for damages for personal injuries the plaintiff claimed loss of earnings whilst he was out of work in consequence of the accident. During part of the period for which he claimed he had received unemployment benefit under the National Insurance Acts.

HELD: As he received the unemployment benefit by virtue of his contributions because he was unemployed the benefit should not be taken into

account in assessing the damages. Neither the defendants' negligence nor
the accident had anything directly to do with his entitlement to the benefit.

Note—But see next case.

Foxley v Olton
[1965] 2 QB 306, [1964] 3 All ER 248, [1964] 3 WLR 1155, 108 Sol Jo 522
(John Stephenson J)
The plaintiff was injured in a road accident due to the defendant's negligence. During a period after the accident when, though capable of doing
some work, he was registered as a disabled person and unable to get a job,
he drew unemployment benefit of £5 16s 6d per week and National Assistance of £4 17s 6d per week, which together exceeded his weekly pre-
accident earnings. The disability which prevented him from getting a job
resulted from his injuries. The defendant contended that the plaintiff was
not entitled to damages for loss or earnings during the period in question
since the unemployment and national assistance payments together extinguished the loss.
HELD: The principle to be applied was that of *Gourley*'s case (p 429, above)
that damages are compensation for net loss. Was the receipt of the
unemployment benefit and of the national assistance too remote to be taken
into consideration in ascertaining the net loss resulting to the plaintiff from
the defendant's wrongful act? With regard to unemployment benefit it was
not: the defendant's negligence caused the plaintiff to be unemployed and
therefore to be entitled to receive the benefit. The unemployment benefit
should therefore be deducted. But the discretionary nature of the payments
of national assistance did not justify the extension of the *Gourley* principle to
those payments and they should not be taken into account in assessing the
plaintiff's loss. *Eldridge v Videtta* (below) followed.

Note—But see, below, *Cackett v Earl, Sanger v Kent and Callow, Plummer v Wilkins* and
Lincoln v Hayman.

Cheeseman v Bowaters United Kingdom Paper Mills Ltd
[1971] 3 All ER 513, [1971] 1 WLR 1773, 115 Sol Jo 931, CA
In a claim for damages for an injury to his back the plaintiff during the
course of trial added a new item for accelerated retirement. The defendants
claimed that in awarding damages for the loss of earnings during the period
of accelerated retirement the amount received by the plaintiff in unemployment benefit should be deducted.
HELD: This was correct.

Nabi v British Leyland (UK) Ltd
[1980] 1 All ER 667, [1980] 1 WLR 529, 124 Sol Jo 83, CA
The plaintiff recovered damages for personal injury sustained in an
accident at work. In calculating the loss of earnings the judge took into
account the sum of £1,062 which the plaintiff had received by way of
unemployment benefit. On appeal it was argued for the plaintiff that
Parson's case (above) was wrongly decided and that the ratio decidendi of

that case could not be supported in the light of the majority conclusions in *Parry v Cleaver* (p 454, above). Unemployment benefit partook partly of the character of insurance and partly of the character of benevolence.

HELD: The question was whether *Parsons's* case was overruled by *Parry's* case. There was no such inconsistency between the two decisions as would entitle the court to depart from its decision in *Parsons's* case. The unemployment benefit should be deducted.

Note—The court said the time had come for *Parsons's* case to be reviewed and gave leave to appeal to the House of Lords. An appeal was not pursued. However, *Parsons v BNM* was approved in the House of Lords in *Westwood v Secretary of State for Employment* [1985] AC 20, [1984] 1 All ER 874, [1984] 2 WLR 418, [1984] ICR 209, [1984] IRLR 209, 128 Sol Jo 221, HL.

Supplementary benefit

Cackett v Earl
(1976) Times, 15 October
In awarding damages to a man injured in a road accident the judge was invited to deduct payments of (1) unemployment benefit, (2) industrial rehabilitation allowance, (3) supplementary benefit, which the man had received as a result of the injuries.

HELD: All three payments should be deducted. *Parsons v BNM Laboratories* (p 481, above) was binding in respect of (1). (2) and (3) were payments which the plaintiff was entitled by statute to receive; they were not discretionary nor did they arise out of contract. The defendant was entitled to credit for them.

Sanger v Kent and Callow
[1978] CLY 788 (Milmo J)
In an action for damages for personal injuries the defendant contended that the plaintiff should give credit for the full amount of supplementary benefit he had received. The plaintiff had made insufficient National Insurance Contributions to qualify for sickness benefit. The defendant's argument was that supplementary benefit was cash for those in need and was not discretionary. If credit was not given the plaintiff would be paid the amount twice over.

HELD: Accepting the defendant's contention, supplementary benefit payments made to the plaintiff were deductible in full from the damages awarded. *Cackett v Earl* (above) followed.

Plummer v P. W. Wilkins & Son Ltd
[1981] 1 All ER 91, [1981] 1 WLR 831 (Latey J)
The plaintiff, injured in an accident at work, was unable to resume his pre-accident work and received unemployment benefit. Subsequently, being still unable to work he received supplementary allowances of £3,424. It was conceded that on assessment for damages *Nabi*'s case (above) was a binding authority for deduction of the unemployment benefit but it was argued for the plaintiff that supplementary allowances should not be taken into account, as in *Foxley v Olton* (p 482, above).

HELD: There is no valid distinction to be drawn between unemployment benefit which ceases after the prescribed period has expired and supplementary allowance which begins after unemployment benefit ceases. The purpose of damages is to compensate the victim for what he has lost; it is not to put the victim in a better position than he would have been had there been no tortious act. Unless the payments concerned were deducted he would be in a better position than if there had been no tortious act. Both unemployment benefit and supplementary allowance should be deducted from the figure for loss of earnings. *Foxley v Olton* not followed.

Gaskill v Preston
[1981] 3 All ER 427 (Stocker J)
After being injured in a road accident the plaintiff was unable to resume his pre-accident work because of a continuing disability and worked at substantially lower earnings. At the time of the trial he was receiving benefit under the Family Income Supplements Act 1970.
HELD: The benefit so far received should be deducted from the loss of earnings to date. It is a state-financed benefit having the same object and effect as unemployment benefit, the replacement of all or part of the earnings lost by the defendant's breach of duty. To this extent and purpose there is no distinction between unemployment benefit and supplementary benefit or family income supplement. But no deduction should be made in this case from the award for future loss, not because of any difference in principle between benefit received before and benefit received after trial, but because, on the facts of the case no value could be put on the expectation of future benefits under the Act.

Lincoln v Hayman
[1982] 2 All ER 819, [1982] 1 WLR 488, 126 Sol Jo 174, CA
On an appeal from an award of damages to the plaintiff for injuries received in a road accident the defendants contended that the sum of £6,888 received by him in supplementary benefit should be deducted from the award for earnings lost to date.
HELD: The amount of the supplementary benefit received should be deducted. A plaintiff is entitled to compensation for the loss he has suffered, no more and no less. On the other hand completely collateral benefits are to be left out of account. Whether benefits are collateral or not depends on whether or not they are too remote. The payments were made to the plaintiff because he was in need as a direct consequence of the injuries he suffered in the accident. They were made as of right and if they were not deducted the plaintiff would achieve double recovery. Following *Parsons v BNM Laboratories* (above) and *Nabi v British Leyland* (above), and agreeing with the judgments in *Plummer's* and *Gaskill's* cases (above) the amount of the benefit should be deducted from the special damage.

Redundancy payment

Rees v British Steel Corpn
(1 May 1981, unreported) cited in [1981] Abr 207 QBD
The plaintiff was injured in an accident at work; his employers were

reducing their workforce and discharged him with a redundancy payment. But for his injury he would have continued in their employment until retirement. He contended that the redundancy payment should not be taken into account in assessing his damages for loss of earnings.

HELD: It would be unjust to assess damages for loss of future earnings on the basis that he would have continued in employment and yet refrain from taking into account the redundancy payment made on the basis that he was going so to continue. It was really a payment for loss of employment which but for the accident would have continued. It should be deducted from the damages for loss of future earnings.

Note—A redundancy payment was held *not* to be deductible where the employment was unrelated to the accident: *Mills v Hassal* (1982) Times, 24 June.

Retirement pension

Hewson v Downs
[1970] 1 QB 73, [1969] 3 All ER 193, [1969] 2 WLR 1169, 113 Sol Jo 309 (Park J)
The plaintiff, aged 66, was seriously injured by the defendant's negligence and had to retire from work. He had intended working until he was 70. On retirement he began to draw the state retirement pension paid by the Ministry of Social Security. The defendant claimed that this pension should be taken into account in assessing damages.

HELD: The retirement pension should not be taken into account. Lords Reid and Pearce had pointed out in *Parry v Cleaver* (p 454, above) that the Fatal Accidents Act 1959 had enacted that no account should be taken of pension money in assessing damages under the Fatal Accidents Acts and that it could not be right in view of this that pensions should be taken into account in common law actions.

Statutory sick pay

Palfrey v Greater London Council
(1984) Times, 19 December, QBD
When assessing damages for loss of earnings statutory sick pay received by the plaintiff should be taken into account. Benefits received from the state should be taken into account whether unemployment or supplementary benefit or statutory sick pay. This was so even though an employer under the Social Security and Housing Benefits Act 1982 could claim it back from the Government.

National insurance contributions

Cooper v Firth Brown Ltd
[1963] 2 All ER 31, [1963] 1 WLR 418, 107 Sol Jo 295 (Lawton J)
The plaintiff's special damage included a claim for loss of wages. The question arose whether the amount of the weekly national insurance contribution should be deducted.

HELD: The plaintiff as a person in employment was bound to pay national insurance contributions and under the National Insurance Act 1946, s 6 the employers were entitled to deduct the amount of his contributions from his wages. What the plaintiff had lost was what would have been in his pay packet when he took it home, and that was what he was entitled to claim. When special damages are being calculated there should be deducted the amount of any national insurance contributions which the plaintiff would have had to make if he had remained at work.

Job release scheme

Crawley v Mercer
(1984) Times, 9 March (Comyn J)
Payments received under the Job Release Scheme fall to be deducted in full from the damages in respect of loss of earnings awarded to the plaintiff in an action for damages for personal injuries sustained by him in a road accident.

Damages in fatal cases

Important — the cases in this chapter relate to fatal accident claims arising from deaths on or after 1 January 1983. Cases relevant to claims arising before that date (when the applicable provisions of the Administration of Justice Act 1982 came into force), and which will become obsolete as pending matters are disposed of, will be found in the Appendix (p 943, below).

Note—At common law no action in tort lay against a man who caused the death of another person. This result arose from two distinct rules:
1 the death of a person gave no cause of action to others either for mental suffering or material loss;
2 the wrong done to the deceased himself died with him — *actio personalis moritur cum persona*.

Relief against the effects of both these rules was given, to a greater or less extent, by statute: in the case of the first rule by the Fatal Accidents Acts 1846 to 1959 and in the case of the second by the Law Reform (Miscellaneous Provisions) Act 1934.

The Fatal Accidents Acts 1846 to 1959 were consolidated in the Fatal Accidents Act 1976. The Administration of Justice Act 1982 made important amendments to the 1976 Act by substituting for the original ss 1-4, the new sections set out below, and has also effectively overruled the case law which enabled actions to be brought under the Law Reform (Miscellaneous Provisions) Act 1934 for loss of expectation of life and loss of earnings during the 'lost years'. In the result the 1982 Act effected the following principal changes in the law relating to fatal accident claims:

1 Abolition of the right to damages for loss of expectation of life (s 1(1)(a)). Thus the award to the estate of a conventional figure for damages for loss of expectation of life of the deceased (as in e g *Benham v Gambling* p 956, below) will cease.

2 Damages for loss of income for any period after death (as in *Gammell v Wilson* (p 960, below) and other recent cases) are no longer claimable. (Law Reform (Miscellaneous Provisions) Act 1934 s 1(2)(a) as substituted by the 1982 Act, s 4)

3 A wider category of those who as 'dependants' are entitled to claim under the Fatal Accidents Act 1976 as amended by the 1982 Act, s 3 (FAA 1976, s 1(3)).

4 The institution of a claim for damages for 'bereavement' for a limited class of claimants (FAA 1976 as amended, s 1A).

5 In assessing FAA damages no deduction to be made of any benefits accruing to the defendant claimant as a result of the death (FAA 1976 as amended, s 4).

---

1 FATAL ACCIDENTS ACTS CLAIMS

FATAL ACCIDENTS ACT

Fatal Accidents Act 1976, ss 1–4 (as substituted by the Administration of Justice Act 1982, s 3).

1 Right of action for wrongful act causing death   (1) If death is caused by any wrongful act, neglect or default which is such as would (if death had not ensued) have entitled the person injured to maintain an action and recover damages in respect thereof, the person who would have been liable if death had not ensued shall be liable to an action for damages, notwithstanding the death of the person injured.

(2) Subject to s 1A(2) below, every such action shall be for the benefit of the dependants of the person ('the deceased') whose death has been so caused.

(3) In this Act 'dependant' means —

(a) the wife or husband or former wife or husband of the deceased;

(b) any person who —

    (i)   was living with the deceased in the same household immediately before the date of the death, and

    (ii)   had been living with the deceased in the same household for at least two years before that date; and

    (iii) was living during the whole of that period as the husband or wife of the deceased;

(c) any parent or other ascendant of the deceased;

(d) any person who was treated by the deceased as his parent;

(e) any child or other descendant of the deceased;

(f) any person (not being a child of the deceased) who, in the case of any marriage to which the deceased was at any time a party, was treated by the deceased as a child of the family in relation to that marriage;

(g) any person who is, or is the issue of, a brother, sister, uncle or aunt of the deceased.

(4) The reference to the former wife or husband of the deceased in sub-s (3)(a) above includes a reference to a person whose marriage to the deceased has been annulled or declared void as well as a person whose marriage to the deceased has been dissolved.

(5) In deducing any relationship for the purposes of sub-s (3) above —

(a) any relationship by affinity shall be treated as a relationship by consanguinity, any relationship of the half blood as a relationship of the whole blood, and the step-child of any person as his child, and

(b) an illegitimate person shall be treated as the legitimate child of his mother and reputed father.

(6) Any reference in this Act to injury includes any disease and any impairment of a person's physical or mental condition.

1A Bereavement (1) An action under this Act may consist of or include a claim for damages for bereavement.

(2) A claim for damages for bereavement shall only be for the benefit —

(a) of the wife or husband of the deceased; and

(b) where the deceased was a minor who was never married —

(i) of his parents, if he was legitimate; and

(ii) of his mother, if he was illegitimate.

(3) Subject to sub-s (5) below, the sum to be awarded as damages under this section shall be £3,500.

(4) Where there is a claim for damages under this section for the benefit of both the parents of the deceased, the sum awarded shall be divided equally between them (subject to any deduction falling to be made in respect of costs not recovered from the defendant).

(5) The Lord Chancellor may by order made by statutory instrument, subject to annulment in pursuance of a resolution of either House of Parliament, amend this section by varying the sum for the time being specified in sub-s (3) above.

2 Persons entitled to bring the action (1) The action shall be brought by and in the name of the executor or administrator of the deceased.

(2) If —

(a) there is no executor or administrator of the deceased, or

(b) no action is brought within six months after the death by and in the name of an executor or administrator of the deceased,

the action may be brought by and in the name of all or any of the persons for whose benefit an executor or administrator could have brought it.

(3) Not more than one action shall lie for and in respect of the same subject matter of complaint.

(4) The plaintiff in the action shall be required to deliver to the defendant or his solicitor full particulars of the persons for whom and on whose behalf the action is brought and of the nature of the claim in respect of which damages are sought to be recovered.

3 Assessment of damages (1) In the action such damages, other than damages for bereavement, may be awarded as are proportioned to the injury resulting from the death to the dependants respectively.

(2) After deducting the costs not recovered from the defendant any amount recovered otherwise than as damages for bereavement shall be divided among the dependants in such shares as may be directed.

(3) In an action under this Act where there fall to be assessed damages payable to a widow in respect of the death of her husband there shall not be taken account the re-marriage of the widow or her prospects of re-marriage.

(4) In an action under this Act where there fall to be assessed damages payable to a person who is a dependant by virtue of s 1(3)(b) above in respect of the death of the person with whom the dependant was living as husband or wife there shall be taken

into account (together with any other matter that appears to the court to be relevant to the action) the fact that the dependant had no enforceable right to financial support by the deceased as a result of their living together.

(5) If the dependants have incurred funeral expenses in respect of the deceased, damages may be awarded in respect of those expenses.

(6) Money paid into court in satisfaction of a cause of action under this Act may be in one sum without specifying any person's share.

4 Assessment of damages: disregard of benefit   In assessing damages in respect of a person's death in an action under this Act, benefits which have accrued or will or may accrue to any person from his estate or otherwise as a result of his death shall be disregarded.

ADOPTED CHILDREN (s 1(3))

Note—The Adoption Act 1976, s 39(2) provides: 'An adopted child . . . shall be treated in law as if he were not the child of any person other than the adopters or adopter'. The meaning of 'adoption' is defined in the Adoption Act 1976, s 38.

CLAIMANT'S RIGHTS

Dodds v Dodds
[1978] QB 543, [1978] 2 All ER 539, [1978] 2 WLR 434, 121 Sol Jo 619 (Balcombe J)

The administrators of the estate of the deceased claimed damages under the Fatal Accidents Act 1846 on behalf of his son as a dependant. The defendant was the child's mother, the deceased's wife whose negligent driving was the cause of his death. It was conceded that she, though also dependant on the deceased, had no claim. The question was raised whether her negligence affected the claim of the child, the other dependant.

HELD: The negligence of one dependant does not affect the rights of other dependants. The remedy under the Fatal Accidents Act was given to individuals, not to the dependants as a group.

ONE ACTION ONLY (s 2(3))

Cooper v Williams
[1963] 2 QB 567, [1963] 2 All ER 282, [1963] 2 WLR 913, 107 Sol Jo 194, CA

In a road accident on 4 December 1959 caused by the negligence of the defendants a man was killed. He left two dependants, (1) his widow (2) an illegitimate daughter aged 10. They instructed separate solicitors to deal with their respective claims under the Fatal Accidents Acts. On 1 March 1960 the daughter by her next friend issued a writ, having reached agreement with the defendants on the amount of damages to be paid to her, subject to the approval of the Court. On 18 May an application to approve the settlement was granted by the District Registrar who made an order by consent staying the proceedings except for such steps as may be necessary to enforce the order. The widow's solicitors had been notified by the daughter's solicitors of the application and the Registrar and the defendants also knew of the widow's existence. By the Fatal Accident Act 1846, s 3 'not more than one action shall lie for and in respect of the same subject-matter of complaint'. In July 1961 the widow issued proceedings claiming damages under the Fatal Accidents Acts but these were met by the defence that only one action was possible and that the daughter's action had barred any further claim. The widow then applied to intervene in the daughter's action and to have the stay set aside.

HELD: A stay of proceedings is not equivalent to a discontinuance or to a judgment. It can be and may be removed if proper grounds are shown. In the circumstances it would lead to a breach of natural justice to allow the consent order to stand and the Court could and should set aside the order of the district registrar, remove the stay and allow the widow to intervene.

DIVORCED WIFE

Note—See FAA 1976, above s 1(3) and (4).

WHAT DAMAGES ARE RECOVERABLE

Note—Section 1A of the 1976 Act (above, added by the Administration of Justice Act 1982) introduces a new head of fatal accident damages — 'damages for bereavement'. Assessment of damages for dependants for loss of support is dealt with separately in s 1 (above), to which the following digested cases remain relevant.

Dependency — mode of calculation

Maylon v Plummer
[1964] 1 QB 330, [1963] 2 All ER 344, [1963] 2 WLR 1213, 107 Sol Jo 270, CA

It has been established, first, that the pecuniary loss to the persons for whose benefit the action is brought is the only damage recoverable, and, secondly, that the pecuniary loss recoverable is limited to the loss of a benefit in money or money's-worth which, if the deceased had survived, would have accrued to a person within the defined relationship to the deceased and would have arisen from that relationship and not otherwise.

The pecuniary loss which the court has to assess is a loss which will be sustained in the future. This involves making [an estimate of the] benefit in money's-worth arising out of the relationship would have accrued to the person for whom the action is brought from the deceased if the deceased had survived but has been lost by reason of his death.

Because in most cases the most reliable guide as to what would happen in the future if the deceased had lived is what did in fact happen in the past when he was alive, the common and convenient way of making the first estimate where the deceased at the time of his death was the breadwinner of the family is (a) to ascertain what annual benefit in money or money's-worth in fact accrued to the person for whom the action is brought from the deceased and arising out of the relationship before the death of the deceased, (b) to assess the extent (if any) to which that benefit would be likely to have increased or diminished in value in the future if the deceased had lived, (c) to assess the number of years for which that benefit would have been likely to have continued if the deceased had not been killed by the tortious act of the defendant, and (d) to apply to the annual benefit, assessed under (a) and (b) and generally called 'the dependency', the appropriate multiplier derived from (c), allowance being made for the present receipt of a capital sum in respect of annual losses which would be sustained in the future. But the fact that it is convenient to have recourse to the past for guidance as to what would have been likely to happen in a hypothetical future which, owing to the death of the deceased, will never occur, must not blind one to the fact that one is estimating a loss which will be sustained in the future: Per Diplock LJ.

Note—For this case see Appendix, below.

Harris v Empress Motors Ltd
[1983] 3 All ER 561, [1984] 1 WLR 212, 127 Sol Jo 647, CA
In the course of time the courts have worked out a simple solution to the problem of calculating the net dependency under the Fatal Accidents Acts in cases where the dependants are wife and children. In times past the calculation called for a tedious inquiry into how much housekeeping money was paid to the wife, who paid how much for the children's shoes etc. This has all been swept away and the modern practice is to deduct a percentage from the net income figure to represent what the deceased would have spent exclusively on himself. The percentages have become conventional in the sense that they are used unless there is striking evidence to make the conventional figure inappropriate because there is no departure from the principle that each case must be decided on its own facts. Where the family unit was husband and wife the conventional figure is 33% and the rationale of this is that broadly speaking the net income was spent as to one-third for the benefit of each and one-third for their joint benefit. Clothing is an example of several benefit, rent an example of joint benefit. No deduction is made in respect of the joint portion because one cannot buy or drive half a motor car. Part of the net income may be spent for the benefit of neither husband nor wife. If the facts be, for example, that out of a net income of £8,000 per annum the deceased was paying £2,000 to a charity the percentage would be applied to £6,000 and not £8,000. Where there are children the deduction falls to 25%, as was the agreed figure in the *Harris* case: per O'Connor LJ.

Note—See also *Dodds v Dodds* p 505, below.

Pevec v Brown
(1964) 108 Sol Jo 219 (Megaw J)
In an action in which damages were claimed under the Fatal Accidents Acts for a child of two whose mother had been killed it was contended that the child had lost the advantage of the loving care of his mother while he was growing up and that it was something in respect of which pecuniary compensation ought to be alllowed. The claim was put forward on the analogy of *Preston v Hunting Air Transport Ltd* [1956] 1 QB 454, [1956] 1 All ER 443, [1956] 2 WLR 526, 100 Sol Jo 150, [1956] 1 Lloyd's Rep 45 where Ormerod J had, under the Carriage by Air Act 1932, awarded damages over and above the quantifiable loss by reason of the loss of a mother.
HELD: There could be no claim under the Fatal Accidents Acts. It was clear law that a husband who had lost his wife could not recover anything for loss of companionship of his wife nor a wife for loss of her husband's companionship. There was no distinction in principle in the case of an infant. No damages could be awarded in respect of any element of the boy

receiving less care than he would have done had his mother survived. It was financial loss, and financial loss only, which was recoverable.

Note—But see now *Regan v Williamson* and *Mehmet v Perry*, p 508, below. See also, in respect of causes of action occuring on or after 1 January 1983, s 1A of the 1976 Act (above).

Cookson v Knowles

[1979] AC 556, [1978] 2 All ER 604, [1978] 2 WLR 978, 122 Sol Jo 386, [1978] 2 Lloyd's Rep 315, HL

The plaintiff's husband, aged 49, was killed in a motor accident on 14 December 1973. He was a woodworker earning £1,820 a year. His wife, aged 45, earned £900 a year as a school cleaner but £300 of this was attributable to the help her husband gave her with certain jobs. Without her husband's help she was unable to do the job and gave it up. At the date of the trial, 27 May 1976, her husband's earnings would, but for his death, have been £2,318 a year and hers £1,056 a year. There were three children aged 16, 13 and 12 at the time of their father's death. The Court of Appeal assessed the damages in two parts: the actual pecuniary loss to date of trial and the future pecuniary loss from the date of the trial onwards. Although the widow could not do her former work she still had an earning capacity which should be taken into account. After allowing for this and adding a notional sum of £200 for services rendered by the husband at home dependency was £1,614 a year at the date of death and £1,980 at date of trial. Actual pecuniary loss to date of trial was thus £4,492 plus interest at $4\frac{1}{2}\%$ (ie half rate) for $2\frac{1}{2}$ years = £4,997 for the first part. A multiplier of 11 less $2\frac{1}{2}$ (number of years from death to date of trial) = $8\frac{1}{2}$ × £1,980 = £16,830 for the second part with no interest. Total award of Fatal Accidents Act damages £21,827.

HELD, ON APPEAL to the House of Lords: The method adopted by the Court of Appeal was correct: (1) In a normal fatal accidents case the damages should be split into two parts, (a) the pecuniary loss which it is estimated the dependants have already sustained from the date of death up to the date of trial, and (b) the pecuniary loss which it is estimated they will sustain from the trial onwards. (2) The pre-trial loss is the total of the amounts assumed to have been lost by the plaintiffs for each week between the date of death and the trial, though as a matter of practical convenience it is usual to take the median rate of wages as the basis for the multiplicand. (3) Interest on the pre-trial loss should be awarded at half the short term interest rates current during that period. (4) For calculating future loss the figure for dependency to be multiplied by a number of years' purchase it to be calculated as at the date of trial. (5) The multiplier will be related primarily to the deceased's age and hence to the probable length of his working life at date of death. The figure selected as appropriate is to be reduced by the number of years between the date of death and trial — in this case reducing 11 to $8\frac{1}{2}$. (6) No increase in the award should be made to make allowance for inflation. Though the theory that investment in equities would give protection against inflation has been exploded, the high interest rates available from fixed interest securities will give protection to persons not subject to a high rate of income tax when the courts continue to use about the same multiplicand and multiplier as formerly. (7) No interest should be awarded on post-trial loss. (8) (Per Lord Salmon): In my view it is impossible to lay down any principles of law which will govern the assessment of damages for all time. We can only lay down broad guidelines for assessing damages . . . where economic factors remain similar to those prevailing.

Graham v Dodds

[1983] 2 All ER 953, [1983] 1 WLR 808, 147 JP 746, HL

The plaintiff claimed damages under the Fatal Accidents (Northern Ireland) Order 1977 for the death of her husband at the age of 41 in a road accident. The Judge suggested to the jury a figure of £14,400 for loss of dependency up to date of trial and that a reasonable multiplier for calculating future loss might be 11 to 14 years. He also suggested a figure of £4,800 as a figure for the annual loss of dependency after the date of trial. The jury awarded £103,000.

HELD, ON APPEAL to the House of Lords: The award implied an excessively high multiplier in the case of a man 41 years old at the date of death. The gross multiplier should be calculated as from the date of death, not trial. It would be wrong to award a sum for loss up to date of trial and then apply a multiplier for the future as if the deceased had survived to trial. The number of years between death and trial should be deducted from the overall figure for the multiplier before applying it to the estimated future loss of dependency per annum. New trial ordered.

Spiers v Halliday

(1984) Times, 30 June, QBD

The decision in *Wright v British Railways Board* (p 438, above) has not qualified *Cookson v Knowles* (p 493, above): the court was not to take prevailing interest rates or inflation into account when assessing the appropriate multiplier.

On a preliminary point, held, that the court would not look at 'Actuarial Tables for use in personal injury and fatal accident cases' published by HMSO unless evidence were adduced as to the correctness of the contents.

Apportionment between widow and child

Eifert v Holt's Transport Co Ltd

[1951] 2 All ER 655, 95 Sol Jo 561, CA

Electrical engineer aged 28 earning £659 per annum with excellent prospects; widow aged 23; child aged one year, award £6,400, Fatal Accidents Acts, plus £350 Law Reform; total £6,750.

After hearing counsel for the widow, Barry J apportioned £2,000 to the widow and £4,400 to the child. Defendants appealed and contended the award to the child was excessive and therefore the amount of the total award should be reduced.

HELD: If the total was proper, the defendants were not concerned with the apportionment between widow and child.

Note—Said in *Clay v Pooler*, p 963, below, to be 'no longer good law'. But possibly rehabilitated by the Administration of Justice Act 1982.

Speculative possibility of future support

Note—See *Taff Vale Rly v Jenkins*, p 503, below, *Wathen v Vernon*, p 503, below, and *Davies v Taylor*, p 500, below.

Child en ventre sa mère

Note—The absence of case law on this point is presumably because the principle is that such a child is entitled if for his benefit. There is one case in the reports which was decided under the Fatal Accidents Acts. See also *Lindley v Sharp*, below, p 501.

The George and Richard
(1871) LR 3 A & E 466, 24 LT 717, 20 WR 245, 1 Asp MLC 50
In a suite for limitation of liability, instituted on behalf of the owners of a brig (lost in a collision), an appearance was entered on behalf of a child of one of the drowned men *en ventre sa mère*. The court reserved leave to the child, *en ventre*, if born within due time, to prefer its claim for damages sustained by the death of its father.

APPEAL ON AMOUNT: PRINCIPLES

Note—See also *Greenfield v LNER* and other cases on p 406, above.

Nance v British Columbia Electric Rly Co
[1951] AC 601, [1951] 2 All ER 448, [1951] 2 TLR 137, 95 Sol Jo 543, PC
The principles which apply are not in doubt. Whether the assessment of damages be by a judge or a jury, the appellate court is not justified in substituting a figure of its own for that award below simply because it would have awarded a different figure if it had tried the case at first instance. Even if the tribunal of first instance was a judge sitting alone, then, before the appellate court can properly intervene, it must be satisfied either that the judge in assessing the damages, applied a wrong principle of law (as by taking into account some irrelevant factor or leaving out of account some relevant one); or, short of this that the amount awarded is either so inordinately low or so inordinately high that it must be a wholly erroneous estimate of the damage (*Flint v Lovell* approved by the House of Lords in *Davies v Powell Duffryn Associated Collieries*). The last named case further shows that when on a proper direction the quantum is ascertained by a jury, the disparity between the figure at which they have arrived and any figure at which they could properly have arrived must, to justify correction by a court of appeal, be even wider than when the figure has been assessed by a judge sitting alone. The figure must be wholly ''out of all proportion': Per Lord Wright in *Davies'* case.

Dolbey v Goodwin
[1955] 2 All ER 166, [1955] 1 WLR 553, 99 Sol Jo 335, CA
It has been established in *Flint v Lovell* (p 406, above) and other cases that where a judge has not given precise reasons or one cannot see from his

judgment exactly what he took into account; whether he took into account something he ought not or omitted something he should, the Court of Appeal can only look at the total amount and consider whether it is excessively high or unreasonably low and so amounts to an erroneous estimate.

ASSESSMENTS AND DEDUCTIONS

Note—Under the Fatal Accidents Acts the claim is limited to pecuniary loss, actual or prospective.

Benefit of receiving lump sum

Whittcome v Coates
[1965] 3 All ER 268, [1965] 1 WLR 1285, 109 Sol Jo 613, CA
The plaintiff was awarded damages under the Fatal Accidents Acts for the death of her husband. At the time of his death he was aged 58, a trade union official earning £1,200 per annum. This salary would have increased at about 6% each year up to retirement at 65, when he would have received a pension. The judge estimated the plaintiff's dependency at £600 a year to the deceased's retirement age and £450 a year after his retirement. The plaintiff was in poor health and her expectation of life was about 12 years. It was assumed that the deceased's was more. The gross dependency over 12 years would be £6,575. Making allowance for the chances and vicissitudes of life and the fact that damages were paid in one sum the judge awarded £5,250. On appeal the defendants pointed out that a little over £4,000, properly invested in 12 years would produce £6,575.
HELD: In a case of this kind the contingencies and circumstances are all uncertain and the Court has to make a reasonable assessment of probabilities. Mathematical calculations are in no way decisive. Assessments in terms of the price of an annuity were not of much assistance since very few people in his class of life would purchase an annuity. The judge had not erred except in not making sufficient allowance for the fact that the damages would be paid in one immediate payment. Deduction of £1,000 should be made for this.

Butler v Amalgamated Removers and Transport Ltd
(1964) 108 Sol Jo 562, CA
In an action brought by a widow, aged 35, with six children dependency was agreed by counsel at £950 per year. The judge awarded £10,500. On appeal it was argued for the widow that the judge had applied too small a multiplier since £10,500, using both capital and interest, would provide £950 for only 16 years.
HELD: The sum awarded was not erroneous. The judge had taken into account the ages of the parties, the fact that the widow was receiving a capital sum now, all future contingencies and the widow's prospects of re-marriage. Counsel had taken a more rigid view of the agreement on dependency and produced tables of interest and of expectation of life. Tables of that sort could not be produced to the Court without some technical evidence to support them. This could lead to complications which

would greatly lengthen the hearing of fatal accidents cases. It was undesirable to bring in a rigidity which would have the effect of guaranteeing the widow and children the sum of £950 a year over a long period.

Note—Prospects of re-marriage are not now to be taken into account. See p 512, below and Fatal Accidents Act 1976, s 3(3).

Effect of inflation

Mallett v McMonagle

[1970] AC 166, [1969] 2 All ER 178, [1969] 2 WLR 767, 113 Sol Jo 207, HL

The plaintiff claimed damages under the Fatal Accidents Acts for herself and her three children aged six, four and two. Her husband was aged 25 at his death in 1964. She was 24. He worked as a machine operator at a net wage of £12 per week and had for six weeks before his death supplemented his earnings by working as a vocalist in a dance band earning £6 to £10 per week. He gave the plaintiff about £10 per week from his wages and about £3.10.0 per week from his earnings with the band. The plaintiff spent about £3.10.0 per week on his food leaving a net dependency of about £10 per week. His employers closed down in January 1967 but evidence was given by a man who said he would have employed the deceased as an asphalter at £22.10.0 per week though this would have called for long hours and much travelling. A jury awarded £21,500 damages.

HELD: By the Court of Appeal in Northern Ireland and by the House of Lords, the award was so excessive that there must be a new trial. The amount awarded, wisely invested, could without resorting to capital produce an income double the rate of dependency at the time of death. This would not necessarily be wrong in the case of a young man with clear prospects of rising high on the ladder of financial prosperity but this was not such a case; there was no evidence that the deceased was likely to rise high on any ladder to success.

Per Lord Diplock: (1) Though sterling has been subject to continuous inflation experience of 20 years of inflation has shown that its effects can be offset to some extent by prudent investment, in buying a home, in growth stock or in short term high interest-bearing securities. The only practicable course for Courts to adopt in assessing damages under the Fatal Accidents Acts is to leave out of account the risk of further inflation on the one hand and the high interest rates which reflect the fear of it and capital appreciation of property and equities which are the consequence of it on the other hand. In estimating annual dependency money should be treated as retaining its value, and in calculating the present value of annual payments which would have been received in future years interest rates appropriate to times of stable currency such as 4 to 5% should be adopted. (2) Having regard to the uncertainties that have to be taken into account 16 years would appear to represent a reasonable maximum number of years' purchase where the deceased died in his twenties.

Note—See also *Cookson v Knowles*, p 493, above. In *Doyle v Nicholls* (1978) 122 Sol Jo 386 (below), Bristow J not following *Mallett v McMonagle* (above), took into consideration in assessing Fatal Accidents Act damages the likelihood of future inflation at not less than 7% per annum.

Young v Percival
[1974] 3 All ER 677, [1974] 1 WLR 17, 119 Sol Jo 33, CA
The deceased, aged 29 at the time of his death, was employed as a sales representative by a travel firm. His annual income net of tax was £1,615 and the dependency of the plaintiff widow and their two children was £1,100. Evidence was given of likely increases in the deceased's earnings. Some of the increases would result from promotion and some would be given to meet the rising cost of living.
HELD: (1) The multiplier of the figure for dependency at death, ie £1,100, should be 14 having regard to all the factors — the ages of the deceased and the plaintiff (both approaching 30), the fact that the deceased had not long been in the job and that it was in a trade of uncertain profitability. (2) By the date of trial, three and a half years after his death, the dependency would probably, but not certainly, have increased to £2,100 per annum on salary increases resulting from promotion. The multiplier for this increased dependency of £1,000 per annum should, because of the imponderable factors, be eight years only. (3) Following *Taylor v O'Connor* (p 947, below) the estimates or forecasts given in evidence of future earnings increases referable solely to anticipations of future inflation must be excluded from the assessment.

Doyle v Nicholls
(1978) 122 Sol Jo 386 (Bristow J)
The plaintiff's claim for damages under the Fatal Accidents Acts was reached in May 1978, six years after her husband's death. His profession had been that of an anaesthetist with a private as well as a National Health Service practice. He was 54 years old.
HELD: There was no uncertainty about the first six years of the ten-year multiplier: for that period the dependency was £32,245. Was future inflation to be taken into account for the remaining four years? On a consideration of *Taylor v O'Connor* (p 947, below), *Young v Percival* (above) and *Cookson v Knowles* (p 493, above) the law now seemed to be that, while the court should not use an addition to the multiplier as a means of taking into account the probability of future inflation, if a dependant's situation would be affected by future inflation the court should take it into account as best it could. It was a proper inference that over the next four years inflation would be at least 7% a year. The deceased's salary would have increased accordingly, so the plaintiff's dependency figure must be increased *pari passu*. Award from 1977: £27,872. Loss of pension rights: £26,760.

Wife's private income

Cruickshank v Shiels
[1953] 1 All ER 874, [1953] 1 WLR 533, 97 Sol Jo 208, HL
Deceased had a salary of £20,000 per annum, of which £17,000 ceased on his death. The widow had a considerable private income.
HELD: The widow's private means could not be taken into account in the assessment of damages.

Note—And see *Taylor v O'Connor*, p 947, below.

Wife's earnings

Higgs v Drinkwater
(1956) Times, 10 May
The husband was 25 earning £550 a year as a maintenance assessor with nylon spinners. The wife was 33 earning about £800 a year as a lecturer with the local authority. The parties had only been married a year during which they were both working and building up a home, getting furniture and so forth. The widow hoped not to continue her work indefinitely but in a year or two to start a family. Approximately £150 to £200 of the husband's earnings was being spent yearly for the wife's advantage.
HELD: The figure of loss of earnings to be taken into account was the £150 to £200, and there was to be added his loss of prospects of promotion and the increased benefit from that to her. The contributory pension scheme would enure to her benefit as well as to his.

Prospect of family

Malone v Rowan
[1984] 3 All ER 402 (Russell J)
The plaintiff's husband was killed in a road accident. She was at the time 25 years old and he 27. Her earnings were about £60 per week and his £76 which by the date of trial would have risen to £102. At the date of death the plaintiff's dependency was 55% of the deceased's earnings. The plaintiff said in evidence that she had wanted to start a family and would then have given up her job. Her dependency would then have increased (as the judge found) to two-thirds of the deceased's earnings. The judge accepted that she would have become pregnant in the very near future and would have given up her job to look after the children.
HELD: The material facts were indistinguishable from those of *Higgs v Drinkwater* (above). In that case Denning LJ: said it was not right to increase the figure for pecuniary loss because of the possibility of the plaintiff having a family. 'She had not suffered any financial loss on that account. . . . We can only award damages for financial loss and she has suffered none through not having a family. On the contrary, she had kept at work earning [her] salary'. This judgment was binding in the present case and the fraction for dependency as at the date of death could not be altered.

Damages not recoverable

INQUEST

Costs of attending are not damages resulting from the death and were disallowed by Hilbery J in *Grice v Tuke* at Winchester Assizes on 1 March 1940.

GRAVESTONE

Note—See also *Hart v Griffiths* and *Stanton v Youlden*, p 506, below.

Death of plaintiff before trial

Williamson v John I Thorneycroft & Co
[1940] 2 KB 658, [1940] 4 All ER 61, 110 LJKB 82, CA
An action brought by a widow under the Fatal Accidents and Law Reform
Acts. She died before trial. The trial judge ignored the death of the widow
before trial.
HELD, by the Court of Appeal: While the damages had to be assessed at the
date of the husband's death, the court was entitled to inform its mind of
subsequent events throwing light upon the realities of the case, such as the
fact that one dependant had only a short tenure of life before her dependence was brought to an end, and that, therefore, only a comparatively
small sum ought to have been allowed to the widow under the Fatal
Accidents Acts.

Note—See also *Voller v Dairy Produce Packers* (p 946, below) and *Rawlinson v Babcock
and Wilcox Ltd*, p 952, below.

Dependency a question of fact

Peters v Overhead Ltd
(1934) 27 BWCC 190, CA
In 1931, a workman deserted his wife and family, who had to be
maintained by the Poor Law Authorities. He was subsequently killed by
accident arising out of and in the course of his employment when working
under an assumed name. The widow, after learning the facts in 1934,
brought a claim on behalf of herself and her children for compensation as
dependants. The county court judge held on the facts that there was no
dependency or any reasonable probability of dependency and made his
award for the employers. The widow appealed.
HELD: The question of dependency was one of fact and could not be
presumed from the legal obligation to support. There was evidence to
support the finding of fact and no misdirection.

Note—A case under the Workmen's Compensation Acts. See next case.

Marriage breaking down

Davies v Taylor
[1974] AC 207, [1972] 3 All ER 836, [1972] 3 WLR 801, 116 Sol Jo 864,
HL
The plaintiff and her husband were married in 1955. From December 1966
to February 1968, unknown to her husband she had an adulterous
association with a man she met at work. In May 1968 she gave up her job
and on the 9 July she left her husband saying she no longer had any feeling
for him. She went to live with her parents. Her husband very much wanted
her to return to him and begged her to do so. On 31 July he went to her and
asked her to return but she told him of her adulterous affair. On 2 August
he instructed solicitors to begin divorce proceedings. On 14 August he met
the plaintiff by chance, in the street, told her he had consulted a solicitor but

again asked her to return to him; she refused, saying she wanted time to think. Later on the same day he was killed in a motor accident. At the trial of the plaintiff's claim for damages under the Fatal Accidents Acts the judge said that on the question of dependency the test he had to apply was whether the plaintiff had discharged the onus of proving that it was more probable than not that there would have been a reconciliation between her and her husband. He said he was not satisfied there was likely to be a reconciliation and that accordingly the plaintiff had not proved any dependency.

HELD: The judge had applied the wrong test. In this case it had to be decided whether there was a reasonable expectation of a reconciliation, not whether a reconciliation was more likely than not. If, although there was a reasonable expectation, the chance of the reconciliation happening was slight then the damages would be such as would reflect that degree of probability. The plaintiff's damages would be scaled down as the possibility became progressively more remote. But a mere speculative or fanciful possibility of a reconciliation was not sufficient. On the evidence the judge had rightly decided that there was no likelihood of a reconciliation and the plaintiff's claim failed. *Taff Vale Rly Co v Jenkins* (p 503, below) applied.

Dependency on proceeds of crime

Burns v Edman
[1970] 2 QB 541, [1970] 1 All ER 886, [1970] 2 WLR 1005, 114 Sol Jo 356 (Crichton J)
The plaintiff sued for damages for herself and her four children under the Fatal Accidents Acts for the death of her husband. He had had no record of honest employment and no capital assets; he had two convictions for felony. He used to give the plaintiff £20 every Friday. The inference was that such support as he gave came from the proceeds of crime.
HELD: The plaintiff was not entitled to damages. What each dependant was in effect saying was 'I have been deprived of my share of other people's goods brought to me by the deceased dishonestly' and in so far as that was the 'injury' within s 2 of the Acts it was a *turpi causa* and therefore no action in respect of it could be maintained.

Illegitimate child dependant

Kelliher v Ground Explorations
[1955] CLY 741 (Byrne J)
Illegitimate child aged three weeks; mother would probably have obtained a bastardy order of about £1 per week until child 16. Award £500.

Lindley v Sharp
(1973) 4 Fam Law 90, CA
The plaintiff, an illegitimate child born on 18 December 1970, sued by his mother as next friend for Fatal Accident damages for the death of the father, killed in a road accident on 12 August 1970. Paternity was accepted.

The deceased was 17 at the time of his death and had not had any steady employment. The judge put a figure of £4 per week on dependency and considered five years' purchase enough.

HELD, ON APPEAL: The question was what would the financial benefit to the plaintiff have been had the father not been killed? Would he have married the mother? Once paternity was established the mother would have been entitled to maintenance whether or not they had married. Five years' purchase was not enough; nine years should have been awarded at £208 a year = £1,872.

Savings

Gavin v Wilmot Breeden Ltd

[1973] 3 All ER 935, [1973] 1 WLR 1117, 117 Sol Jo 681, [1973] 2 Lloyd's Rep 501, CA

The plaintiff and her husband, both aged 19, were married in 1971. A child was born in November; in December the husband was killed. During the three months or so since marriage they had lived with his parents, paying £6 for accommodation. The husband had been earning £30 per week of which they had put aside £10 per week in a bank account in her name alone. On an appeal against an award of £16,848 made by the judge using an agreed multiplier of 18, defendants complained that the judge had made no reduction for the £10 weekly savings in determining the widow's dependency at £18 per week.

HELD: If the £10 per week had been spent instead of saved the standard of living of both spouses would have gone up. Some part of the £10 per week, whether saved or spent, should be regarded as likely to have been spent eventually for the benefit of the husband himself. To that extent the loss was not the widow's. The dependency should be reduced by £3 per week to £15.

Settlement before death

Read v Great Eastern Rly Co

(1868) LR 3 QB 555, 9 B & S 714, 37 LJQB 278, 18 LT 822, 33 JP 199, 16 WR 1040

Declaration by plaintiff as widow of D under Lord Campbell's Act 1846, and Fatal Accidents Act 1864, against a railway company for negligence whereby D, a passenger, was injured, of which injuries he died. Plea, that in the lifetime of D, defendants paid him, and he accepted, a sum of money in full satisfaction and discharge of all the claims and causes of action he had against defendants. Demurrer, on the ground that the accord and satisfaction with D was no accord and satisfaction of the claim arising from his death.

HELD: The cause of action was defendant's negligence, which had been satisfied in deceased's lifetime, and the death of D did not create a fresh cause of action.

Note—And see *Nunan v Southern Rly Co*, p 213, above. In *McCann v Sheppard* (p 410, above) the question was raised whether in the events which happened in that case, the plaintiff's widow could have a cause of action under the Fatal Accidents Acts. Lord Denning and James LJ were of the opinion that the wording of s 1 of the Act 'would appear to put an insuperable obstacle in the path of such proceedings'.

CHILD KILLED: PARENTS' CLAIM

Taff Vale Rly Co v Jenkins
[1913] AC 1, 82 LJKB 49, 107 LT 564, 29 TLR 19, 97 Sol Jo 27, CA
It is not a condition precedent to the maintenance of an action under the Fatal Accidents Act 1846, that the deceased should have been actually earning money or money's worth or contributing to the support of plaintiff at or before the date of the death, provided that plaintiff had a reasonable expectation of pecuniary benefit from the continuance of the life. Where, therefore, an action was brought by a father under the Fatal Accidents Act 1846, for damages for the loss of a daughter, aged 16, who was killed by the negligence of defendants and it was proved that at the date of her death deceased, who lived with her parents, was nearing the completion of her apprenticeship as a dressmaker and was likely in the near future to earn a remuneration which might quickly have become substantial.
HELD: There was evidence of damage upon which the jury could reasonably act.

Wathen v Vernon
[1970] RTR 471, CA
The plaintiff's son aged 17 was killed by negligence of the defendant. He was an apprentice at an engineering works who was paying for his upkeep only £3 pw to his parents out of a wage of £6 10s but who would have probably earned upwards of £19 pw at 21 and £26 per week at 25. The plaintiff, his father, was aged 56: he had suffered s stroke some years earlier and though he had returned to work there was a possibility of a recurrence which would disable him. He had a wife and three other children, two of them grown up. He claimed damages under the Fatal Accidents and Law Reform Acts. The judge, though accepting that the dead boy was a good son who would have helped his parents if there was a recurrence of the plaintiff's illness, held that the deceased would probably have married within about five years and that the possibility of the plaintiff's illness recurring within that time was not sufficiently high to justify an award under the Fatal Accidents Acts.
HELD, on the plaintiff's appeal: *Taff Vale Rly Co v Jenkins* (above) and *Buckland v Guildford Gas Light & Coke Co* (below) were authorities for saying that the court was entitled in proper circumstances to give damages for loss of support where no support had ever been given. Though the chances against the recurrence of the plaintiff's illness within five years were six to one it was right to make some award to cover the possibility. The award under the Fatal Accidents Act should be one of £500 for the deceased's mother, not the plaintiff.
Per Widgery LJ: If we had to decide it on the assumption that the father's health was normal . . . I would not be able to assent that a case had been made out.

Buckland v Guildford Gas Light and Coke Co
[1949] 1 KB 410, [1948] 2 All ER 1086, 93 Sol Jo 41 (Morris J)
Deceased was a bright intelligent girl aged 13 who was competent to look
after a younger child aged eight. She assisted her parents in the home and it
was anticipated that her gifts would later have enabled her to contribute
financially as well as by services to the household, subject to the changes
and chances that might have affected her and her parents.
Award: FAA £500.

Mere speculative possibility insufficient

Barnett v Cohen
[1921] 2 KB 461, 90 LJKB 1307, 125 LT 733, 37 TLR 629 (McCardie J)
In an action under the Fatal Accidents Act 1846, it is not sufficient for
plaintiff to prove that he has lost by the death of deceased a mere speculative
possibility of pecuniary benefit. In order to succeed it is necessary for him
to show that he has lost a reasonable probability of pecuniary advantage.
   The deceased child was four years of age. The boy was subject to all the
risks of illness, disease, accident and death. His education and upkeep
would have been a substantial burden to the plaintiff for many years if he
had lived. He might or might not have turned out a useful young man. He
would not have earned anything till about 16 years of age. He might never
had aided his father at all. He might have proved a mere expense. I cannot
adequately speculate one way or the other in any event. He would scarcely
have been expected to contribute to his father's income, for the plaintiff
even now possesses £1,000 a year by his business and may increase it
further, nor could the son have been expected to do any domestic service.
The whole matter is beset with doubts, contingencies and uncertainties.
HELD: Upon the facts the plaintiff had not proved damage either actual or
prospective. His claim was pressed to extinction by the weight of multiplied
contingencies. The action therefore failed.

PARENTS DEAD: CHILDREN'S CLAIM

Kassam v Kampala Aerated Water Co Ltd
[1965] 2 All ER 875, [1965] 1 WLR 668, 109 Sol Jo 291, PC
In an action in Uganda for Fatal Accidents Acts damages the claimants
were eight children, aged 3 to 23, of the deceased, a shopkeeper aged about
45. Their mother was also killed in the accident. The judge of first instance
awarded £6,000 but did not apportion the sum among the claimants. The
Court of Appeal for Eastern Africa reduced the award to £1,795, holding
that only four of the children were dependant. The deceased's total annual
expenditure on the family had been £572; the Court took four-ninths of this
(for the four children) and multiplied by $11\frac{1}{4}$ representing the average
dependency in years of these four. The Court made deductions to allow for
the advantage of having a capital sum and for the estimated value of the
acceleration of the children's interests in their father's estate.
   The Privy Council considered the award too low. 'Pure arithmetic does
not always . . . lead to a just result where there are so many imponderables.
The aim in assessing damages in a case such as the present is to estimate the
loss of reasonable expectation of pecuniary benefit. This must in most cases

be a matter of speculation and may be conjecture. The more usual method of assessing damages is that adopted by the trial judge of estimating the total dependency as a lump sum and thereafter apportioning it among the various dependants. Another method may be to assess each dependency separately. . . . But if the method of assessing the support for each dependant separately leads to a result which is so out of line with what would be a reasonable estimate of the loss of each individual dependant this suggests that some step in the calculation must be erroneous.' On the evidence there were eight dependants, not four. But the original award of £6,000 was too high because the judge had taken 15 years as the period of dependency, ignoring the fact that not all the children would have been dependant so long. A figure of £3,500 would fairly represent the total loss of dependency among the eight dependants.

Dodds v Dodds

[1978] QB 543, [1978] 2 All ER 539, [1978] 2 WLR 434, 121 Sol Jo 619 (Balcombe J)

The defendant was driving a car with her husband as passenger when there was an accident in which he was killed and for which she was wholly to blame. It was conceded that she could make no claim for herself under the Fatal Accident Act; the only other dependant was her son, aged eight and a half. The deceased, aged 29 at death and earning £3,000 a year, could reasonably have expected rapid promotion and increases in his earnings had he lived and might by the date of trial have had take-home pay of £4,720 a year. The defendant had trained as a typist after her husband's death and her take-home pay at the time of the trial was £2,080.

HELD: (1) The way to assess the child's loss was to divide up the family expenditure into four columns — items benefiting the father exclusively, items benefiting the mother exclusively, items which benefited the child exclusively and finally those which benefited the whole family (ie rent or mortgage instalments, rates, repairs and decoration of the family house, heating and lighting, telephone, TV, garden, house insurance etc). The sum of columns three and four was the child's dependency. (2) As at the date of trial the child's estimated dependency was £2,750 a year and the combined family income would have been £6,800 a year. Of this the father's contribution would have been £4,720 so that the child's loss of the benefit of his father's income was £1,908 a year. (3) The multiplier should not be reduced by the number of years which had elapsed from death to trial — the judgment in *Cookson v Knowles* (p 493, above) must be taken to have been given *per incuriam* on this point — and the multiplier at the date of trial, the child being then $12\frac{1}{2}$, was 5. (4) The pecuniary loss from the death to trial, calculated at £7,628, should be added. Total award under Fatal Accidents Act £17,168.

Funeral expenses

LAW REFORM (MISCELLANEOUS PROVISIONS) ACT 1934, s 2(3)

'2 (3) In an action brought under the Fatal Accidents Acts 1846 to 1908 damages may be awarded in respect of the funeral expenses of the deceased person if such expenses have been incurred by the parties for whose benefit the action is brought.'

Section 2(3) of Law Reform (Miscellaneous Provisions) Act 1934 was replaced in respect of causes of action arising from deaths on or after 1 September 1976 by s 3(3) of the 1976 Act:

'**3** (3) If the dependants have incurred funeral expenses in respect of the deceased, damages may be awarded in respect of those expenses.'

A person can recover damages under the Fatal Accidents Act (by virtue of the Fatal Accidents Act 1976, s 3(5) above) in respect of funeral expenses which he has incurred even though he has no other claim under the Acts, ie even though he can prove no dependency — so held in *Stanton v Youlden*, below.

Hart v Griffith-Jones
[1948] 2 All ER 729 (Streatfeild J)
Funeral expenses of a girl aged four included embalming the body.
HELD: Not unreasonable and allowed as part of the funeral expenses.
By amendment as an afterthought, a claim for £225 was added for a monument over the grave.
Citing *Goldstein v Salvation Army Assurance Society* [1917] 2 KB 291, 86 LJKB 793, 117 LT 63 (per Rowlatt J, that a tombstone was not allowed as a funeral expense for estate duty), the allowance under the Assurance Companies Act 1909, of a stone or tablet on the grave as a reasonable and proper expense in an insurance for funeral expenses including the erection of a tombstone, and the construction of 'funeral expenses' under that Act was irrelevant. The claim for £225 was wholly unreasonable and was disallowed.

Note—But see next case.

Assessment — gravestone

Stanton v Ewart F. Youlden Ltd
[1960] 1 All ER 429, [1960] 1 WLR 543, 104 Sol Jo 368
A claim for funeral expenses included a sum of £194 15s comprising £155 for a marble memorial erected over the grave six months after the death, synagogue fees £34 10s and £5 5s extra letters on the memorial. The claim also included £5 paid to the minister for attending the funeral, £8 for two additional limousine cars at the funeral, and £5 for removing the body to the house (£18 in all).
HELD: (1) The plaintiff was entitled as executor to recover reasonable expenditure on a gravestone for his wife's grave, and, in the circumstances, an amount of £40 would be included in the damages in respect of the stone.
(2) The payments, amounting to £18 as specified would also be included as funeral expenses in the damages recoverable by the plaintiff.

CLAIM FOR DEATH OF WIFE

Wife not earning

Berry v Humm & Co
[1915] 1 KB 627, 84 LJKB 918, 31 TLR 198
Plaintiff, a workman earning 38s a week, sued defendants to recover

damages for the death of his wife, who was knocked down by a motor taxi-cab belonging to defendants and instantly killed. The wife had performed the ordinary household duties of a woman in her position, and in consequence of her death plaintiff had to employ a housekeeper and to incur extra expenses of management by the housekeeper instead of his deceased wife. The jury assessed plaintiff's damages at £50.

HELD: Under Lord Campbell's Act 1846, the damages recoverable in such an action are not limited to the value of money loss, or the money value of things lost, but include the monetary loss incurred by replacing services rendered gratuitously by the deceased where there was a reasonable prospect of their being rendered freely in the future but for the death, and, therefore, plaintiff was entitled to recover the damages assessed by the jury.

Morris v H. Rigby (Road Haulage) Ltd
(1966) 110 Sol Jo 834, CA

The husband, a medical officer earning £2,820 a year, claimed damages under the Fatal Accidents Act for the death of his wife. He had five children aged two to fifteen years. He got his wife's sister to come to take care of them and do the domestic duties his wife had done, paying her a gross wage of £20 per week. The judge awarded £8,000.

HELD, ON APPEAL: The award was not too high. The plaintiff was entitled to the reasonable cost of replacing his wife's services — *Berry v Humm* (above). He had acted reasonably in employing his wife's sister at £20 per week.

Bailey v Barking and Havering Area Health Authority
(1978) Times, 22 July (Pain J)

The plaintiff claimed damages under the Fatal Accidents Acts for the death of his wife. Before her death he was employed as a hospital porter but after her death he gave up work and stayed at home to look after his three daughters. He claimed that damages should be assessed on the basis that he had lost a housekeeper; the wages of a housekeeper were more than the wages of a hospital porter.

HELD: Approaching the matter as a juryman would, it was repugnant that a plaintiff should make a profit out of the situation. Commonsense indicated that a husband should be compensated for his actual loss. That was the measure of the damages.

Jeffery v Smith
(1970) 114 Sol Jo 268, [1970] RTR 279, CA

The plaintiff's wife was killed in a motor accident caused by the negligence of the defendant. There were three children aged, at the time of the trial, nine, six and three. The plaintiff was 51. His mother-in-law had looked after the children since the wife's death but her bad health prevented her from continuing to do so. The plaintiff called evidence from an employment agency that a housekeeper to look after the children would cost at least £10 per week. The judge took a multiplier of 10 years and awarded £5,200.

HELD, ON APPEAL: The award should stand. There was no evidence before the court to indicate that the figure of £10 per week was wrong and it was clear from the judgment that the judge had borne in mind the 'imponderables' such as the possibility of the plaintiff's re-marriage.

Regan v Williamson
[1976] 2 All ER 241, [1976] 1 WLR 305, 120 Sol Jo 217 (Watkins J)
At the time of her death the plaintiff's wife was 37 years of age. There were four children of the marriage, all boys, aged 13, 10, 7 and 2. The plaintiff had, after her death, engaged a relative to come in daily, except weekends, to provide meals and look after the boys when he was out at work; he paid her £16 per week and it cost him a further £6.50 per week for her food, journeys to and from home and national insurance stamp. The plaintiff estimated that his wife had cost him £10 per week to clothe and feed.
HELD: Precedent would suggest that the overall figure of dependency for calculation of the plaintiff's damages under the Fatal Accidents Act was £22.50 less £10 per week, but this would work an injustice. In valuing the loss of the services of a wife and mother the word 'services' in earlier cases has been too narrowly construed. It should include an acknowledgment that she does not work to set hours nor to rule. She may well during those hours give the children instruction on essential matters or on such things as homework. The figure for dependency should be raised from £12.50 to £20 per week and a further £1.50 per week added for her financial contribution to the home had she eventually gone out to work again. The multiplier should be 11 years.

Mehmet v Perry
[1977] 2 All ER 529, QBD
The plaintiff's wife was killed in September 1973 by the negligence of the defendants. There were five children of the marriage aged, at her death, 14, 11, 7, 6 and 3. The two youngest suffered from a serious hereditary blood disease requiring regular medication and frequent visits to hospital. Because of this the plaintiff gave up work after his wife's death and devoted himself full time to the care of the family. Between September 1973 and trial in October 1976 his net average loss of earnings was £1,500 a year. His future net loss would be at the rate of £2,000 a year. By the date of trial he had received a total of £4,197 supplementary benefit.
HELD: (1) In the particular circumstances, including the illness of the youngest children it was reasonable for the plaintiff to have given up work rather than employ a housekeeper and the proper measure of the loss of the general housekeeping services which his wife had undertaken was his net loss of earnings; (2) for loss of the personal attention of their mother the children were entitled to an additional award (following *Regan v Williamson*, above) but within modest limits because their father was acting as a full-time housekeeper; (3) the plaintiff was entitled to damages for the loss of his wife's services to himself but the sum should be quite small because he was now rendering services to the family unit as a whole as full-time house-keeper and damages were being assessed under (1) by reference to those services; (4) the amount received in supplementary benefit should be deducted from the total. Award for loss of housekeeping services £1,500 × 3 years plus £2,000 × 5 years. £1,500 for children for loss of their mother's

care and attention; £3,000 for plaintiff's loss of his wife's care and attention divided as to £1,000 for the first 8 years and £2,000 thereafter. After deduction of supplementary benefit, total award £14,800.

Wife earning

Burgess v Florence Nightingale Hospital
[1955] 1 QB 349, [1955] 1 All ER 511, [1955] 2 WLR 533, 99 Sol Jo 170 (Devlin J)

The deceased became a dancing partner of the plaintiff for amateur purposes in 1942. In July 1948, they started dancing professionally. In 1951 she was divorced by her husband. In September 1952, she married the plaintiff. After the beginning of 1953 they were nearing the peak of professional status. In January 1953, she entered the defendants' hospital and her death resulted from negligent treatment.

The gross income of the plaintiff, who was 38 years of age, was between £1,000 and £1,250 with prospects of increase by £400 or £500. The deceased was 36. The plaintiff was unable to obtain a suitable dancing partner and his estimated income was reduced to £600 per annum. The parties had lived in a flat and the deceased had performed the household duties. After her death the plaintiff had to employ a woman at 25s per week and to have his meals outside. The deceased had contributed towards the househould expenses. The rent was £9 13s 0d monthly and there were expenses for gas and electricity. She had also contributed to the school fees of the child of her previous marriage and had spent money on her clothes. The school fees had been reduced by half and the plaintiff paid them. The wife had paid at least £1 weekly to her widowed mother who was 66 years of age.

The joint ability to earn an income greatly exceeded the ability of either of them individually. The joint earnings were shared and so were the living expenses. The loss to the plaintiff of his wife as a dancing partner was assessed at £2,500. The other assessments were £1,000 for the loss as wife (services); £1,000 for loss of wife's contribution; £350 for loss by child of wife's payment and prospective assistance; £300 for loss of wife's payment to her mother.

HELD: As to loss of £2,500 as a dancing partner, it is necessary to read some limitations into the rather wide and general wording of the 1846 Act. The loss would fall within the mere wording but the decisions showed that if, eg a servant lost his employment by the death of his employer or of a departmental manager; or a junior partner lost business by the death of a senior partner; there would be no claim under the Act. It makes no difference that the junior partner was a son. The loss would be *qua* junior partner, not *qua* son. The benefit here was as partner and not as wife. The relationship was superimposed on the partnership. The £2,500 was therefore not recoverable.

Contributions to household expenses: contributions 50 or 100 years ago, where the husband paid all the joint living expenses, and money earnings of the wife were a kind of pin money, do not apply to modern life. The parties were earning equally and contributing equally. No case of mutual dependence of that sort has been cited but there was no difficulty in principle. Where the living expenses are less than twice the expense of each living separately, the benefit which each confers on the other comes within the Act.

Note—See also *Maylon v Plummer*, p 951, below.

Hurt v Murphy

[1971] RTR 186 (Talbot J)

The plaintiff was aged 45, his wife 42. On her death he was left with five children aged from 22 to nine. She had fulfilled all the normal tasks of housewife and mother and also earned £3 p w in part-time work. The plaintiff's house was a council house with only two bedrooms. He had insufficient money to buy a house.

HELD: It would not be proper that the defendant should have to pay for a house big enough to enable the plaintiff to employ a resident housekeeper. Damages should be based on the cost of a daily help. The hours of domestic help needed would reduce as the children grew older. On a multiplier of nine, award £4,118.

UNMARRIED WIFE: CHILDREN'S CLAIM

Note—In respect of causes of action accruing on or after 1 January 1983 see the Fatal Accidents Act 1976, ss 1(3)(b) and 3(4) substituted by the Administration of Justice Act 1982, s 3, p 488, above.

PAYMENT INTO COURT

Note—In cases where claims were made in the same action both under the Fatal Accidents Acts and under the Law Reform Act it was formerly necessary for a defendant to apportion a payment into Court between the two causes of action unless he first obtained an order from the Court dispensing with apportionment. Since 1 January 1964 this is no longer necessary. See RSC Ord 22, r 1(5) and (6).

PAYMENT OUT OF COURT

RSC Ord 22, r 4 is as follows:

'(1) Where a plaintiff accepts any sum paid into Court and that sum was paid into Court —

(d) in satisfaction either of causes of action arising under the Fatal Accidents Act 1976, and the Law Reform (Miscellaneous Provisions) Act 1934, or of a cause of action arising under the first mentioned Act where more than one person is entitled to the money the money in Court shall not be paid out except in pursuance of an order of the Court, and the order shall deal with the whole costs of the action or of the cause of action to which the payment relates as the case may be.'

Order 80, r 15 provides:

'(2) Where, in action in which a claim under the Fatal Accidents Act 1976, is made by or on behalf of more than one person, a sum in respect of damages is adjusted or ordered or agreed to be paid in satisfaction of the claim, or a sum of money paid into Court under Ord 22, r 1, is accepted in satisfaction of the cause of action under the said Act, then, unless the sum has been apportioned between the persons entitled thereto by a jury, it shall be apportioned between those persons by the Court.'

Control of money in court

Note—Control of money recovered under the Fatal Accidents Act is exercised by the court under RSC Ord 80, r 12. The rule is as follows:

'12 (1) Where in any proceedings —
(a) money is recovered by or on behalf of, or adjudged or ordered or agreed to be paid to, or for the benefit of a person under disability, or
(b) money paid into court is accepted by or on behalf of a plaintiff who is a person under disability,
the money shall be dealt with in accordance with directions given by the Court, whether under s 174 of the County Courts Act 1959, or this rule, or under both that section and this rule and not otherwise.
(2) Directions given under this rule may provide that the money shall, as to the whole or any part thereof, be paid into the High Court and invested or otherwise dealt with there.
(3) Without prejudice to the foregoing provisions of this rule, directions given under this rule may include any general or special directions that the Court thinks fit to give and, in particular, directions as to how the money is to be applied or dealt with and as to any payment to be made, either directly or out of the amount paid into court and whether before or after the money is transferred to or paid into a county court, to the plaintiff, or to the next friend in respect of money paid or expenses incurred for or on behalf of or for the benefit of the person under disability or for his maintenance or otherwise for his benefit or to the plaintiff's solicitor in respect of costs.
(4) Where in pursuance of directions given under this rule money is paid into the High Court to be invested or otherwise dealt with there, the money (including any interest thereon) shall not be paid out, nor shall any securities in which the money is invested, or the dividends thereon, be sold, transferred or paid out of court, except in accordance with an order of the Court'.

A widow over 18 is not a 'person under disability' and is able to enter into a valid settlement or compromise of her own claim without obtaining the approval of the Court under Ord 80, r 11. The Administration of Justice Act 1965, s 19 which formerly enabled the Court to control money recovered by a widow under the Fatal Accidents Acts was repealed as from 1 August 1971 by the Law Reform (Miscellaneous Provisions) Act 1971, s 5(1). 'The power of the Court to control widows' damages recovered under the Fatal Accidents Act 1976 (formerly the Fatal Acccidents Acts 1846 to 1959) has been entirely abolished, whether or not the claim is also made on behalf of an infant' (*Supreme Court Practice 1985*, 80/12/2, p 1156).

Jeffrey v Kent County Council
[1958] 3 All ER 155, [1958] 1 WLR 927, 102 Sol Jo 620 (Paull J)
An agreement for a lump sum requires that (1) each of the dependants who is *sui juris* approves, and (2) the court sanctions the agreement as being for the benefit of each of the dependants who are infants. A dependant who is *sui juris* is bound by the administrator's agreement, but the claim of the other dependants remains to be settled by the court, and the court does not consider the amount paid to the settling dependant unless it affects the loss of any of the other dependants. If a settlement by a widow individually is

far too small a sum to provide the resources which she would otherwise have had to bring up infant children, the court may give to the infants much larger sums than if the widow had received a proper capital sum.

REMARRIAGE OF WIDOW

Not to be taken into account

Note—See the Fatal Accidents Act 1976, s 3(3), p 489, above.

Effect on children's damages

Mead v Clarke Chapman & Co Ltd
[1956] 1 All ER 44, [1956] 1 WLR 76, 100 Sol Jo 51, CA
A welder aged 23, earning £8 10s 0d per week was killed on 15 January 1951, leaving a widow aged 19 and a daughter aged four months. On 27 September 1951, the widow re-married a lorry driver earning at the date of trial, 29 June 1955 (four and a half years after the death) the same figure of £8 10s 0d per week. The deceased gave his wife £6 10s 0d per week. It was accepted that the earnings of the second husband were the same as the first husband. A male child was born of the second marriage and the two children were growing up together. The second husband was very fond of his step-daughter and looked after her nicely.

Donovan J assessed the loss of the family at £5 per week and awarded £180 being £5 per week for the 36 weeks between death and re-marriage, as damages under the Fatal Accidents Acts, apportioned £36 to the infant and £144 to the widow, and held there was no financial loss after the remarriage. The plaintiff appealed in respect of the damages awarded to the child.

HELD, ON APPEAL: It should not be assumed that the position will remain the same for all time. The onus is on the defendants to prove that in all reasonable probability the child cannot suffer any pecuniary loss in the future; that she is provided for during the rest of the time for which she might have been dependent on her father. There might be a large family in years to come. The stepfather might be pressed for money. He might not be able to look after the child as well as her own father would have done. A father can be forced to support his child if he fails to do so, while the stepfather cannot (National Assistance Act 1948, s 42(1)). The father might be willing to assist his own child in education or other ways, which a stepfather might not. The child's claim should be allowed at £200. Appeal allowed accordingly.

Reincke v Gray
[1964] 2 All ER 687, [1964] 1 WLR 832, 108 Sol Jo 461, CA
The plaintiff claimed damages under the Fatal Accidents Acts on behalf of her two children, a boy aged three and a girl aged one, for the death of her husband. He had been in good employment at the time of his death earning £1,800 a year with good prospects. Nine months after his death the plaintiff remarried. Her second husband was a chartered accountant earning

£2,500 a year. He had accepted the two children into the family and had agreed to send the boy to public school as his father had intended. On an assessment of damages the Master, having regard to *Mead v Chapman Clarke & Co Ltd* (above), awarded £2,000 to the boy and £1,750 to the girl.

HELD, ON APPEAL: The awards were excessive. The circumstances in this case were different from those in *Mead's* case, where the widow of a welder married a lorry driver: in that standard of life the fact that there was only a moral and not a legal duty on the second husband to support the children was not immaterial. Moreover the provisions of the Matrimonial Proceedings (Children) Act 1958, s 1(1) now enabled the High Court to impose a legal obligation to provide for the custody, maintenance and education of the children of one party to the marriage who have been accepted into the family by the other party as if they were the children of both parties. Looking at the evidence and considering the probabilities of the future as to financial loss the Court had to consider at what figure the chance of loss should be assessed. The figure of £500 for each child should be substituted for the Master's awards.

Thompson v Price
[1973] QB 838, [1973] 2 All ER 846, [1973] 2 WLR 1037, 117 Sol Jo 468 (Boreham J)

As s 4(1) applies to damages 'payable to a widow' the proportion of damages allotted to a child is to be assessed, where the widow had remarried, having regard to that fact.

Deceased 24 years old at death, widow 22, child 18 months. Widow remarried two or three months later, the second husband being in as good a financial position as the deceased would have been. Dependency of widow £9 per week, multiplier 17 years having regard to ages of deceased and widow. Child entitled to two years three months at £3 per week (£337.50) rounded up to £500 to allow for his receiving perhaps less from stepfather than he would from his own and having to compete with children of second marriage.

DEATH RESULTING FROM ACCIDENT

Pneumonia

Isitt v Railway Passengers Assurance Co
(1889) 22 QBD 504, 58 LJQB 191, 60 LT 297, 37 WR 477, 5 TLR 194

The assured, under a policy granted by the defendant company against 'death from the effects of injury caused by accident', fell and dislocated his shoulder. He was at once put to bed and died in less than a month from the date of the accident, having been all the time confined to his bedroom. In a case stated in a reference under defendants' special Act the umpire found that the assured died from pneumonia caused by cold, but that he would not have died as and when he did had it not been for the accident; that as a consequence of the accident he suffered from pain and was rendered restless, unable to wear his clothing, weak and unusually susceptible to cold, and that his catching cold and the fatal effects of the cold were both due to the condition of health to which he had been reduced by the accident.

HELD: The death of the assured was due to the 'effects of injury caused by the accident' within the meaning of the policy.

Mardorf v Accident Insurance Co
[1903] 1 KB 584, 72 LJKB 362, 98 LT 330, 19 TLR 274

Under a personal accident policy insurers agreed to pay in case of injury by accidental violence if the injury should be the 'direct and sole cause' of death, excluding 'death caused by or arising wholly or in part from disease or other intervening cause, even although the disease or other intervening cause may either directly or otherwise be brought on or result from accident'.

The assured accidentally scratched his leg, which ten days later became inflamed, and erysipelas set in, followed in three days by septicaemia, and soon afterwards by septic pneumonia, of which in less than a week the insured died.

HELD: The erysipelas, septicaemia, and septic pneumonia were not 'intervening causes' and death was caused directly and solely by the injury.

Re Etherington and Lancashire and Yorkshire Accident Insurance Co
[1909] 1 KB 591, 78 LJKB 684, 110 LT 568, 53 SL 266

By the terms of a policy an accident insurance company undertook, if, at any time during the continuance of the said policy, the insured should sustain any bodily injury caused by violent, accidental, external, and visible means, then, in case such injury should, within three calendar months from the occurrence of the accident causing such injury, directly cause the death of the insured, to pay to the legal personal representatives of the insured the capital sum of £1,000. The policy contained the following proviso: 'Provided always and it is hereby as the essence of the contract agreed as follows: that this policy only insures against death where accident within the meaning of the policy is the direct or proximate cause thereof, but not where the direct or proximate cause thereof is disease or other intervening cause, even although the disease or other intervening cause may itself have been aggravated by such accident, or have been due to weakness or exhaustion consequent thereon, or the death accelerated thereby.'

The assured, while hunting, had a heavy fall, and, the ground being very wet, he was wetted to the skin. The effect of the shock and the wetting was to lower the vitality of his system, and being obliged to ride home afterwards while wet, still further lowered his vitality. The effect of this lowering of his vitality was to cause the subsequent development of pneumonia in his lungs, of which he died. The pneumonia was not septic or traumatic, but arose as a direct and natural consequence from the fact that the diminution of vitality caused through the accident, as above-mentioned, allowed the germs called 'pneumococci', which in small numbers are generally present in the respiratory passages, to multiply greatly and attack the lungs.

HELD: The death of the assured was directly caused by accident within the meaning of the policy, and the case did not come within the proviso therein, and the company were consequently liable on the policy.

Shock

Smith v Cornhill Insurance Co

[1938] 3 All ER 145, 54 TLR 869, 82 Sol Jo 625, 61 Lloyd's Rep 122
(Atkinson J)
Policy provided payment for death as the result of bodily injury caused by
violent, accidental, external and visible means. Car found badly damaged
lying on its side some yards below level of road. A very wavy track which
had been forced through bushes near the car, finally led to a river, and
there insured was found standing almost upright with the water a few
inches over her head. There was an overhanging branch by which she could
have pulled herself out. Medical evidence was that she died before or at the
moment her face reached the surface of the water. She had suffered severe
mental and physical shock as a result of the accident and had wandered
aimlessly into the water.
HELD: Death was the result of the accident, as each subsequent event was
due to the brain injury resulting from the accident.

Note—For '*Shock, non-fatal*', p 462, above.

Suicide

Note—This subject is relevant in two connections (1) the death benefit under a
policy and (2) the result of an accident.
   In the case of death by poisoning from the exhaust of a car (asphyxia from carbon
monoxide poisoning) this is prima facie an accident in direct connection with the
insured car, caused by accidental external and visible means, and the onus is on the
insurers to prove the case is suicide within the exception. If it is desired to exclude
this risk from the policy, one method is to exclude death by inhalation.
   Willis' *Workmen's Compensation* dealt with suicide, as follows:

'When it results from insanity or mental derangement (*Dixon v Sutton Heath and Lea
Green Colliery Ltd (No 2)* (1930) 23 BWCC 135) consequent on personal injury by
accident, it is rightly held to be death resulting from the injury (*Malone v Cayzer
Irvine & Co* 1908 SC 479, 45 Sc LR 351, 15 SLT 837, 1 BWCC 27; *Graham v Christie*
(1916) 10 BWCC 486), but suicide of itself is neither proof nor evidence of insanity
(*Grime v Fletcher* [1915] 1 KB 734, 84 LJKB 847, 112 LT 840, 31 TLR 158, 59 Sol Jo
223, 8 BWCC 69).
   The onus of proof is on the applicants and they must show not only that the death
is due to insanity but that the insanity is the direct result of the injury, and it is not
sufficient to show that it is an indirect result, such as that it was caused by brooding
over the accident or worrying over the inability to work. *Withers v London Brighton
and South Coast Rly Co* [1916] 2 KB 772, 85 LJKB 1673, 115 LT 503, 32 TLR 685,
61 Sol Jo 8, 9 BWCC 616, CA.'

Jenkins v Lancasters Steam Coal Collieries

(1923) 16 BWCC 11
The foregoing has been accepted in the Court of Appeal as a correct
statement of the law.

Fuller v Minister of Pensions

(1948) 3 War Pensions Appeal 1623 (Denning J)

The question of causation is always difficult, but suicide is such an overwhelming event in itself that, in the ordinary way, that act is an act of which the cause lies in the man's own individual personality and nothing else. The worries, whether they be personal or whether they be connected with his work are the conditions in which the cause operates and are not a cause at all.

Note—Followed in *Pitt v Minister of Pensions and National Insurance* (1954) Times, 19 January (Ormrod J)

Pigney v Pointers Transporter Services

[1957] 2 All ER 807, [1957] 1 WLR 1121, 101 Sol Jo 851 (Pilcher J)

A workman was injured on 28 July 1955. He brought an action against his employers but on 15 January 1957, before the action had been tried, he committed suicide. His widow and administratrix then commenced proceedings under the Fatal Accidents and Law Reform Acts and the two actions were consolidated.

The injury consisted of a fairly serious cut on the head which had to be stitched and apparently healed perfectly. He was to some extent concussed, was in hospital a few days and made a perfectly good recovery from the physical injury to the scalp. After the accident and up to the time of his death, he suffered from a condition of acute anxiety neurosis with depressive features brought about by the accident. He was not insane under the McNaghten rules. He knew what he was doing and that what he was doing was wrong. He took his life in a fit of depression brought about by a condition of acute anxiety neurosis induced by the accident and injury.

HELD: The case of *Cavanagh v London Transport Executive* (below) and the workmen's cases show that a sane man's death by suicide can in law 'result' from an injury, even though the suicide may not occur until some time after the injury. With regard to the defence of public policy, the last words of s 1 of the Act of 1846 were no doubt introduced so as not to defeat the rights of defendants where no criminal proceedings had been instituted, but the claim, which is a new cause of action created by the Act beyond that which the deceased would have had if he had survived (*Pym v Great Northern Rly Co* (1863) 4 B & S 396, 32 LJQB 377, 8 LT 734), does not depend on that ground but on the ground that the deceased's act did not break the chain of causation. In the case of *Beresford v Royal Insurance Co* (p 891, below), it was held to be against public policy to allow a felon by his crime to benefit his own estate. This is not a case of benefit to the estate of the deceased. The defence of public policy was not raised in the *Workmen's Compensation* case nor in *Cavanagh's* case. The widow is entitled to damages.

Cavanagh v London Transport Executive

(1956) Times, 23 October (Devlin J)

On 25 September 1953, the plaintiff's husband was injured by an omnibus of the defendants. He sustained a fractured skull and other injuries. Some 16 months later he committed suicide. The deceased was a bookmaker a little over 50 years of age, married with two children, now grown up; he had been married 26 years and appeared to have been successful and happy, both domestically and in business. The injuries were severe including a fracture of the vault of the skull which caused concussion and immediate loss of consciousness. On 3 February 1954, his doctor signed him off as fit for work and he went back to his business. His bank account appeared to show that from about May or June 1954, the business was going downhill. The plaintiff said he was a changed man after the accident. The kindliness and his fondness for his children disappeared. Before the accident he had been a reserved man who disliked any sort of swearing. After the accident he became abusive and behaved abominably to her and the children and things got worse when he went back to work. On 23 January 1955 he committed suicide.

The defendant's medical evidence was that it was not a characteristic of head injuries that they led to suicide; there was nothing at the examination; the cause was a depressive psychosis, which was the most common cause of suicide in middle-aged men.

The judge said if the head injuries were ruled out, it must have been depressive psychosis and he did not see any evidence of that. It might be that financial worries operating on the state of mind, contributed to it and was perhaps the immediate cause, but the head injuries might have made him incapable of reacting normally to worries.

HELD: There was no *novus actus*; the business losses were likely to result from his decline in business ability. The plaintiff had discharged the burden of proof of causation.

Farmer v Rash
[1969] 1 All ER 705, [1969] 1 WLR 160, 113 Sol Jo 57 (Willis J)
The Court was asked to approve a settlement of claims under the Fatal Accidents Acts where £2,100 had been paid into Court and apportion the payment between the claimants and the estate under the Law Reform (Miscellaneous Provisions) Act 1934. The deceased was seriously injured by the defendant's negligent driving on 22 February 1965, sustaining fractures of both legs, broken back and broken hip ramus. He was in hospital only two weeks and was sufficiently recovered to attempt a return to work in the summer. Then he began to suffer from depression which by January was so bad that he was admitted to hospital. On 11 February 1966 he committed suicide. A doctor said he thought the accident was an 'important precipitating factor' in causation of the depression. The dependants under the Fatal Accidents Acts were the deceased's wife, from whom he had been separated for many years, their son and an illegitimate son. By his will the deceased had left everything to a woman with whom he had been living for several years and who was the mother of the illegitimate son. The wife was making application in separate proceedings under the Inheritance (Family Provision) Act 1938.

HELD: The likelihood of the executor recovering anything in a contested claim under the Fatal Accidents Acts was so remote that it would be unrealistic to apportion any part of the sum of £2,100 to that head of claim. The whole sum should go to the estate under the Law Reform Act.

ADMINISTRATION CASES

No administrator (FA Act)

Holleran v Bagnell
(1879) 4 LRIr 740 (Ireland)
Curran v Grand Trunk Rly Co
(1898) 25 OAR 407 (Canada)
A action can be sustained by a relative of the deceased, though brought
within six calendar months of the death, unless there be at the time an
executor or administrator of the deceased.

M'Cabe v Great Northern Rly Co of Ireland
[1899] 2 IR 123 (Ireland)
The court will not, in the absence of bad faith, make any order staying an
action under this Act by one of the next of kin within six months and before
administration is taken out, although administration is subsequently taken
out by another of the next of kin, and a second action in respect of the death
of the same deceased is instituted by the administrator.

Note—But see *Cooper v Williams*, p 490, above.

Action before administration

Meyappa Chetty v Supriana Chetty
[1916] 1 AC 603, LR 43 Ind App 113, 85 LJPC 179, 114 LT 1002, PC
Per Lord Parker: As an executor derives his title and authority from the
will, he can institute an action in the character of executor before he proves
the will, and though he cannot carry an action to judgment until he has
obtained probate, that is not because his title depends on probate but
because production of probate is the only way in which, by the rules of the
court, he is allowed to prove his title. On the other hand an administrator
derives his title solely under his grant and cannot, therefore, institute an
action as administrator before he gets his grant. The law on the point is well
settled.

Ingall v Moran
[1944] KB 160, [1944] 1 All ER 97, 113 LJKB 298, 170 LT 57, 60 TLR
120, 88 Sol Jo 68, CA
Deceased was killed by accident on 19 September 1941. On 17 September
1942, the father issued a writ describing himself as administrator. He had
not at that date obtained grant of letters of administration, which grant was
obtained on 13 November 1942. Defendant pleaded the Limitation Act
1939, s 21.
HELD: The description by the plaintiff of himself as administrator in the
writ was false and the writ was a nullity. The defendant could have applied
to strike out the action. The action was incapable of conversion by
amendment into a valid action. Once the 12 months had expired, the cause
of action was barred and could not be resurrected.

Following *Mabro v Eagle Star Insurance Co* [1932] 1 KB 485, where Scrutton LJ said:

'In my experience the court has always refused to allow a party or a cause of action to be added where, if it were allowed, the defence of the statute of limitations would be defeated. The court has never treated it as just to deprive a defendant of a legal defence. If the facts show either that the particular plaintiff or the new cause of action sought to be added are barred, I am unable to understand how it is possible for the court to disregard the statute.'

Note—And see 'Renewal of writ', p 560, below; 'Amendment of proceedings', p 552, below. See also *Austin v Hart*, p 522, below, and note after *Hilton v Sutton Steam Laundry* (below).

Hilton v Sutton Steam Laundry
[1946] KB 65, [1945] 2 All ER 425, 115 LJKB 33, 174 LT 31, CA
The widow of a man who died on 29 October 1942, as the result of an accident, issued a writ on 19 February 1943, in the purported description or capacity of 'administratrix', claiming damages under the Fatal Accidents Act and Law Reform Act, and on 15 March 1943, delivered statement of claim in which such purported description or capacity was repeated. In fact, letters of administration were not obtained until 22 October 1943.

On 19 December 1943, as a result of the decision of *Ingall v Moran*, she applied to amend the writ and statement of claim by striking out the reference to the Law Reform Act and the description 'as administratrix of the deceased's estate', contending that the action would then be in an individual capacity under the Fatal Accidents Acts. If the action went to trial, it was suggested the plaintiff could argue the misdescription was a mere technicality which under the rules of court the judge would have discretion to remedy but it was desired to test the position by applying for amendment.

The defendants objected that this amendment would deprive them of their statutory defence that the action was not commenced within twelve months of the death.

HELD: RSC Ord III, r 4 (now Ord 6, r 3), required that the indorsement must show the capacity in which a plaintiff is suing, and the plaintiff had bound herself to an action in a representative capacity which she did not possess. The amendment could not be allowed as it would deprive the defendants of their rights (as held in *Mabro v Eagle Star Insurance Co*).

Note—But see now *Mitchell v Harris Engineering Co Ltd*, p 559, below, and especially Lord Denning's remarks on the effect of Ord 20, r 5. See also the Limitation Act 1980, s 35(3).

Harries v Ashford
[1950] 1 All ER 427, [1950] WN 177, 94 Sol Jo 193, CA
On 9 August 1944, deceased was killed in a motor accident. On 7 August 1945, a writ was issued by the widow and another, described as administratrices, and the widow in her personal capacity, as plaintiffs, the former claiming under the Fatal Accidents and Law Reform Acts, and the widow under the Fatal Accidents Acts. Grant of administration was made

on 9 August 1945. Statement of claim was delivered on 4 November 1946 and claimed under the Fatal Accidents Acts by the administratrices but not by the widow, although the claim by the widow was in the writ. On 16 December 1949, the plaintiffs applied for leave to amend the writ and statement of claim by deleting the administratrices as parties and consequential alterations, and substituting a claim by the widow under the Fatal Accidents Acts for that of the administratrices.

HELD: The administratrices were improperly joined and should be struck out as plaintiffs with consequential amendments, but the substitution of the widow's claim under the Acts in the statement of claim would not be permitted. Citing *Lewis and Lewis v Durnford* (1907) 24 TLR 64, under Ord XX, r 4 (now Ord 18, r 15), a plaintiff was entitled in his statement of claim to alter, modify, or extend his claim without amending his writ. It had been held in *Cargill v Bower* (1878) 10 ChD 502, 47 LJCh 649, 38 LT 779, that where a plaintiff in his statement of claim omits part of his claim, he will be deemed to have abandoned that part. Having regard to these decisions, the proper course was not to allow the amendment. Even if the court has a discretion, the amendment ought to be refused after such a long lapse of time. *Hilton v Sutton Steam Laundry* followed.

Burns v Campbell

[1952] 1 KB 15, [1951] 2 All ER 965, [1951] 2 TLR 1007, 95 Sol Jo 743, CA

Deceased was domiciled in Northern Ireland and died in England on 23 January 1950. On 12 January 1951, his widow took out letters of administration in Northern Ireland. On 19 January 1951, she issued a writ in England claiming as administratrix for damages under the Fatal Accidents Act 1846. On 20 March 1951, the Northern Ireland grant was re-sealed in England under the Supreme Court of Judicature (Consolidation) Act 1925, s 169(1), as amended. Finnemore J set aside the writ.

HELD, ON APPEAL: Section 169(1) was not retrospective. When the writ was issued the plaintiff had not obtained a grant of administration in England and the action was not properly constituted. At the date of re-sealing more than twelve months had expired from the death and the plaintiff had no claim under the 1846 Act. If the plaintiff had issued the writ on 9 January 1951, in her personal capacity as widow, there would have been a good claim under the 1846 Act but she would not have been able to claim under the Law Reform (MP) Act 1934. *Ingall's* case and *Hilton's* case followed.

Note—Since 1 January 1972 a grant of probate or letters of administration issued in England and Wales in the estate of a person dying domiciled there is recognised in Scotland and Northern Ireland without resealing. Corresponding provisions apply in the case of Scottish confirmations and Northern Irish grants issued in the country of domicil. See Administration of Estates Act 1971. A grant will normally be extracted in that part of the United Kingdom in which the deceased was domiciled.

Stebbings v Holst & Co

[1953] 1 All ER 925, [1953] 1 WLR 603, 97 Sol Jo 727, CA (Donovan J)

The deceased died on 15 June 1951. On 24 January 1952, the widow issued a writ and the title of the action was: Between . . . WMS (widow and administratrix of the estate of AS). The indorsement on the writ was: The plaintiff's claim is for damages under the Fatal Accidents Act and the Law Reform (Miscellaneous Provisions) Act 1934, as widow and administratrix of the estate of JAS deceased. The names of the dependants were not given in the indorsement but were set out in the statement of claim. On 2 February 1952, the plaintiff obtained letters of administration.

HELD: There was no claim under the Law Reform Act. The words 'widow' and 'administratrix' describe the plaintiff's status and not capacity. Order II, r 3 (now Ord 6, r 1), and the form of writ in the Appendix do not expressly require that the plaintiff's personal status should be shown after the name. The contention that the indorsement showed that the plaintiff was suing as administratrix only failed. The plaintiff as widow was entitled to sue under the Fatal Accidents Act 1864. The words 'as widow' were not to be disregarded but the words 'and administratrix' were, because she was not administratrix when the writ was issued and were simply an error. The rule does not require the dependants to be stated in the indorsement. It is sufficient that they are in the statement of claim. *Hilton v Sutton Steam Laundry* distinguished.

Finnegan v Cementation Co Ltd

[1953] 1 QB 688, [1953] 1 All ER 1130, [1953] 2 WLR 1015, 97 Sol Jo 332, CA

Defendants were building a bridge in Ireland and deceased, a workman in their employ, was injured on 16 January 1952, and died as a result on 22 January 1952. His widow took out letters of administration in the Republic of Ireland on 6 May 1952, but she was never granted letters of administration in the United Kingdom. On 10 June 1952, she issued a writ in England. The writ was indorsed 'the plaintiff's claim is as administratrix of the estate of PJF deceased for damages under Fatal Accidents Acts on behalf of the dependants of the said PJF against the defendants for the negligence of themselves their servants or agents as a result of which the deceased lost his life and his dependants suffered damage.' The statement of claim was delivered with the writ on 13 June 1952. Paragraph 1 alleged 'the plaintiff is the widow and administratrix of PJF (hereinafter called "the deceased") and she brings this action for the benefit of the dependants of the deceased under the Fatal Accidents Acts 1846 to 1908, and for the benefit of the deceased's estate'.

On 12 February 1953, the defendants issued a summons to set aside the writ and proceedings on the ground that she had no title to sue as administratrix in England. The Master made an order in terms of the summons which was confirmed on appeal by Parker J. The plaintiff appealed to the Court of Appeal and contended (1) the action was brought by the plaintiff both as widow and as administratrix and her action in her personal capacity as widow was good under the Fatal Accidents Acts; (2) the letters of administration in Ireland were sufficient to satisfy s 2 of the 1846 Act.

HELD: The second submission was wrong. A person who is granted letters of administration in Ireland is not a person empowered to administer the estate in England.

The indorsement of the writ claims as administratrix. There is no mention that the plaintiff is the widow. The statement of claim cannot be treated as extending or modifying the claim indorsed on the writ. Reading the indorsement and the statement of claim together, the plaintiff is claiming both as widow and administratrix. The submission that the words 'as administratrix' are surplusage and should be struck out cannot be allowed. There is no difference between this case and *Hilton's* case. *Stebbings'* case is different. Here the plaintiff's claim is made as administratrix.

Note—See note after *Hilton v Sutton Steam Laundry*, p 519, above.

Austin v Hart
[1983] 2 AC 640, [1983] 2 All ER 341, [1983] 2 WLR 866, 127 Sol Jo 325, PC
Simon Austin was killed in a road accident on 4 May 1974. In his will he had appointed as executor his brother William, who did not obtain probate until May 1976. On the 2 August 1974 four dependants of Simon instituted proceedings by writ for damages against the negligent car driver in their own names. The Compensation for Injuries Ordnance of Trinidad and Tobago, s 8 provided that such an action should be brought by and in the name of the executor but if no action be brought by or in the name of the executor within six months then such action could be brought by and in the names of the intended beneficiaries (cf the Fatal Accidents Act 1976, s 2). By an amendment of the defence on 9 July 1975 the defendant pleaded that the court had no jurisdiction to entertain the claim, since it had been commenced by the plaintiffs in their own names before the six months had elapsed. The courts in Trinidad held the action was a nullity because the plaintiffs were not entitled to issue a writ when they did on 2 August 1974. HELD, ON APPEAL to Privy Council: The action was not a nullity. Section 8 of the ordnance did not expressly invalidate an action by a dependant within six months of the death, even assuming that William Austin was, before probate, 'an executor'. By 4 November 1974 it was certain the dependants were entitled to begin proceedings because by then no action had been started by the executor. *Ingall v Moran* (above) was different as that action was under the Law Reform (Miscellaneous Provisions) Act 1934 and the plaintiff was not the administratrix at the date of the writ. *Finnegan v Cementation* (above) was not in point because the plaintiff sued as administratrix though she never was. In the present case the plaintiffs were entitled to sue in the capacities named in the writ unless the executor intervened within six months of the death, and he had not. The plaintiffs were entitled to proceed with the action.

Bowler v John Mowlem & Co
[1954] 3 All ER 556, [1954] 1 WLR 1445, 98 Sol Jo 820, [1954] 2 Lloyd's Rep 387, CA
Accident and death, 12 February 1951; writ issued 19 October 1951; title of plaintiff, Winifred Bowler (administratrix of Thomas Henry Bowler deceased); indorsement, the plaintiff's claim is for damages for negligence and/or breach of statutory duty under the Fatal Accidents Acts 1846–1908, and under the Law Reform (Miscellaneous Provisions) Act 1934.
   The statement of claim was delivered with the writ and stated the plaintiff was the administratrix and lawful relict and brought the action for the

benefit of the estate under the 1934 Act and for the benefit of the dependants under the Fatal Accidents Acts, the persons under the statute being the widow, a son aged fourteen and a daughter aged seven. Letters of administration were not granted until 10 November 1952. Ormerod J held that the widow was suing as administratrix. The writ was bad and the action could not succeed.

On appeal this decision was reserved.

HELD: Romer LJ, *dubitante*, the writ was valid because by Ord 3, r 4 (now Ord 6, r 3), it was the indorsement on the writ which was the crucial matter. That is where the representative capacity must be shown and there was no mention of representative capacity in the indorsement. It is not stated in the indorsement that the plaintiff claims as administratrix. The statement of claim does not affect the matter. That is a description of status and not representative capacity. The writ is not a nullity. The misdescription in the title and in the statement of claim is not fatal. It may be cured by amendment. Cases of *Ingall, Hilton* (p 519, above), *Burns* (p 520, above), and *Finnegan* (above) distinguished.

---

2 LAW REFORM ACT CLAIMS

LAW REFORM (MISCELLANEOUS PROVISIONS) ACT 1934

'**1 Effect of death on certain causes of action**   (1) Subject to the provisions of this section, on the death of any person after the commencement of this Act all causes of action subsisting against or vested in him shall survive against, or, as the case may be, for the benefit of, his estate. Provided that this subsection shall not apply to causes of action for defamation. [*Remainder of subsection repealed by Law Reform (Miscellaneous Provisions) Act 1970.*]

(1A) The right of a person to claim under section 1A of the Fatal Accidents Act 1976 (bereavement) shall not survive for the benefit of his estate on his death [*added by Administration of Justice Act 1982, s 4(1).*]

(2) Where a cause of action survives as aforesaid for the benefit of the estate of a deceased person, the damages recoverable for the benefit of the estate of that person —

(a) shall not include
   (i)   any exemplary damages:
   (ii) any damages for loss of income in respect of any period after that person's death; [*Subsection (2)(a) substituted by Administration of Justice Act 1982, s 4(2).*]

(b) [*Repealed by Law Reform (Miscellaneous Provisions) Act 1970*];

(c) where the death of that person has been caused by the act or omission which gives rise to the cause of action, shall be calculated without reference to any loss or gain to his estate consequent on his death, except that a sum in respect of funeral expenses may be included.

[*Subsection (3), which required proceedings in tort against a deceased person's estate to be started within six months of the grant of representation, was repealed by the Proceedings Against Estates Act 1970.*]

(4) Where damage has been suffered by reason of any act or omission in respect of which a cause of action would have subsisted against any person if that person had

not died before or at the same time as the damage was suffered, there shall be deemed, for the purposes of this Act, to have been subsisting against him before his death such cause of action in respect of that act or omission as would have subsisted if he had died after the damage was suffered.

(5) The rights conferred by this Act for the benefit of the estates of deceased persons shall be in addition to and not in derogation of any rights conferred on the dependants of deceased persons by the Fatal Accidents Acts 1846 to 1908, or the Carriage by Air Act 1932, and so much of this Act as relates to causes of action against the estates of deceased persons shall apply in relation to causes of action under the said Acts as it applies in relation to other causes of action not expressly excepted from the operation of sub-s (1) of this section.

(6) In the event of the insolvency of an estate against which proceedings are maintainable by virtue of this section, any liability in respect of cause of action in respect of which the proceedings are maintainable shall be deemed to be a debt provable in the administration of the estate, notwithstanding that it is in a demand in the nature of unliquidated damages arising otherwise than by a contract, promise or breach of trust.'

[References to Fatal Accidents Acts 1846 to 1908 include a reference to Fatal Accidents Act 1976 — See Sch 1, para 2.] The new s 1(2)(a)(ii) takes effect from 1 January 1983 in respect of causes of action accruing on or after that date.

It will be seen that, taken with the Administration of Justice Act 1982, s 1(1)(a) (p 443, above) these changes abolish the right of an estate, first established in *Rose v Ford* (below) to recover damages for loss of expectation of life where personal injury has resulted in death. Subsection (2)(a)(ii) also renders obsolete cases such as *Kandalla v British Airways* and *Gammell v Wilson* (below) where damages were awarded for loss of earnings during the years lost by the death.

They do not, of course, affect the right of the estate to recover damages for the injury, pain and suffering inflicted on the deceased and suffered by him between the moment of injury and death; eg the award of £2,000 in *Andrews v Freeborough* (p 474, above) or the awards of £20 and £2 in *Rose v Ford* itself.

In *Gammell v Wilson* [1982] AC 27, [1981] 1 All ER 578, [1981] 2 WLR 248, 125 Sol Jo 116, HL it was held, in the House of Lords, that s 1(2)(c) was not intended to deprive the estate of the right to recover damages in respect of losses when the right to recover damages was already vested in the deceased immediately before his death.

Husband and wife

Note—By the Law Reform (Husband and Wife) Act 1962, s 1, an action is maintainable against a spouse by the personal representatives of a deceased spouse for Law Reform damages or by a third party for a contribution.

See *Re Newsham*, p 527, below.

As a surviving spouse is often the executor or administrator of the deceased spouse it should be remembered that a person cannot be plaintiff and defendant in the same action. The Supreme Court Practice cites *Ellis v Kerr* [1910] 1 Ch 529, 79 LJCh 291, 102 LT 417, 54 Sol Jo 307, and *Re Phillips* [1931] WN 271, 101 LJCh 338, 76 Sol Jo 10. In a case in chambers the driver was killed in an accident, in which the driver's father was injured. The father took out letters of administration to the estate of his deceased son and issued a writ with himself personally as plaintiff and himself as administrator as defendant. The insurers moved to set aside the writ and the Master struck out the action. Plaintiff appealed to the Judge in chambers, who upheld the Master and the plaintiff withdrew the action.

Costs — liability of personal representatives

Note—The contention has been put forward in practice that a legal personal representative who brings an unsuccessful action for Law Reform damages is not personally liable for costs but only the estate.

The position is given in *Halsbury's Laws of England* (4th edn) vol 17, para 1562 as follows:

'In ordinary cases an executor or administrator who sues as such and fails, is personally liable for the costs of the action, and unless the defendant has been guilty of some misconduct inducing the plaintiff to bring the action, the judgment against him will be that the defendant recover the costs to be levied *de bonis propriis* (from his own goods). But this will not preclude the personal representative from indemnifying himself out of the estate if he is entitled to such indemnity under the principles previously stated.'

Similarly when the representatives of a deceased plaintiff obtain an order to carry on the proceedings, they become personally liable for all the costs *ab initio* (vol 17, para 1572).

Volume 24 of the *English and Empire Digest* at p 1050, sets out the cases under the heading of 'Personal liability of representative'.

This is subject to the principle that costs are always in the discretion of the court.

PERSONS ENTITLED TO ESTATE ON INTESTACY

Note—The distribution is provided for by the Administration of Estates Act 1925, s 46, as amended by the Intestates' Estates Act 1952 and the Family Provision Act 1966, s 1. See *Halsbury's Laws of England* (4th edn) vol 17, para 1404 for complete table.

One or more of the same persons is normally entitled to the Grant of Letters of Administration and in the same order.

Intestate leaving	Distribution
1 Wife or husband no issue	Husband or wife takes — If there is surviving a parent, or brother or sister of the whole blood or issue of such brother or sister — (a) personal chattels absolutely; (b) £85,000 free of duty and costs, with interest at such rate as the Lord Chancellor may specify by order under payment or appropriation; (c) half residue absolutely.
2 Wife or husband and issue	Husband or wife takes — (a) personal chattles absolutely; (b) £40,000 on terms of £85,000 above; (c) life interest in half residue; (d) issue take residue on statutory trusts subject to life interests of spouse in one half.
3 Issue only	Issue* take equally.
4 No issue	In order, subject to (1) above — (a) father and mother equally; (b) sole parent; (c) brothers and sisters of whole blood*; (d) brothers and sisters of half blood*; (e) grandparents equally; (f) uncles and aunts of whole blood*; (g) uncles and aunts of half blood*; (h) husband or wife.
5 If no such persons	Crown or Duchy.

*Provided they attain 21 or marry *per stirpes*.

Illegitimate children

The property rights of illegitimate children and their parents are contained in the Family Law Reform Act 1969 of which s 14 sub-ss (1), (2) and (4) are as follows:

'**14 Right of illegitimate child to succeed on intestacy of parents, and of parents to succeed on intestacy of illegitimate child**   (1) Where either parent of an illegitimate child dies intestate as respects all or any of his or her real or personal property, the illegitimate child or, if he is dead, his issue, shall be entitled to take any interest therein to which he or such issue would have been entitled if he had been born legitimate.

(2) Where an illegitimate child dies intestate in respect of all or any of his real or personal property, each of his parents, if surviving, shall be entitled to take any interest therein to which that parent would have been entitled if the child had been born legitimate.

(3) In accordance with the foregoing provisions of this section, Part IV of the Administration of Estates Act 1925 (which deals with the distribution of the estate of an intestate) shall have effect as if —

(a) any reference to the issue of the intestate included a reference to any illegitimate child of his and to the issue of any such child;

(b) any reference to the child or children of the intestate included a reference to any illegitimate child or children of his; and

(c) in relation to an intestate who is an illegitimate child, any reference to the parent, parents, father or mother of the intestate were a reference to his natural parent, parents, father or mother.

(4) For the purposes of sub-s (2) of this section and of the provisions amended by sub-s (3)(c) thereof, an illegitimate child shall be presumed not to have been survived by his father unless the contrary is shown.'

Protection is given to personal representatives who have the task of distributing the estate by s 17 of the 1969 Act:

'**17 Protection of trustees and personal representatives**   Notwithstanding the foregoing provisions of this Part of this Act, trustees or personal representatives may convey or distribute any real or personal property to or among the persons entitled thereto without having ascertained that there is no person who is or may be entitled to any interest therein by virtue of —

(a) s 14 of this Act so far as it confers any interest on illegitimate children or their issue or on the father of an illegitimate child; or

(b) s 15 or 16 of this Act,

and shall not be liable to any such person of whose claim they have not had notice at the time of the conveyance or distribution; but nothing in this section shall prejudice the right of any such person to follow the property, or any property representing it, into the hands of any person, other than a purchaser, who may have received it.'

Adopted children

Note—The status and property rights conferred by adoption are contained in the Adoption Act 1976, s 39. See p 490, above.

Where person entitled may be prejudiced

Re Newshams Estate
[1967] P 230, [1966] 3 All ER 681, [1966] 3 WLR 1207, 110 Sol Jo 621
(Karminski J)
The deceased was killed in a road accident on 25 December 1965 and his wife, who was a passenger in the car he was driving, was injured. She had a claim for damages for her injuries against her husband's estate which was entitled to an indemnity against the claim under a policy of insurance. If the widow became administratrix of the estate her claim might be void against the insurers under the terms of the policy. By virtue of the Supreme Court of Judicature (Consolidation) Act 1925, s 162 as amended by the Administration of Justice Act 1928, the Court had a discretion, where by reason of special circumstances it appeared necessary or expedient, to appoint as administrator some person other than the person by law entitled to the grant. Whilst the Court is slow to pass over the person entitled to the grant, in this case the person so entitled would be prejudiced by such grant and was consenting to being passed over. In these circumstances her stepfather, who was willing to act as administrator, would be so appointed.

Note—For the powers given to the Court by s 162 of the 1925 Act (repealed) see the Supreme Court Act 1981, s 116.

Practice and procedure

CHAPTER 14
Limitations

THE LIMITATION ACTS

Brief historical note—A general rule for limitation of actions in tort and simple contract requiring such actions to be commenced within six years from the cause of action arising was established by the Statute of Limitation of 1623, which remained in force (with some accretion of exceptions and amendments) until supplanted by the Limitation Act 1939. The six-year period was maintained by s 2 of that Act. A proviso was added to that section by the Law Reform (Limitation of Actions) Act 1954 reducing the limitation period to three years in actions of negligence, nuisance and breach of duty for damages in respect of personal injuries. That Act also helpfully abolished or amended to three years a variety of special periods of limitation contained in particular statutes. The Limitation Act 1963 gave the court power to disapply the limitation period of three years so as to enable a plaintiff to pursue an action for damages for personal injury when material facts 'of a decisive character' were proved to have been outside his knowledge, in effect, when the cause of action arose. The Act also by s 4, prescribed a time limit of two years for contribution proceedings. The Limitation Act 1975 simplified the elaborate provisions of the 1963 Act for disapplying or extending the three-year period and, by ss 2A, 2B and 2C added to the 1939 Act, made rules for determining the date from which time began to run in personal injury and fatal accident cases. A further section inserted as 2D in the 1939 Act provided a new and more liberal rule by which to disapply the three-year period in certain cases. The Limitation Act 1980 (into force 1 May 1981) repeals and re-enacts with some amendments and additions, the surviving provisions of the earlier acts so far as they related to the subject matter of this book. The following is a brief destination table:

Limitation Act 1963	Limitation Act 1980
S 4	S 10 (see p 550, below)
Limitation Act 1975	
S 2	S 2 (tort), S 5 (contract)
S 2A	S 11, 14
S 2B	S 12, 14
S 2C	S 13
S 2D	S 33

The relevant sections of the Acts are set out below.

The following points, sometimes overlooked, should be noted:

1 In the case of plaintiffs under age, time does not *begin* to run until the eighteenth birthday (see s 28 p 536, below).

2 A defendant wishing to rely on a statute of limitation must plead it (RSC Ord 18, r 8(1)).

3 'Damage only' claims have a six-year limitation period (s 2).

4 The validity of a writ not yet served will not normally be extended if to do so would deprive the defendant of the benefit of a limitation period (see pp 564 to 569, below).

5 The day on which the cause of action arose is excluded from the computation of the limitation period (see, p 535, below).

Ronex Properties Ltd v John Laing Construction Ltd

[1983] QB 398, [1982] 3 All ER 961, [1982] 3 WLR 875, 126 Sol Jo 727, CA

A writ or third party notice cannot be struck out as disclosing no cause of action merely because the defendant has a defence under the Limitation Acts. 'Where it is thought to be clear that there is a defence under the Limitation Act, the defendant can either plead that defence and seek the trial of a preliminary issue, or, in a very clear case, seek to strike out the claim on the ground that it is frivolous, vexatious and an abuse of the process of the court. But in no circumstances can he seek to strike out on the ground that no cause of action is disclosed' (per Stephenson LJ).

LIMITATION ACT 1980

2 Time limit for actions founded on tort　An action founded on tort shall not be brought after the expiration of six years from the date on which the cause of action accrued.

5 Time limit for actions founded on simple contract　An action founded on simple contract shall not be brought after the expiration of six years from the date on which the cause of action accrued.

Actions in respect of wrongs causing personal injuries or death

11 Special time limit for actions in respect of personal injuries　(1) This section applies to any action for damages for negligence, nuisance or breach of duty (whether the duty exists by virtue of a contract or of provision made by or under a statute or independently of any contract or any such provision) where the damages claimed by the plaintiff for the negligence, nuisance or breach of duty consist of or include damages in respect of personal injuries to the plaintiff or any other person.

(2) None of the time limits given in the preceding provisions of this Act shall apply to an action to which this section applies.

(3) An action to which this section applies shall not be brought after the expiration of the period applicable in accordance with subsection (4) or (5) below.

(4) Except where sub-s (5) below applies, the period applicable is three years from —

(a) the date on which the cause of action accrued; or

(b) the date of knowledge (if later) of the person injured.

(5) If the person injured dies before the expiration of the period mentioned in sub-s (4) above, the period applicable as respects the cause of action surviving for

the benefit of his estate by virtue of s 1 of the Law Reform (Miscellaneous Provisions) Act 1934 shall be three years from —
(a) the date of death; or
(b) the date of the personal representative's knowledge; whichever is the later.
(6) For the purposes of this section 'personal representative' includes any person who is or has been a personal representative of the deceased, including an executor who has not proved the will (whether or not he has renounced probate) but not anyone appointed only as a special personal representative in relation to settled land; and regard shall be had to any knowledge acquired by any such person while a personal representative or previously.
(7) If there is more than one personal representative, and their dates of knowledge are different, sub-s (5)(b) above shall be read as referring to the earliest of those dates.

12 Special time limit for actions under Fatal Accidents legislation (1) An action under the Fatal Accidents Act 1976 shall not be brought if the death occurred when the person injured could no longer maintain an action and recover damages in respect of the injury (whether because of a time limit in this Act or in any other Act, or for any other reason).
  Where any such action by the injured person would have been barred by the time limit in s 11 of this Act, no account shall be taken of the possibility of that time limit being overridden under s 33 of this Act.
(2) None of the time limits given in the preceding provisions of this Act shall apply to an action under the Fatal Accidents Act 1976, but no such action shall be brought after the expiration of three years from —
(a) the date of death; or
(b) the date of knowledge of the person for whose benefit the action is brought; whichever is the later.
(3) An action under the Fatal Accidents Act 1976 shall be one to which ss 28, 33 and 35 of this Act apply, and the application to any such action of the time limit under sub-s (2) above shall be subject to s 39; but otherwise Parts II and III of this Act shall not apply to any such action.

13 Operation of time limit under s 12 in relation to different dependants (1) Where there is more than one person for whose benefit an action under the Fatal Accidents Act 1976 is brought, s 12(2)(b) of this Act shall be applied separately to each of them.
(2) Subject to sub-s (3) below, if by virtue of sub-s (1) above the action would be outside the time limit given by sub-s 12(2) as regards one or more, but not all, of the persons for whose benefit it is brought, the court shall direct that any person as regards whom the action would be outside that limit shall be excluded from those for whom the action is brought.
(3) The court shall not give such a direction if it is shown that if the action were brought exclusively for the benefit of the person in question it would not be defeated by a defence of limitation (whether in consequence of s 28 of this Act or an agreement between the parties not to raise the defence, or otherwise).

14 Definition of date of knowledge for purposes of ss 11 and 12 (1) In ss 11 and 12 of this Act references to a person's date of knowledge are references to the date on which he first had knowledge of the following facts —
(a) that the injury in question was significant; and
(b) that the injury was attributable in whole or in part to the act or omission which is alleged to constitute negligence, nuisance or breach of duty; and
(c) the identity of the defendant; and
(d) if it is alleged that the act or omission was that of a person other than the defendant, the identity of that person and the additional facts supporting the bringing of an action against the defendant;

and knowledge that any acts or omissions did or did not, as a matter of law, involve negligence, nuisance or breach of duty is irrelevant.

(2) For the purposes of this section an injury is significant if the person whose date of knowledge is in question would reasonably have considered it sufficiently serious to justify his instituting proceedings for damages against a defendant who did not dispute liability and was able to satisfy a judgment.

(3) For the purposes of this section a person's knowledge includes knowledge which he might reasonably have been expected to acquire —

(a) from facts observable or ascertainable by him; or

(b) from facts ascertainable by him with the help of medical or other appropriate expert advice which it is reasonable for him to seek;

but a person shall not be fixed under this subsection with knowledge of a fact ascertainable only with the help of expert advice so long as he has taken all reasonable steps to obtain (and, where appropriate, to act on) that advice.

38 Interpretation   'Personal injuries' includes any disease and any impairment of a person's physical or mental condition, and 'injury' and cognate expressions shall be construed accordingly;

'Damages in respect of personal injuries'

Ackbar v C. F. Green & Co

[1975] QB 582, [1975] 2 All ER 65, [1975] 2 WLR 773, 119 Sol Jo 219, [1975] 1 Lloyd's Rep 673 (Croom-Johnson J)

The plaintiff instructed the defendants who were insurance brokers to obtain a policy covering the use of his motor lorry including passenger risks. The defendants omitted to ensure that the policy covered claims by passengers. The plaintiff was injured when riding as a passenger in his own lorry but was unable to recover damages from the driver because the policy did not cover him against passenger claims. More than three years but less than six years after the accident the plaintiff issued a writ against the defendants for failing to obtain passenger liability cover. They pleaded that the action was statute-barred as being one where the damages claimed 'consist of or include damages in respect of personal injuries to any person' (Limitation Act 1980, s 11(1)).

HELD: The action was not statute-barred. The question to ask was 'What is the action all about?' The answer was that it was about an alleged breach of contract by the defendants whereby the plaintiff lost the right to recover his loss either from the driver or from his own insurers. The damages for personal injuries which he might have recovered were only the measure of the damages now claimed. The limitation period was thus six years not three.

When time begins to run

For causes of action to which the Limitation Act 1980, s 2 applies time runs from the date of the accrual of the cause of action, namely, the date when physical damage occurred whether or not the damage could have been discovered with reasonable diligence at that date by the plaintiff (*Pirelli General Cable Works Ltd v Oscar Faber & Partners* below). In cases of personal injury ss 11 and 14 provide alternatives for the date when time begins to run and a distinction is drawn between the date of accrual of the cause of action and the date when time begins to run.

Pirelli General Cable Works Ltd v Oscar Faber
[1983] 2 AC 1, [1983] 1 All ER 65, [1983] 2 WLR 6, 127 Sol Jo 16, 265 Estates Gazette 979, CA
The defendants were consulting engineers who advised the plaintiffs on the construction of a chimney. It was built in July 1969. The material used was unsuitable and cracks occurred not later than April 1970. The damage was not discovered by the plaintiffs until 1977 and they could not with reasonable diligence have discovered it before October 1972. The writ was issued in October 1978.
HELD, ON APPEAL to the House of Lords: The action was statute-barred. In cases of latent defects to buildings the cause of action will not accrue until damage occurs, which will commonly consist of cracks coming into existence as a result of defect even though the cracks or the defect may be undiscovered and undiscoverable. The principle of the decision, in *Cartledge v E Jopling & Sons Ltd* [1963] AC 758, [1963] 1 All ER 341, [1963] 2 WLR 210, 107 Sol Jo 73, [1963] 1 Lloyd's Rep 1, HL was applicable. It was not correct (as had been held in *Sparham-Souter v Town and Country Planning Developments (Essex) Ltd* [1976] QB 858, [1976] 2 All ER 65, [1976] 2 WLR 493, 120 Sol Jo 216, 74 LGR 355, CA) that a plaintiff suffers damage only when he discovers, or ought with reasonable diligence to have discovered, damage to the buildings.

See also *Kensington & Chelsea v Wettern Composites* [1985] 1 All ER 346.

Dove v Banhams Patent Locks
[1983] 2 All ER 833, [1983] 1 WLR 1436, 127 Sol Jo 748, (Hodgson J)
In 1967 the defendants, who were specialists in burglary prevention, fixed a security gate to the basement door of a house which in 1976 was purchased by the plaintiff. In 1979 the door was forced by a burglar who effected entry and stole valuable goods. The judge held the defendants to have been negligent in the way in which the gate had been fitted and that they owed the same duty of care to the plaintiff as they had to the owner of the house in 1967 who had employed the defendants to do the work. The defendants pleaded that the plaintiff's claim was statute-barred.
HELD: The claim was not statute-barred. The cause of action did not accrue until physical damage occurred, namely when the gate was forced. It did not accrue at the time when the defective work was done. *Pirelli General Cable Works Ltd v Oscar Faber & Partners* (above) followed.

Marren v Dawson Bentley & Co Ltd
[1961] 2 QB 135, [1961] 2 All ER 270, [1961] 2 WLR 679, 105 Sol Jo 383 (Havers J)
The plaintiff claimed damages for personal injuries received in an accident. The accident occurred at 1.30 pm on 8 November 1954. The writ was issued on 8 November 1957. The defendants contended that as the plaintiff could have issued a writ on 8 November 1954, the last day on which he would be entitled to do so would be 7 November 1957, and that the action was out of time.
HELD: The day on which the cause of action arose was excluded from the computation of the three years and therefore the plaintiff's action was not statute barred.

ADDED DEFENDANT

Gawthrop v Boulton

[1978] 3 All ER 615, [1979] 1 WLR 268, 122 Sol Jo 297 (Walton J)

The plaintiff in an action started against B in 1975 applied in 1977 to join as a defendant K, who had been B's partner until 1971. K opposed the application on the ground that if in an action begun within the limitation period he was added as a defendant when the six years had already expired he would lose the protection of the Limitation Act.

HELD: Not so. There is nothing to be said for the view that time ceases to run as from date of issue of the writ. Time was still running in K's favour up to the day when the amendment was made. It is different where it is a plaintiff that is proposed to be added or changed.

Note—See also *Liff v Peasley* (p 543, below) and note.

Persons under a disability — s 28

Note—The Limitation Act 1939, s 22 is repealed and replaced by the Limitation Act 1980, s 28 which is as follows:

'**28 Extension of limitation period in case of disability**   (1) Subject to the following provisions of this section, if on the date when any right of action accrued for which a period of limitation is prescribed by this Act, the person to whom it accrued was under a disability, the action may be brought at any time before the expiration of six years from the date when he ceased to be under a disability or died (whichever first occurred) notwithstanding that the period of limitation has expired.

(2) This section shall not affect any case where the right of action first accrued to some person (not under a disability) through whom the person under a disability claims.

(3) When a right of action which has accrued to a person under a disability accrues, on the death of that person while still under a disability, to another person under a disability, no further extension of time shall be allowed by reason of the disability of the second person.

(4) [Recovery of Land].

(5) If the action is one to which s 10 of this Act applies, sub-s (1) above shall have effect as if for the words ''six years'' there were substituted the words ''two years''.

(6) If the action is one to which s 11 or 12(2) of this Act applies, sub-s (1) above shall have effect as if for the words ''six years'' there were substituted the words ''three years''.'

'**38 Interpretation**   (2) For the purposes of this Act a person shall be treated as under a disability while he is an infant, or of unsound mind.

(3) For the purposes of sub-s (2) above a person is of unsound mind if he is a person who, by reason of mental disorder within the meaning of the Mental Health Act 1959, is incapable of managing and administering his property and affairs.'

Kirby v Leather

[1965] 2 QB 367, [1965] 2 All ER 441, [1965] 2 WLR 1318, 109 Sol Jo 357, CA

On 15 May 1959 the plaintiff received serious head injuries in a road accident. He was aged 24, the eldest of seven children, and contributed largely to the support of his widowed mother and his brothers and sisters. He was unconscious in hospital for three weeks after the accident and was not discharged until August 1959 when he returned home. His mind was gravely affected, his behaviour being extremely abnormal: he was incapable of working or of looking after himself. He could not concentrate long enough to appreciate the nature and extent of any claim he might have. His mother made some inquiries about the accident and was told by the police that no one was to blame; her son's employer told her not to start anything; the plaintiff himself told her not to bother. His condition gradually improved on treatment but he remained seriously affected and virtually unemployable. In August 1963 he went to see a solicitor's managing clerk and asked him to help find his motor scooter, damaged in the accident. His strange manner led the clerk to make inquiries into the accident and a writ was issued in October 1963 claiming damages for the plaintiff's personal injuries. The defendant, the driver of the van with whom the plaintiff had collided, contested the proceedings both as to negligence and on the ground that the claim was statute-barred. The judge of assize held the defendant not liable on the issue of negligence but said that if he were the action was not statute-barred since the plaintiff was of unsound mind, applying the test in Ord 80, r 1 — 'a person who by reason of mental disorder is incapable of managing and administering his property and affairs' — and was protected by the Limitation Act 1939, s 22. The Court of Appeal reversed his decision on negligence holding the defendant two-thirds to blame. On the question of limitations:

HELD: The plaintiff became of unsound mind by reason of the accident on 15 May 1959 and was thus so 'on the date when [the] right of action accrued' as required by s 22 of the 1939 Act. The words 'unsound mind' must be construed in relation to the subject matter with which the statute is dealing, which in this case meant incapable of managing his affairs in relation to the accident as a reasonable man would do. He remained so throughout: the action ought to have been started by a next friend but this had been put right at the trial. Accordingly the action was not statute-barred.

Per Danckwerts LJ: On the meaning of unsoundness of mind the words in Ord 80, r 1 'is incapable of managing or administering his property and affairs' are a reasonable statement of the relevant situation.

Per Winn LJ: When the plaintiff suffered the injuries to his head he became and thereafter at all material times remained of unsound mind. Had he merely been unconscious, but there had been lacking evidence that throughout the period of unconsciousness his mental powers had been so affected as to make him in the relevant sense of unsound mind, I would not have thought that there would have been any suspension of the running of the limitation period.

Penrose v Mansfield
(1970) Times, 8 October (Waller J); affd (1971) 115 Sol Jo 309, Times, 19 March, CA
The plaintiff was badly injured by negligence of the defendant on 10 November 1965. The writ was issued on 12 December 1968. He claimed that the action was not out of time because due to his injuries, he was not in a fit state to manage his own affairs until after 12 December 1965 and that

he was entitled to the protection of s 22 as amended.

HELD: Following *Kirby v Leather* (above) the problem for consideration was whether it had been shown on the probabilities that the plaintiff was for some five weeks or more of unsound mind, that is, 'by reason of mental illness incapable of managing his affairs in relation to the accident as a reasonable man would do'. On the evidence, especially the fact that he had himself on 10 December 1965 signed a consent for operative treatment, he had failed to show that his mental state until after 12 December was such as to bring himself within the terms of s 22. The action was statute-barred.

'Fraud' — Limitation Act 1980, s 32

'**32 Postponement of limitation period in case of fraud, concealment or mistake** (1) . . . where in the case of any action for which a period of limitation is prescribed by this Act, either —
(a) the action is based upon the fraud of the defendant; or
(b) any fact relevant to the plaintiff's right of action has been deliberately concealed from him by the defendant;. . . .
the period of limitation shall not begin to run until the plaintiff has discovered the fraud [or] concealment . . . or could with reasonable diligence have discovered it.'

Kitchen v RAF Association
[1958] 2 All ER 241, [1958] 1 WLR 563, 102 Sol Jo 363, CA
A man serving in the Royal Air Force was on leave and on 22 May 1945, was electrocuted when using some electrical equipment in the kitchen of his home. His widow believed the cause was negligence of the electricity company in the wiring of the installation. A voluntary organisation forwarded particulars of her case to the RAF Association and the RAF Association to a firm of solicitors who had offered to help members of the RAF and their dependants, in November 1945. The solicitors allowed the 12 months' limitation under the Fatal Accidents Act (the limit then in operation) to expire without commencing proceedings. On 3 June 1946, the solicitors endeavoured to persuade the electricity company to make an *ex gratia* payment, without success. The widow then herself wrote to the company, and as a result a sum of £100 was paid to the RAF Association through the solicitors as a donation from an unknown source on condition that the widow must not know the source. The company did not accept the suggestion of the solicitors that a payment would be taken as a full settlement of all claims. The solicitors had failed to draw any distinction between the claim under the Fatal Accidents Act and the Law Reform Act.

In 1950 the widow obtained legal aid and an action was commenced against the company by another firm of solicitors under the Law Reform Act and settled for £250.

On 30 September 1955, a third firm of solicitors commenced proceedings against the RAF Association and the original solicitors for damages for negligence. The action failed against the Association, and the solicitors denied the negligence alleged and pleaded that the action was statute barred under the Limitation Act 1939, s 2. By her reply the widow pleaded s 26 of the Act.

HELD: The word 'fraud' is not limited to common law fraud or deceit. No degree of moral turpitude is necessary to establish fraud within the section.

Beaman v ARTS Ltd p 906, below. The relationship of solicitor and client existed and negligence was established. The failure of the solicitors to notify the widow of what the company was proposing, which had the effect of throwing away any case she might have had under the Fatal Accidents Acts, is just enough to say that there was concealment by fraud and so to deprive them of the right to set up the Limitation Act 1939. The widow had acted with reasonable diligence. Judgment for the plaintiff.

Applying s 33 (replacing the Limitation Act 1939, s 2D)

'33 Discretionary exclusion of time limit for actions in respect of personal injuries or death (1) If it appears to the court that it would be equitable to allow an action to proceed having regard to the degree to which —
(a) the provisions of s 11 or 12 of this Act prejudice the plaintiff or any person whom he represents; and
(b) any decision of the court under this subsection would prejudice the defendant or any person whom he represents:
the court may direct that those provisions shall not apply to the action, or shall not apply to any specified cause of action to which the action relates.
(2) The court shall not under this section disapply s 12(1) except where the reason why the person injured could no longer maintain an action was because of the time limit in s 11.
If, for example, the person injured could at his death no longer maintain an action under the Fatal Accidents Act 1976 because of the time limit in Art 29 in Sch 1 to the Carriage by Air Act 1961, the court has no power to direct that s 12(1) shall not apply.
(3) In acting under this section the court shall have regard to all the circumstances of the case and in particular to —
(a) the length of, and the reasons for, the delay on the part of the plaintiff;
(b) the extent to which, having regard to the delay, the evidence adduced or likely to be adduced by the plaintiff or the defendant is or is likely to be less cogent than if the action had been brought within the time allowed by s 11 or (as the case may be) by s 12;
(c) the conduct of the defendant after the cause of action arose, including the extent (if any) to which he responded to requests reasonably made by the plaintiff for information or inspection for the purpose of ascertaining facts which were or might be relevant to the plaintiff's cause of action against the defendant;
(d) the duration of any disability of the plaintiff arising after the date of the accrual of the cause of action;
(e) the extent to which the plaintiff acted promptly and reasonably once he knew whether or not the act or omission of the defendant, to which the injury was attributable, might be capable at that time of giving rise to an action for damages;
(f) the steps, if any, taken by the plaintiff to obtain medical, legal or other expert advice and the nature of any such advice he may have received.
(4) In a case where the person injured died when, because of s 11, he could no longer maintain an action and recover damages in respect of the injury, the court shall have regard in particular to the length of, and the reasons for, the delay on the part of the deceased.
(5) In a case under sub-s (4) above, or any other case where the time limit, or one of the time limits, depends on the date of knowledge of a person other than the plaintiff, sub-s (3) above shall have effect with appropriate modifications, and shall have effect in particular as if references to the plaintiff included references to any person whose date of knowledge is or was relevant in determining a time limit.

(6) A direction by the court disapplying the provisions of s 12(1) shall operate to disapply the provisions to the same effect in s 1(1) of the Fatal Accidents Act 1976.
(7) In this section ''the court'' means the court in which the action has been brought.
(8) References in this section to s 11 include references to that section as extended by any of the preceding provisions of this Part of this Act or by any other provisions of Part III of this Act.'

McCafferty v Metropolitan Police District Receiver
[1977] 2 All ER 756, [1977] 1 WLR 1073, 121 Sol Jo 678, CA
By writ issued in 1974 the plaintiff claimed damages for deafness alleged to be due to his employer's negligence. He had discovered a degree of deafness as a result of an audiogram taken in 1968 but had not then made a claim. He had regarded his deafness at that time merely as 'an irritating nuisance' and had carried on at his work, not thinking of making a claim.
HELD: The discretion of the court could properly be exercised under the Limitation Act 1939, s 2D and his action was not time-barred. The plaintiff had known by 1968 what had happened to his hearing and it was not a case to be dealt with under s 2A. It could be inferred that the plaintiff had carried on in 1968 without making a claim because he did not consider the 'irritating nuisance' to be worth the risk of losing his job by litigating with his employers. That was commendable and could be taken into consideration by the court in considering s 2D.

Cornish v Kearley & Tonge Ltd
(1983) 133 NLJ 870 (Hirst J)
The plaintiff sustained injury at work in July 1975. He felt pains from time to time but did not issue a writ until December 1981.
HELD: The date of knowledge for the purposes of the Limitation Act 1980, s 11 was 1 January 1976 but the court would allow the action to proceed under s 33 because (1) although the delay was a long one the reasons were reasonable; (2) there had not been much reduction in the cogency of the evidence; (3) the plaintiff and his advisers had acted promptly and reasonably; and (4) it was not unreasonable of him not to have taken legal advice until June 1981. *McCafferty v Metropolitan Police District Receiver* (above) followed.

Buck v English Electric Co Ltd
[1978] 1 All ER 271, [1977] 1 WLR 806, 121 Sol Jo 13 (Kilner Brown J)
The plaintiff's husband was first certified as suffering from pneumoconiosis in 1959. In succeeding years his degree of disability was assessed at 100% and he gave up work. He claimed damages and issued a writ in February 1975. In April 1975 he died. The defendants pleaded that his claim was statute-barred.
HELD: On the evidence that by 1963 he knew he suffered from pneumoconiosis and knew of other men who were making claims, the Limitation Act 1939, s 2A gave him no help because of sub-s (6)(a) and sub-s (7). But s 2A could be disapplied by s 2D. The plaintiff had given as his reason for not claiming between 1963 and 1972 that as he was working and receiving a disability pension he thought it would be sponging to make a claim. Although the delay in bringing the claim was inordinate the

section gives a judge the same sort of discretion as the Court of Appeal has exercised in dealing with cases of dismissal for want of prosecution. On the facts the delay was not so extreme as to be conclusive and the claimant had acted reasonably. So far as concerned prejudice to the defendants they had dealt with similar claims since 1963 and must be assumed to have preserved the necessary evidence. It was equitable to allow the action to proceed.

Wood v SKF (UK) Ltd
(7 April 1982, unreported) (Cantley J) (Taken from transcript supplied)
The plaintiff when working as a machine operator in the defendants' employment sustained a burn to his right eyelid from a piece of hot swarf on an occasion in 1936. The injury was treated in the first-aid room; the plaintiff did not cease work and made no kind of claim. For some years the scar at the site of the burn was only a slight nuisance due to occasional throbbing, but became more troublesome in the 1950s. From 1955 to 1957 he received medical treatment including x-ray therapy to a cell carcinoma on the eyelid resulting from the burn. The x-ray treatment cured the carcinoma but caused a hardening of the inner surface of the eyelid and changes in the eye itself, giving rise to ulceration. The plaintiff continued at work throughout but in June 1978 to prevent further trouble the eyelids of his right eye were sewn together permanently, causing him the permanent loss of use of the eye. He consulted solicitors through his trade union and a writ was issued on 12 November 1980 claiming damages. The defendants pleaded that the action was statute-barred.
HELD: (1) The plaintiff could not reasonably have considered the injury sufficiently serious to justify instituting proceedings for damages during the six years from the injury to the end of the then limitation period, but the situation was different by 1957: by that date he had knowledge that his injury was significant as defined in s 2A of the Limitation Act 1939 as amended by the 1975 Act. The claim was barred by s 2A unless it would be equitable to direct under s 2D that 2A should not apply. (2) The delay which fell to be considered was the period after 1957, though until the 1975 Act any action brought would have been defeated by a plea of limitation. Advice if taken before that date would have been that the action was statute barred. When the plaintiff did take advice in 1978 he acted promptly and reasonably on it. As to the defendants, they pleaded prejudice from the long delay by depriving them of evidence of the system of work in 1936 but they had not challenged some of the evidence or countered the evidence of the plaintiff and his three witnesses who were working in the factory in 1936. Taking all the circumstances into consideration as required by s 2D, s 2A should not apply to this action.

Note—The action proceeded and the plaintiff was awarded damages. The gap of 44 years from cause of action to institution of proceedings in an ultimately successful accident claim would seem to be much the longest on record.

SECTION 33 NOT APPLIED

Davies v British Insulated Callender's Cables Ltd
(1977) 121 Sol Jo 203 (Thesiger J)
In November 1970 the plaintiff sustained a back injury when at work. No report of the accident was made nor any statements taken. Though he

obtained Social Security benefit he made no claim for damages until 1975.
A writ was issued in 1976.

HELD: (1) As in *Buck's* case it was right to decide as a preliminary issue
whether the Limitation Act 1939, s 2A should be disapplied under s 2D.
(2) The court's discretion to allow the action to proceed should not be
exercised, since 'the evidence adduced or likely to be adduced [would be]
less cogent than if the action had been brought within the time allowed by
s 2A.' It would be extremely difficult for anyone to remember what had
happened at the time of the accident.

Davis v Soltenpur

(1983) 133 NLJ 720 (Hobhouse J)

On 10 October 1977 the plaintiff was struck and injured by a car driven by
the defendant, who was uninsured. The claim was notified to the Motor
Insurers' Bureau who appointed an insurance company as investigating
office. After a good deal of correspondence the plaintiff's solicitors issued a
writ on 3 November 1980. The defendant pleaded the action was out of
time. As a preliminiary point the plaintiff asked the court to disapply the
Limitation Act 1939, s 2A (now s 11 of the 1980 Act) under the provisions
of s 2D of the 1939 Act (now s 33 of the 1980 Act).

HELD: Section 2D(3) required the court to have regard to all the circumstances of the case. The application must be refused since (a) the balance of
advantage to the plaintiff was that he should sue his solicitors for negligence; (b) the defendant would be prejudiced by continuing to be involved
in the action; it was legitimate and appropriate for the court to take into
account the position of the Motor Insurers' Bureau since it was a composite
unit with the defendant; and (c) a trial was never going to be satisfactory
because of the defendant's character and the plaintiff's injuries (including
amnesia).

Hattam v National Coal Board

(1978) 122 Sol Jo 777, CA

The plaintiff was injured in an accident in 1953. In 1973 he was advised he
may have a claim for damages. In 1976 a writ was issued; nearly a year later
it was served. After delivery of the statement of claim the defendants
applied to dismiss for want of prosecution. The judge applying the tests laid
down in *Birkett v James* (p 633, below) dismissed the application. The defendants appealed.

HELD, allowing the appeal: The delay was such that there could not
possibly be a fair trial. Five of the defendants' officials were dead, the pit
where the accident occurred had closed down and the files destroyed. The
facts were clear to the plaintiff in 1953 and the limitation period prescribed
by s 2A of the 1939 Act expired in 1956. The discretion which the Court
had by virtue of s 2D was not to apply where it would not be equitable in the
present case and the action should be stayed.

Per Lord Denning: The best procedure in future cases of this kind would
be a simple summons to dismiss the action. The court could determine the
matter on affidavit evidence on both sides.

NO DISADVANTAGE — CO-DEFENDANT LIABLE

Liff v Peasley

[1980] 1 All ER 623, [1980] 1 WLR 781, 124 Sol Jo 360, CA

The plaintiff was injured in a road accident on 25 October 1973 by the negligence of the defendant Peasley. He issued a writ against him on 14 August 1975. In 1978 he was required by MIB (Peasley being uninsured) to join another defendant Spinks. The Statement of Claim was amended for this purpose by order of 5 October 1978 and a copy of the amended writ was sent to Spinks's solicitors. They entered unconditional appearance and served a defence which pleaded that the action against Spinks was statute-barred. They then applied for an order under Ord 15, r 6 that Spinks should cease to be a party in that he was joined after the expiry of the limitation period.

HELD: (1) there were no grounds for exercising the discretion of the Court under the Limitation Act 1939, s 2D in favour of the plaintiff since he was not disadvantaged by s 2A: he already had a cast iron case against Peasley; (2) it was an established rule of practice that the court will not allow a person to be added as a defendant to an existing action if the claim sought to be made against him is already statute-barred and he relies on it as a defence; (3) the preferable basis, both on the rules of the court and on the decided cases, on which the rule can be justified is that the action against the added party is deemed to begin against him on the date of the amendment of the writ, not the date of the original writ. (4) Spinks was not precluded from obtaining an order that he cease to be a party by his solicitors having entered unconditional appearance. When it became apparent that he intended to rely on the claim being statute-barred he became a party who had been improperly added, or who had ceased to be a proper party, within the meaning of Ord 15, r 6(2)(a).

Note—'The theory propounded by *Gawthrop v Boulton* (p 536, above) and *Liff v Peasley* that an amendment to add a new defendant as a party to an existing action would not have retrospective effect to the date of the writ but would take effect from the date of the amendment is directly counter to s 35 of the Limitation Act 1980 that an amendment takes effect from the date of the issue of the writ and *not* from the date of the amendment.' (*Supreme Court Practice*, 1985 20/5–8/2).

RELEVANT DELAY AND PREJUDICE

Deeming v British Steel Corpn

(1978) 123 Sol Jo 303, CA

The plaintiff was injured when struck by a motor vehicle driven by L on the defendants' premises on 26 June 1973. He issued a writ against L within the limitation period and obtained interlocutory judgment in default of defence. L applied to set aside the judgment, saying he was an employee of the defendants driving to work, that he had been examined during an internal enquiry carried out by the defendants' works police and was not insured. The plaintiff then issued a writ against the defendants on 8 December 1976. The defendants pleaded that the claim was statute-barred. On trial of the limitation point the judge said the action was not statute-barred by the Limitation Act 1939, s 2A because the plaintiff had not been aware of the facts sworn to by L, but said he would not have exercised his discretion under s 2D in favour of the plaintiff. On an appeal the plaintiff conceded that as the plaintiff's solicitors had received a copy of the report of the defendants' internal enquiry the judge's decision on s 2A could not be supported, but appealed against his decision on s 2D.

HELD: Section 2D should be applied in favour of the plaintiff. The delay that was relevant within s 2D(3)(a) and (b) was the five and a half months' delay between June and December 1976, but that delay did not affect the cogency of the evidence the defendants had to adduce. The prejudice to a defendant which fell for consideration under s 2D(1)(b) was the prejudice flowing from any decision of the court to allow the action to proceed; the prejudice to the defendant caused by the plaintiff's delay within the normal limitation period was not prejudice caused by the court in allowing under s 2D, the action to proceed.

NAME OF DEFENDANT UNKNOWN

Simpson v Norwest Holst Southern Ltd
[1980] 2 All ER 471, [1980] 1 WLR 968, 124 Sol Jo 313, CA

The plaintiff was employed on a building site as a carpenter; the memorandum given to him under the Contracts of Employment Act gave the employers' name as 'Norwest Holst Group', which was not a legal entity. He was injured at work on 4 August 1976. He claimed damages but was unable to tell his solicitors which company in the group employed him, nor did letters from the employers' insurers reveal it until, in reply to a direct enquiry from his solicitors, they wrote on 4 July 1979 giving the defendant company's name. The solicitors issued a county court summons on 17 August 1979. The defendants applied to dismiss the action as being out of time. The court refused the application, exercising its discretion under the Limitation Act 1939, s 2D to disapply s 2A.

HELD, dismissing appeal: (1) As the identity of an employer against whom proceedings could be taken was not known to the plaintiff until the insurers' letter of 4 July 1979 time did not run until he had that 'knowledge' for the purposes of s 2A(4)(b) and the action was not out of time. (2) Section 2D should not be read in any restrictive sense so as to apply only to exceptional cases (following *Firman v Ellis* (below), on this point). (3) It was not correct, as the defendants maintained, that the plaintiff was prejudiced only by his solicitors' delay and not by s 2A. By 4 August 1979 his claim was likely to be barred by a limitation plea and this was due to s 2A not to his solicitors' delays. The defendants were not prejudiced, as they were in no worse position to defend the claim on 17 August 1979 than on the 3rd. There was ample evidence on which the county court judge could properly exercise his discretion under s 2D.

Note—Section 2A(4)(b) has now become the Limitation Act 1980, s 11(4)(b).

Common v Croft
[1980] LS Gaz R 358, CA

In November 1975 the plaintiff was injured in a collision between his motor cycle and the defendant's car. Both were served with summonses and, in April 1976, convicted of driving without due care. The plaintiff issued a writ for damages in April 1979. His excuse for not issuing the writ within three years of the accident was that he had not known the identity of the defendant until the police summonses were served in April 1976 and that he thought his conviction precluded him from civil remedy until he was told otherwise early in 1979. The defendant applied to have the action struck out as being statute-barred. The judge dismissed the summons.

HELD, ON APPEAL: (1) The judge was wrong in holding that time ran only from April 1976, when the plaintiff first had actual knowledge of the defendant's identity at the hearing of the summonses. He should have considered s 2A(8); the Plaintiff could have ascertained the defendant's identity when the summonses were served; but (2) he was right in allowing the action to proceed under s 2D. The delay referred to in s 2D(3) meant unlawful, culpable delay, namely, the delay which occurred from the expiry of the primary limitation period to the issue of the writ. This was the effect of *Deeming's* case.

Note—The section numbers refer to the Limitation Act 1939 as amended. Section 2A(8) now appears as the Limitation Act 1980, s 14(3), and s 2D(3) as s 33(3) of the 1980 Act.

STARTING SECOND ACTION OUT OF TIME

Firman v Ellis
Down v Harvey
Pheasant v Smith (Tyres) Ltd
[1978] QB 886, [1978] 2 All ER 851, [1978] 3 WLR 1, 122 Sol Jo 147, CA
The plaintiffs claimed damages for injuries received in road accidents. In each case no issue arose on liability: the only issue was the amount of damages to be awarded when the plaintiffs should be sufficiently recovered to enable this to be done. In each case the plaintiffs' solicitors issued writs but allowed them by inadvertence to expire before service. When three years had elapsed the defendants' insurers refused to entertain the claims because they had become statute-barred. The plaintiffs began new actions by issuing writs out of time and applied under the Limitation Act 1939, s 2D that the limitation period in s 2A should not apply.

HELD: The court could properly exercise its discretion under s 2D in favour of the plaintiffs. Section 2D was not limited to exceptional cases; it gave a discretion to extend time in all cases where the three-year limitation had expired before the issue of the writ. The solicitors' slip had not prejudiced the defendants at all. On subsidiary points: (1) under the 1975 Act the negligence of the plaintiff's solicitor was an admissible consideration; it might tip the scale where the defendant had been substantially prejudiced by the delay; (2) the words 'the plaintiff' in s 2D(3) included his solicitor or agent except where the context confined to it the plaintiff personally; (3) 'the court' in sub-s (2) meant a judge of the High Court or county court, a judge in chambers or a judge hearing an application as a preliminary issue, but not a master in the High Court or a registrar in the county court.

Note—But see below, *Walkley v Precision Forgings Ltd* and *Chappell v Cooper*.

Walkley v Precision Forgings Ltd
[1979] 2 All ER 548, [1979] 1 WLR 606, 123 Sol Jo 354, HL
In 1966 the plaintiff found himself to be suffering from Reynaud's disease, possibly caused by vibration of machine tools at work. He issued a writ in October 1971 and served it. The employers' solicitors entered appearance.

Nothing more was done because the plaintiff's solicitors advised him that he did not have a good claim. A second firm of solicitors revived the claim in 1973 but the defendants' solicitors wrote saying that if the plaintiff intended to proceed with the action they would apply to dismiss it for want of prosecution. Nothing more was done in the action. In December 1976 a third firm of solicitors issued a new writ for the plaintiff and served it with a statement of claim. The defendants' solicitors applied for the second action to be struck out under Ord 18, r 19 as an abuse of the process of the court. It was conceded by the plaintiff that the first action would be likely to have been dismissed for want of prosecution. On appeal from the master, the judge declined to strike out the second action on the plaintiff's undertaking to discontinue the first action. The Court of Appeal said the judge was right and that the plaintiff was entitled to have the question whether his second action should be allowed to proceed tested under the Limitation Act 1939, s 2D by reference to the criteria there set out.

HELD, on the defendants' appeal to the House of Lords: The second action should be struck out. The affidavit of the defendants' solicitor had been directed to the issue under s 2D and the plaintiff had not answered it; no answer was possible for on the facts before the court it was clear that since the plaintiff had begun an action within the period limited by s 2A he had not been prejudiced by it. *Birkett v James* (p 633, below) had no relevance; all that case decided was that when a plaintiff had allowed an action to go to sleep it would be an improper exercise of the court's discretion to dismiss it for want of prosecution before the expiry of the limitation period: it had no application to a personal injury action after the primary limitation period had expired.

Per Lord Diplock: Once a plaintiff has started an action (the first action) within the primary limitation period it is only in the most exceptional circumstances that he would be able to bring himself within s 2D in respect of a second action brought to enforce the same cause of action. If the first action is still in existence . . . he has not been prevented from starting his action by s 2A or s 2B at all, so the provisions of those sections cannot have caused him any prejudice. Does it make any difference that the first action is no longer in existence at the time of the application under s 2D either because it has been struck out for want of prosecution or because it has been discontinued by the plaintiff of his own volition? In my view it does not. The only exception . . . where it might be proper to give a direction under s 2D . . . would be a case in which the plaintiff had been induced to discontinue by a misrepresentation or other improper conduct by the defendant.

Note—The *Firman v Ellis* cases (above) were not cited.

Deerness v John R. Keeble & Son (Brantham) Ltd

[1983] 2 Lloyd's Rep 260, 133 NLJ 641, [1983] Com LR 221, HL

On 7 October 1977 the plaintiff was very seriously injured in a road accident. The defendants were to blame. Their insurers embarked on negotiations for settlement of the claim. The plaintiff's solicitors issued a writ on 23 August 1979 but did not serve it. On 4 August 1980 the insurers paid by agreement the sum of £5,000 as an interim payment. A few days still remained for service of the writ but it was not served, the plaintiff's solicitors apparently regarding the interim payment as an admission of liability and believing the limitation period would date from that payment. Later, appreciating their error, the solicitors issued a second writ on 23 April 1981 and served it on 12 May: they applied for an order under the Limitation Act 1980, s 33 that the action should be allowed to proceed notwithstanding s 11 of the Act.

HELD: The action could not proceed. The decision in *Walkley v Precision Forgings Ltd* (above) was binding on the court. No waiver or agreement that the limitation period would not be insisted upon could be made out of the fact that an interim payment had been made. An appeal to the House of Lords was dismissed. The fatal obstacle to the application under s 33 of the Limitation Act 1980, s 33 was the fact that the plaintiff's solicitors did cause a writ to be issued within the primary limitation period. The plaintiff had not been prejudiced by s 11 of the Act. She had brought the first action within the normal limitation period; if she suffered any prejudice it was by her own solicitors' inaction and not by operation of the Act.

Wilson v Banner Scaffolding Ltd
(1982) Times, 22 June, QBD (Milmo J)

The plaintiff sustained injury in an accident in September 1975. His solicitors issued a writ against both the first and second defendants on 11 July 1978 and served it on both on 11 September 1978. Later, the plaintiff's solicitors learned that the second defendants, a limited company, had been wound up in August 1976. In September 1979 the plaintiff obtained an order of the county court giving leave to begin an action against the second defendants notwithstanding the winding up order, and in October 1979 an order was obtained by consent of the first defendants to add the second defendants as defendants to the action begun in July 1978. The writ was served on the second defendants who pleaded in their defence that against them the action was statute-barred. On the plaintiff's application under the Limitation Act 1939, s 2D, as amended, that s 2A should be disapplied:

HELD: The Companies Act 1948, s 231 prevented the plaintiff from commencing any proceedings against the second defendants without first obtaining the leave of the court. Thus the writ as served on 11 September 1978 was a nullity in respect of the second defendants. *Walkley v Precision Forgings* (above) did not prevent an order being made under s 2D to disapply s 2A because there was no action in being against the second defendants until the Writ was amended in October 1979, outside the primary limitation period. At the time when the primary limitation period expired neither the plaintiff not his advisers knew or had reason to suspect that the second defendants were in liquidation. The second defendants' insurers had known of the claim within weeks of the accident. On taking into account the matters referred to in s 2D(3) it would be equitable to allow the action to proceed.

Note—For section numbers in the Limitation Act 1980 see note on p 531, above.

Solicitor's negligence

Browes v Jones and Middleton
(1979) 123 Sol Jo 489, CA

The plaintiff was injured in an accident by negligence of the second defendants. Liability was clear. He instructed solicitors (the first defendants) promptly after the accident but after three years they had still not issued a writ and the claim became statute-barred. By other solicitors the plaintiff began an action against his first solicitors for negligence in allowing the claim to go out of time but later joined the original tortfeasors as second defendants, seeking leave under s 2D of the Limitation Act to proceed notwithstanding the provisions of s 2A.

HELD: On the application under s 2D to disapply s 2A, leave should be refused. The plaintiff admitted that he had suffered no prejudice by the first defendants' failure to issue a writ in time since he had a cause of action against them by reason of their negligence. In a case like the present the first vital and preliminary matter to decide before disapplying s 2A was that there was some prejudice to the plaintiff, and here there was none. But the second defendants had suffered prejudice by having to face an action after the three-year period had elapsed — see *Martin v Turner* (p 629, below). It was not 'equitable' that they should be made defendants at the present stage simply because solicitors had been negligent. *Walkley's* case (above) and *Tolley v Morris* (p 637, below) had affected *Firman's* case but it was very strange that *Firman* had not been cited to the House of Lords in either *Walkley* or *Tolley*.

Thompson v Brown Construction Ltd
[1981] 2 All ER 296, [1981] 1 WLR 744, 125 Sol Jo 377, HL

The plaintiff was injured at work by the collapse of a scaffold. He claimed damages from the second defendants, a scaffolding company, who did not dispute liability. The plaintiff's solicitors negotiated for a time and then lost the file. By the time they found it more than three years had elapsed. The writ was issued 37 days out of time. The defendants pleaded the Limitation Act 1939 and denied that it would be equitable to allow the action to proceed under s 2D. The judge considered himself bound by the decision in *Browes's* case (above) to hold as a matter of law that the plaintiff was not prejudiced by the provisions of s 2A because he had a cast iron claim in negligence against his solicitors. He refused to make a direction under s 2D.

HELD: *Browes's* case should not be treated as authority for the proposition of law for which the judge treated it. In deciding whether discretion should be exercised under s 2D a court must have regard not only to the provisions of s 2D(1) but also those of s 2D(3). The onus of showing that in the particular circumstances of the case it would be equitable to make an exception lies on the plaintiff; but subject to that the court's discretion to make or refuse an order is unfettered. The conduct of the parties as well as the prejudice one or other will suffer if the court does or does not make an order are all to be put into the balance. What was said about the unfettered nature of the discretion in *Firman v Ellis* (above) was right though the actual decision in that case must be regarded as having been overruled by *Walkley's* case (above). The judge in the present case had not exercised his discretion and the issue must be remitted to him for a decision.

Chappell v Cooper
[1980] 2 All ER 463, [1980] 1 WLR 958, 124 Sol Jo 544, CA
The plaintiff issued a writ within the three-year limitation period but failed
to serve it. A second writ was issued after the limitation period had expired.
The judge in chambers, following *Firman v Ellis* (above), gave leave under
the Limitation Act 1939, s 2D for the second action to proceed.
HELD, allowing the appeal: Having regard to the speeches in the House of
Lords in *Walkley's* case the decision in *Firman's* case could no longer stand.
It made no difference that in the present case there was no question of
discontinuance of the first action or dismissal for want of prosecution. The
principle was general that if a plaintiff does not for any reason proceed with
the first action he cannot claim to be prejudiced by s 2A in the second
action: the cause of the prejudice is his own failure to proceed with the first
action.

Per Ormrod LJ: The whole of the judgment in *Firman v Ellis* as far as I
can see has gone except perhaps for one remaining point . . . that in the
exercise of the discretion under the 1975 Act in the form as now limited by
the House of Lords, the discretion is one which is to be exercised generally
and not in the restricted fashion which the appellants in *Firman v Ellis* were
arguing for.

JUDGES' DISCRETION

Conry v Simpson
[1983] 3 All ER 369, CA
On 12 January 1973 the plaintiff was injured by the first defendant's car
when standing at the side of the second and third defendants' vehicle. The
injury was to his leg. His solicitor failed to issue a writ within three years.
He instructed other solicitors who issued a writ against the first solicitor for
professional negligence in 1977: that action remained pending. After the
decision in *Firman v Ellis* (p 545, above) was reported in February 1978
the plaintiff revived the claim and issued a writ in November 1979 against
the potential tortfeasors and applied to the court to disapply s 11 of the 1980
Act. The judge made an order disapplying s 11 as against the first defendant (whose insurers had not denied negligence) but not as against the
second and third defendants. The first defendant appealed.
HELD, by the Court of Appeal: The judge had an unfettered discretion, as
originally held in *Firman v Ellis*, to disapply s 11 provided he had regard to
all the circumstances of the case and in particular to the six circumstances
specified in s 33(3). It was not for an appellate court to reverse the
discretion of the judge unless he had gone very wrong. The judge had
considered all the points in issue and there were no grounds for saying that
the judge had fallen into error.

Action for trespass

Note—See *Letang v Cooper*, p 18, above.

NEW CLAIMS IN PENDING ACTIONS

The provisions in respect of counterclaims formerly contained in the Limitation Act 1939, s 28 have been repealed and re-enacted in the Limitation Act 1980, s 35. New provisions already introduced by the Limitation Amendment Act 1980, s 8 have been incorporated in s 35. Transitional Provisions are contained in Sch 2, para 6 of the Act. Sub-ss (1)–(3) read as follows:

'**35 New claims in pending actions: rules of court**   (1) For the purposes of this Act, any new claim made in the course of any action shall be deemed to be a separate action and to have been commenced —
(a) in the case of a new claim made in or by way of third party proceedings, on the date on which those proceedings were commenced; and
(b) in the case of any other new claim, on the same date as the original action.
(2) In this section a new claim means any claim by way of set-off or counterclaim, and any claim involving either —
(a) the addition or substitution of a new cause of action; or
(b) the addition or substitution of a new party;
and 'third party proceedings' means any proceedings brought in the course of any action by any party to the action against a person not previously a party to the action, other than proceedings brought by joining any such person as defendant to any claim already made in the original action by the party bringing the proceedings.
(3) Except as provided by s 33 of this Act or by rules of court, neither the High Court nor any county court shall allow a new claim within sub-s (1)(b) above, other than an original set-off or counterclaim, to be made in the course of any action after the expiry of any time limit under this Act which would affect a new action to enforce that claim.
    For the purposes of this subsection, a claim is an original set-off or an original counterclaim if it is a claim made by way of set-off or (as the case may be) by way of counterclaim by a party who has not previously made any claim in the action.'

In the absence, as yet, of reported cases to illumine this difficult section, reference may usefully be made to the detailed examination of its effect in the *Supreme Court Practice 1985* vol 2, pp 1580–1. See also *Reed Publishing Holdings Ltd v Kings Reach Investments Ltd* [1983] LS Gaz R 1923, CA.

THIRD PARTY CASES

Time limit for contribution proceedings

The Limitation Act 1963, s 4(1) as substituted by the Civil Liability (Contribution) Act 1978, s 9(1) appears now in the Limitation Act 1980, s 10(1)–(4) as follows:

'**10 Special time limit for claiming contribution**   (1) Where under s 1 of the Civil Liability (Contribution) Act 1978 any person becomes entitled to a right to recover contribution in respect of any damage from any other person, no action to recover contribution by virtue of that right shall be brought after the expiration of two years from the date on which that right accrued.
(2) For the purposes of this section the date on which a right to recover contribution in respect of any damage accrues to any person (referred to below in this section as 'the relevant date') shall be ascertained as provided in sub-s (3) and (4) below.

(3) If the person in question is held liable in respect of that damage —
(a) by a judgment given in any civil proceedings; or
(b) by an award made on any arbitration;
the relevant date shall be the date on which the judgment is given, or the date of the award (as the case may be).

For the purposes of this subsection no account shall be taken of any judgment or award given or made on appeal in so far as it varies the amount of damages awarded against the person in question.

(4) If, in any case not within sub-s (3) above, the person in question makes or agrees to make any payment to one or more persons in compensation for that damage (whether he admits any liability in respect of the damage or not), the relevant date shall be the earliest date on which the amount to be paid by him is agreed between him (or his representative) and the person (or each of the persons, as the case may be) to whom the payment is to be made.

(5) An action to recover contribution shall be one to which ss 28, 32 and 35 of this Act apply, but otherwise Parts II and III of this Act (except ss 34, 37 and 38) shall not apply for the purposes of this section.'

George Wimpey & Co Ltd v British Overseas Airways Corporation

[1955] AC 169, [1954] 3 All ER 661, [1954] 3 WLR 932, 98 Sol Jo 686, HL
Littlewood was employed by BOAC and on 28 July 1949, was injured by a motor vehicle of Wimpeys. Writ was issued against both defendants on 26 April 1951. Third-party notice was issued by Wimpeys against BOAC on 8 June 1951. BOAC pleaded in their defence that action was not brought within 12 months (as the law then required), and was barred. This defence succeeded.

With regard to the third-party proceedings, Parker J held that Wimpeys must show that the BOAC was a tortfeasor who is or would if sued have been liable in respect of the damage. The word 'liable' in the Law Reform (Married Women and Tortfeasors) Act 1935, s 6(1)(c) (now replaced by the Civil Liability (Contribution) Act 1978, s 1) means 'held liable', ie successfully sued to judgment. Recovery can also be made against him if he has not been sued but if he had been sued to judgment he would have been held liable. In this case BOAC had been sued and held not liable. The claim for contribution failed.

An appeal to the House of Lords was dismissed.

Per Viscount Simonds and Lord Tucker: The right conferred by s 6(1)(c) to recover contribution from a joint tortfeasor who would, if sued, have been liable, does not extend to a joint tortfeasor who has been sued and held not to be liable. Where the language of a statute is not calculated to deal with a situation to which it has to be applied and the arguments are fairly evenly balanced, that which causes the least alteration in the law should be chosen.

Note—The words 'who would, if sued, have been held liable' do not appear in s 1 of the Civil Liability (Contribution) Act 1978. The single word 'liable' is used, but sub-s (3) excludes liability to contribute where a person has 'ceased to be liable by virtue of the expiry of a period of limitation', thus preserving the effect of the above case.
See also *Southern Water Authority v Carey* [1985] 2 All ER 1077 and *Harper v Gray and Walker* [1985] 2 All ER 507, [1985] 1 WLR 1196.

Nature of limitation defence

Yew Bon Tew (alias Yong Boon Tiew) v Kenderaan Bas Mara

[1983] 1 AC 553, [1982] 3 All ER 833, [1982] 3 WLR 1026, 126 Sol Jo 729, PC

The plaintiffs, injured in a collision with the defendants' bus in Selangor, Malaysia, failed to issue proceedings within the 12 months prescribed by the Public Authorities Protection Ordinance 1948, and their potential claim became statute-barred on 5 April 1973. In June 1974 an amending Act substituted a three-years' limitation period for the 12 months. The plaintiffs issued a writ in March 1975, within the three years. Was the plaintiffs' cause of action finally statute-barred in 1973 or was it revived by the 1974 Act?

HELD: The claim was barred. Whether a statute was retrospective was a question of construction which could not in all cases be decided by classifying it as procedural or substantive. The test was to see whether the 1974 Act, if applied retrospectively, would impair existing rights and obligations. When the plaintiffs failed to bring their action within the 12 months the defendants acquired an accrued right which was designed to give it immunity for acts done in discharge of its public duties. It was in every sense a right even though it arose under an Act which could be classified as procedural. It was not a purpose of the 1974 Act to deprive a potential defendant of a limitation defence which he already possessed. When a limitation period had expired a potential defendant should be able to assume he was no longer at risk and able to part with papers, discard proofs of evidence and discharge his solicitor.

AMENDMENT OF PROCEEDINGS OUT OF TIME

Writ and statement of claim

Batting v London Passenger Transport Board

[1941] 1 All ER 228, CA

A new form of negligence cannot be added by amendment after the expiry of the period of limitation, ie of neglect to maintain tram track to endorsement of negligent driving.

Marshall v London Passenger Transport Board

[1936] 3 All ER 83, 80 Sol Jo 893, CA

The plaintiff issued a writ indorsed simply with the claim for damages for personal injuries and consequential loss sustained by reason of the negligence of the defendants, their servants or agents.

After the expiry of the period prescribed by the Limitation Act, the plaintiff applied to amend by adding a claim for breach of statutory duty under the Tramways Act 1870.

HELD: (1) The writ was lacking in particularity: it did not specify what duty the defendants had failed to perform; but the insufficiency was remedied in the statement of claim under Ord 20, r 4 (now Ord 18, r 15(2)). (2) The amendment sought to set up a new cause of action which was then statute barred and the amendment could not be allowed.

Note—See also *Pathak v James Nourse Ltd* and *Dornan v J. W. Ellis & Co Ltd* (p 557, below). See also RSC Ord 20, r 5(2) and (8) under which *Batting's* and *Marshall's* cases might now be decided differently.

Hall v Meyrick
[1957] 2 QB 455, [1957] 2 All ER 722, [1957] 3 WLR 273, 101 Sol Jo 574, CA

The general rule is quite clear that the plaintiff will not be allowed to amend by setting up fresh claims in respect of causes of action which since the issue of the writ have been barred by the Statute of Limitations. The principle was declared in *Weldon v Neal* (1887) 19 QBD 394.

Stanhope Steamship Co v British Phosphate Comrs
[1956] 2 Lloyd's Rep 331, CA

It is a well settled practice that the Court would not allow an amendment to a pleading which had the effect of depriving the other party of a defence under any Statute of Limitations.

Cases of *Marshall* (above), *Hilton* and *Ingall* (p 518, above) followed.

Weait v Jayanbee Joinery Ltd
[1963] 1 QB 239, [1962] 2 All ER 568, [1962] 3 WLR 323, 106 Sol Jo 369, CA; appeal to House of Lords [1962] 1 WLR 1083, HL

The infant plaintiff was injured in an accident at work and sued his employers. Their insurers had medical examinations by two doctors before proceedings, neither of whom criticised the treatment received by the plaintiff. The writ was issued two and a quarter years after the accident. After proceedings were begun the defendants asked for an examination by a neuro-surgeon. The plaintiff agreed but owing to some delay which was not the fault of the defendants the examination did not take place until three and a half years after the accident. The neuro-surgeon reported that part of the plaintiff's disability was due to negligent medical treatment. The defendants applied to amend the defence to plead this, though the plaintiff would no longer be able to sue those responsible for the treatment because the limitation period had expired.

HELD: The defendants should be allowed to amend. The question was what was the proper amount of damages for the defendants to pay. It was a misfortune if some fact which was not ascertained before the limitation period expired showed that the damages recoverable against the defendants were only part of the loss and that the remainder could have been recovered from a third party had it been known in time; but that misfortune could not be put on the defendants when they had been free from fault.

Turner v Ford Motor Co Ltd
[1965] 2 All ER 583, [1965] 1 WLR 948, 109 Sol Jo 354, CA

The plaintiff, working on a building site, was injured when a brick dropped on his head. He sued two defendants, neither of whom was his employer, alleging that the brick was dropped by a servant of one or the other. Both defendants denied negligence. Discovery in the action was not completed until after the expiration of the limitation period. On information appearing in a document disclosed by one of the defendants the other applied to amend his defence to allege negligence on the part of the plaintiff in not wearing a safety helmet provided by his employers. The plaintiff opposed the amendment on the ground that if he had known within the limitation period that this point was to be taken he would have joined his employers as defendants, a course which was not now open to him, and that he would thus be prejudiced by the amendment.

HELD: In *Weait v Jayanbee Joinery Ltd* (above) the question was discussed whether leave to amend should be granted after the statutory period when the proposed amendment sought to cast blame on some third party. In such a case there was a great deal to be said for refusing leave to amend. This case was different as the proposed amendment sought only to put blame on the plaintiff. It did nothing to encourage the plaintiff to do anything he could not have done within the three years. He must know whether he was issued with a helmet and wore it and it had always been open to him to proceed against his employers if he had wished. There was no good reason for refusing the amendment.

Endorsement defective

Hill v Luton Corpn
[1951] 2 KB 387, [1951] 1 All ER 1028, [1951] 1 TLR 853, 95 Sol Jo 301 (Devlin J)
Accident 28 January 1950; writ issued 17 July 1950; endorsement 'damages for negligence and breach of contract'. The endorsement was admittedly defective for insufficient particularity. Writ served 10 February 1951, with statement of claim which cured the defect in the endorsement. Defendants applied to set aside the writ and service. Defendants admitted that a defective endorsement could be cured by a properly drafted statement of claim and that the defect was cured in this case.

HELD: Order LXX, r 1 (now Ord 2, r 1), provided that non-compliance with any rule shall not render any proceedings void unless the court or a judge shall so direct. The writ was not a nullity. The action had been commenced within twelve months. This was not a case where the action could not be effectively prosecuted without amendment requiring the leave of the court. The principle that a defect in the writ can be cured by a proper statement of claim operates in the same way as a right to amend without leave. *Marshall's* case and *Batting's* case was distinguishable (1) because the plaintiff was not seeking the aid of the court, and (2) the defendant knew what cause of action he had to meet within the permitted period.

Application to set aside dismissed.

Groundsel v Cuthell
[1952] 2 QB 673, [1952] 2 All ER 135, [1952] 1 TLR 1558, 96 Sol Jo 413 (Ormerod J)
Death 12 February 1951; writ issued 22 January 1952; endorsement for damages under Law Reform (Miscellaneous Provisions) Act 1934 and Fatal Accidents Acts 1846 to 1908, in respect of defendant's negligence; writ served 23 April 1952. Defendant entered conditional appearance and applied to set aside service of writ for defective endorsement (which was

admitted). Before hearing of summons, statement of claim delivered which cured the defect.

HELD: The point was left open in *Hill's* case whether decision should be on the position at issue of summons or at the hearing. The decision should be as at the hearing. If this were wrong, plaintiff did not seek discretion of court because he was not seeking the aid of the court. If service set aside, plaintiff could re-serve the writ and deliver statement of claim with the writ and cure the defect and there were some months available to do so. The defendant was not deprived of a defence and *Marshall's* case and *Batting's* case did not apply.

OBITER: If discretion of court was necessary, it should be exercised in favour of plaintiff.

Pontin v Wood

[1962] 1 QB 594, [1961] 1 All ER 294, [1962] 2 WLR 258, 105 Sol Jo 1105, CA

The plaintiffs were injured in an accident on 27 March 1958 and claimed damages against the defendant. They issued a writ on 13 March 1961, endorsed 'The plaintiffs' claim is for damages for personal injuries', a defective endorsement since it did not set out the cause of action. The writ was served on 25 March 1961 but the defendant did not enter an appearance. On 22 July 1961, the plaintiffs delivered a properly drawn statement of claim to the defendant personally. This was procedurally wrong as the defendant had not entered an appearance: it should have been filed with the Court with an affidavit of service. On 4 August 1961 the defendant applied to the District Registrar to have the writ set aside but the application was refused. The defendant entered a conditional appearance and appealed. The judge reversed the order of the District Registrar and set aside the writ on the ground that it was a nullity until cured by a proper statement of claim and that this had not been done within the limitation period.

HELD, by the Court of Appeal: A writ was not a nullity by reason of a defective endorsement (*Hill v Luton Corpn*, p 554, above). At the date of the issue of the defendant's summons and the date of the hearing by the District Registrar the defendant had not appeared and the plaintiffs were entitled to file a statement of claim with an affidavit of service of the writ: the defendant had acquired no right which it required an order of the Court of Appeal to defeat. The cases of *Marshall* and *Batting* (p 552, above) were not a point because in those cases the plaintiffs needed an order of the Court to do something to the detriment of the defendants. Appeal allowed.

Sterman v E. W. and W. T. Moore

[1970] 1 QB 596, [1970] 1 All ER 581, [1970] 2 WLR 386, 114 Sol Jo 90, CA

The plaintiff sustained injury at work in May 1965. He issued a writ against his employers in August 1967 by attending in person at the Royal Courts of Justice. The endorsement on the writ was defective because it did not mention the cause of action. In May 1968 the plaintiff instructed solicitors who applied to amend the endorsement. The master, and on appeal, the judge, refused on the ground that service of a good statement of claim would cure the defect. When the statement of claim was served the defendants applied to strike it out on the ground that the cause of action in the statement of claim was not mentioned in the writ, contrary to Ord 18, r 15(2).

HELD: (1) The writ was defective but the defect was cured when the defendants entered unconditional appearance. (2) Nevertheless in the absence of an amendment to the writ the statement of claim was bad because it did not comply with Ord 18, r 15(2). (3) Although the limitation period had expired it was right to allow the writ to be amended so as to enable the action to proceed. Ord 20, r 5(1) should be given its full width and the amendment allowed because it was just to do so, even though it deprived the defendants of a defence under the Limitation Acts. *Pontin v Wood* (p 555, above) followed.

Note—See also *Brickfield Properties v Newton* [1971] 3 All ER 328, [1971] 1 WLR 862, a case of an alleged breach of contract in which the authorities were considered and discussed.

Collins v Hertfordshire County Council
[1947] KB 598, [1947] 1 All ER 633, [1947] LJR 789, 176 LT 456, 111 JP 272, 63 TLR 317, 45 LGR 263 (Hilbery J)

In an action for negligence against a hospital, the statement of claim alleged (inter alia) the negligence of a house surgeon as a servant of this hospital.

More than 12 months (which was then the limitation period) after the cause of action, an amendment was applied for alleging the negligence of a pharmacist also as a servant of the hospital.

HELD: Not a new cause of action; it was only particulars of the cause of action for negligence of the hospital.

Pathak v James Nourse Ltd
(1961) 105 Sol Jo 1106, [1961] 2 Lloyd's Rep 467, CA

The plaintiff was injured when working as a seaman on the defendant's vessel. He was struck by a rope when the operation of winding the vessel away from the quay was being attempted. The endorsement on the writ claimed damages for 'personal injuries caused by the negligence of the defendants their servants or agents sustained by the plaintiff. . . .' The case reached trial after the limitation period had expired, the statement of claim having alleged that the accident was due to a defective stopper rope. At the trial it soon appeared that this case was false. The judge expressed the view that the accident was due to the negligent way in which those in charge of the ship were conducting the operation. The plaintiff applied and was permitted to amend the statement of claim to allege this negligence. The trial was continued several months later and the defendants held liable to the plaintiff on the grounds set out in the amendment.

HELD: The endorsement on the writ was sufficient to cover the new allegation in the amended statement of claim which did not amount to a new cause of action.

Dornan v J. W. Ellis & Co Ltd
[1962] 1 QB 583, [1962] 1 All ER 303, [1962] 2 WLR 250, 105 Sol Jo 1083,
CA
On 10 April 1957 the plaintiff sustained an eye injury from a piece of a drill
which broke when being used by a fellow-servant of the defendants. He
claimed damages by a writ the endorsement of which alleged 'breach of
statutory duty and/or negligence of the defendants, their servants or
agents'. The statement of claim contained no allegation against the fellow-
workman. On 21 October 1961 (after the limitation period had expired),
the plaintiff applied to amend the statement of claim to allege negligence
against the fellow-workman.
HELD: The amendment should be allowed. The fresh allegations did not
introduce a new cause of action nor a new set of ideas as in *Marshall's* case
(p 552, above) or *Batting's* case (p 552, above). It must be a question of
degree in each case on its particular facts.

Misnomer of defendant

Davies v Elsby Bros Ltd
[1960] 3 All ER 672, [1961] 1 WLR 170, 105 Sol Jo 107, CA
On 20 March 1956, the plaintiff was injured at work. He had been
employed by Elsby Brothers until 1955 when the business of the firm was
taken over by Elsby Brothers Limited by whom he continued to be
employed. When the plaintiff instructed solicitors in March 1959 he told
them he was employed by Elsby Brothers. They found the name in a
current telephone directory and issued a writ for the plaintiff against 'Elsby
Brothers (a firm)'. Nearly 12 months later, just before the writ expired the
solicitors discovered that the name was incorrect and amended it by
striking out '(a firm)' and substituting 'Limited'. They then served the
writ on the last day of the time allowed.
HELD: The defendants were entitled to have the writ set aside. The Court
had no discretion to allow an amendment that would deprive the defendants of a defence that had accrued under the Limitation Act 1939, the
action having become statute-barred before the amendment. The judge's
refusal to amend the writ was upheld in the Court of Appeal. It was not
possible for the defendants to know when looking at the writ that it must
have been intended for the company, as the date of the accident was not
specified. It was not a misnomer but a substitution of one legal person for
the members of the firm. The omission of the word 'Limited' would not
always be fatal if it was clear for whom it was intended but in the present
case the omission of a date prevented this. If there had never been a firm
described as Elsby Brothers the answer might have been different.

Note—See now *Mitchell v Harris Engineering Co Ltd*, p 559, below and RSC
Ord 20, r 5.

Whittam v W. J. Daniel & Co Ltd
[1962] 1 QB 271, [1961] 3 All ER 796, [1961] 3 WLR 1123, 105 Sol Jo 886,
CA
The plaintiff was injured in an accident at work on 10 September 1957

when in the employment of W. J. Daniel & Co Ltd. On 9 September 1960, she issued a writ against 'W. J. Daniel and Company (a firm)'. On 12 October 1960 (after the limitation period had expired) she amended the description of the defendants in the writ by Master's fiat to 'W. J. Daniel & Co Ltd'. After service of the writ the defendants sought to have it set aside on the ground that nobody was sued within the period of limitation and that they were made defendants for the first time on 12 October 1960. The defendants were incorporated on 6 October 1931 taking over a business run by Walter James Daniel which ceased to be carried on with effect from 10 November 1931.

HELD: It was a case of mere misnomer and the amendment was properly allowed. The defendants could be in no doubt from the original description of the defendants in the writ that it was intended for them. The word 'Limited' was not an essential part of the name of a company and its omission did not mean that nobody was sued when the writ was issued.

Evans Constructions Co Ltd v Charrington & Co Ltd
[1983] QB 810, [1983] 1 All ER 310, [1983] 2 WLR 117, 126 Sol Jo 658, 264 Estates Gazette 347, CA

The defendants having served notice on the plaintiffs under the Landlord and Tenant Act 1954 'as agents for Bass Holdings Ltd' to terminate the plaintiffs' tenancy the plaintiffs' solicitors issued an originating application against the defendants in the county court for grant of a new lease. They did so mistakenly believing the defendants to be the landlords. The defendants applied to the court to strike out the application on the ground that they were not the plaintiffs' landlords. The plaintiffs sought to have Bass Holdings joined as defendants.

HELD, in the Court of Appeal: Bass Holdings should be substituted as defendants under Ord 20, r 5(3) and the plaintiffs have 14 days to serve them, the time under the Act having expired. It was important to bear in mind the distinction between suing A in the mistaken belief that he is the party responsible for the matters complained of and seeking to sue B but mistakenly naming him as A. Order 20, r 5(3) is designed to correct the latter and not the former category of mistake. But the party applying must also satisfy the court that the mistake was genuine, the error in the name not misleading and that it is just to allow the correction. In the present case all the criteria were met.

Wrong defendant sued

Rodriguez v Parker
[1967] 1 QB 116, [1966] 2 All ER 349, [1966] 3 WLR 546 (Nield J)

On 30 October 1961, the plaintiff was injured when knocked down by a van owned by R. J. Parker and driven by his son R. S. Parker. On 20 April 1962, solicitors on behalf of the plaintiff wrote R. S. Parker claiming damages for 'your negligent driving'. An insurance company replied acknowledging the letter 'addressed to our insured', their own letter being headed 'R. J. Parker'. Negotiations for settlement were eventually broken off and the solicitors ceased to act. On 28 August 1963, the plaintiff's trade union on his behalf wrote the insurers a letter headed 'Your insured —

R. S. Parker' renewing the claim and in November 1963, fresh solicitors were instructed by or on behalf of the plaintiff. These solicitors obtained an offer which the plaintiff refused and on 11 June 1964, they issued a writ against 'R. J. Parker (male)': the endorsement claimed damages for the 'negligent driving of the defendant'. On 4 January 1965, they served the writ on R. J. Parker. His insurers instructed solicitors who entered appearance. On 14 June 1965, the statement of claim was served alleging 'negligent driving of the defendant'. The insurers' solicitors served a defence denying that the 'defendant was . . . driving any motor vehicle at the time and place alleged'. The plaintiff's solicitors then realised they had sued the wrong defendant and applied to amend the writ to substitute 'R. S. Parker for 'R. J. Parker' and to extend the validity of the writ.

HELD: They were entitled to the order asked for. RSC Ord 20, r 5 allowed the Court to amend a writ so as to correct the name of a party even if the effect was to substitute a new party where the Court was satisfied that the mistake was genuine and not misleading. It was not necessary to show that it was a case of mere misnomer. The mistake was genuine on the part of the plaintiff's solicitors and was not misleading to the insurers or their solicitors because: (1) the letter before the action of 20 April 1962; (2) the union's letter of 28 August 1963, and (3) the references to the defendant's negligent driving in the writ and statement of claim all made it clear that R. S. Parker was the person intended to be sued. It was just to allow the amendment as the claim was first made within six months of the accident and the intended defendant had ample time and opportunity to prepare his case. The amendment being allowed it followed that the validity of the writ should be extended.

Mitchell v Harris Engineering Co Ltd
[1967] 2 QB 703, [1967] 2 All ER 682, [1967] 3 WLR 447, 111 Sol Jo 355, CA

The plaintiff claimed damages from his employers, Harris Engineering Co Ltd, for injury sustained at their works at Tunbridge Wells. The company was registered in Northern Ireland. The plaintiff's solicitors, unaware of this, issued the writ against an associated company Harris Engineering Co (Leeds) Ltd which was registered in England and which they assumed was the correct defendant. The writ was not served until after the limitation period had expired. When the company secretary (who was secretary of both companies) received the writ he sent it to the employers' insurers who told the plaintiff's solicitors they had sued the wrong company. The plaintiff applied to amend writ by substituting Harris Engineering Co Ltd for Harris Engineering Co (Leeds) Ltd.

HELD, ON APPEAL: They could have leave to do so. Order 20, r 5 was not ultra vires the rules committe merely because it might have the effect of depriving a defendant of the benefit of a statue of limitations. Whenever a writ has been issued within the permitted time but is found to be defective the defendant has no 'right' to have it remain so. The Court can permit the defect to be cured by amendment. The circumstances in which a litigant may amend existing proceedings, for example by adding or substituting defendants, are essentially a matter of practice or procedure. Whether it is proper to allow the amendment is a matter for the discretion of the Court within the language of the rule. There was a genuine mistake on the part of the plaintiff's solicitors: it did not mislead the defendants since the secretary could tell from the writ that the accident occurred at the Irish company's works.

Per Lord Denning MR: Rule 5(3) has removed the injustice caused by the decision in *Davies v Elsby Bros Ltd*. Rule 5(4) has removed the injustice caused by *Hilton v Sutton Steam Laundry*. Rule 5(5) has removed the injustice caused by such cases as *Marshall v London Passenger Transport Board*.

Wrong date

Hay v London Brick Co Ltd

[1981] LS Gaz R 974, Times, 12 May, CA

The plaintiff sustained injury in an accident at work. He began proceedings giving 18 November 1974 as the date of the accident. In February 1980 the defendants disclosed documents showing that the date of the accident was in fact 3 December 1975. The plaintiff applied to amend the pleadings to substitute 3 December 1975 for 18 November 1974. The judge refused the amendment on the ground that it introduced a new cause of action.

HELD: Order 20, r 5(5) did not permit an amendment made after expiry of the limitation period if the effect would be to add or substitute a new cause of action, unless it arose out of substantially the same facts. The date of the cause of action was of importance on the question whether the action was statute-barred but that was a procedural matter, not one of substance. The date also affected the special damage but that went only on the measure of damages, not the cause of action. A plaintiff could prove his cause of action without being able to prove its precise date. The proposed amendment did not create a new cause of action: the court therefore had a discretion to allow the amendment and should do so. Appeal allowed.

RENEWAL OF WRIT AFTER LIMITATION OPERATIVE

Note—For date of expiry of writ see p 681, below.

Battersby v Anglo-American Oil Co

[1945] 1 KB 23, [1944] 2 All ER 387, 114 LJKB 49, 171 LT 300, 61 TLR 13, 88 Sol Jo 423, CA

A writ claiming damages under the Fatal Accidents Acts was issued within 12 months of the death, but was not served within 12 months of the issue of the writ. The defendants entered a conditional appearance and applied to set aside the writ and service.

HELD: The case of *Holman v George Elliot & Co* [1944] KB 591, [1944] 1 All ER 639, 113 LJKB 459, 170 LT 373, 60 TLR 394, 88 Sol Jo 289, CA should not be followed. Leave to renew should be refused when the effect of granting leave would be to deprive the defendant of his defence under the statute.

E Ltd v C

[1959] 2 All ER 468, [1959] 1 WLR 692, 103 Sol Jo 472 (Roxburgh J)

The court has jurisdiction to renew a writ at its discretion but, following *Battersby's* case, refused to do so where the renewal was needed to avoid the running of time under the Limitation Act. The Court would not allow a writ to be renewed when the effect of so doing would be to deprive a defendant of a statutory defence.

Sheldon v Brown Bayley's Steel Works Ltd and Dawnays Ltd

[1953] 2 QB 393, [1953] 2 All ER 894, [1953] 3 WLR 542, 97 Sol Jo 570, CA

Fatal accident 12 October 1950; writ issued 3 October 1951, against two defendants; neither defendant served within 12 months as required by Ord VIII, r 1 (see note after *The Prins Bernhard*, p 562, below). First defendants entered conditional appearance and applied for and obtained order setting aside service of writ on them. Second defendants entered an unconditional appearance but on hearing of the first defendants' application, took out a similar application and obtained an order from the Master, upheld by the judge on appeal.

HELD, ON APPEAL to the Court of Appeal: Order VIII, r 1, gives power within 12 months to apply to renew the writ; Ord LXX, r 1, provides for cases of non-compliance with rules; Ord LXIV, r 7, gives power to enlarge the time; Ord XII, r 30 (not called to the attention of the judge) provides that a defendant before appearing may take out a summons to set aside the service on him.

The writ did not become a nullity by non-service within the proper time. It was an irregularity which was waived by the unconditional appearance of the second defendants. Appeal allowed.

Note—Order VIII, r 1, is now replaced by RSC Ord 6, r 8, Ord LXX, r 1, by Ord 2, r 1, Ord LXIV, r 7, by Ord 3, r 5 and Ord XII, r 30, by Ord 12, r 8. See note following *The Prins Bernhard*, below.

Duchin v Swanage UDC, Duchin v Dorset County Council

[1954] 2 QB 308, [1954] 2 All ER 817, [1954] 3 WLR 407, 98 Sol Jo 575 (Havers J)

Writ issued against public authority 7 August 1952; affidavit in support of application for renewal ex parte left with master's secretary 5 August 1953; affidavit indorsed by master 'renew for one month' initialled and dated 5 August 1953; plaintiff's solicitor called 6 August 1953, and asked to see the master; master not available but his secretary stated he would be practice master 7 August 1953; solicitor called 7 August but the master was not practice master that day and would not be till 11 August; solicitor called 11 August and master altered indorsement from one to six months; writ sealed with renewal date 11 August, writ served 4 February 1954; conditional appearance 11 February 1954; summons to set aside writ and service issued 17 February 1954; 31 March 1954, cross-application for rectification by dating 11 August for 5 August or extension to 11 August.

HELD: Under Ord VIII, r 1, the writ must be resealed by 6 August and was no longer in force on 11 August; no grounds for exercising discretion under Ord LXIV, r 7; the writ was incapable of renewal on 11 August. *Nazer v Wade* (1861) 1 B & S 728, 31 LJQB 5, 5 LT 604, 8 Jur NS 134 and

Evans v Jones (1862) 2 B & S 45 31 LJQB 61, 5 LT 673, 8 Jur NS 641, sub nom A applied.

Note—For present numbering of rules see note to preceding case.

The Prins Bernhard
[1964] P 117, [1963] 3 All ER 735, [1963] 3 WLR 1043, 107 Sol Jo 812, [1963] 2 Lloyd's Rep 236 (Hewson J)
In an Admiralty action the plaintiffs issued a writ in rem on 1 February 1962, the last day of the limitation period. The defendants' vessel was within the jurisdiction on three occasions within a year of issue but the plaintiffs did not serve the writ as they were in negotiation with the defendants and thought that to serve the writ might prejudice the negotiations. On 31 January 1963, the plaintiffs applied to the Court and obtained an extension of the writ for six months. It was again renewed on 29 July 1963, and service effected on 9 September 1963. The defendants entered a conditional appearance and applied to set aside the writ and all subsequent proceedings for irregularity.
HELD: The fact that service of the writ might prejudice the negotiations was a 'good reason' within Ord VIII, r 1, for extending the writ even though this would deprive the defendants of the benefit of the time bar. *Battersby's* case was different: in that case the writ had already expired and the defence of limitation had accrued when application was made to the Court for renewal.

Note—But see *Easy v Universal Anchorage*, p 565, below, in which the above case was 'explained' by the Court of Appeal.
    Order VIII, r 1 of the old rules is replaced in the 1965 rules by Ord 6, r 8. The old rule allowed the court to renew only 'if satisfied that reasonable efforts have been made to serve such defendant or for other good reasons'. These words are omitted from the new rule. Despite this it has been held that the Court's discretion to renew a writ has not been widened: see next case and those following.

Heaven v Road and Rly Wagons Ltd
[1965] 2 QB 355, [1965] 2 All ER 409, [1965] 2 WLR 1249, 109 Sol Jo 335 (Megaw J)
In a personal injury claim the cause of action arose on 31 March 1961. A writ was issued on 20 December 1963, but not served. Negotiations were in progress between the parties but had broken down by 15 September 1964. The writ expired on 19 December 1964 but on an ex parte application on 26 January 1965, the master renewed it for three months. It was served on 29 January 1965: the defendants applied for the writ to be set aside and service declared invalid.
HELD: It was not correct that the new Ord 6, r 8 (in effect from January 1964) had widened the discretion of the Court to renew a writ after the period allowed for service had expired. The decisions in *Battersby v Anglo-American Oil Co Ltd* and *Sheldon v Brown Bayley's Steel Works Ltd* (above) are still binding on the court. The rule is that leave will not be given to extend the validity of a writ when application is made retrospectively after the period of 12 months prescribed by the rules has expired if the effect of so doing would be to deprive the defendant of a defence which he would have

had under the relevant statute of limitation had leave to extend not been given and the plaintiff had to serve a fresh writ. To justify the exercise of the discretion there must be exceptional circumstances, e g agreement between the parties to defer service or where the defendant had evaded service. A technical slip by the plaintiff's solicitors is not sufficient. The writ here must be set aside.

Note—In *Brickfield Properties v Newton* [1971] 3 All ER 328, [1971] 1 WLR 862, 115 Sol Jo 307, Sachs LJ said that if it was intended to convey in *Heaven's* case that the courts were not in process of liberalising, insofar as they have a discretion, their view as to what constituted the justice of the case as between the parties he would not agree. Since *Pontin v Wood* (p 555, above) there had been a progressive development to a broader approach which had been encouraged by the amendments of the rules embodied in RSC Ord 20, r 5.

Bernstein v Jackson
[1982] 2 All ER 806, [1982] 1 WLR 1082, 126 Sol Jo 330, CA
In an action based on an agreement to pay £3,000 the writ was issued on 7 December 1977. The writ expired on the 6 December 1978 but the plaintiff did not apply to renew it. In January 1979 without renewing the writ the district registrar made an order for substituted service of the writ by notice served at the address of the defendant's solicitor, and this was done. In May 1981 the plaintiff signed judgment in default of acknowledgement of service. On 13 July 1981 the defendant applied to set aside service and the judgment. The judge held that the writ was not valid for service because not renewed but that he had jurisdiction to cure the irregularity under Ord 2, r 1 and gave liberty to the defendant to defend the action provided she filed acknowledgment of service within 14 days.
HELD, ON APPEAL: This was not right. The writ though not a nullity, was not valid for service after 6 December 1978. The judge could not extend the writ under Ord 6, r 8 (because it had already expired) and the irregularity could not be cured in the discretion of the judge under Ord 2, r 1. Ord 6, r 8 provides a compendious code for extension and renewal of writs. Even if the judge had jurisdiction to exercise his discretion under Ord 2, r 1 he should not have done so to cure such a fundamental defect. Writ and service set aside.

Note—In *Leal v Dunlop Bio-Process International Ltd* [1984] 2 All ER 207, [1984] 1 WLR 874, 128 Sol Jo 471, CA the view was expressed that a failure to get the leave of the court to serve a writ out of the jurisdiction as required by RSC Ord 11, r 1 was an 'irregularity' which could be cured within Ord 2, r 1 though in the circumstances of that case it would be an improper exercise of the court's jurisdiction to do so.

Chappell v Cooper
[1980] 2 All ER 463, [1980] 1 WLR 958, 124 Sol Jo 544, CA
On an application to extend the validity of a writ which had expired it was argued that since 1975, because of the provisions of s 2D of the Limitation Act 1939, there was no longer valid reason for refusing an extension on the ground that it would deprive the defendant of the benefit of a limitation period which had accrued, since the plaintiff can apply to have the limitation period disapplied.

HELD: Not so. Had *Firman v Ellis* (p 545, above) remained good law it might have been otherwise, but having regard to the restrictive interpretation of the relevant provisions of the 1975 Act by the House of Lords in *Walkley v Precision Forgings* (p 545, above) the principles which have long existed upon which extensions of time to serve a writ which had not been timeously served are determined remain unaffected.

Blackman v Eke
[1982] LS Gaz R 142, CA
The plaintiff was injured on 21 April 1977 by the defendant's negligent driving. A writ was issued by the plaintiff's solicitors on 26 October 1979 and sent with a copy for acceptance of service to the defendant's solicitors on 6 October 1980. The original writ was not returned nor appearance entered. The plaintiff's solicitors issued a summons for an interim payment on 25 November 1980 and were then told by the defendant's solicitors that they had never received the writ and letter of 6 October. The summons was treated as an application for extension of time for service of the writ under Ord 6, r 8(2). The judge held that he was bound by *Chappell v Cooper* (p 563, above) not to do so.
HELD, ON APPEAL: The long-established rule of practice that the court would not exercise its discretion to renew the validity of a writ for service when its exercise would defeat the vested rights of the defendant to plead a statute of limitations had not been undermined by s 2D of the Limitation Act 1939, added by the 1975 Act. The Court's rejection of that submission in *Chappell v Cooper* (p 563, above) was not obiter: it was a ground of the decision of Roskill LJ, accepted by the other two members of the court. Appeal dismissed.

Note—The plaintiff's solicitors issued a second writ on 20 February 1981 and applied for leave to proceed with that action under s 2D. The application was rejected on the authority of *Walkley v Precision Forgings* (p 545, above). Section 2D is now replaced by the Limitation Act 1980, s 33.

Street v Bebber
(1965) Times, 6 July, CA
Accident January 1961. Negotiations with insurers, the writ issued December 1963. Writ not served and negotiations continued until, in September 1964 (when writ still operative) plaintiff's solicitors were told that insurers would nominate solicitors to accept service; but writ was still not served until beginning of 1965. The master on an ex parte application granted an extension of time for six months to serve the writ but the judge on appeal set aside the writ and the order granting extension.
HELD: On application to Court of Appeal for leave to appeal out of time against the judge's order, this was not a case in which it would be right to give leave to appeal and extend time. The time under the Limitation Act had passed and to grant relief and encourage the plaintiff to appeal would be to deprive the defendant of his defence under the Act. If the plaintiff consulted other solicitors he had a strong prima facie case for recovering damages against his present solicitors.

Easy v Universal Anchorage Co Ltd
[1974] 2 All ER 1105, [1974] 1 WLR 899, 118 Sol Jo 464, CA
Accident 18 August 1969. Negotiations for settlement of claim started but
became protracted by difficulty in getting instructions from the plaintiff.
Writ issued 17 August 1972. In July 1973 defendants' insurers offered
£3,000. In September 1973, the writ not having been served and the plaintiff having refused the offer, the plaintiff's solicitors applied for renewal.
HELD: No renewal could be permitted. The fact that negotiations were in
progress for a settlement at the time when the writ was about to expire was
not a sufficient reason for not serving the writ.

The World Harmony
[1967] P 341, [1965] 2 All ER 139, [1965] 2 WLR 1275, [1965] 1 Lloyd's
Rep 244 (Hewson J)
Collision at sea, 14 December 1960, writ issued 13 December 1962, almost
the limit of time allowed by the Maritime Conventions Act 1911, renewed
on application 9 December 1963, served May 1964.
HELD: The writ should not have been renewed. The fact that the plaintiff
was abroad was not very material in these days of rapid and easy communication. It was not the duty of the Court to effect a cure where plaintiffs had
been dilatory.

Excelby v Philpott and Philpott
[1969] 2 Lloyd's Rep 234, CA
The plaintiff was seriously injured in a road accident on 21 May 1964.
Only the question of damages was in issue. The plaintiff's solicitors delayed
proceeding with the action because of the difficulty in formulating the
claim. The defendants' insurers wished to negotiate a proper settlement. A
writ was issued in time but the defendants had meanwhile gone to Australia
and the plaintiff's solicitors could not trace them. They obtained an
extension of the writ on 3 August 1968. In August they discovered the
defendants had returned to England. The writ was then served. The defendants applied to set aside the order extending the time for service.
HELD: It was a case in which the plaintiff should have an extension of time.
There was a clear distinction on the facts from *Baker v Bowketts Cakes*
(below).
   Per Winn LJ: In many cases of personal injury litigation there are very
good reasons, as in many others there are no good reasons, for issuing the
writ towards the end of the three years of the Statute of Limitations and
keeping it in cold storage for nearly as long as the end of the year of its
validity before applying to renew. In every case one must look at the
circumstances and events and the conduct of the parties.

Note—The difficulty can be avoided by applying for substituted service of the writ
on the insurers. See the *Supreme Court Practice 1985*, note to Ord 65, r 4 (p 1008
65/4/6). But note *Clarke v Vedel*, p 781, below.

Siksnys v Hanley
(1982) Times, 26 May, CA

The plaintiff was badly injured in a road accident by the negligent driving of the defendant on 30 April 1977. His solicitor issued a writ on 25 January 1980. Despite efforts by the plaintiff and his solicitors the defendant could not be found and his whereabouts were unknown. In February 1981 the writ having expired unserved the plaintiff applied to the Court for an extension and an order for substituted service at the address of the defendant's insurers. The validity of the writ was extended under Ord 6, r 8 on the ground that there were exceptional circumstances. On appeal the defendant argued that exceptional circumstances did not exist: the plaintiff should have applied for an order for substituted service at the insurer's address (as Lord Diplock had recommended in *Gurtner v Circuit* (p 781, below)) before the writ had expired.

HELD: The order should stand. The way in which the defendant had kept out of the way did make the case one of exceptional circumstances.

Hay-Kellie v Michaelides
(1969) 113 Sol Jo 902, CA

Accident 4 June 1964 causing plaintiff serious injuries. Writ issued 1 November 1965, served on second defendant 2 February 1966. Not served on first defendant who was said to have gone to Greece in October 1964. Next friend appointed 8 May 1969, the plaintiff's mental state being such that he was unable to conduct his own affairs. An application was made for leave to renew the writ as against the first defendant.

HELD: It was a doubtful point whether under Ord 6, r 8(2) once the writ had been served on one defendant it might be good. In all the circumstances including the fact that both defendants were covered by the same insurance policy, leave should be given to renew the writ for 12 months and to serve it out of the jurisdiction.

Note—See *Jones v Jones*, p 682, below.

Baker v Bowketts Cakes Ltd
[1966] 2 All ER 290, [1966] 1 WLR 861, 110 Sol Jo 230, CA

The plaintiff contracted dermatitis in the defendants' employment, which he left in January 1962. In April 1962 he consulted solicitors, who made a claim for damages. In October 1962 the employers' insurers denied liability. The plaintiff's solicitors applied for a legal aid certificate for him: this was refused in April 1963 but an appeal was allowed and a certificate limited to taking counsel's opinion granted in January 1964. In May 1964 the certificate was extended to enable a writ to be issued and this was done on 28 May 1964. In June 1965, the certificate was further extended to take the action through the pleadings but meanwhile the plaintiff's solicitors applied on 25 May 1965 to the District Registrar to extend the validity of the writ. He adjourned the application and the solicitors then made an effort to serve the writ before it expired by posting a copy to an address given them by a local director of the defendants: the address was incorrect and the writ was not served. In August 1965, on an ex parte application the judge extended the writ and granted an extension for four months. It was served in September 1965, and the defendants applied to set it aside. The judge reversed his previous decision and held it was not right to extend the writ.

HELD, ON APPEAL: (1) Having regard to the Legal Aid and Advice Act 1949, s 1(7)(b) the difficulty and delay in getting legal aid was irrelevant; (2) a plaintiff ought not to get an extension except for good cause. During the whole of the year from May 1964 to May 1965 the plaintiff's solicitors could and should have got on with the case and there was no sufficient reason why they had not. The fact that at the last minute the local director of the defendants gave a wrong address was not a sufficient reason for extending the writ. Having left it as late as that it behoved the plaintiff's solicitors to make absolutely sure they got it properly served. Appeal dismissed.

The 'Angelina the Great'
[1983] 1 Lloyd's Rep 591, CA
Per Ackner LJ: If an application (for extension of time) is not made until time for service of the writ has already expired then the applicant is in a more serious situation than if he applied to the Court before time has expired, because in the latter situation there must always be some prospect, if the judge refuses to grant him an extension, of still having a prospect of complying with the order.

Stevens v Services Window and General Cleaning Co Ltd
[1967] 1 QB 359, [1967] 1 All ER 984, [1967] 2 WLR 939, 111 Sol Jo 97 (Chapman J)
Accident 9 November 1961. Writ issued 5 November 1964 but not served: 26 October 1965, writ renewed by District Registrar on plaintiff's ex parte application. Writ served 7 July 1966. The defendants' solicitors entered conditional appearance and applied to have the service set aside.

HELD: The fact that the District Registrar had renewed the writ before it expired did not prevent the Court from considering, after the date when the writ would have expired, whether good and sufficient reason had been shown for renewing it. The delays in completing enquiries, corresponding with the legal aid committee and getting counsel's opinion were no reason for not serving the writ before it expired. Renewal should not have been allowed by the District Registrar and service must be set aside.

Osborne v Distillers Co Ltd
(1967) 112 Sol Jo 50, 117 NLJ 1242
In 1961 Mrs Osborne, who was expecting a child, took on prescription a drug containing thalidomide. On 6 July 1962, the child was born without hands. A writ was issued on 28 May 1965, against the manufacturers of the drug. It was not served within 12 months; instead the plaintiff's solicitor applied to the District Registrar for renewal of the writ giving as his reason that there was a test action pending. The date when the cause of action arose was not shown. The District Registrar renewed the writ for 12 months. It was served on 2 May 1967.

HELD: On the application of the defendants, service must be set aside.

Battersby v Anglo-American Oil Co (p 560, above) decided that it was not ordinarily a good cause for renewing a writ that the plaintiff wished to hold up proceedings while some other case was tried. The case came within the general principle that a writ was not to be renewed so as to deprive the defendants of the benefit of the statute [of limitations], save for good reason.

Failure to perfect amendment in time

Braniff v Holland Hannen and Cubitts

[1969] 3 All ER 959, [1969] 1 WLR 1533, 113 Sol Jo 836, CA

In an action for damages for personal injuries the accident occurred on 24 October 1965 and the writ was issued against the first defendants on 25 October 1966. On 24 July 1968, the plaintiff, wishing to join the second defendants, obtained an order for amendment of the writ and statement of claim. By an oversight he failed to amend and reseal the writ within 14 days as required by Ord 15, r 8(4). On 23 October 1968 (after expiry of the limitation period), he obtained an extension of time for making the amendment. When the writ was served the second defendants applied to set aside the writ and service and obtained an order from the judge in chambers to that effect.

HELD, ON APPEAL: The judge rightly exercised his discretion in so ordering. By Ord 15, r 8(4) the added defendant is not to be a party to the action until the amendment is duly completed in accordance with the rule. Thus there was no writ available against the second defendant at all until the amendment was made. To permit the plaintiff an extension of time beyond the expiry of the limitation period deprived the added party of a defence under the Limitation Acts and put the case in the category of those where a plaintiff seeks to renew an expired writ, as in *Heaven v Road and Rly Wagons Ltd* (p 562, above). The fact that under Ord 20, r 5 certain amendments were permitted although the statutory period had run did not mean that in general there had been any relaxation in the principle formerly applying in *Weldon v Neal* (1887) 19 QBD 394.

Renewal by master unasked

Bugden v Ministry of Defence

[1972] 1 All ER 1, [1972] 1 WLR 27, 115 Sol Jo 811, CA

The plaintiffs, passengers injured in a motor accident, sued for damages. They were bound to succeed against one or other of the defendants. Negotiations took a long time. A writ was issued on 23 September 1969, just within the limitation period. On 7 September 1970, they applied to the master for issue of a concurrent writ so that it could be served on the third defendant in Scotland. The master made the order and added, without being asked, 'Liberty to renew for three months'. The plaintiff's solicitors accepted the renewal and did not serve the writ until December 1970. The third defendant then applied to have the renewal set aside.

HELD: The renewal of the writ was valid. Although no application had been made to the master for renewal as required by Ord 6, r 8(2) there were in existence at the time of the master's order good and sufficient grounds for renewing the writ — there was no issue on liability, there was a difficult medical position and negotiations were proceeding — plus the fact that only 12 days remained at the time in which to serve it in Scotland. The plaintiffs' solicitors would have been acting reasonably if they had applied for the extension which was in fact given. The order should stand.

Waiver of defence limitations

Lubovsky v Snelling
[1944] KB 44, [1943] 2 All ER 577, 113 LJKB 14, 170 LT 2, 60 TLR 52, CA
A defence that the action is statute-barred can be waived by agreement or conduct.

In a claim under the Fatal Accidents Acts, the defendants' insurers agreed with the claimant's solicitors before the limitation period expired (1) that they had no defence, and that the negotiations should proceed 'on the basis of admission of liability', but (2) that 'a writ would have to be issued in any event because whether they agreed about the quantum of damages or not, the court would have to approve and apportion it'. This amounted to a contract not to plead the Fatal Accidents Act 1846, s 3.

Appeal from Tucker J (reported 75 Ll L Rep 165) allowed.

Note—The practical result of this decision seems to be that an insurer should never admit liability as distinct from admitting negligence. It was cited and distinguished in the following case, where it was pointed out that in *Lubovsky's* case it was an essential part of the bargain made between the parties that liability for the cause of action was definitely accepted and that the defendants were thereafter precluded from putting forward any defence whatever which would impeach that liability and was a contract not to plead the statute of limitations. They were debarred from raising the point.

The 'Sauria' and the 'Trent'
[1957] 1 Lloyd's Rep 396, CA
The plaintiff's motor vessel was lying moored at a wharf when it was struck and damaged by a barge which was being towed by a tug. Correspondence took place between solicitors of the parties and eventually the solicitors for defendants admitted liability. Attempts were then made to arrange an arbitration to fix the amount of damages, but agreement was not reached, and in January 1957, the plaintiffs began an action. The collision took place on 16 June 1953; the admission of liability was by letter dated 19 January 1955. The defendants took a preliminary objection that the claim was barred by the Maritime Conventions Act 1911, s 8 which required proceedings within two years from the date of damage. Judge Block in the City of London Court held that the action was barred. The plaintiff submitted the admission was qualified and not absolute; while the matter was still under discussion the admission was withdrawn. The plaintiffs appealed.
HELD: There was an admission of liability but there was no undertaking to waive the right of defendants to rely on the section. The case of *Lubovsky v Snelling* was distinguishable on its facts. There was no ground for exercising

the discretion given to the Court by the proviso to the section. Appeal
dismissed.

By entering appearance

Re Chittenden, Chittenden v Doe
[1970] 3 All ER 562, [1970] 1 WLR 1618, 114 Sol Jo 954 (Ungoed-
Thomas J)
The plaintiff issued an originating summons within the time allowed by the
Inheritance (Family Provision) Act 1938 but at the suggestion of the
executors, who were the defendants, did not serve it while negotiations
were pending. More than 12 months later the plaintiff obtained an order ex
parte extending the time for service of the summons. It was then served and
the defendants entered unconditional appearance. More than a year later
the defendants applied to set aside the order and service.
HELD: (1) It would be unjust to refuse to exercise discretion in the plaintiff's favour on the ground that to do so would deprive the defendant of the
benefit of a statute of limitation where the defendant is himself a party to
the withholding of service of the originating process whether by asking or
agreeing to it or otherwise; (2) the effect of Ord 2, r 2(1) is that entry of
unconditional appearance waives any irregularity in the proceedings.
Sheldon's case (above) followed. Application dismissed.

Note—The procedure of entering conditional appearance before applying to set
aside a writ has been replaced by the procedure in RSC Ord 12, rr 7 and 8 — filing
acknowledgment of service followed by an application to the court issued within
the time limited for defence.

By conduct of negotiations

The Owenbawn
[1973] 1 Lloyd's Rep 56 (Brandon J)
Collision between two vessels 28 August 1969. Negotiations for settlement
of claims begun between solicitors 10 September 1970 still continuing on 2
July 1971 when plaintiffs' solicitors issued writ and notified defendants'
solicitors it was 'to protect the two year time limit which would otherwise
expire in August'. Further discussions took place at long intervals. On 3
August 1972 the writ having expired and the latest offer from the defendants being still outstanding, the plaintiffs' solicitors applied ex parte for,
and were granted, a renewal to 27 August 1972. The defendants applied for
renewal to be set aside.
HELD: On the facts, there was an agreement that service of the plaintiffs'
writ should be deferred so long as negotiations were continuing and the writ
was rightly renewed. *Re Chittenden* (above) applied.

Hare v Personal Representatives of Malik
(1980) 124 Sol Jo 328, CA
The plaintiff was injured in July 1976 as a passenger in a car accident in
which the driver was killed. His solicitors notified the deceased's insurers of
the intended claim in July 1976. The parties negotiated. In September

1978 the plaintiff's solicitors issued a writ naming the defendants as 'the personal representatives of the estate' of the deceased. The insurers nominated solicitors who continued to negotiate. There was delay whilst the insurers' solicitors tried to find personal representatives. When in September 1979 the plaintiff's solicitors made application to proceed under Ord 15, r 6A it was pointed out that the writ had expired. An application to renew was refused by the judge on the ground that there was no exceptional circumstances.

HELD, allowing an appeal: There were exceptional circumstances in that negotiations had continued on the basis that both parties agreed that the case should proceed and neither should take technical points against the other. The fact that the plaintiff's solicitors were at fault did not in itself mean that the situation was not exceptional.

CHAPTER 15
Evidence

1 ADMISSIBILITY: HEARSAY EVIDENCE

Note—Rules of the Supreme Court, Ord 38, r 1 reads:

'Subject to the provisions of these rules and of the Civil Evidence Act 1968 and the Civil Evidence Act 1972, and any other enactment relating to evidence, any fact required to be proved at the trial of any action begun by writ by the evidence of witnesses shall be proved by the examination of the witnesses orally and in open court.'

Greenaway v Homelea Fittings (London) Ltd
[1985] 1 WLR 234, 129 Sol Jo 49, QBD
The plaintiff was injured when unloading one of the defendants' vans. He claimed damages and applied for an order that certain statements of the van driver should be admissible in evidence at the trial without calling the driver as a witness. The Master made an order under RSC Ord 38, r 9(2). HELD, ON APPEAL: The order should not have been made. The Master had reasoned that if the driver had been joined as a defendant his statement would have been admissible. But in that event it would have been admissible only against himself and not against the other defendant. In spite of the Civil Evidence Act 1968 the best evidence rule should apply unless there were compelling reasons why not. There was no reason why the driver should not be called.

Note—The Civil Evidence Act 1968 provides for the admissibility of hearsay evidence (whether oral or written) in civil proceedings. It is important in motor claims cases in providing the means by which evidence from the following sources can be conveniently brought before the court whether or not the person making the statement is called as a witness:

1 statements made by parties or witnesses to police officers and recorded in the police report;

2 evidence given orally in proceedings in the magistrates' courts;

3 evidence given at an inquest and recorded by the coroner;

4 statements of fact contained in hospital notes and records.

The machinery for adducing hearsay evidence in the High Court is contained in RSC Ord 38, rr 20 to 32, made in pursuance of s 8 of the Act.

The Civil Evidence Act 1972 makes hearsay statements of opinion admissible in evidence in civil proceedings to substantially the same extent as are hearsay statements of fact under the 1968 Act.

Nicholls v Williams

(1983) Times, 21 May (Mann J)

RSC Ord 25, r 8(1)(d) (which provides that ' . . . the contents of any police accident report book shall be receivable in evidence at the trial . . .') does not make hearsay statements recorded in a police officer's notebook admissible in evidence unless the rules of court made under the Civil Evidence Act 1968 and contained in RSC Ord 38 are complied with. It could not have been intended that Ord 25, r 8(1)(d) should afford an exception to the Ord 38 rules.

CIVIL EVIDENCE ACT 1968

1 Hearsay evidence to be admissible only by virtue of this Act and other statutory provisions, or by agreement (1) In any civil proceedings a statement other than one made by a person while giving oral evidence in those proceedings shall be admissible as evidence of any fact stated therein to the extent that it is so admissible by virtue of any provision of this Part of this Act or by virtue of any other statutory provision or by agreement of the parties, but not otherwise.

(2) In this section 'statutory provision' means any provision contained in, or in an instrument made under, this or any other Act, including any Act passed after this Act.

2 Admissibility of out-of-court statements as evidence of facts stated (1) In any civil proceedings a statement made, whether orally or in a document or otherwise, by any person, whether called as a witness in those proceedings or not, shall subject to this section and to rules of court, be admissible as evidence of any fact stated therein of which direct oral evidence by him would be admissible.

(2) Where in any civil proceedings a party desiring to give a statement in evidence by virtue of this section has called or intends to call as a witness in the proceedings the person by whom the statement was made, the statement —

(a) shall not be given in evidence by virtue of this section on behalf of that party without the leave of the court; and

(b) without prejudice to paragraph (a) above, shall not be given in evidence by virtue of this section on behalf of that party before the conclusion of the examination-in-chief of the person by whom it was made, except —

(i) where before that person is called the court allows evidence of the making of the statement to be given on behalf of that party by some other person; or

(ii) in so far as the court allows the person by whom the statement was made to narrate it in the course of his examination-in-chief on the ground that to prevent him from doing so would adversely affect the intelligibility of his evidence.

(3) Where in any civil proceedings a statement which was made otherwise than in a document is admissible by virtue of this section, no evidence other than direct oral evidence by the person who made the statement or any person who heard or otherwise perceived it being made shall be admissible for the purpose of proving it:

Provided that if the statement in question was made by a person while giving oral evidence in some other legal proceedings (whether civil or criminal), it may be proved in any manner authorised by the court.

Section 3 provides for a witness's previous statement, if proved, to be evidence of any facts stated therein of which direct oral evidence by him would be admissible.

4 Admissibility of certain records as evidence of facts stated (1) Without prejudice to s 5 of this Act, in any civil proceedings a statement contained in a document shall, subject to this section and to rules of court, be admissible as evidence of any fact stated therein of which direct oral evidence would be admissible, if the document is, or forms part of, a record compiled by a person acting under a duty from information which was supplied by a person (whether acting under a duty or not) who had, or may reasonable be supposed to have had, personal knowledge of the matters dealt with in that information and which, if not supplied by that person to the compiler of the record directly, was supplied by him to the compiler of the record indirectly through one or more intermediaries each acting under a duty.

(2) Where in any civil proceedings a party desiring to give a statement in evidence by virtue of this section has called or intends to call as a witness in the proceedings the person who originally supplied the information from which the record containing the statement was compiled, the statement —

(a) shall not be given in evidence by virtue of this section on behalf of that party without the leave of the court; and

(b) without prejudice to paragraph (a) above, shall not without the leave of the court be given in evidence by virtue of this section on behalf of that party before the conclusion of the examination-in-chief of the person who originally supplied the said information.

(3) Any reference in this section to a person acting under a duty includes a reference to a person acting in the course of any trade, business, profession or other occupation in which he is engaged or employed or for the purposes of any paid or unpaid office held by him.

Section 5 deals with statements produced by computers.

6 Provisions supplementary to ss 2 to 5 (1) Where in any civil proceedings a statement contained in a document is proposed to be given in evidence by virtue of s 2, 4 or 5 of this Act it may, subject to any rules of court, be proved by the production of that document or (whether or not that document is still in existence) by the production of a copy of that document, or of the material part thereof, authenticated in such manner as the court may approve.

(2) For the purpose of deciding whether or not a statement is admissible in evidence by virtue of s 2, 4 or 5 of this Act, the court may draw any reasonable inference from the circumstances in which the statement was made or otherwise came into being or from any other circumstances, including, in the case of a statement contained in a document, the form and contents of that document.

(3) In estimating the weight, if any, to be attached to a statement admissible in

evidence by virtue of s 2, 3, 4 or 5 of this Act regard shall be had to all the circumstances from which any inference can reasonably be drawn as to the accuracy or otherwise of the statement and, in particular —

(a) in the case of a statement falling within s 2(1) or 3(1) or (2) of this Act, to the question whether or not the statement was made contemporaneously with the occurrence or existence of facts stated, and to the question whether or not the maker of the statement had any incentive to conceal or misrepresent the facts;

(b) in the case of a statement falling within s 4(1) of this Act, to the question whether or not the person who originally supplied the information from which the record containing the statement was compiled did so contemporaneously with the occurrence or existence of the facts dealt with in that information, and to the question whether or not that person, or any person concerned with compiling or keeping the record containing the statement, had any incentive to conceal or misrepresent the facts:

7 (1) Subject to rules of court, where in any civil proceedings a statement made by a person who is not called as a witness in those proceedings is given in evidence by virtue of s 2 of this Act —

(a) any evidence which, if that person had been so called, would be admissible for the purpose of destroying or supporting his credibility as a witness shall be admissible for that purpose in those proceedings; and

(b) evidence tending to prove that, whether before or after he made that statement that person made (whether orally or in a document or otherwise) another statement inconsistent therewith shall be admissible for the purpose of showing that that person has contradicted himself:

Provided that nothing in this subsection shall enable evidence to be given of any matter of which, if the person in question had been called as a witness and had denied that matter in cross-examination, evidence could not have been adduced by the cross-examining party.

Notice of intention to adduce hearsay evidence

Note—Order 38, r 21 requires any party who wishes to adduce hearsay evidence at the trial to serve notice of his intention to do so on every other party. A party who is served with notice under r 21 may, if he wishes, serve a counter-notice requiring a person mentioned in the notice to be called as a witness. The object is to avoid a party being taken by surprise at the trial. The following cases refer to this procedure.

Ford v Lewis
[1971] 2 All ER 983, [1971] 1 WLR 623, 115 Sol Jo 145, CA
A plaintiff, aged five, was struck and injured by the defendant's vehicle when crossing the road with her parents. At the trial, ten years later, the defendant through mental illness was not available to give evidence. His counsel sought to put in evidence under s 2 of the Civil Evidence Act 1968 a written statement made by the defendant shortly after the accident of which no notice had been served on the plaintiff as required by Ord 38, r 21. The judge, purporting to exercise his discretion under s 8(3)(a) of that Act and Ord 38, r 29, admitted the statement in evidence and found the defendant not liable. At the hearing of the plaintiff's appeal counsel for the defendant said he himself had advised against disclosing the statement before the trial because he thought the plaintiff's parents might in some way adjust or trim

their evidence so as to meet and destroy it if they knew of the statement in advance.

HELD: The judge had been left ignorant of the vital fact that non-compliance by the defendant with the statutory requirement was due, not to inability, inadvertence or slackness on the part of his advisers, but to a deliberate decision not to comply. There could be no valid exercise of the discretion given to the Court by r 29 where there has been a deliberate withholding from the Court of the reason for non-compliance. Even if the judge had known of the reason he would not be acting judicially if he had exercised his discretion in favour of the defendant and thus enabled him to adopt tactics of surprise which the rules as to notice were designed to prevent. There must be a new trial.

Rasool v West Midlands Transport Executive

[1974] 3 All ER 638 (Finer J)

The defendants, sued for damages for injuries sustained by the plaintiff when knocked down by a bus, sought to put in evidence a written statement from a witness highly prejudicial to the plaintiff's case. The defendants served a notice on the plaintiff under RSC Ord 38, rr 21 and 22(3) asserting that the witness could not be called because 'She has left her former address number 225 Charles Road Small Heath Birmingham and cannot at present be found. It is understood that she is now beyond the seas and is probably resident in Jamaica.' The defendants had made extensive enquiries in the Birmingham area to find the witness and had received information from two people that she had gone to Jamaica but they had made no enquiries in Jamaica to find her. The plaintiff served a counter-notice under r 25(2) and claimed the defendants had not shown reasonable diligence in trying to find the witness.

HELD: (1) Of the five reasons given in the Civil Evidence Act 1968, s 8(2)(b) the defendants' notice really invoked only the assertion that the witness could not be found, but the evidence of their enquiries was sufficient to show a probability that she was in fact beyond the seas; (2) the reason given in s 8(2)(b) was disjunctive: if the maker of the statement is beyond the seas it does not have to be proved also that she cannot by reasonable diligence be found; (3) if the Court is satisfied on any of the five specified reasons it has no residuary discretion to exclude the statement by reference to other circumstances; (4) the defendants' notice was out of order: it should have read simply 'because she is beyond the seas'. Order made accordingly.

Note—Approved in *Piermay Shipping Co SA v Chester* [1978] 1 All ER 1233, [1978] 1 WLR 411, 121 Sol Jo 795, CA. 'I agree in its entirety with the reasoning of the judgment of Finer J': per Megaw LJ.

Documents — s 4

H v Schering Chemicals Ltd

[1983] 1 All ER 849, [1983] 1 WLR 143, 127 Sol Jo 88 (Bingham J)

The plaintiffs wished to put in evidence as records under the Civil Evidence Act 1968, s 4 articles from medical journals, documents summarising research and letters from medical journals for the purpose of showing that the administering of a drug caused certain injuries.

HELD: The documents were not records within the meaning of s 4. The intention of that section is to admit in evidence documents which either give effect to a transaction itself or which contain a contemporaneous register of information supplied by those with direct knowledge of the facts. The documents in the present case were not records nor primary or original sources. They were a digest or analysis of records which must exist or have existed but were not themselves records. Nor was RSC Ord 38, r 3 intended to permit the adducing on an issue crucial to the outcome of an action of material which does not rank as evidence even for the purposes of the Act of 1968.

Note—Applied in *Savings and Investment Bank Ltd v Gasco Investments* [1984] 1 All ER 296, [1984] 1 WLR 271, 128 Sol Jo 115, [1984] BCLC 179

Transcript of evidence

Taylor v Taylor
[1970] 2 All ER 609, [1970] 1 WLR 1148, 114 Sol Jo 415, CA
The shorthand writer's transcript of the evidence given in a criminal trial is admissible in evidence in civil proceedings both under the Civil Evidence Act 1968, s 2(1) and under s 4(1) of that Act. The summing-up of the judge might not be admissible under s 2(1) but would probably be under s 4(1) since it is a record compiled by the shorthand writer in his capacity as such.

---

2 PROOF OF EVIDENCE OF CRIMINAL PROCEEDINGS

Proof of convictions (see when in force the Police and Criminal Evidence Act 1984, s 73)

THE CRIMINAL PROCEDURE ACT 1865

6 Proof of conviction of witness for felony or misdemeanour may be given   A witness may be questioned as to whether he had been convicted of any felony or misdemeanour, and upon being so questioned if he either denies or does not admit the fact, or refuses to answer, it shall be lawful for the cross-examining party to prove such conviction; and a certificate containing the substance and effect only (omitting the formal part) of the indictment and conviction for such offence, purporting to be signed by the clerk of the court or other officer having the custody of the records of the court where the offender was convicted or by the deputy of such clerk or officer (for which certificate a fee of five shillings and no more shall be demanded or taken) shall, upon proof of the identity of the person, be sufficient evidence of the said conviction, without proof of the signature or official character of the person appearing to have signed the same.
(The words following 'prove such conviction' are repealed by the Police and Criminal Evidence Act 1984 as from a date to be announced.)

THE PREVENTION OF CRIMES ACT 1871

18 Evidence of previous conviction   A previous conviction may be proved in any legal proceeding whatever against any person by producing a record or extract of such conviction, and by giving proof of the identity of the person against whom the conviction is sought to be proved with the person appearing in the record or extract of conviction to have been convicted.

A record or extract of a conviction shall in the case of an indictable offence consist of a certificate containing the substance and effect only (omitting the formal part of the indictment and conviction), and purporting to be signed by the clerk of the court or other officer having the custody of the records of the court by which such conviction was made, or purporting to be signed by the deputy of such clerk or officer; and in the case of a summary conviction shall consist of a copy of such conviction purporting to be signed by the justice of the peace having jurisdiction over the offence in respect of which such conviction was made, or to be signed by the proper officer of the court by which such conviction was made or by the clerk or other officer of any court to which such conviction has been returned.

A record or extract of any conviction made in pursuance of this section shall be admissible in evidence without proof of the signature or official character of the person appearing to have signed the same.

A previous conviction in any one part of the United Kingdom may be proved against a prisoner in any other part of the United Kingdom.

The mode of proving a previous conviction authorised by the section shall be in addition to and not in exclusion of any other authorised mode of proving such conviction.

(Save for the sentence beginning 'A previous conviction' the whole section is repealed by the Police and Criminal Evidence Act 1984 from a date yet to be announced.)

A certified copy of a conviction is admissible in civil proceedings against the person convicted or anyone claiming under him. *Re Crippen's Estate* [1911] P 108, [1911–13] All ER Rep 207, 80 LJP 47, 104 LT 224, 27 TLR 258, 55 Sol Jo 273, *Mash v Darley* [1914] 1 KB 1, 83 LKJB 78, 109 LT 873, 78 JP 4.

Convictions: admissibility in civil proceedings

Note—It was formerly the rule (propounded in *Hollington v Hewthorn* [1943] KB 587) that evidence of conviction for a motoring offence was inadmissible in subsequent civil proceedings. The opinion of the criminal court was held to be irrelevant.

The rule was abolished by the Civil Evidence Act 1968, Part 2 (ss 11 to 19). The relevant subsections of s 11 are as follows:

'11 Convictions as evidence in civil proceedings   (1) In any civil proceedings the fact that a person had been convicted of an offence by or before any court in the United Kingdom or by a court-martial there or elsewhere shall (subject to sub-s (3) below) be admissible in evidence for the purpose of proving, where to do so is relevant to any issue in those proceedings, that he committed that offence, whether he was so convicted upon a plea of guilty or otherwise and whether or not he is a party to the civil proceedings; but no conviction other than a subsisting one shall be admissible in evidence by virtue of this section.

(2) In any civil proceedings in which by virtue of this section a person is proved to have been convicted of an offence by or before any court in the United Kingdom or by a court-martial there or elsewhere —

(a) he shall be taken to have committed that offence unless the contrary is proved; and

(b) without prejudice to the reception of any other admissible evidence for the purpose of identifying the facts on which the conviction was based, the contents of any document which is admissible as evidence of the conviction, and the contents of the information, complaint, indictment or charge-sheet on which the person in question was convicted, shall be admissible in evidence for that purpose.

(4) Where in any civil proceedings the contents of any document are admissible in evidence by virtue of sub-s (2) above, a copy of that document, or of the material part thereof, purporting to be certified or otherwise authenticated by or on behalf of the court or authority having custody of that document shall be admissible in evidence and shall be taken to be a true copy of that document or part unless the contrary is shown.'

Wauchope v Mordecai
[1970] 1 All ER 417, [1970] 1 WLR 317, 113 Sol Jo 941, CA

The plaintiff was injured when the defendant opened a car door and knocked him off his bicycle. The defendant admitted to the police that he opened the car door: he was charged with the offence and convicted. The plaintiff's action for damages was tried after the Civil Evidence Act 1968, s 11 had come into force. The judge was told of the conviction but said he would ignore it. He found for the defendant.

HELD, ON APPEAL: Section 11(1) of the 1968 Act made the conviction admissible as evidence to prove, where it was relevant, that the offence was committed. When the judge gave judgment he put his decision on the burden of proof; but under s 11(2) the defendant was to be taken to have committed the offence unless the contrary was proved. It was for the defendant to prove he had not opened the car door. If the judge had had the Act in mind he must have found for the plaintiff. Appeal allowed.

Stupple v Royal Insurance Co Ltd
[1971] 1 QB 50, [1970] 3 All ER 230, [1970] 3 WLR 217, 114 Sol Jo 551, CA

Per Lord Denning MR: The Act does not merely shift the evidential burden, as it is called. It shifts the *legal* burden of proof. . . . Take a running down case where a plaintiff claims damages for negligent driving by the defendant. If the defendant had not been convicted, the legal burden is on the plaintiff throughout. But if the defendant has been convicted of careless driving the legal burden is shifted. It is on the defendant himself. At the end of the day, if the judge is left in doubt the defendant fails because the defendant had not discharged the legal burden which is on him. The burden is, no doubt, the civil burden: he must show, on the balance of probabilities, that he was not negligent.

Conviction must be pleaded

Note—Rule 7A to RSC Ord 18 requires any party who, in pursuance of s 11 or s 12 of the 1968 Act wishes to rely on a previous conviction to include in his pleading the particulars of it specified in the rule. A party who wishes to deny the conviction or its relevance to the proceedings must do so in his pleading.

3 MEDICAL EVIDENCE

National insurance doctor

Ward v Shell Mex and BP Ltd
[1952] 1 KB 280, [1951] 2 All ER 904, [1951] 2 TLR 976, 95 Sol Jo 686
(Streatfeild J)
Plaintiff sought to call as a witness a doctor who was a member of a medical
board under the National Insurance (Industrial Injuries) Act 1946,
s 38(1), to testify as to the plaintiff's condition at the time he examined the
plaintiff as such member and his own conclusions as to the cause of that
condition.
HELD: The evidence was not admissible. He was a member of a statutory
body rather than an individual expert. His position was judicial or quasi-
judicial somewhere between that of an arbitrator and that of a judge. He
was a competent witness to prove matters material to the issue but his
evidence was limited to what took place at the hearing before him, what
issues were raised, but not competent, nor was it relevant for him to
explain, and still less vary, the award he had given. That award must stand
on its own footing. He could not give evidence as to the reasons which
prompted him to the conclusion which resulted in the certificate granted.
The certificate stands on its own footing and cannot be contradicted or
explained or varied by a member of that tribunal. The evidence of this
witness ought not to be received.

Agreeing medical reports

Proctor v Peebles
[1941] 2 All ER 80, 57 TLR 375, 85 Sol Jo 281, CA
Order on Summons for Directions that medical reports be agreed and
dispensing with the attendance of doctors as witnesses should not be made
as a matter of form.

Harrison v Liverpool Corpn
[1943] 2 All ER 449, 60 TLR 14, CA
The summons for directions makes provision for an agreed medical report.
In order that a report may be an agreed medical report for this purpose it
must contain a statement of facts and opinions on which the doctors on both
sides who make it are in agreement, or, where the parties agree to accept a
report from one doctor, the facts and opinions stated and given by that
doctor. Independent reports made by doctors on each side without
agreement as to the facts and opinions appearing in them are not agreed
medical reports within the meaning of the form.

In future orders should refer not to 'medical reports', but to 'a medical
report'. This will not preclude the making of more than one agreed report
where different doctors on each side deal with different aspects of the case
e g where two different kinds of injury are dealt with by different specialists.

Where doctors are instructed with a view to obtaining an agreed medical
report it is desirable that the parties should agree on a statement of any
relevant matters to which it is desired that the attention of the doctors

should be directed. For example, in claims at common law or for breach of statutory duty the doctors should be instructed that general disability as well as disability in respect of earning capacity is a relevant matter (*Practice Direction* [1943] WN 221).

Devine v British Transport Commission
[1954] 1 All ER 1025, [1954] 1 WLR 686, 98 Sol Jo 287 (Denning LJ, sitting in QB)
The common form order for directions that unless a medical report be agreed medical evidence be limited to two witnesses on each side does not impose any legal duty to attempt to agree. Mutual disclosure is a matter of arrangement. If the defendant invites the plaintiff's reports, there is an implied understanding to reciprocate. The agreed report should be confined to the medical issues strictly so called. Agreement in most cases is desirable to save costs and the time of medical men but in a serious case the court may be greatly helped by the attendance of medical men.

Note—The Rules of the Supreme Court (Amendment) Order 1974, SI 1974/295, added new rules numbered 36 and 37 to Ord 38, requiring a party to an action to seek directions from the court before adducing expert evidence and dealing specifically with medical evidence.
Rule 37 has been substituted in the following form by SI 1980/1010:

'Expert evidence in actions for personal injuries
37 (1) This rule applies to any claim for personal injuries except:
(a) any Admiralty action; and
(b) any action where the pleadings contain an allegation of a negligent act or omission in the course of medical treatment.
(2) Where an application is made under r 36(1) in respect of oral expert evidence, then unless the Court considers that there is insufficient reason for not doing so, it shall direct that the substance of the evidence be disclosed in the form of a written report or reports to such other parties and within such period as the Court may specify.
(3) Where the expert evidence relates to medical matters the Court may, if it thinks fit, treat the following circumstances as sufficient reason for not giving a direction under para (2), namely that the expert evidence may contain an expression of opinion —
(i) as to the manner in which the personal injuries were sustained; or
(ii) as to the genuineness of the symptoms of which complaint is made
(4) Where the expert evidence does not relate to medical matters, the Court may, if it thinks fit, treat as a sufficient reason for not giving a direction under paragraph (2) any of the circumstances set out in sub-paras (a) or (b) of r 38(2).'

Exchanging medical reports

McGuinness v Fairbairn Lawson Ltd
(1966) 110 Sol Jo 870, CA
On a summons for directions an order was made that a medical report be agreed if possible and, if not agreed, medical evidence should be limited to two witnesses for each side. The plaintiff's solicitors suggested mutual simultaneous exchange of medical reports by posting them the same day but the defendants merely sent copies of two reports and asked for the plaintiff's reports in exchange. The plaintiff sent only one and the

defendants obtained an order from the judge in chambers requiring the plaintiff to produce the other.

HELD, ON APPEAL: The order should not have been made. A doctor's report was protected by legal professional privilege and the other side was not entitled as of right to see it. Only if there was an agreement to produce it could production be enforced and, on the facts, there was no agreement here. A party was not bound to produce an unfavourable report.

Dalton v Clark & Fenn Ltd

(1963) 107 Sol Jo 595 (Glyn-Jones J)

In an action for damages for personal injuries where liability had been admitted the defendants declined to agree medical reports and the parties had not exchanged reports. The judge said he strongly deprecated the keeping back of medical reports. The proper course was for the plaintiff to hand over his medical reports on the terms that, if they were not agreed, he should be entitled to know why by seeing the defendant's reports.

Note—See also *McGuinness v Fairbairn Lawson Ltd*, above.

Worrall v Reich

[1955] 1 QB 296, [1955] 1 All ER 363, [1955] 2 WLR 338, 99 Sol Jo 109, CA

In an action for damages for personal injuries, there in no power under Ord XXX, r 6(1) (now Ord 25, r 6(3)) to order the parties to exchange medical reports. Such a report is a document privileged from disclosure and so is excluded by para (4). The order should be that a medical report be agreed, if possible, and if not, the medical evidence be limited to (two) witnesses for each party. It should follow the printed form of summons. It is a matter of agreement and not the subject of an order.

Kirkup v British Railways Engineering Ltd

[1983] 3 All ER 147, [1983] 1 WLR 1165, 127 Sol Jo 447, CA

Although in many personal injury cases it was convenient and just for there to be simultaneous disclosure of experts' reports because the area of inquiry and possible disagreement was comparatively limited it was different where the case was such that until the defendants knew what the plaintiff was going to say they could not start to prepare their expert evidence. Order that the plaintiff should disclose reports by his experts within 28 days of setting down for trial and reports by the defendants' experts be disclosed within 42 days thereafter confirmed.

Causton v Mann Egerton (Johnsons) Ltd

[1974] 1 All ER 453, [1974] 1 WLR 162, [1974] 1 Lloyd's Rep 197, CA

In the course of a claim against them for damages for personal injuries the defendants asked for medical examinations of the plaintiff and were granted them by the plaintiff's solicitors 'on the usual terms' which was taken to mean merely on payment of the plaintiff's expenses. The plaintiff's solicitors obtained medical reports separately from time to time. The order for directions in the action ordered that a medical report be agreed upon if possible, and if not, medical evidence be limited to two witnesses for each party. The defendants' solicitors asked the plaintiff's solicitors for copies of all the reports they had obtained and were sent them. They then agreed the plaintiff's reports and refused to disclose their own. On the plaintiff's application for disclosure —

HELD: As was clear from *Worrall v Reich* above a medical report was a privileged document and the Court had no power under Ord 5, r 6 to order its disclosure. There was nothing in the correspondence in the present case from which an agreement to exchange reports could be inferred, nor anything amounting to a waiver by the defendants of their privilege. The plaintiff's solicitors could have attached conditions to production of their reports but they did not. An agreement to disclose was not implied in the phrase 'usual terms'; the plaintiff's solicitor should have told the defendants what agreement they were seeking or making so that no dispute could arise.

Agreed medical evidence incomplete

Gravatt v Card
[1957] 1 Lloyd's Rep 19 (Gorman J)
The judge said the amount of damages had given some anxiety because while it was right to agree medical reports, it was not right to agree them where so much was left to guess and conjecture which could be solved either by asking questions about the reports or by arranging for a doctor to attend. There was no evidence whether the man was fit to undergo an operation or evidence that the operation would be successful or otherwise. The parties would not agree to the calling of the doctor; they stood by their agreement that the medical reports should be read. I mention that because it is putting the Court in the position in which a Court should not have to be put when one is concerned to do complete justice to the parties.

Jones v Griffith
[1969] 2 All ER 1015, [1969] 1 WLR 795, 113 Sol Jo 309, CA
In a claim for damages for epilepsy where medical reports had been agreed the Court of Appeal said it was a matter of regret that in such a serious case no doctor was put in the witness box as someone of whom the judge could ask questions even if counsel did not wish to ask them. Where a medical report is agreed the effect is that the words of the report are treated as though they had been given in evidence: argument becomes an argument as to the proper construction of the words used by the doctors when the court should have the opportunity of itself examining the doctors.

Peters v Harding
(1963) Times, 26 October (Willmer LJ)
The judge said some difficulty had been caused by a statement in one of the medical reports: 'as is well known, there was a well-defined history of psychological trouble before the accident'. The doctor who wrote that report had clearly derived that from another doctor's report, but the Court

knew nothing about it. It would be useful when a medical report was being prepared for the purpose of agreement with the other side if a doctor who drew on information obtained from some other doctor were to annexe an extract from that other doctor's report or state in some greater detail what the view expressed by that other doctor was.

Kaiser v Carlswood Glassworks Ltd
(1965) 109 Sol Jo 537, CA
On the hearing of an appeal by the defendants against an award of £3,500 for head injuries Sellers LJ pointed out that there were two medical reports only, the second of which was 12 months old at the date of hearing in the Court below. The judge was entitled to have up-to-date reports otherwise it was more difficult for him to assess developments one way or the other.

Mullard v Ben Line Steamers Ltd
[1971] 2 All ER 424, [1970] 1 WLR 1414, 114 Sol Jo 570, CA
Per Sachs LJ: Where serious damages are in issue and where above all things what purport to be agreed medical reports do not in fact agree, it is essential for oral medical evidence to be adduced before the Court. . . . Parties who do not take the trouble to bring their medical witnesses to Court have only themselves to blame for the results of such difficulties; but I would add that in my view an obligation lies on the trial judge to insist in serious cases that he have oral evidence before he makes an assessment.

Hambridge v Harrison
[1973] 1 Lloyd's Rep 572, CA
Per Edmund Davis LJ: It is thoroughly undesirable, and indeed irregular, for the Court to be called upon to make its own choice between so-called agreed medical reports which are, in fact, in conflict. . . . It is therefore well to sound a note of warning that the day may come when the Court, confronted with so-called agreed medical reports which in fact disagree with each other in a material respect, will have no alternative but to send the matter back for a further hearing.

Malingering

Stojalowski v Imperial Smelting Corpn (NSC) Ltd
(1976) 121 Sol Jo 118, CA
The defendants were the plaintiff's employers from whom he claimed damages for injury sustained at work. They alleged he was malingering. There was a conflict of medical evidence. The judge accepted the written evidence of a hospital registrar in deciding the plaintiff was a malingerer. HELD, ON APPEAL: The judge was wrong to treat the registrar's written evidence as proof of his views. An allegation of malingering was a charge of fraud and any positive evidence from the defendants should be put to the witness. Damages increased from £4,000 to £37,328.

Joyce v Yeomans
[1981] 2 All ER 21, [1981] 1 WLR 549, 125 Sol Jo 34, CA
It is not correct that where expert (ie medical) witnesses are concerned the
trial judge has no significant advantage over an appellate court in forming a
correct judgment between conflicting views: *Stojalowski v Imperial Smelting
Corpn* (above) was not intended to go as far as that. Even when dealing with
expert witnesses, a trial judge has an advantage over an appellate court in
assessing the value, the reliability and impressiveness of the evidence given
by experts called on either side.

No attempt to agree medical evidence — costs

Constanti v Papageorgiou
(1963) 107 Sol Jo 596 (Havers J)
In an action for personal injuries the plaintiff's medical report was not
given to the defendant and the plaintiff called a surgeon to give evidence.
The defendant would have agreed his report. The hearing lasted several
days. Judgment was given for the plaintiff but on a submission from the
defendant that he should not be required to pay the surgeon's fees for
attending Court it was ordered that the question whether the plaintiff was
entitled to recover the costs of calling the surgeon was to be determined by
the taxing master.

Vose v Barr
[1966] 2 All ER 226 n (Lyell J)
The plaintiff was injured in a road accident on 23 April 1964. Liability was
not in issue. His solicitor obtained a medical report on 12 June 1965, and
issued a writ on 17 June. On 2 July, the defendant's solicitors asked for a
copy of the medical report so that they could make an offer in settlement.
The plaintiff's solicitor replied enclosing the statement of claim and said he
would consider the request for a copy of the medical report when the
defence had been served. When the defence was served the plaintiff's
solicitor still withheld the medical report in spite of several requests from
the defendant's solicitors, who could make no offer without it. The medical
report was not disclosed until shortly before trial, several months later,
when an immediate settlement resulted.
HELD: On the defendant's application, it was a proper case in which to
deprive the plaintiff of part of his costs. There was an omission on the part
of the plaintiff's solicitor within the provisions of Ord 62, r 7 to do
something which would have been calculated to save costs. Judgment for
the plaintiff with costs against the defendant down to 12 July 1965, but not
beyond.

Note—The judge made it clear that this is not a decision that a refusal to disclose a
medical report is in every case an omission which should affect the order as to costs.
It was a decision on the facts. The plaintiff had fully recovered and the medical
evidence was entirely contained in the medical report of 12 June 1965. See also
Chetland v Babcock and Wilcox Ltd, p 610, below.

4 MISCELLANEOUS CASES

EVIDENCE AT TRIAL

Driver not agent to admit negligence

Tustin v Arnold
(1915) 84 LJKB 2214, 113 LT 95, 31 TLR 368
An admission by the driver of his vehicle of his liability for a collision is not admissible against his employer, unless he had the express authority of his employer to make admissions, or the admissions were part of the *res gestae*. Words, even spoken words, are not part of the *res gestae* unless made at the time and the natural consequence of the accident, springing spontaneously out of the accident, and germane to it.

Note—And see *Burr v Ware RDC*, p 646, below.

Glasgow Corpn v Muir
[1943] AC 448, [1943] 2 All ER 44, 112 LJPC 1, 169 LT 53, 59 TLR 266, 87 Sol Jo 182, HL
At a church picnic party in a public park of the defendants the manageress of the tea room gave permission for the party to have their tea in the tea room at the park. Two members of the party were carrying a tea urn when hot water was spilled on children. The defendants were sued for the alleged negligence of the manageress who should have anticipated such a risk. The manageress admitted that if she had been told of the arrival of the men with the urn, she 'certainly would have got the children away from the entrance to the doorway'.
HELD: By Lord Macmillan, not an admission binding on the defendants.

Inconsistent with pleadings

Roberts v Dorman, Long & Co Ltd
[1953] 2 All ER 428, [1953] 1 WLR 942, 97 Sol Jo 487, 51 LGR 486, CA
Evidence given which is at variance with further and better particulars of the defence ought not to be admitted even though the opposing party does not take objection.

Earlier statement admissible

Ahmed v Brumfitt
(1967) 112 Sol Jo 32, CA
The plaintiff claimed damages for the injuries he received when he was struck by the defendant's car when crossing the road. At the trial a witness for the defendant was cross-examined about a report of the accident he had given and which was inconsistent with his evidence-in-chief. In re-examination he was allowed by the judge to give evidence of a statement he had given to the police a week after the accident. The plaintiff was held 60% to blame for the accident. He appealed, contending that the judge

should not have allowed the earlier statement to be put in.
HELD: There was nothing wrong in admitting the statement. When in cross-examination a statement is put to a witness which was said to conflict with his examination-in-chief it is always admissible to put to him in re-examination an earlier statement consistent with it for the purpose of rehabilitating his credit in respect of the evidence he had given.

Expert evidence not needed

Hinds v London Transport Executive
[1979] RTR 103, CA
The plaintiff was injured in a collision with the defendants' bus. His solicitors obtained a report from a consulting engineer giving arguments in favour of the plaintiff on the issues of negligence and causation. They sent a copy to the defendants and applied under Ord 38, r 40 on summons for directions. The master refused leave for the report to be given in evidence.
HELD, ON APPEAL: Leave was rightly refused. The report was not expert evidence at all and even if it were it should not be called; it was a case where expert evidence was not needed.

Non-stop motorist — identification

Grew v Cubitt
[1951] 2 TLR 305, 95 Sol Jo 452, Div Ct
A lorry driver was convicted of driving without due care, failing to stop after an accident, and failing to report it, arising out of an alleged collision between the lorry and a car. The car driver could not describe the lorry at all or identify it; his recollection was that it was a browny-red. An eye-witness said the lorry had a little red on it and that he observed its index number and caused his wife to write it down but he did not remember the number himself. The defendant admitted to the police he was the owner of a lorry of that number; that he was driving the lorry on that day at the place concerned, but he denied any accident. The constable did not give any description of the lorry in evidence.
HELD: There was no evidence on which the defendant could be convicted. The wife should have been called or the piece of paper produced. There was no evidence that the lorry involved was the defendant's lorry.

Jones v Metcalfe
[1967] 3 All ER 205, [1967] 1 WLR 1286, 131 JP 494, 111 Sol Jo 563, Div Ct
The defendant was charged with driving a lorry without due care and attention on the evidence of a witness who said he saw an accident caused by the driving of a lorry which did not stop. He had taken the registration number of the lorry and reported it to the police. In a statement to the police the defendant admitted he had driven a lorry of that number on that day. At court the witness could not remember the number. The defendant was convicted.
HELD, ON APPEAL: The conviction must be quashed. There was no

admissible evidence identifying a lorry bearing the number reported to the police since the independent witness had been unable to testify to the number in court and the police evidence as to the number was merely hearsay.

Hampson v Powell
[1970] 1 All ER 929, 134 JP 321, [1970] RTR 293, Div Ct

On a charge of careless driving against the driver of a lorry which did not stop a witness said he stopped his car at traffic lights and felt a bump at the back from a lorry which came out of a side street. He took the number of the lorry but did not say in evidence what it was. He said the collision caused the boot of his car to fly open. Another witness said he saw a lorry come out of a side street and hit a car and the boot lid flew open. He did not know the number of the lorry. A police officer gave evidence of tracing a lorry number HXJ 604 F and of interviewing the defendant who admitted he was driving a lorry HXJ 604 F at the place and time of the accident but said he knew nothing of the collision. The defendant gave no evidence. The magistrates found that the defendant was the driver of the lorry involved in the accident because there was evidence that a lorry collided with the car and also evidence that the defendant was the driver of a lorry at the precise time and place of the accident.

HELD: The magistrates' decision should stand. In *Jones v Metcalfe* (above) the conviction had been quashed because the magistrates had accepted inadmissible evidence. In the present case they had simply accepted that as the lorry driven by the defendant was at the precise spot at the precise time the accident occurred and there was no evidence of any other lorry being present there was sufficient proof that the defendant was the driver concerned.

R v McLean
(1967) 111 Sol Jo 925, 52 Cr App Rep 80, CA

A man who was attacked and robbed made a mental note of the number of the car used by his attackers and dictated it three minutes later to another man who wrote it down. The car bearing that number had been hired under a false name by the defendant, who was convicted of the robbery. The man who had been robbed was unable in evidence to say that the number written by the other man (who had given evidence of it) was right since he had not been shown it at the time.

HELD: The conviction could not stand. Following *Jones v Metcalfe* (above) the evidence of the number of the car contravened the hearsay rule.

Motor car log book ('Vehicle registration document')

R v Sealby
[1965] 1 All ER 701, Liverpool Crown Court (Chapman J)

A motor car log book is not admissible evidence of its contents, in particular of the chassis number and engine number. It is merely hearsay evidence of its contents and is not a 'public document' so as to bring it within the exception in favour of public documents to the rule against hearsay evidence. Although it contains an extract from the registration particulars in the register kept by the county council (which is a public document) it is a private document issued to the owner of the car.

View by judge

Salsbury v Woodland
[1970] 1 QB 324, [1969] 3 All ER 863, [1969] 3 WLR 29, 113 Sol Jo 327, CA

In a case where there was a question whether a driver should have seen a telephone wire which had fallen across a road the trial judge visited the scene in his own car without telling the parties. He had been doubtful before doing so whether the driver could have been expected to see the wire but after making his view came to the conclusion the driver ought to have seen it in time to slow down. On appeal it was suggested that the judge should not have done this and there should be a new trial.

HELD: In general a view is something which should be conducted by the judge by appointment in the presence of representatives of both sides, but where it is merely a case of a judge visiting a public place to see what it looks like there is nothing wrong in it, provided he makes sure there have been no material changes in the locality.

Note—For full facts see p 304, above.

Buckingham v Daily News Ltd
[1956] 2 QB 534, [1956] 2 All ER 904, [1956] 3 WLR 375, 100 Sol Jo 528, CA

A workman was injured by the blade or plate of a rotary machine and sued the employers alleging a failure to provide a safe system of work. The judge, with consent of the parties, inspected the machine before the evidence. The defendants called no evidence. Judgment was given for the defendants. The plaintiff appealed, contending that what the judge did was something forbidden by law.

A note in the *County Court Practice* says: 'A view is merely for the purpose of enabling the tribunal to understand the questions raised and to follow and apply the evidence, and must not be used to supply or take the place of evidence.'

HELD: The view was a matter of evidence and not of opinion. Where the matter is one of ordinary common sense, the judge is entitled to rely on the real evidence of a view, just as much as on the oral evidence of witnesses.

Note—72 LQR 470 points out that models are frequently brought into court and are regarded as evidence on which a conclusion can be based. The judge was acting on the evidence which he had seen with his own eyes. It is surprising that there should have been any doubt on this point, as the introduction of real evidence is a commonplace, and it cannot make any difference whether the evidence is produced in court, or at the site of the accident.

Witness called by judge

Note—The following note appears in the *Supreme Court Practice 1985*, p 565:

Note to Order 38, rule I

Witness called by judge — By the consent of both parties, or even in the absence of objection by either, the judge may call a witness whom neither party proposes to call, and may examine him himself; but since such witness is not the witness of either party, neither has the right to cross-examine him, though the judge may allow either, or (possibly) both parties to do so. (*Fallon v Calvert* [1960] 2 QB 201, [1960] 1 All ER 281, [1960] 2 WLR 346, 104 Sol Jo 106, CA, *Re Enoch and Zaretzky, Bock & Co's Arbitration* [1910] 1 KB 327, [1908–10] All ER Rep 625, 79 LJKB 363, 101 LT 801, CA, limiting dictum of Esher MR in *Coulson v Disborough* [1894] 2 QB 316, 70 LT 617, 58 JP 784, 42 WR 449, 10 TLR 429, 38 Sol Jo 416, 9 R 390, CA)'

WITHOUT PREJUDICE

Hoghton v Hoghton
(1852) 15 Beav 278, 21 LJCh 482, 17 Jur 99
Where letters are written 'without prejudice' with a view to a compromise, they cannot be given in evidence.

Paddock v Forrester
(1842) 3 Man & G 903, 3 Scott NR 715
Where a letter written by one of the parties to a dispute to the other, is expressed to be 'without prejudice', neither that letter not the answer to it can be given in evidence on the part of the writer of the first letter, although the answer is not expressed to be 'without prejudice'.

Re Harris, ex p Harris
(1875) 10 Ch App 264, 44 LJBcy 33, LT 417, 23 WR 531
Where a negotiation for a compromise is commenced by one letter written 'without prejudice', the whole is protected.

Walker v Wilsher
(1899) 23 QBD 335, 58 LJQR 501, 54 JP 213, 37 WR 723, 5 TLR 649, CA
I think the words 'without prejudice' mean without prejudice to the position of the writer of the letter. If the terms proposed in the letter are accepted, a complete contract is established, and the letter, although written without prejudice, operates to alter the position of affairs and to establish a contract. Supposing a letter is written without prejudice, it is taken, according both to authority and good sense, that the answer should also be without prejudice.

India Rubber, Gutta Percha and Telegraph Works Ltd v Chapman
(1926) 20 BWCC 184, CA
Letters following a letter written 'without prejudice' should be treated as

being also inadmissible unless there is a clear break in the chain of correspondence to indicate that the ensuing letters are open.

Note—In *Bray on Discovery*, p 308, it is said:

'The right to discovery may under very special circumstances be lost by contract as where correspondence passed between the parties' solicitors with a view to an amicable arrangement of the question at issue in the suit on a stipulation that it should not be referred to or used to the defendant's prejudice in case of a failure to come to an arrangement.'

Rabin v Mendoza & Co
[1954] 1 All ER 247, [1954] 1 WLR 271, 98 Sol Jo 92, CA
Plaintiff instructed surveyors to advise on the purchase of a house. He claimed from them damages for negligence. Before action was taken, the parties met to discuss a settlement without prejudice. The parties agreed that the report of another surveyor should be obtained by defendants. Later on action was commenced.
HELD: The report was made solely for the purpose of 'without prejudice' negotiations and as the result of an express or tacit agreement that it would not be used to the prejudice of either party and was privileged from production.

Agreement reached 'without prejudice' is binding

Tomlin v Standard Telephones and Cables Ltd
[1969] 3 All ER 201, [1969] 1 WLR 1378, 113 Sol Jo 641, CA
In dealing with a claim for damages for personal injury the defendants' insurers wrote the plaintiff's solicitor a letter marked 'Without Prejudice' saying 'We are only prepared to deal with the case on a 50–50 basis'. The solicitor replied 'my client had instructed me to say that he will agree to settle his case on a 50–50 basis as you propose and accordingly this leaves only the question of quantum to be disposed of'. In subsequent letters the insurers referred to 'the agreement come to between us' and eventually wrote 'It has already been agreed that this is a 50–50 case and accordingly we are prepared to pay £625 in settlement'. All the insurers' letters were marked 'Without Prejudice'. The plaintiff rejected the offer and sued for damages to be assessed, on the basis that there was a concluded agreement to pay him one-half.
HELD: There was a binding agreement. The Court was entitled to look at letters marked 'Without Prejudice' to see if an agreement had been reached. There was a concluded agreement on the issue of liability leaving over for further negotiation the separate and severable question of quantum of damages.

Note—See also *Walker v Wilsher*, above.

DISCOVERY: CROWN PRIVILEGE

Re Grosvenor Hotel London
[1964] Ch 464, [1963] 3 All ER 426, [1964] 2 WLR 184, 107 Sol Jo 1002, (Cross J)
It has been clear law since the decision of the House of Lords in *Duncan v Cammell Laird & Co Ltd* that an objection to production properly taken by a public department on the ground that to produce the documents would be injurious to the public interest is conclusive. Viscount Simon said in *Duncan's* case:

'The essential matter is that the decision to object should be taken by the minister who is the political head of the department and that he should have seen and considered the contents of the documents and himself have formed the view that on grounds of public interest they ought not to be produced either because of their actual contents or because of the class of documents, e g departmental minutes to which they belong.'

When an objection to production is supported by a minister's affidavit the affidavit must (1) contain evidence from which the Court can judge whether the minister came to a fresh decision of his own on the question whether the documents should be withheld, without any regard to a previous decision taken by his subordinates, and (2) specify the class of documents to which those for which he claims privilege belong. It is important that the public should know the principles on which ministers purport to act on these cases.

Note—The whole subject of Crown privilege on discovery of documents was exhaustively considered in proceedings reported as *Re Grosvenor Hotel (London) No 2* [1965] Ch 1210 [1964] 3 All ER 354, [1964] 3 WLR 1009, 108 Sol Jo 674. The Court of Appeal (Lord Denning MR, Harman LJ and Salmon LJ) reached the following conclusions:
1 If Crown privilege is to be successfully claimed the objection must be taken in proper form, in the ordinary way by the minister himself after considering the documents himself.
2 A document may be privileged either because of its contents or because it is one of a class of documents privileged, apart from their contents, by the source from which they proceed.
3 There is a residual power in the courts to override the executive in cases where Crown privilege is unreasonably claimed for a class of document, e g comprising routine communications between civil servants, and the court may ask to see the documents to make a decision.
4 Where a minister is objecting to production of all documents in a particular class which is not privileged by reason of the contents he must justify his objection with reasons, describing the nature of the class and the reason why the documents should not be disclosed.
The subject of Crown privilege was further considered by the House of Lords in *Conway v Rimmer*.

Conway v Rimmer
[1968] AC 910, [1968] 1 All ER 874, [1968] 2 WLR 989, 112 Sol Jo 191, HL
A probationary constable claimed damages from a police superintendent for malicious prosecution. On discovery of documents the defendant

claimed privilege for reports submitted to his superior officer on the ground that they were of a class of documents which it was contrary to the public interest to disclose. The plaintiff submitted that where the objection was to production of a document because of the class to which it belonged as opposed to its own contents the Court might examine the document and, if satisfied that the interests of justice so demanded, overrule the Crown objection. He relied on *Merricks v Nott-Bower* [1965] 1 QB 57, [1964] 1 All ER 717, [1964] 2 WLR 702, 128 JP 267, 108 Sol Jo 116; *Re Grosvenor Hotel* (above) and *Wednesbury Corpn v Ministry of Housing* [1965] 1 All ER 186, [1965] 1 WLR 261, 129 JP 123, 108 Sol Jo 1012.

HELD, in the House of Lords: *Duncan v Cammell Laird* is not an authority for saying that in all cases where privilege is claimed for a document on the grounds that it is one of a class which must be withheld from production for reasons of public interest the certificate of the minister must, as a matter of law, be treated as conclusive. The Court has an inherent right to decide for itself on the information supplied, or if necessary, by inspection of the document itself, whether it comes within a class of document which must as a class be withheld from production.

Note—For the considerations that ought to influence judges in deciding whether to order inspection see *Air Canada v Secretary of State for Trade* [1983] 2 AC 394, [1983] 1 All ER 910, [1983] 2 WLR 494, 127 Sol Jo 205, HL

Oral evidence not privileged

Broome v Broome

[1955] P 190, [1955] 1 All ER 201, [1955] 2 WLR 401, 99 Sol Jo 114, CA
In a divorce suit a wife petitioner issued a *subpoena ad test* to be served on a representative of the Soldiers', Sailors' and Airmen's Families' Association in Hong Kong, and a *subpoena duces tecum* on the Secretary of State for War to produce documents of the Association. The Secretary of State gave a certificate that it was not in the public interest that the documents should be produced or the evidence of the representative given orally.

HELD: Crown privilege could attach to all documents from or to a servant or agent of the Crown, but it was wrong to attempt to prevent the witness giving evidence of any sort. Application to set aside the *subpoena* failed.

CHAPTER 16
Practice

SUMMARY OF HIGH COURT ACTION

Personal injury claim: procedural steps

(*Note*—the page numbers refer to places in this book where relevant case material may be found: the references do not purport to be exhaustive.)

1 Letter before action: it should contain the date, time and place of the accident and sufficient information to identify the event together with the name(s) of the claimant(s). Detailed particulars of the alleged negligence are not requisite. A request to pass the letter to insurers is advisable.

2 If no reply is received from any insurers in claims for personal injuries, details of insurance should be sought before proceeding further. There are the following possible sources or methods:
(1) a police report — write to the appropriate force;
(2) if no police report can be supplied yet, the police may notify insurance details by letter on request;
(3) a letter to the person against whom the claim is being made, drawing attention to the Road Traffic Act 1972, s 151 (p 771, below) and requiring disclosure of the particulars.

3 If and when the identity of the insurers is known but no letter or other acknowledgment has been received from them write them with a copy of the letter before action. If no insurer can be traced write the Motor Insurers' Bureau (see pp 775–802, below).

4 If necessary or desirable, apply for legal aid certificate.

5 Issue of proceedings by writ; necessary points to note:
(a) Time limits for commencement of proceedings (see ch 14, above, especially sections of Limitation Act 1980 dealing with personal injury claims, pp 532–549).
(b) In fatal cases representation of the deceased's estate by probate or letters of administration is needed unless the case is one to which the Fatal Accidents Act 1976, s 2(2) can conveniently apply (p 489, above).
(c) Notice must be given to the insurer of the issue or intended issue of proceedings (pp 763–765, below) or to Motor Insurers' Bureau where there is no traceable insurer (cl 5(1)(a) of the Uninsured Drivers' Agreement, p 776, below) before or within seven days of issue.
(d) ensure endorsement to writ identifies cause of action (pp 554–557, above).
(e) ensure correctness of names of parties and capacity in which they sue or are sued (pp 557–560, above); next friend for plaintiff under age.
(f) In proceedings against the Crown, refer to requirements of Crown Proceedings Act (p 615, below).

6 If writ not served within 12 months of issue, renew before expiry and before expiry of limitation period (pp 560–571, above).

7 Service of writ may be effected by
(a) personal service on individual defendant;
(b) ordinary post at defendant's usual or last known address;
(c) insertion through defendant's letter box;
(d) leaving writ at or posting it to registered office of limited company;
   In case of a defendant abroad, see RSC Ord 11. For service on corporate bodies other than limited companies see Ord 65, r 3. For service on partnership see Ord 81, r 3;
(e) substituted service by order of the court when the defendant cannot be found: if insured, by post at insurer's address, if not insured by post at the address of Motor Insurers' Bureau, or otherwise (pp 681 and 781 below).

8 The defendant's acknowledgment of service and notice of intention to defend are due within 14 days of service. Note:
(a) a defendant applying to set aside the writ or service must issue his application within 14 days of filing acknowledgment of service;
(b) the acknowledgment and notice can be validly filed at any time before the plaintiff signs judgment in default.

9 The plaintiff's Statement of Claim may be endorsed on the writ or may be served with it. If not then it should be served within 14 days after the defendant gives notice of intention to defend (see RSC Ord 18, r 1). Note:
(a) any special damage claimed must be pleaded (pp 456–457, above);
(b) a claim for interest on damages must be pleaded (p 393, above);
(c) possible difficulties in amending out of time (pp 552–557, above).

10 If no acknowledgment of service of the writ with notice of intention to defend is filed by the defendant within 14 days of service, or, after service of the Statement of Claim no defence is served within 14 days, interlocutory judgment can be signed by the plaintiff unless the defendant has obtained an extension of time by consent or by order of the court on a time summons. The defendant may apply to set aside the judgment (see p 675, below) or contest the claim on assessment of damages only. Contributory negligence (e g failure by the plaintiff to wear a seat belt) is not an issue which can be contested on a mere assessment of damages following interlocutory judgment: it is an issue on liability which must be pleaded in a defence.

11 The defence must be served within 14 days of the time limited for acknowledgment of service or service of the Statement of Claim, whichever is the later. Note:
(a) the court will not normally order further and better particulars of the Statement of Claim before service of the defence (pp 657–658, above and RSC Ord 18, r 2(5));
(b) circumstances in which the court will set aside a default judgment (p 675, below)
(c) limitation period for counter-claim (p 550, above);
(d) admission of negligence or liability (p 599, below).

12 The plaintiff may serve a reply (if appropriate) and a defence to a counter-claim within 14 days of defence.

13 Third-party proceedings may be started by the defendant before service of defence without leave; but after defence served leave of the court is required, obtained usually ex parte on affidavit evidence (pp 603–604, below). Note:
(a) between defendant tortfeasors no specific contribution proceedings are needed merely to establish proportions of liability (*Croston v Vaughan*, p 603, below);
(b) new rules on limitations are established in the Limitation Act 1980, s 35 (p 550, above).
(c) third party and contribution proceedings have 'a life of their own' (p 604, below).

14 Application for interim payment of damages. (pp 442–443, above and RSC Ord 29, rr 9–18).Note:
(a) application may be made at any time after service of writ and expiry of time limited for acknowledgment of service;
(b) interim payments must not be disclosed to the court at trial (p 442, above).

15 Automatic directions in personal injury actions (RSC Ord 25, r 8) take effect when pleadings are closed. They deal with discovery (see below), expert evidence, expert witnesses, photographs, sketch plan and police report, setting down and place of trial. See ch 15, above (evidence).

16 Consolidate actions in which common questions of law or fact arise (p 602, below and RSC Ord 4, r 9).

17 Discovery and interrogatories: note
(a) discovery is to be given within 14 days of close of pleadings by list of documents (RSC Ord 24, r 2);
(b) defendant in an action arising from a collision or apprehended collision involving vehicle is not required to make discovery to the plaintiff;
(c) legal professional privilege (p 617, below);
(d) Crown privilege — public policy (p 592, above);
(e) interrogatories may be allowed in 'running down' cases (p 645, below).

18 Payment into Court: note:
(a) addition of interest (p 662, below);
(b) effect on costs (pp 659–662, below);
(c) payment out.

19 Settlement of action: note possible points arising:
(a) inadequate settlements (pp 675–679, below);
(b) 'without prejudice' letters (pp 590–591, above);
(c) binding receipt (p 680, above);
(d) Court approval (RSC Ord 80, r 11).

20 Trial:
(a) solicitors to supply calculation (*Practice Note* 1 August 1984, 81 LS Gaz 2742);
(b) if and when by jury (pp 648–651, below);
(c) adjournments;
(d) medical evidence;
(e) assessment of damages by judge (p 408, above);
(f) award of interest on damages (pp 435–442, above);
(g) unassisted defendant; award of costs (pp 697–699, below).

21 Appeal:
(a) new evidence (pp 641–653, above);
(b) unassisted party — costs from legal aid fund (pp 699–701, above);
(c) appeal from jury (p 408, above);
(d) appeals on amount — principles (pp 406–408, above).

22 judgment:
(a) effect — *res judicata* (pp 670–674, below);
(b) interest on judgment debt (*Supreme Court Practice 1985* p 629).

23 Costs:
(a) Bullock and Sanderson orders (pp 604–607, below);
(b) effect of payment into Court (pp 659–662, below);
(c) claim and counter-claim (pp 608–609, below);
(d) on infant's settlement (p 610, below);
(e) party and party and common fund (p 611, below).

24 Dismissal for want of prosecution:
(a) principles (pp 627–635, below);
(b) special cases (pp 635–640, below).

ADJOURNMENT OF TRIAL

Note—See RSC Ord 35, r 3.

Green v Northern General Transport
(1970) 115 Sol Jo 59, CA

When a personal injury action was listed for hearing at assizes the judge refused an application by the defendants for the case to be stood out; they said a material witness was not then available. The action was heard and judgment given for the plaintiff.

HELD, ON APPEAL: If there was a material witness who was not available and whose presence was desirable the judge should grant an adjournment, where injustice would otherwise be done, provided that any injustice to the other party could be compensated in costs. There should be a new trial.

Plaintiff's failure to attend court

Renge v Collins
(1966) 110 Sol Jo 724, 116 NLJ 1061, CA

The plaintiff, who had a legal aid certificate with a nil contribution, sued in the county court for damages for personal injury alleged to have been sustained on the defendant's premises. On the day fixed for the hearing she could not face going to court and went to see her doctor. He gave her a certificate that she was suffering from nervous debility and was unable to attend court. She took it to her solicitors and then went off. At court where the defendant was ready with his witnesses to contest the case, the plaintiff's counsel produced the certificate and asked for an adjournment. The judge sent for the doctor, who gave evidence that the plaintiff was physically able to come to court but was unbalanced emotionally and might be just the same next time. The judge refused to grant an adjournment and dismissed the case. On appeal it was said for the plaintiff that the judge should have granted either an adjournment or a non-suit.

HELD: The judge had rightly exercised his discretion in not adjourning the case, the defendant being present with all his witnesses. On the question of granting a non-suit, which would have enabled the plaintiff to reinstate the case on paying all the costs, it was for her counsel to elect to have a non-suit if she wanted it. She had a right to non-suit as was shown by *Clark v Arthur's Engineering Ltd* [1959] 2 QB 211. As her counsel had not exercised her right to make the election she could not now come to the Court of Appeal to seek an alteration of the order dismissing the action.

ADMINISTRATOR SUING ALSO PERSONALLY

Note—It has been contended that a claim by a legal personal representative suing in a representative capacity cannot be joined in the same action with a claim by the same person in a personal capacity. It now seems established that this is not the case.

Littlechild v Holt
[1950] 1 KB 1, [1949] 1 All ER 933, [1949] LJR 1299, 65 TLR 270, 93 Sol Jo 387, CA

Per Lord Goddard CJ: It is always the case that a claim by an executor or administrator, as executor or administrator, can be joined with a claim by the executor or administrator personally. So, too, if there is a claim by the executor personally, it can be joined with a claim by him or her as executor. It is open to a person who obtains an order to continue proceedings as administrator or executor to join a claim by himself or herself in his or her personal capacity with the claim that is made in the representative capacity. At any rate, it is within the discretion of the court to allow those two claims to be made at the same time. Where the two claims are of a very similar nature, I see no reason at all why they should not be joined.

ADMISSION OF NEGLIGENCE

Blundell v Rimmer
[1971] 1 All ER 1072, [1971] 1 WLR 123, 115 Sol Jo 15, [1971] 1 Lloyd's Rep 110 (Payne J)
The plaintiff was a passenger in a car when he was injured in a collision with a car driven by the defendant. In his defence the defendant denied the negligence alleged against him, denied the damage alleged and blamed the driver of the car in which the plaintiff was travelling. Later the defendant's solicitors made a payment into Court and sent a letter to the plaintiff's solicitors admitting the defendant's negligence and, though admitting that the plaintiff would be entitled to damages which flowed in law from the negligence, denying that the plaintiff had suffered any damage. The plaintiff applied for interlocutory judgment under RSC Ord 27, r 3; the registrar made the order asked.
HELD, ON APPEAL: The order should not have been made. The letter from the defendant's solicitors was an admission only of negligence and was a denial of damage. Until damage was proved by evidence the plaintiff was not entitled to judgment on the admission because no claim against the defendant had been established; no admissions of fact had been made upon which he became entitled to judgment in pursuance of Ord 27, r 3. The case should be distinguished from judgments in default of appearance or defence or where part of a liquidated claim had been admitted.

Note—See next case for Ord 27, r 3.

Rankine v Garton Sons & Co Ltd
[1979] 2 All ER 1185, 123 Sol Jo 305, CA
RSC Ord 27, r 3 says: 'Where admissions of fact are made by a party to a cause or matter either by his pleadings or otherwise, any other party . . . may apply to the Court for such judgment or order as upon those admissions he may be entitled to without waiting for the determination of any other question . . . and the Court may give such judgment . . . as it thinks just.' The plaintiff claimed damages from the defendants for injury alleged to have been sustained when he slipped on a pool of glucose at the defendants' premises. In their defence the defendants denied the incident alleged, denied the negligence alleged and denied that any negligence resulted in damage. In a letter to the plaintiff's solicitors, however, the defendants' solicitors admitted that the incident resulted from the defendants' negligence and said that the allegations of contributory negligence would not be pursued, the intention being 'to explore the possibilities of amicably terminating the proceedings'. The plaintiff applied under Ord 27, r 3 for judgment for damages to be assessed. The master gave leave for judgment to be entered. The judge in chambers dismissed the defendants' appeal.
HELD, by the Court of Appeal: The judgment should be set aside. Approving Payne J's decision in *Blundell v Rimmer* (above) and following

Lord Reading's statement of the law in *Munday v LCC* [1916] 2 KB 331, two elements were needed for the cause of action (1) the breach of duty, ie negligence, and (2) damage suffered by the plaintiff. The letter from the defendants' solicitors did not in terms admit liability but only negligence, and had preserved the defendants' right to question the causal connection between the plaintiff's injuries and the accident. The admission of negligence did not necessarily involve an admission that some damage had resulted. Appeal allowed.

APPEAL

Principle in running down action

Lofthouse v Leicester Corpn
(1948) 64 TLR 604, CA
Deceased cyclist was killed in collision with a motor omnibus. Oliver J held deceased alone to blame.
HELD, ON APPEAL: The Court of Appeal had a wider power on appeal from a judge than a jury and can reverse the judge on the facts. The judge sees and hears the witnesses and obtains the atmosphere. Although not exhaustive, the Court of Appeal ought not to interfere on a pure question of fact unless the judge did not take all the circumstances and evidence into account, or misapprehended certain of the evidence, or that he had drawn an inference which there is no evidence to support. The judge must decide the case on the evidence given, not on how he thought the accident probably happened.

Lincoln v Hayman
[1982] 2 All ER 819, [1982] 1 WLR 488, [1982] RTR 336, CA
Two lorries collided on a country lane too narrow for them to pass without one or both going on to the grass verge. Immediately after the accident police officers and a press photographer arrived: photographs were taken and a sketch plan made showing the positions of the vehicles and of certain wheel marks on the road and the grass verges. The accounts of the accident from the two drivers differed very widely.
HELD, ON APPEAL: Where, as here, the judge's reasoning was based on inferences from plans and photographs (and not from the demeanour of the witnesses) the Court of Appeal was in as good a position as the judge to draw its own inferences from the undisputed primary material. Judge's finding of blame wholly on the defendant altered to two-thirds on the plaintiff one-third on the defendant.

Inconsistent findings of two judges

Baker v Market Harborough Industrial Co-operative Society
Wallace v Richards (Leicester) Ltd
[1953] 1 WLR 1472, 97 Sol Jo 861, CA
Two vehicles proceeding in opposite directions collided and both drivers were killed. An action by widow of driver A was dismissed by Mr Justice X on the ground that there was no proof of negligence of driver B. An action

by the widow of driver B was afterwards heard and Mr Justice Y held both drivers equally to blame. The Court of Appeal granted leave to appeal out of time in the A action. Facts and references at p 52, above, *res ipsa loquitur*.

Kemshead v British Transport Commission
[1958] 1 All ER 119, [1958] 1 WLR 173, 102 Sol Jo 122, CA
On 6 December 1952, a motor car collided with a train at an accommodation level crossing. One passenger in the car named Bland was killed and another passenger name Kemshead was injured. Bland's widow sued the British Transport Commission and on 4 February 1954, Stable J gave judgment for her. The Commission did not appeal.

Kemshead also sued the Commission and on 10 May 1956, Stable J gave judgment for him. The Commission appealed and the appeal was allowed.

Per Denning LJ: It is very unfortunate that in regard to two different plaintiffs there should be different results in the courts of law. The parties ought to have taken a different course. They ought all to have been plaintiffs in one action or should have agreed on one action being a test action.

The defendants not having appealed and having paid the damages in the first action was a direct encouragement to the second plaintiff and were therefore refused costs.

Fresh evidence on appeal

Note—See p 641, below and ch 12, pp 409–411, above.

Transfer to a different judge

Birch v County Motor and Engineering Co Ltd
[1958] 3 All ER 175, [1958] 1 WLR 980, 102 Sol Jo 632, CA
A was a pillion rider on a motor cycle driven by B which collided with a car driven by C. Both A and B sustained injuries. B brought an action against C in the county court. The only witnesses were B and A. The judge accepted the evidence of C on the only disputed evidence of fact, and found both B and C negligent in the proportions of three-fourths blame to B and one-fourth to C. Later A brought an action in the same court against C, who joined B as third party. C applied under Ord 16, r 1(1) to transfer the action to another county court on the ground that the judge having made up his mind that C was in some degree to blame, the probable result was that A would recover his damages from C, as A was not affected by the apportionment in the former action, and B might not be worth powder and shot. C appealed.
HELD: The question is clearly a matter for the discretion of the judge, and he had not taken into account matters not relevant to the proper exercise of that discretion. It was not a case where the judge formed a very unfavourable view of a witness or his credibility. The grounds stated by the judge for his refusal of the application were not entirely satisfactory, and it must be a real trial. Application to transfer to another court rejected, but the judge must try the second case fairly and fully, listening to the evidence and making a note.

APPEALS — COUNTY COURT

Note—The County Court Appeals Order 1981, SI 1981/1749, requires leave to be obtained to appeal from a county court where the claim (or counter-claim, if larger) is for an amount not exceeding one-half of the limit of the jurisdiction of a county court under the County Courts Act 1984, s 15 (at present £5,000).

ARBITRATION

Note—The Arbitration Acts 1889 to 1934 were repealed and consolidated without any substantial alteration by the Arbitration Act 1950 (14 Geo 6, c 27), which came into force on 1 September 1950. Important reforms in the law and practice of arbitrations were made by the Arbitration Act 1979.

The application of a condition in insurance policies requiring any dispute to be referred to arbitration has become of less importance in view of the decision of insurers not to require compliance with such condition except on a dispute relating to amount when liability is not in issue.

Abandonment of Arbitration

Note—The following statement was issued in January 1957:

'The British Insurance Association and *Lloyd's* announce that their members have entered into an agreement in respect of United Kingdom business, the general effect of which is to allow an assured who prefers to have questions of liability, as distinct from amount, determined by the Courts, to do so notwithstanding that the policy contains an Arbitration Clause.

The insurers have defined their intentions as follows:-
"If in dispute arising under a contract of insurance made in the United Kingdom the assured brings an action in any Court in the United Kingdom, the insurers will, notwithstanding that the contract contains an arbitration clause, not apply to the Court for a stay of action on that ground unless —
(1) the whole of the dispute relates to the amount of the claim, liability being admitted; or
(2) the dispute relates partly to liability and partly to amount and the assured refuses to give an undertaking that, in the event of the insurer being found liable, he will agree to any dispute as to amount being determined in the manner provided in the arbitration clause.
Nothing in the foregoing shall apply —
(a) to a contract of reinsurance; or
(b) to a contract of marine insurance; or
(c) to a contract which is an insurance of all or any of the following risks relating to aviation, namely, loss of or damage to aircraft liability of the assured to third parties or to passengers, and loss of or damage to, or liability in respect of, cargo consigned by air; or
(d) to a contract of credit insurance; or
(3) where the terms of the insurance are set out in a contract or policy which is specially negotiated and in which an arbitration clause has been specifically agreed." '

CONSOLIDATION OF ACTIONS

Note—See RSC Ord 4, r 9.

Healey v A. Waddington & Sons Ltd

[1954] 1 All ER 861, [1954] 1 WLR 688, 98 Sol Jo 286, CA

Arising out of one accident, eight actions were brought against three defendants. Before delivery of pleadings, the three defendants applied to consolidate the actions. The master ordered the actions to be consolidated and tried together; one statement of claim to be delivered to include the special damage of each plaintiff and separate issues as to damages.

The judge in chambers set this order aside and ordered one action to be tried as a test action and the other actions stayed.

HELD, ON APPEAL: The actions should be consolidated up to determination of issue of liability, any issue peculiar to one plaintiff to be separately dealt with; separate particulars of damage and issues of damages separately dealt with; order in terms agreed between counsel.

CONTRIBUTION PROCEEDINGS

Third-party procedure — High Court

The procedure is contained in RSC Ord 16.

Order 16, r 10 enables a written offer of contribution by a third party or one of two or more tortfeasors to be treated as a payment into court without any order to that effect, such offer to be taken into account by the judge at the trial in exercising his discretion as to costs.

The form of letter may be as follows:

'Please take notice that the defendant . . . hereby makes a written offer to contribution of . . . per cent (or $\frac{1}{4}$, $\frac{1}{3}$, $\frac{1}{2}$) of the liability of the defendants to the plaintiff and reserves the right for the purposes of Ord 65, r 5(a) to bring this offer to the attention of the judge at the trial. Please acknowledge receipt of this letter.'

Without fresh proceedings

Croston v Vaughan

[1938] 1 KB 540, [1937] 4 All ER 249, 107 LJKB 182, 158 LT 221, 102 JP 11, 54 TLR 54, 81 Sol Jo 882, 36 LGRI, CA

The court can apportion damages between two defendants in the action brought by the original plaintiffs against those defendants without the necessity of any fresh or further proceedings.

Note—Order 16, r 8, provides for service by one defendant upon another of notice of claim for contribution.

Pride of Derby v British Celanese

[1952] 1 All ER 1326, [1952] WN 227, [1952] 1 TLR 1013, 96 Sol Jo 263 (Harman J)

Plaintiffs as riparian owners obtained an injunction restraining three defendants from allowing effluent to pass into the River Derwent so as to interfere with the plaintiffs' right of fishing, and an inquiry into damages. The defendants were not joint tortfeasors but were severally liable. They applied to the judge to apportion the damages, when certified as the result of the inquiry, in proportions agreed between the three defendants.

HELD: The court had jurisdiction to make the order. *Croston v Vaughan* followed.

Third party proceedings after settlement of main action

Stott v West Yorkshire Road Car Co

[1971] 2 QB 651, [1971] 3 All ER 534, [1971] 3 WLR 282, 115 Sol Jo 568, CA

The defendants' bus collided with the plaintiff on his motor cycle when passing a parked vehicle. He was seriously injured. They brought third-party proceedings against the owners of the parked vehicle for a contribution to any damages awarded to the plaintiff. Before the action reached trial the defendants settled the plaintiff's claim by a payment of £10,000 made expressly 'without any admission of liability whatsoever by' the defendants. On an appeal from a summons for third-party directions the judge held that the third-party proceedings could not continue because (1) the original action being dead there was nothing on which the third-party proceedings could bite, and (2) as they had made the payment to the plaintiff without admission of liability the defendants had no right to contribution at all.

HELD, by the Court of Appeal: This was wrong. (1) Once an action is settled the third-party proceedings can proceed as if they had been started by separate action — RSC Ord 16, r 4(3)(b). (2) It was not necessary that the defendants should have admitted liability to the plaintiff or been held liable to him; it was only in third-party proceedings that they had to show that they would have been held responsible in law to the plaintiff and liable to pay him damages.

Note—See now Civil Liability (Contribution) Act 1978, s 1(4) p 19, above.

Proceedings between defendants

Clayson v Rolls Royce Ltd

[1951] 1 KB 746, [1950] 2 All ER 884, 66 (Pt 2) TLR 827, 94 Sol Jo 741, CA

If one defendant wishes to obtain particulars, or discovery of documents, or interrogatories from his co-defendant, he is entitled to do so under the principle of *Croston v Vaughan* that there is a right of contribution without formal proceedings. He must first issue and serve a notice under Ord XVIA, r 12(1) (now Ord 16, r 8(1)) and issue a summons for directions pursuant to para (2) (now r 4), so that the issues may be clearly defined.

COSTS

Two defendants

BULLOCK ORDER

Bullock v London General Omnibus Co

[1907] 1 KB 264, 76 LJKB 127, 95 LT 905, 23 TLR 62, 50 Sol Jo 66, CA

Where the plaintiff claims damages for personal injuries against two companies for their joint negligence or alternatively against each of them for its negligence, there is jurisdiction to order the plaintiff to pay the costs of the successful defendant and recoupment to the plaintiff by the unsuccessful defendant.

Note—The note to RSC Ord 62, r 2 in the *Supreme Court Practice 1985* p 874 includes the following:

'Where in the opinion of the court, it was reasonable in all the circumstances, for the plaintiff to sue two defendants, making his claim against them in the alternative, and where he succeeds only against one of them, the court has a discretion to order the unsuccessful defendant to pay the successful defendant's costs. This it may do either by ordering payment of those costs direct by the unsuccessful to the successful defendant, or by ordering the plaintiff to pay the latter's costs, and allowing him to include these costs in the costs payable to him by the unsuccessful defendant. Each of these two forms or order is commonly known as a Bullock Order (from *Bullock v London General Omnibus Co*) but the former may be more accurately called a Sanderson Order from *Sanderson v Blyth Theatre Co*. Where the plaintiff may be insolvent, the first mentioned order is generally the more appropriate.'

SANDERSON ORDER

Rudow v Great Britain Mutual Life Assurance Society
(1881) 17 ChD 600, 50 LJCh 504, 44 LT 688, CA
Under the Judicature Acts it is no longer necessary to order a plaintiff to pay the costs of a defendant and have them over against another defendant so that if the second defendant is insolvent plaintiff loses them. The proper form of order now is to order defendant who is liable to them as between himself and his co-defendant to pay them to the co-defendant.

Sanderson v Blyth Theatre Co
[1903] 2 KB 533, 72 LJKB 761, 89 LT 159, 52 WR 33, 19 TLR 660, CA
(Stirling LJ)
The proper form of order was laid down in *Rudow's* case. I think this practice ought to be adhered to wherever it is practicable to do so.

Bullock Order

Mayer v Harte
[1960] 2 All ER 840, [1960] 1 WLR 770, 104 Sol Jo 603, CA
The plaintiff brought an action for damages against two defendants of whom one paid into Court £15. The plaintiff did not accept the payment and later joined a third defendant who, unknown to her, was an undischarged bankrupt. At the trial she obtained judgment for £20 10s 0d against the third defendant, the first and second defendants succeeding in their defence. The judge awarded the first and second defendants' costs against the plaintiff, such costs to be added to the plaintiff's costs recoverable from the third defendant (a Bullock Order). He refused to order the first and second defendants' costs to be paid by the third defendant direct (a Sanderson Order).
HELD, by the Court of Appeal: There was no principle which required that the judge must necessarily order that the successful defendants should recover their costs direct from the unsuccessful defendant. The matter was one for the discretion of the Court provided that the discretion was judicially exercised.

Besterman v British Motor Cab Co Ltd
[1914] 3 KB 181, 83 LJKB 1014, 110 LT 754, 30 TLR 319, 58 Sol Jo 319, CA

Plaintiff was injured as a result of a collision between a motor cab and an omnibus. He sued and recovered against the cab company and failed against the bus company. The cab company before trial had notified the bus company, but not the plaintiff, that they blamed the bus company; they did not blame them in their defence, but did at the trial.

HELD: The plaintiff was entitled to a Bullock Order. The fact that there were two people and either might have been liable makes it reasonable for a plaintiff to join both defendants. A defendant should not be joined unreasonably. If it is reasonable to be in a state of uncertainty and to join both defendants, the costs of both defendants are costs in the action. The test is whether there are reasonable grounds for suing both defendants.

Wickens v Associated Portland Cement Manufacturers
[1951] 1 Lloyd's Rep 162 (Cassels J)

The test is whether plaintiff was reasonable in issuing a writ against both defendants.

Sanderson Order

Ryan v T. F. Maltby Ltd
[1954] 1 Lloyd's Rep 196 (Hilbery J)

The courts have adopted the procedure of the *Sanderson* case and not the Bullock Order. The successful defendant then has a right to be heard on taxation of their costs and this is not left to the plaintiff.

Bullock Order refused

Wong Kwok Hong v A. and R. Brown Ltd
[1948] 1 KB 515, [1948] 1 All ER 185, 64 TLR 132, 92 Sol Jo 124, CA

The plaintiff acting on the old Ord XVI, r 7 (now revoked), that where a plaintiff is in doubt whom to sue, he may sue two or more defendants, sued two defendants. The judge found for the plaintiff against one defendant, but in favour of the other defendant. He awarded plaintiff costs against the unsuccessful defendant, and the successful defendant costs against the plaintiff but did not order the unsuccessful defendant to pay the costs of the successful defendant to the plaintiff. In the case of *Besterman v British Motor Cab Co Ltd* (above), the unsuccessful defendant had contended in the correspondence that the successful defendant was partly to blame although the plaintiff had not been told of the contention, and the judge made a Bullock Order.

By the Supreme Court of Judicature (Consolidation) Act 1925, s 31, there is no right of appeal on a matter of costs only without the leave of the court or a judge. The judge did not give leave.

The plaintiff contended he had a right of appeal without leave on the ground that costs are a matter of discretion and the discretion had not been really exercised, (1) due to the failure to act as a judge should act, ie judicially, or (2) there were no materials on which he could exercise discretion.

HELD: *Besterman's* case did not entitle a plaintiff in this position as of right to a Bullock Order. Order XVI, r 7, had nothing to do with costs, and acting on it did not entitle the plaintiff to any special order as to costs. It only decided that the judge had a discretion. There was no failure to act judicially and there was material on which to exercise discretion. The appeal failed for want of leave to appeal.

Partial Order

Keating v Channel Shipping Ltd
[1961] 1 Lloyd's Rep 264 (Winn J)
The plaintiff issued proceedings against the first defendants for damages for personal injuries. The first defendants denied liability and blamed Astridge & Sons. The plaintiff joined the latter as second defendants only two and a half months before the three-year limitation period expired. The plaintiff failed against the first defendants but succeeded against the second, who in their defence had not blamed the first. He was ordered to bear the first defendants' costs up to joinder of the second defendants, thereafter a Bullock Order for the recovery of the first defendants' costs from the second defendants.

Costs after payment into Court

Note—See pp 659–662, below.

High Court costs refused

Finch v Telegraph Construction and Maintenance Co
[1949] 1 All ER 452, 65 TLR 153, [1949] WN 57, 93 Sol Jo 219 (Devlin J)
A workman sustained an injury to his eye. Two months later the eye became inflamed and painful, and a medical report to his solicitors said it was obviously a very serious matter. The plaintiff recovered £10.
HELD: No 'sufficient reason' for bringing action in High Court to justify costs on High Court scale under the County Courts Act 1934, s 47(3)(a). Costs awarded on county court scale.

Matarazzo v Kent Area Health Authority
(1983) 127 Sol Jo 393, CA
When a minimum award of damages to entitle costs on the High Court scale was £1,200 the plaintiff was awarded £1,000 damages plus interest agreed at £225. He claimed costs on the High Court scale.
HELD: The Law Reform (Miscellaneous Provisions) Act 1934 s 3(1C) as added by the Administration of Justice Act 1969, s 22 showed that interest should be disregarded. The plaintiff was not entitled to High Court costs.

Note—In respect of county court cases the Law Reform (Miscellaneous Provisions) Act 1934 s 3(1C) was replaced by the County Courts Act 1959, s 97A, added by the Administration of Justice Act 1982. Subsection (8) retained the effect of s 3(1C) of the 1934 Act. The County Courts Act 1959, s 97A has been replaced without amendment by the County Courts Act 1984, s 69.

When High Court costs recoverable

Hopkins v Rees and Kirby Ltd

[1959] 2 All ER 352, [1959] 1 WLR 740, 103 Sol Jo 509 (Glyn-Jones J)
Plaintiff, a steel erector, sued his employers for damages for negligence in
respect of an accident at work on 20 November 1955. Writ was issued on 6
May 1957. The defence included a contention of contributory negligence.
On 25 November 1957, trial was ordered at Glamorgan. In March 1958,
defendants paid into Court £250 and plaintiff served notice of acceptance
within the prescribed time. The plaintiff applied for costs on the High
Court scale.
HELD: The question is, is the Court satisfied that at the time the writ was
issued, it was then obvious that it was a county court action, or was it an
action which, when tried by one judge, rather than another, and leaving
out any question of contributory negligence, might have resulted in an
award exceeding £400. Looking at the medical evidence and no more, I am
unable to say that it should have been quite clear to the plaintiff as a
reasonable man that no judge would award more than £400 for that injury.
   I do not accept the contention of the defendants that regard should be
had to all matters that were in dispute in the action, including medical
evidence and the circumstances in which the accident happened.

Costs where two actions tried together

John Fairfax & Sons Pty Ltd v E. C. De Witt & Co Pty Ltd

[1958] 1 QB 323, [1957] 3 All ER 410, [1957] 3 WLR 877, 101 Sol Jo 901,
CA
The order that two actions be listed and tried together does not make them
anything else than two actions. The discretion as to costs of either action
must be confined to the parties to that action. A cannot be ordered to pay
the costs of B incurred in proceedings to which A was not a party. The order
does not have the effect of turning separate proceedings into one set of
proceedings. Appeal from the decision of the trial judge that he had no
jurisdiction to make such an order, dismissed.

Claim and counter-claim

Medway Oil and Storage Co v Continental Contractors

[1929] AC 88, 98 LJKB 148, 140 LT 98, 45 TLR 20, HL
When a claim and counter-claim are both dismissed with costs, upon the
taxation of the costs, the true rule is that the claim should be treated as if it
stood alone, and the counter-claim should bear only the amount by which
the costs of the proceedings have been increased by it. No costs not incurred
by reason of the counter-claim can be costs of the counter-claim. In the
absence of special directions by the court there should be no
apportionment. The same principle applies where both the claim and the
counter-claim have succeeded.

Note—In motor accident cases where there is injury or damage suffered by both
parties and liability is in dispute it may be important on the question of costs to
choose whether to proceed by way of claim or counter-claim.

Cinema Press Ltd v Pictures and Pleasures Ltd
[1945] KB 356, [1945] 1 All ER 440, 172 LT 295, 61 TLR 282 CA
Defendants paid into court £25, with denial of liability. Plaintiffs recovered
£5. The judge awarded costs to the plaintiffs and gave defendants costs on
the issue of damages after payment in.

The taxing master allowed nothing to defendants on the ground that
there is no apportionment in issue cases.
HELD: The principles of costs of claim and counter-claim laid down in
Medway Oil & Storage Co v Continental Contractors (above) applied. There is no
apportionment, but a division of some items common to the issue of negligence and the issue of damages, eg brief fee, instructions for brief,
discovery and correspondence. There is jurisdiction to award to one side
such proportion of the costs as the judge thinks fair. This is the simplest way
and simplicity is desirable.

Lowther v Lewin
(1964) 109 Sol Jo 33 (Sachs J)
In an action arising from a road accident the plaintiff was found 30% to
blame and awarded £1,323; the defendant was found 70% to blame and on
his counter-claim was awarded £103. Each party was insured against third-
party risks. The plaintiff supported by the defendant applied to the Court
not to exercise its discretion under Ord 15, r 2(4) to give judgment for the
plaintiff for the balance of £1,220 but to give judgment for both parties with
appropriate costs so as to avoid difficulties in apportioning costs between
the insurance companies.

The judge said he saw no objection: judgment for the plaintiff for £1,323
with costs of the action save in so far as they were increased by the counter-
claim; judgment for the defendant for £103 with such costs as were solely
referable to the counter-claim.

Costs on dismissal of appeal and cross-appeal

The Stentor
[1934] P 133, [1934] All ER Rep 545, 103 LJP 105, 152 LT 450, 18 Asp
MLC 490, CA
When an appeal and cross-appeal are dismissed with costs, the principle of
no apportionment laid down as to claim and counter-claim in the *Medway*
case is applicable.

Per Scrutton LJ: The matter is not to be dealt with by apportionment.
Only those extra costs which are occasioned by the cross-appeal are the
subject-matter of the order for costs on the cross-appeal.

Exercise of judge's discretion

Jones v McKie and Mersey Docks and Harbour Board
[1964] 2 All ER 842, [1964] 1 WLR 960, 108 Sol Jo 442, CA
The plaintiff's vehicle was damaged by the second defendant's vehicle
owing to the negligent driving of the first defendant, a servant of the second
defendants, whose defence was that he was not acting in the scope of his
employment at the time of the collision. The action was brought in the

Liverpool Court of Passage. The evidence at the trial showed that when the accident occurred the first defendant had been using his employers' vehicle to return home for his house key which he would need when he had finished work. He gave evidence that the second defendants did not forbid drivers to take their vehicles when going hime to dinner and that he and other drivers did so. The judge held that the first defendant was not acting in the scope of his employment at the time of the accident and gave judgment for the second defendants against the plaintiff. He refused to award them costs against the plaintiff on the ground that they exercised no proper control over the use of their vehicles by the drivers. On appeal, held, an appeal on costs was permissible only on the same principle as is provided by the Supreme Court of Judicature (Consolidation) Act 1925, s 31(1)(h), namely, that the Court of Appeal must be able to say that the judge in the court below, however much he may have been purporting to exercise his discretion, has not really exercised his discretion at all, that is, by taking into consideration wholly extraneous and irrelevant matters. It was impossible to say in the present case that, in thinking the second defendants' failure to control their transport was reprehensible, the judge proceeded on grounds which were wholly unconnected with the cause of action. He did exercise his discretion, however wrongly, and it was not open to the Court of Appeal to interfere.

Note—The Supreme Court of Judicature (Consolidation) Act 1925 has been repealed. Section 31(1)(h) of that Act has been substantially re-enacted in the Supreme Court Act 1981, s 18(1)(f).

Infant's costs — taxation

Note—Formerly it was the duty of the solicitors who appeared for the plaintiffs in infants' cases to carry in their bill of costs for taxation and not to enter into agreement with the other side with regard to costs. This is no longer necessary.

See now note to Ord 80, r 12 'Agreeing costs', *Supreme Court Practice 1985* vol 1, p 1161.

Unsatisfactory conduct of action

Chetland v Babcock and Wilcox Ltd
(1966) 110 Sol Jo 430 (Blain J)

The plaintiff was injured at work and claimed damages against the defendants. In correspondence the plaintiff's solicitors alleged that the hospital notes supported the diagnosis of their client's doctor, but on being asked by the defendant's solicitors to grant access to those notes they refused. On the issue of liability the plaintiff's solicitors had statements about the accident from witnesses who would not give statements to the defendants, being prevented, it was said, by the shop steward of the plaintiff's trade union. The defendants denied liability and made no payment into Court. At the hearing the witnesses gave evidence about the accident and the defendants then admitted liability. The hospital notes only partially supported the doctor's diagnosis. The plaintiff was awarded £455 but the defendants opposed his application for costs of the whole action.

HELD: He should have only 75% of his costs. The combination of circumstances on the medical aspects and the question of proof of liability in this case was very unsatisfactory. It was wrong that litigation should be conducted as warfare, since it made a mockery of the opportunity to use the machinery of payment into Court. That machinery was a way not only of saving costs but often a good method of ensuring that an unfortunate injured plaintiff received a fair sum of money very much sooner than by a hearing.

Note—See also *Vose v Barr* p 585, above.

Service by post — default judgment

Peter Cox v Thirwell
(1981) 125 Sol Jo 481 (Forbes J)
The plaintiff served a writ on the defendant by post pursuant to Ord 10, r 1(2)(a). The defendant was abroad and did not receive it; the plaintiffs signed judgment in default. The master on the defendant's application set aside the judgment but ordered that he pay the plaintiff's costs in any event. On the defendant's appeal on the question of costs:
HELD: The previous practice on setting aside a regular judgment of giving the plaintiff his costs in any event was not appropriate where neither party was at fault. In such a case the correct order was costs in cause.

Party and party: common fund

Note—RSC Ord 62, r 28 (assessment of costs) is as follows:

'**28** (1) This rule applies to costs which by or under these rules or any order or direction of the Court are to be paid to a party to any proceedings either by another party to those proceedings or out of any fund (other than a fund which the party to whom the costs are to be paid holds as trustee or personal representative).
(2) Subject to the following provisions of this rule, costs to which this rule applies shall be taxed on the party and party basis, and on a taxation on that basis there shall be allowed all such costs as were necessary or proper for the attainment of justice or for enforcing or defending the rights of the party whose costs are being taxed.
(3) The Court in awarding costs to which this rule applies may in any case in which it thinks fit to do so order or direct that the costs shall be taxed on the common fund basis.
(4) On taxation on the common fund basis, being a more generous basis than that provided for by paragraph (2), there shall be allowed a reasonable amount in respect of all costs reasonably incurred, and paragraph (2) shall not apply; and accordingly in all cases where costs are to be taxed on the common fund basis the ordinary rules applicable on a taxation as between solicitor and client where the costs are to be paid out of a common fund in which the client and others are interested shall be applied, whether or not the costs are in fact to be so paid.'

Layzell v British Portland Cement Manufacturers Ltd
[1961] 1 All ER 244, [1961] 1 WLR 557, 105 Sol Jo 322
In a case in which he was asked to exercise his discretion under sub-rule (3) Paull J dealt with the meaning of 'common fund basis' as follows:

'A query which arises under para (4) of r 28 is whether that means that costs which are taxed on a common fund basis are taxed on what used to be known as solicitor and client basis, or on what used to be known as solicitor and own client basis. As far as I can see and understand the matter, it seems to me that that rule lays down that if costs are taxed on a common fund basis, they should be taxed on the same basis as costs were taxed before the rule came into force if the order made was that costs should be taxed on a solicitor and client basis. Although there is talk of common fund, and although submission has been made that it may be that the use of those words would entail taxation on a solicitor and own client basis, I do not so read the rules. I cannot govern the taxing master, but I think that I ought to indicate that in my judgment, under para (4) of r 28, taxation on the common fund basis is really the same as taxation on the old solicitor and client basis.'

EMI Records Ltd v Ian Cameron Wallace Ltd
[1983] Ch 59, [1982] 2 All ER 980, [1982] 3 WLR 245, 126 Sol Jo 465.
On an application for a review of costs on an indemnity basis, the court's conclusions included the following:

(1) The Judicature Act 1925, s 50(1) gave the court a wide discretionary power over costs which had not been cut down by Ord 62, r 28 so as to confine the court to making orders only on a party and party basis or the common fund basis and no other basis.

(2) The Court had power to order the payment of costs on an indemnity basis, the result being that all the costs incurred would be allowed except those unreasonably incurred or of an unreasonable amount, and is applying those exceptions, the receiving party would be given the benefit of the doubt.

Zaniewski v Scales
(1969) 113 Sol Jo 525, Times, 28 June, (Chapman J)
An agreement by an insurance company with solicitors to pay 'your reasonable costs' is an agreement to pay 'your costs to be taxed if not agreed'.

County court

Pepper v Healey
(1982) 126 Sol Jo 497, [1982] RTR 411, CA
Following a collision between their cars the plaintiff began proceedings against the defendant in the county court for an amount not exceeding £200. The defendant, represented by solicitors instructed by her insurers, denied liability. Both parties proposed to call expert and other witnesses at the trial and have legal representation. The plaintiff applied to the registrar for an order rescinding automatic reference of the claim to arbitration under Ord 19, r 1(4) on the grounds provided by Ord 19, r 1(5)(d) 'that it would be unreasonable for the claim to proceed to arbitration having regard to . . . the circumstances of the parties'. The registrar made the order as asked and was upheld by the judge.
HELD, ON APPEAL: There was no reason to suggest that the judge had applied his discretion wrongly. The contest between the parties was unequal as the defendant had the protection of an insurance company and the plaintiff had not. If there was an arbitration no solicitor's charges would be allowed as between party and party. If, on the other hand, the case was tried in the county court and the plaintiff won she would recover her costs;

as she needed representation the judge was entitled to conclude that the case should be tried by the county court.

Newland v Boardwell
[1983] 3 All ER 179, [1984] 1 WLR 1453, 127 Sol Jo 580, CA

The County Court Rules 1936, Ord 19, r 1(4) provides that when the amount claimed in proceedings does not exceed £500 the action shall on receipt of a defence of the claim be referred for arbitration by the registrar. Order 19, r 1(ii) provides that no solicitors' costs shall be allowed in respect of any proceedings referred to arbitration unless certified by the registrar to have been incurred through the unreasonable conduct of the opposite party.

In an action arising from a collision of two vehicles the defendant in his defence admitted negligence but expressly did not admit the plaintiff's alleged injuries loss and damage. The claim being limited to £500 the registrar referred it for arbitration, since the refusal to admit the injuries loss and damage amounted to a defence on the issue of causation. The plaintiff having later accepted a payment into court the registrar gave a certificate that her costs should be paid by the defendant by reason of his 'unreasonable conduct' in defending the action. If the defendant had submitted to interlocutory judgment for damages to be assessed he could have called evidence and been heard on quantum of damages but would have been liable to an order for costs against him.

HELD, in the Court of Appeal: The denial of liability in the defence was a device to take advantage of Ord 19, r (4) and avoid an order for costs. It was a misuse of the pleading process and justified the registrar's certificate under r 1(ii)(c). But the words 'through the unreasonable conduct of the opposite party' could not affect costs incurred before the unreasonable conduct. When the plaintiff knew from the defence that the case would have to be referred for arbitration she could have withdrawn her retainer to her solicitors and incurred no more costs. Thus her liability for costs after the defence was not the result of the defendant's 'unreasonable conduct' but of her own failure to protect herself. She was entitled against the defendant only to the costs on the summons (ie her costs up to the filing of the defence).

Note—Order 19 of the County Court Rules 1936 is now contained in Ord 19 of the 1981 Rules.

Running-down action: leading counsel

Hosie v Malcolm
[1966] L S Gaz R 404 (McNair J)

In an action arising from a road accident the second defendants, a bus company, briefed leading counsel. The first defendant was man of straw. The second defendants were successful and were awarded costs to be taxed as between party and party. The taxing master allowed the costs of briefing leading counsel on the ground that the plaintiff had only to establish a scintilla of negligence against the second defendants to saddle them with all the damages and all the costs, a liability running well into four figures, with only a worthless remedy over against the first defendant.

HELD, on a review by the judge: It was not a case which justified allowing the fee of leading counsel on a party and party taxation. The taxing master's grounds were not apposite because if the second defendants had been sued alone they would have been exposed to exactly the same risk. There was no complex problem in the case and it was the kind of case commonly dealt with by junior counsel. Appeal allowed.

CROWN, CLAIMS AGAINST

Note—Before the Crown Proceedings Act 1947, the Crown was in general immune from legal process, and the principle that the King could do no wrong was a defence to any government department or official, other than the actual driver, to a claim for damage or injury caused by a government vehicle. The Treasury Solicitor as a matter of grace defended proceedings against the driver and the Treasury met any judgment against him. The Act reversed both rules, that the Crown could not be sued in its own courts, and that 'the Crown could do no wrong'.

The Act and the Rules are set out in the *Supreme Court Practice* and the *County Court Practice*. Sections 2, 4 and 10 of the Act are set out below, together with a short note of other relevant sections to assist reference.

In the High Court the Rules are in Ord 77.

In the county court they are Ord 42, rr 1–14.

CROWN PROCEEDINGS ACT 1947
(10 & 11 Geo 6, c 44)

2 Liability of the Crown in tort   (1) Subject to the provisions of this Act, the Crown shall be subject to all those liabilities in tort to which, if it were a private person of full age and capacity, it would be subject:
(a) in respect of torts committed by its servants or agents;
(b) in respect of any breach of those duties which a person owes to his servants or agents at common law by reason of being their employer; and
(c) in respect of any breach of the duties attaching at common law to the ownership, occupation, possession or control of property:
Provided that no proceedings shall lie against the Crown by virtue of para (a) of this subsection in respect of any act or omission of a servant or agent of the Crown unless the act or omission would apart from the provisions of this Act have given rise to a cause of action in tort against that servant or agent or his estate.
(2) Where the Crown is bound by a statutory duty which is binding also upon persons other than the Crown and its officers, then subject to the provisions of this Act, the Crown shall, in respect of a failure to comply with that duty, be subject to all those liabilities in tort (if any) to which it would be so subject if it were a private person of full age and capacity.
(3) Where any functions are conferred or imposed upon an officer of the Crown as such either by any rule of the common law or by statute, and that officer commits a tort while performing or purporting to perform those functions, the liabilities of the Crown in respect of the tort shall be such as they would have been if those functions had been conferred or imposed solely by virtue of instructions lawfully given by the Crown.
(4) Any enactment which negatives or limits the amount of the liability of any Government department or officer of the Crown in respect of any tort committed by that department or officer shall, in the case of proceedings against the Crown under this section in respect of a tort committed by that department or officer,

apply in relation to the Crown as it would have applied in relation to that department or officer if the proceedings against the Crown had been proceedings against the department or officer.

(5) No proceedings shall lie against the Crown by virtue of this section in respect of anything done or omitted to be done by any person while discharging or purporting to discharge any responsibilities which he has in connection with the execution of judicial process.

(6) No proceedings shall lie against the Crown by virtue of this section in respect of any act, neglect or default of any officer of the Crown, unless that officer has been directly or indirectly appointed by the Crown and was at the material time paid in respect of his duties as an officer of the Crown wholly out of the Consolidated Fund of the United Kingdom, moneys provided by Parliament, the Road Fund, or any other Fund certified by the Treasury for the purposes of this subsection or was at the material time holding an office in respect of which the Treasury certify that the holder thereof would normally be so paid.

4 Application of law as to indemnity, contribution, joint and several tortfeasors, and contributory negligence (1) Where the Crown is subject to any liability by virtue of this Part of this Act, the law relating to indemnity and contribution shall be enforceable by or against the Crown in respect of the liability to which it is so subject as if the Crown were a private person of full age and capacity.

(2) [Replaced by Civil Liability (Contribution) Act 1978, s 9(2) and Sch 2.]

(3) Without prejudice to the general effect of s 1 of this Act, the Law Reform (Contributory Negligence) Act 1945 (which amends the law in relation to contributory negligence) shall bind the Crown.

[Section 5 of the Civil Liability (Contribution) Act 1978 reads:

'Without prejudice to s 4(1) of the Crown Proceedings Act 1947 (indemnity and contribution), this Act shall bind the Crown, but nothing in this Act shall be construed as in any way affecting Her Majesty in Her private capacity (including in right of Her Duchy of Lancaster) or the Duchy of Cornwall.']

10 Provisions relating to the armed forces (1) Nothing done or omitted to be done by a member of the armed forces of the Crown while on duty as such shall subject either him or the Crown to liability in tort for causing the death of another person, or for causing personal injury to another person, in so far as the death or personal injury is due to anything suffered by that other person while he is a member of the armed forces of the Crown if —

(a) at the time when that thing is suffered by that other person, he is either on duty as a member of the armed forces of the Crown or is, though not on duty as such, on any land, premises, ship, aircraft or vehicle for the time being used for the purposes of the armed forces of the Crown; and

(b) the Minister of Pensions certifies that his suffering that thing has been or will be treated as attributable to service for the purposes of entitlement to an award under the Royal Warrant, Order in Council or Order of His Majesty relating to the disablement or death of members of the force of which he is a member;

Provided that this subsection shall not exempt a member of the said forces from liability in tort in any case in which the court is satisfied that the act or omission was not connected with the execution of his duties as a member of those forces.

(2) No proceedings in tort shall lie against the Crown for death or personal injury due to anything suffered by a member of the armed forces of the Crown if —

(a) that thing is suffered by him in consequence of the nature or condition of any such land, premises, ship, aircraft or vehicle as aforesaid, or in consequence of the nature or condition of any equipment or supplies used for the purposes of those forces; and

(b) the Minister of Pensions certifies as mentioned in the preceding subsection;

nor shall any act or omission of an officer of the Crown subject him to liability in tort for death or personal injury, in so far as the death or personal injury is due to anything suffered by a member of the armed forces of the Crown being a thing as to which the conditions aforesaid are satisfied.

(3) A Secretary of State, if satisfied that it is the fact —

(a) that a person was or was not on any particular occasion on duty as a member of the armed forces of the Crown; or

(b) that at any particular time any land, premises, ship, aircraft, vehicle, equipment or supplies was or was not, or were or were not, used for the purposes of the said forces;

may issue a certificate certifying that to be the fact; and any such certificate shall, for the purposes of this section, be conclusive as to the fact which it certifies.

Section 17 provides that proceedings must be instituted against the department, or if this is inappropriate or doubtful, the Attorney-General. A list of the departments and the solicitor who will accept service is published by HMSO.

Section 18 provides that service of documents must be on the solicitor for the department, or, if none, the Treasury Solicitor.

Section 19 gives the Crown the option to appear in London to a District Registry writ, and to trial in London.

Section 20 enables the Crown to transfer an action in a county court to the High Court.

Section 28 deals with discovery of documents and interrogatories subject to right of refusal in the public interest.

Subject to exceptions not relevant to motor claims the Limitation Act 1980 applies to proceedings by or against the crown 'in like manner as it applies to proceedings between subjects' (Limitation Act 1980, s 37).

Full information of the circumstances of the claim is to be given before the Crown is bound to take any step in the action. A form of endorsement of writ is set out below, and this is also suitable in the county court.

The Rules also provide that judgment is not to be entered in default of appearance or pleadings; for service on solicitor; interlocutory proceedings in London; summons necessary for third party notice; and trial in London.

In the county court the summons is to issue where the cause of action arises; the particulars are to show the grounds of liability of the Crown and Department and officers concerned; no date of hearing on plaint note, nor until stay of action ended; and application for third party notice to be served on Crown. Order 42 provides for service by delivery or registered post.

Specimen endorsement of writ in Crown cases

'The plaintiff's claim is for damages for negligent driving on the part of . . . a Crown servant. The circumstances in which it is alleged that the liability of the Crown has arisen are that on the . . . day of . . . the plaintiff's motor vehicle was being driven along . . . Road . . . when a motor vehicle owned by the Crown driven by a Crown servant who was engaged on service for the Crown at the time of the alleged negligent driving collided with and damaged the plaintiff's said motor vehicle.

The Government Department concerned is the [insert Authorised Government Department].'

Crown costs

Note—By the Administration of Justice (Miscellaneous Provisions) Act 1933, s 7, costs in actions or arbitrations are in the discretion of the Court or arbitrator in any civil proceedings to which the Crown is a party.

List of Government Departments and solicitors

Note—Reference should be made to the latest edition of the *Supreme Court Practice* for the up-to-date list of authorised Government Departments and the solicitors and addresses for service.

DIPLOMATIC PRIVILEGE

Dickinson v Del Solar
[1930] 1 KB 376, [1929] All ER Rep 139, 99 LKJB 162, 142 LT 66, 45 TLR 637 (Lord Hewart CJ)
The defendant was First Secretary of the Peruvian Legation, an appointment entitling him to immunity from legal process. The plaintiff obtained a judgment against him for damages for personal injury caused by the defendant's negligent driving. He had not claimed diplomatic immunity because the Minister of the Peruvian Legation had instructed him not to do so, the accident having happened when he was not on official business. The defendant's insurers refused to indemnify him because their policy covered him only against 'legal liability' and he was, they said, under no legal liability.
HELD: The insurers were wrong. Diplomatic agents are not immune from legal liability for wrongful acts. More accurately, they are not liable to be sued in English courts unless they submit to the jurisdiction. Diplomatic privilege does not import immunity from legal liability but only exemption from local jurisdiction. In the present case the privilege was waived. The judgment created a legal liability against the defendant which the insurance company must meet.

Note—Subsequently the Foreign Office obtained from all authorised motor insurers doing business in the UK an assurance, still effective, that they will not attempt to rely on the privileged positions of their diplomatic clients.

DISCOVERY OF DOCUMENTS

Legal professional privilege

Note—RSC Ord 24, r 1, provides that after close of pleadings in an action begun by writ there shall be discovery by the parties of documents relating to matters in question in the action. By r 2(2) of the Order a defendant to an action arising out of an accident on land due to a collision or apprehended collision involving a vehicle shall not make any discovery unless the Court otherwise orders. Thus in respect of motor claims discovery against the defendant can generally be obtained only by order of the Court. Where an order has been obtained the question may arise whether a claim form and correspondence with insurers must be produced to the plaintiff's solicitor.

The Hopper No 13
[1925] P 52, 94 LJP 45, 132 LT 736, 41 TLR 189, Div Ct
The Port of London Authority issued general instructions to masters of their craft to report in triplicate on the form provided 'immediately after every casualty'. The report was made on a printed form headed 'Confidential report furnished for the information of the Authority's solicitor in view of anticipated litigation, in respect of a casualty occurring between the Authority's . . . and the . . . '. The report was sent to a firm of solicitors who invariably acted for the Authority on the instructions of underwriters. In practice the report was sent to the dredging superintendent, who passed it on to the chief harbour master, who in turn passed it on to the manager of the Authority's insurance department, and in every case of collision he sent the report to the solicitors.

The owners of a vessel in collision with a dredger of the Authority, relying on the decision of *Birmingham and Midland Motor Omnibus Co v London and North Western Rly Co* [1913] 3 KB 850, CA, 83 LJKB 474, 109 LT 64, 57 Sol Jo 752, that it was necessary in any large business organisation for written records to be regularly made, and to hold such documents privileged merely because the proprietors of the business organisation had in mind their utility in case of litigation, feared, threatened, or commenced, would be unsound in principle and disastrous in practice, contended the report was not privileged.

HELD: The document was furnished for the information of the solicitors and made bona fide for the purpose of being used by the solicitors in anticipated litigation. There was the almost inevitable certainty of litigation where there is a collision between craft; in default of settlement litigation must inevitably follow. The report was made for the purpose of being submitted to solicitors. The document was obtained for the solicitors in the sense of being procured as materials upon which professional advice should be given in proceedings pending, or threatened, or anticipated. The document was prepared in such a way that it is useful in the case of a claim, and it gives the very information which an experienced person would look for if a claim were to be made.

The document was privileged from production.

Westminster Airways Ltd v Kuwait Oil Co Ltd
[1951] 1 KB 444, [1950] 2 All ER 596, 66 TLR 281, 94 Sol Jo 551, 84 Ll L Rep 297, CA
A motor lorry belonging to defendants ran into an aircraft belonging to the plaintiffs which had been forced to land on a road in Kuwait. The accident occurred on 25 November 1947. Formal notice of a claim for damages was given by the plaintiffs to the defendants on 29 December 1947.

Pursuant to an order for discovery of documents, the defendants made an affidavit which included the following paragraph:

'The defendant company object to produce any of the documents set forth in the schedule hereto upon the ground that they came into existence and were made after litigation was in contemplation and in view of such litigation for the purpose of obtaining and furnishing to the solicitors of the defendant company evidence and information as to the evidence which could be obtained and otherwise for the use of the solicitors to enable them to conduct the defence in this action and to advice the defendants.'

The defendants disclosed (inter alia) the following documents:
1 a letter from defendants' representative at Kuwait to the defendants in London dated 27 November 1947;
2 a similar letter dated 3 December 1947;
3 a letter from the defendants' insurance brokers to the defendants' insurers dated 19 December 1947, which enclosed document 2.

The defendants claimed privilege for documents which included letters from their insurers to their brokers of 22 and 23 December 1947, and from the defendants to the brokers of 31 December 1947.

HELD: The letter of 3 December made it quite clear that there was more than a probability of litigation at that time. It gave details of the accident and stated that the pilot of the aircraft had made a statement of his evidence which resulted in the driver of the motor lorry being found guilty of driving without due care and attention in the political agents' court. It was obvious from the nature of the accident and the letter of 31 December that litigation was anticipated before the actual claim (29 December) was received.

Per Jenkins LJ: Insurers are concerned in the matter only because they have agreed by the contract of insurance to indemnify their assured against claims of the character in question. That being so, the very fact that the insurance company is communicated with at all indicates that a claim is anticipated.

Seabrook v British Transport Commission
[1959] 2 All ER 15, [1959] 1 WLR 509, 103 Sol Jo 351 (Havers J)
The plaintiff was the widow of a workman employed by the defendants who was killed whilst at work. She sued for damages alleging negligence and breach of statutory duty. The summons for directions ordered a list of documents. The defendants claimed privilege for some documents including correspondence between and reports made by the defendants' officers and servants.

The plaintiff called for particulars of the 'reports' and in particular whether they included a statement by James Munro with whom the deceased was working. The defendants replied as follows: 'the reports are accident reports and reports by the defendants' officers and servants on their enquiries into this accident, which reports include a statement of James Munro, with whom the deceased was working.'

HELD: A party may ask the judge to look at the documents but it is entirely a matter for the judge to exercise his discretion on the facts of any particular case. It is not necessary in this case to look at them. The claim for privilege has been established. Appeal dismissed.

Note—The Editorial Note in the All England Report points out that this decision must be considered with that of *Longthorn v BTC*, below. The *Supreme Court Practice 1985* at 24/5/9 says the scope of *Seabrook* and the correctness of *Westminster Airways* and the practice based upon them 'will need reconsideration'.

Longthorn v British Transport Commission
[1959] 2 All ER 32, [1959] 1 WLR 530, 103 Sol Jo 352 (Diplock J)
Plaintiff was injured by accident whilst in the employ of the defendants, and shortly after the defendants held a private inquiry into the cause of the accident, which occured on 21 January 1955, and the inquiry was in March

1955. At the inquiry, in which the plaintiff took part, the object of the inquiry as set out in the defendant's affidavit of documents was as follows:

'It was then explained to the injured man the purpose of the inquiry, that it was not so much convened to establish guilt or attach blame to either himself or any other person who may have been concerned, but rather to ascertain the cause of the accident with a view to safeguarding against any possible similar happening in the future. Longthorn's co-operation was invited to this end, this being willingly promised by him.'

At the time of the inquiry, the defendants did not know that the plaintiff intended to bring the action and first became aware of it by a letter of 5 July 1955. Writ was issued on 29 February 1956. In the proceedings the defendants first filed a list of documents, in which they claimed privilege and later an affidavit of documents, also claiming privilege, on the same grounds as in *Seabrook's* case, subject to the wording of these documents. In *Seabrook's* case the affidavit said that the documents were prepared 'wholly or mainly' for the purpose of being furnished to the solicitor. In *Longthorn's* case there was no such claim. The list of documents used the words 'inter alia' for the appropriate purpose. The judge said he agreed with every word of the judgment of Havers J in *Seabrook's* case. The judge decided to look at the documents and held that the claim for privilege was not established on the ground put forward in the affidavit.

HELD: The document nor any part of it is not privileged, because the inquiry was not to any appreciable extent for the purpose of obtaining for or furnishing to the solicitor. It was for the purpose of safeguarding against a similar occurrence.

If this ground is wrong, I think the defendants are estopped from claiming privilege in respect of that part of the document which contains the plaintiff's evidence. Appeal dismissed.

'DOMINANT PURPOSE'

Waugh v British Railways Board
[1980] AC 521, [1979] 2 All ER 1169, [1979] 3 WLR 150, [1979] IRLR 364, 123 Sol Jo 506, HL

The plaintiff's husband, an engine driver, was killed when two locomotives collided. She claimed damages under the Fatal Accidents Acts. Soon after the accident a joint internal report on it was prepared by two officers of the defendant board as was the board's normal practice after an accident. Its objects were to assist in establishing the cause of the accident and equally for the purpose of providing the board's solicitor with material on which he could advise the board in any proceedings arising out of the accident. Proceedings were to be anticipated in the present case. The report was headed 'For the information of the board's solicitor . . . for the purpose of enabling him to advise the BRB in relation thereto'. The plaintiff sought discovery of the report; the defendants refused on the ground of legal professional privilege.

HELD: Reversing the decision of the Court of Appeal, the report should be disclosed. Unless the purpose of submission to the legal adviser is at least the *dominant* (but not necessarily the sole) purpose for which the relevant document was prepared the reasons which require privilege to be extended to it cannot apply. Here the two purposes for which the report was prepared were of equal rank or weight.

Neilson v Laugharne
[1981] QB 736, [1981] 1 All ER 829, [1981] 2 WLR 537, 125 Sol Jo 202, CA
In an action against the police for, inter alia, damage to property and wrongful arrest the plaintiff sought discovery of statements taken by the police for the purposes of an enquiry under the Police Act 1964, s 49 into a complaint made by the plaintiff arising from the same incidents. The defendants claimed legal professional privilege against disclosure.
HELD, following *Waugh v British Railways Board* (above): The dominant purpose of the police in taking the statements was to carry out the statutory duty to investigate required by s 49 and there was no legal professional privilege in respect of those statements.

Note—Applied in *Hehir v Metropolitan Police Comr* [1982] 2 All ER 335, [1982] 1 WLR 715, 126 Sol Jo 330, CA.

Re Highgrade Traders Ltd
(1983) Times, 20 December, CA
Following a fire at the premises of Highgrade Traders Ltd in suspicious circumstances the fire insurers obtained reports from loss adjustors, accountants and fire investigators at the instance of their solicitors. As a result the insurers refused to meet a claim. The company later went into liquidation. The liquidator applied to the court under the Companies Act 1948, s 268(3) for an order that the insurers' claims officer should produce the reports.
HELD, ON APPEAL: No order should be made. Applying the test in *Waugh v British Railways Board* (above) the dominant purpose of the reports was to discover the cause of the fire so as to ascertain if there had been a fraud. It was clear that if a claim was persisted in there would be litigation. The judge's view that finding the cause of the fire was the main purpose and legal advice only a secondary purpose was a misinterpretation of the relevant authorities. Knowing the cause of the fire was of no use on its own; the insurers had formed a view early on in the dispute that litigation was probable. The documents were privileged.

PLAINTIFF'S STATEMENT

Britten v F. H. Pilcher & Sons
[1969] 1 All ER 491 (Thesiger J)
The plaintiff suffered injury when in the defendant's employment. Three weeks after the accident he gave a statement to the defendants' insurers, and signed it, describing the accident. Later he sued for damages and in the statement of claim gave a different version of the accident. At the trial he was confronted with his signed statement and lost the action. The statement was headed 'This statement is intended for the use of the company's legal advisers in connection with litigation already commenced or anticipated'. It had not been disclosed by the defendants on discovery. The plaintiff opposed the defendants' application for costs on the ground that the statement should have been disclosed and that if it had the action might have been abandoned at an early stage.
HELD: The defendants were not under a duty to disclose it. As Havers J said in *Seabrook v British Transport Commission* (above) the practice on

discovery is a reconciliation of two opposing principles, (1) the need to protect professional legal assistance and advice, and (2) the requirement that in the interests of justice and in order that the parties should not be taken by surprise, all relevant documents should be before the court. In the present case as the statement was admissible against the plaintiff and was in the possession of the defendants there was no risk that it would not be brought to the attention of the court. The plaintiff must have known he had made the statement and could not be taken by surprise by it. It had never been previously suggested that documents under the heading that this document had should be disclosed in advance to plaintiffs so as to enable them to trim their evidence to suit.

INTERROGATORY

Jones v G. D. Searle & Co
[1978] 3 All ER 654, [1979] 1 WLR 101, 122 Sol Jo 435, CA
In an action for damages for alleged medical negligence the plaintiff asked for the discretion of the court to be exercised in her favour under the Limitation Act 1939, s 2D (now the Limitation Act 1980, s 33). She revealed that she had taken counsel's opinion. The defendants sought to interrogate whether the opinion had been favourable or not. The plaintiff refused to answer on the ground of legal professional privilege.
HELD: Section 2D(3)(f) required the court to have regard to the steps taken by the plaintiff to obtain 'medical legal or other expert advice and the nature of any such advice'. As the court is under a duty to consider the advice it must be able to demand evidence as to what the nature of the advice was. The defendants were entitled to have the interrogatory answered.

Birmingham v Kelly
(26 April 1979 unreported) (Jupp J in chambers)
The plaintiff alleged he was injured in a motor accident on 8 June 1973. As the proposed defendants' whereabouts could not be ascertained, the plaintiff's solicitors notified his claim to Motor Insurers' Bureau on 22 May 1975. The Motor Insurers' Bureau appointed an insurance office to investigate the claim who communicated with the plaintiff's solicitors. On 17 August 1977 the investigating office denied liability on the Motor Insurers' Bureau behalf as no writ had been issued. The plaintiff instructed new solicitors who issued a writ and applied in due course for specific discovery of correspondence and recorded notes of telephone conversations between the Motor Insurers' Bureau and the investigating office from 22 May 1975 to 24 February 1978.
HELD: The documents were privileged: although the Motor Insurers' Bureau had not instructed solicitors during the period in question everything they did was to prepare the case for settlement or defence, whichever would prove appropriate. The Limitation Act 1939, s 2D did not justify overriding the privilege. Prejudice to the defendants had not been averred and *Jones v Searle* (above) which dealt with interrogatories, did not apply.

Note—The Limitation Act 1939, s 2D has now become the Limitation Act 1980, s 33.

Medical reports

Schneider v Leigh
[1955] 2 QB 195, [1955] 2 All ER 173, [1955] 2 WLR 904, 99 Sol Jo 276, CA

The doctor examined a plaintiff claiming damages for personal injuries sustained in a motor accident on the instructions of the defendants' solicitors and reported to the solicitors, who wrote to the plaintiff's solicitors and in their letter quoted two paragraphs of the report. The plaintiff's solicitors showed the letter to the plaintiff. The plaintiff by the same solicitors, whilst the action for personal injuries was still pending, issued a writ against the doctor claiming damages for libel alleging the two paragraphs were defamatory and that the doctor was guilty of malice. In his defence in the libel action the doctor pleaded privilege. The plaintiff applied in the libel action for discovery of the whole report and of the other documents passing between the doctor and the defendants' solicitors in the first action. Plaintiff by his counsel contended that an order for inspection should take effect only after the first action had been disposed of.
HELD: By Hodson and Romer LJJ, Singleton LJ dissenting, the documents were not privileged in the libel action.

Per Romer LJ. The privilege which exists in the first action is that of the company and of no one else; and the company can at any time waive the privilege without the defendant's consent. ['The company' were the defendants in the first action.]

Note—71 LQR 316 points out that the person making the report must take the risk that it may thereafter be disclosed and subject him to an action for libel. Whether he can protect himself by obtaining from his employers a guarantee that the report will be kept secret in all circumstances is uncertain (cf *Weld-Blundell v Stephens* [1920] AC 956, [1920] All ER Rep 32, 89 LJKB 705, 123 LT 593, 36 TLR 640, 64 Sol Jo 529, HL).

Patch v United Bristol Hospital Board
[1959] 3 All ER 876, [1959] 1 WLR 955, 103 Sol Jo 833 (Streatfeild J)

The plaintiff had an operation to his hand at the defendants' hospital, and following the operation he developed an infection. Pursuant to the recommendation in a circular issued by the Ministry of Health, and before the plaintiff had intimated any intention of making a claim, written statements were made by the consulting surgeon, the senior registrar, house surgeons and nurses at the hospital, and were sent to the solicitors to the hospital. Subsequently the plaintiff commenced proceedings against the hospital. The hospital claimed that the statements were privileged. The judge ruled that although no action had been commenced, the statements were not made in the ordinary course of hospital treatment, but in order to provide the legal adviser of the hospital with the necessary material to advise, if such a claim should be made.

Watson v Cammell Laird & Co
[1959] 2 All ER 757, [1959] 1 WLR 702, 103 Sol Jo 470, [1959] 2 Lloyd's Rep 175, CA

Plaintiff's affidavit of documents contained a document described as 'Copy

of Birkenhead Hospital Management Committee Case Notes relating to'
the plaintiff.

HELD: Although it was no more than a verbatim copy of a document which
was itself not privileged, it was entitled to legal professional protection as
the copy had been prepared by the plaintiff's solicitors for the purposes of
the action.

Mechanical defects — reports of earlier complaints

Blakebrough v British Motor Corpn Ltd
(1969) 113 Sol Jo 366, CA

The plaintiffs claimed damages for injuries received when an 1100 car
made by the defendants overturned. They alleged that the car was
dangerous and that other 1100 cars made by the defendants had crashed in
circumstances suggesting the existence of manufacturing defects. On an
application for discovery of documents relating to reports investigations
and complaints of uncontrollability for unknown causes in 1100 cars it was
held by the Court of Appeal the plaintiffs should have an order to include all
complaints relating to sudden uncontrollability of steering for unknown
causes in the defendants' 1100 cars. A party was entitled to discovery of
every document relating to the matters in question in the action containing
information which might directly or indirectly enable him to advance his
own case or damage his adversary's.

Cross-examination of witness

Burnell v British Transport Commission
[1956] 1 QB 187, [1955] 3 All ER 822, [1956] 2 WLR 61, 100 Sol Jo 33,
[1955] 2 Lloyd's Rep 549, CA

A witness made and signed a statement to defendants and at the trial was
called by the plaintiff. With the statement in his hands, defendants' counsel
asked the witness whether he had not given a statement and made certain
statements in it.

HELD: Plaintiff's counsel was entitled to call for production of the whole
document.

Although the defendants might have been entitled to claim privilege at
one stage not to produce the document, having used it in part and waived
privilege as to part, it is waived as to the whole.

Note—See also *General Accident Assurance v Tanter* [1984] 1 All ER 35.

Discovery before proceedings

Note—The Administration of Justice Act 1970, s 31 gave the Court power to order
discovery and production of documents before proceedings against 'a person who
appears to the court to be likely to be a party to the proceedings' in which a claim in
respect of personal injuries 'is likely to be made.' The Section now appears as the
Supreme Court Act 1981, s 33(2) as follows:
'(2) On the application, in accordance with rules of court, of a person who appears
to the High Court to be likely to be a party to subsequent proceedings in that court

in which a claim in respect of personal injuries to a person, or in respect of a person's death, is likely to be made, the High Court shall, in such circumstances as may be specified in the rules, have power to order a person who appears to the court to be likely to be a party to the proceedings and to be likely to have or to have had in his possession, custody or power any documents which are relevant to an issue arising or likely to arise out of that claim —
(a) to disclose whether those documents are in his possession, custody or power; and
(b) to produce such of those documents as are in his possession, custody or power to the applicant or, on such conditions as may be specified in the order —
    (i) to the applicant's legal advisers; or
    (ii) to the applicant's legal advisers and any medical or other professional adviser of the applicant; or
    (iii) if the applicant has no legal adviser, to any medical or other professional adviser of the applicant.'

Dunning v Board of Governors of the United Liverpool Hospitals
[1973] 2 All ER 454, [1973] 1 WLR 586, 117 Sol Jo 167, CA

A patient who entered hospital for investigations became gravely ill and her family suspected a wrong diagnosis and treatment. She obtained a legal aid certificate to get a medical opinion. She was examined by a specialist who said the hospital was probably not at fault but that his assessment of the medical aspect was considerably hampered by the absence of the hospital notes, and that he ought to see them. The hospital board refused to disclose them.

HELD: The claimant was entitled to an order for disclosure of the notes. 'Likely to be made' in the Act means 'may well be made' dependent on the outcome of the discovery. The fact that the only basis for saying that a claim is not 'likely' is the absence of the documents for which discovery is sought does not preclude the court from ordering their production; but the applicant must disclose the nature of the claim and show there is a reasonable basis for making it.

Shaw v Vauxhall Motors Ltd
[1974] 2 All ER 1185, [1974] 1 WLR 1035, 118 Sol Jo 347, CA

A factory worker was injured when a fork lift truck failed to stop, as it should, when he took his foot off the pedal. He applied to the Court for an order against his employers under the Administration of Justice Act 1970, s 31 for discovery of maintenance reports on the machine. The judge in chambers refused an order, considering discovery should be made in the ordinary course of an action, if brought.

HELD: Allowing the appeal, one of the objects of s 31 is to enable a plaintiff to find out before he starts proceedings whether he has a good cause of action or not. That object would be defeated if he had to show in advance that he already had a good cause of action. He should set out the substance of his case in an open letter or other document which could if necessary be used at the subsequent trial, if any. An important aspect of the matter was that legal aid should not, in the public interest, continue beyond the point at which it is reasonably clear that the plaintiff had no prospect of success. Counsel in the present case had conceded that if the reports showed nothing wrong the applicant could not succeed in an action and litigation would be avoided.

Deistung v South West Metropolitan Regional Hospital Board
[1975] 1 All ER 573, [1975] 1 WLR 213, 119 Sol Jo 13, CA
When an order is made under s 31 against a hospital for production of the
hospital notes and records to the plaintiff's medical adviser only, the plaintiff is not bound by his report but can write him for further advice or have
him seen by counsel in conference as an expert witness.

COSTS

Hall v Wandsworth Health Authority
(1985) 125 Sol Jo 188, Times, 16 February (Tudor Price J)
Normally where application is made to the court under s 33(2) the defendant's costs are paid by the plaintiff since it is fair and right that the party
put to expense and who may never be sued should be reimbursed (see RSC
Ord 62, r 3(12)); but the words 'unless the court otherwise directs' enable
the court to order the defendant to pay the plaintiff's costs where there had
been misconduct in the disclosure proceedings. In personal injury and
medical negligence cases delay is to be avoided: where there had been
failure to disclose before and after the Master's hearing the defendants
could be denied their costs and there was jurisdiction to award costs against
them.

Discovery against a person not a party

Note—The Supreme Court Act 1981, s 34 gives the Court power in an action in
respect of personal injuries to order a person who is not a party to the proceedings
to disclose and produce documents which are in his possession, custody or power
and which are relevant to an issue arising from the claim. The relevant subss are as
follows:

'**34 Power of High Court to order disclosure of documents, inspection of
property etc in proceedings for personal injuries or death**   (1) This section
applies to any proceedings in the High Court in which a claim is made in respect of
personal injuries to a person, or in respect of a person's death.
(2) On the application, in accordance with rules of court, of a party to any
proceedings to which this section applies, the High Court shall, in such
circumstances as may be specified in the rules, have power to order a person who is
not a party to the proceedings and who appears to the court to be likely to have in
his possession, custody or power any documents which are relevant to an issue
arising out of the said claim —
(a) to disclose whether those documents are in his possession, custody or power,
    and
(b) to produce such of those documents as are in his possession, custody or power
    to the applicant or, on such conditions as may be specified in the order —
    (i)   to the applicant's legal advisers; or
    (ii) to the applicant's legal advisers and any medical or other professional
          adviser of the applicant; or
    (iii) if the applicant has no legal adviser, to any medical or other professional
          adviser of the applicant.'

Paterson v Chadwick
[1974] 2 All ER 772, [1974] 1 WLR 890, 118 Sol Jo 169 (Boreham J)
The plaintiff issued proceedings against solicitors claiming damages for

professional negligence in failing to bring proceedings within the limitation period against a hospital where, she alleged, she had suffered personal injury during medical treatment. In the action against the solicitors she applied under the Administration of Justice Act 1970, s 32(1) (now the Supreme Court Act 1981, s 34, p 626, above) for an order against the hospital management committee for discovery of the hospital records of her treatment. The committee opposed the application on the ground that her claim against the solicitors was not 'in respect of personal injuries'.

HELD: An order for discovery should be made. 'In respect of' conveys some connection or relation between the claim and the personal injuries. The nature and extent of her personal injuries formed an essential ingredient in the proof of her claim; unless she could prove the injuries she would fail. The connection was clear.

DISMISSAL FOR WANT OF PROSECUTION

Note—Before 1967 orders to dismiss for want of prosecution were rarely made on a first application without giving the plaintiff an opportunity of keeping the action in being. The successful applications to dismiss in *Reggentin's* and *Fitzpatrick's* cases (below) led to a flood of similar applications. Three were dealt with together after full argument and are reported under the title of *Allen v Sir Alfred McAlpine & Sons Ltd* at [1968] 2 QB 229. The Court of Appeal made the following general observations:

1 The Court will do all in its power to enforce expedition, if need be by striking out actions when there has been excessive delay.

2 There is no rule or practice that the court should never on first application dismiss the action. When the delay is prolonged and inexcusable and is such as to do grave injustice the Court may in its discretion dismiss the action straightaway, leaving the plaintiff to his remedy against his own solicitors.

3 Mere inactivity on the part of the defendant will not amount to acquiescence in delay and prejudice his application to dismiss but he cannot rely on delay for which he has been responsible e g in failing to comply with a procedural step.

4 The court must consider whether the plaintiff will himself be prejudiced by the dismissal when he is not personally to blame for the delay, i e whether his solicitors (if they were the cause of the delay) are good for the damages. But see *Rowe v Tregaskes* and *Martin v Turner*, pp 000 and 000, below.

In *Bremer Vulkan v South India Shipping* [1981] AC 909 ([1979] 3 All ER 194, [1979] 3 WLR 471, 123 Sol Jo 504) Donaldson J after commenting that the law had developed considerably in the past 12 years summarised the guidelines as follows:

1 The power to dismiss for want of prosecution should be exercised only where the court is satisfied that either: (a) the default has been intentional and contumelious, e g disobedience to a peremptory order of the court or conduct amounting to an abuse of the process of the court; or (b)(i) there has been inordinate and inexcusable delay on the part of the plaintiff or his lawyers, and (ii) such delay (1) either will give rise to a substantial risk that it is not possible to have a fair trial of the issues in the action, or (2) is such as is likely to cause or to have caused serious prejudice to the defendants either as between themselves and the plaintiff or between each other or between them and a third party.

2 Only in exceptional cases should an action be dismissed before the relevant limitation period has expired, at least if it is likely that the plaintiff will issue a new writ.

3 The action of a plaintiff in delaying for almost all or any part of the limitation period cannot be relied on as constituting inordinate or inexcusable delay, but such delay is far from being irrelevant. It will have an important bearing on the degree of expedition required of the plaintiff once the proceedings have been instituted; delay which would be acceptable if the proceedings had begun promptly may

become inordinate and inexcusable after a late start, and the degree of prejudice to the defendant may be greatly heightened.

4 Prejudice to the defendant may take many forms; witnesses may die, become untraceable or their recollections may dim. More than that, the very fact of having a large unquantified claim hanging over the defendant's head for a long period may itself be highly prejudicial.

5 The defendant will lose his right to have the action dismissed if he induces in the plaintiff a reasonable belief that, notwithstanding the delay, he is willing for the action to proceed, and the plaintiff does work or incurs further expenses as a result. But acquiescence in delay is not a permanent bar to obtaining a dismissal after further delay. Each case will have to be considered in the light of its own particular facts.

6 Mere inactivity on the part of the defendant is not to be construed as acquiescence in delay by the plaintiff.

Illustrations of the 'guidelines' are to be found in the following cases:

Application for dismissal granted

Reggentin v Beecholme Bakeries Ltd

[1968] 2 QB 276 n, [1968] 1 All ER 566 n, CA
Accident October 1961. Claim made: medical examination January 1963. Widow issued writ January 1964. Order for Directions June 1964. Interrogatories November 1964. Inspection of *locus in quo* August 1965. Nothing then done until November 1966 when plaintiff applied for further interrogatories and defendants applied to dismiss for want of prosecution. HELD: The action should be dismissed. It was the duty of the plaintiff's solicitors to get on with the action and when it went to sleep for 13 months the defendants were entitled to apply for dismissal. Public policy demanded that actions should be brought on speedily.

Fitzpatrick v Batger & Co Ltd

[1967] 2 All ER 657, [1967] 1 WLR 706, 111 Sol Jo 276, CA
Accident 13 December 1961. Legal aid certificate October 1962. Writ issued 7 February 1963. Defence served 19 April 1963. In June 1963 defendants offered £300 in settlement which was refused. Nothing more was done until February 1965 when further negotiations took place ending without result in May 1965. Nothing more happened until February 1967 when the plaintiff's solicitors wrote seeking to revive the claim. The defendants thereupon applied to dismiss for want of prosecution. The master and the judge in chambers allowed the plaintiff to continue on payment of £30 into Court as security for costs.
HELD, ON APPEAL: The action should be dismissed forthwith. Public policy demands that the business of the courts should be conducted with expedition. It is impossible to have a fair trial six years after the accident. It was immaterial that the defendants could have taken out an application to dismiss earlier: they were justified in letting sleeping dogs lie. The plaintiff would have his remedy against his solicitors in negligence.

Allen v Sir Alfred McAlpine & Sons Ltd
[1968] 2 QB 229, [1968] 1 All ER 543, [1968] 2 WLR 366, 112 Sol Jo 49,
CA
Accident February 1959. Writ 13 July 1960. Pleadings closed January
1961. Discovery 1965. February 1967 plaintiff's solicitors wrote saying
they were ready to proceed. April 1967 defendants applied to dismiss. Only
two witnesses out of six could still be traced.
HELD: Impossible to have fair trial.

Clough v Clough
[1968] 1 All ER 1179, [1968] 1 WLR 525, 112 Sol Jo 154, CA
Accident 7 October 1961. Writ 2 October 1964. No statement of claim
served until defendants issued summons to dismiss on 1 September 1967.
Before summons was heard plaintiffs served statement of claim.
HELD: Delay prolonged and inexcusable. Under Ord 19, r 1 court had a
discretion to dismiss for failure to serve statement of claim even if it was
served before hearing of summons.

Gloria v Sokoloff
[1969] 1 All ER 204, 112 Sol Jo 422, CA
Accident 8 November 1961. Writ 6 November 1964. Statement of claim
next day. Defences January 1965. August 1966 issue of liability disposed of
between defendants, who asked for particulars of special damage but did
not get them. April 1967 defendants issued summons for directions and got
order for particulars which were not delivered until December 1967 and
even then were hopelessly vague and imprecise. January 1968 defendants
applied to dismiss.
HELD: Delay inexcusable. Having regard to plaintiff's complaints of
anxiety, depression, etc and of a continuing loss of £40 per week earnings
defendants were seriously prejudiced by it and fair trial was impossible.

Rowe v Tregaskes
[1968] 3 All ER 447, [1968] 1 WLR 1475, 112 Sol Jo 764, CA
Accident 23 November 1962. Plaintiff reported it to his trade union who
made no claim until March 1965. Writ September 1965. Defendant's
insurers denied liability March 1966. Trade union instructed solicitors to
carry on. They served writ August 1966 and did a great deal of work on
investigation. They were just about to serve statement of claim in March
1968 when defendant applied to dismiss.
HELD: Delay had made it impossible to have a fair trial. The fact that the
plaintiff may not be able to prove negligence against the solicitors was not
sufficient reason for refusing order to dismiss.

Martin v Turner
[1970] 1 All ER 256, [1970] 1 WLR 82, 113 Sol Jo 817
Accident 29 May 1960. Liability not in dispute. Writ issued 25 April 1963,
served 2 April 1964. Plaintiff's solicitors were unable to get from him the
information they required to deal with his claim. Surgeons had said in

February 1964 that he was fit for work but he insisted he was not fit and could never work again. A psychiatrist reported that he had become neurotically obsessed about the consequences of the accident.

HELD: The action should be dismissed for want of prosecution even though the solicitors were not to blame and it meant the plaintiff would get nothing from anyone. The defendants had been prejudiced by the delay. The test of the plaintiff's conduct was an objective one: he had acted unreasonably and the delay was therefore inexcusable.

Samuel Butler & Co Ltd v Mills Scaffold Co Ltd
(1970) 114 Sol Jo 912, CA

Accident February 1959 in which four men were killed in the course of building a bridge. Thorough inquest in March 1959 for which an expert made a full report. Evidence of a witness taken on commission in early 1960. In 1962 the plaintiffs who were subcontractors for the erection of heavy steel girders, settled the claims of the widows of the four men. In April 1963 the plaintiffs issued a writ against the defendants, who were scaffolders, for damages for negligent design or erection of scaffolding towers. After two extensions writ served in March 1966: statement of claim for £58,000 damages served March 1967. Defence and counter-claim for £6,000 served October 1967: reply and defence to counter-claim February 1968. March 1970 defendants applied to strike out for want of prosecution. The plaintiffs conceded there had been inordinate and inexcusable delay but contended a fair trial was still possible because of the full inquest and contemporaneous reports.

HELD: The action should be struck out and the counter-claim too. Such an action could not be tried by reading the evidence of witnesses at an inquest or the reports of experts. It was impossible to have a fair trial after 12 years.

Paxton v Allsopp
[1971] 3 All ER 370, [1971] 1 WLR 1310, 115 Sol Jo 446, CA

Plaintiff, 20, injured February 1957. Writ issued October 1957 and statement of claim served. November 1957 defence served. After medical examinations and negotiations, offer of £2,050 made in May 1960 to plaintiff's solicitors which they reported to the plaintiff's father who did not tell the plaintiff and did not answer the letter or reminders. 1964, plaintiff's father died; she found letter of 1960 reporting offer but did nothing about it until 1967. She then consulted solicitors who obtained some information from plaintiff's doctor but did not communicate with defendant's insurers until March 1970. Insurers said if any attempt was made to revive action they would apply to dismiss, but later offered £500. Plaintiff refused on counsel's advice. May 1970 plaintiff served notice of intention to proceed. Defendant applied to dismiss for want of prosecution. There was a hysterical element in the plaintiff's condition due partly to the accident. To avoid prejudice to defendant by delay plaintiff's counsel offered to limit damages to £2,050.

HELD: (1) The action should be dismissed. Though negligence was admitted and contemporaneous medical records were available the defendant was prejudiced because oral examination of medical witnesses was no longer possible to deal with hysterical element in the case. (2) It was not practicable to limit the claim to £2,050. (3) Per Davies LJ: The question whether the plaintiff will have a claim in negligence against her solicitors was irrelevant. *Martin v Turner* (above) approved.

Mordi v LEC Refrigeration Ltd
(1971) 115 Sol Jo 812, CA
Accident (cause of action) 28 January 1966. Writ 22 March 1968. Pleadings closed July 1968. Application to dismiss in default of summons of directions October 1970 when master further short period for summons for directions and setting down. Summons heard 11 November 1970 but action not set down. On 20 April 1971 action dismissed for want of prosecution.
HELD: Master's order upheld. All the delay had to be looked at, not merely the period from November 1970 to second application.

Vaughan v R. Parnham Ltd
[1972] 1 Lloyd's Rep 519 CA
Accident August 1964 causing plaintiff very serious injuries. Writ issued, statement of claim served November 1966; defence and request for particulars January 1967. Then nothing until plaintiff changed to other solicitors in September 1970. Application for legal aid: from November 1970 to April 1971 plaintiff's solicitors were obtaining statements: wrote to defendants' solicitors showing active steps being taken; in August 1971 they delivered the particulars asked for in 1967. Defendants' solicitors acknowledged their letters and said they looked forward to receiving a plan referred to in the particulars. In November 1971 they applied to dismiss for want of prosecution. The judge in chambers ordered dismissal.
HELD, ON APPEAL: The order was rightly made. The defendants' attitude in merely acknowledging letters and doing nothing did not amount to conduct conducing to the delay or acquiescing in it. Following *Allen v McAlpine* (p 629, above) to sit quiet and do nothing was not a waiver of rights which had accrued.

Application for dismissal refused

Bostic v Bermondsey Management Committee
[1968] 2 QB 229, [1968] 1 All ER 543, [1968] 2 WLR 366, 112 Sol Jo 49, CA
Accident 25 September 1958. Solicitors instructed November 1958. Writ 21 February 1961. Statement of claim July 1961. Defendants asked for further and better particulars but did not deliver a defence. Plaintiff's solicitor struck off roll October 1962, but the plaintiff did not find out until August 1965 when she instructed another solicitor who pressed defendants for a defence. They asked for extensions but had still not delivered one when they applied to dismiss for want of prosecution in 1967.
HELD: The defendants' own conduct in not serving a defence and in inducing the plaintiff to incur costs in providing particulars was such as to debar them from being granted a dismissal of the action. Justice was not impossible because they still had all the records.

Hood v Concrete (Midlands) Ltd

(1968) 112 Sol Jo 844, CA

Accident 11 May 1963. Claim August 1964. Writ 5 April 1966. Defendants' insurers repeatedly answered plaintiff's enquiries by saying their enquiries were not yet complete. A technical report was not revealed by them to plaintiff's expert until 1967. Application to dismiss October 1968.

HELD: The insurers should have got on with the case. It did not lie in their mouths to apply for the action to be struck out.

Spriggs v Norrard Trawlers Ltd

[1969] 2 Lloyd's Rep 627, CA

Per Harman LJ: The overriding question is always whether justice can still be done despite delay in prosecuting a claim. There have been a great number of such cases in the past year or so and it is a pity they have got into the Law Reports, for each depends on its own particular facts. It is impossible to have a calender, so to say, and rule that 18 months is inordinate delay and 15 months is not. Except in very general terms no one case is an authority for another.

Akhtar v Harbottle (Mercantile) Ltd

(1982) 126 Sol Jo 643, Times, 4 August 1982, CA

Writ for breach of contract issued and served March 1976. Plaintiff arrested and imprisoned in Burma April 1977. Case listed for hearing on 2 April 1979 but taken out of list on plaintiff's application and adjourned generally as he was still in prison. Application to dismiss July 1980 adjourned twice and heard on 20 April 1982 when plaintiff still in prison awaiting trial. Judge held defendants prejudiced and delay inexcusable.

HELD, ON APPEAL: The delay was not inexcusable as the plaintiff had given a complete excuse for it and the trial could not proceed without his evidence.

Dutton v Spink and Beeching (Sales) Ltd

[1977] 1 All ER 287, 120 Sol Jo 488, CA

Per Stamp LJ: The law, as I understand it, is this. The Court in the exercise of its inherent jurisdiction, may dismiss an action on the ground of the plaintiff's delay in prosecuting it but will not do so unless the delay is inordinate, inexcusable and prejudicial to a fair trial . . . but it does not follow because those conditions are satisfied the jurisdiction ought to be exercised as a matter of course. If one finds that, as the result of the passage of time, the recollection of witnesses is likely to be so dimmed that a fair trial of the action is likely to be prejudiced the temptation to dismiss the action is, I think, rather greater . . . but the court does not strike out an action merely on the ground that there has been such delay that the recollection of witnesses has become impaired. If it were so a multitude of actions would not be tried.

Sayle v Cooksey
[1969] 2 Lloyd's Rep 618, CA
Plaintiff injured January 1960, writ issued August 1960. Defendant and his insurers then began an arbitration to determine whether the insurers were entitled to refuse indemnity. The plaintiff's solicitors, knowing of the dispute, waited to see the outcome. The award was not made until January 1966 and was in favour of the defendant whose insurers now said they were prepared to handle the claim. After some negotiations the plaintiff's solicitors did nothing from December 1966 to November 1967. In January 1968 they obtained opinion of counsel who advised a new medical examination. The doctor instructed did not produce a report until May 1969. Meanwhile in April 1969 the District Registrar made an order to dismiss for want of prosecution.
HELD, ON APPEAL: The action should not be dismissed. The delay from 1961 to 1966 while waiting for the defendant's arbitration to be decided was excusable. The delay from January 1968 was due to the doctor. The delay from December 1966 to November 1967 was inexcusable but had not given rise to any substantial risk that it would make a fair trial of the issues impossible nor would cause serious prejudice to the defendant.

Effect of delay before issue of writ

William Parker Ltd v Ham & Son Ltd
[1972] 3 All ER 1051, [1972] 1 WLR 1583, 116 Sol Jo 903, CA
Cause of action (breach of contract) April 1963. Writ issued December 1967. Pleadings closed December 1968; then no step by plaintiffs until notice of intention to proceed in February 1972.
HELD: Inordinate and inexcusable delay after issue of writ but no prejudice to the defendants by this delay because their situation from the point of view of getting information had not deteriorated since about 1969.

Per Buckley LJ: Delay before the issue of the writ in an action or before the action once commenced ceases to be actively or timeously pursued, may have a bearing on whether delay which follows thereafter is to be regarded as inordinate and inexcusable but cannot itself be inordinate or inexcusable delay. If the facts are such that no additional prejudice to the defendant has arisen as the result of delay after the end of that period in which delay can be said to be excusable it cannot be right in my judgment, for the court to dismiss the action.

Note—But see the following cases and *Birkett v James*, below.

Birkett v James
[1978] AC 297, [1977] 2 All ER 801, [1977] 3 WLR 45, 121 Sol Jo 444, HL
In a claim for payment of a sum of money alleged to be due from the defendant under an oral agreement made in 1969 the plaintiff issued a writ in July 1972. The action proceeded at a reasonable pace until July 1973 when an order was made to set down within 28 days. This was not done and for reasons relating to costs and legal aid nothing further was done until new solicitors gave notice to proceed in July 1975. The defendant applied to dismiss for want of prosecution. The limitation period did not expire until March 1976.

HELD, ON APPEAL to the House of Lords: (1) Non-expiry of the limitation period is generally a conclusive reason for not dismissing an action that is already pending. Insofar as *Spring Grove Services v Deane* (p 636, below) is an authority for saying that a second writ asserting the same claim can be struck out as an abuse of the process it was wrong. (2) As the time elapsed before the issue of a writ within the limitation period cannot of itself constitute inordinate delay the delay relied on by the defendant as prejudicial must relate to the time which the plaintiff allows to elapse unnecessarily after the writ has been issued. *William Parker Ltd v Ham & Son Ltd* (p 633, above) was rightly decided despite later comments on it by the Court of Appeal. The additional prejudice resulting from delay after issue of the writ need not be great but it must be more than minimal. If the delay is not excusable after proceedings are launched but does not worsen the position of the defendant then it is not a case for dismissing for want of prosecution. (3) Whether or not the plaintiff may have an action for negligence against his solicitor responsible for the delay is irrelevant. *Martin v Turner* (p 629, above) approved.

Tabata v Hetherington
(1983) Times, 15 December, CA
'Inordinate' delay means a period of time which has elapsed which is materially longer than the time usually regarded by the courts and the profession as an acceptable period of time.

President of India and Union of India v John Shaw & Sons (Salford) Ltd
(1977) 121 Sol Jo 795, CA
Actions for damages were begun by writs in 1971 and 1972 on contracts alleged to have been breached several years earlier. Statements of claim were served in January 1972 but did not quantify the claim. Only in a postscript to a letter of 7 March 1974 did the plaintiffs' solicitors mention that the claim was 'in the region of £1m'. In October 1974 the plaintiffs said the action would proceed but on their giving notice of intention to proceed in May 1976 the defendants applied to dismiss.
HELD: They were entitled to have the action dismissed. *Birkett v James* (above) had made the decisive delay that which arose after the issue of the writ to cause prejudice but defective memory was only one cause of prejudice to be taken into account. It was a matter of great prejudice to a commercial concern like the defendants to have such unquantified claims hanging over their heads. Additional prejudice had been created by the delay since issue of the writs.

Abouchalache v Hilton International Hotels (UK) Ltd
(1982) 126 Sol Jo 857, Times, 15 November, CA
The plaintiff was badly injured in a bomb explosion at the Hilton Hotel, London, in 1975. He issued a writ but discontinued in 1976 so as to begin proceedings against the defendant's parent company in New York where damages would be higher. After three years of those proceedings, however, it was decided that England was the *forum conveniens* and the action was

dismissed on the terms that the defendants would not plead the Limitation Act if an action was started before 12 December 1979. A writ was then issued in England before that date, but nothing more was done for two years. The defendants applied to have the action dismissed for want of prosecution.

HELD: The action should not be dismissed. The defendants, unlike those in the *Biss* case (p 638, below) were part of a large international undertaking whose servants were not fearful of the outcome of the litigation. No records had been destroyed and there was no prejudice additional to any present at the time when the writ was issued within the agreed time limit.

Special cases

THIRD-PARTY PROCEEDINGS

Hart v Hall and Pickles Ltd
[1969] 1 QB 405, [1968] 3 All ER 291, [1968] 3 WLR 744, 112 Sol Jo 786, CA

The plaintiff was injured in 1962 when unloading a lorry. He sued his employers who blamed haulage contractors and joined them as third parties. The plaintiff then joined the haulage contractors as second defendants. These steps were completed by July 1965. Nothing more was done and in March 1968 the second defendants successfully applied for an order dismissing the action against them for want of prosecution. The first defendants then made a similar application but it was refused. The action went on to trial where the third parties (formerly second defendants) claimed to be dismissed from the action on the ground that there could not longer be a claim against them for contribution under the Law Reform (Married Women and Tortfeasors) Act 1935 as they were parties who had been sued but were not liable, the action against them having been dismissed for want of prosecution.

HELD: The third parties were not entitled to be dismissed from the action. The words in s 6(1) 'who is, or would if sued have been, liable' mean sued to judgment. To be exempted from contribution a person must have been sued to judgment and found not to be liable. When an action has been dismissed for want of prosecution the defendant has not been sued to judgment. It is only an interlocutory order, a matter of procedure, which does not affect substantive rights. The case as between the defendant and third parties must be tried as if there had been no dismissal at all.

Note—See also Civil Liability (Contribution) Act 1978, s 1(3).

CLAIM AND COUNTER-CLAIM

Zimmer Orthopaedic Ltd v Zimmer Manufacturing Co
[1968] 2 All ER 309, [1968] 1 WLR 852, 112 Sol Jo 335 (Cross J)

In an action relating to trade marks and passing off neither party did anything for nearly five years after close of pleadings. Then the defendants applied to dismiss: the plaintiffs applied to dismiss the counter-claim.

HELD: It is for the plaintiff and his advisers to get on with the action and the defendant is normally under no duty to stimulate him into action, but in the circumstances of the present case the defendants having done nothing to secure that the counter-claim should be heard as soon as possible should not have an order to dismiss the claim unless they submitted to a similar order dismissing the counterclaim.

Janata Bank v Noor
(1983) Times, 18 November, CA
Although a defendant is in the same position in respect of pursuing a counter-claim as the plaintiff is in pursuing the main action he is not precluded thereby from applying to strike out the main action. Zimmer's action (above) was not authority for precluding a counter-claiming defendant from applying to dismiss the main action for want of prosecution, though the plaintiff might equally succeed in an application to dismiss the counter-claim on the same grounds.

LIMITATION PERIOD NOT EXPIRED

Spring Grove Services Ltd v Deane
(1972) 116 Sol Jo 844, CA
Writ issued 7 October 1969 claiming £1,564 for hire of linen. After unsuccessful application for judgment under Ord 14 plaintiffs took no further step. October 1971 on defendant's application action dismissed for want of prosecution, defendant saying on affidavit that he had been told claim had been abandoned. November 1971 plaintiffs issued new writ for £1,564; defendant applied to strike out writ as an abuse of the Court.
HELD: The second action should be struck out. Though a new action could be started on the same cause of action it was always subject to the inherent jurisdiction to dismiss it as an abuse of the court. In the present case the plaintiffs had given no explanation for the new claim; it was an attempt to resurrect something that was dead and buried.

Department of Health and Social Security v Ereira
[1973] 3 All ER 421, CA
The plaintiffs sued the defendant for £9,000 arrears of National Insurance contributions by writ issued 15 November 1967. Nothing more was done until April 1972 when the plaintiffs gave notice of intention to proceed. On defendant's application the action was struck out for want of prosecution. Plaintiffs then issued a new writ on 27 July 1972 for the proportion of the £9,000 not already statute-barred. Defendant applied to strike out second action as an abuse of the Court.
HELD: It should not be struck out. *Spring Grove Services v Deane* did not mean that a second action would automatically be struck out. In that case there were good reasons for doing so. In the present case in which the defence was of the thinnest possible character and the defendant was not prejudiced in his defence there were not.

Note—In *Maxwell v Raeburn* (1973) 117 Sol Jo 527 in the Chancery Division, where the facts were somewhat similar to *Ereira's* case, the second action was likewise allowed to continue. No reference was apparently made to either *Spring Grove Services v Deane* or *Ereira's* case.

Janov v Morris
[1981] 3 All ER 780, [1981] 1 WLR 1389, 125 Sol Jo 641, CA
An action for breach of contract was dismissed for want of prosecution
when the plaintiff failed, without giving any reason, to comply with a
peremptory order of the court to issue a summons for directions. There
were still four years of the limitation period remaining. He issued a new
writ based on the same cause of action as the first.
HELD: Where an action had been struck out for failure to obey a
peremptory order of the court, the court had a discretion to strike out the
second action as being an abuse of the process of the court under Ord 18,
r 19(1)(d). Order accordingly.

Approved in *Palmer v Birks* (1985) Times, 21 November.

Bailey v Bailey
[1983] 3 All ER 495, [1983] 1 WLR 1129, 127 Sol Jo 551, CA
The plaintiff was injured in a motor accident on 28 September 1973 by her
husband's negligent driving. She dealt personally with his insurers
claiming damages for her injuries and accepted £325 in settlement, a sum
substantially less than the value of her claim. Later she instructed solicitors
who issued a writ against her husband on the 24 September 1976 for
damages for his negligence. A defence was served pleading accord and
satisfaction. The statement of claim was amended to allege fraudulent
misrepresentation on the part of her husband's insurers in letters sent to
her before the settlement. Some delay followed and in April 1980 the defendant issued an application to strike out for want of prosecution. The
hearing being adjourned until August the plaintiff issued a new writ in July
1980 four days before the limitation period expired, against her husband
and the insurers for fraudulent misrepresentation. On the 12 August 1980
the registrar dismissed the first action for want of prosecution. The defendants applied to strike out the second action as being an abuse of process.
HELD, by the Court of Appeal: There is a distinction in principle between
a situation in which an action has been struck out for disobedience of an
order of the court (as in *Janov v Morris*, above) and where an action has been
dismissed for want of prosecution. The plaintiff may have failed in the first
action to obey the rules of the court but she had issued her second writ quite
lawfully within the limitation period. It was impossible to say that the
second action constituted an abuse of the process of the court. *Birkett v James*
(p 633, above) and *Tolley v Morris* (below) applied. *Janov v Morris*
distinguished.

Tolley v Morris
[1979] 2 All ER 561, [1979] 1 WLR 592, 123 Sol Jo 353, HL
The plaintiff was born on 12 November 1961; injured in an accident 21
May 1964. Writ issued 3 May 1967, served 20 April 1968; then nothing
more done until notice of intention to proceed followed by statement of
claim 19 August 1977. The defendant applied to have the action dismissed.
HELD: The Limitation Act 1939, s 22 as amended by the Limitation Act
1975 enabled the plaintiff to bring an action for personal injuries until 3
years after her eighteenth birthday, ie until 12 November 1982. The facts
brought the case within the rule laid down in *Birkett v James* (above). If the
action were dismissed the plaintiff could bring a fresh action and the

defendant would be even more seriously prejudiced. *Biss v Lambeth* (below) was distinguishable; in that case the court was dealing with cases (e g under the Limitation Act, s 2D) where the plaintiff had only a defeasible, not an absolute, right to begin a fresh action. The action should go on.

Note—The provisions of the Limitation Act 1939, s 22 as amended by the Limitation Act 1975 are now contained in the Limitation Act 1980, s 28. Section 2D of the 1939 Act has become s 33 of the 1980 Act.

LIMITATION ACT 1975

Biss v Lambeth, Southwark and Lewisham Area Health Authority
[1977] 2 All ER 125, [1978] 1 WLR 382, 122 Sol Jo 32, CA
The plaintiff was treated in the defendant's hospital in 1965. She complained of the treatment and claimed damages. After an adverse opinion from counsel her legal aid certificate was discharged. In 1973 she got legal aid again and in 1975 obtained leave under the Limitation Act 1963 to begin proceedings out of time ((1975) Times, 13 February). In December 1975 the defendants served a request for further and better particulars. Her solicitors did nothing for nine months. New solicitors were unable to get a new medical opinion. In March 1977 the defendants applied to dismiss for want of prosecution.
HELD: The action should be dismissed. Though the crucial delay was the nine months after issue of the writ from which no extra prejudice could be shown, the reasoning in *Birkett v James* (p 633, above) could not have been intended by the House of the Lords to apply to actions which under the Limitation Act 1975 could be started more than three years after accrual of the cause of action.

COUNTY COURT

Kirkpatrick v Salvation Army
[1969] 1 All ER 388, [1969] 1 WLR 1955, 112 Sol Jo 823, CA
In a personal injury action in the county court the defendant applied to the registrar to dismiss for want of prosecution. The registrar made an order accordingly but on appeal the judge held that though the registrar has power to strike out an action under Ord 13, r 4(4) (now the County Court Rules 1981, Ord 13, r 3) there was no power in the county court to strike out an action for want of prosecution on an application by the defendants.
HELD, by the Court of Appeal: This was not right. There was no reason for thinking that because the Court has power to act on its own motion to strike out an action the defendant should be deprived of making an application himself to dismiss for want of prosecution.

Kerr v National Carriers Ltd
[1974] 1 Lloyd's Rep 365, CA
Road accident July 1968. Letter before action June 1970, particulars of claim filed November 1970, defence three days later then action adjourned generally to allow defendant to join a third party. January 1971, leave to join third party then further adjournment. Hearing fixed by Court for June 1972, but further adjournment when third party died; his executors were joined November 1972. Court gave notice in June 1973 of intention to strike out unless hearing date applied for. Hearing fixed for 9 August 1973

but adjournment again applied for by parties' consent on 2 August. On 9 August judge struck it out of his own motion.

HELD: Dismissing plaintiff's application for leave to appeal out of time from the judge's order, the delay had been quite shocking. In running down actions the memory of witnesses of matters which frequently happen in seconds deteriorates with the passing years. The rules of the Court are there to be observed and parties cannot by mutual cordiality agree to prolong the trial by agreeing to adjournments in the interlocutory stage. There is a supervising duty vested in the Court of scrutinising cases such as the present.

COSTS OF PRELIMINARY ISSUE

Teheran Europe Co Ltd v S. T. Belton (Tractors) Ltd (No 2)
[1971] 2 QB 491, [1971] 3 All ER 1121, [1971] 2 WLR 1113, 115 Sol Jo 207, CA

In an action begun in 1959 preliminary issues were ordered to be tried and in 1967 were decided in favour of the plaintiffs, with costs ordered against the defendants. In 1968 an order was made for discovery. The plaintiffs then did nothing more and in 1969 the action was dismissed for want of prosecution. The defendants claimed that the plaintiffs were not entitled to tax the costs awarded to them in the interlocutory proceedings because (1) the dismissal of the action precluded any further step in the action and taxation of costs was a step, and (2) loss of the costs was a part of the sanction against undue delay.

HELD: Neither contention could be accepted. There was no rule or authority that on dismissal of an action a party should be prohibited from taking any further step. Though dismissal was a sanction it was a heavy sanction in itself and there was no cause to add to it a forfeiture of an existing order for costs.

FAILURE TO COMPLY WITH ORDER

Pryer v Smith
[1977] 1 All ER 218, [1977] 1 WLR 425, 120 Sol Jo 839, CA

Accident 16 August 1971. Claim made 24 March 1972 by solicitors who, after some correspondence with defendant's insurers, ceased to act. The plaintiff then acted in person, issuing a writ on 8 August 1974 and serving statement of claim on 14 January 1975. Further and better particulars delivered 12 April 1975, defence served 18 June 1975. Order for directions 6 October 1975 required action to be set down in 56 days but it was not. Plaintiff instructed other solicitors on 31 December 1975 who came on the record in March 1976. Defendant issued summons to dismiss for want of prosecution on 23 March 1976; heard by district registrar on 20 April 1976 and order made to dismiss. Plaintiff's appeal to judge in chambers on 7 May 1976 was allowed, but conditionally upon the plaintiff setting action down for trial within 10 days and taking certain other steps within specified time limits, otherwise action dismissed. None of the steps ordered were complied with in time. On 25 May the defendant drew up the order dismissing the action. The plaintiff appealed to the judge on 2 July, for extension of time limits but the judge held he had no jurisdiction to do so. The plaintiff appealed to the Court of Appeal against orders of 7 May, and 2 July.

HELD: Even assuming the judge was wrong in holding he had no jurisdiction to extend time after the order of 7 May had been drawn up, he had correctly exercised his discretion on 7 May, to dismiss the action if the time limits set down were not complied with. It was not correct, as the plaintiff maintained, that the judge must be satisfied before making such an order that there has been, not merely inordinate and inexcusable delay, but also the likelihood of serious prejudice to the defendant. The judge has jurisdiction in an application to dismiss for want of prosecution, if the circumstances in his view warrant it, to made an order which prescribes time conditions and to provide that on failure to take those further steps within the time limits the action shall be dismissed, even though he is not satisfied at that moment of time that there is a likelihood of serious prejudice to the defendant.

FOREIGN TORTS

Hart v Gumpach
(1873) LR 4 PC 439, 9 Moo PCCNS 241, 42 LJPC 25, 21 WR 365
By the law of England actions for personal wrongs arising in foreign countries may be brought in an English court.

Phillips v Eyre
(1870) LR 6 QB 1, 10 B & S 1004, 40 LJQB 28, 22 LT 869
An act committed abroad, if valid and unquestionable by the law of the place cannot, so far as civil liability is concerned, be drawn in question elsewhere. As a general rule, in order to found a suit in England for a wrong alleged to have been committed abroad, two conditions must be fulfilled. (1) The wrong must be of such a character that it would have been actionable if committed in England; (2) the act must not have been justifiable by the law of the place where it was done.

Carr v Fracis, Times & Co
[1902] AC 176, 71 LJKB 361, 85 LT 144, 50 WR 257, 17 TLR 657
A tort that has been committed abroad is not actionable in the English courts unless two conditions are satisfied. In the first place, the wrong must be of such a character that it would have been actionable if committed in England; and secondly, the act must not have been justifiable by the law of the place where it was committed.

Damages

Chaplin v Boys
[1971] AC 356, [1969] 2 All ER 1085, [1969] 3 WLR 322, 113 Sol Jo 608, HL
The defendant was injured in a road accident in Malta. The defendant admitted negligence. Maltese law limits damages for personal injuries to actual financial loss and allows no damages for pain and suffering. Both parties were British servicemen and the plaintiff brought this action in England. The defendant claimed that questions of remoteness of damage

fell to be decided by the *lex loci delicti*, i e Maltese law, and that the plaintiff
was entitled only to his special damage.
HELD: Following *Machado v Fontes* ([1897] 2 QB 231, 66 LJQB 542, 76 LT
588), when there is a right of action in this country for a tort committed
abroad the question what damages are to be awarded falls to be decided by
English law just as if the tort had been committed in this country. The
plaintiff was entitled to recover both the general damages of £2,250 and the
special damage of £53.

Appeals to the Court of Appeal and to the House of Lords were
dismissed. All the Law Lords were agreed in dismissing the appeal but
differed on the reasons for doing so.

Lord Hodson: The right to damages for pain and suffering is a
substantive right. Controlling effect in determining the questions between
the parties should be given to the law of that jurisdiction which because of
its relationship with the occurrence and the parties has the greater concern
with the issue raised in the litigation. The law of England is applicable since
even though the occurrence took place in Malta this was overshadowed by
the identity and circumstances of the parties, British subjects temporarily
serving in Malta.

Lord Guest: To justify an action in England for a tort committed abroad
the conduct must be actionable by English law and by the laws of the
country in which the conduct occurred. Whatever relates to the remedy to
be enforced must be determined by the *lex fori* but there is a distinction
between the kind of damage for which a remedy will be given and the
method of compensating the plaintiff for his loss. The kind of damage is a
matter of substantive law to be decided by the *lex loci delicti* but the method
of compensation is a procedural matter to be determined by the *lex fori*.
Damages for pain and suffering were merely an element in the
quantification of the total compensation and therefore a matter for the *lex
fori*, i e English law.

Lord Donovan: I am content with the rule enunciated by Willes J in
Phillips v Eyre (p 640, above) and would leave it alone. I would not
substitute 'actionable' for 'not justifiable'. An English court was competent to entertain this action under the rule in *Phillips v Eyre* and once it
had done so it was right that it should award its own remedies.

Lord Wilberforce: The broad principle should be that a person should
not be permitted to claim in England in respect of a matter for which civil
liability does not exist, or is excluded, under the law of the place where the
wrong was committed. Provisions of the *lex delicti* denying or limiting
recovery of some head of damage (such as pain and suffering) should be
given effect to but some qualification of the rule is required in certain
individual cases. The principle to be applied is whether with respect to a
particular issue some other jurisdiction has a significant relationship with
the occurrence and the parties. In the present action between two British
subjects the question of damages for pain and suffering must be segregated
and when this is done it is seen that an English court should apply its own
rules.

Lord Pearson: The English authorities show that the Willes formula (in
Phillips v Eyre) has been accepted. The first of his conditions gives the
predominant role to English substantive law and the second of his
conditions does not require actionability by the law of the place where the
act was committed. I can see no reason for discarding this established rule

and it was right for the trial judge in accordance with it to apply the English substantive law, the *lex fori*.

Accident in France — action in England

Kohnke v Karger
[1951] 2 KB 670, [1951] 2 All ER 179, [1951] 2 TLR 40
The plaintiff was a passenger in a car driven by the defendant in France when there was a collision with a lorry and she was injured. A French court awarded her £1,400 damages in correctional proceedings against the lorry driver, which were paid. The defendant was held one-third to blame in those proceedings, and reimbursed the lorry driver in that proportion. The plaintiff considering herself inadequately recompensed began proceedings against the defendant in the present action in England undertaking to give credit for the amount already recovered. The defendant contended that as she had already recovered from the lorry driver in France she could not have damages against the defendant.
HELD: If the plaintiff obtains abroad a judgment which is satisfied against a defendant and then sues him in his country for the same debt or damages the plaintiff cannot succeed: *Barber v Lamb* (1860) 8 CBNS 95, 29 LJCP 234, 2 LT 238, 6 Jur NS 981, 8 WR 461 but it may be different if there are separate causes of action against different defendants for the same damage. On the evidence the plaintiff was not adequately compensated by the award of £1,400. The award of an amount against the lorry driver in France could not avail the present defendant except to the extent that the damages were in part satisfied by the lorry driver. Award £2,200 less the £1,400 recovered from the lorry driver.

Note—This case is discussed at p 309 of 101 LJ (8 June 1951), that it is well settled that if a foreign judgment has been satisfied the creditor will be considered to have elected to take it in discharge of the whole cause of action, and will be debarred from suing in this country on the original cause of action, even if, owing to a difference between the laws of the two countries, the amount of the foreign judgment is less than he might have recovered if the action had been brought in this country: *Barber v Lamb* (1860) 8 CBNS 95, 29 LJCP 234, 2 LT 238, 6 Jur NS 981, 8 WR 461; *Taylor v Hollard* [1902] 1 KB 676, 71 LJKB 278, 86 LT 228, 50 WR 558, 18 TLR 287.

FRESH EVIDENCE ON APPEAL

Ladd v Marshall
[1954] 3 All ER 745, [1954] 1 WLR 1489, 98 Sol Jo 870, CA
Per Denning LJ: In order to justify the reception of fresh evidence [on appeal] or a new trial, three conditions must be fulfilled: first, it must be shown that the evidence could not have been obtained with reasonable diligence for use at the trial; second, the evidence must be such that, if given, it would probably have an important influence on the result of the case, although it need not be decisive; third, the evidence must be such as is presumably to be believed, or in other words, it must be apparently credible, although it need not be incontrovertible.

Note—See also pp 409–411, above.

House v Haughton Bros (Worcester Ltd)
[1967] 1 All ER 39, [1967] 1 WLR 148, 110 Sol Jo 891, CA
In the plaintiff's claim for damages for injury received at work an important issue was the number of scaffold boards available to him at the time of the accident. The judge accepted the evidence of the defendants' main witness that no further boards had been provided after the accident before the factory inspector's visit; he dismissed the action. Afterwards three men tendered statements that additional boards had been delivered in the interval before the factory inspector's visit. These men had all been present at the trial and two had given evidence for the plaintiff but had not been asked any questions on that issue.
HELD: The plaintiff was entitled to have a new trial. The requirements in *Ladd v Marshall* (above) that the new evidence could not have been obtained with reasonable diligence for use at the trial can be amplified by saying that where the situation is that although a witness is called at the trial and gives evidence on other matters but had not told the plaintiff's solicitors what he was able to say on that issue then if the solicitors are not shown to have been neglectful or dilatory in the way in which they had interviewed him his evidence 'could not have been obtained with reasonable diligence'. Insofar as the evidence he could have given was not known to them then *quoad* such evidence neither he nor that evidence was available.

Roe v Robert MacGregor & Sons Ltd
[1968] 2 All ER 636, [1968] 1 WLR 925, 112 Sol Jo 235, CA
At 1 am Roe was driving a van with his wife and others as passengers. They were going home from an RAF mess function. Roe failed to see a 'road closed' sign, crashed through a barrier and went over an embankment. He and his wife were injured. They sued contractors who were doing the road works and who, he alleged, had not lighted the obstacle. At the trial Roe said he had drunk only three half-pints of beer during the evening. The judge treated him as having been quite sober and awarded him damages. On hearing of the case and the result another passenger told the contractors' solicitor that to his knowledge Roe had been hopelessly drunk and that that was the cause of the accident. The solicitor also found a publican who said (contrary to what Roe had said in evidence) that Roe and other members of his party had been drinking heavily before they went to the RAF mess. The contractors appealed and applied for leave to adduce further evidence.
HELD: (1) It would be hopelessly inconvenient merely to allow the new evidence to be adduced: the only course, if the Court was to do anything was to order a new trial, since evidence in rebuttal must also be admitted. (2) The three conditions required by *Ladd v Marshall* (p 641, above) were duly satisfied. The defendants' solicitor could not reasonably have sought the evidence from the passenger before the trial since he might himself have had a claim. The evidence would certainly have a most important effect on the judge's view of contributory negligence. It could not be said it was not credible: the word 'credible' in this connection means that on the face of it the evidence was not worthy of any credence. In the present case one could not go as far as that. New trial ordered.

Delaney v Douglas (No 1)
[1969] 3 All ER 1454n, CA
At an early stage in the investigation of a road accident claim the question
arose whether or not a car had been parked opposite a public house at the
material time. The plaintiff's solicitor had evidence from some witnesses
that a car was so parked but did not enquire at the public house itself until a
considerable time after the accident: by that time the licensee had moved
and could not be found. At the trial the judge held there was no car there.
The former licensee was then found and was prepared to say that there was
a parked car. The plaintiff sought leave to adduce this evidence on an
appeal.
HELD: Leave must be refused. Reasonable and due diligence on the part
of the plaintiff's solicitor should require him when the story was being
originally investigated to enquire at the house immediately opposite the
relevant scene. This was not done until too late.

HUSBAND AND WIFE

Note—With effect from 1 August 1962, the common law rule by which spouses
were precluded from suing each other in tort was abolished. This is the effect of the
Law Reform (Husband and Wife) Act 1962, s 1 of which is as follows:

'**1 Actions in tort between husband and wife**   (1) Subject to the provisions of
this section each of the parties to a marriage shall have the like right of action in tort
against the other as if they were not married.
(2) Where an action in tort is brought by one of the parties to a marriage against
the other during the subsistence of the marriage, the Court may stay the action if it
appears —
(a)   that no substantial benefit would accrue to either party from the
            continuation of the proceedings; or
(b)   that the question or questions in issue could more conveniently be
            disposed of on an application made under s 17 of the Married Women's
            Property Act 1882 (determination of questions between husband and wife
            as to the title to or possession of property);
and without prejudice to para (b) of this subsection the Court may, in such an
action, either exercise any power which could be exercised on an application under
the said section seventeen, or give such directions as it thinks fit for the disposal
under that section of any question arising in the proceedings.'

When dealing with such an action reference should be made to RSC Ord 89, r 2
for the special rules relating to such actions in tort.
By s 3(3) of the Act 'parties to a marriage' includes parties to a marriage which has
been dissolved.

INSURANCE — DISCLOSURE TO COURT

Gowar v Hales
[1928] 1 KB 191, [1927] All ER Rep 631, 96 LJKB 1088, 137 LT 580, CA
It is an established rule of practice that, in an action for personal injuries,
the fact that the defendant is insured should not be disclosed to the jury, and
it is within the discretion of the judge to discharge the jury and order the
plaintiff to pay costs.

Note—See also *Askew v Grimmer* (1927) 43 TLR 354; *Wright v Hearson* [1916] WN 216; *Grinham v Davies* [1929] 2 KB 249, 98 LJKB 703, 139 LT 379, 44 TLR 523, 72 Sol Jo 303, Div Ct; *Jones v Birch Bros Ltd* [1933] 2 KB 597, [1933] All ER Rep 251, 102 LJKB 746, 149 LT 507, 49 TLR 586, CA. As appears from the following cases the 'established rule of practice' is virtually a dead letter, even in those rare cases tried before a jury.

Morey v Woodfield
(1961) Times, 12 July, [1961] CLY 2333
The plaintiff, a child of nine, suffered a dislocation of the cervical vertebrae causing complete paralysis of her body and legs and almost complete paralysis of her arms. Little improvement could be expected in her condition. Her injuries were received in a motor accident for which the defendant admitted liability. Her action for damages was tried by a judge sitting with a jury who awarded her £50,000. In his summing-up the judge (Glyn-Jones J) said: 'I am not going to be bound by the old-fashioned rule which has long out-lived its usefulness and pretend these damages are going to be paid by the defendant. They are not and you all know it.'

Harman v Crilly
[1943] KB 168, [1943] 1 All ER 140, 112 LJKB 224, 168 LT 42, 59 TLR 96, 87 Sol Jo 76, CA
The plaintiff brought an action against the driver, Crilly, and the owners, A. W. Robey Ltd, of a motor vehicle for damages for personal injuries. Both defendants issued a third-party notice claiming indemnity against the insurers of the motor vehicle. The insurers contended the policy was issued to A. W. Robey, who had assigned his business, including the vehicle, to the limited company, and therefore the policy was not available to the defendants. The insurers contended that the disclosure of the insurance would prejudice or embarrass the fair trial of the action.
HELD: The rule of practice of non-disclosure of insurance to a jury (*Gowar v Hales* [1928] 1 KB 191; *Jones v Birch Bros Ltd* [1933] 2 KB 597; and *Carpenter v Ebblewhite* [1939] 1 KB 347, [1938] 4 All ER 41, 108 LJKB 110, 159 LT 564, 55 TLR 17, 82 Sol Jo 889, CA) does not apply to trial by judge alone. It was left open whether it still applies in jury trials of motor cases since the Road Traffic Acts.

Note—See *Morey v Woodfield*, above.

Murfin v Ashbridge and Martin
[1941] 1 All ER 231, CA
Although the insurers have control over the proceedings, they are not parties to the action and cannot therefore make an application in their own name.

Note—And see *Semtex v Gladstone* [1954] 2 All ER 206, [1954] 1 WLR 945, 98 Sol Jo 438.

INTERROGATORIES

Griebart v Morris
[1920] 1 KB 659, 89 LJKB 397, 122 LT 736, 64 Sol Jo 275, CA

The plaintiff was seriously injured when hit by the defendant's car and had little recollection of the accident, nor were there any witnesses. She sought leave to interrogate the defendant on the positions of the vehicles at the moment of the accident.

HELD: She was entitled to interrogate. There was no rule of practice in running-down cases not to allow interrogatories. There is a right to interrogate in order to obtain an admission if necessary for disposing fairly of the action, subject to two limitations (1) interrogatories are not permissible if of a 'fishing' nature nor (2) if they seek to obtain the names of the opponents' witnesses.

Marskell v Metropolitan District Rly Co
(1890) 7 TLR 49, CA

In an action for personal injuries against a railway company, an interrogatory was disallowed which was directed to ascertaining which of the company's servants saw plaintiff at the time of the accident and what plaintiff's position then was.

Note—The *Law Times Journal* of 13 September 1947, p 142, cites this case as authority for the statement that 'An interrogatory in an action for personal injuries as to the number and names of the defendants' witnesses of the accident will not be allowed'.

Potter v Metropolitan District Rly Co
(1873) 28 LT 231, 37 JP 696

A passenger on the railway of defendants having been hurt by a train, was accompanied to her home by two of their servants under the direction of a third, an inspector. Subsequently bringing an action for damages in respect of the injury received, she sought to administer certain interrogatories to defendants.

HELD: They might be interrogated as to the names of their inspector, of their other servants who accompanied plaintiff home and of the driver of the engine driving the train by which she was a passenger, but might not be asked whether any of the servants of the company witnessed the accident, and, if so, what were their names.

Legal professional privilege

Conlon v Conlons Ltd
[1952] 2 All ER 462, [1952] WN 403, [1952] 2 TLR 343, 96 Sol Jo 547, CA

Plaintiff claimed damages for personal injuries from defendants. His solicitors wrote to defendants' insurers without prejudice offering terms of settlement. Later plaintiff issued a writ. Defendants pleaded that terms of settlement had been agreed and that the plaintiff's claim had been compromised by way of accord and satisfaction. Plaintiff in his reply denied any agreement to compromise and pleaded that if any agreement had been entered into, his solicitors had no authority to enter into it.

Defendants administered interrogatories asking —
1 Were the solicitors at the dates of the letters acting on his behalf.
2 Had he not authorised the solicitors to negotiate or to hold themselves out as having authority to do so.
3 Had he not authorised the solicitors to make the offers.
4 At what date were their instructions withdrawn.

The Court of Appeal suggested it would be legitimate and proper to put a question — Did you authorise your solicitors to accept £1,000 and costs, or to settle the case for £1,000 and costs.

The plaintiff declined to answer on the ground that they related to communications between him and his solicitors confidentially and in their professional character, and were privileged.

HELD: Citing *Welsh v Roe* (1918) 87 LJKB 520, [1918–19] All ER Rep 620, 118 LT 529, 34 TLR 187, 62 Sol Jo 269 after issue of writ a solicitor had implied general authority to settle the action which could not be limited unless brought to the notice of the other side; and *Macauley v Polley* [1897] 2 QB 122, 66 LJQB 665, 76 LT 643, 45 WR 681, CA that a solicitor could not compromise before writ issued where actual authority must be proved; the rule as to privilege did not extend to communications which the client instructed the solicitor to repeat to the other party. Such communications were not confidential. Order to answer the interrogatories upheld.

Note—As to interrogatories between co-defendants in a contribution case, see *Clayson v Rolls Royce Ltd* p 604, above. For interrogatories in an action calling for leave under the Limitation Act 1980, s 33 see *Jones v Searle*, p 622, above.

Fatal case

Sloan v Hanson
[1939] 1 All ER 333, 55 TLR 417, 83 Sol Jo 174, [1939] WN 28, CA
'Did you at an inquest held by Dr Lord, one of His Majesty's coroners for the County of Surrey, at the Guildhall, Kingston, in the said county, on 4 and 11 April 1938 (in answer to questions or otherwise), make any and if so which of the statements contained in the document served herewith?' A copy of the deposition of the defendant at the inquest on Adam Sloan was served with the interrogatory. Interrogatory allowed.

Burr v Ware RDC
[1939] 2 All ER 688, CA
An interrogatory will not be allowed in a fatal case asking for the admission of the statement of the driver at the inquest, where the driver is the defendant's servant, and there was no proof that the driver was an agent with authority to made admissions.

Note—And see *Tustin v Arnold*, p 586, above. The Civil Evidence Act 1968 has largely eliminated the need for interrogatories of this kind.

ISSUE, TRIAL OF

Note—The Court has power under RSC Ord 33, r 4 to order trial of different questions or issues in an action at different times or places. Thus there may be separate trials of the issues of liability and damages. See the comments of Winn LJ in *Hawkins v New Mendip Engineering* [1966] 3 All ER 228, [1966] 1 WLR 1341, 110 Sol Jo 633, CA (above, p 425) and the note 33/4/7 'Separate Trials of Issues of Liability and Damages' in the *Supreme Court Practice*. A r 4A has been added to Ord 33 by SI 1980/1010. It provides that where an order is made under r 4(2) for a split trial a party against whom a finding of liability is sought may make a written offer to the other party to accept liability up to a specified proportion. The rule seems intended in respect of costs to have a similar effect to that of a payment into Court.

Coenen v Payne
[1974] 2 All ER 1109, [1974] 1 WLR 984, 118 Sol Jo 499, CA
Cars driven by the plaintiff and defendant collided head-on, injuring both. The plaintiff, a German veterinary surgeon, claimed heavy damages including large sums for potential loss of earnings. Trial would be likely to be extended by four days by the evidence on damages. The defendant counter-claimed in respect of his own injuries and applied for separate trials on the issues of liability and damages. The judge refused separate trials on the ground that the plaintiff was entitled to choose the normal method of trying liability and quantum at the same time.
HELD, ON APPEAL: This was not right. The Winn Committee had recommended a less restrictive approach to separate trials. Winn LJ himself had alluded to separate trials in *Hawkins*'s case, (above, p 425). RSC Ord 33, r 4(2) gives the courts power to grant separate trials and they should be ready to do so wherever it is just and convenient. In the present case much time and expense in trying the issue of damages would be wasted if the plaintiff were to fail on the issue of liability. The plaintiff could not claim the right to choose merely by agreeing to pay for the extra expense. Appeal allowed.

JOINDER OF PARTIES

After amendment of defence

Brittain v Martin
(1965), 109 Sol Jo 76, Times, 14 January, CA
The plaintiff was struck and injured by a rear wheel of the defendants' lorry which had broken away from the lorry as a result of the rear axle fracturing. The statement of claim pleaded *res ipsa loquitur*. In the defence it was pleaded, on the basis of expert advice, that the fracture was due to metal fatigue which the defendants could not have discovered. At the trial the defendants' expert made it clear he had abandoned the theory of metal fatigue and was now attributing the fracture to a hair-line crack arising from the way in which the axle had been manufactured. After hearing other expert evidence the judge allowed an amendment of the defence to give effect to the new evidence but refused an application by the plaintiff to add the manufacturers of the lorry as defendants.
HELD, ON APPEAL: There was no good ground why the judge, once having admitted the evidence of the defendants' experts and granted leave to amend the defence, could resist the application. The evidence criticised, whether consciously or not, the method of manufacture of the axle casing.

The plaintiff must be entitled to join any defendant on whom the original defendant sought to cast responsibility, even though she may have no means of her own of determining where the fault lay.

JURY

Hope v Great Western Rly Co
[1937] 2 KB 130, [1937] 1 All ER 625, 106 LJKB 563, 156 LT 331, 53 TLR 399, 81 Sol Jo 198, CA
It is completely within the discretion of the judge to order an action to be tried either with or without a jury.

Pease v George
[1960] 1 All ER 709 n, [1960] 1 WLR 427, 104 Sol Jo 328, CA
An infant plaintiff claimed damages for injuries received in a road accident which he alleged was due to the defendant's negligence. In his summons for directions the plaintiff asked for an order that the trial should be with a jury. His injuries, according to the statement of claim, were such that he was a total invalid and would remain so mentally and physically for the rest of his life. The master ordered trial by judge alone and, on appeal, the judge in chambers upheld the master's order.
HELD, by the Court of Appeal: There might be much to be said for having a jury in so serious a case, but under RSC Ord 36, r 1(3) it is in the discretion of the Court or the judge to decide one way or the other and that is an absolute discretion. The master and judge in chambers had each refused a jury and there were no grounds for interfering. *Hope v Great Western Rly Co* followed.

Note—The present rule for determining the mode of trial is Ord 33, r 4. It omits para (3) of the former Ord 36, r 1, but the Court still has a discretion in making an order for mode of trial and the following cases are still effective. See Supreme Court Act 1981, s 69(3) and notes to Ord 33, r 5 in the *Supreme Court Practice*.

Hennell v Ranaboldo
[1963] 3 All ER 684, [1963] 1 WLR 1391, 107 Sol Jo 829, CA
The plaintiff claimed damages for injuries to his right leg including a fracture, a dislocation of the knee and amputation of two toes. He was off work six months but had made quite a good recovery. On the summons for directions the master made an order for trial by a jury: on appeal to the judge the order was upheld.

The Court of Appeal ordered trial by judge alone. It was an ordinary case of personal injuries. Though the matter was completely in the discretion of the judge (*Hope v Great Western Rly Co*, above) he had not properly exercised it, having indicated that he thought it desirable to have a case tried by jury occasionally as a sample. The Court could therefore exercise its own discretion. Trial by judge alone has the advantages (1) that judges know the sort of scale of damages which are awarded in these cases: this secures uniformity and (2) that if a judge makes an award wholly out of proportion it can be corrected in the Court of Appeal: it could not be done so easily in the case of a jury award. Trial by jury causes costs for the parties and extra work for the public and was not warranted in these circumstances.

Sims v William Howard & Sons Ltd
[1964] 2 QB 409, [1964] 1 All ER 918, [1964] 2 WLR 794, 108 Sol Jo 174, CA
The plaintiff suffered injury to his spinal cord in a factory accident as a result of which he was confined to a wheelchair. He applied for trial by jury and on appeal from the master the judge in chambers so ordered.
HELD, ON APPEAL: It was not correct that cases of serious injury were particularly suitable for trial by jury. In personal injury cases there should be some degree of uniformity. The judges have evolved a scale of awards which is well known, but it can never be applied by a jury since they cannot be told of it. *Hope v Great Western Rly Co* (p 648, above) did not mean that the discretion of the judge was so absolute that no appeal lay from it. It can be reviewed on appeal if he fails to take into account what ought to be taken into account. The principle of uniformity is so important that it is a relevant consideration for the judge to take into account: he must have failed to do so in this case and trial should be by judge alone.

Watts v Manning
[1964] 2 All ER 267, [1964] 1 WLR 623, 108 Sol Jo 257, CA
The plaintiff was injured when she was struck by a scooter ridden by the defendant. She began an action for damages for personal injuries. Her husband began a separate action for loss of consortium. The plaintiff's most serious injury was to her pelvis, causing, she alleged, inability to have sexual intercourse or conceive a child. On her application the master ordered trial by jury: in her husband's action he ordered trial by judge alone. On appeal in the plaintiff's action the judge in chambers decided it should also be tried by judge alone since the defendant ought to be entitled to consolidate the two actions and this would not be possible if there were different modes of trial; he also said there was a complicated medical issue fit for a judge alone. The plaintiff appealed. Immediately before the hearing of the appeal the husband discontinued his action.
HELD: The judge's decision should not be disturbed. In exercising the discretion there should, in fairness to both plaintiffs and defendants, be some accepted maxims which should be applied. In order to achieve uniformity, even in a case of serious injury, there should be trial by judge alone. The main disadvantages of jury trial are (1) extra time and expense; (2) impossibility of securing uniformity of awards; (3) no reference can be made to awards in similar cases; (4) difficulty in putting right a jury award on appeal; (5) unsuitability of jury for dealing with complicated issues. These factors should be borne in mind when a decision is to be made whether or not jury trial is to be ordered.

Ward v James
[1966] 1 QB 273, [1965] 1 All ER 563, [1965] 2 WLR 455, 109 Sol Jo 111, [1965] 1 Lloyd's Rep 145, CA
As a result of a road accident for which he alleged the defendant was to blame the plaintiff was a permanent quadraplegic, both arms and legs being paralysed. In July 1963 the master and, on appeal the judge in chambers, ordered trial by jury. In October 1964, following the reported decisions in *Sims v Howard* and *Watts v Manning* (above), the defendant applied for leave to appeal against the order out of time. The Court of

Appeal gave leave to appeal and decided that the appeal should be heard by the full court, the point not having been considered by a full court since *Hope v Great Western Rly Co* (p 648, above).

Judgment was delivered in the appeal by Lord Denning MR (the other members of the court concurring) dealing with the following matters:

Hope's case decided that the mode of trial was in the discretion of the court or a judge without being fettered by an *presumption of law* in favour of or against a jury.

The Court of Appeal can and will interfere with the discretion of the judge if it can see that the judge has given no weight (or not sufficient weight) to those considerations which ought to have weighed with him. Even if he has given no reasons, the Court may infer he has gone wrong and reverse his decision.

In the great majority of personal injury cases trial by judge alone is acceptable to the parties. The judges set the standard for awards and thus there is uniformity of decision. If a party asks for a jury it is often because he has a weak case or desires to appeal to sympathy. Serious injuries have been said in the past to afford a good reason for ordering trial by jury but recent experience has led to doubts on this score. In very serious cases scales and conventional figures have been worked out by the judges which juries do not know of and cannot be told.

The lessons of recent cases are that three things are desirable (a) assessability, ie, the award in very serious cases must basically be a conventional figure; (b) uniformity: unless similar decisions are given in similar cases there is dissatisfaction with and criticism of the administration of justice; (c) predictability: if awards are predictable with some measure of accuracy settlements are encouraged. None of these desiderata is achieved when damages are left at large to the jury.

The Court of Appeal can interfere with a jury award if it is 'out of all proportion to the circumstances of the case' and with a judge's award if it is, 'a wholly erroneous estimate of the damage suffered'. In practice the Court has been much less willing to interfere with a jury award than with a judge's. In future the court will not feel the same hesitation as it formerly did. If it is 'out of all proportion' it will be set aside and the Court may order a new trial by judge alone, or by consent of the parties, substitute its own figure.

Note—It was announced a fortnight after the judgment of the Court of Appeal was delivered that the action had been settled ((1965) Times, 11 February).

Hodges v Harland and Wolff Ltd
[1965] 1 All ER 1086, [1965] 1 WLR 523, 109 Sol Jo 178, [1965] 1 Lloyd's Rep 181, CA

The plaintiff's injuries in an accident at work included the tearing off of the penis and of the scrotal skin. He applied for trial by jury but the master felt himself bound by authority to order trial by judge alone. On appeal the judge in chambers considered the cases and the principle of uniformity but nevertheless thought it was a case for a jury and so ordered. On appeal to the Court of Appeal, held, the judge had taken into account all the considerations he ought to bear in mind and none that he should not; there was no ground for disturbing this exercise of his discretion.

Per Lord Denning MR: It is a mistake to suppose *Ward v James* took away the right to trial by jury. . . . What *Ward v James* did do was this: it laid down the considerations which should be borne in mind by a judge when exercising his discretion; and it is apparent that, on those considerations, the result will ordinarily be trial by judge alone. It will not result in trial by jury save in exceptional circumstances . . . I think the judge was well entitled to take the view that this was an exceptional case.

MEDICAL EXAMINATIONS

Note—Halsbury's Laws (4th edn) vol 30, para 38, p 34 says:

'A medical practitioner who examines a person against his will and without statutory authority to do so, and a surgeon who performs an operation without his patient's express or implied consent, are each liable in trespass.'

Beven on *Negligence in Law* (3rd end), p 997, says:

'Outside this enactment (Regulation of Railways Act 1868) there appears to be no power to order an examination of a person injured and whose injuries are the subject of legal proceedings; though the strong comment that a refusal to submit to examination would elicit at the trial is a considerable safeguard against the want of such a power working practical injustice.'

McDowell v Strannix
[1951] NI 57, [1952] CLY 2768
Plaintiff's advisers refused medical examination except upon terms that evidence limited to damage and no evidence given to statements made by plaintiff to defendant's doctor as to liability.
HELD: Terms reasonable.

Pickett v Bristol Aeroplane Co Ltd
[1961] CLY 7183, (1961) Times, 17 March, CA
In an action for damages for dermatitis the plaintiff was examined by doctors instructed by the defendants. One of the doctors having died the defendants asked for a further examination by a dermatologist. The plaintiff refused. On an interlocutory application by the defendants for an order that the action be stayed until the plaintiff submitted to examination —
HELD: The Court has an inherent jurisdiction to make such an order, but this was not a case in which it ought to be exercised. The defendants could have no possible right to a direct order compelling the plaintiff to submit to examination; and to order a stay until he submitted to examination would be an indirect method of achieving the same result. Such an order would be an improper interference with the plaintiff's civil liberty and with his right to present his case in his own way.
Per Donovan LJ: It would be wrong to shut out a plaintiff from the Seat of Justice even if he refused any examination at all, still less where, as in the present case, he had refused to be examined only by one particular doctor.

*Note—*See *Starr v National Coal Board* and *Lane v Willis*, p 653, below.

Edmeades v Thames Board Mills Ltd
[1969] 1 QB 67, [1969] 2 All ER 127, [1969] 2 WLR 668, 113 Sol Jo 88,
[1969] 1 Lloyd's Rep 221, CA
In an action for damages for personal injuries the defendants were given
facilities for a medical examination of the plaintiff by Dr A. When reports
were exchanged the defendants saw that the plaintiff's doctor was saying
that there was a condition of osteoarthritis not alleged in the statement of
claim and therefore not considered by Dr A. They asked for a new
examination by a specialist, naming six specialists from whom the plaintiff
could choose. The plaintiff's solicitors refused to grant any facilities for a
further examination except by Dr A who was not one of the six. The defendants applied to the Court for an order that the action be stayed unless the
plaintiff submit to examination by one of the six.
HELD: The Court had ample jurisdiction to grant a stay whenever it was
just and reasonable so to do. The request of the defendants was reasonable
and if not granted would result in the court being unable to do justice to
their case. *Pickett*'s case (above) was different in that only one name was put
forward. The defendants were entitled to the order sought.

Murphy v Ford Motor Co Ltd
(1970) 114 Sol Jo 886, CA
In an action for damages for pneumoconiosis the defendants asked for a
medical examination by a named doctor. The plaintiff's solicitors refused
on the ground that that doctor made reports only for insurance companies.
This allegation was shown to be untrue and the plaintiff's solicitors
withdrew it but still declined to agree to the examination. The defendants
sought a stay as in *Edmeades*'s case.
HELD: They were entitled to have a stay. If the defendants in a personal
injury case made a reasonable request for the plaintiff to be medically
examined by a doctor whom the defendants have chosen, then the plaintiff
should accede to such a request unless he has a reasonable ground for
objecting to that particular doctor. If the plaintiff has any reasons he should
give them so that the Court can see what they are: a mere refusal does not
put the onus on the defendant to show that his choice was justified. Having
nominated a fit and proper person the defendants were entitled to the
examination.

Starr v National Coal Board
[1977] 1 All ER 243, [1977] 1 WLR 63, 120 Sol Jo 720, CA
The plaintiff claimed damages for injury to the elbows by ulnar nerve
compression alleged to have been sustained over a period of time at work.
After receiving an indeterminate report from a surgeon the defendants
asked for an examination by Dr X a neurologist. The plaintiff's solicitors
refused, saying, in effect, 'Any consultant neurologist other than Dr X, but
under no circumstances Dr X.' The defendants applied for a stay unless
and until the plaintiff submitted to examination by Dr X.
HELD: They were entitled to a stay. In exercising its discretion the Court
must have regard to the fundamental right of the plaintiff to personal
liberty but also of the defendant to defend himself in litigation as he and his
advisers think fit. The principles to be followed were those indicated in
Edmeades's and *Murphy*'s case (above), *Pickett*'s case (p 651, above) cannot

stand against those two cases. The Court's discretion cannot be exercised unless each party exposes the reason for his action. The plaintiff had sought to prove that he and his advisers entertained a reasonable apprehension that Dr X might produce a misleading report which might make a just determination of the cause more difficult. On the evidence adduced he had failed to do this.

Hall v Avon Health Authority
[1980] 1 All ER 516, [1980] 1 WLR 481, 124 Sol Jo 293, CA
The defendants to an action for damages for personal injury asked for a medical examination of the plaintiff to be carried out by their specialist medical adviser. The plaintiff's solicitors had no personal objections to the specialist but asked as a term of agreement to the examination that a doctor nominated by them on behalf of the plaintiff should be present.
HELD: The term could not be insisted upon. The court ought to have good and substantial reasons put before it if it is to impose conditions of this kind on a reasonable request for a medical examination. It was not an adequate reason to say that the plaintiff was a woman of 52, or that in other cases plaintiffs had been upset by the way in which they had been examined by other doctors for other defendants. An FRCS of good standing should be given credit for being fair and considerate in his examination and report on an opposite party.

Lane v Willis
[1972] 1 All ER 430, [1972] 1 WLR 326, 116 Sol Jo 102, CA
The plaintiff received injuries in a road accident in 1968. In the statement of claim they were given as 'bruising of chest, contusion of left knee, nervous shock and depressive anxiety state'. In February 1971 these particulars were considerably extended by amendment to include severe depression requiring treatment in a sanatorium and possibly early retirement. The defendants had two examinations by a neurologist after the amendment and then asked the plaintiff's solicitors for examination by a psychiatrist. The request was refused. They applied for a stay of the action unless the plaintiff should submit to examination by a named psychiatrist.
HELD: The defendants were entitled to the order asked. In *Pickett*'s case (above) Lord Donovan had expressed doubt whether the court had jurisdiction to make the order but the real point there was that the defendants were insisting on examination by one doctor to whom the plaintiff objected. In the present case there was no objection to the particular doctor nominated but to any further examination. The correct test was that laid down in *Edmeades*'s case, that the court had jurisdiction to grant a stay whenever it was just and reasonable so to do and could do so where the plaintiff's refusal was such as to prevent the just determination of the cause.
   Per Sachs LJ: There was a heavy onus on the defendant to show why a further examination was needed. In future cases medical evidence should be produced to show that the further examination was required in the interests of justice.

Aspinall v Sterling Mansell Ltd
[1981] 3 All ER 866 (Hodgson J)
The plaintiff claimed damages for industrial dermatitis allegedly contracted in the defendants' employment. They asked for a medical examination at which their doctor administer a patch test. She refused to undergo an examination which would include a patch test. The defendants applied for an order that the action be stayed unless and until the plaintiff submitted to such examination.
HELD: No stay would be granted. There was a slight risk of a major recrudescence of dermatitis from a patch test. There is a difference not of degree but of kind between an ordinary examination and one which includes such procedures as patch testing. It is not the reasonableness of the defendants' request which is in question but the reasonableness of the plaintiff's refusal. It cannot ever be unreasonable for a plaintiff to refuse to undergo a procedure which carries with it a risk, however slight, of serious injury.

Prescott v Bulldog Tools Ltd
[1981] 3 All ER 869 (Webster J)
The plaintiff claimed damages for alleged industrial deafness contracted in the defendants' employment. He underwent a number of medical examinations from some of which it appeared that the deafness was in part due to causes other than his employment. The defendants asked for a further examination by a specialist who intended to carry out a caloric test, x-ray photographs and an electrocochleography. The plaintiff refused to undergo the tests. The defendants applied for a stay unless and until the plaintiff submitted to the examination and tests. There was evidence that the caloric test induces a degree of discomfort and the electrocochleography involves risk and discomfort.
HELD: In cases of this kind the court should examine objectively the weight of reasonableness of the defendant's request as seen by the defendant and the weight of the reasonableness of the plaintiff's objections as seen by him and balance the one against the other. Although it is extremely unlikely that a court would hold it unreasonable for the plaintiff to refuse a test which carried a risk of serious injury the court should (despite the view expressed in *Aspinall*'s case (above)) consider the matter without introducing any presumption one way or the other. In the present case the reasonableness of the plaintiff's objections to the electrocochleography and x-rays outweighed the reasonableness of the defendant's request, but as the plaintiff had already undergone a caloric test by his own expert the reasonableness of the defendants' request for that test outweighed the reasonableness of his refusal.

Supplying copy of medical report

Clarke v Martlew
[1973] QB 58, [1972] 3 All ER 764, [1972] 3 WLR 653, 116 Sol Jo 618, CA
The second defendant asked for a medical examination of the plaintiff by two named doctors. The plaintiff agreed subject to her solicitors being supplied with copies of the reports. The second defendant objected to this

requirement and applied for a stay until the plaintiff should grant facilities for the examination.

HELD: The plaintiff's stipulation was fair. It was reasonable and just as a condition of being granted a medical examination that the defendant should make available the doctor's report to the plaintiff. If and when the plaintiff got further reports on her own she must reciprocate and show those to the defendant.

Megarity v D. J. Ryan & Sons Ltd

[1980] 2 All ER 832, [1980] 1 WLR 1237, 124 Sol Jo 498, CA

The defendants, against whom the plaintiff claimed damages for personal injury, applied for an order that the action be stayed until the plaintiff submitted to medical examination by the defendants' medical adviser. The district registrar refused an order except on condition that the defendants supplied a copy of the report to the plaintiff as required by *Clarke v Martlew* (above). An appeal to the judge in chambers succeeded.

HELD, by the Court of Appeal: The judge was right. When *Clarke v Martlew* was decided RSC Ord 38, rr 36 and 37 did not exist. Those rules established a complete code dealing with the conditions which attach to the adducing of expert evidence at the trial. The 'fairness' which Lord Denning required in *Clarke*'s case was secured by the new rules. A condition calling for disclosure of the defendant's report should not be imposed.

McGinley v Burke

[1973] 2 All ER 1010, [1973] 1 WLR 990, 117 Sol Jo 488, [1973] 2 Lloyd's Rep 508

In an action for damages for personal injuries the defendant's solicitors asked permission to have the plaintiff medically examined. The plaintiff's solicitors stipulated that they must be supplied with a copy of the report. Defendant's solicitors were agreeable to this provided the plaintiff's solicitors supplied copies of all their own reports. They refused; the defendant's solicitors applied for a stay of the action.

HELD: The plaintiff must at least offer reciprocity. If the plaintiff's solicitors require to see a copy of the defendant's medical report immediately they must be prepared to offer an equivalent report of their own in exchange but they are not obliged to disclose all their reports. The Court is only concerned with those on which the plaintiff intents to rely at the trial. As an alternative to immediate disclosure the parties can agree to eventual exchange before trial.

Note—Present-day practice under RSC Ord 25, r 8 (automatic directions) requires parties to disclose the substance of any medical or other expert evidence as a condition of being allowed to call such evidence.

Fatal Accidents Acts claim

Baugh v Delta Water Fittings Ltd

[1971] 3 All ER 258, [1971] 1 WLR 1295, 115 Sol Jo 485 (Lawson J)

The plaintiff, aged 54, was the widow of a man killed in an accident at work. She claimed damages as administratrix of her husband's estate under the Law Reform (Miscellaneous Provisions) Act 1934 and for herself as his dependant under the Fatal Accidents Acts. The defendants required her to be medically examined: she refused. The defendants applied for a stay of the action as in *Edmeades*'s case (p 652, above). They had no reason to believe her health was other than normal.

HELD: (1) The plaintiff's expectation of life was irrelevant to the claim under the Law Reform (Miscellaneous Provisions) Act 1934 and there could be no grounds for a stay of proceedings under that Act. (2) Even if the view of the Court of Appeal in *Edmeades*'s case was right that the Court can order a stay when an injured plaintiff refuses examination, the same considerations do not apply when the plaintiff is a dependant suing under the Fatal Accidents Acts. In such a case no order should be made unless the defendant can show substantial grounds for making the application, e g that the widow has a grave disease. That was not the case here and there was no reason to compel her to submit to examination.

Plaintiff's doctor's fee

Bram v Ponsford and Devenish
[1953] CLY 3463, Mayor's Court

Defendants' solicitors requested a medical examination of plaintiff and by letter agreed that it should take place 'on the usual terms'.

HELD: The solicitors were liable for the attendance fee of the plaintiff's specialist but not for any sum referable to his travelling expenses in the absence of express subsequent agreement.

Note—On presence of plaintiff's doctor at examination see *Hall v Avon Area Health Authority* (above, p 653).

Sequential disclosure of experts' reports

Kirkup v British Railways Engineering Ltd
[1983] 3 All ER 147, [1983] 1 WLR 1165, [1983] 1 All ER 855, [1983] 1 WLR 190, 126 Sol Jo 730

On a summons for directions in a personal injury action the master ordered disclosure of the plaintiff's expert's reports within 28 days after setting down and of the defendants' experts' reports within 42 days thereafter. The plaintiff appealed against the order.

HELD: The basic rule was that experts' reports obtained for the purpose of the litigation were privileged. Ord 25, r 8(1)(b) provided for disclosure by mutual exchange. On applications relating to calling expert evidence Ord 38, r 37(2) required the court to order disclosure unless it considered there was 'sufficient reason for not doing so'. The question in issue was the extent of the Court's discretion. The instances given in Ord 38, r 37(3) and (4) were guidelines but not the only circumstances in which disclosure may be withheld. Mutuality, and fairness were not the only matters to be considered; there were also the saving of costs, the avoidance of surprise and the need to avoid amendments at trial. It would not be unreasonable in appropriate circumstances to require the plaintiff to show his hand by sending his expert's report first so that the defendant might consider the issues raised in it. Appeal dismissed.

Order 14

Dummer v Brown
[1953] 1 QB 710, [1953] 1 All ER 1158, [1953] 2 WLR 984, 97 Sol Jo 331, CA
A judge has a discretion to permit this procedure though the suitable cases must be very small indeed. In this case the defendants had not filed any answer to the affidavit of the plaintiff reciting a plea of guilty to dangerous driving by the driver and alleging there was no defence.
SEMBLE: If the defendants by affidavit had given even a slight indication of some real defence, the judge's decision might have been different.

PARTICULARS BEFORE DEFENCE

Monk v Redwing Aircraft Co
[1942] 1 KB 182, [1942] 1 All ER 133, 111 LJKB 277, 166 LT 42, 58 TLR 94, CA
Order XIX, r 7(b) provided that further and better particulars of the statement of claim shall not be ordered before defence unless necessary or desirable to enable the defendant to plead or for any special reason. The defendant is entitled to particulars of special damage before defence to enable him to decide whether or not to make a payment into court, and if so, the amount.

Note—Order XIX, r 7, is now replaced by Ord 18, r 12. Paragraph (5) of r 12 provides that the Court shall not order particulars 'before service of the defence unless, in the opinion of the Court, the order is necessary or desirable to enable the defendant to plead or for some other special reason'.

Tarbox v Pancras Borough Council
[1952] 1 All ER 1306, [1952] WN 254, [1952] 1 TLR 1293, 96 Sol Jo 360, CA
Plaintiff alleged that whilst walking on the footpath a servant of the defendants swept rubbish, including a tin lid, into his path and under his feet so that he slipped and fell and was injured. The master ordered particulars of the place where the plaintiff was walking; the position of the defendants' servant when sweeping and the position of the plaintiff when he fell and that the particulars should be marked on a scale plan. The judge in chambers affirmed the order. Plaintiff's appeal was dismissed.
HELD: There was discretion to make the order. It was a reasonable method to adopt in the circumstances of the case.

An article by Sir William Ball in the *Law Times* of 10 June 1949 calls attention shortly to some general principles including the following. The court will not sanction an attempt to deliver interrogatories under the guise of seeking particulars: *Lister v Thompson* (1890) 7 TLR 107. A summons for particulars will be dismissed if it appears that the application is a mere attempt to ascertain the names of witnesses: *Temperton v Russell* (1893) 9 TLR 321. But particulars in a proper case may be ordered although they involve disclosure of evidence which will be relied on at the trial: *Marriott v Chamberlain* (1886) 17 QBD 154, 55 LJQB 448, 54 LT 714, 34 WR 783, 2

TLR 640, CA and although the applicant must know the true facts better than his opponent, because he is entitled to know the case that opponent intends to set up: *Harbord v Monk* (1878) 38 LT 411.

In an action for damages for personal injuries caused by negligence, it is now common form to give particulars of the negligence alleged.

'Special damage' must always be particularised. Care should be taken to avoid extravagance as the special damage may have to be proved. The plaintiff should not omit to give particulars of anything to which he is justly entitled as the plaintiff may be held bound by his particulars, and the point is also important if defendant makes a payment into court. An extravagant claim in an item of special damage may discredit the plaintiff at the trial.

FORM OF NOTICE FOR FURTHER AND BETTER PARTICULARS IN COUNTY COURT

TAKE NOTICE —

That pursuant to Ord 6, r 7, the defendant hereby requires you to file and deliver further and better particulars of the plaintiff's particulars of claim herein as follows:

Under para

(a) By stating by and to whom the several sums of £   , and £
were paid and on what date or dates and identifying all accounts and receipts.
(b) By stating the date of purchase, from whom purchased and the price paid for the (e g clothing) and identifying the account and receipt.

Under para

Of the contract of service under which the loss of wages (salary) claimed is payable; if in writing, identifying the document; if oral, by stating by and with whom the same was made and on what date and setting out fully the material terms thereof.

Income tax

Phipps v Orthodox Unit Trusts Ltd
[1958] 1 QB 314, [1957] 3 All ER 305, [1957] 3 WLR 856, [1957] TR 277, CA

The plaintiff brought an action for damages for wrongful dismissal from his position of sole managing director. The defendant company applied for further and better particulars as follows: 'Of the alleged damage stating whether the plaintiff received any taxable income in any of the tax years from 1948–9 onwards, and if so then (1) the amount of such income from every source in each of such years; (2) the amount of any and all assessments to income tax and surtax respectively in each of such years showing how such amounts are made up; and in any event giving full particulars of any facts which entitled or would have entitled the plaintiff to tax allowances in respect of each of the said years.'

HELD: Applying the principles established in the case of *British Transport Commission v Gourley* (p 429, above) and applying the decision in *Monk v Redwing Aircraft Co* (p 657, above), the particulars must be supplied.

Per Jenkins LJ: Our decision, unless applied with caution and common sense, may well result in a great waste of time and expense. Particulars should be limited to what is really reasonably necessary to enable the party seeking them to know what case he has to meet.

Per Parker LJ: Particulars should generally be confined to the broad facts, such as 'The plaintiff is a married man', 'He is entitled to an allowance in respect of two children', 'His unearned income is £100 a year', matters of that sort, and in the ordinary case that can give rise to no difficulties.

PAYMENT INTO COURT

Note—The rules relating to payment into court are in RSC Ord 22.

Corby District Council v Holst & Co
[1985] 1 All ER 321, [1985] 1 WLR 427, 129 Sol Jo 172, CA

The defendants wrote a letter headed 'Without prejudice' to the plaintiffs offering a sum of money in full and final settlement of the action and sought an interlocutory order that the offer be treated for all purposes as a payment into Court pursuant to RSC Ord 22, r 1. The Official Referee declined to make an order.

HELD, ON APPEAL: It was questionable whether the Court had any jurisdiction to make such an order but even if it had, the Official Referee was right to refuse to make an order. Costs were by statute left to the discretion of the judge which had to be exercised in accordance with the rules. Whether such an offer as the one in the present case was to be treated as a payment into court was itself a matter for the trial judge and could not be legislated for in advance in interlocutory proceedings.

Costs when plaintiff fails to recover more than amount in court

Note—The Rules of the Supreme Court, Ord 62 provide by r 5 'The Court in exercising its discretion as to costs shall, to such extent, if any, as may be appropriate in the circumstances take into account . . . any payment of money into Court and the amount of such payment.'

Findlay v Railway Executive
[1950] 2 All ER 969, [1950] WN 570, 66 (Pt 2) TLR 836, 94 Sol Jo 778, CA

An accident causing personal injury occurred on 24 October 1947, and before February 1948, the defendants in correspondence admitted liability. Defence was delivered on 23 March 1948, and admitted negligence, leaving the only issue of quantum of damages. Medical examination took place in March 1949, and in June 1949, defendants paid £920 into court, which was not accepted. Trial took place on 27 April 1950. Special damages were agreed at £117 5s 1d and the judge awarded £750 as general damages making £867 5s 1d in all. The judge awarded the plaintiff the costs of the action, and gave leave to appeal on the question of costs.

HELD, ON APPEAL: per Somervell LJ: Order LXV, r 6 [now revoked but see RSC Ord 62, r 5] provides that the judge in exercising his discretion as to costs takes into account both the fact that money has been paid into court and the amount of such payment. In *Donald Campbell & Co v Pollak* [1927] AC 732, 96 LJKB 1132, 137 LT 656, 43 TLR 495, 787 it was stated that there was a settled practice of the courts or reasonable expectation that in the absence of special circumstances a successful litigant should receive his costs and that it was necessary to show some grounds for exercising discretion to refuse such costs. The discretion was absolute and unfettered but must be exercised judicially and a discretion exercised on no grounds could not be judicial nor should it be exercised except for some reason connected with the case. The defendant was a successful litigant and there were no circumstances entitling the judge to deprive him of costs.

Hultquist v Universal Pattern and Precision Engineering Co Ltd
[1960] 2 QB 467, [1960] 2 All ER 266, [1960] 2 WLR 886, CA
The defendants denied liability but paid a sum of money into Court in satisfaction of the plaintiff's claim. At the trial the plaintiff succeeded on the issue of liability but was awarded less damages than the amount in Court. The plaintiff asked for the costs of the issue of liability.
HELD, ON APPEAL: The matter was one for the discretion of the judge but it is very rare that a plaintiff in such a case and in such circumstances is awarded the costs of the issue of liability. The action of tort consists of wrong-doing and damage resulting therefrom and the plaintiff must prove both to obtain judgment. On the face of it there can be no complaint and no ground for an order for costs on the issue of liability where the plaintiff has been called upon to prove a case to establish his right to damages and has failed to get more than the amount in Court.

Wagman v Vare Motors Ltd
[1959] 3 All ER 326, [1959] 1 WLR 853, 103 Sol Jo 600, CA
The plaintiff commenced an action for damages. The defendants paid a sum of money into Court. The plaintiff did not accept it. The case proceeded and the only issue was damage. The amount awarded by the judge was the exact sum paid into Court. The defendants applied for costs from the payment in, when the amount was disclosed. The plaintiff asked the judge to exercise the discretion given to him by the rule. The judge awarded the plaintiff his costs up to the date of payment in, but ordered that there should be no order as to costs thereafter, on the ground that he had been inclined at one time to give a larger sum than he had finally awarded. The defendants appealed.

The Court of Appeal held that the discretion had not been really exercised at all, and therefore the exercise of discretion did not arise. The fact that the judge had at one time thought of giving a larger sum did not constitute any material on which his discretion could be exercised. The Court of Appeal decided that the judge's decision must be disturbed and the costs after the date of payment in should be the defendants'.

McGuckin v Cammell Laird
(1962) 106 Sol Jo 547, [1962] 1 Lloyd's Rep 635, CA

In an action under the Fatal Accidents Acts in which the defendants admitted liability, the judge awarded the plaintiff £4,548 damages. He arrived at this sum by multiplying the figure of weekly loss by the number of years purchase, making a total of £4,004; increased this to £4,500 by estimating and allowing for a sum in respect of the deceased's probable increase of earnings, and finally added the funeral expenses of £48. The defendants had made a payment into Court earlier in the action of exactly the same sum. The judge declined to give the defendant costs against the plaintiff after payment in on the ground that he had reached the figure of £4,500 merely as a round sum and that it was not a precise valuation. He made no order as to costs after date of payment in.

HELD, ON APPEAL (following *Wagman v Vare Motors*, above): There was no material on which the judge could exercise his discretion in this way. The defendants were entitled to costs after the date of payment in.

Bettaney v Five Towns Demolition Co Ltd
(1971) 115 Sol Jo 710, CA

The defendants paid into Court £50 on 28 January, £21 on 29 January, and £30 on 1 February. On 1 February the defendants' solicitor telephoned the plaintiffs' solicitors and told him there was £101 in court: he replied that the least his clients would accept was £150 and the action continued. Trial began on 2 February, continued on 16 March, and finished on 23 March. The plaintiffs recovered only £76. On costs the judge said that his discretion was unfettered because the prescribed notice of the third payment in could not have been received by the plaintiffs' solicitors before 2 February. He awarded the costs to the plaintiffs.

HELD: On the defendants' appeal, the judge had founded himself on the language of Ord 11, r 9 of the County Court Rules [now Ord 11, r 3 of the 1981 Rules] and had apparently concluded that the plaintiffs had been prejudiced because they could not give notice of acceptance of the payment in before the trial began. But all r 9 meant was that unless the plaintiff gave notice of acceptance as specified the action would not be automatically stayed. The plaintiffs had known of the payment in of £101 by 1 February, and had elected to go on. The judge was bound to take the payment into Court into account and, if he had, could not have deprived the defendants of their costs as from the date of the final payment in.

Nominal damages recovered

Alltrans Express Ltd v CVA Holdings
[1984] 1 All ER 685, [1984] 1 WLR 394, 128 Sol Jo 47, CA

The plaintiffs obtained judgment under Ord 14, the defendants contesting only the amount of the plaintiffs' loss. The action was transferred to the Official Referee for assessment of damages. He held the plaintiffs had not proved any loss and awarded £2 nominal damages. He awarded the costs of the trial to the plaintiffs on the ground that they had been awarded £2 assessed damages and there was no payment in Court by the defendants.

HELD: This was not right. The judge had attached far too much weight to the absence of any payment into Court. If the defendants had paid in £2 it would not have been accepted. The truth was that it was the defendants who were the successful party. Costs of the trial to the defendants.

Claim increased at trial

Cheeseman v Bowaters (UK) Paper Mills Ltd
[1971] 3 All ER 513, [1971] 1 WLR 1773, 115 Sol Jo 931, CA
As pleaded in the statement of claim the plaintiff's claim was for damages for a back injury and loss of earnings for three periods off work. The defendants paid £750 into Court three weeks before trial. At Court the plaintiff claimed a further sum for a fourth period off work and damages for accelerated retirement caused by his injury. The judge awarded damages for both these items. Without them the award would have been less than the amount in Court.
HELD, by the Court of Appeal: As the additional award which brought the total above the amount in Court was on a new case calling for amendments to the statement of claim at the trial the defendants should have their costs from the date of payments in i e the standard order when the plaintiff fails to recover as much as the amount in court.

Interest

RSC Ord 22, r 1(8) says: 'For the purposes of this rule, the plaintiff's cause of action in respect of a debt or damages shall be construed as a cause of action, also, of such interest as might be included in the judgment, whether under s 35A of the Act or otherwise, if judgment were given at the date of the payment into Court'. Thus a payment into court should also include interest on the damages up to the date of payment in.

Two causes of action

The Talamba
[1965] P 433, [1965] 2 All ER 775, [1965] 3 WLR 562, 109 Sol Jo 631, [1965] 2 Lloyd's Rep 128 (Hewson J)
The plaintiffs were the owners, masters and crews of nine tugs four of which rendered salvage services to the *Talamba* and the others to the *Troll*. The *Talamba* and the *Troll* were both owned by the defendants who paid into court a sum of money in respect of the services to each vessel. On an application to apportion the sums as between each tug:
HELD: The owners, masters and crews had a separate cause of action in respect of each tug. Under the new rule if a plaintiff was embarrassed by the defendants' payment the court might order apportionment. Embarrassment meant being put in a difficulty. The plaintiffs were in difficulty until they knew how the services of each tug were regarded by the defendants in terms of money. The overall amount offered to each tug in respect of the services should be designated in such a case as this.

Tingay v Harris
[1967] 2 QB 327, [1967] 1 All ER 385, [1967] 2 WLR 577, 110 Sol Jo 926, CA
The plaintiff, an architect, sued the defendant in the county court for fees which he put at £166 for work done, including preparing plans. The defendant paid into court £75 in satisfaction of the amount claimed. The plaintiff did not accept it. Subsequently the plaintiff obtained leave of the court to add another defendant and claimed damages against both for conversion of the plans. At the trial the judge awarded the plaintiff £75 for fees and £2 nominal damages for the conversion. The case against the second defendant was dismissed. He awarded the plaintiff the costs of the action against the first defendant, purporting to apply Ord 11, r 3 and Ord 15, r 1 of the County Court Rules [now Ord 11, r 1 and Ord 15, r 1 of the 1981 Rules]. The defendant appealed against the award of costs.
HELD: The judge was wrong. The payment into court of £75 had been made before the plaintiff added the further cause of action and he could not have been in any doubt as to the cause of action in respect of which it was paid in, namely, the claim for the fees. As only £75 was awarded for that claim the defendant was the successful party and entitled to costs after date of payment in. The award of £2 for the conversion being *de minimis* should not carry any costs for the plaintiff.

Payment in by one of two defendants

Parkes v Knowles
[1957] 3 All ER 600, [1957] 1 WLR 1040, 101 Sol Jo 816 (Lynskey J)
Plaintiff was injured whilst a passenger in the car driven by the first defendant which collided with the omnibus of the second defendants. Plaintiff commenced proceedings in the High Court against both defendants, and each defendant in his defence blamed the other for the cause of the accident. The first defendant paid £100 into court under RSC Ord 22, r 1. Plaintiff gave notice of acceptance and thereupon, as provided by r 4(3) (now r 3(4)) all further proceedings were stayed, and the money could not be paid out except pursuant to an order dealing with the whole costs of the action. Plaintiff applied for an order under r 4(3) to deal with the amount in court, and contended it was not money recovered in the action under the County Courts Act 1955, s 1(2) [now the County Courts Act 1984, s 1(2)] which provides that where an action is commenced in the High Court which could have been commenced in the county court, if the plaintiff recovers a sum of less than £300 unless there was reasonable ground for supposing the amount of the plaintiff's claim would exceed the amount recoverable in the county court.
HELD: (1) It was money recovered in the action under the County Courts Act 1955, s 1(2) [now the County Courts Act 1984, s 1(2)]. (2) As to costs, the acceptance of the £100 showed that the plaintiff thought the amount was fair and there were no reasonable grounds for supposing the claim would exceed the county court limit. The plaintiff was only entitled to recover from the first defendant costs on scale 3 of the county court. So far as the second defendant was concerned, there was no further issue to be tried, and he was entitled to judgment against the plaintiff with costs on the High Court scale. On the question whether the plaintiff was entitled to add

in his costs against the first defendant the costs he had to pay the second defendant: from the very start the car driver blamed the bus driver and in view of a letter written to the plaintiff, and the allegations in the pleadings, the plaintiff was reasonable in suing both defendants and in fact was bound to do so. He was entitled to recover from the first defendant the costs which he has to pay to the second defendants. A Bullock Order would involve double taxation and the proper order is, first defendant to pay plaintiff's costs on scale 3 of the county court, and the first defendant to pay the second defendant's costs on the High Court scale.

Note—For limitation of recoverable costs of actions in contract and tort see now the County Courts Act 1984, ss 19 and 20.

Two plaintiffs

Smith v Schilling
[1928] 1 KB 429, 97 LJKB 276, 138 LT 475, 44 TLR 109, CA
If there are two plaintiffs, such as an infant and his father, a payment into court must be divided and appropriated to the cause of action of each plaintiff or the payment in is bad.

Note—Followed in *Emcee Ltd v Sunday Pictorial Newspapers (1920) Ltd* [1939] 2 All ER 384, 83 Sol Jo 456 (Singleton J).

Wrong amount paid in

H v L
(1982) Times, 1 July, QBD (McCullough J)
In an action for damages the defendants made a payment into court which the plaintiff accepted by the usual notice to the defendants' solicitors. All proceedings were consequently stayed. A month later the defendants issued a summons for an order removing the stay and for repayment of the money accepted on the ground that the payment into court had been made in error. It was not alleged that the plaintiff or his solicitors realised that any mistake had been made.
HELD: The court had an inherent jurisdiction to set aside a stay and to order repayment of money paid out of court if proper grounds were shown. It was not restricted to cases of fraud or mistake. The existence of the power was evidenced by such authorities as *Derrick v Williams* (p 678, below), *Cooper v Williams* (p 490, above) and *Lambert v Mainland Market Deliveries* (p 686, below). It was a matter of discretion for the court. In the present case the plaintiff had done nothing wrong and the defendants had made a careless mistake. The plaintiff was an old man and some anxiety would be imposed by ordering repayment. Order refused.

Discretion to alter judgment

Millensted v Grosvenor House (Park Lane), Ltd
[1937] 1 KB 717, [1937] 1 All ER 736, 106 LJKB 221, 156 LT 383, CA
Judge of High Court gave judgment for £50 with costs on county court scale. He was then informed that £20 had been paid into court.

Next day he altered the damage to £35 and by formal judgment ordered payment of £35 and county court costs.

HELD: Judge had discretion to allow case to proceed after being told of sum in court, and to alter his judgment at any time before it was drawn up and perfected.

Withdrawal of money paid in

Garner v Cleggs
[1983] 2 All ER 398, [1983] 1 WLR 862, 127 Sol Jo 347, CA

In an action for damages for professional negligence the defendants paid into Court £25,655 and served notice of payment in on the 11 August. The plaintiff did not serve notice of acceptance within 21 days or at all. Having obtained some evidence which they considered showed a change of circumstance the defendants applied to the court to be allowed to take the money out of court: an order to that effect was made on the 26 February. Trial began on 16 March and lasted eight days. Judgment was given for the plaintiff for less than the sum that was originally in court. The judge gave the plaintiff all his costs against the defendants on the ground that at the date of the trial there was no money in court which he could take to avoid the trial. The defendants appealed against the order claiming all the costs of the action from the date of payment in.

HELD: As the defendants had applied simply for all the costs from date of payment in and no other apportionment had been sought from the judge he was entitled to exercise his discretion in the way he had. Nevertheless it would have been wrong to disregard altogether the fact that a payment into court had been made. From the expiry of the 21 days after payment in until the notice of payment in was withdrawn by the defendants the plaintiff was at risk as to costs and the costs incurred during that period should ordinarily be borne by him.

No mention in notice of appeal

Phillips v Gordon
(1966) 110 Sol Jo 189, CA

Per Davies LJ: Whatever the rights and wrongs of the Court of Appeal knowing that there was money paid into court, and how much it was, it was undesirable that that should be underlined by being mentioned in the notice of appeal.

Thornton v Swan Hunter (Shipbuilders) Ltd
[1971] 3 All ER 1248, [1971] 1 WLR 1759, 115 Sol Jo 832, CA

In an appeal by the defendants against the amount of damages it was ordered by the Court of Appeal, on the defendants' application, that in the transcript of the evidence and judgment in the Court below (1) the discussion after the award (which included references to the amount paid into court by the defendants) should be deleted, but (2) a passage in the evidence which showed that an offer had been made, and a reference in the judgment to a payment into court without mentioning the amount, should not be deleted.

Note—Followed in *Beaumont v British Uralite Ltd* (1973) 117 Sol Jo 914.

PAYMENT OUT OF COURT

Cumper v Pothecary
[1941] 2 KB 58, [1941] 2 All ER 516, 110 LJKB 577, 165 LT 243, 57 TLR 503, CA

A defendant who has paid money into court is not entitled as of right to have it paid out to him if not accepted in the time allowed. The court has a discretion for good reasons, eg the discovery of a complete defence (*Frazer and Haws v Burns* (1934) 49 Ll L Rep 216, *Williams v Boag* [1941] 1 KB 1, [1940] 4 All ER 246, 109 LJKB 913, 165 LT 56, CA), or the change caused by the decision of the House of Lords in *Benham v Gambling* [1941] AC 157, [1941] 1 All ER 7, 110 LJKB 49, 164 LT 290, HL (p 956, below). The proper procedure is to apply to withdraw the notice of payment in and for payment out, or to substitute a notice for a reduced amount and payment out of the difference.

Note—For effect of withdrawal see *Garner v Cleggs* p 665, above.

DURING TRIAL

Gaskins v British Aluminium Co Ltd
[1976] QB 524, [1976] 1 All ER 208, [1976] 2 WLR 6, 119 Sol Jo 848, CA

The plaintiff claimed damages for an injury at work. A writ was issued in December 1973. The defendants paid into court £5,500 on 23 January 1975. The trial began on 24 March 1975. The plaintiff's case did not go well and on the following morning he applied under Ord 22, r 5 to take the £5,500 out of court. The defendant opposed the application. The judge refused the plaintiff's application and adjourned the case to be heard by another judge.

HELD, dismissing the plaintiff's appeal: (1) An application to take money out of court during a trial should not be granted when the defendant opposes it. (2) It would also be right to refuse the application if, on the facts, the position had altered since the money was paid in. (3) RSC Ord 22, r 7 forbidding disclosure to the trial judge that money has been paid into court is directory, not compulsive. If he is made aware of the payment in by inadvertence or otherwise, the judge has a discretion to decide whether to continue to hear the case or not. Leave was given to apply to the judge to continue the hearing.

County court

Gold v Introductions Ltd
[1963] 2 All ER 279, [1963] 1 WLR 517, 107 Sol Jo 252, CA

In an action for £307 commission due to the plaintiff the defendant made payments into Court amounting to £83, the last of these on 2 October. On 29 November, ie more than the four days limited by Ord 11, r 9(a) [now Ord 11, r 3 of the 1981 Rules] of the County Court Rules the plaintiff gave notice of acceptance. The judge refused to award the plaintiff his costs up to the date of payment in on the ground that Ord 11, r 11 [now Ord 11, r 5 of the 1981 Rules] of the County Court Rules did not empower him to do so.

HELD: Rules 7 and 9 should be read with r 11. The plaintiff was entitled to his costs up to the date of payment in but the money was not to be paid out without an order of the Court, who could order the plaintiff to pay any costs reasonably incurred by the defendant after date of payment in.

Note—See also *Seacroft Hotel (Teignmouth) Ltd v Goble* [1984] 3 All ER 116, [1984] 1 WLR 939, 128 Sol Jo 499, CA on late notice of acceptance and limits of judge's discretion on costs.

White v Harding
(1976) 120 Sol Jo 590, CA

In an action for damages in the county court in which the hearing date was 17 October, the defendant paid an amount into Court on 9 October. Notice was given by the registrar to the plaintiff on the 10th, so that the plaintiff had until the 17th to accept. On the 17th before the hearing began she agreed to accept but the defendant would not agree to payment out unless his costs were paid after the 9th. The trial then proceeded but the plaintiff was awarded only the same amount as was in court, with costs up to the 9th.

HELD, ON APPEAL: The operative notice of the payment in was that of the registrar and by RSC Ord 11, r 9 [now Ord 11, r 3 of the 1981 Rules] she could accept on the 17th before the hearing; but the rule also provided that notice had to be given to the registrar and every defendant. As no such notice had been given the costs were within the judge's discretion and he had exercised it correctly. Appeal dismissed.

Infant's damages

Note—RSC Ord 80, r 12, gives to the Court control of money paid into court for an infant whether under a settlement or judgment. (For the text of the rule see p 511, above).

By the Family Law Reform Act 1969, s 1 a person on and after 1 January 1970 attains full age at 18 instead of 21. He may be called a minor (s 12) until of full age.

M v Lester
[1966] 1 All ER 207, [1966] 1 WLR 134, 110 Sol Jo 53 (Lawton J)

As a result of a brain injury received in a road accident the infant plaintiff would be unable to work and would require constant care and supervision, though his condition was not such that he would need to be detained in hospital. After the court had approved a settlement of his claim at £15,000 an application was made to decide how the money should be dealt with.

The judge ordered that the money be transferred to the Court of Protection. In the ordinary way the Court of Protection was not concerned with looking after the affairs of infants but in some cases, such as this, it would do so. It has full powers of investment, expert investment advice available and long experience in dealing with people who are incapable of looking after themselves. It would do the job better than trustees, and would provide continuity.

Morey v Woodfield (No 2)
[1964] 1 QB 1, [1963] 3 All ER 584, [1963] 3 WLR 486, 107 Sol Jo 651
(Megaw J)
Costs incurred in the preparation and approval of a trust deed settling
£50,000 damages awarded to an infant for personal injuries were not
chargeable to the defendants under the Supreme Court Rules 1959, r 28(2)
(ie on a taxation on a party and party basis); they were not incurred for the
attainment of justice between the plaintiff and defendant. They were costs
incurred, perfectly properly, in providing for the disposition of damages
paid by the defendant.

Note—This decision was accepted by the Court of Appeal as 'obviously right' in the
similar case of *Warren v King* [1964] 1 WLR 122n, 108 Sol Jo 114, CA. The rule is
now Ord 62, r 28.

PROCEEDINGS AGAINST ESTATE OF DECEASED TORTFEASOR

Under the Supreme Court Act 1981, s 87(2) (replacing the Proceedings against
Estates Act 1970, s 2) the Court has power to make rules to enable proceedings to
be commenced against the estate of a deceased person where no grant of probate or
letters of administration had been made, or to enable an action started against a
person already dead to be treated as having been started against his estate, or for
enabling proceedings started against an estate to be maintained against personal
representatives to whom a grant had been made or a person appointed by the
Court to represent the estate. The rules are contained in RSC Ord 15, r 6A to
which reference should be made for details of the appropriate procedures.
Proceedings can be started before the issue of a grant. An application must then be
made for an order appointing a person to represent the deceased's estate for the
purpose of the proceedings. The defendants can be named as 'the personal
representatives of A B deceased'.

Pratt v London Passenger Transport Board
[1937] 1 All ER 473, 156 LT 265, 53 TLR 355, 81 Sol Jo 79, CA
The plaintiff applied in a pending action to add the Official Solicitor under
Ord XVI, r 46 (now Ord 15, r 15), without the consent of the Official
Solicitor.
HELD: An order could not be made without his consent.

Re Amirteymour
[1978] 3 All ER 637, [1979] 1 WLR 63, 122 Sol Jo 525, CA
An Iranian died indebted to the plaintiff bank. The bank issued a writ
against the estate described as 'The personal representatives of' the
deceased. There had been no grant of probate or letters of administration
in this country. With the consent of the Official Solicitor the plaintiffs
obtained an order from the court under Ord 15, r 6A appointing him as
representative of the estate limited to accepting service of the writ. He
refused consent to an order which extended to his taking any further step in
the proceedings. He accepted service of the writ. The bank signed
judgment in default of appearance and sought to enforce it by garnishee
proceedings.

HELD: Proceedings against the estate of a deceased person were actions *in personam*. In all such actions there had to be a natural or artificial person whom the law could recognise as a defendant against whom steps in the action could be taken. The appointment of the Official Solicitor to act as defendant was strictly limited and lapsed as soon as he had accepted service of the writ. No one else had been appointed to take his place and the judgment was a nullity.

Note—Where a person dies intestate, his real and personal estate, until administration is granted, shall vest in the President of the Family Division of the High Court in the same manner and to the same extent as formerly in the case of personal estate it vested in the Ordinary.

APPLICATION UNDER RSC Ord 15, r 15

Watts v Official Solicitor
[1936] 1 All ER 249, 80 Sol Jo 204, CA
Plaintiff issued writ on 11 May 1935, against two defendants. On 5 June 1935, one defendant died. The deceased was insured. Plaintiff required judgment against deceased's estate to sue insurers under the Road Traffic Act 1934, s 10 (now the Road Traffic Act 1972, s 149). The Official Solicitor consented to act and was appointed representative of deceased's estate under Ord XVI, r 46 (now Ord 15, r 15), plaintiff undertaking to pay his costs. Insurer's solicitors had appeared for deceased before his death. The Official Solicitor nominated his own solicitors and served notice of change. Insurers' solicitors objected, and although the Official Solicitor offered to employ them, they contended under the policy the Official Solicitor was bound to do so and notice of change was unnecessary.

   Atkinson J ordered the notice of change to be removed from the file and that insurers' solicitors should remain on the record.
HELD, ON APPEAL: Insurers had no *locus standi* and could not be heard. The Official Solicitor was entitled to conduct and to select his own solicitors.

Lean v Alston
[1947] KB 467, [1947] 1 All ER 261, [1947] LJR 559, CA
A pillion passenger was injured in a collision between a motor cycle and a car. The motor cyclist was killed in the collision. The pillion passenger issued a writ against the car owner, who wished to serve a third-party notice on the deceased's representative, but no administrator had been appointed and the widow declined to act. Defendant applied under Ord XVI, r 46 (now Ord 15, r 15), to appoint a representative of deceased's estate, who could be made a third party in the action, and the master made the appointment. Denning J allowed an appeal, taking the view that there was no power to make the order or if he had a discretion he ought not to make the appointment.
HELD, ON APPEAL, per Morton LJ: If the judge exercised his discretion because he thought the widow, being a person beneficially interested in the estate, should not have this representation imposed on her, the discretion was exercised on a wrong principle. Granting the application would possibly save the estate the expense of an application to the Probate Division to appoint a personal representative. The Court understanding

that the person appointed was to be indemnified for costs by the defendant, there was power to make the order and in the exercise of the discretion it was obviously right to do so because the defendant had a right to claim contribution and it would save the expense of a second trial and unfairness to the defendant if a material witness died in the interval.

PLAN OF SCENE OF ACCIDENT

Davey v Harrow Corpn
[1958] 1 QB 60, [1957] 2 All ER 305, [1957] 2 WLR 941, 101 Sol Jo 305
Judicial notice may be taken of a practice of the Ordnance Survey.

Note—The order for directions in a motor accident case usually contains an order for a plan or sketch plan, which is usually agreed. In view of the above case, it seems possible that an ordnance map may be put in without evidence, but the practice will probably remain of submitting to the opponents for agreement. An ordnance map to scale of 50 inches to the mile is suitable for most cases. Such maps can be obtained from Edward Stanford Ltd, 12 Long Acre, London WC 2.

RES JUDICATA

Brunsden v Humphrey
(1884) 12 QBD 141, [1881–5] All ER Rep 357, 53 LJQB 476, 51 LT 529, 49 JP 4, 32 WR 944, CA
The rule of the ancient common law is that where one is barred in any action real or personal by judgment, demurrer, confession or verdict, he is barred as to that or the like action of the like nature for the same thing for ever. It is a well settled rule of law that damages resulting from one and the same cause of action must be assessed and recovered once for all. One wrong was damage to property. A further wrong was injury to the person.

Note—See also p 684 and *Sanders v Hamilton*, p 687, below.

Two actions, same accident

Marginson v Blackburn Borough Council
[1939] 2 KB 426, [1939] 1 All ER 273, 108 LJKB 563, 160 LT 234, 55 TLR 389, 83 Sol Jo 212, CA
Car of A driven by A's wife, with A and his daughter as passengers, collided with bus of B and as a result there was damage to property of C. C sued A and B in the county court. B served third-party notice on A and counter-claimed against A for damage to bus. A served third-party notice on B. The judge found A and B equally to blame. Afterwards A sued B in the High Court for damages for injury to himself, his daughter and death of his wife.
HELD: The plaintiff was estopped from proceeding with his personal claims but not with claims in representative capacity as it had been necessary to decide in the first action the question of negligence as between the parties to the second action.

Townsend v Bishop

[1939] 1 All ER 805, 160 LT 296, 55 TLR 433, 83 Sol Jo 240 (Lewis J)
A motor car was driven by the son as servant of the owner and collided with
a lorry. The father brought an action in the High Court against the lorry
owner for the father's damage in negligence, which was sent to the county
court. The judge found the son was negligent and the action failed. The son
then brought an action in the High Court against the lorry owner for the
son's own damage.
HELD: No *res judicata*. The defendant had failed to prove that the matter
now in issue was the same as that previously litigated and between the same
parties. The son was not a party, but an agent, in the previous litigation.

Johnson v Cartledge and Matthews

[1939] 3 All ER 654 (Cassels J)
A was a passenger in car of B which collided with taxicab of C. C brought a
county court action against B, and C was held by the county court judge
alone to blame. Afterwards, A sued B and C in High Court and Cassels J
found B alone to blame. B had issued third-party proceedings against C in
the action. B contended issue of negligence between B and C was *res judicata*
and he was entitled to indemnity on this ground.
HELD, Per Cassels J: C had been found in the High Court proceedings not
to be a tortfeasor, and B could not therefore recover indemnity or contribution from C. Furthermore this was not a case of *res judicata*, as the damage in
the two cases was different. For the doctrine of *res judicata* to apply the
parties must be the same, and the damage must be the same, and the issues
of law and of fact must be the same. (*Marginson v Blackburn Borough Council*
(above) distinguished.)
   The action in the county court was for damage to property; in the High
Court for personal injuries and in the third-party proceedings the claim
would not have been possible before the Law Reform (Married Women
and Tortfeasors) Act 1935.

Bell v Holmes

[1956] 3 All ER 449, [1956] 1 WLR 1359, 100 Sol Jo 801 (McNair J)
A motor car driven by A collided with a motor car driven by B which had a
passenger X on 26 March 1955. On 18 August 1955, A issued a writ
against B for personal injuries and B counter-claimed for his own personal
injuries. On 7 October 1955, X issued a summons against both A and B as
defendants in the county court. The pleadings in the two actions were
substantially identical. In the county court action each defendant blamed
the other and adopted the allegations made by the plaintiff against the
other. No formal notice of contribution was filed by either defendant
against the other but the judge was requested by both defendants to deal
with the matter of apportionment between the defendants. On 17 February
1956, the judge found against both defendants and held A five-sixths to
blame and B one-sixth. Both judgments were satisfied and the time for
appeal had long expired when the action between A and B came on for
hearing. By his amended defence B pleaded A was bound by the county
court judgment and A by his reply denied that he was so bound. McNair J
directed this issue be tried as a preliminary issue.

HELD: (1) It was plain on the authorities, and was common practice, that the court as to apportionment had power to determine the question of contribution between defendants without any formal notice of contribution; (2) as to *res judicata*, this was a matter of evidence, and included a case where judgment had been given after the issue of the writ, and was a good plea in this case; (3) as to the plea that the issues were not the same, the issues of fact were identically the same and the fact that they were technically different was immaterial; (4) as to the contention that a plea of estoppel by record could only be proved by production of the record under the County Court Rules 1936, Ord 24 [now Ord 22 of the 1981 Rules] whilst not satisfied that this was necessary, A had waived this form of proof by his pleadings. The apportionment was *res judicata*.

Randolph v Tuck
[1962] 1 QB 175, [1961] 1 All ER 814, [1961] 2 WLR 855, 105 Sol Jo 157 (Lawton J)

The plaintiff received injuries on 19 July 1957, when riding in a car owned and driven by the first defendant which collided with a car owned by the second defendants and driven by their servant the third defendant. In a county court action heard on 13 July 1958, in which the first defendant had sued the second and third defendants for damages for his own personal injuries he was found wholly to blame. The plaintiff issued her writ on 15 October 1959 and on 1 January 1960 the second and third defendants by third-party notice claimed indemnity from the first defendant in the event of their being found liable to pay damages to the plaintiff. The claim was based on the Law Reform (Married Woman and Tortfeasors) Act 1935. They pleaded that the issue between them and the first defendant had been determined by the county court judge and that his decision was binding on the first defendant. The plaintiff's action was heard on 6 February 1961, when Lawton J held that the damage suffered by the plaintiff was caused by the negligence of both the first and third defendants and that they were equally to blame.

HELD, in the third-party proceedings: (1) The second and third defendants were not entitled to claim indemnity as persons entitled to be indemnified under the Law Reform (Married Women and Tortfeasors) Act 1935, s 6(1)(c) since to do so would be to base a cause of action on an estoppel by record. At common law this cannot be done and s 6(1)(c) does not allow that which common law would not. (2) The first defendant was not estopped by the judgment in the county court from denying his own sole responsibility for the damage suffered by the plaintiff, since the precise issue decided in the county court was not the same as in the plaintiff's action. In the county court the issue decided was that the damage suffered by the first defendant was caused, not by any breach of duty owed him by the third defendant, but by his own failure to take proper care for his own safety. In the present action the issue decided was whether the damage suffered by the plaintiff had been caused by breach of duty owed to her by the first or the third defendant or either of them. These duties were similar but nevertheless separate and distinct (*Hay (or Bourhill) v Young*, p 6, above). Moreover the extent of the respective responsibilities of the first and third defendants for the damage suffered by the plaintiff, ie blameworthiness as distinct from causation, had never been before the county court. (3) *Marginson v Blackburn Borough Council* (p 670, above) was distinguished on the ground that in that case the county court judge had made a separate decision in the damage claim between Marginson and the bus company. *Bell v Holmes* (above) not followed.

Note—For the Law Reform (Married Women & Tortfeasors) Act 1935 s 6(1)(c) see now Civil Liability (Contribution) Act 1978, p 19, above.

Wood v Luscombe

[1966] 1 QB 169 [1964] 3 All ER 972, [1965] 3 WLR 996, 109 Sol Jo 833, (Streatfeild J)

L and W, both riding motor cycles, collided. L was injured and so also was W's father who was riding pillion on W's machine. L sued W for damages: at the trial of the action Phillimore J held them both to blame equally for L's injuries. W's father then sued L for damages for his own injuries and L joined W as third party, claiming a contribution. L contended that, as Phillimore J in the previous action had held L and W equally to blame, W was estopped from denying in the present proceedings that they were equally to blame.

HELD: The contention was correct. W's father being an innocent passenger the thing actually in dispute, namely, who was to blame for the damage done in the accident had already been determined by Phillimore J and was *res judicata*. The issue was precisely the same in both actions and the same evidence would support both. *Bell v Holmes* followed: *Randolph v Tuck* not followed. *Marginson v Blackburn Borough Council* not applicable because the facts were different.

Scope of doctrine

Greenhalgh v Mallard

[1947] 2 All ER 255, CA

Res judicata is not confined to the issues which the court is actually asked to decide, but covers issues of facts which are so clearly part of the subject matter of the litigation and so clearly could have been raised that it would be an abuse of the process of the court to allow a new proceeding to be started in respect of them. In *Green v Weatherill* [1929] 2 Ch 213 at 221, Maugham J quoted some observations by Wigram VC in *Henderson v Henderson* (1843) 3 Hare 100 at 114:

'I believe I state the rule of the court correctly when I say, that where a given matter becomes the subject of litigation in, and of adjudication by, a court of competent jurisdiction, the court requires the parties to that litigation to bring forward their whole case, and will not (except under special circumstances) permit the same parties to open the same subject of litigation in respect of matter which might have been brought forward as part of the subject in contest, but which was not brought forward only because they have, from negligence, inadvertence, or even accident, omitted part of their case. The plea of *res judicata* applies, except in special cases, not only to points upon which the court was actually required by the parties to form an opinion and pronounce a judgment, but to every point which properly belonged to the subject of litigation and which the parties, exercising reasonable diligence, might have brought forward at the time.'

In *Brunsden v Humphrey* (p 670, above) there were two separate causes of action, — trespass to the person and trespass to goods.

Re Waring, Westminster Bank Ltd v Burton-Butler

[1948] Ch 221, [1948] 1 All ER 257, [1948] LJR 705, 64 TLR 147, (Jenkins J)

Where a decision of the Court of Appeal is overruled by a later case in the House of Lords, a person who was a party to the proceedings in the Court of Appeal is bound by the decision of the Court of Appeal on the principle of *res judicata*, but a person who was not a party is not bound and is entitled to take advantage of the decision of the House of Lords.

Wright v Bennett

[1948] 1 All ER 227, 92 Sol Jo 95, CA

The issues need not be identical. The plea will succeed if the issues and facts are in substance the same.

Winnan v Winnan

[1949] P 174, [1948] 2 All ER 862, [1949] LJR 345, 65 TLR 22, 92 Sol Jo 688, 47 LGR 10, CA

The observations by Wigram VC in *Henderson v Henderson* quoted above were also quoted by Lord Shaw in *Hoysted v Taxation Commrs* [1926] AC 155, 9 LJPC 79, 134 LT 354, 42 TLR 207, PC and adopted in this case.

Issue estoppel

Note—In *Mills v Cooper* [1967] 2 QB 459 at 468 Diplock LJ said the doctrine of issue estoppel so far as it affects civil proceedings may be stated thus; a party to civil proceedings is not entitled to make, as against the other party, an assertion, whether of fact or of the legal consequences of facts, the correctness of which is an essential element in his cause of action or defence, if the same assertion was an essential element in his previous cause of action or defence in previous civil proceedings between the parties or their predecessors in title and was found by a court of competent jurisdiction in such previous civil proceedings to be incorrect, unless further material which is relevant to the correctness or incorrectness of the assertion and could not by reasonable diligence have been adduced by that party in the previous proceedings has since become available to him.

Miller v British Railways Board

(1968) 112 Sol Jo 595 (Browne J)

The plaintiff, a railway passenger, lost the tip of a finger in the door of a carriage after an altercation with the station manager. He was charged by a police constable of British Railways under byelaw 14(1) and (3) with opening the carriage door and entering the train when it was in motion, and convicted. He sued British Railways for damages for slamming the door on his finger when the train was stationary. Without pleading it the defendants contended at trial that the conviction raised an issue estoppel which prevented the plaintiff from giving evidence that the train was not in motion when he entered it.

HELD: The prosecution could not be regarded as being between the same parties as the action as the constable was not the same party as the defendants. The principle stated in *Mills v Cooper* was limited to a finding in civil proceedings. A finding in previous criminal proceedings did not give rise to issue estoppel in subsequent civil proceedings.

Note—The final sentence in the above case may call for reconsideration; see *Mcllkenny v Chief Constable of the West Midlands* [1980] QB 283, [1980] 2 All ER 227, [1980] 2 WLR 689, 144 JP 291, CA. *Miller's* case was not cited there but Sir George Baker said of *Mills v Cooper* that it was not an 'authority for the proposition that an issue of fact affirmatively decided in a criminal case cannot be used as conclusive, that is, as an issue estoppel, in a subsequent civil case.'

SETTING ASIDE DEFAULT JUDGMENT

Burns v Kondel
[1971] 1 Lloyd's Rep 554, CA
The plaintiff was injured in a traffic collision with the defendant, who was then charged by the police with careless driving and pleaded guilty. The plaintiff's solicitors issued a writ and served it on the defendants personally on 21 October. On 29 October, they wrote to the defendant saying that unless appearance was entered within four days they would sign judgment. The defendant replied that he handed the writ to his insurers. His letter reached the solicitors on 3 November just after they had signed judgment. The insurers applied to set aside the judgment.
HELD: The Court does not set aside a judgment in default unless there is an affidavit showing a defence on the merits, but that does not mean the defendant must show a *good* defence. He need only show a defence which discloses an arguable or triable issue. In an accident case it is sufficient if he shows that there is a triable issue of contributory negligence. The insurers, who are the people who have to pay should not be shut out altogether from having contributory negligence investigated.

SETTLEMENT OF CLAIM

Inadequate settlement

Martin v Bannister
(1933) 47 Ll L Rep 270
To constitute a binding settlement the mind of the claimant must go with the apparent settlement.
   An injured man whilst in hospital settled his claim through a solicitor acting on his behalf with an insurance company for £100 and 35 guineas costs without proceedings. Later the man instructed a fresh solicitor who issued a writ. The company in the name of their assured applied to stay the action on the ground that the cause of action had been settled.
HELD, by the Court of Appeal: As on the face of the receipt no mention was made of the 35 guineas costs and it was doubtful whether plaintiff had assented to a compromise whereby the solicitor was to receive what was relatively such a large sum for costs, the action must proceed and the stay was refused.

Note—See also *Taylor v Walker*, p 678, below.

Roberts v Eastern Counties Rly Co
(1859) 1 F & F 460
Plaintiff accepted £2 for damage to clothes, not supposing he had sustained any serious injury.
HELD: Not an accord and satisfaction for a patent and severe injury.

Ellen v Great Northern Rly Co
(1901) 17 TLR 453, CA
Plaintiff signed receipt for money paid by defendants as compensation for accident in full settlement for all claims. His eyesight soon began to fail and he became totally blind as a result of the accident. He brought action and defendant pleaded action not maintainable.
HELD: Action maintainable, it being a question for the jury.

Saunders v Ford Motor Co
[1970] 1 Lloyd's Rep 379 (Paull J)
On 10 April 1964 the plaintiff suffered a severe injury to his eye at work. On his return to work he was sent by his employers to see E, a representative of their insurers who had an office at the works, to settle a claim for compensation. The plaintiff accepted an offer of £200, believing from the conversation that it was for pain and suffering and loss of wages only and that if the eye got worse he could go back for more. He signed a receipt for the £200 'in settlement of all claims, whether now or hereafter to become manifest, arising directly or indirectly from' the accident. He could not read the receipt because of bad sight; it was filled in by E. When asked at court what 'manifest' meant the plaintiff did not know.
HELD: He was not bound by the receipt. There was attached to the payment of £200 an understanding that if his eye deteriorated he could come back; alternatively the parties were not *ad idem* because he signed the receipt believing he would be able to come back. The form of receipt used should not be used between employers and a workman who had no professional advice. The receipt ought to make it clear in simple language that whatever happens to him he can receive no more money.

Horry v Tate & Lyle Refineries Ltd
[1982] 2 Lloyd's Rep 416 (Pain J)
The plaintiff sustained a hernia by accident at work; there was a 15% chance of recurrence. He accepted £1,000 in settlement of his claim for damages. The employers' insurers negotiated the settlement; the plaintiff was not professionally represented nor independently advised. He signed what purported to be a final discharge. Later, following a recurrence, he sought advice and in proceedings based on the original accident the employers by their insurers pleaded a release by way of accord and satisfaction based on the settlement.
HELD: The plaintiff was not bound by the settlement. He had relied on the insurers' advice and they knew it. They had a fiduciary duty of care which they could have discharged by asking him to obtain independent advice. There was a duty on them to specify what deduction was made for contributory negligence. They should have supplied him with a copy of the

medical report and ensured he understood that no further claim could be made. Their interest conflicted with his. The relationship imposed on them a fiduciary duty. *Lloyd's Bank Ltd v Bundy* ([1975] QB 326, [1974] 3 All ER 757, [1974] 3 WLR 501, CA) and *Saunders v Ford Motor Co* (above) applied.

Arrale v Costain Civil Engineering Ltd
(1975) 119 Sol Jo 527, [1976] 1 Lloyds Rep 98, CA

The plaintiff, an Arab labourer working in Dubai for the defendants, sustained a serious injury at work resulting in the loss of his left arm. The law of Dubai provides for payment of compensation to a workman by the employer on a fixed scale. The amount due for the plaintiff's injury was £490. The defendants paid to him this amount and he signed a receipt which referred to the compensation law and continued with the same words as were used in the receipt in *Saunders v Ford Motor* (above). Later the plaintiff came to England and sued the defendants for damages at common law. They pleaded that all liability had been discharged by the receipt.

HELD: (1) As the plaintiff was entitled to the payment of compensation of £490 there was nothing else the receipt could apply to; (2) there was no true accord and satisfaction — no one had told the plaintiff when he signed the receipt that he might have a claim at common law. He was not prevented by the receipt from proceeding with the claim.

Rideal v Great Western Rly Co
(1859) 1 F & F 706

If the mind of the plaintiff went with the terms of settlement and he understood their effect when he assented to them, agreement binding.

Lee v Lancashire and Yorkshire Rly Co
(1871) 6 Ch App 527, 25 LT 77, 35 JP 726, 19 WR 729

A mere receipt in writing is simply an acknowledgment of money paid, and may be impeached or explained by parol evidence.

Lovell v Williams
(1938), 62 L1 L Rep 249, CA

Plaintiff brought an action in the county court and accepted £35 in full settlement and the action was withdrawn. He afterwards discovered he had sustained a fractured skull and was permanently disabled. He issued writ and defendant applied to stay the action as being frivolous and vexatious and an abuse of the process of the court.

HELD: Not a case for a stay. The question whether there had been a settlement of all future claims must be decided in the action.

Taylor v Walker
[1958] 1 Lloyd's Rep 490 (Havers J)

The plaintiff was crossing the road when he was struck and injured by a motor cycle ridden by W. He was introduced by a so-called claims service to a claims assessor B, who made a claim against W. B did not fully investigate the facts and did not obtain a medical report, though he saw one obtained by W's insurers. He received an offer of £300 from the insurers and asked them for 40 guineas costs. He strongly recommended the plaintiff to accept, saying nothing about the fee, and the plaintiff did so. The insurers paid the fee of 40 guineas to B by a separate cheque from the damages. Later the plaintiff by a next friend sought to rescind the settlement.

HELD: He was entitled to do so. As an agent B had to act in good faith in the interest of his principal. In obtaining payment of 40 guineas for himself without telling the plaintiff he had not so acted. It was not necessary for the plaintiff to prove a corrupt motive on the part of the insurers in paying the 40 guineas. On the facts the payment was a bribe since it was a payment to B himself without disclosure to B's principal, the plaintiff. The settlement was therefore voidable by plaintiff.

Derrick v Williams
[1939] 2 All ER 559, 160 LT 589, 55 TLR 676, 83 Sol Jo 397, CA

On 26 July 1935, the infant child of the respondent was killed by a motor lorry belonging to the appellant. The respondent, as the personal representative of the infant, thereupon brought an action claiming damages under the Law Reform (Miscellaneous Provisions) Act 1934, and in October 1935, the appellant, as defendant in that action, paid into court £50 with a denial of liability, and that sum was taken out by the respondent. At the time, in reliance upon the decision of the Court of Appeal in *Rose v Ford* it was thought that damages could not be recovered in respect of loss of expectation of life, but that decision was in 1937 reversed in the House of Lords. The respondent on 27 September 1938, brought the present action, based upon the same facts as the previous action, and claimed damages for loss of expectation of life. The appellant took the preliminary point that the acceptance of the sum paid into court in the previous action was a bar to the present proceedings. The court decided this point in favour of the appellant but gave the respondent leave to amend his statement of claim in the first action, without, however, defining the terms of the amendment. The respondent in his amended statement of claim, claimed to be entitled to withdraw his acceptance of the sum of £50 or, alternatively, to have the agreement by which he accepted the sum set aside, on the ground that it was made under a mistake of fact or a mistake of law. The appellant appealed against the order so far as it allowed an amendment of the statement of claim.

HELD: (1) As the effect of the acceptance of the money paid into court was to stay the proceedings the respondent's proper course was to apply in the action to have the stay removed and to have liberty to withdraw his consent. This was not, however, a case in which such an application would have been granted. (2) A litigant whose claim has been satisfied by money paid into court cannot afterwards contend that that money was accepted under a mistake in law, on the ground that the law was not as then laid down by the Court of Appeal, but as subsequently enunciated by the House of Lords. (3) Where leave to amend is asked for, the actual amendment should be formulated before leave is given.

Indemnity — compromise

Biggin & Co Ltd v Permanite Ltd

[1951] 2 KB 314, [1951] 2 All ER 191, [1951] 2 TLR 159, 95 Sol Jo 414, CA

The Dutch Government bought mastic from the plaintiffs, who had bought it from the defendants. The Dutch found it unsatisfactory and refused to pay the plaintiffs for it. The dispute went to arbitration where, at the hearing, on the advice of counsel the plaintiffs settled the £55,000 claim for £43,000. They then sued the defendants for the amount of £43,000 as a reasonable settlement of the Dutch claim. The judge treated the figure of £43,000 as irrelevant in the action and required the plaintiffs to prove the loss.

HELD, allowing the appeal, the law encourages reasonable settlements especially where strict proof would be an expensive matter. To establish reasonableness the plaintiff must first lead evidence so that the court can conclude whether the sum paid was reasonable. It is also relevant to prove that the settlement was made under legal advice. If the defendants fail to shake that case the amount of the settlement can properly be awarded as damages.

Order to stay

McCallum v Country Residences Ltd

[1965] 2 All ER 264, [1965] 1 WLR 657, 109 Sol Jo 293, CA

In an action for moneys due to the plaintiff for work and labour done the parties carried on negotiations for settlement in 'without prejudice' correspondence which amounted in the result to an agreement that the defendants would pay £900 and costs. The defendants did not pay, however, but made further complaints about the plaintiff's work. The plaintiff's solicitors then issued a summons to stay the action on the terms that (1) the defendants pay the plaintiff £900 within seven days, (2) the defendants pay the plaintiff's costs to be taxed as between party and party, and (3) the plaintiff's costs be taxed on a common fund basis pursuant to the Third Schedule of the Legal Aid and Advice Act 1949. On the hearing of the summons the official referee was told by the defendant's representative that the compromise was not fully agreed but he read the correspondence and then made an order in the terms of the summons. On appeal by the defendants.

HELD: the official referee was probably right in concluding that there was a binding agreement to settle at £900 and costs, but he was not entitled to make an order embodying the terms without the defendant's consent. A Tomlin order (which this was) can only be made by consent. The plaintiff's correct course to obtain a judgment was to sue on the agreement. In the absence of consent to an order, as distinct from consent to the agreement, the court had no jurisdiction to make an order.

Receipt not binding

Note—See *Saunders v Ford Motor Co* p 676, above.

Neuchatel Asphalte Co Ltd v Barnett

[1957] 1 All ER 362, [1957] 1 WLR 356, 101 Sol Jo 170, CA

Defendant employed the plaintiff company to do work for him, and the company's account was £259. He claimed allowances of £14 or £15. On 26 October 1955, he sent a cheque for £125, and stated in a covering letter that the sum was 'on account' pending the company's reply on outstanding queries. On 21 December 1955, he wrote — 'With further reference to your account, in spite of repeated requests for allowance to which I am entitled, you have failed to advise me in the matter. I am therefore enclosing my further cheque for £75 in respect of this work.' On the back of the cheque he had typed — 'In full and final settlement of account.' The cheque was endorsed by the rubber stamp of the company and signed by the secretary. On 2 January 1956, the company wrote the defendant about the complaints and offered a credit of £4 10s 0d in respect of his queries. The defendant replied that his cheque of 21 December 'was in "full and final settlement of your account" and was endorsed accordingly and accepted by you . . . the matter must therefore now be considered as concluded'. The company sued for the balance.

HELD: The words on the back of the cheque were inconsistent with the main object and intention of the transaction because (1) the letter of 21 December imported the payment was only on account, and (2) the company had not agreed to a reduction of £50, the amount of the balance, and the words should be rejected. The company was entitled to the balance.

Citing an unreported case of *George A. Woodman & Sons v Linden* in the Court of Appeal on 13 April 1956, the court does not allow printed forms to be made a trap for the unwary; and this is so, even though they are typed and not printed.

Haigh v Lawford

(1964) 114 LJ 208, Salisbury Cty Ct (Judge Bulger)

The plaintiff's car was damaged in a collision with the defendant's car on 1 September. The plaintiff's insurers paid for the repairs and wrote the defendant's insurers on 5 November for 'reimbursement'. Meanwhile the plaintiff who had a £10 excess, wrote the defendant's insurers claiming this amount. On 13 December the defendant's insurers paid him £10 and sent him a form of receipt which he signed and returned 'in full satisfaction of all claims' against the defendant arising out of the accident. On 25 January the plaintiff's insurers pressed their claim for the cost of repairs. The defendant's insurers repudiated it, relying on the form of discharge signed by the plaintiff.

HELD: On the facts the receipt did not conclude the matter because the correspondence showed that the plaintiff in accepting the £10 was concerned only to recover his uninsured loss. The receipt was a standard printed form and was not intended to be a contractual document. But apart from this, once the plaintiff's insurers had paid out under the policy and given notice to the wrongdoer, their right to recover against the latter by action in the assured's name could not be defeated by any compromise subsequently made by the assured with the wrongdoer. Once the insurer's right of subrogation had crystallised the wrongdoer with the knowledge of payment to the assured should not be allowed to prejudice that right by release or compromise with the assured.

Note—See also *Taylor v Wray*, p 685, below.

Cashing cheque

Bell v Galynski and A. Kings Loft Extensions Ltd
[1974] 2 Lloyd's Rep 13, CA

Some damage was done to the party wall between the plaintiff's and the first defendant's houses by contractors (the second defendants) employed by the first defendant. The plaintiff had the damage repaired and wrote the first defendant saying the repair had been done and that he would send him a copy of the account, adding 'any further deterioration of my property . . . will result in a claim for compensation in addition . . .'. Later he sent a copy of the account for the repairs at £18.15 'without prejudice to any further claim from the building work . . .'. The second defendants sent the plaintiff a cheque for £18.15 'in full and final settlement of your claim against Mr Galynski with regard to damage caused to the party wall'. The plaintiff cashed the cheque.

HELD: He had compromised the matter and had no legal claim for any further compensation.

SERVICE OF WRIT

Date of expiry of writ

Trow v Ind Coope (West Midlands) Ltd
[1967] 2 QB 899, [1967] 2 All ER 900, [1967] 3 WLR 633, 111 Sol Jo 375, CA

Accident 11 September 1962; writ issued 10 September 1965; writ served on 10 September 1966 though earlier in the day than when the writ was issued a year before. The defendants applied to set aside service on the ground that the writ had not been served within '12 months beginning with the date of its issue' (Ord 6, r 8(1)).

HELD: (1) 'Date' means the whole day of the date of issue. The time of day of issue or service is immaterial. (2) The words 'beginning *with* the date of its issue' means that the day of the date of issue is to be included in the period of 12 months: the words must be taken to have been used to avoid the application of the general rule which might otherwise have applied that the first day of a specified period should be excluded in determining whether the period has elapsed. The period having begun with 10 September 1965 expired at the end of 9 September 1966. Service on the following day was bad and should be set aside.

Note—Contrast *Marren v Dawson Bentley & Co* (p 535, above) where the operative words were 'The following actions shall not be brought after the expiration of three years from the date on which the cause of action accrued' (Limitation Act 1939, s 2(1) as amended: now the Limitation Act 1980, s 2).

Pritam Kaur v S. Russell & Sons Ltd
[1973] QB 336, [1973] 1 All ER 617, [1973] 2 WLR 147, 117 Sol Jo 91, CA

The plaintiff's husband was killed at work on 4 September 1967. She issued a writ on 7 September 1970. 5 and 6 September 1970, were a Saturday and Sunday when the Court office was closed for business.

HELD: (1) Following *Marren v Dawson Bentley & Co Ltd* (p 535, above) the day on which the cause of action arose was to be excluded from the computation of the three years limitation period. (2) When a time is prescribed by statute for doing any act which can only be done if the Court office is open on the day when the time expires then if that day is a Sunday or other *dies non* the time is extended to the next day on which the court office is open. Thus by issuing on 7 September 1970 the plaintiff was in time.

Note—Applied in *The Clifford Maersk*, [1982] 3 All ER 905, [1982] 1 WLR 1292, 126 Sol Jo 446, [1982] 2 Lloyds Rep 251.

Two defendants

Jones v Jones
[1970] 2 QB 576, [1970] 3 All ER 47, [1970] 3 WLR 20, 114 Sol Jo 374, CA
On 19 July 1965 the plaintiff was a passenger in one of two cars which collided. He was injured. A writ was issued on 13 June 1968 against both drivers. The first was served with the writ on 12 June 1969. The second was served on 3 July 1969. He applied to the Court to set aside service on the ground that the writ had expired. The plaintiff's solicitor, who had relied on Ord 6, r 8 as meaning that after service on one defendant the writ did not need renewal, consulted the practice master, who expressed the same view. When the second defendant's application came before another master he ordered service to be set aside. On the plaintiff's appealing to the judge he merely exercised his discretion to extend the time for service and the writ was re-served on the second defendant, who then appealed to the Court of Appeal.
HELD: (1) Order 6, r 8(2) did not and could not be taken to mean that if one defendant had been properly served the writ remains valid for service after 12 months from the date of issue without renewal; (2) in the present case the judge was justified in using his discretion to extend the writ, because the plaintiff's solicitor was not unreasonable in his interpretation of the rule as was evidenced by the fact that the practice master had taken the same view; (3) nevertheless that view was mistaken and in the unlikely event of a solicitor making the same mistake again it will be no sufficient reason for renewing the writ.

Service on manager

Willmott v Berry Bros (a firm)
(1981) 126 Sol Jo 209, [1982] LS Gaz R 536, CA
The defendants, a firm, became a limited company in 1979 without any change in the business carried on or the principal place of business. The change of status was not publicised. The plaintiffs, alleging negligence between 1973 and 1976 began proceedings against 'Berry Bros (a firm)' and served the writ by giving it to a manager, employed since March 1980, at the principal place of business in August 1980 in accordance with Ord 81, r 3(1)(b).
HELD: The plaintiffs had acted reasonably under Ord 18, r 1 in using on the writ the name 'Berry Bros' since the business was generally known by

that name. 'Business of the partnership' in r 3(1)(b) included a business which was a partnership at the time the cause of action accrued, the ownership of which had changed by the time of service of the writ, if identifiable as the same business. The person having control or management for the purpose of service did not have to be one who had been a servant of the partners at the date of accrual of the cause of action. The writ had been validly served.

Service by post — county court

White v Weston
[1968] 2 QB 647, [1968] 2 All ER 842, [1968] 2 WLR 1459, 112 Sol Jo 217, CA

After a motor accident the plaintiff and defendant exchanged addresses. Subsequently the plaintiff claimed for the damage to his car and had correspondence with the defendant's insurers. Some months later the plaintiff issued a summons in the county court. By this time the defendant had moved to a different address. The bailiff was unable to serve the defendant but as he thought him to be still at the old address the registrar ordered service at that address by post. The summons did not reach the defendant who was quite unaware of it when the plaintiff obtained judgment. When he did learn of it the defendant applied to set aside the judgment. The judge made an order setting aside the judgment but made the costs of the first hearing to be costs in the cause.

HELD, ON APPEAL: This was not correct. As the summons had not been served on the defendant (since he no longer lived at the address to which it was sent) he was *ex debito justitiae* entitled to have the judgment set aside without terms being imposed.

A CONTRASTING CASE

Cooper v Scott-Farnell
[1969] 1 All ER 178, [1969] 1 WLR 120, 112 Sol Jo 945, CA

The plaintiff issued a county court summons on 24 April, which, by the procedure for service set out in Ord 8, r 8(2) was sent by post to the defendant's address. But the defendant had gone abroad on holiday on 31 March and did not return until 22 June. Meanwhile the plaintiff had obtained judgment against him. It was set aside because obtained without his knowledge but the judge made the costs of the abortive hearing costs in the cause.

HELD, ON APPEAL against the order as to costs: *White v Weston* (above) was not an authority for saying that there could be no service where the defendant had not received the summons. In *White's* case the summons was wrongly addressed and therefore not served. In the present case the summons was properly served by post in accordance with the code for service of documents contained in Ord 8. The judge therefore had a discretion as to costs and had exercised it properly.

Note—The County Court Rules Ord 8, r 8 has been replaced by Ord 7, rr 9 and 10 of the 1981 Rules.

SHORTHAND NOTE

Theocharides v Joannou
[1953] 2 All ER 52, [1955] 1 WLR 296, 99 Sol Jo 205 (Roxburgh J)
A judge has a right to require a shorthand note which is unfettered subject
to appeal to the Court of Appeal. His discretion is not affected by the Legal
Aid (General) Regulations, reg 14(3). Case adjourned until transcript
available.

Dixon v City Veneering Mills Ltd
[1953] 2 All ER 1112 n, [1953] 1 WLR 1369, 97 Sol Jo 780, CA
It is the duty of parties to consider whether it is enough for part only of the
transcript of the shorthand note of the evidence to be copied and not the
whole. Certain of the costs may be disallowed.

SPLITTING THE CAUSE OF ACTION

Note—A plaintiff may bring two separate actions in respect of the very same
circumstances provided there are two causes of action, ie (1) personal injuries,
(2) damage to property.

Brunsden v Humphrey
(1884) 14 QBD 141, 53 LJQB 476, 51 LT 529, 49 JP 4, 32 WR 944, CA
Damage to goods and injury to the person give rise to distinct causes of
action, although occasioned by the same wrongful act.
The plaintiff brought an action against the defendant in the county court
for damage to his goods (in that case a cab) and recovered the amount he
claimed. He later brought an action in the High Court against the same
defendant in respect of the same act of negligence for personal injuries.
HELD: The action was maintainable and was not barred by the previous
proceedings in the county court.
The test is not whether he had the opportunity of recovering in the first
action what he claims in the second, but whether he sought to do so.
Per Bowen LJ: Two separate kinds of injury were in fact inflicted and
two wrongs done. . . . One wrong was done as soon as the plaintiff's
enjoyment of his property was substantially interfered with. A further
wrong arose as soon as the driving also caused injury to the plaintiff's
person. . . . The wrong consists in the damage done without lawful
excuse, not the act of driving, which (if no damage had ensued) would have
been legally unimportant.

Note—The relevance of this point is that damage to vehicle and loss of use are parts
of the same cause of action.
In *Buckland v Palmer* (p 686, below) Griffiths LJ said 'I take it to be settled by the
decision of this court in *Brunsden v Humphrey* that if as a result of a car accident a
plaintiff suffers both personal injury and damage to his car he has two distinct
causes of action, one for his personal injuries and the other for damage to his
property. I confess that I have always had difficulty in following the reasoning of
the majority in *Brunsden v Humphrey* and I observe that it has not been followed in
either the United States or Canada'.

Taylor v O. Wray & Co Ltd
[1971] 1 Lloyd's Rep 497, CA

The plaintiff when driving his car collided with the defendants' lorry. He sustained some personal injury and through his own solicitors claimed damages. They issued a county court summons and included in the claim the £10 excess under the plaintiff's comprehensive policy. Meanwhile his insurers had written to the defendants' insurers notifying a claim for the balance of the cost of repairs to the car amounting to about £180. In the plaintiff's action the defendants paid into court £30 which the plaintiff after further negotiations accepted 'in full settlement of his claims in this action'. His insurers then instituted fresh proceedings in his name to recover the balance of the costs of repairs to his car. The defendants pleaded that as the plaintiff had already claimed in respect of the cause of action for damage to the car (by claiming his £10 excess) disposal of that claim had ipso facto put an end to that cause of action and barred all further proceedings.

HELD: The defence was a technical one of no merit. The principle underlying *Brunsden v Humphrey* (above) was that if a party prosecutes a cause of action to judgment he cannot start all over again and sue for further relief in respect of that same cause of action; but notwithstanding that decision the same cause of action can in certain circumstances be the subject of more than one set of proceedings. In the present case the plaintiff's solicitors had made it clear that acceptance of the £30 was in settlement only of the claims in the first action. Moreover the defendants' insurers already knew that the plaintiff's insurers were claiming from them the balance of the repair charges. The cogency of the maxims *Nemo bis debet vexari* and *Interest reipublicae ut sit finis litium* depends on the facts: the plaintiff and his insurers had not acted vexatiously or oppressively in pursuing the present claim nor were they prevented from doing so.

Note—See also *Haigh v Lawford*, p 680, above.

Lambert v Mainland Market Deliveries Ltd
[1977] 2 All ER 826, [1977] 1 WLR 825, 121 Sol Jo 477, [1978] 1 Lloyd's Rep 245, CA

The plaintiff's parked car was struck by a vehicle driven by the defendants' driver and damaged beyond repair. There was no knock-for-knock agreement between the respective insurers. The plaintiff's insurers paid him £982.37 for the total loss value of his car less his £30 excess. They claimed the amount of their outlay from the defendants' insurers who, pleading inevitable accident, offered 50%. Meanwhile the plaintiff acting in person issued a summons in the county court for his uninsured losses of £72.80 including the £30 excess. On service of the summons the defendants' insurers immediately paid into court the £72.80 plus costs on the summons and wrote the plaintiff's insurers withdrawing the offer of 50% of the claim. The county court paid out the £72.80 to the plaintiff, the action being thereby stayed under the County Court Rules Ord 11, r 7(2): 'Where the amount paid into court is the whole amount of the claim together with the costs stated on the summons the action shall be stayed'.

The plaintiff's insurers in the name of the plaintiff applied for a removal of the stay to enable them to continue with the action for recovery of their own outlay. The county court judge held that he had a discretion to remove the stay but that it was not a case in which he should do so.

HELD, ON APPEAL: (1) The court had jurisdiction in a proper case to remove a stay which has resulted from the operation of Ord 11, r 7(2), though it is a jurisdiction which should be exercised with very great care. When an action is stayed it does not come to end but loses its inherent ability to go forward; but it can be started up again by order of the court. Dicta in *Derrick v Williams* (p 678, above) and *Cooper v Williams* (p 490, above) adopted. (2) This was one of the probably few and rare cases in which a stay ought to be set aside. The defendants' insurers, at the time when they made the payment into court, were well aware that the plaintiff's claim was only a small part of the whole claim which was intended to be prosecuted against them. They were seeking to take advantage of the procedure to bar any further claim against them.

Note—It was accepted by the plaintiff's insurers that they could not start a fresh action in the plaintiff's name for the amount of their claim. *Taylor v Wray*, above, is not mentioned in the judgments. The County Court Rules Ord 11, r 7 has been replaced by Ord 11, rr 2, 3 and 4 of the 1981 Rules.

Buckland v Palmer
[1984] 3 All ER 554, [1984] 1 WLR 1109, 128 Sol Jo 565, CA

After a damaging collision between her car and the defendant's the plaintiff issued a summons against him in the county court for £50 being the excess not covered by her policy. He paid the whole amount into court, though denying liability, and she accepted it. The action was thereby automatically stayed by operation of Ord 11, r 3(3) of the then County Court Rules. Subsequently her insurers began proceedings in her name against the defendant for the balance of the cost of repairs which they had paid for. The defendant applied to the court that the second action be struck out on the ground that it was an abuse of the process of the court. The county court judge, relying on *Taylor v O. Wray & Co Ltd* (above) refused to strike out the action.

HELD, on the defendant's appeal: *Taylor's* case was distinguishable and out of line with the general stream of authority. It was in the public interest that there should be finality in litigation. On principle and on the authorities (including *Derrick v Williams* (p 678, above) and *Lambert v Mainland Market Deliveries* (above)) (1) it is an abuse of the process of the court to bring two actions in respect of the same cause of action, and (2) where there has been no judgment in the first action it can, when appropriate, be revived and amended to include the whole claim. The second action should be struck out without prejudice to an application to remove the stay on the first action and amend the particulars of claim in that action.

Note—Sir John Donaldson MR said the decision left open the problem of what is to happen if the first action has proceeded to judgment, but he said he 'would expect the courts to reappraise the circumstances in which a judgment could be set aside if justice so required'.

County Courts Act 1959, s 69 [now the County Courts Act 1984, s 35]

Vines v Arnold
(1849) 8 CB 632, 7 Dowl & L 277, Rob L & W 180, Cox M & H 320
Adkin v Friend
(1878) 38 LJCP 277, 38 LT 393
'It shall not be lawful for any plaintiff to divide any cause of action for the purpose of bringing two or more actions in one or more of the county courts.'

It would seem that if a plaintiff divides his causes of action, and sues for part of his claim, and the defendant does not raise the objection at the trial of the first action, the plaintiff can afterwards sue for the rest of his claim, and the defendant is not protected by the above section.

Sanders v Hamilton
(1907) 96 LT 679, 23 TLR 389
But where the plaintiff by mistake claims too small a sum and the defendant admitting liability pays that amount into court, and it is taken out by the plaintiff, the plaintiff cannot, when leave to amend his claim has been refused, maintain a new action for the larger amount both on the principle of *res judicata* and by reason of the provisions of this section.

In an action in detinue in the county court, plaintiff by mistake claimed too small a sum. Defendant paid into court the amount claimed without denial of liability and it was taken out by plaintiff. Upon discovering his mistake, plaintiff asked leave to amend his particulars, which was refused, and judgment was given in the action for defendant. Plaintiff then began a new action for the larger amount, giving credit to defendant for the sum previously paid into court.
HELD: The matter was *res judicata*, and the action was not maintainable.

In High Court

Poulett v Hill
[1893] 1 Ch 277, 62 LJ Ch 466, 68 LT 476, 41 WR 503
If two actions are commenced, the second asking for relief which might have been obtained in the first, the second is prima facie vexatious, and may be stayed.

Alfred Rowntree & Sons Ltd v Frederick Allen & Sons
(1936) 41 Com Cas 90
Plaintiff cannot bring two actions for different parts of damage arising from the same breach.

SUING DISSOLVED COMPANY

Note—The Companies Act 1948, s 352(1) reads as follows:

'Where a company has been dissolved, the court may at any time within two years of the date of the dissolution, on an application being made for the purpose by the liquidator of the company or any other person who appears to the court to be interested, make an order, upon such terms as the court thinks fit, declaring the dissolution to have been void, and thereupon such proceedings may be taken as might have been taken if the company had not been dissolved.'

Re Roehampton Swimming Pool Ltd
[1968] 3 All ER 661, [1968] 1 WLR 1693, 112 Sol Jo 670 (Megarry J)
On 30 August 1965 an infant sustained injury when diving into a swimming pool in the occupation of a limited company. In July 1967 the company went into voluntary liquidation and on 12 April 1968, the company was deemed to have been dissolved. No writ had been issued against the company. In August 1968 the infant's solicitor applied in her own name to resuscitate the company under s 352 so that it could be sued. HELD: If the application had been made by the claimant himself there would have been no difficulty in granting it since he, with a claim for damages against the company, plainly fell within the words 'any other person who appears to the court to be interested'. But the solicitor was not a 'person . . . interested', since those words mean a person having a pecuniary or proprietary interest.

Re BBH (Middletons) Ltd
(1970) 114 Sol Jo 431 (Plowman J)
31 December 1965: company passed special resolution for voluntary winding-up; 15 February 1966: applicant, an employee of the company, injured in road accident when driving company's van; 21 March 1968: company dissolved; 14 February 1969: applicant issued writ against company for damages for personal injury; 19 March 1970: applicant began proceedings to have company's dissolution declared void under s 352(1). HELD: Assuming time under the Limitation Acts was running in favour of the company during the period until the dissolution it could not have continued to run after 21 March 1968, because the company had been dissolved and there was no one in whose favour it could have run. As the claim was not necessarily statute-barred, or would be barred if an order were made under the section, the dissolution should be declared void but without prejudicing any defence the company cared to put forward in any further action the applicant might bring against it.

Note—The Companies Act 1948, s 353(6) reads as follows:

'If a company or any member or creditor thereof feels aggrieved by the company having been struck off the register, the court on an application made by the company or member or creditor . . . may, if satisfied that the company was at the time of the striking off carrying on business or in operation, or otherwise that it is just that the company be restored to the register, order the name of the company to be restored to the register . . .'. The application may be made within twenty years of the striking off.

Re Harvest Lane Motor Bodies Ltd
[1969] 1 Ch 457, [1968] 2 All ER 1012, [1968] 3 WLR 220, 112 Sol Jo 518 (Megarry J)
The widow of a man killed in a road accident on 16 July 1961 issued a writ on 26 April 1963 claiming damages under the Fatal Accidents and Law Reform Acts against the limited company whose servant she alleged was to blame. In June 1965 whilst the action was still proceeding the company's name was struck off the register under the Companies Act, s 353 as being a defunct company.
HELD: She was for the purpose of s 353(6) a 'creditor' and entitled to apply. The subsection is concerned with a grievance on the part of some

person whether a company, a member or a creditor. The petitioner had an action in being when the company was struck off. The Act could not have intended to differentiate between those creditors whose debts are fixed and ascertained and those whose debts are contingent and prospective. The company's name should be restored to the register.

Note—It is not necessary that there should be an action in being against a company at the date of its being struck off for an application under s 353(6) to succeed. In *Re Regent Insulation Co Ltd* ((1981) Times, 5 November) the company was struck off the register in May 1976 for non-compliance with provisions of the Companies Act. A former employee who had worked for the company from November 1964 to January 1967 using asbestos was found in 1976 to be suffering from asbestosis. He applied in January 1981 that the company be restored to the register to enable him to institute proceedings against it. The registrar made an order in February 1981 restoring the company to the register and directing that the period between its being struck off in 1976 and its restoration should not be counted for the purposes of any Statute of Limitation. An appeal in the name of the company by its insurers was dismissed.

TRANSFER FROM COUNTY COURT TO HIGH COURT

Note—The County Courts Act 1984 s 42, gives this right to a plaintiff on the footing that there is reasonable ground for supposing the amount recoverable in respect of his claim to be in excess of the amount recoverable in the county court. The county court judge must make the order if he is satisfied that reasonable ground exists.

The defendant also has the right if he gives security approved by the registrar for such amount as the registrar may determine; and the judge certifies that in his opinion some important question of law or fact is likely to arise.

VISITING FORCES

Visiting Forces Act 1952

Note—By s 9 of the Act the Secretary of State for Defence may arrange for the settlement of claims against visiting forces.

The International Headquarters and Defence Organisations Act 1964 applies the provisions of the Visiting Forces Act 1952 to any headquarters or organisation designated by an Order in Council.

Claims procedure

STATEMENT TO BE ISSUED BY THE SECRETARY OF STATE FOR DEFENCE IN PURSUANCE OF S 9(2) OF THE ACT

Part 1
(Claims against a visiting force)

1 The claims to which the arrangements relate are:
    (a) Claims arising out of tortious acts committed on land in the United Kingdom by any member of one of the said Visiting Forces or its civilian component or any other act on land for which a Visiting Force or its

civilian component is responsible in tort and claims other than contractual claims arising out of or in connection with the operation over the territory of the United Kingdom or the territorial waters thereof of an aircraft owned or controlled by a Visiting Force.

(b) Maritime claims.

2 The arrangements apply to claims arising out of acts done on or after the dates shown against the countries listed in the Schedule.

3 Claimants must address their claims as follows:

(a) Claims other than maritime claims should be addressed to:
The Ministry of Defence, Claims Commission, York House, Kingsway, London WC 2.

4 If the alleged tortious act was committed in the performance of an official duty, the claim will be dealt with in the same manner as it would have been if such tortious act had been committed by a member of the British Armed Forces. If a settlement of the claim is reached by negotiation any sum due under that settlement will be paid by the Secretary of State for Defence. If a settlement of the claim cannot be reached by negotiation it is open to the claimant to bring proceedings in the British Courts in respect of his claim against the individual wrongdoer concerned and any sum due under any judgment of the Court obtained by the claimant will be paid to him (provided notice of the intention to start proceedings against the wrongdoer has been given to the authorities referred to in paragraph 3).

5 If on investigation of a claim it is ascertained that the act complained of was not done in the performance of an official duty, no responsibility for settlement will be accepted by the Secretary of State for Defence. The claim will, however, be investigated by the appropriate United Kingdom authority and a report prepared and submitted to the appropriate authority of the Visiting Force concerned so that the latter may consider whether or not an *ex gratia* payment might be made to the claimant direct by the particular Force concerned. A claimant, if he so desires, may institute proceedings against the individual concerned in respect of any act outside the scope of his official duty, but responsibility for satisfying a judgment obtained in these circumstances will not be accepted by the Secretary of State of Defence.

6 If a dispute arises whether a tortious act of a member of a Visiting Force or civilian component was committed in the performance of official duty the question may be submitted to a legal Arbitrator whose decision will be binding and conclusive upon all the parties concerned. The same course will be followed where a claimant is unable to identify the wrongdoer.

Part II of the Statement makes similar arrangements for claims against International Headquarters or Defence Organisations.

The Schedule referred to in para 2 of Part I is as follows:

Canada	
Belgium	
France	
The Netherlands	12 June 1954
Norway	
The United States of America	
Luxembourg	
Turkey	
Greece	1 January 1957
Denmark	
Portugal	
Italy	
Federal Republic of Germany	14 August 1961

CHAPTER 17
Legal aid

ASSISTED PERSON'S COSTS

Legal aid

Note—The Legal Aid and Advice Act 1949 has been repealed and replaced by the Legal Aid Act 1974 which, with minor exceptions, came into force on 8 May 1974. The current regulations are the Legal Aid (General) Regulations 1980 which came into force 1 January 1981.

Right of assisted person to costs from fund

Page v Page, Metcalfe v Wells
[1953] Ch 320, [1953] 1 All ER 626, [1953] 2 WLR 432, 97 Sol Jo 150, CA
A party who has been granted a legal aid certificate is entitled as of right to an order for taxation of his costs under the Act. There is no discretion in the court to withhold an order, although no order is made as to the costs of the proceedings.

Appeal on costs

Starkey v Railway Executive
[1951] 2 All ER 902, [1951] WN 546, 95 Sol Jo 710, CA
The plaintiff, an assisted person, recovered damages from the defendants. Stable J made an order for costs against the defendants 'for such costs as an assisted person pays the state'. As the plaintiff had a nil contribution this meant the defendants were not required to pay any of the plaintiff's costs. The plaintiff appealed.
HELD: This was wrong; the 1949 Act, s 1(7) [now s 2(5) of the 1974 Act],

providing that the rights and liabilities of the parties should not be affected, was conclusive. Order for costs varied and defendants ordered to pay the costs.

Law Society's charge

LAW SOCIETY'S GAZETTE, FEBRUARY 1959, p 95

General Council of the Bar
Legal Aid Fund Costs out of Sum Recovered by Assisted Plaintiff

At page 19 of the *Annual Statement* of the General Council of the Bar for 1954, the attention of members of the Bar was drawn to s 3(4) of the Legal Aid and Advice Act 1949 [now s 9(6) of the 1974 Act] and to the case of *R v Judge Fraser Harrison, ex p Law Society* [1955] 1 QB 287, [1955] 1 All ER 270, [1955] 2 WLR 220, 99 Sol Jo 79. It was there stated that when settling actions, counsel are reminded that s 3(4) of the Act creates a charge for the benefit of the Legal Aid Fund on any property recovered or preserved for the assisted person and on any damages recovered to the extent of any unpaid costs of the proceedings and that this charge operates even where the assisted person's contribution is nil.

The Bar Council are aware that there were at one time exceptional cases in which this charge had been waived. They are also aware that there have been cases in which counsel for parties to a settlement have sought and obtained the approval of the judge to the settlement subject to a recommendation by the judge that those responsible should consider refraining from enforcing the statutory charge.

The Bar Council have now been informed that as the statute creating the charge provides no exception, The Law Society cannot obtain any waiver of the charge in future cases.

In these circumstances the Bar Council have issued a circular to the Bar drawing attention to the position of counsel acting for an assisted plaintiff who is offered some sum by way of settlement on behalf of the defendant. Unless such an offer contains a provision to pay an adequate sum to the assisted plaintiff by way of costs the charge will reduce and may exceed the sum offered.

Particular attention is drawn to the effect of the charge where there has been a payment into court and advice is sought upon the question of acceptance.

The Bar Council are of the opinion that in such circumstances counsel are bound to draw the attention of the assisted person and of the instructing solicitor to these matters and should themselves clearly appreciate that any recommendation from the Bench which may have been sought or volunteered is incapable of effecting any waiver of this statutory charge.

DEFENDANT'S COSTS AGAINST ASSISTED PERSON

Deduction from damages

Nolan v C. and C. Marshall
[1954] 2 QB 42, [1954] 1 All ER 328, [1954] 2 WLR 285, 98 Sol Jo 108, CA
Defendants paid £763 into court. Plaintiff awarded £504 1s 11d at trial. Disposable capital and contribution assessed at nil.
ORDER: Plaintiff to recover costs up to payment in; defendants to recover their costs after payment in; defendants to deduct excess of their costs over plaintiff's costs from damages (McNair J).
HELD, ON APPEAL: Section 4(3) of the 1949 Act (now s 11(3) of the 1974

Act) deals with contribution by the assisted person. When the award was made, the case had passed that stage. There is nothing in the Act or Regulations to show that the costs could not be deducted from damages.

Bloomfield v British Transport Commission
[1960] 2 QB 86, [1960] 2 All ER 54, n, [1960] 2 WLR 693, 104 Sol Jo 329, CA

The plaintiff appealed against an award of £1,500 damages on the ground that it was insufficient. The appeal was dismissed. The defendants asked for the costs of the appeal though the plaintiff was an assisted person under the Legal Aid and Advice Act 1949.

HELD: There was no good ground why the full costs of the appeal should not be awarded and they would have to come out of the damages. They would be assessed at £75.

Cook v S
[1967] 1 All ER 299, [1967] 1 WLR 457, 110 Sol Jo 964, CA

In an action for negligence against a solicitor the defendant paid into court £1,500. At trial the plaintiff, who was legally aided, was awarded only £1,110. The defendant's costs after payment in amounted to £1,400 but the judge gave him only £200 costs.

HELD, ON APPEAL: As the legal aid fund had a charge on the damages for the plaintiff's costs (*Bloomfield v British Transport Commission*, above) and as the balance of the damages (£910) would be wholly absorbed by the plaintiff's costs the contest was between the defendant and the legal aid fund. As the legal aid fund was maintaining the plaintiff's action and as the defendant had made a successful payment into court he should have all his costs, at least up to £1,110, but the plaintiff should not be ordered personally to pay any of the excess. Appeal allowed.

Order for costs against assisted person

Blatcher v Heaysman
[1960] 2 All ER 721, [1960] 1 WLR 663, 104 Sol Jo 545, CA

The plaintiffs were successful in an action against the defendants for fraudulent misrepresentation and were awarded £350 damages. On finding that both parties were legally aided, the judge refused to make an order for costs against the defendants.

HELD, ON APPEAL: An order for costs should be made against the defendants since if no parties had been legally aided the defendants would have been ordered to pay costs. An award of costs was to be made subject to the provisions of the Legal Aid and Advice Act 1949, s 2(2) (now s 8(1) of the 1974 Act) that the amount should be reasonable 'having regard to all the circumstances'. The duty of considering who is to pay must be fulfilled in accordance with the same principles on which discretion is normally exercised.

Mercantile Credit Co v Cross
[1965] 2 QB 205, [1965] 1 All ER 577, [1965] 2 WLR 687, 109 Sol Jo 47,
CA
The plaintiff, an assisted person with a nil contribution, failed in his action
against the defendants. The county court judge ordered him to pay the
whole of the defendants' costs.
HELD: Section 2(2) of the 1949 Act requires the judge to award not more
than an amount which is a reasonable one for the assisted person to pay. As
against a defendant with a nil contribution the order made here was a
wholly unreasonable one and one which did not amount to a proper
exercise of the judge's discretion. The contribution would be restricted to
£25.

Barling v British Transport Commission
[1955] 2 Lloyd's Rep 393 (Devlin J)
I think the same amount as the plaintiff is asked to contribute to her costs
should be the same amount towards the costs of the defendant if the
defendant is successful. Order £35 10s 0d payable by the same instalments.

THE MOTOR INSURERS' BUREAU DEFENDING

Godfrey v Smith
[1955] 2 All ER 520, [1955] 1 WLR 692, 99 Sol Jo 419 (Donovan J)
A motor cyclist with a pillion passenger collided with another motor cyclist,
who was uninsured. The two first named, who were not legally assisted,
sued the uninsured motor cyclist, who obtained legal aid. The action
succeeded and the usual order for costs was made against the defendant. At
that time the legal aid certificate was not available, but was later obtained,
and application was made on his behalf for the costs to be assessed in
accordance with the certificate.
　　The judge said that, apart from the fact that the defendant was represented by the Motor Insurers' Bureau, he would have made an order for
£50 costs by instalments. It was largely a matter of discretion whether a
court took the Motor Insurers' Bureau agreement into account. It would
be unjust that the plaintiff should be out of pocket because the defendant
was legally aided and could not pay the costs. The Motor Insurers' Bureau
agreement was relevant on the question of a full order for costs, and the
judge ordered payment of the taxed costs in the ordinary way.

Limited certificate

Dugon v Williamson
[1964] Ch 59, [1963] 3 All ER 25, [1963] 3 WLR 477, 107 Sol Jo 572, CA
After judgment against him in the High Court the defendant served notice
of appeal. He then obtained a legal aid certificate for the appeal limited to
obtaining a transcript of the judgment and obtaining counsel's opinion on
the prospects of the appeal. While the appeal was in the warned list the legal
aid committee discharged the certificate after considering counsel's
opinion. The defendant continued the appeal on his own resources and
lost. On an application by the plaintiff for costs it was held that whilst the
certificate was in force even though for a limited purpose the defendant was

an 'assisted person' so that his liability for costs during that period was not to exceed an amount which was reasonable in the circumstances (the Legal Aid and Advice Act 1949, s 2(2)(e)). In the present case the amount was nil.

Note—Section 2(2)(e) of the 1949 Act is re-enacted as s 8(1)(e) of the 1974 Act.

Impecunious defendant submitting to judgment

Ranson v Burns
(1964) 108 Sol Jo 676 (Sachs J)
The plaintiff was awarded £800 damages for personal injuries, the defendant having admitted negligence. After judgment given counsel for the defendant applied for a stay of execution: the defendant was not insured against this claim, had no means and had a legal aid certificate limited to defending on the amount of damages only. The plaintiff and her advisers knew this before trial.

The judge said that where a legally-aided defendant was not in a position to pay money into court he was nonetheless in a position to submit to judgment for some specific sum. For an impecunious defendant to take advantage of legal aid to proceed without making some offer to submit to judgment was certainly wrong. He ordered the defendant to pay the costs of the action.

Security for costs — foreign plaintiff

Jackson v John Dickinson & Co (Bolton) Ltd
[1952] 1 All ER 104, [1952] WN 9, CA
Plaintiff, an assisted person, was ordinarily resident in Dublin. Defendants applied for security for costs under Ord LXV, r 6 (now Ord 23, r 1), on the ground of residence abroad. The district registrar took into consideration the fact that the plaintiff was an assisted person and made an order fixing the security at £25. His order was reversed by the commissioner of assize.
HELD, ON APPEAL: Security is ordered as a matter of course under Ord LXV, r 6, against a plaintiff out of the jurisdiction because an order for costs may be ineffective unless he had property within the jurisdiction, and this applies to an assisted person although a full order for costs will probably not be made against the plaintiff. The order for security was right, and there was no reason to interfere with the sum fixed. *Conway v George Wimpey* (p 164, above) did not apply. No regulations had been made under ss 1(7) or 12(2)(b)(ii) of the 1949 Act.

Wyld v Silver (No 2)
[1963] 1 QB 169, [1962] 2 All ER 809, [1962] 1 WLR 863, 106 Sol Jo 409, CA
Although the Court will not ordinarily make an order to give security for costs of an appeal against a legally-aided person (*Conway v George Wimpey*, p 164, above) it has jurisdiction to do so. The defendant had disposable capital of £323 and his contribution to the legal aid fund was £207. He was required to give security for £100 before prosecuting an appeal.

DEFENDANT'S COSTS FROM LEGAL AID FUND

Payment of costs to unassisted opponents

Note—The Legal Aid Act 1964 provided for the payment out of the legal aid fund of costs incurred by successful opponents of legally-aided litigants. It has been repealed and replaced by the Legal Aid Act 1974, ss 13 and 14 without amendment. The Court may make an order for payment of such costs provided the following requirements are satisfied:

1 The proceedings must be 'finally decided' in favour of the unassisted party. They are to be treated as finally decided (a) if no appeal lies against the decision; (b) if an appeal lies with leave and the time for applying for leave has expired without leave being granted; (c) if no leave is required, or leave to appeal has been granted and no appeal is brought within the time limited for appeal.

2 The Court must be satisfied that it is just and equitable in all the circumstances that the costs should be paid.

3 The Court must in every case first consider what orders should be made for costs against the party who has legal aid and for determining his liability in respect of the costs.

4 The proceedings in the court of first instance must have been instituted by the party receiving legal aid.

5 The Court must be satisfied that the unassisted party will suffer severe financial hardship unless the order is made.

6 The proceedings are not such that, apart from the Act, no order would be made for payment of the unassisted party's costs.

Only the court by which the proceedings are 'finally decided' can make the order. Costs means party and party costs but includes the costs of applying for the order. Appeal against an order lies only on a point of law.

See also the Legal Aid (General) Regulations 1980, SI 1980/1984, regs 127–140.

Nowotnik v Nowotnik

[1967] P 83, [1965] 3 All ER 167, [1965] 3 WLR 920, 109 Sol Jo 632, CA

In a case in which a wife who had a legal aid certificate unsuccessfully sued for divorce from her husband who had not, the Court of Appeal decided that no order could be made for payment of the husband's costs from the legal aid fund for three reasons:

1 Apart from the Act no order would have been made for costs against the wife, since it had not been the practice in the Divorce Court even before 1949 to make an order for costs against a wife without means. (See requirement 6 above.)

2 The husband would not suffer 'severe financial hardship' if no order were made. He earned about £1,200 a year and had about £10 in hand per week after paying ordinary living expenses.

3 It was not 'just and equitable' to make an order: even if the husband had earned £500 a year less and had thus qualified for a legal aid certificate himself his contribution would have exceeded the amount of his costs and the Legal Aid Fund would have paid nothing. He could not be allowed to be better off by having no legal aid certificate.

Note—Held wrongly decided in next case.

Hanning v Maitland (No 2)

[1970] 1 QB 580, [1970] 1 All ER 812, [1970] 2 WLR 151, 114 Sol Jo 14, CA

In a dark lane at night the plaintiff, a cyclist, collided with the defendant, a pedestrian, and was injured. He succeeded in getting a legal aid certificate to sue for damages. The defendant was aged 54; his net wage was about £18 per week but he was thrifty and had saved about £2,700 with which he hoped to buy a house. He did not apply for legal aid and would not have got it if he had because of his savings. The action was fought and the plaintiff's claim was dismissed. When the defendant applied for payment of his costs out of the Legal Aid Fund under the 1964 Act the trial judge said the litigation was a waste of time and it would be a wicked thing if the defendant had to pay anything. Despite this the taxing master refused any payment; on appeal the judge (not the trial judge) also refused, considering himself bound by *Nowotnik v Nowotnik* (above).

HELD, ON APPEAL to the Court of Appeal: *Nowotnik*'s case was wrongly decided in giving emphasis to 'severe' in the phrase 'severe financial hardship'. The word should be construed to exclude insurance companies, commercial organisations and wealthy folk who can meet the costs without feeling it. It should not be construed to exclude people like the defendant of modest income or capital who would find it hard to bear his own costs of £325 out of his hard-earned savings. *Nowotnik*'s case was also wrong in holding that an unassisted person should not get more out of the legal aid fund than he would if he were an assisted person. If the legally-aided plaintiff loses his case it is 'just and equitable' that the fund should pay every penny of his taxed costs. Appeal allowed.

Kelly v London Transport Executive

[1982] 2 All ER 842, [1982] 1 WLR 1055, 126 Sol Jo 262, CA

On 21 October 1974 the plaintiff sustained a trivial injury in the defendants' employment. He returned to work but gave up work in March 1975 complaining of depression, eye trouble and deafness. He consulted solicitors in March 1977 who got opinions from two counsel, obtained a legal aid certificate and from time to time amassed 19 medical reports. They also with counsel's opinions obtained unlimited leave from the legal aid committee to go on with the action. The defendants engaged five medical specialists. They paid £750 into court on 28 July 1980 which was not accepted and offered £4,000 on 24 September 1980 because they would be unable to recover costs from the legally-aided plaintiff. This was also refused on the advice of counsel. At trial in October 1980 the judge rejected the claim as bogus: the symptoms complained of were due to chronic alcoholism. He awarded £75 for the original small injury. The defendants applied under the Legal Aid Act 1974, s 13(1) to recover their costs of £8,000.

HELD: No order could be made because they could not show 'severe financial hardship'. They were a huge corporation 'hopelessly and continuously' in deficit almost to £175 m, supported by a grant from the GLC. It would not be 'severe financial hardship' for them to meet a bill for £8,000. They could (per Lord Denning) proceed against the solicitors and counsel personally.

CLAIM AND COUNTER-CLAIM

Millican v Tucker
[1980] 1 All ER 1083, [1980] 1 WLR 640, 124 Sol Jo 276, CA
The plaintiffs, unassisted litigants, claimed against legally-aided defendants who counter-claimed on substantially the same issues. The action was settled at the hearing on terms which amounted to a total surrender by the defendants. The plaintiffs applied for an order for payment of their costs out of the Legal Aid Fund under the Legal Aid Act 1974, s 13. The judge ordered payment by the Fund of the plaintiffs' costs of the counter-claim and directed that in taxing those costs the costs on issues common to both claim and counter-claim should be divided equally between the costs of the claim and those of the counter-claim. The Legal Aid Fund appealed.
HELD: The judge had no jurisdiction to make such an order. If it had been made inter partes it would have been well within the judge's discretion, but as it was made pursuant to a statutory power only and against the legal aid fund, which was not a party, the judge had no power to do it.

Where a court orders that claim and counter-claim be dismissed, or allowed, with costs, the rule of taxation is that the claim should be treated as if it stood alone and the counter-claim should bear only the amount by which the costs of the proceedings had been increased by it. A judge has a wide discretion to make a special order inter partes if he thinks fit, and can make such order as he likes, but however the costs may be dealt with by the judge's order, costs incurred in connection with the claim can never be appropriated to the counter-claim so as to become part of the costs of the counter-claim.

Note—See also *R & T. Thew Ltd v Reeves* [1982] QB 172, [1981] 2 All ER 964, [1981] 3 WLR 190, 125 Sol Jo 358, CA

Costs of appealing

Parker v Thompson
[1966] 3 All ER 766n, [1967] 1 WLR 28, 110 Sol Jo 772, CA
The requirement of 'severe financial hardship' does not apply to costs in the Court of Appeal.

The defendant successfully contested an action for damages against him at assizes, incurring costs of £271 in so doing. An appeal failed completely, the defendant incurring costs of £120 in fighting it. He was uninsured but could not show severe financial hardship. The plaintiffs were legally aided. An order was made to pay the defendant £120 out of the legal aid fund to meet the costs of the appeal since it was 'just and equitable in all the circumstances'.

Saunders v Anglia Building Society
[1971] AC 1004, [1970] 3 All ER 961, [1970] 3 WLR 1078, 114 Sol Jo 885, 22 P & CR 300, HL
In an action against a building society the assisted person succeeded in the court of first instance but failed in the Court of Appeal and in the House of Lords. On the society's application for costs to be paid out of the legal aid fund under the Legal Aid Act 1964—

HELD: (1) The court must first be 'satisfied that it is just and equitable in all the circumstances' that the unassisted party should get relief. The phrase was a composite phrase conveying one idea and it would be useless and might be misleading to seek to split it up. (2) A distinction had to be drawn between costs in the court of first instance, where the means of the unassisted person had to be considered, and costs in an appeal, where there was no means test. (3) The society had not been taken to the Court of Appeal by the assisted litigant: there was no sufficient reason why they should recover from public funds costs which they themselves chose to incur. But it was right that they should have their costs in the House of Lords from the legal aid fund, the assisted litigant having obtained legal aid to appeal to the House.

Note—See also *General Accident Fire and Life Assurance Ltd v Foster* [1973] 1 QB 50, [1972] 3 All ER 877, [1972] 3 WLR 657, [1972] 2 Lloyd's Rep 288, CA

Clifford v Walker
[1972] 2 All ER 806, [1972] 1 WLR 724, 116 Sol Jo 275, CA
Saunders's case did not decide that an unassisted litigant who appeals to the Court of Appeal and wins is barred from recovering costs from the legal aid fund. He can recover his costs against the legal aid fund if it is just and equitable for him to do so, even though it was he who was the appellant. The fact that the unassisted party is of relatively limited means is a consideration that may be sufficient to justify an order.

Note—But see *Davies v Taylor (No 2)*, below.

Lewis v Averay (No 2)
[1973] 2 All ER 229, [1973] 1 WLR 510, 117 Sol Jo 188, CA
In the county court both parties had legal aid, but in the Court of Appeal the appellant Averay was unable to get legal aid and was supported by the Automobile Association whose solicitors acted for him. He applied under s 1(2) of the 1964 Act for his costs to be paid out of the legal aid fund.
HELD: An order should be made to that effect. Averay was the litigant and the costs were 'incurred by him'. It was just and equitable that he should have them because he was a member of the AA and was in honour bound to reimburse the AA so far as he recovered the costs against the other side.

Davies v Taylor (No 2)
[1974] AC 225, [1973] 1 All ER 959, [1973] 2 WLR 610, 117 Sol Jo 246, HL
The respondent, successful both in the Court of Appeal and the House of Lords (in both of which the appellant was legally aided) applied for an order under s 1(1) of the 1964 Act that his costs on the appeal should be paid out of the legal aid fund (see *Davies v Taylor*, p 500, above). He was insured under a motor policy and his insurers would pay his costs.
HELD: An order should be made. The costs were 'incurred by him in the proceedings' within s 1(1) even though the insurers agreed to pay them,

unless there was an agreement between him and his solicitors that he would not pay their costs; it had not been proved there was. The fact that the order would benefit the insurers did not prevent it from being 'just and equitable'. The court had a very wide discretion under the Act; success in the appeal alone (contrary to the view expressed by the Court of Appeal in *Clifford v Walker* [1972] 2 All ER 806 (p 700, above)) could be a sufficient justification for an order. But the court should not usually give its reasons.

Note—See also two applications similarly dealt with on the same occasion: *Shiloh Spinners Ltd v Harding (No 2)* and *O'Brien v Robinson (No 2)* [1973] 1 All ER 966 and 969n. For s 1(1) of the 1964 Act see now s 13(1) of the 1974 Act.

Megarity v D. J. Ryan & Sons Ltd (No 2)
[1982] AC 81, [1981] 1 All ER 641, [1981] 2 WLR 335, 125 Sol Jo 167, HL
The plaintiff made an unsuccessful interlocutory appeal (see *Megarity v Ryan*, p 655, above) and the Court of Appeal ordered the unassisted defendants costs of the appeal to be paid out of the legal aid fund. The Law Society objected that 'proceedings' meant the whole action and that the court had no power to award costs of an interlocutory appeal since the action was not yet 'finally decided'.
HELD: Not so. An interlocutory appeal is 'proceedings' and the court was entitled to make the order.

DUTY OF LEGAL ADVISERS

Duty of solicitor

Minkley v Minkley
[1953] 1 All ER 1176n, Div Ct
It may be the duty of a solicitor for an assisted person to inform the Legal Aid Committee of any facts coming to his knowledge after the grant of a certificate which might affect the continuance of the certificate.

Hopeless cases — penalty in costs

Edwards v Edwards
[1958] P 235, [1958] 2 All ER 179, [1958] 2 WLR 956, 102 Sol Jo 402 (Sachs J)
A wife obtained legal aid and commenced proceedings for wilful neglect to maintain. In the proceedings it became clear that the chances of success did not really exist at all. The husband's solicitors wrote with information to the area committee and sent a copy to the wife's solicitor, who attended before the committee; the certificate was not revoked, and the case proceeded to trial. The husband applied for an order that the wife's solicitors should personally bear the costs incurred by him.
HELD: The Court has inherent powers over solicitors in their capacity as officers of the court. The duty is to conduct litigation with due propriety and is due to the court and to all those against whom they are concerned. It is not enough to invoke the jurisdiction that the case failed, or error of

judgment even of an order equivalent to negligence. It must be a serious dereliction of duty but need not amount to *mala fides* or other obliquity. Unreasonably to initiate or continue an action when it has no or substantially no chance of success may give jurisdiction. The fact that the solicitor is acting under a legal aid certificate does not affect the position. Section 1(7)(b) of the 1949 Act (now s 2(5)(b) of the 1974 Act) preserves the rights of other parties.

Order for payment by the solicitors personally of all costs from and after the issue by them of the summons for directions.

Kyle v Mason
(1963) Times, 3 July
An order to pay costs personally was made by the Court of Appeal in a case in which the plaintiff's appeal, for which he had obtained a legal aid certificate, was dismissed. The Court said there were no grounds at all for the appeal, which arose from a claim for damages for injuries received in a road accident. The certificate had been granted on the basis of a letter from the plaintiff's solicitor and on seeing the letter the Court required the solicitor to show cause why he should not personally pay the costs. Through counsel the solicitor agreed that the letter was misleading though written under an honest mistake as to the effect of the evidence. He agreed to pay all the costs himself and an order was made accordingly.

Per Ormerod LJ: This case underlined the care which must be taken when supplying information to legal aid committees. Misleading information made their task difficult if not impossible. The information given by the solicitor was misleading and therefore the Court felt impelled to take the course which it had adopted.

Holmes v National Benzole Co Ltd
(1965) 109 Sol Jo 971, Times, 30 November (Lyell J)
In an action for damages in which the plaintiff was legally aided all the claims were abandoned in the course of the trial in February 1964 and the action withdrawn. The taxing master reported after an enquiry that there was evidence of costs having been incurred without reasonable cause. On an application for the plaintiff's costs to be taxed under the Third Schedule of the Legal Aid and Advice Act 1949 the judge refused any costs to the plaintiff's solicitor after 1 March 1962. It was implicit (he said) from the judgment of Lord Maugham in *Myers v Elman* [1940] AC 282, [1939] 4 All ER 484, 109 LJKB 105, 162 LT 113, 56 TLR 177, 84 Sol Jo 184, HL that a solicitor who without any investigation of his client's claim allowed or encouraged a client to pursue a claim which proper investigation would at an early stage have shown to be a hopeless one was in breach of his duty to his client for he would be causing his client to incur costs without reasonable cause. Where the client was legally aided the sanction of the client's displeasure where money was spent on fruitless litigation was not so present as in the case of a private client but the absence of that sanction should not be an excuse to exercise a lesser degree of care. There was a heavy duty on counsel and solicitors to test their client's case with the same anxious care as they would bring to one where they looked to their clients for the costs.

Note—Regulation 23(1) of the 1971 regulations provides that 'any costs wasted by failure to conduct the proceedings with reasonable competence and expedition shall be disallowed or reduced'.

MISCELLANEOUS

Costs of winding up proceedings

Re Peretz Co Ltd
[1965] Ch 200, [1964] 3 All ER 633, [1964] 3 WLR 1159, 108 Sol Jo 840
(Buckley J)
The petitioner's legal aid certificate authorised him to prosecute an action against a company for damages for trespass and nuisance and included enforcement proceedings in respect of any order or judgment obtained in the action. It was held that the certificate was effective to cover winding-up proceedings founded on a judgment debt.

Solicitor and client costs

Gibbs v Gibbs
[1952] P 332, [1952] 1 All ER 942, [1952] 1 TLR 1143 (Havers J)
Paragraph 4(1) of the Third Schedule to the 1949 Act (now Sch 2, para 4(1) of the 1974 Act) provides for taxation of costs as between solicitor and client. This does not justify a taxation as between solicitor and own client.

Sharing counsel with unassisted party

Howson v M. A. Forte
(1965) 109 Sol Jo 702, CA
Two plaintiffs, one legally aided, the other not, brought a joint action against the defendants for breach of contract. They came to the trial represented by separate counsel. The defendants objected and the judge upheld the objection, applying the ordinary rule that there should be only one representation. They appealed. The grounds on which they applied for separate representation were that the plaintiff who had legal aid had a certificate for leading counsel; if the other plaintiff's name appeared on leading counsel's brief he might be liable for half the fee, which he could not afford. HELD: This was no ground for granting the application. If neither party had been legally aided they would have had to make their own financial arrangements; the fact that one of them was legally aided did not make any difference.

PART 4
Insurance

CHAPTER 18

Third-party insurance

COMPULSORY THIRD-PARTY INSURANCE

Note—The statutory provisions relating to compulsory insurance against third-party risks are contained in the Road Traffic Act 1972, Part VI which re-enacts, with some amendments, the provisions on the same topic formerly contained in the Road Traffic Act 1960. The 1972 Act came into force on 1 July 1972, but provision for compulsory passenger insurance was deferred until 1 December 1972 (see pp 748–749, below).

Road Traffic Act 1972, ss 143, 144

143 Use of motor vehicles to be insured or secured against third-party risks
(1) Subject to the provisions of this Part of this Act, it shall not be lawful for a person to use, or to cause or permit any other person to use, a motor vehicle on a road unless there is in force in relation to the use of the vehicle by that person or that other person, as the case may be, such a policy of insurance or such a security in respect of third-party risks as complies with the requirements of this Part of this Act; and if a person acts in contravention of this section he shall be guilty of an offence.
(2) A person charged with using a motor vehicle in contravention of this section shall not be convicted if he proves that the vehicle did not belong to him and was not in his possession under a contract of hiring or of loan, that he was using the vehicle in the course of his employment and that he neither knew nor had reason to believe that there was not in force in relation to the vehicle such a policy of insurance or security as is mentioned in sub-s (1) above.
(3) This Part of this Act shall not apply to invalid carriages.

144 Exceptions from requirement of third-party insurance or security
(1) Section 143 of this Act shall not apply to a vehicle owned by a person who has deposited and keeps deposited with the Accountant General of the Supreme Court the sum of £15,000, at a time when the vehicle is being driven under the owner's control.
(2) The said s 143 shall not apply—
(a)   to a vehicle owned by the council of a county, county borough or county district in England or Wales, the Common Council of the City of London, the council of a London borough, the Greater London Council, a county, town or district council in Scotland, or by a joint board or joint committee in England or Wales, or joint committee in Scotland, which is so constituted as to include among its members representatives of any such council, at a time when the vehicle is being driven under the owner's control;
(b)   to a vehicle owned by a policy authority or the Receiver for the Metropolitan Police District, at a time when it is being driven under the owner's control, or to a vehicle at a time when it is being driven for police purposes by or under the direction of a constable, or by a person employed by a police authority, or employed by the said Receiver; or
(c)   to a vehicle at a time when it is being driven on a journey to or from any place undertaken for salvage purposes pursuant to Part IX of the Merchant Shipping Act 1894;
(d)   to the use of a vehicle for the purpose of its being furnished in pursuance of a direction under para (b) of s 166(2) of the Army Act 1955 or under the corresponding provision of the Air Force Act 1955;
(e)   *(Repealed by the London Regional Transport Act 1984, s 71(3), Sch 6, para 10.)*
(f)   to a vehicle which is made available by the Secretary of State to any person, body or local authority in pursuance of s 11 or s 13 of the National Health Service Reorganisation Act 1973 at a time when it is being used in accordance with the terms on which it is so made available.

By s 198(5) of the 1972 Act tramcars and trolley vehicles are excluded from the provisions of Part VI of the Act (ss 143 to 158).
Sections 143 and 144 replace respectively ss 201 and 202 of the Road Traffic Act 1960.
Sub-section 2(f) of s 144 was added by the National Health Service (Vehicles) Order 1974, SI 1974/168.

'Using' a motor vehicle

Brown v Roberts
[1965] 1 QB 1, [1963] 2 All ER 263, [1963] 3 WLR 75, 107 Sol Jo 666, [1963] 1 Lloyd's Rep 314 (Megaw J)
A van owned and driven by the defendant was drawing up at the kerb when the passenger, to whom he was giving a lift, opened the nearside door. It struck and injured the plaintiff who was on the pavement. She claimed damages against the defendant on the grounds that the passenger was 'using' the vehicle within the meaning of the Road Traffic Act 1930, s 35(1) (which was in similar terms to s 143 of the 1972 Act) and that, as the defendant's policy did not cover negligence of a passenger, he was in breach of the statutory duty as in *Monk v Warbey* (p 716, below).
HELD: The passenger though negligent was not 'using' the vehicle within

the meaning of the section and the defendant was not under a duty to provide insurance against that negligence. Although there may be more than one person 'using' a vehicle at any given time and though the element of driving the vehicle is not an essential element of 'using' (*Elliott v Grey*, p 709 below) a person, does not 'use a motor vehicle on the road' for the purposes of s 35(1) of the 1930 Act unless there is present in the person alleged to be the user an element of controlling, managing or operating the vehicle at the relevant time. The mere relationship of a passenger to a motor vehicle or to a particular part of a motor vehicle is not 'use' for the purposes of the Act.

See also *Thomas v Hooper* (1985) Times, 25 October.

Leathley v Tatton
[1980] RTR 21, Div Ct
The defendant went to an address with two friends intending to look at a car with a view to buying it. The owner did not turn up. One of the friends had a key which fitted the car. The car would not start so one of the friends got into the driving seat and the defendant pushed the car: when it started he jumped into the passenger seat. He took no part in the driving of the car. He was charged with using the car when uninsured contrary to s 143 of the 1972 Act.
HELD: There was a case to answer. It was a clear situation in which the defendant and his friend were acting in concert, a joint enterprise for the purpose of setting the car in motion and to see how the car functioned. The defendant was 'using' it, and the fact that someone else was driving it was irrelevant.

Note—*Brown v Roberts* (above) was cited but distinguished on the ground that it was a case which concerned civil liability and did not reflect on the meaning of 'use' in the present case.

B v Knight
[1981] RTR 136, QBD
O'Nion took a van without the owner's consent. He drove it to a place where he met the defendant, B, a minor. B got into the van and O'Nion drove off. During the journey, but not before, B learned that O'Nion had taken the van without the owner's consent. He did not ask to be allowed to get out as he 'did not fancy the idea of walking home'. He was convicted of using the van uninsured contrary to s 143 of the RTA 1972.
HELD, allowing his appeal: He was not 'using' the vehicle. A passenger merely letting himself be driven where there is no element of joint enterprise does not 'use' the vehicle. B was simply getting a lift from O'Nion in the course of O'Nion's 'use'.

Cobb v Williams
[1973] RTR 113, [1973] Crim LR 243, Div Ct
The defendant was being brought home from work in his own car driven by a woman who was not his servant when an accident occurred. Neither of them was insured. The defendant was charged with 'using' his car when not insured, contrary to the Road Traffic Act 1960, s 201 (now s 143 of the 1972 Act). The magistrates dismissed the charge on the ground that the

meaning of 'use' should not be extended beyond driving and that the charge should have been one of 'permitting'.

HELD: This was not right. The word 'use' is wider than 'drive'. The defendant was using his own car for his own purposes and in person in being driven home, though the driver was somebody else.

Bennett v Richardson
[1980] RTR 358, QBD

The defendant, a registered blind person, was charged with, inter alia, using a motor vehicle without insurance in force contrary to the Road Traffic Act 1972, s 143. At the time in question he was a passenger sitting in the back of an ice cream van driven by his partner. The van was hired, the two partners being equally liable under the hire terms. The defendant's job in the business was cleaning the van and helping to serve ice cream. It was being used on partnership business. The justices applied Lord Parker's principle in *Windle v Dunning* (p 731, below) and dismissed the charge.

HELD, on the prosecutor's appeal: The justices' decision was right. Per Lord Widgery: I would be anxious to see that [the] principle was adhered to and not easily jettisoned for some alternative. The principle to which I refer is this. A man cannot be convicted for using a motor vehicle which he is not personally driving unless he is the employer of the driver. If the owner is driving the vehicle then, good enough, he can be charged with using it. If the owner's employee, in the strict sense of the master-servant relationship, is driving the vehicle, again the employer can be regarded as vicariously being responsible. . . . But if the relationship between driver and would-be defendant is any other than those to which I have referred, then it is not possible to convict the person not driving of these offences. . . . The fact that [the defendant] was blind was quite irrelevant . . . the fact that the driver and the defendant were partners is also irrelevant because there is authority which shows that the mere relationship of partnership between driver and the would-be driver or passenger is not enough. *Cobb v Williams* (above) distinguished.

Garrett v Hooper
[1973] RTR 1, [1973] Crim LR 61, Div Ct

A co-partner does not 'use' a vehicle merely because it is driven by his partner on partnership business.

Passmoor v Gibbons
[1979] RTR 53, [1978] Crim LR 498, QBD

On the other hand a partner who did not take part in the day-to-day running of the company nonetheless 'uses' a vehicle when it is being driven by an employee in the course of his business on behalf of the company.

SERVANT DRIVING
Mickleborough v BRS (Contracts) Ltd
[1977] RTR 389, [1977] Crim LR 568

The defendants were owners of a vehicle hired out with driver for five years to a hirer who alone decided what journeys to do and what loads to carry. Having found the vehicle overloaded a traffic examiner prosecuted the defendants for 'using' the vehicle when overloaded. The loading had been done by the hirers. The justices held the defendants were not 'using' the vehicle since the hirers had control of the vehicle.

HELD: This was not right. Citing Lord Parker, in *Windle v Dunning* (p 731, below) where there is an alternative of 'causing or permitting' then 'using' has a restricted meaning. It is not to be extended to cover persons other than the owner and the driver, provided the driver is his servant and engaged at the material time on his employer's business. The driver was driving on his employer's, the defendants', business of hiring out motor lorries and therefore the defendants were 'using' the vehicle at the material time.

Richardson v Baker

[1976] RTR 56, [1976] Crim LR 76

An employee of the defendant without the defendant's knowledge and without his express or implied authority took a tractor unit on to a road to convey a load for the purposes of the defendant's business as a haulage contractor.

HELD: The defendant was guilty of 'using' the vehicle in contravention of the Vehicles (Excise) Act 1971. Even if 'using' was limited to the narrow meaning given when there was an alternative of 'causing or permitting' then prima facie a vehicle was being used by a master when it was on a road driven by his servant about his master's business. Absence of any authority from him for such use made no difference.

VEHICLE NOT BEING DRIVEN

Elliott v Grey

[1960] 1 QB 367, [1959] 3 All ER 733, [1959] 3 WLR 956, 124 JP 58, 103 Sol Jo 921, 57 LGR 357

Defendant's car broke down on 20 December 1958, and defendant placed it outside his house in the road. Before 7 February 1959, he had jacked up the wheels, removed the battery and terminated his insurance cover. On 7 February 1959, he had unjacked the wheels, cleaned the car, and sent its battery to be recharged, but the car could not be mechanically propelled because the engine would not work. He had no intention of driving it on 7 February 1959, or of removing it from its position in the road. He was convicted of using the car whilst uninsured contrary to the Road Traffic Act 1930, s 35(1). The defendant appealed.

HELD: The words 'to use' meant 'to have the use of a motor vehicle on a road' and, as the car could be moved on 7 February 1959, even though it could not be driven, the appellant had the use of it on a road, within the meaning of s 35(1). Appeal dismissed.

Note—The Road Traffic Act 1930, s 35(1) was in similar terms to s 143 of the 1972 Act.

Napthen v Place

[1970] RTR 248, Div Ct

A motor car was bought at an auction and subsequently stood on the roadway outside the defendant's premises for several weeks untaxed and uninsured. He was charged with using a vehicle on a road uninsured and unlicensed. The prosecution sought to prove that he was the owner but justices did not accept that he was and dismissed the charges.

HELD: On a case stated, it is not essential for either of the charges that the person charged should have been the owner or proved to be the owner of the vehicle in question.

Gosling v Howard
[1975] RTR 429, Div Ct (1968)
The defendant's car was parked on a grass verge of a rural road well off the carriageway and had not been moved for three months. The justices dismissed summonses against him for 'using' a vehicle on a road uninsured and without a test certificate.
HELD, on the prosecutor's appeal: This was wrong. There was no evidence that the car was not in running order and as in *Elliott v Grey* (above) the defendant had the use of the vehicle.

Williams v Jones
[1975] RTR 433, Div Ct (1969)
The defendant used his employer's trade plates to bring a vehicle back to his premises to do it up for sale. On the way it broke down and the defendant left it on a part of the highway that was no longer used because of road improvements. He removed the trade plates and abandoned the vehicle. He was charged with using the vehicle on a road uninsured, his employer's policy being effective only when the trade plates were on. The justices dismissed the charge, holding there had been no user of the vehicle after removal of the trade plates.
HELD: Following *Elliott v Grey* (above) that notwithstanding that the vehicle was abandoned and the trade plates removed, the defendant was thereafter 'using' the vehicle within the meaning of the Road Traffic Act 1960, s 201 (now the Road Traffic Act 1972, s 143).

Eden v Mitchell
[1975] RTR 425, [1975] Crim LR 467, Div Ct
The defendant was charged with using his car on a road with tyres which did not comply with the Motor Vehicles (Construction and Use) Regulations. It was parked outside his house but he had not driven it for some time and had no intention of doing so having been ill. The justices accepted that his sickness and intention not to drive was as sufficient as if the vehicle itself had been immobilised and dismissed the charge.
HELD, on the prosecutor's appeal: This was the wrong test. The intention of the defendant was immaterial. The true test was whether or not such steps had been taken as to make it impossible for anyone to use the vehicle.

MOTOR VEHICLE

Note—The Road Traffic Act 1972 s 190(1) and the Road Traffic Regulation Act 1984, s 136(1) define 'motor vehicle' as a mechanically propelled vehicle intended or adapted for use on roads.

Lawrence v Howlett
[1952] 2 All ER 74, 116 JP 391, [1952] WN 308, [1952] 1 TLR 1476, 96 Sol Jo 397, 50 LGR 531, [1952] 1 Lloyd's Rep 483, Div Ct
A bicycle was fitted with an auxiliary engine but could be used as an ordinary pedal cycle. The auxiliary motor was not in working condition, the cylinder, piston, and connecting rod having been removed, and it was being used as a pedal cycle. The rider was charged with using a motor vehicle without insurance and convicted.
HELD, ON APPEAL: It could not be mechanically propelled. A motor car is designed so that it has only a mechanical means of propulsion and would

therefore be classified whether in working order or not as a mechanically propelled vehicle, but a dual-purpose machine may depend on its working condition and purpose of use. It was not at the material time a 'motor vehicle' and did not require third party insurance.

It was an exceptional case not to be extended beyond its particular facts.

Floyd v Bush
[1953] 1 All ER 265, [1953] 1 WLR 242, 117 JP 88, 97 Sol Jo 80, 51 LGR 162, [1953] 1 Lloyd's Rep 64, Div Ct
A pedal cycle with an auxiliary motor the engine of which is in working order is a mechanically propelled vehicle within s 1 of the 1930 Act although the driver pedals the cycle without using the engine, and requires an insurance policy; distinguishing *Lawrence v Howlett* where the engine had been dismantled. *Shimmell v Fisher* [1951] 2 All ER 672, 115 JP 526, [1951] 2 TLR 753, 95 Sol Jo 625, 49 LGR 813, 35 Cr App Rep 100 followed.

R v Tahsin
[1970] RTR 88, Div Ct
The defendant was riding a moped by using the pedals as on an ordinary bicycle. The engine was not working and he said a temporary defect had prevented him from starting it.
HELD: Even if a moped was to be treated as falling within a different class from that of cars and lorries a temporary defect which prevented the engine from being started did not exclude it from being a 'mechanically propelled vehicle' within the meaning of the Road Traffic Act 1960, s 253(1) and therefore a 'motor vehicle' for the purposes of the 1960 Act. *Floyd v Bush* applied; *Lawrence v Howlett* distinguished.

Note—Section 253(1) of the 1960 Act was in the same terms as s 190(1) of the Road Traffic Act 1972

McEachran v Hurst
[1978] RTR 462, [1978] Crim LR 499, Div Ct
The defendant was riding a moped on a public road by pedalling it. The engine was not in working order and there was no petrol in the tank. The defendant had bought it for £5 and had never used the engine. He was taking it to a friend to be repaired.
HELD: Following *R v Tahsin* (above) the test is whether the vehicle is constructed so that it can be mechanically propelled, not whether it has an engine in working order at the relevant time. There must be a conviction.

Newberry v Simmonds
[1961] 2 QB 345, [1961] 2 All ER 318, [1961] 2 WLR 675, 125 JP 409, 105 Sol Jo 324, 59 LGR 309, Div Ct QBD
The respondent's car was parked on a public road for a month without a road fund licence in force. The outward appearance of the car was normal but at the material time it had no engine. A charge under the Vehicles (Excise) Act 1949, s 15 of using on a public road a mechanically propelled vehicle for which no licence under the Act was in force was dismissed by the justices on the ground that if there were no engine in the car it was not a mechanically propelled vehicle.
HELD: On a case stated, there must be a conviction. The words 'mechanically propelled vehicle' have the same meaning in the Vehicles (Excise)

Act 1949, as in the Road Traffic Act 1930, and the same decisions are relevant to both Acts. Following *Floyd v Bush* (above) and *Lawrence v Howlett* (above) a motor car does not cease to be a mechanically propelled vehicle on the mere removal of the engine if the evidence admits the possibility that the engine may shortly be replaced and the motive power restored.

Note—The Vehicles (Excise) Act 1949, s 15, is now replaced by the Vehicles (Excise) Act 1971, s 8. 'Mechanically propelled vehicle' is not defined in either Act.

Smart v Allan
[1963] 1 QB 291, [1962] 3 All ER 893, [1962] 3 WLR 1325, 127 JP 35, 106 Sol Jo 881, 60 LGR 548, Div Ct QBD
The defendant bought a Rover car for £2 for scrap and left it parked on a public highway. The engine was incomplete and did not work. It had no gearbox, one tyre was missing and the other flat; it had no battery and could be moved only by towing on two wheels. It could have been put in running order only at a cost out of all proportion to its value. It was not taxed or insured and the defendant was charged with using the car on the road within the meaning of the Road Traffic Act 1960, s 201 (now the Road Traffic Act 1972, s 143), when not insured.
HELD: Some limit must be put and some stage reached when one says of a vehicle, 'This is so immobile that it has ceased to be a mechanically propelled vehicle'. In the present case, unlike *Newberry v Simmonds* (above) there was no reasonable prospect of the vehicle ever being made mobile again. It had ceased to be 'a mechanically propelled vehicle' within the meaning of the Road Traffic Act 1960, s 253(1) (which was in the same terms as the Road Traffic Act 1972, s 190(1)), and was therefore not a 'motor vehicle' for the purposes of s 201.

McNeill v Ritchie
1967 SLT (Sh Ct) 68
The accused's car, parked on a public road, had the gear-box removed together with the overdrive and propeller shaft which he sold as scrap. It would have cost more to replace these parts than the car was worth. He had no intention of putting the car in running order and was hoping to find someone to buy it for spares. He was charged with using it without insurance and a test certificate. He contended it was not a 'motor vehicle' within the meaning of the Road Traffic Act 1960, s 253 (now s 190 of the 1972 Act).
HELD: The test was whether the car had reached the stage where there was no reasonable prospect of ever making it mobile again. The facts that it was uneconomic to restore the missing parts and that the accused was only keeping it for spares raised sufficient doubt as to remove the car from the class of 'mechanically propelled vehicles'.

Law v Thomas
(1964) 108 Sol Jo 158, 62 LGR 195, Div Ct
The defendant's car was left standing in the roadway for three months untaxed and uninsured. It could not be driven because of a defect which the defendant thought was a cracked cylinder block. When the car was inspected it was found that the fault was merely a blown core plug. When the plug was replaced the car was in working order. On a charge against the owner of using a vehicle on a road when uninsured contrary to s 201 (of the

1960 Act — now the Road Traffic Act 1972, s 143) the justices, having been referred to *Smart v Allan* (above) held that the car was not 'a mechanically propelled vehicle intended or adapted for use on the roads' and dismissed the charge.

HELD, ON APPEAL: *Smart v Allan* was an extreme case. In the present case the car could be made mobile in a matter of minutes. It was at all times a mechanically propelled vehicle which the owner was using on a road without the necessary insurance cover. There must be a conviction.

Note—Followed and applied in *Binks v Department of Environment* [1975] RTR 318 (an excise case).

Intended or adapted

Note—For 1972 Act section numbers, see, p 706, above.

Burns v Currell
[1963] 2 QB 433, [1963] 2 All ER 297, [1963] 2 WLR 1106, 127 JP 397, 107 Sol Jo 272, 61 LGR 356, Div Ct

The appellant drove a 'go-kart' on one occasion on a road to which the public had access. He was convicted by justices of unlawfully using a motor car contrary to the Road Traffic Act 1960, s 201 (now the Road Traffic Act 1972, s 143) and the Motor Vehicles (Construction and Use) Regulations 1955. The go-kart had a tubular frame on four small wheels, an engine, single seat and steering column. It had no horn, springs, parking brake, driving mirror or wings and had rear wheel brakes only. There was no policy of insurance in force.

HELD, ON APPEAL: The real question was whether the go-kart was a motor vehicle within the meaning of the Road Traffic Act 1960, s 253(1) (now the Road Traffic Act 1972, s 190(1)) ie 'a mechanically propelled vehicle intended or adapted for use on the roads'. 'Intended' does not mean intended by the manufacturer or retailer or by the user at the moment of the offence. The test is whether a reasonable person looking at the vehicle would say that one of its uses would be some general use on the road. There was no evidence before the justices to satisfy this test. 'Adapted' means 'fit and apt' for use on the road and the go-kart was not. Appeal allowed.

Chalgray Ltd v Apsley
(1965) 109 Sol Jo 394, Div Ct

The defendants were the owner and driver of a 15 cwt dumper. On a number of occasions it was driven along the pavement and roadway of a public highway for distances up to 100 yards for the purpose of carrying building materials for work being carried on at an adjoining building site. The defendants were charged with using a motor vehicle on a road when not covered by insurance contrary to the Road Traffic Act 1960, s 201.

HELD: On a case stated, the sole issue was whether the dumper was a motor vehicle within s 253(1). The present case fell within the ambit of those cases where there was only occasional use of the dumper on the highway as part of the construction plant. *Burns v Currell* (above) showed that the real test was whether some general use on the road was intended. The mere intention of the driver to use the plant on the highway could not without further evidence turn the dumper as a whole by way of general use into a motor vehicle. There was no evidence of that type of general use which would justify a conviction. There were many pieces of plant used for constructional work that were self-propelled and yet were not motor vehicles merely because they might, from time to time, emerge on the highway.

Note—Section 201 of the 1960 Act was effectively the same as s 143 of the Road Traffic Act 1972 set out at p 704, above.

Brown v Abbott
(1965) 109 Sol Jo 437, Div Ct
The defendant steered along a road a Ford car which was being towed by another car. He was charged with using the Ford on a road whilst uninsured. The Ford had been adapted for racing by substitution of a different engine, removal of front and rear passenger seats and replacement of glass by perspex. There was no silencer and no number plates; the lights did not operate and the battery and propeller shaft had been removed. The justices, applying *Burns v Currell* (above), held that it was not 'intended or adapted for use on roads' and thus not within s 201 (now the Road Traffic Act 1972, s 143).
HELD, on a case stated: The justices' decision should stand.

Per Lord Parker CJ: Counsel for the prosecutor sought to say that, although the justices had applied the latest test in *Burns v Currell* they must have misdirected themselves. Although he might have come to a different conclusion if he had heard the case, and thought it was not a piece of building plant or equipment nor a go-kart, and it might well have been said that the vehicle still remained a vehicle for use on the road notwithstanding the alteration, that was not the test. It could not be said, bearing in mind the onus of proof on the prosecution, that the justices could not as a reasonable tribunal be satisfied that the car had not at the material time been intended or adapted for use on the roads.

Nichol v Leach
[1972] RTR 476, Div Ct
The defendants were prosecuted for using a motor vehicle on a road without insurance. The vehicle was a mini which the defendants had bought as scrap and had rebuilt for autocross racing, removing the windows, passenger seat and number plates and substituting a rev. counter for the speedometer. They towed it on public roads to a meeting, one defendant driving the towing vehicle and the other steering the mini. They contested the charge on the ground that the mini was not 'intended or adapted for use on roads' within s 253(1) of the 1960 Act (now s 190(1) of the Road Traffic Act 1972), since they had no intention of using it on roads nor had they adapted it for that purpose.
HELD: A car does not cease to be a vehicle intended for use on roads merely because its present owner sees no prospect of driving it on a road under its own power. The mini had retained its character as a motor car intended to run on roads and was within s 253(1).

Note—*Burns v Currell*, p 713, above, and *Brown v Abbott*, above, were not cited.

Local authority — s 144(2)(a)

R v Urmston UDC and Jones
(1953) Times, 29 July
An urban district council were summoned for permitting the use of an uninsured motor lorry and the driver for using the uninsured lorry. The lorry was drawing a trailer and the certificate of insurance did not cover the use of the lorry with a trailer. The Manchester county magistrates dismissed the summonses. Local authorities need not insure their motor vehicles when they were being driven by council employees in the course of their employment. The insurance of their vehicles by a local authority was quite voluntary.

Disabled vehicle

Police v Turton
(1953) *Post Magazine* 2 May, 488
A haulage contractor towed a lorry belonging to a friend to a garage. The towed lorry had had the engine removed and the tow was for a new engine to be fitted. The policy did not cover the drawing of a trailer other than a disabled mechanically propelled vehicle. He was prosecuted for having no effective insurance. The police relied on *Lawrence v Howlett* (p 710, above). Insurers gave evidence that they would regard the towed vehicle as being mechanically disabled and they would have accepted liability for an accident.

The magistrates (Holmfirth) convicted.

Note—See also *Elliott v Grey*, p 709, above.

Trailers attached

Leggate v Brown
[1950] 2 All ER 564, 114 JP 454 [1950] WN 379, 66 (Pt 2) TLR 281, 94 Sol Jo 567, 49 LGR 27, 84 Ll L Rep 395, Div Ct
The defendant's motor policy covered a tractor with an endorsement which enabled the tractor to be used with two trailers. The defendant used the tractor on a road towing two laden trailers. The Road Traffic Act 1930, s 18(1) (now replaced by s 65(1) of the 1972 Act without material amendment), makes it an offence for a tractor to draw two laden trailers. The defendant was prosecuted for driving uninsured, and the prosecution contended that as the defendant was using the tractor in an illegal manner, the policy was void because an indemnity against the consequences of an illegal act was void as being against public policy. The magistrates convicted the defendant.
HELD, ON APPEAL: The policy insured the defendant, as the Act required, against the consequences of the negligent driving of the tractor. It said nothing about laden trailers. It simply allowed the vehicle to be used with two trailers. If the policy had insured the defendant against using the tractor illegally, to that extent it would have been ineffective, but that had nothing to do with injury to third persons. The policy was an insurance

against the consequences of negligent driving of the vehicle, because a third party can only claim if there has been negligent driving. If there has been negligent driving, it does not matter whether there were two trailers or none. If the tractor was driven negligently, an injured person has a right to compensation, and this policy indemnified against negligent driving. Conviction quashed.

Kerridge v Rush
[1952] 2 Lloyd's Rep 305, Div Ct

The policy of insurance on an agricultural motor tractor excluded indemnity when the vehicle was drawing a greater number of trailers in all than permitted by law. The Road Traffic Act 1930, s 18(1) (now s 65(1) of the 1972 Act) provides that a motor tractor shall not draw on the highway more than one laden trailer or two if unladen. The tractor was drawing a four-wheel laden trailer and a tumbril, constructed and intended to be drawn by a horse, laden with a horse-hoe frame.

HELD: The tumbril was a trailer. The tractor was drawing a greater number of trailers than was permitted by law and was not insured.

BREACH OF STATUTORY DUTY TO INSURE

Note—In the case of *Monk v Warbey* it was held s 143 imposes a statutory duty similar to that recognised in the case of unfenced machinery in the decision of *Groves v Lord Wimborne* (1898) 2 QB 402, 67 LJQB 862, 79 LT 284, 14 TLR 493, 34 Dig 218. *Monk v Warbey* was followed in *Richards v Port of Manchester* (1934) 152 LT 413, 50 Ll L Rep 88, CA. If, therefore, the owner of a car insured owner-driver only permits another person to drive his car, and that person being so uninsured has not the means to meet a third-party claim the owner is liable for damages for personal injury sustained by a third party.

Monk v Warbey
[1935] 1 KB 75, 104 LJKB 153, 152 LT 194, 51 TLR 77, 78 Sol Jo 783, 50 Ll L Rep 33, CA

The owner of a motor car who in contravention of the Road Traffic Act 1930, s 35(1) (now replaced by s 143 of the 1972 Act), permits his car to be used by a person who is not insured against third-party risks is liable in damages to a third party who has been injured by the negligent driving of the uninsured person. In such a case the object and purview of the Act show that the penalties prescribed by s 35(2) were not intended to be the sole remedy for the breach of the owner's statutory duty. Where a person uninsured against third-party risks is permitted by the owner to use a car, and injury is caused by his negligent driving to a third party the latter may, where the uninsured person is without means, sue the owner of the car directly for damages for breach of statutory duty and need not first sue the uninsured person.

Gregory v Ford
[1951] 1 All ER 121 (Byrne J)

A lorry owned by the first defendant was driven by their servant, the second defendant, and injured the plaintiff, a motor cyclist. The plaintiff obtained judgment against both defendants.

The lorry at the time was uninsured. The first defendant claimed indemnity from the second defendant on the ground of his negligence. The second defendant claimed indemnity from the first defendant on the ground that it was an implied term of the employment that the servant should not be required to do an unlawful act.

The judge referred to the observation of Singleton J in *Blows v Chapman* [1947] 2 All ER 576, 112 JP 8, 63 TLR 575, 46 LGR 13 Div Ct: 'It is not, I think, the duty of a workman to ask his employer each day, is this vehicle insured.'

HELD: The second defendant was entitled to indemnity from the first defendant on this ground. The first defendant was not entitled to indemnity from the second defendant because, although the servant was negligent, it was owing to the breach of statutory duty of the first defendant that the damages fell upon him.

Lister v Romford Ice and Cold Storage Ltd Co
[1957] AC 555, [1957] 1 All ER 125, [1957] 2 WLR 158, 121 JP 98, 101 Sol Jo 106, [1956] 2 Lloyd's Rep 505, HL

Per Lord Morton of Henryton, speaking of *Gregory v Ford*: I agree that it was an implied term of the employment that the servant should not be required to do an unlawful act but there is no implied term that the driver is entitled to be personally indemnified by a policy.

Note—For references see p 176, above.

Implied indemnity

Road Transport and General Insurance Co v Adams; Irwin (third party)
[1955] Crim LR 377

The defendant had hired a car from the third party and had asked whether it was insured, to which the third party answered in the affirmative. In fact the car was not covered if the defendant drove it. After a collision, he was convicted of driving uninsured. In the present action the plaintiffs obtained judgment against both the defendant and the third party for the amount expended by the insurers in settling claims arising from the accident. The defendant claimed indemnity from the third party who pleaded that as the damages the defendant had had to pay arose out of a crime the court should not grant relief.

HELD: The defendant was entitled to be indemnified by the third party, as he had been led by him to believe in the existence of a fact, which, if it had been true, would have been an answer to any imputation of illegality (applying *Burrows v Rhodes* [1899] 1 QB 816, 68 LJQB 545, 80 LT 591, 63 JP 532, 48 WR 13, 15 TLR 286).

Policy avoided

Goodbarne v Buck

[1940] 1 KB 771, [1940] 1 All ER 613, 109 LJKB 837, 162 LT 259, 56 TLR 433, 84 Sol Jo 380, CA
The fact that a policy is avoided by insurers does not bring into operation the principle of *Monk v Warbey*.

Motor Insurers' Bureau not a defence

Corfield v Groves

[1950] 1 All ER 488, [1950] WN 116, 66 (Pt 1) TLR 627, 94 Sol Jo 225 (Hilbery J)
A third party was fatally injured by an uninsured car. The driver was not the servant or agent of the owner. The administratrix, who was the widow and the only dependant, sued the driver for negligence and the owner for breach of statutory duty under *Monk v Warbey*, alleging that the driver was without means to satisfy any judgment against him. A witness from the Motor Insurers' Bureau expressed the opinion that under the Motor Insurers' Bureau agreement the Bureau would satisfy any judgment against the driver. The owner pleaded that as the Bureau would pay the damages, the plaintiff would suffer no loss by reason of the lack of means of the driver or her breach of statutory duty. The driver was found guilty of negligence.
HELD: The breach of statutory duty was a continuing breach operative at the time of the accident (the time of the tortious act), and the cause of action arose at the moment of the tortious act. On the death the widow's right of action under the Fatal Accidents Acts immediately accrued and an enforceable claim against the owner for any damages which she then sustained by reason of the breach of statutory duty which existed at the time of the tortious act. The damage accrued because at the time the driver was uninsured and financially nothing was obtainable from him even by bankruptcy proceedings. Greer LJ in *Monk v Warbey* pointed out that it does not matter, even if it were the fact, that at the time of the tort her damages could not be quantified. In theory, of course, her damages are quantified as on the day of the accruing of her complete cause of action. If the judgment was satisfied by the Bureau, no difficulty arises, because the damages cannot be taken twice by the plaintiff. Judgment against both defendants.

Note—Apparently the point dealt with in *Fleming v McGillivray*, below, was not taken.

Fleming v McGillivray

1945 SLT 301 (Lord Mackintosh)
An action under *Monk v Warbey* is not competent against the owner of the car until it is known that the wrongdoer cannot pay and there is no effective policy. It must be established—
  1 that the driver could not pay; and
  2 that the insurers could not be made to pay.

Note—See also *Martin v Dean*, below.

Damage not result of breach

Daniels v Vaux
[1938] 2 KB 203, [1938] 2 All ER 271, 107 LJKB 494, 159 LT 459, 54 TLR
621, 82 Sol Jo 335 (Humphreys J)
Defendant bought car and allowed her son to use it, though not insured.
About 21 June 1934, plaintiff injured. On 29 December 1936, the son died.
No action had then been commenced. The son had substantial means.
HELD: (1) The son was not servant or agent; (2) the defendant was guilty
of breach of statutory duty; (3) no legal damage from breach. The damage
was due to the delay in commencing the action and not to the defendant's
breach of her duty to insure.

Note—The limitation in the Law Reform (MP) Act 1934, that an action is not
maintainable unless the cause of action arose not earlier than six months before the
death was repealed by the Law Reform (Limitation of Actions & c.) Act 1954, s 4.

Driver unable to meet judgment

Martin v Dean
[1971] 2 QB 208, [1971] 3 All ER 279, [1971] 2 WLR 1159, 115 Sol Jo 369,
[1971] RTR 280 (John Stephenson J)
Dean lent his motor cycle to Kirby, who was not insured for riding it. The
plaintiff was knocked down and injured as a result of Kirby's negligence.
He sued both Kirby and Dean, alleging against the latter a breach of s 201
of the 1960 Act. He alleged he had suffered loss by the breach in that Kirby
might be impecunious and unable to satisfy a judgment promptly or at all.
Kirby was a single man, a bus driver earning £23 per week, and had no
savings.
HELD: The plaintiff had to show not only that Dean had committed a
breach of s 201 but that the breach had caused him loss. It was right that the
plaintiff should sue both defendants in the same action so that the rights of
the defendants *inter se* could be disposed of but if it was shown that the
borrowing driver could pay in full there would be no liability on the owner
except for nominal damages. If the borrowing driver could pay some of the
damages the lending owner could be liable only for the remainder. The
question was how much the borrower could pay, not over a long period or
after being made bankrupt, but within a few weeks of judgment. In the
present case the amount Kirby could pay was minimal and there should be
judgment against both defendants for the whole sum awarded.

Note—Section 201 was in the same terms as s 143 of the 1972 Act.

DRIVER: WHETHER POLICY EFFECTIVE

Servant driving

Sutch v Burns
[1943] 2 All ER 441, 60 TLR 1, 87 Sol Jo 406, 76 Ll L Rep 203
(Atkinson J)
A lorry driver delivered goods to a customer. The customer asked the

driver to carry some goods of the customer across the road to another branch of the customer's works. The driver agreed. The customer's goods were loaded on to the lorry, and the customer's workmen got on the lorry. The driver turned to the left where the road was wide enough to turn. In turning, some goods were dislodged and knocked one of the workmen off the lorry, and he was killed. The widow brought proceedings against the lorry owner and the driver, and obtained judgment against the driver but not the owner. The widow sued insurers under s 10 of the 1934 Act (now the Road Traffic Act 1972, s 149).

Insurers conceded that the policy was to be treated as one which complied with s 35(1) of the 1930 Act. It was admitted that deceased was a passenger by reason of or in pursuance of a contract of service with the customer. Insurers contended that the legal obligation of the section only arose where there was liability of the policy holder, and that the driver was only indemnified where his employer was liable. The third party contended that the policy must cover any permitted driver and that there was no limitation on the use of the vehicle.

HELD: The section did not limit user by a permitted driver to the authority given by the employer. The policy must insure against any liability incurred by the driver to third parties. A person giving permission must insure against all claims of third parties arising out of the user on a road. A policy which purported to insure the employer or the driver to a less extent did not comply with the Act.

Note—In the Court of Appeal the judgment was set aside on the ground that a decision had been sought on a hypothetical policy and a court had no jurisdiction to do this.

The Divisional Court disagreed with the decision of Atkinson J in the following case.

John T. Ellis Ltd v Hinds
[1947] KB 475, [1947] 1 All ER 337, [1947] LJR 488, 176 LT 424, 63 TLR 181, 91 Sol Jo 68, 45 LGR 118, 80 Ll L Rep 231, Div Ct

A company owned a motor vehicle which was driven by a lad of 17 who was not himself entitled to be treated as insured under the policy. The facts are set out at p 836, below.

HELD: The company was not in breach of the section. The section refers to the use of the vehicle and says nothing about driving. The statute uses the word 'Drive' in ss 5, 9 and 15.

If the car is being driven by a servant on the employer's business so that the owner is liable to a third person, and the liability of the owner is covered by insurance, there is in force in relation to the user of the vehicle whether by the owner or driver a policy of insurance.

We cannot agree with the decision of *Sutch v Burns*. An owner is bound to take out a policy which covers the user of the vehicle by his servant but only whilst on his business. If a servant is driving without authority, his master has not caused or permitted the use of the vehicle. The owner of a car is not bound to cover the liability of his chauffeur on a 'joy ride', or in circumstances which absolve the master from liability. There was no obligation on the facts in *Sutch v Burns* for the employer of the driver to have a policy which would cover the driver when he was not driving on the employer's business.

Note—In *Sutch v Burns* in the Court of Appeal the case was argued on its merits, and the court took time to consider its verdict. Meanwhile the case of *Sun Life Assurance of Canada v Jervis* [1944] AC 111 had been decided in the House of Lords, and in consequence of that decision, it became unnecessary to deal with the arguments.

It was pointed out in argument that if, e g an owner of a motor car insured for pleasure purposes but not for carriage of goods, lent his car to a friend for pleasure use, and the friend used it for the carriage of goods, this could not mean that insurers were liable under the policy, nor that the owner was liable on the principle of *Monk v Warbey*.

The point has now been settled by *Ellis v Hinds*, above.

Lees v Motor Insurers' Bureau

[1952] 2 All ER 511, [1952] WN 409, [1952] 2 TLR 356, 96 Sol Jo 548, [1952] Lloyd's Rep 210 (Lord Goddard CJ)

The owner of a motor lorry had a policy which indemnified him but did not indemnify the driver personally. The policy excluded liability where the accident to the third party arose out of and in the course of his employment by the owner. On 5 May 1948, a servant of the owner was killed by the negligence of the driver in an accident which arose out of and in the course of the employment of the deceased by the owner. The widow sued the driver and obtained a judgment by default against him. She then sued the Motor Insurers' Bureau contending that the judgment was in respect of a liability required to be covered by s 35(1) and s 36(1)(b) of the 1930 Act (now s 143(1) and s 145(3)(a) of the 1972 Act), being a liability incurred by the driver caused by the use by the driver of a vehicle on a road; that the Act required the policy to cover the driver personally and that the Bureau had incurred a liability to satisfy the judgment under the terms of the agreement.

HELD: On a special case stated by an arbitrator, the contention that the policy was required to insure the driver personally is exactly what was held in *Sutch v Burns* which was overruled in *John T. Ellis Ltd v Hinds*. Section 35(1) required a person to insure because he is the owner, the person who uses or permits the use. What has to be covered is the use of the vehicle not the person using the vehicle. *Ellis v Hinds* (above) and *Marsh v Moores* (p 722, below). In *Richards v Cox* [1943] 1 KB 139, [1942] 2 All ER 624, 112 LJKB 135, 168 LT 313, 59 TLR 123, 87 Sol Jo 92, CA following *Digby*'s case (p 860, below) there were in effect two policies in one document, a policy insuring the owner and a policy insuring the driver. There was no such term in this policy. The policy complied with the Act and covered all the persons whom the Act required to be covered. It excluded employees of the insured in cases arising out of and in the course of the employment, and underwriters are entitled to exclude that liability under the Act. A policy had been taken out by the owner to cover the use of the vehicle and therefore the vehicle was an insured vehicle and the liability which was incurred was not one which was required to be covered by insurance. The respondents were under no liability to the claimant.

Note—The accident occurred before the abolition of common employment on 5 July 1948. After that date a third party would presumably sue the employers without reference to a motor policy or to the Bureau.

Driver retaining control when teaching

Marsh v Moores

[1949] 2 KB 208, [1949] 2 All ER 27, [1949] LJR 1313, 113 JP 346, 65
TLR 318, 93 Sol Jo 450, 47 LGR 418, Div Ct

A policy issued to a limited company covered the company against third-party risks for social, domestic and business purposes. There was an exception from liability if the car with the company's consent was being driven by a person who to the knowledge of the company was a disqualified person or had never been licensed. A servant of the company who was the son of the managing director on the latter's instructions was making a journey in the car. As a servant of the company he was entrusted by the company with the control, driving and management of the vehicle. He had as passenger his cousin, a girl of 17 who to the son's knowledge had not and never had had a licence. The son allowed the cousin to take over the wheel, whilst he himself retained control of the hand-brake.

HELD: There was an effective policy. The test whether the car was being used uninsured was not whether the son or cousin was insured in respect of his or her personal liability, but whether the company would have been liable to a third party. The son still remained the driver; in allowing his cousin to take the wheel he was still acting within the scope of his employment although in an unauthorised and improper way, and the company would have been liable to a third party. The only person driving with the general consent of the company was the son, who held a licence; the cousin was not driving with the company's consent or knowledge. The policy complied with the requirements of s 35(1) (s 143(1) of the 1972 Act), which does not require a policy covering the driver's personal liability. *Ellis v Hinds* followed.

Langman v Valentine

[1952] 2 All ER 803, 116 JP 576, [1952] WN 475, [1952] 2 TLR 731, 96 Sol
Jo 712, 50 LGR 685, Div Ct

The owner of a motor car had a policy which covered him and also any person driving with his permission who had or had held and was not disqualified from holding a licence. The owner was teaching a passenger to drive on a road. The passenger had not and had never had a licence. The passenger was sitting in the driver's seat and was steering the car under the guidance of the owner and using the accelerator and the footbrake. The owner was in the passenger's seat with his left hand on the steering wheel and his right hand on the handbrake. He was able to steer the car, stop it and start it, the ignition switch being within his reach and the hand-brake under his control. The passenger was summoned for using a motor car uninsured and for driving without a licence. The owner was summoned for permitting the former and abetting the latter. The justices held the owner was the driver and dismissed the summonses.

HELD, ON APPEAL, Lord Goddard CJ and Finnemore J: (1) The passenger was a driver and should have been convicted for driving without a licence; (2) there was no evidence that the owner knew the passenger did not have a licence; (3) though not 'the driver' the owner was 'a driver' and an injured person could have brought an action against him and he would have been liable as a driver and there was therefore an effective policy. There could be two drivers at the same time.

Per McNair J dissenting: The passenger was a user of the car and there was no effective policy in relation to her.

Ellis v Hinds and *Marsh v Moores* followed.

Note—The case of *Rubie v Faulkner* (p 70, above) is not mentioned in the reports, nor *Sampson v Aitchison* (p 179, above).

Evans v Walkden

[1956] 3 All ER 64, [1956] 1 WLR 1019, 120 JP 495, 100 Sol Jo 587, 54 LGR 467, Div Ct

A son 15 years old and therefore unlicensed was in the driving seat and his father was seated with him. The car was being driven in bottom gear at not more than 4 or 5 mph for a total distance of about 200 yards. The father was in a position to control the driving of the son and was doing so and could have stopped the car immediately. The steering wheel was within the father's reach and also the brake and clutch pedals, the ignition key and the gear handle on the steering wheel. The handbrake was on the right-hand side of the driver and was not accessible to the father. The father's policy excluded liability whilst driven by an unlicensed driver. The justices found that the father was at the same time a driver of the car and dismissed summonses against the son and father for driving without insurance and for permitting respectively.

HELD: There was no evidence to support the finding that the father was in control of the car or that he was a driver of the car. The insurance policy permitted use for tuition provided — 'There shall be present in the insured car as a tutor a person under whose supervision the holder of a provisional licence would be entitled to drive.' This did not affect the exclusion of liability if driven by an unlicensed driver. *Langman v Valentine* (above) distinguished. Case remitted to justices to convict.

Tyler v Whatmore

[1976] RTR 83, [1976] Crim LR 315, Div Ct

The defendant was charged with 'actually driving a motor vehicle' when in such a position that she could not have proper control. She was sitting beside a man who was in the driving seat operating the pedals. She had both hands on the steering wheel; he made no attempt to steer and his hands were not on the wheel.

HELD: Following *Langman v Valentine* (above) she was 'driving'. It was a question of fact. Both were driving, since he was able to control the propulsion and she was controlling the steering.

Note—See also *R v Wilkins*, p 838, below.

Paid driver

Bryan v Forrow

[1950] 1 All ER 294, 114 JP 158, 48 LGR 347, sub nom *Forrow v Bryan* [1950] WN 91, 94 Sol Jo 194, Div Ct

The owner of a motor lorry was insured by a cover note, under which the person or persons allowed to drive were—

1 the above-named proposer only;
2 the above-named proposer or his paid driver;
3 the above-named proposer or his paid employee or any friend or relative of the proposer driving with his unremunerated permission provided such person holds a licence to drive such motor vehicle or has held and is not disqualified by order of a court of law from holding or obtaining such licence.

The lorry owner contracted with a customer to transport goods of the customer. The lorry owner was ill and arranged for the lorry to be driven by a driver in the regular employ of the customer.

The owner was prosecuted for permitting the use of the lorry without an effective policy of insurance. It was contended that the customer's driver was not the paid driver of the owner.

HELD: The contrast was between the professional and the non-professional driver — the paid driver and the paid employee. The words 'paid driver' are capable of two constructions, (1) the driver paid by the owner; (2) a driver driving for the owner who is a paid driver. The latter construction is right and the cover note was effective to cover third-party risks and insurers would be liable under it.

Disqualified driver

Saycell v Bool
[1948] 2 All ER 83, 112 JP 341, 64 TLR 421, 92 Sol Jo 311, 46 LGR 447, Div Ct
Respondent was the owner of a motor van and was disqualified from holding a licence. The van was standing in a road outside his premises which was on an incline. His garage was 100 yards lower down. He pushed the van down the incline and when in motion, got into the driving seat and steered it towards the garage. There was no petrol in the tank and the engine was not running.
HELD: Respondent was 'driving' the van, and being disqualified, there was no third party insurance in force.

Note—And see *Floyd v Bush*, p 710, above. See also *R v MacDonagh* and *Blayney v Knight*, pp 838, 839 below.

Driver not in employ

Lyons v May
[1948] 2 All ER 1062, 113 JP 42, [1948] WN 483, 65 TLR 51, 93 Sol Jo 59, Div Ct
A garage proprietor who had repaired a motor lorry drove it at the owner's request to the owner's premises. The owner's policy covered only the owner or 'any duly authorised person in his employ'. The policy of the garage proprietor did not cover the risk. The justices held the garage proprietor was temporarily in the owner's employ for the purpose of delivering the lorry.
HELD: (1) The garage proprietor was not in the owner's employment. (*Burton*'s case, p 833, below, is not mentioned in the report.) (2) The owner had given 'permission'. He had not asked the garage proprietor if he had an effective policy.

Ballance v Brown
[1955] Crim LR 384, [1955] CLY 2451, Div Ct
A policy provided that the company would 'treat as though he were the insured any person in the insured's employ who is driving such a vehicle on the insured's order or with his permission for the purpose of the business of the insured'. The insured, who from time to time bought scrap from the defendant, instructed him to take the insured's car to the defendant's house and to pick him up the next morning to go on a business trip; he also told him to do any business he could.
HELD: The car was insured while being driven by the defendant. *Lyons v May* (above) distinguished.

Tapsell v Maslen
(1966) 110 Sol Jo 853, [1967] Crim LR 53 Div Ct
The respondent allowed Williams to use his motor scooter when there was no policy of insurance in force. When he lent the scooter to Williams he honestly believed Williams had an insurance certificate. The justices dismissed a charge of permitting the use of the scooter when there was no policy in force.
HELD, ON APPEAL: The justices must convict. Section 201 (s 143 of the 1972 Act) was expressed in terms whereby all the prosecution had to do was to show first that permission to use had been given and next that there was no insurance cover. *Lyons v May* (above) and *Morris v Williams* (p 728, below) were binding authorities for this.

Named driver

Goodwin v Leckey
[1946] NI 40, (1946) LR Dig 118 (MacDermott J)
A taxi was insured under a policy which indemnified only when driven by the insured or two named drivers. A driver not named was driving with the permission of and in the course of the employment of the insured.
HELD: The policy was inoperative. A policy complies with the Northern Ireland Act although it does not cover any driver with permission. *Sutch v Burns* (p 719, above) not followed.

No heavy goods vehicle licence

Police v Hepper
[1978] CLY 2591, Knightsbridge Crown Ct
The defendant was charged with driving a heavy goods vehicle when not insured. There was a policy in force allowing any person to drive who 'holds a licence to drive the vehicle or has held and is not disqualified from holding or obtaining such a licence'. The defendant had held and was not disqualified from holding an ordinary driving licence but had never held a heavy goods vehicle licence.
HELD: The policy did not cover him.

Hired vehicle

Sands v O'Connell
[1981] RTR 42, QBD
The defendant was aged 20. Anticipating difficulty in hiring a car to drive whilst under 21 she induced a friend aged 23 to hire a car for her. He did so by a contract of hire which stipulated 'Drivers must be aged between 21 and 70 years'. He also completed a 'supplementary proposal form' for insurance declaring 'I am not under 21 or over 70 years of age', and that 'the above declaration applies also in respect of all persons who will drive'. The insurance policy covering the vehicle was issued to the company hiring out the vehicle and extended to indemnify any person driving the vehicle 'on the order or with the permission of the policyholder'. The friend lent the vehicle during the hire period to the defendant who drove it for herself. She was charged with driving whilst uninsured.
HELD: (1) The contract of hire by referring to 'drivers' authorised the friend to permit other persons to drive limited to those between 21 and 70; but (2) the defendant was not driving on the order or with the permission of the policyholder since she had no direct permission from them and the friend's authority was limited to drivers between 21 and 70; (3) though by an unusual indorsement the policy extended to treat a person driving the vehicle as if he or she was in the employment of the policyholder under a contract of service the defendant did not receive authority from the friend within the scope of his employment and such decisions as *Marsh v Moores* (p 722, above) were not applicable. Her appeal against conviction was dismissed.

Crown servant — private use

Salt v MacKnight
1947 JC 99, 1947 SLT 327, High Ct of Justiciary
The Road Traffic Act 1930, s 121(2) (which provides that Parts I and III of the Act shall apply to the Crown) is no warrant for the suggestion that Part III of the Act (in which falls s 35) does not apply to servants of the Crown irrespective of what they are doing nor to Crown vehicles irrespective of the purpose for which they are being used, and consequently a departmental official who is using a Crown vehicle for his own business is not immune from prosecution under s 35 (which requires a third-party insurance to be in force).

Note—The equivalent provision to s 121(2) in the 1972 Act is s 188(1):

'**188 Application to Crown**   (1) Subject to the provisions of this section—
(a)   Part I of this Act,
(b)   Part II of this Act, except ss 56, 57, 58, 59 and 61,
(c)   Part III of this Act, except s 100,
(d)   Part IV of this Act, and
(e)   in this Part, ss 159, 160, 161, 164, 165, 174, 175 and 179,
shall apply to vehicles and persons in the public service of the Crown.'

Sections 143 and 144 of the 1972 Act which contain equivalent provisions to s 35 of the 1930 Act are in Part VI of the Act.

CAUSE OR PERMIT

Note—For s 35(1) of the 1930 Act see now the Road Traffic Act 1972, s 143(1), p 704, above.

McLeod v Buchanan
[1940] 2 All ER 179, 84 Sol Jo 452, 1940 SC (HL) 17, 1940 SN 20, 1940 SLT 232, HL

A solicitor owned a poultry farm which was managed by his brother. A private car owned by the solicitor was registered and insured in the name of the brother for private and business use of the brother. The solicitor knew that his brother used the car for his private purposes. This car was replaced by a van which was registered and insured in the name of the solicitor for commercial use only. The certificate was sent from the solicitor's office to the brother without any comment, and the brother did not notice that it was limited to commercial use. The solicitor never gave the brother any permission to use the van for private purposes and did not know of this use, nor did he tell the brother that the insurance was restricted or make any conditions as to the use of the van. The brother used it for private purposes. HELD: The solicitor had permitted the brother to use an uninsured vehicle and was liable on the principle of *Monk v Warbey*.

Per Lord Wright: To 'cause' involves some express or positive mandate, or some authority. To 'permit' is a looser and vaguer term. It may denote an express permission, general or particular, as distinguished from a mandate. The other person is not told to use the vehicle in the particular way, but he is told that he may do so if he desires. It includes cases where permission is merely inferred. If the other person is given control of the vehicle, permission may be inferred if the vehicle is left at the other person's disposal in such circumstances as to carry with it a reasonable implication of a discretion or liberty to use it in the manner in which it was used.

In order to prove permission, it is not necessary to show knowledge of similar user in the past, or actual notice that the vehicle might be, or was likely to be, so used, or that the accused was guilty of a reckless disregard of the probabilities of the case, or a wilful closing of his eyes. He may not have thought of his duties under the section. The sending of the insurance certificate without any further intimation was not sufficient notice to his brother of the change. . . . In my opinion the necessary permission is established.

Watkins v O'Shaughnessy
[1939] 1 All ER 385, 161 LT 144, 83 Sol Jo 215, CA

At a public auction held by the second defendants, the first defendant bought a motor car. He drove it away, although, to the knowledge of the servants of the second defendants, the car was uninsured and unlicensed. In fact, the servants of the second defendant lent the first defendant the company's trade number plates for the purpose, and supplied him with a slip, referring to a different car, but altered by them to appear to refer to the car in question, and assured him that such a proceeding was quite in order. The plaintiff was injured by the alleged negligent driving of the first defendant, but, as a judgment against him would be useless, the plaintiff did not ask for judgment against him, but did ask for judgment against the second defendants, alleging that they had caused or permitted the first defendant to use a motor vehicle in respect of which there was not in existence a policy of insurance in accordance with the Road Traffic Act 1930, s 35.

HELD: As the sale had been completed before the driving of the car by the first defendant, the second defendants had no control over him, and could not, therefore, be said to have 'caused or permitted' him to drive, and, in any event, the acts of the servants of the second defendant were quite unauthorised by them.

For A to permit B to do anything, the relation between A and B must be such that it is not open for B lawfully to do the thing in question without such permission. It must be open for A to withhold that permission without which B cannot lawfully do the thing in question. Permission to do that thing must be necessary for the thing's performance.

Goodbarne v Buck

[1940] 1 KB 771, [1940] 1 All ER 613, 109 LJKB 837, 162 LT 259, 56 TLR 433, 84 Sol Jo 380, CA

Cause or permit are two different verbs. To make a person liable for 'permitting' another person to use, he must be in a position to forbid the other person to use the vehicle, ie where he is the owner of the car. The fact that one person assisted another to get a worthless piece of paper in place of an effective policy, did not 'cause' him to use the vehicle on the road without an effective policy.

Note—See also *Thompson v Lodwick* p 71, above.

Lloyd v Singleton

[1953] 1 QB 357, [1953] 1 All ER 291, [1953] 2 WLR 278, 117 JP 97, 97 Sol Jo 98, 51 LGR 165, Div Ct

A company owned a motor car which was insured in the name of the managing director of the company and covered persons who had his permission to drive. The respondent, the assistant general manager of the company, had full discretion himself to use the vehicle for his work or to allow other employees of the company to use it in the course of the company's business. The respondent permitted his brother, who was not an employee of the company, to drive, and was charged with permitting the use without insurance. The justices dismissed the charge on the dictum of MacKinnon LJ in *Goodbarne v Buck* (above).

HELD: The part of that judgment which stated that the person permitting must be in a position to forbid the other person to use, followed. The court was unable to agree with the further statement that the only person who could forbid was the owner, which must have been *per incuriam*.

Morris v Williams

(1951) 50 LGR 308, Div Ct

A company owned four vehicles, one of which was a van which was uninsured. The manager of the company instructed an employee to go by car. The employee used the van. The manager was summoned for permitting a vehicle to be used when uninsured. The magistrates convicted.

HELD, ON APPEAL: The employee was permitted by the manager to use the van. There was implied, if not express, authorisation. Conviction upheld.

Note—See also *Kelly v Cornhill Insurance Co Ltd*, p 834, below.

Newbury v Davis
(1974) 118 Sol Jo 222, [1974] RTR 367, Div Ct
The defendant gave permission to Jarvis to borrow his car and use it provided he insured it. Jarvis failed to insure it and was convicted of using the car without insurance. The defendant was charged with 'permitting' Jarvis to use the car uninsured.
HELD: He was not guilty. Permission given subject to a condition which is unfulfilled is no permission at all.

Baugh v Crago
[1975] RTR 453, [1976] 1 Lloyd's Rep 563, Div Ct
The policy of insurance covering the defendant's vehicle was effective only when the driver held a driving licence. He allowed a man to drive who had no licence, though he thought he had.
HELD: The defendant was guilty of a breach of the Road Traffic Act 1972, s 143. It was not the same as in *Newbury v Davis* (above). A distinction must be drawn between a case where the owner of a car grants permission to another to drive believing that the other is covered by insurance when he is not and a case where a person allows another to drive making it a condition that he shall not drive unless and until he is covered by insurance.

Clydebank Co-op Society v Binnie
1937 JC 17
A business firm kept cars for hire. A customer hired a car for 13s and arranged with five friends to pay 2s 6d each. Defendant's manager knew other passengers were to be carried, but did not know of the separate payments. The passengers were joining together to make frequent journeys, picked up at different places. Defendants were put on their guard and had a duty to enquire.
HELD: Defendants guilty of 'permitting'.

Churchill v Norris
(1938) 158 LT 255, 82 Sol Jo 114, 31 Cox CC 1
Defendant told his driver not to drive with too heavy a load, put instructions in the cabin of his vehicle, and instructed driver if in doubt to weigh the laden vehicle. Defendant knew the weight of timber was by custom measured in a rough and ready way by size, which might be erroneous. He had not ordered his servants specifically never to start a journey without weighing. Having knowledge of the prevailing method, he had connived at conduct which might well lead to commission of the offence, and had therefore 'permitted'. 'Permit' may mean no more than a failure to take proper steps to prevent.

Sidcup Building Estates Ltd v Sidery
(1936) 24 Ry & Can Tr Cas 164
Defendants had threatened drivers with instant dismissal if they worked more than the legal number of hours. They did not dismiss a driver who disobeyed.
HELD: Guilty of 'permitting'.

Note—And see *Cox & Son Ltd v Sidery* (1935) 24 Ry & Can Tr Cas 69.

Grays Haulage Co Ltd v Arnold
[1966] 1 All ER 896, [1966] 1 WLR 534, 130 JP 196, 110 Sol Jo 122, Div Ct
The defendants were convicted by magistrates of 'permitting' their driver to drive for continuous periods amounting in the aggregate to more than 11 hours contrary to the Road Traffic Act 1960, s 73. He had driven their vehicle from Carlisle to London from 10 am to 10.30 pm with only one hour's rest. They had failed to take steps which would or might have prevented the driver doing as he did such as providing a recorder on the vehicle or making arrangements for the driver to telephone them during the journey by reversing the charges.
HELD, ON APPEAL to the Divisional Court: This was not 'permitting'. In *James & Son Ltd v Smee* (p 732, below) it had been pointed out that knowledge is of two kinds, actual knowledge, and knowledge which consists of shutting one's eyes to the obvious, that is, failing to do something or doing something not caring whether contravention takes place or not. Here there was no question of actual knowledge nor was it a case of shutting one's eyes to the obvious. There was no evidence that the defendants had any knowledge of circumstances which they had allowed to go on without caring whether an offence had been committed or not. Knowledge is not imputed by mere negligence. Conviction quashed.

Fransman v Sexton
[1965] Crim LR 556, Div Ct QBD
The defendant, who operated a self-drive car hire service, was held not guilty of 'permitting' the use of a car with an inadequate braking system where one of the rear brakes was defective and did not work but where new parts had been provided about a year before and the defendant did not know the brake was inoperative. Knowledge is an essential element in 'permitting' something. It is not to be imputed by mere negligence, but by something more, such as recklessly sending out a car not caring what would happen.

Goldsmith v Deakin
(1933) 150 LT 157, 98 JP 4, [1933] WN 255, 50 TLR 73, 31 LGR 420, 30 Cox CC 32.
The dictionary definition of 'to permit' is to give leave to; allow; to afford means. The offence of 'permitting user' arises where, to quote the words of Lawrence J: 'Although the respondent may not have known affirmatively the way in which the vehicle was being used, if in fact he allowed it to be used, and did not care whether it was being used in contravention of the

statute or not, he did, in my view, permit its use under Road Traffic Act 1930.'

Distinguished in next case.

Evans v Dell
[1937] 1 All ER 349, 156 LT 240, 101 JP 149, 53 TLR 310, 81 Sol Jo 100, 35 LGR 105, Div Ct

A vehicle was hired by the organisers of a dance to take persons attending the dance from A to C. This intention had been advertised in a newspaper without the respondent's knowledge. At the dance it was announced that passengers must take tickets and contribute not less than sixpence. A number bought tickets which were collected in the coach. Neither the respondent nor his driver knew of the payments.

HELD: That as the respondent had no knowledge of the advertisement or the payments, and had not deliberately shut his eyes to what was being done, he had not 'permitted'.

Per Goddard J: Mens rea is an essential ingredient in offences under the Road Traffic Acts.

Shave v Rosner
[1954] 2 QB 113, [1954] 2 All ER 280, [1954] 2 WLR 1057, 18 JP 364, 98 Sol Jo 355, Div Ct

A motor car repairer reshoed the brakes of a motor van and drove it to the owner, who drove the repairer back to his garage, testing the brakes himself. A little later the same day the owner was driving the van when a wheel came off and injured a pedestrian. The wheel came off because the repairer's servants had not properly fastened the hub nuts. The repairer was prosecuted for 'using or causing or permitting to be used' a vehicle 'causing or likely to cause danger to any person'.

HELD: In one sense it might be said the repairer 'caused' the van to be used by delivering it in a dangerous condition and the owner unwittingly using it. He did not 'use' it himself; he did not 'permit' because he could not give permission to the owner to use his own car. When 'causes or permits' are found in contrast, 'permits' means giving leave and licence to somebody to use the car, and 'causes' means ordering or directing someone to use it. The repairer had ceased to have control or dominion over the van, and had not caused its use, and was not criminally liable under the Regulations.

Note—70 LQR 453 points out that the words 'cause' and 'causation' have various meanings depending on the circumstances and that it is clear in a civil action for injuries to the passer-by the defendant would have been liable on the ground that he had caused the accident as it was his negligence which had caused the wheel to break off from the car.

Windle v Dunning & Son Ltd
[1968] 2 All ER 46, [1968] 1 WLR 552, 132 JP 264, 112 Sol Jo 196, 66 LGR 516, Div Ct

Lorries hired to the respondents but loaded by them were found by an inspector of weights and measures to be overloaded. The respondents were convicted of 'using' the lorries on a road carrying loads exceeding that

allowed by the Construction and Use Regulations, contrary to the Road
Traffic Act 1960, s 64(2) (now s 45 of the 1972 Act). The drivers were not
the respondents' servants but were hired with the lorries.

HELD, ON APPEAL: The respondents were not 'using' the lorries.

Per Lord Parker: 'Using' when used in connection with causing and
permitting has a restricted meaning. It certainly covers the driver; it may
also cover the driver's employer if he, the driver, is about his master's
business, but beyond that I find it very difficult to conceive that any other
person could be said to be using the vehicle as opposed to causing it to be
used.

Swan v MacNab

[1977] JC 57, High Ct of Justiciary

A vehicle driven by an employee was found to have a defective braking
system. His employers were charged with 'using' the vehicle when it did
not comply with the Road Traffic Act 1972, s 40(5). They contended that
they could not be convicted of 'using' but only of 'causing or permitting'
the use of the vehicle.

HELD: The offence of 'using' a vehicle could be committed both by the
driver of the vehicle and by the company on behalf of whom the vehicle was
being driven.

Note—See also *Carmichael & Sons Ltd v Cottle* (1971) 114 Sol Jo 867, [1971] RTR 11
and *Crawford v Haughton* [1972] 1 All ER 535, [1972] 1 WLR 572, 116 Sol Jo 125,
[1972] RTR 125. Also *Balfour Beatty v Grindey* [1975] RTR 156 and *Howard v G. T.
Jones & Co Ltd* [1975] RTR 150.

James & Son v Smee

[1955] 1 QB 78, [1954] 3 All ER 273, [1954] 3 WLR 631, 118 JP 536, 98
Sol Jo 771, 52 LGR 545, Div Ct

A motor lorry and trailer left the owner's premises with the brakes
complying with the regulations. At the premises of third parties, the driver
with a boy assistant, uncoupled the trailer to enable loading. After loading,
the driver left the boy to couple the trailer to the lorry. The boy failed to
connect the brakes of the trailer properly and the driver took no steps to
check the connections. The owners were prosecuted for 'permitting'.

HELD: They had not permitted; conviction quashed. The question should
be: 'Has the permitter authorised the very thing which happened?' If so, or
if he had more than a very shrewd idea of what would happen, then he
should be found guilty. If not, no case has been proved against him. A
permission to use it is not, unless more is proved, a permission to use in
contravention.

L. F. Dove Ltd v Tarvin

(1964) 108 Sol Jo 404, Div Ct

A firm of motor engineers lent one of their cars to a customer to use whilst
they were repairing his own. He drove it to London and as a result a charge
was brought against the motor engineers that they did unlawfully use the
car all the tyres of which were not maintained in safe condition contrary to
the Motor Vehicles (Construction and Use) Regulations 1955, reg 78. The

defendants contended that as they had parted with possession and control of the car to the customer for his use, they were not using it at the time of the offence.

HELD: The point was a good one. The defendant had not been charged with causing or permitting the use of the car. The word 'use' was found in many regulations and there was a clear distinction between 'use' for oneself by oneself or a servant or agent and causing or permitting someone not a servant or agent to use. Here the defendants had not used the car at the time of the offence.

ROAD

Definition

Note—'Road' is defined in s 196(1) of the Road Traffic Act 1972 as any highway and any other-road to which the public has access, and includes bridges over which a road passes.

The definition in the Road Traffic Act 1930, s 121 and s 257(1) of the 1960 Act was in similar terms.

Purves v Muir
1948 JC 122, 1948 SLT 529, 98 LJ 413, High Ct of Jus, Scot
A courtyard not on the same level as the adjoining road which could be used for turning or parking vehicles only and was not a means of vehicular communication and not a road in the ordinary sense, although the public had access to it, is not a 'road' within the meaning of the section.

Bugge v Taylor
[1941] 1 KB 198, 110 LJKB 710, 164 LT 312, 104 JP 467, 85 Sol Jo 82, 39 LGR 100, Div Ct
The forecourt of an hotel was the private property of the owners. It was about 60 feet long and varied in width from 20 feet to 10 feet and was bounded on the west side by an island public pavement but open to the street at both ends. There was no obstruction to prevent the public, on foot or vehicles, from going over the forecourt, or to separate it from the street, and the public used it without let or hindrance to reach the hotel and to cut the corner. On occasions, public service and other vehicles had been over and through it.

HELD: It was a road within the Act.

R v Shaw
[1974] RTR 225, [1974] Crim LR 672, CA
An alley 8 ft 6 in wide led to a path 10 feet wide. Together they joined two public roads, and though contained within council property, were used by pedestrians as a short cut between the two roads. The Council did not object to people using it in this way.

HELD: The evidence was quite sufficient to entitle the jury to make the finding that the public had access and that the alley and path were a 'road'.

O'Brien v Trafalgar Insurance Co
(1945) 109 JP 107, 61 TLR 225, 78 Ll L Rep 223, CA
A road in a fenced-in factory within a protected area is not a road within the
Road Traffic Act 1930, s 121(1). There was no access and it was not open
to the public.

R v Lynn
[1963] 1 QB 164, [1963] 3 All ER 659, [1963] 3 WLR 946, 128 JP 48, 107
Sol Jo 833, CCA
The appellant was charged with driving a vehicle on a road in a manner
dangerous contrary to the Road Traffic Act 1960, s 2(1) (now s 7(1) of the
1972 Act). The incident giving rise to the charge occurred in the Tuesday
Market Place, King's Lynn, which was laid out as a car park with herring-
bone markings.
HELD: The particular issue whether the place where the car was driven
was a road was essentially one of fact for the jury and they must have been
satisfied that the place was a road within the meaning of the Road Traffic
Act 1960. Appeal dismissed.

Harrison v Hill
1932 JC 13, Scot
A road was part of a farm and led only to the farmhouse, where it terminated. It had no other houses on it, and it was not maintained by any public
authority but by the farm tenant in terms of his lease. There was no gate at
the entrance to it, and no intimation that it was not open to the public; and
except at times in summer, when the farmer placed a pole across it to
prevent the straying of cattle, there was no obstacle to prevent the public
having access to it. The road was used by the public as an access to the
farm, and members of the public, not having business there also frequently
walked on it. They had, on several occasions, been turned off by the farmer
when there were growing crops in the adjoining fields.
HELD: The road was a road to which the public had access within the Road
Traffic Act 1930, s 121(1).

Note—See also p 736, below.

Harrison v Co-operative Insurance Co Ltd
(1968) 118 NLJ 910 (Hinchcliffe J)
The plaintiff was injured in a collision between his motor cycle and a car on
a private roadway within factory premises. The insurers of the car refused
to meet a judgment for damages the plaintiff obtained against the car driver
on the ground that the place was not a 'road' within the meaning of s 203.
The road was used by members of the general public as well as by vehicles
having no business at the factory to gain access to a weighbridge and to
avoid other congested highways. There had once been a 'private road' sign
at the entrance to the road but it had been removed a considerable time
before the date of the accident from causes unknown.
HELD: It was a question of fact whether the road was ' a highway . . . to
which the public had access'. The absence of the 'private road' sign

was important; the public had access to adjacent roads and in the absence of any prohibition express or implied or any obstruction would not have any reason to suppose that access to the particular road in question was restricted in any way. The plaintiff was entitled to succeed.

Note—Section 203 — see now the Road Traffic Act 1972, s 145.

R v Beaumont
[1964] Crim LR 665, CCA

B was charged with being in charge of a motor vehicle on a road when unfit to drive through drink. The road in question was an occupation road leading to a farm and to part of the farmer's land occupied by 200–250 caravans in one of which B lived. The road also led to a river and by leave of the farmer was used by anglers and picnickers. At the entrance to the road was a gate (always kept open), and two notices which read: 'Trespassers will be prosecuted' and '10 mph'. B contended there was not sufficient evidence that the road came within the definition in the Road Traffic Act 1960, s 257. The prosecution relied on the number of people using the road; the persons living in the caravans, their visitors, anglers, etc.
HELD: There was no evidence that the general public used the road. The Court was unable to accept the contention that where a particular class of persons uses a road the number of persons in the class makes the road one to which the public has access. *Harrison v Hill* (above) applied.

Thomas v Dando
[1951] 2 KB 620, [1951] 1 All ER 1010, 115 JP 344 [1951] 1 TLR 1067, 49 LGR 793, Div Ct

Respondent occupied a shop with a forecourt and unpaved area between the pavement and kerbstone of the highway and the garden attached to the shop. The forecourt and area were his private property. There was no physical interruption between the surface of the unpaved area and that of the road, but the only people who used the unpaved area were respondent's customers going to the shop. Respondent left his car unlighted at night on the unpaved area. He was prosecuted for having an unlighted vehicle on a road contrary to the Road Transport Lighting Act 1927, s 1(1).
HELD: The statement in *Harrison v Hill*, above, that the class of road in s 121 of the Road Traffic Act 1930 is wider than the class of public roads to which the public has access in virtue of a positive right belonging to the public, and flowing either from statute or from prescriptive user, was held by Lord Caldecote CJ in *Bugge v Taylor* (p 733, above) to be applicable to the definition of 'road' in the 1927 Act. This was not a 'road' within the 1927 Act. *Bugge v Taylor* distinguished.

Note—The Road Transport Lighting Act 1927, s 15 is now repealed and replaced by the Road Traffic Act 1972 which in s 196 defines 'road' as set out on p 733, above.

The cases of *Bugge v Taylor* and *Thomas v Dando* are decisions under the 1927 Act but, as mentioned in those cases, are applicable to the 1960 Act.

Note—The following quotations from the judgment in *Harrison v Hill* (p 734, above) were quoted by McNair J in the case of *Buchanan v Motor Insurers' Bureau*

[1955] 1 All ER 607, [1955] 1 WLR 488, 119 JP 227, [1954] 2 Lloyd's Rep 519.
He said that they seemed to him to give very clear guidance as to the proper way of
approaching the question.

Harrison v Hill
1932 JC 13, Scot
Per Lord Clyde: It is plain, from the terms of the definition, that the class of
road intended is wider than the class of public roads to which the public has
access in virtue of a positive right belonging to the public, and flowing
either from statute or from prescriptive user. A road may therefore be
within the definition (1) although it belongs to the class of private roads,
and (2) although all that can be said with regard to its availability to the
public is that the public 'has access' to it. I think that, when the statute
speaks of 'the Public' in this connection, what is meant is the public
generally, and not the special class of members of the public who have
occasion for business or social purposes to go to the farmhouse or to any
part of the farm itself; were it otherwise, the definition might just as well
have included all private roads as well as all public highways. I think also
that, when the statute speaks of the public having 'access' to the road, what
is meant is neither (at one extreme) that the public has a positive right of its
own to access, nor (at the other extreme) that there exists no physical
obstruction, of greater or less impenetrability, against physical access by
the public; but that the public actually and legally enjoys access to it. It is, I
think, a certain state of use or possession that is pointed to. There must be,
as matter of fact, walking or driving by the public on the road, and such
walking or driving must be lawfully performed — that is to say, must be
permitted or allowed, either expressly or implicitly, by the person to whom
the road belongs. I include in permission or allowance the state of matters
known in right of way cases as the tolerance of a proprietor.
  Per Lord Sands: In my view, any road may be regarded as a road to
which the public have access upon which members of the public are to be
found who have not obtained access either by overcoming a physical
obstruction or in defiance of prohibition express or implied.

Kreft v Rawcliffe
(1984) Times, 12 May, QBD
The defendant was charged with offences on a 'road' as defined in s 196(1).
The only evidence that members of the public had access to the road was
that of a farmer of the land on which the road ran, that in 55 years he had
seen members of the public on the land very rarely. A police constable
patrolling the road, merchants and postmen visiting the farms down the
road, the borough engineer realigning footpaths near the road and
customers to a wholesaler fronting the road were not members of the public
for the purposes of the statute.
HELD: Not a 'road'.

Knaggs v Elson
(1965) 109 Sol Jo 596, Div Ct
The defendant parked his car without lights in a private road the ownership

of which was vested in trustees. It was a cul-de-sac having 36 houses: there were no gates or other barriers but there was a notice 'Private Road — No Parking'. The trustees had taken steps to try to prevent parking. A police officer gave evidence of driving his car into the road, turning and reversing without restriction. The prosecution contended it was a 'road to which the public has access'.

HELD: It had long been held, deriving from *Harrison v Hill* (above) that the public might have access to a road, whether or not they had the right of access, if their presence was tolerated by the owners, but not if they entered by overcoming an obstruction or in defiance of a prohibition expressed or implied. Here there was a sign which on the face of it prohibited members of the public from entering; but it was not conclusive that their presence was not tolerated. Steps had been taken to prevent parking and no member of the public was likely to enter it for any other purpose; the police officer's evidence did not prove otherwise. No doubt the road was used by the inhabitants and their visitors but they were a limited class. Applying *R v Beaumont* (above) and *R v Waters* (1963) 107 Sol Jo 275, 47 Cr App Rep 149 (which showed that if only a restricted class was admitted the road would be private but if a restricted class was excluded the road would be public) this was not a 'road to which the public had access'.

Deacon v A. T. (a minor)
[1976] RTR 244, Div Ct

The defendant aged 15 was driving a car on a road within a housing estate the property of the Greater London Council. There were gates to the estate normally kept open and no signs either restricting or permitting the public or any class of the public from entering the estate on foot. The justices found that the roads of the estate were used by residents on the estate and visitors to them.

HELD: Without any evidence that members of the public in the wide sense, that is to say, persons who were not residents and were not visitors to residents, used the road of this estate it was not a 'road' as defined in the Road Traffic Act 1972, s 196(1).

Note—In *Cox v White* [1976] RTR 248, Lord Widgery CJ said 'I would invite . . . justices charged with this same question (whether a road on an industrial estate was within the definition in s 196(1)) to look at the very brief statement of Lord Sands in *Harrison v Hill* (quoted at p 736, above) . . . I think that in 99 cases out of 100 that direction is all the justices need to decide whether a road is a "road" for current purposes.'

Adams v Metropolitan Police Comr
[1980] RTR 289 (Jupp J)

The plaintiffs were residents in houses in Aberdeen Park, Highbury, London, a private estate built in Victorian times. The estate road was originally gated at both points of access and there was no access to the public except on business. In the course of time one of the gates disappeared but notices remained saying access was limited to residents and their authorised callers only. Nevertheless the road was in regular daily use by persons entering the estate to pass through to places on the other side. Motorists and motor cyclists used the road as a kind of free race track or as a car park. The police refused to prosecute for offences under the Road Traffic Acts because they were advised the road was not one to which the public had access within the meaning of s 196 because of the notices. In November 1970 the notices forbidding access to unauthorised persons were removed by the estate company. The plaintiffs sued for a declaration that the road was one to which the public had access within the meaning of the section.

HELD: There was ample evidence that the public had access, especially by the pedestrians from properties outside the estate who passed through it to shops and a public open space on the other side. They had access without 'either by overcoming a physical obstruction or in defiance of prohibition express or implied' following Lord Sands's test in *Harrison v Hill* (p 736, above). The public use of Aberdeen Park, notwithstanding the signs, was tolerated by the owners of the road. The road was therefore one coming within s 196(1). Even so it was not a case for making a declaration the notices having now been removed and the police acknowledging that they would accept the view of the Court.

Kellett v Daisy
[1977] RTR 396, Div Ct

The justices found that the defendant had driven without due care and attention on Elles Road, Farnborough, a road to which the public had access but which was a Crown road as defined by the Transport Act 1968, s 149(5)(b). The defendant maintained that he could not be convicted because the prosecution had not shown that the Road Traffic Act 1972 bound the road.

HELD: That approach was false. The question was not whether the road was bound by the Act but whether the defendant was. He was driving without due care on a road as defined by the Road Traffic Act 1972, s 196 and he was bound by the Act.

Chapman v Parlby
(1963) 108 Sol Jo 35, 62 LGR 150, Div Ct

A cyclist was struck by the defendant's car when riding along a road connecting a public highway with a War Department depot. The road was 49 feet long and had a solid white line across it half-way along. The cyclist was between the highway and the white line when struck. Justices dismissed a charge of careless driving on the grounds that the road was not a 'road' within the Road Traffic Act 1960, s 3 (now s 3 of the 1972 Act).

HELD: Following *Harrison v Hill* the road was a 'road' for the purposes of the section as it was one on which members of the public were to be found and which had no obstacle to prevent them from using it. A member of the public would meet with no physical obstruction and would meet with no prohibition express or implied until he reached the solid white lines.

Houghton v Schofield
[1973] Crim LR 126, Div Ct

A local authority made a traffic control order prohibiting waiting in a road giving access to a car park. There was an adjoining loading area and a cul-de-sac, not separated from the road by any physical barrier: the double yellow lines on the road included the area and cul-de-sac. The defendants were lessees of a shop from the authority on terms which gave them some right over the cul-de-sac but not a right to exclude the public. The defendants parked a vehicle in the cul-de-sac and were prosecuted for contravening the traffic order. They contended that the cul-de-sac was not a 'road'.

HELD: Following *Buchanan v MIB* (above pp 735–736) the test was whether there was any physical obstruction for the public to overcome or any prohibition express or implied to public access. The magistrates were justified in holding on the evidence that the cul-de-sac was a road.

Lorry crossing pavement

Randall v Motor Insurers' Bureau
[1969] 1 All ER 21, [1968] 1 WLR 1900, 112 Sol Jo 553, [1968] 2 Lloyd's Rep 553 (Megaw J)
The plaintiff in the course of his duty tried to prevent a lorry from leaving a building site. The lorry ran him down at the entrance to the site, the rear wheel passing over his leg and severely injuring it. He was just inside the boundary when this occurred; the front of the lorry was crossing the pavement of the street which the site adjoined. The plaintiff obtained judgment against the driver for damages which was not satisfied. He sued the Motor Insurers' Bureau for satisfaction of the judgment. They resisted the claim on the ground that the lorry was not being used 'on a road' within the meaning of the Road Traffic Act 1960, s 203(3)(a) (now s 145 of the 1972 Act).

HELD: The fact that the plaintiff was still on private property and therefore not 'on a road' at the time of the injury was immaterial. The defendants did not deny that the pavement was a part of the road. At the time when the lorry wheel ran over the plaintiff's leg the greater part of the lorry was on the road and the lorry was using the road. It was the use of the lorry on the road — the fact that it was being driven further on to the road in order to drive away along the road — which caused the injury.

Quayside

Walton v Newcastle-upon-Tyne Corpn
[1957] 1 Lloyd's Rep 412, Div Ct
A quayside road was vested in the defendants under various local statutes that all public rights of way or passage over the road were extinguished. The road joined a public highway at each end. There was no hindrance or obstruction to prevent members of the public walking or proceeding along it and no notice boards or other indication to the public that they did not use it as of right. It was distinguished from the highway by marks on the road and was private property not repaired or maintained by any highway authority. In fact many motor vehicles, both motor cars and lorries, frequently proceeded in either direction and members of the public were free to walk or motor along the roadway in either direction and did so. It was used by the public just in the same way as any other road.

HELD: The road was within the definition of 'road' in s 121(1) of the 1930
Act (now in the Road Traffic Act 1972, s 196(1)).

Dock roads

Note—Roads on dock property are not normally within the definition in s 196(1)
since they are not places to which the general public has access as a matter of legal
right (*Buchanan v Motor Insurers' Bureau* [1955] 1 All ER 607, [1955] 1 WLR 488, 119
JP 227, 99 Sol Jo 319 [1954] 2 Lloyd's Rep 519). But the Port of London Act 1968,
s 199, as substituted by the Port of London Act 1982, s 4 extends many of the
provisions of the Road Traffic Acts to 'dock roads', including the requirements of
ss 143 and 144 of the Road Traffic Act 1972. Section 199 has the following
definitions:
> 'dock road' means any road, pier, wharf, quay, bridge or other work which, or
> any land which is:
> (1) vested in or the property of the Port Authority; and
> (2) situate within the customs wall or fence bounding any dock of the Port
> Authority; and
> (3) accessible to motor vehicles;
> 'motor vehicle' has the same meaning as in the Road Traffic Act 1972.

In respect of docks of the British Transport Docks Board see the British Transport Commission Act 1961, s 26(2) (as amended): 'The Road Traffic Act 1972
shall have effect as if, in the provisions thereof referred to in this section, the
expression ''road'' included a dock road'. Section 143 of the 1972 Act is one of the
provisions referred to. By s 26(1) a 'dock road' means 'any road, pier, wharf,
quay, bridge, works or land which is situate within any dock or harbour premises
of the Docks Board (not being a road as defined by the Road Traffic Act 1972,
s 196) . . .'

Aerodromes

Note—The Civil Aviation Act 1982, s 37 applies the road traffic enactments to
roads within a designated aerodrome to which the public does not have access to the
same extent as they apply in relation to roads to which the public has access.

Car park

Griffin v Squires
[1958] 3 All ER 468, [1958] 1 WLR 1106, 123 JP 40, 102 Sol Jo 828, 56
LGR 442, Div Ct
A car park owned and maintained by the urban district at the public
expense, had a frontage to the main road of 123 feet and a depth of 80 feet.
The south side abutted on the pavement of the main road, with two
entrances each 11 foot wide; the east side was bounded by a wall; the west
side by railings and a privet hedge; and the north side by a fence. At the
north-west corner there was an opening 15 feet wide abutting on a private
footpath leading to a bowling club and council allotments. The allotment
users had to cross the car park to get to their gardens.

An unlicensed and uninsured woman driver drove a car from a stationary position in the car park for a distance of 10 yards, in the course of
which the car crossed through the privet hedge and came to rest on a lawn

outside the council buildings. She was prosecuted under the Road Traffic
Act 1930, ss 4(1) and 55.

HELD: The question whether the car park as a part of the footpath was a
'road' was a question of fact for the magistrates, and so was the question
whether the car park was a road. It is not enough alone that the public have
access, but that it is a road. There was evidence to justify the finding that it
was not a road. Appeal dismissed.

Note—The provisions of s 4(1) of the Road Traffic Act 1930 are now contained in
the Road Traffic Act 1972, ss 84(1) and (2); those of s 35 of the 1930 Act in s 143 of
the 1972 Act.

Oxford v Austin
[1981] RTR 416, QBD

In determining whether a car park can be a road within the Road Traffic
Act 1972, s 196(1) there is a well established process founded on findings of
fact. The first question to be asked is whether there is in the ordinary understanding of the word a road ie a definable way between two points over
which vehicles can pass, a way of communication ordinarily to be thought
of as a road. The second question is whether or not the public or a section of
the public has access to that which has the appearance of a definable way. If
one or two members of the public demonstrate as a fact that the public has a
right of access it is irrelevant that the area is privately owned. Even a
private car park may be one to which the public has access. If both
questions can be answered affirmatively then there is a road for the
purposes of the various Road Traffic Acts and Regulations.

Note—See also *R v Lynn*, p 734, above.

Paterson v Ogilvy
1957 SLT 354, [1957] CLY 3147, High Ct of Justiciary

A field, used as a parking place at an agricultural show, held a 'place'
within the Road Traffic Act 1930, s 15.

Note—The relevant provisions of the Road Traffic Act 1930, s 15 are now
contained in the Road Traffic Act 1972, s 5.

Private property

Norton v Hayward
(1968) 112 Sol Jo 767, Div Ct QB

An area of ground consisting partly of an entrance to a passageway giving
access to the rear of business premises and a street was designated a 'double
yellow line' road under the Road Traffic Act 1960, s 26. Part of it was
demised to the defendant whose business premises adjoined it. He parked
his car in the area and was prosecuted.

HELD: Although part of the relevant area was private land in the sense of
forming part of the demise that did not prevent it from being a 'road'
within s 257 of the Act.

Note—The Road Traffic Act 1960, s 26 has been replaced by the Road Traffic Regulation Act 1984, s 2. In that act 'road' is defined as in the Road Traffic Acts 1960 and 1972.

REQUIREMENTS OF POLICY

Road Traffic Act 1972, s 145

145 Requirements in respect of policies of insurance   (1) In order to comply with the requirements of this Part of this Act, a policy of insurance must satisfy the following conditions.

(2) The policy must be issued by an authorised insurer, that is to say, a person or body of persons carrying on insurance business within the Insurance Companies Act 1982, Sch 2, Pt II, Group 2 [and being a member of the Motor Insurers Bureau, a company limited by guarantee and incorporated under the Companies Act 1929 on 14 June 1946].

(3) Subject to sub-s (4) below, the policy—

(a)   must insure such person, persons or classes of persons as may be specified in the policy in respect of any liability which may be incurred by him or them in respect of the death of or bodily injury to any person caused by, or arising out of, the use of the vehicle on a road [in Great Britain]; and

(aa) must insure him or them in respect of any liability which may be incurred by him or them in respect of the use of the vehicle and of any trailer, whether or not coupled, in the territory other than Great Britain and Gibraltar of each of the member states of the communities according to the law on compulsory insurance against civil liability in respect of the use of vehicles of the State where the liability may be incurred; and

(b)   must also insure him or them in respect of any liability which may be incurred by him or them under the provisions of this Part of this Act relating to payment for emergency treatment.

(4) The policy shall not, by virtue of sub-s (3)(a) above, be required to cover—

(a) liability in respect of the death, arising out of and in the course of his employment, of a person in the employment of a person insured by the policy or of bodily injury sustained by such a person arising out of and in the course of his employment; or

(b) any contractual liability.

This section replaces s 203 of the 1960 Act which replaced s 36(1) of the 1930 Act. The words in square brackets in sub-s 2 were added by the Road Traffic Act 1974, s 20(1). Those in sub-s 3(a) and the whole of 3(aa) were added by the Motor Vehicles (Compulsory Insurance) (No 2) Regulations 1973; the words from 'insurance business' to '1982' in sub-s (2) were substituted by the Insurance Companies Act 1982.

SUBSECTION (3)(a): 'ANY PERSON'

Cooper v Motor Insurers' Bureau
[1985] QB 575, [1985] 1 All ER 449, [1985] 2 WLR 248, 129 Sol Jo 32, CA
Killacky bought an old motor cycle and took it to Cooper, who he knew had

expert knowledge of motor cycles, to try it out. Cooper mounted the machine and rode off. On approaching a major road he applied the brakes and they failed to operate. He collided with a car and was seriously injured. He sued Killacky in negligence for failing to warn him that the brakes were defective and obtained judgment for £214,207. Killacky was not insured and unable to satisfy the judgment. Cooper sued the Motor Insurers' Bureau, claiming that Killacky's liability was a 'relevant liability' within the definition in cl 1 of the Motor Insurers' Bureau Uninsured Driver's Agreement 'a liability in respect of which a policy of insurance must insure a person in order to comply with Part VI of the Road Traffic Act 1972'. It was argued on his behalf that 'any person' in s 145(3)(a) of the 1972 Act included the plaintiff even though he was driving. For the Bureau it was argued that s 143 was vital and that it was the use of the vehicle causing damage to others which was the only liability to be covered. The judge held the Motor Insurers' Bureau not liable. Section 143 spoke first of a person using and second of one who caused or permitted the use; the section was not intended to insure against personal injury to the person actually using the vehicle.

HELD, ON APPEAL: The judge was right. Section 145(3)(a) was not the end of the story. Consideration had to be given to s 143(1). The obligation imposed by that subsection is an obligation to abstain from using, or from causing or permitting any other person to use, a motor vehicle on the road unless there is in force in relation to the use of the vehicle by that person or that other person a policy of insurance complying with the requirements of Part VI of the Act. A policy covering him 'in respect of third-party risks' clearly does not include the actual driver of the vehicle at the time of the use of the vehicle which gives rise to the damage. The scope of the phrase 'any person' in s 145(3)(a) is limited by s 143(1) so as to exclude the driver of the vehicle.

SUBSECTION (4)(a): ARISING OUT OF AND IN THE COURSE OF

Vandyke v Fender
[1970] 2 QB 292, [1970] 2 All ER 335, [1970] 2 WLR 929, 134 JP 487, 114 Sol Jo 205, CA

Vandyke and Fender were moulders employed by the second defendants at a foundry 30 miles from their homes. The second defendants arranged with Fender to lend him a car in which he could drive to work, bringing Vandyke and two other employees. Although the arrangements for providing the car and paying him an allowance for petrol was part of Fender's contract of service neither he nor Vandyke was obliged to use the car if they did not wish to do so. It was not a term of their contract of service that they must use it. When riding as a passenger in the car on the way to work Vandyke was injured in an accident for which Fender was held to blame.

HELD: Vandyke was in the vehicle 'by reason of . . . a contract of employment' but not 'in the course of' his employment. The test whether Vandyke was in the car 'in the course of' his employment was the same as in the leading cases under the Workmen's Compensation Acts, namely, whether he was under an obligation as a term of his employment to travel in the car, and he was not. The words injury 'arising out of and in the course of his employment' were used in the old Workmen's Compensation Acts from 1897 to 1945. The selfsame words have been used in the Road Traffic Acts 1930 and 1960. They have also been used in employers' liability policies. In my opinion they should receive the same interpretation in all three places; for they are all so closely connected that they ought, as matter of commonsense, to receive the same interpretation in each. The words were construed and applied in thousands of cases under the Workmen's Compensation Acts: and I think we should follow those cases. The two leading cases, most apposite for present purposes are *St Helens Colliery Co Ltd v Hewitson* [1924] AC 59, 93 LJKB 177, 130 LT 291, 40 TLR 125, 68 Sol Jo 163 and *Weaver v Tredegar Iron and Coal Co Ltd* [1940] AC 955. They show, to my mind quite conclusively that when a man is going to or coming from work, along a public road, as a passenger in a vehicle provided by his employer, he is not then in the course of his employment — unless he is *obliged* by the terms of his employment to travel in that vehicle. It is not enough that he should have the right to travel in the vehicle, or be permitted to travel in it. He must have an *obligation* to travel in it. Else he is not in the course of his employment. That distinction must be maintained; for otherwise there would be no certainty in this branch of the law: per Lord Denning.

St Helens Colliery Co v Hewitson
[1924] AC 59, 93 LJKB 177, 130 LT 291, 40 TLR 125, 68 Sol Jo 163, 16 BWCC 230, HL

A workman employed at a colliery travelled by a special train provided by an agreement between his employers and a railway company. The employers paid the railway company and the workman agreed to a deduction from his wages of half the fare paid by his employers and to waive all claims against the railway company.

HELD: The workman was under no obligation or duty to be there, he was not doing something in discharge or performance of a duty to his employers directly or indirectly imposed upon him by or arising out of his contract of service. There was only a right and not an obligation. Not 'arising out of and in the course of his employment'.

Note—Hewitson's case was distinguished (except by Viscount Maugham who considered it indistinguishable) in the following case.

Weaver v Tredegar Iron and Coal Co
[1940] AC 955, [1940] 3 All ER 157, 109 LJKB 621, 164 LT 231, 56 TLR 813, 84 Sol Jo 584, HL

A railway line passed through the premises of a colliery company. There was a halt station used only by the colliery workmen. The access to the station was the property of the railway company. Workmen obtained tickets from the colliery company, who arranged with the railway company for the trains. The workmen were not compelled to use the trains, but practically all did so. A workman was injured on the platform.

HELD: The employment continued whilst the workman was on any private exit which he was only entitled to use by reason of his status of a workman. The accident arose out of and in the course of the employment.

Craw v Forrest
1931 SC 634, 24 BWCC Supp 67, Ct of Sess
A girl accepted employment as a weeder and picker on a fruit farm on condition that the employer conveyed her a distance of eight miles each day to her work. The time occupied in this conveyance was not paid for as working time. The workman was neither expressly bound by her contract, nor ordered by her employer or by anyone on his behalf, to use the means of conveyance provided, which was a motor lorry belonging to the employer and under the control of his son. The lorry was the only practicable means by which the workman could get to her work in time to start at the prescribed hours, and but for the offer of the conveyance to her work the workman would not have accepted the employment.
HELD: The workman was neither bound by her contract of service nor ordered by her employer to use the means of transport provided. Not 'arising out of and in the course of'.

Black v Aitkenhead
(1938) 31 BWCC Supp 73, Ct of Sess
A labourer, while engaged on work at a distance from his home, was conveyed over part of the distance on a motor lorry which was provided by his employers. There was no express contract between the workman and his employers for the use of this conveyance; but, before accepting the job, the workman knew that the lorry would be provided free of cost, and he would not have accepted the offer of employment if it had not been available. This free conveyance was entirely optional, but it was used by employees who resided at a distance from the work. There was no direct transport connection between the workman's home and place of work, and travel by the ordinary route would have materially increased both the cost and the time of the journey. While being conveyed to his work, the workman fell from the lorry and was killed.
HELD: As the workman was not under any contractual obligation to use the lorry, his death while he was proceeding to his work on that conveyance was not the result of an accident arising in the course of his employment within the Workmen's Compensation Act 1925, s 1(1).

Netherton v Coles
[1945] 1 All ER 227, 37 BWCC 165, CA
A workman was employed at a job 11 miles from his home. He had travelling allowances and free travelling facilities by voucher or otherwise. He left the place of work on a motor cycle and met with an accident on the public road.
HELD: Not 'out of'; the workman outside working hours was at liberty to choose his own time and method of transport.

Allen v Siddons
(1932) 25 BWCC 350
A foreman was employed at a fixed weekly wage of £3 and his hours of work were from 7 am-5 pm. On one job he had to be at work at 7.30 am. He left home at 7 am on his motor cycle and met with an accident on his way to

work. The employer argued that he was not concerned with what the man did before 7.30 am. The county court judge held the accident arose out of and in the course of. The Court of Appeal said that although the employer might have had the right to give orders to the workman at any time after 7 am he did not on this occasion exercise that right, and the workman's employment in fact began at 7.30 am. The accident having happened merely when the workman was going to work, it did not arise out of and in the course of.

Alderman v Great Western Rly Co
[1938] AC 454, 30 BWCC 64, HL
A travelling ticket collector signed on for duty at Oxford in the morning, travelled by train to Paddington and there joined a train to Swansea where he signed off duty for the night. The next morning he had to sign on at Swansea and return via Paddington to Oxford where his duties ended. Whilst spending the night at Swansea, he was under an obligation to lodge within a reasonable distance of the station and to leave his address in case of emergency. He was injured on his way from his lodgings to sign on for duty at Swansea station. The House of Lords held that the accident did not arise out of and in the course of the employment.

Blee v London and North Eastern Rly Co
[1938] AC 126, [1937] 4 All ER 270, 107 LJKB 62, 158 LT 185, 54 TLR 71, 81 Sol Jo 941, 30 BWCC 364, HL
A platelayer was liable to be called on at any time for emergency work for which he received overtime commencing from the time he left his home. At 10.30 pm after retiring to bed, he was called up on an emergency. On his way from his home to the railway siding, he met with an accident. The House of Lords held that the employment commenced at the time he left home and the accident arose out of and in the course of his employment.

Dunn v A. G. Lockwood & Co
[1947] 1 All ER 446, 40 BWCC 60, CA
A workman who lived at Whitstable was employed as a plasterer by a firm of builders at Margate. Work began each day at 8 am but the workman was permitted to catch the 7.40 am train from Whitstable arriving at Margate at 8.15 am and was paid from 8 am. He was permitted to take the train on condition that he started work as soon as possible after he arrived at Margate station. On his way from the station to his work he met with an accident. The Court of Appeal held that the permission to the workman to take a train which caused him to be late for work placed upon him the contractual duty to go from the station to his place of work as quickly as possible. It was in performing this duty to his employers that the accident happened and it accordingly arose out of and in the course of his employment.

Patterson v Costain and Press (Overseas) Ltd
(1979) 123 Sol Jo 142, 2 Lloyd's Rep 204, CA
The defendants were carrying out constructional work at Bid Boland

170 km from Abadan in Persia. They provided transport in their own vehicles for their employees, of whom the plaintiff was one, from Abadan to Bid Boland where the plaintiff both worked and was housed. The only other way of making the journey was by taxi, very rarely done because expensive. After a short holiday in Kuwait the plaintiff returned to Abadan to make the remainder of the journey by road to Bid Boland; the defendants had arranged for a Landrover to be available. On the journey to Bid Boland he was injured in an accident. If the accident arose 'in the course of' his employment the defendants would be indemnified by their employers' liability insurers; if not, then by their public liability insurers.

HELD: Applying *St Helens Colliery v Hewitson* (p 744, above) the accident arose 'in the course of' the employment. There had to be on the part of the plaintiff an obligation and not merely a right to use the transport provided but on the facts there was an obligation. It was not a case of a man going from his home to his place of work. It was part of the sphere of his employment to travel on the employer's vehicle from Abadan to the site of his work and his home 170 km away at Bid Boland: [1978] 1 Lloyd's Rep 86 (Talbot J).

An appeal was dismissed. The accident had occured in Iran; the contract showed that virtually from the time of getting off the aircraft at Abadan the plaintiff was in the defendants' employment. It was clearly distinguishable from the English cases.

Directors

Note—A question may arise in the case of a director of an insured company who is a passenger in the company's vehicle driven by the company's servant whether there is 'employment' of a director under sub-s (4), and whether a director can sue the company of which he is a director.

A director is not (except in an exceptional case) a servant, ie he is not employed under a contract of service, but if he is engaged on the business of the company, he may be 'employed' by the company. He may therefore come within a term in the policy excluding accidents arising out of and in the course of the employment.

In a case in practice, one of the two directors of a private limited company was travelling in a company's car driven by a servant of the company on the way to Scotland for an exhibition of the company's goods on the following day. He was at liberty to travel by any other means if he wished. He was killed in an accident caused by the driver's negligence. His personal representatives sued the company. The issue was contested between the motor insurers and the employer's liability insurers whether, at the time of the accident, his death arose 'out of and in the course of his employment' by the company. It was held, in the Queen's Bench Division, that it did. It was not disputed by either insurer that he was, even though a director, an employee: the only question was whether the accident was 'out of and in the course of'; ie the same issue as in *Vandyke v Fender* (p 743, above).

Normandy v Ind Coope & Co
[1908] 1 Ch 84, 77 LJ Ch 82, 97 LT 872, 24 TLR 57
Re Lee Behrens & Co
[1932] 2 Ch 46, 101 LJ Ch 183, 147 LT 348
A director, as such, is not an employee of the company.

Hutton v West Cork Rly Co
(1883) 23 ChD 654, 52 LJ Ch 689, 49 LT 420, 31 WR 827, CA
Nor, as such, is he a servant of the company.

R v Stuart
[1894] 1 QB 310, 63 LJMC 63, 58 JP 299, 42 WR 303
He may, however, be employed as a servant.

Trussed Steel Concrete Co v Green
[1946] Ch 115, 115 LJ Ch 123, 174 LT 122, 110 JP 144
And a managing director with a contract of service may be an employee of
the company.

Lee v Lees Air Farming Ltd
[1961] AC 12, [1960] 3 All ER 420, [1960] 3 WLR 758, 104 Sol Jo 969, PC
In 1954 the appellant's husband formed a company for the purpose of
conducting an aerial top-dressing business. The nominal capital was 3,000
shares of £1 each of which he held 2,999. He was governing director. By the
articles of the company it was provided that the company should employ
him as the chief pilot and that the relationship of master and servant should
apply. In 1956 he was piloting the company's aircraft on top-dressing
operations when it crashed and he was killed.
HELD: He was a 'person who has entered into or works under a contract of
service with an employer' for the purposes of the New Zealand Workers
Compensation Act 1922. The contractual obligations in the articles were
not invalidated by the circumstance that the deceased was the sole
governing director in whom was vested the full government and control of
the respondent company.

Road Transport Industry Training Board v Reader's Garage Ltd
(1969) 113 Sol Jo 125, Times, 31 January, Div Ct
The managing director of a garage company having seven employees held
$99\frac{1}{2}\%$ of the shares and drew £1,450 p a from the business, in which he took
an active part.
HELD: The fact that he held the overwhelming majority of the shares,
decided what was to be done and who was to do it and how much money he
could draw out on his own account did not preclude him from being also an
employee of the company. If his main work was that of a director and he
only occasionally stepped into the shoes of his workmen that was one thing.
But if he spent many hours in the filling station or in the garage for repairs
with only short periods on director's duties a tribunal might come to a
different decision. It was a question of fact whether a contract of service
could be implied.

PASSENGER INSURANCE

Note—Neither the Road Traffic Act 1960 nor its predecessor the 1930 Act required
users of motor vehicles to be insured in respect of liability for death or bodily injury

to passengers in the vehicle being used except a vehicle in which passengers were carried for hire or reward or by reason of or in pursuance of a contract of employment. Subsection 203(4) of the 1960 Act was as follows:

'(4) The policy shall not . . . be required to cover—
(a) liability in respect of the death of, or bodily injury to, persons being carried in or upon, or entering or getting on to or alighting from, the vehicle at the time of the occurrence of the event out of which the claims arise; or
(b) liability in respect of the death, arising out of and in the course of his employment, of a person in the employment of a person insured by the policy or of bodily injury sustained by such a person arising out of and in the course of his employment; or
(c) any contractual liability.

Provided that para (a) of this subsection shall not have effect in the case of a vehicle in which passengers are carried for hire or reward or by reason of or in pursuance of a contract of employment.'

The Motor Vehicles (Passenger Insurance) Act 1971 made insurance cover for passenger liability compulsory by repealing para (a) and the proviso of sub-s 203(4). The 1971 Act was to come into force on 1 December 1972, but was repealed in advance by the Road Traffic Act 1972. The effect of the 1971 Act was retained in s 145 of the 1972 Act (p 000, above) but delayed until 1 December 1972 by para 5 of Sch 8.

Thus compulsory passenger insurance has been required since 1 December 1972.

It will be noted that insurance against claims by passengers arising out of and in the course of their employment by the person insured by the policy is still not required even after 1 December 1972 (1972 Act, s 145(4)(a)).

For s 148(3) see p 704, above.

In the case of *Vandyke v Fender* [1969] 2 QB 581, [1969] 2 All ER 1291, [1969] 3 WLR 217, 113 Sol Jo 467, [1969] 2 Lloyd's Rep 164 the facts of which are set out on p 743, above the second defendants who were the plaintiff's employers had an employer's liability policy indemnifying them against liability arising from accidents arising out of and in the course of the plaintiff's employment with them. Paull J held that the National Insurance (Industrial Injuries) Act 1946, s 9 (now replaced by the Social Security Act 1975, s 53) which deems accidents occurring when an employee is travelling to work by vehicle with the permission of the employer to arise out of and in the course of his employment is of general application and is not limited to claims for benefit under the Act.

The Court of Appeal said this was wrong; s 9 altered the interpretation of 'arising out of and in the course of his employment' only for the special purposes of the 1946 Act. It changed neither the common law nor the ambit of the responsibilities imposed by the Road Traffic Act: [1970] 2 QB 292, [1970] 2 All ER 335, [1970] 2 WLR 929, 134 JP 487, 114 Sol Jo 205.

INSURANCE CERTIFICATE

Road Traffic Act 1972, s 147

147 Issue and surrender of certificates of insurance and of security (1) A policy of insurance shall be of no effect for the purposes of this Part of this Act unless and until there is delivered by the insurer to the person by whom the policy is effected a certificate (in this Part of this Act referred to as a 'certificate of insurance') in the prescribed form and containing such particulars of any conditions subject to which the policy is issued and of any other matters as may be prescribed.

(3) Different forms and different particulars may be prescribed for the purposes of sub-s (1) or (2) above in relation to different cases or circumstances.

(4) Where a certificate has been delivered under this section and the policy or security to which it relates is cancelled by mutual consent or by virtue of any provision in the policy or security, the person to whom the certificate was delivered shall, within seven days from the taking effect of the cancellation, surrender the certificate to the person by whom the policy was issued or the security was given or, if the certificate has been lost or destroyed, make a statutory declaration to that effect; and a person who fails to comply with this subsection shall be guilty of an offence.

Section 147 replaces s 205 of the Road Traffic Act 1960. Subsection (2) refers to securities (s 146).

Starkey v Hall
[1936] 2 All ER 18, 80 Sol Jo 347, 55 Ll L Rep 24, Div Ct
A policy is not in force until delivery of the certificate to the assured and delivery of the certificate to a hire purchase company is not delivery to the assured and the assured is liable for an offence under s 35(1).

Note—Section 35, ie of the 1930 Act. See s 143 of the 1972 Act.

Egan v Bower
(1939) 63 Ll L Rep 266, Div Ct
A certificate contained limitation of use to policy holder's business under C licence not covering carrying passengers for hire or reward. Policy holder was carrying his wife and children not on business. Insurers wrote to the police that they would indemnify for private pleasure purposes.
HELD: The policy did not cover the risk and the policy holder had committed an offence under s 35(1).

Carnill v Rowland
[1953] 1 All ER 486, [1953] 1 WLR 380, 117 JP 127, 97 Sol Jo 134, 51 LGR 180, [1953] 1 Lloyd's Rep 99, Div Ct
A proposal form for motor cycle insurance restricted the cover to use when a sidecar or box carrier was permanently attached. A cover note with temporary certificate was issued restricted to use of the motor cycle to which a sidecar was permanently attached. The permanent certificate would have contained the words 'use of the cycle is only permitted when a sidecar or box carrier is attached'. The insured removed the sidecar body and drove with only the sidecar chassis and the wheel, and was summoned for driving uninsured. The insurers gave evidence that for the purposes of the policy they regarded what was attached as a sidecar and would have held covered.
HELD: The meaning of the cover note may be a question of doubt. The construction put on it by the insurers was not impossible and the justices were entitled to accept the insurers' construction.

A decision by justices or on appeal of a Divisional Court does not bind the insurers or the insured and the fact that justices have to decide a question of insurance law in the absence of the insurers, who are the parties most interested, makes it desirable to make use of an arrangement that has been entered into with the approval of the appropriate authorities for consultation between the police and insurance companies whether insurers hold covered. If a respectable insurance company consider themselves on risk, the mischief aimed at by the Act does not arise.

Note—The existence of such an 'arrangement' is a matter of doubt. See *Boss v Kingston*, p 842, below.

Certificate does not enlarge policy

Note—A question which was for some time unsettled was whether a certificate of insurance which contains terms which are different from the terms of the policy has any legal effect at all as regards third parties, or between the insurer and the assured, or whether the conditions of the policy are the only test. It has now been settled in *Spraggon*'s case, below.

In *Gray v Blackmore* (p 759, below) a policy excluded use for any purpose in connection with the motor trade, and the certificate contained a similar limitation. The argument for the insurers was that there was no estoppel by the certificate because it stated on its face the limitations to which it was subject.

Per Branson J: It is obvious from s 36(5) relating to the certificate of insurance that the policy may contain conditions the nature of which is left completely open. So it clearly contemplates conditions, and unless they are to be conditions limiting the liability of the underwriter, what possible reason can there be for their inclusion in the certificate, the object of which is to make clear to whom it may concern the conditions, if any, subject to which the policy has been issued.

McCormick v National Motor Accident Insurance
(1934) 50 TLR 528, 78 Sol Jo 633, 40 Com Cas 76, 49 Ll L Rep 361, CA

Insurers discovered just before the trial of an action brought by a third party against their assured that they were entitled to avoid the policy for false statement in the proposal form. It was contended for the third party that the issue of the certificate prevented insurers from asserting that the policy was avoided.

Per Greer LJ: The effect and need of the certificate is this, that it enables the assured to say: 'Here is my certificate of insurance, and I am not liable as long as I have got an insurance.' It is not a document which is supposed to be addressed to all the world, including people who have never seen it and may never have heard — and a great many people never have heard — either of the Act of Parliament or of the certificate. It is only issued for the purpose of enabling the assured to produce that document when he is on the road, which will show that he has complied with the Act to the extent of getting a policy of insurance; but it is not intended to be a representation that the policy which he has got will in any event become a policy on which he will be entitled to recover in the event of an accident happening and damages resulting.

Per Slesser LJ: The certificate is merely giving the means of enabling a man to drive a motor car. It has no greater effect than that.

Note—For s 36(5) see now s 147 of the Road Traffic Act 1972.

Spraggon v Dominion Insurance Co Ltd

(1940) 67 Ll L Rep 529 (Stable J), (1941) 69 Ll L Rep 1, CA

Tomrley hired a car from Warnes. Insurers had issued a policy to Warnes providing indemnity to drivers hiring cars unless within the category of excluded drivers. Excluded drivers included any who had not (1) satisfied the insured (Warnes) by an actual driving test, (2) completed a proposal form, (3) a current driving licence for 12 months free from endorsements, (4) forwarded the proposal form immediately after the driving test to insurers by registered post. Insurers had issued a certificate to Warnes insuring any driver who holds a licence and is not disqualified. Tomrley held a licence and was not disqualified. He was therefore within the wording of the certificate. He had a provisional licence from 25 November 1937, to 22 February 1938, and thereafter an annual licence, which was indorsed with a conviction for speed on 24 March 1938. He did not post the proposal form he signed to insurers. He never had a driving test.

He was therefore not within the wording of the policy. Warnes assured Tomrley that he was covered. An action was brought by a third party against the insurers.

HELD: Insurers were not liable, because it is only where there is a policy of insurance in respect of which the certificate has been issued that the third party had a cause of action against insurers. The accident was not covered by the policy, and the certificate was therefore of no effect: Per Stable J.

HELD, ON APPEAL: Tomrley was not insured by the policy; the CA made no reference to the certificate.

Note—It follows that the opinion previously widely held by insurers that the insurer is bound by the wording of the certificate as distinct from the policy is without foundation. It is now made perfectly plain that the policy is the only document which creates any liability on insurers, and the certificate is (in this respect) merely a piece of paper to produce to the police to show that there is a policy in existence, without affecting in any way the limitation contained in the policy.

Some policies expressly incorporate the certificate in the policy, and in that case different considerations may arise as between insurers and the assured.

Biddle v Johnston

(1965) 109 Sol Jo 395, [1965] 2 Lloyd's Rep 121, Div Ct

A policy of insurance insured C Ltd and four other named associated companies in respect of the use of a motor vehicle owned by C Ltd, but did not insure R Ltd, a company some of whose shareholders were directors of C Ltd. There had been some co-operation between C Ltd and R Ltd until a receiver of C Ltd was appointed when it largely ceased. The certificate issued under the policy was expressed to cover use by C Ltd 'and/or associated companies', without naming them, in connection with the policy-holder's business. The appellant, a director of R Ltd, caused an employee of R Ltd, to drive the vehicle on an occasion after the appointment of the receiver of C Ltd. He was charged with causing him to use the vehicle when uninsured contrary to the Road Traffic Act 1960, s 201 (now s 143 of the 1972 Act). He contended that R Ltd was 'an associated company' covered by the certificate. The justices convicted on the ground that since the appointment of the receiver, who had control of C Ltd, R Ltd and C Ltd were no longer associated companies.

HELD: On a case stated, there was evidence to support the justices' finding. Apart from this, under s 201 of the 1960 Act there must be an enforceable contract of insurance; a cover note referred to in s 216(1) was such a contract, but a certificate, which was not in itself a contract at all, could not comply with the requirements of the Act. By s 205(1) a policy of insurance was of no effect unless and until a certificate were delivered, but that did not affect the position. The difficulty here was that the policy and certificates did not agree with each other.

Note—

1960 Act	1972 Act
section 201	section 143
section 205(1)	section 147(1)
section 216(1)	section 158(1)

SPECIMEN CERTIFICATE OF INSURANCE FOR PRIVATE CAR

*Note—*This certificate complies with the provisions of the Road Traffic Act 1972 and the Motor Vehicles (Third Party Risks) Regulations 1972.
1 Index Mark and Registration Number of Vehicle
2 Name of Policyholder
3 Effective date of the Commencement of Insurance for the purposes of the Act.
4 Date of Expiry of Insurance
5 Persons or Classes of Persons entitled to drive*
(a) The Policyholder
    The Policyholder may also drive a Motor Car (or Motor Cycle) not belonging to him and not hired to him under a hire purchase agreement.
(b) Any other person who is driving on the Policyholder's order or with his permission.
Provided that the person driving holds a licence to drive the vehicle or has held and is not disqualified for holding or obtaining such a licence.
6 Limitations as to use*
Use only for social, domestic and pleasure purposes and by the Policyholder in person in connection with his business or profession. The Policy does not cover use for hiring, racing, pace-making, speed testing, commercial travelling, the carriage of goods or samples in connection with any trade or business or use for any purpose in connection with the Motor Trade.
    The towing (not for reward) of one disabled mechanically propelled vehicle is covered.
    I Hereby Certify that the Policy to which this Certificate relates is issued in accordance with the provisions of Part VI of the Road Traffic Act 1972.

Authorised Insurers

    * Limitations rendered inoperative by the Road Traffic Act 1972, s 148, are not to be included under this heading.
    An 'open' certificate is one which in place of the index mark and registration number of the insured vehicle specifies 'any motor car the property of the policy holder or hired to him under a hire purchase agreement'. The certificate remains effective when the insured changes his vehicle but the cover provided by the policy is limited to Road Traffic Act liability until particulars of the replacement vehicle have been accepted by the insurer.

SPECIMEN FORM OF RENEWAL NOTICE AND TEMPORARY CERTIFICATE

The renewal premiums on the above Insurance Policy fall due on the renewal date above-mentioned and the Company will issue to the insured after the payment of the premium a new Certificate of Insurance as prescribed by the Road Traffic Act 1972. As the certificate cannot be issued until the premium has been received, payment should be made in time to allow of the certificate being in the hands of the Insured not later than the renewal date of the policy.

The object of the covering note on the reverse side of this renewal notice is to protect you under the above Acts should the new permanent Certificate of Insurance not reach you by the renewal date. It is, therefore, most important that you should retain this notice until the permanent certificate reaches you.

You are reminded that it is an offence to use a motor vehicle on a road without a certificate of insurance.

The cover referred to in the Covering Note hereon which is given solely to enable the policyholder to comply with the provisions of the Road Traffic Acts operates only if and when such Acts require the issue of a certificate to the policyholder.

TEMPORARY COVERING NOTE

Insurance is hereby granted in terms of the policy referred to in this notice until and including the fifteenth day from the renewal date referred to in this notice, but only in respect of such insurance as is necessary to comply with the requirements of the Road Traffic Act 1972, Part VI, subject otherwise to the terms and conditions and exceptions of the said policy and in accordance with the particulars of the certificate of insurance relating to the said policy current on the said renewal date and provided that an insurance covering the aforesaid liability has not been effected with any other Authorised Insurers.

I Hereby Certify that this Covering Note is issued in accordance with the provisions of Part VI of the Road Traffic Act 1972.

Authorised Insurers

Taylor v Allon
[1966] 1 QB 304, [1965] 1 All ER 557, [1965] 2 WLR 598, 109 Sol Jo 78, [1965] 1 Lloyd's Rep 155, Div Ct
The defendant's car was insured under a policy which expired on 6 April. The insurance company had sent him the usual renewal notice on the back of which was printed a 'temporary cover note' giving third-party cover for 15 days from the date of expiry. This was expressed to be for the purpose of protecting the policyholder on renewal until his new certificate arrived. In fact the plaintiff had no intention of renewing the policy as he proposed to change his insurance to another company. He did not become insured by the new company until 16 April though he used his car on the 15th. He was charged with using his car on that day when not insured, contrary the Road Traffic Act 1960, s 201. He produced the temporary cover note sent him by the old company, whose representative gave evidence that they considered themselves liable and in the case of an accident would have paid.
HELD: (1) In the definitions in s 216 of the Act 'insurance' means insurance pursuant to an enforceable contract and therefore 'covering note' must mean a cover-note enforceable as a contract; (2) the evidence of the insurance company's representative could not help the court when the

issue was whether there was an enforceable contract; (3) if there was any contract embodied in the temporary cover note it could arise only by offer and acceptance. As there was no provision in the policy for an extension of the cover the temporary cover note must be an offer to insure for the future which could be accepted by paying the renewal premium. Even if the policyholder did not communicate his acceptance in this way there might be an implied acceptance from conduct if he took his car out in reliance on the temporary cover, and there would then be liability on him to pay the renewal premium or a premium for the period of cover. But this was not the position in the present case. The defendant had no intention of renewing the policy and had not given evidence that he was relying on the temporary cover note at the time of the offence. The magistrates were right in convicting him.

Note—For section numbers see note following *Biddle*'s case, p 753, above.

COVER NOTE

Roberts v Warne
[1973] RTR 217, Div Ct
Roberts, a hire-car driver, made an agreement with Davies, who ran a hire-car booking office, that he would drive Davies's car when required on bookings provided by Davies, who would ensure that Roberts was covered by Davies's insurance. As the car, when the agreement was made, was insured only for named drivers of whom Roberts was not one, they went to the insurance brokers through whom Davies's insurance was placed, where Davies in Roberts's presence asked the brokers that the policy should be varied to cover any driver. The brokers telephoned the insurers who specifically authorised them to give insurance cover for any driver of the car. The brokers thereupon issued a 60-day cover note to Davies providing for such cover. The insurers later decided not to provide 'any driver' cover but their letters to the brokers on the subject were delayed by a postal strike and did not reach them. More than 60 days after the issue of the cover-note Roberts was stopped and charged with driving when uninsured.
HELD, ON APPEAL by case stated: Roberts was rightly convicted. The Road Traffic Act 1960, s 201, requires that there shall be a policy of insurance in force in relation to the persons using the vehicle. The cover note was in itself a policy of insurance (though an insurance certificate is not) albeit a temporary one and there was a certificate printed on it; but the policy had not been amended when the cover note expired and did not cover Roberts. The telephone conversation between brokers and insurers did not amount to an oral variation of the existing written policy. The fact that the insurers might in the circumstances have been estopped as against Roberts from denying that he was entitled to be indemnified did not make up for the lack of a policy on the relevant date so far as s 201 was concerned, since a policy is something which has to be in writing and requires stamping, and no amendment to include Roberts expressly had been done when the cover note expired.

Note—Section 201 of 1960 Act now s 143 of 1972 Act.

Cartwright v MacCormack; Trafalgar Insurance Co Ltd, Third Party
[1963] 1 All ER 11, [1963] 1 WLR 18, 106 Sol Jo 957, [1962] 2 Lloyd's
Rep 328, CA
The defendant claimed to be indemnified by the third party, an insurance
company, against damages awarded to the plaintiff for injuries sustained in
a road accident. The cover note was on the third party's printed form with
some entries in handwriting. It contained the words 'This cover note is
only valid for 15 days from the commencement date of risk'. The 'effective
time and date of commencement of risk' was entered at '11.45 am' and
'2.12.59'. The accident giving rise to the claim occurred at 5.45 pm on 17
December 1959. The third party claimed that the cover note had expired
before the accident happened.
HELD: 'Time' and 'date' were used on the cover note as separate terms
and the duration of the insurance company's liability was expressed at 15
days from the commencement date. The commencement date was 2
December and the policy therefore expired 15 days from 2 December. On
the ordinary rules of construction these words excluded the first date and
began at midnight on that date: the defendant was still insured when the
accident happened.

A cover note cannot be ante-dated or the certificate is false in a material
particular. At the Huddersfield Police Court on 23 March 1939, the
Prudential Assurance Co were fined £30 and £10 10s 0d costs for issuing,
and the agent Sam Whitehead £3 for aiding and abetting, a cover note
which was ante-dated ((1939) Times, 24 March).

London and Scottish v Ridd
(1940) 65 Ll L Rep 46, Div Ct
The issue of cover notes, even though £3 is paid on account of premium of
£37, does not require insurers to issue a certificate for 12 months, and they
cannot be convicted of failing to issue a certificate of insurance under the
Motor Vehicle (TP Risks) Regulations 1933.

Neil v South East Lancashire Insurance Co
1932 SLT 29
'Subject to the usual terms of the company's policy' referred only to the
general conditions and did not incorporate the warranty contained in the
proposal form.

Broad v Waland
(1942) 73 Ll L Rep 263 (Atkinson J)
But if the cover note is granted on the faith of a statement in the proposal
form, which is a material misrepresentation or non-disclosure, the policy
contained in the cover note can be set aside in a declaration action.

INEFFECTIVE RESTRICTIONS IN POLICY

Road Traffic Act 1972, s 148(1)

148 Avoidance of certain exceptions to policies or securities and of certain agreements, etc, as to risks requested to be covered thereby   Where a certificate of insurance or certificate of security has been delivered under section 147 of this Act to the person by whom a policy has been effected or to whom a security has been given, so much of the policy or security as purports to restrict, as the case may be, the insurance of the persons insured by the policy or the operation of the security by reference to any of the following matters, that is to say—

(a) the age or physical or mental condition of persons driving the vehicle, or

(b) the condition of the vehicle, or

(c) the number of persons that the vehicle carries, or

(d) the weight or physical characteristics of the goods that the vehicle carries, or

(e) the times at which or the areas within which the vehicle is used, or

(f) the horsepower or cylinder capacity or value of the vehicle, or

(g) the carrying on the vehicle of any particular apparatus, or

(h) the carrying on the vehicle of any particular means of identification other than any means of identification required to be carried by or under the Vehicles (Excise) Act 1971

shall, as respect such liabilities as are required to be covered by a policy under s 145 of this Act, be of no effect:

Provided that nothing in this subsection shall require an insurer or the giver of a security to pay any sum in respect of the liability of any person otherwise than in or towards the discharge of that liability, and any sum paid by an insurer or the giver of a security in or towards the discharge of any liability of any person which is covered by the policy or security by virtue only of this subsection shall be recoverable by the insurer or giver of the security from that person.

Note—For sub-s (2) see below; for sub-s (3), see p 213, above.

This is a most important section, but of course it only operates in respect of Act liability. The conditions remain effective in respect of damage to property. It replaces s 206(1) of the 1960 Act.

It is important to observe that the proviso gives an absolute statutory right to the insurer to recover from the assured irrespective of any express condition in the policy.

Passengers

Note—From and after 1 December 1972 a user of a vehicle cannot restrict or exclude his liability to a passenger in respect of bodily injury or death by any antecedent agreement *with the passenger*. See s 148(3) of the Act and 'Exclusion of passenger liability ineffective', p 213, above.

Physical condition of driver

National Farmers' Union Mutual Insurance Society Ltd v Dawson
[1941] 2 KB 424, 111 LJKB 38, 166 LT 245, 70 Ll L Rep 167 (Caldecote LCJ)
A policy contained a condition that the assured should use all care and diligence to avoid accidents and to employ only steady and sober drivers. The assured drove his car under the influence of drink and injured third parties. Insurers settled the claims of third parties and brought arbitration proceedings against the assured to recover the sums so paid. The Arbitrator found that the assured did not use all care and diligence to avoid accidents and to employ only steady and sober drivers.
HELD, on a special case stated: Although the case did not come within any of the restrictions mentioned in s 12 of the 1934 Act (now the Road Traffic Act 1972, s 148(1), above), and the proviso to the section had therefore no application, the finding of the Arbitrator that the assured did not use all reasonable care and diligence to avoid accidents was supported because he had driven in a state when, through having consumed so much alcoholic liquor, he was unfit to have proper control over the vehicle, and distinguishing *Concrete Ltd v Attenborough* (1939) 83 Sol Jo 946, 65 Ll L Rep 174 the insurers were entitled to recover for breach of condition.

BREACH OF CONDITION AFTER ACCIDENT

Road Traffic Act 1972, s 148(2)

148 (2) A condition in a policy or security issued or given for the purposes of this Part of this Act providing that no liability shall arise under the policy or security, or that any liability so arising shall cease, in the event of some specified thing being done or omitted to be done after the happening of the event giving rise to a claim under the policy or security, shall be of no effect in connection with such liabilities as are required to be covered by a policy under s 145 of this Act:

Provided that nothing in this subsection shall be taken to render void any provision in a policy or security requiring the person insured or secured to pay to the insurer or the giver of the security any sums which the latter may have become liable to pay under the policy or security and which have been applied to the satisfaction of the claims of third parties.

Note—This section relates to breach of policy conditions after accident, such as failure to report an accident, but does not affect breaches before or at the time, such as not having a driving licence in force. It replaces without alteration s 206(2) of the 1960 Act.

Bright v Ashfold
[1932] 2 KB 153, 101 LJKB 318, 147 LT 74, 96 JP 182, 48 TLR 357, 76 Sol Jo 344, Div Ct
A motor cycle policy contained a condition exempting from liability if carrying a passenger unless a sidecar was attached. The assured drove the motor cycle with a pillion passenger without a sidecar, and was charged with driving without an effective policy.

HELD: Section 38 only applied to a breach of condition after accident, whereas in this case the condition circumscribed the operation of the policy from the beginning. Therefore there was no policy in force.

Note—Section 38 of the 1930 Act is now s 148 of the 1972 Act.

There is nothing in the Road Traffic Act 1972, apart from s 148(2) to prevent an underwriter and an insured from agreeing that a motor car policy against third-party risks shall contain any conditions which they think fit. If the insured uses the car on the road without complying with the Act he will be liable to a penalty, but this cannot lay a greater burden on the underwriter. The object of s 148(2) is that where, at the time when an accident happened, the person using the car was properly insured, so that the liability of the underwriter arose when the accident happened, the underwriter should not be allowed to escape from that liability owing to something which the insured did or omitted to do after the happening of the accident.

Gray v Blackmore
[1934] 1 KB 95, 103 LJKB 145, 150 LT 99, 50 TLR 23, 47 Ll L Rep 69
(Branson J)
The plaintiff made to the defendant and other underwriters a proposal for insurance of a motor car, and disclosed the fact that he was a garage proprietor. The underwriters issued a policy which provided (inter alia) for indemnity against liability to third persons in respect of bodily injury in the event of accident arising out of the use of the car. The policy also expressly provided that it should not cover liability caused, sustained or incurred while the car was being used otherwise than for 'private purposes', which were defined as meaning 'social, domestic and pleasure purposes and use by the assured in person in connection with his business or profession. The term ''private purposes'' does not include . . . use for any purposes in connection with the motor trade.' A certificate of insurance under Part II of the Road Traffic Act 1930, containing a similar limitation was also issued to the plaintiff. While using the car, as the judge found, for a purpose in connection with the motor trade, the plaintiff had an accident, as a result of which a third party claimed damages for personal injuries. The underwriters having refused to indemnify the plaintiff, he claimed a declaration that they were bound to do so.
HELD: (1) That there was no inconsistency in the clause defining 'private purposes' between the words 'use by the assured in person in connection with his business' and the words excluding 'use for any purposes in connection with the motor trade', and the fact that plaintiff had disclosed that he was a garage proprietor did not entitle him to rely on the first part of the clause and ignore the second. The true construction was that the second half took out of the protection of the policy something which, but for it, the first half would have brought in, namely, use by a garage proprietor personally for the purposes of his business. (2) That, in view of the limitation appearing on the certificate, the issue of the certificate created no estoppel. (3) That the Road Traffic Act 1930, s 36 merely defines the cover which a driver must obtain in order to escape the penal consequences of driving without a policy under s 35. Section 38 does not avoid a condition limiting the cover under a policy: it merely prevents an underwriter escaping liability to a third party by reason of some act or omission of the assured after the claim has arisen. The effect of a breach of the conditions in

the policy is not to throw on the underwriter a burden which he has never agreed to undertake, but merely to put the assured, so far as the insurance provisions of the Road Traffic Act 1930, are concerned, in the same position as if he had never taken out a policy at all.

Note—For ss 35 and 36 of the Road Traffic Act 1930 see Road Traffic Act 1972, s 143 (p 704, above) and s 145 (p 742, above). For s 38 see s 148(2) of the 1972 Act.

PERSON INSURED NOT NAMED IN POLICY

Road Traffic Act 1972, s 148(4)

148 (4) Notwithstanding anything in any enactment, a person issuing a policy of insurance under section 145 of this Act shall be liable to indemnify the persons or classes of persons specified in the policy in respect of any liability which the policy purports to cover in the case of those persons or classes of persons.

Note—For s 145 of the Act, see p 742, above.

This subsection replaces s 206(3) of the 1960 Act which replaced s 36(4) of the Road Traffic Act 1930 without material amendments.

Tattersall v Drysdale
[1935] 2 KB 174, 104 LJKB 511, 153 LT 75, 51 TLR 405, 79 Sol Jo 418, 52 Ll L Rep 21 (Goddard J)
A policy provided 'the insurance shall extend to indemnify any person who is driving on the assured's order or with his permission'. These words (s 36(4) of the 1930 Act — now s 145 of the 1972 Act) mean that, notwithstanding the provisions of the Life Assurance Act 1774, as to insurable interest and as to the absence of any name in the policy other than that of the assured the insurers shall indemnify everyone whom they have said they will indemnify.

Note—The question whether this subsection operates in a case other than of compulsory insurance has been a matter of discussion among insurers since the Act was passed.

The history of the subsection begins with the case of *Williams v Baltic Insurance Association* [1924] 2 KB 282, 93 LJKB 819, 131 LT 671 (Roche J), where the policy was issued to Williams, and his sister, who was not named in the policy, was driving the car. The insurance company took the point that the Life Assurance Act 1774, required the insured to be named in the policy or it was void as a gaming transaction. The court held against the company on two grounds: (1) That it was an insurance of goods, and (2) alternatively, the policy holder was trustee for his sister.

In a case in the Privy Council of *Vandepitte v Preferred Accident* [1933] AC 70, 102 LJ PC 21, 148 LT 169, 49 TLR 90, the suggestion that the policyholder was a trustee was disapproved.

Until the case of *Austin v Zurich Insurance Co* (p 855, below), this point does not seem to have been the subject of express decision. The point arose in *Digby v General Accident* (p 860, below), but was not taken. Insurers generally have probably taken the view that it would be inequitable to say in the policy that they indemnify the driver, though not named, and when a claim arises that they are not bound to do so because he is not named.

Tucker J in *Austin's* case (1944) held that the subsection applies to all cases and is not limited to cases where indemnity is compulsory. The Court of Appeal was not required to deal with the point but expressed no dissent from the judge's view. See p 855, below.

Road Traffic Act 1972, s 148(5)-(7).

For the purpose of enabling a vehicle covered by a private car policy to be used under car-sharing arrangements the following subsections have been added to s 148 by the Transport Act 1980, s 61:

(5) To the extent that a policy or security issued or given for the purposes of this Part of this Act—

(a) restricts, as the case may be, the insurance of the persons insured by the policy or the operation of the security to use of the vehicle for specified purposes (for example, social, domestic and pleasure purposes) of a non-commercial character; or

(b) excludes from, as the case may be, that insurance or the operation of the security—

  (i)   use of the vehicle for hire or reward; or

  (ii) business or commercial use of the vehicle; or

  (iii) use of the vehicle for specified purposes of a business or commercial character, then, for the purposes of that policy or security so far as it relates to such liabilities as are required to be covered by a policy under s 145 of this Act, the use of a vehicle on a journey in the course of which one or more passengers are carried at separate fares shall, if the conditions specified in sub-s (6) below are satisfied, be treated as falling within that restriction or as not falling within that exclusion, as the case may be.

(6) The conditions referred to in sub-s (5) above are—

(a) the vehicle is not adapted to carry more than eight passengers and is not a motor cycle;

(b) the fare or aggregate of the fares paid in respect of the journey does not exceed the amount of the running costs of the vehicle for the journey (which for the purposes of this paragraph shall be taken to include an appropriate amount in respect of depreciation and general wear); and

(c) the arrangements for the payment of fares by the passenger or passengers carried at separate fares were made before the journey began.

(7) Subsections (5) and (6) above apply however the restrictions or exclusions described in sub-s (5) are framed or worded; and in those subsections 'fare' and 'separate fares' have the same meaning as in s 2(4) of the Transport Act 1980.

DUTY OF INSURERS TO SATISFY JUDGMENTS

Road Traffic Act 1972, s 149

149 Duty of insurers or persons giving security to satisfy judgment against persons insured or secured against third-party risks   (1) If, after a certificate of insurance or certificate of security has been delivered under s 147 of this Act to the person by whom a policy has been effected or to whom a security has been given, judgment in respect of any such liability as is required to be covered by a policy of insurance under s 145 of this Act (being a liability covered by the terms of the policy or security to which the certificate relates) is obtained against any person who is insured by the policy or whose liability is covered by the security, as the case may be, then, notwithstanding that the insurer may be entitled to avoid or cancel, or may have avoided or cancelled, the policy or security, he shall, subject to the provisions of this section, pay to the persons entitled to the benefit of the judgment any sum payable thereunder in respect of the liability, including any amount payable in respect of costs and any sum payable in respect of interest on that sum by virtue of any enactment relating to interest on judgments.

(2) No sum shall be payable by an insurer under the foregoing provisions of this section—

(a) in respect of any judgment, unless before or within seven days after the commencement of the proceedings in which the judgment was given, the insurer had notice of the bringing of the proceedings; or

(b) in respect of any judgment, so long as execution thereon is stayed pending an appeal; or

(c) in connection with any liability, if before the happening of the event which was the cause of the death or bodily injury giving rise to the liability, the policy or security was cancelled by mutual consent or by virtue of any provision contained therein, and either—

  (i) before the happening of the said event the certificate was surrendered to the insurer, or the person to whom the certificate was delivered made a statutory declaration stating that the certificate had been lost or destroyed, or

  (ii) after the happening of the said event, but before the expiration of a period of fourteen days from the taking effect of the cancellation of the policy or security, the certificate was surrendered to the insurer, or the person to whom it was delivered made such a statutory declaration as aforesaid; or

  (iii) either before or after the happening of the said event, but within the said period of fourteen days, the insurer has commenced proceedings under this Act in respect of the failure to surrender the certificate.

(3) No sum shall be payable by an insurer under the foregoing provisions of this section if, in an action commenced before, or within three months after, the commencement of the proceedings in which the judgment was given, he has obtained a declaration that, apart from any provision contained in the policy or security, he is entitled to avoid it on the ground that it was obtained by the non-disclosure of a material fact, or by a representation of fact which was false in some material particular, or, if he has avoided the policy or security on that ground, that he was entitled so to do apart from any provision contained in it:

Provided that an insurer who has obtained such a declaration as aforesaid in an action shall not thereby become entitled to the benefit of this subsection as respects any judgment obtained in proceedings commenced before the commencement of that action unless before, or within seven days after, the commencement of that action he has given notice thereof to the person who is the plaintiff in the said proceedings specifying the non-disclosure or false representation on which he proposes to rely; and a person to whom notice of such an action is so given shall be entitled, if he thinks fit, to be made a party thereto.

(4) If the amount which an insurer becomes liable under this section to pay in respect of a liability of a person who is insured by a policy or whose liability is covered by a security exceeds the amount for which he would, apart from the provisions of this section, be liable under the policy or security in respect of that liability, he shall be entitled to recover the excess from that person.

(5) In this section—

(a) 'insurer' includes a person giving a security;

(b) 'material' means of such a nature as to influence the judgment of a prudent insurer in determining whether he will take the risk and, if so, at what premium and on what conditions; and

(c) 'liability covered by the terms of the policy or security' means a liability which is covered by the policy or security or which would be so covered but for the fact that the insurer is entitled to avoid or cancel, or has avoided or cancelled, the policy or security.

Note—This section replaces without amendment s 207 of the 1960 Act which replaced the Road Traffic Act 1934, s 10. Section 158(2) of the 1972 Act provides that in relation to policies under which more than one certificate is issued or a copy certificate, references in the Act to a certificate shall be construed as references to all the certificates or to the copy.

Under the proviso to sub-s (3) of s 149 the procedure is to take out a summons in the action 'For an order that [TP] a party served with notice pursuant to s 149(3) of the Road Traffic Act 1972, be added as a defendant and be at liberty to appear in the said proceedings pursuant to the said Act.'

NOTICE TO INSURERS — s 149(2)(a)

Note—Pursuant to sub-s (2)(a) of s 149 a plaintiff's solicitor should give formal notice to the insurer of the commencement of proceedings. The subsection speaks of commencement of proceedings, not the service of the writ. Presumably it is intended to protect the insurers where an insured fails to send on the writ to insurers and judgment is signed in default, rendering the insurers liable without having had the opportunity to defend.

Similar notice is required to achieve for the plaintiff the protection of the MIB Uninsured Drivers Agreement: see p 776, below.

Express notice necessary

McGoona v Motor Insurers' Bureau and Marsh
[1969] 2 Lloyd's Rep 34, QBD
Per Lawton J: What is a notice for the purpose of sub-s (2)(a) [of s 149]? Now, 'proceedings' in that sub-clause, in my judgment, must mean the beginning of legal proceedings. Notification that a claim may be made is not notification of the commencement of proceedings and there is obviously good reason why the commencement of proceedings is the material time. . . . It is important from the insurers' point of view, too, that they should have notice not later than seven days after commencement

of proceedings because of the danger of judgment in default of appearance being given against the defendant assured.

Herbert v Railway Passengers Assurance Co
[1938] 1 All ER 650, 158 LT 417, 60 Ll L Rep 143 (Porter J)
Notice under sub-s (2)(a) must be something more formal than a casual mention of the proceedings in a conversation. There must be something which indicates that notice is being given.

Weldrick v Essex and Suffolk Equitable Insurance Society
(1950) 83 Ll L Rep 91, erratum p 477 (Birkett J)
On 11 July 1947, solicitors acting for a passenger wrote to the insurers of the car as follows: 'We have been consulted by Mrs Eva Weldrick of 42a High Street, King's Lynn, who is a partner in the business of a drapery peddling carried on by Mr Jan Mahomed, who, we are advised, sustained injuries as a result of an accident which occurred as long ago as 11 March 1947, as a result of Mahomed's car in which she was travelling in connection with the said business, coming into collision with a stationary lorry. We understand your Society has repudiated liability, and we shall be grateful to have your confirmation thereof in writing, because you will appreciate, we shall have to take proceedings as against Mahomed, and as against the owner of the other vehicle, and at the same time give notice to the Motor Insurers' Bureau of your repudiation of liability.'

The insurers replied on 18 July as follows: 'We are in receipt of your letter of the 11th inst, and in reply have to confirm that we have repudiated liability in respect of the unfortunate accident.'
HELD: The insurers had notice that proceedings would almost inevitably be brought but that was not sufficient to satisfy the requirements of s 10(2)(a) of the 1934 Act (now s 149 of the 1972 Act). Adopting Porter J in *Herbert v Railway Passengers Assurance Co* (above) formality was necessary for such a notice and a statutory requirement of this kind must be pretty strictly fulfilled. There was no evidence that defendants had notice of the proceedings either before or within seven days after they had been brought. What they did have was an intimation that in certain circumstances proceedings might be brought, but not necessarily that they would be brought. The requirements of s 10 had not been fulfilled. Insurers did not have notice of the bringing of the action. Judgment for insurers.

Ceylon Motor Insurance Association v Thambugala
[1953] AC 584, [1953] 2 All ER 870, [1953] 1 Lloyd's Rep 289, PC
The Motor Car Ordinance of Ceylon contains provisions in the same terms as s 149(2)(a) of the 1972 Act.

On 21 May 1946, claimant's solicitors wrote to insurers that they were instructed to file an action on behalf of T of (address) for the recovery of damages against K of (address) caused by car No X 4851 on 1 September 1945; that the claim was Rs 15,000; that they understood the car was insured with insurers; and that unless the claim was settled on or before the 31st inst, they were instructed to file action against the owner of the car. HELD: The notice was sufficient. The name of the court was not required, and the words 'unless the claim is settled' did not affect the notice. *Weldrick*'s case not relevant.

Counter-claim: notice

Cross v British Oak Insurance Co Ltd

[1938] 2 KB 167, [1938] 1 All ER 383, 107 LJKB 577, 159 LT 286, 60 Ll L Rep 46 (du Parcq J)

Fowler, insured by defendants, was driving a motor vehicle on 7 January 1936, and injured Cross and Baker. In March 1936, Baker commenced an action against Fowler in county court. Fowler brought in Cross on a third-party notice. Cross filed a counter-claim in county court against Fowler. Cross recovered £90 damages and £28 9s 9d costs against Fowler. The company were served with notice of the third-party proceedings but not of the counter-claim.

HELD: The counter-claim was the commencement of separate proceedings and notice of those proceedings, not having been given within seven days, the company was not liable on the certificate. Proceedings means the proceedings begun by a person who may for this purpose be regarded as a plaintiff, which results in the judgment upon which reliance is placed as against the insurers.

No notice must be pleaded

Baker v Provident Accident and White Cross Insurance Co Ltd

[1939] 2 All ER 690, 83 Sol Jo 565, 64 Ll L Rep 14 (Cassels J)

Absence of notice, if relied on, should be pleaded by insurers.

Setting aside default judgment

Windsor v Chalcraft

[1939] 1 KB 279, [1938] 2 All ER 751, 107 LJKB 609, 159 LT 104, 54 TLR 834, 82 Sol Jo 432, 61 Ll L Rep 69, CA

Third party issued writ against assured and gave notice to insurers under s 10 (now s 149 of the 1972 Act). The writ was served and assured did not inform insurers and allowed judgment to go by default. Damages were assessed by a Master. Third party sued insurers on the certificate. No notice was given by third party to insurers that writ served or case set down. HELD: (Slesser LJ dissenting): Insurers were entitled under Ord XXVII, r 15 (now Ord 13, r 9), which empowers the court to set aside a judgment by default on terms, to have the judgment set aside on the ground that they had an actual interest by reason of the liability imposed by statute and were injuriously affected by it. (*Jacques v Harrison* (1883) 12 QBD 136 followed.)

Cancellation

J. H. Moore & Co v Crowe

[1972] 2 Lloyd's Rep 563, Mayor's and City of London Court

The plaintiffs' fleet of 82 vehicles was insured under a policy issued by the defendant underwriters containing a provision that they were entitled to cancel the policy on seven days' notice and in such event they would refund a proportion of the premium on surrender of the insurance certificate. The defendants supplied the plaintiffs with six copies of the certificate all identical except for the numbers. After receiving notice of cancellation the plaintiffs returned three of the copies but could not find the others. The defendants refused to make a refund of premium until all should be returned.

HELD: The plaintiffs were entitled to a refund. The defendants had not issued six certificates but one only with five additional copies. By returning the certificate numbered 1 the plaintiff had complied with the terms of the policy. The provisions of the Road Traffic Act (ie ss 147 and 149 of the 1972 Act) were irrelevant.

Note—Notice of cancellation given by Lloyd's Underwriters to brokers. A summons was issued and defendant refused to surrender certificate on the ground that the necessary notice had not been served upon him.

Defence upheld, Lord Mayor, at Mansion House, *City Press*, 3 June 1938.

Form of statutory declaration

I, . . . (name) of . . . (address) in the County of . . . (occupation) DO SOLEMNLY AND SINCERELY DECLARE that the certificate of insurance delivered to me by . . . (Insurers) under s 147(1) of the Road Traffic Act 1972, pursuant to Policy No . . . in respect of . . . (make) motor car registration number . . . (which policy has been cancelled) has been lost or destroyed.

AND I MAKE THIS SOLEMN DECLARATION conscientiously believing the same to be true and by virtue of the provisions of the Statutory Declarations Act 1835.

DECLARED at

             in the County

of   this

day of   19. . .

    Before me,

                                     A Commissioner for Oaths

Form of summons for failure to surrender certificate

In the City of London

    To   of

Information has been laid this day by . . . for and on behalf of . . . solicitor to the . . . Insurance Co Ltd for that you on the . . . day of . . . 19. . at . . . (address of insurers) in the said City being a person to whom a certificate of insurance had been delivered under s 147(1) of the Road Traffic Act 1972, and the Policy in relation to such certificate having been cancelled on and from the . . . 19. . by virtue of a provision therein, did unlawfully fail within seven days to surrender the certificate to the insurers, to wit, the . . . Insurance Co Ltd or if it had been lost or destroyed, to make a statutory declaration to that effect. Contrary to s 147(4) of the Road Traffic Act 1972.

You are therefore hereby summoned to appear before the Court of Summary Jurisdiction, sitting at . . . in the . . . on the . . . day of . . . at the hour of eleven in the forenoon to answer to the said information.

    Dated the . . . day of . . . 19. .

ACTION FOR DECLARATION

An action under s 149(3) for a declaration is still essential for an insurer in cases where liability arises under s 149(1) and where it is sought to make the insurers of a potential co-defendant who is only fractionally to blame entirely liable for the judgment by operation of the provisions of the MIB Domestic Agreement.

Indorsement of writ for declaration

The plaintiffs claim—
    1 A declaration that they were entitled to avoid a policy of insurance, dated . . . No . . . issued by them to the defendant, apart from any provision contained in the said policy on the ground that it was obtained by non-disclosure of a material fact or facts and/or representations of fact which were false in some material particular or particulars.
    2 Further or other relief.
    3 Costs.

Notice to third party

As solicitors for and on behalf of (insurers) we hereby give you notice in pursuance of sub-s 3 of s 149 of the Road Traffic Act 1972, that the said (insurers) as the Insurers under Policy No . . . , dated . . . issued by them to one (assured) have commenced an action (19   ) No . . . in the Queen's Bench Division of the High Court of Justice on the . . . day of . . . against the said (assured) for a declaration in pursuance of sub-s 3 of s 149 of the Road Traffic Act 1972, that the said (insurers) were entitled to avoid the said policy on the ground that it was obtained by the said (assured) by non-disclosure of material facts and/or representations of fact which were false in material particulars, and that they propose to rely on the following representations and non-disclosure.

Representations

By a written proposal, dated . . . the said (Assured) represented (1) that . . . when in truth it was . . . and (2) . . .

Non-disclosure

The said (Assured) failed to disclose that . . . Dated . . .
To (Third Party).

Declaration action before third party action

Zurich General Accident and Liability Insurance Co v Livingston
1938 SC 582, 1938 SLT 441, Scot
Insurers brought proceedings for a declaration and third parties, who had not commenced proceedings against the assured before the commencement of the action for a declaration, applied for leave to be joined as defendants.
HELD: That the third parties were entitled to be added as defendants, in

respect that while they had not a statutory title by virtue of the proviso to s 10(3) they had at common law a title to defend an action which might deprive them of the statutory right conferred upon them by s 10(1).

Note—For s 10(1) and s 10(3) of the 1934 Act, see now the Road Traffic Act 1972 s 149(1) and (3) (p 761, above).

Rights limited to notice

Contigency Insurance Co v Lyons
(1939) 65 Ll L Rep 53, CA
Insurers issued writ for declaration and served notice on third party on the ground that the car, insured for private pleasure, was being used for hiring. In the statement of claim they added grounds, not mentioned in the notice, of non-disclosure of material facts in the proposal form. The third party applied to strike out the additional grounds from the statement of claim.

The Court of Appeal declined to strike out and held the questions should be dealt with at the trial.
SEMBLE (per MacKinnon LJ): It is doubtful if grounds not stated in the notice are open to the insurer.

Note—This point was afterwards decided in the following case.

Zurich General Accident and Liability Insurance Co v Morrison
[1942] 2 KB 53, [1942] 1 All ER 529, 111 LJKB 601, 167 LT 183, 58 TLR 217, CA
A declaration cannot be made against a third party on grounds not stated in the notice. The court cannot vary the section of the Act.

Per MacKinnon LJ: The grounds are limited to those specified in the notice.

Delay in declaration action

Trafalgar Insurance Co Ltd v McGregor
[1942] 1 KB 275, 111 LJKB 193, 166 LT 213, 71 Ll L Rep 107, CA
Insurers on 4 October 1939, issued a writ for a declaration for non-disclosure of all motoring convictions. On 11 March 1940, the third party wrote for particulars. On 15 March 1940, on motion by insurers for judgment in default against assured, Charles J adjourned the motion until trial and ordered the particulars. The assured disappeared and insurers were unable to obtain the information required for the particulars. After 18 months the third party applied for dismissal of the action for non-compliance with the order for particulars.
ORDERED: That insurers be precluded at the trial from giving evidence in support of certain parts of the statement of claim. The judge at the trial has discretion to admit evidence on terms.

Declaration action: position of MIB

Note—See *Fire Auto and Marine Insurance Co Ltd v Greene*, p 786, below.

Discovery of documents

Merchants' and Manufacturers' Insurance Co v Davies

[1938] 1 KB 196, [1937] 2 All ER 767, 106 LJ KB 423, 156 LT 524, 53 TLR
717, 81 Sol Jo 457, 58 Ll L Rep 61, CA
In a declaration action by motor insurers to avoid a policy for non-
disclosure of convictions the defendant applied for discovery of documents
against the insurers to show cases where non-disclosure of convictions had
not been relied on as a ground for refusing insurance cover. The application was refused.

Agreement in lieu of action

Note—It is frequently desirable to deal with a case whilst denying liability under the
policy to avoid the expense of declaration. In such a case a written authority should
be taken.

To . . . (insurers)
I hereby authorise and request you to instruct a solicitor on my behalf to defend the
action brought against me by . . . and I agree that your so doing is entirely without
prejudice to all questions under the policy issued by you to me and without
prejudice to your right to apply for a declaration under s 149(3) of the Road Traffic
Act 1972, and that the repudiation of all liability under the policy by you remains
in full force and effect.

Liability covered by the terms of the policy

Campbell v McFarland and Armagh UDC

[1972] NI 31
In a collision between McFarland's car and a refuse lorry a dustman was
injured. He sued McFarland and his own employers, the owners of the
lorry, and obtained judgment for £12,500 against both. The judgment allocated 25% blame to McFarland and gave a right to contribution as
between the defendants. McFarland's insurers had refused to indemnify
him under their policy on the ground of misrepresentation and took no part
in the action. The plaintiff demanded that his employers should satisfy the
whole of the judgment and they did so. They then applied to the Court to
order direct reimbursement to them from McFarland's insurers of one-
quarter of the damages by virtue of the Motor Vehicles and Road Traffic
Act (Northern Ireland) 1934, s 18 (which was similar in effect to s 207 of
the Road Traffic Act 1960 (now s 149 of the Road Traffic Act 1972)).
HELD. The application failed. The question was whether a policy issued
for the purposes of that part of the Act requiring compulsory insurance
against third-party risks is required to cover liability under an order for
contribution. There were two distinct liabilities facing McFarland (1) his
liability at common law to the plaintiff for which he was obliged to have
compulsory insurance, and (2) his liability under the Law Reform
(Miscellaneous Provisions) Act (Northern Ireland) 1937, s 16 (which was
to the same effect as the Law Reform (Married Women and Tortfeasors)
Act 1935, s 6, p 17, above). The first was a liability to meet in full a
judgment obtained against him by the plaintiff, and he was bound by
statute to insure against it; but the second was a separate liability created by

the Law Reform Act. Though the policy did give cover against the liability
to contribute it was not a liability the policy was required to cover by the
compulsory insurance provisions of the Road Traffic Act. Following
Lockerbie's case (below) a liability which was covered by the policy but
which was not required to be covered did not come within the scope of s 18
of the 1934 Act.

Lockerbie v Eagle Star Insurance Co
20 March 1936 (Lord Jamieson)
The pursuer was a passenger (not within the category of passengers
required to be covered) in a motor car belonging to one Lee and was
injured in an accident to the car. She obtained a judgment for damages
against Lee and then sued Lee's insurers under s 10(1) of the Road Traffic
Act 1934 (now s 149 of the 1972 Act).

The words 'being a liability covered by the terms of the policy' did not
apply. That would bring within the scope of the section any liability
covered by the policy whether required to be covered or not. That is clearly
not the meaning of the section. It is limited to cases in which liability is
required to be covered. The words quoted are necessary to protect insurers
who are not liable unless the liability is in fact covered by the policy.

W. R. Chown & Co Ltd v Herbert
(1950) 100 LJ 597, Wandsworth Cty Ct (Judge Hodgson)
The Trafalgar insured the defendant under a motor policy containing the
condition 'the insured shall repay to the company all sums paid by the
company in discharge satisfaction or settlement of the liability' required by
the Road Traffic Act to be covered by insurance 'incurred to a third party
by the insured . . . which the company would not have been liable to pay
but for the provisions of the Act'. After a collision between the insured's car
and a cab the Trafalgar refused indemnity because of a mis-statement in
the proposal form but settled the cab driver's claim for damages for
personal injury at £75 and also paid the hospital charges of £15. The plaintiffs sued the defendant for damage to the cab; the defendant joined the
Trafalgar as third parties in the action, claiming indemnity and the
Trafalgar counterclaimed for the £90 they had paid to the cab driver. The
judge held that the Trafalgar were entitled to refuse indemnity because of
the mis-statement, but on the counterclaim:
HELD: The Trafalgar could not recover the £75 paid to the cab driver from
the defendant. The liability to pay the cab driver under the Road Traffic
Act 1934, s 10 (now s 149 of the 1972 Act) did not arise until there was a
judgment and there had been no judgment. The condition in the policy
covered an existing liability only, not a contingent one. The payment of
hospital charges was a statutory liability, however, and the Trafalgar were
entitled to be repaid the £15 by the defendant under the terms of the
condition.

Intentional injury

Note—See *Hardy v MIB*, p 784, and *Gardner v Moore*, p 785, below.

Policy covering owner but not driver

Note—See *Lees v Motor Insurers' Bureau*, p 721, above.

BANKRUPTCY OF INSURED

Road Traffic Act 1972, s 150

150 Bankruptcy, etc, of insured or secured persons not to affect claims by third parties (1) Where, after a certificate of insurance or certificate of security has been delivered under s 147 of this Act to the person by whom a policy has been effected or to whom a security has been given, any of the following events happens, that is to say,—

(a) the person by whom the policy was effected or to whom the security was given becomes bankrupt or makes a composition or arrangement with his creditors;

(b) the said person dies, and an order is made under s 130 of the Bankruptcy Act 1914, for the administration of his estate according to the law of bankruptcy;

(c) if the said person is a company, a winding-up order is made with respect to the company or a resolution for a voluntary winding up is passed with respect thereto, or a receiver or manager of the company's business or undertaking is duly appointed or possession is taken, by or on behalf of the holders of any debentures secured by a floating charge, of any property comprised in or subject to the charge.

the happening of that event shall, notwithstanding anything in the Third Parties (Rights Against Insurers) Act 1930, not affect any such liability of the said person as is required to be covered by a policy of insurance under s 145 of this Act, but nothing in this subsection shall affect any rights conferred by that Act on the person to whom the liability was incurred, being rights so conferred against the person by whom the policy was issued or the security was given.

DUTY TO GIVE PARTICULARS OF INSURANCE

Road Traffic Act 1972, s 151

151 Duty to give information as to insurance or security where claim made (1) A person against whom a claim is made in respect of any such liability as is required to be covered by a policy of insurance under section 145 of this Act shall, on demand by or on behalf of the person making the claim—

(a) state whether or not, in respect of that liability, he was insured by a policy having effect for the purposes of this Part of this Act or had in force a security having effect for those purposes, or would have been so insured or would have had in force such a security if the insurer or, as the case may be, the giver of the security had not avoided or cancelled the policy or security, and

(b) if he was or would have been so insured, or had or would have had in force such a security, give such particulars with respect to that policy or security as were specified in [any certificate of insurance or security delivered in respect of that policy or security, as the case may be, under s 147 of this Act, or where no such certificate was delivered under the said section the following particulars, that is to say, the registration mark or other identifying particulars of the vehicle concerned, the number or other identifying particulars of the insurance policy issued in respect of the vehicle, the name of the insurer and the period of the insurance cover].

(2) If without reasonable excuse, a person fails to comply with the provisions of the sub-s (1) above or wilfully makes a false statement in reply to any such demand as aforesaid, he shall be guilty of an offence.

Note—The words in square brackets in sub-s (1)(b) were inserted by the Motor Vehicles (Compulsory Insurance) (No 2) Regulations 1973, SI 1973/2143.

Road Traffic Act 1972, s 154

Note—See 'Hospital charges', p 426, above.

EMERGENCY MEDICAL TREATMENT

Road Traffic Act 1972, s 155

155 Payment for emergency treatment of traffic casualties   (1) Where medical or surgical treatment or examination is immediately required as a result of bodily injury (including fatal injury) to a person caused by, or arising out of, the use of a motor vehicle on a road, and the treatment or examination so required (in this Part of this Act referred to as 'emergency treatment') is effected by a legally qualified medical practitioner, the person who was using the vehicle at the time of the event out of which bodily injury arose shall, on a claim's being made in accordance with the provisions of s 156 of this Act, pay to the practitioner, or, where emergency treatment is effected by more than one practitioner, to the practitioner by whom it is first effected—
(a) a fee of £1.25 in respect of each person in whose case the emergency treatment is effected by him; and
(b) a sum, in respect of any distance in excess of two miles which he must cover in order to proceed from the place whence he is summoned to the place where the emergency treatment is carried out by him and to return to the first-mentioned place, equal to $2\frac{1}{2}$ new pence for every complete mile and additional part of a mile of that distance.
(2) Where emergency treatment is first effected in a hospital, the provisions of sub-s (1) above with respect to payment of a fee shall, so far as applicable, but subject (as regards the recipient of a payment) to the provisions of s 156 of this Act, have effect with the substitution of references to the hospital for references to a legally qualified medical practitioner.
(3) Liability insured under this section by the person using a vehicle shall, where the event out of which it arose was caused by the wrongful act of another person, be treated for the purposes of any claim to recover damage by reason of that wrongful act as damage sustained by the person using the vehicle.

In respect of accidents occurring on or after 1 August 1981 £10.00 is substituted for £1.25 and 18 pence for $2\frac{1}{2}$ pence by the Road Traffic Accidents (Payments for Treatment) (England and Wales) Order 1981 SI 1981/929. SI 1982/1194 increases £10 to £10.90 as from 20 September 1982. The Road Traffic Act 1972, s 156 contains supplementary provisions as to payments for treatment.

CHAPTER 19
Motor Insurers' Bureau

Historical note — The Third Parties (Rights Against Insurers) Act 1930 and the Road Traffic Acts 1930 and 1934 enabled persons injured in road accidents to enforce against motor insurers judgments obtained against motorists who were in breach of policy conditions or whose policies were voidable. This still left effectively uncompensated persons injured by motorists who had no insurance at all. In 1937 the Cassel Committee recommended that a Central Fund should be set up from which victims of motor accidents caused by uninsured motorists could obtain compensation. The war having intervened it was not until 1946 that such a fund was set up by the motor insurance market, including Lloyds. It was done by forming a company, limited by guarantee, known as the Motor Insurers' Bureau to hold and administer the Central Fund, which was and is funded by the motor insurers themselves. Most motor insurers and Lloyds motor syndicates became members of the Bureau. Since 1974 all authorised insurers as defined in the Road Traffic Act 1972, s 145 are required to be members (Road Traffic Act 1974, s 20) The Bureau is not itself an insurance company. The means by which uninsured claims were to be satisfied were laid down in an agreement with the Minister of Transport of 17 June 1946. This was replaced from time to time by similar agreements. The current Uninsured Drivers Agreement is that of 22 November 1972 (below), entered into between the Bureau and the Secretary of State for the Environment.

The 1946 agreement still left uncompensated the victim of a 'hit-and-run' driver ie a driver whose identity was unknown, except that by note 6 of the agreement the Bureau undertook to give 'sympathetic consideration to the making of an ex gratia payment to the victim'. This loose arrangement was replaced in 1969 by an Untraced Drivers Agreement establishing a detailed procedure by which to deal with such cases. The current

Untraced Drivers Agreement, dated 22 November 1972 is set out below at pp 789–796.

The Bureau deals also with personal injury claims

1 against foreign motorists visiting Britain (p 801, below), and

2 where the user of the vehicle was insured but the insurer has become insolvent (p 783, below).

THE UNINSURED DRIVERS' AGREEMENT

Note—The current agreement set out below is dated 22 November 1972 and is effective in respect of accidents occurring on and after 1 December 1972. It replaced the agreement of 1 February 1971 which itself replaced the original agreement of 17 June 1946. The Agreement and the Notes is an official publication and is Crown copyright. It is reproduced by permission of the Controller of HM Stationery Office, from which copies can be bought.

The parties to the agreement are the Motor Insurers' Bureau and the Secretary of State for the Environment. There is thus no privity of contract between the Bureau and a claimant, nor between the Bureau and the uninsured driver. Nevertheless the Bureau allows itself to be sued if a breach of the terms of the agreement is alleged (see p 782, below). The whole of the Bureau's duties and liabilities in respect of a claim against an uninsured driver arise from the agreement. Thus the first essential for anyone conducting such a claim is to READ THE AGREEMENT and the notes appended to it.

Text of an Agreement dated 22 November 1972 between the Secretary of State for the Environment and the Motor Insurers' Bureau together with some notes on its scope and purpose.
In accordance with the Agreement made on 31 December 1945 between the Minister of War Transport and insurers transacting compulsory motor vehicle insurance business in Great Britain (published by the Stationery Office under the title 'Motor Vehicle Insurance Fund') a corporation called the 'Motor Insurers' Bureau' entered into an agreement on 17 June 1946 with the Minister of Transport to give effect from 1 July 1946 to the principle recommended in July 1937 by the Departmental Committee under Sir Felix Cassel, (Cmd 5528), to secure compensation to third party victims of road accidents in cases where, notwithstanding the provisions of the Road Traffic Acts relating to compulsory insurance, the victim is deprived of compensation by the absence of insurance, or of effective insurance. That Agreement was replaced by an Agreement which operated in respect of accidents occurring on or after 1 March 1971. The Agreement of 1971 has now been replaced by a new Agreement which operates in respect of accidents occurring on or after 1 December 1972.

The text of the new Agreement is as follows—

MEMORANDUM OF AGREEMENT made the 22nd day of November 1972 between the Secretary of State for the Environment and the Motor Insurers' Bureau, whose registered office is at Aldermary House, Queen Street, London, EC4N 1TR (hereinafter referred to as 'MIB') SUPPLEMENTAL to an Agreement (hereinafter called 'the Principal Agreement') made the 31st day of December 1945 between the Minister of War Transport and the insurers transacting compulsory motor vehicle insurance business in Great Britain by or on behalf of whom the said Agreement was signed in pursuance of paragraph 1 of which MIB was incorporated.

IT IS HEREBY AGREED AS FOLLOWS—
DEFINITIONS
1 In this Agreement—
    'contract of insurance' means a policy of insurance or a security;
    'insurer' includes the giver of a security;

'relevant liability' means a liability in respect of which a policy of insurance must insure a person in order to comply with Part VI of the Road Traffic Act 1972.

Note—For Part VI of the Road Traffic Act 1972 see pp 704 to 772, above, especially ss 143 and 145; for a relevant decision see *Cooper v MIB*, p 742, above. It is also a necessary factor that the accident should have occurred on a 'road' within the definition in s 196(1) of the 1972 Act, pp 733 to 741, above.

SATISFACTION OF CLAIMS BY MIB

2 If judgment in respect of any relevant liability is obtained against any person or persons in any court in Great Britain whether or not such a person or persons be in fact covered by a contract of insurance and any such judgment is not satisfied in full within seven days from the date upon which the person or persons in whose favour the judgment was given became entitled to enforce it then MIB will, subject to the provisions of Clauses 4, 5 and 6 hereof, pay or satisfy or cause to be paid or satisfied to or to the satisfaction of the person or persons in whose favour the judgment was given any sum payable or remaining payable thereunder in respect of the relevant liability including any sum awarded by the Court in respect of interest on that sum and any taxed costs or any costs awarded by the Court without taxation (or such proportion thereof as is attributable to the relevant liability) whatever may be the cause of the failure of the judgment debtor to satisfy the judgment.

Note—See notes 2 and 3 appended to the agreement (p 779, below). As there is no privity of contract between a claimant and the Bureau the claimant has, at law, no cause of action but in practice the Bureau submits to being sued without taking the point. See p 782, below, 'Enforcing judgment: proceedings against the Motor Insurers' Bureau'.

PERIOD OF AGREEMENT

3 This Agreement shall be determinable by the Secretary of State at any time or by MIB on twelve months' notice without prejudice to the continued operation of the Agreement in respect of accidents occurring before the date of termination.

RECOVERIES

4 Nothing in this Agreement shall prevent insurers from providing by conditions in their contracts of insurance that all sums paid by them or by MIB by virtue of the Principal Agreement or this Agreement in or towards the discharge of the liability of their assured shall be recoverable by them or by MIB from the assured or from any other person.

Note—This clause relates to recovery of sums paid to a claimant by or on behalf of an 'insurer concerned' (see p 787, below). A usual form of words in a policy is 'The insured shall repay to the Company all sums paid by the Company which the Company would not have been liable to pay but for the provisions of the law of any territory in which the policy operates'.

CONDITIONS PRECEDENT TO MIB'S LIABILITY

5 (1) MIB shall not incur any liability under Clause 2 of this Agreement unless—
Notice of proceedings
(a) notice of the bringing of the proceedings is given before or within seven days after the commencement of the proceedings—
    (i) to MIB in the case of proceedings in respect of a relevant liability which is either not covered by a contract of insurance or covered by a contract of insurance with an insurer whose identity cannot be ascertained, or
    (ii) to the insurer in the case of proceedings in respect of a relevant liability

which is covered by a contract of insurance with an insurer whose identity can be ascertained;

Note—'Notice'. See note 4 at the end of the agreement. The requirement of notice is in similar terms to that of notice to insurers in the Road Traffic Act 1972, s 149(2)(a) and the cases under the Act (pp 763–765, above) would seem equally applicable to cl 5(1)(a) of the Motor Insurers' Bureau agreement.

It should be observed that this condition, like the others in cl 5, is a condition precedent to the Bureau's liability. Any failure to comply precludes ab initio enforcement against the Bureau of an unsatisfied judgment obtained against a tortfeasor.

Supply of information
(b) such information relating to the proceedings as MIB may reasonably require is supplied to MIB by the person bringing the proceedings;
Judgment against all persons liable
(c) if so required by MIB and subject to full indemnity from MIB as to costs the person bringing the proceedings has taken all reasonable steps to obtain judgment against all the persons liable in respect of the injury or death of the third party and, in the event of such a person being a servant or agent, against his principal;

Note—Another tortfeasor liable. As the Bureau is required by the agreement only to meet unsatisfied judgments it will not meet or contribute to any judgment which another tortfeasor is liable for and is able to satisfy. This is so even where the uninsured driver is partly to blame. If some degree of blame might conceivably be attached to another driver who is insured then a claimant can be required under cl 5(1)(c) to join the insured driver as a defendant and pursue the claim against him. However, the requirement should be properly worded so as to make clear that cl 5(1)(c) is being referred to and the indemnity for costs mentioned. If the insurer of the other tortfeasor is a motor insurer and therefore a party to the Domestic Agreement (see p 787, below) then the liability of the insurer to the Bureau is provided for by that agreement. If the other tortfeasor is not insured (e g a highway authority) or is insured in respect of a liability other than vehicle insurance then, it is submitted, a contribution judgment obtained by such a party against the uninsured driver cannot be enforced against the Bureau in separate proceedings or otherwise (see *Campbell v McFarland*, p 769, above for an analogous situation under the Road Traffic legislation). As to costs on a full indemnity basis see *EMI Records Ltd v Ian Cameron Wallace Ltd*, p 612, above).

Assignment of judgment
(d) the judgment referred to in Clause 2 of this Agreement and any judgment referred to in paragraph (c) of this Clause which has been obtained (whether or not either judgment includes an amount in respect of a liability other than a relevant liability) and any order for costs are assigned to MIB or their nominee.

Note—This condition (which must be fulfilled by the claimant on request as a condition precedent to any payment by the Bureau of an unsatisfied judgment) is to enable the Bureau to execute the judgment against the uninsured driver. It also may, it is submitted, operate to give the Bureau (or an 'insurer concerned') the rights of a judgment creditor under the Road Traffic Act 1972, s 149 against the insurer of the judgment debtor under a driving-other-vehicles extension who has declined to meet the judgment for breach of a condition which is void or of no effect under s 148.

(2) In the event of any dispute as to the reasonableness of a requirement by MIB for the supply of information or that any particular step should be taken to obtain

judgment against other persons it may be referred to the Secretary of State whose decision shall be final.

(3) Where a judgment which includes an amount in respect of a liability other than a relevant liability has been assigned to MIB or their nominee in pursuance of para (1)(d) of this Clause MIB shall apportion any monies received in pursuance of the judgment according to the proportion which the damages in respect of the relevant liability bear to the damages in respect of the other liabilities and shall account to the person in whose favour the judgment was given in respect of such monies received properly apportionable to the other liabilities. Where an order for costs in respect of such a judgment has been so assigned monies received pursuant to the order shall be dealt with in the same manner.

EXEMPTIONS

6 (1) MIB shall not incur any liability under Clause 2 of this Agreement in a case where—

(a) the claim arises out of the use of a vehicle owned by or in the possession of the Crown, except where any other person has undertaken responsibility for the existence of a contract of insurance under Part VI of the Road Traffic Act 1972 (whether or not the person or persons liable be in fact covered by a contract of insurance) or where the liability is in fact covered by a contract of insurance;

(b) the claim arises out of the use of a vehicle the use of which is not required to be covered by a contract of insurance by virtue of s 144 of the Road Traffic Act 1972, unless the use is in fact covered by such a contract;

(c) at the time of the accident the person suffering death or bodily injury in respect of which the claim is made was allowing himself to be carried in a vehicle and—

    (i) knew or had reason to believe that the vehicle had been taken without the consent of the owner or other lawful authority except in a case where—

        (A) he believed or had reason to believe that he had lawful authority to be carried or that he would have had the owner's consent if the owner had known of his being carried and the circumstances of his carriage; or

        (B) he had learned of the circumstances of the taking of the vehicle since the commencement of the journey and it would be unreasonable to expect him to have alighted from the vehicle; or

    (ii) being the owner of or being a person using the vehicle, he was using or causing or permitting the vehicle to be used without there being in force in relation to such use a contract of insurance as would comply with Part VI of the Road Traffic Act 1972, knowing or having reason to believe that no such contract was in force.

Note—'Knowing or having reason to believe' (Clause 6(1)(c)(ii)). See *Porter v Addo, Porter v Motor Insurers' Bureau*, p 783, below.

(2) The exemption specified in sub-para (1)(c) of this Clause shall apply only in a case where the judgment in respect of which the claim against MIB is made was obtained in respect of a relevant liability incurred by the owner or a person using the vehicle in which the person who suffered death or bodily injury was being carried.

(3) For the purposes of these exemptions—

(a) a vehicle which has been unlawfully removed from the possession of the Crown shall be taken to continue in that possession whilst it is kept so removed;

(b) references to a person being carried in a vehicle include references to his being carried in or upon or entering or getting on to or alighting from the vehicle.

(c) 'owner' in relation to a vehicle which is the subject of a hiring agreement or a hire-purchase agreement, means the person in possession of the vehicle under that agreement.

AGENTS

7 Nothing in this Agreement shall prevent MIB performing their obligations

under this Agreement by Agents.

Note—See note 4 appended to the agreement. Where there is no policy or the identity of the insurer is unknown the Bureau for the purpose of investigation appoints an insurance office, the 'investigating office' to make enquiries and, where appropriate, negotiate settlement. This function does not, of course, mean that the office is question is an 'insurer concerned', as to which see p 787, below. This should be self-evident, but the mistake is often made.

OPERATION

8 This agreement shall come into operation on the first day of December 1972 in relation to accidents occurring on or after that date. The agreement made on 1 February 1971 between the Secretary of State and MIB shall cease and determine except in relation to claims arising out of accidents occurring before the first day of December 1972.

IN WITNESS etc

NOTES

The following notes are for the guidance of those who may have a claim on the Motor Insurers' Bureau under the Agreement, and of their legal advisers, but they must not be taken as rendering unnecessary a careful study of the Agreement itself. Communications on any matter connected with the Agreement should be addressed to the Motor Insurers' Bureau whose address is Aldermary House, Queen Street, London, EC 4.

1 The agreement, which operates from 1 December 1972, supersedes earlier agreements made on 17 June 1946 (which was operative from 1 July 1946) and on 1 February 1971 (which was operative from 1 March 1971) in relation to claims arising out of accidents occurring on or after 1 December 1972.

2 If damages are awarded by a court in respect of death or personal injury arising out of the use of a motor vehicle on a road in circumstances where the liability is one which was, at the time the accident occurred, required to be covered by insurance and such damages, or any part of them, remain unpaid seven days after the judgment becomes enforeable, the Bureau will, subject to the exceptions in Clause 6 of the agreement, pay the unrecovered amount (including any interest awarded by the court and costs) to the person in whose favour the judgment has been given against an assignment of the judgment debt. This applies whether the judgment debtor is a British resident or a foreign visitor.

3 Nothing in the Agreement affects the position at law of the parties to an action for damages arising out of the driving of a motor vehicle. The Bureau's liability under the Agreement can only arise when the plaintiff has successfully established his case against the person or persons liable in the usual manner and judgment has been given in his favour. There is, of course, nothing to exclude the acceptance of compensation by the plaintiff under a settlement negotiated between the plaintiff and the alleged person liable or the Bureau.

4 WHERE THERE IS A POLICY. In cases where it is ascertained that there is in existence a policy issued in compliance with the Road Traffic Act 1972, the insurer concerned will normally act as the agent of the Bureau and, subject to notice being given as provided for in Clause 5(1)(a)(ii), will handle claims within the terms of the Agreement. This will apply even if the use of the vehicle at the time of the accident was outside the terms of the policy or the insurer is entitled to repudiate liability under the policy for any other reason. (In the latter connection, victims and those acting on their behalf are reminded of the requirements as to the giving of notice to the insurer if the protection afforded to third parties by s 149 of the Road Traffic Act is sought.) This arrangement is, of course, without prejudice to any rights insurers may have against their policy holders and, to avoid any possible misapprehension, it is emphasised that there is nothing in this Agreement affecting any obligations imposed on a policy holder by his policy. Policy holders are not released from their contractual obligations to their insurers, although the scheme

protects THIRD PARTY VICTIMS from the consequences of failure to observe them. For example, the failure of a policy holder to notify claims to his insurers as required by his policy, although not affecting a victim's right to benefit under the scheme, may leave the policy holder liable to his insurers.

WHERE THERE IS NO POLICY OR THE IDENTITY OF THE INSURER CANNOT BE ASCERTAINED. In cases where there is no policy, or for any reason the existence of a policy is in doubt or where there is a policy but the identity of the insurer cannot be ascertained, the victim or those acting on his behalf must notify the Bureau of the claim. It is a condition of the Bureau's liability that they should receive notification before or within 7 days after the commencement of proceedings against the alleged person liable. In practice, however, it will be preferable to notify the Bureau in all cases where the name of the insurer is not speedily forthcoming.

5 Claims arising out of the use of uninsured vehicles owned by or in the possession of the Crown will in the majority of cases be outside the scope of the Bureau's liability (see Clause 6 of the Agreement). In such cases the approach should be made to the responsible authority in the usual way. The same benefits in respect of compensation will be afforded by the Crown to the victim in such cases as they would receive were the accident caused by a private vehicle except where the victim is a serviceman or servicewoman whose death or injury gives rise to an entitlement to a pension or other compensation from public funds.

6 The Bureau have no liability UNDER THIS AGREEMENT to pay compensation in respect of any person who may suffer personal injuries or death resulting from the use on a road of a vehicle, the owner or driver of which cannot be traced. However, in relation to accidents occurring ON OR AFTER 1 May 1969 and before 1 December 1972, an agreement dated 21 April 1969 between the Minister of Transport (now the Secretary of State for the Environment) and the Bureau for the Compensation of Victims of Untraced Drivers applies. In relation to accidents occurring on or after 1 December 1972, an Agreement dated 22 November 1972 between the Secretary of State and the Bureau applies.

LIABILITY TO CLAIMANTS

Road Traffic Act liability only

Note—See Note 2 to the agreement, p 779, above. It follows that the Motor Insurers' Bureau will meet claims arising only from personal injury or death resulting from the use of a motor vehicle on a 'road' as defined in the Road Traffic Act 1972, s 196. Loss resulting from the injury, such as loss of earnings, is claimable, but not loss or damage which, though resulting from the same accident, is not the result of the personal injury. See cl 5(3) of the agreement. See *Cooper v Motor Insurers' Bureau*, p 742, above.

Where there is a policy

Note—See Note 4 to the 1971 agreement. Where there is a policy in force on a vehicle even though the policy was not effective to cover the driver at the time of the accident, or was voidable or for some reason unenforceable, the insurer who issued the policy (the 'Insurer concerned': see p 787, below) will deal with the claim. In such cases Motor Insurers' Bureau itself is not normally concerned with the claim at all, unless there is disagreement with the insurer concerned whether the claim comes within the agreement. See p 782, below, 'Enforcing judgment'.

Notice of proceedings

Note—See cl 5(1)(a)(i) and (ii) and Note 4. See also cases under heading 'Notice to insurers', p 776–7, above.

Defendant disappeared — substituted service

Note—Claims against a driver whose identity has never been established (ie a hit-and-run driver) are not within the agreement set out above but come within the agreement on untraced drivers, p 789, below. But a driver whose identity is known but who has disappeared is not an 'untraced' driver and judgment must be obtained to create liability on the Bureau. In such a case substituted service of proceedings can be effected at the address of the Bureau as in *Gurtner*'s case (below) and set out in the *Supreme Court Practice* in the note 65/4/6 to Ord 65, r 4.

Plaintiffs' solicitors sometimes attempt to serve a disappeared defendant by posting the writ to his 'last known address' (RSC Ord 10, r 1(2)), and then proceed to sign judgment in default of notice of intention to defend. It would seem that if it can be shown that, at the time of posting, the address in question was no longer the defendant's address and that the writ could not have reached him there service is bad and the judgment will be set aside. See *White v Weston* (p 683, above).

Gurtner v Circuit
[1968] 2 QB 587, [1968] 1 All ER 328, [1968] 2 WLR 668, 112 Sol Jo 73, [1968] 1 Lloyd's Rep 171, CA

The plaintiff's solicitors issued a writ against the defendant but were unable to serve it personally because he had gone to Canada and could not be traced. Although it appeared from the police report that the defendant had produced a valid insurance certificate after the accident the insurers could not be identified. The plaintiff's solicitors applied to the Motor Insurers' Bureau who instructed the Royal Insurance Company to investigate. The solicitors obtained an order for substituted service of the writ on the defendant by sending it to the Royal Insurance Company by ordinary prepaid post.

HELD, ON APPEAL: It was obviously wrong to order service on the defendant at the address of the Royal Insurance Company, since the affidavit did not show that the writ was likely to reach the defendant or come to his notice. The order could be set aside if it would serve any useful purpose. If there was any possibility of tracing the defendant in Canada, substituted service should be ordered by advertisement but that seemed useless in the present case and the order should be allowed to stand. Where it is not possible to ascertain the insurers an order might be made for service at the address of the Bureau but such an order should not be made except on evidence that all reasonable efforts have been made by the plaintiff to trace the defendant and effect personal service.

Clarke v Vedel
[1979] RTR 26, CA

The plaintiffs were injured in a collision with a motor cycle. The motor cyclist gave his name as David Vedel. He disappeared after the accident and could not be traced. The address he gave turned out to be false; he produced no insurance or other documents to the police. The motor cycle, bearing false number plates, had been stolen from its lawful owner some months earlier. The records of the Registrar of Births and Deaths showed no entry for any person named David Vedel at the time of the date of birth he gave. The plaintiffs issued a writ against 'David Vedel' and obtained an order for substituted service at the address of the Motor Insurers' Bureau. The 'insurers concerned' under the Domestic Agreement applied in the name of the Bureau to set aside the order.

HELD: The order should be set aside. *Gurtner v Circuit* (above) was not an authority for saying that it is proper in every case where the Bureau may be involved to make an order for substituted service on the defendant at the address of the Bureau. The order could not possibly bring the proceedings to the notice of whoever was the motor cyclist. It was an Untraced Drivers Agreement case and should be dealt with under that agreement.

Per Stevenson LJ: This court recognises that there may be cases where a defendant who cannot be traced and, therefore, is unlikely to be reached by any form of substituted service, can nevertheless be ordered to be served at the address of the insurers or the Bureau in a road accident case. But . . . I am not satisfied that it applies to this case.

Enforcing judgment: proceedings against the Motor Insurers' Bureau

Note—Cases can, and do, arise where the Motor Insurers' Bureau or the 'insurer concerned' (see p 787, below) dispute their liability under the agreement on the ground that the case is outside the Road Traffic Act, e g that the place of the accident was not a 'road' or (in cases arising before 1 December 1972) that the claimant was a passenger not carried for reward or by reason of or in pursuance of a contract of employment. In such cases where a judgment had already been obtained against the uninsured motorist and is unsatisfied proceedings can be taken against the Bureau. The Bureau is a corporation and therefore a legal *persona* capable of being sued in its own name. Theoretically the claimant cannot claim the benefit of the Motor Insurers' Bureau agreements because he is not a party, but•in practice the Bureau does not take the point by way of defence. Lord Donovan mentioned the point in *Albert v Motor Insurers Bureau* ([1972] AC 301, [1971] 2 All ER 1345):

'The question immediately suggests itself as to how the appellant as a third party can claim the benefit of this agreement. The point was looked at in *Hardy v Motor Insurers' Bureau* (p 784, below) where Lord Denning remarks that the agreement is on the face of it a contract between two parties for the benefit of a third, and that no point was taken by the Bureau that the agreement was not enforceable by the third person. Diplock LJ also considered the matter in *Gurtner v Circuit* (p 786, below) saying that on a number of occasions the Court had turned a blind eye to the position; and that unless the point were specifically raised the court was "entitled to proceed on the assumption that the Bureau has, before action is brought, contracted for good consideration with the plaintiff to perform the obligations specified in its contract with the Minister or has by its conduct raised an estoppel which would bar it from relying on absence of privity of contract". In the present case the Bureau has likewise raised no point . . . and in the circumstances I say no more on the matter.'

For examples of cases in which the Bureau has been sued, see the cases of *Lees* (p 721, above) and *Hardy* (p 784, below). For cases where the Bureau's right to be joined was considered see p 786, below.

When suing an uninsured driver plaintiffs sometimes add MIB as second defendants for a declaration of liability under the Uninsured Drivers' Agreement even where no issue on the applicability of the agreement has been raised. As the following decision shows this is not a maintainable nor permissible procedure.

Carpenter v Ebblewhite
[1939] 1 KB 347, [1938] 4 All ER 41, 108 LJKB 110, 159 LT 564, CA
The plaintiffs, injured in a road accident by a car driven by B, sued E as
being vicariously liable for B's negligence. They also joined E's insurers for
a declaration that they were liable to meet a judgment against E. E's
defence was that he had sold the car to B, who was not his servant or agent.
The insurers applied to strike out the claim against them on the ground that
it disclosed no reasonable cause of action.
HELD: The insurers were entitled to be struck out of the action. They were
not saying E was not entitled to indemnity under the policy if he was found
liable. In an action by a plaintiff against a defendant there cannot be a claim
by the plaintiff for a declaration of liability against a third person for the
relief claimed in the action where no dispute has yet arisen between the
plaintiff and that person.
   Per Greer LJ: The claim against the insurance company was frivolous
and vexatious, as there could not be any claim for a declaration in view of
the fact that there was not at that time any dispute between the plaintiffs
and the insurance company.

Note—This decision, though arising from an insurance policy is equally relevant to
the Uninsured Drivers' Agreement.

Passenger claims — cl 6(1)(c)(ii)

Porter v Addo: Porter v Motor Insurers' Bureau
[1978] 122 Sol Jo 418, [1978] 2 Lloyd's Rep 463, [1978] RTR 503,
(Forbes J)
Mrs Porter bought a car in Holland and brought it to England. She was
told by the Customs she must not drive the car because it was not insured.
She told Mr Addo, a television engineer who she knew used a car in the
course of his work, about her difficulties and he offered to drive the car for
her from Harwich to London. She did not ask him if he was insured to drive
but as she had told him the Customs had said she must get an insured driver
to drive it she assumed his insurance policy covered him to drive other
people's cars including hers. On the journey an accident occurred caused
by his negligence and she was injured. He was not in fact insured to drive
her car. She sued Addo for damages and the Motor Insurers' Bureau for a
declaration that the Bureau should pay an unsatisfied judgment against
Addo. The Bureau relied on cl 6(1)(c)(ii) of the 1972 agreement, saying
that as owner she was permitting the vehicle to be used 'having reason to
believe' there was no contract of insurance in force.
HELD: She was entitled to a declaration. 'Having reason to believe' is not
the same as 'having reasonable belief' nor as 'having no reason to believe' a
contract was in force. 'Having reason to believe' is a reference to a rational
process of thought. It placed the onus quite differently. What reason could
Mrs Porter have to believe no contract was in force? On the facts as found
she could have none.

Claims against liquidated insurance companies

Note—As the uninsured drivers' agreement requires the Motor Insurers' Bureau

to meet any judgment obtained in a Road Traffic Act claim if it has not been satisfied within seven days the obligation extends to judgments obtained against
motorists who were insured at the time of the accident but whose insurers have
subsequently gone into liquidation. In dealing with such claims the Bureau does
not attempt to recover from policy holders.

In respect of liquidations by resolution or presentation of a winding-up petition
after 29 October 1974, the Policyholders Protection Act 1975, s 7 provides for
payment by the Policyholders Protection Board of the full amount of a sum payable
to a person entitled to the benefit of judgment under the Road Traffic Act 1972,
s 149 as soon as reasonably practicable after the beginning of the liquidation.

Wilful injury

Hardy v Motor Insurers' Bureau

[1964] 2 QB 745, [1964] 2 All ER 742, [1964] 3 WLR 433, 108 Sol Jo 422,
[1964] 1 Lloyd's Rep 397, CA

The plaintiff was chief security officer at a large metal works. Having seen a
stolen road fund licence in a van belonging to a fitter named Phillips he
waited at the place where the private road leading from the works joined the
main road and stopped the van as it came out. He put his head in at the
window and asked Phillips to pull in to the nearside. Instead Phillips drove
forward at a fast rate on to the main road dragging the plaintiff along and
injuring him. The plaintiff obtained judgment against Phillips for £300
damages but the judgment was unsatisfied. Phillips was uninsured and
the plaintiff, having given notice of the proceedings against Phillips to the
Motor Insurers' Bureau began this action against the Bureau for the
amount of the unsatisfied judgment. It was argued for the defendants that
liability for a criminal act was not a liability which the Road Traffic Act
1960 required or could require to be covered by insurance.

HELD: Applying the test in *DPP v Smith* [1961] AC 290, [1960] 3 All ER
161, [1960] 3 WLR 546, 124 JP 473, 104 Sol Jo 683 Phillips must be taken
to have intended to injure the plaintiff and was guilty of a felony under the
Offences against the Person Act 1861, s 18. The Road Traffic Act 1960,
s 203(3)(a) required Phillips to be covered by a policy of insurance 'in
respect of any liability which may be incurred by him in respect of the death
of or bodily injury to any person caused by, or arising out of, the use of a
vehicle on a road'. This included any use by him of the vehicle, be it an
innocent use or a criminal use, or be it a murderous use or a playful use.
Such a policy would be good in its inception but the question arises whether
the motorist can enforce it when he had made criminal use of the vehicle.
Clearly he could not, since no person can claim reparation or indemnity for
the consequences of a criminal offence of which his own wicked intent is an
essential ingredient — *Beresford v Royal Insurance Co Ltd* (p 891, below).
There is a broad rule of public policy that no person can claim reparation or
indemnity for his own wilful and culpable crime. Thus if Phillips had
himself met the plaintiff's judgment he would have been unable to claim
indemnity from an insurer if he had been insured. But this rule of public
policy affected only the wrongdoer and would not prevent an innocent
third party from claiming the benefit of such a policy against an insurer.
Part VI of the Act gave a third party a direct right of action under s 207
against insurers where there was a liability against which the statute
required a motorist to insure. It followed that where, as here, the motorist

was not insured the liability was one which the plaintiff could require the defendants to meet under the Motor Insurers' Bureau agreements.

Gardner v Moore
[1984] AC 548, [1984] 1 All ER 1100, [1984] 2 WLR 714, 128 Sol Jo 282, [1984] 2 Lloyds Rep 135, HL
The defendant Moore, when driving his car without any insurance cover, deliberately drove on to the pavement, striking and injuring the plaintiff. It was an intentionally criminal act for which Moore was convicted and sentenced to imprisonment. Gardner sued Moore for damages in an action in which Moore took no part. Judgment was given against him for £15,526 damages. The Motor Insurers' Bureau (joined as second defendants) denied liability to meet the judgment, maintaining that *Hardy*'s case (above) was wrongly decided.
HELD, *Hardy*'s case had been correctly decided and the Bureau was liable to satisfy the judgment. The general principle that no person can claim indemnity for his own wilful and culpable crime cannot be invoked against an innocent third party whose claim is not through that of the wrongdoer. The Motor Insurers' Bureau agreement was intended to protect an innocent third party where the wrongdoer was not covered by a relevant policy of insurance; for the Bureau to invoke the doctrine of public policy that a man may not profit by the consequences of his own wrong doing was contrary both to the object and grammatical sense of the agreement.

THE MOTOR INSURERS' BUREAU AND DEFENDANT

Motor Insurers' Bureau's authority to act for uninsured driver

Note—As the Bureau is not an insurer and has no contractual relationship with the uninsured driver it cannot file acknowledgment of service of a writ on behalf of an uninsured driver without express authority. In this respect an 'insurer concerned' is in the same position as MIB. When the uninsured driver is available he may, and often does, give an authority coupled with an agreement to indemnify the Bureau. A suitable form of authority and indemnity is the following:

I . . . (name) consent to Motor Insurers' Bureau taking over and conducting in my name the defence of the plaintiff's claim against me in this action arising from the accident of the . . . (date).
  It is understood that the cost of the defence of the plaintiff's claim will be borne by Motor Insurers' Bureau. I hereby give Motor Insurers' Bureau full authority to effect a settlement of the plaintiff's claim on my behalf and I hereby agree to indemnify them against and to repay to them all sums paid by them in respect of such settlement, including the costs of the plaintiff.
  I undertake to give Motor Insurers' Bureau all information and assistance in my power.
  This agreement is determinable at any time by Motor Insurers' Bureau or myself by notice in writing and I agree that after such determination by either of us Motor Insurers' Bureau will have no obligation to conduct my defence and will not be responsible for any costs incurred after such determination.

  Dated this . . . day of . . . 19 . .
  Signed . . .

With such authority the Bureau can then file acknowledgment of service and conduct a defence in the name of the defendant. In a proportion of cases, however, the uninsured driver either cannot be found by the time a claim falls to be dealt with or refuses to sign an authority. In such cases the Bureau may, when proceedings have been instituted against the uninsured driver, apply to the Court under RSC Ord 15, r 6(2)(b) to be joined as a defendant in the action with liberty to exercise the rights of the uninsured defendant. This procedure evolves from the following case.

When Motor Insurers' Bureau entitled to be joined as defendant

Gurtner v Circuit
[1968] 2 QB 587, [1968] 1 All ER 328, [1968] 2 WLR 668, 112 Sol Jo 73, [1968] 1 Lloyd's Rep 171, CA
The plaintiff was struck and injured by a motor cycle in 1961. The police took particulars of the accident, including the motor cyclist's name and address and the number of his insurance certificate but no writ was issued against him by the plaintiff until 1964. By that time he had gone to Canada and could not be traced. The particulars of his insurance certificate in the police report did not enable the insurers to be identified. After two renewals of the writ the plaintiff in June 1966 obtained an order for substituted service on the motor cyclist at the office of the insurance company handling the matter for the Bureau. As the motor cyclist could not be found no appearance could be entered for him. The Bureau then applied to be joined as defendants in the action.
HELD: They were entitled to be joined as defendants. Order 15, r 6 provides that the court may order any person to be added as a party 'whose presence before the court is necessary to ensure that all matters in dispute . . . may be completely and effectively determined and adjudicated upon'. When two parties were in dispute in an action and the determination of that dispute would directly affect a third person in his legal rights or in his pocket the court had a discretion to allow him to be added as a party on such terms as it thought fit. The Bureau were directly affected not only in their legal rights but also in their pocket. They ought to be allowed to come in as defendants.

Declaration action: position of the Motor Insurers' Bureau

Fire Auto and Marine Insurance Co Ltd v Greene
[1964] 2 QB 687, [1964] 2 All ER 761, [1964] 3 WLR 319, 108 Sol Jo 603, [1964] 2 Lloyd's Rep 72 (John Stevenson J)
The plaintiff company were motor insurers but were not members of the Motor Insurers' Bureau. After an accident from which claims arose by injured persons against a policyholder the plaintiffs began this action against him under the Road Traffic Act 1960, s 207(3) for a declaration that they were entitled to avoid the policy on the ground of non-disclosure of a material fact. The Motor Insurers' Bureau applied under RSC Ord 15, r 6 to be added as a defendant in the action, since they would be required under Bureau agreements to meet any judgment obtained by an injured party against the policyholder if the plaintiffs succeeded in obtaining the declaration. Order 15, r 6 provides that the court may order

any person to be joined as party whose presence before the court is necessary to ensure that all matters in dispute in the cause or matter may be effectually and completely determined and adjudicated upon.

HELD: The Bureau were not entitled to be joined as a party. A person who applies for an order under Ord 15, r 6 to be added as a defendant must at least be able to show that some legal right enforceable by him against one of the parties to the action or some legal duty enforceable against him by one of the parties to the action will be affected by the result of the action. These plaintiffs were not parties to the domestic agreement. Moreover, even if the Bureau were legally liable to satisfy an injured claimant's judgment against the policy-holder it would be liable to the Minister, not to the injured person himself. Its liability is not statutory but contractual and its agreement with the Minister confers no rights except on him. The fact that Bureau has never taken this point against a claimant makes no difference and did not prevent the plaintiffs in this action from taking the point against them.

Note—The Road Traffic Act 1974 by s 20 now requires all authorised insurers as defined in s 145(2) of the 1972 Act to be members of the Motor Insurers' Bureau. In any event the basis of the decision must be regarded as inconsistent with, and superseded by, the decision in *Gurtner v Circuit* (above).

Costs where the Motor Insurers' Bureau defend — legal aid

Note—See *Godfrey v Smith*, p 695, above.

THE MOTOR INSURERS' BUREAU AND INSURERS

The Domestic Agreement

Note—The 'Domestic Agreement' is an agreement between Motor Insurers' Bureau and its members, namely those insurance companies and members of underwriting syndicates at Lloyd's transacting compulsory motor vehicle insurance business in the UK. The purpose of the agreement is financial: to establish and maintain a central fund from which payments can be made when there is no 'insurer concerned' and secondly to determine when a liability falls to be met by a member as 'insurer concerned'.

The general principle established by the agreement is that if there is a policy in existence in respect of the vehicle being used at the time of the relevant accident, even though the tortfeasor is not himself insured by it, the insurer issuing the policy will meet the claim. In cases where there is no such policy the claim will be met from the Bureau's central fund. The definition of 'insurer concerned' is thus of importance and is as follows.

'Insurer concerned

"The insurer concerned" means the insurer who at the time of the accident which gave rise to the Road Traffic Act liability was providing any insurance against such liability in respect of the vehicle arising out of the use of which the liability of the judgment debtor was incurred. An insurer is concerned within the meaning of this Agreement notwithstanding that:
(i) the insurance has been obtained by fraud, misrepresentation, non-disclosure of material facts or mistake; or

(ii) some term, description, limitation, exception or condition (whether express or implied) of the insurance or of the proposal form on which it is based expressly or by implication excludes that Insurer's liability whether generally or in the particular circumstances in which the judgment debtor's liability was incurred; or

(iii) the judgment debtor was in unauthorised possession of the vehicle arising out of the use of which the liability of the judgment debtor was incurred

and only ceases so to be concerned:

 (i) in the case of an insurance expressed to be for a term of twelve months at least, after the expiry of fifteen days from the date on which the insurance by its terms lapsed;

(ii) in the case of an insurance expressed to be for a term of twelve months or more, but which by provision in the policy or by notice in writing by either party is not intended to be renewed, from the date on which the insurance by its terms lapsed;

(iii) in the case of an insurance for a term of less than twelve months, when the term thereof expires;

(iv) when the insurance has been cancelled before the date on which the Road Traffic Act liability was incurred by agreement of the parties to the insurance or under a power of cancellation contained therein;

 (v) when the insurance has ceased to operate by reason of a transfer of interest in the vehicle which the insurance purports to cover;

(vi) when before the date on which the Road Traffic Act liability was incurred the Insurer has obtained a declaration from a Court of competent jurisdiction that the insurance is void or unenforceable.'

When a driver or user of a vehicle is not covered by the policy issued in respect of the vehicle and the insurer deals with the claim only as 'insurer concerned' under the Domestic Agreement then the insurer cannot claim the benefit of any of the terms of the policy (e g in defending the action in the name of the defendant driver) but is in precisely the same position as MIB would be if there were no policy at all; the insurer cannot file notice of acceptance of service of the writ without obtaining the defendant's express authority or by application to the Court under Ord 15, r 6 in the name of the Motor Insurers' Bureau (see p 786, above). On the other hand the 'insurer concerned' has the protection of the Bureau agreement e g under cll 5 and 6 (see pp 776–778, above).

It will be seen from the definition of 'insurer concerned' that the insurance has to be in respect of the vehicle involved. Thus an insurer cannot become an 'insurer concerned' by reason of a 'driving other cars' clause in a policy covering another vehicle.

UNTRACED MOTORISTS

Note—Under an agreement with the Minister of Transport dated 21 April 1969 the Motor Insurers' Bureau undertook to make payments of compensation to persons injured by motor vehicles when the owner or driver could not be traced. This agreement has been replaced by an agreement of 22 November 1972.

An 'untraced' driver is one whose identity is unknown and has not been established; hence proceedings against him in a court of law are not possible. But a driver whose name and address or other necessary details sufficient to establish his identity and enable a writ or summons to be issued against him are known does not become an 'untraced' driver merely because he has disappeared or cannot be found when a claim is made. However, a driver who, having given fictitious particulars at the time of the accident, cannot be traced is 'untraced'; see *Clarke v Vedel*, p 781, above.

Motor Insurers' Bureau (compensation of victims of untraced drivers)

Text of an Agreement dated 22 November 1972, between the Secretary of State for the Environment and the Motor Insurers' Bureau together with some notes on its scope and purpose.

On 21 April 1969 the Minister of Transport and the Motor Insurers' Bureau entered into an agreement to secure compensation for third party victims of road accidents when the driver responsible for the accident could not be traced. That agreement has now been replaced by a new agreement which operates in respect of accidents occurring on or after 1 December 1972. The text of the new agreement is as follows.

AN AGREEMENT made 22 November 1972 between the Secretary of State for the Environment and the Motor Insurers' Bureau, whose registered office is at Aldermary House, Queen Street, London, EC4N 1TR (hereinafter referred to as 'MIB').

IT IS HEREBY AGREED as follows:—

1 (1) Subject to paragraph (2) of this clause, this agreement applies to any case in which an application is made to MIB for a payment in respect of the death of or bodily injury to any person caused by or arising out of the use of a motor vehicle on a road in Great Britain and the case is one in which the following conditions are fulfilled, that is to say, — (a) the event giving rise to the death or injury occurred on or after the 1 December 1972; (b) the applicant for the payment either — (i) is unable to trace any person responsible for the death or injury, or (ii) in a case to which clause 5 hereof applies where more than one person was so responsible, is unable to trace one of those persons; (any person so untraced is hereby referred to as 'the untraced person'); (c) the death or injury was caused in such circumstances that on the balance of probabilities the untraced person would be liable to pay damages to the applicant in respect of the death or injury; (d) the liability of the untraced person to pay damages to the applicant is one which is required to be covered by insurance or security under Part VI of the Road Traffic Act 1972, it being assumed for this purpose, in the absence of evidence to the contrary, that the vehicle was being used in circumstances in which the user was required by the said Part VI to be insured or secured against third party risks; (e) the death or injury was not caused by the use of the vehicle by the untraced person as a weapon, that is to say, in a deliberate attempt to run the deceased or injured person down; (f) the application is made in writing within three years from the date of the event giving rise to the death or injury.

(2) This agreement does not apply to a case in which — (a) the death or bodily injury in respect of which such application is made was caused by or arose out of the use of a motor vehicle which at the time of the event giving rise to the death or bodily injury was owned by or in the possession of the Crown, unless the case is one in which some other person has undertaken responsibility for the existence of a contract of insurance under Part VI of the Road Traffic Act 1972; (b) at the time of the accident the person suffering death or bodily injury in respect of which the application is made was allowing himself to be carried in a vehicle and — (i) knew or had reason to believe that the vehicle had been taken without the consent of the owner or other lawful authority, except in a case where — (A) he believed or had reason to believe that he had lawful authority to be carried or that he would have the owner's consent if the owner had known of his being carried and the circumstances of his carriage; or (B) he had learned of the circumstances of the taking of the vehicle since the commencement of the journey and it would be unreasonable to expect him to have alighted from the vehicle; or (ii) being the owner of or being a person using the vehicle he was using or causing or permitting the vehicle to be used without there being in force in relation to such use a policy of insurance or

such security as would comply with Part VI of the Road Traffic Act 1972, knowing or having reason to believe that no such policy or security was in force.

(3) The exemption from the application of this agreement specified in sub-para (2)(b) of this clause shall apply only in a case where the application is made to MIB in respect of a liability arising out of the use of the vehicle in which the person who suffered death or bodily injury was being carried.

(4) For the purpose of para (2) of this clause — (a) a vehicle which has been unlawfully removed from the possession of the Crown shall be taken to continue in that possession whilst it is kept so removed; (b) references to a person being carried in a vehicle include references to his being carried in or upon, or entering or getting on to or alighting from the vehicle; (c) 'owner' in relation to a vehicle which is the subject of a hiring agreement or a hire purchase agreement means the person in possession of the vehicle under that agreement.

2 (1) An application to MIB for a payment in respect of the death of or bodily injury to any person may be made either by the person for whose benefit that payment is to be made (hereinafter called 'the applicant') or by any solicitor acting for the applicant or by any other person whom MIB may be prepared to accept as acting for the applicant.

(2) Any decision, award or payment given or made or other thing done in accordance with this agreement to or by a person acting as aforesaid on behalf of the applicant, or in relation to an application made by such a person, shall, whatever may be the age, or the circumstances affecting the capacity, of the applicant, be treated as having the same effect as if it had been done to or by, or in relation to an application made by, an applicant of full age and capacity.

3 Subject to the following provisions of this agreement, MIB shall, on any application made to them in a case to which this agreement applies, award to the applicant in respect of the death or injury in respect of which the application is made a payment of an amount which shall be assessed in like manner as a court, applying English law in a case where the event giving rise to the death or injury occurred in England or Wales or applying the law of Scotland in a case where that event occurred in Scotland, would assess the damages which the applicant would have been entitled to recover from the untraced person in respect of that death or injury if proceedings to enforce a claim for damages in respect thereof were successfully brought by the applicant against the untraced person.

4 In making an award in accordance with clause 3 hereof — (a) MIB shall not be required to include in the payment awarded any amount in respect of any damages for loss of expectation of life or for pain or suffering which the applicant might have had a right to claim under the Law Reform (Miscellaneous Provisions) Act 1934, or, as the case may be, under any corresponding rule of law in force in Scotland nor, in a case where the application is made in respect of a death, shall MIB be required to include in the payment awarded any amount in respect of solatium for the grief of any relative of the deceased which the applicant might have had a right to claim under any enactment or rule of law in force in Scotland; and (b) in assessing the amount to which the applicant is entitled in respect of loss of earnings if the applicant has received his wages or salary in full or in part from his employer, whether or not upon an undertaking given by the applicant to reimburse his employer if he recovers damages, he shall be not to the extent of the amount so received be regarded as having sustained a loss of earnings.

5 (1) This clause applies to any case to which this agreement applies where the death or bodily injury in respect of which an application has been made to MIB under this agreement (hereinafter in this clause referred to as 'the relevant death or injury') was caused partly by the untraced person and partly either by an identified person, or by identified persons, or by some other untraced person or persons

whose master or principal can be identified and was so caused in circumstances making the identified person or persons or any such master or principal as aforesaid liable to the applicant in respect of the relevant death or injury.

(2) If in a case to which this clause applies one or other of the conditions specified in the next following paragraph is satisfied, the amount to be awarded by MIB to the applicant in respect of the relevant death or injury shall be determined in accordance with the provisions of para (4) of this clause and their liability to the applicant shall be subject also to the provisions of para (7) of this clause and to clause 6 hereof.

(3) The conditions referred to in the last foregoing paragraph are — (a) that the applicant has obtained a judgment in respect of the relevant death or injury against the identified person or against one or more of the identified persons or against any person liable as their master or principal or the master or principal of any other person which has not been satisfied in full within three months from the date on which the applicant became entitled to enforce it; or (b) that the applicant — (i) has not obtained and has not been required by MIB to obtain a judgment in respect of the relevant death or injury against the identified person or persons or against any person liable as the master or principal of any such identified person or persons or as the master or principal of any other person, and (ii) has not received any payment by way of compensation from any such person or persons.

(4) The amount to be awarded by MIB to the applicant in a case to which this clause applies shall be determined as follows: (a) if the condition specified in para (3)(a) of this clause is satisfied and the judgment mentioned in that paragraph is wholly unsatisfied within the period of three months therein referred to, the amount to be awarded shall be an amount equal to the untraced person's contribution to a full award; (b) if the condition specified in para 3(a) of this clause is satisfied but the judgment mentioned in that paragraph is satisfied in part only within the period of three months therein referred to, the amount to be awarded — (i) if the unsatisfied part of the said judgment is less than the untraced person's contribution to a full award, shall be an amount equal to that unsatisfied part, or (ii) if the unsatisfied part of the said judgment is equal to or greater than the amount of the untraced person's contribution to a full award, shall be an amount equal to the untraced person's said contribution; (c) if the condition specified in para (3)(b) of this clause is satisfied, the amount to be awarded shall be an amount equal to the untraced person's contribution to a full award.

(5) The following provisions of this paragraph shall have effect in any case in which an appeal from or any proceeding to set aside any such judgment as is specified in para (3)(a) of this clause (hereinafter in this clause referred to as 'the original judgment') is commenced within a period of three months beginning on the date on which the applicant became entitled to enforce the original judgment: (a) until the said appeal or proceeding is disposed of the foregoing provisions of this clause shall have effect as if for the period of three months referred to in said para (3)(a) there were substituted a period expiring on the date when the said appeal or proceeding is disposed of; (b) if as a result of the said appeal or proceeding the applicant ceases to be entitled to receive any payment in respect of the relevant death or injury from any of the persons against whom he has obtained any such judgment as is specified in the said para (3)(a), the foregoing provisions of this clause shall have effect as if he had neither obtained nor been required by MIB to obtain a judgment against any person or persons; (c) if as a result of the said appeal or proceeding, the applicant becomes entitled to recover an amount which differs from that which he was entitled to recover under the original judgment, the foregoing provisions of this clause shall have effect as if for the reference in the said para (3)(a) to the original judgment there were substituted a reference to the judgment under which the applicant became entitled to the said different amount; (d) if as a result of the said appeal or proceeding the applicant

remains entitled to enforce the original judgment the foregoing provisions of this clause shall have effect as if for the period of three months referred to in the said para (3)(a) there were substituted a period of three months beginning on the date on which the appeal or other proceeding was disposed of. The foregoing provisions of this paragraph shall apply also in any case where any judgment given upon any such appeal or proceeding is itself the subject of a further appeal or similar proceeding and shall apply in such a case in relation to that further appeal or proceeding in the same manner as they apply in relation to the first mentioned appeal or proceeding.

(6) In this clause — (a) 'full award' means the amount which would have fallen to be awarded to the applicant under clause 3 thereof in respect of the relevant death or injury if the untraced person had been wholly responsible for that death or injury; and (b) 'untraced person's contribution' means that proportion of a full award which on the balance of probabilities would have been apportioned by a court as the share to be borne by the untraced person in the responsibility for the event giving rise to the relevant death or injury if proceedings to recover damages in respect of that death or injury had been brought by the applicant against the untraced person and all other persons having a share in that responsibility.

(7) MIB shall not be under any liability in respect of the relevant death or injury if the applicant is entitled to receive compensation from MIB in respect of that death or injury under the agreement providing for the compensation of victims of uninsured drivers entered into between the Secretary of State and MIB on 22 November 1972.

6 (1) The following shall be conditions precedent to any liability falling upon MIB upon an application made to them under this agreement in respect of any death or injury, that is to say, — (a) the applicant shall give all such assistance as may reasonably be required by or on behalf of MIB to enable any investigation to be carried out under this agreement, including, in particular, the furnishing of statements and information either in writing, or, if so required, orally at an interview between the applicant and any person acting on behalf of MIB; (b) if so required by MIB at any time before MIB have communicated their decision upon the application to the applicant, the applicant shall, subject to the following provisions of this clause, take all such steps as in the circumstances it is reasonable to require the applicant to take to obtain judgment against any person or persons in respect of their liability to the applicant in respect of the death or injury as having caused or contributed to that death or injury or as being the master or principal of any person who has caused or contributed to that injury; (c) if so required by MIB the applicant shall assign to MIB or to their nominee any judgment obtained by him (whether or not obtained in pursuance of a requirement under subparagraph (b) of this paragraph) in respect of the death or injury to which his application to MIB relates upon such terms as will secure that MIB or their nominees shall be accountable to the applicant for any amount by which the aggregate of all sums recovered by MIB or their nominee under the said judgment (after deducting all reasonable expenses incurred in effecting such recovery) exceeds the amount payable by MIB to the applicant under this agreement in respect of that death or injury.

(2) If MIB require the applicant to bring proceedings against any specified person or persons: (a) MIB shall indemnify the applicant against all costs reasonably incurred by the applicant in complying with that requirement unless the result of those proceedings materially contributes to establish that the untraced person did not cause or contribute to the relevant death or injury; and (b) the applicant shall, if so required by MIB and at their expense, furnish MIB with a transcript of any official shorthand note taken in those proceedings of any evidence given or judgment delivered therein.

(3) In the event of a dispute arising between the applicant and MIB as to the reasonableness of any requirement by MIB under para (1)(b) of this clause, or as to whether any such costs as are referred to in para (2)(a) of this clause were reason-

ably incurred, that dispute shall be referred to the Secretary of State whose decision thereon shall be final: Provided that any dispute arising between the applicant and MIB as to whether MIB are required to indemnify the applicant under para (2)(a) of this clause shall, in so far as it depends on the question whether the result of any proceedings which MIB have required the applicant to bring against any specified person or persons have or have not materially contributed to establish that the untraced person did not cause or contribute to the relevant death or injury, be referred to the arbitrator in accordance with the following provisions of this agreement, whose decision on that question shall be final.

7 MIB shall cause any application made to them for a payment under this agreement to be investigated and, unless MIB decide that the application should be rejected because a preliminary investigation has disclosed that the case is not one to which this agreement applies, they shall cause a report to be made on the application and on the basis of that report MIB shall decide whether to make an award and, if so, the amount of the award which shall be calculated in accordance with the foregoing provisions of this agreement.

8 MIB may before coming to a decision on any application made to them under this agreement request the applicant to furnish them with a statutory declaration to be made by the applicant, setting out to the best of his knowledge, information and belief the facts and circumstances upon which his claim to an award under this agreement is based, or such of those facts and circumstances as may be specified by MIB.

9 (1) MIB shall notify their decision to the applicant and when so doing shall — (a) if the application is rejected because a preliminary investigation has disclosed that it is not one made in a case to which this agreement applies, give their reasons for the rejection; or (b) if the application has been fully investigated furnish him with a statement setting out — (i) the circumstances in which the death or injury occurred and the evidence bearing thereon, (ii) the circumstances relevant to the assessment of the amount to be awarded to the applicant under this agreement and the evidence bearing thereon, and (iii) if they refuse to make an award their reasons for that refusal; and (c) in a case to which clause 5 of this agreement applies specify the way in which the amount of that award has been computed and its relation to those provisions of clause 5 which are relevant to its computation.
(2) Where MIB have decided that they will not indemnify the applicant against the costs of any proceedings which they have under clause 6(1)(b) hereof required the applicant to bring against any specified person or persons on the ground that those proceedings have materially contributed to establish that the untraced person did not cause or contribute to the relevant death or injury, they shall give notice to the applicant of that decision and when doing so they shall give their reasons for it and furnish the applicant with a copy of any such transcript of any evidence given or judgment delivered in those proceedings as is mentioned in clause 6(2)(b) hereof which they regard as relevant to that decision.

10 Subject to the provisions of this agreement MIB shall, — (a) on being notified by the applicant that MIB's award is accepted; or (b) if at the expiration of the period during which the applicant may give notice of an appeal under clause 11 hereof there has not been given to MIB either any such notification as aforesaid of the acceptance of MIB's award or a notice of an appeal under the said clause 11, pay the applicant the amount of that award, and such payment shall discharge MIB from all liability under this agreement in respect of the death or injury in respect of which that award has been made.

11 The applicant shall have a right of appeal to an arbitrator against any decision notified to him under clause 9 hereof on any of the following grounds, that is to say,

— (a) that the case is one to which this agreement applies and that his application should be fully investigated by MIB with a view to their deciding whether to make an award to the applicant and, if so, the amount of that award; or (b) where the application has been fully investigated — (i) that MIB were wrong in refusing to make an award, or (ii) that the amount they have awarded to the applicant is insufficient; or (c) in a case where a decision not to indemnify the applicant against the costs of any proceedings has been notified under clause 9(2) hereof, that that decision was wrong, if within six weeks from the date when notice of the decision against which he wishes to appeal was given him, the applicant, not having previously notified MIB that their decision is accepted, gives notice to MIB that he wishes to appeal against their decision.

12 A notice of appeal under clause 11 hereof shall state the grounds of the appeal and shall be accompanied by an undertaking to be given by the applicant or by the person acting on his behalf as provided in clause 2 hereof, that — (a) the applicant will accept the decision of the arbitrator; and (b) the arbitrator's fee shall be paid to MIB by the applicant or by the person giving the said undertaking in any case where MIB are entitled to reimbursement of that fee under the provisions of clause 22 hereof.

13 The applicant may, when giving notice of his appeal or at any time before doing so, make comments to MIB on their decision and may supply them with such particulars as the applicant may think fit of any other evidence not contained in the written statement supplied to the applicant by MIB which he considers is relevant to the application and MIB may, before submitting the applicant's appeal to the arbitrator, cause an investigation to be made into this further evidence and shall report to the applicant the result of that investigation and of any change in their decision which may result from it. The applicant may, within six weeks from the date on which this report was sent to him, unless he withdraws his appeal, make such comments thereon as he may desire to have submitted to the arbitrator.

14 (1) In a case where MIB receive from the applicant a notice of appeal in which the only ground of appeal which is stated is that the amount awarded to the applicant is insufficient MIB may before submitting that appeal to the arbitrator give notice to the applicant that if the appeal proceeds they will request the arbitrator to decide whether the case is one in which MIB should make an award at all and if they do so they shall at the same time furnish the applicant with a statement setting out such comments as they may consider relevant to the decision which the arbitrator should come to on that question.
(2) Where MIB give a notice under para (1) of this clause, the applicant may within six weeks from the date on which that notice is given make such comments to MIB and supply them with such particulars of other evidence not contained in any written statement furnished to him by MIB as he may consider relevant to the question which the arbitrator is by the notice requested to decide, and clause 13 hereof shall apply in relation to any comments made or particulars supplied by the applicant under this paragraph as it applies in relation to any comments made or particulars supplied under the said clause 13.

15 MIB shall, where they receive notice of an appeal from the applicant under the foregoing provisions of this agreement, unless the appeal is previously withdrawn, submit that appeal (but in a case where they cause such an investigation to be made as is mentioned in clause 13 hereof, not until the expiration of six weeks from the date on which they sent the applicant a report as to the result of that investigation and, in a case where they gave such notice to the applicant as is mentioned in clause 14(1) hereof, not until the expiration of six weeks from the date on which they gave that notice and, if they have caused an investigation to be made into any evidence supplied under clause 14(2) hereof, not until the expiration of six weeks from the

date on which they sent the applicant a report as to the result of that investigation) to an arbitrator for a decision, sending to the arbitrator for that purpose the application made by the applicant, a copy of their decision thereon as notified to the applicant and of all statements, declarations, notices, undertakings, comments, transcripts, particulars or reports furnished, given or sent under this agreement either by the applicant or any person acting for him to MIB or by MIB to the applicant or a person so acting.

16 On any such appeal — (a) if the appeal is against a decision by MIB rejecting an application because a preliminary investigation has disclosed that the case is not one to which this agreement applies, the arbitrator shall decide whether the case is or is not one to which this agreement applies and, if he decides that it is such a case, shall remit the application to MIB for full investigation and for a decision by MIB in accordance with the foregoing provisions of this agreement; (b) if the appeal is against a decision by MIB given after an application has been fully investigated by MIB (whether before the appeal or in consequence of its being remitted for such investigation under para (a) of this clause), the arbitrator shall decide, as may be appropriate, having regard to the grounds stated in the notice of appeal and to any notice given by MIB to the applicant under clause 14 thereof, whether MIB should make an award under this agreement to the applicant and, if so, the amount which MIB should award to the applicant under the foregoing provisions of this agreement; (c) if the appeal relates to a dispute which has arisen between the applicant and MIB which is required by the proviso to clause 6(3) hereof to be referred to the arbitrator, the arbitrator shall also give his decision on that dispute.

17 The arbitrator shall decide the appeal on the documents submitted to him as set out in clause 15 hereof and no further evidence shall be produced to him: Provided that — (a) the arbitrator shall be entitled to ask MIB to make any further investigation which he considers desirable and to submit a written report of their findings to him for his consideration; and (b) MIB shall send a copy of any such report to the applicant who shall be entitled to submit written comments on it to MIB within four weeks of the date on which that copy is sent to him; and (c) MIB shall transmit those comments to the arbitrator for his consideration.

18 The arbitrator by whom any such appeal as aforesaid shall be decided shall be an arbitrator to be selected by the Secretary of State from two panels of Queen's Counsel appointed respectively by the Lord Chancellor and the Lord Advocate for the purpose of determining appeals under this agreement, the arbitrator to be selected from the panel appointed by the Lord Chancellor in cases where the event giving rise to the death or injury occurred in England or Wales and from the panel appointed by the Lord Advocate where that event occurred in Scotland.

19 The arbitrator shall notify his decision on any appeal under this agreement to MIB and MIB shall forthwith send a copy of the arbitrator's decision to the applicant.

20 Subject to the provisions of this agreement, MIB shall pay the applicant any amount which the arbitrator has decided shall be awarded to the applicant, and such payment shall discharge MIB from all liability under this agreement in respect of the death or injury in respect of which that decision has been given.

21 Each party to the appeal will bear his own costs.

22 MIB shall pay the arbitrator a fee approved by the Lord Chancellor or the Lord Advocate, as the case may be, after consultation with MIB: Provided that the arbitrator may in his discretion, in any case where it appears to him that there were no reasonable grounds for the appeal, decide that his fee ought to be paid by the

applicant and, where the arbitrator so decides, the person giving the undertaking required by clause 12 hereof shall be liable to reimburse MIB the amount of the fee paid by them to the arbitrator except in so far as that amount is deducted by MIB from any amount which they are liable to pay to the applicant in consequence of the decision of the arbitrator.

23 If in any case it appears to MIB that by reason of the applicant being under the age of majority or of any other circumstances affecting his capacity to manage his affairs it would be in the interest of the applicant that all or some part of the amount which would otherwise be payable to him under an award made under this agreement should be administered for him by the Family Welfare Association or by some other body or person under a trust MIB may establish for that purpose a trust of the whole or part of the said amount to take effect for such period and subject to such provisions as may appear to MIB appropriate in the circumstances of the case.

24 This agreement may be determined at any time by the Secretary of State or by MIB by either of them giving to the other not less than 12 months previous notice in writing: Provided that this agreement shall continue to have effect in respect of any case where the event giving rise to the death or injury occurred before the date on which this agreement terminates in accordance with any notice so given.

25 This agreement shall come into operation on 1 December 1972 in relation to accidents occurring on or after that date, and the agreement made on 21 April 1969 between the Secretary of State and MIB shall cease and determine except in relation to applications arising out of accidents which occurred on or after 1 May 1969 and before the said 1 December 1972.
IN WITNESS etc.

NOTES
The following notes are for the guidance of those who may wish to make application to the Motor Insurers' Bureau for payment under the agreement, and for the guidance of their legal advisers, but they must not be taken as rendering unnecessary a careful study of the agreement itself. Communications connected with the agreement should be addressed to the Motor Insurers' Bureau, whose address is Aldermary House, Queen Street, London, EC4N 1TR.

1 This agreement replaces a previous one dated 21 April 1969 which put on a formal basis the arrangements which have existed since 1946 under which the Bureau have made ex gratia payments in respect of death or personal injuries resulting from the use of a motor vehicle the owner or driver of which cannot be traced. Provision is made for an appeal against the Bureau's decision in such cases.

2 The agreement dated 21 April 1969 applies to a death or bodily injury arising out of an accident occurring on a road in Great Britain on or after 1 May 1969, and before 1 December 1972. This agreement applies in relation to accidents occurring on or after 1 December 1972.

3 Subject to the terms of the agreement, the Bureau will accept applications for a payment in respect of the death of, or bodily injury to, any person resulting from the use of a motor vehicle on a road in Great Britain in any case in which — (a) the applicant for the payment cannot trace any person responsible for the death or injury (or, in certain circumstances, a person partly responsible) (clause 1(1)(b); and (b) the death or injury was caused in such circumstances that the untraced person would be liable to pay damages to the applicant in respect of the death or injury (clause 1(1)(c)); and (c) the untraced person's liability to the applicant is one which at the time the accident occurred, was required to be covered by insurance or

security (clause 1(1)(d)). The Bureau will not, however, deal with deliberate 'running down' cases (clause 1(1)(e)) nor with certain other cases relating to Crown vehicles and certain categories of 'voluntary' passenger (clause 1(2) — (4)).

4 Application for a payment under the agreement must be made in writing to the Bureau within three years of the date of the accident giving rise to the death or injury (clause 1(1)(f)).

5 Under clause 3, the amount which the Bureau will award will (except for the exclusion of those elements of damages mentioned in clause 4) be assessed in the same way as a court would have assessed the amount of damages payable by the untraced person had the applicant been able to bring a successful claim for damages against him.

6 Clause 5 relates to cases where an untraced person and an identified person are each partly responsible for a death or injury, and defines the conditions under which the Bureau will in such cases make a contribution in respect of the responsibility of the untraced person.

7 Under clause 6(1)(b), the Bureau may require the applicant to bring proceedings against any identified person who may be responsible for the death or injury, subject to indemnifying the applicant as to his costs as provided in clause 6(2) and (3).

8 On receipt of an application, the Bureau will, if satisfied that the application comes within the terms of the agreement, investigate the circumstances and, when this has been done, decide whether to make a payment and, if so, how much (clause 7).

9 The Bureau may request the applicant to make a statutory declaration setting out all, or some, of the facts on which his application is based (clause 8).

10 The Bureau will notify the applicant of their decision, setting out the circumstances of the case and the evidence on which they base their decision and, if they refuse to make a payment, the reasons for that refusal (clause 9).

11 If the applicant does not exercise his right to appeal against the Bureau's decision, the Bureau's decision will be final and the applicant will be entitled to be paid the amount awarded by the Bureau (clause 10).

12 If the applicant wishes to appeal against the decision on the grounds specified in clause 11, he must notify the Bureau within six weeks of being notified of the decision, and give the undertakings set out in clause 12.

13 The Bureau may, as a result of comments made by the applicant on their decision, investigate the application further, and if so they will communicate with the applicant again. In such a case, the applicant will have six weeks from the date of that further communication in which to decide whether or not to go on with his appeal (clause 13).

14 Where the applicant appeals only on the grounds that the amount awarded to him is too low, the Bureau may give him notice that if the matter proceeds to appeal, they will ask the arbitrator to decide also the issue of the Bureau's liability to make any payment. The applicant will have six weeks from the date of any such notice in which to comment to the Bureau on this intention (clause 14).

15 Appeals will be decided by an arbitrator who will be a Queen's Counsel

selected by the Minister of Transport from one of two panels to be appointed by the Lord Chancellor and the Lord Advocate respectively (clause 18).

16 All appeals will be decided by the arbitrator on the basis of the relevant documents (as set out in clause 15) which will be sent to him by the Bureau. If the arbitrator asks the Bureau to make a further investigation, the applicant will have an opportunity to comment on the result of that investigation (clause 17).

17 The arbitrator may, at his discretion, award the cost of his fee against the applicant if he considers the appeal unreasonable; otherwise, each party to the appeal will bear their own costs, the Bureau paying the arbitrator's fee (clauses 21 and 22).

18 In certain circumstances, the Bureau may establish a trust for the benefit of an applicant of the whole or part of any award (clause 23).

[Reproduced by permission of the Controller of HM Stationery Office].

Note—The agreement provides a complete code of practice for such applications. So long as MIB complies with the procedure provided by the agreement its decisions cannot be the subject of litigation.

Persson v London Country Buses

[1974] 1 All ER 1251, [1974] 1 WLR 569, 118 Sol Jo 134, [1974] 1 Lloyd's Rep 415, CA

The plaintiff, a bus conductor, was injured when the bus pulled up sharply. He claimed damages from his employers on the ground that the driver was negligent, but they denied liability; they said the accident was caused by the negligence of a motorist who could not be identified or traced. The plaintiff applied to the Motor Insurers' Bureau for an award under the 1969 (untraced drivers) agreement. After investigation the Bureau decided that no award should be made because the plaintiff had not satisfied cl 1(1)(c). He then began proceedings in the county court against his employers and the Bureau, alleging a failure by the Bureau to compensate him in accordance with the 1969 agreement. The county court judge ordered the claim against the Bureau to be struck out on the ground that it disclosed no cause of action.

HELD, ON APPEAL: The judge was right. The agreement is enforceable by the Minister and (by consent of the Bureau) by an applicant, but only in accordance with the terms of the agreement. An award under cl 3 in favour of an applicant is expressly made subject to the provisions of the following clauses, including cl 7, which prescribes what the Bureau has to do and, when done, requiring the Bureau to decide whether to make an award. The process under cl 7 is subject to a right of appeal under cl 11, but if there is no award there is no right to payment. The Bureau's decision to reject the application was in fulfilment of the terms of the agreement and not a repudiation of it. An applicant cannot bring an action against the Bureau alleging breach of the agreement upon a basis of fact which is reserved by the agreement for the Bureau's decision.

Elizabeth v Motor Insurers' Bureau

[1981] RTR 405, CA

The appellant was injured when riding his motor-cycle behind a van. The van braked and the appellant ran into it. The van did not stop and was not traced. In an appeal under the Motor Insurers' Bureau Untraced Drivers Agreement the arbitrator said he found it impossible to say that the appellant had proved on the balance of probabilities that the van driver did anything negligent.

HELD, on appeal from the decision of a judge refusing to remit the case to an arbitrator: The burden of proof in circumstances was not on the appellant. Having regard to the fact that all the evidence was contained in documents a judge should be ready to inquire closely into the proceedings before the arbitrator. The decision in *Gussman v Gratton-Storey* (p 57, above) was relevant and was worthy of consideration. Award remitted.

Suing possible joint tortfeasor — cl 6(1)(b)

White v London Transport Executive

[1971] 2 QB 721, [1971] 3 All ER 1, [1971] 3 WLR 169, 115 Sol Jo [1971] RTR 326, CA

The plaintiff was in a bus when it pulled up sharply and she was injured. The bus driver said the accident was due to the negligence of the driver of a vehicle which had not stopped and could not be traced. The plaintiff applied to the Motor Insurers' Bureau under the 1969 agreement. The Bureau then required the plaintiff under para 6(1)(b) of the agreement to take proceedings against the bus driver and his employers the LTE. When she did so the Bureau applied under Ord 15, r 6(2)(b) to be joined as a party.

HELD: The application should be rejected. The 1969 agreement gave the Bureau considerable powers of control over the litigation which it required the plaintiff to conduct e g cll 6(1)(a) and (b), 6(2) and 8. Since the plaintiff was bringing this action on the direction of the Bureau she was bound to pursue it with all vigilance and skill to make the defendants liable, so that all matters in the claim against the LTE would be properly and fully investigated without joining the Bureau. Joinder of the Bureau was not 'necessary' within the opening words of Ord 15, r 6(2)(b).

Note—The 1969 Untraced Drivers' Agreement has been replaced by the 1972 Agreement. See p 789, above.

Short procedure

Note—A Supplemental Agreement dated 7 December 1977 has been made the object of which is to provide for speedier disposal of certain types of application. It enables the Bureau at its discretion to offer an award in a specified sum furnishing the applicant with particulars of the circumstances and of the evidence on which the offer is based. The applicant can accept the offer at that stage foregoing the right of appeal and discharging the Bureau from all liability. The agreement relates to applications on or after 3 January 1978. There is an upper limit for the operation of the accelerated procedure. As from 19 July 1982 the limit is £20,000. Before that date the limit was £10,000.

Supplemental Agreement between the Secretary of State for Transport and the Motor Insurers' Bureau

Text of an Agreement dated 7 December 1977, between the Secretary of State for Transport and the Motor Insurers' Bureau together with some notes on its scope and purpose.

AN AGREEMENT made 7 December 1977 between the Secretary of State for Transport and the Motor Insurers' Bureau, whose registered office is Aldermary House, Queen Street, London, EC4N 1 TR (hereinafter referred to as 'MIB') SUPPLEMENTAL to an Agreement (hereinafter referred to as the 'Principal Agreement') relating to compensation of victims of untraced drivers and made 22 November 1972 between the Secretary of State for the Environment and MIB.

IT IS HEREBY AGREED as follows:—

1 (1) In any case in which an application has been made to MIB in pursuance of clause 2(1) of the principal agreement on or after the 3 January 1978 and in which a preliminary investigation in pursuance of clause 7 thereof has disclosed that the case is one to which that agreement, but not clause 5 thereof, applies MIB may, instead of causing a report to be made on the application as provided by the said clause 7, make, or cause to be made, to the applicant an offer to settle his application in a specified sum, assessed in accordance with clause 3 of the principal agreement. (2) Where an offer is made in pursuance of paragraph (1) above, there shall be furnished to the applicant (at the same time) in writing particulars of (i) the circumstances in which the death or injury occurred and the evidence bearing thereon, and (ii) the circumstances relevant to the assessment of the amount to be awarded to the applicant and the evidence bearing thereon.

2 On receipt by MIB or its agent of an acceptance of the offer referred to in the foregoing clause, in the form specified in the Schedule hereto and duly completed by the applicant: (a) the principal agreement shall have effect in relation to the application as if in clause 7 the words 'and unless MIB decide' to the end of that clause, and clauses 9 to 22 inclusive were omitted; and (b) MIB shall pay to the applicant the amount specified in the offer, and such payment shall discharge MIB from all liability under this and the principal agreement in respect of the death or injury in relation to which the payment has been made.

3 In clause 4(a) of the principal agreement after the words 'solatium for the grief of any relative of the deceased' there shall be inserted the words 'or a loss of society award to a member of the immediate family of the deceased under s 1(4) of the Damages (Scotland) Act 1976'.

4 In clause 16 of the principal agreement there shall be added at the end the following proviso: 'Provided that where the arbitrator has dealt with an appeal under paragraph (a) of this clause all the foregoing provisions of this agreement shall apply as if the case were an application to which this agreement applies upon which MIB had not communicated a decision'.

5 This agreement shall be construed as one with the principal agreement and, without prejudice to the operation of clause 6 thereof, shall cease to have effect on the date that that agreement terminates in accordance with clause 24 thereof, and subject to the proviso there mentioned.

6 Clauses 1 and 2 of this agreement may be determined at any time by the Secretary of State or by MIB, by either of them giving to the other not less than 12 months previous notice in writing: Provided that the said clauses shall continue to have effect in respect of any case where the event giving rise to the death or injury occurred before the date on which those clauses terminate in accordance with any notice so given.

SCHEDULE (referred to in clause 2)
Form of Acceptance (under Supplemental Agreement dated 7 December 1977) I, [*full name of applicant*] of [*address*] HEREBY ACCEPT the sum of £. . . offered, in pursuance of clause 1 of an agreement made between the Secretary of State for Transport and the Motor Insurers' Bureau (hereinafter called 'MIB') and dated 7 December 1977, by or on behalf on MIB in settlement of the application made by me or on my behalf on [*date*] to MIB in pursuance of clause 2(1) of an agreement made between the Secretary of State for the Environment and MIB and dated 22 November 1972 relating to compensation of victims of untraced drivers in respect of: [*particulars of, and circumstances giving rise to, injuries*] AND UNDERSTAND that payment of that sum will discharge MIB from all liability under the afore-mentioned agreements, and that I shall have no further rights under those agreements (in particular any right of appeal to an arbitrator under clause 11 of the agreement of 22 November 1972).

Name and address and description   Signature of applicant:
of witness: Date:
IN WITNESS etc.
NOTES
1 This agreement supplements the agreement dated 22 November 1972 concerning compensation for personal injuries suffered by victims of untraced drivers.

2 The following notes are for guidance only and must not be taken as rendering unnecessary a careful study of this supplemental agreement itself together with the main agreement to which it relates. Communications concerning these agreements should be addressed to the Motor Insurers' Bureau, whose address is Aldermary House, Queen Street, London EC4N 1TR.

3 Clause 1 of the supplemental agreement provides for the use of a shorter form of procedure than that stipulated in the main agreement with the object of securing speedier disposal of certain applications to the Bureau. Except in a case where both an untraced person and an identified person may each partly be responsible for the injuries giving rise to an application, the Bureau may, at its discretion, make an offer of an award in a specified sum furnishing the applicant at the same time with particulars of the circumstances of the case and of the evidence on which the offer is based. If the applicant is prepared to accept the offer and undertake, on payment by the Bureau, to discharge them from all liability and forego any right of appeal to an arbitrator the Bureau will pay the sum offered forthwith. If the offer is not acceptable the application will thereafter be dealt with in accordance with the full procedure as set out in the main agreement.

4 The purpose of clause 4 of the supplemental agreement is to make clear that the Bureau remain entitled to require any applicant to take proceedings against a known person in accordance with clause 6(1)(b) of the main agreement, notwithstanding that the applicant had successfully appealed against a decision by the Bureau to reject the application after a preliminary investigation.

FOREIGN MOTORISTS IN ENGLAND

*The Motor Vehicles (International Motor Insurance Card)
Regulations 1971, SI 1971/792*

1 Regulations come into operation 10 June 1971.

2 Revokes the Motor Vehicles (International Insurance Card) Regulations 1969, SI 1969/668.

3 Interpretation 'British Bureau' is the MIB. 'Foreign Bureau' is a central organisation set up by motor insurers in any country abroad (ie outside the UK the Isle of Man and the Channel Islands) having an agreement with the British Bureau for third-party insurance of motorists. Description and meaning of 'insurance card'.

4 Sets out requirements for the validity of the insurance card.

5 As respects the use of a motor vehicle specified in a valid insurance card s 201 of the Road Traffic Act 1960 shall have effect as though the said card were a policy of insurance.

6(1) The insurance card shall have the effect of an insurance certificate. Duty to give information as to insurance under s 209(1) of the Road Traffic Act 1960 to be fulfilled by giving particulars of serial number, name of Bureau and name and address of person specified on card as the insured.
(2) Person making a claim shall give notice in writing to British Bureau as soon as practicable after the accident, specifying the nature of the claim and against whom it is made.
(3) When an accident occurs and the insurance card is produced to a police constable he may detach the duplicate page from the card for the purposes of recording the insurance particulars.

7 Production of duplicate page of insurance card in civil proceedings is evidence of holder having signed authority to Bureau to accept service of proceedings and handle claims.

8 Holder of insurance card may produce it on application for motor vehicle licence for purposes of reg 9 of Motor Vehicles (Third Party Risks) Regs 1961.*

9 Police to furnish to the British Bureau on request (or to an authorised insurer at the Bureau's request) any information relating to the contents of a duplicate page detached by a police constable under reg 6(3) and forward it to the Bureau or the authorised insurer.

10 Special provision for motor vehicles from Northern Ireland — effective policy and certificate required.

* Now replaced by the Motor Vehicles (Third Party Risks) Regulations 1972, SI 1972/1217. Sections 201 and 209(1) of the Road Traffic Act 1960 are now replaced by ss 143 and 151(1) respectively of the Road Traffic Act 1972.

CHAPTER 20
Motor policies

1 FORMATION: PROPOSAL AND MATERIALITY

MATERIAL FACT

Uberrimae fidei

Brownlie v Campbell
(1880) 5 App Cas 925, HL
Per Lord Blackburn: In policies of insurance, whether marine or life insurance there is an understanding that the contract is *uberrima fides*.

Note—Followed in *Regina Fur Co v Bossom*, p 807, below.

Proudfoot v Montefiore
(1867) LR 2 QB 511, 36 LJQB 225, 16 LT 585, 15 WR 920
Per Cockburn LJ: The insurer is entitled to assume, as the basis of the contract between him and the assured, that the latter will communicate to him every material fact of which the assured has, or, in the ordinary course of business, ought to have, knowledge.

W. Pickersgill & Sons Ltd v London and Provincial Marine and General Insurance Co Ltd

[1912] 3 KB 614, 82 LJKB 130, 107 LT 305, 28 TLR 591, 57 Sol Jo 11
The duty to make a full disclosure proceeds from an implied term in the contract precedent to the insurer's liability.

Greenhill v Federal Insurance Co

[1927] 1 KB 65, 95 LJKB 717, 135 LT 244, 70 Sol Jo 565, 31 Com Cas 289, 17 Asp MLC 62, CA
Per Scrutton LJ: Now insurance is a contract of the utmost good faith, and it is of the gravest importance to commerce that this position should be observed. The underwriter knows nothing of the particular circumstances of the voyage to be insured. The assured knows a great deal, and it is the duty of the assured to inform the underwriter of everything that he is not taken as knowing, so that the contract may be entered into on an equal footing.

What is material

Zurich General Accident and Liability Insurance Co v Morrison

[1942] 2 KB 53, [1942] 1 All ER 529, 111 LJKB 601, 167 LT 183, 58 TLR 217, 86 Sol Jo 267, 72 Ll L Rep 167, CA
Materiality must always be a question of degree to be determined by the court. It is a question of fact in each case.

Note—Followed by Atkinson J in *Broad v Waland* (1942) 73 Ll L Rep 263, at 628 and 679. See further p 815, below.

Merchants' and Manufacturers' Insurance Co v Hunt

[1940] 4 All ER 205, 57 TLR 32, 84 Sol Jo 670 (Stable J)
The right to avoid the policy for misrepresentation depended on equity and not implied term of the contract.

Note—See further p 814, below.

Locker and Woolf Ltd v Western Australian Insurance Co

[1936] 1 KB 408, 105 LJKB 444, 154 LT 667, 52 TLR 293, 80 Sol Jo 185, CA
The obligation on a person making a proposal for insurance (against fire) to disclose all material facts is not limited to matters exclusively relating to fire risks, but extends to any matters which would influence the judgment of the insurance company in deciding whether to take or refuse the risk. Proposal for fire insurance in November 1931:
   '*Q*. Has this or any other insurance of yours been declined by any other company? *A*. No.'
   L & W when trading in partnership in 1930, had applied to the N Co for a policy covering their motor vehicles, and the N Co had declined such proposal.

HELD, in the Court of Appeal: The non-disclosure of this refusal of the motor car insurance was the non-disclosure of a material fact in the proposal for the fire insurance which therefore entitled the fire insurance company to avoid the policy.

The Marine Insurance Act 1906, s 18(2), provides that every circumstance is material which would influence the judgment of a prudent insurer in fixing the premium or determining whether he will take the risk. This definition is applicable to all classes of insurance: per Scott LJ.

It is elementary that one of the matters to be considered by an insurance company in entering into contractual relations with a proposed insurer is the question of the moral integrity of the proposer — what has been called the moral hazard: per Slesser LJ.

Note—Followed in *Regina Fur Co v Bossom*, p 807, below. And see *Condogianis v Guardian Assurance Co*, p 822, below.

Container Transport International Inc and Reliance Group Inc International v Oceanus Mutual Underwriting Association (Bermuda) Ltd

[1984] 1 Lloyd's Rep 476, CA
Under the Marine Insurance Act 1906 ss 18(2), 20(2) any circumstance was material if it would 'influence' the judgment of a prudent insurer. 'Influence' meant that the disclosure would have had an impact on the prudent insurer's opinion and on his decision-making process; it was not necessary that he would actually have been induced to refuse the risk or alter the premium. The test was whether the presentation of the risk to the insurer had been fair, so that a prudent insurer could form a proper judgment whether to accept the proposal and, if so, on what terms.

March Cabaret Club and Casino Ltd v London Assurance

[1975] 1 Lloyd's Rep 169 (May J)
The plaintiff company owned and ran a club and casino and was itself controlled and directed by S and his wife. In 1967 the defendant insurers issued a policy covering the contents against fire risks, extended on renewal to cover the company's buildings. On 14 June 1969 S was arrested on a charge of handling stolen goods and on 28 November 1969 was committed for trial. The policy fell due for renewal on 20 April 1970; when renewing S did not disclose his arrest and committal to the insurers. On 22 June 1970, he was convicted and fined £2,000. On 14 September 1970, there was a fire at the club premises causing £27,024 damage. The insurers, after investigation in which they learned of S's prosecution and conviction declared the policy void on the ground of material non-disclosure when the policy was renewed in April 1970.
HELD: There had been a material non-disclosure entitling the insurers to avoid the policy. The duty to disclose material facts arises outside the contract of insurance and not by way of implied term. The test of materiality was whether the facts would, on a fair consideration of the evidence, influence a reasonable insurer to decline the risk. Whether a particular circumstance is material or not is a question of fact in which the moral integrity of the proposer is important. S should, before renewal in

April 1970, have disclosed that he had committed the crime referred to; even if he had subsequently been acquitted he ought to have disclosed the fact of his arrest, charge and committal, but not if he had been acquitted before the renewal.

Note—In *Reynolds and Anderson v Phoenix Assurance Co Ltd* [1978] 2 Lloyd's Rep 440 (noted at p 808, below), another fire insurance case, Forbes J disagreed with a comment by May J that the fact of the arrest, charge and committal should have been disclosed even though in truth S was innocent. He said the most relevant circumstance for disclosure is that the proposer had actually committed an offence of a character which would in fact influence the insurer's judgment; the material circumstance is the commission of the offence.

Lambert v Co-operative Insurance Society
[1975] 2 Lloyd's Rep 485, CA
The defendants issued an 'All-risks' policy to the plaintiff covering jewellery belonging to herself and her husband. When proposing for the policy in 1963 she had not disclosed her husband's conviction for receiving stolen goods a few years earlier nor, on renewing the policy in 1972, did she disclose her husband's conviction on charges of conspiracy and theft in 1971. When she made a claim under the policy for loss of some items of jewellery the defendants repudiated on the grounds that she had failed to disclose material facts, namely, the convictions. Evidence was given by the defendants' branch manager that if he had known of the 1971 convictions he would not have invited renewal.
HELD: The defendants were entitled to repudiate. The test of materiality set out in the Marine Insurance Act 1906, s 18 that 'every circumstance is material which would influence the judgment of a prudent insurer in fixing the premium or determining whether he will take the risk' was the general rule of all insurance law. There is no difference in this respect between marine and other forms of insurance. The same test had been adopted in the Road Traffic Act 1934, s 10(5) and was applied in *Zurich Insurance Co v Morrison* (p 804, above). The suggestion that it is only what a reasonable proposer would consider relevant that has to be disclosed is not the law.

Note—Followed in *Woolcott v Sun Alliance and London Insurance Ltd* [1978] 1 All ER 1253, [1978] 1 WLR 493, 121 Sol Jo 121, 744.

Godfrey v Britannic Assurance Co Ltd
(1963) 107 Sol Jo 536, [1963] Lloyd's Rep 515 (Roskill J)
In a proposal form for life insurance the assured was required to say what illness or accidents he had had or medical advice or treatment. He did not disclose, because he thought them immaterial, the following: (1) he had been twice sent to hospital by his doctor for a check-up on his kidneys, (2) there had been a small area of infection in his lung, (3) five attacks of pharyngitis in two or three years, (4) general bad health for the last two and a half years.
HELD: The assured was required to disclose every material circumstance of which he knew or ought to have known: a material circumstance was one which would influence the judgment of a prudent underwriter in fixing the

premium or in determining whether or not he would take the risk. The opinion of the assured whether or not a particular fact was material was irrelevant. The defendants were entitled to repudiate the contract of insurance.

Rose Lodge Ltd v Castle

(1966) 110 Sol Jo 705, [1966] 2 Lloyd's Rep 113 (McNair J)
The plaintiffs diamond merchants, insured their diamonds against all risks with defendant underwriters. The proposal form did not contain any question about previous convictions of employees. The plaintiffs did not disclose: (1) that in 1946 their managing director (the effective principal of the company) had been convicted of giving a bribe of five shillings to a police officer and had been fined £75; (2) that their sales manager had in 1956 (before entering the plaintiff's employment) been convicted of smuggling diamonds into the USA. On 31 January 1965 in Hatton Garden the managing director was robbed of diamonds worth £300,000. The plaintiffs claimed to be indemnified under the policy. The defendants refused to pay, claiming that the policy was void for non-disclosure of material facts known to the plaintiffs, namely, the two convictions. On the evidence the judge found that the robbery had actually occurred as alleged and that there was no suggestion that the sales manager had anything to do with it.

He nevertheless held that the plaintiffs could not succeed. It was not sufficient that a proposed insured should disclose to the insurer what he, the proposer, thought was material the insurer should know. There was the further duty that he should do it to the extent that a reasonable man would have done it. The disclosure must be of all he ought to have realised would be material, not merely of that which he in fact realised to be material (*Joel v Law Union and Crown Insurance Co* [1908] 2 KB 863, 77 LJKB 1108, 99 LT 712, 24 TLR 898, CA). Expert evidence of materiality may be given by underwriters but the issue as to disclosability was still one to be determined by the view of reasonable men. On the facts of the present case the managing director's offence and conviction were not material and need not have been disclosed, but the sales manager's conviction was different. He had been a party to a dishonest transaction and a reasonable man would appreciate that he remained or might remain a security risk. His conviction was a material fact which ought to have been disclosed.

Regina Fur Co v Bossom

[1957] 2 Lloyd's Rep 466 (Pearson J)
Burglary claim by limited company; directors Waxman and Freeman; The company failed to disclose that Waxman had been convicted 20 years before of receiving a quantity of fur skins knowing the same to have been stolen.
HELD: The test was that disclosure must be of all that a proposer ought to have realised to be material. A first impression would naturally be that an isolated conviction more than 20 years old must be too ancient and too remote. When the first policy was issued Waxman held a predominant position in the company. Evidence is admissible on the point whether the conviction affected the moral hazard to such an extent as to be material (*Yorke v Yorkshire Insurance Co Ltd* [1918] 1 KB 662 at 670). Expert evidence

that it was was given by two underwriters, and a witness for the plaintiff was unable to say that it was not. On the special facts of this case, and not based on any decision in any other case, the court found it was material.

Note—An appeal was dismissed [1958] 2 Lloyd's Rep 425.

Rehabilitation of Offenders Act 1974

Reynolds v Phoenix Assurance Co Ltd
(1978) 122 Sol Jo 161, [1978] 2 Lloyd's Rep 22, CA
The plaintiffs sued the defendant insurers under a fire policy for payment of a loss caused by a fire at the insured property. In the course of the proceedings the defendants learned that one of the insured plaintiffs had been convicted of an offence 16 years earlier. They applied to amend the defence to plead that the conviction should have been disclosed when proposing for the policy and that the non-disclosure was material.
HELD, ON APPEAL: Though the Rehabilitation of Offenders Act 1974, s 4 excluded the possibility of bringing evidence of a spent conviction it was subject to s 7(3) which enabled a judge to admit evidence of such a conviction if satisfied 'that justice cannot be done in the case except by admitting' the evidence. The amendment should be allowed so that the issue could be brought before the court, when the judge could hear evidence and decide whether the conviction was a material matter without evidence of which justice could not be done.

Note—At the subsequent trial of the action Forbes J held that evidence of the conviction should be admitted. Injustice would otherwise be done to the defendant insurers since they would be prevented from avoiding a policy which on the evidence it would be the universal practice of insurers to avoid: [1978] 2 Lloyd's Rep 440.

Evidence

Thames and Mersey Marine Insurance Co v Gunford
[1911] AC 529, 80 LJPC 146, 105 LT 312, 27 TLR 518, 55 Sol Jo 631, HL
Ionides v Pender
(1874) LR 9 QB 531, 43 LJQB 22, 30 LT 547
Expert evidence may be given on the question of fact that knowledge of particular circumstances affecting acceptance might be material.

Note—Cited in *Merchants' and Manufacturers' Insurance Co v Davies*, p 814, above. See *Regina Fur Co v Bossom*, above, and *Rose Lodge Ltd v Castle*, above.
      In *Locker's* case (p 804, above), Swift J cited *Carter v Boehm* (1766) 3 Burr 1905 (*Smith's Leading Cases* (13th edn) vol I, p 546), in which Lord Mansfield held the evidence of insurance experts as to materiality was improper and the court must decide the question without it. To the opposite effect he cited *Becker v Marshall* (1922) 12 Ll L Rep 413, where the judge admitted evidence, as is now the established custom, of experts as to materiality, *Glasgow Assurance Corpn v Symondson & Co* (1911) 104 LT 254, 27 TLR 245, 16 Com Cas 109, that in recent practice evidence had frequently been admitted of underwriters, and *Glicksman's* case [1925] 2 KB 593, where it was argued that before a court can find that a fact is material, somebody must give evidence of the materiality. He said this was entirely

contrary to the whole course of insurance ligitation; 'it is so far contrary that it is frequently objected that a party is not entitled to call other people to say what they think is material; that is a matter for the courts on the nature of the facts'.

Waiver of materiality on proposal

Glicksman v Lancashire and General Assurance Co

[1927] AC 139, 136 LT 263, 43 TLR 46, 70 Sol Jo 1111, 26 Ll L Rep 69, HL

In a proposal form for burglary insurance insurers asked the proposer whether he had previously applied for burglary insurance to another office and been refused.

HELD: The fact that a question of this sort was asked showed that the insurance company thought it was material whether a proposal had been refused or not and thus brought it to the knowledge of the proposer that it was a material fact.

Arterial Caravans Ltd v Yorkshire Insurance Co

[1973] 1 Lloyd's Rep 169 (Chapman J)

The duty is on the assured to disclose any material information which he has, and it is only if, as the cases indicate, the insurers are put on enquiry about some particular matter that it can be said that they have waived the obligation, the requirement, as to disclosure. As Banks LJ put it in the case of *Mann MacNeal v Capital and Counties Insurance Co* [1921] 2 KB 300, 90 LJKB 846, 124 LT 778, 37 TLR 247, 5 Ll L Rep 203, CA quoting Lord Esher:

'it is not necessary to disclose mu nutely every material fact; assuming that there is a material fact which [the assured] is bound to disclose, the rule is satisfied if he disclosed sufficient to call the attention of the underwriters in such a manner they can see that if they require further information they ought to ask for it.'

Jester-Barnes v Licenses and General Insurance Co

(1934) 49 Ll L Rep 231

Per MacKinnon J: If they had asked him the question 'have you or your driver during the past five years been convicted of any offence' and he had said 'no' and that was true, I should have come without hesitation to the conclusion that they were not entitled after asking that question and receiving that answer to take it to mean that he had failed to disclose that he had been convicted eight years ago and that it was a material fact.

Waiver by approbating policy

West v National Motor and Accident Insurance Union

[1954] 2 Lloyd's Rep 461 (Lord Goddard CJ)

Insurers repudiated a claim under a burglary policy for non-disclosure as to value, but did not repudiate the policy.

HELD: Having approved the policy they could not repudiate the claim.

Note—An appeal was dismissed [1955] 1 All ER 800, [1955] 1 WLR 343, 99 Sol Jo 235, [1955] 1 Lloyd's Rep 207, CA

Waiver by dealing with claim

Note—See also *Greenwood v Martin's Bank*, p 890, below.

M'Cormick v National Motor and Accident Insurance Union Ltd
(1934) 50 TLR 528, 78 Sol Jo 633, 40 Com Cas 76, 49 L1 L Rep 361, CA
During the course of the trial of an action between a third party and the
assured, it came out in evidence that the assured had been previously
convicted for dangerous driving. He had stated on the proposal form that
he had not been convicted. Insurers continued to defend the action, and
five days later repudiated liability under the policy.
HELD: This did not amount to waiver. The insurers were entitled to
continue to defend the action.
   Whether you treat it as an election or whether you treat it as a ratification
or whether you treat it as a decision simply to act on the knowledge you
have acquired, the duty to take action does not arise (1) unless you know all
the facts — being put on enquiry is not sufficient; you must know the facts
— and (2) unless you have a reasonable time to make up your mind. You
are not bound the moment the statement is made to you to make up your
mind at once; you are entitled to a reasonable time to consider — to a
reasonable time to make enquiries: Per Scrutton LJ.
   There must be an irresistible inference that the parties intended to adopt
one of two courses open to them and to discard or waive the other and in
such a manner as to represent to other persons definitely and unequivocally
that he has taken that view whereby it may act to their detriment: Per
Slesser LJ.

Evans v Employers' Mutual Insurance Association Ltd
[1936] 1 KB 505, 105 LJKB 141, 154 LT 137, 52 L1 L Rep 51, CA
If it is established by evidence that the duty of investigating and
ascertaining facts has been delegated in the ordinary course of a company's
business to a subordinate official, the company will, in law, be bound by his
knowledge in the same way as it is affected by the knowledge of the board of
directors. The claimant said in the proposal form that he had been driving
for five years, which was untrue. An accident occurred and in the claim
form he stated he had been driving six weeks. The claim form and proposal
form were handed to the respondents' claims superintendent, who was
authorised to deal with such matters, and was passed on by him in
accordance with the practice of the office, to a clerk for the purpose of
checking the statements they contained and noting any discrepancies
therein. The clerk noticed the discrepancy, but did not call attention to it,
considering it of no importance. Thereafter the respondents paid for
damage to car and medical expenses, and negotiated claims by third
parties. Before settling those claims the claims superintendent became
aware of the untrue statement, whereupon the respondents repudiated
liability.
HELD: The respondents had waived their right to repudiate liability.

Locker and Woolf Ltd v Western Australian Insurance Co Ltd
[1936] 1 KB 408, 105 LJKB 444, 154 LT 667, 52 TLR 293, 80 Sol Jo 185
(Swift J)
On a fire loss the company's assessors sold the salvage. The policy
contained a condition that the company may, without thereby incurring
any liability and without diminishing the rights of the company to rely on
conditions of this policy, take possession of the property insured and deal
with it for all reasonable purposes and in any reasonable manner.
HELD: There was no waiver.

Stone v Licenses and General Insurance Co Ltd
(1942) 71 Ll L Rep 256 (Birkett J)
16 May, 4 am : accident involving lorry carrying load in breach of policy
condition. 8 am : driver telephoned assured who informed insurers. 6.30
pm : branch manager of insurers visited accident and saw the
unauthorised load. 17 May: driver made full disclosure at insurer's office.
Insurers then had full knowledge of all material facts. 23 May: Branch
manager gave instructions to remove debris and sell it for £1. The assured
was not consulted. 7 June: Insurers wrote repudiating liability under policy
and sent their own cheque for £1 to assured who refused to accept the
cheque.
HELD: The breach of condition had been waived.

Mutual mistake

Magee v Pennine Insurance Co Ltd
[1969] 2 QB 507, [1969] 2 All ER 891, [1969] 2 WLR 1278, 113 Sol Jo 303,
[1969] 2 Lloyd's Rep 378, CA
The plaintiff took out a motor insurance policy with the defendants in 1961.
There were serious misstatements of fact in the proposal which would
entitle the defendants to repudiate liability under the policy or declare it
void. In 1964 the car was damaged in an accident. After an inspection by an
engineer the defendants wrote to the plaintiff saying it was damaged
beyond repair, that its value according to the engineer was (after salvage)
£385 and offering him that amount 'in settlement of your claim'. The
plaintiff accepted but the insurers then discovered the inaccuracy of the
statements in the proposal form and refused to pay. The county court judge
found that the plaintiff had not been fraudulent and that the defendants'
letter was a binding offer which had been accepted.
HELD: There had been a common mistake of fact, namely, that there was a
valid policy of insurance. Accepting that the agreement to pay £385 was a
separate contract the defendants were entitled to avoid it on the ground of
mutual mistake in a fundamental and vital matter.

Agent is agent of proposer

Newsholme Bros v Road Transport and General Insurance Co Ltd
[1929] 2 KB 356, 98 LJKB 751, 141 LT 570, 45 TLR 573, 73 Sol Jo 465,
CA
With regard to misstatements in a proposal form the insurance agent is the

agent of the assured and not of the insurer. A proposal form for the insurance of a motor-bus was signed by the person wishing to effect the insurance, but the answers to the questions therein, which were warranted to be true and to form the basis of the contract, were filled in by the insurance company's agent, who, although told the true facts, wrote, for some unexplained reason, answers which were untrue in a material respect. The agent was not authorised by the insurance company to fill in proposal forms and it did not appear that the company knew that he had in fact done so. His duties were to procure persons to effect insurance and to see, so far as he could, that proposal forms were correctly filled up; he was not authorised to give a cover note or to enter into a policy of insurance. A policy was issued to the person who had signed the proposal form and during its currency he made a claim under it, but the insurance company repudiated liability on the ground of the untrue statements in the proposal form.

HELD: The agent of the insurance company in filling in the proposal form was merely the *amanuensis* of the proposer, that the knowledge of the true facts by the agent could not be imputed to the insurance company, and, therefore, that the insurance company was entitled to repudiate liability on the ground of the untrue statements in the proposal form.

Facer v Vehicle and General Insurance Co Ltd
[1965] 1 Lloyd's Rep 113 (Marshall J)
The plaintiff signed a proposal form which was filled in for him by a Mr Bonham, a sub-agent or servant of Mr Braun, who was an agent of the defendants. The answer 'No' was written on the proposal form to the question 'Do you suffer from any defective vision or hearing or from any physical infirmity?' though the plaintiff had disclosed to Bonham that he had only one eye. The proposal form ended 'I agree that this proposal and declaration shall be the basis of the contract between the company and myself' and also said 'If this proposal is written by another it shall be deemed he shall be my agent and not an agent of the company'.

HELD: The vital question was whether Bonham, when he inaccurately answered the question about defective vision by putting in the word 'No' was the agent of the plaintiff in filling in the form or the agent of the defendants. The case was governed by *Newsholme Brothers v Road Transport & General Insurance Co Ltd* (above) with this further strengthening factor that in the present case there was an express declaration in the proposal that the person filling in the form was to be deemed the agent of the proposer and not of the company. The defendants were entitled to avoid the policy.

A CONTRASTING CASE

Stone v Reliance Mutual Insurance Society Ltd
[1972] 1 Lloyd's Rep 469, CA
In 1966 the plaintiff insured his house with the defendants under a fire and theft policy. In 1967 there was a fire and the defendants paid him £280. The policy then lapsed. In 1968 the defendants' district inspector called with a view to getting the plaintiff to take out a new policy. He called only on people who had previously held policies and it was the company's practice that for the proposal form he should put the questions orally and write down the answers himself. He filled in a proposal form without asking any

questions and plaintiff's wife signed it without reading it. The form contained a declaration by the proposer that the person writing down the answers did so as the proposer's agent. Two of the answers in by the inspector were to the effect that the plaintiff had not previously held a policy with the defendants and that he had not previously made any claims in respect of the risks proposed. Later a burglary took place for which the plaintiff claimed, disclosing on the claim form the earlier fire claim. The defendants refused to indemnify on the ground of non-disclosure of the fire claim in the proposal form.

HELD: Though the proposal form was expressed to be filled in by the inspector as the plaintiff's agent his express evidence had been that it was company practice that he should put the questions and write down the answers. The proper inference was that it was his duty, owed to his employers, to take proper care. It was quite different from *Newsholme's* case (above); it was far more like *Bawden's* case (referred to below). The inspector knew of the earlier policy and of the fire claim: it was his mistake and not the proposer's. The company could not rely on it to avoid the policy.

AGENT'S AUTHORITY

Notice of loss to agent

Brook v Trafalgar Insurance Co Ltd
(1946) 79 Ll L Rep 365, CA

The plaintiff's motor car was insured with defendants. The fulfilment of the policy conditions was a condition precedent to the right to recover. Notice of loss had to be given in writing to the head office immediately, and if not given within seven days, all benefits under the policy were forfeited.

The motor car was destroyed by fire on 17 December 1943.

On 18 December 1943, the plaintiff called at the office of the agent and obtained a claim form which the plaintiff signed on 3 January 1944, and handed back to the agent.

Stable J held the condition was waived by notice to the agent.

HELD: Allowing the appeal waiver had not been pleaded and could not be considered. An agent has no authority to waive the express condition of the policy.

The company were not liable.

Note—A different position may arise where the agent is acting as the agent of the insurer and not of the proposer. In *Newsholme's* case, Scrutton LJ said: 'In my view, the important question for the decision of this case is whether the knowledge of the agent, acquired in filling up the proposal for the assured, is to be taken as the knowledge of the company. If the person having authority to bind the company by making a contract in fact knows of the untruth of the statements and yet takes the premium, the question may be different. Even then I see great difficulty in avoiding the effect of the writing signed by the proposer that the truth of the statements is the basis of the contract.' (Decision of *Bawden v London, Edinburgh and Glasgow Assurance Co* [1892] 2 QB 534, 61 LJQB 792, 57 JP 116, 8 TLR 566, CA where the company were held liable, distinguished.)

The insurer has been held liable in:
Thornton-Smith v Motor Union Insurance Co Ltd
(1913) 30 TLR 139
Ayrey v British Legal and United Provident Assurance Co
[1918] 1 KB 136, 87 LJKB 513, 118 LT 255, 34 TLR 111 (distinguished in
Newsholme's case)
Holdsworth v Lancashire and Yorkshire Insurance Co
(1907) 23 TLR 521
Golding v Royal London Auxiliary Insurance Co
(1914) 30 TLR 350
Kaufmann v British Surety Insurance Co Ltd
(1929) 45 TLR 399

Insurer has been held not liable in:
Dunn v Ocean Accident and Guarantee Corpn Ltd
(1933) 50 TLR 32, 47 Ll L Rep 129, CA

Broker's implied authority

Stockton v Mason
[1978] 2 Lloyd's Rep 430, CA
The policyholder had a policy covering a Ford Anglia car. He exchanged
the car for an MG. His wife telephoned the brokers on 8 April and told
them; she asked that the MG be substituted for the Anglia as the car
insured under the policy. The broker said 'Yes, that will be all right. We
will see to that.' On 18 April at 3.30 pm the plaintiff was seriously injured
when travelling as a passenger in the MG driven by the policy holder's son.
The policy covered driving by any authorised driver. At 5.15 pm on the
18th the policyholder received a letter from the brokers written on the 17th
saying cover for the MG was limited to himself only. The judge held that
the brokers' remark was merely a statement that they would seek to
negotiate a contract of insurance on the MG; the insurers were not liable
and the brokers were liable in negligence to the policy holder's son for
failing to notify the policyholder of their failure to get insurance on the
desired terms.
HELD, ON APPEAL: There was a valid contract of interim insurance. A
broker had implied authority to issue on behalf of the insurer or enter into
as agent for the insurer contracts of interim insurance normally recorded in
cover notes. In making the remark quoted the brokers were acting as agents
for the insurers and not for the person wishing to be insured. Such an
interim contract of insurance can be made orally and in informal colloquial
language. The insurers were liable.

CASES OF MATERIAL MISREPRESENTATION

Age of driver

Merchants' and Manufacturers' Insurance Co Ltd v Hunt
[1940] 4 All ER 205, 57 TLR 32, 84 Sol Jo 670 (Stable J)
A proposal form which had the usual declaration and warranty contained

the following questions: '*Q*. Have you or any person who to your knowledge will drive the car ever been convicted of an offence in connection with a motor vehicle or motor cycle, or is any prosecution pending? *A*. No'.

The proposer knew that his son was likely to drive the car, and the son had been convicted of three motoring offences.

HELD: The representation of fact is material. The answer of an unqualified negative is an assertion (1) that the proposer has the knowledge which he purports to impart, and (2) that that knowledge is what he is imparting. The answer does not mean 'No, to the best of my knowledge and belief'.

'*Q*. Will the car be driven by any person under twenty-one? *A*. No'.

The proposer knew that the car would be driven quite frequently by his son, who was 17. The question of age is 'material'. Although each representation was innocent, the information was in fact false.

Note—In the Court of Appeal the case was decided on a different point but Scott LJ agreed with the construction of the questions and answers in the proposal form.

Zurich General Accident and Liability Insurance Co v Leven
1940 SC 406, 1940 SN 33, 1940 SLT 350

A question in a proposal form was as follows: '*Q*. Have you or has any other person who to your knowledge will drive been convicted of any offence in connection with any motor vehicle; if so, state nature of the offence, date and amount of the fine, and if licence was indorsed or suspended? *A*. No.'

HELD: The answer was a double statement of fact: firstly, I know the answer to the question and, secondly, the answer to the question is 'No'.

Age of proposer

Broad v Waland
(1942) 73 Ll L Rep 263 (Atkinson J)

A cover note was issued on the faith of proposal that proposer was 21 years of age. The brokers had clear and definite instruction not to issue a cover note to any person under 21. The proposer was 19 years 6 months and 2 weeks.

HELD, in an action for a declaration: (1) The misrepresentation was material; (2) the policy had been 'obtained' by the misrepresentation. The declaration was granted.

Alien

Horne v Poland
[1922] 2 KB 364, 91 LJKB 718, 127 LT 242, 38 TLR 357, 66 Sol Jo 368, 10 Ll L Rep 175, 275 (Lush J)

Where an alien takes out a burglary insurance policy, the fact that he is an alien may be a circumstance the non-disclosure of which to the insurers will avoid the policy.

Conviction — motor offences

Bond v Commercial Assurance Co
(1930) 35 Com Cas 171, 36 Ll L Rep 107
Appellant took out with respondents a motor car policy of insurance in respect of a car of which he was the owner. Appellant employed more than one driver in the course of his business and at the time when the insurance was effected the agent of respondents told him that if he paid an extra premium the policy would protect him whoever might be driving the car, and appellant paid the extra premium accordingly. During the currency of the policy the car, while being driven by a son of appellant, came into collision with a cyclist. The cyclist brought an action against appellant for damages, and appellant referred the claim to respondents, who repudiated liability on the ground that at the time when the policy was taken out appellant had failed to disclose a material fact. It appeared that before the insurance was effected appellant's son had been convicted several times of motoring offences, chiefly in relation to a motor cycle, and respondents contended that this was a material fact which ought to have been disclosed by appellant. Before the policy was issued appellant had received a proposal form from respondents and had answered all the questions in that form fully and truthfully and he did not know that any further information was required. At that time he had not his son in mind. Appellant's claim against respondents was referred to arbitration as required by the policy and the arbitrator awarded in favour of respondents on the ground that a material fact had not been disclosed. Appellant now appealed to the Divisional Court to have the award set aside.
HELD: The arbitrator had decided rightly and the award must be confirmed.

Butcher v Dowlen
(1980) 124 Sol Jo 883, [1981] RTR 24, 1 Lloyd's Rep 310, CA
The plaintiff claimed money due under a policy of motor insurance issued by the defendant to her husband who had been killed in an accident. The defendant served a defence denying liability under the policy on the ground that her husband had failed to disclose criminal charges and a conviction in the proposal form. The plaintiff, who said she had no knowledge of any conviction, obtained an order for further and better particulars specifying the alleged offences and charges with dates and other details. The defendant was unable to say more in reply than that the deceased had 'been convicted of offences on several occasions' without any details. The plaintiff applied to strike out the defence for failure to supply the particulars ordered.
HELD, dismissing an appeal from a judge: The defence should be struck out. It was not good enough for the defendant to say the action should go to trial so that a police officer could produce evidence from the Criminal Records Office which at present the defendant did not have. The burden of proof was on the defendant and there was not enough to justify the allegations made in the defence going to trial.

Other offences

Cleland v London General Insurance Co Ltd
(1935) 51 Ll L Rep 156, CA

The defendants repudiated liability on the ground of the non-disclosure of material facts on the proposal form. They relied upon the following statement in the proposal form: 'I have withheld no information which would tend to increase the risk or influence the acceptance of this proposal'. It was said that the insured had answered 'No' to the question on the proposal form: 'Have you or your driver ever been convicted or had a motor licence indorsed?' when in fact there were convictions against him as follows. 10 January 1922: Breaking and entering a garage and stealing a motor cycle and sidecar. Released on recognisances. 17 July 1922: Forging a cheque. Five months' imprisonment. 26 September 1922. Breach of recognisances. Nine months' imprisonment. 19 July 1926: Breaking and entering shop and stealing parcels and other articles. Eighteen months' imprisonment with hard labour. Stealing a fur stole and other articles to the value of £1,000. Three years' penal servitude.

It was submitted that the insured had accurately and truthfully answered the question on the proposal form, because the convictions had no relation to motor car offences. Counsel also contended the insured was under no common law liability to disclose to the London General his past bad character except so far as that character was material to the subject matter of the policy.

HELD, in the Court of Appeal (affirming Horridge J): A person entering into such a contract was bound to disclose the fact that he had been convicted although those convictions had nothing at all to do with motor offences, and therefore the insurance company were entitled to repudiate liability.

Taylor v Eagle Star Insurance Co Ltd
(1940) 67 Ll L Rep 136 (MacNaghten J)

A question in a proposal form was as follows: '*Q*. Have you or has your driver been convicted of any offence in connection with the driving of any motor vehicle? *A*. No'.

An accident occurred on 20 April 1937. The assured had been convicted of the following offences. 7 June 1927: Drunk and disorderly; fined £2. Assaulting the police; one month imprisonment. Throwing a glass bottle to the public danger; fined £2. 23 October 1931: Permitting use of uninsured car; fined £2. 27 March 1933: Driving car without road fund licence; fined 10s. 13 June 1933: Drunk on licensed premises; fined 10s. 7 December 1935: Drinking during prohibited hours; fined 15s.

Following *Revell*'s case, the answer in respect of the motoring offences was not untrue, but the other convictions were facts material to be known to insurers and not having been disclosed, insurers were not liable on the ground of non-disclosure.

Note—See *Revell v London General Insurance*, p 823, below.

Declinature by previous insurer

Cornhill Insurance Co Ltd v Assenheim

(1937) 58 Ll L Rep 27 (MacKinnon J)

The failure to disclose a previous refusal to renew is 'material'.

Holt's Motors Ltd v South East Lancashire Insurance Co Ltd

(1930) 36 Ll L Rep 17 (Horridge J), (1930) on appeal 35 Com Cas 281, 37 Ll L Rep 1, CA

An intimation by a previous insurer that they would not invite renewal is a material fact which should be disclosed by a proposer.

Owner — proposer not

Guardian Assurance Co Ltd v Sutherland

[1939] 2 All ER 246, 55 TLR 576, 83 Sol Jo 398, 63 Ll L Rep 220 (Branson J)

On 17 March 1938, Sutherland signed a proposal form for Mercedes Benz BXD 1 and plaintiffs issued cover notes until policy issued on 26 May 1938. On 20 May 1938, Sutherland telegraphed to plaintiffs to transfer to a Lancia car, confirmed on 10 June by application form signed by Sutherland for substitution, and policy endorsed accordingly. On 17 June 1938, at request of Sutherland an employee of Green Park Motors Ltd telegraphed to insurers 'Please cover me on Mercedes EYT 114 as well as Lancia' and insurers issued cover note. On 20 June 1938, Sutherland signed a form that EYT 114 should be substituted for the Lancia and stating Sutherland was the owner of EYT 114 and that it was registered in his name. On 20 June 1938, before the form signed on 20 June by Sutherland had reached insurers car EYT 114 driven by one Sidebotham was involved in an accident causing personal injuries to third parties. EYT 114 was the property of Green Park Motors. Sidebotham introduced one Chang, a Chinese, as purchaser, and on 17 June Chang agreed to purchase. Chang, owing to his foreign nationality, could not get cover without delay. Sidebotham had a policy from 15 August 1937, to 15 August 1938, but he had not revealed in his proposal form a number of convictions for dangerous driving and driving without due care, and some of his previous accidents, and had mis-stated his age as over 21 when in fact it was nineteen and a half and his policy was avoided in October 1938. Sutherland had no interest in EYT 114.

HELD: It was all one contract and was obtained by mis-statement and concealment. If the cover note for EYT 114 was a new contract it was obtained by material misrepresentation. The telegram represented that EYT 114 was Sutherland's property. It was material for insurers to know that Sutherland had nothing to do with the car, but that it was sold to Chang and about to be driven by Sidebotham with his bad record of offences and accidents. A policy obtained by misrepresentation insures no one and is not a policy within s 36(4) of the 1930 Act. Following *McCormick v National Motor and Accident Insurance Union Ltd* (pp 751 and 810, above) (1) the opening words of the subsection were inserted to get rid of the difficulty created by the Life Assurance Act 1774; (2) the function of the subsection was to get over the difficulty that nobody who was not a party to a contract could sue upon it (compare *Vanderpitte v Preferred Accident* (p 760, above)).

Sidebotham was not driving EYT 114 on the assured's order or with his permission. Sutherland had no interest whatever in EYT 114 and had no right to give or refuse permission. Application for declaration granted.

Note—Section 36(4) of the 1930 Act has now been replaced by s 148(4) of the 1972 Act.

Zurich General Accident and Liability Insurance Co Ltd v Buck

(1939) 64 Ll L Rep 115 (Branson J)

A, a greengrocer carrying on business at No 56 Brewery Road on 1 September 1936, took out a policy, and two subsequent policies, with the X Co, each of which policies lapsed for non-payment of premium. On 4 October 1937, A took out a policy with plaintiffs subject to termination if hire-purchase agreement terminated except if due to purchase by A. On 9 December 1938, A was fined for speeding. On 15 March 1938, the hire-purchase agreement terminated and the policy was cancelled. Judgment was obtained against A by the motor trader and was unsatisfied.

On 15 March 1938, B, the brother of A, who had a butcher's business next door to A, bought a motor van and lent it to A for use in A's business. It was registered in B's name. Plaintiffs' agent received proposal forms and issued cover notes. A informed the agent that the van belonged to A but he wished it to be insured in the name of B, but A would use it in his business and it would be driven by A only. The proposal stated that the proposer was B; that B's business was at No 56 and was a greengrocery business; that no person who would drive had been convicted of a motoring offence; that proposer had been insured with the Co-operative; that no company had cancelled his policy. A had been insured with the Employers' Liability and the plaintiffs.

HELD: Cancelled or refused to renew does not mean allowed to lapse by non-payment. The conviction and some of the mis-statements taken by themselves were not very material, but the proposal as a whole quite obviously did not in the least represent a true state of the facts, and some of the mis-statements would have led an underwriter to consider whether to accept the proposal or at least to make further enquiries. B had nothing to do with A's use of the van, and a third party could have no possible claim against B and B had no insurable interest and the policy was valueless. Application for declaration granted.

Goodbarne v Buck

[1940] 1 KB 771, [1940] 1 All ER 613, 109 LJKB 837, 162 LT 259, 56 TLR 433, 84 Sol Jo 380, CA

The third party in the previous case afterwards sued B on the principle of *Monk v Warbey*.

HELD: B was never the owner of the van and could not prevent A, who was the owner, from driving it. The policy was voidable, not void; it was valid and subsisting unless and until insurers elected to avoid it. This did not mean that for all purposes of s 35 of the 1930 Act the policy must be regarded as never having been in existence at all. There was a policy in force at the time which satisfied the section and the fact that it was subsequently avoided did not prevent there having been a policy in force at the material time.

Void or voidable

Durrant v Maclaren
[1956] 2 Lloyd's Rep 70, Div Ct
The defendant obtained insurance to drive a hired car by giving replies in a proposal form which were untrue and would have entitled the insurer to avoid the policy *ab initio*. He was prosecuted for driving an uninsured car on the argument that if a policy can be avoided *ab initio* it is not a policy in force.
HELD: The argument could not succeed. The Road Traffic Act 1934, s 10 (now s 149 of the 1972 Act) provides that the insurer must pay if judgment is obtained in respect of an accident unless proceedings are taken under subs (2). No such proceedings having been taken the insurance was in force at the time when the alleged offence occurred.

Adams v Dunne
[1978] RTR 281, [1978] Crim LR 365, Div Ct
The defendant obtained a cover note from insurers by concealing the fact that he was disqualified from driving. He was prosecuted for driving uninsured; on the relevant date the insurers had not taken any steps to avoid the contract though they would not have given cover had they known he was disqualified. The prosecution conceded that if the contract was merely voidable the case would be covered by *Durrant v Maclaren* (above) but argued that as the contract was void *ab initio* the case was different; a contract of insurance purporting to insure a disqualified driver was an illegal contract.
HELD: The insurers had been misled and had not, with open eyes, entered into a contract to insure a disqualified driver. Until the insurers took steps to avoid it the contract remained a contract of insurance for the purposes of the Road Traffic Act 1972, s 143. The case was covered by *Durrant v Maclaren*.

Note—See also *Evans v Lewis*, p 840, below.

CASES WHERE MISREPRESENTATION WAS NOT MATERIAL

Cost price — part exchange

Brewtnall v Cornhill Insurance Co Ltd
(1931) 40 Ll L Rep 166
An insured car was destroyed by fire. A claim was made, the defence being that there had been a concealment of a material fact in the proposal form. The question was: '*Q.* Cost price to proposer. *A.* £145.'
There was evidence that proposer gave £45 and another car (agreed price £100) in part exchange — should exchange of car have been disclosed?
HELD: The defence of concealment failed. Judgment for assured.

Driving 12 months regularly; provisional licence

Zurich General Accident and Liability Insurance Co Ltd v Morrison

[1942] 2 KB 53, [1942] 1 All ER 529, 111 LJKB 601, 167 LT 183, 58 TLR 217, 86 Sol Jo 267, 72 Ll L Rep 167, CA

A question in a proposal form for motor insurance asked 'Have you driven cars regularly and continuously in the UK during the past 12 months?' HELD: The question was most embarrassing and if taken literally no one could answer it other than in the negative. If the insurers want to know how long a man has driven on the road or for how long he had held a licence they should ask the questions in plain terms. The proposer had done some driving on a provisional licence and some on works roads during the 12 months preceding the proposal and it could not be said his answer to the question, 'Yes', was untrue. The failure to reveal that he had only a provisional licence to drive and had failed one driving test was not a material non-disclosure since there was no evidence that the insurers would not have issued a policy on the same terms had those matters been disclosed. In a case of this kind the insurers must establish two propositions in order to avoid the policy: (1) that the matter relied on was 'material' in the sense that the mind of a prudent insurer would be affected by it, and (2) that in fact the underwriter's mind was so affected and the policy thereby obtained. The insurers had not established these propositions.

Note—Followed by Atkinson J in *Broad v Waland* (1942) 73 Ll L Rep 263 at 628 and 679.

Conviction for inefficient brakes

Note—See *Mackay v London General*, p 822, below.

CASES WHERE MISREPRESENTATION IS MADE MATERIAL BY DECLARATION

Note—A statement not material *per se* is made material as against the insured (though not against third parties under the Road Traffic Act) by incorporation of the proposal form and declaration. This principle still operates in respect of claims not within the Road Traffic Acts.

Provincial Insurance Co Ltd v Morgan

[1933] AC 240, 102 LJKB 164, 49 TLR 179, 44 Ll L Rep 275, sub nom **Morgan v Provincial Insurance Co Ltd** (1932) 148 LT 385, HL

Answers to questions in the proposal form are converted into conditions of the policy by the declaration that the answers shall be the basis of the contract.

Note—For facts see p 832, below.

Followed in *Beauchamp v National Mutual Indemnity Insurance Co Ltd* [1937] 3 All ER 19.

The effect of the warranty on a proposal form of the truth of its contents and the statement that it forms the basis of the contract is shown in the case *Dawson's Ltd v Bonnin*, below.

Garaged elsewhere

Dawsons Ltd v Bonnin
[1922] 2 AC 413, 91 LJPC 210, 128 LT 1, 38 TLR 836, 11 Ll L Rep 57, 12
Ll L Rep 237, HL
A firm of contractors in Glasgow insured a motor lorry at Lloyds against
damage by fire and third-party risks. The policy recited that the proposal
should be the basis of the contract and be held as incorporated in the policy,
and it was expressed to be granted subject to the conditions at the back
thereof. By the fourth condition 'material mis-statement or concealment of
any circumstances by the insured material to assessing the premium
herein, or in connection with any claim, shall render the policy void'. In
reply to a question in the proposal form, 'State full address at which the
vehicle will usually be garaged', the answer given was 'Above address',
meaning thereby the firm's ordinary place of business in Glasgow. This
was not true, as the lorry was usually garaged at a farm on the outskirts of
Glasgow. The inaccurate answer in the proposal was given by
inadvertence. The lorry having been destroyed by fire at the garage, the
insured claimed payment under the policy.
HELD: (1) This mis-statement in the proposal was not material within the
meaning of condition 4. (2) The recital in the policy that the proposal
should be the basis of the contract made the truth of the statements
contained in the proposal, apart from the question of materiality, a
condition of the liability for the insurers; the effect of this recital was not cut
down by the special conditions on the back of the policy; and the claim
failed.

Excess of £2 10s 0d

Mackay v London General Insurance Co Ltd
(1935) 51 Ll L Rep 201 (Swift J)
A proposal form contained the following questions and answers: '*Q*. Has
any office or underwriter refused, cancelled or declined to accept or renew
such insurance, or required an increased premium or special condition? *A*.
No. *Q*. Have you or your driver ever been convicted or had a motor licence
endorsed? *A*. No.'
    The proposer three years before, when aged 18, had insured a motor
cycle with an excess of £2 10s 0d, and he had been fined 10s because a nut
had become loose on the brakes and he was driving without efficient
brakes. Both these answers were quite immaterial, but the proposer had
contracted that the proposal and declaration were the basis of the contract
and he had made two inaccurate answers.

Partial disclosure of previous claims

Condogianis v Guardian Assurance Co
[1921] 2 AC 125, 90 LJPC 168, 125 LT 610, 37 TLR 685, 3 Ll L Rep
40, PC
Appellant sued respondents upon a policy issued by them insuring certain
laundry premises against fire. A proposal form filled up by appellant when

applying for the policy contained the following question: 'Has proponent ever been a claimant on a fire insurance company in respect of the property now proposed, or any other property? If so, state when and name of company.' Appellant's answer was, 'Yes. 1917. Ocean.' That answer was literally true, as in 1917 he had claims against the Ocean Insurance Co in respect of the burning of a motor car, but in 1912 he had made a claim against another company in respect of a similar loss. The proposal form stated that it was the basis of the policy, and that the particulars given by appellant were to be express warranties. The policy contained a condition that if there was any misrepresentation as to any fact material to be known in estimating the risk, respondents were not to be liable upon the policy. HELD: (1) The answer was untrue, since the question could not reasonably be read as being intended to have the limited scope which would render the answer true. (2) There was a breach of warranty, whether or not the misrepresentation was as to a material fact. (3) Applicant could not recover on the policy.

Driving offences

Revell v London General Insurance Co Ltd
[1934] 1 All ER 744, 152 LT 258, 50 Ll L Rep 114 (MacKinnon J)
A proposal form contained the following question: '*Q*. Have you or any of your drivers ever been convicted of any offence in connection with the driving of any motor vehicle? *A*. No.'

Driver in fact previously convicted: (1) Of unlawfully driving a car without a suitable reflecting mirror; (2) of unlawfully using a car without having in force an insurance policy covering third party risks.
HELD: Question might reasonably mean carefulness of driver and answer was not untrue.

Previous theft

Farra v Hetherington
(1931) 47 TLR 465, 75 Sol Jo 542, 40 Ll L Rep 132
Proposal form was declared the basis of the contract. Proposal form asked for previous losses of motor vehicles during past three years. Proposer did not disclose that within three years a car had on three occasion been abstracted or stolen, though on each occasion it was recovered a few hours later.
HELD: Insurers not liable.

Description of occupation — bookmaker

Holmes v Cornhill Insurance Co Ltd
(1949) 82 Ll L Rep 575 (Morris J)
Proposer orally asked an insurance company for insurance of a motor car for use in his business as a commission agent. The company told him they did not insure bookmakers. Proposer stated he was not a bookmaker but was a commission agent dealing in furniture. He had had a furniture shop

for a short time three or four years before but for two years had no shop,
warehouse or business premises in connection with furniture dealing and
kept no books or records of any such dealing. His main occupation was that
of a bookmaker and not that of a dealer. He signed a proposal form stating
his occupation as dealer. The proposal form contained the usual
declaration and warranty.

The arbitrator made his award in the form of a special case. His findings
were:

1 The description of dealer was untrue.
2 The failure to disclose that he was a bookmaker was material.
3 That (1) and (2) each constituted a breach of the warranty which was
made the basis of the policy.
4 The policy was induced by the false representation that he was not a
bookmaker.

The arbitrator found the company not liable. The finding was upheld.

2 LIMITS OF COVER

Note—There is nothing in the compulsory insurance sections of the Road Traffic
Act to make an insurer liable when the vehicle is being used outside the limits of the
policy. But the insurer may be the 'insurer concerned' for the purposes of the
Motor Insurers' Bureau agreements (see p 787, above).

USE OF VEHICLE

Business sold to company

Levinger v Licenses and General Insurance Co Ltd
(1936) 54 Ll L Rep 68 (Eve J)
Proposer insured car to cover use in her business of milliner. Her business
was taken over by a limited company of which she was chief shareholder.
HELD: Car at time of accident was on the business of the company, which
had no interest in the policy. The company was not insured, nor its
business.

Description of use clause

Passmore v Vulcan Boiler and General Insurance Co Ltd
(1935) 154 LT 258, 52 TLR 193, 64 Ll L Rep 92, 80 Sol Jo 167, (du
Parcq J)
Policy covered assured whilst using car for the purpose of her business.
Exception not liable if used otherwise than in 'description of use' clause, ie
business of assured of representative and no other. Assured and another
representative both employed by same company were using car on

employer's business. The car was not being used for the business of the assured alone, but also the business of other employee.

HELD: Policy covered business use of assured only, and insurers not liable when used for business of any other person whether also used for business of assured or not. The business of the other person might have been of a different kind and insurers were entitled to know exactly what business risk they were covering and the extent of the risk they were undertaking.

If the policyholder extended a courtesy to a friend or acquaintance or stranger who was carrying on some business and was assisted in carrying on that business by the use of the car, and the assured gave a lift as a matter of kindness, courtesy or charity, I think the proper view would be that the car was being used for a social purpose.

Note—See also *D. H. R. Moody Ltd v Iron Trades*, p 830, below. In *Seddon v Binions* (below) the passage in du Parcq J's judgment summarised in the second paragraph above was considered and explained by all three members of the court. Roskill LJ said that nothing in his judgment in *Seddon's* case was intended to cast any doubt upon the applicability of that passage to a case to which it is appropriate.

Browning v Phoenix Assurance Co Ltd
[1960] 2 Lloyd's Rep 360 (Pilcher J)

The owner of a car asked the plaintiff, a garage foreman, to take his car for a long run to get the back axle oil well warmed so that it could be drained and changed: he said that if the plaintiff cared to do this on a Sunday and take his wife and family with him, he had no objection. The owner's insurance policy covered any other person who drove with his permission provided that such person should be subject to the exceptions and conditions of the policy as if he were the insured. A general exception excluded liability of the insurers while the vehicle was being used otherwise than in accordance with the 'description of use'. The latter was set out in a schedule and excluded 'use for any purpose in connection with the Motor Trade'. After the oil had been changed in the back axle the plaintiff took the car out with his brother and brother-in-law as passengers partly, as he alleged, for the pleasure of the ride and partly to check the car for any defects. Whilst on this run there was a collision with another vehicle due to his admitted negligence. The defendant company refused to indemnify him.

HELD: On the facts the plaintiff was not driving with the owner's permission since the long run which the owner asked him to make was for the purpose of draining the oil from the back axle, and that had already been done. But even if the plaintiff had been driving with the owner's permission the policy would not have covered him: he was driving for two purposes (1) the permitted purpose of taking his family for a ride, (2) a second purpose which would have been a purpose in connection with the motor trade. The plaintiff's user would thus have been for a permitted purpose and a specifically excluded purpose. In these circumstances, following *Passmore v Vulcan Boiler and General Insurance Co Ltd* the plaintiff would not be entitled to recover from the defendant.

Seddon v Binions
(1977) 122 Sol Jo 34, [1978] 1 Lloyd's Rep 381, [1978] RTR 163, CA
The defendants were father and son. The son carried on the business of
carpet layer. The father helped the son in the business but was not his
employee. The son had an employee named Hale. When the son was
working on a job some miles from home the father brought Hale in the
son's van. Hale claimed he had toothache and wanted to go home at
lunchtime. It was the son's normal practice to take Hale to and from jobs.
The father intended going home for lunch so it was arranged that he would
take Hale in the son's Triumph car. On the journey there was a collision
with another vehicle in which the plaintiff was injured. The father had a
policy on a car of his own covering him when driving other cars, restricted
to use for social, domestic and pleasure purposes or in connection with his
own business.
HELD: He was not covered by his policy at the time of the accident. He was
driving his son's car for two purposes — his own social and domestic
purposes and, in driving Hale home, for purposes of his son's business. An
alternative test to apply was to look for the primary purpose, or essential
character, of the journey; and in the present case it was to take the son's
employee home and was not social, domestic or pleasure.
    Per Megaw LJ: If there be such a primary purpose, or essential
character, then the courts should not be meticulous to find some possible
secondary purpose, or some inessential character, the result of which could
be suggested to be that the use of the car fell outside the proper use for the
purposes of which cover was given by the insurance company. If, however,
there are cases in which there are, in the proper sense of the word, two
'purposes', as was the case in *Passmore v Vulcan Boiler and General Insurance Co
Ltd* (above) on the finding of the arbitrator, then I have no reason to
disagree in any way with the conclusion in that case as to the results that
would follow.

FRIEND'S EMPLOYER — BUSINESS OF

Pailor v Co-operative Insurance Society Ltd
(1930) 38 Ll L Rep 237, CA
Car driven by employee of insured's friend on friend's business — 'The
Society will also similarly indemnify any relations or friend of the insured
. . . whilst driving . . . with the insured's knowledge and consent.' 'The
Society shall not be liable while the car is being used for other than private
pleasure or professional purposes or for driving to and from the insured's
place of business or for making personal business calls (excluding
commercial travelling) or personal visits to the scene of his business
operations.'
CONSTRUCTION: Arbitrator's finding of fact that employee was a friend
of the insured.
HELD: That a 'general knowledge and consent' was sufficient to bring the
friend within the ambit of the policy, but that the friend's use of the car on
his own employer's business did not come within the exception to the
exception clause, and that the company were therefore not liable. Appeal
and cross-appeal dismissed.

USE UNDER A 'C' LICENCE

Croucher v Wolfe and S A Wise & Co (1955) Ltd

[1961] 1 Lloyd's Rep 139 (Howard J)

The plaintiff recovered damages against the defendants for the negligent driving of their employee. The lorry which the defendants were using was hired from the third party under an agreement that so long as the defendants were using the lorry the third parties should keep it properly insured. The third parties were a limited company and Art 3(s) of the Articles of Association described one of the objects of the company as being 'to run or let out on hire motor cars and lorries, steamwaggons or other commercial vehicles'. A policy of insurance had been issued in respect of the lorry containing a warranty that the vehicle was to be used only for the following purposes 'Use in connection with the policy holders' business . . . under a "C" Licence'. The insurance certificate in force at the time of the accident contained the following paragraph: 'Limitations as to use. Use in connection with the policyholder's business as builders and contractors under a "C" Licence'.

HELD: The policy of insurance in respect of the vehicle did not cover it while it was being used on the day of the accident by the driver employed by the defendants on the defendants' business.

Allen v John

[1955] 1 Lloyd's Rep 27, Div Ct

A motor lorry owned by a firm A was insured under a Lloyd's Commercial Motor Vehicle policy. It was a condition that underwriters were not liable whilst the lorry was on hire or being used for purposes other than stated in the schedule. The schedule limited cover to use in connection with the insured's business under 'C' hiring licence including social, domestic and pleasure purposes with insured's consent. The lorry was hired to B Co and the policy was indorsed to extend to cover the B Co and also holders of relative 'C' hiring licences whilst the vehicle was being used on their behalf. The lorry was hired out for reward by the B Co and was being used by and on behalf of the B Co. The Road and Rail Traffic Act 1933, s 2(4) prohibits a vehicle under 'C' licence from use for the carriage of goods for hire or reward. The lorry driver and the two partners in the A firm were convicted of driving and permitting use whilst uninsured.

HELD: Although underwriters probably never intended the position to be covered, the indorsement covered the B Co and was not vitiated because the use was contrary to s 1(1) of the 1933 Act. The indorsement gave a complete cover to the B Co. Convictions quashed.

MOTOR ENGINEER — USE OF CAR FOR SHEEP FARMING

Jones v Welsh Insurance Corpn Ltd

[1937] 4 All ER 149, 157 LT 483, 54 TLR 22, 81 Sol Jo 886, 59 Ll L Rep 13 (Goddard J)

Assured was a motor mechanic who earned £2 14s 0d per week. He ceased work at 5 pm. He bought five sheep and rented two acres to keep them. He had a private car policy excepting liability if used otherwise than in accordance with 'description of use' clause, ie private purposes and use by assured in person in connection with his business . . . of motor engineer and no other . . . excluding use for carriage of goods in connection with any trade or business. Assured's brother took car and brought two sheep and two lambs to the father's house.

HELD: Assured was not keeping sheep for pleasure or for food for himself and family, but was a sheep farmer in a small way as a sideline, and it was a business, and the car was being used for carriage of goods in connection with business of sheep farming. It was not a case of physical characteristics of the goods under s 12(d) but the use of the car for business purposes and carriage of goods in connection with a business.

Use for 'hire or reward'

PAYMENT BY PASSENGER

Wyatt v Guildhall Insurance Co Ltd

[1937] 1 KB 653, [1937] 1 All ER 792, 106 LJKB 421, 156 LT 292, 53 TLR 389, 81 Sol Jo 358, 57 Ll L Rep 90 (Branson J)

Policy was for private use excluding use for hiring. Assured agreed to take a passenger for 25s on an isolated occasion.

HELD: User not within terms of policy.

Bonham v Zurich General Accident and Liability Insurance Co Ltd

[1945] KB 292, [1945] 1 All ER 427, 114 LJKB 273, 172 LT 201, 61 TLR 271, 78 Ll L Rep 245

A proposal form contained the question 'Will passengers be carried for hire or reward?' and the answer was 'No'. The answers in the proposal were made the basis of the contract. The policy excluded use for hiring.

The assured habitually and regularly carried three passengers who worked at the same place. Two passengers paid 1s 2d or 1s 3d per return journey calculated on the cost of railway fares. The other never did pay.

The assured never asked the passengers for payment but the two passengers voluntarily offered him the money. He would have carried them if they had not paid anything. The assured paid for petrol, oil, tyres, insurance and other expenses of the car. The assured would have made the journeys if there were no passengers. An accident occurred and one of the passengers was killed.

HELD, ON APPEAL, per du Parcq LJ and Uthwatt J (MacKinnon LJ dissenting): Insurers were not liable. A distinction is to be drawn between 'hire' and 'reward' or the words 'or reward' would not be necessary. The assured intended to accept from the passengers a payment which he expected to be tendered and which they intended to tender. He took from them each day a sum which they never failed to pay and which he expected to receive. This was carrying passengers for reward.

The reward need not be payable under an agreement enforceable at law. 'Hire' imports an obligation to pay. 'Reward' included cases where there is no obligation to pay. All the judges in the Court of Appeal agreed the car was not being used for hire.

Note—See also *McCarthy v British Oak Insurance Co*, below, and cases cited in note following it.

See now s 148, sub-ss (5) to (7) of the Road Traffic Act 1972, (p 761, above).

PAYMENT FOR PETROL AND OIL — WHETHER 'HIRED'

McCarthy v British Oak Insurance Co Ltd

[1938] 3 All ER 1, 159 LT 215, 82 Sol Jo 568, 61 Ll L Rep 194 (Atkinson J)
Assured, a garage proprietor, without receiving any payment, lent a car for
the evening to a driver (who had at times driven a coach for him and done
odd jobs for him as a mechanic) for private purposes excluding use for hire.
The driver paid the assured 10s or 12s for the petrol and oil but nothing
more, and the driver took two friends as passengers, and the passengers
paid the driver what he had paid for the petrol and oil, and for two quarts of
beer which was for the use of the driver and passengers.
HELD: Hire meant a genuine business contract for a stipulated reward. In
Wyatt's case the passenger agreed to pay for conveyance and the money was
clear profit for the assured. Here the driver did not make anything for
himself and there was nothing to constitute a legal contract for hire, and the
insurers were liable.

Note—And see *Bonham v Zurich General Accident and Liability Insurance Co Ltd*, p 828,
above; *Wyatt v Guildhall Insurance Co*, p 828, above and *Lyons v Denscombe*, below.
See also the Road Traffic Act 1972, s 148(5), (6) and (7).

PRIVATE HIRE

Lyons v Denscombe

[1949] 1 All ER 977, 113 JP 305, [1949] WN 257, 47 LGR 412, 93 Sol Jo
389, Div Ct
A mineworker drove his car to the colliery each morning and in the evening
drove home four fellow workmen under an agreement or contract with one
of them to pay 8s per week (2s each) whether they used the car or not. The
car was licensed for private hire and hackney purposes. The insurance
policy did not cover use for hire or reward other than private hire; which
was defined as the 'letting of the vehicle supplied direct from the policy
holder's garage'. He was prosecuted for (1) not being insured, (2) not
holding a licence for an express carriage, and (3) not holding a road service
licence. The justices found there was one contract for one fare of 8s paid
weekly and not four contracts for 2s each.
HELD: The car was not used as an express carriage under s 61(1) of the
1930 Act and did not require a public service vehicle licence under s 67(1)
or a road service licence under s 72(1).
'Private hire' means hire for a defined journey at a defined time as
distinct from plying for hire like a taxicab and included the picking up of
passengers away from the garage even though the car went to the place
some hours before the hirers got into it. Every person who hires a private
hire car expects the car to pick him up somewhere. He need not go to the
garage; it might meet him at a railway station. If so, it is supplied direct
from the garage.
The use was covered by the policy.

Note—See also *Orr v Trafalgar Insurance Co*, below; *McCarthy v British Oak Insurance
Co*, above, and cases cited in note following it.
Sections 67(1) and 72(1) of the 1930 Act have now been replaced in effect by the
Road Traffic Act 1960. Section 67(1) is replaced by s 127(1)-(4) and s 72(1) by
s 134(1). Section 61 of the 1930 Act was already repealed.

Social, domestic and pleasure purposes

Note—See also *Samuelson v NIG*, p 837, below.

Wood v General Accident Fire and Life Assurance Corpn Ltd

(1948) 65 TLR 53, 92 Sol Jo 720, 82 Ll L Rep 77, [1948] WN 430
(Morris J)

A Daimler car was insured for 'social, domestic and pleasure purposes'.
The insured, a garage proprietor, used the car for a journey to interview a
firm with the object of negotiating a contract in connection with his garage
business. He was 67 years old and it was more convenient to travel in his
own Daimler which was immediately available than a hired car.

The arbitrator found it was a more comfortable, pleasurable and restful
way of making the journey than in a hired car, but held it was not covered
by the policy.

On appeal by special case stated, the insured argued that the test was the
reason for the use of the journey and not what might happen at the end, and
the reason was use in a comfortable and pleasurable way.

HELD: The words were well known and well used, and in their natural,
ordinary, normal and reasonable meaning, did not cover the journey.
Appeal dismissed.

Orr v Trafalgar Insurance Co Ltd

(1948) 82 Ll L Rep 1, CA

The insurance policy on a motor car indemnified whilst being used solely
for the purposes in the schedule — the schedule stated 'Private purposes
only'. The policy defined 'Private purposes' as social, domestic and
pleasure purposes and use by the insured in person travelling to and from
his permanent place of business. The policy excluded liability if being used
for private or public hire.

The insured was in the house of one Gallagher who carried on a private
hire business when Gallagher received a telephone request for a hire.
Gallagher asked the insured to do the job for him. Whilst doing so the
insured's car met with an accident. The insured telephoned Gallagher who
went in his car and finished the journey. The passenger asked what the
charge would be and Gallagher did not make a charge because the accident
caused the passenger to miss his train.

Pritchard J held that he should draw the inference that there was an
implied obligation on the passenger to pay; that the use was private hire
and insurers were not liable.

Upheld in Court of Appeal.

D H R Moody (Chemists) Ltd v Iron Trades Mutual Insurance Co Ltd

(1970) 115 Sol Jo 16, 69 LGR 232, [1971] 1 Lloyd's Rep 386, [1971] RTR
120 (Wrangham J)

The Clacton Urban District Council entertained some visitors from the
French town of Valence with which Clacton was 'twinned'. At the end of
the visit the clerk of the council took the visitors to Heathrow airport in a car
lent to the council by a councillor to see them off. On the return journey the
car was damaged. The defendant insurers claimed that the car was not
being used for a social purpose.

HELD: The activities of an individual could be divided into those which he pursued because he had to earn a living and those which he pursued of his own free will such as social or domestic pleasures. Similarly a local authority's activities could be so divided into those duties that they were compelled by statute or convention to carry out and voluntary activities which might be of a social character. The council's activities in arranging contact with Valence were social. The car was being used by the council for a social purpose; the fact that the actual driver, the clerk, was fulfilling a duty to his employer by driving it did not prevent its use from being a social purpose.

Whitehead v Unwins (Yorks)
(1962) Times, 1 March, [1962] Crim LR 323
A vehicle was used for carrying food for consumption by cows. The policy covered use for 'social and domestic' purposes. The justices dismissed a charge under the Road Traffic Act 1960, s 201, of using the vehicle when not covered by insurance.
HELD: On a case stated, there must be a conviction. The argument that as cows are domestic animals the carrying of food for cows is a domestic use is a complete fallacy. The fact that the vehicle was lent did not itself make the use social.

Towing cement mixer

J R M (Plant) Ltd v Hodgson
[1960] 1 Lloyd's Rep 538
A motor lorry was engaged in carting rubble from a contractor's site. The contractor's foreman asked the driver as a favour to tow a cement mixer a short distance to another site along a public road. The policy had a provision excluding cover when the lorry was used for drawing a trailer 'except the towing of any one disabled mechanically propelled vehicle or any farm implement or machine not constructed or adapted for the conveyance of goods'.
HELD: 'Farm implement or machine' meant 'farm implement or farm machine' and since the cement mixer was neither the policy did not cover the use of the lorry when towing the mixer.

Use within description of risk

TAXI-CABS DRIVEN IN TWO SHIFTS

Farr v Motor Traders' Mutual Insurance Society
[1920] 3 KB 669, 90 LJKB 215, 123 LT 765, 36 TLR 711, CA
Plaintiff was the owner of two taxicabs which he insured with defendants in February 1918, for one year against damage caused to either of them by accidental external means. In the proposal for the policy plaintiff, in answer to a question, stated that each cab was to be driven in one shift per 24 hours. At the foot of the proposal form plaintiff stated that the above statement was true, and the policy provided that the statements in the proposal were to be the basis of the contract, and to be considered as

incorporated therein. In August 1918, while one of the cabs was undergoing repair, the other cab was driven in two shifts per 24 hours for a very short time, and from that time until the accident hereinafter mentioned happened, the two cabs were driven in one shift only. In November 1918, the cab which had been driven in two shifts in August was damaged by an accident. It was at that time being driven in one shift only. In an action on the policy to recover in respect of the damage so caused, defendants contended that the statement in the proposal that the cab was to be driven in one shift per 24 hours was a warranty, and upon breach thereof the insurance came to an end.

HELD: The statement was not a warranty, but was merely descriptive of the risk, indicating that the cab, whilst being driven in more than one shift per 24 hours, would cease to be covered by the policy, but would be covered whilst being driven in one shift; and defendants were liable.

COMMERCIAL TRAVELLER CARRYING PASSENGERS

Roberts v Anglo-Saxon Insurance Association
(1927) 36 Ll L Rep 154 (Salter J), (1928) 96 LJKB 590, 137 LT 243, 43 TLR 359, 27 Ll L Rep 313, CA

A statement in a proposal form that a motor car was to be used only for commercial travelling was a statement descriptive of the risk covered by the insurance, and the insurers were not liable for an accident which happened while the motor car was being used to carry passengers, carrying passengers not being within the description.

COAL LORRY CARRYING TIMBER

Provincial Insurance Co Ltd v Morgan
[1933] AC 240, 102 LJKB 164, 49 TLR 179, 44 Ll L Rep 275, 38 Com Cas 92, Sub nom **Morgan v Provincial Insurance Co Ltd** (1932) 148 LT 385, HL

A proposal form contained the following questions and answers: 'Q. State (a) the purposes in full for which the vehicle will be used, and (b) the nature of the goods to be carried. A. (a) the delivery of coal; (b) coal'. The premium was less than it would have been for general haulage. The vehicle was used for carrying a load of timber and 5 cwt of coal. The timber had been delivered and 3 cwt of the coal, and the vehicle was on the way to deliver the remaining 2 cwt of coal.

HELD, in the Court of Appeal: The questions defined the risk. They were not a warranty going to the root of the contract that the vehicle would never be used except for coal. The vehicle was covered whilst carrying coal, but not covered whilst carrying a load other than coal. Carrying a load of timber did not avoid the policy.

HELD, in the House of Lords: Whilst not dissenting from the conclusion of CA that it was a description of the risk and not the intention to warrant that the vehicle would never be used for any other purpose, the questions and answers were intended to ascertain the intentions of the assured with regard to the user of the lorry and the goods to be carried therein, and the answers were true, correct and complete, and there was no breach of warranty or of any condition precedent to liability.

CAR CARRYING TIMBER FOR PRIVATE PURPOSES

Piddington v Co-operative Insurance Society Ltd

[1934] 2 KB 236, 103 LJKB 370, 151 LT 399, 50 TLR 311, 78 Sol Jo 278
(Lawrence J)

The insurance of a private car excluded liability when used for other than
private pleasure: or for conveying goods other than personal luggage. The
insured was a designer for a firm of brassworkers, and drove home from
work at noon with two laths, 12 or 14 feet long, fastened lengthwise on top
of the car, intended for the repair of some trellis work in his garden. The
same afternoon, without removing the laths, he went on a pleasure run,
and met with an accident causing fatal injuries to a pedestrian. Insurers
declined liability under the policy, contending that the use was otherwise
than 'solely for private purposes' as set out in the proposal form, and was
'conveying goods other than personal luggage'.

HELD: The word 'pleasure' was in contradistinction to 'business' and
'personal luggage' to 'merchandise' and the insured's garden was his
pleasure and not his business, and the laths were personal luggage and not
merchandise. The case of *Buckland v R* (p 871, below) which construed
personal luggage, related to a railway rate and was not applicable to a
policy of insurance. Both grounds of denial failed.

Lee v Poole

[1954] Crim LR 942, [1954] CLY 2948, Div Ct
Insured carried some furniture for a friend without payment.
HELD: Within the policy cover.

Driver 'in the insured's employ'

Burton v Road Transport and General Insurance Co Ltd

(1939) 63 Ll L Rep 253 (Branson J)

Cross, a motor dealer, was insured under a Motor Traders' policy which
covered, as if he were the insured, 'any person in the insured's employ'.
Cross had a car to sell; in pursuance of a pre-existing arrangement between
them, Westwood told Cross of a possible purchaser, Goulding. Cross then
commissioned Westwood to take Goulding on a demonstration run.
Westwood would be, and was, paid £1 by Cross for doing the
demonstration for him, whether or not he succeeded in selling the car.
During the run there was a collision in which the plaintiff, a motor cyclist,
was injured. Cross's insurers refused to pay damages awarded against
Westwood on the ground that he was not in Cross's employment.

HELD: It was not necessary in order to give a business effect to the policy,
to restrict the meaning of 'employment' to employment under a contract of
service. Cross was using Westwood to try to sell the car to someone
introduced by him: in so doing he was 'employing' him. The insurers were
liable under s 10 of the 1934 Act (now the Road Traffic Act 1972, s 149,
p 761, above).

DRIVER NOT WITHIN POLICY

Consent — driving with

Paget v Poland
(1947) 80 Ll L Rep 283 (Lewis J)
The daughter of the owner of a car working for the Ministry of Information
had to drive a van of the Ministry from St Albans to Cambridge and
obtained the loan of her mother's car to enable her to return. This required
that a driver should take the car to Cambridge. The daughter suggested a
friend Miss P, but the mother refused to allow her car to be driven by Miss
P, and the mother suggested Miss M, a friend of the mother. Miss M
started as driver and on the way changed places with Miss P. An accident
occurred while Miss P was driving and Miss M was injured.

Miss M recovered judgment against the daughter and Miss P.
Presumably the daughter was liable because Miss P was treated as her
agent.

Section 1 of the policy on the mother's car read: The underwriters will
indemnify under this section any licensed driver personally driving with
the insured's consent any motor vehicle hereby insured.
HELD: In an action against underwriters, Miss P was not personally
driving with the consent of the insured, and underwriters were not liable on
the policy.

Herbert v Railway Passengers Assurance Co
[1938] 1 All ER 650, 158 LT 417, 60 Ll L Rep 143 (Porter J)
Insured (OOD) with friend in sidecar, fell ill, and allowed friend to drive.
Company not liable.

Permission to drive — insured dead

Kelly v Cornhill Insurance Co Ltd
[1964] 1 All ER 321, [1964] 1 WLR 158, 108 Sol Jo 94, [1964] 1 Lloyd's
Rep 1, HL (Sc)
On 11 April 1958 Michael Kelly proposed for insurance to the Cornhill
Insurance Co Ltd in respect of his own car. In the proposal form he said the
car would be driven by his son Kevin Kelly and that he himself had no
licence to drive and did not intend having one. Insurance was granted on
26 April 1958 and was renewed for a further year on 26 April 1959. On 2
June 1959 Michael Kelly died. Neither his executrix nor anyone else told
the insurers of his death until after 4 February 1960, on which date damage
was caused to the car and other property in an accident whilst Kevin Kelly
was driving. The latter claimed indemnity under the policy as a person
'driving the insured car . . . with the permission of the insured'. It was
admitted that whilst Michael Kelly was alive Kevin had permission from
him to drive the car without limitation.
HELD: The question for decision was simply whether Kevin Kelly was
driving on 4 February 1960 with the permission of his father who had died
on 2 June 1959: did a permission to use the car which could at any time be
revoked lapse on the death of the person giving it? It had been argued for

the respondents that permission necessarily involved a continuing power of control but it could not be said that continuing opportunity or ability to control was necessary, because prolonged absence or illness might negative that. In the absence of any express provision in the policy there was no reason to hold as a matter of law that a permission should automatically lapse on death of the permittor. The son was entitled to the benefit of the policy on 4 February 1960.

Disqualification of driver

General Accident Assurance Corpn v Shuttleworth
(1938) 60 Ll L Rep 301 (Humphreys J)
The condition in a policy that the assured shall not be disqualified or the company will not be liable is a limitation of the insurance cover and is outside the purview of the policy or certificate. The insured signed a proposal on 10 June 1936, and declared he had not been convicted of a motoring offence. On 5 August 1936, the assured was convicted of driving a motor cycle without an insurance certificate and disqualified for 12 months. On 11 August 1936, the assured applied to transfer the insurance to another car and signed a declaration that he had not been convicted of a motoring offence. On 5 September 1936, the company issued a cover note and insurance certificate for 14 days, instead of a certificate for 12 months as a means of obtaining payment of the additional premium of £4, in terms of the company's usual form of policy. On 16 September 1936, a third party was injured.
HELD: Risk was outside policy.
SEMBLE: (1) A motor car covers a motor cycle; (2) the false declaration invalidated the cover note.

Edwards v Griffiths
[1953] 2 All ER 874, [1953] 1 WLR 1199, 117 JP 514, 97 Sol Jo 592, 51 LGR 549, [1953] 2 Lloyd's Rep 269, Div Ct
The respondent had passed a driving test and obtained a driving licence for motor cycles and tractors in October 1951. In 1952 he was informed by the licensing authority that as he was under supervision under the Mental Deficiencies Act, he must not drive a motor cycle. The respondent's application for renewal of driving licence was refused. His employer's certificate of insurance provided for use by any person driving with permission provided such person held a licence or had held and was not disqualified from holding or obtaining a licence.
HELD: 'Disqualified' in the certificate meant disqualified by an order of the court and not prohibited from obtaining a licence by mental or physical disability.

Mumford v Hardy
[1956] 1 All ER 337, [1956] 1 WLR 163, 100 Sol Jo 132, 54 LGR 150, [1956] 1 Lloyd's Rep 173, Div Ct
A youth born on 7 June 1939 (ie under 16) obtained a provisional licence to drive a car on 13 April 1955, expiring 12 July 1955, by falsely stating that

he was born on 22 January 1938. His father permitted him to drive a car which was insured to indemnify any driver with consent holding a licence to drive such a car. The son was charged with driving uninsured on 23 April 1955, and 1 June 1955. The father was charged with permitting on 1 June 1955.

The insurers told the justices they would have considered themselves liable by reason of *Edwards v Griffiths* (above). The justices accordingly dismissed the informations.

By the Road Traffic Act 1930, s 9(2) a person under 17 years of age is prohibited from driving a car; by s 9(5) such a person shall be deemed disqualified for holding or obtaining such a licence; s 7(4) provides that a licence obtained by a disqualified person shall be of no effect.

HELD: An offence was proved on each of the three informations.

Note—The subsections of the 1930 Act were repealed and are now replaced without material amendment by the Road Traffic Act 1972 as follows:

1930 Act	1972 Act
Section 9(2)	Section 4(1)
Section 9(5)	Section 96
Section 7(4)	Section 98(2)

Limited company — servant without licence

John T Ellis Ltd v Hinds

[1947] KB 475, [1947] 1 All ER 337, [1947] LJR 488, 176 LT 424, 63 TLR 181, 91 Sol Jo 68, 45 LGR 118, 80 Ll L Rep 231, Div Ct

A company owned a motor vehicle which was driven by a lad under 17 years of age who did not hold and never had held a driving licence and by reason of his age was not qualified to obtain one. The company had no express knowledge of these facts. The driver told the company that he held a licence and that he had already driven for several firms including one that he named. A request to the driver to produce his licence and an investigation would have disclosed the facts and the company recklessly omitted to make these enquiries.

The policy exempted from liability if a person driving with consent did not to knowledge of the insured or his representative who gave consent hold a licence unless he had held and was not disqualified from obtaining one. HELD: if a man deliberately shuts his eyes to the obvious, he had as much knowledge as if he were expressly told the facts to which he had closed his eyes, but it is quite another thing to say that because a man has means of knowledge of which he does not avail himself, therefore, he has knowledge. If he does not know of something which it is his duty to know, and which, therefore, ought to have known, he cannot plead lack of knowledge, but knowledge and means of knowledge are not the same thing. This is an exception clause which is construed strictly. It would be for insurers to prove that the company knew the driver was unlicensed. It does not impose a duty to make enquiries. In the circumstances the policy was effective.

Lester Bros (Coal Merchants) Ltd v Avon Insurance Co Ltd

(1942) 72 Ll L Rep 109 (Atkinson J)

A commercial motor policy issued to a limited company (1) indemnified the insured, (2) extended to cover anybody driving on the insured's order or with his permission.

The insurers were not liable if the vehicle was: (a) being driven by the insured unless he (i) holds a licence to drive such vehicle or (ii) has held and is not disqualified for holding or obtaining such a licence; (b) being driven with the general consent of the insured or his representative by any person who to the knowledge of the insured or of such representative does not hold a licence to drive such vehicle unless such person has held and is not disqualified for holding or obtaining such a licence.

The arbitrator was not satisfied that the assured knew the driver did not have a licence. A servant of the company who did not have and never had a licence was driving when an accident occurred.

HELD: As the insured was a limited company, and giving the policy a commercial meaning, ie by himself or his servants, clause (a) and not clause (b) applied. Insurers were not liable.

O.O.D. policy — repairer driving

Samuelson v National Insurance and Guarantee Corpn Ltd
[1984] 3 All ER 107, Q B D
The motor policy issued by the defendants to the plaintiff gave indemnity against theft. The 'limitations as to use' were 'social domestic and pleasure' only, though by General Exception 1(a)(i) 'the exclusion of use for any purpose in connection with the Motor Trade' was not to prejudice the indemnity whilst the car was 'in the custody or control of a member of the Motor Trade' for repair. General exception 1(c) excluded indemnity when the car was 'being driven by or for the purpose of being driven' in charge of any person other than the authorised driver. By reference to the certificate of insurance the only authorised driver was 'the policy holder'. A repairer who had the car for some necessary work on it drove it to the manufacturers' agents for some spare parts. He needed to take the car to the agents to ensure that the parts did fit. He parked it nearby but whilst he was away for a few minutes getting the parts the car was stolen and was never recovered. The plaintiff claimed under the policy for the loss.

The judge held that he was not entitled to indemnity. Paragraph 1(a)(i) simply declared that the limitation of use was not breached by delivering it into the custody or control of a member of the motor trade for repair. The exception 1(c) related to driving and was not affected by this. At the time of the theft the car was, for the purpose of being driven, in the charge of a person other than the authorised driver.

HELD, ON APPEAL: The judge was right in saying that clause 1(c) was not cut down by 1(a). But on the facts of this case, namely, that the repairer needed to take the car to the agents to ensure that the new parts would fit, it was, at the moment it was stolen, in the repairer's charge for the purpose of repair and not for the purpose of driving, and the indemnity was restored by General Exception 1(a)(i). Appeal allowed.

Provisional licence holder unaccompanied

Rendlesham v Dunne
[1964] 1 Lloyd's Rep 192, CC (Herbert J)
Dunne, who held only a provisional licence to drive, was driving Griffin's

car with his permission. He was unaccompanied and the car was without 'L' plates. Griffin's insurance policy was expressed to indemnify any person driving with his permission provided that 'such person holds a licence to drive' the car. An accident having occurred, the insurers refused to indemnify Dunne.

HELD: They were bound to indemnify him. (1) It was impossible to construe the policy so as to restrict the meaning of the word 'licence' to that of a full licence. The Road Traffic Act 1960 uses the word 'licence' to include both types of licence. It cannot be said that a man has not got a licence to drive a car on the road merely because he has failed to comply with a condition upon which he has been granted a licence. (2) A condition of the policy requiring the insured to take all reasonable steps to safeguard the car from loss and damage was not broken by allowing Dunne to drive. That condition was concerned with the physical condition of the car and did not cover damage caused by negligent driving or driving by somebody in contravention of the terms of his licence.

Driver and driving

R v Wilkins
(1951) 115 JP 443, [1951] CLY 9109, Berkshire Quarter Sessions
Section 121(1) of the 1930 Act provided:

' "Driver," where a separate person acts as steersman of a motor vehicle, includes that person as well as any other person engaged in the driving of the vehicle and the expression "drive" shall be construed accordingly.'

There may, therefore, be more than one driver of a vehicle. If one of such drivers holds a licence to drive, the exceptions clause in the insurance policy providing that the insurers shall not be liable if the insured vehicle is driven by a person not holding a driving licence, does not apply, and the vehicle remains insured under the policy.

The appellants, brother and sister, were on a public road on a tractor. The sister, who had no driving licence, was seated in the driving seat. The brother, who had a licence, was standing behind her. Both were charged and convicted of driving a vehicle which was uninsured by reason of the fact that it was being driven by a person who did not hold a driving licence.

HELD: There were two drivers, and since one held a licence, the exceptions clause did not apply and the vehicle was insured.

Note—Section 121(1) of the 1930 Act is replaced by s 196(1) of the 1972 Act in which 'driver' is similarly defined.

R v MacDonagh
[1974] QB 448, [1974] 2 All ER 257, [1974] 2 WLR 529, 118 Sol Jo 222, CA
A motorist pushing his car with his shoulder against the door pillar and both feet on the road, controlling movement by his hand on the steering wheel, is not 'driving' within the meaning of the Road Traffic Act 1972.

McQuaid v Anderton
[1980] 3 All ER 540, [1981] 1 WLR 154, 144 JP 456, 125 Sol Jo 101, [1980] RTR 371, Div Ct
A motor vehicle was being towed by another vehicle by means of a tow

rope. The appellant was sitting in the driver's seat of the towed vehicle steering by means of the steering wheel and able to operate the brakes.
HELD: He was 'driving' the vehicle within the meaning of the Road Traffic Act 1972, s 99.

Caise v Wright, Fox v Wright
[1981] RTR 49, QBD
Caise was driving a car which was towing another car of which Fox was in the driver's seat able to slow, stop and steer it to a limited extent.
HELD, following *McQuaid v Anderton* (above): Fox was 'driving' the towed car.

Burgoyne v Phillips
(1983) 147 JP 375, [1983] RTR 49, [1983] Crim LR 265 QBD, Div Ct
The defendant was sitting at the wheel of his car after dropping a friend off. Assuming the ignition key was still in the ignition lock he released the handbrake and let the car roll forward preparatory to driving away. He then realised he had no keys. The steering was locked and the engine not running. He hastily applied the brakes but the car collided with a vehicle in front, having rolled forward about 30 feet.
HELD: He was 'driving' the car. The essence of driving is the use of the driver's control to direct the movement of the car however produced. An important factor was that he had himself deliberately set the vehicle in motion.

Jones v Pratt
[1983] RTR 54, QBD
A front seat passenger, seeing a small animal run across the road, grabbed the steering wheel causing the car to go off the road and crash.
HELD, he was not 'driving' the car.

Blayney v Knight
[1975] RTR 279, 60 Cr App Rep 269, [1975] Crim LR 237, Div Ct
A taxi driver drove his car to a club to pick up a fare. He got out of the car leaving the engine running and the driver's door open; the automatic transmission lever was in 'drive' but the handbrake was on. He went to the door of the club to speak to his fare and, on turning round, saw the defendant sitting in the driver's seat talking to two men who had got into the rear seat. He went to the car and tried to pull the defendant out of the driver's seat. There was a struggle and the car moved forward along the road. The driver fell off on to the road and the rear wheel passed over his legs. The defendant was charged with various offences including careless driving and driving when not insured. The justices accepted the defendant's evidence that he had not intended to drive and that his foot must accidentally have pressed the accelerator.
HELD, ON APPEAL: He was not 'driving'. Following the test applied in *R v MacDonagh* (above) an activity was not 'driving' if it was not driving in any ordinary sense of the word. It was not a case where a person was consciously seeking the movement of the car in some way and it was thus not 'driving'.

Car hirer's policy

Haworth v Dawson
(1946) 80 Ll L Rep 19 (Lewis J)
Insurers issued a policy to G & K Hire, indemnifying them and any person hiring a car who completed a proposal form which was the basis of the contract and who was not an excluded hirer. A hirer was excluded unless (1) he was a person whom G & K Hire had satisfied themselves by an actual driving test was a qualified, careful and competent driver; (2) he had completed a proposal form; (3) he held a current driving licence which was continuous for at least 12 months and free from any endorsements. The proposal form required that the hirer should never have been prosecuted under the Motor Car or Road Traffic Acts for any offence thereunder; had never had a licence endorsed or suspended; had not been involved in any motor accidents of any kind whatever during the prior 12 months; and had never been refused insurance nor the renewal of any policy issued. The proposal form required G & K Hire to warrant that (1) they had tested the hirer and satisfied themselves of his capability to drive by causing him to drive the car on the highway in their presence; (2) to examine the hirer's driving licence and warrant it had been issued for more than twelve months and was free from endorsements; and (3) that the car was in sound condition and working order. One Dawson hired a car from G & K Hire, and injured a third party, who sued Dawson and G & K Hire. Judgment was given against Dawson and the action was adjourned to join the insurers as defendants. It was admitted Dawson was a man of straw, and G & K Hire admitted they were liable under *Monk v Warbey*. Dawson's licence was endorsed for speeding in 1937 and again in 1938; he had had two accidents; G & K Hire did not give him any test.

Insurers denied that Dawson or G & K Hire were covered by the policy and that s 10 of the 1934 Act therefore did not apply.
HELD: Dawson was an excluded hirer and insurers were not liable.

On the question of costs, G & K Hire contended that the insurers had been wrongly joined, as there could have been no cause of action against them at the date of the writ, and the plaintiff ought to have issued a fresh writ, but the court held they had been party to the proceedings without raising any objection, and made an order in the Sanderson form that G & K Hire pay the costs of insurers.

Note—And see *Bowmaker v Wycombe Motors*, p 337, above. Section 10 of the 1934 Act is now replaced by s 149 of the 1972 Act.

Evans v Lewis
(1964) 108 Sol Jo 259, [1964] 1 Lloyd's Rep 258, Div Ct
The defendant was charged with using a motor vehicle on a road without there being in force a policy of insurance in respect of third party risks contrary to the Road Traffic Act 1960, s 201 (now s 143 of the 1972 Act). At the time of the offence he was driving a car hired from a car-hire garage. There was a policy in force issued by insurers to the garage to cover their vehicles when out on hire. It included the words 'This policy is only to cover any vehicle . . . subject . . . to the following conditions (a) that the insured shall verify . . . that the hirer is not among the excluded persons

enumerated below . . . (8) publicans . . . (e) the Company's form of proposal for hirer driving insurance shall be completed and signed by each hirer'. The defendant was a publican but declared in the proposal form that he was a printer. Relying on *Durrant v MacLaren*, (p 820, above) he claimed that he was insured by virtue of s 207 of the Act (s 149 of the 1972 Act) until proceedings had been taken under the section by the insurer and this had not been done.

HELD, ON APPEAL from a dismissal of the charge: This case was not the same as *Durrant's*. Here there was no contract of insurance between the defendant and the insurance company and the document he completed was wrongly called a proposal form. The defendant was never covered by the insurance policy, for it specifically excluded publicans: in such circumstances s 207 did not apply.

SALE OF VEHICLE

Car sold

Rogerson v Scottish Automobile and General Insurance Co Ltd
(1931) 146 LT 26, 48 TLR 17, 75 Sol Jo 724, 41 Ll L Rep 1, HL
Defendants contracted by a policy of insurance to indemnify plaintiff against 'all sums which the assured shall become legally liable to pay as compensation for . . . bodily injury . . . caused to any person or persons by a motor car described in the schedule hereto'. The car was thereinafter referred to as 'the insured car'. The policy further provided that 'this insurance shall cover the legal liability as aforesaid of the assured in respect of the use by the assured of any motor car (other than a hired car) provided that such car is at the time of the accident being used instead of the insured car'. Plaintiff exchanged the insured car for a new car of a similar type. While plaintiff was using the new car an accident occurred, causing injury to a third person, and plaintiff referred the claim to defendants, who repudiated liability on the grounds that plaintiff was not using the new car 'instead of' the old one and that when the insured car was sold the insurance ceased. An action for a declaration that defendants were liable to indemnify plaintiff against the claim was brought.

HELD: The policy necessarily implied that the insured car should be the subject-matter of the insurance at the time of the accident and therefore the action failed.

Note—See p 753, above, on 'open' certificate.

Tattersall v Drysdale
[1935] 2 KB 174, 104 LJKB 511, 153 LT 75, 51 TLR 405, 79 Sol Jo 418, 52 Ll L Rep 21 (Goddard J)
A policy (third party) contained the following clause: 'Subject to the terms and conditions of this policy, this section is extended to cover: The insured whilst personally driving for private purposes any other private motor car not belonging to the insured in respect of which no indemnity is afforded the insured by any other insurances applying to such car, provided always that the car or cars hereby insured shall not be in use at the same time'.

The insured sold the car referred to in the policy, and after the sale had an accident whilst driving a car lent to him.

HELD: The policy was in respect of the ownership and use of a particular car, and the clause was expressly stated to be an extension clause; the insured had ceased to be interested in the subject matter of the insurance and the extension fell with the rest of the policy.

Wilkinson v General Accident Insurance Corpn Ltd
[1967] 2 Lloyd's Rep 182, Manchester Assizes

Middleton, a motor dealer, acted as agent of the defendants to procure insurance business. He had authority to issue cover notes; insurance certificates and policies would be issued by the defendants themselves. The plaintiff had a car insured under a policy issued by the defendants through Middleton's agency. The policy had the usual extension to cover the holder when driving a car not owned by him. In October 1961 he sold the car and Middleton witnessed the hire purchase agreement. In December 1961 Middleton told the plaintiff that his policy would expire if a further premium was not paid. Thereupon the plaintiff paid a year's premium and received in due course a new certificate, which referred to the car which he had sold in October. He did not buy another car but occasionally used his brother-in-law's car. In September 1962 he had an accident whilst doing so. He claimed indemnity under the policy. In this action his counsel conceded that in the ordinary way where an insured parts with the car insured the policy ceases to have effect (*Tattersall v Drysdale*), but he contended that as Middleton, the defendants' agent, had known of the sale of the car and yet had invited renewal some weeks later the defendants were estopped from denying that the plaintiff was covered.

HELD: This was not correct. Middleton had obtained knowledge of the sale of the car in his capacity as a motor dealer, not insurance agent, and his knowledge so obtained was not to be imputed to the defendants. Once the car was sold the policy was void: the plaintiff knew Middleton's authority was limited to issuing cover notes and receiving premiums. It would not be possible for such an agent to effect so fundamental a change in the policy as to give general cover to the plaintiff when driving cars belonging to others after he had disposed of his own.

Boss v Kingston
[1963] 1 All ER 177, [1963] 1 WLR 99, 106 Sol Jo 1053, 61 LGR 109, Div Ct QBD

Boss was driving Hansford's motor cycle with Hansford on the pillion. Hansford's insurance was effective only when Hansford was driving. Boss had a policy in respect of a Triumph motor cycle which he had sold a fortnight before. This policy afforded cover to Boss when riding 'any motor cycle described in the schedule' and also whilst riding any other motor cycle 'not belonging to him . . . as though such motor cycle were a motor cycle described in the schedule'. The schedule contained particulars of the Triumph motor cycle only. They were charged with using a motor cycle on a road when there was not in force a policy of insurance in relation to the user of that vehicle contrary to the Road Traffic Act 1960, s 201 (now s 143 of the 1972 Act). The justices convicted on the ground that Boss's policy lapsed when he sold the Triumph because he then ceased to have an insurable interest in the vehicle to which the policy related.

HELD: On a case stated: (1) As Boss's policy, unlike those considered in *Rogerson v Scottish Automobile* (above) and *Tattersall v Drysdale* (above), was in respect of third-party risks only there was no need for him to have an insurable interest in the vehicle and the justices' reasoning was wrong. (2) The decisive question was whether the policy provided two wholly independent indemnities, ie one when riding the Triumph and the other when riding another motor cycle, or whether the second was dependant on the first and lapsed with it. For three reasons the policy could not be construed as providing two separate indemnities: (a) the premium was fixed by reference to the named vehicle; (b) the natural interpretation of the second indemnity was to effect temporary cover whilst the named vehicle was out of use; (c) condition 5 of the policy requiring the insured to keep the Triumph in efficient condition was a condition precedent to liability. (3) Section 201 requires the driver of a motor vehicle to have a legally binding policy of insurance in force. It was no defence to bring evidence, as was done in this case, that the insurers would have met any claim. The conviction was right though for the wrong reasons.

Peters v General Accident Fire and Life Assurance Corpn Ltd
[1938] 2 All ER 267, 158 LT 476, 54 TLR 663, 82 Sol Jo 294, 36 LGR 583, 60 Ll L Rep 311, CA

A sold his van to B and handed over the insurance policy which covered any person driving with assured's consent or permission. Plaintiff obtained judgment against B and took proceedings against insurers under s 10. Part of the purchase price remained owing on sale.

HELD: (1) Purchaser was not driving with consent or permission of assured, as the van was purchaser's own property. (2) Assured was not entitled to assign the policy. It is a contract of personal indemnity and insurers cannot be compelled to accept responsibility of a person who may be quite unknown to them. The policy was one in which there was inherent a personal element of such a character as to make it quite impossible to say that it was assignable at the volition of the assured.

The risk that A is going to incur liability by driving his motor car, or persons authorised by A, is one thing. The risk that B will incur or persons authorised by B may be a totally different thing. Insurers make enquires as to the driving record of proposer. A good record may be accepted. A bad record may be refused, or a higher premium required.

Smith v Ralph
[1963] 2 Lloyd's Rep 439, Div Ct

On 15 March 1963 the respondent bought a car from Davies, who handed him a certificate of insurance issued by motor insurers to Davies valid from 25 February 1963 to 24 February 1964. The respondent was charged with using the car on 13 April 1963 when uninsured. He produced the certificate issued to Davies which was expressed to cover not only the policyholder but any other person who was driving on the policyholder's order or with his permission.

HELD: Any permission or authority given by the policyholder Davies could not extend beyond the time of the sale when he ceased to be a policyholder in the sense of having any insurable interest. The respondent was not covered and there must be a conviction.

Car bought on approval

Bullock v Bellamy
(1940) 67 Ll L Rep 392 (Cassels J)
On 12 May Borrett paid £10, whilst negotiating with one Elliott, a salesman in the employ of one Gray, for the purchase of a Chrysler car belonging to Gray, and was given a receipt by Elliott and told by Elliott that he was driving the Chrysler with the owner's consent, and that Borrett was covered by Borrett's policy but to make doubly sure he should ask for a transfer of his insurance to the Chrysler. On 12 May Borrett wrote his insurance brokers asking for a transfer of the insurance from his Morris car to the Chrysler and saying that he would call at the office and see them. On the afternoon of 12 May Borrett met with an accident whilst driving the Chrysler and injured the third parties. On 13 May Elliott brought the log book of the Chrysler to Borrett. On Elliott's instructions, Gray's office wrote the registration authority that Borrett had purchased the car, and afterwards wrote that Gray had repurchased it. On 14 May Borrett tried the car again and was not satisfied and wrote to Elliott that he did not intend to keep the car, and the next day, Sunday, Elliott collected it and the following day, Monday, it was back in Gray's stock for sale. On 14 May Borrett sold the Morris to one Barnes with whom he had been negotiating. Subsequently, towards the end of May, Borrett bought a Wolseley car from Gray and received credit for the £10. Borrett told the police when the accident occurred he had only bought the car that morning and had posted a letter to transfer the insurance. He was in a fainting condition at the time and did not know what he told the police. Mrs Borrett said at the time, 'You have not bought it'.
HELD: The car did not belong to Borrett. He was only trying it. If he did not like it, the £10 would be taken off the price of any other car bought from Gray. It was a sale on approval and there was no approval and therefore no sale. Borrett was driving a car not belonging to him, and his insurers were liable to the third parties who had obtained judgment against Borrett.

---

3 BREACH OF CONDITION

ONUS OF BREACH OF CONDITION

Levy v Assicurazioni Generali
[1940] AC 791, [1940] 3 All ER 427, 56 TLR 851, 84 Sol Jo 633, 67 Ll L Rep 174, PC
The general rule is that the onus of proving that a condition has been broken rests upon insurers. By express words in the policy this onus of proof may be placed upon the assured.

Bond Air Services Ltd v Hill

[1955] 2 QB 417, [1955] 2 All ER 476, [1955] 2 WLR 1194, 99 Sol Jo 370, [1955] 1 Lloyd's Rep 488 (Lord Goddard CJ)

An aircraft insurance policy by condition 7 provided that the insured should comply with all statutory requirements, and by condition 8 that performance of the policy conditions was of the essence of the contract and conditions precedent to the insured's right to recover. Insurers contended the onus of proof was on the insured to prove compliance with three specific statutory requirements and a further condition to produce and verify documents and information, and further alleged specific breaches of these conditions.

HELD: It is for the insurer to prove a breach of condition where he is not relying on a breach of condition precedent to the formation for the policy, and it is also for him to prove an exception. A condition places some duty or responsibility on the insured; an exception restricts the scope of the policy. It is axiomatic in insurance law that as it is always for an insurer to prove an exception, so it is for him to prove the breach of a condition which would relieve him of liability in respect of a particular loss. The contention that by providing that the observance of conditions is to be a condition precedent to liability to pay shifts the onus on to the claimants is wrong. The parties could use words to shift the onus but much clearer words than those used here would be necessary. The burden of proof of failure to comply with the conditions was on the insurers.

CONDITION OF VEHICLE

Damaged or unsafe condition

Trickett v Queensland Insurance Co Ltd

[1936] AC 159, 105 LJPC 38, 154 LT 228, 52 TLR 164, 80 Sol Jo 74, 53 Ll L Rep 255, PC

A general exceptions clause in a private motor vehicle insurance policy provided that: 'No liability shall attach to the company under this policy in respect of . . . any personal accident to the insured occurring: (1) While any motor vehicle in connection with which indemnity is granted under this policy is: (e) Being driven in a damaged or unsafe condition'.

The insured, while driving at night a motor car covered by the policy, was involved in a collision with another motor car and was killed. At and about the time of the accident the lights of his motor car were not shining. On a claim under the policy by the insured's daughter as assignee of the rights under the policy from the legal personal representative of the insured:

HELD: At the time of the accident the motor car driven by the insured was in a damaged or unsafe condition within the meaning of the exceptions clause, and that the insurance company was accordingly relieved from liability under the policy irrespective of whether or not the insured was aware at the time of the accident of the damaged or unsafe condition of the car. The terms of the exceptions clause were unambiguous and plain, and there was no justification for supplementing them by adding 'to the knowledge of the driver', or for reforming the contract into which the insured had entered.

The position of a motor car on land cannot be assimilated to that of a ship at sea and the same code of law rigidly applied to both cases so as to make the exceptions clause to the policy only applicable where the motor vehicle was in a damaged or unsafe condition at the beginning of its journey. Such an argument based on the identity of the conditions which govern the seaworthiness of a ship at sea and the roadworthiness of a motor car on land is unsound.

Reasoning of Goddard J to the contrary in *Barrett v London General Insurance Co Ltd* [1935] 1 KB 238 (p 848, below) disapproved. Judgment of the Court of Appeal of New Zealand (1932) NZLR 1727 affirmed.

Note—See also *Clarke v National Insurance and Guarantee Corpn*, p 849, below.

Liverpool Corpn v T. and H. R. Roberts
[1964] 3 All ER 56, [1965] 1 WLR 938, 109 Sol Jo 510, [1964] 2 Lloyd's Rep 219 (Cumming-Bruce J)
The defendant firm, who were motor coach proprietors and operators, were insured against third-party risks under a policy containing the following condition: 'The insured shall take all due and reasonable precautions to safeguard the property insured and to keep it in a good state of repair. The underwriters shall not be liable for damage or injury caused through driving the motor vehicle in an unsafe condition either before or after the accident.' An accident occurred due to the brakes of the defendants' motor coach failing to stop the vehicle within a reasonable distance. A motor engineer inspected the vehicle and found the brake linings worn and the servo mechanism defective due to neglect over a period of months. The firm's business was managed by T. Roberts who relied on a qualified mechanic G. Roberts to deal with maintenance. The firm had no system of written reports on maintenance and no instructions were given for periodical inspection or overhaul of braking systems.
HELD: (1) The two sentences of the condition were not separate obligations so as to create an absolute obligation by the second sentence to keep the vehicle in safe condition. The second sentence was merely an expression of the consequences of a failure to fulfil the duty imposed by the first sentence. The wording of the condition in *Trickett v Queensland Insurance Co* (above) was quite different. In the present case the fact that the vehicle was objectively in an unsafe condition irrespective of knowledge or want of precautions on the part of the insured would not be enough to constitute a breach. (2) Applying *Woolfall and Rimmer v Moyle* (p 856, below) the duty under the policy to keep the vehicle in a good state of repair was personal to the defendants and a casual act of neglect by an employee would not amount to a breach of it: but on the facts the defective condition of the vehicle was due to the failure of T. Roberts to impose or exercise any system for periodical inspection and the condition had been broken.

Salmon Contractors Ltd v Monksfield
[1970] 1 Lloyd's Rep 387, Mayor's and City of London Court
The plaintiffs' lorry was carrying a load of bundles of plywood when two bundles fell off, injuring a woman pedestrian. The defendant, who was the insurer, declined to indemnify the plaintiffs on two grounds: (1) the policy excluded claims due to 'the spreading of material or substance from the insured vehicle or load carried by such vehicle'; (2) there was a breach of

condition 4 of the policy which excluded liability if the vehicle was 'driven or used in an unsafe condition'.

HELD: (1) 'Spreading' meant a deliberate diffusion or dissemination of material, not an unintentional displacement; (2) this case was not, like *Clarke v National Insurance & Guarantee Corpn* (p 849, below), a case of overloading which made the vehicle unsafe but of a load which was itself unsafe. The unsafe loading did not put the vehicle itself into an 'unsafe condition'. The defendant was not entitled to refuse indemnity.

Efficient condition

Brown v Zurich Accident and Liability Insurance Co

[1954] 2 Lloyd's Rep 243 (Sellers J)

The claimant was the owner of a Fordson van insured with the respondents under a comprehensive motor car policy. The van was involved in a collision in December 1950. The tyres of both front wheels were completely devoid of tread though not worn down to the canvas at any point. The collision was due to the van going into an uncontrollable skid on an icy road. The tyres were inspected by the police after the accident but no proceedings were taken by the police under reg 71 of the 1947 regulations. The skid might have occurred even if the front tyres had adequate treads. The respondents contended that the claimant was in breach of the condition requiring him to maintain the vehicle in an efficient condition and was therefore not entitled to recover. Fulfilment of the policy condition was a condition precedent to liability. The arbitrator held that the policy requirement was to take all reasonable steps to safeguard from loss or damage and maintain the vehicle in efficient condition; that the smooth state of the front tyres made the vehicle inefficient and the claimant had failed to take reasonable steps to maintain in efficient condition.

HELD: 'Efficient condition' meant 'roadworthy'. The finding of fact by the arbitrator that the tyres were dangerous and made the vehicle unsafe and inefficient in condition, could not be disturbed by the court. 'Vehicle' includes tyres. *Woolfall & Rimmer v Moyle* (p 856, below) not applicable. Award for respondents upheld.

Conn v Westminster Motor Insurance Association Ltd

[1966] 1 Lloyd's Rep 407, CA

The plaintiff was driver and owner of a taxicab for the use of which the defendants issued an insurance policy covering third-party claims and damage. Condition 5 of the policy said 'The Policyholder shall take all reasonable steps to safeguard from loss or damage and maintain in efficient condition the vehicle' insured. Condition 1 made the due observance and fulfilment of the conditions of the policy a condition precedent to the insurers' liability under the policy. The plaintiff was driving the cab when it veered off the roadway into some railings and was damaged beyond repair. After the accident the police found both front tyres were bare of tread and one brake shoe was worn down to the metal. The defendants refused to meet claims under the policy, relying on condition 5. The cause of the accident was not established but there was no evidence that it was due to the condition of the brakes or tyres.

HELD: (1) The words 'efficient condition' in the context of condition 5 meant 'roadworthy condition'. (2) On the plaintiff's evidence that he noticed no symptoms of wear in the brakes, and bearing in mind that the actual state of the brakes could not be ascertained without dismantling them, the defendants had not shown a failure on the part of the plaintiff to take all reasonable steps to maintain his brakes. (3) Unlike the brakes the state of the tyres was plain for anyone to see: having no tread they were unroadworthy and the plaintiff was in breach of condition 5. (4) It was irrelevant whether any breach of condition 5 caused the accident. The only question was whether there was a breach of the condition. There was a breach and the plaintiff could not succeed.

McInnes v National Motor and Accident Insurance Union
[1963] 2 Lloyd's Rep 415, 1963 SLT (Sh Ct) 52, Sheriff Ct
The defendants had issued a policy of motor insurance to the plaintiff of which condition 5 read 'The insured shall take all reasonable steps to safeguard from loss and damage and maintain in efficient condition the vehicle . . .'. They refused to indemnify the plaintiff after an accident, alleging that it was due to worn tyres and defective brakes. He contended that the words of the condition were so indefinite as to be unenforceable. HELD: The question was, what did the words 'efficient condition' mean? The limited meaning suggested by Sellers J in *Brown v Zurich Insurance Co* that when used of a vehicle they meant 'roadworthy', was not justified. 'Efficient' can have no precise meaning any more than the word 'reasonable'. Yet both are capable of enforcement by legal means. 'Efficient condition' means capable of doing what is normally and reasonably required of it. In the case of a motor vehicle it should not be difficult to decide whether the use wherein it failed was one within the reasonable contemplation of the parties to the policy. The condition was not too indefinite to be enforceable.

Jones and James v Provincial Insurance Co Ltd
(1929) 46 TLR 71, 35 Ll L Rep 135 (Rowlatt J)
The policy contained a condition that 'the assured shall take all reasonable steps to maintain such vehicle in efficient condition', and it provided that the observance of the conditions should be a condition precedent to the liability of the insurers. The claimants removed the foot-brake from the vehicle, leaving only a hand-brake, and in this state of affairs the vehicle caused damage, and was itself damaged, in an accident, but the exact cause of the accident could not be ascertained. HELD: The condition was a condition precedent and as it had been broken, the insurers were not liable on the policy.

Barrett v London General Insurance Co
[1935] 1 KB 238, 104 LJKB 15, 152 LT 256, 51 TLR 97, 78 Sol Jo 898, 50 Ll L Rep 99 (Goddard J)
By a policy of motor car insurance the defendants agreed to indemnify the assured against third party risks, 'liability in respect of any accident while driving the car in an unsafe or unroadworthy condition' being excluded. HELD: Applying the principle of marine insurance that there is an implied warranty that a ship is seaworthy at the time of sailing, but no warranty

that she shall continue seaworthy throughout the voyage, the policy must be taken to mean that, for the assured to be covered by it, the car must be roadworthy when it set out on its journey but need not continue to be roadworthy throughout the journey. An assignee of the assured was, therefore, entitled to recover in an action against the defendants on the policy where the defendants (on whom lay the onus of proving unroadworthiness) failed to prove that the car was unroadworthy when it began its journey and only showed that, by reason of a defective brake, it was unroadworthy at the time of the accident.

Note—This reasoning was disapproved in *Trickett v Queensland Ins Co*, p 845, above.

'Safeguard from loss or damage'

New India Assurance Co Ltd v Yeo Beng Chow
[1972] 3 All ER 293, [1972] 1 WLR 786, 116 Sol Jo 373, [1972] 1 Lloyd's Rep 479, [1972] RTR 356, PC

Insurers issued a motor policy to the respondent insured. It was in the form of a comprehensive policy, but cover was restricted to third party liability only by deleting section I of the policy which indemnified against loss of or damage to the insured vehicle. The remaining section indemnified against liability in respect of personal injury to any person or damage to property of third parties. The policy contained conditions of which condition 3 required the insured to 'take all reasonable steps to safeguard the vehicle from loss or damage and to maintain the vehicle in efficient condition . . .'. After a collision in which a motor cyclist was killed the insured's vehicle was found by a vehicle examiner not to have been kept in an efficient and roadworthy condition. The insurers, in conformity with the compulsory insurance legislation, paid the damages and costs awarded against the insured for the death of the motor cyclist and then claimed these sums from the insured for breach of condition 3. It was argued on his behalf, and accepted by the Federal Court of Malaysia, that, section I of the policy having been deleted, condition 3 could not survive unaffected; that as loss or damage was not covered by the policy, so much of the condition as required the insured to safeguard the vehicle from loss or damage could have no application and that the condition had been 'mutilated'.

HELD: This was not right. It did not follow from a limitation of the cover provided by the policy that any alteration was to be implied in the conditions precedent contained in the policy. Insurance companies can insert such conditions as they choose and if the conditions inserted are accepted by the insured, they are binding on him. There is no obligation on an insurance company to relate the conditions to particular aspects of the policy.

Overloading — passengers

Clarke v National Insurance and Guarantee Corpn Ltd
[1964] 1 QB 199, [1963] 3 All ER 375, [1963] 3 WLR 710, 107 Sol Jo 573, [1963] 2 Lloyds Rep 35, CA

The plaintiff was the owner of a Ford Anglia four-seater car for which a motor policy was issued to him by the defendants, an insurance company.

A term of the policy excluded liability whilst the car was 'being driven in an unsafe or unroadworthy condition'. The plaintiff was driving the car with eight adult passengers in it when it collided with another car whilst descending a steep hill. The judge found that by reason of the overloading the steering, braking and control of the car were seriously impaired. The defendants refused to meet claims arising from the accident.

HELD, ON APPEAL: The defendants were not liable under the policy. Maritime cases dealing with the warranty of seaworthiness, though by no means governing the matter, are of some assistance; in such cases it has been held that overloading or bad stowage can render a vessel unseaworthy. At the time of the accident the vehicle was unroadworthy through being overloaded and the exception clause applied.

Per Harman LJ: I think that one must regard the car as it was as it proceeded along the road, not look at it empty before it was loaded up and say: This was a safe and mechanically sound car. The words which are important for this purpose are 'being driven' and, when it was being driven it was, by reason of overloading, just as in the ship cases, rendered unsafe and unroadworthy.

Note—See also *Salmon Contractors v Monksfield*, p 846, above.

Houghton v Trafalgar Insurance Co Ltd

[1954] 1 QB 247, [1953] 2 All ER 1409, [1953] 3 WLR 985, 97 Sol Jo 831, [1953] 2 Lloyd's Rep 503, CA

On 10 March 1951, plaintiff bought a 1939 Morris private saloon car. He signed a proposal form which contained a marginal note that 'All policies exclude legal liability to passengers', and obtained a cover note containing the words 'Full comprehensive' which incorporated the proposal form and was subject to the terms and conditions of the company's policy of insurance. The car had two bucket seats at the front. The back seat was for two passengers but had a centre arm which could be raised to make room for a further passenger. An accident occurred on 18 March 1951, involving damage to car, damage to property of third parties and injury to passengers. At the time of the accident there were five passengers and the driver. The policy was issued on 9 April 1951, and excluded passenger liability. Insurers contended (1) that the car was conveying a load in excess of that for which it was constructed, in which case liability was excluded by the policy; and (2) the insurance did not cover liability to passengers. There was no evidence from the makers of the load the car was constructed to carry. The car had a boot but was not carrying any luggage. The weight of the six persons in the car was 62 stones 4 lbs.

HELD: As to (1) the words were inapt for a private car or in relation to passengers. Overloading was not the same thing as overcrowding. The dictionary meanings of 'load' are — 'weight, carriage, act of loading, that which is laid on either a person or an animal to be carried'. The load is not in excess of the load for which the car was constructed unless the load carried, whether it be passengers, luggage or both, is in excess of the total load for which the car is constructed. Here it was not. Verdict for plaintiff on this point.

As to (2), the marginal words were part of the proposal form and the cover note incorporated the proposal form and the proposal was for an insurance excluding legal liability to passengers. Defendants succeeded on this point. Plaintiff was entitled to indemnity in respect of damage to car to the building but not passenger liability: [1953] 2 Lloyd's Rep 18 (Gorman J).

The company appealed on the first point. Appeal dismissed.

Per Somervill LJ: It would need the plainest possible words if it were desired to exclude the insurance cover by reason of the fact that there was at the back one passenger more than the seating accommodation. I hope any company will print their definition in red ink when the policy is inapplicable when an extra passenger is carried.

Per Denning LJ: If the clause had the meaning contended for, I would regard it was almost a trap.

Per Romer LJ: If this provision is applied to a private motor car, I have not the least idea what it means.

DUTY TO NOTIFY INSURERS

Failure to notify insurers of prosecution

Lickiss v Milestone Motor Policies at Lloyds

[1966] 2 All ER 972, [1966] 1 WLR 1334, 110 Sol Jo 600, [1966] 2 Lloyd's Rep 1, CA

Motor insurers issued to a motor cyclist a policy covering third-party risks only. Section 1 said the insurers would at the insured's request or at their own option pay the costs of defending proceedings in the magistrates' court. Condition 1 required the insured to forward immediately to the insurers any notice of prosecution, summons or process relating thereto. Condition 13 made the fulfilment of the terms and conditions of the policy a condition precedent to their liability to make any payment under the policy.

On 17 May, the motor cyclist collided with a taxi. He did not at once report it to the insurers but the taxicab driver's solicitors did so and the insurers wrote to the motor cyclist on 25 May enclosing a claim form for completion. He filled it in and returned it but did not tell the insurers he had received notice of prosecution from the police nor that he had received a summons for hearing on 2 July. On 18 June, the police told the insurers of the pending proceedings and the insurers wrote the motor cyclist on 23 June: 'It would be appreciated if you would let us know why you have not notified us of these proceedings since we wish to arrange your defence'. The motor cyclist replied to this but the insurers did not receive his reply. He wrote the court pleading guilty to the charge and was fined £5. He wrote the insurers telling them this but they eventually wrote him repudiating all liability for paying for the damage to the taxi: they said their position with regard to the third-party claim had been prejudiced by his action. The county court judge held the insurers were not entitled to insist on conducting the motor cyclist's defence in the magistrate's court: it would be contrary to public policy that an accused should not be allowed to have his own solicitor. But he held the failure to send the notice of prosecution or the summons was a breach of a condition precedent and the insurers were entitled to succeed.

HELD, ON APPEAL: The county court judge was clearly right on the first point but not on the second. It was unnecessary for the motor cyclist to send the documents to the insurers since they had all the relevant information from the police by their letter of 18 June. Moreover, the insurers' letter of 23 June was a waiver of the condition. When they heard from the police on 18 June, they could have asked their insured for the notice of prosecution and summons, but they did not. They merely asked him why he had not notified them of the proceedings and by not asking for the documents as good as said they did not want them. Apart from this, condition 1 was to afford protection to the insurers so that they should know of any proceedings in good time: as they obtained all material knowledge from another source they were not prejudiced and could not reply on the condition to defeat the claim. Appeal allowed.

Cox v Orion Insurance Co Ltd
[1982] RTR 1, CA
The plaintiff was issued with a motor insurance policy by the defendants whereby it was a condition precedent to their liability that he should give notice and deliver detailed particulars of any accident, loss and damage. Whilst the plaintiff was driving the car it collided with another vehicle and was damaged. He claimed under the policy but declared that someone else was driving the car at the time of the collision. Later he made a claim for theft in respect of the same incident. The defendants repudiated liability under the policy. The plaintiff had been convicted of various road traffic offences as being the driver at the time of the collision.
HELD: The defendants were entitled to repudiate. The plaintiff was in breach of the condition precedent in that they had not been given detailed particulars of the collision. *Lickiss v Milestone Motor Policies* (above) distinguished.

Giving notice 'as soon as possible'

Verelst's Administratrix v Motor Union Insurance Co Ltd
[1925] 2 KB 137, 94 LJKB 659, 133 LT 364, 41 TLR 343, 69 Sol Jo 412 (Roche J)
A policy of insurance covering (inter alia) the death of the insured by accident, contained the following condition: 'In the case of any accident, injury, damage or loss . . . the insured or the insured's representative for the time being shall give notice . . . in writing to the head office of the company of such accident, injury, damage or loss as soon as possible after it has come to the knowledge of the insured or of the insured's representative for the time being.'

During the currency of the policy, namely, on 14 January 1923, the insured was killed in a motor accident in India. Knowledge of her death reached her personal representative in England within a month, but the personal representative did not know of the existence of the policy of insurance till January 1924. Notice was given to the insurance company as soon as possible thereafter. The insurance company repudiated liability on the ground that notice was not given 'as soon as possible' within the meaning of the condition.
HELD: In considering whether notice was given 'as soon as possible'

within the meaning of the condition, all existing circumstances must be taken into account, including the available means of knowledge of the insured's personal representative of the existence of the policy and the identity of the insurance company; and the arbitrator, to whom the dispute had been submitted, was entitled to find that notice had been given 'as soon as possible'.

Berliner Motor Corpn and Steiers and Sports Inc v Sun Alliance Assurance
[1983] 1 Lloyd's Rep 320 [1983] Com LR 9 (Bingham J)
A product and public liability insurance policy required the insured to notify the insurers promptly of any event which might give rise to a claim. A claim arose out of an accident in America. The insured did not notify the insurers until ten months later.
HELD: The insured's delay was a gross breach of condition. The insurers were not liable.

Adamson & Sons v Liverpool and London and Globe Insurance Co Ltd
[1953] 2 Lloyd's Rep 355 (Lord Goddard CJ)
A 'money in transit' policy contained a condition that the company should be under no liability in respect of any loss which had not been notified to the company within fourteen days of its occurrence. A clerk was handed money once a week to purchase National Insurance stamps. Over a period between October 1949 and June 1951 he had retained a total sum of £2,366 2s 9d. The policy limited the liability to £25 for any one loss.

The insured became aware of the loss on 28 June 1951, and notified insurers the following day. They contended a loss did not occur until it was discovered. Insurers contended that a loss occurred at the time of each theft and their liability was limited to the two thefts within the fortnight before notification.
HELD: The sum of £2,366 2s 9d represented a series of 78 losses as each separate theft constituted a separate loss, and the liability was limited to £50.

Impossibility of compliance

Re Coleman's Depositories and Life and Health Assurance Association
[1907] 2 KB 798, 76 LJKB 865, 97 LT 420, 23 TLR 638, CA
On 28 December 1904, the assured signed a proposal form for an Employer's Liability policy and a cover note was issued which did not contain any conditions. On 3 January 1905, a policy was issued, and delivered to the assured on 9 January 1905, in force from 1 January. The policy contained a condition requiring immediate notice of accident which was of the essence of the contract. On 2 January 1905, an accident occurred to a workman which was believed slight, and no notice given. Dangerous symptoms supervened. Notice was given on 14 March, and the workman died on 15 March.
HELD: The assured did not know and had no opportunity of knowing of the existence of the condition at the date of the accident, the condition was

one with which it was impossible to comply, and the policy did not impose a condition on the assured in respect of this accident, and the assured was entitled to indemnity.

Note—It is now common practice for the cover note to contain a statement that it is issued subject to the conditions of the policy.

Stoneham v Ocean Railway and General Accident Insurance Co
(1887) 19 QBD 237, 57 LT 236, 51 JP 422, 3 TLR 695
A policy of insurance covered death caused by accident happening within the UK, and was made subject to a condition that in case of fatal accident notice thereof must be given to the insurers within seven days. The assured was accidentally drowned in Jersey. It was impossible to give notice within seven days. An action was brought on the policy.
HELD: The accident happened within the UK and notice was not a condition precedent to the right to recover, and the insurers were liable.

Cassell v Lancashire and Yorkshire Accident Insurance Co
(1885) 1 TLR 495
Personal accident policy contained a proviso that the assured should give the insurers notice of the occurrence of the accident and of the injuries received within 14 days of the date of the accident.

The assured met with an accident in July, but was not aware that he had received injury until the March following, when he at once gave notice to the company.
HELD: This was not notice within the time limited by the policy, and assured not entitled to recover.

Hiddle v National Fire and Marine Insurance Co of New Zealand
[1896] AC 372, 65 LJPC 24, 74 LT 204
The longer the time between the event causing the loss and the claim, the more difficult it is for the insurer to enquire into the circumstances of the loss and assess his liability. The defence in *Stoneham's* case failed and in *Cassell's* case succeeded depending on the wording of the policy.

Re Williams and Lancashire and Yorkshire Accident Insurance Co's Arbitration
(1902) 51 WR 222, 47 Sol Jo 110
A workmen's compensation policy provided that the employer was 'to give immediate notice to the company of any accident causing injury to a workman' and that 'time should be of the essence of this condition'. At the foot of the policy there was a notification that every notice to be given by the assured should be in writing sent by post to, or delivered at, the head office of the company.

An accident occurred to a workman on 10 October 1900, and on 16 October the assured notified the accident by telephone to the insurance agent. On 1 December the insured received written notice of claim from the workman and forwarded it to the company on 4 December.

HELD: The giving of immediate notice of the accident was a condition precedent to liability; the communication to the agent was not notice to the company and company not liable.

Note—*Cassell's* case and *Williams'* case were cited by the company's counsel in *Verelst's* case but not referred to in the judgment.

A repudiation based upon a breach of condition precedent to liability may fail because the condition is in fact a condition subsequent.

See also *Pioneer Concrete (UK) Ltd v National Employers Mutual Insurance Association Ltd* [1985] 2 All ER 395, QBD.

A MOTOR POLICY

Allen v Robles
[1969] 3 All ER 154, [1969] 1 WLR 1193, 113 Sol Jo 484, [1969] 2 Lloyd's Rep 61, CA

The defendant took out an insurance policy with the third party, a French insurance company, for the use of his motor car. On 9 April he collided with the plaintiff's house, causing damage. The policy contained a condition which relieved the company of liability to the insured if he failed to give notice within five days of having knowledge of a claim. The defendant received a letter from the plaintiff on 18 April claiming damages, but he did not report the claim to the company until some date in August. The company's solicitors wrote the defendant's solicitors on 10 August, saying their clients reserved their position under the policy. Shortly afterwards they wrote the plaintiff's solicitors that the company was not indemnifying the defendant but did not write the defendant's solicitors to this effect until 29 November.

HELD: There was a breach of condition and the insurers had not lost their right to rely on it merely by their delay in notifying the defendant. The position was that when the insurers discovered in August (1) that there was a claim and (2) that the defendant was in breach of his condition they were in a position then either to elect whether to repudiate or accept liability or it was open to them to delay their decision particularly in view of the letter of 10 August. Mere lapse of time would only operate against them if the insured was thereby prejudiced or if rights of third parties intervened or the delay was so long as to be evidence that they had accepted liability. None of these possibilities arose in the present case.

Condition binds a driver who is not the policy-holder

Austin v Zurich General Accident and Liability Insurance Co Ltd
[1945] KB 250, [1945] 1 All ER 316, 114 LJKB 340, 172 LT 174, 61 TLR 214, 78 Ll L Rep 185, CA

The plaintiff, Austin, was insured with the Bell Assurance Association, and was driving a car belonging to Aldridge, who was insured with the Zurich Insurance Co. Aldridge and one Nicholson were passengers in the car which met with an accident. Aldridge was killed and Nicholson injured. The accident occurred on 23 May 1938. By two informations dated 22 June 1938, Austin was charged with dangerous driving and careless driving. The summonses were returnable on 20 July. Austin gave no notice to the Zurich Co of these impending prosecutions.

The Bell settled a claim by Aldridge's executors for £4,000 and costs and a claim by Nicholson for £305 and costs. The Bell in the name of Austin as plaintiff sued the Zurich for these sums, claiming in right of subrogation.

The Zurich policy provided indemnity to any person driving the vehicle with the insured's (ie Aldridge's) permission subject to the terms of the policy. It was a condition of the policy that notice should be given to the insurers as soon as possible after an accident or of an impending prosecution.

HELD: (1) There was a right to sue in subrogation, apart from the right of one insurer to claim in contribution from another. (2) Austin was entitled to sue the Zurich though not named in their policy. Subsection 4 of s 36 of the 1930 Act applied. This subsection did not include the words 'in respect of a liability required to be covered by a policy issued under this section', which appear in s 10 of the 1934 Act, and is not confined to a liability required to be covered by s 36. (3) Each insurer (subject to (5) below) was liable for 50%. (4) The Zurich cover was subject to the fulfilment of the policy conditions by Austin, and one condition required notice in writing immediately if the insured shall have knowledge of any impending prosecution. Austin could have obtained information of the provisions of the Zurich policy, and he had not fulfilled the condition. On this ground only, judgment was for the Zurich with one-third of the costs: [1944] 2 All ER 243, 77 Ll L Rep 409 (Tucker J).

ON APPEAL: As to subrogation and double insurance: the plaintiff having been completely indemnified by one insurer, was not entitled to claim on the principle of subrogation. The claim would be by and in the name of that insurer against the other insurer for contribution on the principle of double insurance.

As to s 36(4): the subsection gave Austin a right to sue the Zurich company but in so doing he was claiming a benefit under a document to which he was not a party. A person who claims the benefit of a document in that way is bound to take it as he finds it. He cannot claim the benefit of anything which the document gives him without complying with its terms.

Note—Section 36(4) of the 1930 Act is now s 148(4) of the Road Traffic Act 1972; s 10 of the 1934 Act is s 149 of the 1972 Act; and s 36 is now s 145 of the 1972 Act.

REPUGNANCY OF CONDITION

Woolfall and Rimmer Ltd v Moyle
[1942] 1 KB 66, [1941] 3 All ER 304, 111 LJKB 122, 166 LT 49, 58 TLR 28, 86 Sol Jo 63, CA

An employer's liability policy issued to a limited company contained the condition: 'The assured shall take reasonable precautions to prevent accidents and to comply with all statutory obligations.'

The purchase and supply of timber for scaffolding was left entirely to the foreman, who was competent and skilled. Scaffolding was erected and a ledger broke, injuring workmen. The foreman admitted he had no suitable timber available.

HELD, in the Court of Appeal: The assured had taken reasonable precautions by employing a competent foreman. Insurers could not say, I will insure you against negligence on condition that you are not negligent. They could not grant an indemnity with one hand and take it away with the other, but could say the assured should not carry on business in a reckless manner. The contention that the condition applied to the negligence of the foreman was a complete misconception. The condition was not a warranty that everybody employed by the assured, or in fact anybody except the assured, would take reasonable precautions. In appointing the foreman the assured were not delegating their duty under the condition, but performing it.

Maltby (T. F.) Ltd v Pelton Steamship Co Ltd
[1951] 2 All ER 954 n, [1951] WN 531, 95 Sol Jo 834, [1951] 2 Lloyd's Rep 332 (Devlin J)

Shipowners indemnified stevedores against claims by workmen arising from use of gear, provided they took reasonable precautions to prevent accidents and to comply with statutory requirements, and that their gear was regularly and properly tested, and did not use improper or inadequate gear. On a claim by stevedores for indemnity under the contract, the court found the foreman of the stevedores was negligent.

HELD: The decision in *Woolfall's* case made it impossible to contend that the negligence of the foreman brought them within the first part of the stipulations.

With regard to the gear, the words must be construed as meaning 'You the owner of the business shall not use improper or inadequate gear'. It did not mean 'You through your foreman, shall not use improper or inadequate gear'. The claim for indemnity succeeded.

Note—See also *London Crystal Window Cleaning Co Ltd v National Mutual Indemnity Insurance Co Ltd* [1952] 2 Lloyd's Rep 360.

Fraser v B. N. Furman (Productions) Ltd
[1967] 3 All ER 57, [1967] 1 WLR 898, 111 Sol Jo 471, [1967] 2 Lloyd's Rep. 1, CA

The defendants were found liable in damages to the plaintiff, their employee, for negligence and breach of statutory duty in failing to guard a welding machine in which she sustained injury. It had originally had a guard but they had removed it. They sued insurance brokers in third-party proceedings for an indemnity against these damages for breach of contract in having failed to insure them against the plaintiff's claim. The policy which it had been intended to obtain for the defendants was an Eagle Star employers' liability policy which contained the condition 'The insured shall take reasonable precautions to prevent accidents'. The brokers denied liability on the ground that if the policy had been issued the insurers would have been entitled to repudiate liability under it for breach of the condition.

HELD: (1) Following *Woolfall and Rimmer v Moyle* (above) the obligation to take precautions is on the insured personally: failure by an employee to do so would not be a breach of the condition. (2) 'Reasonable precautions' means reasonable as between insurer and insured, without being repugnant to the commercial purpose of the contract. By this test what is reasonable is that the insured must not deliberately court a danger by taking measures which he knows are inadequate to avert it. It is not enough that his omission to take some precaution is negligent: it must be reckless, not caring, though aware of the danger, whether it is averted or not. The purpose of the condition is to ensure that the insured will not refrain from taking precautions simply because he is covered. That was not the case here: the defendants had not appreciated the risk to which they were exposing the plaintiff. (3) It was not a defence to show merely that the insurers would have been entitled to repudiate. It must be shown that they would in fact have done so. The good repute of the company in question and the absence of any evidence that they would have sought to rely on the alleged breach of condition made it impossible to hold that they would have done so. The brokers were liable to indemnify the defendants.

W. and J. Lane v Spratt

[1970] 2 QB 480, [1970] 1 All ER 162, [1969] 3 WLR 950, 113 Sol Jo 920, [1969] 2 Lloyd's Rep 229 (Roskill J)

The plaintiffs, haulage contractors, were insured under a goods in transit policy issued by the defendant, an underwriter at Lloyd's. It contained the condition 'the Insured shall take all reasonable precautions for the protection and safeguarding of the goods . . .'. The plaintiffs engaged a driver after interviewing him and after making one abortive attempt to follow up a reference by telephone. On his first day at work he drove off with a lorry load of merchandise and was not seen again. The defendant refused to indemnify the plaintiffs on the ground that there had been a breach of condition.

HELD: In failing to take up references the plaintiffs had failed to take the elementary precautions which were usual in the trade and if the only duty was to take reasonable care they had failed in that duty. But that did not put them in breach of the condition. Following *Fraser v B. N. Furman (Productions) Ltd* (above) it is not enough that the omission to take a particular precaution should be negligent, it must be at least reckless, not caring whether the danger was averted or not. That was not true of these plaintiffs and they were entitled to indemnity.

CHAPTER 21
Other insurance points

1 INTERPRETATION OF POLICY

Admission in breach of policy condition

Terry v Trafalgar Insurance Co
[1970] 1 Lloyd's Rep 524, Mayor's and City of London Court
The defendants issued to the plaintiff a policy of motor insurance containing the condition 'No liability shall be admitted nor any offer promise or payment made to third parties without the company's written consent'. After a collision between his car and another he wrote to the other driver later on the same day 'As damage to your vehicle was not severe I will pay for the making good. Technically the blame for the accident falls on me . . .'. Afterwards, the third party's damage proving more severe than he had thought, the plaintiff claimed indemnity from the defendants, who refused cover on the ground that there had been a breach of the condition. HELD: The letter was an admission of liability. The condition was not void as being contrary to public policy since it merely required the insured to refrain from admissions; it did not require him to lie. It was a necessary and proper condition for the protection of insurance companies. *Lickiss's* case (p 851, above) was not an authority for the proposition that an insurer cannot rely upon a breach of condition unless he has suffered an actual prejudice. In any event the defendants were in fact prejudiced: by the plaintiff's admission on the day of the accident they were deprived of a possible chance of a favourable settlement. Judgment for the defendants.

Age of insured

Lloyds Bank Ltd v Eagle Star Insurance Co Ltd

[1951] 1 All ER 914, [1951] 1 TLR 803, [1951] 1 Lloyd's Rep 385 (Jones J)
A policy contained a clause — Personal Accidents. If the insured shall
sustain any personal injury caused by violent, accidental, external and
visible means . . . and if such injury shall be the sole and immediate cause
of death within ninety days . . . (a) death of insured — £1,000; provided
the company shall not be liable to pay compensation in respect of personal
injuries . . . if under the age of 16 years or over the age of 65 years. The
deceased insured was 65 years and seven months.
HELD: (1) The contention that the proviso only applied to injuries which
did not result in death failed. The fact that the policy under the heading of
'Personal Accidents' also provided for compensation in respect of personal
injuries resulting either in death or in certain disablements did not have this
effect. (2) The proviso means a person who has reached his sixty-fifth
birthday and applies to anyone who has lived beyond the attainment of the
sixty-fifth birthday.

Assured as a third party

Note—There was formerly a difference of opinion on the question whether an
assured of a policy could claim against insurers under the policy for personal injury
caused to him whilst a passenger in his own car driven by his own servant, or other
person driving on his order or with his permission.
    The point was the subject of an award by Lord Robertson in an arbitration
under the Scottish procedure. The policyholder was injured whilst a passenger in
her own car driven by a person with permission. It was admitted the driver was
entitled to indemnity if there was a liability to 'Third Parties', but denied that the
policyholder was a third party. The section in the policy was headed 'Liability to
Third Parties'. Lord Robertson held that the policyholder was not a third party
within the meaning of the policy and there was no liability under it (reported 73
Lloyd's Rep 189). The same question came before the courts in *Digby v General
Accident Fire and Life Assurance Corpn Ltd*, where in the House of Lords, a conclusion
was reached to the contrary.

Digby v General Accident Fire and Life Assurance Corpn

[1943] AC 121, [1942] 2 All ER 319, 11 LJKB 628, 167 LT 222, 58 TLR
375, 87 Sol Jo 29, 73 Ll L Rep 175, HL
The policyholder was a passenger in her own car, driven by her servant.
Owing to his negligent driving, she was injured and was awarded damages
against him (*Thompson v Bundy* (1938) Times, 5 May). He then brought an
action against her insurers, claiming indemnity. The judge (Atkinson J)
held that the driver was entitled to be indemnified ([1940] 1 All ER 514, 66
Ll L Rep 89). In the Court of Appeal his decision was reversed ([1940] 2
KB 226, [1940] 3 All ER 190, 109 LJKB 740, 163 LT 366).
HELD, ON APPEAL to the House of Lords (Lord Atkin, Lord Wright and
Lord Porter, Viscount Simon LC and Viscount Maugham dissenting):
The insurers were liable to indemnify the driver against the claim of the
assured.

The policy contained six sections of which section 2 (described in the margin as dealing with 'Third-party liability') gave the assured indemnity against '(1) all sums which the policy-holder shall become legally liable to pay in respect of any claim by any person (including passengers in the automobile) for loss of life or accidental bodily injury . . . caused by, through, or in connexion with such automobile . . .'. The same section further provided '(3) The insurance under this section shall also extend to indemnify in like manner any person whilst driving [the car] on the order or with the permission of the policy-holder, provided . . . that such person shall as though he were the policy-holder observe fulfil and be subject to the terms, exceptions and conditions of this policy in so far as they can apply'.

Per Lord Atkin: There was no justification for transferring the words from the margin to the body of the document and saying that 'any claim by any person' must be read as 'any claim by any third party'. 'Any person' means any member of the public. In section 2(1) 'any person' cannot include the policy holder because he cannot be liable to pay himself, but in section 2(3) which begins anew with a fresh promise of indemnity the driver is to be indemnified 'in like manner', and on this occasion the policy holder is plainly 'any person'.

Per Lord Wright: By section 2(3) the insurers undertake in favour of the driver a separate insurance against third-party liability so that he becomes the assured whilst the policyholder becomes *pro hac vice* the third party. There is no warrant for extending the meaning of 'any person' in section 2(1) to 'any person other than the policy-holder' when the words are brought over into section 2(3).

Per Lord Porter: 'Third-party' is merely a useful description of a particular type of insurance and does not mean that 'any claim by any person' must be confined to a third person who is not a party to the contract. In a policy such as this there is not one contract of insurance only; there is one with the policy holder and one also with each person driving on her order and with her permission. For the purposes of a claim made by her against him, he is the assured, the company are the insurers and she is the third party.

Civil commotion — riot

Levy v Assicurazioni Generali

[1940] AC 791, [1940] 3 All ER 427, 56 TLR 851, 84 Sol Jo 633, 67 Ll L Rep 174, PC

The court approved the definition of 'Civil commotion' in *Welford & Otter v Barry's Fire Insurance* — as follows:

This phrase is used to indicate a state between a riot and civil war. It has been defined to mean an insurrection of the people for general purposes, though not amounting to rebellion; but it is probably not capable of any very precise definition. The element of turbulence or tumult is essential; an organised conspiracy to commit criminal acts, where there is no tumult or disturbance until after the acts, does not amount to civil commotion. It is not, however, necessary to show the existence of any outside organisation at whose instigation the acts were done.

London and Lancashire Fire Insurance Co v Bolands Ltd
[1924] AC 836, 93 LJPC 230, 131 LT 354, 40 TLR 603, 68 Sol Jo 629, HL
Four armed men entered the assured's premises on a summer evening
while it was still daylight, held up the employees with revolvers, and took
possession of all the money they could find in the cashier's office. There was
no disturbance in the neighbourhood at the time.
HELD: The priviso was not confined to the case where the theft was
facilitated by an antecedent or simultaneous riot, but included a case where
the theft itself in the manner in which it was conducted constituted a riot at
law. The finding of the arbitrators that the circumstances constituted a riot,
upheld.

Munday v Metropolitan Police District Receiver
[1949] 1 All ER 337, 113 JP 177, 65 TLR 145, 93 Sol Jo 72, 47 LGR 196
(Pritchard J)
Damage to the extent of £175 was done to houses and property of the plaintiff which were adjacent to the football ground by a crowd unable to obtain
admission to the match between Chelsea and Moscow Dynamos. The
crowd invaded the property, climbed on to a garage, broke fences, gates,
gutters and drain pipes, and damaged chimney stacks, roofs and glass. The
plaintiff claimed under the Riot (Damages) Act 1886, for damage caused
by persons riotously and tumultuously assembled together.
HELD: Adopting *Ford v Metropolitan Police District Receiver* [1921] KB 344,
125 LT 18 and *Field v Metropolitan Police Receiver* [1907] 2 KB 853, 76 LJKB
1015, 97 LT 639, 71 JP 494, 23 TLR 736, 51 Sol Jo 720, five elements were
necessary to constitute a riot: a number of persons not less than three; a
common purpose; execution or inception of the common purpose; and
intent on the part of the number of persons to help one another by force if
necessary, against any person who might oppose them in the execution of
the common purpose; and force or violence, not merely used in and about
the common purpose, but displayed in such a manner as to alarm at least
one person of reasonable firmness and courage.
   The judge found each of these elements proved. There was a riot, and
plaintiff was entitled to recover.

R v Sharp; R v Johnson
[1957] 1 QB 552, [1957] 1 All ER 577, [1957] 2 WLR 472, 121 JP 227, 101
Sol Jo 230, 41 Cr App Rep 86
Per Lord Goddard: It may be that the fifth element referred to in *Field's*
case may require reconsideration at some future time.

Continuing warranty

Note—The theory that answers in a proposal form import a warranty which
continues during the insurance did not receive any support in the case of *Woolfall &
Rimmer v Moyle*.

Woolfall and Rimmer Ltd v Moyle

[1942] 1 KB 66, [1942] 3 All ER 304, 111 LJKB 122, 166 LT 49, 58 TLR 28, 86 Sol Jo 63, CA

A proposal form for Employers' Liability contained the question: Are your machinery, plant and ways properly fenced and guarded and otherwise in good order and condition? The answer was 'Yes'. It was contended by insurers that the question was not limited to the date of the proposal form but continued during the currency of the policy. The Court of Appeal said that it was to enable insurers to find out the character of the risk. There was not a particle of justification for reading into it any element of futurity whatsoever.

Note—Also noted with reports at p 856, above. And see 'Renewal — implied warranty', p 897, below.

Pim v Reid

(1843) 6 Man & G 1, 6 Scott NR 982, 12 LJCP 299, 1 LTOS 230

A policy of insurance was made subject, amongst others, to the following condition: 'In the insurance of goods, wares, or merchandise, the building or place in which the same are deposited is to be described, the quality and description of such goods, also whether any hazardous trade is carried on or any hazardous articles deposited therein; and, if any person or persons shall insure his or their buildings or goods, and shall cause the same to be described otherwise than as they really are, to the prejudice of the company, or shall misrepresent or omit to communicate any circumstance which is material to be made known to the company in order to enable them to judge of the risk they have undertaken or are required to undertake, such insurance shall be of no force.'

HELD: This condition applies only to misrepresentations or omissions to communicate circumstances existing at the time of effecting the policy; and the insurance was not avoided by the carrying on a more hazardous trade upon the premises, or the placing hazardous goods thereon, pending the current year of the insurance.

Sweeney v Kennedy

(1948) 82 Ll L Rep 294, Eire Div Ct

A proposal dated 4 March 1946, for insurance of a motor lorry contained the question. 'Are any of your drivers under 21 years of age or with less than 12 months' driving experience?' and was answered 'No'.

The policy was issued on 18 March 1946. At that date the answer was true and the assured had no intention of employing a driver under 21. A son of the assured was first employed as a driver on 17 June 1946, and occasionally employed as driver until 2 February 1947, after which date he was regularly so employed. On 7 October 1947, an accident occurred when the son, who was under 21, was driving.

The declaration in the proposal form was stated to be 'promissory and so form the basis of the contract'.

HELD: (1) No such alteration of risk as to avoid policy. (2) No continuing warranty that no driver under 21 would be employed. (3) 'Promissory' read with the following words, did not refer to the future. It signified a positive declaration. 'I promise you that it is so.' Underwriters held liable.

Kirkbride v Donner

[1974] 1 Lloyd's Rep 549, Mayor's and City of London Court

Miss Kirkbride filled in a proposal form for insurance of her car. In answer to the question 'Will the car to your knowledge be driven by any person under 25 years of age?' she put merely 'Yes, self'. She signed the usual declaration at the end of the form containing the words 'this declaration signed by me is promissory'. The policy when issued provided that the underwriters would not be liable in respect of loss whilst the car was 'being driven by or in charge for that purpose of any person in whose record there is to the knowledge of the policy holder a prejudice existing such as would amount to material information to be known to the underwriters'. On an occasion when she intended to visit a theatre club she allowed her younger brother to drive there in her car on an arrangement that she would use it to drive him back at the end of the visit. Her brother drove the car there, parked it and handed her the keys. During the evening the car was stolen and not recovered. The underwriters refused to meet the loss.

HELD: They were not entitled to decline liability under the policy, because (1) on the facts Miss Kirkbride's brother was not in charge of the car when it was stolen, since the purpose for which he had driven the car had come to an end and Miss Kirkbride was herself at the club; (2) the use of the word 'promissory' in the declaration did not mean that she was warranting that the situation implied or expressed in the proposal form would continue into the future: all it meant was, 'At the time of signing the form those are my intentions'. When she signed the proposal form Miss Kirkbride did not intend that the car would be driven by anyone under the age of 25 other than herself.

Note—See also *Kennedy v Smith*, p 869, below.

Contra proferentes

Thomson v Weems

(1884) 9 App Cas 671, HL (Lord Watson)

The question must be interpreted according to the ordinary and natural meaning of the words used, if their meaning be plain and unequivocal, and there is nothing in the context to qualify it. On the other hand, if the words used are ambiguous, they must be construed *contra proferentes*, and in favour of the assured.

Cornish v Accident Insurance Co

(1889) 23 QBD 453, 58 LJQB 591, 54 JP 262, 38 WR 139, 5 TLR 733 (Lindley LJ)

In a case on the line, in a case of real doubt, the policy ought to be construed most strongly against the insurers; they frame the policy and insert the exceptions. But this principle ought only to be applied for the purpose of removing doubt, not for the purpose of creating a doubt or magnifying an ambiguity when the circumstances of the case raise no real difficulty.

Ejusdem generis

Sun Fire Office v Hart

(1889) 14 App Cas 98, 58 LJPC 69, 60 LT 337, 53 JP 548, 37 WR 561, 5 TLR 289, PC

Per Lord Watson: It is well-known canon of construction, that when a particular enumeration is followed by such words as 'or other', the latter expression ought, if not enlarged by the context, to be limited to matters *ejusdem generis* with those specially enumerated. The canon is attended with no difficulty, except in its application. Whether it applies at all, and if so, what effect should be given to it, must in every case depend upon the clause under construction.

Note—The phrase is chiefly used in cases where general words have a meaning attributed to them less comprehensive than they would otherwise bear, by reason of particular words preceding them.

One line of authority is to give all the words their common meaning unless it is reasonably plain on the face of the document itself that they are not used with that meaning.

The other line of authority is that the general words which follow particular and specific words of the same nature as themselves take their meaning from them and are presumed to be restricted to the same genus as those words.

The phrase was considered by Devlin J in the following case citing *Scrutton on Charterparties* (15th edn) p 239:

'It must be remembered that the question is whether a particular thing is within the genus that comprises the specified things. It is not a question (though the point is often so put in argument), whether the particular thing is like one or other of the specified things.'

Chandris v Isbrandtsen-Moller Co Inc

[1951] 1 KB 240, [1950] 1 All ER 768, 66 TLR 971, 94 Sol Jo 303, 83 Lloyd's Rep 385 (Devlin J)

The rule is merely, as I think, an aid to ascertaining the intention of the parties.

If there is something to show that the literal meaning of the words is too wide, then they will be given such other meaning as seems best to consort with the intention of the parties. In some cases it may be that they will seem to indicate a genus; in others that they perform the simpler office of expanding the meaning of each enumerated item. If a genus cannot be found, doubtless that is one factor indicating that the parties do not intend to restrict the meaning of the words. But I do not take it to be universally true that whenever a genus cannot be found the words must have been intended to have their literal meaning, whatever other indications there may be to the contrary. I see no reason why, if it accords with the apparent intention of the parties, the words should not be treated, as suggested by Lord Macnaghten in *Thames and Mersey Marine Insurance Co Ltd v Hamilton, Fraser & Co* ((1887) 12 App Cas 484 at 501), as being 'inserted in order to prevent disputes founded on nice distinctions' and 'to cover in terms whatever may be within the spirit of the cases previously enumerated'.

Note—Followed in *Coates v Diment* [1951] 1 All ER 890 (Streatfeild J).

False representation

Brown, Jenkinson & Co Ltd v Percy Dalton (London) Ltd
[1957] 2 QB 621, [1957] 2 All ER 844, [1957] 3 WLR 403, 101 Sol Jo 610,
[1957] 2 Lloyd's Rep 1, CA

Shipowners at request of owners of goods shipped on their vessel and on a
promise by owners to indemnify, issued bills of lading stating the goods
were shipped in apparently good order and condition. Both parties knew
that statement was false. Shipowners had to pay a loss to consignees and
sued owners for indemnity.

HELD: By Morris and Pearce LJJ, Lord Evershed MR dissenting:
Although shipowners did not desire or intend that anyone should be
defrauded, they had made a representation of fact which they knew to be
false with intent that it should be acted on, and had committed the tort of
deceit, and the indemnity was unenforceable.

Garage

Barnett and Block v National Parcels Insurance Co
[1942] 1 All ER 221, 166 LT 147, 58 TLR 144, 86 Sol Jo 140 (Atkinson J);
[1942] 1 All ER 55 n, 58 TLR 270, 86 Sol Jo 233, 73 Ll L Rep 17, CA

Policy insured against theft from van 'whilst left in a garage'. It was in a
yard at the back of a private hotel; there were two gates to the yard, both
fastened by bolts on the inner side; it was completely enclosed, partly by
buildings and partly by a wall over 12 feet high, but there was no roof.

HELD: Applying the test of plaintiff's counsel 'a garage is a place where
one can get reasonable protection and shelter for a car' the yard was not a
garage. 'Garage' means a building with a roof and is not applicable to an
unroofed yard.

Affirmed in CA.

It is a pure question of fact. If the arbitrator had found the other way, I
do not think we should have interfered with his finding: Per Goddard LJ in
the Court of Appeal.

Goods in trust

Engel v Lancashire and General Assurance Co Ltd
(1925) 41 TLR 408, 69 Sol Jo 447, 30 Com Cas 202, 21 Ll L Rep 327

Applicants insured claimant, who was a furrier, against burglary, the
policy covering not only goods belonging to claimant but goods which were
on his premises and were in his possession on trust or on commission and
for which he was 'responsible'. A burglary took place, and claimant lost
both goods of his own and goods which were in his custody as a bailee.
Claimant had not been guilty of any negligence as a bailee, and so was not
liable to the owners of the bailed goods for their loss.

HELD: 'Responsibility' in such a connection meant legal liability only,
and therefore, claimant could not recover on the policy in respect of the
bailed goods.

John Rigby (Haulage) Ltd v Reliance Marine Insurance Co Ltd
[1956] 2 QB 468, [1956] 3 All ER 1, [1956] 3 WLR 407, 100 Sol Jo 528,
[1956] 2 Lloyd's Rep 10, CA
Plaintiffs, road transport contractors, conducted business through
subcontractors. They agreed with customers to carry goods lying at a
Liverpool dock to Birmingham. A man driving a lorry called on plaintiffs
and stated he was employed by and the lorry belonged to sub-contractors
on the plaintiffs' list. He was given a collection order for the goods. He was
not a servant of the sub-contractors and the lorry did not belong to them.
Neither he nor the goods were ever heard of again. Plaintiffs' insurance
policy covered 'goods belonging to the assured or held by the assured in
trust for which the assured are themselves responsible'.
HELD: The words 'in trust' were not used in a policy in a strict technical
sense, and should be construed according to their ordinary meaning. The
collection order was as between the plaintiffs and the man wholly invalid,
but as between the plaintiffs and the owners of the goods it was an offer to
undertake the carriage of their goods if they would deliver them to the
person holding the collection order. The plaintiffs were entrusted with the
goods, and liable for their loss, and were entitled to indemnity under their
policy.

Waters and Steel v Monarch Fire and Life Assurance Co
(1856) 5 E & B 870, 25 LJQB 102, 26 LT OS 217, 2 Jur NS 375, 2 WR 245
A, a wharfinger and warehouseman, effected with a company a policy
against fire on goods in trust or on commission. A was merely responsible
to the owners for due diligence in their custody. The company contracted
with him to make good any damage by fire to the property insured. He had
in his warehouse goods belonging to his customers which were deposited
with him in that capacity, and on which he had a lien for the charges for
cartage and warehouse rent, but no further interest of his own. No charge
was made to the customers for insurance, nor were they informed of the
existence of the policy. His warehouse was consumed by fire, with all the
goods in it. The company paid the value of his own goods, and the amount
of his lien on his customers' goods, but refused to pay the value of the
customer's interest in the value of the goods beyond the lien.
HELD: That A was entitled to recover the full value of his customers' goods
notwithstanding that he was not liable to them to make good the loss.

Hepburn v A. Tomlinson (Hauliers) Ltd
[1966] AC 451, [1966] All ER 418, [1966] 2 WLR 453, 110 Sol Jo 86,
[1966] 1 Lloyd's Rep 309, HL
The plaintiffs were road hauliers who regularly carried cigarettes for the
Imperial Tobacco Co. The goods carried were insured by the plaintiffs
under a policy binding the underwriters 'to pay or make good to the
assured . . . or to indemnify them against . . . all risks of loss or damage
however arising'. The goods covered included 'Tobacco . . . the property
of the Imperial Tobacco Co'. The goods were stolen whilst in the plaintiff's
lorry, though in circumstances which did not make the plaintiffs liable to
the owners for the loss. The plaintiffs claimed against the underwriters
under the policy for the value of the goods lost. The underwriters refused to

pay on the grounds that the policy was a contract of indemnity and the plaintiffs had suffered no loss.

HELD: The plaintiffs were entitled to succeed. A bailee has an insurable interest beyond his own personal loss if the goods are destroyed. This has never been regarded as in any way inconsistent with the overriding principle that insurance of goods is a contract of indemnity. The question is whether the bailee has insured his whole insurable interest — a goods policy — or whether he has only insured against personal loss — a personal liability policy. The policy wording in this case was appropriate to a goods policy and the underwriters must pay the full value of the goods to the plaintiffs, who must account to the owners for the money so recovered. *Waters v Monarch Life Assurance Co* (p 867, above) approved and applied. The intention of the assured at the time of entering into the policy is irrelevant.

Per Lord Reid: The principle preventing *jus quaesitum tertio* has been firmly established for at least half a century, but I do not think we are bound to be astute to extend it on a logical basis so as to cut down an exception, if it be an exception, which has stood unchallenged since the decision of *Waters'* case more than a century ago.

Household

English v Western
[1940] 1 KB 145, [1939] 4 All ER 345, 109 LJKB 55, 62 LT 15, 56 TLR 107, 84 Sol Jo 114, 65 Ll L Rep 80 (Branson J); [1940] 2 KB 156, [1950] 2 All ER 515, 109 LJKB 728, 162 LT 370, 56 TLR 380, 84 Sol Jo 465, 67 Ll L Rep 45, CA

A policy excluded members of the assured's household. The assured and his sister, an infant, lived with their father. Neither made any contribution to the upkeep of the home, but both were in receipt of allowances from their father. The sister whilst a passenger in the assured's car, being driven by the assured, was injured. It was contended the assured must be the householder.

The judge held that a member of the assured's household was a member of the same household to which the assured belonged and that there was no liability under the policy.

HELD, ON APPEAL, by Slesser and Clauson LJJ, Goddard LJ dissenting: The words were equivocal and capable of either construction and the phrase was ambiguous, and applying the principle of *contra proferentes*, the insurers were liable. Appeal allowed.

Per Clauson LJ: A man may be related to a household in two ways. He may be a member of the household, or he may be the head of the household. Either meaning is possible and natural; it is therefore ambiguous.

Influence of intoxicating liquor

Louden v British Merchants Insurance Co Ltd
[1961] 1 All ER 705, [1961] 1 WLR 798, 105 Sol Jo 209, [1961] 1 Lloyd's Rep 154 (Lawton J)

A private motor car policy issued by the defendants provided that they would pay compensation for injury or death caused to the policyholder whilst travelling in a motor car not belonging to him, subject to the proviso that the defendants should not be liable for injury sustained by him 'whilst under the influence of drugs or intoxicating liquor'. The plaintiff's husband, the holder of the policy was killed whilst travelling in a car owned and driven by someone else. The alcohol content of his blood was found to be such as would cause some degree of inco-ordination of movement and a tendency to stagger.

HELD: (1) Following the test in *Mair v Railway Passengers Assurance Co Ltd* (1877) 37 LT 356 the words 'under the influence of intoxicating liquor' meant such influence as would disturb 'the quiet calm, intelligent exercise of his faculties' and, on the facts, the defendants had proved such influence. (2) The word 'whilst' had a temporal, not a causative, meaning. The exemption clause did not call for any causal connection between the bodily injury sustained and the influence of intoxicating liquor. The defendants were not liable under the policy.

Kennedy v Smith
1976 SLT 110

After drinking a pint and a half of lager with friends the defender gave them a lift in his car. On a straight section of a dual carriageway road the car crossed the central intersection and collided with a sign. The two passengers were killed. The defender's motor policy contained a condition exempting the insurers from liability for any claim arising when the insured was driving and was under the influence of intoxicating liquor. The defender had signed a declaration when proposing for insurance that he was a total abstainer from birth and would notify the insurers if this ceased to apply.

HELD, ON APPEAL: (1) The phrase 'under the influence of intoxicating liquor' meant under such influence as to disturb the balance of the mind; on the evidence this was not the case here. (2) The declaration of abstinence was not an undertaking by the defendant as to future conduct and the insurers were not excepted from liability by a breach of the declaration.

Lorry — includes removed engine

Seaton v London General Insurance Co Ltd
(1932) 48 TLR 574, 76 Sol Jo 527, 43 Ll L Rep 398 (du Parcq J)

Assured removed the engine of his motor lorry to his carpenter's shop 150 yards away for repair, and while there it was destroyed by fire. The proposal form stated the lorry would be garaged on assured's own premises.

HELD: Insurer liable. The engine and the rest of the lorry together were still the lorry insured.

'Loss or damage': unauthorised driver

Greenleaf Associated Ltd v Monksfield
[1972] RTR 451, [1972] 2 Lloyd's Rep 79

A policy issued by the defendant underwriter to the plaintiff indemnified against 'loss of or damage to the insured car'. A general exception excluded liability in respect of 'any accident injury loss damage or liability . . . caused sustained or incurred while (the car) is being driven by any person' not specified in the statutory certificate 'which is deemed to be incorporated herein'. The only persons specified in the certificate were Mr and Mrs B. The car was damaged when being driven by a mechanic who had taken it on a joy ride without the insured's consent.

HELD: The plaintiffs were not entitled to indemnity for the damage to the car. It had been argued that if the car was being driven without the insured's consent the exception did not apply because the words 'with the consent of the insured' ought to be read into it; but there was no reason for inserting in the policy words that were not there. There was no ambiguity in regard to 'loss' while the vehicle was being driven by an unauthorised person even though the policy covered theft, since there could be no 'loss' by theft in the way of damage to the vehicle because the theft occurred at the moment of taking: 'loss' meant physical not financial loss.

Motor car

Laurence v Davies
[1972] 2 Lloyd's Rep 231 (Dunn J)
The defendant was insured for use of his motor car by a policy which extended cover to him additionally against third-party claims arising from accidents caused by or in connection with 'the driving by the insured of any motor car . . . not belonging to him . . .'. He was driving a Ford Transit van not belonging to him when there was an accident in which the plaintiff was injured. The defendant's insurers refused to indemnify him on the ground that the van was not a 'motor car'. The defendant relied on the definition in the Road Traffic Act 1960, s 253(2) (now s 190(2) of the 1972 Act): ' "motor car" means a mechanically propelled vehicle, not being a motor cycle or invalid carriage, which is constructed itself to carry a load or passengers and the weight of which unladen . . . does not exceed three tons'.

HELD: The van was a motor car. The words had to be considered in the context of motor insurance. If motor insurers wished to put some meaning on words like 'motor car' other than those contained in the Road Traffic Act they should make it abundantly clear in the policy; if they failed to do so the words would be deemed to have the statutory meanings.

Non-compliance with condition

Walker v Pennine Insurance Co Ltd
[1979] 2 Lloyd's Rep 139 (Sheen J) affd, [1980] 2 Lloyd's Rep 156, CA
On 5 August 1970 Miss W, a passenger in the plaintiff's car, was seriously injured in an accident. The plaintiff was insured under a policy issued by the defendants indemnifying him against liability at law for damages in respect of bodily injury to any person. The policy contained a condition. 'If the company shall disclaim liability to the insured for any claim hereunder and if within 12 calendar months from the date of such disclaimer legal proceedings have not been instituted . . . in respect thereof by the insured . . . then the claim shall for all purposes be deemed to have been

abandoned . . .'. In November 1970 Miss W's solicitors wrote the plaintiff claiming damages for her but he did not reply nor tell the defendants. The solicitors then wrote notifying the claim to the defendants themselves who on making investigations decided not to indemnify the plaintiff because, they maintained, he was in breach of a policy condition as to the roadworthiness of the car at the time of the accident. They notified him through the brokers on 3 February 1971 that they would not meet the claim. On 17 February 1971 the plaintiff's solicitors wrote the defendants denying the alleged breach of condition and saying the plaintiff expected to be indemnified. The defendants replied on 22 March 1971 maintaining their refusal. They nominated solicitors to accept service of proceedings against themselves but the plaintiff took no further step to enforce indemnity for nearly four years. Meanwhile Miss W took proceedings against the plaintiff who did nothing about them until she had obtained judgment in default of appearance and in 1975 was about to have damages assessed. In July 1975 the plaintiff's solicitors wrote the defendants seeking to revive the claim for indemnity. The defendants denied liability on the ground that he had not instituted proceedings against them within one year of their refusal to indemnify.

HELD: (1) The defendants' letter of the 22 March 1971 quite clearly disclaimed liability under the policy and no proceedings had been started against them within a year thereafter. It was not a breach of the contract. The refusal to indemnify was on the terms of the contract. (2) It was not necessary that the amount of the claim should be known before it constituted a claim under the policy. The defendants were not liable. An appeal was dismissed. 'I would be content in this case wholly to adopt the judgment of the Learned Judge upon which . . . I could not hope to improve' (per Roskill LJ).

Personal luggage

Buckland v R

[1933] 1 KB 329, 49 TLR 39, 76 Sol Jo 850 (McCardie J); affd [1933] 1 KB 767, 102 LJKB 404, 148 LT 557, 49 TLR 244, CA

There is no distinction between 'ordinary luggage' and 'passengers' luggage' and 'personal luggage'.

The court called attention to various decisions which are difficult to reconcile as follows:

Held to be personal luggage: All articles of apparel, whether for use or ornament, the gun case or fishing apparatus of the sportsman, the easel of the artist on a sketching tour, the books of the student, officer's revolver and binoculars.

Held not to be personal luggage: Title deeds carried by a solicitor; truck containing six pairs of sheets, six pairs of blankets, and six quilts; violin-cello carried for professional purposes; the pencil sketches of an artist; hamper containing professional costumes and property of a comedian; sewing machine, invalid chair, bicycle.

The definition adopted by the court was 'articles intended for the traveller's personal use and convenience as distinct from merchandise carried for purposes of business'.

Note—Compare with *Piddington v Co-operative Insurance*, p 833, above.

Records — trader's policy

Laycock v Road Transport and General Insurance Co
(1940) 67 Ll L Rep 250 (Singleton J)
A motor trader's policy and certificate were subject to a proviso that the
make, horse power, registered number and date and time of departure
have been prior to each and every departure of such vehicle from the
premises or garage recorded in a special register kept by the policyholder
for the purposes of the policy. Some or all of the said particulars were not so
recorded.
SEMBLE: Insurers were not liable to a third party.

Written words in printed document

Where an instrument is in a printed form with written additions or
alterations, the written words (subject always to be governed in point of
construction by the language and terms with which they are accompanied)
are entitled, in case of reasonable doubt as to the meaning of the whole, to
have a greater effect attributed to them than the printed words: *Halsbury's
Laws of England* (2nd edn) vol 10, p 279. Cited in *Addis v Burrows* [1948] 1
KB 444, [1948] 1 All ER 177, [1948] LJR 1033, 64 TLR 169, 92 Sol Jo
124, CA. See now *Halsbury* (4th edn) vol 12, p 634.

---

2 DOUBLE INSURANCE

Note—The right of contribution in a case of double insurance is said to be part of
the general law relating to guarantees. In *Halsbury's Laws of England* (4th edn)
vol 20, p 120, in dealing with Guarantees and the Right to Contribution, the rule
is given as follows:

'A surety who has paid more than his share of the common liability is entitled to
compel contribution from his co-sureties, whether they are bound jointly and
severally, or severally, and by the same or different instruments, and whether the
surety claiming contribution did or did not know, when he became bound as such,
that he was co-surety with others. The right to contribution is not founded on
contract, but is the result of the general equity arising at the inception of the
contract of guarantee on the ground of equality of burden and benefit. In
determining whether a relationship is that of principal and surety, giving rise to
contribution among co-sureties, the substance of the transaction must be
considered and the form of the instrument creating it may in a proper case be
wholly disregarded. Where parties are not liable to a common demand there is no
right of contribution between them' (paras 220 and 221).

The rule in non-marine insurance is given at p 266 of vol 22 of *Halsbury's Laws of
England* (3rd edn) (repeated in substantially the same terms at p 285 of the 4th edn,
vol 25) as follows:

'The assured is at liberty subject to any policy conditions to the contrary to effect as
many policies as he pleases, but, where the contract is one of indemnity, he cannot,

however numerous the policies may be, recover more than the amount of his loss. Apart from any condition in the policy, he is entitled to claim payment in full under any of the policies, leaving the insurers under that policy to claim contribution from their co-insurers. Most policies of non-marine insurance contain a contribution clause limiting the liability of the insurers to their rateable proportion of the loss. In this case the assured cannot claim payment in full under any of the policies; each policy is liable for its rateable proportion only. To give rise to a right of contribution, each policy must cover the loss of the same property by the same peril; there is no contribution unless there is a common loss caused by a peril common to the policies' (paras 527 and 528).

In a case in practice a building contractor employed by a local authority gave an indemnity to the authority on similar lines to the indemnity clause in *London and North Eastern Rly Co v Furness Shipbuilding Co* (1934) 103 LJKB 180, 150 LT 382, 48 Ll L Rep 1, HL. A workman employed by the contractor was injured by the negligence of the driver of a motor vehicle of the authority. The workman claimed damages from the authority and the claim was paid by the motor insurers, who by right of subrogation claimed indemnity from the contractor under the indemnity clause. It was agreed that this was a case of double indemnity and the insurer was entitled to a rateable contribution (agreed at one-half) and not reimbursement of the full amount.

See also *Austin v Zurich Insurance Co*, p 855, above.

Pro rata contribution clause

If at the time of loss or damage happening to any property insured by this policy, there be any other subsisting insurance or insurances, whether effected by the insured, or by any other person, covering the same property or any part thereof, this policy shall not be liable to pay or contribute in respect of such loss or damage more than its rateable proportion of the aggregate liability under all the insurances covering such property.

Non-contribution clause

This insurance does not cover any loss or damage which at the time of the happening of such loss or damage is insured by or would, but for the existence of this policy, be insured by any other existing policy or policies except in respect of any excess beyond the amount which would have been payable under such other policy or policies had this insurance not been effected.

Gale v Motor Union Insurance Co Ltd
Loyst v General Accident Fire and Life Assurance Corpn Ltd
[1928] 1 KB 359, 96 LJKB 199, 38 LT 712, 43 TLR 15, 70 Sol Jo 1140, 26 Ll L Rep 65 (Roche J)

G took with the M Co a motor car insurance policy covering himself and any friend driving with G's consent and providing as follows: 'Condition 6. The extension of the indemnity to friends or relatives of the insured is conditional upon such friend or relative being a licensed and competent driver and not being insured under any other policy. Condition 10. If at the happening of any accident, injury, damage or loss covered by this policy there shall be subsisting any other insurance or indemnity of any nature whatever covering same, whether effected by insured or by any other person, then the company shall not be liable to pay or contribute towards any such damages or loss more than a reateable proportion of any sum payable in respect thereof for compensation.' L, G's brother-in-law, took out with the G Co a similar policy, providing that 'insured will also be indemnified hereunder while personally driving a car not belonging to him provided that there is no other insurance in respect of such other car whereby insured may be indemnified', and that 'if at the time of the occurrence of any accident, loss or damage, there shall be any other indemnity or insurance subsisting, whether effected by insured or by any other person, the corporation shall not be liable to pay or contribute more than a rateable proportion of any sums payable in respect of such accident, loss or damage'. While L was driving G's car with G's consent it had a collision and L had to pay damages. G, as trustee for L, claimed against the M Co and L, on his own behalf, claimed against the G Co.

HELD: In each policy the provision as to rateable contribution qualified the preceding clause, and each company was liable to pay claimants half the amount claimed.

Portavon Cinema Co v Price and Century Insurance Co Ltd
[1939] 4 All ER 601, 161 LT 417, 84 Sol Jo 152, 65 Ll L Rep 161 (Branson J)
This clause (non-contribution) should be applied only to cases which are strictly cases of double insurance.

Weddell v Road Transport and General Insurance Co Ltd
[1932] 2 KB 563, 101 LJKB 620, 146 LT 162, 48 TLR 59, 75 Sol Jo 852, 41 Ll L Rep 69 (Rowlatt J)
A motor car accident policy issued by the respondent company to J. R. W. extended the insurance to a relative driving the car provided that the latter was not entitled to indemnity for the same risk under another policy. L. W. W., a relative of J. R. W., while driving the car, injured a third party, who claimed damages. L. W. W. was himself insured with the C insurance company against claims for injuries caused by him while driving a car not belonging to him, provided that he was not entitled to an indemnity in respect thereof from another company. The respondents denied liability on the ground of the proviso in their policy exempting them where the claimant was entitled to indemnity under another policy.

HELD: On the proper construction of the policies, the insurance clause in each policy expressed to be cancelled by the co-existence of a similar clause in the other policy should be excluded from the category of co-existing cover, and that therefore the respondents, not being protected by their proviso, were liable.

Note—Weddell's case and *Gale's* case (above) were approved in *Steelclad Ltd v Iron Trades Mutual Insurance Co Ltd* 1984 SLT 304.

National Employers Mutual General Insurance Association Ltd v Hayden
[1979] 2 Lloyd's Rep 235 (Lloyd J); [1980] 2 Lloyd's Rep 149, CA
A firm of solicitors were covered, in respect of a claim against them for

professional negligence, by two policies of insurance. The first, issued by the plaintiff company, contained a clause: 'This policy does not indemnify the insured in respect of any claim made against him for which the insured is or would but for the existence of this policy be entitled to indemnity under any other policy except in respect of any excess beyond the amount payable by such other policy.' The second had a provision: 'This insurance shall not indemnify the assured in respect of any loss arising out of any claim in respect of any circumstance or occurrence which has been notified under any other insurance.'

HELD: There was dual insurance. Both clauses were exceptions clauses even though one was narrower than the other, but even if they were not exclusion clauses in the strict sense but clauses restricting cover, it would still be impossible to distinguish between them. By giving effect to both clauses neither policy would pay. In those circumstances the principle in *Weddell's* case (above) should be applied: if each policy would cover but for the existence of the other then the exclusions are treated as cancelling each other out. The plaintiffs were entitled to contribution.

Note—The defendant appealed and the appeal was allowed. The principle of *Weddell's* case, said the Court, was not in doubt but it could only apply where an insured is covered by both policies, were it not for the excluding clauses. On the construction of the policies in the present case, however, there was no co-existing cover. The two policies were not concurrent but consecutive. The NEM were alone liable. ([1980] 2 Lloyd's Rep 149, CA).

See also the decision of Tucker J on this point in *Austin v Zurich Insurance Co*, p 855, above.

A case in practice arose where the assured had failed to give notice of the loss to one insurer and that insurer was in consequence not liable to the assured. The question was whether that insurer was nevertheless liable on the principle of dual insurance.

The case went to arbitration. The arbitrator held there does not appear to be any direct authority and considered the question to be 'Is the right of contribution an independent right arising as between insurers or merely a benefit accruing to the insurer who pays by subrogation?' The principle does not seem to have been dealt with since *Newby v Reed* (1763) 1 Wm Bl 416, and *Rogers v Davies* (1777) 2 Park *Marine Insces* 8th Edn 601. He considered that the principle of natural justice as between co-insurers was the principle to be applied and not subrogation, and that the right of contribution is an independent right of the insurer against his co-insurer which arises as a contingent right when the loss occurs though not enforceable until payment is made. This view is supported by the Marine Insurance Act 1906, s 80. Being an independent right, the failure of the assured to comply with a policy condition cannot take away that right. On the basis of apportionment, he referred to *American Surety Co of New York v Wrightson* (1910) 103 LT 663, 27 TLR 91, 16 Com Cas 37. But see next case.

Breach of condition of one policy — effect

Monksfield v Vehicle and General Insurance Co Ltd

[1971] 1 Lloyd's Rep 139, Mayor's and City of London Court

P was involved in an accident when driving a car belonging to W. He was insured under a policy issued to himself by the plaintiff, a member of Lloyds, who dealt with and paid the third party claim. W had a policy issued by the defendants which extended to cover P but neither P nor W reported the claim to them nor claimed indemnity under that policy. Each policy had a term excluding cover if the driver was entitled to indemnity under any other policy, so that, other considerations apart, there was dual insurance as in *Weddell's* case (above). A condition in W's policy required the insured to give notice in writing to the company as soon as possible after the occurrence of any accident, but the defendants did not hear of the accident until eight months later.

HELD: The fact that there had been a breach of condition of their policy by failing to report the accident relieved the defendants of the liability to make contribution. They would clearly have been in a position to repudiate a claim by W; it could not be an equitable result that insurers who had no notice of the accident and had no say in the handling of the claim should be called upon to make a contribution when they would have been entitled to repudiate if the claim had been brought under the terms of their own policy.

---

3 INSURER, INSURED AND THIRD PARTIES

Excess clause

Beacon Insurance Co Ltd v Langdale
[1939] 4 All ER 204, 83 Sol Jo 908, 65 Ll L Rep 57, CA

A motor policy covering third party risks contained a condition that the company should be entitled, if it so desired, to take over and conduct in the name of the assured the defence or settlement of any claim and should have full discretion in the settlement of any claim. The policy was subject to a £5 excess.

The company settled a third-party claim by a cyclist without the express sanction of the assured and also against his view of the rights of the matter, as he wished to claim against the third party. The company made what they believed to be, in his interests and theirs, an advantageous settlement, and they were at pains to show that the settlement should be made with a denial of liability, so that no one could say that they had admitted any culpability whatever on his behalf. The assured contended that the company were not entitled to settle the claim without notice to him and that they had not acted reasonably in the exercise of their authority.

HELD (distinguishing *Groom v Crocker*, p 898, below): The policy gave the company power to settle the claim without consulting the assured, and the assured was liable to pay the company the £5 excess.

Knock for knock agreement

Morley v Moore
[1936] 2 KB 359, [1936] 2 All ER 79, 105 LJKB 421, 154 LT 646, 52 TLR 510, 80 Sol Jo 424, 55 Ll L Rep 10, CA

The plaintiff was insured for damage to his car bearing a £5 excess. The car damage was £33 2s 8d, and his insurers paid the £28 2s 8d. Plaintiff sued for £33 2s 8d. Defendants pleaded the 'knock for knock' agreement and that plaintiff only entitled to receive £5.

HELD: Plaintiff entitled to recover £33 2s 8d, but he would hold £28 2s 8d as trustee for his insurers, they being subrogated in his rights. The 'knock for knock' agreement does not prevent a plaintiff who has been paid for damage to his car by his own insurers from suing the negligent party for such damage in spite of a direction from his own insurers that they do not want him to claim it. The insurers are entitled to be subrogated but had no right to forbid the assured from exercising his common law right against the wrongdoer.

Bourne v Stanbridge
[1965] 1 All ER 241, [1965] 1 WLR 189, 108 Sol Jo 991, CA
In an action in the county court the plaintiff claimed £230 being the cost of repairs to his car, damaged in a collision with the defendant's car. His driver being found two-thirds to blame he recovered only £76 being one-third of the amount claimed. When the judge was considering costs, counsel for the defendant revealed that, as the plaintiff knew before proceedings, there was a knock for knock agreement between the plaintiff's and defendant's insurers and that the only sum in respect of repairs for which the plaintiff was liable was his excess of £10. The judge then awarded the plaintiff his costs only on Scale 2 and not on Scale 3.

HELD: Though the judge had a discretion under the County Court Rules, Ord 47, r 1 he had not exercised it on a right principle. The plaintiff was quite entitled to bring an action for the whole amount of the damage as *Morley v Moore* (above) shows; the knock for knock agreement between insurers was not a matter which he should have considered as of any relevance in respect of the award of costs.

Note—But see next case.

Hobbs v Marlowe
[1978] AC 16, [1977] 2 All ER 241, [1977] 2 WLR 777, 121 Sol Jo 272, [1977] RTR 253, HL
The plaintiff's car was damaged in a collision for which the defendant was wholly to blame. The cost of repairs at £237.59 (less the excess) was paid by the plaintiff's insurers, who were parties to a knock for knock agreement with the defendant's insurers. The plaintiff's uninsured loss amounted to £73.53 which was not enough under the County Court Rules to entitle him to an award of costs (except the court fee) in an action against the defendant. His solicitors, solely to obtain an award of their costs, sued on his behalf for the whole of the cost of the repairs and uninsured losses, ie £301.12. On payment of a judgment for the whole amount the defendant's insurers would be entitled under the knock for knock agreement to payment of £227.59 from the plaintiff's insurers who would then recover that sum from the plaintiff. In county court proceedings the defendant (by his insurers) admitted liability and paid into Court £73.53. The judge, following *Morley v Moore* (above) gave judgment for the whole amount claimed but in awarding costs held that the inflation of the claim solely for

costs was an abuse of the process of the court and awarded only the costs appropriate to an award of £73.53, ie the court fee of £7.50.

HELD, ON APPEAL to the House of Lords: (1) *Morley v Moore* was rightly decided and the plaintiff was not precluded from suing for the full amount of the damages by reason of the fact that he had already received a large part of that sum from his insurers. (2) The judge's exercise of his discretion on the award of costs was a proper one and there were no grounds for an appellate court to interfere with it. *Bourne v Stanbridge* (above) should be regarded as wrongly decided.

Limited indemnity — costs

Note—If a policy indemnity is limited to a named figure, and litigation is begun, and the damages are likely to exceed the indemnity, the business plan is to pay over the limit, otherwise the costs of litigation must also be paid.

Allen v London Guarantee and Accident Co Ltd
(1912) 28 TLR 254

By a policy of insurance, defendants insured the assured in respect of accidents caused by his employees when in charge of his horse-drawn vehicle. The total liability of defendants was limited to £300 for all claims for compensation and costs, charges and expense, paid or payable in respect of or arising out of any accident or occurrence, and defendants were to be entitled, in the name and on behalf of the assured, to take over and have the absolute control of all negotiations and proceedings which might arise in respect of any accidents or claim. There was a further provision that defendants might pay the maximum to the assured in the case of any one accident or occurrence or occurrences and thereupon their liability in respect of that accident or occurrence should cease; but if the assured wished defendants to continue the defence he should pay and make good all costs and expenses incurred thereby. Two persons who had been injured by an accident caused by a cart belonging to the assured brought actions against him claiming damages. The assured gave notice thereof to defendants, and they defended the actions, the assured, not being consulted having nothing to say as to the advisability of defending the actions. The actions resulted in verdicts against the assured for £200 and £175, respectively. The costs in these actions recoverable by two plaintiffs against the assured amounted to £218; and as he did not pay those costs an execution was levied on his goods and to get rid of this he had to pay the £218, which he now claimed from the defendants.

HELD: Although there were two accidents there was only one 'occurrence' within the meaning of the policy, and therefore defendants' limit of £300 applied; but defendants having defended the actions in the name of the assured without his consent they incurred a common law liability for the costs, and were therefore liable to repay the £218, which the assured had been compelled to pay.

Knight v Hosken
(1943) 75 Ll L Rep 74

Underwriters issued to an estate agent a policy indemnifying against negligence limited to £2,000. An action was brought against the assured claiming £3,700. Underwriters by their solicitors defended the action, and invited the assured to contribute seventeen-thirty-sevenths of the costs of defence. The assured agreed to contribute towards the costs of defence in the event of damages being awarded in excess of £2,000 which event happened.

HELD, by Atkinson J (72 Ll L Rep 206) and upheld in the Court of Appeal: There was no promise for a consideration and the assured was under no liability to contribute. Underwriters defended the action primarily for their own benefit.

Subrogation

Burnand v Rodocanachi
(1882) 7 App Cas 333, 51 LJQB 548, 47 LT 277, 31 WR 65, 4 Asp MLC 576, HL

Castellain v Preston
(1883) 11 QBD 380, 52 LJQB 366, 49 LT 29, 31 WR 557, CA

The general rule of law is that when there is a contract of indemnity and a loss happens, anything which reduces or diminishes that loss reduces or diminishes the amount which the indemnifier is bound to pay, and if the indemnifier has already paid it then if anything which diminishes the loss comes into the hands of the person to whom he has paid it, it becomes an equity that the person who has already paid the full indemnity is entitled to be recouped by having that amount back.

John Edwards & Co v Motor Union Insurance Co
[1922] 2 KB 249, 91 LJKB 921, 128 LT 276, 38 TLR 690, 16 Asp MLC 89, 27 Com Cas 367. McCardie J said:

The doctrine of subrogation was derived by our English Courts from the system of Roman law, and has been widely applied in our English body of law, e g to sureties and to matters of ultra vires as well as to insurance. In connection with insurance it was recognised ere the beginning of the eighteenth century. In *Randal v Cockran* (1784) 1 Ves Sen 98, it was held that the plaintiffs' insurers after making satisfaction stood in the place of the assured as to goods, salvage, and restitution in proportion for what they paid. As the Lord Chancellor (Lord Hardwicke) said: 'The plaintiffs had the plainest equity that could be.'

It is curious to observe how this doctrine of subrogative equity gradually entered into the substance of insurance law and at length became a recognised part of several branches of the general common law. In *Mason v Sainsbury* (1782) 3 Doug KB 61 at 64 Lord Mansfield said: 'Every day the insurer is put in the place of the insured', and Buller J, in the same case, in approving judgment for the plaintiff insurer, said: 'Whether this case be considered on strict legal principles, or upon the more liberal principles of insurance law, the plaintiff is entitled to recover.' These more liberal principles were based on equitable considerations, and in the well-known case of *Burnand v Rodocanachi* (1882) 7 App Cas 333 at 339, Lord Blackburn said in reference to a marine policy: 'If the indemnifier has already paid it, then, if anything which diminishes the loss comes into the hands of the person to whom he has paid it, it becomes an equity that the person who has already paid the full indemnity is entitled to be recouped by having that amount back.' This equity springs I conceive solely from the fact that the ordinary and valid contract of marine insurance is a contract of indemnity only. The point was put most clearly by Brett LJ in *Castellain v Preston* (1883) 11 QBD 380 at 386, when he said: 'The very foundation, in my opinion, of every rule which has been applied to insurance law is this, namely, that the contract of insurance contained in a marine or fire policy is a contract of indemnity, and of indemnity only.' That is the principle embodied in the Marine Insurance Act 1906, s 79.

If then subrogation is based on indemnity it is well to consider the features flowing from subrogation. This matter is neatly stated in *Porter on Insurance* (6th edn) p 236, as follows: 'This right rests upon the ground that the insurer's contract is in the nature of a contract of indemnity, and that he is therefore entitled, upon paying a sum for which others are primarily liable to the assured, to be proportionably subrogated to the right of action of the assured against them.' See, too, *Arnould on Marine Insurance* (10th edn) vol ii, s 1226, and *MacGillivray on Insurance* p 733. If once the claim be paid then as a matter of equity the rights to recover against third persons pass from the assured to the insurer although the legal right to compensation remains in the assured and although actions at law must be brought in the name of the assured and not of the insurer: see *London Assurance Co v Sainsbury* (1783) 3 Doug KB 245 at 254; *King v Victoria Insurance Co* [1896] AC 250, 65 LJPC 38, 74 LT 206, 44 WR 592, 12 TLR 285. As pointed out in *MacGillivray* p 740, it follows from this equity that if the assured upon tender of a proper indemnity as to costs refuse the use of his name the insurer can by proceedings in equity compel him to give the use of his name. This has long been settled law.

Morris v Ford Motor Co Ltd
[1973] QB 792, [1973] 2 All ER 1084, [1973] 2 WLR 843, 117 Sol Jo 393, [1973] 2 Lloyd's Rep 27, CA
As a term of a contract to perform cleaning services for the Ford Motor Company, Cameron Industrial Services agreed to indemnify Fords against all claims made by inter alios their own employees arising from negligence on the part of Ford's employees. Morris, an employee of Cameron was injured by the negligence of Roberts, an employee of Fords. His claim was met by Fords, who claimed indemnity from Cameron. Admitting their liability to indemnify Fords, Cameron sued Roberts, claiming to do so in right of subrogation to the rights of Fords to claim against their employee as in *Lister's* case. Evidence was given that Fords never sued their servants because to do so would be to court industrial action in the form of strikes: serious industrial repercussions would follow if they entered into contracts under the terms of which their servants might be sued by others in their name.
HELD: A right of subrogation arises from the very nature of the contract of indemnity itself and not from any implied term in the contract, but it can be excluded expressly or by implication. In the present case of an agreement operative in an industrial setting in which employers never sue their servants because of likely industrial repercussions a term of the contract was to be implied that the right of subrogation was excluded.

Scottish Union and National Insurance Co v Davis
[1970] 1 Lloyd's Rep 1, CA

The plaintiffs insured the defendant's car under a comprehensive policy. It was damaged by a third party and was sent to coachbuilders for repair. They did not do the work well and the defendant twice returned the car for them to make good the repair without the job being done satisfactorily. An engineer advised that the work done was so bad that it would cost more to put right than the original estimate. The defendant complained several times to the plaintiffs' branch representative and did not sign a satisfaction note. Despite this the plaintiffs paid the repairers' bill of £409. Later the defendant recovered £350 from a third party in respect of the original damage. The plaintiffs claimed this sum on the principle of subrogation. HELD: The only basis on which the alleged subrogation could be put forward was that the plaintiffs had fully indemnified the defendant; but they had done nothing of the kind. The attempts to repair the car had been quite valueless and the payment of £409 by the plaintiffs to the repairers was not a payment for the successful doing of the repairs under the policy at all. Even if it was unreasonable of the defendant not to allow the repairers to make yet another effort to make good their work (and it could not be held that he was) it was irrelevant to the right of subrogation. Judgment for the defendant.

Note—See also *Haigh v Lawford*, p 680, above.

Yorkshire Insurance Co Ltd v Nisbet Shipping Co Ltd
[1962] 2 QB 330, [1961] 2 All ER 487, [1961] 2 WLR 1043, 105 Sol Jo 367, [1961] 1 Lloyd's Rep 479 (Diplock J)

The 'Blairnevis' became a total loss after a collision with the 'Orkney' in 1945. The insurers paid the owners the agreed value of £72,000 for a total loss. The owners then sued the owners of the 'Orkney' in Canada and recovered $336,000 being the value of the 'Blairnevis' in 1945 at $4.45 to the £1 sterling which was the rate of exchange at that time. The sum was paid to the owners in Canada in 1958 and when transmitted to England realised £127,000 at the current rate of exchange. The insurers claimed to be entitled to the whole sum of £127,000 from the owners and not merely to the £72,000 they had paid under the policy. HELD: The insurers were entitled to the amount they had paid under the policy and no more.

Indemnity or insurance

Solicitors' and General Life Assurance Society v Lamb
(1864) 2 De G J & Sm 251, 4 New Rep 313, 33 LJCh 426, 10 LT 702
Dane v Mortgage Insurance Corpn Ltd
[1894] 1 QB 54, 63 LJQB 144, 70 LT 83, 10 TLR 86

The principle operates when there is a contract of indemnity but does not apply to insurances which are not contracts of indemnity.

Meacock v Bryant
[1942] 2 All ER 661, 167 LT 371, 59 TLR 51, 74 Ll L Rep 53 (Atkinson J)
The question whether a contingency policy was one of indemnity or not
was contested and it was held that subrogation applied.

Note—And see decision of Tucker J in *Austin v Zurich Insurance Co,* p 855, above.

Motor repairs — insurer not agent of insured

Godfrey Davis Ltd v Culling and Hecht
[1962] 2 Lloyd's Rep 349, 106 Sol Jo 918, CA
The defendants, insured by the Brandaris Insurance Company, sustained
damage to their car. They delivered the car to the plaintiffs, motor
repairers, who sent them an estimate for repairs costing £160 and invited
instructions from them or their insurers. The defendants sent the estimate
to the Brandaris who instructed assessors to inspect the damage. The
assessors wrote the plaintiffs saying they would make an examination 'on
behalf of [the defendants'] insurers' and after inspection wrote the plaintiffs
confirming that it would be in order for them to proceed with the repairs in
accordance with the estimate and to send the final account for the repairs to
the Brandaris. When the repairs were done the defendants collected the car
from the plaintiffs who charged them only the £10 excess under the policy
and an agreed payment for a new tyre. The Brandaris went into liquidation
and the plaintiffs received no payment from that company for the work
done. They then sought in this action to make the defendants liable for the
whole cost of the repairs.
HELD: An insurer is not by necessary implication an agent of the insured
in arranging for repairs to be done. On the letters which passed in this case
it was clear that the insurers had themselves made a contract with the plaintiffs to do the repairs. There was no holding out and no circumstances from
which an agency could be implied. There is no general rule of law that
when an insured person surrenders or subrogates to the insurer all his
rights and liabilities over a particular accident giving rise to a claim that
what the insurer thereafter does he does as agent of the insured person: that
depends entirely on the terms of the policy or some express or ostensible
authority. The defendants were not liable.

Cooter and Green Ltd v Tyrrell
[1962] 2 Lloyd's Rep 377, CA
The defendant's car was damaged in an accident. His father asked the
plaintiffs, who were motor repairers, for an estimate of the cost of
the repairs. The plaintiffs sent a provisional estimate which was sent on to
the defendant's insurers. The plaintiffs knew the estimate was required for
the insurers, who instructed assessors to inspect the car. As a result and at
the request of the assessors, a revised estimate was prepared and sent to
them by the plaintiffs. The assessors wrote in reply confirming their
inspection on behalf of the insurers, approving the estimate, and
confirming that repairs might proceed accordingly. The letter asked the
insurers to collect the excess of £15 from the defendant and said the
insurers' net liability would be £241: they asked for a satisfaction note and

account to be forwarded to them. The repairs were shortly afterwards completed: they had been started before the assessors' letter was received because the plaintiffs knew the defendant and his father personally and the defendant had frequently telephoned asking them to expedite the work. He eventually signed the satisfaction note after trying the car. The insurers shortly afterwards became insolvent and failed to pay the plaintiffs' account for the repairs. The plaintiffs then sued the defendant for the whole cost of the repairs. The policy contained a provision: 'The company may at its own option repair . . . such motor car . . . or may pay in cash the amount of loss or damage . . . .'.

HELD: The defendant was not liable. The letter from the assessors was an offer which was accepted by the conduct of the plaintiffs in completing the repairs and complying with the request for the satisfaction note and account to be sent to the assessors. There was a binding contract between the plaintiffs and the insurers and no one else. The insurers had exercised their choice under the policy by electing to place their own contract for the repairs. The father's request for an estimate was not the same as an order for the work: the final estimate was not discussed with the defendant at all and his telephone calls gave rise to no inference which could affect the contract.

Brown and Davis Ltd v Galbraith

[1972] 3 All ER 31, [1972] 1 WLR 997, 116 Sol Jo 545, [1972] 2 Lloyd's Rep 1, [1972] RTR 523, CA

The owner of a car damaged in an accident took it to repairers telling them it was comprehensively insured and asking for an estimate of the cost of repair. The estimate was sent to him a few days later. He also notified his insurers who sent their assessor to see the repairers. Agreement was reached between assessor and insurer on the cost of repairs and a printed form was filled in by the assessor which inter alia notified the repairers of the need for them to collect the £25 excess from the owner. The repairs were then carried out and an invoice sent by the repairers to the insurers, though without a signed satisfaction note from the owner, as he was not satisfied with the work done. He had some work done to the car elsewhere (the cost of which he deducted from the excess) and then took the signed satisfaction note to the repairers. By that time the insurers had gone into liquidation and the repairers were not paid. They sued the owner for the whole cost of the repairs.

HELD: There were two contracts involved, one between the repairers and the insurers whereby the insurers undertook to pay for the repairs and one between the owner and repairers (to be implied from his having taken the vehicle to them for repair) by which the repairers undertook to carry out the work expeditiously (as in *Charnock v Liverpool Corpn*, p 884, below). But there was nothing from which in the contract between the owner and repairers a term could be implied that the owner had a liability to pay for the repairs beyond the amount of the excess. The facts of the case were clearly parallel with those in *Godfrey Davis Ltd v Culling and Hecht* (p 882, above) and *Cooter and Green v Tyrrell* (above) and there was nothing in the judgments in *Charnock's* case to controvert the principles applied in either of those cases.

Kirklands Garage (Kinrose) Ltd v Clark
1967 SLT (Sh Ct) 60

The pursuers carried out repairs to the defender's car on the instructions of insurance assessors after the defender had filled in a claim form from his insurers. He signed a satisfaction note and collected the car. The insurers did not pay for the repairs and subsequently went into liquidation. The pursuers claimed that as the defender's name appeared on documents passing between them, the assessors and the insurers, it proved that the insurers were acting as the defender's agents in ordering the repairs.

HELD: So far as the documents went the defender's name appeared only as a reference; the insurers appeared to be acting as principals and made no disclosure that they were to be treated as agents of the defender. That being so the pursuers could not succeed unless there was a general rule of law that insurers are always acting as agents for the insured in instructing repairs. *Godfrey Davis Ltd v Culling and Hecht* and *Cooter and Green v Tyrrell* (above) show that there is no such rule.

A contrary decision

Martin v Stannard
[1964] CLY 585, Cty Ct (Judge Dow)

The plaintiff carried out repairs to the defendant's motor vehicle at the defendant's request after his insurance company had sent an assessor to inspect the damage and had intimated by telephone through the defendant's insurance brokers, that the work could proceed on the plaintiff's estimate of £138. After carrying out the work the plaintiff released the vehicle to the defendant on receiving an assurance over the telephone from the insurance brokers that if the defendant signed a satisfaction note the insurance company would pay. On the insurers becoming insolvent without paying, the plaintiff claimed the £138 from the defendant.

HELD: The contract for the repairs was between the plaintiff and the defendant (who had received the benefit of them), the insurance company being merely in the position of a guarantor. The plaintiff was entitled to recover the £138 from the defendant.

REPAIRER'S LIABILITY TO INSURED

Charnock v Liverpool Corpn
[1968] 3 All ER 473, [1968] 1 WLR 1498, 112 Sol Jo 781, [1968] 2 Lloyd's Rep 113, CA

The plaintiff's car was damaged in an accident by negligence of the first defendant's servant. He took the car to a garage where he wanted the repairs done and by arrangement met his insurer's assessor there. The repairers prepared an estimate and eventually the insurers wrote them: 'We confirm it is in order to proceed with the repairs as per your estimate. . . . Please forward your final account to this office on completion, together with a signed satisfaction note.' A reasonable period for doing the repairs was five weeks but the repairers took eight. The plaintiff hired a car for the whole of the eight weeks and sued the first defendants and the repairers for the costs. The first defendants were admittedly liable for five weeks' hire charges: the judge held the repairers liable for the other three on the ground that they had impliedly contracted with the plaintiff to do the repairs within a reasonable time and were in breach of that contract. HELD, ON APPEAL, by the repairers: The judge was right. The decisions in *Cooter and Green v Tyrrell* and *Godfrey Davis Ltd v Culling and Hecht* (above) did not decide that there was no contract of any sort between the owner and repairer. In those cases the question was whether the contract to pay for the repairs was made between the insurers and the repairers or between the owner and repairers. In the present case there was a clear contract to be inferred from the facts between the repairers and the plaintiff that in consideration of his leaving his car with them for repair they would carry out the repairs with reasonable expedition and care and that they would be paid by the insurance company. The repairers were in breach of this contract.

Note—See also *Hargreaves Vehicle Distributors v Holbrook*, p 366, above.

INSURER'S LIABILITY TO INSURED

Davidson v Guardian Royal Exchange Assurance
[1979] 1 Lloyd's Rep 406, Ct of Sess

Insurers issued a comprehensive motor policy covering 'loss of or damage to the vehicle' and containing a provision in the case of damage: 'The company may at its own option repair the vehicle'. There was an exemption from liability to pay for 'loss of use'. The insured's car was damaged by fire; the insurers elected to repair it and sent it away for this purpose. It was not returned repaired until 40 weeks had elapsed. A reasonable time for repair would have been eight weeks. The insured claimed damages for loss of use of the car.

HELD: (1) Having undertaken to repair the car the insurers were bound to do so within a reasonable time. There was a breach of this implied term for the period beyond the eighth week. (2) If there was any ambiguity in the policy the construction had to be *contra proferentem*. (3) The insured's claim in this action was based on breach of contract; the policy was not concerned with breach of contract and the exemption clause did not apply.

Total loss

Page v Scottish Insurance Corpn
(1929) 33 Ll L Rep (Scrutton J) 134, 98 LJKB 308, 140 LT 571, 45 TLR 250, 73 Sol Jo 236, CA

A condition of the assured's right to claim as for total loss is his obligation to surrender the subject matter of the insured risk to his insurers.

On abandonment the property and all its incidents pass to the underwriter to whom it is abandoned. I have known cases myself in my own practice where underwriters have made an extremely good thing by accepting abandonment because they have got something more than the amount they had to pay.

Third Parties (Rights against Insurers) Act 1930

The effect of the two decisions in *Re Harrington Motor Co Ltd* [1928] Ch 105, 97 LJCh 55, 138 LT 185, 44 TLR 58, and *Hood's Trustees v Southern Union General Insurance Co of Australasia* [1928] Ch 793, 97 LJCh 467, 139 LT 536, [1928] B & CR 95, CA was that the right of indemnity contained in a policy was property of the assured and passed to the liquidator or trustee on liquidation or bankruptcy. A third party who obtained a verdict from the assured did not obtain his damages, but the liquidator or trustee collected the money from the insurer and it was assets for distribution between all the creditors, and the third party had to share his claim with the other creditors.

These decisions resulted in the Third Parties (Rights against Insurers) Act 1930, as follows:

'**1 Rights of third parties against insurers on bankruptcy, etc of the insured**   (1) Where under any contract of insurance a person (hereinafter referred to as the insured) is insured against liabilities to third parties which he may incur, then —

(a) in the event of the insured becoming bankrupt or making a composition or arrangement with his creditors; or

(b) in the case of the insured being a company, in the event of a winding-up order being made, or a resolution for a voluntary winding-up being passed, with respect to the company, or of a receiver or manager of the company's business or undertaking being duly appointed, or of possession being taken, by or on behalf of the holders of any debentures secured by a floating charge, of any property comprised in or subject to the charge;

if, either before or after that event, any such liability as aforesaid is incurred by the insured, his rights against the insurer under the contract in respect of the liability shall, notwithstanding anything in any Act or rule of law to the contrary, be transferred to and vest in the third party to whom the liability was so incurred.

(2) Where an order is made under s 130 of the Bankruptcy Act 1914, for the administration of the estate of a deceased debtor according to the law of bankruptcy, then, if any debt provable in bankruptcy is owing by the deceased in respect of a liability against which he was insured under a contract of insurance as being a liability to a third party, the deceased debtor's rights against the insurer under the contract in respect of that liability shall, notwithstanding anything in the said Act, be transferred to and vest in the person to whom the debt is owing.

(3) In so far as any contract of insurance made after the commencement of this Act in respect of any liability of the insured to third parties purports, whether directly or indirectly, to avoid the contract or to alter the rights of the parties thereunder upon the happening to the insured of any of the events specified in para (a) or para (b) of sub-s (1) of this section or upon the making of an order under s 130 of the Bankruptcy Act 1914, in respect of his estate, the contract shall be of no effect.

(4) Upon a transfer under sub-s (1) or sub-s (3) of this section, the insurer shall, subject to the provisions of s 3 of this Act, be under the same liability to the third party as he would have been under to the insured, but —

(a) if the liability of the insurer to the insured exceeds the liability of the insured to the third party, nothing in this Act shall affect the rights of the insured against the insurer in respect of the excess; and

(b) if the liability of the insurer to the insured is less than the liability of the insured to the third party, nothing in this Act shall affect the rights of the third party against the insured in respect of the balance.

(5) For the purposes of this Act, the expression 'liabilities to third parties', in relation to a person insured under any contract of insurance shall not include any liability of that person in the capacity of insurer under some other contract of insurance.

(6) This Act shall not apply —

(a) where a company is wound up voluntarily merely for the purposes of reconstruction or of amalgamation with another company; or

(b) to any case to which sub-s (1) and (2) of section seven of the Workmen's Compensation Act 1925, applies.

2 Duty to give necessary information to third parties (1) In the event of any person becoming bankrupt or making a composition or arrangement with his creditors, or in the event of an order being made under s 130 of the Bankruptcy Act 1914, in respect of the estate of any person, or in the event of a winding-up order being made, or a resolution for a voluntary winding-up being passed, with respect to any company or of a receiver or manager of the company's business or undertaking being duly appointed or of possession being taken by or on behalf of the holders of any debentures secured by a floating charge of any property comprised in or subject to the charge it shall be the duty of the bankrupt, debtor, personal representative of the deceased debtor or company, and, as the case may be, of the trustee in bankruptcy, trustee, liquidator, receiver, or manager, or person in possession of the property to give at the request of any person claiming that the bankrupt, debtor, deceased debtor, or company is under a liability to him such information as may reasonably be required by him for the purpose of ascertaining whether any rights have been transferred to and vested in him by this Act and for the purposes of enforcing such rights, if any, and any contract of insurance, in so far as it purports, whether directly or indirectly, to avoid the contract or to alter the rights of the parties thereunder upon the giving of any such information in the events aforesaid or otherwise to prohibit or prevent the giving thereof in the said events shall be of no effect.

(2) If this information given, to any person in pursuance of sub-s (1) of this section disclosed reasonable ground for supposing that there have or may have been transferred to him under this Act rights against any particular insurer, that insurer shall be subject to the same duty as is imposed by the said subsection on the persons therein mentioned.

(3) The duty to give information imposed by this section shall include a duty to allow all contracts of insurance, receipts for premiums, and other relevant documents in the possession or power of the person on whom the duty is so imposed to be inspected and copies thereof to be taken.

3 Settlement between insurers and insured persons Where the insured has become bankrupt or where, in the case of the insured being a company, a winding-up order has been made or a resolution for a voluntary winding-up has been passed, with respect to the company, no agreement made between the insurer and the insured after liability has been incurred to a third party and after the commencement of the bankruptcy or winding-up, as the case may be, nor any waiver, assignment, or other disposition made by, or payment made to the insured after the commencement aforesaid shall be effective to defeat or affect the rights transferred to the third party under this Act, but those rights shall be the same as if no such agreement, waiver, assignment, disposition or payment had been made.'

Note—This section does not include a composition or arrangement with creditors or appointment of receiver or manager or possession by debenture holders. Presumably this is to enable the insured's business to be carried on.

4 In the application of this Act to Scotland —
(a) the expression 'company' includes a limited partnership;
(b) any reference to an order under s 130 of the Bankruptcy Act 1914, for the administration of the estate of a deceased debtor according to the law of bankruptcy, shall be deemed to include a reference to an award of sequestration of the estate of a deceased debtor, and a reference to an appointment of a judicial factor, under s 163 of the Bankruptcy (Scotland) Act 1913, on the insolvent estate of a deceased person.

5 Short title This Act must be cited as the Third Parties (Rights against Insurers) Act 1930.

Note—An infant cannot be made bankrupt. A married woman formerly could not, but can now.

It is to be noted that this Act is not limited to motor accidents but is general in its application, and that only the rights which the assured possesses against the insurer pass to the third party. The third party is therefore bound by the policy conditions, except as is mentioned later. If, therefore, there is an arbitration clause in the policy, this binds the third party. A similar position arose under the Workmen's Compensation Acts, and this point was decided in the case of *King v Phoenix Assurance Co* [1910] 2 KB 666, 80 LJKB 44, 103 LT 53, 3 BWCC 442, CA. The same point has been decided in motor cases.

Post Office v Norwich Union Fire Insurance Society Ltd
[1967] 2 QB 363, [1967] 1 All ER 577, [1967] 2 WLR 709, 111 Sol Jo 71, [1967] 1 Lloyd's Rep 216, CA

Contractors carrying out drainage works damaged a buried telephone cable. The Post Office claimed from them the cost of making good the damage. The contractors did not pay, alleging that the damage was due to wrong information given to them by a Post Office engineer. A year after the incident and before any proceedings had been started they went into liquidation. The Post Office thereupon sued their insurers (the defendants) claiming that under the Third Party (Rights against Insurers) Act 1930, s 1 they were entitled to recover the amount of the damage.

HELD: The Post Office could not claim against the insurers until it had first obtained a judgment against the contractors. The Act transfers to the third party the wrongdoer's rights against the insurers under the policy. In the present case those rights were to be indemnified 'against all sums which the insured shall become legally liable to pay as compensation in respect of loss of or damage to property'. The right to indemnity would not arise until the insured's liability to pay the third party had been ascertained and brought into existence by a judgment of the Court or by agreement. It was not open to the plaintiff to establish its right to damages from the contractors in the present proceedings against the insurers: the liability must first be established by a judgment in a separate action against the contractors.

Freshwater v Western Australian Assurance Co Ltd
[1933] 1 KB 515, 102 LJKB 75, 148 LT 275, 49 TLR 131, 76 Sol Jo 888, 44 Ll L Rep 282, CA

Plaintiff was injured in a motor accident and recovered judgment against C & H for £300 damages for negligence. H subsequently became bankrupt. At the time of the accident H was insured with defendant company against third-party risks. The policy of insurance contained the usual arbitration clause making an award a condition precedent to bringing an action on the policy. Plaintiff issued a writ against defendant company contending that under the Third Parties (Rights against Insurers) Act 1930, s 1, and the Road Traffic Act 1930, s 36(4) (now replaced by the Road Traffic Act 1972, s 148(4)), they were accountable to him for the amount of the judgment. The defendant company thereupon took out a summons to stay the action on the ground that under the arbitration clause the obtaining of an award was a condition precedent to bringing the action.

HELD: The rights of the defendant company under the policy were not

affected by either of the Acts of 1930 and it was therefore entitled to rely on
the arbitration clause, which made it a condition precedent to bringing an
action that an award should first be obtained.

Hassett v Legal and General Assurance Society Ltd
(1939) 63 Ll L Rep 278 (Atkinson J)
The third party served a writ on the assured company by registered post.
The company had ceased to exist and the writ was ignored. The third party
signed judgment in default and damages were assessed at £1,050.

The assured had failed to fulfil the policy condition requiring them to
give notice to insurers of the commencement of proceedings. No notice of
the claim was given to insurers. The assured company were to blame and
(*semble*) the third party's solicitors, who had not informed insurers of plaintiff's claim against assured. The third party had no greater rights than the
assured would have had. Insurers not liable.

Farrell v Federated Employers Insurance Association Ltd
[1970] 3 All ER 632, [1970] 1 WLR 1400, 114 Sol Jo 719, [1970] 2 Lloyd's
Rep 170, CA
The plaintiff was injured in November 1962. He claimed damages against
the employers who were insured by the defendants. In September 1964 a
receiver was appointed by the employers' secured creditors. In September
1965 the plaintiff issued a writ against the employers and served it by
registered post at their registered office on 6 January 1966. There was no
one there to deal with it, the employers having ceased to trade. The plaintiff's solicitors signed judgment in default of appearance on 28 February
1966. On 2 March 1966 they notified the defendant insurers of the
judgment: this was the first the defendants knew of the issue and service of
proceedings. They refused to satisfy the judgment on the ground that there
had been a breach of a condition of the policy requiring the insured to notify
and forward any writ immediately on receipt. The plaintiff accepted that
for the purposes of the Third Parties (Rights against Insurers) Act 1930 he
stood in the shoes of the employer as against the insurers but claimed
(1) the burden of proof was on the insurers, to show that the condition was
binding on the employers, (2) that he had complied with the condition,
(3) that if there was a breach the insurers had not been prejudiced.
HELD: (1) On the case as pleaded the burden of proof was not on the
insurers but even if it was they had discharged it by showing that in the
usual course of business the employers would have received the policy
document; (2) notification of the service of the writ eight weeks later and
after signing judgment was not 'immediately on receipt'; (3) the insurers
had been prejudiced by signing judgment before notifying them. They
were not liable to meet the judgment.

Murray v Legal and General Assurance Society Ltd
[1970] 2 QB 495, [1969] 3 All ER 794, [1970] 2 WLR 465, 113 Sol Jo 720,
[1969] 2 Lloyd's Rep 405 (Cumming-Bruce J)
The plaintiff was injured at work in March 1963. In July 1963 his
employers went into voluntary liquidation. They were insured against

liability to employees by the defendants to whom they owed £1,708 in respect of adjusted premiums. The plaintiff obtained judgment against his employers in 1966 for £1,750. He claimed against the defendants under the Third Parties (Rights against Insurers) Act 1930 for payment of this amount. The insurers claimed to set off against the amount of the judgment the sum owed for premiums on the ground that the 1930 Act vested in the plaintiff a statutory right of subrogation whereby he was in no better position that the person whose rights he had acquired.

HELD: They could not do so. It is not all the rights and liabilities of the insured under the contract of insurance which are transferred to the third party but only those in respect of the liability incurred by the insured to the third party. There is no express transfer of liabilities of the insured to the insurer in the Act, but if there is under the policy a defence by way of condition available against the insured (as in *Hassett's* case) that defence would be available against the third party. Rights which were not referable to the particular liability of the insured to the particular third party were not transferred.

---

4 MISCELLANEOUS CASES

Estoppel

Greenwood v Martins Bank Ltd
[1933] AC 51, 101 LJKB 623, 147 LT 441, 48 TLR 601, 75 Sol Jo 544, HL (Lord Tomlin)

The essential factors giving rise to an estoppel are, I think:

1 A representation or conduct amounting to a representation intended to induce a course of conduct on the part of the person to whom the representation is made.

2 An act or omission resulting from the representation whether actual or by conduct by the person to whom the representation is made.

3 Detriment to such person as a consequence of the act or omission.

Mere silence cannot amount to a representation, but when there is a duty to disclose deliberate silence may become significant and amount to a representation.

Insurance Companies Act 1958

Department of Trade and Industry v St Christopher Motorists Association Ltd
[1974] 1 All ER 395, [1974] 1 WLR 99, 117 Sol Jo 873, [1974] 1 Lloyd's Rep 17, ChD

The defendant company ran an association to protect the interests of motorists. Members could pay an annual sum and, subject to the decision of a committee could be provided with a chauffeur if they became legally unable to drive because of, e g becoming disqualified on conviction of a road traffic offence. The decision of the committee was final and an applicant had to satisfy certain requirements but the committee's discretion was not absolute: if the member fulfilled the requirements he was entitled to the services offered by the association.

HELD: Contracts of insurance were not confined to contracts for payment of a sum of money but included contracts for some benefit corresponding to the payment of a sum of money. The defendants were an insurance company to which the Insurance Companies Act 1958 applied.

Note—The Insurance Companies Act 1958 has been repealed and replaced by the Insurance Companies Act 1974 (consolidated in the Insurance Companies Act 1982), which, though it does not reproduce the 1958 Act, fulfils the same function.

Public policy

Beresford v Royal Insurance Co Ltd

[1938] AC 586, [1938] 2 All ER 602, 107 LJKB 464, 158 LT 459, 54 TLR 789, 82 Sol Jo 431, HL

A man who had insured his life for £50,000 shot himself. He did so to enable his creditors to have some benefit from the proceeds of the policies. HELD: A man is not to be allowed to have recourse to a Court of Justice to claim a benefit of his crime whether under a contract or a gift. Deliberate suicide, *felo de se*, has always been regarded in English law as a crime. It is contrary to public policy for a court of law to enforce a contract to pay a sum of money to a person's representatives in the event of his committing *felo de se*. His administrator claims as his representative and as such falls under the same ban.

Note—See also *Hardy v Motor Insurers' Bureau* and *Gardner v Moore*, pp 784–785, above.

Ashmore, Benson, Pease & Co Ltd v A. V. Dawson Ltd

[1973] 2 All ER 856, [1973] 1 WLR 828, 117 Sol Jo 203, [1973] 2 Lloyd's Rep 21, [1973] RTR 473, CA

The plaintiffs arranged with the defendants, who were hauliers, to carry two pieces of machinery each weighing 25 tons from Stockton to Hull. The defendants sent two articulated lorries each of 10 tons unladen weight to collect the machinery which was loaded on the lorries in the presence of the plaintiffs' transport manager, who knew that when loaded each vehicle would weigh 35 tons. He was aware of the regulation in the Motor Vehicles (Construction and Use) Regulations 1966 limiting the permissible loaded weight of an articulated lorry to 30 tons. On the journey one of the lorries overturned damaging the machinery.

HELD: The plaintiffs were barred from suing the defendants for the damage. Even if the contract was lawful when made (in that it could have been performed by using the right kind of vehicle) the performance of it was illegal. The plaintiffs' transport manager who knew the weight of the two loads and the regulations failed to stop the loading when he went to watch it being done: he was a participator in the illegality.

St John Shipping Corpn v Joseph Rank Ltd
[1957] 1 QB 267, [1956] 3 All ER 683, [1957] 3 WLR 870, 100 Sol Jo 841,
[1956] 2 Lloyd's Rep 413 (Devlin J)
Shipowners contracted with a company of millers to carry wheat from
Alabama to Liverpool. The ship was overloaded and the master was
convicted under statute for the offence of overloading. The millers declined
to pay the freight contending illegality.
HELD: The shipowners had only to prove that they delivered the goods.
The rights which could not be enforced had to be those directly resulting
from the crime, but no claim for freight could be clearly identified as being
the excess illegally earned, consequently, the shipowners were entitled to
recover the freight.
　Beresford v Royal Insurance Co distinguished

Archbolds (Freightage) Ltd v S. Spanglett Ltd
[1961] 1 QB 374, [1961] 1 All ER 417, [1961] 2 WLR 170, 105 Sol Jo 149,
CA
The plaintiffs claimed £3,674 damages for loss of a consignment of whisky
which was stolen from the defendants while they were transporting it as
carriers for the plaintiffs. The defendants pleaded that the plaintiffs could
not recover damages because the contract of carriage was illegal. The
defendants' vehicle had only a 'C' licence though an 'A' licence was
required (Road and Rail Traffic Act 1933, s 1(1)). The plaintiffs were
unaware that the defendants' vehicle had no 'A' licence.
HELD: The object of the Road and Rail Traffic Act 1933 was not to
interfere with the owner of the goods or his facilities for transport but to
control those who provided the transport. The penalties provided by the
Act applied to those using the vehicle but not to the goods owner. Thus a
contract of carriage was collateral to the use of the vehicle and not impliedly
forbidden by the statute. The plaintiffs were entitled to recover the amount
of their loss. *St John Shipping Corpn v Joseph Rank Ltd*, applied.

Bedford Insurance Co v Instituto de Resseguros do Brasil
[1984] 3 All ER 766, [1984] 3 WLR 726, 128 Sol Jo 701, [1984] 1 Lloyd's
Rep 210 (Parker J)
By the Insurance Companies Act 1974, s 2 no person might carry on in
Great Britain business of a class listed in s 1 without authorisation from the
Secretary of State. The plaintiffs were an insurance company operating
through brokers in London who entered into insurance contracts of a
specified class listed in s 1 in respect of which they obtained reinsurance
cover from the defendants. The plaintiffs had no authorisation from the
Secretary of State. Any person carrying on business in contravention of the
Act was guilty of an offence punishable by fine or imprisonment. The
plaintiffs sued the defendants under the reinsurance contract for amounts
due under the primary contracts.
HELD: What was prohibited was both the making and performance of any
contract of insurance of the relevant class by way of business. Though it
was the insurer who committed the offence, not the insured, no enforceable
right under the prohibited contract was acquired by the insured, for under
the Act it would be an offence for the insurer to pay him. The contracts

written by the plaintiffs' agents were null and void. Quoting Denning LJ in *Marles v Philip Frant* (p 895, below) 'if the plaintiff requires any aid from an illegal transaction to establish his cause of action, then he shall not have any aid from the court'. The plaintiffs were not entitled to recover under the reinsurance contract because the primary contracts were unenforceable.

Stewart v Oriental Fire & Marine Insurance Co
[1984] 3 All ER 777, [1984] 3 WLR 741, 128 Sol Jo 645, [1984] 2 Lloyd's Rep 109 (Leggatt J)

The plaintiffs were underwriters at Lloyds claiming sums due on risks reinsured by the defendants, a foreign company doing insurance business in London through sub-agents. The defendants were not authorised for any relevant business by the Department of Trade under the Insurance Companies Act 1974 (see *Bedford Insurance Co v Instituto de Resseguros do Brasil*, above). If the *Bedford* case were rightly decided the plaintiffs could not recover under the reinsurance contract. It was submitted that what the Act rendered illegal was business of effecting and carrying out particular classes of contracts of insurance, not individual contracts.

HELD: It was important to consider the purpose of the statute: it was principally designed to protect the public by ensuring the financial soundness of insurers. To render individual contracts of insurance void would be repugnant to the policy of the Act. There was no express prohibition of contracts of insurance in the Act; it deliberately maintained a distinction between carrying on insurance business and making individual contracts of insurance. It did not intend to go further and prohibit contracts of insurance, the effecting and carrying out of which constituted the carrying on of insurance business. Judgment for the plaintiffs. *Bedford Insurance Co v Instituto de Resseguros do Brasil* (above) not followed.

Criminal negligence

James v British General Insurance Co Ltd
[1927] 2 KB 311, 96 LJKB 729, 137 LT 156, 43 TLR 354, 71 Sol Jo 273, 27 Ll L Rep 328 (Roche J)

Tinline v White Cross Association Insurance Co
[1921] 3 KB 327, 90 LJKB 118, 125 LT 632, 37 TLR 733 (Bailhache J)

Insurers are liable even though the assured is guilty of criminal negligence amounting to manslaughter. A policy covered liability of the assured for accidental injury caused by his negligence, even though gross and attended by criminal consequences; the policy, by covering these liabilities, was not void as against public policy, and the assured was entitled to the indemnity which he claimed.

Note—Both these decisions were cases of motor car manslaughter, and policies against third party liability were enforceable.

These cases were questioned in *Haseldine v Hosken* [1933] 1 KB 822, 102 LJKB 441, 148 LT 510, 49 TLR 254, 45 Ll L Rep 59, CA (insurance against solicitors's negligence, where solicitor guilty of champerty).

Alexander v Rayson
[1936] 1 KB 169, 105 LJKB 148, 154 LT 205, 52 TLR 131, 80 Sol Jo 15, CA
The court will not enforce transactions tainted with fraudulent or immoral purposes or objects.

Note—Untrue statement of rent in lease to avoid stamp duty.
   Applied in *Edler v Auerbach* [1950] 1 KB 359, [1949] 2 All ER 692, 65 TLR 645, 93 SK 727 (Devlin J)

Beresford v Royal Insurance Co Ltd
[1938] AC 586, [1938] 2 All ER 602, 107 LJKB 464, 158 LT 459, 54 TLR 789, 82 Sol Jo 431, HL
But in the case of a crime, such as *felo de se*, which is a deliberate felony akin to murder, the court will not allow the criminal or his representatives to recover.

Note—See (p 891, above). But by the Suicide Act 1961, s 1 suicide is no longer a crime.

Gray v Barr
[1971] 2 QB 554, [1971] 2 All ER 949, [1971] 2 WLR 1334, 115 Sol Jo 364, [1971] 2 Lloyd's Rep 1, CA
The defendant was insured against liability to pay 'damages in respect of . . . bodily injury to any person . . caused by accidents'. Being suspicious one night that his wife was at the house of a neighbour, Gray, with whom she was having an affair he went to find her and took with him a loaded shotgun. In Gray's house he fired a shot at the ceiling to frighten him; the other barrel then discharged accidentally, killing him. Gray's widow sued for damages under the Fatal Accidents Acts; the defendant in third party proceedings claimed to be covered by the policy.
HELD, ON APPEAL: (1) The policy did not cover, because the events leading to Gray's death were not an 'accident' but arose from the defendant's deliberate act in taking a loaded gun to enforce his search; (2) the further question arose of public policy. In *Tinline's* and *James's* cases (p 893, above) the act indemnified was one intended by the law that people should insure against; so far as manslaughter on the road by gross negligence is concerned public policy does not prevent the enforcement of an indemnity. The present case, in which the person seeking indemnity was guilty of deliberate, intentional and unlawful violence or threats of violence, was not of that type. As in *Beresford's* case (above) the rule of public policy applied that no person can claim indemnity for his own wilful and culpable crime. The defendant was not entitled to indemnity under the policy.

Marcel Beller Ltd v Hayden
[1978] QB 694, [1978] 3 All ER 111, [1978] 2 WLR 845, 122 Sol Jo 279, [1978] 1 Lloyd's Rep 472, [1978] RTR 344 (Judge Edgar Fay QC)
The plaintiffs took out a personal accident policy on the life of their employee John McCredie issued by the defendant. Compensation was

payable under the policy if McCredie sustained 'accidental bodily injury which shall solely and independently of any other cause . . . result in his death'. McCredie was killed when a car he was driving at high speed crashed out of control on a bend. His blood alcohol content at the time was 261 milligrammes per 100 millilitres. Liability under the policy was excluded if death resulted from 'deliberate exposure to exceptional danger . . . or the insured person's own criminal act'.

HELD: (1) McCredie's death was accidental; (2) driving the car knowing he had consumed an excessive amount of alcohol, though negligent, was not deliberately exposing himself to exceptional danger; (3) the offences of dangerous driving and driving under the influence of drink were sufficiently serious to qualify as criminal acts within the meaning of the exemption. Judgment for the defendant.

Marles v Philip Trant & Sons Ltd; Mackinnon, (third party)

[1954] 1 QB 29, [1953] 1 All ER 645, [1953] 2 WLR 564, 97 Sol Jo 189, CA

A sold to B wheat which was in breach of condition regarding description. B sold to C under the same description but failed to deliver to C the particulars prescribed by the Seeds Act 1920, s 1. C sued B, who added A as third parties claiming indemnity.

HELD: By Singleton and Denning LJJ, Hodson LJ dissenting: B was entitled to indemnity from A.

Per Denning LJ: In *Beresford's* case and *Haseldine's* case the plaintiff was seeking to get reparation for the consequences of his own culpable crime. *Tinline's* case and *James'* case were rightly decided.

Per Hodson LJ: I share the doubts expressed in *Haseldine's* case in so far as the cases of *Tinline* and *James* may tend to support the proposition that an assured can get indemnity from his insurers against his own intentional acts of illegality.

Note—69 LQR 293 suggests that there is no ground for the reasoning of Denning LJ that there is a distinction between illegality which destroys a cause of action and illegality which affects only the damages recoverable, and that the insurance cases have been doubted in *Haseldine v Hosken*.

Rectification of policy

Sun Life Assurance of Canada v Jarvis

[1943] 2 All ER 425, CA

Plaintiff applied for a policy in the terms of the company's Illustration. The policy issued was less favourable to the assured.

HELD: The plaintiff was entitled to the benefits of the Illustration and to rectification of the policy.

Whiteside v Whiteside

[1949] Ch 448, [1949] LJR 1117, 65 TLR 438, 93 Sol Jo 350, [1949] TR 111 (Harman J); [1950] 1 Ch 65, [1949] 2 All ER 913, 66 (Pt 1) TLR 126, CA

Per Harman J: I take the law to be correctly stated in *Kerr on Fraud and Mistake* (6th edn) at p 620:

'Though the court will rectify an instrument which fails through some mistake of the draftsman in point of law to carry out the real agreement between the parties, it is not sufficient in order to create an equity for rectification that there has been a mistake as to the legal construction or the legal consequences of an instrument.'

Quoting Turner LJ in *Stone v Godfrey* (5 De G M & G 76 at 90):

'I assume . . . that this court has power (as I feel no doubt that it has) to relieve against mistakes in law as well as against mistakes in fact.'

ON APPEAL, per Evershed MR: I do not read that passage as meaning that if the mistake made is in using language to perfect an agreement which in law has some result different from the common intention, that is not a case in which there can be rectification. I think that would be too wide. I think it may well be that if the mistake has arisen from the legal effect of the language used that may provide a ground for the exercise of the court's reforming power. Subject, however, to that qualification, I think that the passage cited is correct.

As has been said, this discretionary remedy of rectification must be cautiously watched and jealously exercised.

George Cohen Sons & Co v Docks and Inland Waterways Executive (1950) 84 Ll L Rep 97, CA

The defendants cannot be heard to say that they misapprehended their own document; still less to say that they did not misapprehend it, but sought to gain an advantage over the plaintiffs by getting past the plaintiffs without them being made aware of it a change in the obligation as to repairs.

Citing Lord Chelmsford LC in *Fowler v Fowler* (1859) 4 De G & J 250:

'The power which the court possesses of reforming written agreements where there has been an omission or insertion of stipulations contrary to the intention of the parties and under a mutual mistake, is one which has been frequently and most usefully exercised. But it is also one which should be used with extreme care and caution. To substitute a new agreement for one which the parties have deliberately subscribed ought only to be permitted upon evidence of a different intention of the clearest and most satisfactory description.'

LLOYD'S: SLIP PART OF CONTRACT

The contract is made on the issue of the policy and the policy is not therefore a memorandum of an antecedent contract. In *MacKenzie v Coulson* (1869) LR 8 Eq 368, James VC at 375: 'Courts of Equity do not rectify contracts; they may and do rectify instruments purporting to have been made in pursuance of the terms of contracts. But it is always necessary for a plaintiff to show that there was an actual concluded contract antecedent to the instrument which is sought to be rectified; and that such contract is inaccurately represented in the instrument.' *MacKenzie v Coulson* was concerned with an attempt to rectify a policy of insurance to accord with the terms of a 'slip'.

The nature of the cover is defined in the contract of insurance with the assured. There are two documents: the policy itself and the brokers' 'slip'. The 'slip' identifies briefly the type of cover required and the parties to the contract. It is addressed from the brokers to the underwriters; and for this purpose the broker is treated as the agent of the assured. It may be suggested the 'slip' is in the nature of a proposal and to have a similar effect.

The policy on the other hand, is a contractual document and is presumed to embody the terms agreed by the parties. Lord Wright in *Izzards* case ([1937] AC 773) dealing with a proposal and the policy said: Though the warranties and conditions expressed in the proposal are declared to be the basic conditions of the policy, that must be subject to their being overriden by any express terms to the contrary effect in the actual policy. The documents must be read together and reconciled so that every part of the contract may receive effect, but if there is a final and direct inconsistency, the positive and express terms of the policy must prevail. The 'slip' should therefore be admissible in any consideration of the effect of the policy.

Renewal — implied warranty

Re Wilson and Scottish Insurance Corpn
[1920] 2 Ch 28, 89 LJCh 329, 123 LT 404, 36 TLR 545, 64 Sol Jo 514
(Astbury J)
It may be very material to the insurer on renewal to know of any change in the extent of the risk to enable them to determine whether or not they will continue the insurance, and that if on the renewal the assured had informed the insurers of the alteration, the premium would have been increased or the renewal refused.

EXPRESS DECLARATION ON RENEWAL

I declare that the particulars given above are true and that the motor car is and shall be kept in good condition, and I also declare that since the issue of the above-numbered policy neither I nor any other person who will ordinarily drive the car has been declined insurance by any other insurance company or association, nor has any stipulation been made that I or such other person should bear the first portion of any loss. I further declare that neither I nor such other person has developed any physical infirmity, defective vision or hearing or been convicted of any offence in connection with the driving of any motor car: *Re Wilson and Scottish Insurance Corpn* [1920] 2 Ch 28, 89 LJCh 329, 123 LT 404, 36 TLR 545, 64 Sol Jo 514.

In *Law Accident Insurance Society v Boyd* 1942 SC 384, a proposal was made and policy issued in 1935. It was renewed, and the last renewal was in February 1940. In July, 1939, the assured was convicted of an offence under the Road Traffic Act 1930, s 15. He did not disclose this conviction on renewal in February 1940. Insurers took proceedings for a declaration. The defendants moved the court for a ruling that there was no prima facie case. Lord Stephenson negatived the motion. Defendants appealed. The appeal was dismissed.

The Lord Justice Clerk said that on each renewal there at once arose an obligation on the insured to make such disclosure or correct any statement in his original proposal form which may be material to the risk for which he seeks cover during the year still to come. He considered the rule stated on p 429 of *Macgillivray* (2nd edn) as follows, to be true:

'In fire policies and similar risks where the insurers may decline to renew a policy at the expiration of the original period each renewal is made on the faith of the continued truth of the original representations and if there has been any material change adverse to the interests of the insurers which has not been disclosed on or before payment of the renewal premium the insurers may repudiate liability or limit their liability to the amount for which they would have been liable if there had been no change.'

I think it is quite clear that there was a duty upon the proposer for renewal to disclose all the material facts in exactly the same way as at the date when the policy was originally taken up: Per Lord Wark, Lord Mackay and Lord Jamieson concurring.

And see 'Continuing warranty', pp 862, above.

Solicitor's duty to insured

Groom v Crocker

[1939] 1 KB 194, [1938] 2 All ER 394, 108 LJKB 296, 158 LT 477, 54 TLR 861, 82 Sol Jo 374, 60 Ll L Rep 393, CA

A passenger in a car belonging to his brother was injured in a collision with a lorry. The lorry driver was convicted of dangerous driving. The car owner took proceedings against the lorry owner, whose insurers paid £100 into court with denial which was accepted. The passenger brought proceedings against the lorry owner, and at the request of the lorry owners, joined his brother as defendant. Insurers of the car instructed solicitors who advised that the car owner was not negligent. The two insurers agreed to share the passenger claim. Negligence was admitted on behalf of the car owner in the defence and the action dropped against the lorry owner. The car owner's solicitors wrote a letter to the passenger's solicitors that the car owner admitted negligence. The insurer's branch office wrote a letter to the agent discussing this admission. The policy gave insurers absolute conduct and control of proceedings, and contained the *Scott v Avery* ((1856) 5 HL Cas 811, 25 LJEx 308, 28 LTOS 207) clause.

The car owner sued insurers and solicitors for negligence and/or breach of duty and libel. The car owner alleged the letters were written without his consent; that he had not been negligent; that the letters were defamatory; that he had suffered damage because he would not be able to obtain insurance at normal rates; that it was an implied term of the policy and also the duty of insurers that insurers would act as plaintiff's agents with due regard to his interests; that the admission of negligence was a device to reduce damages which would not be assessed so high against a brother as against a stranger. The jury found for the plaintiff on all points.

HELD: As against insurers — (1) letter was not defamatory and (2) the arbitration clause was a good defence.

As against the solicitors — there was a relationship of solicitor and client following *Walsh v Julius White and Bywaters* (1927) Times, 13 July and in *Re Crocker Re Taxation of Costs* [1936] Ch 696, [1936] 2 All ER 899, 105 LJCh 276, 155 LT 344, [1936] WN 192, 52 TLR 565. £1,000 damages for negligence awarded. The letter was defamatory, and plea of privilege failed because there was malice, ie indirect motive. £1,000 damages for libel awarded.

HELD, ON APPEAL: Insurers cannot in terms admit that the assured has been negligent contrary to the fact without their solicitor incurring a liability for breach of duty and possibly also the insurers, unless the assured consents. The right given to the insurers is to have control of proceedings in which they and the assured have a common interest because he is the defendant and the insurers because they are contractually bound to indemnify him. Each is interested in seeing that any judgment to be recovered against the assured shall be for a small a sum as possible.

The assured is not entitled to complain of anything the insurers require the assured to submit to provided it falls within the policy, properly construed. Insurers have the right to decide upon the proper tactics to pursue in the conduct of the action, provided it is in what they bona fide consider to be the common interest of themselves and the assured, but not to be influenced by matters altogether outside the litigation with which the assured has no concern. The policy is subject to the implied term that the solicitor shall act reasonably in the interests of both the assured and the insurers.

Note—See also *Meah v McCreamer*, p 455, above.

Although the relationship of solicitor and client exists between the insurer's solicitor and the insured, the solicitor must not say he is instructed by the insured or call him his client, or he may find the insured and his personal solicitor protesting it is not the fact. The personal solicitor may, as has happened, report the insurer's solicitor to the Law Society, who will uphold his protest. Insurer's solicitor should say they are instructed 'on behalf of'.

Re Crocker
[1936] WN 192

An insured is entitled to production and inspection of the documents in the possession of his insurers' solicitors relating to the defence of his action by the insurers.

Note—Where it is impracticable to obtain the permission of the assured to the admission of negligence, a form of defence designed to avoid the incurring of costs on the issue of negligence, as distinct from damage, is the following. It is useful where the insurers of two defendants have a sharing agreement.

DRAFT DEFENCE

1 The defendants admit that subject to proof of the alleged injury loss and damage the plaintiff is entitled to damages against one or other or both of them in this action, and do not contest the issue of liability.
2 The defendants do not admit the alleged or any personal injury loss or damage.

ALTERNATIVE SHORT FORM WITH ASSURED'S CONSENT

The defendants for the purposes of this action only and not further or otherwise and reserving all rights between themselves, jointly admit negligence.

Brokers' negligence

Osman v Ralph Moss Ltd
[1970] 1 Lloyd's Rep 313, CA

The plaintiff, a Turk having only a limited knowledge of English asked the defendants, insurance brokers, to provide him with motor insurance. They recommended a policy underwritten by a company which they knew was of doubtful stability. The plaintiff accepted their recommendation and paid a year's premium. Shortly afterwards the insurers went into liquidation and the plaintiff was uninsured. He did not realise this. A letter the defendants sent him was misleading and inadequate to warn him. A few weeks later he had an accident as a result of which he was prosecuted for having no insurance, fined £25 and incurred 30 guineas costs. In addition he was sued by the other party in the accident and judgment given against him for £207 and £37 costs which being uninsured, he had to meet himself.

HELD: The defendants were liable for negligence in failing properly to acquaint him that he was uninsured. He was entitled to be repaid the amount of the premium and (1) the damages he had to pay plus £5 of the costs, (2) the amount of the fine and the costs in the magistrate's court. It was foreseeable that by reason of the defendants' breach of duty and negligence he might incur liability for damages but he should have mitigated the loss of costs by submitting to judgment when the claim was made. It was not against public policy that he should be indemnified against the fine because there had been no mens rea and no personal negligence.

Bromley London Borough Council v Ellis
[1971] 114 Sol Jo 906, [1971] 1 Lloyd's Rep 97, CA
In July Mrs D sold a car to E and agreed to have insurance transferred to him. E asked her brokers to do this and they agreed. They filled up a proposal form, which he signed, but failed to send it off until November. The insurers wrote asking a question which the brokers did not answer. The insurers wrote in December saying that in the absence of a reply within seven days the insurance would be cancelled. The brokers did nothing and did not tell E. The insurers cancelled the policy. In February E collided with the plaintiff's car and was found liable for £805 damage and loss. Only after the accident did he discover he was not insured. He claimed indemnity from the brokers.

HELD: The brokers, though agents for the insurance company and not for E, were under a duty of care to look after his interests. They had failed to use reasonable care and were liable to indemnify him.

Warren v Henry Sutton & Co Ltd
[1976] 2 Lloyd's Rep 276, CA
The plaintiff, about to go abroad with his car, telephoned his insurers and asked for his insurance to be extended to cover a friend whom he knew to have a bad driving record. He gave his insurers the name of his broker; the insurers telephoned the broker for details and were told by him that the plaintiff's friend had 'no accidents, no conviction and no disabilities'. A bad accident occurred whilst the friend was driving and on discovering his bad record the insurers refused indemnity to the plaintiff, who then sued the broker.

HELD: It was the duty of the broker when obtaining extension of the cover to make such enquiries about the friend's record as would enable him to make a truthful statement to the insurers. His recklessness in making the statement he did was the cause of the insurers' repudiation and he was liable to the plaintiff in damages.

McNealy v Pennine Insurance Co Ltd
(1978) 122 Sol Jo 229, [1978] 2 Lloyd's Rep 18, [1978] RTR 285, CA

The plaintiff's main occupation was the repair of property, but he was also an expert guitarist and sometimes played in a band. Before going abroad with a band he went to brokers to get insurance for his car. The policy suggested by the brokers excluded cover for part-time musicians and they knew this. They asked the plaintiff what his occupation was and he said 'property repairer'. A policy was issued. When an accident occurred the insurers refused indemnity; it was conceded they were entitled so to do. The plaintiff sued the brokers.

HELD: The plaintiff was entitled to succeed. It was the duty of the brokers to use all reasonable care to see that the assured was properly covered. They should have gone through the list of excluded categories and asked the plaintiff if he was or had been a part-time musician. It was their duty to ensure as far as possible that he came within the list of categories acceptable to the insurance company. They were in breach of their duty of care.

Broker not liable to insured

O'Connor v B. D. B. Kirby & Co
[1972] 1 QB 90, [1971] 2 All ER 1415, [1971] 2 WLR 1233, 115 Sol Jo 267, [1971] 1 Lloyd's Rep 454, [1971] RTR 440, CA

The plaintiff having bought a car went to the defendant, an insurance broker, to take out an insurance policy. The broker filled in a proposal form for him for the T company. He told the plaintiff the premium would be higher if he did not have a garage for the car, and he also told the plaintiff to check the proposal form to see if it was correct before signing it. On the form the broker had shown incorrectly that the car would be kept in a private garage. The plaintiff signed the form and in due course a policy was issued. Subsequently the insurers on finding that the car was parked in the street refused to indemnify the plaintiff against a loss he sustained. The plaintiff claimed damages against the broker alleging breach of a contractual duty to fill in the form properly.

HELD: It was the duty of a proposer for insurance to see and make sure that the information in the proposal form was accurate and he cannot be heard to say that he did not read it properly or was not fully appraised of its contents. The plaintiff should have read the form: he signed it and if he was so careless as not to read it properly he had only himself to blame. Judgment for the defendant.

CHAPTER 22
Conversion

Note—The majority of motor policies indemnify in respect of the loss of or damage to the car insured, without any qualification or limitation, so that they are somewhat similar to an all risks policy in this respect. Other policies limit the indemnity, so far as conversion is concerned, to loss by theft.

A common cause of claims for loss of car arises where the insured takes a cheque in payment on the sale of the car and the cheque is dishonoured on presentation. In the absence of circumstances such as in the cases of *Cundy* and *Pearson*, this is a case of loss of the proceeds of sale and not of loss of the car.

Where insurers are liable and have paid the loss, they are subrogated to the rights of the insured in respect of recovery of the car or of damages, and this involves tracing the property, as distinct from the possession, in the car. It is therefore necessary to consider the subjects of theft, sale of goods and hire purchase.

Where the car is in the possession of the police, there is a right to proceed in the magistrates' court for its return (p 939, below).

If the car is not in police possession, the proceedings are in the civil court for delivery up of the car or payment of its value and damages for detention. There is also the right to claim damages for conversion against any intermediate purchaser. The question is whether the title has passed to a subsequent purchaser.

Definition of conversion

Lancashire and Yorkshire Rly Co v MacNicoll
(1918) 88 LJKB 601, 118 LT 596, 34 TLR 280, 62 Sol Jo 365
Dealing with goods in a manner inconsistent with the right of the true owner amounts to a conversion, provided that it is also established that there is an intention on the part of the defendant in so doing to deny the

owner's right or to assert a right which is inconsistent with the owner's right.

Note—Approved in *Oakley v Lyster* [1931] 1 KB 148, 100 LJKB 177, 144 LT 363, CA

'LOSS' OF PROPERTY

Loss — meaning of

Holmes v Payne
[1930] 2 KB 301, 99 LJKB 441, 143 LT 349, 46 TLR 413, 37 Ll L Rep 41
Jewellery was missed on 24 November; reported as a loss to insurers the following day; on 4 December an agreement for replacement was suggested, and in December and the following February articles in replacement were selected. On 27 February the jewellery was found. Underwriters were held bound by the agreement, and, *semble*, there was a loss within the meaning of the policy.

Per Roche J: 'Uncertainty as to recovery of the thing insured is, in my opinion, in non-marine matters the main consideration on the question of loss. In this connection it is, of course, true that a thing may be mislaid and yet not lost, but, in my opinion, if a thing has been mislaid and is missing or has disappeared and a reasonable time has elapsed to allow of diligent search and of recovery and such diligent search has been made and has been fruitless, then the thing may properly be said to be lost. The recovery of the thing is at least uncertain, and I should say, unlikely.'

Subsequent discovery or recovery of the thing assured is, of course, of itself no disproof of the loss.

Loss — all risks

British and Foreign Marine Insurance Co v Gaunt
[1921] 2 AC 41, 90 LJKB 801, 125 LT 491, 37 TLR 632, 65 Sol Jo 551
There are, of course, limits to 'all risks'. They are risks, and risks insured against. The expression does not cover inherent vice or mere wear and tear. It covers a risk, not a certainty. It does not cover a loss which the insured brings about by his own act, for then he has injured them himself.

Note—Quoted in *London and Provincial Leather Processes v Hudson* [1939] 2 KB 724, [1939] 3 All ER 857, 109 LJKB 100, 62 LT 140, 55 TLR 1047, 83 Sol Jo 733 (Goddard LJ)

Loss — Webster's case

Webster v General Accident Assurance Corpn
[1953] 1 QB 520, [1953] 1 All ER 663, [1953] 2 WLR 491, 97 Sol 155, [1953] 1 Lloyd's Rep 123, (Parker J)
A comprehensive policy on a motor car included the following words: 'Section 1 Loss of or damage to the insured motor car. The corporation

will indemnify the policyholder against loss of . . . any motor car described in the schedule hereto.'

The car owner entered his car for sale with a reserve of £325, which was not reached. He was about to collect his car, when Taylor (who had arranged the auction) said to him — 'Don't go' and told him he had an offer to buy the car privately for £335. The owner then left the car with Taylor on the understanding that it would be sold as soon as Taylor had communicated to the private buyer that his offer was accepted. There was no such buyer. Taylor sent the car to another auction sale the car was sold to A at auction and afterwards by A to B. Taylor sent cheques for varying amounts in purported payment, all of which were dishonoured, and the last returned 'account closed'. The arbitrator found that there was no larceny by a trick nor larceny by a bailee, but that the owner had been swindled out of the car by the fraud and false pretences of Taylor. The arbitrator found that the purchaser had acquired a good title and it was not unreasonable for the owner to refrain from attempting to claim the car from the purchaser. He considered that 'loss' could be fairly defined as 'an effective deprivation in circumstances making recovery uncertain'.

If a chattel is handed over to an agent, whether or not as a result of a fraudulent misrepresentation, and the agent then proceeds to deal with the chattel in a way which amounts to a conversion of the chattel, there may be a loss. The claimant had taken all reasonable steps to recover his car and recovery was, to say the least, uncertain. There was a loss within the meaning of the policy.

The judge declined the argument that the loss was of the proceeds of sale and not the loss of the chattel. Following *London and Provincial Leather Processes Ltd v Hudson* (p 903, above), award affirmed.

Note—69 LQR 163 points out that the fact that the plaintiff had voluntarily handed the car to T did not mean that a loss could not be established. If the owner of a chattel hands it over to X for sale, X having honestly represented that he has a buyer, and the chattel is duly sold by X who misappropriates the proceeds, there would not be a loss of the chattel but a loss of the proceeds of sale. Here, however, the loss occurred when T sent it to the auction for sale, for at that moment he deprived the plaintiff of his title without authority.

Eisinger v General Accident Fire and Life Assurance Corpn Ltd
[1955] 2 All ER 897, [1955] 1 WLR 869, 99 Sol Jo 511, [1955] 2 Lloyd's Rep 95 (Lord Goddard CJ)

The owner of a motor car agreed to sell the car to a purchaser and accepted a cheque in payment and parted with the car and the log book. The purchaser never had any intention of paying for the car and the cheque was worthless. The car was insured against loss or damage and the owner claimed from insurers for a loss of the car.

HELD: The car had been obtained by false pretences and the property in the car had passed to the purchaser. The consent of the owner was real consent induced by fraud and not an appearance of consent induced by fraud produced by a trick. The transaction amounted to obtaining a car by false pretences and not that of larceny by a trick. The loss was the value of the cheque and not the loss of the car. Parting with the property as well as the possession distinguished it from *Webster's* case (above). The owner had not lost the car. He had lost the proceeds of sale. There was no loss within meaning of the policy.

Agent

Note—See under heading '*Servant or agent*', p 917, below.

Finding lost goods

Farquharson Bros & Co v King & Co
[1902] AC 325, 71 LJKB 667, 86 LT 810, 51 WR 94, 18 TLR 665, 46 Sol
Jo 584, HL
The finder of lost goods acquires no title as against the true owner, and can
give none except by a sale in market overt.

Infant

Ballett v Mingay
[1943] KB 281, [1943] 1 All ER 143, 112 LJKB 193, 168 LT 34, CA
The plaintiff loaned goods to an infant who agreed to pay a weekly sum for
the loan. Plaintiff demanded the return of the goods. Defendant had
meanwhile parted with possession of the goods. Plaintiff sued the infant in
detinue ie in tort. The infant pleaded that the claim was for breach of
contract and infancy was a defence.
HELD: The terms of the bailment did not permit the infant to part with the
possession of the goods. The action of the infant in parting with the goods
fell outside the contract altogether. The act was one of tort, distinct from
the contract, and the infant was liable in tort.

LIMITATIONS

RB Policies at Lloyd's v Butler
[1950] 1 KB 76, [1949] 2 All ER 226, [1949] WN 229, 65 TLR 436, 93 Sol
Jo 553, 82 Ll L Rep 841, (Streatfeild J)
A motor car registration number JD 6412 was stolen by some person
unknown on 27 June 1940. In January 1947, the car, bearing the
registration number ALN 765 was found in the possession of the defendant, having passed to him through a line of intermediate purchasers
during the previous seven years. Insurers had paid for loss by theft and
acquired the title and sued for possession. The defendant pleaded the
statute of limitations.
   The Limitation Act 1939, s 2(1) provides that no action shall be brought
after the expiration of six years from the date on which the cause of action
accrued. The defendant was an innocent purchaser for good consideration
in good faith.
   Section 3(1) provides:

'Where any cause of action in respect of the conversion or wrongful detention of a
chattel has accrued to any person and, before he recovers possession of the chattel,
a further conversion or wrongful detention takes place, no action shall be brought
in respect of the further conversion or detention after the expiration of six years
from the accrual of the cause of action in respect of the original conversion or
detention.'

Section 3(2) provides:

'Where any such cause of action has accrued to any person and the period prescribed for bringing that action and for bringing any action in respect of such a further conversion or wrongful detention as aforesaid has expired and he has not during that period recovered possession of chattel, the title of that person to the chattel shall be extinguished.'

Halsbury's Laws of England (2nd edn) vol 20, p 618, said (cf 4th edn, vol 28, p 279): 'A cause of action cannot accrue unless there be a person in existence capable of suing and another person in existence who can be sued.'

HELD: The fact that a person is not traceable or is not known, does not mean that he is not in existence and cannot be sued. The fact that the plaintiffs could not find a defendant whose name they could insert in a writ does not mean that there is not in existence a person who can be sued. The provision that the period of limitation shall not 'begin to run' under s 26 until discovery in the case of fraud shows that time runs even though a plaintiff is ignorant that he has a cause of action. The cause of action 'accrued' in 1940 when the car was stolen. The plaintiff's claim was therefore barred by the statute.

Note—The subsections referred to have been repealed and substantially re-enacted by the Limitation Act 1980, ss 2 and 3. In s 3 the words 'or wrongful detention' and 'or detention' have been omitted wherever they appeared in s 3(1) and (2) of the 1939 Act, the tort of detinue having been abolished.

Limitation Act 1939, s 26 — fraudulent concealment

Beaman v ARTS Ltd
[1949] 1 KB 550, [1949] 1 All ER 465, 65 TLR 389, 93 Sol Jo 236, CA
The Limitation Act 1939, s 26 provides that where the right of action has been concealed by fraud the period of limitation shall not begin to run until the plaintiff has or could with reasonable diligence have discovered it. In 1935 the plaintiff, who was going abroad, deposited four packages with the defendant company, and paid storage charges on them until 1938. In January 1940, she wrote to the company from Turkey to send the packages to her at Athens where she would go to collect them but this was not possible owing to war conditions. Six months later the company desiring to close down their business and being of opinion that the contents of the packages were worthless, gave the packages to the Salvation Army. No communication was sent to the plaintiff, and it was not until her return to England towards the end of 1946 that she was informed of the position. She thereupon brought proceedings against the company more than six years after the date of the conversion.

HELD: The plaintiff had placed confidence in the company, who had disposed of the packages in its own interest and made no attempt to communicate with the plaintiff and kept no adequate record of what had been done with the goods. These acts were calculated to keep the plaintiff in ignorance of the wrong that had been committed and amounted to a fraudulent concealment of the cause of action.

Note—The Limitation Act 1939, s 26 has been replaced by s 32 of the 1980 Act without relevant alteration.

MEASURE OF DAMAGES

Caxton Publishing Co v Sutherland Publishing Co
[1939] AC 178, [1938] 4 All ER 389, 108 LJCh 5, 160 LT 17, 55 TLR 123, 82 Sol Jo 1047, HL
Per Lord Roche: The measure of damages for conversion is the value of the thing converted at the date of conversion. In *Reid v Fairbanks* (1853) 13 CB 692, 43 Dig 509, there was a list of value available, because the true owner had contracted to sell a ship under construction for £x. It was held, or rather, agreed (because the actual decision was on another point) that the damage was £x-£y representing the cost of finishing the construction. I entirely accept the view that expenses incurred after the conversion should come off [the damages]. As the appellants in fact used the material, the proper inquiry is as to its fair value.

Per Lord Porter: Damages to the full value of the property converted may be given against two person for successive conversions of the same chattel, and, until payment in full of the sum awarded is made by one of the defendants, the judgment remains in force against the other. In neither case, however, would the plaintiff be permitted to recover more than the sum awarded for the injuries received or the value of the chattel, as the case might be, because the law will not permit any greater sum to be recovered than that representing the actual damage suffered. Mere possession of the property of others is not conversion, since, by a fiction, the original possession is regarded as lawful.

F. R. Evans (Leeds) Ltd v British Trailer Co Ltd
Unreported; discussed 102 Sol Jo 241 (Streatfeild J)
Defendants purchased from the Government shortly after the war generating sets for about £35 each, and resold to a third party, who resold them in 1951 to plaintiffs for £110 each. The goods were left on defendants' premises notwithstanding their requests to remove them. In 1952 plaintiffs sold 13 sets at £150 each, which were removed, leaving seven sets still on defendants' premises. In 1956 the defendants, having forgotton they belonged to the plaintiffs, sold them for scrap at £16 each. Six months later the plaintiffs were offered £195 each f. o. b. by an overseas customer.

In an action for conversion, the judge said the test was the value at the date of conversion, and as there was a buyer at £195 in October 1956, the indication was that the value had not fallen since 1952, and awarded £150 per set, less a deduction for transport costs.

The Mediana
[1900] AC 113, 69 LJP 35, 82 LT 98, 48 WR 398, HL
Even the loss of the use for a time of chattel which the owner would not have used during that time may give rise to substantial damages, whether in an action for damages or in an action for conversion.

Sachs v Miklos
[1948] 2 KB 23, [1948] 1 All ER 67, [1948] LJR 1012, 64 TLR 118, CA
While the measure of damages for conversion is usually the value of the goods at the date of judgment, if the bailor knew or ought to have known at

an earlier date that the conversion had taken place or was about to take place and took no immediate steps to recover the goods, the measure of damages was the value of the goods at the date of his knowledge or supposed knowledge.

Note—But see Diplock LJ's comment below and *Winfield and Jolowicz on Tort* (12th edn) p 500.

General and Finance Facilities Ltd v Cooks Cars (Romford) Ltd
[1963] 2 All ER 314, [1963] 1 WLR 644, 107 Sol Jo 294, CA (Diplock LJ)
Per Diplock LJ: The judgment (in an action in conversion) is for a single sum of which the measure is generally the value of the chattel at the date of conversion together with any consequential damage flowing from the conversion and not too remote to be recoverable in law. With great respect to the dictum of Lord Goddard LJ in *Sachs v Miklos* this is not necessarily the same as the measure of damages for detinue where the same act constitutes detinue as well as conversion although in many cases this will be so.

Note—See facts on p 913, below.
The Torts (Interference with Goods) Act 1977, s 2 (into force 1 June 1978) is as follows:

'2 Abolition of detinue   (1) Detinue is abolished.
(2) An action lies in conversion for loss or destruction of goods which a bailee has allowed to happen in breach of his duty to his bailor (that is to say it lies in a case which is not otherwise conversion, but would have been detinue before detinue was abolished).'

London and Provincial Motor and Tractor Co Ltd v Boundary Garage
[1948] WN 267, 92 Sol Jo 499 (Birkett J)
B bought A a motor car for £350 on the faith of statements made with utter recklessness and without any enquiry whether they were true or false and therefore fraudulent. B entered into a hire-purchase agreement with C. The car was a stolen car and had to be returned to the true owner.
HELD, in an action by B against A: B was entitled to recover the £350 from A and a declaration (following *Household Machines Ltd v Cosmos Exporters Ltd* [1947] KB 217, [1946] 2 All ER 622, [1947] LJR 578, 176 LT 49, 62 TLR 757) that the plaintiffs are entitled to recover from the defendants such damages as the plaintiffs may be held liable to pay and/or may reasonably pay to C in consequence of any breach by plaintiffs of the hire purchase agreement with C, in so far as such breaches are attributable to the breach of contract or tortious acts found in the judgment in the action.

Strand Electric Co v Brisford Entertainments Ltd
[1952] 2 QB 246, [1952] 1 All ER 796, [1952] 1 TLR 939, 96 Sol Jo 260, CA
Defendants, the owners of a theatre, allowed possession to a prospective purchaser, who obtained lighting equipment from the plaintiffs on hire at £9 6s 8d per week. The prospective purchaser was unable to complete and notified the plaintiffs to collect the equipment. Defendants refused to allow

plaintiffs to take possession of the goods. The judge assessed damages on the prospective receipts from hire if the goods had been returned.

HELD, ON APPEAL: The defendants had used the goods for their own benefit and were liable for the payments payable under the hire agreement.

Per Denning LJ: If a car used in business is detained, and the owner has to hire another car at an increased rate, he can recover the cost of the substitute, ie the actual loss. If a car is put out of action during repair, the wrongdoer is only liable for the loss suffered by the plaintiff.

Hillesden Securities Ltd v Ryjak Ltd

[1983] 2 All ER 184, [1983] 1 WLR 959, 127 Sol Jo 521, [1983] RTR 491 (Parker J)

R, the owner of a Rolls Royce car, leased it on the 11 June 1979 to V for a term of 36 months. On 13 September 1980 V purported to sell the car to E and a company of which E was a director and shareholder. V paid no leasing instalments after October 1980 and R accordingly sought the return of the car. Having failed he assigned his rights in the car to the plaintiffs who began proceedings against E and his company. On 11 March 1982 E ceased to be a director or shareholder in the company. The action came on for trial on 30 November 1982. The car was returned to the plaintiffs on 3 December 1982. On the issue of damages it was argued on behalf of E that s 3 of the Act had no application as he had not been in possession and control of the car after 11 March 1982.

HELD: E. plainly converted the car on the 13 September 1980 and was liable for conversion. The parties had agreed that a proper figure for the use of the car which the defendants had enjoyed was £115 per week. Section 3 of the 1977 Act referred to relief which may be given 'in proceedings . . . against a person who is in possession or control of the goods'. This meant persons who were in possession and control of the goods when the proceedings were launched. Following the decision in *Strand Electrical Co v Brisford Entertainments* (above), in the case of a profit-earning chattel which a defendant has used for his own benefit the owner can recover by way of damages a hire charge plus either the return of the chattel or, if there has been a subsequent conversion by disposal, the value of the chattel at the date of such conversion. The plaintiffs had lost the use of the car over the whole period from the original conversion to the 3 December 1982. Though E had ceased to have any connection with the company on the 11 March 1982 he could not be heard to say that by putting it out of his power to return the car he terminated his liability. Judgment against both defendants for the hire charge at the agreed weekly figure for the whole period to 3 December 1982, namely, £13, 280, plus interest from 23 February 1981 the date when R first made a written demand for return of the car.

Note—For s 3 see p 912, below.

Mason v Burningham

[1949] 2 KB 545, [1949] 2 All ER 134, [1949] LJR 1430, 65 TLR 466, 93 Sol Jo 496, CA

Plaintiff bought a second-hand typewriter from defendant for £20 and paid £11 10s 0d to have it overhauled. The typewriter had been stolen, and plaintiff sued defendant for £31 10s 0d. The Sale of Goods Act 1893, s 12 provides (1) an implied warranty of the vendor's right to sell; and (2) an implied warranty for quiet possession. Section 53(2) provides that the measure of damages for breach of warranty is the estimated loss directly and naturally resulting, in the ordinary course of events, from the breach of warranty.

The court below, citing *Victoria Laundry (Windsor) Ltd v Newman Industries* [1949] 2 KB 528, [1949] 1 All ER 997, 65 TLR 274, 93 Sol Jo 371, CA found that plaintiff behaved in a common-sense way and did the ordinary and natural thing and what was right and proper. What was reasonably foreseeable at the time of the contract depends on the knowledge imputed or actually possessed by the party in breach. Everyone is taken to know the ordinary course of things and consequently what loss is liable to result from a breach of that ordinary course.

HELD, ON APPEAL: The damages claimed flowed directly and naturally from the breach; it resulted in the ordinary course of events. The plaintiff was entitled to recover the £31 10s 0d claimed.

Note—The Sale of Goods Act 1893, s 12 has been repealed and replaced in similar terms by the Sale of Goods Act 1979, s12. S 53(2) is repeated in the 1979 Act.

ALLOWANCE FOR IMPROVEMENT OF GOODS

Note—The Torts (Interference with Goods) Act 1977 provides by s 6:

'**6 Allowance for improvement of the goods**   (1) If in proceedings for wrongful interference against a person (the ''improver'') who has improved the goods, it is shown that the improver acted in the mistaken but honest belief that he had a good title to them, an allowance shall be made for the extent to which, at the time as at which the goods fall to be valued in assessing damages, the value of the goods is attributable to the improvement.

(2) If, in proceedings for wrongful interference against a person (''the purchaser'') who has purported to purchase the goods —

(a) from the improver, or

(b) where after such a purported sale the goods passed by a further purported sale on one or more occasions, or any such occasion,

it is shown that the purchaser acted in good faith, an allowance shall be made on the principle set out in sub-s (1).

For example, where a person in good faith buys a stolen car from the improver and is sued in conversion by the true owner the damages may be reduced to reflect the improvement, but if the person who bought the stolen car from the improver sues the improver for failure of consideration, and the improver acted in good faith, sub-s (3) below will ordinarily make a comparable reduction in the damages he recovers from the improver.

(3) If in a case within sub-s (2) the person purporting to sell the goods acted in good faith, then in proceedings by the purchaser for recovery of the purchase price because of failure of consideration, or in any other proceedings founded on that failure of consideration, an allowance shall, where appropriate, be made on the principles set out in sub-s (1).

(4) This section applies, with the necessary modifications, to a purported bailment or other disposition of goods as it applies to a purported sale of goods.'

For rules of court see RSC Ord 42, r 1A.

Munro v Willmott
[1949] 1 KB 295, [1948] 2 All ER 983, [1949] LJR 471, 64 TLR 627, 92 Sol
Jo 662 (Lynskey J)
Defendant allowed plaintiff to leave her car in the yard of the premises of
which he was licensee without charge in 1942. In 1945 he wanted the car
moved. He tried but failed to get in touch with the plaintiff. The car was not
roadworthy and he had it repaired at a cost of £85, and sold it by auction for
£105. In 1946 the plaintiff sued for the full value of the car without any
allowance for the £85 spent on repairs.
HELD: The defendant was not an agent of necessity and was liable. He was
entitled to credit, not because he had made the payment, but to ascertain
the true value of the property which the plaintiff had lost. If the car had not
been repaired, it would at the time of the judgment have realised something
in the nature of £25 as scrap. Judgment for £35, being value of car, £120,
crediting the £85.

Greenwood v Bennett
[1973] QB 195, [1972] 3 All ER 586, [1972] 2 WLR 691, [1972] RTR 535,
CA
Bennett wishing to have some work done to a car to prepare it for sale
entrusted it to Searle to do the work. Searle used the car for his own
purposes and in doing so damaged it. He wrongfully 'sold' it in its
damaged state to Harper who in good faith paid him £75 for it. Harper
spent £226 on it to put it in good order and then sold it for £450 to a finance
company. When Searle's misdealing with the car was discovered the police
seized the car and brought interpleader proceedings to determine the
ownership. The judge ordered the car to be delivered up to Bennett and
held that Harper was not entitled to be paid by Bennett for the £226 worth
of work done to the car.
HELD: The judge should have required Bennett to pay Harper the £226 as
a condition of being given delivery of the car. The principle that lay to hand
to meet the case was derived from the law of restitution — that the owners
should not be allowed to enrich themselves at the expense of a person who
has done work to a property of which he honestly believes himself to be the
owner.

Possessory title only

Wilson v Lombank Ltd
[1963] 1 All ER 740, [1963] 1 WLR 1294 (Hinchcliffe J)
The plaintiff, a dealer, bought a car and took it for repairs to a garage where
he had a monthly account. After the repairs were done the garage staff put
the car on the forecourt to await collection. A representative of the defendants, a finance company, saw it there and took it away. Both parties
thought themselves to have a good title to the car but neither in fact was the
owner: it really belonged to another finance company to whom the defendants delivered it when satisfied that this was so. The plaintiff sued for
damages for trespass on the ground that he had possession of the car and the
defendants had no right to take it away.
HELD: The plaintiff was entitled to immediate possession of the car at the

time when it was on the forecourt since he could at any moment demand its return. The garage had no lien for the costs of repairs having regard to the course of dealing, ie the monthly account. The plaintiff having never lost possession of the car the defendants had wrongfully taken it and must pay damages. Delivery to the true owner did not defeat the plaintiff's claim. The measure of damages was the full value of the car at the time the tort was committed, namely, the price the plaintiff paid for the car plus the cost of repairs.

Finance company

Wickham Holdings Ltd v Brooke House Motors Ltd
[1967] 1 All ER 117, [1967] 1 WLR 295, CA

When a finance company sues in conversion (eg when the hirer under a hire-purchase agreement wrongfully sells the goods or the benefit of the agreement) it can recover its actual loss and no more. It does not recover the full value of the goods but only the balance outstanding on the hire-purchase price.

Note—Followed in *Belvoir Finance Co Ltd v Stapleton* [1971] 1 QB 210, [1970] 3 All ER 664, [1970] 3 WLR 530, 114 Sol Jo 719, CA. Both *Wickham* and *Belvoir* were considered in *Chubb Cash Ltd v John Crilley & Son* [1983] 2 All ER 294, [1983] 1 WLR 599, 127 Sol Jo 153, CA. Per Bush J: these cases decided that the measure of damages was the market value of the goods, or the amount still owing under the hire-purchase agreement, whichever was the lower as at the date of the conversion. It was a limited decision, not a decision which entitled the plaintiffs, if the amount outstanding on the hire-purchase agreement was greater than the value of the goods, to claim that.

REMEDIES OF OWNER

Note—The Torts (Interference with Goods) Act 1977, provides by s 3:

'**3 Form of judgment when goods are detained** (1) In proceedings for wrongful interference against a person who is in possession or in control of the goods relief may be given in accordance with this section, so far as appropriate.
(2) The relief is —
(a) an order for delivery of the goods, and for payment of any consequential damages, or
(b) an order for delivery of the goods, but giving the defendant the alternative of paying damages by reference to the value of the goods, together in either alternative with payment of any consequential damages, or
(c) damages.
(3) Subject to rule of court —
(a) relief shall be given under only one of paras (a), (b) and (c) of sub-s (2).
(b) relief under para (a) of sub-s (2) is at the discretion of the court, and the claimant may choose between the others.
(4) If it is shown to the satisfaction of the court that an order under sub-s (2)(a) has not been complied with, the court may —
(a) revoke the order, or the relevant part of it, and
(b) make an order for payment of damages by reference to the value of the goods.
(5) Where an order is made under sub-s (2)(b) the defendant may satisfy the order by returning the goods at any time before execution of judgment, but without prejudice to liability to pay any consequential damages.

(6) An order for delivery of the goods under sub-s (2)(a) or (b) may impose such conditions as may be determined by the court, or pursuant to rules of court, and in particular, where damages by reference to the value of the goods would not be the whole of the value of the goods, may require an allowance to be made by the claimant to reflect the difference.

For example, a bailor's action against the bailee may be one in which the measure of damages is not the full value of the goods, and then the court may order delivery of the goods, but require the bailor to pay the bailee a sum reflecting the difference.

(7) Where under sub-s (1) or sub-s (2) of s 6 an allowance is to be made in respect of an improvement of the goods, and an order is made under sub-s (2)(a) or (b), the court may assess the allowance to be made in respect of the improvement, and by the order require, as a condition for delivery of the goods, that allowance to be made by the claimant.

(8) This section is without prejudice —

(a) to the remedies afforded by s 133 of the Consumer Credit Act 1974, or

(b) to the remedies afforded by ss 35, 42 and 44 of the Hire-Purchase Act 1965, or to those sections of the Hire-Purchase Act (Northern Ireland) 1966 (so long as those sections respectively remain in force), or

(c) to any jurisdiction to afford ancillary or incidental relief.'

For rules of court see RSC Ord 42, r 1A.

Delivery up

Whiteley Ltd v Hilt

[1918] 2 KB 808, 87 LJKB 1058, 119 LT 632, 34 TLR 592, 62 Sol Jo 717, CA

If a plaintiff sues for wrongful detention and seeks judgment for the return of a car, the court can order that execution shall issue for the return of the car, but this is discretionary, and instead may merely award the value to the plaintiff.

General and Finance Facilities Ltd v Cooks Cars (Romford) Ltd

[1963] 2 All ER 314, [1963] 1 WLR 644, 107 Sol Jo 294, CA

The plaintiffs obtained a judgment by default 'that the plaintiff do have return of the mobile crane OMF 347 or recover against the defendants its value and damages to be assessed'. Assessment of damages was referred to the master who simply ordered that the amount of damages be assessed at £150. On being asked by the parties whether the plaintiffs were to have the crane returned to them he said 'No'. The plaintiffs appealed.

HELD: The judgment was one which gave the defendant the option of returning the crane but it also gave the plaintiffs the right to apply to the court to enforce specific restitution of the chattel. It was essential to the exercise of this right that the judgment should specify separate amounts for the value of the chattel at the date of assessment and for the damages for its detention. The matter must go back to the Master for separate assessments.

Note—See now the Torts (Interference with Goods) Act 1977, s 3(2) and (3), p 912, above.

Hirer's duty on termination of hire

Capital Finance Co Ltd v Bray

[1964] 1 All ER 603, [1964] 1 WLR 323, 108 Sol Jo 95, CA

The defendant hired a car from the plaintiffs under a hire-purchase agreement. He fell behind with his instalments and the plaintiffs repossessed themselves of the car by taking it from outside his house in the middle of the night. This was unlawful since the contract was one within the Hire-Purchase Act 1938 and the defendant had paid more than one-third of the hire-purchase price. Perhaps realising the error the plaintiffs returned the car on the following day. The defendant paid no further instalments though there was evidence that he made some use of the car. The plaintiffs wrote the defendant requiring him to return the car by delivering it to one of three specified addresses. The defendant did not do so: the plaintiffs then sued him for instalments due and for damages in detinue for the period subsequent to their letter demanding a return of the car.

HELD: (1) The hire-purchase agreement was determined by the illegal retaking of the car and was not revived by returning it, since this was merely an implied offer to revive it which the defendant had not accepted. (2) The defendant's failure to return the car, following the plaintiff's requiring him to deliver it to one of the specified addresses, did not give them any cause of action in detinue. He was not bound to take the car to them but only to let them have it if they came for it. No one, except by contract, is under a duty to take a chattel to its owner. In this case the contract, that is, the hire-purchase agreement, was already at an end.

Recaption

An owner can lawfully reclaim and take possession of a car wrongfully detained wherever he happens to find it, so long as it is not in a riotous manner or attended with breach of the peace, and may even justify an assault to recapture the car if the person in possession refused to return it (*Blades v Higgs* (1861) 10 CB(NS) 713 at p 720 per Erle CJ). In that event it seems that if the person wrongfully in possession has spent money on improving the car, this money might not be recoverable from the owner.

Note—See *Greenwood v Bennett* (p 911, above) and the Torts (Interference with Goods) Act 1977, s 6 (p 910, above).

In the report of the next case the following abbreviations are used: HP — Bowmaker Ltd. R — Rudolph, 5th party. K — Kennedy, 4th party. H — Hayton, 3rd party. M — Kingsway Motors, defendants. B — Butterworth, plaintiff.

Butterworth v Kingsway Motors

[1954] 2 All ER 694, [1954] 1 WLR 1286, 98 Sol Jo 717 (Pearson J)

A hire-purchase company as owners hired a car to R on a usual hire-purchase agreement on 3 January 1951. Before R had paid all the instalments or exercised the option to purchase, she purported on 1 August 1951, to sell the car to a motor dealer, K for £350 cash and a car valued at

£650. On 11 August 1951 K sold the car to H for £1,015. The same day H sold it to M for £1,030. On 15 August 1951, M sold it to B for £550 cash and a car valued at £725 (£1,275). B continued to use the car until but not after 16 July 1952. R meanwhile continued to pay the instalments until she learned she had no right to sell and she then informed the HP Co of the position. On 15 July 1952, the HP company wrote to B stating that the car was their property and calling for its delivery up, adding without prejudice, that they would accept £175 14s 2d to validate the title. On 17 July 1952, B's solicitors wrote to K claiming the return of the money paid for the car, and to the HP company for a copy of the HP agreement. On 23 July 1952, the HP company's solicitors wrote to B's solicitors that they had received a cheque from R which when met would discharge their interest. The cheque was met on 25 July. On 9 August, B's solicitors wrote to M for the return of the purchase price of £1,275 and for instructions with regard to the return of the car. On 14 August the HP company wrote to B's solicitors that their interests had been completed and on 18 August M's solicitors wrote to the same effect to B's solicitors, who on 22 August wrote to B's solicitors referring to their letter of 17 July. The reply was on 22 August that they had nothing to add to their letter of 18 August. On 12 September 1952, a specially indorsed writ was issued claiming £1,275.

M issued a third-party notice against H; H issued a fourth-party notice against K; and K issued a fifth-party notice against R.

HELD: B had effectively rescinded the contract of sale and was entitled to recover £1,250: *Rowland v Divall* [1923] 2 KB 500, 92 LJKB 1041, 129 LT 757, 67 Sol Jo 703. On 25 July 1952 R had acquired a good title and this fed the previously defective title of the subsequent buyers: *Whitehorn Bros v Davison* [1911] 1 KB 463, 80 LJKB 425, 104 LT 234, CA, *Blundell-Leigh v Attenborough* [1921] 3 KB 235, 90 LJKB 1005, 125 LT 356, 37 TLR 567, 65 Sol Jo 474, CA, *Robin and Rambler Coaches v Turner* (p 931, below). M was entitled to damages from H assessed on the value of the car in July 1952, assessed by the court at £800; judgment for £475. H was entitled to £475 from K and K to £475 from R.

Recovery over

Rowland v Divall
[1923] 2 KB 500, 92 LJKB 1041, 129 LT 757, 67 Sol Jo 703, CA
But if the person wrongfully in possession has purchased the car from a third party, he can recover his full loss from the third party.

Mason v Burningham
[1949] 2 KB 545, [1949] 2 All ER 134, [1949] LJR 1430, 65 TLR 466, 93 Sol Jo 496, CA
This would be limited to money expended in the ordinary course of events and not fancy expenditure at the buyer's whim.

Note—See p 909, above.

If the owner sues for delivery up, but the court does not order the return of the car and awards damages, then on recovery over from a third party of all the damage suffered, the car would of course become the property of the third party. See the Torts (Interference with Goods) Act 1977, s 5(1):

'5 Extinction of title on satisfaction of claim for damages   (1) Where damages for wrongful interference are, or would fall to be, assessed on the footing that the claimant is being compensated —
(a) for the whole of his interest in the goods, or
(b) for the whole of his interest in the goods subject to a reduction for contributory negligence, payment of the assessed damages (under all heads), or as the case may be settlement of a claim for damages for the wrong (under all heads), extinguishes the claimant's title to that interest.'

Sale by sheriff

Curtis v Maloney
[1951] 1 KB 736, [1950] 2 All ER 982, [1950] WN 525, 66 (Pt. 2) TLR 869, 94 Sol Jo 761, CA
The owner of a motor cabin cruiser left it in the care of a firm of boatwrights. In execution of a writ of *fieri facias* against the boatwrights, the sheriff seized the boat and sold it by public auction. The sale was advertised, and no claim was made to the sheriff in respect of the boat before the sale. The owner sued the purchaser for the return of the boat or its value and damages for detention.
The Bankruptcy and Deeds of Arrangement Act 1913, s 15 provides:

'Where any goods in the possession of an execution debtor at the time of seizure by a sheriff, high bailiff, or other officer charged with the enforcement of a writ, warrant, or other process of execution, are sold by such sheriff, high bailiff, or other officer, without any claim having been made to the same, the purchaser of the goods so sold shall acquire a good title to the goods so sold, and no person shall be entitled to recover against the sheriff, high bailiff, or other officer, or anyone lawfully acting under the authority of either of them, except as provided by the Bankruptcy Acts 1883 and 1890, for any sale of such goods or for paying over the proceeds thereof, prior to the receipt of a claim to the said goods unless it is proved that the person from whom recovery is sought had notice, or might by making reasonable inquiry have ascertained that the goods were not the property of the execution debtor: Provided that nothing in this section contained shall affect the right of any claimant who may prove that at the time of sale he had a title to any goods so seized and sold to any remedy to which he may be entitled against any person other than such sheriff, high bailiff, or other officer as aforesaid.'

The plaintiff contended that as he had a title to the goods at the time of the sale and as the purchaser was a person other than such sheriff, high bailiff, or other officer, the proviso preserved the plaintiff's rights.
The defendant contended that the first part of the section gave a good title to the purchaser, and the proviso reserved the rights against the execution creditor.
HELD: By Finnemore J [1950] 2 All ER 201, 66 (Pt. 2) TLR 147, the purchaser acquired a good title and the action failed.
The decision was upheld on appeal.
Per Somervell LJ: A good title means a good title against everybody. The proviso cannot be read so as to contradict and make these express words meaningless by excluding from them the true owner at the time of the sale.
Per Cohen LJ: The proviso preserves the true owner's rights against the execution creditor, and removes any doubts as to the right of the true owner to sue the execution creditor for money he had received.

Per Denning LJ: The proviso preserves the rights of the original owner against the execution creditor of any wrongdoer who had converted the goods prior to the sale.

Note—Approved in *Dyal Singh v Kenyan Insurance Ltd* [1954] AC 287, [1954] 1 All ER 847, [1954] 2 WLR 607, 98 Sol Jo 231, PC. On 'notice' and 'reasonable inquiry' see *Observer Ltd v Gordon* [1983] 2 All ER 945, [1983] 1 WLR 1008, 127 Sol Jo 324.

Servant or agent

Note—*Halsbury's Laws of England* (1st edn) vol 22, p 2, states:

'A servant who acquires possession (*o*) of the property of another, and deals with it in such a manner as to constitute a conversion of it (*p*) is personally guilty of conversion (*q*).
- (*o*)   *Cochrane v Rymill* (1879) 40 LT 744, 43 JP 572, 27 WR 776, CA
- (*p*)   *Barker v Furlong* [1891] 2 Ch 172, 60 LJCh 368, 64 LT 411, 39 WR 621, 7 TLR 406
- (*q*)   *Cary v Webster* (1721) 1 Stra 480
    Greenway v Fisher (1824) 1 C & P 190.'

(See now 4th edn vol 1, para 862.)

Re Samuel (No 2)
[1945] 2 All ER 71 (Evershed J)

Jewellery was handed to a solicitor acting for an undischarged bankrupt with a letter of authority from the bankrupt to place the same at a bank in the name of Mrs M. Later some of the jewellery was handed to the bankrupt, the rest remaining with the bank. It was contended the solicitor was liable for conversion.

HELD: The cases such as *Hollins v Fowler* (1875) LR 7 HL 757, 44 LJQB 169, 33 LT 73, 40 JP 53; *Salmond* (9th edn) pp 302, and 313; *Bowstead on Agency* (10th edn) pp 269, 270, show that provided certain conditions are fulfilled an innocent agent is liable, eg auctioneers as in *Consolidated Co v Curtis & Son* [1892] 1 QB 495, 61 LJQB 325, 56 JP 565, 40 WR 426, 8 TLR 403. But where one deals with goods at the request of the person who has the actual custody in the bona fide belief that the custodier is the true owner, or has his authority, he should not be held liable.

If the act of the agent is purely ministerial, it would not amount to conversion, eg a servant transferring goods from one place to another, or from one servant to another on the same premises. In the case of auctioneers they disposed of the property altogether by selling and delivering it, which could not be called ministerial, nor excused if done by the authority of a person merely entrusted with custody. The solicitor had received them as agent or minister for the bankrupt. His act was ministerial and did not amount to a conversion by him.

An appeal was dismissed, [1945] 1 Ch 408.

Waiver

United Australia Ltd v Barclays Bank Ltd
[1941] AC 1, [1940] 4 All ER 20, 109 LJKB 919, 164 LT 139, 57 TLR 13,
46 Com Cas 1, HL
A party who sues one tortfeasor for conversion does not waive his rights
against another tortfeasor unless he has obtained judgment and
satisfaction.

OWNER'S RIGHTS AGAINST PURCHASER IN GOOD FAITH

Note—See also cases under headings 'Hire purchase', pp 928–933, below, and
'Registration Document', pp 933–938, below.

Sale of Goods Act 1979

21 Sale by person not the owner   (1) Subject to this Act, where goods are sold
by a person who is not their owner, and who does not sell them under the authority
or with the consent of the owner, the buyer acquires no better title to the goods than
the seller had unless the owner of the goods is by his conduct precluded from
denying the seller's authority to sell.
(2) Nothing in this Act affects —
(a) the provisions of the Factors Acts, or any enactment enabling the apparent
     owner of the goods to dispose of them as if he were their true owner;
(b) the validity of any contract of sale under any special common law or statutory
     power of sale, or under the order of a court of competent jurisdiction.

22 Market overt   (1) Where goods are sold in market overt, according to the
usage of the market, the buyer acquires a good title to the goods, provided he buys
them in good faith and without notice of any defect or want of title on the part of the
seller.

23 Sale under voidable title   When the seller of goods has a voidable title to
them, but his title has not been avoided at the time of the sale, the buyer acquires a
good title to the goods, provided he buys them in good faith and without notice of
the seller's defect of title.

24 Seller in possession after sale   Where a person, having sold goods,
continues or is in possession of the goods, or of the documents of title to the goods
the delivery or transfer by that person, or by a mercantile agent acting for him, of
the goods or documents of title under any sale, pledge, or other disposition thereof,
to any person receiving the same in good faith and without notice of the previous
sale, has the same effect as if the person making the delivery or transfer were
expressly authorised by the owner of the goods to make the same.

25 Buyer in possession after sale   Where a person, having bought or agreed to
buy goods, obtains, with the consent of the seller, possession of the goods or the
documents of title to the goods, the delivery or transfer by that person, or by a
mercantile agent acting for him, of the goods or documents of title, under any sale,
pledge or other disposition thereof, to any person receiving the same in good faith
and without notice of any lien or other right of the original seller in respect of the
goods, has the same effect as if the person making the delivery or transfer were a
mercantile agent in possession of the goods or documents of title with the consent of
the owner.

26 Supplementary to sections 24 and 25   In ss 24 and 25 above 'mercantile agent' means a mercantile agent having in the customary course of his business as such agent authority either —
(a) to sell goods, or
(b) to consign goods for the purpose of sale, or
(c) to buy goods, or
(d) to raise money on the security of goods.

Note—See *Lambert v G. and C. Finance Corpn Ltd* and *Newtons of Wembley Ltd v Williams*, pp 924–925, below.

THEFT ACT 1968, s 31(2)

(2) Notwithstanding any enactment to the contrary where property has been stolen or obtained by fraud or other wrongful means, the title to that or any other property shall not be affected by reason only of the conviction of the offender.

The Factors Act 1889

1 Definitions   For the purposes of this Act —
(1) The expression 'mercantile agent' shall mean a mercantile agent having in the customary course of his business as such agent authority either to sell goods, or to consign goods for the purpose of sale, or to buy goods, or to raise money on the security of goods.

Obtaining good title

Nanka-Bruce v Commonwealth Trust
[1926] AC 77, 94 LJPC 169, 134 LT 35, PC
The law upon this branch of the contract of sale is thus expressed by Lord Cairns LC in *Cundy v Lindsay* (p 921, below):

'Now, with regard to the title of personal property, the settled and well-known rules of law may, I take it, be thus expressed: by the law of our country the purchaser of a chattel takes the chattel as a general rule subject to what may turn out to be certain infirmities in the title. If he purchases the chattel in market overt, he obtains a title which is good against all the world; but if he does not purchase the chattel in market overt, and if it turns out that the chattel has been found by the person who professed to sell it, the purchaser will not obtain a title against the real owner. If it turns out that the chattel has been stolen by the person who professed to sell it, the purchaser will not obtain a title. If it turns out that the chattel has come into the hands of the person who professes to sell it by a de facto contract, that is to say, a contract which has purported to pass the property to him from the owner of the property, there the purchaser will obtain a good title, even although afterwards it should appear that there were circumstances connected with that contract, which would enable the original owner of the goods to reduce it, and to set it aside, because these circumstances so enabling the original owner of the goods, or of the chattel, to reduce the contract and to set it aside, will not be allowed to interfere with a title for valuable consideration obtained by some third party during the interval while the contract remained unreduced.'

Market overt

Bishopsgate Motor Finance Corpn Ltd v Transport Brakes Ltd
[1948] 1 All ER 408, [1948] LJR 1000, 64 TLR 163, 92 Sol Jo 246,
(Humphreys J); on appeal [1949] 1 KB 322, [1949] 1 All ER 37, [1949]
LJR 741, 65 TLR 66, 93 Sol Jo 71, CA
A obtained a car from plaintiffs under a hire-purchase agreement under
which the property in the car remained in the plaintiffs. A instructed a firm
of auctioneers to offer the car in their auction sale at Maidstone market,
where under statutory powers a cattle and general market, which was a
long established public market, is held every Tuesday. The auctioneers
paid on behalf of A the toll of 1s (which was repaid by A) payable on every
vehicle put up for sale. The car was put up in its turn at the auction, which
was held about 11.45 am, but did not reach the reserve price and later with
a lower reserve, which again was not reached, and was withdrawn. B was in
the market at the auction but did not bid. Later in the day B was looking at
the car and was approached by A, and after negotiation A sold the car to B
about 2.30 pm.
    B at a later date sold the car to C.
HELD: The sale was in market overt and B acquired a good title under the
Sale of Goods Act 1893, s 22 (now replaced by s 22 of the 1979 Act). The
test laid down by Blackburn J in *Crane v London Dock Co* ((1864) 5 B & S 313,
4 New Rep 94, 33 LJQB 224, 10 LT 372, 28 JP 565, 10 Jur NS 984, 12 WR
745), applied, that the vendor must buy the goods under circumstances
such as would induce him to think the sale was a good sale in the market
overt: namely, he must buy a thing which is openly exposed in market overt
under such circumstances that he might say to himself no person but the
owner would dare expose them for sale here, and therefore I have a right to
assume that the shopkeeper has a right to sell them. The goods must be
corporally present and exposed in the market.
ON APPEAL: It was contended (1) market overt could only rest upon a
grant, and not upon a statute; (2) a toll, if payable, must be paid by the
person who effects the sale; (3) the goods must be put up for sale by a trader
in the market; and (4) a sale by private treaty was not a sale according to
the usuage of the market.
HELD: As to (1) market overt extended to markets established by statute;
there was no authority for the proposition; as to (2) A had paid the 1s toll by
the auctioneers to the corporation's collector; as to (3) it was not necessary
that goods must be put up for sale by a trader in the market; the sale could
be made by the possessor himself; and as to (4) there was no proof of usage
that a car could only be sold in the market by public auction. Appeal
dismissed.

Reid v Metropolitan Police Comr
[1973] QB 551, [1973] 2 All ER 97, [1973] 2 WLR 576, 117 Sol Jo 244,
[1973] Lloyd's Rep 518, CA
At 7 in the morning of 13 February Cocks bought a silver candelabra from a
stall-holder who was just erecting his stall in the New Caledonian Market,
Bermondsey. The candelabra had been stolen from the plaintiff by a person
unknown.
HELD: Cocks did not obtain a good title. Though the market overt rule

extended to statutory markets such as the New Caledonian a sale which would give a good title against the true owner must be made 'between the rising of the sun and the going down of the same' (Coke, 2 Inst 713). Sunrise being at 8.19 am on 13 February, the sale was not one made in market overt.

The *Post Magazine* of 31 July 1948 (p 735), reports the case of a stolen car entered in an auction sale of motor vehicles in the market place of a country town where it was eventually purchased by the garage proprietor who ran the sale. He sold the car to A, who sold it to B, who applied for registration. It then transpired that the registration plates of the vehicle had been changed. The true owner claimed from B. The thief could not be prosecuted to conviction for lack of evidence. The garage proprietor pleaded market overt.

An old grant in Latin in the town's museum from the Lord of the Manor had constituted the market on the appointed day of the week (Wednesday). The auction was on Monday.

HELD: Not market overt.

No contract

Cundy v Lindsay
(1878) 3 App Cas 459, 47 LJQB 481, 38 LT 573, 42 JP 483, 26 WR 406, HL
L was a manufacturer in Ireland; Alfred Blenkarn, who occupied a room in a house looking into Wood Street, Cheapside, wrote to L, proposing a considerable purchase of L's goods, and in his letter used this address— '37 Wood Street, Cheapside' and signed the letters, without any initial for a Christian name, with a name so written that it appeared to be 'Blenkiron & Co'. There was a respectable firm of that name, 'W. Blenkiron & Co' carrying on business at 123 Wood Street. L sent letters, and afterwards supplied goods, the letters, the goods, and the invoices accompanying the goods, being all addressed to 'Messrs Blenkiron & Co, 37 Wood Street'. The goods were received by Blenkarn at that place, and disposed of to defendants who were entirely ignorant of the fraud.
HELD: No contract was made with Blenkarn, even a temporary property in the goods never passed to him, so that he never had a possessory title which he could transfer to defendants, who were consequently liable to plaintiffs for the value of the goods.

Ingram v Little
[1961] 1 QB 31, [1960] 3 All ER 332, [1960] 3 WLR 504, 104 Sol Jo 704, CA
The plaintiffs were the owners of a car which they advertised for sale. A swindler called on them and made an offer which they were willing to accept, but on its appearing that he intended to pay by cheque the plaintiffs said that they would accept only cash. The swindler then said he was a Mr P. G. M. Hutchinson of Stanstead Road, Caterham. Whilst the matter was being discussed, one of the plaintiffs went to the Post Office nearby and

found that there was Mr P. G. M. Hutchinson at the address mentioned. She returned and told the co-plaintiff and as a result the plaintiffs agreed to accept a cheque. The swindler took the car away in exchange for the cheque and sold it to the defendants. He was not P. G. M. Hutchinson of Caterham and the cheque was dishonoured.

HELD: There was no contract for sale between the plaintiffs and the swindler and the property in the car had not passed to him. The plaintiffs were the offerors and the swindler was the offeree. In making their offer to sell the car not for cash but for a cheque the plaintiffs were under the belief that they were dealing with, and therefore making their offer to, the honest Mr P. G. M. Hutchinson of Caterham. The swindler knew what was in the minds of the plaintiffs for he had put it there and he knew that their offer was intended for Mr P. G. M. Hutchinson of Caterham and not for him. There was no offer which he (the swindler) could accept and therefore there was no contract.

Note—See note following next case.

Voidable contract

Lewis v Averay
[1972] 1 QB 198, [1971] 3 All ER 907, [1971] 3 WLR 603, 115 Sol Jo 755, CA

The plaintiff advertised his car for sale. A man came to see it: he said he was Richard Green and led the plaintiff to believe he was a well-known film actor of that name. Eventually he said he would like to buy the car and proffered a cheque for the price. The plaintiff agreed to sell but was unwilling to let the man take the car until the cheque had been cleared. He asked if he had anything to prove he was Richard Green. The man produced a pass of admission to a film studio bearing his photograph and the name 'R. A. Green'. The plaintiff was satisfied and let the man take the car and log book in exchange for the cheque. On presentation the cheque was found to be from a stolen cheque book and was worthless. A day or two later the man, under the name of the plaintiff, sold the car to the defendant who bought it in good faith. The plaintiff, on discovering what had happened, sued the defendant for a return of the car and damages for its retention.

HELD: The plaintiff could not succeed. The facts were very similar to those in *Ingram v Little* (above) and *Phillips v Brooks* (p 924, below) but those two cases could not be reconciled with one another. The true principle is that when two parties have come to what appears to be a contract the fact that one party is mistaken as to the identity of the other does not mean that there is no contract, but merely that the contract is voidable and liable to be set aside provided it is done before a third party has in good faith acquired rights under it. The plaintiff had made a contract with the man who was before him: the misrepresentations as to his identity merely made the contract voidable and it had not been avoided when the defendant acquired the car.

Note—Megaw LJ said he found it 'difficult to understand the basis, either in logic or in practical considerations, of the test laid down by the majority of the court in

Ingram v Little' by which the validity of the offer 'is made to depend on the view which some rogue should have formed . . . as to the state of mind of the opposite party . . . who does not know that he is dealing with a rogue'.

See also *Dennant v Skinner*, p 926, below.

Milford Mutual Facilities Ltd v H. W. Hidson Ltd
(1962) *Guardian*, 7 December

The defendants were motor dealers. A man came to them with a Ford car and asked to exchange it for an Austin which was in their showroom. He said he was R. Ashworth of Cheadle. He produced a log book for the car in that name and a driving licence in the same name. He was allowed to take away the Austin and collected the log book of that car four days later. The defendants sold the Ford but it was later found to be a stolen car and the defendants had to reimburse the purchaser. Meanwhile the man had offered the Austin for sale to a Mr Wright. As the latter required hire-purchase facilities both he and the man (who was still representing himself to be R. Ashworth of Cheadle) went in person to the office of the plaintiffs, a hire-purchase company. The log book of the Austin showed the defendants as owners and the man produced a receipt showing the exchange for the Ford. The plaintiffs then bought the Austin for £480, entering into a hire-purchase agreement with Wright. The defendants, having found that the Ford was stolen traced the Austin to Wright and repossessed themselves of it by driving it away from outside his house. In this action the plaintiffs claimed its return and damages for detinue and conversion. The defendants contended that the car was not the property of the plaintiffs as there had been no contract of sale: the plaintiffs had intended to contract with R. Ashworth of Cheadle and not with the man who had brought the car for sale. There was a real R. Ashworth of Cheadle but he was entirely unconnected with the transactions.

HELD: The court was bound by *Ingram v Little* (above) which had to be applied to this case. When parties contracted in each others' presence there was a presumption that the offeror intended to contract with the person physically before him and it was a difficult presumption to rebut. The vital question was whether the persons contracted with the man or with the real Mr Ashworth. Did the physical presence in their offices preponderate over the personality of the real person who was fraudulently misrepresented? On the facts of this case they were contracting with the person present before them: not a man who represented himself to be Mr R. Ashworth but a man who represented himself as owner of the car. There was accordingly a voidable, not a void, contract and the property passed. The plaintiffs were entitled to succeed.

Owner parting with log book

Note—See pp 933–938, below.

Contract must be dis-affirmed

Phillips v Brooks Ltd

[1919] 2 KB 243, 88 LJKB 953, 121 LT 249, 35 TLR 470, 24 Com Cas 263

If A fraudulently assuming the name of a person of credit and stability, buys, in person, and obtains delivery of, goods from B, the property in the goods passes to A, and he can therefore give a good title thereto to a third party who, acting bona fide and without notice, has given value therefor, unless in the meantime B has taken steps to dis-affirm the contract with A.

Note—See *Lewis v Averay*, p 922, above and *Ingram v Little*, p 921, above.

Repudiation of sale by conduct

Car and Universal Finance Co Ltd v Caldwell

[1965] 1 QB 525, [1964] 1 All ER 290, [1964] 2 WLR 600, 108 Sol Jo 15, CA

On 12 January the defendant sold his car to a swindler, Norris, accepting for it a cheque for £975. On the following day he presented the cheque to the bank and was told it was worthless. He at once went to the police so as to recover the car and telephoned the AA for the same purpose. On 20 January the police found the car in the possession of Motobella Ltd, who claimed to have bought it in good faith and to have sold it on 15 January to G. & C. Finance Corpn Ltd, a finance company. On 29 January Norris was arrested and pleaded guilty to obtaining the car by false pretences. On 13 August the car was transferred from G. & C. Finance to the plaintiffs, another finance company. After the defendant had obtained judgment against Motobella Ltd by default for the return of the car the plaintiffs claimed in this action that the title in the car was vested in them.

HELD: The question was whether G. & C. Finance obtained a good title to the car from Norris. The sale to Norris was voidable by the defendant: could he avoid it without communicating his rescission to Norris? Normally the rule is that an election to avoid a contract is not complete until the decision has been communicated to the other party, but in the circumstances of the present case where a fraudulent rogue would know that the defendant would want his car back as soon as he discovered the fraud it would not be right to hold that such a man could claim to have the rescission communicated to him. The position has to be viewed as between Norris and the defendant, who could not have made his position plainer. In circumstances such as the present case the innocent party may evince his intention to disaffirm the contract by overt means falling short of communication or repossession. The plaintiffs had not obtained any title to the car as against the defendant.

Note—See also next case.

Mercantile agent—Factors Act 1889

Newtons of Wembley Ltd v Williams

[1965] 1 QB 560, [1964] 3 All ER 532, [1964] 3 WLR 888, 108 Sol Jo 619, CA

On 15 June the plaintiffs sold a car to Andrew who gave them a cheque for

£735 for it. He drove it away and registered it in his name on the same day. On 18 June the plaintiffs heard from the bank that the cheque would not be met. They at once made extensive though unsuccessful enquiries to find Andrew, sent a 'Stop' notice to the Hire-Purchase Information Bureau and informed the police. On 6 July in Warren Street, London, Andrew sold the car to Biss, a dealer, for £550 cash. Biss took the car to Wincanton and on 12 July sold it to the defendant for £505, which was all the defendant would give him for it. Later in July as a result of an effort by the defendant to sell the car, the Hire-Purchase Information Bureau became aware of its whereabouts and told the plaintiffs. On 14 September, Andrew pleaded guilty at Middlesex Sessions to a charge of obtaining the car by false pretences. The plaintiffs claimed the return of the car or its value on the ground that like the defendant in *Car and Universal Finance Co v Caldwell* (above) they had rescinded the contract before the car was sold by the fraudulent party who could thus pass no title to it.

HELD: The unequivocal acts of the plaintiffs on finding that the cheque would not be met were effective to rescind the contract as in *Caldwell*'s case so that after 20 June at latest Andrew had at common law no title to pass. But the Factors Act 1889, s 9 provided that when a buyer of goods obtained possession of them with the seller's consent delivery of the goods on sale to any person acting in good faith without notice of the original seller's rights in respect of them had the same effect as if the person making the delivery were a mercantile agent in possession of the goods with the consent of the owner. Section 2 of the Act provides that a sale of goods by a mercantile agent in possession of the goods with the consent of the owner (which has not, to the knowledge of the person taking under the sale, been determined) shall be valid if made when acting in the ordinary course of business of a mercantile agent. Biss took the car in good faith without notice of the plaintiffs' rights. Andrew was acting in the ordinary course of business of a mercantile agent in that the sale to Biss was made at the well-known kerbside market for cash dealing in second hand cars in Warren Street. Accordingly Biss received a valid title to the car which he later passed to the defendant.

Lambert v G. and C. Finance Corpn Ltd
(1963) 107 Sol Jo 666 (Havers J)

The plaintiff advertised his car for sale. E agreed to buy it and offered a cheque in payment of the price. The plaintiff was unwilling to let E have the car except for cash but eventually agreed to let E take the car away in exchange for the cheque on the terms that he, the plaintiff, retained the log book, which he would send on when the cheque was cleared. In fact the cheque was dishonoured and the plaintiff reported the matter to the police. The car was subsequently sold by a dealer to the defendants, a hire-purchase company. The plaintiff sued for damages for its conversion. The defendants contended that he was not the owner, having sold it to E.

HELD: The Sale of Goods Act 1893, s 18(1) provides that unless a different intention appears the property in specific goods passes when the contract is made. Section 25(2) provides that where a person agrees to buy goods and is given possession of them by the owner he has the same power to give a good title as a mercantile agent under the Factors Act 1889 (see above). In the present case a different intention was shown for the purposes of s 18(1) by the plaintiff's retaining the log book. The defendants could not rely on s 25(2) because a sale of a car without a log book is not a sale in the ordinary course of business. The plaintiff was still the owner and was entitled to damages.

Note—The Sale of Goods Act 1893, s 18(1) is repeated in the Sale of Goods Act 1979, s 18(1) and s 25(2) of the 1893 Act in s 25(1) of the 1979 Act.

Auction

R. H. Willis & Son v British Car Auctions Ltd
[1978] 2 All ER 392, [1978] 1 WLR 438, 122 Sol Jo 62, [1978] RTR 244, 246 Estates Gazette 134, CA
Where goods are sold by the intervention of an auctioneer, under the hammer or as a result of a provisional bid, then if the seller has no title, the auctioneer is liable in conversion to the true owner.

Dennant v Skinner and Collom
[1948] 2 KB 164, [1948] 2 All ER 29, [1948] LJR 1576 (Hallett J)
The plaintiff carried on business as the South London Motor Auctions and was a certified auctioneer. He held an auction sale of 35 vehicles and knocked down six vehicles to a man named King. When the first vehicle, a Commer van, was knocked down, the plaintiff asked the buyer his name. The man said it was King; that he was from King's Motors of Oxford and the son of the proprietor. This firm was known to the plaintiff as of high repute. A later vehicle was a Standard car. When King went to the plaintiff's office after the sale, plaintiff asked how he meant to pay, and King said he would like to pay by cheque. Plaintiff said he did not accept cheques from people he did not know. King was in possession of trade plates and had drivers there to drive away the vehicles. He repeated that he was the son of the proprietor of King's of Oxford and said he was running the Portsmouth branch and produced a cheque book showing by the counterfoils he had been paying large sums to other auctioneers. Plaintiff believed these representations and accepted the cheque on King signing a form certifying that the cheque would be met on presentation and agreeing that the ownership of the vehicles would not pass until the cheque was met. The cheque was dishonoured and King was convicted of obtaining the vehicles by false pretences and with intent to defraud.

King had meanwhile sold the Standard car to Collom, who sold it to Skinner. Plaintiff sued Skinner for possession of the car on the ground that the transaction was larceny by a trick. Skinner brought in Collom as third party.
HELD: The sale was complete on the fall of the hammer (Sale of Goods Act 1893, s 58(2)). The property passed on the sale (s 18, r 1). It was not a case of larceny by a trick but obtaining goods by false pretences. The distinction stated in *Archbold* is that in larceny the owner does not intend to part with the property but only the possession; in false pretences he intends to part with the property. Citing Lord Haldane in *Lake v Simmons* [1927] AC 487 at 501, HL adopting Fry J in *Smith v Wheatcroft* (1878) 9 ChD 223, 47 LJCh 745, 39 LT 103, 27 WR 42 when consideration of the person is an element in the contract, error with regard to the person destroys consent and annuls

the contract, but where it does not and the vendor is willing to sell to any person, the contract stands. Here the sale was irrespective of the identity of the buyer. Plaintiff did not sell to King because of the false statements. The car was sold before King's identity was mentioned. The case was indistinguishable from *Phillips v Brooks Ltd* (p 924, above). In *Lake v Simmons* the goods were handed to the swindler as bailee and the vendor did not intend to enter into any contract of sale. In *Heap v Motorists Advisory Agency Ltd* [1923] 1 KB 577, 92 LJKB 553, 129 LT 146, 39 TLR 150, 67 Sol Jo 300, the plaintiff never intended to part with the property to the fraudulent person but merely the custody to sell to a person who was imaginary.

By parting with the property, the plaintiff lost his rights of lien or re-sale (the Sale of Goods Act 1893, s 39(1)(a) and (c)), but the property had already passed. The signed agreement that the property would not pass could not affect the fact that the property had already passed. It did not divest King of the property and re-vest it in the plaintiff.

The defendant was acting reasonably in joining the third party.

Judgment for the defendant, and for the third party against the defendant with costs; defendant's costs against plaintiff to include all costs of third-party proceedings.

Note—See also *Lewis v Averay*, p 922, above. The Sale of Goods Act 1893, s 58(2) has been replaced in the same terms by the Sale of Goods Act 1979, s 57(2) and s 18 of the 1893 Act by s 18 of the 1979 Act. Section 39(1)(a) and (c) of the 1893 Act was repeated in s 39(1)(a) and (c) of the 1979 Act.

Sale by intermediary with no authority to sell

Jerome v Bentley & Co
[1952] 2 All ER 114, [1952] WN 357, [1952] 2 TLR 58, 96 Sol Jo 463 (Donovan J)

Plaintiff handed to T a diamond ring on approval to try and sell the ring and if sold to pay the plaintiff £550, and if not sold within seven days to return it to the plaintiff. After the seven days T representing himself as owner, sold the ring to defendants. T shortly afterwards sent a cheque for £50 to the plaintiff, which was dishonoured. T. was charged with larceny as a bailee and pleaded guilty and was convicted. Plaintiff sued defendants for damages for conversion.

HELD: At the time of sale T had no authority to deal with the ring at all. It was not a case of a servant as in *Farquharson v King* (p 905, above), but of a person without authority to deal with the thing except for safe custody (*Mercantile Bank of India v Central Bank of India* [1938] AC 287, [1938] 1 All ER 52, 107 LJPC 25, 158 LT 269, PC). T became a thief of the ring as in *R v Henderson* (1871) 23 LT 628, 35 JP 325, 11 Cox CC 593. There was no representation as agent with authority to sell. In *Commonwealth Trust v Akotey* [1926] AC 72, 94 LJPC 167, 134 LT 33, 41 TLR 641, PC, the owner sent the goods and the consignment note to L, and so had permitted L to be in possession of all the insignia of possession and apparent title, and L passed them on to the purchaser from L. The owner could not contend the title had not passed. In the dictum in *Lickbarrow v Mason* (1787), cited in *Akotey*'s case, that the loss falls on the person who has 'enabled' a third party to occasion the loss, 'enabled' means doing something by one of the innocent parties which misled the other.

Judgment for plaintiff for the value of the ring. *Akotey*'s case not followed.

Sale by intermediary with authority to sell

Eastern Distributors Ltd v Goldring (Murphy, third party)
[1957] 2 QB 600, [1957] 2 All ER 525, [1957] 3 WLR 237, 101 Sol Jo 553, CA

The owner of a motor van authorised a motor dealer to sell the van to a hire-purchase finance company, to obtain an agreement by the company to sell it to him on hire-purchase terms and to apply the proceeds of sale in paying the deposits on the van and on a car which he desired to purchase from the dealer. He signed in blank a proposal form and memorandum of hire-purchase agreement in respect of both vehicles and gave them to the dealer to complete. The dealer certified in the proposal form that the van was his (the dealer's) absolute property. The dealer sold the van to the plaintiffs, a hire-purchase finance company, who accepted the owner's proposal and sent him a counterpart of the agreement. The hire-purchase transaction in respect of the car was not implemented and the dealer told the owner that the whole transaction was cancelled. The owner afterwards sold the van, believing it to be his own property, to a third party who bought it in good faith and without knowledge of the dealer's action. The owner made no payments under the hire-purchase agreement to the plaintiffs, who terminated the agreement and claimed the van or its value from the third party.

HELD: The plaintiffs were entitled to recover. (1) The owner had clothed the dealer with apparent authority to sell and was precluded from denying authority within the Sale of Goods Act 1893, s 21(1); (2) although the agreement had not been 'made and signed by the hirer' as required by the Hire-Purchase Act 1938, s 2(2)(a), neither that section nor s 17 of that Act took away their rights against any person other than the hirer; (3) the judge assumed the owner to be the seller under s 25(1) of the 1893 Act and he had not remained in possession; the hire-purchase agreement was effective to change his possession as seller to possession as bailee.

Note—For sections of Sale of Goods Act see note above.

HIRE PURCHASE

'Sale' by hirer

North Central (or General) Wagon and Finance Co v Graham
[1950] 2 KB 7, [1950] 1 All ER 780, 66 (Pt 1) TLR 707, CA

The plaintiffs, a hire-purchase company, let a motor car on hire purchase under an agreement which contained obligation on the hirer:

1 not to do anything prejudicially to affect the ownership or financial position of the owner;
2 not to attempt to sell or otherwise dispose of the car;
3 (a) if the hirer shall fail to pay any sum due or to observe or perform any

stipulation on his part herein contained the owner may terminate the hiring; (b) if this hiring be terminated for any reason the owner may by written notice put an end to the hiring under any other agreement between the parties;

4 this agreement is only a contract of bailment.

The hirer instructed an auctioneer to sell the car, and the auctioneer sold it. Plaintiffs sued the auctioneer for damages for conversion.

Lewis J dismissed the action, being influenced by the absence of a clause that breach ipso facto put an end to the agreement. He held the plaintiffs were not entitled to possession at the time of sale.

HELD, ON APPEAL: It was essential for the plaintiffs to show that they were entitled at the time of the sale to immediate possession. The case was similar to *Jelks v Hayward* [1905] 2 KB 460, 74 LJKB 717, 92 LT 692, 53 WR 686, except that the right to determine the hiring and take possession did not include the words 'without previous notice'. There could be no implied term requiring notice, because such notice was required in the case of other agreements. There is, apparently, no direct authority on the construction of the words 'may terminate the hiring', and it is a little startling that there should not be because it is the commonest form of expression in hire-purchase agreements. The plaintiffs could terminate the hiring without notice and the moment a breach occurred, the owner had the right to immediate possession. The plaintiffs therefore had the right to terminate the hiring at will the moment after the breach occurred. They therefore had an immediate right to possession and could sue the defendant in conversion.

The general principle of law is that a bailee who does something inconsistent with the terms of the contract, or any act or disposition which is wholly repugnant to or an absolute disclaimer of the holding as bailee, terminates the bailment and re-vests the bailor's right to possession. Here that general law does not apply because the contract makes special provision.

Appeal allowed.

Union Transport Finance v British Car Auctions Ltd
[1978] 2 All ER 385, 246 Estates Gazette 131, CA

Smith took a car on hire-purchase from the plaintiffs. The contract gave the plaintiffs the right at any time to declare the hiring terminated on breach of its terms or default in rental payments on notice given to the hirer at his last known address. Smith took the car to the defendant auctioneers without disclosing the hire-purchase contract and they sold it at auction to an innocent purchaser. The plaintiffs sued the defendants in conversion for damages. The defendants contended that the plaintiffs had no right to immediate possession of the car at the time of the sale, not having served notice, and could not sue in conversion. It was not disputed that for a bailor or lessor on hire purchase to sue in conversion he must show that he is entitled at the time of the sale to immediate possession of the goods.

HELD: The defendants could not succeed. At common law a bailor becomes entitled at once to bring the contract to an end and acquire the right to immediate possession if the bailee acts in a way which destroys the basis of the contract. The express term of the contract enabling the plaintiffs to terminate the hiring by notice did not oust the common law rule and deprive the plaintiffs of their rights at common law. Smith had torn up the contract of bailment by fraudulently selling the car through an auctioneer to an innocent third party. It would require very clear language to deprive the bailor of his common law rights in such circumstances and the language used in the present contract was nothing like strong enough. *North Central Wagon Co v Graham* (above) applied.

Moorgate Mercantile Co Ltd v Finch
[1962] 1 QB 701, [1962] 2 All ER 467, [1962] 3 WLR 110, 106 Sol Jo 284, CA

The plaintiffs were a finance company who let a car on hire purchase to the first defendant. At a time when he was in arrear with payments under the agreement he lent the car to the second defendant at his request though without knowing for what purpose it was required. The second defendant loaded the car with uncustomed watches and was subsequently caught by customs men with the watches in the car. As a result he was convicted and the car was forfeited to the Customs authorities under the relevant statutory provisions. The plaintiffs claimed damages for conversion of the car by the second defendant. The hire-purchase agreement contained the words 'in case of any and every breach of any term or condition hereof the owners shall forthwith without notice or demand become entitled immediately to recover possession of the vehicle'.

HELD: (1) The second defendant knew that forfeiture of the car was a natural and probable consequence of his conduct and there was a conversion of the car. (2) As the first defendant was in arrear with payments under the hire-purchase agreement this was a breach which entitled the plaintiffs to immediate possession (following *North Central Wagon & Finance Co v Graham*, above) and the second defendant was therefore liable to the plaintiffs for conversion of the vehicle.

United Dominion Trust (Commercial) Ltd v Parkway Motors
[1955] 2 All ER 557, [1955] 1 WLR 719, 99 Sol Jo 436 (McNair J)

On 8 October 1952, a hire-purchase company hired a van to Williams by an agreement which contained a condition that the hirer should keep the van in his possession and should not sell, offer for sale, assign or charge the van or the benefit of the agreement; a further condition provided that default in payment of an instalment or any breach or act which in the opinion bona fide formed of the hire-purchase company would jeopardise their rights, gave them the right by notice forthwith to terminate the agreement and retake possession; and a further clause after all payments had been made and provided the hirer had not committed any breach of agreement, the hirer had the option to purchase for 10s.

On 8 December 1953, the instalment was not paid. On 23 December 1953, Williams advertised the van for sale and the following day sold the van to Trotter for £410. Two days after this, Trotter sold the van to Parkway Motors for £410 10s 0d, Trotter undertaking to see that £96 the balance due under the agreement and the 10s option money, was paid to the hire-purchase company. Trotter's cheque to Williams was not met, and Williams on 28 December 1953, reported the position to the hire-purchase company and paid the instalment due on 8 December. On 4 January 1954, the hire-purchase company served Williams with a notice terminating the agreement. On the same day Parkway Motors tendered to the hire-purchase company by cheque, and on 12 January in cash, £96 10s 0d the balance of hire and the 10s option money. The hire-purchase company refused to accept either the cheque or cash and sued for the return of the van.

HELD: Williams was prohibited from assigning and therefore unable to pass any rights. Parkway Motors had no rights to cut down the hire-purchase company's prima facie right to recover the van. The case of a pledge of goods is irrelevant. Earlier decisions differed because there was an assignable interest. Judgment for the hire-purchase company for the return of the van or £350 its value.

Note—The Hire-Purchase Act 1964 provides protection for private purchasers of motor vehicles which are subject to hire-purchase contracts. Part 3 of the Act (substituted by the Consumer Credit Act 1974 as from 19 May 1985) provides that where a hirer of a motor vehicle under a hire-purchase agreement disposes of that vehicle to a private purchaser who buys in good faith and without notice of the hire-purchase agreement the disposition shall have effect as if the title of the owner to the vehicle had been vested in the hirer immediately before that disposition, ie the purchaser gets a good title. Where a hirer disposes of the vehicle to a trade or finance purchaser who disposes of it to a private purchaser in good faith without notice the same result follows. Where the 'first private purchaser' takes the vehicle under a new hire-purchase agreement from the original purchaser in good faith and without notice of the original hire-purchase agreement he still gets a good title under the provisions of the agreement (eg when he has paid all the instalments) even though by that time he can no longer satisfy the requirement of taking in good faith without notice of the original agreement. The Act has effect notwithstanding anything in the Sale of Goods Act 1979, s 21 or the Factors Acts. It does not exonerate the hirer from any liability, civil or criminal, to which he would otherwise be subject nor does it protect any trade or finance purchaser who takes from the hirer or from another trade or finance purchaser who is not claiming under the 'first private purchaser's' title. The Act applies to dispositions made on or after 1 January 1965. For a detailed account of the provisions of the Act see *Halsbury's Laws of England* (4th edn) paras 121, 122, 268 and 269 and the extensive notes to those paragraphs.

A 'trade or finance purchaser' within the meaning of the Act (s 29(2)) does not receive the protection of a 'private purchaser' under s 27 merely because in a particular transaction he buys a car for his own private use: *Stevenson v Beverley Bentinck Ltd* [1976] 2 All ER 606, [1976] 1 WLR 483, 120 Sol Jo 197, [1976] RTR 543, CA

Car on hire purchase in part exchange

Robin and Rambler Coaches Ltd v Turner
[1947] 2 All ER 284 (Hilbery J)
B obtained a Hillman car on hire purchase from W, paying £200 deposit. He paid one instalment of £40 10s 0d.

B sold the Hillman car to plaintiffs for £275 cash and a Jaguar car in part exchange.

B sold the Jaguar car to defendants for £525. Defendants sold it to F for £550.

W claimed the Hillman car from plaintiffs, and plaintiffs paid to W the balance due under the hire-purchase agreement, and costs, to obtain the title to the Hillman.

Plaintiffs claimed the Jaguar car from defendants.

HELD: The contract was voidable by the fraud of B but was not void; and was not avoided before the sale to defendants; defendants bought in good faith and the property in the Jaguar car passed to the defendants.

Finance company with no title

Warman v Southern Counties Car Finance Corpn

[1949] 2 KB 576, [1949] 1 All ER 711, [1949] LJR 1182, 93 Sol Jo 319 (Finnemore J)

In September 1947, a hirer entered into a hire-purchase agreement, paying £155 down and agreeing to pay £9 18s 0d 'rent' each month. After paying the instalments the hirer was to have the option of purchasing the car for 1s. In January, February and March 1948, the hirer received letters from a company claiming that the car was their property, which he ignored, but did not inform the hire-purchase company of the claim. He made the final payment of rent in April 1948, and on the same day was served with a writ by the owner of the car. The hirer handed over the car to the true owners and claimed damages from the hire-purchase company.

HELD: The hirer was entitled to rely on the warranty of ownership, which became effective at the date of the agreement and not when the final payment was made. The plaintiff was entitled to recover. The hire-purchase company were not entitled to any counterclaim or set off for the use of the car.

HP Information Ltd

Moorgate Mercantile Co Ltd v Twitchings

[1977] AC 890, [1976] 2 All ER 641, [1976] 3 WLR 66, 120 Sol Jo 470, HL

In about 1938 a number of finance companies set up an organisation called HP Information Ltd to obtain and register details of hire-purchase contracts and supply it to dealers and finance houses who were concerned to know whether a vehicle was the subject matter of a hire-purchase agreement. By 1971 98% of all such agreements were registered with HPI. The plaintiff company was a member and the defendant, a motor dealer, was an associate member. The plaintiffs let a vehicle on hire purchase to McLorg but negligently failed to register the transaction with HPI. McLorg offered the car for sale to the defendant who enquired of HPI whether there was any hire-purchase agreement and was told that no hire-purchase agreement was registered in relation to that car. The defendant then bought the car from McLorg and resold it. When the plaintiffs heard of it they sued the defendant for damages for conversion.

HELD: They were entitled to succeed. The plaintiffs were not estopped from claiming title to the car by reason of their failure to register the agreement because (1) the reply given by HPI to the defendant's enquiry was not a representation that no hire-purchase agreement existed but only that no such agreement had been communicated to them. Moreover their reply was not made as agents for the plaintiffs. (2) There was no legal duty of care owed by the plaintiffs to the defendant to register the agreement with HPI and estoppel by negligence could not arise in the absence of a duty of care.

Loan on security

Polsky v S and A Services Ltd
[1951] 1 All ER 185 (Lord Goddard CJ); appeal dismissed [1951] 1 All ER 1062 n, [1951] WN 256, 95 Sol Jo 414, CA
Plaintiff purchased a motor car from a dealer for £895 and paid by cheque. Next day, to obtain £400 to pay into his bank to meet the cheque, he arranged with defendants, a hire-purchase company, to advance £400. By the documents, defendants purported to buy from plaintiff the car and let it to him on hire purchase. The value of the car was stated to be £895; that an initial payment of £495 had been made, leaving £400, plus £50 for charges, as 'balance of hire' payable by instalments. Plaintiff signed a receipt saying 'Received cheque £400 payment for the car', and a document that he clearly understood he was selling the car to defendants.
HELD: Not a genuine sale and re-hire, but a loan of £400 on the security of the car and void for non-registration as a bill of sale.

R v Deller
(1952) 36 Cr App Rep 184, CCA
Defendant entered into a transaction with a hire-purchase company which purported to buy the defendant's car and to let the car back to him on hire-purchase terms. The documents were not registered as a bill of sale. Before he had paid all the instalments, he exchanged the car with C for the car of C, representing to C that he, the defendant, was the owner of the first car free from incumbrances and that there was no money owing on it. He was prosecuted for obtaining the car of C by false pretences.
HELD: It is a question of fact for the jury whether it was a genuine sale and re-hiring or a transaction of loan on the security of the car. If the latter, and void for non-registration as a bill of sale, the first car remained the property of the defendant and he was not guilty of any false pretence. *Polsky*'s case followed.

REGISTRATION DOCUMENT ('Log Book')

Not a document of title

Joblin v Watkins and Roseveare (Motors) Ltd
[1949] 1 All ER 47, 64 TLR 464 (Croom-Johnson J)
Plaintiff entered into an agreement on 4 November 1945, with one Smith whereby plaintiff purchased from Smith a second-hand motor car for £275 with option to Smith to re-purchase for £300 on or before 6 December 1945. Smith handed plaintiff the registration book of the car and a cheque post-dated to 6 December 1945, for £300. The registration book showed one Adams as the last owner. The plaintiff never saw the car and never took delivery. Earlier in 1945 the defendants had employed Smith as an agent to

buy cars in their name, but had ceased to do so in April 1945. The car had been bought by defendants from Adams but remained in Adams' possession for repairs for defendants. The cheque was dishonoured on presentation, and plaintiff was unable to obtain the money or the car from Smith. He sued defendants alleging Smith was a mercantile agent of defendants in possession of the document of title to goods under the Factors Act 1889, s 2(1).

By s 1(4) document of title includes any document authorising or purporting to authorise the possessor of the document to transfer the goods.

The Road Vehicles (Registration and Licensing) Regulations 1949, reg 9(1) (now reg 12(1) of the 1971 Regulations), provides that on sale of a car the then owner shall deliver the registration book to the new owner and forthwith notify the change to the authority.

HELD: The true transaction was a loan; it was not a disposition under the 1889 Act.

OBITER: (1) Smith was not a mercantile agent. (2) The registration book was not a document of title. The primary object was to show who was liable to pay the tax. It might indicate the right of the seller to be dealing with the vehicle, when the licence fell due, and the position generally, and that it was duly registered. It showed Adams as the owner.

Bishopsgate Motor Finance Corpn Ltd v Transport Brakes Ltd

[1949] 1 KB 322, [1949] 1 All ER 37, [1949] LJR 741, 65 TLR 66, 93 Sol Jo 71, CA

Per Denning LJ: Whilst the log book was not a document of title, it was the best evidence of title and a transfer was open to suspicion if the log book was not handed over. If not produced, or containing the wrong name, or if obviously tampered with, the buyer was put on enquiry, and purchased at his own risk. The plaintiffs here did not keep the log book in their own hands or in their own name. They were a finance company who allowed the hirer to have the car and take the log book in his own name. By reason of that fact, he was able to dispose of the car to an innocent purchaser.

Note—Also noted at p 920, above, 'Market overt'.

These observations do not seem to have regard to the Road Traffic Act 1930, s 121, which provides that 'owner' in relation to a vehicle which is the subject of a hire agreement or a hire-purchase agreement, means the person in possession of the vehicle under that agreement. This section is now replaced by the Road Traffic Act 1972, s 196, in which 'owner' is defined in the same terms. The vehicle registration document contains a warning notice: 'The Registered Keeper is not necessarily the legal owner'.

Car = car and log book

Bentworth Finance Ltd v Lubert

[1968] 1 QB 680, [1967] 2 All ER 810, [1967] 3 WLR 378, 111 Sol Jo 272, CA

The defendant signed a hire-purchase agreement with the plaintiffs, a finance company for a car. The car was delivered to her house but not a log book. She did not use the car, not being able to tax it, and did not pay any instalments. The plaintiffs took possession of the car and sued for arrears of instalments.

HELD: There was an implied condition that there should be a log book and as no log book had been supplied the contract of hire purchase had never come into effect and the plaintiffs could not sue on it.

Per Lord Denning MR: It is the common understanding of people that, if a car is bought or is taken on hire purchase, the log book will be provided. There is a great difference between the price of a car *with* the log book and the price of a car *without* the log book. The absence of it gives rise to the suspicion that the seller has a doubtful title. In short, the log book, though not a document of title, is very good evidence of title.

Owner parting with log book — sale

Central Newbury Car Auctions Ltd v Unity Finance Ltd (Mercury Motors, third parties)

[1957] 1 QB 371, [1956] 3 All ER 905, [1956] 3 WLR 1068, 100 Sol Jo 927, CA

In July 1947, a new car was registered with the index number CFX805 and a registration book issued. In October 1948, a change of ownership was registered which continued until 23 January 1955, when the car was bought by one Ashley and registered in his name but he did not sign the book. In September 1955, the car was sold at an auction to the plaintiffs, motor dealers, who did not register as owners. On 4 November 1955, a man giving the name of Cullis agreed with plaintiffs to take the car on hire purchase and left a Hillman car in part purchase. Cullis signed the forms for a hire-purchase agreement giving a fictitious address and a fictitious name and address as his employers. Plaintiffs recommended Cullis to the hire-purchase company as a suitable and responsible person. Without waiting for the completion of the hire-purchase agreement, plaintiffs allowed Cullis to take the car and the registration book. The next day the finance company declined the proposed agreement because of these fictitious statements. Plaintiffs then made enquiries about the Hillman car and found it was on hire purchase and paid £100 to the finance company concerned to validate their title. On 7 November 1955, a man who was probably Cullis but gave the name of Ashley, the name in the book, sold the Morris car to dealers in a distant town for £200, and these dealers sold it to the first defendants, a finance company, who let it on hire purchase to the second defendant. Plaintiffs sued both defendants for damages for conversion. The county court judge dismissed the action, holding that the plaintiffs were estopped by conduct. The plaintiffs appealed.

HELD, per Hodson LJ: It was a case of larceny by a trick by Cullis. The plaintiffs were not estopped by their negligent conduct from claiming as true owners. The case fell to be determined, not on a consideration of negligence, but on what is the nature of the representation made by the delivery of the registration book. The book itself is not a document of title: its terms negative ownership.

Per Morris LJ: By parting with the car and registration book the plaintiffs did not give an authority to sell. The registration book does not prove legal ownership. It proclaims a clear warning and intimation that it does not. Plaintiffs made the mistake of being deceived by a plausible trickster but the case does not depend on their carelessness in parting with the car and the book, but on the effect of their so acting. The plaintiffs are not estopped by their negligent conduct.

Appeal allowed by a majority; judgment against both defendants for damages agreed at £240.

Note—'Larceny': see Theft Act 1968, p 938, below.

J. Sargent (Garages) Ltd v Motor Auctions (West Bromwich) Ltd
[1977] RTR 121, CA

The plaintiffs, father and son, were car dealers. They bought a Jaguar E-type car for eventual resale but, pending sale, the son used it himself. A business acquaintance, Spencer, had become friendly with the plaintiffs. He owned and ran a business for providing special registration numbers. He suggested that he might get a special number for the car: the son agreed and gave him the log book for that purpose. A few days later, having sold a car of his own to the plaintiffs, Spencer asked to borrow the Jaguar for a couple of days. The plaintiffs rather reluctantly agreed. Spencer took the car and did not return. He took it a few days later to the first defendants who were auctioneers and it was sold at auction to the second defendant. The plaintiffs sued for damages for conversion.

HELD: The plaintiffs were not estopped from denying Spencer's authority to sell by their conduct in allowing Spencer to have both car and log book. *Central Newbury Car Auctions Ltd v Unity Finance* (p 935, above) was still good law. The log book was not a document of title. The plaintiffs, on the facts, had not been negligent but even if they had it would not have created an estoppel because they owed no duty of care to the general public.

Log book obtained without consent — Factors Act 1889

Pearson v Rose and Young Ltd (Little, third party; Marshall, fourth party)
[1951] 1 KB 275, [1950] 2 All ER 1027, 66 (Pt 2) TLR 886, 94 Sol Jo 778, CA

The plaintiff on 15 March 1949, was told by a mercantile agent that the agent could obtain a new motor car for the plaintiff for £467 in six months, but required a deposit of £100. Three days later plaintiff saw the agent and discussed whether the plaintiff could sell his car because of the covenant against resale, and to clear up this point the plaintiff produced his log book and handed it to the agent. Whilst the agent had it, he asked the plaintiff to accompany the agent's wife to hospital, which the plaintiff did and forgot about the log book. Later the same day the agent sold the plaintiff's car and handed the log book to the purchaser. The purchaser sold the car, and his purchaser in turn also sold it. The agent was afterwards convicted of fraud in connection with this and other cars. The plaintiff sued the ultimate purchaser for damages for conversion.

Devlin J held the agent was in possession of the car with the consent of the plaintiff, that the agent had tricked the plaintiff out of possession of the log book, and dismissed the plaintiff's claim.

HELD, ON APPEAL: On the sale of a second-hand car the purchaser would ordinarily require delivery of the log book. Cars could be sold without a log book but the price would be substantially reduced, and the sale of a car without a log book was not a sale in the ordinary course of business. The sale of a car with its log book is a more valuable subject matter than a car without its log book. The agent was never in possession of the log book with the consent of the plaintiff.

Appeal allowed with costs.

George v Revis
(1966) 111 Sol Jo 51 (Megaw J)

The plaintiff advertised his car for sale. A man named Robinson called and agreed to buy it, subject to a satisfactory engineer's report. He was allowed by the plaintiff to take the car away for an engineer's inspection. After he had gone the plaintiff discovered he had taken the log book also, though the plaintiff had not consented to his having possession of it. Robinson did not return and a month later sold the car to the defendant, who bought in good faith.

HELD: The Factors Act 1889 protected an innocent purchaser if (1) there had been a agreement by the owner to sell; (2) the original purchaser (here Robinson) had obtained the goods with the consent of the seller; (3) the ultimate purchaser (the defendant) had acted in good faith and without notice of any right of the original seller. Conditions (1) and (3) were fulfilled. Condition (2) was fulfilled as far as the car alone was concerned if the facts as to the log book were disregarded, but the log book was of vital significance in the sale of a car. *Pearson v Rose & Young* (above) was clear authority for this and was sufficient to decide the case. The plaintiff had not consented to Robinson having possession of the log book: he was entitled to a return of the car or damages.

Note—See also *Bentworth Finance Ltd v Lubert*, p 934, above.

Stadium Finance Ltd v Robbins
[1962] 2 QB 664, [1962] 2 All ER 633, [1962] 3 WLR 453, 106 Sol Jo 369, CA

The defendant was the owner of a car which he wished to sell. He took it to a dealer who agreed to put it in his showroom and to report any enquiries. The defendant kept the ignition key but, probably by accident, left the log book locked in the glove box. The dealer obtained an ignition key and also opened the glove box, finding the log book. He arranged for his salesman to take the car on hire-purchase and sold it to the plaintiffs, a hire-purchase company. The salesman failed to make the first monthly payment and the plaintiffs sought to take possession of the car. They found that the defendant had already seized it as his property. They claimed the return of the car or its value and damages.

HELD: The plaintiffs could succeed only if they could show that the sale of the car to them by the dealer was made by him when acting in the ordinary course of business of a mercantile agent, ie within the terms of the Factors Act 1889, s 2(1). The car, with or without the ignition key and the log book, was 'goods' within the meaning of the Act but the dealer was not acting in the ordinary course of his business as a mercantile agent. The car had been put in possession of the dealer with no key and no registration book easily available: a dealer who sells motor cars in the ordinary course of his business sells those which are in a condition to be used as cars and the sale of a car deficient both of log book and ignition key could not be in the ordinary course of business of a mercantile agent. The provision in s 2(4) of the Act that consent of the owner shall be presumed in the absence of evidence to the contrary did not affect the case because the defendant's retention of the key was evidence of his intention to control the sale.

Note—See also *Lambert v G. C. Finance Corpn Ltd*, p 925, above.

Owner giving possession of log book

Du Jardin v Beadman Bros Ltd
[1952] 2 QB 712, [1952] 2 All ER 160, [1952] 1 TLR 1601, 96 Sol Jo 414
(Sellers J)
On 12 May 1951, G obtained possession from the defendants of a Standard car on payment of £10 and a cheque for £700 leaving a Hillman car as security for the cheque, stating he wanted to take the car right away to show to a prospective buyer. Defendants handed him the registration book and receipt. Shortly afterwards, G or another man, in the absence of defendants, drove the Hillman car away. On 15 May 1951, plaintiff purchased the Standard car from G. The cheque for £700 was worthless and subsequently the police took possession of the Standard car from the plaintiff. G was convicted of obtaining the car by false pretences, and the Standard car returned to the defendants.
HELD: Though G had obtained possession of the car by larceny by a trick, he had possession with consent. The fact that there was only an agreement for sale and not a sale was immaterial. *Pearson*'s case followed; *Lake*'s case not followed. There was no inconsistency in *Pearson*'s case. The question was whether possession was with consent and this depended on the knowledge of the owner or seller. The defendants consented to possession. Order for car to be returned to plaintiff.

THEFT

Note—The Larceny Act 1916 was repealed by the Theft Act 1968 (in force 1 January 1969) and the term 'larceny' is obsolete. The Theft Act 1968, s 1 defines theft as follows:

'(1) A person is guilty of theft if he dishonestly appropriates property belonging to another with the intention of permanently depriving the other of it; and "theft" and "steal" shall be construed accordingly.'

Section 12 creates a particular offence of taking a motor vehicle without authority.

Section 15 deals with obtaining property by deception and should be contrasted with the Larceny Act 1916, s 32. It is as follows:

'(1) A person who by deception dishonestly obtains property belonging to another, with the intention of permanently depriving the other of it, shall on conviction on indictment be liable to imprisonment for a term not exceeding ten years.
(2) For purposes of this section a person is to be treated as obtaining property if he obtains ownership, possession or control of it, and "obtain" includes obtaining for another or enabling another to obtain or to retain.
(3) For purposes of this section "deception" means any deception (whether deliberate or reckless) by words or conduct or as to fact or as to law, including a

deception as to the present intentions of the person using the deception or any other person.'

Orders for restitution are dealt with in s 28.

For meaning of 'theft' in insurance policies see *Grundy (Teddington) v Fulton*, p 173, above.

Procedure for recovery of stolen property in police custody — Police (Property) Act 1897

1 Where the police have recovered stolen property from an innocent holder they will not normally deliver it to the person from whom it was stolen unless the person from whom the property was recovered expressly disclaims ownership. If that person fails or refuses to give such a disclaimer the owner can proceed against the police in a court of summary jurisdiction by virtue of the provisions of the Police (Property) Act 1897, for an order for delivery of the property to him.

2 *Venue.* This will depend on the person sued. If the property is held by the Metropolitan Police the defendant will be the Commissioner of Police, New Scotland Yard. The powers of a court of summary jurisdiction under the section are to be exercised by a metropolitan magistrate or by lay justices for the inner London area, and the venue can be agreed with the police. In other parts of the country than the Metropolitan Police District presumably the Chief Constable of the police force holding the property should be made defendant and the summons should be taken out in the court of summary jurisdiction within the district of which his office is situated.

3 *Procedure.* (a) Application is made by the owner (or by his solicitor on his behalf without his attendance) to a magistrate for issue of a summons against the Commissioner of Police or Chief Constable as the case may be in accordance with para 2 above. On the application being granted the summons (form below) is issued in the court office. The summons can forthwith be handed to the warrant officer of the police at the court. It is suggested that before the application is made a date for the hearing be agreed with the police officers who have charge of the property.

(b) Notice of the summons is served by the police on any other claimant to the property so that he may attend at the hearing to dispute the title to the property if he wishes.

(c) On the hearing of the summons evidence of identification and ownership of the property is adduced by the owner. The police or any other claimant may raise such matters or give such evidence relating to the ownership of the property as they may think fit and the court makes its order accordingly. It is open to any person to dispute the order made and to reopen the matter within six months. If not challenged within six months, however, the order becomes indefeasible.

(d) Where the owner at the time of theft has been paid the full value of the property under a policy of insurance the information should nevertheless be laid in his name. When an order has been made for delivery of the property to him he should then sign an authority to the police authorising them to deliver the property to the insurers. In the absence of this the police will not recognise the rights of the insurers to the property.

IN THE METROPOLITAN POLICE DISTRICT

To *The Commissioner of Police, New Scotland Yard*
WHEREAS application has this day been made to the undersigned, one of the Magistrates of the Police Courts of the Metropolis, sitting at the Bow Street Police Court, by . . . of . . . to make an order under the provisions of the 'Police

(Property) Act 1897', respecting certain Property, to wit, . . . which Property has come into the possession of the Police under the circumstances mentioned in the said Act:

You ARE THEREFORE HEREBY SUMMONED to appear before me, or such other of the said Magistrates as may then be sitting at the said Police Court on . . . day, the . . . day of . . . at the hour of . . . in the . . . noon if you desire to show cause why an order should not then be made for the delivery of the said Property to the person appearing to be the owner thereof, or such other order as to me, or such other Magistrate as aforesaid, may seem meet.

Dated the . . . day of . . . , 19 . .

(Signed)

One of the Magistrates of the Police Courts of the Metropolis

Irving v National Provincial Bank Ltd

[1962] 2 QB 73, [1962] 1 All ER 157, [1962] 2 WLR 503, 126 JP 76, CA
Where an order has been made by a magistrate under the Police (Property) Act 1897, for delivery of property to a claimant and the physical possession has passed to him, the former possessor of the goods is in no better position than any other person if he takes proceedings within six months to re-open the matter (see para 3 (c) above). He can no longer rely on a presumption from his previous possession and the onus of proving his title to the goods is on him.

R v Uxbridge Justices ex p Metropolitan Police Comr

[1981] QB 829, [1981] 3 All ER 129, [1981] 3 WLR 410, 146 JP 42, 125 Sol Jo 445, CA
1 An application under s 2(1) of the 1897 Act need not be made by complaint, but can be made by application only, that being the practice in the metropolitan magistrates courts: in that case magistrates have no power to order costs.
2 On a complaint it is inappropriate to make an order for costs against the police where the police do not object to the order sought.

APPENDICES

Fatal accident cases

Note—This appendix contains fatal accident cases which have been made largely obsolete by the provisions of the Administration of Justice Act 1982, but are relevant to pending claims arising before January 1983. They do not purport to comprise an exhaustive selection of cases on the old law.

FATAL ACCIDENTS ACT 1976, ss 1–3 (as enacted)

1 Right of action for wrongful act causing death (1) If death is caused by any wrongful act, neglect or default which is such as would (if death had not ensued) have entitled the person injured to maintain an action and recover damages in respect thereof, the person who would have been liable if death had not ensued shall be liable to an action for damages, notwithstanding the death of the person injured.
(2) Every such action shall be for the benefit of the dependants of the person ('the deceased') whose death has been so caused.
(3) In this Act 'dependant' means —
(a) the wife or husband of the deceased,
(b) any person who is a parent or grandparent of the deceased,
(c) any person who is a child or grandchild of the deceased, and
(d) any person who is, or is the issue of, a brother, sister, uncle or aunt of the deceased.
(4) In deducing any relationship for the purposes of sub-s (3) —
(a) any relationship by affinity shall be treated as a relationship by consanguinity, any relationship of the half blood as a relationship of the whole blood, and the stepchild of any person as his child, and
(b) an illegitimate person shall be treated as the legitimate child of his mother and reputed father.
(5) Any reference in this Act to injury includes any disease or any impairment of a person's physical or mental condition.

2 Persons entitled to bring the action (1) The action shall be brought by and in the name of the executor or administrator of the deceased.
(2) If —
(a) there is no executor or administrator of the deceased, or
(b) no action is brought within six months after the death by and in the name of an executor or administrator of the deceased,
the action may be brought by and in the name of all or any of the dependants.
(3) Not more than one action shall lie for and in respect of the same subject matter of complaint.
(4) The plaintiff in the action shall be required to deliver to the defendant or his solicitor full particulars of the dependants for whom and on whose behalf the action is brought, and of the nature of the claim in respect of which damages are sought to be recovered.

3 Assessment of damages   (1) In the action such damages may be awarded as are proportioned to the injury resulting from the death to the dependants respectively, and the amount so recovered, after deducting the costs not recovered from the defendant, shall be divided among the dependants in such shares as may be directed.

(2) In assessing damages payable to a widow in respect of the death of her husband in an action under this Act there shall not be taken into account the remarriage of the widow or her prospects of remarriage.

(3) If the dependants have incurred funeral expenses in respect of the deceased, damages may be awarded in respect of those expenses.

(4) Money paid into court in satisfaction of a cause of action under this Act may be in one sum without specifying the dependants' shares.

Divorced wife not a dependant

Payne-Collins v Taylor Woodrow Construction Ltd
[1975] QB 300, [1975] 1 All ER 898, [1975] 2 WLR 386, 119 Sol Jo 49 (O'Connor J)
The plaintiff claimed damages under the Fatal Accidents Acts for the death of her husband. She was the second wife of the deceased, whose first marriage was dissolved in 1967 and custody of the children of that marriage was awarded to the first wife. In the present action the first (ie former) wife applied to the Court to be joined as a dependant in the widow's action.
HELD: The former wife was not a dependant within the meaning of the Fatal Accidents Acts. Neither s 2 of the 1846 Act nor s 5 of the 1959 Act in defining the class of dependants made any provision which included a divorced husband or wife as a person on whose behalf an action could be brought.

ASSESSMENTS AND DEDUCTIONS

Effect of inheritance

Bradburn v Great Western Rly Co
(1874) LR 10 Exch 1, 44 LJEx 9, 31 LT 464, 23 WR 48
The statute has laid down no rules as to mode of calculating the damages to be given in respect of the right of action which it created. The rule was first laid down in this court, and that rule was, that the damages were to be a compensation to the family of the deceased equivalent to the pecuniary benefits which they might have reasonably expected from the continuance of his life. If, therefore, the person claiming damages was put by the death of his relative into possession of a large estate, there was no loss; he was the gainer by the event; and similarly, whatever comes into the possession of the family who have suffered by the death of their relative by reason of his death must be taken into account.

Daniels v Jones
[1961] 3 All ER 24, [1961] 1 WLR 1103, 105 Sol Jo 568, CA
The plaintiff claimed damages under the Fatal Accidents Act, for the death of her husband, the managing director of a private company. He was aged 51 at the time of his death and she 54. There were five children of whom two

were married. The deceased's net average earnings were £3,300 per year for three years before his death and were increasing. He was a frugal man in his personal requirements and provided generously for his family. The value of his estate was £30,750. The judge adopted 13 years as the period for capitalising the annual loss and estimated the net annual earnings over that period at £4,600. He took 9.9 as the multiplier, being the present value of an annuity for 13 years. He found that the net amount the plaintiff received from her husband's estate after payment of death duties was £20,750 but held that she already had an expectancy based on her chances of surviving him which he put at $12\frac{1}{2}\%$. The amount to be set off in respect of the acceleration of her expectancy against the gross capital value of the dependency was £18,200, being £20,750 less $12\frac{1}{2}\%$. The net award was thus £14,600.

On appeal the defendant raised several criticisms of the judge's method of assessment: if all the defendant's contentions were right the plaintiff would appear to have lost nothing by her husband's death. The appeal was dismissed.

Per Holroyd Pearce LJ: It is difficult to believe that the widow has sustained no loss when she found herself in possession of his capital of £40,000 (to take counsel for the defendant's figure) less upwards of £10,000 death duties, and when his high earnings were no longer available for the family. If counsel's arguments are correct and if arithmetically the conclusion must be that there is no loss in this case, arithmetic has failed to provide the answer which common sense demands. Since the question is one of actual material loss, some arithmetical calculations are necessarily involved in an assessment of the injury. But they do not provide a substitute for common sense.

ESTATE DUTY

Davies v Whiteways Cyder Co Ltd
[1975] QB 262, [1974] 3 All ER 168, [1974] 3 WLR 597, 118 Sol Jo 792, [1974] 2 Lloyd's Rep 556, [1974] STC 411 (O'Connor J)
The first plaintiff's husband, a successful businessman, had over the years made various dispositions of his money for her benefit and that of their son. He was killed in a road accident by negligence of the defendant's driver before the period of seven years had elapsed; as a result nearly £40,000 was brought back for estate duty and £17,000 duty was paid.
HELD: In the claim by the widow and son under the Fatal Accidents Acts, the sum of £17,000 (less £500 to cover the small chance of the deceased's not surviving the remainder of the seven years had the accident not happened) was recoverable from the defendants as damages for the death. It was (1) a financial loss which the plaintiffs had suffered and would suffer as a result of death, and (2) arose from the relationship of husband and father, and was accordingly within the words of s 2 of the 1846 Act.

DEDUCTIONS

Pym v Great Northern Rly Co
(1863) 4 B & S 396, 36 LJQB 377, 8 LT 734, 10 Gur N S 199, 11 WR 922
Apart from statutory exceptions, from the assessed loss must be deducted any pecuniary advantage received by the dependants in consequence of the death.

Yelland v Powell Duffryn Associated Collieries Ltd

[1941] 1 KB 154, [1941] 1 All ER 278, 110 LJKB 401, 164 LT 401, 57 TLR 172, 85 Sol Jo 177, CA

Per Luxmoore LJ: There can be no question that apart from any statutory provision to the contrary, the damages to be awarded under the Fatal Accidents Acts are to be ascertained with due regard to any benefits accruing to the person entitled to participate in them by reason of the death which gives rise to such damages (citing *Hicks v Newport, Abergavenny and Hereford Rly Co* (1857) 4 B & S 403 n).

Accelerated benefits by succession

Voller v Dairy Produce Packers Ltd

[1962] 3 All ER 938, [1962] 1 WLR 960, 106 Sol Jo 550 (Nield J)

The father of two children aged ten and six was killed in a road accident due to the negligence of the defendants. He was aged 36: the dependency of his wife and children at the time of his death was assessed at £19 per week. He died intestate leaving £985 and a house valued at £3,500 less mortgage of £779. Two years later his wife died. In claims under the Fatal Accidents and Law Reform Acts in respect of his death —

HELD: (1) A proper award under the Law Reform Act was £320. (2) The wife's claim under the Fatal Accidents Acts must be assessed on the short period of dependency up to the time of her own death (following *Williamson v Thorneycroft*, (p 500, above)). Subject to matters mentioned below, this was £612. (3) The estate of £985 was a benefit to the wife consequent on her husband's death since it was received sooner than it would otherwise have been, coupled with certainty. A proper amount to be deducted in the present case in respect of this acceleration was £150. The Law Reform damages from her husband's estate must also be deducted leaving a net award of £142. (4) The children would have been dependant to the age of 18. A proper award in the present case was £1,908 to the older and £2,376 to the younger, subject to deductions mentioned below. (5) No deduction should be made from the widow's award in respect of the value of the house as she lived in it until her death (*Heatley v Steel Co of Wales*, p 950, below) but in the case of the children (who had been taken into the home of an aunt after their mother's death) the position was different. There was an accelerated benefit coming to the children from the sale of the house. It was immaterial that it came to them through their mother's estate and not directly from their father's. A proper deduction in respect of the accelerated benefit was £150 from the elder child's award and £225 from the younger child's leaving totals of £1,758 and £2,151 respectively.

Note—See also 'effect of inheritance', p 944, above.

Daniels v Jones

[1961] 3 All ER 24, [1961] 1 WLR 1103, 105 Sol Jo 568, CA

Per Willmer LJ: I do not at all assent to the proposition that, in the particular circumstances of this case, the value of the estate is to be set off pound for pound against the loss of income as a matter of precise arithmetical calculation. . . . The reality of the situation is that for all practical purposes the widow (and her family) were enjoying the benefit of it almost as much before the death of the deceased as they do now.

Note—For facts, see p 944, above. See also *Taylor v O'Connor*, below.

Taylor v O'Connor

[1971] AC 115, [1970] 1 All ER 365, [1970] 2 WLR 472, 114 Sol Jo 132, [1970] TR 37, 49 ATC 37, HL

The plaintiff's husband was aged 53 at his death, a partner in a firm of architects. In the year before his death his earnings were £14,890 and would have been £21,000 for the next 12 years — about £7,500 per annum after tax. £1,500 of this would have had to be left in the firm for capital and there would have been some savings from the remaining £6,000, he would have spent about £3,000 p a in a manner beneficial to the plaintiff and their daughter. £10,000 came to the plaintiff from the estate. The judge awarded £54,196 damages.

HELD: Though the judge's method of assessment might be varied in some details, his figure was within the reasonable range of possible awards and should be upheld. On individual items: (1) In valuing the dependency the judge's method of allowing for the fact that the widow would receive £10,000 from the husband's estate was to deduct £200 from the annual value of the dependency to allow for acceleration of her interest in the estate; this was a proper deduction. (2) Although it would be unrealistic to refuse to take inflation into account at all, the judge's method, which was to increase the multiplier of the annual dependency from 10 to 12 was not a valid one. The lump sum of damages should be assessed on the basis that it will be invested with the aim of getting some capital appreciation to offset the probable arise in the cost of living. Having regard to the incidence of tax and surtax and the widow's expectation of life of 21 years, however, 12 was not an unreasonably high multiplier. (3) In taking the incidence of tax into account any private income of the widow's should be ignored.

PAYMENTS NOT TO BE TAKEN INTO ACCOUNT — FATAL ACCIDENTS ACT 1976, s 4

Note—The Fatal Accidents Act 1959, s 2 was repealed and replaced as respects causes of action arising from deaths on or after 1 September 1976, by the Fatal Accidents Act 1976, s 4 as follows:

'4 Assessment of damages: disregard of certain benefits (1) In assessing damages in respect of a person's death in an action under this Act, there shall not be taken into account any insurance money, benefit, pension or gratuity which has been or will or may be paid as result of the death.
(2) In this section —
'benefit' means benefit under the enactments relating to social security, including enactments in force in Northern Ireland, and any payment by a friendly society or trade union for the relief or maintenance of a member's dependants,
'insurance money' includes a return of premiums, and
'pension' includes a return of contributions and any payment of a lump sum in respect of a person's employment.'

Humphrey v Ward Engineering Services Ltd
(1975) 119 Sol Jo 461 (Latey J)

The deceased was killed a month before his sixtieth birthday when he would have received a lump sum from his employers. Had he then worked to 65 he would have received another lump sum and a pension. His widow had now received from the employers a lump sum and a widow's pension. If these were to be disregarded in assessing damages because of the provisions of the Fatal Accidents Act 1959, s 2 she would be better off than if her husband had survived. It was argued for the defendants that she had first to prove pecuniary loss to claim damages under the 1846 Act and if because of the benefits she had received she had no loss the 1959 Act did not apply.

HELD: That was not right. The wording of s 2(1) of the 1959 Act was very clear: the benefits to the widow by reason of her husband's death were to be disregarded in deciding whether or not there had been a loss and what should be the damages by way of compensation.

Estate duty on insurance moneys

Baker v T. E. Hopkins & Son Ltd
[1958] 3 All ER 147, [1958] 1 WLR 993, 102 Sol Jo 636 (Barry J)

Deceased was a medical practitioner aged 41. He left a widow of the same age, a boy of 12 and a girl of 10. The widow was also a qualified doctor and was in partnership with her husband in the practice, having one-fifth share of the profits. The husband had very many panel patients, but the wife had only a few, being largely occupied as an anaesthetist at hospital. The net annual gain accruing to the family from Dr Baker's earnings was probably somewhat more than £1,000 per annum. He left estate of £36,827 gross, made up of £15,370 insurances, £2,725 house and furniture, £8,236 government stock, £1,488 in a trustee savings bank and reversions valued at £629. Excluding the insurance moneys and the house and furniture, which were to be disregarded in assessing damages, the total estate was £10,353. The amount of the medical practice gratuity paid by the Ministry of Health on his death was £5,540 and the death gratuity under the health service scheme was £3,592.

The amount of the estate duty was £8,897. The defendants contended that the widow benefited by the amount of the estate less the insurance moneys and less only such portion of the total estate duty as was attributable to that part of the estate other than the £15,378 received under the insurance policies.

HELD: It would be infringing the real meaning of the provisions of the Act to deal with death duties or estate duties in that way. The estate duty is a debt; and it is a debt against the estate as a whole. It is not possible without infringing the provisions of the Act to subdivide it and treat some part of that sum of £8,897 as being attributable and payable out of the insurance moneys and the balance as being attributable to and being payable out of the remainder of the estate.

Award, £12,000.

Law reform damages must be taken into account

Ellis v Raine

[1939] 2 KB 180, [1939] 1 All ER 104, 108 LJKB 292, 161 LT 234, 55 TLR 344, 83 Sol Jo 152, CA

It will, of course, be open to, and indeed the duty of, the learned judge who presides at the new trial to point out to the jury that as in this case the dependants who claim under Lord Campbell's Act are the same persons as the beneficiaries of the estate of the deceased who claim under the Law Reform Act, any recovery under the latter Act may diminish, and may well extinguish, any claim under the former Act, and that those dependants or claimants must not to any extent be allowed to have their claim for damages twice over: Per MacKinnon LJ.

With regard to the relation which the damages given under one head should bear to those under the other, I do not think there is any real difficulty at all. I have always directed juries somewhat in this way. The Fatal Accidents Act deals with pecuniary loss only. If the parties who will benefit from the damages awarded under the Fatal Accidents Act are the same as those who will benefit from the damages awarded under the Law Reform Act, the damages under the Fatal Accidents Act must be reduced by the amount which is given as loss under the Law Reform Act. If the amount given under the Law Reform Act is equal to or exceeds what the jury may give under the Fatal Accidents Act, they give nothing under the Fatal Accidents Act at all. If, on the other hand, in any particular case a jury (as well may happen) should consider that the damages under the Fatal Accidents Act exceed the damages given under the Law Reform Act, then it may be necessary to assess both.

If in the present case the jury come to the conclusion, as ordinarily speaking they would, that the loss of the child's expectation of life was greater than the loss under the Fatal Accidents Act, then they would give no damages under that Act.

Yelland v Powell Duffryn Associated Collieries Ltd

[1941] 1 KB 154, [1941] 1 All ER 278, 110 LJKB 401, 164 LT 401, 57 TLR 172, 85 Sol Jo 177, CA

Damages under the Law Reform Act recovered by a widow reduce her pecuniary loss under the Fatal Accidents Acts and must be taken into account in estimating that loss. The Court of Appeal rejected the contrary contention based on the words of s 1(5) of the 1934 Act that the rights are in addition to and not in derogation of the rights under the Fatal Accidents Acts, and pointed out that the 1934 Act did not contain language similar to the 1908 Act that sums paid under a contract of assurance shall not be taken into account.

Davies v Powell Duffryn Associated Collieries Ltd

[1942] AC 601, [1942] 1 All ER 657, 111 LJKB 418, 167 LT 74, 58 TLR 240, 86 Sol Jo 294, HL

In assessing damages awarded under the Fatal Accidents Acts, damages under the Law Reform Act must be taken into account in the case of dependants who will benefit under the latter Act. The balance of loss and gain to a dependant by the death must be ascertained, the position of each dependant being considered separately. If at the time of assessing the damages under the Fatal Accidents Acts no proceedings have been taken under the Law Reform Act, the authority assessing the damages could always take into account the possibility of such proceedings and make allowance accordingly.

A difficult matter, no doubt, and quite incapable of accurate valuation. In some circumstances the extent of loss depends upon data which cannot be ascertained with certainty, and must necessarily be matters of estimate, and, it may be, partly of conjecture. The deceased might have willed away from the widow his estate in whole or in part, or the estate might be insolvent.

Murray v Shuter
[1976] QB 972, [1975] 3 All ER 375, [1975] 3 WLR 597, 119 Sol Jo 712, [1975] 2 Lloyd's Rep 470, CA

In an action carried on under the 1934 Act the administrators of the estate of J. M. Murray claimed damages for injuries and loss of earnings he sustained as a result of a road accident in January 1969. He remained in a coma until he died in April 1973. After his death the administrators began an action under the Fatal Accidents Acts on behalf of his widow and children. The actions were consolidated. In the first action the net damages awarded for injuries and loss of amenities were £7,837 and for loss of earnings £4,613. In the FAA action the provisional figure for damages was £76,800. The question to be decided was by how much, if any, the gross damages in the FAA action should be reduced by deducting damages awarded to the estate in the first action.

HELD: (1) As the sum of £7,837 awarded to the estate for loss of amenities would pass to the widow and children as beneficiaries under the intestacy the provisional FAA damages should be reduced by that amount. (2) Deduction of the loss of earnings was different: had Mr Murray earned that amount he would have used it for their benefit in his lifetime. It would be unjust to reduce the compensation paid to the dependants for loss of his support after his death because of the belated receipt of money which, but for the dependant's wrongdoing, would have been used for their financial support in the four years or so preceding his death. None of it should be regarded as deductible.

House and furniture, value of

Heatley v Steel Co of Wales Ltd
[1953] 1 All ER 489, [1953] 1 WLR 405, 97 Sol Jo 149, CA

Deceased, locomotive driver aged 43 owned leasehold house worth £1,450 less £260 on mortgage.

HELD, ON APPEAL: The value of the house should not be deducted. The widow was living in it with the family exactly as before. If sold, she would have to find another house.

Voluntary payments

Peacock v Amusement Equipment Co Ltd

[1954] 2 QB 347, [1954] 2 All ER 689, [1954] 3 WLR 288, 98 Sol Jo 533, CA

The plaintiff as husband claimed damages under the Fatal Accidents Acts in respect of the death of his wife. The deceased by her will left her property, chiefly a grocery business to her two children by a previous marriage, and nothing to the plaintiff. The business was sold and the two children voluntarily paid over to the plaintiff the sum of £575 which was said to represent about one-third of the estate.

HELD: The case of *Redpath v Belfast and County Down Rly Co* (p 415, above), was not a case under the Fatal Accidents Acts but the statements of Andrews LCJ are applicable that money publicly subscribed should not be 'directed' to reduce the damages payable by the wrongdoer. Why should the defendants' burden be lightened by the generosity of the public? It would only be in very unusual circumstances that a voluntary payment would be taken into account when there was no expectation of it at the time of the death. In this case there is a *nova causa interveniens* and the payment was not made in consequence of or as a result of the death. It was a voluntary gift out of generosity or affection.

Birkett LJ citing Lord Wright in *Davies v Powell Duffryn Associated Collieries* (above):

'Section 2 of the Act of 1846 provides that the action is to be for the benefit of the wife, or other member of the family, and the jury (or judge) are to give such damages as may be thought proportioned to the injury resulting to such parties from the death. The damages are to be based on the reasonable expectation of pecuniary benefit or benefit reducible to money value. In assessing the damages all circumstances which may be legitimately pleaded in diminution of the damage must be considered. The actual pecuniary loss of each individual entitled to sue can only be ascertained by balancing, on the one hand, the loss to him of the future pecuniary benefit, and, on the other, any pecuniary advantage which from whatever source comes to him by reason of the death.'

The payment in this case was not money paid by reason of the death. Appeal allowed.

Note—See also *Rawlinson v Babcock and Wilcox*, p 952, below.

A voluntary gift to a dependant might, since the 1959 Act, be regarded as being included in the term 'gratuity' in s 2 of the Act (s 4 of the 1976 Act).

Maylon v Plummer

[1964] 1 QB 330, [1963] 2 All ER 344, [1963] 2 WLR 1213, 107 Sol Jo 270, CA

The plaintiff's husband died on 6 January 1961 following a road accident caused by the defendant's negligence. The plaintiff (aged 41 at the date of the trial) claimed damages under the Fatal Accidents Acts for herself and her two children aged 13 and nine. The deceased was 40 years of age. He had been conducting his own business since 1955. It was a limited company of which he held all the shares except one, which was owned by the plaintiff. The whole business was run by the deceased with some casual help from the plaintiff. She was allotted a salary each year from the profits: during the last financial year before the accident she was allotted £800, her husband's salary from the company being £1,800. These salaries together comprised practically the whole profit of the company. The plaintiff proved in evidence that £1,328 per year was spent on herself and the two children. The judge raised this to £1,375 to allow for increased income which the deceased would probably have attained had he lived and took a multiplier of 13, having regard to the ages of the plaintiff and the deceased. This made a total of £17,875 which the defendant sought to reduce on two grounds (1) that as the plaintiff received a salary which she spent on herself and the children, the figure of £1,375 should be reduced by the amount of her salary, (2) the company had received the sum of £2,000 under a life policy taken out by the company on the deceased's life. As a result the company's share capital was increased in value by that amount. The plaintiff had received the benefit of this because she had inherited her husband's shareholding and it should be deducted from the £17,875.

HELD: (1) The loss must result from one of the specified relationships in the Acts. In the present case the relationship which gave rise to the salary was not superimposed on that of marriage as in *Burgess v Florence Nightingale Hospital* (p 509, above), but arose from it, since the plaintiff and her husband had already been married eight years when he started his business: but for the relationship of husband and wife the plaintiff would never have received the salary. Its loss was therefore to be included in assessing damages. (2) The question was whether the benefit which had accrued to the plaintiff in the enhanced value of the shares by reason of the liability of the insurance company to pay the £2,000 to the company the plaintiff's inheritance of the shares under the will came within the words 'insurance money' in the Fatal Accidents Act 1959, s 2 (now s 4 of the 1976 Act, p 947, above). A liberal interpretation should be put on the words and in the special facts of this case the £2,000 was 'insurance money' not to be set off against the figure of lost dependency.

The defendant appealed.

HELD: (1) The fact that in law the plaintiff was employed by the company should not be allowed to hide the reality of the matter, namely, that the excess of her actual salary over the market value of her services was a benefit which arose from the relationship of husband and wife. It was only this excess, however, and not the whole salary, which could be counted as a loss in assessing the damages. That portion of her salary which represented the market value of the work she performed (and which could be put at £200 per annum) should be deducted from the calculation of her loss. Damages reduced to £14,748. (2) The insurance payment was covered by the Act and should not be deducted.

Rawlinson v Babcock and Wilcox Ltd
[1966] 3 All ER 882, [1967] 1 WLR 481, 111 Sol Jo 76 (Chapman J)

The plaintiff's father, aged 45, was killed in an accident at work on 4 September 1962; her mother, his widow, died on 23 January 1964. The plaintiff, 14 years old at the time of her father's death, was taken care of by her uncle after her mother died, living as a member of his family and paying 30s per week towards her keep; at the time of the hearing of the action in 1966 she was earning £5 13s 6d per week as a typist. Another uncle gave her presents of £5 or more every two or three months. Her father had been earning £22 per week at the time of his death and the total dependency of his wife and daughter was agreed to have been £700 a year of which £200 could be allocated to the plaintiff. The defendants urged that her damages under the Fatal Accidents Act should be evaluated at no more than support until she left school at which time she would have ceased to be financially dependant on her father, and that living with her uncle she was now no worse off financially than if her father had been still alive.

HELD: (1) Contributions to the plaintiff's upkeep arising from motives of charity and benevolence must be ignored in assessing damages under the Fatal Accidents Acts since the operative cause of such contributions unlike insurance monies is not the fact of death but motives of compassion. (2) If her father had not been killed he would very probably after her mother's death have expected the plaintiff to keep house for him but in return would have lavished everything upon her. £400 a year would be a likely dependency figure plus the value of a substantial advancement on marriage.

Award, £2,450 including £283 for the period before her mother's death.

Note—See also *Voller v Dairy Produce Packers*, p 946, above.

Hay. v Hughes

[1975] QB 790, [1975] 1 All ER 257, [1975] 2 WLR 34, 118 Sol Jo 883, [1975] 1 Lloyd's Rep 12, CA

Mr and Mrs Hay, aged 29 and 24, were killed in a road accident. Their children, aged four and a half and two and a half, were then taken by their maternal grandmother, Mrs Toone, into her own home and cared for by her. She did so without thought of being paid and intended to continue to bring them up. Mr Hay was a welder at the time of his death who would, at the date of trial, have been earning £40 per week. Mrs Hay did not work. In assessing damages for the children under the Fatal Accidents Acts the judge adopted a figure of £1,000 per annum as the amount by which they were worse off by the loss of their father and £1,000 per annum by the loss of their mother. The latter figure was based on the assumed cost of providing the housekeeper or nanny. He took a multiplier of 8 and, after deducting £2,500 representing the value of the parents' estates, awarded £16,400 damages. On appeal it was argued for the defendant (1) the replacement of the deceased's mother's services not having taken place no award for the pecuniary loss of those services should be made; (2) the services rendered by Mrs Toone in looking after the children for nothing were 'benefits resulting from the death' and should be taken into account.

HELD: The award was right. On (1) the fact that a widower decided to manage for himself after the death of his wife would not disentitle him to sue for and recover damages for the pecuniary loss he had nevertheless sustained. Similarly the fact that the orphaned children had not incurred the expense of a housekeeper did not destroy or diminish their right to be compensated. On (2) it is not possible to discover from the decided cases any established principle to determine whether the benefits conferred by Mrs Toone on the children should be taken into account or not. It was a jury question to which the judge addressed himself and decided in a way which seemed fair, namely, that Mrs Toone's care conferred no benefit which should be taken into account. The principle that the assessed loss of a plaintiff should be reduced by any pecuniary advantage coming to him by reason of the death has been so seriously eroded by legislation that in the light of history the court should hesitate to extend the principle to classes of benefit not directly covered by binding authority.

Grzelak v Harefield and Northwood Hospital Management Committee
(1968) 112 Sol Jo 195 (Megaw J)
The plaintiff's wife died four days after a surgical operation. The defendants admitted liability. She was 37 years of age, a school-teacher earning £1,100 a year net: the salary in the same job at the date of trial four years later would have been £1,300 pa. The plaintiff was 43, a tailor; his contribution to the matrimonial income was less, sometimes much less, than his wife's. He gave her £2 10s 0d per week. She contributed £4 per week to the support of her parents aged 80 and 76. Her bank balance had increased from £750 to £1,400 in three years up to her death.

Award: Law Reform Act — for loss of expectation of life £500, funeral expenses £88. Fatal Accidents Acts — the wife had built up a balance to buy a car for their joint use and it could not be assumed that there would not have been similar expenditure for their joint benefit. The annual figure the husband could have expected was £200 after allowing credit for the £2 10s 0d per week he was not now paying her. The appropriate multiplier was 15. Allowing both for likely increases in the wife's income and that payment would be made now the gross figure was £3,000. The sum of £1,648 the plaintiff had received from his wife's estate must be deducted and the Law Reform damages of £550, leaving £802 FAA damages for the husband. £225 should be awarded to the parents.

UNMARRIED WIFE — CHILDREN'S CLAIM

Phipps v Cunard White Star Co Ltd, The Queen Mary
[1951] WN 118, [1951] 1 TLR 359, 95 Sol Jo 188, [1951] 1 Lloyd's Rep 54, (Willmer J)
Deceased, an AB aged 39, had lived since 1934 with a woman to whom he was not married, and left three illegitimate children by her. Deceased contributed £3 per week to the support of three children and of the plaintiff (the woman) and to the upkeep of the home.

The Admiralty Registrar found that the plaintiff ran the home and maintained the children and was certainly dependant on the deceased but she was not a dependant under the Fatal Accidents Acts and could not claim, and the amount to the children could not be assessed on the basis of what she could claim if she had been entitled to claim. The children shared in the benefit of the deceased's contribution to her. He awarded £500 divided between the three children — boy aged 15, £100; girl aged 13, £150; girl aged 8, £250. The usual evidence was given with regard to the pensions. HELD, on objection to the report. The Court would not vary the report unless it was erroneous by a very considerable margin. The judge would have arrived at a figure somewhat, but not very much, in excess, but the difference was so small that it would be wrong to interfere. The loss to each child was probably about 15s per week until approximately 16 years of age.

Objection dismissed.

K v JMP Co Ltd
[1976] QB 85, [1975] 1 All ER 1030, [1975] 2 WLR 457, 119 Sol Jo 188, CA

The plaintiffs sued under the Fatal Accidents Acts for damages for the three children of a self-employed labourer, killed in an accident. The deceased and the unmarried mother of the three children had lived as man and wife for a number of years and their children at his death were aged six, five and three. The mother continued to look after the children, drawing supplementary allowance of £10.40 per week for herself and £8.70 for them. The deceased's earnings had been about £2,800 per annum. In addition to usual living expenses he had paid for holidays in Ireland, toys for the children and family outings. The judge awarded damages on the basis that the children were entitled to awards which would enable the mother to provide the same standard of living as the deceased had provided, that is, including the cost of the mother's upkeep: he assessed the children's loss at a figure which included all the deceased's expenditure other than that on himself. The judge applied the number of years' purchase from the date of the trial to 16 years of age for each child. The defendants appealed.
HELD: (1) As the mother was now receiving supplementary allowance for herself the amount awarded to the children in respect of her share of upkeep and benefits from the deceased's income should be reduced by the amount of her necessary living expenses paid for by her supplementary allowance; (2) contrary to the contention of counsel for the children the mother would not lose her entitlement to supplementary benefit by reason of the aggregation of the damages awarded to the children since she would not be 'a person [who] has to provide for the requirements of another person' within the meaning of the Ministry of Social Security Act 1966, sch 2 when the children's needs were provided for by the awards of damages; (3) the judge was not in error in fixing 16 as the age at which the children would have ceased to be dependent on the deceased but the years of purchase should have been calculated from the date of death, not from the date of trial. Awards increased to £3,836 for eldest child, £4,384 for middle child and £5,480 for the youngest.

LAW REFORM DAMAGES

Loss of expectation of life

Note—The right to damages for loss of expectation of life in fatal cases was established by the House of Lords in *Rose v Ford* (below). The damages awarded in subsequent cases varied from nothing, the estimate of a jury, to £2,000, the award of a judge. The measure of damages was then dealt with by the House of Lords in *Benham v Gambling* (p 956, below) the effect of which was to reduce awards to sums between £100 to £500 a decision reinforced in 1967 by *Yorkshire Electricity Board v Naylor* (p 957, below), but more recently higher awards were made: see p 959, below. Where the person entitled to the estate also has a claim under the Fatal Accidents Acts the amount of the Law Reform damages becomes largely immaterial since those damages merge in the Fatal Accidents Acts damages.

Rose v Ford

[1937] AC 826, [1937] 3 All ER 359, 106 LJKB 576, 157 LT 174, 53 TLR 873, 81 Sol Jo 683, 58 Ll L Rep 213, HL

The deceased, a young woman aged 23, was injured on 4 August 1934. On 6 August the right leg was amputated. On 8 August she died. For those four days she was in a state of coma.

In the House of Lords it was argued the damages for loss of expectation of life would take into account the enjoyment of life, the amenity value of life, the pleasure of life and the earning power. The House of Lords upheld the award of a sum of £20 for four days' pain and suffering and a nominal sum of £2 for two days' loss of the leg, in addition to £300 awarded under the Fatal Accidents Acts. As to loss of expectation of life, they upheld the decision in *Flint v Lovell* ([1935] 1 KB 354, 104 LJKB 199, 152 LT 231, 51 TLR 127, 78 Sol Jo 860) that a cause of action existed for loss of normal expectation of life (apart from any question of mental suffering), and that this cause of action passed to the legal personal representative and accepted the assessment of the Court of Appeal of £1,000.

Lord Wright said that normal expectancy of life was a thing of temporal value, so that its impairment was something for which damages should be given. Special cases might occur, such as that of an infant or an imbecile or an incurable invalid or a person involved in hopeless difficulties.

Lord Roche said it did not involve the question of rich and poor and pays regard to the normal and the average. A rich miser living in squalor or a very poor man deeply sunk in misery might require special treatment.

Benham v Gambling

[1941] AC 157, [1941] 1 All ER 7, 110 LJKB 49, 164 LT 290, 57 TLR 177, 84 Sol Jo 703, HL

An infant aged two and a half was killed in a motor accident on 1 June 1938. The father as administrator of the child's estate claimed damages. The only question apart from funeral expenses was for diminution of the child's expectation of life. The child was living in modest but otherwise favourable circumstances.

HELD: The statistical or actuarial is not the proper test. The thing to be valued is not the prospect of length of days, but the prospect of a predominantly happy life. The age of the individual may, in some cases, be a relevant factor. For example, in extreme old age, the brevity of the expectation may be relevant, but the damages are not to be calculated solely, or even mainly, on the life expectation. The problem seemed more suitable for discussion in an essay on Aristotelian ethics than in a judgment of a court of law. Were the circumstances, on balance, calculated to lead to a positive measure of happiness, or to a future of unhappiness or despondency? It is an objective estimate of what kind of future on earth the victim might have enjoyed. In the case of a very young child there is uncertainty about the future. At an age of settled prospects the future is more definite. The social position is not a factor. Happiness does not depend on wealth or status. It is an attempt to equate incommensurables. In assessing damages, whether in the case of a child or an adult, very moderate figures should be chosen.

The proper figure in this case would be £200, and even this amount would be excessive if it were not that the circumstances of the infant were most favourable.

Note—Discussed and re-affirmed by House of Lords in *Yorkshire Electricity Board v Naylor*, below.

Instantaneous death

Morgan v Scoulding
[1938] 1 KB 786, [1938] 1 All ER 28, 107 LJKB 299, 158 LT 230, 54 TLR 253, 81 Sol Jo 1041 (Lewis J)
Deceased, a motor mechanic, aged 23, was killed instantaneously.
HELD: The injury occurred before the death, although there might be only a split second between the accident and the death.

Measure of damages under Law Reform (cases since Benham v Gambling)

Burns v Edman
[1970] 2 QB 541, [1970] 1 All ER 886, [1970] 2 WLR 1005, 114 Sol Jo 356, [1970] 1 Lloyd's Rep 137 (Crichton J)
In a case in which the deceased aged,32 had been a convicted felon and had lived on the proceeds of crime the judge said the court was entitled to take judicial notice that the life of a criminal was not a happy one and awarded Law Reform damages of £187 only.

Fall in the value of money

Hart v Griffiths-Jones
[1948] 2 All ER 729 (Streatfeild J)
Deceased girl aged four lived in a slum area. The mother had deserted the father and the child had to accompany the father when he went out as a hawker. The prospects of a happy life were such that the award would have been less than £200 in *Benham*'s case. It was argued for the plaintiff that the difference in the value of money between 1941 and 1946 should be taken into account. No evidence of the depreciation of the value of the pound was given but the judge was asked to act upon his own knowledge.
HELD: It was obvious that the pound was worth more in 1941 than it is now, and taking the difference into account, the judge awarded £200, plus funeral expenses.

Yorkshire Electricity Board v Naylor
[1968] AC 529, [1967] 2 All ER 1, [1967] 2 WLR 114, 111 Sol Jo 278, HL
The plaintiff's son, aged 20, was killed instantly by electric shock. The defendants admitted liability. He had been a jointer's mate by occupation and would probably have become a jointer at 21. He was a healthy happy young man living with his parents. His recreations were football and hiking. The defendants offered (and paid into Court) £500 Law Reform damages but the plaintiff did not accept. A statistician gave evidence that the purchasing power of the pound had fallen by two-and-a-half times since 1941. The Judge of Assize awarded £500 Law Reform damages.
    The plaintiff appealed. The Court of Appeal increased the award to £1,000, saying that in *Benham v Gambling* (above) in 1941 the House of

Lords had limited damages for this type of claim to a figure somewhere between a minimum of £200 and a maximum of £500. If £200 was the correct award of damages for the prospective happiness of a very young child (as in *Benham v Gambling*) in 1941 then £1,000 was the right figure in 1966 in the case of a young man in the circumstances of the deceased.

HELD: On the defendants' appeal to the House of Lords, the Judge's award of £500 should be restored. There was nothing in Lord Simon's judgment in *Benham v Gambling* to the effect that the minimum award should be £200 and the maximum £500. Lord Simon had said very moderate figures should be chosen whether in the case of a child or an adult: he also said the £200 awarded in that case (a child of two and a half years old) would be excessive were it not that the child's circumstances were most favourable. Though he said damages in the case of a very young child should be reduced he did not say they should be substantially less than those awarded to an adult. In awarding £500 the judge quite properly had regard to the fall in the value of money and to his knowledge of awards in other cases in the last 10 years. His award should not be interfered with.

Per Lord Devlin: Except for the extremities of childhood and old age, prospective length of years makes no difference. Social position and worldly possessions are also irrelevant. . . . While the law remains as it is, I think it is less likely to fall into disrespect if judges treat *Benham v Gambling* as an injunction to stick to a fixed standard than if they start revaluing happiness, each according to his own ideas.

Per Lord Upjohn: In relation to the assessment of damages for loss of expectation of life, I do not think that evidence as to the fall in the purchasing power of the pound has much relevance. For my part, though not questioning its technical admissibility, I deprecate the submission of such evidence in these circumstances.

Cain v Wilcock

[1968] 3 All ER 817 n, [1968] 1 WLR 1961, 112 Sol Jo 844, [1968] 2 Lloyd's Rep 440, CA

£500 was awarded for loss of expectation of life of a small child, a girl aged two and a half. The defendant appealed on the ground that the award did not take into account the tender years of the deceased and was the conventional award appropriate to an ordinary adult person.

HELD: There was no error in the award: it was substantially in line with what members of the House of Lords had said was appropriate in *Benham v Gambling* (p 956, above).

Per Willmer LJ: I think it would be disastrous if this appeal succeeded to the extent of persuading us to enter into minute calculations in a case of this character. If we were to take that course I can only forsee that there would be a flood of litigation, perhaps carried to this court, seeking to draw minute distinctions between the circumstances of deceased persons. That, I think, would be a wholly unwholesome development, and generally speaking it seems to me that it would be wise to stick (except in very exceptional circumstances) to that which may be regarded as the conventional although admittedly artificial figure.

Per Russell LJ: Having considered the complicated attitudes adopted on this subject by members of the House of Lords, it seems to me that it would lead to highly desirable certainty, without much harm to insurance

companies, if judges listened in silence to argument, and simply awarded
£500 without giving any reasons at all.

R v Johal
[1973] QB 475, [1972] 2 All ER 449, [1972] 3 WLR 210, 136 JP 519, 116
Sol Jo 195, 56 Cr App Rep 348, CA (Hollings J)
The deceased was a youth aged 17. Actuarial evidence was given (July
1972) that the pound sterling had depreciated 40% in value since 1966.
HELD: General damages for loss of expectation of life £700; the time had
come for the conventional figure of £500 to be increased.

Note—In *McCann v Sheppard* (p 411, above) the Court of Appeal awarded £750 for
loss of expectation of life without mentioning earlier decisions.

In *Ashraf v West Midlands Passenger Transport Executive and Dillon* [1977] CLY 734,
Chapman J though maintaining that mathematical calculations should not be
applied to the conventional figure to allow for inflation, awarded £1,100 for loss of
expectation of life to a boy aged six, and indicated that he would have awarded
more had the child not been so young. An award of £1750 in *Gammell v Wilson* was
reduced to £1,250 on appeal: p 960, below.

Following the House of Lords' decision in *Pickett v British Rail Engineering* (p 444,
above) the concept of a claim for earnings lost during years following the claimant's
death was extended in a number of decisions to fatal cases. *Kandalla v British Airways
Board* a decision at first instance was the earliest reported example, confirmed by
the House of Lords in *Gammell v Wilson*. Later decisions were concerned to
establish the correct principle for assessing such claims under the Law Reform
(Miscellaneous Provisions) Act 1934. Two issues calling for attention were
(1) what deductions should be made from the deceased's gross amount of lost
earnings in calculating the damages payable, and (2) the effect of the rules of
devolution in cases of an intestacy on the total amount of damages to be paid under
both the Fatal Accidents and Law Reform Acts. Relevant reported cases are set out
below. For a detailed break-down of the effects on the rules on intestacy as between
widow and children where damages were recovered under both Acts see 'The Fatal
Windfall' (R. M. Nelson-Jones) in the Law Society's Gazette, 7 October 1982, at
p 1249.

Kandalla v British Airways Board
[1980] 1 All ER 341, [1980] 2 WLR 730 (Griffiths J)
The plaintiffs were husband and wife aged, at trial in 1979, 74 and 68.
Their two daughters, when aged 31 and 27, were killed in an aeroplane
accident in 1972. They were medical practitioners practising in London.
The plaintiffs lived in Iraq but intended coming to live in England where
they would have received financial support from their daughters. They
claimed damages under the Fatal Accidents Acts for themselves and under
the Law Reform (Miscellaneous Provisions) Act 1934 on behalf of the
daughters' estates.
HELD: (1) on the available evidence the damages payable under the Fatal
Accidents Acts (before taking into account anything inherited from the
daughters' estates) amounted to £54,000. (2) The award to each estate in
respect of loss of expectation of life was £750. (3) following indications
given in speeches of the Law Lords in *Pickett's* case (p 444, above) there
must be an award to each estate in respect of loss of earnings during the
years lost. There was no reason in principle why this should not be so, nor

could the argument be accepted that such damages were excluded by virtue of s 1(2)(c) of the 1934 Act [set out in *Gammell*'s case below]. The award is not to include sums that the deceased would have spent for themselves: on the evidence before the court the award for the 'lost years' could not be assessed at more than that assessed for the parents' support ie £54,000. (4) As the parents would receive more from the estates than the value of the Fatal Accidents Acts claims, the latter were therefore extinguished.

Gammell v Wilson
[1982] AC 27, [1981] 1 All ER 578, [1981] 2 WLR 248, 125 Sol Jo 116
A boy of 15 was killed in a road accident for which the defendants admitted liability. His parents claimed damages for his estate under the Law Reform (Miscellaneous Provisions) Act 1934 for loss of expectation of life and damages for loss of earnings during the 'lost years'. They also claimed for themselves under the Fatal Accidents Act. The judge awarded £6,656 for loss of future earnings and £1,750 (reduced on appeal to £1,250) for loss of expectation of life. He would have awarded £2,000 under the Fatal Accidents Act but as the plaintiffs were entitled to the whole of the estate he made no award under that Act. The defendants appealed against the £6,656 for loss of future earnings on the grounds that (1) such damages were not recoverable, being excluded by the Law Reform Act, s 1(2): 'Where a cause of action survives as aforesaid for the benefit of the estate of a deceased person, the damages recoverable for the benefit of the estate of that person . . . (c) where the death of that person has been caused by the act or omission which gives rise to the cause of action, shall be calculated without reference to any loss or gain to his estate consequent on his death . . .; and (2) that if such damages were recoverable the award was excessive. The Court of Appeal rejected both contentions: s 1(2)(c) was not intended to deprive the estate of the right to recover damages in respect of losses when the right to recover was already vested in the deceased immediately before his death. As to the amount of damages, the estimate should be based on evidence and should not be a merely nominal sum.
HELD, ON APPEAL to the House of Lords: The Court of Appeal was right. (1) The cause of action for damages for the lost years vests in the deceased when he is injured and if he be killed instantaneously, immediately before his death. 'Losses' in s 1(2)(c) refer to such matters as capital transfer tax; 'gains' to eg the proceeds of life insurance; that is, to such matters as the deceased, had he lived, could neither have experienced nor collected. A loss for which the deceased had a cause of action immediately before his death was not excluded by the subsection. (2) On assessment of damages, the loss was pecuniary and must on the facts be found to be at least capable of being estimated. In the case of a young child the lost years of earning capacity will ordinarily be so distant that no estimate is possible and no award should be made. But in the case of a teenager there could be actual employment or real prospects. In the present case the deceased was already in some kind of work at £20 a week and would progress. Taking a multiplier of 16 for the lost years and £8 per week for the surplus over living expenses the award was reasonable and should not be reduced.

Benson v Biggs Wall & Co Ltd

[1982] 3 All ER 300 [1983] 1 WLR 72 n (Pain J) (Judgment 19 June 1980)
The plaintiff's husband was killed in an accident at work. The defendants
admitted liability. The plaintiff claimed damages for herself and her infant
son under the Fatal Accidents Act 1976 and for her husband's estate under
the Law Reform (Miscellaneous Provisions) Act 1934. Her husband was
21 at the date of death. At the date of trial she was 26 and the child 17
months. In respect of the Fatal Accidents Act claim it was agreed that the
husband's own living expenses amounted to 30% of his earnings and the
family's dependency to 70%; the claim was agreed at £49,000.
HELD: (1) On apportionment of the FAA damages, as the function of the
court is to safeguard the child his portion should be assessed on his genuine
dependency and not on a 'pocket money' dependency. The right figure was
£5,000, having regard to his extreme youth. (2) In assessing Law Reform
Act damages for the 'lost years' the same yard stick should be used for
calculating living expenses as under the FAA, namely, by deducting 30%,
thus arriving at the same overall figure of £49,000. (3) The deceased's
estate fell to be divided on intestacy as to one-half to the plaintiff plus a life
interest in half of the remainder, and as to the other half of the remainder to
the son on the statutory trusts. By agreement of the figures the Law Reform
damages of £49,000 were to be divided as to £36,750 to the widow and
£12,250 to the son. The Law Reform damages fell to be deducted from the
FAA damages and as she was entitled to £42,500 under the FAA her share
of those damages was reduced to £5,750. The son's FAA damages were
wholly extinguished by his share of the Law Reform damages. Thus the
total award exceeded the award under either of the Acts alone by £6,000.

Note—In *Lawrence v John Laing Ltd* (5 May 1982, unreported) Cantley J assessed the
compensation in respect of the lost years at the same sum as that at which he
assessed the Fatal Accidents Act claim. He said it would be wrong to deduct from
the notional net earnings all sums which were expended by the deceased for the
benefit of himself and his family in the family home. 'To deduct an artificially
calculated proportion of the cost of maintaining the family home could leave a Mrs
Pickett unable to maintain the house which had been provided for her or anything
like it. In the present case most of the cost of the deceased's house was expended for
his dependants'.

White v London Transport Executive

[1982] QB 489, [1982] 1 All ER 410, [1982] 2 WLR 791, 126 Sol Jo 277
(Webster J)
The deceased was 25 when killed in an accident caused by the defendant's
negligence. He was single man who had been living with his mother and
stepfather. He had an illegitimate son aged six not living with him and to
whose support he made no contribution. The deceased's mother was his
only dependant and it was agreed that her claim under the Fatal Accidents
Act 1976 was for £2,500 only. He earned an average of £75 per week after
tax, most of which he spent on himself. He left no estate. The issue was to
determine the deductions to be made from the deceased's prospective net
earnings to arrive at the damages recoverable for the lost years' earnings. It
was contended by the defendants that the loss to be assessed was loss to the
estate ie the amount of the estimated net surplus which could have been
expected in the deceased's estate at the end of his natural life: alternatively,

that the whole of the deceased's prospective expenditure should be deducted, including any amounts the deceased would have spent on his dependants.

HELD: (1) The defendants' contentions were not supported by authority. The loss to be assessed was not to the estate but to the deceased for his lost years' earnings. Moreover *Pickett*'s case was compelling authority for the proposition that no deduction was to be made to take account of the money a deceased person would have spent on his dependants. (2) The loss to be assessed was the amenity of earning more than was needed to live a reasonably satisfying and potentially enjoyable life, taking into account the particular circumstances of the deceased. Thus the amounts to be deducted were not only the cost of maintaining himself, including housing, heating, food, clothing, necessary travelling expenses, insurance premiums etc., but also other expenditure appropriate to a man in his circumstances. In the present case such deductions would leave one-third of his net earnings for the first five years and one-quarter of the remaining ten years of the 15 years' purchase. Award £2,500 for his mother (under the Fatal Accidents Act); for the estate £23,273 for the lost years, £1,250 for loss of expectation of life and £300 funeral expenses.

Nutbrown v Rosier
(1982) Times, 1 March, QBD

The plaintiff was the widow and administratrix of the estate of her husband killed in a road accident. She claimed for herself and her two children under the Fatal Accidents Act and for the estate under the Law Reform Act 1934. Her husband was a scientist earning £11,475 at date of death and would have been earning £18,755 per annum three years later. The question to be decided was whether in assessing damages for loss of potential earnings during the 'lost years' only the deceased's living expenses solely attributable to his own purposes should be deducted or whether there should be an additional deduction representing costs incurred by the deceased for housing, food or other incidental costs of living and leading a satisfactory life.

HELD: preferring the view of Webster J in *White v London Transport* (above) and of Mustill J in *Sullivan v W. Yorkshire Passenger Transport* (unreported) to that of Peter Pain J in *Benson v Biggs Wall* (p 961, above), the deduction should embrace all the costs associated with any individual's particular lifestyle ie the cost of living a reasonably satisfying and enjoyable life having regard to his particular circumstances.

Smith v MacKay
(27 May 1982, unreported) (Halsbury's Laws October Monthly Review)

A private soldier aged 20 was killed in an accident. In a claim for loss of future earnings:

HELD: The 'living expenses' which had to be deducted from gross loss (on a multiplier of 16) did not comprise all expenditure other than investment in savings or capital assets. Living expenses meant only the reasonable expenses of keeping alive in reasonable comfort, including the cost of reasonable pleasures. No deduction should be made of money the deceased would have spent on prospective dependants.

Clay v Pooler
[1982] 3 All ER 570 (Hodgson J)
The plaintiff's husband was killed in a road accident. She claimed damages for herself and her daughters aged 15 and 14 under the Fatal Accidents Act and for her husband's estate under the Law Reform Act 1934. His income would, at date of trial, have been £5,933 per annum: his use of a company car for private purposes was assessed by the judge to be worth £800 pa. It was contended by counsel for the defendant that in assessing the Law Reform claim for loss of earnings the expenditure of the deceased to be deducted was not the same amount as the living expenses deducted for the purpose of the Fatal Accidents Act claim: it should include also those items of expenditure which although part of his 'living expenses' would continue to be necessary expenses of his dependants after his death.
HELD: (1) It seemed clear from the speeches in *Pickett*'s case (p 444, above) that the House of Lords was saying that, in cases where the victim has dependants, money expended on those dependants was not to be taken to be part of his own living expenses. On this point *Benson v Biggs Wall* (above, p 961) followed, *Nutbrown v Rosier* (above) not followed. The 'living expenses' to be deducted were the same for both the Fatal Accidents Act and Law Reform claims. (2) Where there is insurance money coming into the estate which by s 4(1) of the 1976 Act is not to be taken into account in assessing Fatal Accidents Act damages it should be taken into account in the Law Reform Act claim proportionally among the beneficiaries and not by deduction from the whole estate before applying the rules on intestacy.

Note—See also *Ashley v Vickers* (1983) Times, 18 January, in which Croom Johnson J, declining to follow those decisions which automatically equated Law Reform damages for 'lost years' with Fatal Accidents Act dependency, said it was a question of guessing how the situation at death would have developed.
    Other reported decisions on damages for loss of earnings during the 'lost years' include:
Lolley v Keylock (1984) 128 Sol Jo 471, 81 LS Gaz R 1518
Warwick v Jeffery (1983) Times, 21 June

Harris v Empress Motors Ltd
[1983] 3 All ER 561, [1984] 1 WLR 212, 127 Sol Jo 647, CA
The plaintiff's husband was killed in an accident caused by the negligence of the defendants. There were two dependant children of the marriage. The net loss of earnings during the 'lost years' on a multiplier of 16 was £107,500. The judge made the same deduction in respect of the deceased's 'living expenses' as he had for the Fatal Accidents Act claim, namely 25%, making an award for 'lost years' earnings of £82,325. On appeal,
HELD: The question to be decided was how the deduction from the net loss of earnings for the lost years should be determined. One solution was the judge's method — deduction of the same amount as for assessing Fatal Accidents Act dependency. A second solution was deduction of all expenditure except savings. A third was the 'available surplus' solution as in *White v London Transport Executive* (p 961, above) ie deducting from the net earnings the cost of maintaining the deceased in his station in life. Both the Fatal Accidents Act method and the 'savings only' method should be rejected. The *White*'s case solution should be applied save that the deceased should not be treated as an eternally single man. In the present case there

was much less speculation than in *White*'s case and what was not to be deducted could be seen with reasonable clarity. In the result the amount to be deducted would in general be greater than the percentage used for calculating the dependency under the Fatal Accidents Act.

SUBSTANTIAL UNEARNED INCOME

Adsett v West
[1983] QB 826, [1983] 2 All ER 985, [1983] 3 WLR 437, 127 Sol Jo 325 (McCullough J)
The deceased was a man of 26 years, the son of a successful businessman with whom he was in partership, owning shares. At the time of his death on the 8 March 1980 his partnership capital was £33,000 yielding an income which continued after his death. He also had an income of earnings from his work in the business. He was unmarried but there was a likelihood that he would have married in the near future. The administrator of his estate (his father) claimed damages for loss of anticipated earnings and loss of income from the capital.
HELD: A distinction must be drawn between income from earnings and income from capital. The income from capital continues after death and involves no loss to the deceased: the deceased's estate was entitled to damages for the lost earnings based on the anticipated earnings, (taking 16 years as a suitable multiplier) less the amounts he would have been likely to spend on his own living expenses and pleasures. Taking into account the rather slight possibility of marriage 25% of his total net income (including income from capital) should be taken as the surplus after deduction of expenditure on himself. On the evidence his net income attributable to capital owned at death during the 16 years would amount to £44,698. Over the same period the 'surplus' of total income at 25% would be £31,800. There could therefore be no award for loss of the 'surplus' in the lost years. At the moment before the deceased died there remained in existence capital which the deceased owned and which would, after his death, continue to earn more money than would have been needed to provide his 'surplus' had he lived. His death obviated the expenditure of that part of his total income which he would have devoted to his own living expenses and pleasures; as a result more 'surplus' money became available in the 'lost years' not less. The only damages to be awarded were the conventional £1,250 for loss of expectation of life and the funeral expenses.

Note—The full report of the judgment is valuable for the very full discussion of the earlier decisions.

Personal injury damages — specimen awards

MULTIPLE INJURIES

Burton v De La Rue (Crosfield) Ltd
(5 December 1984 unreported)
Warehouseman, 20, knocked off motor cycle, sustained extensive bruising and lacerations. Left with minor scars on leg and thigh, where a pin was inserted, and diminishing discomfort in the hip. General damages £4,000.

Kazimierski v Sharp
(2 February 1984 unreported)
Plaintiff, 78, knocked down whilst crossing road. Fracture of frontal bone of skull, fractures of right radius and ulna, pubic rami, the wing of the ilium and the right ischial. He had been fit and active but now walked with difficulty and he had lost the ability to concentrate and speak succinctly. His arm movement is limited. General damages £15,150 including £3,650 for financial expenses.

Plumridge v Ayers
(3 May 1984, unreported)
Lorry driver, 34: comminuted and displaced fracture of right wrist, a less serious injury to the left wrist and extensive bruising. Left with a reduction of grip in the right hand and the possibility of osteo-arthritis in the left hand. His right wrist is likely to deteriorate. General damages £6,000.

Johnson v Gilbert
(7 February 1984, unreported)
Labourer, 41, struck by car which mounted the pavement. Fractures to seven ribs with lung complications, right collarbone, right shoulder blade, left femur and several bones in the right foot. He now has limitation of movement in the right shoulder, difficulty in walking, pain in his foot and a deformity in the rib cage which reduces his lung power. General damages £28,000 including £10,000 for future loss of earnings.

Aneja v Jessey
(20 July 1983, unreported)
Schoolboy, 7, hit by car sustained fractures to right humerus, right

collarbone, left femur, concussion and lacerations. A nerve paralysis has left him with a slight squint. He has made a good recovery apart from unsightly scarring on the knee and a 1% risk of epilepsy. General damages £4,000.

Sully v Doggett
(5 December 1984, unreported)
Teacher, 23: multiple fractures to skull, face and mandible and fractures in right arm, right leg, left tibia and left hip, she also suffered a gross laceration to the right heel. She is left with restricted jaw movement and no useful vision in the left eye. Brain damage has left her with weakness in the left fingers and an inability to judge the position of hand and arm. Her left leg is 1 inch shorter than the right and she is likely to get osteo-arthritis in the left hip which will need replacing. She walks with a limp and has considerable scarring. Her chances of marriage have been diminished. General damages £39,500 including £3,000 for disadvantage on the labour market and £5,000 for future loss of earnings.

Davies v Rickersey
(6 July 1983, unreported)
Schoolboy, 14, suffered comminuted fracture to left femur, left pubic rami and right medial malleolus, laceration to scalp and liver, a large contaminated wound to perineum and bruising to head and pancreas. Now has slight shortness of left leg and restricted movement of the knee and scarring. Other minor difficulties will resolve. General damages £6,500.

Cheshire v Maidstone Borough Council
(2 December 1983, unreported)
Cleaner, 54, suffered bruising and swelling to left arm, hip and knee. She has recovered except for possible carpal tunnel syndrome which should resolve in a few months. General damages £2,250.

Hollands v Cutting
(7 March 1984, unreported)
Air stewardess, 28, car forced off the road into a lamp post. Fractures to odontoid peg and second cervical vertebra, dental injuries, extensive contusions and abrasions and a crush fracture to the right heel. Now has permanent deformity to the right heel and walks with a limp. Her previous sporting activities are denied to her. General damages £16,295 including £1,500 for disadvantage on labour market and £6,295 for future expenses.

Lisney v Hamilton
(3 February 1984, unreported)
Schoolgirl, 6, asleep in car involved in accident, sustained concussion, shock, loss of memory, a paralytic ileus, lacerations to head, arm, leg and mouth, a fracture with gross displacement of the right femur, a double jaw fracture and the loss of nine teeth. The right leg is now bent and slightly

shorter though the latter may resolve. There is a risk of osteo-arthritis. She has stopped growing. There are unsightly scars on the forehead arm and thigh. General damages £16,500 including £3,150 for future dental treatment.

Devine v Hazelwood
(14 February 1984, unreported)
Office cleaning supervisor, 62, displaced fracture to medial femoral condyle, a left-sided haemothorax, shock, concussion bruising and lacerations. She had pain in the knee and walks with a limp. Degenerative changes will increase her disability. General damages £16,050 (after deducting 25% from the compensation for the chest injury for failing to wear a seat belt), including £4,500 for future loss of earnings and £1,050 for the costs of a home help.

Nicholls v Williams
(1983) Times, 21 May
Horsetrainer, 55, unconscious for one week after a road accident; fractured sternum, several ribs, left and right femur, tibia, tibula two fingers and dislocated right hip. Now has occasional chest pains restricted movement in fingers and left foot and stiffness in the right hip and left knee. There is a risk of osteo-arthritis. His right leg is 2 inches shorter and he uses crutches and a caliper with a heel raise. General damages £47,875 including £23,875 for loss of future earnings.

Copeland v Otis Elevator Co Ltd
(20 July 1983, unreported)
Lift and elevator fitter, 49, suffered fractures to two ribs, three lumbar vertebrae and the left humerus, multiple bruising and a haematoma in the right loin. Now has pain in the lumbo-sacral spine and wears a supporting belt. He can no longer do heavy lifting. General damages £5,500 including £1,000 for loss of earnings capacity.

Pritchard v Armer
(15 November 1984, unreported)
Tractor driver, 55, injured when lorry ran into back of his tractor. Whiplash injury to neck, capsular injury to left shoulder and an inguinal hernia. The hernia, to which he was susceptible, has healed with a 15% chance of recurrence. He is left with a shoulder which is painful and restricted in movement and he wears a neck collar when gardening. General damages £5,000 including £1,000 for the hernia.

AMPUTATIONS

Coupland v Arabian Gulf Petroleum Co
(22 June 1983, unreported)
Senior maintenance technician, 37, caught leg in an unguarded fan.

Amputation below the knee and he now wears an artificial leg. He could not carry on his pre-accident work and now does a job which puts stress on the stump. He still has a lot of pain. General damages £69,000 including £23,500 for the injury itself.

Napolitan v British Railways Board, Parker and Hertfordshire County Council
(2 December 1983, unreported)
Mentally retarded man, early 20s, suffered traumatic amputation of right leg below the knee. He has adapted well to the artificial leg. He is unable to continue what few hobbies he had. General damages £22,000.

Underwood v Gains Transport Services Ltd
(27 January 1984, unreported)
Motor fitter, 60, left arm amputated five inches below elbow. The end of the stump is tender and he still suffers pain and pins and needles. These conditions make his artificial arm of little use. He cannot do any heavy lifting. General damages £45,000 including £20,000 for future loss of earnings.

TRUNK

Davies v Delanair Ltd
(4 December 1984, unreported)
Factory worker, 43, hit by a forklift truck, which triggered off asthma. She is permanently unable to work, resistant to drugs and very short of breath. She cannot walk more than 100 yards, has difficulty with stairs and sexual intercourse is virtually impossible. Minor colds become serious illnesses. General damages £54,600 including £37,100 for future loss of earnings.

Williams v Tibbs
(29 June 1983, unreported)
Works supervisor, sustained double fractures of the second to the ninth ribs, a right pneumothorax and a fracture of the right clavicle. He had painful thoracotomy and tracheostomy operations and four operations to remove tubes from his throat and wires from his chest. He has been able to go back to work but movement in the shoulder is restricted, the ribs are tender and he has become increasingly prone to depression and agitation. His hobbies are restricted. General damages £9,000.

HEAD

Williams v M. Margolis
(29 April 1983, unreported)
Salesman, 64, sustained fissure fracture to skull, exacerbated symptomless osteoarthritis in the knees and suffered a deep vein thrombosis of the left leg. His knees symptoms have been advanced two years by the accident.

His senses of smell, hearing in the right ear and sight in the right eye have been slightly reduced. There is an 8% chance of epilepsy. His memory, concentration and temperament have been affected. General damages £24,000 including £4,000 for loss of earning capacity.

Youill v Dotchon
(2 August 1984, unreported)
Systems engineer, 27, suffered severe penetrating wound to left frontal region of the skull. His intellectual faculties only slightly affected but his ability to use his intelligence has been damaged permanently due to the impoverishment of his verbal short-term memory. He is easily depressed and short tempered and his enjoyment of life has been considerably affected. General damages £116,400 including £30,000 for the injuries themselves.

Mahoney v Frank Harris Coaches Ltd
(21 December 1983, unreported)
Schoolboy (10, 12 at date of trial), knocked down by bus. Suffered very severe brain damage. Unconscious for six months and now in a state of mute quadriparesis with no chance of improvement. Very little control over the muscles of the body and he has frequent epileptic fits. His life expectancy is 15 years. General damages £223,496 inclusive of £179,946 for future financial losses and expenses.

Seaman v McFarlane
(26 May 1983, unreported)
Bus driver, 34, suffered multiple skull fractures and rupture of middle meningeal artery causing internal bleeding and pressure on the brain. He suffers from double vision, impairment of memory and personality change. There is a small risk of epilepsy. General damages £28,200 including £18,200 for future earnings loss.

O'Keeffe v London Borough of Tower Hamlets
(16 April 1984, unreported)
Schoolboy, 7, compound fracture of left frontal bone. Left with a slight dent over eyebrow and a 5% risk of epilepsy. General damages £6,500 comprised of £1,500 for the head injury £1,000 for the cosmetic defect and £4,000 for the risk of epilepsy.

Wood v Putman
(12 April 1984, unreported)
Schoolgirl, 16, sustained severe facial damage and minor injuries in a road accident. Made a good recovery but left with multiple facial scarring. Associated serious psychological effects are subsiding. Her eyes have been slightly affected and she lost a tooth. General damages £9,500 including consideration of an educational disadvantage resulting from the accident.

Jacobs v Hampshire County Council
(15 May 1984, unreported)
Supervisor, 46, thrown off bicycle and suffered fracture to left occipital bone, lacerations and contusions. He now has neck pain, permanent loss of sense of smell and impaired sense of taste. General damages £8,500 including £2,000 for disadvantage on the labour market.

Peel v Palmers Scaffolding Ltd
(17 February 1984, unreported)
Scaffolder, 26, fell 40 feet and sustained moderately serious head injuries. Now has dizziness, headaches, trembling and loss of memory which should all improve. He cannot work at heights. General damages £35,800 including £30,800 for loss of earnings.

English v Upwell Internal Drainage Board
(1 March 1984, unreported)
Agricultural drainage worker, 60, fractured cheekbone and laceration to top left side of skull. He had severe pain for several months and a neuroma had to be removed. General damages £2,500.

Kent v Maidment
(27 February 1984, unreported)
Invoice Clerk, 25, fractured skull with brain and nerve injury. Extensive lacerations and two fractures in pubic area. Her right eye is only 10% effective, there is a 10% risk of epilepsy and her short term memory ability to learn, compose in writing and spell are poor. She reacts badly to stress. General damages £36,500 including £11,500 for financial losses and expenses.

Dhillon v Thames Case Ltd
(1 July 1983, unreported)
Machine operator, sustained fractured jaw, loss of two teeth, damage to two others and cuts. Now has permanent nerve loss in right lower lip, the skin below and the inside of lip affecting taste mechanism. General damages £1,750.

Kaye v Alfa Romeo (Great Britain) Ltd and Motorway Sports Cars Ltd
(6 December 1983, unreported)
General manager, 35, sustained severe head injuries, flexion injuries to neck and minor leg injuries. A large part of bone of the skull was lost and a prothesis and then another one was fitted. There is a slight risk of infection. He has severe headaches, an over sensitive right eye and somewhat impaired mental facilities. There is a 5% epilepsy risk. The neck injuries have caused degenerative arthritic changes which will increase. General damages £20,000.

Butcher v Kaluza
(21 November 1983, unreported)
Schoolboy, 17, bilateral fractures of mandible, damage to teeth, laceration to left side of face and other minor injuries. A good recovery but he is left with a permanent scar and a sensitive jaw. General damages £7,500 including a small allowance for loss of employment prospects.

EYES

Hill v John Mowlem & Co
(16 October 1984, unreported)
Workman, 60, blinded in one eye although can appreciate light. General damages £12,000.

Liberty v Tyler
(17 February 1984, unreported)
Trainee hairdresser, 16, almost blind in right eye. She has a noticeable squint which could probably be corrected by an operation. There is a 10% risk of detachment of the retina and a 5% risk of glaucoma which might result in removal of the eye. The left eye now tires easily. General damages £17,500 including £14,000 for the loss of the eye itself.

Cox v Dixon
(19 December 1983, unreported)
Police Officer, 27, lost an eye and has marked facial scarring and headaches and depression. General damages £44,000 including £17,500 for the injuries themselves.

Wilshir v Essex A. H. A.
(21 December 1984, unreported)
Boy, blinded in left eye and limited sight in the right. 15–20% risk of total blindness. General damages £101,970 including £50,000 for the injuries themselves.

White v Goss
(24 February 1983, unreported)
Woman sustained right eye injury and is now 90% blind in that eye. She has pain and discomfort in the eye. General damages £13,500.

FACE

Flaherty v Reed
(5 June 1984, unreported)
Police officer, 30, involved in motor cycle accident sustained a broken nose, cuts and bruises. There was a blockage of the nose and his sense of smell was affected both of which would be cured by operation. His headaches were improving. General damages £3,500.

Minter v D and H Contractors (Cambridge) Ltd
(1983) Times, 30 June
Schoolboy, 9, went head first over handlebar of bicycle when he hit an obstruction. He lost two front teeth and sustained multiple facial lacerations. He now has extensive scarring on the forehead and occasional headaches. General damages £2,500.

Caldwell v Addressograph Multigraph Ltd
(26 October 1982, unreported)
Press operator, received a blow to the face. Bruising, black eye general malaise and pains in neck and shoulder. Previous nervous condition aggravated. General damages £2,000.

Hines v Brown
(14 January 1983, unreported)
Civil engineer, 2 inch-long laceration above eye and quarter-inch laceration to nose, bruising to ribs and abrasion to wrist. He suffered from paresthesia and numbness to the forehead scar. General damages £1,000.

NECK

Gravett v Bonners of Welling Ltd
(26 July 1984, unreported)
Man, 56, dustcart driver. Whiplash injuries to neck, continuing pain and restricted movements in neck and shoulders and headaches. His headaches will disappear but his neck will be vulnerable. General damages £3,000.

Monteith v Rycroft
(13 January 1984, unreported)
Man, 60, welding engineer, whiplash injuries causing avulsion fractures to fifth and sixth vertebrae. Pain in neck and left arm likely to continue: neck movement restricted. He has given up swimming and does less gardening. General damages £6,500 including £1,500 for disadvantage on labour market.

Bambridge v Marshall
(20 May 1983, unreported)
Nursing sister, 33, suffered whiplash to the cervical spine causing severe cervical disc prolapse. Further acute episodes provoked by relatively trivial strains. Neck movement slightly limited and has pain in left side of neck and left shoulder at the end of the day. She tires easily and wears a cervical collar in bed and to drive. Enjoyment of dancing and boating affected. Damages £8,750 including £3,000 for future earnings loss and disability on labour market.

Jenkinson v Police Comr
(26 October 1983, unreported)
Policeman, injured interspinus ligament of the back of neck causing scar tissue to form and trap a nerve. He suffers a gradually worsening pain in the neck which interferes with his enjoyment of life but should decrease as the trapped nerves die. General damages £3,000.

White v Dowman
(17 June 1983, unreported)
Steel erector, in a vehicle hit from behind; neck sprain with immediate pain and stiffness. Still has intermittent minor pain which is improving. Possible minor future discomfort. General damages £2,500.

Patience v Andrews
(19 November 1982, unreported)
Undergraduate, 19, crush fracture of seventh cervical vertebra and minor skull fractures. He recovered well from initial partial tetraplegia a fusion operation on the neck was performed. He is left with a residual reduction in grip and of sensation in arms and down the left side. General damages £12,000.

SPINE

Miller v National Institute for Research in Dairying
(21 November 1983, unreported)
Farm labourer, 51, hit in back and thrown 10 yards. Lumbar spine damaged. He was unable to do heavy lifting and has continuous low back pain and numbness. General damages £6,000.

Lake v Greater London Council
(17 April 1984, unreported)
Fireman, 22, thrown to ground from fire engine. Back pains prevented him returning to work for five months. Full recovery apart from slight ache. General damages £2,000.

Hunt v O'Riordan
(3 February 1984, unreported)
Personal assistant, 21, sustained fracture dislocations of three dorsal vertebrae resulting in complete paraplegia below that level. She has lost all voluntary movement and sensory information in the lower part of her body. General damages £200,605 including £55,000 for the injury itself.

Aylett v Avon A. H. A.
(30 November 1984, unreported)
Nursing auxiliary, 33, suffered severe back pain which developed into right sided sciatica — now has constant low level pain but the prognosis is good.

She now does lighter work and has given up gardening, decorating, and tennis. General damages £10,384.39 including £4,884.39 for future loss of earnings.

Kelly v Evans
(14 December 1983, unreported)
Student, 17, fractured second lumbar vertebra. Recovered from partial paralysis but legs are weaker and he limps. Paralysis of spinal nerves had led to risk of loss of bowel control. Sexual function is greatly impaired. There is a risk of recurrent urinary infection and of the paralysis returning. He has bouts of depression and is self-conscious of the scarring. He is severely restricted in the activities he can undertake. General damages £90,000 including £30,000 for sexual difficulties.

Austin v Farmer
(13 November 1984, unreported)
Farm labourer, suffered chronic lumbar strain. Has recovered but experiences backache two or three times a week. He is fit for light work only. General damages £6,500 including £2,500 for loss of earning capacity.

Burgess v Bovis International Civil Engineering Ltd
(22 February 1984, unreported)
Civil engineering foreman, 39, sustained whiplash type injury to his lumbar spine. He is now a chronic back pain invalid with altered sensation in the legs and right arm. He has limited leg raising ability. General damages £38,500 including £30,000 for loss of earnings capacity.

Cherry v Kadri
(13 June 1983, unreported)
Fireman, sustained a back injury leading to frequent pain in back and left buttock. The pain is worse after lifting and bending. His hobbies are restricted. The condition should improve leaving mild backache and vulnerability. General damages £5,250 including £3,500 for the injury itself.

Gorman v Ford Motor Co Ltd
(15 July 1983, unreported)
Machine operator, 55, injured back now has pain on occasion in lower back, which was diminishing. He has given up active pastimes and cannot have sexual intercourse. General damages £2,750.

Gray v Burton
(15 November 1982, unreported)
Architectural assistant, 35, sustained a whiplash injury to cervical spine and soft tissue injury to the lumbar spine. He now suffers from occasional

pain and wears a corset periodically. Hobbies of swimming, cycling, gardening have been affected. General damages £3,500.

Lynch v Glacier Metal Co Ltd
(11 October 1982, unreported)
Bookkeeper, 47, sustained a hairline fracture of the interior articular facet of the third lumbar vertebra. After a year of severe backache the pain became spasmodic. He can no longer jog or play tennis and he worries about his back weakness. General damages £5,000.

Saunders v Warburton
(7 March 1983, unreported)
Insurance representative, 45, in a car hit from behind. Suffered mild retrospondylolisthesis of the fifth lumbar vertebra and multiple minor injuries. The accident aggravated previous back trouble and he can no longer play snooker or decorate. General damages £4,000 including £500 for loss of future earning capacity.

Rehnsi v Record Tower Cranes Ltd
(21 February 1983, unreported)
Fitter, 48, sustained a lower lumbar disc rupture causing regular pain for which he takes medication. He can do no heavy lifting and cannot drive for more than two to three hours per day. He wears a back support. General damages £6,000 including £2,500 for disadvantage on the labour market.

UPPER LIMBS/SHOULDER

Goldstone v Winchelow
(8 June 1984, unreported)
Welder, suffered severe strain to right shoulder accompanied by a frozen shoulder. He has great pain when raising his right arm above his head. Sleep affected. Symptoms should subside over 6 to 12 months and he should recover fully. Meanwhile golf and decorating affected. General damages £1,650.

McGowan v Berger, Jenson & Nicholson Ltd
(21 December 1983, unreported)
Paint grinder, 38, severe strain to left upper arm. Still suffers stabbing pain in the shoulder on occasion. The condition could be cured by an operation. General damages £3,000.

Vincer v Greater London Council
(25 October 1982, unreported)
Fireman, 46, received a blow to shoulder and is now permanently disabled and has considerable pain. Upwards and downwards movements from the shoulder are affected, there are signs of tendonitis and there is muscle

wasting in the shoulder blades. He is unfit for work involving heavy lifting, pushing or pulling. His hobbies, including international standard archery, are restricted. Damages for the injury itself £6,000.

UPPER LIMB/ARM

Kellman v Macy
(16 January 1985, unreported)
Actor, 23, sustained fracture of upper end of ulna and dislocation of head of radius. Prosthesis inserted in elbow. Now has full range of movement in arm but sensation in lower arm not normal and reduced power in hand restricts its use for heavy physical tasks. Possibility of future operation. General damages £13,500 including £1,500 for disability on labour market and £2,000 for future expenses.

Fowler v Northamptonshire Area Health Authority
(25 July 1984, unreported)
Widow, 71, right-handed suffered comminuted fracture of right humerus where it articulates in the shoulder joint. Left with considerable and permanent disability, restriction of movement in shoulder causing difficulty in some jobs, eg lifting a kettle. General damages £4,000.

Sturley v Police Comr
(18 June 1984, unreported)
Plaintiff, 46, suffered fracture to middle and lower third of left ulna. Left with constant dull ache and a slight loss of movement in elbow and shoulder. General damages £2,000.

Wright v Mockett
(2 May 1984, unreported)
Lance-bombardier, 35, sustained fracture of left ankle and fracture to humerus. He had eight operations on elbow but is now left with no bone in the arm from half-way down the upper arm to the top of the forearm. There is the possibility of future amputation. He experiences pain in the arm. General damages £15,000 including £2,500 for loss of future earning capacity.

Ayres v Crowthrone Transport Co Ltd and Barefoot
(7 March 1983, unreported)
Plaintiff, involved in motor cycle accident. Injuries to chest with almost full recovery and to both arms leaving him with unsightly scarring on left arm and a one inch shortening to the right arm. He has a loss of sensation in the left arm and numbness in right hand. General damages £8,000.

Wiles v Molins Ltd
(21 February 1983, unreported)
Clerk-messenger, fractured right elbow and had operation to screw

fragments of ulna together. His enjoyment of bowls is impaired. General damages £2,500.

UPPER LIMBS/WRIST/HAND

Rogers v London Co-operative Society Ltd
(8 March 1983, unreported)
Dairy processor/assistant, 22, cut right wrist on glass. Tendon and nerve damage causing numbness in fingers loss of grip and difficulty in picking up small objects and writing. General damages £10,000 including £3,000 for loss of earning capacity.

Hogg v SLP Fabricating Engineers Ltd
(14 April 1983, unreported)
Plater, 28, fracture to lower end of left radius. He is left handed. Left with minor loss of grip and aching after heavy work. General damages £2,500.

Greenfield v Tower Ships Ltd (The Tower Duchess)
(18 November 1982, unreported)
Seaman, 27, sustained comminuted fracture of base of left thumb metacarpal with subluxation at base of trapezio and metacarpal joint. Off work two and a half months and on light duties for five months. Thumb now 1 cm shorter, now has minor discomfort which could be relieved by operation and minor restriction in movement. Damages for the injury itself £1,100.

Hunt v Austin Packaging Group Ltd
(18 March 1983, unreported)
Skilled fitter, 35, amputation of area under nail of right thumb which is now $1\frac{1}{2}$ cms short with a bulbous skin graft. There is little sensation in the thumb tip. He has had to give up his tennis and badminton and his handyman activities are restricted. General damages £7,000.

King v Camden London Borough
(21 July 1982, unreported)
Carpenter, 45, (now 49) sustained traumatic amputation of left little finger and ring finger and an injury to middle finger. General damages £5,000 including £2,500 for loss of employment prospects.

Botley v Department of the Environment
(21 June 1982, unreported)
Fitter, 48, sustained injuries to his left hand. The index and middle fingers are now deformed and scarred and flexion is reduced. The ring finger had to be amputated through the middle phalanx leaving a tender stump. All three fingers tend to be painful and the dexterity and grip of the hand are greatly reduced. General damages £10,500 including £2,500 for loss of prospects on labour market.

Craddock v J. H. Dewhurst Ltd
(10 February 1984, unreported)
Butcher, 34, sustained transverse laceration to right wrist severing median nerve and four tendons to the middle and ring fingers. Left with limited grasping facility, less manipulative skill in his hand and reduced sensations. A nerve graft from the left leg left a scar there and rendered the leg much weaker especially in cold weather. He had to give up work and his hobbies of gardening, painting, darts and making models. In addition he gave up driving and can only walk half a mile without discomfort. General damages £14,000 for pain suffering and loss of activity and £32,780 future loss of earnings.

Brummitt v Aibbert Shipping Co Ltd
(29 July 1983, unreported)
Crewman on boat, 17, sustained crush injury to right hand. Index and middle fingers amputated remaining fingers stiff attenuated and hyper-sensitive. Left with large scar on abdomen from skin graft. The hand is of very limited use. General damages £68,500 including £50,000 for loss of earnings capacity.

LOWER LIMBS/HIP/THIGH

North v Sandell Perkins Ltd
(20 June 1984, unreported)
Insurance broker, 20, sustained compound fracture dislocation of the left hip and compound fracture of left tibia and fibula in a motor cycle accident. He still suffers pain in hip after standing or walking or running more than 150 yards. Movement of the hip and ankle restricted and the leg is slightly painful and he has stiffness of the foot and clawing of the toes. The leg and hip are scarred. Osteoarthritis in the hip is expected. His sporting activities are restricted. General damages £22,000.

Crisp v Taylor
(30 March 1984, unreported)
Record company supervisor, 42, sustained a double fracture of left side of pelvis and bruising to knees. She will continue to have pain in back, groin and left thigh, necessitating pain killing drugs. She has difficulty in her domestic chores and in gardening. She also suffers psychological symptoms. General damages for the hip injury £5,500.

Hogben v McKenna
(27 May 1983, unreported)
Plaintiff, 57, sustained minimally displaced subcapital fracture of the left femur. Now has occasional pain and occasional limp. She also suffers from severe depression. General damages £2,750.

Dearlove v North London Polytechnic
(8 February 1984, unreported)
Cleaner, 46, fractured left femur the head of which was replaced by a steel ball. However, she will require a complete hip replacement which will give ninety per cent chance of some recovery. She now has a limp and walks with a stick. She requires assistance in standing up and sitting down. General damages £12,000.

Hill v British Telecommunications
(14 February 1984, unreported)
Technical Officer, 61, Sub-capital displaced fracture of left femur. A prosthesis was fitted giving nearly full movement. Standing and walking are affected and he no longer does the decorating or gardening. He is nervous and afraid of falling. He takes pain killers. General damages £7,000.

Sendall v Balfour Beatty Power Construction Ltd
(23 June 1983, unreported)
Canteen assistant, 56, suffered fractured neck of the right femur which would not unite causing pain and disablement until the hip was replaced. However, the operation left her still in pain and the hip is immobile. She needs help to get on a bus and can do little housework. She may get some improvement. General damages £9,000 including £1,000 for future loss of earnings.

LOWER LIMBS/KNEE

Drew v Drew
(26 April 1983, unreported)
Housewife, 58, suffered depressed fractures of left lateral tibial plateau. On crutches for six months then used a stick. The leg is still swollen and she is hampered in her pre-accident activities. It is likely that she will suffer from osteoarthritis. General damages £4,500.

Jennings v British Railways Board
(30 January 1984, unreported)
Delivery van driver, early 60s, compound fracture of left patella. The kneecap had to be removed. Now has aching knee and a loss of power. He finds heavy lifting, climbing stairs and squatting difficult and he cannot run, dance or garden. General damages £6,000.

Haines v Wells
(5 October 1984, unreported)
Trainee accountant, 22, riding motor cycle which collided with car. Various superficial injuries leaving him with a scar on the left knee. The right knee suffered a compound fracture and now causes discomfort and sometimes gives way. He will eventually have to have the knee cap replaced. He can no longer play football, squash and badminton. General damages £7,500.

Scott v Biffa Ltd
(10 May 1984, unreported)
Self-employed builder, injured in a motor-cycle accident, comminuted fracture of right leg and superficial injuries. Good recovery but leg half an inch shorter and there is some stiffness. General damages £4,000.

Orchard v Williams & Son Ltd
(14 March 1984, unreported)
Dock worker, 42, comminuted fracture of right tibia and fibula. His leg now bows backwards and is 1 inch shorter. He is unfit for heavy work. General damages £10,000 including £4,000 for disadvantage in the labour market.

Brophy v McLennon
(8 June 1984, unreported)
Plaintiff, sustained internal injuries to his knee in a motor cycle accident. The knee is unstable and the plaintiff can no longer pursue sports. Osteoarthritis is likely to occur. General damages £5,000.

Tillotson v London Borough of Harrow
(17 January 1984, unreported)
Schoolgirl, 11, fractured right tibia and fibula. A long period of enforced immobility caused muscle wasting. She made a gradual improvement and a full recovery is expected in 12 months. She has been unable to participate in sports and cannot stand for long. General damages £6,500.

Taylor v Kent County Council
(17 January 1984, unreported)
Fireman, 24, suffered detachment of a horn of medial meniscus. Good recovery apart from some loss of sensation and the possibility of future arthritic changes. General damages £3,000.

Martin v Chloride Automotive Batteries
(25 June 1984, unreported)
Maintenance fitter, 48, suffered tear to medial meniscus in right knee. He is left with a mild residual ache and discomfort in kneeling and squatting. General damages £5,000 including £1,500 for loss of earning capacity.

LOWER LIMBS/ANKLE/FOOT

Murphy v Van Praagh
(18 April 1984, unreported)
Dustman, 44, sustained compound fracture of right tibia and fibula. His ankle swells up and is affected by cold and damp; it is restricted in movement. His leg is five-eights of an inch shorter. Osteoarthritis may occur in the future. General damages £5,500.

Brady v G & S Formwork Ltd
(10 May 1983, unreported)
Carpenter, 48, fractured right os calcis damaging the joint below the ankle. Movement now restricted and there is a risk of osteoarthritis. He experiences pain after use of the limb and is restricted in walking and climbing ladders. General damages £6,500 including £2,000 for loss of earning capacity.

Caine v Inner London Education Authority
(30 July 1984, unreported)
Schoolboy, 15, fractured both ankles in a go-cart accident and is now permanently disabled. He is barred from many sports and types of work. There is a risk of deterioration in the right ankle and of osteoarthritis in the left foot. General damages £99,800 including £79,800 for future earnings loss and disability on labour market.

Coleman v GKN Mills Building Services Ltd
(21 February 1984, unreported)
Chargehand scaffolder, 36, sustained a serious injury to the left os calcis and other minor injuries. He cannot now climb or walk on uneven ground. General damages £34,314.71 including £24,314.71 for future earnings loss.

Bond v Blue Circle Industries Ltd
(23 June 1983, unreported)
Welder, 25, suffered serious crush injuries to left foot including several fractures and then amputation of the first and second toes. A skin graft was necessary and the remaining toes are clawed. He has pain on walking and his sporting activities are restricted. General damages £25,000 including £7,500 for future disability on the labour market.

Gohill v General Refrigeration Ltd
(21 May 1984, unreported)
Refrigeration engineer, 40, suffered a grossly comminuted fracture of the left ankle. He will remain considerably disabled, he walks with an inverted foot and cannot run. His heel and foot are deformed. General damages £16,000 including £6,000 for disadvantage on the labour market.

Index